S0-BAP-852

MARKETING MANAGEMENT

Text and Cases

Seventh Edition

Douglas J. Darymple
Indiana University

Leonard J. Parsons
Georgia Institute of Technology

JOHN WILEY & SONS

New York • Chichester • Weinheim • Brisbane • Singapore • Toronto

ACQUISITIONS EDITOR   Brent Gordon
MARKETING MANAGER   Jessica Garcia
SENIOR PRODUCTION EDITOR   Patricia McFadden
SENIOR DESIGNER   Karin Gerdes Kincheloe
PHOTO EDITOR   Lisa Gee
ILLUSTRATION EDITOR   Anna Melhorn
PRODUCTION MANAGEMENT   Hermitage Publishing Services

This book was set in 10/12 Times Roman by Hermitage Publishing Services
and printed and bound by Von Hoffmann Press. The cover was printed by Phoenix Color, Inc.

This book is printed on acid-free paper.

Copyright 2000 © John Wiley & Sons, Inc. All rights reserved.

No part of this publication may be reproduced, stored in a retrieval system or transmitted in
any form or by any means, electronic, mechanical, photocopying, scanning or otherwise,
except as permitted under Secion 107 or 108 of the 1976 United States Copyright Act, without either the prior written permission of the Publisher, or authorization through payment of
the appropriate per-copy fee to the Copyright Clearance Center, 222 Rosewood Drive, Dan-
vers, MA 01923, (978) 750-8400, fax (978) 750-4470. Requests to the Publisher for permission should be addressed to the Permissions Department, John Wiley & Sons, Inc., 605 Third
Avenue, New York, NY 10158-0012, (212) 850-6011, fax (212) 850-6008, E-
Mail:PERMREQ@WILEY.COM. To order books please call 1(800) 225-5945

ISBN 0-471-33238-0

Printed in the United States of America

10 9 8 7 6 5 4 3 2 1

PREFACE

This combination text and casebook is designed to help students learn marketing management concepts and apply them to solve business problems. Marketing is the driving force that helps firms succeed in the new era of information explosion, instant Internet communications, and global competition. Students must appreciate the key role that marketing plays in the creation and distribution of goods and services to business and consumer buyers. The importance of marketing to business prosperity means that marketing has become an important pathway for students to move to the top of the executive career ladder.

Marketing works closely with other functional areas. Business problem-solving and planning today is multidisciplinary. Students must understand the linkages among the functional areas.[1] Taking a flexible multidisciplinary approach in thinking and problem solving prepares the student for not only that first position in marketing but also for the ultimate move to general managment.

Approach and Objectives

The 7th edition of *Marketing Management* focuses on the activities of managers who make the everyday decisions that guide the marketing of goods and services. To operate successfully in a business environment, students need to understand what marketing executives do and how marketing builds sales and profits. This book provides in-depth coverage of all elements of the marketing mix and shows how they are used in the business world. Our approach to marketing management is comprehensive, up-to-date, and practical. We use many real-world examples and present them in an easy-to-read style. Stories in boxes highlight recent applications of marketing management (Marketing in Action boxes) and unique marketing strategies (Marketing Strategy boxes). The 7th edition of *Marketing Management* is unique because it is one of only two marketing books that devote half their space to text material and half to cases. We place cases at the end of each chapter so students can take the principles they learn in each chapter and apply them directly to solve a relevant case problem. Students get a complete marketing management text and a marketing casebook all in

---

[1] Rhett H. Walker, Dallas Hanson, Lindsay Nelson, and Cathy Fisher, "A Case for a More Integrative Multidisciplinary Marketing Education," *European Journal of Marketing,* Vol. 32, No. 9/10, 1998, pp. 803–812.

one package. Thus students who take courses using this text have only one book to buy and carry around.

We believe that the new edition offers instructors flexibility to emphasize text or case material, as they prefer, and to employ different methods of instruction. Some instructors may want to supplement this book with specialized readings or to add some of their own cases. We encourage the instructor to have students subscribe to *The Wall Street Journal,* read general business publications such as *Business Week* and *Fortune,* and get exposure to specialized marketing publications such as *Admap* and *Promo* magazines.

We have suppressed some of the citations that appeared in earlier editions. Our objective is to simplify the appearance of the book, not to claim the ideas of our colleagues as our own. Readers looking for source material are encouraged to seek out earlier editions of our book. Much of the theoretical material embedded in the book first appeared in the academic publications such as the *Journal of Marketing* and the *Journal of Marketing Research.* At the end of each chapter we include Suggested Readings and References. Suggested Readings are usually articles that help flesh out and illustrate the material in the book. References are often books containing details about the material contained in a chapter, since each chapter topic could be given as a course by itself!

Changes in This Edition

The most important content change in the new edition is our expanded coverage of electronic commerce and the Internet. We now have extensive discussions of the impact of the Internet on marketing activities in the distribution, direct marketing, advertising, and promotion chapters. To highlight our increased focus on interfunctional coordination, we added "Applying to" and "Integrating with" icons in the margins to point out relevant text discussions. We have also updated eighty-five percent of the boxed inserts to provide students with newer and more interesting examples. To help make students more aware of the social environment, we have included a business ethics question at the end of each of the chapters. The case section of the book has been strengthened by the addition of 27 new cases out of a total of 39. In recognition of the growing importance of global marketing, we have included 28 international cases. Now that services account for over half of GDP, we selected 15 service marketing cases for the new edition. One question at the end of most chapters, as well as some of the cases, have databases that encourage the use of SPSS statistical software for student analysis.

We have chosen to reduce the length of the new edition to make it easier for students to use. Our goal was to shorten the book by eliminating secondary material without hurting coverage of important topics. For example, the forecasting material was integrated with the product development chapter so the book now has 16 chapters. We would note that although all the chapters have been shortened, they have been thoroughly revised with new material, updated tables, figures, and references.

Supplements

Successful marketing management courses require a well-written text and an effective set of supplementary teaching materials. We have assembled an outstanding package of these aids to support *Marketing Management.*

- Instructors Resource Guide. Includes suggested course syllabi, chapter outlines, lecture notes, case notes, and answers to chapter-end questions.

- SPSS Student Version for Windows 9.0. This software is available to package with the text to help students analyze the data in The High Museum of Art, Del Monte Foods, and other cases.
- PowerPoint Files and NBR videos. A topic outline and key figures from the text are now available in PowerPoint files that can be downloaded from the book's Web site for use in class. The Web site is www.wiley.com/college. At this point, users can access the site in two primary ways:

  1. Search for Book Site by Author Name:

  |A|B|C|D|E|F|G|H|I|J|K|L|M|N|O|P|Q|R|S|T|U|V|W|X|Y|Z|

  Selecting "D" will provide you a listing of Web sites of lead authors with last names beginning with D.

  2. By selecting:
  Business
  Marketing
  Marketing Management

The Web site will be open access except for the Instructor's resources. Secured Instructor Resources (PowerPoint files, Instructor's Manual, and the like) can be accessed only by using a password. Instructors can register for the password online. They will simply need to follow the registration instructions.

NBR stands for Nightly Business Report (PBS). The Wiley Nightly Business Report video series contains segments from the highly respected Nightly Business Report, which have been selected for their applicability to marketing management principles and for their reinforcement of key concepts in the text. Each of the segments is approximately three-to-five-minutes long and can be used to introduce topics to the students, enhance lecture material, and provide real-world context for related concepts. The videotape is available to adopters of the text. Please see your Wiley representative for details.

Acknowledgements

This book could not have been published without the spirited comments and suggestions from a host of colleagues and reviewers. Although we don't have room to mention everyone, we would like to express our appreciation to the following professors who provided valuable tips for the seventh edition: Craig Andrews, Marquette University; Connie Rae Bateman, University of North Dakota; Terry Bristol, University of Arkansas at Little Rock; Kevin Coulson, Northeastern Illinois University; Susan Dann, Queensland University of Technology, Australia; Craig Kelley, California State University, Sacramento; Eldon Little, Indiana University Southeast; Charles L. Martin, Wichita State University; Richard M. Reese, Clemson University; Dennis Rosen, University of Kansas; and Nader H. Shooshtari, University of Montana.

We would like to thank the people from John Wiley & Sons for their guidance and support: our editor, Brent Gordon and his (then) editorial assistant, Jennifer LiMarzi; our senior production editor, Patrician McFadden; our photo editors, Marge Graham and Lisa Gee; and our assistant editor for supplements, Cynthia Rhoads. The quality of the educational package was enhanced by Larry Meyer of Hermitage Publishing Services (editing and production), by Diane Hambley, University of South Dakota, and Tracy Clark, Multimedia Lab, DuPree College of Management, Georgia Institute of Technology (PowerPoint presentation), and by Stan Maddock, Maddock Illustration (jpeg files of figures). In addition, we would like to belatedly thank Stephen Walsh, State University of New York, Oneonta, who prepared several hundred unsolicited multiple-choice questions for the 6th edition after its *Instructor's Manual* was published.

We express our appreciation to those who made case materials available for the new edition. We note than sometimes figures in the author's original cases have not been reproduced in our book because the appropriate case clearinghouse did not provide our publisher with camera-ready copy.

We are especially indebted to Linda Sharp for typing countless drafts and revisions. Last, but certainly not least, we thank our wives, Nancy and Julie, for their help and encouragement.

Douglas J. Dalrymple
Leonard J. Parsons

ABOUT THE AUTHORS

Douglas J. Dalrymple is Professor of Marketing in the School of Business at Indiana University. He received his DBA degree in marketing from Michigan State University and his MS and BS degrees from Cornell University. Professor Dalrymple has taught at the University of California, Los Angeles, the Georgia Institute of Technology, the University of San Diego, and the University of North Carolina, Greensboro. His research emphasizes forecasting and sales force issues. Publications in which his articles have appeared included *Journal of Personal Selling & Sales Management, Decision Sciences, Industrial Marketing Management, International Journal of Forecasting, Journal of Business Research, Business Horizons, California Management Review,* and *Applied Economics.* Professor Dalrymple is the author or coauthor of 24 marketing books including *Basic Marketing Management* (2nd ed.), *Sales Management: Concepts and Cases* (6th ed.), *Cases in Marketing Management,* a computerized *Sales Management Simulation* (4th ed.) and two retailing texts. His books and articles have been translated into Spanish, Chinese, Japanese, and Hebrew.

Leonard J. Parsons is professor of marketing at Georgia Institute of Technology's Dupree College of Management. He received his S.B. degree in chemical engineering from the Massachusetts Institute of Technology and his M.S.I.A. and Ph.D. degrees in industrial administration with a specialization in marketing from Purdue University's Krannert School. He has taught at Indiana University and the Claremont Graduate School, and has been a visiting scholar at M.I.T., a Fulbright-Hays Senior Scholar at Katholieke Universiteit Leuven (Belgium), a visiting professor at INSEAD (France), the Norwegian School of Marketing (Oslo), and U.C.L.A., an Advertising Educational Foundation Visiting Professor at Anheuser-Busch, and an Intercollegiate Center for Management Science Visiting Professor at the Center for Research on the Economic Efficiency of Retailing of the Facultés Universitaires Catholiques de Mons (Belgium) and at the European Institute for Advanced Studies in Management (Brussels). He has been a member of the European Marketing Academy's Executive Council, a member of the Graduate Management Admission Council's Research and Test (GMAT) Development Committee, chair of the American Statistical Association's Section on Statistics in Marketing, and a member of the

Advisory Board of the American Marketing Association's Marketing Research Special Interest Group. He has served as marketing departmental editor of *Management Science* and associate editor of *Decision Sciences,* and has been on the editorial boards of the *Journal of Marketing Research,* the *Journal of Marketing,* and the *Journal of Business Research.* He has coedited special issues of the *International Journal of Forecasting* and the *International Journal of Research in Marketing.* He has coauthored or coedited five books, and *Market Response Models: Econometric and Time Series Analysis,* two programmed learning texts, seven chapters in books, and articles in journals such as the *Journal of Marketing Research, Management Science, Operations Research, and Applied Economics.* He has received several awards from the American Marketing Association, including the first place award in its National Research Design Competition, and a grant from the American Association of Advertising Agencies. He is a member of Beta Gamma Sigma and Phi Kappa Phi and is listed in *Who's Who in America.* He is an expert on market response models, and his main interest is in marketing productivity.

CONTENTS

THE ROLE OF MARKETING IN ORGANIZATIONS AND SOCIETY

> Marketing today is not a function; it is a way of doing business.
>
> REGIS McKENNA

The field of marketing in the new millennium is full of challenges and risks. Domestic firms in every country find that they can no longer ignore foreign competition and foreign markets. Organizations that let their costs and prices get out of line with the rest of the world see their market shares plummet. Companies also learn that they cannot ignore emerging technologies and new forms of organizational structure.

Some firms seize market opportunities and grow while others fade away. Why? We believe that one reason is vision. Another reason some organizations grow is that they choose chief executive officers with marketing backgrounds. Research has shown that more top executives come out of marketing than any other field. A marketing emphasis can make the difference between organizational success and disaster. We believe it is essential that you acquire strong marketing skills so that you can operate in today's competitive environment. This book has been specifically designed to show you how to develop and implement marketing strategies and tactics for organizations of the new millennium.

WHAT IS MARKETING?

Marketing is one of the most powerful tools employed by organizations in their never-ending struggle for survival and growth. One definition of marketing is

the process of planning and executing the conception, pricing, promotion, and distribution of ideas, goods, and services to create exchanges that satisfy individuals, organizations, and society.[1]

This definition points out that the objective of marketing is to satisfy customers' needs. Thus, the first challenge is to find a set of customers and identify their needs so that appropriate goods and services can be developed. Once an organization has a product, marketing personnel design pricing, promotion, and distribution plans to make these items leap into the hands of the customer. Executives are responsible for meeting organizational goals while ensuring that the customer and the public are not harmed by marketing activities. When we speak of exchanges, we do not restrict ourselves to the onetime, arm's-length transaction between a buyer and a seller.

In a single-event transaction, all that counts is the sale.[2] Price is the most important factor. More often, instead of only one transaction, there are repeated transactions between parties. This is true for some industrial components and most consumables: frequently purchased consumer goods and business supplies. Advertising and sales promotions are used to gain and retain customers. Concepts such as brand loyalty now have meaning. Nonetheless, there may be little direct contact between the marketer and the customer in many consumer markets. When we examine business-to-business markets, we often see long-term agreements among parties. Frequently, a buyer has a list of qualified vendors. The buyer encourages competition among these vendors, perhaps by using a competitive bidding process, to get the best price. The buyer monitors product quality by inspection on delivery. Thus, although this is a long-term relationship, its basis is adversarial. However, the picture we have painted of the marketplace so far, which could be called *transactional marketing,* is changing.

Relationship marketing emphasizes the interdependence between buyer and seller. Even for frequently purchased consumer products, you need to move beyond a repeat transaction mentality to relationship marketing. This has been made possible by the technical ability to create large databases, which identify customers and their needs. You can reach specific customers through direct selling or direct marketing. This approach to relationship marketing is known as *database marketing.* It could also be considered a form of transactional marketing but one that allows you to get somewhat closer to your customer. When using advanced information technology based on individually addressable and interactive media, database marketing is known as *interactive marketing.*

INTEGRATING *... with Information Techonology Management*

Facing new pressures, once contending parties, especially in business-to-business markets, are realizing the value of cooperation. Quality, delivery, and technical support as well as price, enter into negotiations. Quality is built into the production process. Product design becomes a collaborative process. Individuals in the seller organization interact with their counterpart in the buyer organization in a process known as "customer partnering." Thus, social exchange (i.e., personal interactions) to create value for both parties is paramount. This approach to relationship marketing is known as *interaction marketing,* and should not be confused with interactive marketing.

In today's world, it's important to develop long-term, mutually supportive relationships with your customers—whether they are channel members or end users. This approach can be extended to embrace suppliers and, at times, competitors as well. In some cases, the relationship takes the form of a partnership or a strategic alliance. For example, the Coca-Cola Company and Nestlé S.A. have a joint venture, Coca-Cola Nestlé Refreshments Company. Among other things, this joint venture sells a canned beverage, Nestea Iced Tea. The product is produced and distributed by Coca-Cola bottlers in various countries. This approach to relationship marketing, which is known as *network marketing,* takes into account the totality of the relationships in a market or industry, and it is a more holistic view of interaction marketing. Interaction marketing emphasizes the focal relationship of the firm in the network as indicated in Figure 1-1.

APPLYING *... to Consumer Beverages Marketing*

A perceptual map showing transactional marketing and the three types of relationship marketing is shown in Figure 1-2. Certain types of marketing practice are more common in some sectors than others (as indicated in Figure 1-2). While one type of marketing may be predominant in a firm, others are also practiced. A comparison of the characteristics of the four types is given in Table 1-1.

In sum, a contemporary view of the purpose of marketing is

to identify and establish, maintain, and enhance relationships with customers and other stakeholders, at a profit, so that the objectives of the partners involved are met; and this is achieved by mutual exchange and fulfillment of promises.[3]

Nonetheless, for most organizations, transactional marketing remains relevant and is practiced concurrently with various types of relationship marketing. Some of the interplay that

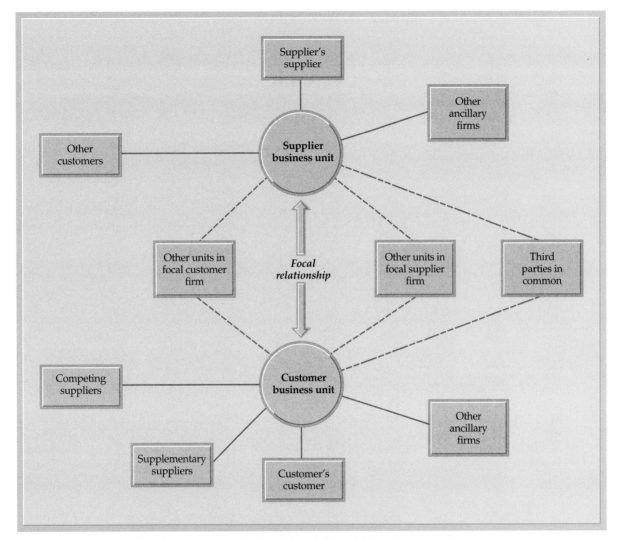

FIGURE 1-1   Focal Relationship Within a Network
(From James C. Anderson, Håkan Håkansson, and Jan Johanson, "Dyadic Business Relationships Within a Business Network Context," *Journal of Marketing,* Vol. 58, No. 4 [October 1994], p. 3)

takes place is hinted at in the Ocean Spray example given in the Marketing in Action box 1-1.

The role marketing plays in an organization varies by organizational level (Table 1-2). At the corporate level, *marketing as culture* is emphasized; at the strategic business unit level, *marketing as strategy;* and at the operating level, *marketing as tactics.* This chapter emphasizes marketing as culture: the basic set of values and beliefs about the central importance of the customer that guide the organization, as articulated by the marketing concept.

WHO IS THE MARKETING MANAGER?

A marketing manager is anyone responsible for making significant marketing decisions. Except in the case of very small firms, no single person is accountable for all the decisions described in this book. The responsibility for marketing is diffused throughout the organiza-

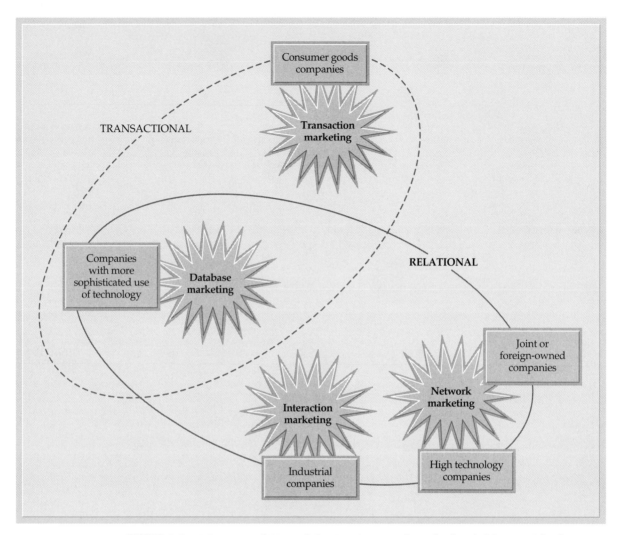

FIGURE 1-2   A Perceptual Map of the Four Types of Marketing (with exemplars).
(Constructed from information in Roderick J. Brodie, Nicole E. Coviello, Richard W. Brookes, and Victoria Little, "Toward a Paradigm Shift in Marketing? An Examination of Current Marketing Practices," *Journal of Marketing Management,* Vol. 13, No. 5 [July 1997], pp. 383–406.)

INTEGRATING
. . . with
Engineering
and Finance

tion. Senior managers are continually making pricing and strategic marketing decisions. But engineers are also involved in marketing because they have to design products that meet customers' needs, wants, and quality standards, as are corporate treasurers who oversee the credit terms and credit availability that directly affect buying decisions.

Several managers in an organization specialize in marketing decision making. These include *brand and product managers,* who make the day-to-day decisions for individual items and prepare the annual marketing plan. The brand manager is charged with managing and further developing the brand equity. *Category managers* coordinate the marketing strategies of related products and brands. The evolution of the brand manager system at Procter & Gamble is described in Marketing in Action box 1-2. There are also line sales managers who guide the implementation of the marketing plan by the field sales force. In addition to these line managers, there are a variety of staff managers. Advertising and promotion managers control the preparation of print ads, TV commercials, direct-mail

TABLE 1-1   Types of Marketing

	Transactional Perspective	Relational Perspective		
	Transactional Marketing	Database Marketing	Interaction Marketing	Network Marketing
Managerial intent[a]	Customer attraction (to satisfy a customer at a profit)	Customer retention (to satisfy the customer, increase profit, and attain other objectives such as increased loyalty or decreased customer risk)	Interaction (to establish, develop, and facilitate a cooperative relationship for mutual benefit)	Coordination (interaction between sellers, buyers, and other parties across multiple firms for mutual benefit, resource exchange, market access)
Decision focus[a]	Product or brand	Product/brand and customers in targeted market	Relationships between individuals	Connected relationships among firms (in a network)
Relational exchange focus[b]	Economic transaction	Information and economic transaction	Interactive relationships between a buyer and a seller	Connected relationships among firms
Parties involved[b]	A firm and buyers in the general market	A firm and buyers in a specific target market	Individual sellers and buyers (a dyad)	Sellers, buyers, and other firms)
Communication pattern[b]	Firm "to" market	Firm "to" individual	Individuals "with" individuals (across organizations)	Firms "with" firms (involving individuals)
Type of contact[b]	Arm's-length, impersonal	Personalized, yet distant	Face-to-face, interpersonal (close, based on commitment, trust, and cooperation)	Impersonal – interpersonal (ranging from distant to close)
Duration[b]	Discrete (yet perhaps over time)	Discrete and over time	Continuous (ongoing and mutually adaptive, may be short or long-term)	Continuous (stable yet dynamic, may be short-or long-term)
Formality[b]	Formal	Formal (yet personalized via technology)	Formal and informal (i.e., at both the business and social level)	Formal and informal (i.e., at both the business and social level)
Balance of power[b]	Active seller–passive buyers	Active seller–less passive buyers	Seller and buyer mutually active and adaptive (interdependent and reciprocal)	All firms active and adaptive
Managerial investment[a]	Internal marketing assets (focusing on product/service, price, distribution, promotion capabilities)	Internal marketing assets (emphasizing communication, information, and technology capabilities)	External market assets (focusing on establishing a relationship with another individual)	External market assets (focusing on developing the firms position in a network of firms)

(continued)

TABLE 1-1   Continued

	Transactional Perspective	Relational Perspective		
	Transactional Marketing	Database Marketing	Interaction Marketing	Network Marketing
Managerial level[a]	Functional marketers	Specialist marketers (e.g., customer service manager, loyalty manager)	Managers from across functional areas	General manager
Time frame[a]	Short-term	Longer-term	Short or long-term	Short or long-term

[a] Managerial dimension
[b] Relational exchange dimension

Source: Nicole E. Coviello, Roderick J. Brodie, and Hugh J. Munro, "Understanding Contemporary Marketing," *Journal of Marketing Management,* Vol. 13, No. 6 (August 1997), pp. 501–522.

MARKETING IN ACTION *1-1*

APPLYING
. . . to
Consumer
Beverages
Marketing

Ocean Spray, the Number One Cranberry Brand

Ocean Spray, a farmer's cooperative, markets cranberry juice. Traditionally, Ocean Spray considered its product an all-family beverage. It viewed Mom buying a big bottle for the whole family to drink at home. More recently, it realized it should view each family member as buying a different product outside the home. For example, a 13-year-old might get off a school bus and hit a convenience store on the way home. Ocean Spray expected bigger growth from away-from-home and international than in-home. Consequently, it formed three strategic marketing groups to tackle away-from-home, in-home, and international campaigns. It also set up a brand development group to serve as a resource.

Ocean Spray was eager to break into the broader beverage category to establish the same status as Coke and Pepsi in consumers' minds. To this end, Ocean Spray and Pepsi began a joint venture in 1992. However, the relationship was downgraded to that of distribution agreement in 1995, leaving each company free to develop its own new products and marketing. Ocean Spray didn't give Pepsi as much control over the brand as Pepsi wanted. Pepsi then decided to buy its own juice company so that it could be in control without having to please a farmer's coop. In 1998, Pepsi proposed buying Tropicana. This deal could eventually edge Ocean Spray off Pepsi trucks. Ocean Spray could lose as much as half of its single-serve sales, the portion now handled by Pepsi-owned bottlers. This would kill its momentum in single-serve products—its main vehicle to reach younger consumers. Pepsi maintained that it would honor the current distribution contract. Nonetheless, Ocean Spray filed suit against its distribution partner to block the purchase of Tropicana. The relationship has been contentious but it expanded Ocean Spray's single-serve sales from 1.5 million cases to 22 million cases in five years.

In the meantime, Ocean Spray took its eye off the juice aisle and lost ground with grocers and consumers. Ocean Spray growth historically relied on new products but few had been forthcoming. The trade asked Ocean Spray, "Where are you? We need you spending money and bringing us new products." Grocers wanted help in growing the shelf-stable juice business. While Ocean Spray was not paying attention, newcomer Northland Cranberries made inroads with its 100 percent cranberry juice. Ocean Spray responded by bringing out Wellfleet Farms, an upscale line of 100 percent fruit blends with flavors such as Georgia Peach. In addition, although predominately broker sold, Ocean Spray began to rely more on its own sales staff as grocer consolidations expanded accounts beyond the territory of individual brokers. The company centralized customer sales reps at headquarters from seven scattered plants.

— *Marketing is an interpersonal process based on ongoing contact, mutual goals, trust, and commitment.*

Source: Betsy Spethmann, "Second Wave," *Promo,* October 1998, pp. 38–40, 170–172.

TABLE 1-2 Marketing's Role in the Organization

Organizational Level	Role of Marketing	Name
Corporate	To promote a customer orientation by being a strong advocate for the customer's point of view, as called for by the marketing concept. To assess market attractiveness by analyzing customers' needs and requirements, as well as competitive offerings in the markets potentially available to the firm, to assess potential competitive effectiveness. To develop the firm's overall value proposition in terms reflecting customers' needs and to articulate it to the marketplace and throughout the firm.	Corporate marketing
Strategic business unit	To determine how to compete (market segmentation, targeting, and product positioning) in your chosen business through a more detailed and careful analysis of competitors and of the firm's resources and skills for competing in specific market segments. To decide when and how to partner.	Strategic marketing
Operating	To formulate and implement marketing programs based on the marketing mix—products, pricing, distribution, and marketing communications. To manage customer and reseller relationships.	Marketing management

Source: Developed from Frederick E. Webster, Jr., "The Changing Role of Marketing in the Corporation," *Journal of Marketing,* Vol. 56, No. 4 (October 1992), pp. 1–17.

MARKETING IN ACTION *1-2*

APPLYING ... to Consumer Goods Marketing

Procter & Gamble Redefines the Brand Manager

The Procter & Gamble Co. is generally credited with developing the brand management system. Brand managers had near absolute power and responsibility to run their brands. Being a P&G brand manager was one of the greatest jobs in the world. Over time, however, the brand managers' clout has eroded. This can be seen in the evolution of P&G's brand management:

1931	brand management system approved
1979	customer business teams instituted
1987	category management implemented
1990	everyday low pricing started
1993–95	marketing staff cut through restructuring
1995	global success models sought
1997	media buying and planning consolidated

The managers of P&G brands within the same category once competed fiercely against each other, even to the extent of refusing to share data. The implementation of category management to stop this fratricide naturally took away some the brand manager's power. The introduction of value pricing meant that slower moving brands and stock-keeping units as well as promotional budgets were trimmed. Restructuring cut the marketing staff by 30 percent by eliminating brand assistant and assistant brand manager positions for some smaller brands. Needless variations in products and packaging internationally were weeded out. Global strategic teams, made up of brand and category managers worldwide, were made responsible for identifying "global success models" in product development and ad copy. Once a model is in place, brand managers have little authority to change it. Seeking to improve cost effectiveness in media spending worldwide, ad planning and buying was centralized in an ad agency, shifting media responsibility away from brand managers. Thus, while brand managers still have responsibility for positioning of brands based on consumer needs and for developing broad media strategy, they have lost their grip on such areas as new product development, advertising copy, media planning, and promotions. The brand managers have become more tactical and get more involved in account-by-account, store-by-store marketing.

— *The brand manager today is no longer the final decision-maker but must be brand champion and multi-functional team captain.*

Source: Jack Neff, "P&G Redefines the Brand Manager," *Advertising Age,* October 13, 1997, pp. 1, 18, 20.

brochures, and contests that help to boost the sales of goods and services. Larger firms also have managers of product development and marketing information.

WHAT DOES A MARKETING MANAGER DO?

A marketing manager is, first and foremost, someone who has control or direction of an organization or organizational unit, that is, a manager. There are fundamental aspects of a manager's job that apply across functional areas. Managers have been shown to play 10 roles: figurehead, leader, liaison, monitor, disseminator, spokesperson, entrepreneur, disturbance handler, resource allocator, and negotiator. These roles can be classified as interpersonal, informational, or decisional. Table 1-3 describes these roles and gives examples of how they might apply specifically to a marketing manager. For example, a national account manager for a health and beauty aids company often negotiates sales and promotional terms with the central purchasing offices of large national supermarket chains. As you can see, many of these roles require not only knowledge of marketing concepts and practices, but the exercise of interpersonal skills as well.

The full range of marketing activities in the firm is described in Figure 1-3. Note that the marketing manager is in the center of interactions with a host of people both inside and outside the organization. Marketing talks to customers, research and development, production, finance, suppliers, ad agencies, and marketing research firms. The net result of these interactions is products delivered to satisfied buyers plus profits to fuel innovations for tomorrow. Your most important role is to understand customers.

Customer Contact

Marketing people continually interact with customers. Customers must be your first and most enduring concern. Close attention to their needs is essential for success. Some of the

TABLE 1-3   The Marketing Manager's Job

Role	Description	Example
Interpersonal		
Figurehead	Performs some duties of a ceremonial nature.	Takes important customer to lunch.
Leader	Assumes responsibility for work of subordinates.	Motivates the sales force.
Liaison	Makes contacts outside the vertical chain of command.	Meets with an account executive from a direct marketing firm.
Informational		
Monitor	Scans the environment for information.	Hears from a supplier about a competitor's new product.
Disseminator	Shares information with others, especially subordinates.	Provides feedback from meetings with prospective clients at their locations.
Spokesperson	Sends some information to people outside the organizational unit.	Makes a speech to lobby for favorable legislative treatment.
Decisional		
Entrepreneur	Seeks to improve the unit, adapting it to changing conditions in the environment.	Assigns a new idea to the product development team.
Disturbance handler	Responds to high-pressure disturbances.	Address a consumer boycott initiated by a special interest group.
Resource allocator	Decides who will get what in the organizational unit.	Determines the allocation of promotion budget across brands.
Negotiator	Bargains with others.	Negotiates sales terms with a channel member.

Source: Developed from Henry Mintzberg, *Mintzberg on Management,* New York: The Free Press, 1989, pp. 7–24.

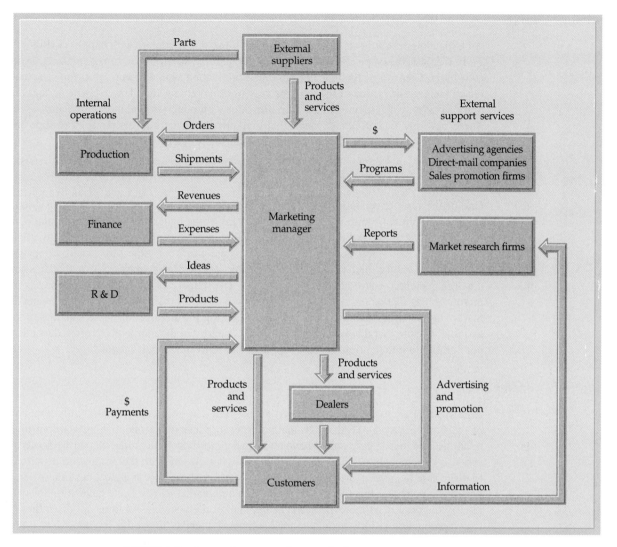

FIGURE 1-3   **Operating Areas for Marketing Managers**

ways that marketing managers relate to customers are shown in Figure 1-3. The diagram shows marketing managers interacting with two types of customers: dealers who resell your products to others and final users. Both types have unique needs that demand specialized marketing programs. Because these customers are typically located some distance from the office, you have to go into the field to talk with them. You also have to set up distribution systems to make goods and services available when and where they are needed.

The marketing manager has responsibility for directing persuasive communications to dealers and ultimate customers and arranging for payment for purchases. In the case of fast-moving consumer goods companies that face the growing power of the retail trade, *customer business teams,* made up of sales, finance, logistics, and perhaps brand management staff, often work with major retail accounts to develop promotion strategy. In this situation, promotions are funded through a single business development fund for each retail account. In addition, marketing managers have responsibility for collecting information on customer satisfaction, customer loyalty, and future needs. Managing customer relations is a tremendous responsibility and can represent the difference between achieving the goals of the organization and failure.

Supplier Contact

An expanding role for marketing managers is more direct contact with suppliers (Figure 1-3). In the past, the emphasis was on vertical integration, whereby the firm produced all of its own parts. Companies thought that in-house production would lower costs, but it actually raised them. Today some of the most successful firms rely on suppliers for parts and production so that they can focus on core activities such as product design, marketing, and service. These new *strategic alliances* mean that marketing managers must spend more time with suppliers to make sure product quality is maintained and delivery dates are met.

Buying External Services

One of the least understood facts about marketing is that much of the work is assigned to external suppliers (Figure 1-3). In the past, many firms had their own in-house marketing research, advertising, and promotion staffs. Today most companies hire outside advertising agencies to create their advertising and a separate firm to handle direct-mail campaigns. Contests and display materials are developed by special organizations, and market research data are gathered by still another organization. The reliance on outside suppliers means that in your job as marketing manager, you become a buyer of these services. It also means that marketing managers spend a lot of time coordinating the activities of these separate groups and making sure that the work is done on time. Victory in the marketplace often depends on your ability to hire the right service suppliers and to evaluate their output.

Internal Coordination

A third challenge to marketing managers stems from their role as coordinator with other areas of the firm (Figure 1-3). Although marketing is responsible for maintaining good customer relations, as a manager you often have no formal control over the production of the goods and services customers buy. Thus marketing has to work closely with the production department to make sure that orders are filled on time, at an affordable price, and meet customers' specifications. Sometimes this means that production and marketing personnel have to find ways to modify the product to meet the needs of the market. Less successful firms are often those in which production and marketing are unable to work together to get this job done.

Another key interaction for marketing managers involves their ability to work with the research and development department (Figure 1-3). Marketing often comes up with good ideas for new products, but R&D is responsible for turning them into salable products. Thus your success as a marketer may depend on the relationship you develop with the R&D staff. Marketing managers also have to interact with the financial managers of the firm (Figure 1-3). Marketing activities are often expensive, and marketing managers have to meet with financial managers to prepare budget requests. If funds are tight, marketing managers have to find ways to reorganize their activities to make them more efficient. Some of the areas that require financial support are advertising, product development, maintenance of dealer inventories, and credit lines to finance customers' purchases.

If you take a position in marketing, some of the work-related tasks you will encounter are illustrated in Marketing in Action box 1-3. Marketing is much more than a list of things to do; it is a natural sequence of events that leads to greater sales and profits.

THE MARKETING MANAGEMENT PROCESS

Marketing managers plan and implement a sequence of activities that help the firm achieve its goals. The precise actions taken vary with the product or service to be promoted, but a

APPLYING
. . . to
Consumer
Food
Marketing

MARKETING IN ACTION *1-3*

Marketing Activities of One Manager

The Australian biscuit (cracker/cookie) company Arnott's is the giant in its marketplace, with a dominant 60 percent share in its home country. It has manufacturing plants all over Australia. Arnott's New Zealand also does a big biscuit business. Here, Arnott's turnover is some $85 million a year, though they rank second in this market to Griffins. In 1996, its South Auckland, New Zealand, plant was in need of a major upgrade to bring it up to the year 2000. Because of that extra expense and Arnott's new state of the art factory recently completed in Sydney, the company decided to close the New Zealand plant and supply all of its product from Australia.

When Arnott's decided to close its manufacturing base in New Zealand and concentrate entirely on a sales and marketing force, it needed a savvy, new-wave manager to drive the operation. Enter Janine Smith as general manager for Arnott's New Zealand. After years of manufacturing, her big challenge was to refocus Arnott's on marketing. There was great complexity in gradually closing down 150 different product lines and at the same time gradually reducing staff numbers. Smith had to manage that closure before she could begin a new culture, which brought some special management challenges. "The company had always had strong marketing but because of the sheer weight of numbers involved in manufacturing, you can't help but be dominated by that arm of the business," said Smith. "With the manufacturing gone, we can now concentrate solely on the service and marketing arm."

"The first important lesson was having to manage through other people rather than manage direct," said Smith. "In the past, if we ran short of one line we simply cranked up production. But with supply coming from Australia that doesn't work. Now we're constantly in communication with each other so situations like that don't get out of hand. We have lots of partnerships with people, and we have to understand that we are managing through other people."

But the transformation wasn't without its glitches. Arnott's in Australia received extortion threats during 1997 and was forced to pull 40 percent of its stock off the shelves. This directly impacted on the New Zealand operation, as Arnott's struggled to supply its home market, let alone New Zealand. Some lines went out of supply until Australia could make the product and that lost some market share points. Yet overall the company has retained its 32 percent share of the market, something Smith can point to as a credit to her management skills.

Forecasting demand has become an integral part of the new culture. Smith's team has to make sure they don't have any repeats of undersupplying their customers, mostly the supermarkets. A lot of time and energy now goes into accurately judging supply and demand.

Another deliberate strategy was to recruit an almost entirely new team. Seventy percent of the 30 management staff under Smith's control have been in the job less than a year. Many of the former management staff were repatriated to Australia or left of their own volition, something that suited Smith. "We are building a whole new company culture and when you're doing that it's easier to start from scratch," she said. "To generate a 'can-do' culture you need consistency, and if you have someone who's been there, done that, bored with their job, that can affect the whole culture. A lot of the people here are in their particular role for the first time, and there's a terrific energy about that, a willingness to take risks and go the extra mile. Of course that's the upside, the downside is that we did lose knowledge—a little too fast in the short term."

With so many new recruits Smith uses more than just instinct when hiring. Potential recruits are tested with an occupational personality questionnaire—the Saville and Holdsworth OPQ. This details areas of potential strength and weakness of people in areas such as strategy, problem solving and customer service. Though Smith agreed that such tests are not always 100 percent accurate, she said they identify focus, energy and drive. It also identifies team styles that the company uses to develop teams more effectively.

Smith's own style is energetic and one suspects she would score highly on the "can-do" scale of her own questionnaire. She doesn't spend time agonizing over problems, preferring to move on to the solution. "The way I look at life, these are the cards we've been dealt and now we have to rise to the occasion and make it work. I believe you only go after what you can change; if you can't change it then you forget worrying about it."

(continues)

MARKETING IN ACTION *1-3*   (continued)

INTEGRATING
... with
Cross-
Functional
Terms

Smith is also fluent in modern management styles. "Cross-functional teams" is part of her everyday vocabulary. "I like to encourage people to look at the bigger picture. We'll get teams from various disciplines together to solve a problem, and we get a wealth of perspectives. People understand their own job best, and if you ask them to think about it they have the greatest opportunity to see ways of doing it better."

And while they're doing that, Smith provides the overview. With the experience of 20 years of management, she likes to think outside the square. "As a manager, more and more, you have to become a very good listener. You have to objectively listen and work out the consistency and logic of a particular argument." Smith said that's also a skill that requires asking the right questions. Often, she says, junior managers will be trying to make decisions on imperfect information. When you ask the right questions you can open minds to a new direction or solution. Management, she says, is about more thinking and less doing—the ability to see the big picture and understand the wider implications of decisions.

Hierarchical management is not her style and as she strolls around the office, greeting staff and popping her nose round doors, it's obvious she's no stranger to the impromptu meeting. She believes in talking directly to her staff as well as a regular monthly meeting with everyone in which they discuss what went wrong and celebrate their wins. Smith also likes to get out with the salespeople—some 100 of them—so on a monthly basis she gets in the car with the territory managers and goes out with them, calling on customers. The new management team had to accept working without a lot of processes to begin with. Initially there were few structures in place and so, again, it demanded people with faith in their own ability.

INTEGRATING
... with
Suppliers

Part of Smith's philosophy of managing through people also means building partnerships with suppliers. "Some people treat their suppliers as dependent on them, but I believe suppliers are part of our business. When you involve them you get them thinking about your business from your point of view, and their contribution can be all the greater." Smith invites suppliers to corporate functions because she believes she's in partnership with them as much as her clients. It's a move that has apparently taken some of the suppliers by surprise, but enriched their relations with Arnott's.

In the long term, Smith said her company is looking to make significant inroads into the "share of mouth." Throughout the restructuring the company held its category share, and Smith says that's a positive in the face of the upheavals of any restructuring. Closer contact with the parent company has its advantages. In the past six months Arnott's has introduced new lines without having to go through complex research and development because it's already been done in Australia.

What has not changed throughout the transition is a focus on brands. The "Farmbake" brand is now, as before, the biggest biscuit brand in New Zealand and Smith doesn't intend to let that slip. Growth in the future will come from nurturing other key brands, and to that end Smith is fostering a culture of "loving the brand." Underscoring the lot is service to the customer, which mostly means the big supermarkets.

Looking back on the change in the culture, Smith says most of it went exactly right, the result of planning and the commitment of people to make it work. It's also a reflection of the ability of the general manager.

— *Senior management is responsible for creating the enabling conditions that ensure future decisions generate value for both customers and shareholders.*

Source: Wendy Colville, "Taking the Biscuit," *Management-Auckland*, October 1998, pp. 22–26.

general idea can be obtained from the flowchart shown in Figure 1-4. This diagram provides a basic framework for the book. First, managers need to adopt a marketing philosophy. This chapter explains why organizations should be customer driven and in tune with the goals of society. Although you are charged with promoting the sale of goods and services, you must also learn to balance these objectives against the long-term needs of society for a safe and healthy environment. In addition, you need to know which marketing activities are ethical and which violate current business standards.

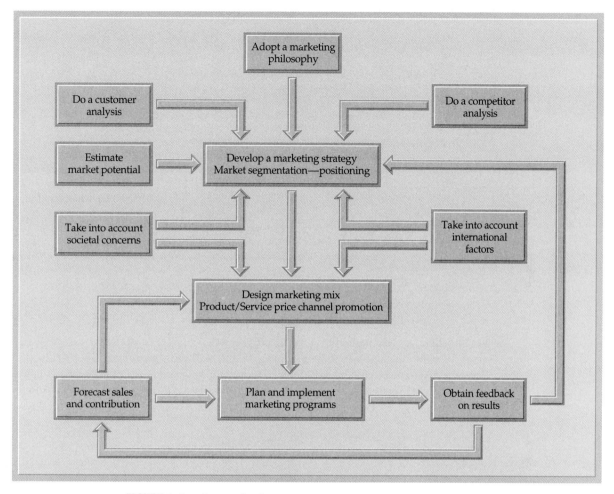

FIGURE 1-4 The Marketing Management Process

Second in the management process is a concern with marketing strategy (Chapter 2): our emphasis is on achieving a sustainable competitive advantage for the organization. A problem-solving approach is used throughout the book and the cases at the end of the chapters provide opportunities to apply what you have learned.

Customer Focus

Before sound marketing strategies can be created (Figure 1-4), you have to know who your potential and/or existing customers are and why they behave as they do (Chapter 3). In developing marketing strategies, the manager must select appropriate market segments to be targets of the marketing effort (Chapter 4). You also have to understand your competitors and where they are going (Chapter 5). A critical decision here is how your organization's offerings should be positioned against those of your competitors. Perhaps the most creative and challenging step in marketing is designing the right mix of marketing activities to tap the target segments. The *marketing mix* is the specific collection of actions and associated instruments employed by an organization to stimulate acceptance of its ideas, products, or services (Table 1-4). The basic functions included in the mix are product development and policymaking, pricing, channel selection and control, and marketing communications—per-

TABLE 1-4   Marketing Mix

Element	Description	Examples
Product	Instruments that mainly aim at the satisfaction of the prospective exchange party's needs	Product characteristics, options, assortments, brand name, packaging, quantity, factory guarantee
Price	Instruments that mainly fix the size and method of payment for goods or services	List price, usual terms of payment, usual quantity discounts, terms of credit
Distribution	Instruments that determine the intensity and manner in which goods or services will be made available	Different types of distribution channels, density of distribution system, trade relation mix, merchandising advice
Marketing communications		
Personal selling	Face-to-face, personal communication efforts	Amount and type of selling, compensation plans
Direct marketing	Other one-to-one communication efforts	Number of direct-mail pieces and telephone calls
Advertising	Mass communication efforts	Theme advertising in various media, permanent exhibits

Source: Based on Walter van Waterschoot and Christophe Van den Bulte, "The 4P Classification of the Marketing Mix Revisited," *Journal of Marketing,* Vol. 56, No. 4 (October 1992), pp. 83–93.

sonal selling, direct marketing, and advertising. The term *marketing mix* can be used to describe either the activity, such as pricing, or the marketing instrument, such as list price. When trying to determine the best marketing mix for your product, you face a large number of alternatives. The only way to reduce these alternatives to a manageable number is to take a strategic focus. That is one reason why we emphasize strategy in a marketing management book.

New Products

Product development activities focus on the conversion of customers' wants into real products or services (Chapter 6). Since existing products and services lose their attractiveness over time, product development is essential to the survival of all organizations. Marketing managers are responsible for designing the systems needed to find, screen, and evaluate new ideas. Product policy (Chapter 7) emphasizes the management of a product over its life cycle. This involves reformulating old products and getting rid of some of them. Since more money is being spent in highly industrialized countries of the world on services than on manufactured goods, the special marketing needs of intangible merchandise are discussed (Chapter 8).

A critical dimension of your job as marketing manager is making decisions on what prices to charge for goods and services to generate desired levels of sales (Chapter 9). Marketing also has the task of organizing brokers, wholesalers, and retailers into channels of distribution so that merchandise and services will be available where customers need and want them (Chapter 10). Personal selling (Chapter 11) is required for many products, and marketing managers have the job of hiring, training, and deploying the right number of salespeople to meet the needs of potential buyers. Direct marketing (Chapter 12) has become increasingly important with the creation of large databases. Direct marketing includes telephone marketing, direct mail, and the Internet. Advertising (Chapter 13) focuses on nonpersonal communication through measured media. This means that you have to choose among newspapers, radio, television, billboards, direct mail, and magazines. Sales promotions and public relations (Chapter 14) support the basic marketing mix. You must determine budgets for point-of-purchase displays, contests, and other promotional activities.

Building the Plan

After an appropriate marketing mix has been selected, it is your job as marketing manager to prepare and implement a detailed marketing plan. Vital to developing marketing strategies and tactics today is the international dimension (Chapter 15). The production and marketing of many goods are now on a global basis, which leads firms to consider the impact of such things as cultural differences and currency exchange rates on pricing and distribution plans. Responsibility for implementing marketing programs (Chapter 16) rests with brand managers, who continually monitor the results of marketing activities and recommend program improvements.

Although we have shown marketing management as a sequence of steps that follow the chapters of this book, you should realize that brand managers often work on several of these activities at the same time. Also, feedback in terms of results and customer reactions provides continuous inputs for strategy revisions and updated sales forecasts (Figure 1-4). Marketing management is a highly interactive process, and your success as a marketing professional will depend on your ability to coordinate and work through others.

The marketing management process begins with the adoption of the marketing philosophy. We will now focus on what makes a firm marketing driven.

THE MARKETING CONCEPT

Organizations must adapt to changing economic environments and meet competitive threats to prevent loss of market share, stagnation, and perhaps even bankruptcy. Some companies take an operations orientation. They are primarily concerned with cost cutting and production. Others are technology driven. They want to do something new and exciting. Both may founder because they ignore their customers or their competition.

The belief that organizational goals can be reached by satisfying customers has grown so much in importance among managers that it has become known as the *marketing concept.* The marketing concept is a business philosophy that maintains that the key to achieving organizational goals is to determine the needs of target markets and deliver the desired merchandise more efficiently than do competitors. This idea of focusing a whole organization on attending to customer needs has gained widespread acceptance among managers. Three important dimensions of the marketing concept that you must understand are these:

1. A customer orientation
2. An integrated company effort
3. Goal-directed behavior

Although these three factors interact to help improve marketing activities, they will be discussed separately.

A Customer Orientation

The basic idea of the marketing concept is to give customers what they want. This means that organizations must decide who their target customers are and then determine their wants and needs. The net result should be the creation of goods and services that satisfy customers' expectations.

The advantages of a customer orientation seem so obvious that it is hard to understand why the concept has not been more widely adopted. However, some organizations still take a very narrow view of their mission, a problem that has been called *marketing myopia.* Banks, for example, once thought of themselves as protectors of their customers' money. They hid behind bars, and their hours were from 10:00 A.M. to 3:00 P.M. a few days a week.

Following the marketing concept, banks have added branch locations that are open on Saturdays, have extended weekday hours, and feature drive-up windows. They have also installed 24-hour teller machines that dispense cash and perform other services to serve customers better. Now you can even do your banking over the Internet.

An Integrated Company Effort

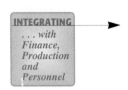

A second dimension of the marketing concept suggests that marketing activities should be closely coordinated with each other and with the other functional areas of the organization. Under the marketing concept, sales, finance, production, and personnel all work together to satisfy customers' needs. With the production orientation, production emphasizes rigid schedules so that costs could be kept low through long production runs. If the sales department said that a customer needed 21-day delivery of 100,000 cases of perfumed, two-color facial tissues in boutique boxes, the likely answer was that it couldn't be done because it would raise costs. Under the marketing concept, the major task of the production department is to learn how to rearrange schedules to meet customers' needs at an acceptable cost. One result has been the emergence of flexible manufacturing systems.

In the past, marketing has emphasized sales goals, production has attempted to minimize costs, and R&D has been concerned with unique ways to apply technology. Although these objectives may be useful performance standards for individual departments, they are incompatible with the marketing concept, and it is unlikely that the goals of the firm will be achieved when they are pursued separately. The objective should be to operate each part of the firm in order to reach overall targets. The marketing concept has been a useful mechanism in helping to unify the independent functional areas to increase customer satisfaction and improve profits.

Goal-Directed Behavior

The third objective of the marketing concept is that behavior should be directed at achieving the goals of the organization.[4] This means that marketing plans and corporate goals must be closely coordinated. Firms are focusing more and more on creating value for shareholders rather than simply accumulating profits. Nonetheless, short-term profitability remains a key objective for most firms. Activity based costing (ABC) expressly links the true cost of marketing, selling, and servicing each customer to determine how much profit each produces. One consequence is that firms do not treat all customers equally, as illustrated in Marketing in Action box 1-4.[5]

In the case of nonprofit organizations, objectives are usually stated more broadly. For example, one goal of the U.S. Army is to get recruits and reenlistments, municipal bus lines try to make their services as convenient as possible to maximize the number of passengers, and the goal of Big Brother – Big Sister programs is to get volunteers to contribute their time.

Organizations often have multiple goals. While community orchestras seek to enhance their audiences' appreciation of music, they also must sell enough seats to meet their operating expenses. This means that they need to offer young people's concerts to make sure that future generations will support the orchestra. Also community orchestras must balance their programs with a mix of new selections to educate customers and enough traditional favorites to maintain financial support.

Implementing the Marketing Concept

One of the most successful advocates of the marketing concept is the highly profitable Wal-Mart retail chain. At Wal-Mart, customers come first and are welcomed at the door

MARKETING IN ACTION *1-4*

The Non-Egalitarian Approach to Customers

APPLYING
. . . to
Financial
Services
Marketing

Fielding phone calls at First Union Corp.'s huge customer-service center in Charlotte, North Carolina, Amy Hathcock is surrounded by reminders to deliver the personal touch. Televisions hang from the ceiling so she can glance at the Weather Channel to see if her latest caller just came in from the rain; a bumper sticker in her cubicle encourages, "Practice random kindness and senseless acts of beauty." But when it comes to answering yes or no to a customer who wants a lower credit card interest rate or to escape the bank's bounced-check fee, there is nothing random about it. The service all depends on the color of a tiny square—green, yellow or red—that pops up on Ms. Hathcock's computer screen next to the customer's name. For customers who get a red pop-up, Ms. Hathcock rarely budges—these are the ones whose accounts lose money for the bank. Green means the customers generate hefty profits for First Union and should be granted waivers. Yellow is for in-between customers; there's a chance to negotiate. The bank's computer system, called "Einstein," takes just 15 seconds to pull up the ranking on a customer, using a formula based on minimum balances, account activity, branch visits and other variables.

INTEGRATING
. . . with
Information
Technology
Management

"Everyone isn't all the same anymore," says Steven G. Boehm, general manager of First Union's customer-information center where agents will handle about 45 million customer calls this year. After years of casting a wide net to lure as many consumers as possible, banks and many other industries are becoming increasingly selective, limiting their hunt to "profitable" customers and doing away with "loss-leaders." Wielding ever-more-powerful computer systems, they are aggressively mining their vast databases to weed out losers, or at least to charge them more, and to target the best customers for pampering.

For banks, a typical "bad" customer makes frequent branch visits, keeps less than $1,000 in the bank and calls often to check on account balances. The most profitable customers, who keep several thousand dollars in their accounts, use a teller less than once a month and hardly ever use the call center. And while favored customers generate more than $1,000 in profits apiece each year, the worst customers often cost the bank money—a minimum of $500 a year.

What's more, the top 20 percent of typical bank customers produce as much as 150 percent of overall profit, while the bottom 20 percent of customers drain about 50 percent from the bank's bottom line, according to Market Line Associates, an Atlanta bank-consulting firm.

First Union, the sixth-largest bank in the United States, estimates its Einstein system will add at least $100 million in annual revenue, or less than one percent of its 1997 total revenue of about $12 billion. About half of that increase is expected to come from extra fees and other revenue from unprofitable customers, and from holding on to preferred customers who might otherwise leave the bank if not for the extra pampering.

First Union acknowledges that it is still figuring out how to track profits generated by its new strategy. "It's not so much that it can't be done, but we need to refine the mechanism," says Sandy Deem, a First Union spokeswoman. Part of the problem is that most banks haven't married their disparate computer systems. While one database may track how many times a customer visits ATMs, how much the bank spends on marketing to get that person there might be in another system, with a third system estimating how much interest income an account generates.

The profit obsession, of course, has many risks. For one, future profits are hard to predict. A high-school student on his way to an engineering degree, a master's degree in management of technology, and a plum job in a high technology industry might be worth courting. So might an unprofitable customer who suddenly inherits a lot of money and wants to purchase certificates of deposit or other financial products

— *A policy of bending over backwards for your most profitable customers pays off, but at the risk of straining relations with nonpreferred customers.*

Source: Rick Brooks, "Alienating Customers Isn't Always a Bad Idea, Many Firms Discover," *Wall Street Journal,* January 7, 1999, pp. A1,A12.

APPLYING
. . . to
Retailing

by people greeters; once inside, hourly employees (called associates) approach customers and ask how they can help, and checkout lines are kept short. The whole operation is designed to be responsive to customers' needs. In addition, most senior managers spend four days a week on the road making sure that the 1300 stores are clean and operating smoothly. Wal-Mart helps to integrate company activities by sharing cost, freight, and profit margin data with department heads and hourly associates. Also, when a store's profit goal is exceeded, the hourly associates share in the additional profit. To help control losses from damage and theft, Wal-Mart has instituted a shrinkage bonus when employees keep store losses below company goals. Group harmony is fostered by encouraging troubled employees to talk about their problems with management. Wal-Mart has shown that when employees work together to meet customers' needs, they are better able to meet company sales and profit goals.

Marketing-driven firms must always keep in mind the interests of all the players with whom they interact: customers, channel members, competitors, regulators, and society as a whole. The ultimate success of a firm rests on obtaining sustainable competitive advantages based on long-run customer and channel franchises.

MARKETING AND SOCIETY

Some people question whether the marketing concept is an appropriate organizational theme in an era of environmental deterioration, poverty, and neglected social services. Is society better off when firms sell goods to satisfy individual wants and needs or should marketing managers adopt a longer-run goal of maximizing human welfare? Perhaps we should use a broader definition of the marketing concept:

> The societal marketing concept holds that the organization's task is to determine the needs, wants, and interests of target markets and to deliver the desired satisfactions more effectively and efficiently than competitors in a way that preserves or enhances the consumer's and the society's well-being.[6]

This definition asks marketers to balance customers' wants, company profits, and the public interest. Instead of just maximizing profits, marketing managers are beginning to consider the interests of society when they make decisions. The relative positions of marketing and several environmental variables are highlighted in Figure 1-5. We show marketing plans surrounded by the marketing mix variables under your control. However, most of the factors in the outer ring cannot be changed by individual organizations. You are generally at the mercy of economic conditions and international trade agreements. You also have little control over changes in consumer tastes and the actions of competitors. Two areas that are influenced by marketing activities are responsible marketing conduct, such as environmental responsibility, and business ethics.

Responsible Marketing Conduct

In our rush to create products that sell, we sometimes select packaging that is bulky and does not degrade over time. Marketing is often blamed for the mountains of trash that are filling up landfills, polluting our rivers, and desecrating the landscape. The "green" movement believes that the answer is for business to produce more environmentally safe products. However, sales of products that help the environment have been slow. One problem is that recycled paper and other green items often cost more. Although people say they will pay 7 to 20 percent more for green merchandise, this sentiment has not held up at the cash register. Also, some people do not like the performance or texture of recycled paper and other household products. Some tissue, for instance, isn't as soft.

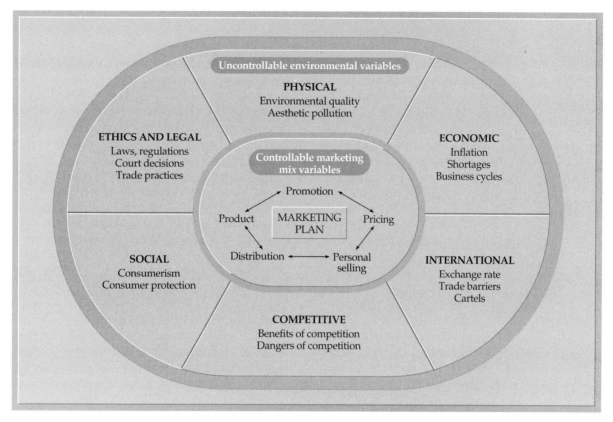

FIGURE 1-5   **Societal & Environmental Factors Impacting Marketing Programs**

APPLYING
... to
Consumer
Packaged
Goods
Marketing

The dilemma for marketers is to find ways to help the environment, satisfy customers, and make a profit. A popular solution is to make packages smaller. This is not as easy as it appears because smaller packages are harder to see in the store and offer less space for promotional messages. Procter & Gamble (P&G) has had some success in Europe with refills for cleaners and detergents that come in throwaway pouches. These have not worked in the United States and the trend is to a reduction in package sizes. For example, P&G has devised a concentrated Ultra Tide powdered detergent that provides savings for both the manufacturer and the retailer. Consumers get a smaller box to carry around, but the cost per wash is somewhat higher. Other successful green programs include the replacement of Styrofoam hamburger containers with cardboard boxes by McDonalds. Also, P&G has eliminated the cartons from Secret and Sure deodorants, keeping 80 million cartons from going to the landfill. These examples show that creative managers can find ways to balance customer wants, environmental needs and profitability. This approach is known as *green marketing*.

Environmentalism is only one aspect of responsible marketing conduct. Yes, you should design your products for recyclability where possible. Also, products should be reusable without discarding, but they also must be built with integrity and quality for safety, accessibility by the disabled, longevity, and more. A second problem area is knowing what marketing tactics are ethically acceptable.

Business Ethics

Business ethics is a set of standards governing the conduct of members of the business community. These standards evolve from interactions among businesspeople and reflect how firms expect to be treated by others. In recent years, the drive for short-term profits has been a major threat to American business ethics. When the next quarter's bottom line outweighs all other considerations, ethical shortcuts lead to insider trading and payoffs.

You should understand that companies are not unethical; people are unethical. This implies that if you hire the right employees—people with principles—you are ahead of the game. However, even the right people can go wrong if they are not given proper guidance in moral decision making. A common problem is that standard company solutions simply do not work. Often there are no applicable laws or court decisions to guide you in specific situations, and actions must be taken in the "twilight zone" between the clearly right and the clearly wrong.

SUMMARY

Our book is concerned with showing you how managers develop marketing plans and manipulate marketing variables to meet long-run customer needs in the presence of business rivals. We believe marketing managers are the driving entrepreneurial force that allows organizations to compete successfully in the race for customer acceptance.

This chapter has introduced you to the role of the marketing manager in business and non-profit organizations. The basic functions of marketing have been described as planning, pricing, promoting, and distributing goods and services to customers. We suggest that organizations must have a marketing focus if they expect to succeed. One such philosophy, called the marketing concept, helps organizations achieve their goals by emphasizing customer satisfaction through close coordination of marketing with the other operating areas of the institution.

Marketing activities must also be coordinated with a number of environmental factors that are largely outside the control of individual organizations. This means that organizations need to spend more time educating their employees about which marketing activities are ethical and making sure that products are safe before they are introduced.

Marketing is a creative and ever-changing occupation with few rules. The position of marketing manager is stimulating because you associate with a wide variety of people in a continuously changing environment. Moreover, marketing management is an excellent training ground for advanced assignments within any organization. Because marketing managers have to work with so many areas of the firm, they are often tapped for positions as general managers. Research has shown that marketing jobs offer the fastest route to the top. Today organizations are turning away from the financial executives, engineers, and lawyers once favored for CEOs and are looking to marketing managers to provide leadership for the future. We believe that marketing is the path to your own marketability.

NOTES

1. Adapted from the official definition of marketing prepared by the American Marketing Association.
2. This section draws heavily on Frederick E. Webster, Jr., "The Changing Role of Marketing in the Corporation," *Journal of Marketing,* Vol. 56, No. 4 (October 1992), pp. 1-17 and Roderick J. Brodie, Nicole E. Coviello, Richard W. Brookes, and Victoria Little, "Toward a Paradigm Shift in Marketing? An Examination of Current Marketing Practices," *Journal of Marketing Management,* Vol. 13, No. 5 (July 1997), pp. 383–406.
3. C. Gronroos, "The Rebirth of Marketing: Six Propositions about Relationship Marketing," Swedish School of Economics and Business Administration, working paper 307, Helsinki, 1995.
4. Selection of goals determines success criteria. See Tom Ambler and Flora Kokkinaki, "Measures of Marketing Success," *Journal of Marketing Management,* Vol. 13, No. 7 (October 1997), pp. 665–678.

5. Bob Donath, "Fire Your Big Customers? Maybe You Should," *Marketing News,* June 21, 1999, p. 9.

6. Philip Kotler, *Marketing Management,* 9th ed., Prentice-Hall, 1997, p. 27.

SUGGESTED READING

Berthon, Pierre, James M. Hulbert, and Leyland F. Pitt. "Brand Management Prognostications," *Sloan Management Review,* Vol. 40, No. 2 (Winter 1999), pp. 63–65.

de Mortanges, Charles P., Jan-Willem Rietbroek, and Cort M. Johns. "Marketing Pharmaceuticals in Japan: Background and the Experience of U.S. Firms," *European Journal of Marketing,* Vol. 31, No. 8 (1997), pp. 36–51.

Han, Jin K., Namwoon Kim, and Rajendra K. Srivastava. "Market Orientation and Organizational Performance: Is Innovation a Missing Link?" *Journal of Marketing,* Vol. 62, No. 4 (October 1998), pp. 30–31.

Homburg, Christian, John P. Workman Jr., and Harley Krohmer, "Marketing's Influence within the Firm," *Journal of Marketing,* Vol. 63, No. 2 (April 1999), pp. 1–17.

van Waterschoot, Walter, and Christophe Van den Bulte. "The 4P Classification of the Marketing Mix Revisited," *Journal of Marketing,* Vol. 56 (October 1992), pp. 83–93.

Webster, Jr., Frederick E. "The Changing Role of Marketing in the Corporation," *Journal of Marketing,* Vol. 56, No. 4 (October 1992), pp. 1–17.

REFERENCES

Hankinson, Graham and Philippa Cowling. "Branding in Practice: The Profile and Role of Brand Managers in the U.K." *Journal of Marketing Management,* Vol. 4 (May 1997), pp. 239–264.

Partridge, Mike and Lew Perren. "An Integrated Framework for Activity-Based Decision Making," *Management Decision,* Vol. 36, No. 9 (1998), pp. 580–588.

Srivastava, Rajendra K, Tasadduq A. Shervani, and Liam Fahey. "Market-Based Assets and Shareholder Value: A Framework for Analysis," *Journal of Marketing,* Vol. 62, No. 1 (January 1998), pp. 2–18.

Turner, Gregory B. and Barbara Spencer. "Understanding the Marketing Concept as Organizational Culture," *European Journal of Marketing,* Vol. 31, No. 2 (1997), pp. 110–121.

Wethey, David. "Is It Really Marketing versus Finance?" *Admap,* Vol. 34, No. 1 (January 1999), pp. 46–48.

QUESTIONS

1. Why has the emphasis in marketing moved from exchanges to relationships?

2. Alitalia Airlines and Starwood Hotels & Resorts Worldwide teamed up with a cross promotion backed by a $1 million ad campaign. For three months (January through March), a print ad featuring the stained glass dome above the posh lobby of Madrid's Palace Hotel ran in a dozen upscale publications including *Architectural Digest, Bon Appetit, W,* and *Town & Country* with the headline, "No Wonder the Rich Get Richer." Body text explained that travelers who flew Alitalia Magnifica class to Europe, Africa, and the Middle East and stayed three nights in any participating hotel in Starwood's Luxury Collection would receive a fourth night free. The deal included breakfast, hotel taxes, and tips. Magnifica is the Italian carrier's new brand for its in-flight service and vacation packages. Amenities include chauffeur service from the airport, leather seats with lots of legroom, and gourmet Italian food and wine. The Luxury Collection is Starwood's roster of more than 50 tony hotels such as the St. Regis in New York. What is the purpose of this tie-in for each company?

3. Give another marketing example of each of the 10 roles a manager plays.

4. Is media selection a good use of a brand manager's time?

5. The marketing concept defines a specific organizational culture—a shared set of beliefs and values centered on the importance of the customer in the organization's strategy and operations. How can managers create, preserve, or change organizational values and behaviors to implement the marketing concept?

6. Social critics have charged that "Marketers are the primary source of false consciousness. This is because they refocus people's thoughts away from reinforcing personal bonds toward acquiring material possessions, from community sharing resources to selfishly hoarding them, and from feeling empathy with other persons to wanting to feel superior to them." How would you respond?

7. Prepaid cellular phone service plans have caught on with drug dealers and other criminals. With no contract and no bills, there is no paper trail—a feature that also makes the service attractive to tax evaders. What is the responsibility of marketers when making products that may facilitate illegal activities?

8. Not long ago, Nestlé Company, of White Plains, New York, became the target of a U.S. consumer boycott sponsored by a group called the Infant Formula Action Coalition (INFACT). INFACT was concerned about the sales techniques used to sell powdered infant formula in third world countries. INFACT claimed that Nestlé's baby product division used uniformed "milk nurses" to promote the product together with free samples and magazine and radio ads. INFACT believed that the general lack of pure water in third world countries made the powdered infant formula more dangerous than mother's milk. Because the infant formula is not sold in the United States, should Nestlé Company of White Plains be concerned about INFACT? If so, how should Nestlé respond to the boycott?

9. Pager Networks Inc., a paging service provider, for several years essentially gave away its pagers in a race to build market share. In the process, it attracted heavy users who receive a flurry of messages but often pay only a rock-bottom monthly fee. How should PageNet address this situation?

10. Nabisco, in a cost-cutting mode, killed its slow-selling Crown Pilot cracker. The cracker was sold only in New England, where it was mostly munched with New England clam chowder. Consumers protested with more than 3,500 angry calls and letters. What should Nabisco do?

CASE 1-1   THE CASE METHOD

The objective of the case method is to introduce a measure of realism into business education. A case approach forces you to deal with problems as they actually occur in a for profit or a not-for-profit organization. Each case is simply a written description of the facts surrounding a particular business situation. With the case approach, it is your responsibility to develop solutions to the problem. Instructors, for example, may set the stage for the case discussion by providing background material or by helping you gain insight into the problem. They may also act as devil's advocates and as critics to test arguments and proposals that you put forth. Finally, they evaluate your performance, assign grades, and make suggestions for improvement.

BENEFITS AND LIMITATIONS

The case method becomes an effective teaching device when students are encouraged to analyze the data presented and to formulate their own sets of recommendations. Because each case is different, the solution that is developed for one case cannot be randomly applied to another. This raises the question of what you actually learn by working with business cases. One obvious benefit is that preparation and discussion of case studies helps you improve your skills in oral and written expression. In addition, the case method provides an easy way to learn about current business practices. Perhaps the most important advantage of the case method is the experience it provides in thinking logically about different sets of data. The development of your analytical ability and judgment is the most valuable and lasting benefit derived from working with business cases.

Most cases, including those in this book, are drawn from the experiences of real firms. The names and locations may be disguised to protect the interests of the companies involved. In addition, final decisions are usually omitted to enhance the problem-solving orientation of the cases, thus permitting you to reach your own conclusions without being forced to criticize the actions taken by others. The case method departs from the typical business situation in that the business executive usually does not have the facts presented as clearly and as neatly as they are in casebooks. Problem solving in business usually involves extensive data collection, something that has been essentially completed for you.

A FRAMEWORK FOR ANALYSIS

You can approach the analysis of business cases in many different ways. Each instructor has his or her own ideas on the number and nature of the steps involved. We believe the following six-step procedure is a logical and practical way to begin.

1. Define the problem.
2. Formulate the alternatives.
3. Analyze the alternatives.
4. Recommend a solution.
5. Specify a plan of action.
6. Prepare contingency plans.

Defining the Problem

Once you are familiar with the facts of the case, you should isolate the central problem. Until this is done, it is usually impossible to proceed with an effective analysis. Sometimes instructors provide questions to help you start your analysis. You should look at questions as guides for action rather than as specific issues to be resolved. All cases should be considered as problems in the management of the marketing mix, not as specific issues concerned only with some narrow phase of management.

We use the term *problem* loosely and employ it to indicate a state of nature that may involve either a negative situation possibly requiring corrective action or simply a situation needing opportunity assessment. You must distinguish between problems and symptoms of problems. Declining sales, market share, or profits are symptoms of more fundamental underlying

problems that are their cause. Any business situation may pose multiple problems. The key to solving unstructured problems is to identify the one that must be solved first, the one whose solution will either eliminate other problems or permit their solution. We are usually interested in solving the most immediate critical problem. For example, we may have problems with the introduction of a new product, problems that have been created by a poor new product development process. Our immediate concern, however, is with addressing the difficulties of the newly launched product. We may well recommended an evaluation of the firm's new product development process, but we will leave that for future study. Note that the central problem is a state of nature. A statement of it should not contain any action verbs (i.e., *to do* is part of the plan of action). Nor should it contain the words *or* and *and,* which are, respectively, part of the statement of alternatives, and an indication of compound problems and lack of identification of *the* central problem.

Selecting the Alternatives

The second step is to define possible alternatives available to resolve the problem. Some of these alternatives may be obvious from the material supplied in the case and from the statement of the main issue. Others may have to be supplied from your own review of the situation. You should be careful to limit your analysis to a reasonable number of alternatives. Three or four alternatives are usually sufficient for a typical case. One alternative that should always be considered is the maintenance of the status quo. Sometimes doing what you have been doing is the best course of action.

Analyzing the Alternatives

The heart of the case method is the analysis of alternatives. To analyze is to separate into parts so as to find out the nature, proportion, function, and underlying relationships among a set of variables. Thus, to analyze is to dig into, and work with, the facts to uncover associations that may be used to evaluate possible courses of action. Your analysis should begin with a careful evaluation of the facts presented in the case. You should be sensitive to the problem of sorting relevant material from that which is peripheral or irrelevant. In reviewing a case, you must be careful to distinguish between fact and opinion. You must also make sure that the facts are consistent and reliable. Some cases may contain errors, and the instructor may prefer to remain silent.

You are expected to base your analysis on the evidence presented in the case, but this does not mean that other information cannot be used. You should utilize facts that are available to the trade and information that is general or public knowledge. You should incorporate relevant concepts from other disciplines, such as accounting, statistics, economics, psychology, and sociology. The criterion in using outside material is that it must be appropriate to the particular situation. For example, do not use census data for 2000 to make decisions in a case dated 1995. For this book we have attempted to select cases that provide you with enough information to complete the analysis. In some situations, however, you may wish to collect additional materials from the library.

Sometimes the most important facts in the case are buried in some chance remark or seemingly minor statistical exhibit. Be careful to sift through the data to uncover all the relationships that apply to the alternatives being considered. This means that the quantitative information must be examined using a variety of ratios, graphs, tables, or other forms of analysis. Rarely are the data supplied in the case in the form most appropriate to finding a solution, and instructors expect students to work out the numbers.

Marketing analyses are usually based on incomplete information. Assumptions must be made.[1] However, they should be made only when necessary and must be clearly labeled as such. Moreover, a rationale should be given for any assumption made. For example, a retail chain stops carrying one of your product lines but continues carrying another. You are interested in what your sales of the dropped product line would have been. You might note that over the past few years the ratio of the sales of the two product lines had been relatively constant. You could assume that the ratio would have remained the same for the current year as well, and multiply this ratio by the current year's sales of the continuing product line to estimate sales of the discontinued line in that chain. Or perhaps you would calculate the lowest and highest ratios over recent history to calculate conservative and optimistic estimates of lost sales. In any case, at the end of any decision-making exercise, you always want to review your assumptions to see how dependent your conclusions are on the assumptions made. (At one extreme, you could assume away the problem!) You should make contingency plans in the event that major assumptions do not hold.

You should realize that a complete analysis is not one-sided. A review of a business situation is not sound unless both sides of important issues are examined. This does not necessarily mean that every point must be mentioned, but major opposing arguments should be addressed where possible. You will find it helpful to explicitly list the pros and cons or advantages and disadvantages of each alternative.

Making Recommendations

After you have carefully analyzed the data and alternatives, you are in a position to make recommendations. Sometimes more than one course of action will look attractive. This is not an unusual situation, as most cases do not have a single right answer. Still, you must come up with a concrete proposal. To arrive at a solution, you should judge the relative risks and opportunities offered by the various alternatives. The optimum choice is the one that provides the best balance between profit opportunities and the risks and costs of failure. Make a clear-cut decision, and avoid qualifications and other obvious hedges. Instructors are much more concerned with how a particular decision was reached than with what alternative was selected.

Students sometimes review the facts and decide that they do not have enough information to reach a decision. They recommend that the decision be postponed pending the results of further research. Usually, "get more information" is not an acceptable solution to a business case. Decisions cannot wait the length of time necessary to conduct good research. In addition, it is unlikely that you will ever have all the information you think you need. Because of the cost of research and the penalties of delay, business decisions are almost always made under conditions of uncertainty.

Specifying a Plan of Action

Having made your decision, how are you going to implement it? You should suggest, in as much detail as the case allows, what actions you would take, when they would be taken, and how much they would cost. You may want to provide pro forma income statements, and other relevant supporting material. Once you have proposed your actions, you would do well to reflect on the potential market reactions to them, especially competitive reactions. These possible reactions might lead you to modify your actions.

If you judge that collecting additional information is the only feasible means of solving a case, you must provide support for this decision. First, you should

---

[1] In most large companies, a corporate planning group provides certain forecasts, assumptions, and planning premises so that everyone in the company is using the same numbers, for instance, on future inflation rates. These tend to be long documents and are not included in casebooks.

state exactly what the research will show and how this information will be used. In addition, you should indicate the research methodology to be followed and the anticipated cost of the study. After you have completed these tasks, you will be in a better position to decide whether additional research is needed. Remember, managers should have a predisposition to act and then adapt, rather than to procrastinate.

Preparing Contingency Plans

When you make a decision, it is based on the facts at hand, as well as on your expectations about the future that you hold at that point in time. Since the future does not always unfold as we expect or wish, we must be prepared for any significant alternative future scenario. You must ask yourself what you will do if the market does not respond to your marketing actions as you anticipate, if competitors take actions that deviate from their usual behavior, if the economy is different than economists have forecasted, and so on.

WRITING THE REPORT

We believe that students who prepare written reports do a better job of analyzing business problems. Writing a good report takes a certain skill, and we would like to suggest a few ideas that may be of help.

When instructors read reports, they check to see whether students fully understand the situation and whether student interpretations of the facts are reasonable. They also like to see papers that are objective, balanced, consistent, and decisive. Perhaps the most common error made by students in writing case reports is to repeat the facts that have been provided. Instead of analyzing the data in light of alternatives, students frequently repeat statements that appear in the cases, with no clear objective in mind. Nothing upsets an instructor more than reading a paper that devotes sev-

eral pages to explaining what he or she already knows about the case.

Another deficiency often observed in writing reports is lack of organization. Students who make this error begin with the first thought that enters their minds and continue, in almost random fashion, until they run out of ideas. The end result is a paper that has no beginning and no end, and often consists of one long paragraph. To avoid this problem, some instructors require that reports be presented in outline form. However, the condensed nature of such reports sometimes makes them hard to follow. Therefore, we prefer the more readable narrative approach.

There is no optimal length for a written case analysis. It depends on the amount of data provided, the preferences of the instructor, and the number of case reports the student turns in during the course. The report should be long enough to cover the subject adequately. It is fairly obvious that written reports must be neat, legible, and free of grammatical and spelling errors. Business professors are not hired to teach English composition, but they do expect certain minimal standards of performance in written expression. Their standards for written work reflect what the business community expects from college graduates.

SUMMARY

Case analysis is designed to give you an opportunity to develop a productive and meaningful way of thinking about business problems. The case method helps train you to use logic to solve realistic business issues. Remember, however, that solutions are worthless unless they can be sold to those who are in a position to act on the recommendations. The case approach provides you with practical experience in convincing others of the soundness of your reasoning.

CASE *1-2* SKYWARD AVIATION–ROUTE EXPANSION*

IVEY

O n Monday, June 6, 1995, Frank Behrendt, president of Skyward Aviation (Skyward), laid out the task for J. M. Smith, manager of business and corporate development:

> Calm Air is making a lot of money and Canadian North may be pulling jet service out of Thompson. Business travellers are sick and tired of getting up really early to catch a 7:00 a.m. flight out of Winnipeg to Thompson. Consumers are also tired of paying exorbitant fares. I think we should offer scheduled service into Winnipeg and other communities in Manitoba. I want you to see if this will work and present your findings and a marketing plan at the July 15 Board of Directors' meeting.

Skyward Aviation was a regional aviation company providing scheduled, charter and aeromedical service. Skyward was based in Thompson, Manitoba, Canada, with additional aircraft and offices in Winnipeg, Manitoba; Norway House, Manitoba; and Rankin Inlet, Northwest Territories.

COMPANY HISTORY

Thompson, Manitoba, was a city of 22,000 people, located in central northern Manitoba and known as "the Hub of the North." The main industries of Thompson included a large nickel mine (International Nickel Company, Inco), transportation and government.

Skyward was founded January 2, 1987, when three partners purchased a small local air service that was almost bankrupt. Skyward began with five aircraft, a hangar, a small office building and fifteen employees. Frank Behrendt, one of the partners and a pilot in northern Canada for a number of years, was appointed president. Prior to the purchase, the company provided an air charter service for passengers, carried freight and performed the occasional medical evacuation from outlying communities around Thompson.

Because of the company's poor reputation, the new partners wanted to deal with some of the obvious weaknesses of its operations. Customers had been unhappy with the level of service, the aircraft were aging, and the aircraft came from three different manufacturers. This had resulted in plummeting revenue, high maintenance costs and high inventory carrying loss. The partners immediately began a fleet renewal process, expanding the fleet with fewer aircraft from one manufacturer.

SCHEDULED SERVICE

After seeing a significant turnaround in customers' acceptance of the company, management decided to provide scheduled service to a number of communities where they had previously done a high volume of charter work. Scheduled service differed from charter service, in that a scheduled flight left a specific community on a predetermined date and time and customers reserved seats on the aircraft. Charter service required customers to reserve an aircraft for their specific use. From a business perspective, scheduled service had more risk since revenue was not guaranteed for all seats on the aircraft. Skyward began scheduled service on September 1, 1988, from Thompson (Manitoba) to York Landing (Manitoba) and to Gods River (Manitoba).

Currently, Skyward served fifteen communities in northern Manitoba and the Northwest Territories (see Exhibit 1 for the company's brochure and the system schedule for Manitoba). With the introduction of new communities, Skyward used an entry pricing strategy of 30 to 40 percent below the competition. Skyward management rationalized that prices were very high due to a lack of competition and Skyward wanted to give consumers a break. The competition responded and closed the price gap very quickly but Skyward was able to pick up a small market share.

In the spring of 1994, Skyward purchased two Embrear Banditerantes (Bandits), 15-seat aircraft. A Bandit had short takeoff and landing characteristics with a high useable weight for an aircraft in its class, ideal for the conditions in northern Manitoba. Each Bandit had a

---

* This case was prepared by Paul Peters under the supervision of Elizabeth M.A. Grasby, Pre-Business Program Director, solely to provide material for class discussion. The author does not intend to illustrate either effective or ineffective handling of a managerial situation. The author may have disguised certain names and other identifying information to protect confidentiality. One time permission to reproduce granted by Ivey Management Services on February 1, 1999. Copyright (c) 1996, The University of Western Ontario. The University prohibits any form of reproduction, storage, or transmittal without written permission from the Richard Ivey School of Business. This material is not covered under authorization from CanCopy or any other reproduction rights organization.

EXHIBIT 1   **Company Brochure and System Schedule for Manitoba**

CHARTER SERVICES:

Whether you want a fifteen minute skytour, a week long sales trip through the arctic, or to move a ton of freight, Skyward's charter services face the challenge of meeting Northern Manitoba's varied transportation needs, from freight delivery to executive transport. Skyward Aviation is there for you:

- **Freight forwarding**
- **Group charters**
- **Fly out fishing**
- **Emergency services**

SKYCARE SERVICES:

At Skyward we know the importance of professional Medevac service. Our specially trained crews, stationed in Thompson and Norway House, and our **Citation Jet** and **Cessna 421** are dedicated to provide this emergency service to the North. SkyCare is privileged to assist Northern Manitoba's health care agencies by providing a vital link to remote communities. SkyCare offers:

- **Dedicated aircraft**
- **Specialized equipment**
- **24 hour availability**
- **Aeromedically trained flight nurses & crew**

For more information on our services in Manitoba or the Keewatin district call our offices in:

Rankin Inlet

PH: 819-645-3200
FAX: 819-645-3208

Winnipeg

PH: 204-888-8664
FAX: 204-888-8665

Norway House

PH: 204-359-4900

**SKYWARD
AVIATION**

SERVING NORTHERN MANITOBA

778-7088

or

1-800-665-0638

Thompson Airport
P.O. Box 1207
Thompson, Manitoba
R8N lP1
Fax: 204-677-5945

SCHEDULE SERVICES:

DEPART FROM		ARRIVING IN		FREQUENCY
THOMPSON	08:30	OXFORD HOUSE	09:20	MON-SAT
OXFORD HOUSE	09:40	THOMPSON	10:20	
THOMPSON	14:00	OXFORD HOUSE	14:50	MON-SAT
OXFORD HOUSE	15:10	THOMPSON	16:00	
THOMPSON	10:00	YORK LANDING	10:30	MON-SAT
YORK LANDING	10:50	THOMPSON	11:20	
THOMPSON	17:15	YORK LANDING	17:45	
YORK LANDING	18:00	THOMPSON	18:30	FRI & SAT
THOMPSON	09:00	LAC BROCHET	10:20	
LAC BROCHET	10:40	BROCHET	11:00	MON, WED, FRI
BROCHET	11:15	THOMPSON	12:25	
THOMPSON	09:00	LYNN LAKE	09:55	
LYNN LAKE	10:15	BROCHET	10:50	TUES & THURS
BROCHET	11:05	LAC BROCHET	11:25	
LAC BROCHET	11:45	LYNN LAKE	12:30	
LYNN LAKE	12:50	THOMPSON	13:45	
THOMPSON	13:00	LAC BROCHET	14:20	
LAC BROCHET	14:40	BROCHET	15:00	SAT
BROCHET	15:20	THOMPSON	16:30	
THOMPSON	10:45	TADOULE	12:05	MON-SAT
TADOULE	12:25	THOMPSON	13:35	

<u>Check-in</u>: 30 prior to flight.
Skyward provides complimentary lunches on all flights over 1 hour.

SPRING 95

DEPART FROM		ARRIVING IN		FREQUENCY
THOMPSON	12:00	GODS NARROWS	13:00	
GODS NARROWS	13:20	GODS RIVER	13:45	TUES, THURS
GODS RIVER	14:00	THOMPSON	15:00	& SAT
THOMPSON	12:00	GODS RIVER	13:00	
GODS RIVER	13:20	GODS NARROWS	13:45	MON, WED, FRI
GODS NARROWS	14:00	THOMPSON	15:00	
THOMPSON	13:00	GARDEN HILL	14:10	
GARDEN HILL	14:30	ST. THERESA	14:45	MON, WED, FRI
ST. THERESA	15:00	THOMPSON	16:10	
THOMPSON	15:30	SHAMATTAWA	16:45	TUES, THURS,
SHAMATTAWA	17:05	THOMPSON	18:20	& SAT
THOMPSON	15:30	SHAMATTAWA	16:45	MON, WED, FRI
SHAMATTAWA	17:05	GILLAM	17:50	
GILLAM	18:10	THOMPSON	19:05	
THOMPSON	16:30	SOUTH INDIAN	17:05	MON-SAT
SOUTH INDIAN	17:25	THOMPSON	18:00	

<u>Baggage allowance</u>: 70 lbs per ticket
Skyward has complimentary shuttle service from your flight into Thompson

large cargo door in the back and was sent out in a configuration utilizing both freight and passengers. The freight was sent on standby so that the airplane usually realized very high load factors because the freight "topped off" the aircraft. Freight generated less revenue than passengers, but Skyward could guarantee next-day delivery into remote communities because of its daily service and could, therefore, charge a much higher per pound rate than its competitors.

It was at this time that Skyward began to focus on increasing the number of passengers and revenue per flight (yield management). By the summer of 1994, Skyward had a significant market share of scheduled traffic in and out of northern Manitoba communities and had done this with no formal advertising.

In early 1995, Skyward purchased two more Bandits. The purchase of these last two aircraft complemented the first two, because all routes could be served by Bandits. This helped enhance passenger appeal, and by June 1995, passengers carried were on target for 25 percent growth over the 1994 level of 35,000.

Skyward's growth in the scheduled service market was also attributed to aircraft flexibility and exceptional customer service. Skyward was currently operating seven types of aircraft, sixteen aircraft in total. Because of the different types of aircraft, smaller aircraft could be substituted and costs reduced if passenger and cargo loads were down on certain days.

The customer base in and out of Thompson was small and 90 percent of business was repeat customers. The employees and management of Skyward were committed to serving the customer and customers often returned to Skyward in response to that commitment. Skyward was the first carrier in Thompson to provide food on flights, offer free shuttle service into town from the airport and run errands for out-of-town customers at no charge.

Skyward's existing reservation system was very inefficient and much of the work was done manually. Skyward required all reservations and all data processing to go through the head office. If a travel agent wanted to book a passenger on a flight from Thompson to Shammattawa, the travel agent had to call Thompson and ask a Skyward agent to check availability and make the reservation. The system also did not provide the necessary marketing information for management to make effective and timely decisions.

THE MANITOBA MARKET

Over the years, Frank Behrendt had toyed with the idea of providing scheduled service to Winnipeg from Thompson, but as other opportunities had presented themselves, resources were directed to those opportunities.

Scheduled air transportation in Manitoba was currently served by four main regional carriers: Canadian North Airlines, Calm Air Ltd., Perimeter Airlines and Skyward Aviation. There were also a number of other carriers which provided scheduled service to a few communities.

Canadian North Airlines, based in Edmonton, Alberta, was a division of Canadian Airlines that provided Boeing 737 jet service (125 passengers) to a number of communities in northern Canada (Alberta, Manitoba, Northwest Territories, Quebec) (see Exhibit 2 for Canadian North system schedule for Manitoba). Because of Canadian Airlines' cash flow problems, Canadian Airlines was continually reviewing operations and restructuring to cut marginal services and reduce expenses. Routes were being turned over to regional connectors to be served with smaller turboprop aircraft. It was believed that, within the year, the routes in Manitoba would no longer be served by Boeing 737 service.

Calm Air, based in Thompson, Manitoba, was a Canadian Airlines Connector (45% ownership by Canadian Airlines) and was the largest passenger carrier in Manitoba (see Exhibit 3 for Calm Air system schedule for selected routes in Manitoba). Calm Air had had very limited competition for almost 20 years and the owners enjoyed a healthy financial position.

Perimeter Airlines served communities in southern Manitoba out of its Winnipeg base operation which was similar to Skyward Aviation. Perimeter Airlines operated 15–19 passenger aircraft and moved approximately 20,000 more passengers than Skyward.

Air transportation customers in the north could be divided into two groups: business and leisure customers. Business travellers made up 65 to 75 percent

EXHIBIT 2   Canadian Airlines North System Schedule—Manitoba

Days of the week	Origin	Destination	Times
12345	Winnipeg	Thompson	07:00–08:15
12345	Thompson	Flin Flon	08:40–09:20
12345	Flin Flon	Winnipeg	09:40–10:40
135	Winnipeg	Gillam	11:20–12:40
135	Gillam	Churchill	13:05–13:45
135	Churchill	Winnipeg	14:15–16:25
123457	Winnipeg	The Pas	17:55–19:00
123457	The Pas	Thompson	19:25–20:05
123457	Thompson	Winnipeg	20:35–21:40

EXHIBIT 3 Calm Air System Schedule—Selected Routes in Manitoba

Days of Week	Origin	Destination	Times
123456	Winnipeg	The Pas	07:30–08:59
12345	The Pas	Winnipeg	09:25–10:34
6	The Pas	Flin Flon	09:25–09:46
6	Flin Flon	Winnipeg	10:05–11:25
12345	Winnipeg	Thompson	14:20–16:05
12345	Thompson	Winnipeg	16:35–18:00
6	Thompson	Winnipeg	08:40–10:24
6	Winnipeg	Thompson	12:00–13:45
7	Winnipeg	Thompson	14:20–16:17
7	Thompson	Winnipeg	16:35–18:00
12357	Winnipeg	Flin Flon	18:30–20:00
12357	Flin Flon	Winnipeg	20:25–21:45

EXHIBIT 4 Mileage Between Selected Communities in Manitoba and the Northwest Territories

Destination	Miles
Winnipeg – Thompson	409
Winnipeg – Flin Flon	388
Winnipeg – The Pass	326
Winnipeg – Gillam	458
Winnipeg – Churchill	627
Winnipeg – Rankin Inlet	923
Thompson – Flin Flon	171
Thompson – Le Pas	207
Thompson – Gillam	127
Thompson – Churchill	249
Thompson – Rankin Inlet	526

of passengers on the considered routes. Most passengers (70 percent) travelling from Winnipeg to Thompson flew the direct flight in the morning and evening. More information needed to be gathered but it was known that passengers considered price, departure times, on-time departure, flight time, connections, food and other amenities, aircraft (size, cleanliness, appearance), employee courteousness, baggage handling and extra baggage charges as important factors in their decision. Leisure travellers usually made travel plans well in advance of flight date.

RECENT DEVELOPMENTS

In February 1995, Calm Air replaced its aging Hawker Siddely 748 (48-passenger prop aerocraft) aircraft with brand new SAAB 340B Plus (30-passenger turboprop aircraft, which were fast and comfortable) aircraft. Three more SAAB 340B Plus's were on order along with one SAAB 2000 (50-seat turboprop aircraft, the fastest turboprop on the market). With the new aircraft, Calm Air offered direct flights from Winnipeg (Manitoba) to Thompson (Manitoba), Flin Flon (Manitoba), and The Pas (Manitoba), complementing Canadian North's service. It was estimated by Skyward's management that Calm Air would realize a profit of $750,000/year on the SAAB 340. Calm Air's new afternoon flights from Thompson to Winnipeg had been successful and the Thursday and Friday flights were always full. Exhibit 4 shows the mileage between selected communities in Manitoba and the Northwest Territories. Fares and passenger loads for Calm Air and Canadian North are shown in Exhibit 5.

Calm Air was involved heavily in the community-supporting races, radio programs and other community

events. Calm Air heavily promoted the new direct service with the SAAB 340B Plus aircraft. Calm Air used the reservation system of its parent, Canadian Airlines, and American Airlines (Sabre system). This system had features such as interactive display and sell which allowed travel agents to inquire and make reservations without the requirement of personal contact with Calm Air.

The federal government, currently run by the Liberal party, as part one of its promises to aboriginal peoples of Canada in the 1994 election "Red Book," was proposing the Strategic Procurement Initiative (SPI). SPI stated that "the program is intended to apply to all procurement (purchases) by all federal government departments and agencies … as long as there is at least one qualified and available aboriginal supplier (50%-owned by aboriginal individuals), no further competition would be sought".[1] Skyward's owners were not aboriginal people. Forty percent of Skyward's current revenue was from direct federal government purchases.

EXPANDED ROUTE CONSIDERATIONS

There were a number of options to consider before making a decision to proceed with the expanded route structure.

Aircraft Decision

One alternative, which would require only minimal adjustment to existing operations, would be to use one of the Embrear Banditerantes on the Thompson to

---

[1] Public Works and Government Services document (Briefing SPI, January 1995, pp. 10,11)

EXHIBIT 5   **Fares and Passengers Boarded for Selected Routes in Northern Manitoba and Northwest Territories**

Winnipeg–Thompson

Fares (return ticket not including taxes)

Full Fare	$576
7 day Advance Fare	$495
14 day Advance Fare	$317
Average Fare	$524
*(70% full/15% 7 day/15% 14 day)	

Passengers Boarded (one way)

**Canadian North	29000
*Calm Air	12000
Total Boardings	41000

Winnipeg–The Pas

Fares (return ticket not including taxes)

Full Fare	$498
7 day Advance Fare	$428
14 day Advance Fare	$274
Average Fare	$440
(60% full/20% 7 day/20% 14 day)	

Passengers Boarded (one way)

Canadian North	7500
Calm Air	4500
Total Boardings	12000

Winnipeg–Flin Flon

Fares (return ticket not including taxes)

Full Fare	$538
7 day Advance Fare	$463
14 day Advance Fare	$296
Average Fare	$475
(60% full/20% 7 day/20% 14 day)	

Passengers Boarded (one way)

Canadian North	5200
Calm Air	7000
Total Boardings	12200

Winnipeg–Gillam

Fares (return ticket not including taxes)

Full Fare	$626
7 day Advance Fare	$538
14 day Advance Fare	$344
Average Fare	$571
*(70% full/15% 7 day/15% 14 day)	

Passengers Boarded (one way)

**Canadian North	5000
*Calm Air	1500
Total Boardings	6500

Winnipeg–Churchill

Fares (return ticket not including taxes)

Full Fare	$778
7 day Advance Fare	$669
14 day Advance Fare	$428
Average Fare	$340
(40% full/30% 7 day/30% 14 day)	

Passengers Boarded (one way)

Canadian North	7000
Calm Air	4000
Total Boardings	11000

Winnipeg–Rankin Inlet

Fares (return ticket not including taxes)

Full Fare	$1,262
7 day Advance Fare	$1,010
14 day Advance Fare	$618
Average Fare	$993
(40% full/30% 7 day/30% 14 day)	

Passengers Boarded (one way)

Canadian North	3500
Calm Air	7000
Total Boardings	10500

* Casewriter estimate
** 1993 Statistics Canada

Winnipeg route. Prior to launching this service, the aircraft would need a new interior at a cost of $10,000. This renovation could be completed in one month.

Another alternative would entail Skyward purchasing a new aircraft. Manufacturers required a lead time of four to six months for delivery of aircraft. Exhibit 6 lists cost and performance information for four appropriate turboprop aircraft, as well as Calm Air's SAAB 340B Plus and the Embrear Banditerante. With a new aircraft purchase, a number of variables would have to be considered: cost, performance, payload, and the ease with which a new aircraft could fit into existing operations.

Other Costs

A number of things would happen once a decision was made to purchase a new aircraft.

Approval from the National Transportation Agency for a "transport" category aircraft (greater than 12,500 lbs) would be needed since the aircraft would be larger

EXHIBIT 6   Aircraft Information

AIRCRAFT	DORNIER 328-110	BA JETSTREAM J41	BEACHCRAFT 1400D	SAAB 340B	EMBREAR BANDITER. "BANDIT"
Payload Passengers	30	29	19	34	15
Payload (lbs)	8118	7220	6430	7000	4664
Speed (knots)	345	250	284	272	225
Direct Operating Cost	$4.02/mile	$3.29/mile	$3.76/mile	$4.23/mile	$2.50/mile
Purchase Price Cad $	$12.0 MM	$8.1 MM	$5.4 MM	$12.5 MM	—

Note: Yearly fixed costs (include only insurance and financing costs as a percentage of purchase price) were 12.5 percent of the purchase price.

than any of Skyward's existing aircraft. Second, certain operations procedures would need to be rewritten because different regulations applied. This would also require revisions to the operations manual.

Third, the maintenance department would need to hire engineers with qualifications to maintain this type of airplane as well as purchase specialized maintenance equipment at a cost of $50,000 to $75,000. For each of the new communities Skyward would serve, Winnipeg being the exception, the company would need to invest $25,000 in ground support equipment such as ground power units, de-icing equipment and boarding/deboarding aids.

Fourth, the flight department would need to recruit and/or train pilots that would have the qualifications to fly the new aircraft. If one aircraft was purchased, five pilots and three flight attendants would need to be recruited and trained. If two aircraft were purchased, eight pilots and six flight attendants would need to be recruited and trained. Training contracts would need to be negotiated with training schools in the United States. A three-week program would cost $25,000 per crew member. The average salary with benefits for a pilot would be $52,150 and for a flight attendant would be $22,000.

With new scheduled service, the following other costs would be incurred: landing and terminal fees at all airports would be $50 per flight; food for passengers could be contracted out at $5.00 per passenger; newspapers and magazines would cost $1.00 per passenger. In Winnipeg, passenger check-in, boarding and baggage handling could be contracted from Air Canada for $120 per flight. Terminal operations in Thompson (rental, computer, communications, supplies, etc.) would cost approximately $75,000 annually, if boarding was moved from Skyward's building to the main terminal. Terminal operations in other communities would be approximately $35,000 annually.

AUTOMATING THE RESERVATION SYSTEM

Skyward was considering upgrading and automating the reservation system. Skyward had contacted Advantis Canada Ltd. to provide automation service. Advantis provided distribution (via computer) of an airline's flight schedules, gave fare information to travel agencies through the Galileo network and managed inventory (seats). The system allowed travel agents to enquire about specific seats on flights, reserve those seats and take payment from customers. With Advantis, collection of fares was done through a central banking group. Travel agents took an eight and one half percent commission for a sale. To contract Advantis costs would include a $50,000 initial one-time setup cost and communication, hardware and miscellaneous costs of $25,000 per year, $1.20 per passenger for all passengers booked (by Skyward agent or travel agent) and an additional $1.20 per passenger for passengers booked on Galileo system (travel agent). Advantis required a lead time of five months to implement the system.

The Manager of Business and Corporate Development began to review the above information to evaluate its feasibility and the time needed before beginning this new scheduled service. Skyward Aviation was a profitable company, but the size of the expansion and investment would require the majority of financing to be debt-financed. He had decisions to make about what communities to serve, the schedule, design and the pricing and promotional strategy to be implemented (Exhibit 7 gives cost information). The average North American airline spent three percent of revenue on advertising on established routes.

EXHIBIT 7   **Advertising and Promotion Costs**

Free Press
These prices were based on running an ad on the business page that is 2 columns wide (4.25″)
and 3.5″ high.

   Casual/Open Rates:

Sunday	$325.00
Monday to Friday	$625.00 per day
Saturday	$790.00

Bus Stop Benches
  $100.00 per bench per month (3-month contract required)
  $125.00 per bench for artwork/setup/installation

Hook Billboards
  $650.00 per billboard per month (drops to $600.00 for 4 billboards)
  $700.00 for artwork/set-up/installation for 2 color billboard ($900.00 total for 4 billboards)

Gallop + Gallop
It did transit-related advertising

21″ × 70″

25 GRPs (31)	$4255.00
50 GRPs (62)	$8165.00

30″ × 139″

25 GRPs (27)	$4945.00
50 GRPs (53)	$9315.00

Mediacom
It did outdoor advertising. Its rates were as follows:

Transit Shelters	4′ × 5′	$ 350.00
Billboard	10′ × 20′	$ 700.00
Superboard	10′ × 44′	$1500.00

There were the production costs on top of that. For example, the superboard would be about
$2250.00 + $11.00 per square foot for anything that juts outside of the 10′ × 44′ space.

Manitoba Business Magazine
Circulation is 8,000. For one-time advertising its rates were as follows:

1/6 page	$ 515.00 (b&w)	$ 735.00 (color)
1/3 page	$ 990.00 (b&w)	$1415.00 (color)
1/2 page	$1640.00 (b&w)	$2350.00 (color)

Weetamah
It published every two weeks. Its circulation is 9,000 in Manitoba.

1/8 page	$132.00
1/4 page	$264.00
1/3 page	$360.00
1/2 page	$540.00

Neechee Culture
It published every 2 months. Total circulation is 300,000 with 10,000 in Winnipeg and 20,000 in
Manitoba. Its rates for black & white ads were as follows:

1/8 page	$250.00
1/4 page	$460.00
1/3 page	$650.00
1/2 page	$900.00

CASE 1-3 LOBLAWS*

"*I*t's been a year since we introduced green products at Loblaws and the decisions still are not getting any easier." In early July 1990, Scott Lindsay was reflecting upon his decision as to which, if any, of three possible products he would recommend for the G·R·E·E·N line: an energy-efficient light bulb, toilet tissue made from recycled paper, or a high-fiber cereal.

As Director of International Trade for Intersave Buying & Merchandising Services (a buying division for Loblaws), it was Scott's job to source and manage about 400 corporate brands (No Name, President's Choice, G·R·E·E·N)[1] for Loblaws in Canada. In four days Scott would have to make his recommendations to the buyers' meeting.

The "green line" for which Scott was sourcing products was a new concept for Loblaws and its customers. Launched in 1989 as part of the corporate President's Choice brands, green products had characteristics that were less hazardous to the environment and/or contributed to a more healthy lifestyle. At issue for Scott was deciding what was green and balancing the financial requirements of the company with the socially responsible initiative of the green line.

As well, his most pressing concern was his ability to convince the president, Dave Nichol, of the merits of his recommendations. Nichol was the driving force behind the corporate brands, and he maintained involvement and final authority on these important product decisions.

In preparation for the buyers' meeting, Scott had to have his written recommendations on Dave Nichol's desk that day. Dave Nichol required that recommendations include retail price and cost data, projected annual sales in units and dollars, as well as the total gross margin expected. In addition to the expected results, best-and worst-case scenarios were required. As well, primary reasons for and against the proposal needed to be given. Typically, the recommendations were made based on the Ontario market, as it was the proving ground for new products.

The first product Scott was considering was a new energy-efficient light bulb, which had been successfully marketed in Germany. The bulb lasted at least 10 times longer than a regular lightbulb but was substantially more expensive. There was no question in Scott's mind that the energy-efficient bulb had strong green characteristics and would enhance Loblaws green image. However, a potential consumer price of $20 and low retail margins were a troubling combination. He knew that store managers, who were measured on sales volume and profits, would not be enthusiastic about a product that would not deliver sales or profits. These store managers controlled the individual products and brands that were carried in their stores.

The second new product was, in fact, not a new product at all. Loblaws had been selling a toilet tissue manufactured with 100 percent recycled material under its No Name corporate label. The existing product could be repackaged under the G·R·E·E·N label and sold beside the No Name line of products. The green packaging might alert consumers sensitive to the recycled feature, thereby generating greater volumes for the product. Further, Scott realized there was an opportunity to price the green toilet tissue at a higher price than the No Name, providing a higher profit margin.

The final product under consideration was a new corn flake product for the very crowded breakfast cereal category. The new cereal had an unusually high fiber content. The "body-friendly" nature of the cereal was the basis for considering it for the green line. Its additional feature was that it could be sourced at a cost much lower than that of the national brands.

LOBLAW COMPANIES LIMITED

Loblaw Companies Limited is part of George Weston Ltd., a conglomerate of companies that operate in three basic areas: food processing, food distribution, and natural resources. George Weston is the sixth largest company in Canada, with sales of $10.5 billion and net income of $98 million in 1989. The Loblaw Companies, an integrated group of food wholesaling and

---

* This case was prepared by Gordon H. G. McDougall of Wilfrid Laurier University in Waterloo, Ontario, and Douglas Snetsinger of the University of Toronto. Copyright © 1991 by Gordon H. G. McDougall. Reproduced by permission.

[1] No Name, President's Choice, and G·R·E·E·N are all trademarks, owned by Loblaw Companies Limited.

retailing companies, had total sales and net earnings in 1989 of $7.934 billion and $70 million respectively (Exhibit 1).

At the wholesale level, divisions such as Kelly, Douglas & Company and Atlantic Wholesalers supplied over 1280 corporate and franchise stores as well as over 12,300 independent retailers through its 54 company-owned warehouses. At the retail level, Loblaws operated both company-owned (corporate) stores including Loblaws, Zehrs, Superstore, and Real Canadian Superstore, and franchised operations including No Frills, Mr. Grocer, and Value Mart. Loblaws retail operations are spread across Canada, except in the province of Quebec, and in New Orleans and St. Louis in the United States. Eastern Canada generates approximately 50 percent of retail sales, western Canada approximately 33 percent, and the United States approximately 16 percent (Exhibit 1).

Two divisions within Loblaws coordinated the purchasing from outside suppliers for the corporate brands. Loblaw International Merchants under the direction of its president, Dave Nichol, was responsible for the development and merchandising of the corporate brand throughout the organization. There were approximately 3000 corporate brands with about 200 new brands added each year. Intersave Buying and Merchandising Services was responsible for the procurement of goods from both foreign and domestic suppliers for the corporate brand program.

THE RETAIL FOOD INDUSTRY

Loblaws operated in the extremely competitive retail food business, an industry that was both highly concentrated and fragmented. Over 13,000 retail stores competed for the Canadian consumer's food dollar, yet 50 percent of the $41 billion sales in 1989 went through only 4 percent of the outlets—the supermarket chains—including Loblaws, Provigo, A&P, Oshawa, Safeway, and Steinberg. The approximately 4800 convenience stores in Canada—Becker's, 7 Eleven, Mac's, and others—had sales of $2.3 billion.

EXHIBIT 1   Loblaws—Selected Financial Highlights (1985–1989)

	1989	1988	1987	1986	1985
Operating results ($ millions)					
Sales	7,934	8,308	8,631	7,839	6,931
Trading profit*	291	258	290	249	225
Operating income	191	160	190	163	152
Net earnings	70	26	74	74	67
Return on sales (percent)					
Operating income	2.4	1.9	2.2	2.1	2.2
Earnings before income taxes	1.4	.8	1.5	1.5	1.7
Per common share ($)					
Net earnings	0.80	0.41	0.87	0.91	0.85
Earnings ratios (percent)					
Return on common equity	11.7	5.9	12.5	14.6	15.6
Return on capital employed	13.8	11.2	13.6	14.3	17.0
Regional sales ($ millions)					
Eastern Canada	3,988	3,705	3,602	3,070	2,781
Western Canada	2,650	2,340	2,087	2,028	1,887
United States	1,296	2,263	2,942	2,741	2,263
Total	7,934	8,308	8,631	7,839	6,931
Regional operating income ($ millions)					
Eastern Canada	90	76	106	74	72
Western Canada	67	56	47	56	45
United States	34	28	37	33	35
Total	191	160	190	163	152
Sales by segment ($ millions)					
Retail	5,025	4,921	4,777	4,430	3,940
Wholesale	2,909	3,387	3,854	3,409	2,991
Total	7,934	8,308	8,631	7,839	6,931

* Trading profit is defined as operating income before depreciation.
Source: Company records.

The over 8000 independent retailers, ranging from small "mom and pop" corner stores to large independent supermarkets, generated sales of about $12.8 billion in 1989. The remaining industry sales, about $5.4 billion, were generated by specialty stores, such as bakeries and seafood stores ($3.2 billion) and a host of other types of stores, including drugstore retail outlets.

When adjusted for inflation, growth in the retail food industry was near zero for the past 5 years and forecasts for the early 1990s suggested a similar pattern. The low industry growth was due, in part, to little growth in the Canadian population and to increased expenditures by Canadians in fast-food and other restaurants. The intense competition within a mature industry meant that average net profit margins (pretax profits/sales) in the industry were low, averaging less than 2 percent in the past 5 years and only 1.5 percent in 1988. Consequently, the major chains were constantly examining new marketing and merchandising innovations, as well as promotion incentives from manufacturers to build value for their customers and create store switching and preference.

The retail food business has seen a number of changes throughout the years, including the following:

- While chain stores' share of the market had been relatively stable, the sales per store had increased as some chains merged and closed stores during the past decade. For example, in early July 1990, Steinberg announced it was selling 69 Ontario stores (58 Miracle Food Marts and 11 Ultra Mart food and drug stores) to A&P. A&P already operated 194 stores in Ontario under the A&P and Dominion names.
- A variety of store formats had been introduced in response to changing consumer preferences, competitive pressures, and economic conditions. For example, "box" stores, warehouse stores, combination stores (selling both food and nonfood products), and superstores had been developed in the past 15 years.
- Specialty stores, with their emphasis on quality and freshness, were increasing their market share.
- Generic (no-name) and store brands were increasing their share at the expense of national brands.
- Control in the industry had been shifting to the large chains, from the manufacturers. This trend was likely to continue as new sources of supply became available through free trade and as the chains reduced their emphasis on nationally branded products.

Six chains—Loblaws, Provigo, Oshawa, Steinberg, Safeway, and A&P—were the major competitors in the Canadian food business. In 1989, Loblaws was the largest of the six, with total sales, wholesale and retail, of $7.9 billion, followed by Provigo ($7.4 billion), Oshawa ($4.9 billion), Steinberg ($4.5 billion), Safeway ($3.5 billion), and A&P ($2.2 billion).

While retail market share data were difficult to obtain because most of the chains operated both wholesale and retail divisions, industry sources estimated that Loblaws held the largest retail share in Canada at around 19 percent. Provigo held a 16 percent share, and it was estimated that the remaining chains held 10 percent or less of the market. Competition was regional in nature, with Provigo strong in Quebec, Safeway strong in western Canada, Loblaws and A & P with strengths in Ontario, and Sobey's (part of the Empire conglomerate) strong in the Maritimes.

The intense competition for market share was reflected by industry experts, who, over the past year, made the following observations:

- Food retailers are locked in a cutthroat industry, scrambling to hold on to a shrinking market. The population is aging, leaving smaller appetites to whet.
- The grocery business is a treacherous one, characterized by low margins and dominated by giant companies. Niche players crowd the corners.
- The economic slowdown has hit supermarkets as consumers cut down on grocery spending. Consumers are buying more food on special and switching to cheaper foods.

LOBLAWS' CORPORATE STRATEGY

Against this background of intense competition, changing consumer preferences, and changing economic conditions, Loblaws has been guided by a corporate strategy that had led to dramatic alterations in the way it did business. Loblaws envisioned the road to sustainable competitive advantage through innovative marketing, low costs, and a large network of suppliers. Traditionally, retailers in the food industry relied on price discounting to generate increased volume sales, thereby increasing market share. Loblaws viewed this way of thinking as valid but narrow. Loblaws' umbrella strategy was to be the best low-cost, high-quality food distributor in the industry. This strategy led to four substantial changes at Loblaws: (1)

the introduction of generics, (2) the development of the President's Choice corporate product line, (3) a broad-scale investment program, and (4) a new marketing strategy.

The Introduction of Generics

First sold in the United States in 1977, generics are unbranded, plainly packaged, less expensive versions of common products such as spaghetti, paper towels, and canned peaches. Loblaws and a competing chain, Dominion, introduced generics in early 1978. Loblaws quickly became the leader in generic sales. In 15 months Loblaws expanded the line, called "No Name," from 16 to 120 products; by 1983, Loblaws carried over 500 generic products which accounted for about 10 percent of Loblaws' total sales. The generics appealed to price-sensitive consumers during a downturn in the Canadian economy.

Loblaws' strategy with their generic line differed from competitors such as Dominion. Most food distributors positioned their generics as lower-priced products with lower quality than competing national brands. Loblaws produced a generic product that was of a higher quality. The quality of No Name products, coupled with lower prices, attractively packaged in an eye-catching yellow with heavy advertising against national brands, led to the success of the line.

Development of the President's Choice Line

With the introduction of No Name, Loblaws recognized another unique marketing opportunity. Through internal market research in the early 1980s on the corporate brand philosophy, the company discovered that the target market for quality corporate products was the more affluent and educated consumer. It was found that this consumer did not require a national brand product to discern product quality and thus acceptability for purchase. It was at this time that Canada was also emerging from a recession. As consumer incomes rose, Loblaws saw an opportunity to meet the demands of this consumer. In 1984, President's Choice was introduced as a higher-quality, high-value brand.

The President's Choice line was positioned directly against national brands. Loblaws' plan was to develop consumer brand loyalty for this corporate line to such an extent that consumers would switch supermarkets to acquire President's Choice. An example of a very successful President's Choice product was the "Decadent" chocolate chip cookie. Based on product tests, Loblaws identified a lack of quality in the leading national brand chocolate chip cookie. The Decadent was made with a higher percentage (40 percent) of chocolate chips and

real butter, and within a few months of its launch it was the best-selling cookie in Ontario.

The increasing activity of Loblaws in developing corporate brands led to the establishment of the Weston Research Center, a product testing laboratory. The center was involved in the research and development of new products, quality control testing, and quality assurance programs. These activities were carried out on behalf of companies within the Weston and Loblaws group. By the late 1980s, the center had 100 employees and spent over $20 million each year to ensure product quality for corporate brands. Typically, a buyer for Loblaws would identify a possible product for inclusion in the corporate line. The buyer would then find a manufacturer to produce the product, and the manufacturer would work with experts from the Weston Research Center to meet the required product quality standards. The product would then be launched as part of the President's Choice or No Name line.

The corporate line was well received by consumers. By 1989, approximately 2200 No Name brands and 700 President's Choice brands made up 30 percent of Loblaws' total grocery sales. President's Choice and No Name brands earned an average 15 percent higher margin than the national brands. Approximately 200 new corporate brands were introduced annually, with three-quarters of them being successful, compared to a 10 percent success rate for national brands.

The Broad-Scale Investment Program

In 1984, Loblaws began a broad-scale investment program that, over the next 5 years, involved expenditures of approximately $1.8 billion on systems and market expansion through store developments. This included an information system to use store-level scanner data to measure every product's sales. This made it possible to monitor the effectiveness of their merchandising strategy, as sales, promotion, and pricing information could be examined weekly to determine individual product profitability and to support inventory management.

Market expansion was accomplished through substantial expenditures to upgrade existing stores, as well as to build new stores in strategic locations. To put this massive investment program in perspective, between 1985 and 1989, Loblaws opened 174 new stores, closed 130 stores, transferred 90 company-owned stores to franchise operations, and transferred 40 franchised stores to company-owned operations (Exhibit 2). Thirty-two of the new stores opened during this period were superstores. Loblaws had identified superstores, also called *combination stores* or *supercenters*,

EXHIBIT 2   Retail Operations—Selected Highlights (1985–1989)

	1989		1988		1987		1986		1985	
	Stores	sq ft (millions)	Stores	sq ft (millions)	Stores	sq ft (millions)	Stores	sq ft (millions)	Stores	sq ft (millions)
Stores										
Beginning of year	311	10.6	361	11.3	380	10.8	363	9.2	381	9.2
Opened	55	1.2	21	1.2	20	1.2	60	2.4	18	0.6
Closed	(18)	(0.2)	(58)	(1.7)	(23)	(0.4)	(46)	(0.9)	(26)	(0.4)
Franchised:										
Transfer to:	(22)	(0.4)	(18)	(0.3)	(18)	(0.4)	(13)	(0.2)	(19)	(0.4)
Transfer from:	8	0.1	5	0.1	2	0.1	16	0.3	9	0.2
End of year	334	11.3	311	10.6	361	11.3	380	10.8	363	9.2
Average store size (in thousands)	33.9 sq ft		34.1 sq ft		31.4 sq ft		28.4 sq ft		25.3 sq ft	
Analysis by size										
>60,000 sq ft	40		33		26		18		10	
40,000–60,000	48		44		47		46		33	
20,000–39,999	148		154		176		179		171	
10,000–19,999	64		68		93		112		129	
<10,000 sq ft	34		12		19		25		20	
Total	334		311		361		380		363	
Sales										
Annual sales (in millions)	$5,025		$4,921		$4,777		$4,430		$3,940	
Annual average sales per gross sq ft	$458		$440		$440		$457		$432	

as the wave of the future and the key to future success in the retailing industry. Superstores (typically over 130,000 square feet) were up to four times the size of conventional supermarkets. Approximately one-third of the space was devoted to nonfood items. For example, Real Canadian Superstore, which opened in Calgary in late 1988, was over 135,000 square feet, larger than two football fields, and stocked over 45,000 items.

Throughout the aggressive expansion program, Loblaws' management stressed that they would maintain the company's financial objectives, including (1) to increase earnings per common share at an average of 15 percent per year over any 5-year period, (2) to provide an average return on common shareholders' equity of 15 percent per year over any 5-year period, and (3) to have less total debt than total equity in the business.

Through all this activity, the company was able to maintain a debt-equity ratio of 1:1 and shareholder returns averaging 12 percent. Although Loblaws did not meet its goals of a 15 percent average shareholder return and a 15 percent average annual increase in earnings per share over the 1984–1989 period that coincided with the repositioning and investment program, the results were still impressive compared to those of many firms in the industry.

The New Marketing Strategy

Dave Nichol, the president of Loblaw International Merchants, was the driving force behind the No Name and President's Choice concepts. He traveled the world to identify new product opportunities for Loblaws. While market research was used to assist in the selection and launch of new products, it was Dave Nichol's innate sense of customer likes which underlay the selection—and success—of many of the corporate brands.

The communication campaign for the corporate brand was unique. From the beginning of the No Name launch, Dave Nichol was involved in advertising these products, often appearing in television campaigns to promote the No Name line. As a result, he became well known to many Canadian consumers. Nichol also introduced the *Insider's Report,* a multicolored, comic-book-size booklet that featured corporate brands and offered consumers shopping tips. Ten million copies of each issue were circulated four times a year as an insert with newspapers across Canada in areas where Loblaws or its affiliates had stores.

The main goals of the *Insider's Report* were to provide news of product availability and to highlight promotions. By consolidating advertising expenditures through the use of the *Insider's Report,* Loblaws spent considerably less on their advertising campaigns than did the national brands. The advertising-to-sales ratio for Loblaws brands was about 3 percent, less than half of that spent by many national brand manufacturers.

THE GREEN IDEA

The G·R·E·E·N line launch had its origins in one of Dave Nichol's buying trips to Germany in 1988, where he was struck by the number of grocery products that were being promoted as environmentally friendly. He discovered that *The Green Consumer Guide,* a how-to book for consumers to become environmentally responsible, had become a best-seller in England. In late 1988, Loblaws began collecting information on Canadian attitudes about the environment. The results suggested that an increasing number of Canadians were concerned about environmental issues, and some expressed a willingness to pay extra to purchase environmentally safe products. Further, many said they were willing to change supermarkets to acquire these products (Exhibit 3).

As well, increased attention was being drawn to Canada's environmental problems. The news media and environmental groups such as Greenpeace and Pollution Probe were providing Canadians with many disturbing facts. For example, Canadians used more energy per capita than any other nation in the world. Canadians also produced approximately 15 tons of carbon dioxide per person per year, the primary cause of the greenhouse effect (the warming of the world's atmosphere). On a per capita basis, Canadians were found to be one of the world's greatest contributors to acid rain, air and water pollution, and the degeneration of the ozone layer.

THE G·R·E·E·N LAUNCH

Armed with these supportive data, in late January 1989, Loblaws' management decided to launch by July 1989 a line of 100 products that were either environmentally friendly or healthy for the body. These products would be added to the family of the corporate line and called G·R·E·E·N. Although the task was considered ambitious, the corporation believed it had the requisite size, strength, influence, network, imagination, and courage to be successful. Loblaws contacted a number of prominent environmental groups to assist in the choice of products. These groups were requested to make a "wish list" of environmentally safe products. Using this as a guide, Loblaws began to source the products for the G·R·E·E·N launch.

EXHIBIT 3   Consumer Attitudes on the Environment

1. National survey on issues.
What is the most important issue facing Canada today?

Issues	1985	1986	1987	1988	1989
Environment	*	*	2	10	18
Goods and services tax	*	*	*	*	15
Inflation/economy	16	12	12	5	10
Deficit/government	6	10	10	6	10
National unity	*	*	*	*	7
Free trade	2	5	26	42	7
Abortion	*	*	*	*	6
Employment	45	39	20	10	6

Source: Maclean's/Decima Research.
* Not cited by a significant number of poll respondents.
Note: Survey conducted in early January of each year.

2. National survey on willingness to pay for cleaner environment.

Would you be willing to pay:
50% more to clear garbage (67%)[1]
10% more for groceries (66%)
$1,000 more for a car (63%)
5¢ a liter more for gas (63%)
$250 more to clean sewage (58%)
10% tax on energy (57%)

Source: Angus Reid Group.
[1] The numbers in parentheses represent the percent of those surveyed who agreed with each statement.
Note: Survey conducted in early 1989.

3. Loblaws customers surveys.

How concerned are you about the environment? (%)
Extremely (32), Quite (37), Somewhat (24), Not Very (5), Don't Care (2)
How likely is it that you would purchase environmentally friendly products?
Very (49), Somewhat (43), Not too (2), Not at all (4)
How likely is it that you would switch supermarkets to purchase environmentally friendly products?
Very (2), Somewhat (45), Not too (24), Not at all (10)

Note: Survey conducted in early 1989.

A few products, such as baking soda, simply required repackaging to advertise the already existing environmentally friendly qualities of the product. Inter-save Buying and Merchandising Services was able to source some products through foreign suppliers, such as the Ecover line of household cleaning products, to be marketed under the G·R·E·E·N umbrella. All G·R·E·E·N products were rigorously tested, as well as screened by environmental groups such as Pollution Probe and Friends of the Earth. This collaboration was developed to such an extent that a few of the products were endorsed by Pollution Probe.

The G·R·E·E·N product line, consisting of about 60 products, was launched on June 3, 1989. Initial G·R·E·E·N products included phosphate-free laundry detergent, low-acid coffee, pet foods, and biodegradable garbage bags (Exhibit 4). A holistic approach was taken in selecting these initial products; for example, the pet food products were included because they provided a more healthful blend of ingredients for cats and dogs. The G·R·E·E·N products were offered in a distinctively designed package with vivid green coloring. When the package design decisions were being made, it was learned that 20 percent of the Canadian population was functionally illiterate. Management felt that the distinct design would give these consumers a chance to readily identify these brands.

The G·R·E·E·N launch was supported with a $3 million television and print campaign. Consumers were informed of the new product line using the June 1989 issue of the *Insider's Report*. In an open letter to consumers, Nichol addressed Loblaws' motivation for the G·R·E·E·N launch (Exhibit 5). Part of this motivation was also to offer consumers a choice which could, in the longer term, provide educational benefits for consumers on specific green issues. As well, by offering the choice, consumers could "vote at the cash register" and, in a sense, tell Loblaws what they were willing to buy and what green products they would accept.

The *Report* provided descriptive statements for many of the G·R·E·E·N products (Exhibit 6) and noted that Loblaws would continue to carry a broad range of products including national brands and President's Choice. The G·R·E·E·N line was to be typically priced below national brand products. The G·R·E·E·N introduction was not without its problems. Shortly after the launch, members of Pollution Probe rejected their previous endorsement of the G·R·E·E·N disposable diaper. These members felt that the group should not support a less than perfect product. The G·R·E·E·N diaper was more environmentally friendly than any other disposable brand. However, it was not, in Pollution Probe's

EXHIBIT 4 The Initial G·R·E·E·N Products

Food	*Pet Food*
Just Peanuts Peanut Butter	Low Ash Cat Food
Smart Snack Popcorn	Slim & Trim Cat Food
"The Virtuous" Soda Cracker	All Natural Dog Biscuits
Cox's Orange Pippin Apple Juice	
White Hull-less Popcorn	*Cooking Products*
Reduced Acid Coffee	"The Virtuous" Canola Oil
Boneless and Skinless Sardines	"The Virtuous" Cooking Spray
"Green" Natural Oat Bran	Baking Soda
Naturally Flavored Raisins: Lemon, Cherry, Strawberry	
"Green" Turkey Frankfurters	*Paper-Based Products*
100% Natural Rose Food	Bathroom Tissue
Norwegian Crackers	"Green" Ultra Diapers
Turkey Whole Frozen	"Green" Foam Plates
Gourmet Frozen Foods (low-fat)	Swedish 100% Chlorine-Free Coffee Filters
"If the World Were PERFECT" Water	"Green" Baby Wipes
	"Green" Maxi Pads
Cleaning/Detergent Products	
	Oil-Based Products
All-Purpose Liquid Cleaner with Bitrex	Biodegradable Garbage Bags
"Green" Automatic Dishwasher Detergent	Hi-Performance Motor Oil
Ecover 100% Biodegradable Laundry Powder*	Natural Fertilizer
Ecover Dishwasher Detergent	Lawn and Garden Soil
Laundry Soil and Stain Remover with Bitrex	
Drain Opener with Bitrex	*Other Products*
Ecover Fabric Softener	Green T-Shirt/Sweatshirt
Ecover 100% Biodegradable Toilet Cleaner	Green Panda Stuffed Toy
Ecover 100% Biodegradable Wool Wash	Green Polar Bear Stuffed Toy
Ecover Floor Soap	Cedar Balls
"Green" 100% Phosphate Free Laundry Detergent	

* The Ecover brands are a line of cleaning products made by Ecover of Belgium. These products are vegetable oil based and are rapidly biodegradable. Loblaws marketed these products under the G·R·E·E·N umbrella.

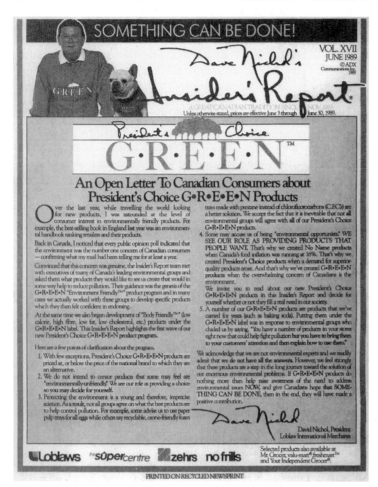

EXHIBIT 5   *The Insider's Report—Open Letter*

opinion, environmentally pure. Further, it was felt that endorsing such products compromised the integrity and independence of the organization. This prompted the resignation of Colin Issac, the director of Pollution Probe. The group subsequently discontinued its endorsement of the diaper but continued its support of six other G·R·E·E·N products.

Controversy also arose around the introduction of the G·R·E·E·N fertilizer. Greenpeace, a prominent environment group, rejected Loblaws' claims that the fertilizer had no toxic elements and therefore was environmentally pure. The group did not know that Loblaws had spent substantial funds to determine that the product was free of toxic chemicals.

Both incidents, although unfortunate, focused the attention of Canadians on the G·R·E·E·N product line. The media highlighted Loblaws as the only North American retailer to offer a line of environmentally friendly products. This publicity also prompted letters of encouragement from the public who supported Loblaws' initiative. Surveys conducted 4 weeks after the

line introduction revealed an 82 percent awareness of the G·R·E·E·N line, with 27 percent of the consumers actually purchasing at least one of the G·R·E·E·N products. In Ontario alone, the G·R·E·E·N line doubled its projected sales and sold $5 million in June 1989.

THE FIRST YEAR OF GREEN

The launch of G·R·E·E·N was soon followed by a virtual avalanche of environmentally friendly products. Major consumer goods companies like Procter & Gamble, Lever Brothers, and Colgate-Palmolive introduced Enviro-Paks, phosphate-free detergents, and biodegradable cleaning products. Competing supermarket chains had varied responses from launching their own green lines (Miracle Mart introduced three "Green Circle" products, Oshawa Foods introduced about 10 "Greencare" products) to highlighting environmentally sensitive products in their stores (Safeway) to improving their internal practices through recycling and other activities (Provigo).

EXHIBIT 6   Examples of Promotion for the G·R·E·E·N Line in *The Insider's Report*

As well, companies from McDonald's to Labatt's positioned themselves in one way or another as environmentally responsible. These marketing activities created some consumer skepticism about whether some of these products were truly environmentally friendly. In addition, various companies had different ideas about what was environmentally friendly, which also created some consumer confusion. Part of the problem was that it was very difficult to determine what was and wasn't environmentally safe. Serious environmentalists argued that to accurately assess the environmental impact of a product, it was necessary to conduct a "cradle-to-grave" analysis—a detailed review of the product, how it was manufactured, how it was used, and how it was disposed of. Others argued that if a product was environmentally better than other brands (for example, a biodegradable disposable diaper versus a regular disposable diaper), then the consumer should be offered that choice.

It appeared that Loblaws' actions had an impact on corporations and consumers. For example, in a national survey of 1500 Canadians conducted in November 1989, 56 percent of respondents answered "yes" to the question "Over the past year, have environmental concerns influenced your purchase decisions?" Of those who answered "yes" and were than asked "In what way?," it was found that 23 percent purchased environmentally friendly products, 21 percent avoided the purchase of hazardous products, 11 percent didn't purchase pesticides, and 7 percent boycotted certain products.

During the year, Loblaws continued to develop and promote the G·R·E·E·N product line. In the first year of G·R·E·E·N, Loblaws sold approximately $60 million worth of G·R·E·E·N products and broke even on the line.

THE DECISIONS

As Scott began to make his decisions on the three products, he reflected on the past year. He thought that $60 million in sales for the G·R·E·E·N line was reasonable, but he had hoped the line would do better. He remembered some of the products that just didn't fit in the line, such as "green" sardines. "I don't think we sold 20 cans of that stuff." Scott and the other buyers at Intersave were very concerned when a product didn't sell. Individual store managers, who were held accountable for the sales and profits of their store, did not have to list (that is, stock in the store that he or she managed) any product, including any in the G·R·E·E·N line. If a store manager thought the product was unsuitable for the store, it wasn't listed. As well, if a buyer got a product listed and it didn't sell, his or her reputation with the store managers would suffer.

One thing that had changed was the product opportunities. When the G·R·E·E·N line was launched, Scott and the other buyers had to actively search to find products that could qualify as green. Now it seemed that all kinds of suppliers were jumping on the environmental bandwagon. However, the environmental advantages of many of these product proposals were difficult to verify. Some, despite good sales potential, could only be considered *pale green,* a term used to describe products that had debatable or small positive impacts on the environment.

Light Bulb

The proposal by Osram, a well-known German manufacturer, was a true green product. The Osram light bulb was a compact fluorescent bulb that could replace the traditional incandescent light bulb in specific applications. The unique aspect of this product was that while fluorescent light technology was commonplace (these long-tube lights were common in office buildings), only recently had the product been modified for use as a replacement for traditional light bulbs. The major benefits of fluorescent light bulbs were that they used considerably less energy than incandescent light bulbs (for example, a 9 watt fluorescent bulb could replace a 40 watt incandescent bulb and still provide the same lighting level, while using only 22.5 percent of the energy) and lasted at least 10 times longer (an estimated 2000 hours versus 200 hours for the incandescent bulb). To date the major application for compact fluorescents had been in apartment buildings in stairwells where lights remained on 24 hours a day. Apartment building owners purchased them because the bulbs lowered both energy costs and maintenance costs (less frequent replacement).

The compact fluorescent had limited applications in the home. Because of its unique shape it could not be used with a typical lampshade (Exhibit 7). The main

EXHIBIT 7   The Osram Light Bulb

application was likely to be in hallways where it was difficult to replace a burned-out bulb. Even in these situations, a new fixture (that is, an enclosure) might be required so that the compact fluorescent would fit.

The bulb's energy efficiency and long-lasting features were well tested and it had been sold for specialized industrial use for several years. The bulb was making satisfactory inroads in Germany even though it was priced at the equivalent of $40 Canadian.

Loblaws sold a variety of 60 and 100 watt No Name and Phillips light bulbs in packages of four. In total the light bulb category generated over $1 million in gross margin for Loblaws in 1989 (Exhibit 8).

The initial Osram proposal was to sell the product to Loblaws at $19.00 per bulb. Even if the markup was set at 5 percent, Loblaws' retail price would be $19.99. Scott talked this over with a number of people at Loblaws and concluded that the price was too high to be accepted by Canadian consumers. At this time, Ontario Hydro entered the picture. Ontario Hydro was extremely concerned about its ability to meet the power demands of its customers in the next decade and was engaged in aggressive energy conservation programs. Ontario Hydro was prepared to offer a $5 rebate for every light bulb that was sold in Ontario in the three months following the launch. Although it meant that customers would have to request the rebate by mail, it reduced the effective price of the bulb to the consumer to $14.99.

Scott felt that the combination of the rebate, a retail price only half of that paid by German consumers, and a strong environmental message had strong merchandising appeal that could be exploited in the launch of the bulb. Nevertheless, the sales potential was still unclear. Loblaws' annual sales in Ontario were nearly 4 million bulbs or $2.7 million. Because this product was unique and new, Scott had difficulty estimating its

EXHIBIT 8   Light Bulbs (1989)

	Average Retail Price[1] ($)	Average Cost ($)	Annual Sales ($000)	Total Gross Margin ($000)	Market Share (%)
Lablaws					
60 Watt	2.25	1.25	470	209	18
60 Watt Soft	2.75	1.50	426	193	16
100 Watt	2.25	1.25	294	130	11
100 Watt Soft	2.75	1.50	279	127	11
Total Lablaws			1,468	659	56
Phillips					
60 Watt	2.40	1.50	367	138	14
60 Watt Soft	3.20	1.65	341	165	13
100 Watt	2.40	1.50	236	88	9
100 Watt Soft	3.20	1.65	210	102	8
Total Phillips			1,153	493	44
Total			2,621	1,152	100

[1] Based on four packs (that is four light bulbs in a package). Total unit sales were 1,019,000 (four packs).

sales potential. His best guess was that Loblaws might sell anywhere from 10,000 to 50,000 Osram bulbs in one year. Scott thought that half the sales would come from regular customers and the other half from customers coming to Loblaws specifically to buy the bulb. Scott also felt that after 3 months, the price should be raised to $24.99 retail to generate a reasonable margin for Loblaws.

Scott thought that if half of the volume were generated at the higher price, it would certainly be easier to maintain the support of the store managers. At the $24.99 price, the margin would be $5.99 per bulb. Even considering the cannibalization issue, the margin on the higher-priced Osram would be about four times higher than the margin for a four-pack of regular bulbs. However, it would be necessary to calculate the contribution for the year to see what the net effect would be for the line. The shelf space required for these bulbs was minimal and could be handled by some minor changes to the layout of the existing bulbs.

BATHROOM TISSUE

The bathroom tissue category was a highly competitive, price-sensitive market. The category was one of the largest in the Loblaws lineup, generating over $31 million in retail sales in Ontario and $7 million in contribution (Exhibit 9). Bathroom tissue was more important to Loblaws than just a volume generator. It was one of the few product categories that would draw price-conscious buyers into the store. Loblaws listed 40 different sizes and colors from various manufacturers. There were six Loblaws' brands in the category.

Loblaws was aggressive at delisting any competitive or corporate brand that did not meet turnover or profitability goals. Manufacturers were just as aggressive at providing allowance and merchandising incentives to ensure satisfactory margins for Loblaws and to facilitate retail price reductions, which in turn would enhance turnover and maintain volume goals. Two national brands—Royale and Cottonelle—held shares of 45 percent and 30 percent, respectively.

For 1989, Loblaws' brands held 16 percent of the market, with No Name White providing a total gross margin of over $1 million. Loblaws' No Name White was sourced for an average cost of $1.15 for a four-roll package. These lower costs were largely based on the fact that the tissue was manufactured with totally recycled material. This product feature made it a candidate for G·R·E·E·N line consideration. The existing product could simply be repackaged with the distinctive G·R·E·E·N labeling and an emphasis placed on the recycled character of the product. No development or testing costs would be required, and artwork and new labeling costs would be minimal.

Several decisions needed to be considered with respect to the repackaging of the No Name product. Should the new product replace the old or simply be added to an already crowded category? Should the price of the new product be set higher than that set for the old? Should the product be launched at all? If it was launched should it get prominence in the quarterly *Insider's Report?* Should it be positioned against some national brands? How much inventory should be ordered, and what was the expected profitability?

EXHIBIT 9   Bathroom Tissue (1989)

	Average Retail Price[1] ($)	Average Cost ($)	Annual Sales ($000)	Total Gross Margin ($000)	Market Share (%)
Loblaws[2]					
President's Choice	2.50	1.95	1,542	339	5
No Name White	1.75	1.15	3,084	1,052	10
No Name Color	1.80	1.35	386	96	1
Loblaws total			5,012	1,487	16
Royale					
White	1.85	1.55	10,795	1,751	34
Color	2.00	1.60	3,855	771	12
Royale total			14,650	2,522	46
Cottonelle					
White	1.85	1.45	4,627	1,000	15
Color	1.95	1.50	4,627	1,068	15
Cottonelle total			9,254	2,068	30
Other Brands					
Capri	1.50	0.90	945	378	3
April Soft	1.40	0.95	721	232	2
Jubilee	1.35	0.70	386	186	1
Dunet	2.45	1.60	405	140	1
White Swan	1.55	1.00	463	164	1
Other Brands total			2,920	1,100	8
Total			31,836	7,177	100

[1] Statistics for the prices, costs and sales have been collapsed over the various sizes and reported in equivalent four-roll packs. Total unit sales were 17,125,000 (four-roll packs).

[2] Loblaws was offered in six different size and color combinations. Most major brands provided a similar variety of sizes and colors.

READY-TO-EAT CEREAL

Loblaws sold more than $14 million worth of family cereals (that is, cereals targeted at the family market) in Ontario in 1989 (Exhibit 10). Loblaws' corporate brand share of the family cereal segment, at 14 percent, was lower than corporate objectives for this category. One of Scott Lindsay's goals was to increase Loblaws' share for this category. The major obstacle was the dominance of the well-known national brands marketed by Kellogg's, Nabisco, General Mills, and Quaker Oats (Exhibit 10). The brand leaders, such as Kellogg's Corn Flakes, Nabisco Shreddies, and General Mills' Cheerios, were as familiar to shoppers as any other product or brand in a store. With decades of advertising and promotional support, these brands had become thoroughly entrenched in the minds and pantries of generations of Canadians.

The brand names of these market leaders provided the manufacturers with strong protection against competitors. However, the manufacturing process did not. The manufacturing processes were well known in the industry, and many firms could produce identical products at favorable costs. Loblaws had found sev-

eral products from domestic sources that appeared to be as good as if not better than the national brands. One such product was a corn flake product which had a very high fiber content. The new product would appeal to those customers who had been primed by the health claims of high fiber diets. In sensory tests it had proven to have an excellent taste and texture profile, and was equal to or preferred in blind taste tests to some of the market leaders. Moreover, the product could be obtained for $1.40 per 500 g package.

The President's Choice brands were beginning to make inroads in this market, and this new product could increase the share. However, it was not clear how to position the high-fiber corn flake product. Should it go in the regular President's Choice line as a line extension of the current corn flake product or should it be packaged as a G·R·E·E·N product? As a regular President's Choice product, it would be positioned directly against Kellogg's as an all-round cereal with extra value. As a G·R·E·E·N product it would be positioned less against Kellogg's and much more towards a health/"good-for-you" claim. G·R·E·E·N positioning might also minimize any cannibalization of the President's Choice corn flakes. The lower sourcing

EXHIBIT 10   Family Cereals (1989)

	Average Retail Price[1] ($)	Average Cost ($)	Annual Sales ($000)	Total Gross Margin ($000)	Market Share (%)
President's Choice					
Bran with Raisins	2.35	1.50	1,051	380	7.4
Honey Nut Cereal	3.00	1.40	324	173	2.3
Toasted Oats	3.00	1.45	221	114	1.5
Corn Flakes	1.75	1.20	193	60	1.4
Crispy Rice	3.20	1.50	263	139	1.8
Loblaws total			2,052	866	14.3
Kellogg's					
Corn Flakes	2.30	1.80	1,436	312	10.1
Raisin Bran	2.75	2.00	1,236	324	8.7
Honey Nut Corn Flakes	3.95	2.70	460	141	3.2
Rice Krispies	3.95	2.52	899	315	6.3
Common Sense	4.40	2.70	433	167	3.0
Mini-Wheat	3.30	2.00	326	129	2.3
Variety Pack	5.90	3.90	309	105	2.2
Other Kellogg's	3.41	2.26	258	87	1.8
Kellogg's total			5,357	1,580	37.5
Nabisco					
Shreddies	2.35	1.70	2,725	754	19.1
Apple/Cinnamon	2.25	1.50	169	57	1.2
Raisin Wheat	3.30	2.10	139	50	1.0
Nabisco total			3,033	861	21.2
General Mills					
Cheerios	3.80	2.60	1,171	370	8.2
Cheerios/Honey Nut	3.90	2.60	1,017	339	7.1
General Mills total			2,188	709	15.3
Quaker					
Corn Bran	3.50	2.25	389	139	2.7
Life	3.15	2.10	358	119	2.5
Oat Bran	4.10	2.80	281	89	2.0
Muffets	2.65	1.60	92	36	0.6
Quaker total			1,120	383	7.8
Others	2.40	1.45	573	227	4.0
Total			14,323	4,626	100.0

[1] Based on 500 gram size. Total unit sales were 4,950,000 (500 gram size).
Cereals are packaged in several different sizes. Some brands like Kellogg's Corn Flakes could have four different sizes (e.g., 350g, 425g, 675g, 800g) on the shelf at one time. To facilitate comparisons, all figures have been converted to a standard 500 g size and where brands had multiple sizes, the figures are reported as averages, weighted by the sales volume of the size.

costs provided some flexibility on pricing. It could be priced as low as $1.75, like the current President's Choice corn flakes, and still maintain good margins or it could be priced as high as Kellogg's Corn Flakes at $2.30 and generate superior margins.

Having reviewed the three proposals, Scott began the process of preparing his recommendations. "I'll start with the financial projections," thought Scott, "then consider the pros and cons of each proposal. Then it's decision time."

MARKETING STRATEGY

> Results are gained by exploiting opportunities not by solving problems.
>
> PETER DRUCKER

Marketing strategy is concerned with finding sustainable ways for organizations to compete in a continuously changing world. This chapter is concerned with helping you select marketing strategies to exploit the opportunities of tomorrow. Organizations that fail to plan for the future will find themselves fading into the sunset.

WHAT IS MARKETING STRATEGY?

A strategy is a plan of action designed to achieve the long-run goals of the organization. Marketing strategies evolve from more general business objectives. Marketing strategies usually include the following dimensions:

1. The product or service market in which you expect to compete.
2. The level of investment needed to grow, maintain, or milk the business.
3. The product line, positioning, pricing, and distribution strategies needed to compete in the selected market.
4. The assets or capabilities to provide a sustainable competitive advantage (SCA).

APPLYING
... to
Consumer
Marketing

Successful marketing strategies are based on *assets* that are strong relative to those of competitors. These assets include brand equity, the scale, scope, and efficiency of operations, financial condition, location, and government support. For example, Nestlé, a Swiss company that is the world's largest food company, has performed well in the marketplace with strong brand names including the Perrier and L'Oréal lines. Some companies believe that, as the world opens up to business, the operating model for today's exemplary companies no longer needs to include ownership of significant manufacturing assets. For example, Sara Lee Corp., whose stable of famous brands includes Legg's hosiery, Sara Lee frozen desserts, Wonderbras, Coach briefcases, and Kiwi shoe polish to name a few, has moved to contract out its production.

Strategies also spring from *capabilities* to do a good job. Capabilities are complex bundles of skills and accumulated knowledge, exercised through organizational processes, that enable firms to coordinate activities and make use of their assets.[1] The capabilities of market-driven organizations are classified in Figure 2-1. Marketing strategies take assets and capabilities and forge them into sustainable competitive advantages. For example, see Marketing Strategies box 2-1.

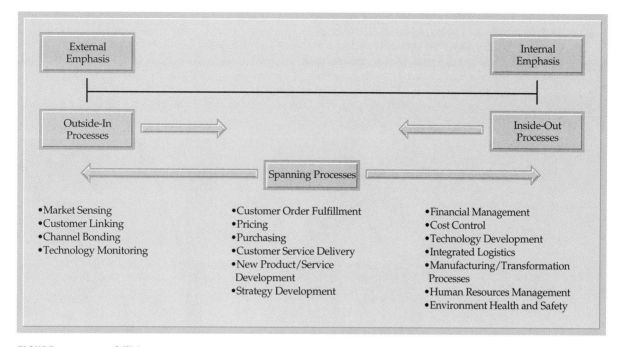

FIGURE 2-1 Capabilities
(From George S. Day, "The Capabilities of Market-Driven Organizations," *Journal of Marketing,* Vol. 58, No. 4 [October 1994], p.41)

Searching for SCAs

Organizations are continuously looking for ways to achieve SCAs. Some of the most important SCAs in a survey of businesses are shown in Table 2-1. Note that a wide variety of SCAs are mentioned, and the top few do not dominate the list. The average business reports 4.6 SCAs, suggesting that it is probably foolish to base your marketing strategy on a single SCA. Table 2-1 reveals some interesting differences in SCAs across industries. High-tech firms, for example, favor technical superiority, quality, and customer service. This often applies to less high-tech industrial firms as well, as illustrated in Marketing Strategies box 2-2. Service companies build their success around quality, good management, name recognition, and customer service. Firms in the "other" category are most interested in SCAs based on quality, name recognition, and low-cost production. On the other hand, technical superiority and low-cost production are not key SCAs for service companies.

Although two of the most important SCAs have been thought to be differentiation and low costs, these SCAs are ranked fifth and twelfth in Table 2-1. Differentiation strategies enhance profits by developing products with unique design, performance, quality, or service characteristics. The objective is to make your product different from that of your competition. Once customers perceive your product as unique, they are less sensitive to price and you can charge more for the product or service.

Low-cost strategies seek to build volume by achieving SCA in the areas of production or marketing. Low costs can be captured through economies of scale, access to raw materials, automated equipment, or outsourcing. (With regard to outsourcing, see Solectron's strategy for growth in Marketing Strategies box 2-3 near the end of this chapter.) Firms with low costs can charge low prices to build market share, or they can use the margins to increase profits. Low costs elsewhere may also allow firms to spend more on advertising and promotion.

Two organizations with low-cost SCAs are Goodyear in tires and Whirlpool in appliances. Goodyear has reduced costs through volume and vertical integration and Whirlpool

APPLYING
. . . to
Industrial
Marketing

MARKETING STRATEGIES *2-1*

Building on Innovation and Customer Loyalty

Although United Knitting has only been in operation less than two decades, the firm has made its mark as a leader in some major niche markets—specializing in performance fabrics. The firm started out producing gussets for hosiery. [A gusset is a small, triangular piece of material inserted in a clothing item to improve the fit or for reinforcement.] Even though United has gone on to new markets and

(continues)

Keeps you warm while you shiver with fear.

Courtesy United Knitting

MARKETING STRATEGIES 2-1 (continued)

more exotic products, those gusset operations continue today as one of the company's niche markets, accounting for 10 to 15 percent of production. "We have some of the most loyal customers in the hosiery industry." From gussets United expanded into liners, primarily swimwear in 100% nylon. Early on, the main customer was Jantzen. A highlight was development of the CoolMax lining, which currently has a widespread distribution. United continues to build products around DuPont's CoolMax fiber.

The last decade or so has solidified the foundation of United: performance fabrics. "We have built this company on performance. Our ability to provide stretch and recovery—and to repeat those characteristics in literally thousands of rolls of fabric, has established our niche in this marketplace."

Key to United's business approach is developing friendships with customers. "We want to talk to them." Typical of management's commitment to working with the customer was the relationship United built in development of the popular JogBra. Convinced of the growing market demand for a bra for female runners, two women began searching the industry for a fabric with stretch and recovery properties that would enable a runner to jog comfortably with the appropriate support. Given United's developmental talents, this challenge was right down its alley. After some experimentation and several sample runs, the plant shipped the women a 10-yd piece of fabric. This was rapidly followed by ongoing modifications, accompanied by increasing production volume. Today, JogBra is a staple in women's sportswear. Champion (a division of Sara Lee) owns the product, but United is still JogBra's principal fabric supplier.

Other products have mushroomed. United worked with DuPont, Glen Raven, and Danskin to develop a fabric using Supplex nylon. Beginning in body aerobics wear, it has grown to the point its applications now include sportswear, fashion and children's wear. Along with this growth in applications has come increasing sophistication in marketing techniques. "Performance hangtags are important. The objective is convincing consumers they are looking at a garment that's made of fabric that performs with the objective of having products that think."

INTEGRATING ... *with Production* ▶ A tour of United's manufacturing operations underscores management's drive for quality and efficiency. For example, most knitting machines operate in clean rooms to offset fly contamination. Commitment to preventive machinery maintenance is evident. Fabric testing is also crucial to operations. Included in the full-service laboratory is a sophisticated system for testing fabric stretch and recovery. These characteristics are critical in United's performance products. United performs 100% inspection of finished fabrics. An Error Source Analysis program quickly provides summary and analysis of any problems.

Recent mergers have greatly expanded United's technical expertise, production capabilities, and markets. The mergers allowed United to tell a common color story that correlates across all fabrics. Finally, the mergers provided United with greater purchasing leverage, from raw materials and dyestuffs to machinery. "Although United is growing in many markets, we don't lose focus on the necessity of giving the customer products that perform, while providing value, quality, speedy delivery and service."

— *Developing and supplying innovative and inspired products ensures customer loyalty.*

Source: Walter N. Rozelle, "United Builds on Innovation and Customer Loyalty," *Textile World*, August 1998, pp. 29–31.

through the use of automated equipment. At the same time, Michelin and Maytag have had success in the same industries with differentiation strategies. Michelin is well known for the safety of its steel belted radial tires and Maytag for the durability of its appliances. For these firms, differentiation has led to a sustainable price premium.

Other successful marketing strategies include focusing on special classes of customers and preemptive strikes. With focus strategies, a clothes retailer might focus on the needs of hard-to-fit buyers or a limited line of sportswear. A preemptive move stakes out new territory, and it is often difficult for competitors to make an appropriate response. Coca-Cola built a

TABLE 2-1   **Most Important Sustainable Competitive Advantages**

Rank	SCA	Type of Firm		
		High-Tech	*Service*	*Other*
1	Reputation for quality	**2**	**1**	**1**
2	Customer service/product support	**3**	**4**	5
3	Name recognition/high profile	16	**3**	**2.5**
4	Retain good management and engineering staff	6	**2**	17
5	Low-cost production	5	14.5	**2.5**
6	Financial resources	12	5.5	6
7	Customer orientation/feedback/market research	7	5.5	11
8	Product-line breadth	12	20	7.5
9	Technical superiority	**1**	6.2	11
10	Installed base of satisfied customers	4	9.5	18.5
11	Segmentation/focus	17	9.5	4
12	Product characteristics/differentiation	9	14.5	9
13	Continuing product innovation	9	12.5	14
14	Market share	9	12.5	11
15	Size/location of distribution	14.5	17.5	7.5
16	Low price/high value offering	18	11	14
17	Knowledge of business	20	7	18.5
18	Pioneer/early entrant in industry	12	17.5	14
19	Efficient, flexible production/operations adaptable to customer	19	16	18.5
20	Effective sales force	14.5	19	18.5
	Average number of SCAs	4.63	4.77	4.19

Source: David A. Aaker, "Managing Assets and Skills: The Key to a Sustainable Competitive Advantage," *California Management Review* (Winter 1989), p. 94.

MARKETING STRATEGIES *2-2*

A Niche for a Quality Supplier

APPLYING ... to Industrial Marketing

Over the past few years, Greer Steel Co., Dover, Ohio, has invested over $21 million to improve quality, shore up its niche in cold-rolled strip, and drum up new business. A subsidiary of privately-held Greer Industries, Greer Steel views itself as "a mill that happens to own a service center." Its Dover cold-rolling mill operation is the primary focus of its efforts. The mill produces carbon and alloy cold-rolled strip steel, flat wire, and flat bar for applications ranging from home appliances to automotive and hardware. It is "really a specialized service center dealing in products that most service centers don't handle. There are a few that do. But, by virtue of flat wire, narrow slit product (under 1 in.), round edging, and things of this nature, we're somewhat unique. We think it's a growth situation, and we're certainly tuning it up in anticipation."

Because Greer views its Dover facility as a mill, it approaches the mill's market much differently than it does Ferndale's service center market. "In some arenas, many service centers are handling business that rightfully should be produced or distributed by a mill. Many are fortunate to secure a position with tonnages that are not historically service center tonnages; they're way too big to be considered service center business. There are instances where that business has reverted back to mill-direct distribution, and that means growth for Dover. The customer is only going to pay so much for your product. By going to the service center, the product gets marked up, so they're paying healthy premiums for services on larger orders which are available in Dover via JIT and stocking programs.

INTEGRATING ... with Production/ Operations Management

We perform JIT where it is necessary and feasible. It costs a lot of money, and has to be carefully managed. At Dover, we put in a lot of stocking programs this past year with our major accounts to ensure on-time delivery. We'll continue in that posture, and add more and more accounts." However, at Dover, JIT is usually limited to customers that buy in larger lot sizes and can forecast usage on a quarterly basis. "We don't necessarily want to stock 1,000 lb. of an item here. It becomes totally unmanageable—and it's really a service center function at that level."

(continues)

MARKETING STRATEGIES 2-2 (continued)

With Ferndale organized to handle smaller orders, JIT is more of a factor in its operations. "More of its business depends on the ability to satisfy those JIT customers. We carry more inventory up there than we'd like to, but we have to do it. It's not quite as feasible for a mill as it is for a service center. With the pressure on suppliers to hold and ship material in a very timely manner, we feel that on a long-term basis, Ferndale will continue to grow, and that the need for the JIT services they provide will grow. JIT, of course, is nothing new. But, we are feeling it more and more every year in performing and aligning ourselves to satisfy customers. We are going to do whatever is economically feasible to service our customers."

Although Greer's Dover cold-rolling mill handles orders that are usually larger than service-center-sized shipments, its niche is in shipping loads smaller than those typically handled at an integrated mill or larger processor. "There is a trend now where larger processors are partnering up with mills to perform finishing and distribution. In most cases, those are very large tonnage items. We try to work at our Dover mill on a minimum of 6,000-lb. orders; we'll take a 500-lb. order at our service center. Larger processors and producing mills will typically handle orders over 20,000 lb. Many of our competitors are not oriented toward specialty products, which we are. So, there is a niche there, we feel. And that market is quite substantial. Most of these outfits are bigger than we are."

Greer sells to many large manufacturers, including Black & Decker, Harley Davidson, Toastmaster, Caterpillar, as well as divisions and suppliers of General Motors, Ford, and Chrysler. But it also has a number of small customers: job shops, and spring, fastener and bearing manufacturers. "With the precision product we have and because most of these companies buy in medium quantities, we have a lot of customers. We're not selling '10,000 tons' to one company. We're covering a large cross section."

INTEGRATING
. . . with
Suppliers

Naturally, suppliers are also important to Greer. The company has about seven suppliers with a concentration on three. "But we're constantly qualifying new sources looking for better product, better gauge control, chemistry, and competitive pricing. This is an ongoing thing that really doesn't stop. We're buying low carbon steel, high carbon steel, alloy, and a little stainless."

Greer's suppliers include integrated mills and minimills; representatives from a new minimill startup were recently at Greer's facility seeking qualification. "We've worked very hard in developing our supply line. We have a very strict qualification procedure for materials. We have a General Motors-approved lab. So, we really react like a fully-integrated mill—except we don't make steel."

Overall, Greer Industries is content with the niche its steel subsidiary fills. But market pressures are forcing the unit to expand its niche in cold-rolled strip. Greer deals heavily in the highly competitive appliance and automotive sectors. For instance, automotive has become particularly tough in recent years; manufacturers have continually reduced their supplier bases, while boosting quality and delivery requirements. "Anytime you are dealing direct with automotive, the cost pressure is very intense," the president adds. "We are very cognizant of that. Staying on the cutting edge of technology is the only way we or any company can remain competitive in that environment. So, we have to spend money to do that. We are, and that will allow us to continue to compete."

One of Greer's major expenditures was the upgrading of its cold reduction/reversing mills in Dover. Greer needed to improve on its gauge control and surface conditioning for its customers' sake; defects have costly effects on overall material yields. "A big factor is the continuity of their processing operations (presses and roll formers); they don't want to experience downtime trying to work material that varies in gauge. They want to set up and go. We need to provide a product that will allow them to do that, coil after coil, day after day, without requiring them to tweak their equipment to make it work. It is a cost savings for the customer with more productivity and a better product."

Packaging is an extremely important function at Greer. "We're on the jewelry end of the steel business, if you will. So, we're dealing with very sophisticated surfaces that can be easily ruined. Our packaging reflects the nature of the product. We're very careful about the way we handle material: pack it, ship it, etc."

But Greer has been making more than just physical changes in Dover and Ferndale. The company has made quality and labor changes as well. For instance, in 1994, Greer established its Employee

(continues)

MARKETING STRATEGIES 2-2 **(continued)**

Involvement Team (EIT) program, which empowers workers and management to address production, quality, and service problems jointly, as a team. "We have union folks and management people attacking problems by department to get to the root cause and make suggestions on how to correct them. EIT is now part of Greer's corporate culture. Team play and working together to make things happen."

INTEGRATING ... *with Quality Improvement* ▶

Quality improvement has been another priority of the new president. Greer established its Greer Quality Plus (GQ+) total quality management program in 1994, which was viewed by the company as the first step toward ISO and QS certification. In November, Greer's Dover plant was recommended for ISO 9002 certification, and it did it without the use of an outside consultant. Instead, Greer used its EITs to make it happen.

"To get any benefit out of it, the people have to do it," states Greer's manager of quality assurances. "There is no right, no wrong; it's what works best for your company. We were fortunate in that we had actually started putting together quality procedures a number of years ago, so we had the baseline items done. We utilized our EITs, and had them start by looking at the work instructions in their particular areas. We had all the resources here, and used our teams." Greer's employees, therefore, have a better understanding of ISO procedures and documentation because they were the ones who actually developed the system; "They're not just memorizing stuff."

Consistency is the number one benefit of ISO. For example, before ISO, inside salespeople were not asking the same questions of customers, using the same forms, et cetera. Now, salespeople are performing their jobs similarly, and that should be the most immediate benefit for customers. Down the line, he says, deliveries and quality should improve further. He notes that for Greer, ISO is an extension of GQ+, which had emphasized accuracy, good service, and quality. ISO, he notes, has more to do with record keeping.

Ferndale will eventually be ISO-certified as well. After that, Greer will target QS 9000, the automotive quality standard. "Quite honestly, we have a long way to go before we achieve QS 9000; it would take a year of concerted effort. It's a monumental leap over and above ISO." QS requires, for instance, more sector-specific requirements, documented strategic planning, a functioning preventive maintenance program, and proven effective use of statistical process controls.

INTEGRATING ... *with Information Technology Management* ▶

Greer is also experimenting with electronic commerce and performs bar coding. Its systems are in compliance with the Automotive Industry Action Group, which sets standards and specifications for the automotive sector. "We currently service about six accounts on an EDI basis. We feel that that will intensify. There is no question about it: the more sophisticated we are in this arena, the better we are going to be able to service our customers who are demanding these kinds of services and communication."

— *Bigness is not necessarily the goal for a niche player; it can be being a high-quality producer and performer.*

Source: Kevin Nolan, "Greer Steel's CR Strip Growth Shows No Sign of Waning," *Metal Center News* (January 1997), pp. 74–83.

dominant position in the Japanese beverage market by signing up all the best distributors. Pepsi and other firms were preempted and had to make do with weaker sales organizations.

Advantages of Strategic Marketing

A strategic approach to marketing has a number of advantages. First, a strategic emphasis helps organizations orient themselves toward key external factors such as consumers and competition. Instead of just projecting past trends, the goal is to build market-driven strategies that reflect customer concerns. Strategic plans also tend to anticipate changes in the environment rather than just react to competitive thrusts.

Another reason strategic marketing is important is that it forces you to take a long-term view of the world. Many people believe that the problems of U.S. automobile and steel companies are due to their obsession with short-term quarterly profits. The Japanese, on the other hand, have had great success in the U.S. electronics and auto markets using a long-run focus. The ability of the Japanese to penetrate U.S. markets also shows that marketing strategy must have an international dimension. Today firms with global marketing strategies are better able to meet customer needs and the growth of international competition.

Strategy-Building Process

The basic dimensions of strategy development are described in Figure 2-2. The first step is to establish a comprehensive mission for the organization. Then a detailed assessment of each strategic business unit must be performed. This usually includes both external and internal analyses of current strengths and weaknesses. Next, appropriate marketing strategies are identified for each business unit. The remainder of Figure 2-2 shows how basic strategies are converted into detailed marketing plans for implementation.

We strongly believe that you first decide what you want to do, your strategy; then you decide how to do it, your tactics. The elements of the marketing mix are highly interrelated, and the best mixes are achieved when you take a strategic approach. For example, a new product might be positioned as a soap with lotionlike properties or as a lotion with soaplike properties. The appropriate price and advertising appeal depend on this positioning. One price level might cause consumers to perceive the product as a soap, while another price level might cause them to perceive it as a lotion. Of course, market strategy itself must be based on a sustainable advantage on one or more elements of the marketing mix.

WHAT IS OUR MISSION?

A well-defined organization provides a sense of direction to employees and helps guide them toward the fulfillment of the firm's potential. Managers should ask, "What is our business?" and "What should it be?" The idea is to extract a purpose from a consideration of the firm's history, resources, distinctive abilities, and environmental constraints. A mission statement should specify the business domains in which the organization plans to operate.[2] These are usually spelled out in product terms, such as "we are a copy machine company," or more broadly as "we are an office productivity company." The firm should try to find a purpose that fits its present needs and is neither too narrow nor too broad.

Effective mission statements should cover the following areas:

1. Product line definition
2. Market scope
3. Growth directions
4. Level of technology

Marketing strategies often involve decisions on which products to add, which to drop, which to keep, and which to modify. Thus it is logical to construct mission statements around product dimensions. For example, Famous Amos is in the cookie business rather than in the more general bakery business. Individual products can lose favor, and some firms prefer to define their mission in terms of customer needs. AT&T can be viewed as being in the communications business rather than in the telephone business. Xerox, best known for its copiers, advertises itself as being in the document business.

Organization missions must also be defined in terms of the market for their products or services. This can be expressed in geographical terms or as customer groupings. For example, Coors beer is not pasteurized, so the company has been limited to markets within refrigerated

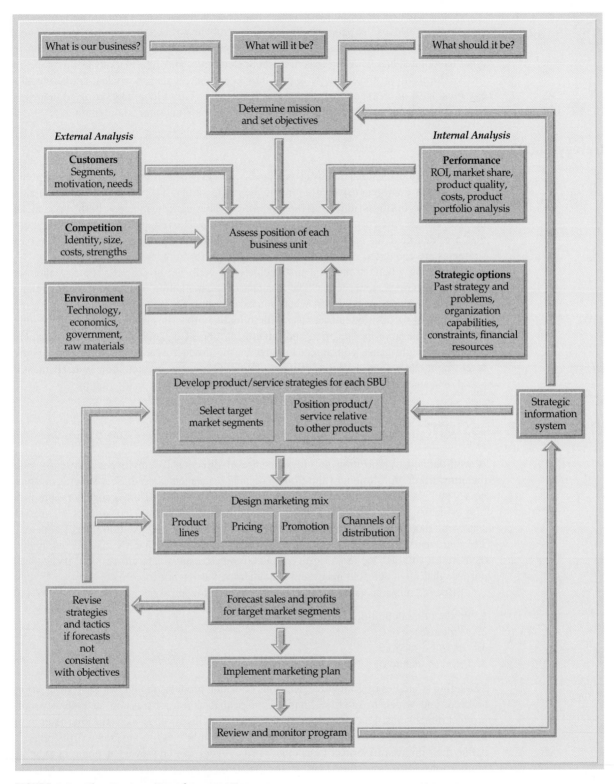

FIGURE 2-2   The Strategy Development Process

trucking distance of its breweries. Pontiac dealerships, on the other hand, are located everywhere but focus on the performance and sports-minded segment of the automobile market.

Technology has become so important to business success that mission statements need to indicate the types and levels of technology that will be emphasized. For example, American steel mills were slow to adopt continuous casting and to see the advantages of melting scrap in minimills. Their inability to recognize and seize new technology has depressed their profits and growth potential.

Finally, mission statements should give management direction on areas for growth. Some firms expand by penetrating existing markets, others by expanding product lines, or by building up present markets, by diversifying, or by growing with new technology or distribution methods. The mission statement tells management what it should not be doing, as well as what it should be doing. Once an organization has a mission, the next step is to focus on the activities of individual business units.

ANALYZING STRATEGIC BUSINESS UNITS

Marketing strategies are designed for use by strategic business units (SBUs) (Figure 2-2). An SBU is any organizational unit that has a business strategy and a manager with sales and profit responsibility. In a small company the SBU would include all operations. SBUs can also be a division of a larger company, product lines, or even selected products. General Electric popularized the SBU concept as a way to foster entrepreneurial spirit in a diversified firm.

Marketing planners operate on the principle that individual business units should play different roles in achieving organizational objectives. Some units are expected to grow faster than others, some units will be more profitable, and not all units will generate the same cash flow. The concept that the organization is a collection of business units with different objectives is a central belief of modern management. These collections of business units are often described as *portfolios*.

Product Life Cycles

The life-cycle concept helps managers keep track of their product portfolios. This proposition suggests that products are born, grow to maturity, and then decline much like plants and animals (Figure 2-3). During the introductory period, sales grow rapidly but high expenses

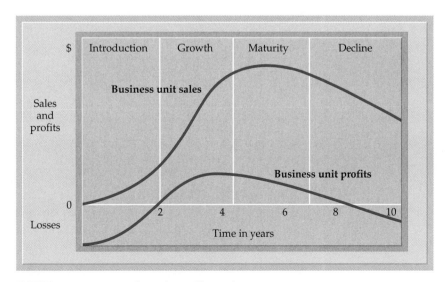

FIGURE 2-3   Impact of Product Life Cycle on Strategy

keep profits negative. Near the end of the growth stage, the rate of expansion of sales begins to slow down and profits reach a peak. During the maturity phase, sales reach their peak and profits are slowly eroded by increased competition. If something is not done to revive declining products, they eventually have to be dropped from the product line.

The life-cycle concept helps managers think about their product line as a portfolio of investments. Ideally, the firm wants to have some business units in each phase of the life cycle. If most of the items are in the mature and declining phases, the company will have trouble reaching its growth objectives. Similarly, if all the products are bunched in the introductory and declining phases, the firm is likely to experience serious cash flow problems. The best plan is to have enough business in the growth and maturity stages spinning off cash to finance the introduction of new products and the reformation of products in decline. The advantage of the product life-cycle analysis is that it makes executives realize that products do not last forever and must eventually be replaced. On the other hand, it is sometimes difficult to know when a product is leaving one stage and entering the next.

Portfolio Matrix

SBUs can be evaluated by positioning them on a diagram that compares relative market shares with market growth rates. Figure 2-4 shows a portfolio matrix developed by the Boston Consulting Group. Each circle in Figure 2-4 represents a business unit in a firm's product portfolio. The size of the circles shows the dollar sales being generated by each unit. The horizontal position of the circles shows their market share in relation to their competitors. A logarithmic scale is used for relative market share that goes from $1/10$ to 10 times the size of the next largest competitor. Thus, business units located to the right of the value 1.0 are smaller than the competition and those to the left are larger.

Portfolio matrices are often divided into four separate quadrants for analysis purposes. The positions of the lines separating the sectors are arbitrary. In Figure 2-4, high growth rates would include all businesses expanding faster than the overall economy. SBUs in each

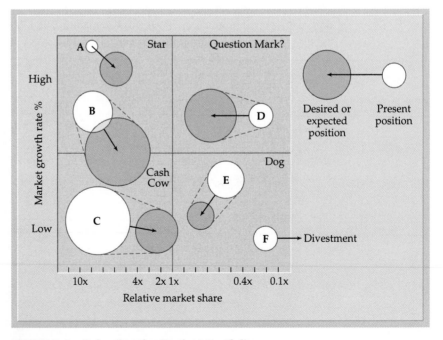

FIGURE 2-4　Balancing the Product Portfolio

corner of the portfolio matrix have sharply different financial requirements and marketing needs.

Stars Products that fall into the *star* category have strong market positions and high rates of market growth. The primary objective with stars is to maintain their market positions and to increase their sales volumes. Stars are the keys to the future because they provide growth, technological leadership, and enhanced respect in the business community. Although stars increase revenues to the firm, they tend to use more money than they generate from earnings and depreciation. To maintain their high rates of growth, stars require extra cash for expanded plant and equipment, inventories, accounts receivable, field salespeople, and advertising programs. Thus, stars are both a blessing and a curse because of the strain they put on the firm to constantly expand working capital.

Another problem with stars is that their high growth rates attract competition. The entry of other firms can help expand a market, but eventually the market will become saturated, and growth rates will decline.

Cash Cows Business units described as *cash cows* are low-growth, high-relative-market-share operations (Product C, Figure 2-4). These products are likely to be in the mature stage of their life cycles and do not require extensive funds for production facilities or inventory buildup. Cash cows also have established market positions and do not need large advertising expenditures to maintain their market shares. As a result, their high earnings and deprecia-tion allowances generate cash surpluses that can be used to invest in other growing products, to support research and development, or to buy into new lines of trade. Cash cows thus pro-vide the basic fuel on which portfolio management of business units depends.

Question Marks Products with low relative market shares in fast-growing markets are called *question marks.* These products have the potential to become stars of the future or to fade into oblivion. Because question marks have such small market shares, they usually absorb more cash than they generate. Thus, in the short run, question marks just eat money, and when their market growth slows, they become dogs.

The preferred approach with question marks is to increase their relative market shares and move them into the star category (Product D, Figure 2-4). However, this often takes a pile of cash, sophisticated marketing plans, and a good measure of luck. If the prospects for improving the market position of a business are not attractive, the firm must consider phas-ing the business out. Large multinational companies are often concerned not only with weaker brands but also with otherwise successful brands that don't have the potential for global reach. One popular approach is simply to sell the business to a competitor. Another technique is to withdraw all promotional support and try to make a few dollars as the product withers away.

Dogs Businesses that fall into the low-growth, low-relative market share quadrant are called *dogs.* These products are often in the decline phase of their life cycles and show little prospect for gaining market position or generating much cash flow. Even worse, dogs can become *cash traps* and absorb more money than they generate as firms try to revive a lost cause. The usual approach with dogs is to sell them when the opportunity occurs or to deem-phasize marketing activities (Products E and F, Figure 2-4).

APPLYING
. . . to
Consumer
Beverages
Marketing

Quaker Oats, for example, sold its Snapple juice and iced-tea business for a fraction of what it paid for this business only three years before. While adding Snapple to its Gatorade sports drink lineup made Quaker the number three beverage company in the United States after Coca-Cola Co. and PepsiCo Inc., Quaker's timing could not have been more inopportune. The fast-growing market for "New Age" uncarbonated drinks such as water, lemonade, and tea began to plateau. Coke and Pepsi got into the game under the Lipton and Nestea brand names. Snapple fell to third place with only an 18 percent share compared with leader Lipton's 33 percent share. The impact on relative share was even more devastating. Quaker thought it was buying a star and found itself being bitten by a dog.

The most common criticism of the portfolio matrix approach is that it does not have enough dimensions to assess a product portfolio accurately. Despite these limitations, the terms *dog, star,* and *cash cow* have become a standard part of the vocabulary of business planning.

Multifactor Methods

Other approaches to strategic planning include those by Arthur D. Little, Shell Chemical, PIMS (Profit Impact of Marketing Strategy), and future scenario profiles. Arthur D. Little has a 24-sector grid. It uses a four-stage product life-cycle concept and stresses that risks increase as products age and market positions weaken. Shell compares prospects for business sector profitability with company competitive capabilities. PIMS uses historical evidence collected across industries on factors contributing to performance. This information permits assessment of the current performance and future strategy options of a business unit. Future scenario profiles focus on projections of what the future may hold given different strategies that might be adopted by a business unit. In addition, some firms have developed their own in-house approaches.

General Electric, for example, has developed a nine-cell matrix based on industry attractiveness and company strength in each business. Units with the best scores are candidates for further investment, and those with the lowest scores are harvested or sold off. Business units in the middle fall into a hold or cash cow category and are used to finance growth. Business units chosen for additional investments have included microwave ovens and industrial plastics. On the other hand, lamps and large appliances followed a hold strategy, and small appliances were sold off.

One survey of industrial firms found that heavy equipment manufacturers preferred the Arthur D. Little and PIMS approaches, light equipment manufacturers preferred the Boston Consulting Group and market attractiveness approaches, and component parts manufacturers preferred the Arthur D. Little approach. Arthur D. Little's 24-sector grid has the most satisfied users.

SELECTING MARKETING STRATEGIES

Once a portfolio of business units has been evaluated, you are ready to assign strategic roles for the future management of each business. This requires creative thinking on your part. You also can consider what businesses like yours usually do by examining what are known as *generic marketing strategies.* The objective is to come up with strategies that lead to sustainable competitive advantages.

Creative Strategic Thinking

Managers must be able to step back from the existing situation and view the product and the market from another angle. This is easier said than done. Some approaches that have been suggested to encourage strategic thinking include the following:

1. Challenge the present strategy.
2. Look for strategic windows.
3. Play on the vulnerabilities of competitors.
4. Change the rules of the game.
5. Enhance customer value.

We elaborate on these approaches in later chapters, especially Chapter 5, which stresses looking for strategic windows and playing on competitors' vulnerabilities. Throughout the book enhancing customer value is emphasized.

Generic Marketing Strategies

The nature of marketing strategies may be seen in what companies actually do.[3] Empirical research based on marketing factors—marketing objectives, strategic focus, market targeting, and quality and price positioning—has shown that many businesses follow one of five strategies.

1. Companies have aggressive growth or market dominance goals. The targeting approach aims at the whole market. The *scope* of the target market in this case is said to be broad. Positioning involves marketing high-quality products at prices similar to those of competitors. This may be considered a differentiation strategy.

2. Companies seek steady sales growth through either market share gain or market expansion. Selected segments are targeted through higher-quality products at higher prices than those of competitors. This may be considered a focused differentiation strategy. *Focus* means narrow market scope.

3. Companies pursue steady sales growth through an emphasis on market share by concentrating on selected segments of the market. Their positioning is average quality at average prices. This may be considered a stuck-in-the-middle strategy, as no real advantage through quality differentiation or low costs is created.

4. Companies strive for steady growth, with a focus on total market expansion or on winning market share by targeting selected segments or individuals. The positioning is higher quality at the same prices. This resembles a variant of a focused differentiation strategy that emphasizes value. It provides a powerful incentive for the expansion of the market as a whole.

5. Companies have defensive objectives, with a focus on cost reduction and productivity improvement. Very selective targeting of individuals is coupled with a positioning of similar quality at similar prices.

While not all firms exactly match one of these profiles, they are usually similar to one of them. As you would expect, differences in deployment of the five strategies correspond to different stages of market maturity (Table 2-2).

Some believe that "All successful strategies are differentiation." The implication is that all strategies are based on some form of differentiation. Where one firm will differentiate on the basis of costs, another will use products, or size of market, or distribution, or some other dimension. If you think of differentiation as the common denominator, then it is easier to see how marketing strategies blend together to achieve the goals of the firm.

STRATEGY EXECUTION

APPLYING
. . . to Healthcare Products Marketing

Having a good strategy is a necessary but not sufficient condition for success. You must ably implement your strategy. For example, the 100-year-old bandage maker Johnson & Johnson (J&J) has pursued a strategy of constantly pushing into new areas to cater to evolving customer needs. J&J views itself as a healthcare company. Its major consumer products are Tylenol painkillers, Band-Aids, baby products, and Nutrogena skin products. Its major professional products are coronary stents—tiny metal scaffoldings that prop open arteries, minimally-invasive surgery products, and wound closure products. Its major pharmaceutical products include Risperdal for schizophrenia, Levaquin for infections, and

TABLE 2-2   Generic Marketing Strategies

	Aggressors	Premium Position Segments	Stuck-in-the-Middlers	High-Value Segmenters	Defenders
Strategic objective	Aggressive sales growth/ domination	Steady sales growth	Steady sales growth	Steady sales growth	Defend/pre-vent/decline
Strategic focus	Win share/ expand market	Win share/expand market	Win share	Win share/expand market	Cost reduction/ productivity improvement
Market targeting	Whole market	Selected segments	Selected segments	Selected segments	Individual customers
Competitive positioning	Higher quality/same price	Higher quality/higher price	Same quality/same price	Higher quality/same price	Same or higher quality/same price
Market type	New, growing; fluid competition; rapid change in customer needs	Mature and stable	Mature and stable	New, growing	Mature and stable
Corporate attitudes	Pro-active NPD;* marketing important; take on any competition	Pro-active NPD; marketing important; take on any competition	Imitate/lead in NPD; take on/avoid competition	Pro-active NPD; take on/avoid competition	Follower in NPD; marketing of limited importance; take on/avoid competition
Performance	Best across financial and marketing based criteria	Good across most criteria	Mediocre	Mediocre, esp. on profit criterion	Worst performance overall

* NPD = new product development.

Source: Graham J. Hooley, James E. Lynch, and David Jobber, "Generic Marketing Strategies," *International Journal of Research in Marketing,* Vol. 9, No. 1 (March 1992), p. 87.

MARKETING STRATEGIES *2-3*

Solectron's Strategy Execution

APPLYING ... to Industrial Marketing

Solectron Corp. is a "stealth manufacturer" of computers, printers, cellular phones, and other high-tech gear. Its American-based factories produce products stamped with famous names such as IBM, Hewlett-Packard, and Mitsubishi Electric. This allows Solectron's customers to become "virtual firms" that do little besides design and market products. Solectron is a leader in the global contract manufacturing business—a business that is growing almost twice as fast as the electronics industry it serves.

Solectron lands orders because it is considered among the world's most efficient manufacturers. It keeps assembly lines running 24-hours a day, spreading the costs of its buildings and machines across more products. Every line looks exactly the same everywhere in the world. Thus, Solectron can shift jobs or add capacity quickly. Moreover, as a massive purchaser of electronic components, it gets low prices and precisely scheduled deliveries that minimize inventory.

Somewhat surprisingly, Solectron's biggest plant is not in Asia but in California's Silicon Valley. This proximity to its customers is prized because it facilitates quick product development. Speed is crucial because high-tech products have short life spans—and the first to market often reaps the

(continues)

MARKETING STRATEGIES 2-3 (continued)

Bob Day/Courtesy Solectron Corp.

largest rewards. As Solectron expands it risks the nimbleness behind its success. Thus, in order to manage its growth, it sometimes turns away a prospective customer.

Solectron relies on high volume and low overhead. Its profit margins are thin. It tracks every efficiency and every expense carefully. It has little room for error. Thus, it must emphasize quality. It asks 150 customers each week to grade it on quality, responsiveness, communication, service, and technical support. These grades are posted inside factories and help determine bonuses for both workers and managers. Solectron is a two-time winner of the Malcolm Baldrige National Quality Award for manufacturing.

— *One strategy is to be the low cost producer; nonetheless, quality is a must.*

Source: Scott Thurm, "Some Firms Prosper by Facilitating the Rise of the 'Virtual' Firm," *The Wall Street Journal,* August 18, 1998, pp. A1, A6.

Procrit for anemia. In the late 1990s, Johnson & Johnson encountered numerous woes. Six experimental drugs fell through late in development. Rivals of the company's coronary stent grabbed 90 percent of its market. Plans for a cholesterol-lowering margarine suffered a regulatory setback. And the company lost a critical battle over rights to a future version of a top-selling anemia drug. J&J suffered setbacks in executing its strategy. In contrast to J&J, an example of a successful implementation of strategy is given in Marketing Strategies box 2-3.

SUMMARY

Marketing strategy is concerned with forging assets and capabilities into sustainable competitive advantages. Strategies are created for portfolios of business units using multifactor evaluation matrices. Remember that your job is to manage product portfolios so that cash cows generate funds for rising stars and dogs are harvested or sold off. We will pursue our discussion of marketing strategy in more detail after we have covered customer and competitive analysis and the crucial concepts of market segmentation, product differentiation, and product positioning.

NOTES

1. Definition from George S. Day, "The Capabilities of Market-Driven Organizations," *Journal of Marketing,* Vol. 58, No. 4 (October 1994), p. 38.
2. The mission statement is sometimes called a *business statement.*
3. This section is taken from Graham J. Hooley, James E. Lynch, and David Jobber, "Generic Marketing Strategies," *International Journal of Research in Marketing,* Vol. 9, No. 1 (March 1992), pp. 75–89. The authors relate their research to that of two other well-known works: R. E. Miles and C. C. Snow, *Organization Strategy, Structure, and Process* (New York: McGraw-Hill, 1978) and Michael E. Porter, *Competitive Strategy* (New York: The Free Press, 1980).

SUGGESTED READING

Cravens, David, Gordon Greeley, Nigel F. Piercy, and Stanley F. Slater. "Mapping the Path to Market Leadership," *Marketing Management,* Vol. 7, No. 3 (Fall 1998), pp. 29–39.

Day, George S. "The Capabilities of Market-Driven Organizations," *Journal of Marketing,* Vol. 58, No. 4 (October 1994), pp. 37–52.

Hooley, Graham J., James E. Lynch, and David Jobber. "Generic Marketing Strategies," *International Journal of Research in Marketing,* Vol. 9, No. 1 (March 1992), pp. 75–89.

Menon, Anil, Sundar G. Bharadwaj, Phani Tej Adidam, and Steven W. Edison, "Antecedents and Consequences of Marketing Strategy Making," *Journal of Marketing,* Vol. 63, No. 2 (April 1999), pp. 18–40.

Williams, Jeffrey R. "How Sustainable Is Your Competitive Advantage?" *California Management Review,* Vol. 34, No. 3 (1992), pp. 29–51.

REFERENCES

Aaker, David A. *Strategic Market Management,* 5th ed. New York: Wiley, 1998.

Day, George S. *Market Driven Strategy: Processes for Creating Value.* New York: The Free Press, 1990.

Douglas, Susan. *Global Marketing Strategy.* New York: McGraw-Hill, 1995.

Jagpal, Sharan. *Marketing Strategy and Uncertainty.* New York: Oxford University Press, 1999.

Jain, Subhash C. *Marketing Planning & Strategy,* 5th ed. Cincinnati: South-Western, 1996.

Schnaars, Steven P. *Marketing Strategy,* 2d rev. ed. New York: The Free Press, 1997.

QUESTIONS

1. KeyCorp is one of the top 15 largest banks in the United States with assets of about $65 billion. KeyCorp is the market share leader in northern metropolitan areas such as Cleveland and Seattle. For a number of years it followed a "snowbelt strategy" of acquiring small, cheap branches in the northern half of the country. Many of the acquired banks are in small towns. Is this strategy consistent with KeyCorp doing targeted selling by market

segmentation? With it being a supermarket of financial services? Would you shift Key-Corp's strategy away from the snowbelt strategy? If so, how?

2. Procter & Gamble is the world's largest consumer products company. P&G sells more than 300 brands to 5 billion consumers in 140 countries. Nonetheless, P&G recently reorganized, shifting product management from four geographical regions to seven essentially self-contained global business units, ranging from baby care to food products. Each unit is completely responsible for generating profits from its products and controls product development, manufacturing, and marketing. Why did P&G restructure its operations?

3. More and more firms have the policy that "marketing will never be constrained by manufacturing." What is the role of manufacturing as a weapon in the ever-present battle for market share? Give an example.

4. Hudson Bay is Canada's largest retailer. Hudson Bay owns The Bay general department store chain and the Zellers discount chain. Hudson Bay has been slow to respond to new competitors, and has been hobbled by dated information systems and poor customer service. One result was that Wal-Mart Stores surpassed Zellers to become Canada's biggest discount chain. Hudson Bay has responded by acquiring K-Mart Canada, Canada's third-largest discount retailer. What did Hudson Bay gain with this purchase?

5. International Business Machines abandoned giant, "bipolar" machines to move to a new technology, CMOS (complementary metal oxide semiconductor). The move resulted in mainframes that are much smaller and consume a lot less power, which allows them to be cooled by air instead of chilled water. This means they cost customers less money to run. They are also cheaper for IBM to make, resulting in higher profit margins. There has been one big drawback—they are slower than the old-style machines that they replaced. Customers who needed high-end machines switched to competitors. In particular, Hitachi Data's Skyline series, which combines the older bipolar technology with some new CMOS technology, became a big hit. IBM's world-wide mainframe share fell from 81 percent in 1995 to about 67 percent in 1998. IBM's new mainframe, System 390 G5 (for fifth generation) for the first time matches the processing speed of the bipolar machines it abandoned. Nonetheless, there is still a performance gap between IBM and Hitachi: 125 MIPS (millions of instructions per second) to 150 MIPS. Assess IBM's strategic decision.

6. Zippo Manufacturing makes lighters. Zippo became a legend by wisely taking up World War II correspondent Ernie Pyle's suggestion that it send lighters to GIs free of charge. The move won Zippo good feelings from an entire generation. Now, however, anti-smoking groups have made lighting up a social no-no. A historic settlement between states and tobacco companies has ended a barrage of marketing that has inadvertently assisted the company. How should Zippo address its evolving marketplace?

CASE 2-1   PCS: THE NEXT GENERATION OF WIRELESS COMMUNICATIONS*

George Thompson was cautiously optimistic about the possibilities. His decision to go forward was an expensive one, laden with a great deal of risk. He had spent days wading through documentation on the various wireless communications technologies and had learned a great deal about the opportunities and pitfalls of each. The technology debate had been raging in the industry for several years, and the jury was still out. One thing, however was clear: the technology decision was a vital one. The path he decided to take could make or break his business.

In addition to his technology dilemma, Thompson was faced with an even more fundamental decision. The 1995 Personal Communications Services (PCS) auctions being held by the Federal Communications Commission were rapidly approaching, and George Thompson still had questions regarding the future of PCS. Should he enter this risky business? If the industry grew as predicted, he and his partners could become rich beyond their expectations; however, the risks were high. If he made the wrong choice the financial and service implications could spell disaster.

As an industry, PCS promised to deliver to the marketplace many features that cellular had not. Wireless communications—namely cellular—had experienced dramatic growth in the past decade due to its increased acceptance as both a productivity tool for business and a convenience for personal use. Based on the trends in the cellular industry, many believed that PCS would demonstrate significant growth in its initial 10 years. Despite the successes of cellular, consumers were demanding better service, lower prices, and increased capabilities. Was PCS the wireless opportunity of the future? Marketplace information was scarce, and the licenses were expensive (see Exhibit 1). This was a decision not to be ventured into lightly. Thompson's partners were counting on him to decide regarding whether or not they would bid for a license, and what type of technology they would employ to bring PCS service to their targeted market of 8.4 million people in the Chicago area.

HISTORY

The mass market for wireless communications began with the introduction of cellular technology in the late 1970s. Wireless communication is similar to radio and television transmission using radio waves to transmit communications instead of electrical impulses traveling through wire or cable. At the time of cellular deployment, the Federal Communications Commission (FCC) divided the country geographically into a number of major service areas (MSAs) and limited the granting of licenses to two cellular service providers per MSA.

The electromagnetic spectrum upon which virtually all forms of telecommunication travels is divided into segments. The government has designated that certain entities and technologies use certain segments of the spectrum. The cellular technology in widespread use today resides in the 850MHz range of the radio spectrum. Cellular service, first offered to the American

---

* This case was prepared by Jennifer M. Griffin under the supervision of Robert E. Spekman, Tayloe Murphy Professor of Business Administration. Copyright (c) 1997 by the University of Virginia Darden School Foundation, Charlottesville, VA. Reproduced by permission.

EXHIBIT 1   Example Results of Round 66 PCS MTA Auction

MTA	BID (#M)	$/POP	Population	% Urban
New York	$346.9	$13.13	18,051,000	100%
Los Angeles	330.0	17.24	14,550,000	97
Houston	55.9	10.77	4,054,000	83
Detroit	78.1	7.81	4,705,000	98
Boston	121.7	12.87	4,134,000	100
Washington	130.0	16.71	4,119,000	97
Richmond	33.0	8.59	1,091,000	74
Denver	27.5	7.08	2,074,000	83
Kansas City	11.1	3.83	1,840,000	73
Milwaukee	$27.6	$6.08	1,752,000	87%
Average		$10.41		

consumer in 1983, had captured 29.3 percent of the wireless technology market ten years later. Its market penetration jumped from 6.7 percent in 1987 to an estimated 33.9 percent in 1994. Cellular's rapid subscription growth rate reveals that it has achieved acceptance more quickly than many other familiar household items including televisions and video cassette recorders.[1] As can be seen in Exhibits 2 and 3, revenues grew from a low of $300 million in 1985 to $3.2 billion by 1990, with expert predictions hovering around $15 billion by 1995.

THE FCC AUCTIONS

In 1994, the FCC decided to relegate a new portion of the radio spectrum to enable the commercial use of PCS. Rather than give away spectrum frequency, a finite resource, the FCC decided to auction the PCS service provider licenses as allowed by the Omnibus Act passed in August of 1993. PCS will reside in the 1.8GHz range of the spectrum. For the new PCS, the FCC has again divided the country into geographical regions to establish areas in which the service providers will operate and compete.[2] The country has been divided into 50 major trading areas (MTAs) and 500 basic trading areas (BTAs). MTA licenses are significantly more expensive than BTA licenses since they cover much larger geographic areas. They are designed for the large players, such as current cellular providers, long-distance carriers or large cable-TV

operators; BTA licenses are targeted at the smaller regional players, such as Thompson and his partners. Thus, the establishment of the different sized areas promotes competition and allows smaller entrepreneurs to enter the industry. The FCC will auction licenses to two service providers per MTA and four service providers per BTA. A small portion of the frequency has been reserved for unlicensed operations.

CURRENT CELLULAR SERVICES

The cellular technology that is in use today is either analog or digital. Most existing U.S. systems are analog, and little conversion to digital has occurred due to its prohibitive costs. Cellular systems are considered high powered (or high tier) and consist of a honeycomb of very large cells, known as macrocells. For the current cellular service, as seen in Exhibit 4, a signal is sent from a mobile telephone to a large radio tower along the 850MHz frequency bandwidth. After reaching the radio tower, the signal is sent along wires to a base station controller to a mobile telephone switching office and on into the public switched telephone network that is operated by the Regional Bell Operating Company (RBOC) for delivery to the recipient.

Although cellular has achieved fairly widespread acceptance in the marketplace, it lags behind traditional wireline phone usage by a factor of 20, in terms of number of minutes of use per month per subscriber. Some of the reluctance towards cellular may be caused by technology problems. The main problems with the existing cellular service are the voice quality of the transmission and its cost. Other concerns include security and system capacity. Callers in some high-volume markets such as Los Angeles or New York have reported having to wait several minutes before obtaining a dial tone. In addition, reports show that about 20 percent of rush-hour callers

---

[1] Teisberg, Elizabeth Olmsted and Sarah R. Collins, "McCaw Cellular Communications, Inc. in 1990," Harvard Business School, 1991, p. 1.
[2] The geographical regions known as MSAs that were established for cellular service are not the same as the MTAs and BTAs established for PCS.

EXHIBIT 2   Wireless Growth 1987–1994

	1987	1988	1989	1990	1991	1992	1993	1994
Cellular	1,231	2,069	3,509	5,283	7,557	11,033	16,009	24,134[a]
SMR	628	763	904	1,063	1,197	1,343	1,477	1,625[b]
Paging	5,900	6,900	8,100	9,900	11,800	15,300	18,700	22,253[b]
Microwave	10,635	11,609	12,444	13,368	14,176	15,042	15,945	17,061[b]
Total	18,394	21,341	24,957	29,614	34,730	42,718	52,131	65,073
% Cellular	6.7%	9.7%	14.1%	17.8%	21.8%	25.8%	30.7%	37.1%

Note: [a] = 1994 actual
[b] = 1994 projected

Source: Personal Communications Industry Association (PCIA) and Cellular Telecommunications Industry Association (CTIA).

EXHIBIT 3   Cellular Industry Growth 1984–1994

Date	Subscribers	Six-Month Revenues	Roamer Services	Cell Sites	Employees	Cumulative Capital Investment	Number of System	Average Monthly Bill	Avg. Call Length (in min.)
Dec 1, 1984	91,600	$178,085,000		346	1,404	$354,760,500	32		2.33
Jun 1, 1985	203,600	176,231,000		599	1,697	588,751,000	65		2.25
Dec 1, 1985	340,213	306,197,000		913	2,727	911,167,000	102		2.26
Jun 1, 1986	500,000	360,585,000		1,194	3,556	1,140,163,000	129		2.35
Dec 1, 1986	681,825	462,467,000		1,531	4,334	1,436,753,000	166		2.48
Jun 1, 1987	883,778	479,514,000		1,732	5,656	1,724,348,000	206		2.32
Dec 1, 1987	1,230,855	672,005,000		2,305	7,147	2,234,635,000	312	$96.83	2.20
Jun 1, 1988	1,608,697	886,075,000		2,789	9,154	2,589,589,000	420	95.00	2.20
Dec 1, 1988	2,069,441	1,073,473,000	$89,331,000	3,209	11,400	3,274,105,000	517	98.02	2.38
Jun 1, 1989	2,691,793	1,406,463,000	121,366,800	3,577	13,719	3,675,473,000	559	85.52	2.38
Dec 1, 1989	3,508,944	1,934,132,000	173,199,000	4,169	15,927	4,480,141,752	584	89.30	2.58
Jun 1, 1990	4,368,686	2,126,362,000	192,350,000	4,768	18,973	5,211,765,025	592	83.94	2.38
Dec 1, 1990	5,283,055	2,422,458,000	263,660,000	5,616	21,382	6,281,596,000	751	80.90	2.41
Jun 1, 1991	6,380,053	2,653,505,000	302,329,000	6,685	25,545	7,429,739,000	1,029	74.56	2.36
Dec 1, 1991	7,557,148	3,055,017,000	401,325,000	7,847	26,327	8,671,544,000	1,252	72.74	2.24
Jun 1, 1992	8,892,535	2,633,285,000	436,725,000	8,901	30,595	9,276,139,000	1,483	68.51	
Dec 1, 1992	11,032,753	4,189,441,000	537,146,000	10,307	34,348	11,262,070,000	1,506	68.68	
Jun 1, 1993	13,067,318	4,819,259,000	587,347,000	11,551	26,501	12,775,967,000	1,523	67.31	
Dec 1, 1993	16,009,461	6,072,906,000	773,269,000	12,805	39,775	13,946,406,629	1,529	61.48	
Jun 1, 1994	19,283,306	6,519,030,599	778,115,600	14,740	45,606	16,107,920,531	1,550	58.65	
Dec 1, 1994	24,134,421	$7,710,890,665	$1,052,666,300	17,920	53,902	$18,938,677,819	1,581	$56.21	

Source: Cellular Telecommunications Industry Association (CTIA).

in such markets were unable to place calls on the first try. Furthermore, the service fees of cellular phones are substantially higher than traditional wireline phones, and the usage charges are different. The recipient of a cellular phone call must always pay for the call, and if the call originates from a cellular phone, the caller must pay too. Finally, many subscribers often keep their handsets turned off to conserve battery life for their less frequent, but more important, calls. As a result of these issues and more, many in the industry, over the past ten years, have been looking for a new technology to replace the inefficiencies of traditional cellular services. Many observers believe that the first company to offer service unencumbered by such problems might win a large share of the market and establish a loyal customer base.

PCS

According to the Personal Communications Industry Association (PCIA), Personal Communications Services (PCS) are defined as "a broad range of individualized telecommunications services that enable people or devices to communicate independent of location."[3] Personal Communications Services provide a number

---

[3] The PCIA actually groups a number of technological services under the category name "PCS." These include satellite, paging, cellular, dedicated data, SMR/ESMR, and the "new" PCS described in this case.

of benefits for the consumer. Primarily, PCS offers *terminal* mobility or access to the service from differing locations or while in motion. Second, PCS offers *personal* mobility—it allows the subscriber to make and receive calls at any location, at any time, on the basis of a unique personal number, as long as the region is covered by a PCS service provider's network. With PCS, each subscriber has a personal phone number; with this number she is able to make or receive phone calls any time, anywhere. Rather than have a home, business, fax, and car phone number, a PCS subscriber can have one PCS phone number to be used everywhere. With PCS, consumers will be able to call *people, not locations.*

PCS offers the promise of delivering what cellular traditionally has not: more variety (such as advanced forms of video and data applications), lower costs, better quality, and improved service, including increased portability (due to smaller handsets), increased reliability (due to extended battery lives), and convenience (due to a single personal phone number per subscriber). Expectations for later developments include multi-media applications. In addition, proponents expect PCS technology to eliminate the dropped calls, reception of unwanted conversations, and other interruptions that still plague many cellular users. Because PCS will operate in a higher frequency range than cellular, the range of transmission of the radio waves is more limited, thus requiring more transmitters per square mile to ensure complete coverage. This means that less powerful, smaller handsets would be used.

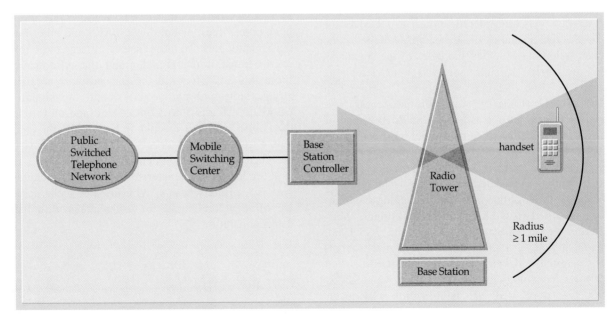

EXHIBIT 4   Cellular/High-Tier PCS

THE PCS TECHNOLOGY OPTIONS

There are several new PCS technologies emerging in the marketplace. During his research, Thompson learned that they could be categorized as (1) either high-tier or low-tier technologies or (2) as either CDMA- or TDMA-type technologies. The first segmentation refers to network architecture. High-tier technologies were the most similar to current cellular services in that they required a similar architecture including large radio towers to transmit the signals. Low-tier technologies required much smaller and less expensive devices known as radio ports. Radio ports are basically radio transmitters and receivers about the size of a shoe box that are much smaller than the large radio towers used in either high-tier PCS or cellular systems. High-tier technologies use very large cells, known as macrocells usually covering at least one mile in radius. In comparison, low-tier technologies use much smaller cells, known as microcells, and are often less than a quarter mile in radius. With a low-tier network composed of microcells, rather than the macrocells found in high-tier networks, there are many more cells per square mile. Smaller (and therefore, more) cells increase system capacity because the same airwave channel can be used simultaneously for different calls in different cells nearby.

The second segmentation scheme for the technologies dealt with the manner in which the data were carried. With every phone call, the signal (voice, data, etc.) must be carried from the location of the person who places the phone call to the intended location or person. Each of the technologies Thompson was reviewing was considered either a CDMA- or TDMA-type technology. This simply refers to the actual ordering of the bits and bytes of the signals as they are carried over the radio waves and telephone lines from one location to another. Developed in 1989, CDMA (Code Division Multiple Access) was originally intended for use at the 850MHz range of the spectrum (cellular's territory) but has been modified to work at the 1.8GHz range. It was developed by QualComm, is marketed under the name CDMA IS-95, and is considered a high-tier technology. A second high-tier option is another technology that has been modified to work in the 1.8GHz range. Marketed in the United States under the name DCS-1900, this technology is a modification of a digital technology originally developed in Europe. GSM is an 850MHz technology and the base from which DCS-1900 was developed. The modification was developed by Ericsson and uses the TDMA (or Time Division Multiple Access) form of interface. GSM, or the Global System for Mobile Communication (the TDMA option), *has* been commercially tested, unlike QualComm's CDMA option. Each manufacturer contends that its technology is superior; they both claim their technology costs less to deploy, and offers better coverage and greater capacity.

Those in the industry hold opinions, as well. Some argue that since GSM has been commercially tested and has achieved widespread acceptance throughout Europe, that DCS-1900 (the technology derived from GSM) is the superior technology. Others argue that the CDMA technology, although not commercially tested, is superior because it is a newer technology that uses the finite spectrum space more efficiently.

High-tier technologies require network architectures very similar to that of traditional cellular networks; since both of the above technologies are high tier, they require much of the costly capital outlays associated with the building of a traditional cellular network.

Another possible solution for Thompson is a technology developed by Bell Communications Research (Bellcore).[4] Bellcore's technology, known as Personal Access Communications Service (PACS), is considered a low-power or low-tier option and thus uses a very different architecture from the traditional high-powered cellular architecture described above. As Exhibit 5 depicts, in a low-tier architecture, such as a PACS architecture, a signal is sent from the small mobile phone handset to a radio port (along the 1.8GHz frequency). Radio ports are small, relatively inexpensive devices that can be deployed on top of lamp poles, trees, or buildings. PACS and other low-tier technologies use these instead of large radio towers to transmit the signal along the microwaves. From this point forward the transmission is carried along traditional phone wires, and the signal is passed to a Radio Port Control Unit and on through the Public Switched Telephone Network to the recipient. PACS uses TDMA technology and is primarily designed for use in high density areas. The small cell size (microcells) characteristic of low-tier technologies is a primary reason why low-tier technologies are often better suited for urban areas with their dense population.

---

[4] Bellcore is a leading provider of communications software and consulting services to telecommunications carriers, businesses, and governments worldwide.

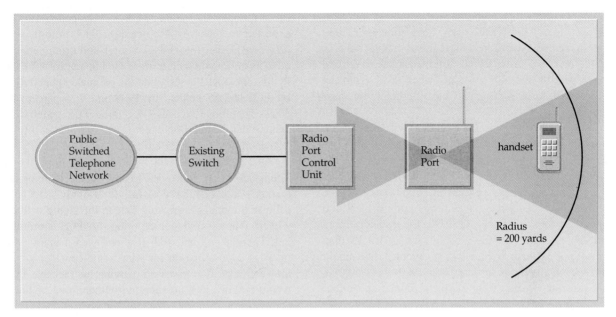

EXHIBIT 5   Low-Tier PCS

HIGH-POWER VERSUS LOW-POWER TECHNOLOGIES

The chart below summarizes the main differences between high- and low-tier technologies.

Characteristics of Technologies

	High-Tier Technologies	Low-Tier Technologies
Cell Size	Large (> 1 mile)	Small (< .25 miles)
Base stations (deployment)	Radio towers; large and expensive ($ million)	Radio ports; small and inexpensive (~ $3000)
Coverage	Ubiquitous	Limited
Handset	Larger	Smaller
Capacity/ geographical area or a city	Low to medium	Very high
Talk time for portables	Short (~ 1 hour)	Long (> 4 hours)
Vehicular service	> 70 mph	~ 35 mph
Quality	< wireline	~ wireline
Principal "designed for"	Outdoor and vehicular	Indoor/outdoor and pedestrian
Expected usage	Low	High

THE EXPECTED MARKET

It was the PCIA's opinion that PCS services would revolutionize the way people communicate, and bring wireless communications to the mass market through lower priced equipment and service charges. Market research indicates that there is a high amount of unmet demand for personal communications, and that the decreasing prices, advanced technologies, and creation of PCS licenses will enable service providers to fill the demand gap through PCS offerings. As seen in Exhibit 3, the prices for cellular service have fallen steadily over the past decade; industry observers expect PCS prices to realize a similar decrease over time as competition heats up within the market. In addition, in its 1994 PCS Market Demand Forecast, the PCIA concluded that despite expectation for increased competition, PCS services will continue to grow. This predicted period of dynamic growth is expected to continue for the next decade. Among other predictions, the PCIA also predicted that the new PCS will be heavily oriented toward consumer, rather than business, service. This forecast suggests that PCS may not necessarily follow in the footsteps of cellular in terms of market penetration. When cellular was introduced in 1983, it exhibited a pattern in which business users first used and accepted cellular, followed by nonbusiness and residential users. In 1990, the average use of cellular was reported to be 75 percent business calls and 25 percent personal. Presently, the U.S. residential market consists of more than 95 million households with an average phone bill per household of approximately $50 per month. The view that PCS will follow a nontraditional penetration pattern is supported by the findings of the National Regulatory Research Institute (NRRI) which predicts that the market for off-site PCS is largely residential, unlike the initial market for cellular service. The NRRI does note, however, that employees who work in critical job functions such as executives, sales, or technical/professional roles and who spend 8 hours or more per week away from the office will form a separate, and important, business market.

All in all, it is expected that PCS will appeal to a broader range of buyers than cellular, which has depended heavily on two market segments (1) the white-collar, college-educated and married subscribers with annual incomes in excess of $50,000 and (2) the blue-collar work force that depends upon the cellular phone as a working tool. In 1990, for instance, more cellular phones were installed in pick-up trucks than any other type of vehicle.[5] The average household income of a cellular subscriber in 1990 was $60,000, but just three years earlier a typical cellular subscriber would have been described as a 55-year-old executive earning more than $90,000, who used her cellular phone 89 percent of the time for business and only 11 percent of the time for personal use.

PCS is expected to add new value to the industry. Rather than replacing existing services, it is expected that the total pie for wireless communications will grow, and the new PCS services will be able to coexist alongside cellular rather than compete. In February 1995, the cellular customer base in the United States reached 10 percent national penetration. In the past decade, the cellular industry has posted record revenue gains, capital investment, and new jobs. In 1994 alone, the total number of cellular customers grew 50 percent—more than eight million new customers—to reach a total of more than 24 million by the end of the year. Cellular industry observers do not expect this growth to drop off; they contend that by 2002 cellular subscriptions will have grown to 52 million customers.

PCS market forecasts indicate that within 10 years, over 50 percent of households will subscribe to cellular or PCS. The timing of service deployment (the rate at which the networks are built and ready for full-scale operation) for PCS, however, is expected to significantly affect demand for service. With service deployment of PCS services anticipated for sometime in 1995, total market penetration predicted by PCIA is expected to grow to 3.1 percent by 1998 or 8.5 million

subscriptions.[6] By 2003, PCS market penetration is expected to reach 10.4 percent or 31.1 million subscriptions. Other forecasts, although still bright, are not quite as optimistic long term as the one put forth by the PCIA. The NRRI asserts that the estimated penetration for PCS is 3.55 percent by 1998 and 8.75 percent by 2003. The above forecasts for rapid PCS penetration assume that penetration occurs after full availability of PCS facilities (i.e., fully built PCS networks).

As if he did not already have enough to think about, Thompson knew he needed to address the issue of the market. With cellular growing so strongly, and with cellular providers promising that in the future cellular will be able to provide everything that PCS is promising, Thompson wondered: Is there even a market for PCS? Is there a market for what some consider a "me too" cellular? There was no denying the fact that PCS would be born in a hostile environment, one of fierce competition among the many current cellular providers. Thompson knew that a "me too" product would simply die in the competitive telecommunications market.

THE TARGETED MARKET AND THEIR BUYING PROCESS

Thompson expected a likely PCS buyer to have a typical new, high-tech product adopter profile. The majority of expected PCS buyers tend to be young, falling in the "under 35 years" age bracket. They are expected to be single, high income, and have attended some college. Men are considered more likely to buy PCS than women. Exhibit 6, which categorizes the age distribution of possible PCS penetration, estimates the long-run penetration that is possible by age group. As such, it suggests possible target markets for Thompson to consider. The distribution, however, may be expected to change as buyers and possible buyers gain experience, as imitators move from the possible buyers category to the buyers category, and as nonbuyers migrate to the buyers and possible buyers categories.[7]

Additionally, studies showed that predicted penetration for people with incomes of $40,000 or over exceeds the penetration for people with incomes under

---

[5] Teisberg, Elizabeth Olmsted and Sarah R. Collins, "McCaw Cellular Communications, Inc. in 1990," Harvard Business School, 1991, p. 4.

[6] Total subscriptions will always be greater than total subscribers because many individuals will subscribe to multiple services (i.e., a consumer who uses both paging and cellular).

[7] Davis, Vivian, Hans Kruse, William Pollard, and Catherine E. Reed, "Competition and Interconnection: The Case of Personal Communications Services," National Regulatory Research Institute, July 1994, p. 60.

EXHIBIT 6   Age Distribution of Possible PCS Penetration

Age Group	Buyers	Possible Buyers	Nonbuyers	Total
Under 35 years	19%	43%	38%	100%
35 to 44 years	16%	39%	45%	100%
45 to 54 years	12%	32%	56%	100%
Over 55 years	9%	28%	63%	100%

Source: Barry E. Goodstadt, "Personal Communications Services in the United States: A Survey of User Interest," *Spectrum* (Burlington, MA: Decision Resources, Inc., July 17, 1991): 27–4.

$40,000 in the buyer and possible buyer categories. In addition, from marketplace research, Thompson could expect that the average American customer would use their PCS phone in their car 53 percent of the time, in addition to still using other phones 33 percent of the time, as a substitute for their home phone 18 percent of the time, as a substitute for an office phone 9 percent of the time, and for other reasons a remaining 9 percent of the time.

Expected Nationwide Method of PCS Use

	Total Users	Current Cellular	Current Non-Cellular
In-car	53%	64%	48%
In addition to other phone	33%	32%	33%
Substitute for home phone	18%	17%	19%
Substitute for office phone	9%	12%	7%
Other	9%	5%	10%

Source: Encompass, Inc., "American Wireless Communication Corporation: Broadband PCS Conference for Designated Entities," June 1994.

From industry contacts, market research, and trends exhibited by the cellular market, Thompson deduced that the generally accepted market requirements for PCS included a service which operates everywhere and is affordable. Being able to operate everywhere does not mean that Thompson has to physically install networks nationwide for his customer base, but it does make his technology choice all the more important. He must be able to offer his customers interoperability with other systems when they travel outside their local area. Most of all, however, the service must be priced competitively. Current national averages for cellular service are approximately $0.50 per minute, and as the cellular market has shown by its significant decrease in prices over the past decade, customers will be very price sensitive. The existing market is very competitive and there is not much room for development of a long-standing competitive advantage. Similar to the

airline industry which is known for its price wars, the telecommunications industry has open competition, high fixed costs, and low variable costs. Market estimates for variable operating costs incurred by PCS service providers are expected to average around $5.00 per subscriber per month, and network development capital expenditures are expected to average around $600 per subscriber. As well, today's telecommunications customer is sophisticated and demanding; George feels he will have to offer all the basics at a very competitive price. He knows that in order for him to gain market share at the expense of the cellular operators in his market area, he must offer voice quality that is better than cellular and, at a minimum, equal to landline. He must be able to guarantee security and privacy of communications, and the handsets must not only be portable but intuitive and easy to use. He needs to offer not only the basic features now, but also the newer, more sophisticated features as they become available. Exhibit 7 compares cellular and PCS features.

THE LOW-TIER OPTION

Since low-tier technologies represent an alternative to the older and more traditional high-tier networks, George had spent a fair amount of time researching them. Because he was considering purchasing a license in an urban market, it was appealing that low-tier systems were primarily designed for high-density markets. And because the low-tier technologies use microcells, the switching from one cell to another would need to occur more frequently if the user moved outside the radius of the microcell. However, the speed at which a user could switch from one microcell to another was limited to approximately 35 miles per hour. How would that affect vehicular users? Given

EXHIBIT 7   Comparison of Cellular and Personal Communications Services

	Cellular	PCS
Power requirements	High	Low
Cell size	Macrocells: up to several miles	Microcells: 200–1,000 feet
Battery size	Large	Small
Poor performance locations	Enclosed spaces	Automobiles
Price	High	Low

Source: Davis, Vivian, Hans Kruse, William Pollard, and Catherine E. Reed, "Competition and Interconnection: The Case of Personal Communications Services," The National Regulatory Research Institute, July 1994, p. 15.

the predictions for the much expanded use (i.e., beyond just in-car use) of wireless communications in the future, was this a significant consideration?

With a low-tier technology he would not have to invest in the costly radio towers typical of traditional cellular networks. The existing networks were all high-tier cellular networks, however, and he was unsure what technologies other future PCS providers were considering. If he chose a low-tier technology and the majority of other PCS service providers chose high tier (and vice versa), he would not be able to offer his customers convenient interoperability. Such a situation would undermine his ability to attract customers and build market share. Another consideration involved the cost of the handsets. Since the handsets required by low-tier systems would not need to be as powerful as those required for a high-tier system, they were also less expensive. The estimated average cost to a service provider for a low-tier handset was approximately $150 compared to approximately $350 for a high-tier system. There were obviously a number of issues to consider. Is a low-tier technology the best choice for the market in which he hoped to bid for a license? His research left him undecided.

Looking to markets outside the United States, low-tier systems have met with mixed results. From market information Thompson surmised that the survival of low tier in France appears dependent on subsidies, and he discovered that trials in several other European countries had been discontinued. However, the low-tier systems have been much more successful in Asia. Success in Asia is thought to be a result of the large highly concentrated population which allows for high coverage and scale benefits and the limited need for vehicular mobility.

All in all, the degree of success in low-tier technology applications appears to be driven by factors such as the ability to offer a significant price gap between the low-tier and high-tier services available to consumers, significant coverage in the served markets, very densely populated markets, and intensive marketing.

CONCLUSION

The cost of bidding for a PCS license was substantial. Estimates were ranging around the $1 mark per MHz per potential customer. As of Round 66 of the auctions which were completed in early February 1995, the average value per potential customer (or POP) was $10.41. For a BTA license in a major metropolitan area such as Chicago, with a population of approximately 8.4 million, this translates into a cost of around $84 million for a 10MHz BTA license. It was an expensive proposition for an unproved product. Would the seemingly increased mobility of American society translate into increased market demand—above and beyond that which exists for cellular? Which technology should Thompson choose? Given that the current national average for landline (regular phone) service averaged around $50 per month and the national average for a cellular customer was approximately $56 per month, at what price should he enter the market with PCS service? And finally, how much of the market would he need to garner in order to be a profitable, ongoing concern?

 **DRYPERS CORPORATION (A)***

When Walter (Wally) Kemp had assumed the title of Chairman of the Board and Co-Chief Executive Officer of Drypers Corporation, a maker of disposable diapers, on January 1, 1995, he had looked back at 1994 with some satisfaction. Operating income was up almost 50 percent (Exhibit 1). Drypers had consolidated the operations of three regional companies into the Drypers Corporation, had begun the process of unifying four regional brands under the Drypers name to create the first national value brand, had increased domestic sales and market share (Exhibit 2), and had built a strong foundation for international growth. Nonetheless, Wally had anticipated that 1995 would be a difficult year for the company as plans for the year centered on the national consolidation from four regional brands to a single national identity under the Drypers brand name. The consolidation was aimed at gaining more distribution in mass merchandiser accounts.

As he sat in his Houston office in early 1995, Wally found that the year was turning out to be much more difficult than even he could have imagined. Drypers

---

* Research by Erin Wieckert. Compiled and edited by Leonard Parsons.

EXHIBIT 1 Drypers' Consolidated Statement of Earnings (in thousands)

| | Year ended December 31 | | |
	1992	1993	1994
Net sales	$77,719	$156,079	$173,552
Cost of goods sold	48,338	95,295	106,130
Gross profit	29,381	60,784	67,422
Selling, general and administrative expenses	23,423	46,231	48,081
Unusual expenses		2,376	1,141
Nonrecurring acquisition-related expenses	300	0	0
Operating income	5,658	12,177	18,200
Related party interest expense	1,763	378	375
Other interest expense	2,367	10,737	7,310
Other income	0	0	434
Income before taxes and extraordinary item	1,526	1,062	10,949
Income taxes			
current	0	565	861
deferred	866	805	3,290
Income (loss) before extraordinary item	660	(308)	6,798
Extraordinary item	(2,898)	0	(3,688)
Net income (loss)	(2,238)	(308)	6,798

was being buffeted by price cuts and promotional battles between Procter & Gamble and Kimberly-Clark. P&G had just repositioned its Luvs brand once again—after having reduced its prices 27 percent in the last 18 months—with a reduction in the number of diapers per package and a reduction in price per package. Concurrently raw material prices were surging.

These developments were putting severe pressure on Drypers' strategy of offering high-quality products at value prices in the narrow niche between premium and private label brands. Drypers was directly challenging P&G's Luvs for that position. Now P&G had just cut Luvs' prices by 11 percent. Wally wondered about the soundness of Drypers' strategy and its execution. He

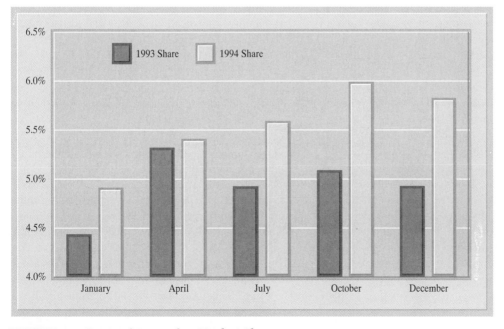

EXHIBIT 2 Drypers' Improving Market Share
Source: A. C. Nielsen Company (52 weeks ended December)

knew that Drypers had to respond to Luvs' latest action.

COMPANY HISTORY[1]

Prehistory

In 1984, Dave Pitassi and two friends—Tim Wagner, whom he had known in high school, and Wally Klemp, a buddy from Lewis and Clark College, in Portland, Oregon—launched a diaper company called VMG Products. As college students a few years earlier, Dave and his friends had kicked around a number of entrepreneurial notions. Ultimately, they hoped to launch a business. As a rebuttal to all the classmates and professors who pooh-poohed their ideas, they printed up a T-shirt proclaiming, "All I want is a chance to fail."

Despite their skepticism toward the corporate world, all three took big-company jobs in the Portland area (Dave with P&G, Wally with Coopers & Lybrand, and Tim with an adhesives company). But nobody wanted to put down roots. Within a year and a half the trio had a business plan they couldn't wait to execute. Operating out of Vancouver, Washington, they would enter the disposable-diaper industry, use local materials to become a low-cost producer, and sell a quality product to supermarkets in the Pacific Northwest. At the time, three national brands—Pampers and Luvs (by P&G), and Huggies (by Kimberly-Clark)—had around 85% of the market; the rest was carved out by private-label producers. If the new company, VMG, could raise around $1 million, the founders reckoned they could build a $15-million regional business within four or five years.

A Seattle-based investment banker liked the plan so much that he wanted to fund it. But to make it more attractive for investors and to preserve equity for the founders, he came up with an interesting approach: instead of selling stock, what about setting up a limited partnership and letting the investors own the production equipment? Initially, the limited partners would get virtually all of VMG's net income. Over time, however, if the business met its plan, the investors' interest would trail off and the founders' percentage would escalate.

Dave, Tim, and Wally saw no problem with the structure. They were thrilled to find any money at all. "When you're 23 years old and trying to raise money

for a diaper business," said Dave, "do you really dictate the terms?" By June 1985 they were running diapers off their state-of-the-art production line and selling them in supermarkets right next to the national brands. But soon a fundamental design weakness of the deal came into focus. The product was being accepted much faster than anyone's wildest dreams would have suggested. In the first few months of production, the founders hit their projected sales volume for year five. Eager to keep up with demand, they began thinking about ordering production equipment. But where would they get another $2 million? Not from the limited partners, who made it clear they had no interest in putting up new money or, for that matter, in seeing their cash payouts diverted to fuel the growth.

The disagreements between the young founders and the investors smoldered over the next few months, during which time VMG wrestled with production snags and inventory snafus. By fall the company was running out of cash, but negotiations with the limited partners (who needed to approve any new financing) were going nowhere. Slowly but surely, moreover, some of the investors were losing confidence in VMG's management. One week before Thanksgiving a group of limited partners took a vote. With no dissenters, they decided to throw the founders out.

On the day of the vote, Tim Wagner broke ranks with his fellow founders and negotiated a new job for himself (temporary, as it turned out) at VMG. Dave and Wally stuck together; neither of them could imagine going to work for people they couldn't trust. Their first impulse after hearing of the vote was to talk to their attorney. When they returned to the plant, the locks had been changed. "One day," Dave said, "we were young guys at the top of everything. We were being interviewed on TV and in the newspapers and were driving identical white Cadillacs. And then we became nobodies overnight."

The New Business

To get beyond their feelings of bitterness and defeat, Dave and Wally wanted to immerse themselves in something else. So they set up a couple of folding tables in Wally's unfinished basement, installed a phone, and started exploring possibilities for another business. While doing some consulting in the consumer-products area, they soon began writing a new business plan. The business? Another diaper company. The place? This time, they'd head for Houston. It was well placed for raw materials and distribution by land and by sea. What's more, no regional diaper brand had yet staked out the South.

---

[1] Taken from company records and from Bruce G. Posner, "Targeting the Giant," *Inc.*, Vol. 15, No. 10 (October 1993), pp. 92–100. Republished with permission of *Inc.* magazine, Goldhirsh Group, Inc. 38 Commercial Wharf, Boston, MA 02110. "Targeting the Giant" (excerpts), Bruce G. Posner, Vol. 15, No. 10. Reproduced by permission of the publisher via Copyright Clearance Center, Inc.

On the face of it, it made a lot of sense. Between them, Dave and Wally had amassed a huge amount of knowledge about the disposable-diaper market. And if they had proved anything in their short tenure at VMG, it was that there truly was a niche in this industry for quality products priced $1 or so beneath the national brands. Consumers liked getting competitive products for less money, particularly when family budgets were being squeezed. Retailers, meanwhile, found that they really could use the regional brand to make money in a category that was usually a money loser. "We had given birth to this concept," Dave noted. "And nobody we knew could articulate it as well as we could."

But could Dave and Wally really do the same thing twice? On some days they had their doubts. They wondered if their naivete hadn't been a huge asset the first time around, more important, perhaps, than any experience. "We worried," says Wally, "that we knew too much." As they approached prospective investors, they pitched their formula for doing business. "Investors weren't interested in a revenge story," notes Wally. "They wanted a good investment." Everyone they met with asked the same basic question: how could they sell against the likes of Procter & Gamble and Kimberly-Clark? Using industry data and the record of VMG, Dave and Wally would present their case: just as they'd done in the Pacific Northwest, they'd create a "smart-shopper choice" for diapers in the South.

Startup It took them more than a year to fund the business, during which time their anxieties ebbed and flowed. A couple of times a month they'd drive 12 hours from Portland to San Francisco for meetings with venture capitalists or individual angels. "We must have done it 30 times," notes Dave. A lot of people simply weren't attracted to the deal. Even if they were, Dave and Wally didn't hesitate to turn prospects away. "We had learned the words due diligence, and we thought a lot about how we wanted the company structured," notes Wally. Some investors wanted too much equity for their money; others had a bent toward getting too involved in management, a red flag if there ever was one. Finally, after Dave and Wally had spent almost a year shopping the deal around, Ron Keil, the former owner of a Portland grocery chain, made the decision to invest $500,000. Because of his background, the investment gained instant credibility. By August 1987 the new company had raised $2.4 million from a total of about 60 individuals.

The moment Dave and Wally had their initial funding, the new company, originally named Veragon Corp., was a blur of activity. The first diapers wouldn't be produced for 10 months, but the challenges the company needed to meet before then seemed endless. There was a facility to rent, a production line to design and order, a broker network to establish, and retail relationships to cultivate. All would have to be done on a thin budget. And in the meantime, both Dave and Wally had to relocate to Houston.

One of their first official acts was to recruit an operations manager from P&G, Terry Tognietti, to become the third partner. Terry, then 31 (with 9 years of diaper experience), had recently spearheaded a P&G development effort that resulted in the first differentiated boy and girl products for Luvs. P&G didn't let him slip away easily; Terry had to sign an inch-thick agreement prohibiting disclosure of critical information for two years. Once Terry was in place as Drypers' operations chief, the three partners (Dave was in charge of sales and marketing; Wally headed finance) spent several months laying down the key planks of their strategy.

Strategy In some areas, they could retrace the pattern from VMG; in others, they needed to be flexible. From day one, for instance, they knew they had to have the right product—a diaper with all the important features of the big brands. The exact specifications were a moving target, however, dictated by the evolving standards P&G and Kimberly-Clark set for baby dryness and comfort.

The pricing goals were clearer: the partners wanted Drypers to be positioned at least $1 a package less than Pampers, Luvs, and Huggies. And beyond that, they wanted to give retailers room for profit they didn't have selling the national brands. The potential for boosting store profits was the main lever they hoped would win them a footing in Texas supermarkets. During the 1980s many retailers had seen their margins on Pampers and the other brands evaporate as mass merchandisers like Wal-Mart and Kmart promoted them at, or near, cost. In Texas and elsewhere, supermarkets treated those brands as "loss leaders"—items they needed on the shelves to pull parents into the stores. The hope was that, once there, customers would drop money on other things, like baby food, where there was higher profit. Chains had already moved toward increasing profits in the expanding diaper category by adding their own lower-priced "store" brands, which were gaining rapidly in the market. By early 1988 store executives in Houston and other parts of Texas began to hear the Drypers pitch.

The Sell-in   Drypers didn't have the money to pay the stores slotting fees for space on their shelves. But Dave and his brokers pledged they'd make up for it by supporting their product with TV and newspaper advertising, along with store inserts and lots of coupons. Whereas P&G ran inflexible national programs on Pampers and Luvs, which didn't bend to the special needs of individual stores, Drypers, they vowed, would collaborate with retailers on a more customized basis. Based on the Drypers game plan, stores could expect to make two to three times the profit they'd normally make on the national brands. As Dave explained, "We wanted to be the retailer's friend."

Some chains, like Kroger and Randall's, agreed to take the product immediately, partly out of support for a new local company. Others, such as Safeway, worried that Drypers might cannibalize their profitable private-label business and elected to wait and see.

Competitive Reaction and Drypers' Solution

When the first packages of Drypers hit the supermarket shelves in late July 1988, Dave, Wally, and Terry suspected it was only a matter of time before they saw a response from P&G. But what form would the response take? And how aggressive would it be? All along Dave had considered the possibility that P&G might use coupons in an effort to garble the Drypers' message. After all, if the price gap between Drypers and P&Gs Pampers and Luvs shrank to less than $1, there would be less reason for consumers to try a new brand. But the blitz of P&G coupons-in ads, stuck on packages, in the mail—took everyone by surprise. In the past Pampers and Luvs had used coupons for 75¢ or less; this latest crop of P&G coupons (distributed only in and around Texas) were worth $2—and were instantly redeemable. Kimberly-Clark, meanwhile, discounted its prices. It was obvious to Dave that Drypers doing nothing would lead to a quick and ugly death.

Dave had just been reading a book about judo, and the thought occurred to him as Drypers was being attacked: what if he found a way to redirect P&G's momentum and furious spending to work against it? He huddled with one of his advertising firm's partners and eventually pieced together a campaign that would put Drypers on the map. In newspaper and magazine ads throughout Texas, Drypers invited consumers to "Pamper, Hug, and Luv Us." Parents could apply any coupon to buy a package of Drypers at $2 off its normal price of $7.99, and Drypers would thus preserve the targeted gap. Retailers, of course, could easily have refused to make the price adjustments at the cash register and to process the paperwork (which involved gath-

ering all the coupons together and then sending them to Drypers for payment). If they had, that would have been the end of it. "But store executives loved it," Dave said. "Everyone likes the underdog."

Within weeks the P&G assault was blunted as thousands of shoppers agreed to give Drypers a try. "The volume," Dave remembered, "just went, pow! After two months we were throwing off cash." Drypers' production ran at capacity—three shifts a day, seven days a week—until new equipment arrived. In some Houston supermarkets Drypers' share of the market hit 15 percent and held firm. Through its independent brokers, meanwhile, the company was beginning distribution in other parts of the South.

The coupon deluge died down, but the Drypers' partners knew that the war would go on. Given the magnitude of the stakes—in 1990 alone, P&G's market share in diapers dropped from 51.5 percent to 49.1 percent—new battles could flare up at any moment. What could Drypers, whose sales were running at around $14 million annually, do to fight off its multibillion-dollar rivals? The only thing they could really do, the founders decided, was to build an organization that was focused like a laser beam on value to the customer and retailer profit. Drypers had to provide all the bells and whistles of the major brands—and sell them for less. As Wally explained, "Every decision we made had to be based on that." It started with staffing.

Organizational Structutre

In contrast with P&G, where there were levels and levels of specialists and middle managers reporting up a pyramid, Drypers aimed to be as flat as possible. To keep general and administrative costs down, all employees from the partners on down would wear multiple hats and share what they knew. "It was designed to breed broad learning," said Dave. Production engineers, for example, would help do the specs for the equipment they eventually installed and ran; and if the equipment broke down, they'd be the ones to fix it. Purchasing people wouldn't just specialize in pulp or tape, as they did at P&G; each would learn to buy a dozen or more materials—everything that went into the making of a diaper. "We expected them to understand the complete production picture," explained Terry. They'd get materials at the same basic cost as Drypers' competitors did—in some cases even for less—with the added benefit of furthering teamwork.

Acquisitions and Consolidation

By the fall of 1991 there were plenty of reasons to think that approach was on track. As Drypers moved its diapers throughout the South, sales were heading for around $35 million, and the company was making handsome operating profits. For the partners, the burning issue of the day was how best to expand into other parts of the country so they might be less of a target for their better-heeled rivals. If Drypers sold its products across the United States, the big brands would have to commit a lot more money to fight, Dave and others thought, which would make Drypers less exposed.

Ultimately, the partners decided that, rather than spending a lot of money slugging it out with regional brands similar to theirs, they'd join forces with them. So, fortified with $11.6 million in new equity raised from Texas buyout funds and venture-capital partnerships, along with $26 million in additional debt, they negotiated two deals that tripled the size of their business. The first one, ironically, was to buy VMG, the Washington company Wally and Dave had been booted from five years earlier. The second, completed in November 1992, was for a company in Marion, Ohio, named UltraCare Products. The CEOs of the two acquired companies were brought in as partners at the top management level. Suddenly, from relative obscurity, Drypers would now claim a nearly 6 percent market share of all the diapers sold in America's supermarkets.

The year 1994 saw the completion of the consolidation of operations of the three regional companies into Drypers Corporation. The first steps were taken to unify four regional brands—Cozies, WeeFits, Baby's Choice, and Drypers—to create the first national value brand under the Drypers' banner. This unification allowed Drypers to streamline its packaging operations. Convenience packs alone went from 21 different packages to only four. Drypers anticipated that its advertising expenditures would be more efficient when supporting one brand instead of four.

Public Offering

Drypers' sales had increased more than 500 percent in the last five years. In October 1993, *Inc.* magazine named Drypers the fastest growing privately-held company in America. Taking advantage of good news, Drypers went public in March 1994 at $14.50 a share. Analysts at the time assigned the stock a 12-month target price of $22.

Management Restructuring

Because of Drypers' entrepreneurial nature, it had always had a flat corporate structure and a lean management team. This encouraged employee productivity

and allowed senior management to stay close to day-to-day developments. Drypers believed that its streamlined management team allowed for closer coordination of overall corporate strategy, while permitting each major area of the company to receive a specialized management focus appropriate to its needs and opportunities.

Achieving the ambitious goal of building a successful national brand would require well-defined strategies and well-executed implementation. For this reason, Drypers decided to adopt a more formalized, sharply delineated management structure. On October 12, 1994, Drypers announced that, effective January 1, 1995, Walter V. Klemp, previously Managing Director-Finance, had been named Chairman of the Board. Terry A. Tognietti, Managing Director-Domestic Operations, had become President of Drypers North America. Raymond M. Chambers, Managing Director-International Operations, was now President of Drypers International. Wally, Terry, and Ray also would hold the title of Co-Chief Executive Officer in order to maintain the focus on teamwork, with clear accountability at all levels of the company. Wally and Terry retained their seats on the Board of Directors, with Ray assuming co-founder Dave's seat. Dave elected to serve as a special advisor to Drypers with focus on identifying new growth opportunities for it. The five-year assignment would allow Dave to pursue mergers, acquisitions and strategic marketing opportunities for Drypers. Randy C. Schaaf, former Managing Director-Business Development, became a consultant to the company.

MARKETING STRATEGY AND 1995 MARKETING PLAN

Competitive Situation

Disposable diapers are a $3.8 billion industry in the United States. This represents the third largest category in the Health and Beauty Aid (HBA) segment of the retail industry. While the diaper category is large, the field of competitors is small. While most HBA categories have between eight and ten brands competing for market share, disposable diapers has only four national brands—even with the addition of Drypers. Yet as the diaper category matures, it is becoming more segmented and more cost-competitive.

What does a giant company like P&G do when the market share in its biggest product category (one that, by itself, would be a Fortune 500 company) drops from 47 percent to 42 percent in a single year as happened in the early 1990s? In Cincinnati, P&G's

hometown, there was lots of handwringing. And to be sure, the worries weren't just over Pampers and Luvs. During 1992 many of P&Gs other top brands—its Downy fabric softener, for example, and its Crest toothpaste—were losing altitude as well. Across the country the private labels and "value" brands, like Drypers, were moving up. Even Kimberly-Clark was holding steady (at around 37 percent of the market). Not surprisingly, P&G wanted its business back. The first salvo came in May 1992, when P&G lowered prices to retailers on both Pampers and Luvs by about 5 percent. Kimberly-Clark quickly got in step, matching the decrease. Then, P&G went further, cutting prices by another 7 percent, and abandoned use of coupons in favor of more consistent everyday prices. In May 1993, Procter & Gamble repositioned its Luvs product as a mid-price brand by eliminating promotional coupons, reducing other promotional expenditures, and lowering Luvs' list price by 16 percent. It also trimmed Pampers' price by 5 percent. In response to these changes, Drypers repositioned its premium brand products in the third quarter of 1993 by substantially reducing the average package price in order to maintain a favorable pricing spread between its premium brand products and those of its premium priced competitors. In mid-July 1993, P&G announced an unprecedented drive to streamline overhead and to cut its costs (partly by laying off 12,000 employees), suggesting there could be more price cuts down the road. Procter & Gamble's 1993 Luvs' repositioning appears to have been unsuccessful. In 1994, Luvs' sales dropped 9.1 percent.

Target Markets

Drypers appeals to consumers who demand the quality and features of the leading brands at a better price and to retailers who appreciate Drypers' higher margins.

Consumer   Drypers' consumer is value-conscious and demanding. She wants a diaper that performs well, has all the features that go along with a premium-quality diaper, and doesn't cost a fortune. She knows it's possible to get all three. Drypers calls her the "Drypers Smart Mom." Drypers' research shows that moms with two or more children are more likely to buy Drypers. While first-time mothers may be swayed by the leading brands' TV advertising, experienced moms recognize they can keep their babies just as dry for less.

The number of Drypers Smart Moms is growing. The '90s consumer is increasingly reluctant to pay premium prices for disposable diapers—especially as value brands like Drypers continue to demonstrate

comparable quality. The segment of diaper shoppers who are value-driven has grown more than 100% in the last five years as shown in Exhibit 3. Terry believed that "15 percent of shoppers are 'price buyers' and 35 percent of all diapers are sold on promotion—with coupons or other incentives."

Retail   Grocers' margins on the leading national brands historically have been slim. As a value brand, Drypers offers retailers higher margins on fewer, more efficient items. By building retailer profits unparalleled by the leading national brands, Drypers will continue to forge strong retailer relationships.

Drypers anticipated that growth would come from greater domestic penetration among merchandisers and drug chains as well as from a largely untapped international market.

Domestic Growth Opportunities

Drypers' total domestic diaper volume was up 13.6 percent (excluding private label) in 1994. Drypers' future domestic growth opportunities include grocery stores, mass merchandisers, chain drug stores and private label.

Increased Grocery Market Share   Grocery stores represent 60 percent of the total volume of diaper sales in the United States. Drypers' unit share in 1994 grew from 4.9 percent to 5.5 percent in food stores nationally, and in 10 major markets, Drypers enjoyed market share of more than 15 percent.[2] New accounts

---

[2] Nielsen Scantrack, 52 weeks ended December.

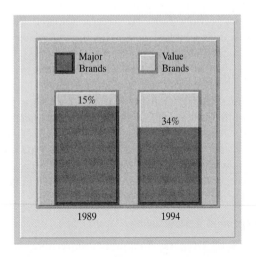

EXHIBIT 3   Growth of Value Segment
Source: A. C. Nielsen Company (52 weeks ended December)

helped fuel that growth. Major retailers like Vons, Delchamps, Raley's and Lucky began carrying Drypers in 1994.

More Mass Merchandisers Mass merchandisers and the non-food class of trade, including drug chains and toy stores, are among the fastest-growing segment of the diaper industry. Today non-food stores represent $1.5 billion in sales, 40 percent of the total U.S. market for diapers. Mass merchandisers typically carry only national brands. So Drypers' unique position as the only national value brand will give it a distinct advantage over regional brands. Drypers already gained distribution through several key mass merchandisers, including Kmart (Super Kmart Centers), Meijer, Venture, Bradlees, and CALDOR.

Private Label Expansion Private label is a $700 million diaper market segment in the United States. The last few years have seen a significant increase in overall private label sales as consumers demand a better value. Drypers is leveraging its branded relationships with retail partners to create opportunities to gain their private label business.

Private label sales are helping Drypers diversify its sales base, build on current relationships with retailers, and gain new distribution. In fact, Drypers' private label unit sales grew nearly 50 percent during 1994. In 1994 Drypers obtained approval from a major grocery buying group, Federated Foods, to sell private label product to its members: Grocers Supply, General Trading, Dearborn Wholesale, and Grocers L.P. Drypers also is now supplying Western Family. With Drypers' retailer relationships, product development, and production capabilities, it is believed that there is plenty of room to grow.

International Expansion

Industry sources estimate the international diaper market to represent about $12 billion in annual sales, while only being 10 percent penetrated. Currently Drypers distributes to 26 countries and territories, and its global penetration is growing rapidly. While Drypers recognized the risk inherent in doing business in countries with emerging economies, some present excellent growth opportunities. Accordingly, Drypers' course for international growth is to be carefully plotted. Central and South America are expected to account for 20 percent of all growth in diaper sales internationally in the next few years. Because of Drypers' proximity and experience, that's where it was focusing much of its effort. In 1994 Drypers

upgraded production facilities, which will significantly increase capacity and efficiency.

Puerto Rico: Gateway to Latin America In 1995 Drypers expected to significantly increase distribution throughout Latin America. Drypers' goal is to become the third largest diaper manufacturer in Latin America. Since Drypers started Puerto Rico's first-ever diaper production facility in February 1993, its annualized sales from that facility have leaped nearly 59 percent. In 1994 Drypers became Puerto Rico's third leading diaper brand, with distribution in four of the country's largest retail chains, including Wal-Mart. And, Drypers began exporting product from its Puerto Rican facility to 14 countries and territories in Central and South America.

Argentina Fueled by its successful experience in Puerto Rico, Drypers entered into a venture with Seler, S.A., an Argentine diaper manufacturer, in 1994. The venture already has begun improving Drypers' bottom line. Only 40 percent penetrated, the Argentine market is estimated to represent $300 to $350 million in annual diaper sales, according to industry experts. The country's high growth rate and relatively steady economic outlook have made this a superior base for further expansion to other Latin American markets, especially within the Mercosur trading pact countries of Brazil, Uruguay, Paraguay, and Argentina.

Mexico While Mexico is Latin America's third largest diaper market, Drypers' progress will be tempered by economic developments there. Drypers changed Mexican distributors in 1994. Now, AlEn Industries, a substantial local producer and distributor of consumer products, is charged with helping Drypers to better tap this important Latin American economy.

Marketing Mix

Drypers' budget for marketing and promotion in 1995 was $20 million. Highlights of the 1995 Marketing Plan are given in Exhibit 4.

Product Development Somehow Drypers had to find a low-cost way to shadow its competitors, step for step, on product innovation and quality. How could the company do it? With clever copying. As a general strategy, the partners didn't aim to be market leaders—that was too costly. Instead, they'd watch P&G and Kimberly-Clark for significant moves, then follow suit, pronto, with their own version. P&G's gender-specific Pampers made their debut in January

EXHIBIT 4   Drypers' 1995 Marketing Plan Highlights

Product

▶ Introduce Jumbo Packs.

▶ Complete development of ultra-thin diaper design and launch.

▶ Improve Drypers Training Pants with regard to absorbency and fit. Specific improvements will include improved contouring in the core for better absorbency, Lycra Tummy Snugs for better fit around the waist, and a new crotch design to eliminate "bunching" and prevent leakage.

Media Advertising

▶ Conduct the first national print advertising campaign in April. The media will be four parenting magazines. The advertisement emphasizes that Drypers, unlike the leading brands, is perfume free.

▶ Sponsor, along with 15 other major brands, Ronald McDonald Children's Charities by producing an advertisement that mentions the Ronald McDonald House and donating a portion of our proceeds. Dypers will receive additional exposure with its logo on placemats in McDonald's restaurants across the country.

▶ Run first trade advertisement in national publications.

Sales Promotions

▶ Drop a Sunday coupon insert in conjunction with Baby Fresh Wipes and Gerber Baby Foods to celebration of National Baby Week. The FSI features six coupons for various baby-related products, including a dollar-off offer from Drypers.

▶ Send direct mailings to new mothers, with coupons to encourage trial.

▶ Participate in a leading in-store coupon program with exclusive placement on retail shelves.

▶ Provide ongoing trade support for Drypers' retail partners.

1990, for instance. "We had ours by that June," Terry said. In fact, Drypers had them in some cities before P&G did.

For technical punch, Drypers didn't feel the need for a research-and-development staff of its own—indeed, it initially had no one working full-time on development. Rather, it leaned on suppliers like 3M and Du Pont, who, Terry argued, stood ready to help. By combining its resources with those of its suppliers, Drypers tries to ensure that its product advancements are cost-effective.

In the early 1990s, Drypers came up with a marketing innovation that gave it a modest edge in the day

care market. It put space for labels on diaper packages so parents could mark them with their babies' names. A perfume-free diaper followed. Most diapers are scented to cover the smell of glue. Even though the perfume was perfectly safe, Drypers has been able to convince nervous parents that their baby deserved better. Drypers' research showed that eight of 10 mothers would prefer a perfume-free diaper.

Drypers was the second entrant into the $450 million training pants (for children who are preparing to move beyond diapers) category. Drypers' training pants were introduced in August 1992. Drypers was the first manufacturer in the United States to introduce the full-stretch continuous waistband and all-around leg gathers that make Drypers' training pants look and feel like real underwear. These improvements helped increase Drypers' training pants unit volume 16.9 percent in 1994 (Exhibit 5) and grocery share 26.7 percent,[3] in spite of the new product launch of a major competitor.

Since then, Drypers has continued to make improvements, resulting in a patent-pending design. Drypers' unique Tummy Snugs elastic system gives

---

[3] A. C. Nielsen, average share of grocery volume (52 weeks ended December 1994 vs. 1993).

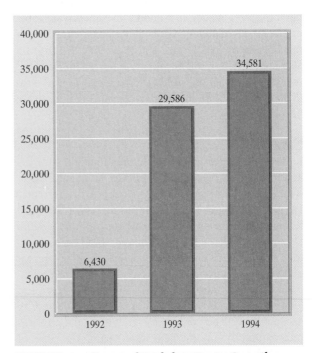

EXHIBIT 5   Drypers' Training Pants Growth

its training pants a better fit. Drypers added a contoured core for better absorbency, and it gave them alphabet graphics, so they're fun and educational (Exhibit 6).

Advertising In a huge and competitive market—during 1994 Kimberly-Clark spent $55 million on Huggies and P&G put $45 million behind Pampers[4]—Drypers' challenge is obvious: how to get attention with much less? Drypers has tried to piggyback on the resources of its competitors. Drypers, for instance, didn't need to spend millions of dollars telling the world why boys and girls would benefit from different products or why thin could be as good as thick; it leaves the expenses of educating the market to P&G and Kimberly-Clark. Drypers invests its ad dollars where they packed the most punch—in local and in-store ads that stressed the value of its products over national brands. Its first-ever national-print advertising and promotion plan is scheduled to be implemented in 1995 to support Drypers' national brand roll-out.

Sales Promotion One highlight of the 1995 Marketing Plan was the formation of promotional alliances with leading names in the baby products industry. Drypers intended to use strategic product partnerships to add value to the Drypers brand in two ways. First, by pooling its promotional funds with other companies, Drypers extended its marketing budget and gar-

---
[4] Competitive Media Reporting

nered greater exposure with more cost efficiency. Second, by joining forces with highly respected, well-established names, Drypers will be able to leverage their brand equity, enhancing its reputation by association. Drypers' 1995 marketing efforts were to include joint promotions with Gerber Products Company and the Ronald McDonald House.

CURRENT SITUATION

These days the relative positioning of the various products is in a state of flux. In some stores, for instance, you see Luvs at the same price as Drypers. In light of the massive pricing pressure, lots of people are speculating that Drypers' best days may be over. Are they? Things are happening so fast that the market data are inconclusive. Different scenarios seem to crop up almost every day. Some retail experts speculate, for example, that the P&G pricing squeeze will backfire—and that whatever Luvs gains in the market may be at the expense of Pampers, not Drypers. "What will P&G do then?" asks Paul Shilling, a broker at Acosta Sales, in Atlanta. Others think it's a good bet that supermarket chains will start to drop prices on their private labels, even if it hurts their profits—thus giving Drypers new room to price below other brands. And then there's this rosy prediction: that stores will stop selling Luvs altogether in favor of products that make them money—with Drypers at the top of their lists. "The Luvs strategy isn't particularly popular with retailers," notes John Bolt, a merchandiser with Houston's 49-store Appletree chain. "Stores see it as predatory."

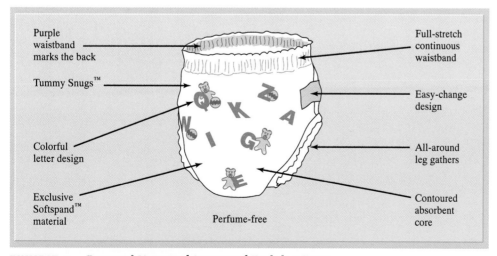

EXHIBIT 6 **Drypers' New and Improved Training Pant**

DECISION TIME

Walter Kemp knew that Drypers' ability to succeed against long odds was once again being severely tested. As 1994 ended, the industry faced dramatic increases in raw material prices that were increasingly impacting profit margins. In addition, Drypers' two major national competitors have triggered a new round of price-cutting. And the potential of the Latin Ameri-can market appears uncertain in the near term due to the economic troubles of Mexico. While Wally believed that Drypers' strategy was sound, he knew that he should reflect on it. Perhaps, positioning Drypers as "a high-quality, low-price, me-too brand" was not sustainable. In the meantime, he would have to discuss with Terry and Ray the immediate actions that Drypers should take.

CUSTOMER ANALYSIS

> The purpose of an enterprise is to create and keep a customer.
>
> THEODORE LEVITT

*T*he most important ingredient in the success of any organization is a satisfied customer. Indeed, some believe that an "obsession with customers" can lead to a sustainable competitive advantage. This means more than getting close to the customer.

WHY ARE CUSTOMERS IMPORTANT?

Customers are essential because this is where the life of an organization begins. Until customers place orders, nothing really happens. Once customers think enough about your goods or services to buy them, you are in business. Also, when customers stop placing orders your organization starts to die. Customers thus have a great deal to do with the success or failure of an enterprise. We believe that customers are the engine, the critical driving force that powers a market economy.

When executives were asked what were the most important issues managers will face, customer wants was second only to product quality. The implication is that marketing managers can never know too much about customers and their needs. This chapter is concerned with answering seven questions you must ask yourself about your customers, their motivations, and your relationship to your customers.

1. Who are my customers?
2. Where are my customers?
3. When do customers buy?
4. What do my customers want?
5. How do customers buy?
6. How do you learn about customers?
7. How does a firm become customer oriented?

Once you understand customers and develop a customer focus, you are ready to design products and marketing programs to fill their requirements.

WHO ARE MY CUSTOMERS?

The issue of who customers are seems at first to be an easy question. After all, we can look at our current invoices and identify everyone to whom we ship. These firms can be classified

APPLYING
. . . to
Industrial
Marketing

by size and industry to give a detailed picture of who buys. Consider the case of McElwee Paper Company.

McElwee Paper Company is a prototypical independent corrugated packaging manufacturer. It faces an ongoing challenge of remaining competitive and profitable in a price-sensitive business dominated by commodity-oriented purchasers. It has developed a sensitive acuity to the needs of its customers. It has been successful by thinking of itself as not just a corrugated box company but as a "packaged solution provider"—even if that solution involves a material other than corrugated. This is not to say that McElwee Paper yielded market to plastic, flexible packaging, and other forms of alternative packaging without a fight. It has stressed one major area of market impact—the environment—where corrugated has the upper hand. McElwee Paper has developed bulk containers or bins, improved coating for increased water resistance, used stronger adhesives for joining and forming, and improved graphics with multicolor flexographic printing. This has allowed it to elevate the status of its corrugated product from that of a basic shipping container to an effective merchandising tool that can be used in point-of-purchase displays and in club stores, warehouse-style stores, and large discount stores. McElwee Paper's goal is to serve its customers' needs efficiently and profitably. To help achieve this goal, McElwee Paper tracks its end-use markets. Nondurable goods consume about 80 percent of its shipments. Of this group, food and beverages make up the largest end-use market with a share of nearly 40 percent, followed by paper and printing at more than 20 percent. A detailed breakdown is given in Table 3-1.

Although customer shipping point data may be useful, they can give a distorted view of who your customers really are. The problem is that deliveries may go to fabricators or channel intermediaries that resell your products to others. This raises the difficult question of whether your most important customer is the OEM, the distributor, the retailer, or the ultimate user. The results also suggest it may be useful to distinguish between business and consumer buyers.

Consumer Customers

Consumer buyers include everyone who purchases goods for their own or family members' consumption. Firms that sell low-priced products such as paper towels often focus their attention on the final buyer. After all, paper towels are branded products that are presold with a heavy use of magazine and television advertising. This suggests that paper towel manufacturers must understand consumer preferences for features such as wet strength, durability, color, number of plys, and price. Firms that accurately measure these preferences are in a better position to create products and ads that will draw customers to grocery stores.

An alternative argument is that towel *brand loyalty,* or the degree customers repurchase, is really low. Can you, for example, name five brands of paper towels? The answer is no and neither can the authors or most anyone. The truth is that all brands of paper towels are similar and buyers do not have strong emotional attachments to items in this product class. Most consumers of fast-moving consumer products have *split loyalties* to several

TABLE 3-1 Corrugation Customer Identification at the McElwee Paper Company

	Proportion of Shipments to				
Year	Food and Beverages	Paper and Printing	Chemical	Rubber	Other
Current	39.1%	22.5%	5.0%	5.3%	28.1%
Last	40.6	21.4	5.0	5.2	27.8
Previous	39.6	22.5	5.1	5.1	27.7

brands; that is, they are multi-brand buyers. Consumers buy from brands in their idiosyncratic repertoires of one or more individual brands.[1] Under these conditions, the marketing activities of grocery stores may be more important than the preferences of the final buyer. Retail stores determine shelf locations, number of shelf facings, final selling prices, the existence of end aisle displays, and whether a brand of towels is "featured" in the weekly store ad. Thus manufacturers that cater to the grocery store buyer with special deals, discounts, display racks, signs, banners, cooperative advertising support, and contests may be able to sell more paper towels than firms that advertise only to the final user.

Okay, this may work for low-priced paper towels, but does the same concept hold true for higher-priced consumer durables? With durables the costs of development and manufacturing are so high that companies surely focus on the final users and their preferences. The answer is yes. When manufacturers ask customers to spend $1,000 or more they usually make an effort to tailor the product to their needs. However, customer contact can be expensive and there may be a cheaper way. For example, a Japanese camera manufacturer wanted to expand its position in the U.S. high-priced camera market. Instead of asking users what features they wanted in new cameras, the firm sent a vice president to America to visit a number of retail camera stores. The executive observed customers buying cameras and then held in-depth conversations with store managers about what features were desirable. He then returned to Japan and developed a new line of cameras that were very successful in the U.S. market. Why did a focus on retail store employees work so well? The answer is that people do not buy $500 cameras off the shelf; retail salespeople sell them cameras in this price range. Thus a key factor was the manufacturer's ability to include features that the clerks could use to sell the cameras to the final buyer. Much of consumer marketing is *transaction marketing*.

APPLYING
. . . to
Consumer
Semi-durable
Marketing

Business Customers

The issue of customer identity is even more complicated with products sold to businesses. Remember that business goods and services are used to create merchandise that is then sold to final users. This means that the demand for business products is *derived* from the demand for the final product. Thus the identity of components and services is often lost when selling to business buyers. As a result, the importance of brands is reduced and the role of specifications, timely delivery, and price is increased. Under these conditions, identifying the "right customer" is extremely difficult.

A common approach with goods sold to businesses is to treat the purchasing agent as the "customer." After all, purchasing agents often select qualified suppliers and negotiate contract terms. However, purchasing agents usually rely on engineers and company scientists for technical expertise. This means that the most "important" customer may actually be some obscure technician who uses the product in the plant or laboratory. Other key business customers are plant managers and the controller. Production managers typically have some input on the type of equipment installed in their plants. Also, controllers pay for supplies and equipment, and they have to approve orders before they can be sent out to vendors. Obviously, business marketing involves satisfying a large number of different customers. Here you often encounter *interaction marketing*.

Another complication with business markets is that buying committees frequently make purchasing decisions. Because membership on these committees may be secret and meetings are usually off-limits to outsiders, the identity and the buying criteria of key business customers may not be readily available.

Firms selling engines for commercial airplanes provide an example of business customer identification problems. The most logical customer for engine manufacturers is the airframe builder such as Boeing or McDonald-Douglas. Engines are a key component and have to be matched carefully with the airframe to give the desired lift, range, and capacity.

APPLYING
. . . to
Business-to-
Business
Marketing

However, engine manufacturers have begun to sell directly to the airlines using features such as durability and low fuel consumption. If this were not complicated enough, a third customer, the leasing firm, has entered the picture. Airplanes have become so expensive that they are commonly sold to a finance company and are then leased to the operating airline. This means the engine supplier has to satisfy the sometimes conflicting demands of three customers: the airframe manufacturer, the financing company, and the airlines. The engine supplier may work together with the airframe manufacturer and financing company to meet the requirements of the airlines. This is an example of *network marketing.*

Nonprofit Customers

Another important class of customer is the not-for-profit sector. This includes community orchestras, the United Fund, public radio and TV stations, credit unions, hospitals, and schools. Each of these organizations is managed by a local board of directors. As a result, purchase orders for supplies and equipment often go to firms that maintain offices in the community. In addition, it is not uncommon for nonprofit groups to place orders with companies associated with friends, relatives, or members of particular political parties. Marketers who expect to sell to nonprofit organizations need a great deal of information on how customers make purchase decisions.

Choosing the Right Customer

Our discussion has shown that consumer, business, and not-for-profit suppliers are often expected to serve multiple customer constituencies. This can complicate product design and the creation of marketing programs. Firms that try to be all things to all customers may fail because they lack the resources to get the job done. Some organizations focus on specific groups of customers and succeed by becoming specialists. Most firms need to cater to the ultimate users as well as dealers and other channel intermediaries. Polaroid sells to retailers (its customers) and markets to instant camera and film users (its consumers). Certainly an ability to set priorities helps put the issue of customer identification in proper focus. Perhaps the best solution to the dilemma of customer emphasis is to take guidance from the strategic plan. A good strategic plan should identify who the company expects to work with not only now but in the future. The relative importance of intermediate and final buyers may change over time. See Marketing in Action box 3-1.

WHERE ARE MY CUSTOMERS?

Knowing where customers are located can be very useful to marketing managers. Existing customers are sometimes traced through invoice data. Service Merchandise catalog stores, for example, make it a point to ask for the address of each customer who makes a store purchase. These addresses are stored in the computer and used to select newspaper and radio media to cover their customer base. They are also used to send catalogs and sales notices directly to customers' homes.

Another way to locate customers is through the use of *warranty cards.* These cards are enclosed with merchandise and customers are asked to fill them out and return them to the manufacturer. Warranty cards are primarily used to notify customers in case of recalls and safety updates, but they can also be used for marketing purposes. Some firms use these names for telephone solicitations for extended warranties and for mailing direct mail offers. Unfortunately, only about 20 percent of warranty cards are returned and large numbers of customers are still unidentified. One solution is to use postage paid warranty cards so customers are more likely to return them.

MARKETING IN ACTION *3-1*

The Impact of Changing Buying Patterns

APPLYING
. . . to
Consumer
Toy
Marketing
and
Retailing

For much of the past 15 years, the toy industry's "Big Three" players—the retailing chain Toys "Я" Us and the manufacturers Mattel (Barbie) and Hasbro (G.I. Joe)—grew together. Toys "Я" Us pioneered the category-killer retailing philosophy of building big stores with huge selections and great prices that wiped out traditional smaller toy stores. Even two superstore imitators, Child World and Lionel, could not compete with Toys "Я" Us and went out of business. Toys "Я" Us swooped down to pick up these chains' best locations. The two big manufacturers acquired smaller ones, cut new toy development, boosted spending on movie- and TV-licensed products and relied on Toys "Я" Us to move the goods while spurning smaller stores.

But over the past three years, a number of trends have started to chip away at these strategies. First, lots of time-strapped parents no longer make Toys "Я" Us a destination for routine toy buying, opting instead to use the increasingly well-stocked toy aisles at Wal-Mart stores and other discounters. A recent national online survey by Digital Research showed a pronounced migration away from toy superstores. Over 40% of the households responding shopped at toy superstores less often than they did four years ago. Second, many upper income parents are turning to specialty-toy retailers for more service or for toys that are marketed for education and enrichment value rather than for instant appeal. The president of one chain of stores promoting higher-end, specialty merchandise has said, "Today, with both parents working, there is a desire to give children the best they can give them. You could define it as guilt." Third, buying surveys, such as by the NPD Group, show that children are outgrowing toys earlier, moving on to computers and electronic games. Toy spending in the U.S. now peaks with three-year-olds! Toy spending steadily drops after that for each age category, with 12-year-olds receiving about half as much. Parents who work longer hours have less time, and so do the kids. Between computer tutoring, after-school activities, organized sports programs, and homework at lower grade levels, children have less time to do what they want. They are even watching less television than five years ago. Toys are playing a smaller role in the time budget of kids.

Age compression is taking place. A survey of households with children under 12 showed that while 46 percent of seven- and eight-year-olds listed playing with toys as a favorite pastime, only 24 percent of 9- and 10-year-olds did, and a mere five percent of 11- and 12-year-olds did. The older groups list reading, going to the park, playing video games, and listening to music higher on their preference lists. Where once girls were interested in Barbie until they were nine years old, they now leave Barbie at five or six. A lot of toys consequently face a compressed product life cycle.

Toys "Я" Us remains the nation's largest toy retailer and most sought after outlet during the holiday season. Nonetheless, it has had to cope with stalled growth rates, falling market share, and earnings that peaked in 1995. Toys "Я" Us is planning to alter its operations to deal with market changes.

(continues)

Courtesy Toys "Я" Us

It believes that there are a number of categories in which it would be possible to extend the age groups to older children. It plans merchandising initiatives to respond to customers' desires for convenience and more educational products. To deal with customers' time pressures, Toys "Я" Us has started selling toys over the Internet rather than only through stores. It is coping with the age compression problem by expanding its demographics by emphasizing baby needs at one end of the spectrum and looking seriously into electronics at the other end. It acquired the largest baby products retailer and renamed it—surprise—Babies "Я" Us.

— *Changing buying patterns impact the relative importance of intermediate and final buyers.*

Source: Joseph Pereira, "Toy-Buying Patterns Are Changing and That Is Shaking the Industry," *The Wall Street Journal,* June 16, 1998, pp. A1, A8.

A locational breakdown of the McElwee Paper Company is shown in Table 3-2. A conservative reaction would be to focus the efforts of your salespeople, distributors, and advertising on the growing South Central market. This approach seeks to make money by concentrating on areas where the firm currently does well. A more aggressive reaction would be to ask why your organization is showing slippage in some areas. Is there something wrong with your product or is it just a marketing problem? Perhaps customers expect local production facilities to assure quick delivery. Perhaps the firm is using the wrong mix of pricing, distribution, and promotional activities.

A further complication for marketing managers is a customer who operates from multiple locations. For example, a plant manager in Oklahoma may want to buy your product but the order may require approval from a parent organization located in New York City. This means selling efforts have to be coordinated and conducted in two widely separate environments. An even more difficult situation occurs when the Oklahoma plant wants to buy your corrugated product and the Florida plant wants another brand. Under these conditions, the New York parent is likely to demand standardization on one product and suppliers will have to sell at three or more locations if they expect to land the order. These examples suggest sellers need to know where customers are located and they must be prepared to conduct extensive marketing activities at a variety of sites.

WHEN DO CUSTOMERS BUY?

At first glance the question of when customers buy does not seem to be a serious problem. If these are the periods when customers want to order, then the marketing concept suggests the marketing manager should adapt production and distribution systems to meet these customer demands.

TABLE 3-2   Location of McElwee Paper's American Customers

Year		Proportion of Shipment to				
	Northeast	Southeast	East Central	North Central	South Central	West
Current	15.8%	19.3%	14.1%	12.0%	21.7%	17.1%
Last	15.4	19.6	14.2	12.2	21.6	17.0
Previous	15.8	19.6	14.0	12.1	21.2	17.3

Adapting to Customer Buying Patterns

Demand variation exists for many products. When enough customers want to rent videos at 10 P.M. or on Sundays, alert stores adjust their hours to fill this need. In a similar fashion innovative banks have added teller machines so customers can withdraw cash 24 hours a day, and mail order firms have toll-free numbers so customers can order at night and on weekends. Even financial service companies have toll-free numbers so customers can trade securities 24 hours a day. The success of these activities depends on knowing a great deal about when customers want to buy.

Changing Customer Buying Patterns

Perceptive marketers not only know when customers buy, they take advantage of those times when they do *not* buy. For example, airlines, resorts, and telephone companies build capacity to meet peak seasonal demands. This means that they have excess capacity sitting idle during the off-season. Marketing managers can help utilize this capacity by implementing special pricing and promotional programs to attract new customers when demand is low. The trick is to see the opportunity to expand sales even though customers do not seem to be interested.

A classic example of extending the period customers will use a product occurred with that old American favorite the turkey. Turkeys were traditionally served during the Thanksgiving and Christmas holidays and were not eaten the rest of the year. An entire industry was created to grow and process turkeys for sale during a two-month period. Although turkey is low in fat and economical, the birds are packaged in 15–20 pound units and take a great deal of time and effort to cook. This is not a problem during holidays when friends gather to celebrate, but turkey is inconvenient during the week when family members may be working. The key to extending turkey sales beyond the normal holiday season is to make it easier for the customer to prepare. Turkeys are now sold year round in pieces, slices, and as breasts for even the smallest buying unit. This example shows that the time when customers buy products can be extended with careful attention to marketing activities.

WHAT DO MY CUSTOMERS WANT?

Determining customer wants seems simple enough, just monitor current sales to see what they are buying. A somewhat more sophisticated approach would record sales by price range, size, and color so that product offerings could be matched with customer preference. While an analysis of internal sales data is straightforward, what do you do if you are not currently selling the item? This problem can be resolved by buying the sales figures for your competitors from independent research firms (ACNielsen) or send observers into their stores to count the number of purchases being made.

There is, of course, more to determining customer wants than just checking out what sells. The main reason is that many new concepts and products have yet to be invented and are not currently for sale. In these cases market research may help you understand customer tastes (see Marketing in Action box 3-2).

You must be careful not to let your preconceptions about customers cloud your thinking. Experienced managers frequently misjudge what customers really want. For example, the Reflective Products Division of 3M sells reflective materials to a wide variety of city, county, and state governments and to sign and barricade manufacturers. 3M is a major player in this market and they have a good idea what product characteristics, delivery times, prices, and services are important. However, when they asked each group of customers to rank these criteria they were stunned by the results. While all the customers' rankings

APPLYING
. . . to
Business-to-
Business
Marketing

MARKETING IN ACTION 3-2

Carmakers Use Research to Cater to Weekend Warriors

APPLYING
. . . to
Consumer
Durables
Marketing

Early on in the car-as-home-trend, Toyota researchers measured every possible drink size—even camping out to watch people's drinking habits in their cars and trucks. Other carmakers were doing their own research, and the cup-holder war began. General Motors Corp.'s Chevy Venture boasted 17 cup holders, or nearly two cup holders for every passenger.

While another cup holder might be too much of a good thing, a superabundance of pockets is something else. Car companies say market research told them that having a map pouch in the door, a glove compartment, and maybe a hidey-hole in the console just didn't provide enough places to stash the necessities of life. In focus groups and surveys, drivers said they were tired of tennis balls rolling around the gas pedal or skis poking out of the trunk. They wanted a place for everything and everything in its place. Toyota's product manager found that younger and more active customers were easygoing about how storage spaces should look. Netting and mesh were fine.

Hoping to distinguish its new vehicle from the competition, Nissan equipped its new small sport utility vehicle with pockets upon pockets. The new Nissan has a cubbyhole in the rear tailgate that can house dirty soccer cleats, wet snowshoes, or a kid's filthy backpack. Under the carpeting in the rear cargo area, there is a hidden compartment for small objects, like tools or tent stakes. And in the rear cargo space are hooks for various different types of storage nets. For sports equipment and other bulky items, Nissan added an overhead cargo area on the roof of the vehicle.

— *You can use market research to understand consumer preferences.*

Source: Emily R. Sendler, "Car Makers Cram Vehicles with Pockets Pouches," *The Wall Street Journal,* August 11, 1998, p. B1

Courtesy Toyota Motor Corp.

included the same factors, there was *no* agreement on which was most important. This meant that the same appeals could not be used for different reflective customers as had been done in the past. 3M was forced to revise its marketing program to emphasize separate criteria for each customer group. Customer wants in this case were not as generic as the managers believed.

HOW DO CUSTOMERS BUY?

By far the most complex issue in customer analysis is figuring out how customers buy. The problem for marketers is that much of the decision-making process takes place inside the buyers' heads, which makes it difficult to observe exactly how choices are made. Fortunately, extensive research has revealed the basic dimensions of the decision process.

A simplified model of the customer buying process is shown in Figure 3-1. Note that the procedure is sequential and time constrained. Also purchase decisions are influenced by a variety of internal and external factors. The first step is for the buyer to recognize that a problem or need exists. In a common situation, the buyer is reminded by the computer that the inventory of parts or supplies is low and needs to be replenished. Sometimes needs arise from the breakdown of the old product or from a constant demand for repairs. Also, advertising or store displays can make people aware of unfilled wants. Social interaction with friends or associates can often lead to buyer interest in new products. Finally, many consumer needs arise from internally generated desires for food, shelter, and clothing.

The second step in the buying process involves a search for alternative ways of solving the problem or filling the need. The inclusion of a detailed search process in Figure 3-1 means the customer is engaged in extended problem solving. Many routine purchases are much simpler than Figure 3-1 suggests. If you just want a candy bar, for example, you are likely to pick one up from the next available vending machine or candy counter rather than shop around at different stores. In the case of depleted business inventory, search may be limited to rebuying the item from a regular supplier. If an item is broken, can it be repaired? How much will repairs cost compared to the cost of buying a new unit? If a new product is needed, what brands are available? What features are offered by the different models? The information search phase of the process is important because this is where marketing can help the buyer gather necessary data. Marketing helps train the salespeople so they will have the information necessary to answer customer questions. Marketing prepares the tags and brochures that inform buyers about the merchandise. Marketing also designs the point-of-

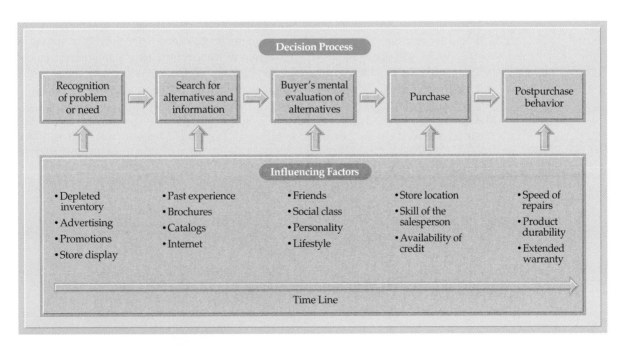

FIGURE 3-1   Customer Buying Process

purchase displays, newspaper ads, TV ads, radio commercials, and Web sites that give customers information on prices, product availability, and desirable product features.

The third step in the buyer's decision process is the evaluation of the alternatives. This part of the process involves little action for the seller; it occurs primarily in the customer's brain. The buyer weighs the advantages and disadvantages of the various alternatives and eventually makes a decision. Because this part of purchase behavior is a mental process, it is hard to observe and, consequently, is more difficult for marketing people to influence.

Once the customer has decided to buy, the next step is to complete the purchase transaction. The job of marketing is to make the product conveniently available so customers do not have to travel great distances or wait in lines for it. Also, marketing can help complete the purchase by simplifying credit arrangements, packaging, and delivery. It is not enough just to interest customers in your product; you must make the product easily available if you expect to sell in any volume.

The final step of the buying process deals with postpurchase behavior. Most products wear out or are used up and have to be replaced. This means that it is important to keep customers satisfied with the purchase so they will buy the item again. Marketing people carefully monitor postpurchase activities of customers so that interest in the product is maintained. The way customers are treated on returns, repairs, and warranty service will influence the decision process for subsequent purchases. A firm that handles postpurchase doubt and anxiety properly is more likely to build a loyal cadre of repeat buyers.

Problem Recognition

The buyer decision process begins with problem recognition. This occurs when a person perceives a difference between what he or she has (poor TV reception) and what he or she would like (a sharp, clear picture). Problem recognition can be awakened by information on past experiences stored in memory, basic motives, or cues from reference groups (Figure 3-2). Motives are enduring predisposition toward specific goals that both start and direct behavior. For example, some people must have the very latest equipment, and others like to avoid uncertainty caused by mechanical breakdowns. Problem recognition also can be activated by an outside stimulus such as advertising.

You should realize that not every difference between actual conditions and the ideal state will lead to purchase. Threshold differences must be exceeded before decision making is started. Buyers will often put up with minor inconveniences for a long time prior to actually becoming aware of their needs and starting to search for a solution. For example, many people will endure a headache for many hours before they go to the drugstore to choose a remedy.

Motivation   Needs tend to be arranged in a hierarchy and consumers usually satisfy their needs on one level before they move to higher levels. Once consumers have satisfied their

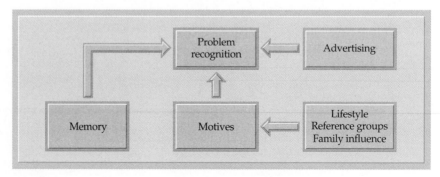

FIGURE 3-2   **Factors Influencing Problem Recognition**

requirements for food and shelter, they become more concerned with safety and products such as health insurance and radial tires. At the next level, a need for belonging is filled by churches, clubs, and family associations. The fourth level in the hierarchy is concerned with status, and some people satisfy this need by buying paintings or jewels. The highest need level is for self-actualization; this implies doing something to develop the talents of the individual, such as taking art lessons or working toward a new occupation.

Although basic needs influence many purchase decisions, we all buy things for other reasons. Some people have an unusually strong concern for their health, for example, and stock up on vitamins and nutrition books. Others are anxious in small groups and purchase quantities of deodorants and mouthwash. Still others crave excitement and take up skydiving and travel to exotic locales. Marketing managers can also appeal to pride in personal appearance or possessions to sell soap, cosmetics, and house paint. Another powerful motivating factor in buying situations is economy.

Reference Groups   One factor that influences the awakening of customer needs is membership in various social groups. Customers often buy products similar to what their friends and business associates own, so it is important to study membership in social groups.

For consumer goods, buyers are sometimes grouped into social classes based on occupation, source of income, type of housing, and residence location. The important thing to remember is that social class membership often determines when people buy products and what they buy. Research has shown that the middle classes are good markets for insurance and travel and the lower classes are prime customers for appliances and automobiles. The upper class is small in numbers, but it controls a lot of wealth that can be steered into various investment opportunities.

Family Influences   The role and influence of family members in consumer decision making vary depending on the product and family characteristics. For example, the six major stages of the family life cycle are (1) young single people, (2) young married couples with no children, (3) young married couples with dependent children, (4) older married couples with dependent children, (5) older married couples with no dependent children, and (6) older single people. The consumer's arrival at each stage of the life cycle initiates needs for new classes of products. When single persons move into their own apartment, they need to buy basic household equipment. When these persons marry, there is a need for more furnishings, and the arrival of children triggers a host of infant-related purchases. Thus, each stage of the family life cycle opens new vistas of needs that can be met by marketing managers who watch for these opportunities.

Joint decision making by the husband and wife tends to decline over the family life cycle as each of the partners becomes more aware of what the other considers acceptable. Usually, one partner will be responsible for decisions concerning a given product class. For example, the husband may be an expert in insurance whereas the wife may be more knowledgeable about children's clothing. This division of responsibility is based on relative expertise. Joint decision making is more important where large expenditures are involved.

Search for Alternatives

Once buyers become aware of their needs, the next step in the decision process is to gather information on products and alternative solutions to the customer's problem. A diagram explaining the search process is shown in Figure 3-3. The search usually begins when buyers consult their memories for information that might solve their current problem. Previous experiences of the buyer with similar merchandise can be reviewed to see what product solutions worked in the past. Memory can also be consulted for recommendations of friends, articles, and advertisements. If memory does not provide enough, buyers start to consult out-

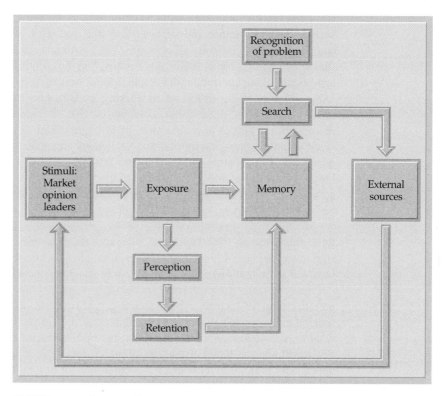

FIGURE 3-3   The Search Process

side sources of information. These include both market-oriented sources such as reading newspaper ads and talking with salespeople and nonmarketing sources such as articles in *Consumer Reports* magazine and conversations with friends.

For outside sources to be effective, buyers have to be exposed to their messages. This means the buyer has to own a radio or TV set, subscribe to magazines and newspapers, read trade journals, see billboards, and be close enough to visit and talk with dealers. After the buyer is exposed to market information, some of the data are sent directly to memory, where it is processed for decision making. However, most of the information goes through a series of filters, where it is often distorted or discarded. This process of interpreting data is called perception.

Perception   In a marketing setting, perception means values attached to communications about products received from salespeople, friends, advertisements, and independent test reports. Variations in the behavior of buyers in the marketplace can be explained partly by individual differences in the way products and services are perceived.

The perceptual process controls both the quantity of information received through attention and the quality or meaning of information as it is affected by bias. Attention is the mechanism governing the receptivity of the buyer to ads and other stimuli to which the buyer is exposed. Bias, on the other hand, is distortion of incoming data caused by previous exposure to the product, other promotional material, or family background. Two aspects of the perceptual process that have important marketing implications are selective attention and perceptual bias.

In the case of selective attention, consumers have frames of reference that they use to simplify the information they are continually receiving from their friends and marketing communications. Although the sorting-out process prevents consumers from being overwhelmed by their experiences, it does mean that they are sensing only part of their environment. For example, people can sit in front of a TV set and read in a room full of children. When they are called to dinner, they often do not hear the summons because they have effectively "tuned out" all sound messages and are receptive only to what they see in magazines or newspapers. In addition, they are likely to notice only some of the ads depending on their preferences for articles or news coverage.

An example of perceptual bias can be described by referring to some research showing that brand names influence taste perception. One brewer asked consumers to explain their preferences for beer and found the answers centered on the physical attributes of the product, such as flavor. Then an experiment was conducted to determine whether the beer drinkers could distinguish among major brands when they were not labeled. The consumers failed this test, and when these same consumers were subsequently asked to rate labeled beers, their ratings differed from those in the unlabeled experiment. These results suggest that brand names influence preference, and the success of a brand of beer may be highly dependent on the effectiveness of its marketing effort. The sense of taste is especially subject to bias and distortion, and product development for items in which flavor is an important attribute must be designed to accommodate this phenomenon.

Perceived Risk   The amount of risk buyers believe is associated with a purchase decision also affects behavior. The degree of risk varies with the costs at stake in a decision and the buyers' degree of certainty that the outcome of the decision will be satisfactory. The costs of a bad decision include monetary loss, time loss, ego loss, social risks, and losses related to the failure to satisfy the aroused need.

Individuals often pursue different risk reduction strategies. Some buy only for cash; others buy the most expensive items as an assurance of quality; still others buy the least expensive to minimize dollar investment. Some risk reduction actions by consumers are inconsistent. Frequently, the amount of deliberation for an expensive product is *less* than for an inexpensive one. Some buyers seem uncomfortable with decisions involving high perceived risk and act hastily. This suggests that perceived risk interacts with the amount of *time* that can be used for decision making.

Opinion Leaders   The search for nonmarket information (Figure 3-3) often involves interpersonal communications with friends, neighbors, relatives, or people at work or school. Individuals who provide others with information for the buying process are called opinion leaders, influentials, or change agents. These nonmarket sources can have a positive effect on purchase, or they can discourage people from buying a product. Research has shown that interpersonal communications are influential in the purchase of durable goods, food items, soaps, motion picture selection, makeup techniques, farming practices, clothing, selection of doctors, retail stores, and new products.

The term *opinion leader* must be used carefully because it is often interpreted as meaning that influence trickles down from members of higher social classes to members of lower social classes. However, influence usually occurs horizontally within strata. Influentials tend to be more gregarious and possess more knowledge in their area of influence. Often this knowledge has been obtained through greater exposure to relevant mass media.

According to the two-step flow of communication, the firm directs its advertising at the influentials in its product category, and these people influence their followers by word-of-mouth communication. The amount of word-of-mouth communication varies according to adopter categories. The purchaser of a product can be classified into one of five groups on the basis of the time of his or her adoption in relation to that of other buyers, as shown in Figure 3-4. The five categories are innovators, early adopters, early majority, late majority, and laggards.

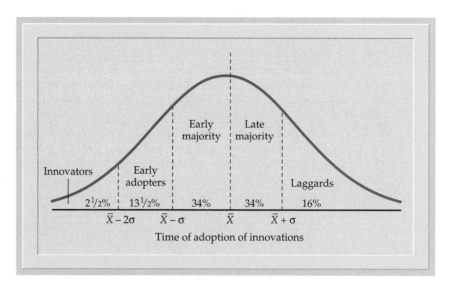

FIGURE 3-4 **Adopter Category as a Function of the Relative Time of Adoption**

Innovators are important in new product introductions because they affect later adopters and retail availability. However, innovators are usually not influentials. They are too innovative to be credible. They do help create awareness of a new product, however, and perform a product testing function which is observed by the influentials. The most important group of opinion leaders are the 13 percent classified as early adopters (Figure 3-4). These people are highly respected and have the most extensive social networks. The early majority also have some value as opinion leaders. However, the late majority and laggards are slow to adopt and have no value as influentials.

Evaluation of Alternatives

The evaluation phase of the customer decision model is the most complex and the least understood part of the process. A great many factors influence individual decision making, and it is difficult to observe what is going on inside the buyer's head. However, a general outline of the evaluation phase is shown in Figure 3-5. Sometimes evaluation occurs as a buyer is searching for information, as when he or she is flipping through a rack of clothes. In other cases, evaluation takes place after the search process is complete. The first stage involves a comparison of the data with the buyer's evaluative criteria. The buyer asks whether various brands would deliver the benefits sought in the product. The outcome of this process is a set of beliefs about the brands available for purchase. These beliefs are stored in memory and tell the buyer the consequences of different purchases based on the evaluative criteria. As a rule, you should view the buyer's evaluative criteria as a given and learn to adapt your product, price, promotion, and distribution elements to these key buying determinants.

The next step occurs when the buyer's beliefs and evaluations are combined to form attitudes (Figure 3-5). Attitudes are mental states of readiness to purchase that are organized through experiences and influence behavior. In general, prospects will purchase items when attitudes toward the product are favorable. If attitudes are negative, the purchase is likely to be postponed, whereas positive attitudes are associated with a strong intention to act. Measurement of intentions is important because it tells you the probability that a purchase will be made. This discussion has described the basic steps of evaluation, and we will now move on to some of the details of the process.

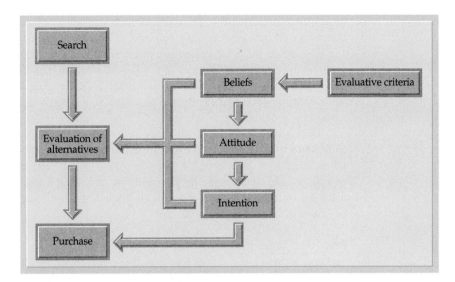

FIGURE 3-5   Alternative Evaluation

Learning   Buyer evaluation of product alternatives is enhanced through learned behavior. Learning can be defined as changes in response tendencies due to the effects of experience. Learning occurs when buyers respond to a stimulus and are rewarded with need satisfaction or are penalized by product failure. For example, a consumer might see an ad for beverages on a hot day and respond by trying different brands such as 7-Up, Slice, or Sprite. If Sprite satisfies the taste, then on future occasions he or she will buy Sprite again. The customer has learned. Theories that explain this adaptive behavior include problem solving, stimulus response, and reinforcement.

Advertising programs are often built on stimulus response theory. For example, a TV commercial of a pleasant outdoor boy–girl situation is shown as a stimulus to the prospect. The idea is to elicit a positive emotional response that can be sent into memory when the brand name "Sprite" is presented in a voice over the commercial.

Marketers also use a learning theory called *operant conditioning,* which says that the probability of a favorable response (read the ad) can be increased by following up with reinforcement or a reward. A print ad might show a person performing an unpleasant household chore (cleaning the oven) with a new spray product. People who read the ad are rewarded with a 50-cents-off store coupon that is placed at the end of the ad copy. Other examples of the use of learning theory in marketing include techniques such as giving out samples of new products and refund offers that are designed to achieve product trial.

Consistency Paradigm   Consistency is another useful concept that helps explain how customers make decisions. Buyers attempt to maintain consistency in their attitudes, behaviors, and the interaction of the two. Exposure to conflicting information produces internal strain. Customers seek to find solutions that minimize this tension. Conflict reduction alternatives include (1) changing behavior to conform to new information, (2) changing attitudes, (3) discrediting the source of the conflict-causing new information, (4) acquiring additional information to reinforce their original position, (5) avoiding the information sources that contribute to the dissonance (selective exposure), (6) distorting the new information, and (7) forgetting the content of the new information (selective recall).

Consistency theory also provides insight for planning new product prices. Often a new product is temporarily offered at a low introductory price. This is done to encourage trial of the product. Although many marginal users will be lost when the price is raised, it is hoped that some of these consumers, who would not have tried the product at the regular price, will be retained. Although this reasoning seems plausible, consistency theory suggests that the effort may be counterproductive and lead to lower rather than higher eventual sales.

The higher the price consumers pay for a new product, the greater will be the pressure on them to justify their purchase by liking the product. The greater liking will, in turn, produce greater repeat purchases. On the other hand, consumers who buy the product on a cents-off promotion can justify the purchase as a bargain and need not alter their attitude toward the product.

Thus, attempts to change attitudes by first changing behavior must involve commitment to product trial. This suggests that sampling a new product would be ineffectual in cases where consumers have established preferences. In one case, housewives resisted cold-water detergents and stated that they would not use a free sample. Some commitment was achieved by using cents-off coupons in the initial advertising and forcing the consumer to pay most of the purchase price.

Fear   One motivating force that is risky to use in marketing communications is fear. The problem is that high levels of fear may cause consumers to distort advertising messages and thus may actually reduce the sales of the product. To sell antilock brakes, for example, auto manufacturers could use films of cars in accidents being smashed and burned. However, consumers might be so horrified by the pictures that they would refuse to consider that accidents might occur. Lower levels of fear help sales by creating interest in the product message, a facilitating effect. The inhibiting and facilitating effects of fear appeals may balance each other out. In this case, a moderate level of fear is optimal. One successful use of fear to sell products has been the publication of personal experiences with household fires to help sell smoke alarms. An example of a fear appeal is given in Marketing in Action box 3-3.

Attitude Formation and Change

Attitudes may affect the buyer's decision-making process (Figure 3-5), and you must understand attitude formation and change if you expect to direct marketing activities to influence sales. *Attitude* is a mental state of readiness, organized through experience, exerting a directive influence on the individual's response to objects, and situations with which it is related. This implies that attitude is a hypothetical construct that intervenes between marketing communications and product purchase. Most discussions of attitude recognize three components: cognitive (perceptual), affective (like-dislike), and conative (intentions).

An interesting synthesis of the relationships among the components of attitude and behavior suggests that at least three alternative sequences of cognitive, affective, and conative (behavioral) change may exist. These may be summarized as follows.

1. The Standard Learning Hierarchy
   Sequence of Change: Cognitive   →   Affective   →   Conative
                             (Perceptual)   (Like-Dislike)   (Purchase)
   Conditions: Buyers are highly involved.
                             Alternative products are clearly differentiated.
                             Mass media promotion is heavy.
                             Product is in early stages of its life cycle.
2. The Dissonance-Attribution Hierarchy
   Sequence of Change: Conative   →   Affective   →   Cognative
                             (Purchase)   (Like-Dislike)   (Perceptual)
   Conditions: Buyers are highly involved.
                             Products are similar.
                             Personal selling is more important than mass media promotion.
                             Product is in early maturity stages of life cycle.

MARKETING IN ACTION 3-3

Soothing the Fear of Germs

APPLYING
. . . to
Consumer
Packaged
Goods
Marketing

Soap used to be a social thing, but now it is a selfish thing. This explains why Dial soap, a 50-year-old brand, is struggling and has pulled the plug on its long-running campaign: "Aren't you glad you use Dial?" in an effort to appeal to a younger crowd. Famous as the old slogan was, Dial decided that it wasn't relevant any longer because of what is going on inside of soap users' heads: When we lather up, we aren't simply primping or worrying about offending others in the outside world. Rather we want to scrub the outside world away. "People are looking at germs in a very different way," says the group account director for Dial's advertising agency, which created the new Dial campaign after talking to consumers. "It used to be, 'I'm trying to make myself presentable to you.' Now it's more about 'Hey, I've got to wash you off of me.'"

In focus groups, Dial discovered that many consumers know Dial as the famous "gold bar" but view the soap as a masculine product, a big drawback in a category where women primarily make the purchase decisions. In addition, Dial users tend to be older, a less-appealing demographic target than young families, whose grimy kids and outdoor activities simply require more soap. Hence, Dial decided on an emotional appeal to women 25 to 49 years old with families. "You might feel your very best when you get out of the shower in the morning, and after that, you start to come into contact with a world that has germs. We can restore you to a safe haven, that area of comfort when you are clean and feel very good about yourself."

A new black-and-white spot, which debuted on NBC's "Today" show, begins with a little girl climbing into a bathtub. A voice-over evokes a scene from "The Wizard of Oz" movie, with the voice of the late Judy Garland wondering if there might be "someplace where there isn't any trouble … far, far away." As she begins to sing "Somewhere Over the Rainbow," a soothing woman's voice tells viewers: "You can get there and feel clean, healthy, restored." The tagline: "Doesn't that feel better?" Although Dial won't discuss the campaign's cost, the budget is nearly three times what the company spent on Dial soap last year, and more than it has spent on any single product campaign in seven years.

The commercial is part of a broader effort to suds up sales of Dial, the first antibacterial soap. While Dial is the No. 2 brand in the bar-soap category, its sales last year fell eight percent despite a growing consumer craze for antibacterial products. Sales of bar soaps were flat last year as many consumers switched to shower gels and liquid soaps, which increased about seven percent, according to Information Resources Inc. But sales of Dial liquid soaps and shower gels also plummeted last year, even as bar-soap competitors cleaned up at the checkout. Sales of market leader Dove, from Unilever, rose 5.5 percent, while Unilever's Lever 2000, the third-ranked soap, increased 6.5 percent. In the No. 4 slot, Colgate-Palmolive's Irish Spring jumped 14 percent.

Dial, like other aging brands, must walk a fine line between updating its image and alienating its core consumers. That is what happened in the late 1970s when Dial, feeling pressure from Procter & Gamble's Coast soap, abandoned the "Aren't you glad you use Dial?" slogan. It switched to "A new Dial morning," promoting Dial as an invigorating soap with a refreshing scent. Market share tumbled, and the company returned to its famous old slogan. But this time, Dial says the slogan change capitalizes on the soap's heritage, but still broadens its appeal. "It's good heritage and that's fine, but this is intended to be a departure. We're making a strong attempt to change the way people feel about Dial."

— *Fear appeals can be effective.*

Source: Tara Parker-Pope, "Dial Soap Aims at Soothing Fear of Germs," *The Wall Street Journal,* January 20, 1998, p. B7.

3. The Low-Involvement Hierarchy

Sequence of Change:	Cognitive	→	Conative	→	Affective
	(Perceptual)		(Purchase)		(Like-Dislike)

Conditions: Buyers have low involvement.

Products are similar.

Broadcast media are important.

Product is in late maturity stage of life cycle.

Attitudes may be positive; yet no sales result. You probably have extremely positive attitudes toward Rolls Royce cars and Steinway pianos, but do not own either, and probably never will. It is even worse than this. Scanner data, which provide irrefutable evidence of buyer choice behavior, are showing direct contradictions to attitude measurements. For example, those consumers who have the highest positive attitude toward healthful living and diet are the same people buying the fattening, creamy deserts. Since the link between attitude and behavior is tenuous, attitude research is giving way to behavior research. "If you want to know what your favorite product is, look through your trash can."

Purchase

Once consumers have selected a product alternative, the next step in the behavioral model is to complete the purchase (Figure 3-6). The purchase part of the transaction is influenced by the buyer's intentions and other special conditions that exist in the marketplace. A buyer may intend to purchase a Sony TV, but if this brand is out of stock, he or she may end up with an RCA. Also, the buyer may want the remote control console model but can only afford to buy a portable TV.

A number of other in-store conditions can influence purchase decisions. The buying process is advanced if the product or service is readily available to the buyer. Consumers may prefer your product, but if they have to travel 50 miles to the nearest dealer, they are not likely to buy it. Similarly, dealers who are open at nights and on weekends have advantages over stores with limited hours, where customers wait in line and in which credit or check-cashing services are not offered. For example, emergency medical clinics that do not require appointments and are open evenings and weekends have siphoned off substantial business from regular doctors and hospital emergency rooms.

In-store displays are another special condition that influences buyer choice. When customers encounter a large display of a new soft drink and are given a free sample, they are more likely to switch brands and try the new item. The display provides new information so that the consumer reevaluates established beliefs and the intention to buy is modified.

A special price at the store level is also a strong inducement to get customers to switch brands. Price is particularly effective when the buyer believes that all brands in a product category are about equal in quality. Under these conditions, a price reduction may temporarily shift customer choice, and then it will revert back when the raided brand makes a counter

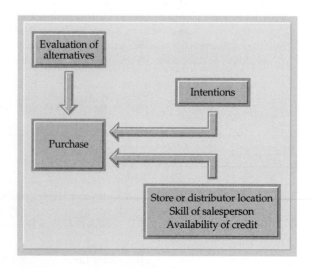

FIGURE 3-6   The Purchase Decision

price adjustment. For example, automobile tires, batteries, and shock absorbers fail on a random basis, and the buyer rarely has time to shop for preferred brands. Thus, the buyer frequently purchases the item that is on sale when he or she comes in for a replacement.

Knowledgeable and helpful personnel at the point of sale are often the key factor that sways a customer toward a particular brand. Salespeople who can explain product features and demonstrate benefits are often able to trade customers up to higher-profit merchandise. One study revealed that three-fourths of those interviewed in five cities said quality of salespeople was a factor in the choice of a shopping center. Clearly, retailers and manufacturers who do the best job of selecting and training salespeople enhance their customer purchase probabilities.

Postpurchase Behavior

Customer postpurchase activity provides several inputs to our model of buyer behavior (Figure 3-7). A major concern is that purchase allows customers to learn more about products or services. Customer expectations are compared with actual product experience; the degree of satisfaction or dissatisfaction assessed; and possible further customer behavior projected. Highly satisfied customers, for example, will alter their beliefs about a product in a favorable direction. These satisfied consumers are likely to be "converted" to repeat buyers and may become advocates of the product in their conversations with others.

Dissatisfaction   Products or services that do not live up to the buyer's expectation for durability or performance result in customer dissatisfaction (Figure 3-7). The most common reaction to product problems is for the customer to return to the dealer and ask for an exchange, refund, or repairs. If the problem is handled properly by the dealer, the buyer's

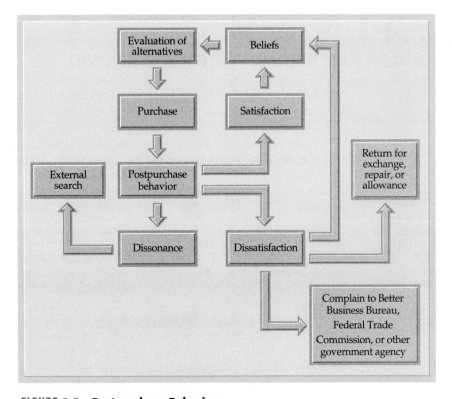

FIGURE 3-7   **Postpurchase Behavior**

positive attitude toward the product will be restored, and the customer will probably buy again. When customer complaints are rebuffed, a negative attitude structure is formed, and repeat purchase probabilities decline. In the case of low-value goods, dissatisfied customers usually do not return to the dealer for an adjustment and simply show their resentment by not buying again.

When customers' complaints are not handled properly, they may result in appeals to outside agencies. The ensuing publicity can lead to lawsuits, product recalls, loss of goodwill, and reduced market shares. For example, research has shown that customer dissatisfaction is high for services such as employment agencies, auto repairs, nursing homes, moving and storage, and appliance repairs. This suggests that some firms could benefit by improving the quality of their services and providing better methods for handling complaints. Firms that fail to deal with dissatisfied customers may end up having to deal with increased government regulation and decreased revenue.

Cognitive Dissonance   Another important area of postpurchase behavior is cognitive dissonance or postpurchase doubt (Figure 3-7). A purchase decision usually does not eliminate dissonance, for the consumer remains aware of the favorable features of the unchosen brands and must reconcile this knowledge with his or her own decisions. The process of reconciliation often involves a search for new information.

The likelihood that consumers will search for information after a purchase increases with the importance of the decision, with the number of negative attributes of the chosen alternative, and with the number of positive attributes of the unchosen alternatives. The kind of information sought depends on consumers' confidence in their initial decisions. Consumers who are confident that they have made the correct decision are more likely to try to find differing information and refute it. On the other hand, less confident consumers are more likely to seek only information that supports their decision. You should engage in activities designed to give buyers more product information, reduce postpurchase doubt, and turn customers into product advocates.

HOW DOES A FIRM BECOME CUSTOMER ORIENTED?

Many firms say they are customer oriented, but often this is just slogans and window dressing. Some managers profess to be interested in customers just to protect their own departments and chances for promotion. For example, managers of a flow controls company gathered to discuss declining sales, earnings, and market share. The president suggested that the only way to solve their problems was to become more customer driven. Everyone agreed and proceeded to give their version of a customer orientation. First the sales VP said they needed more salespeople to get closer to the customers. Then the manufacturing VP said they needed more automatic machinery so they could deliver better quality. The research and development VP called for more expenditures on research to generate more new products. One division manager asked for separate sales forces for each division and another wanted a special engineering group to tailor designs to customer needs. Although all of the managers displayed a customer orientation, they were primarily interested in using this theme to protect their own functional areas rather than to integrate a customer mentality throughout the firm.

In today's competitive environment, everyone in the firm is involved with marketing. Factory workers, people who answer phones, service people, and clerks in the back room all contribute to customer satisfaction. Thus one job of marketing is to make sure these employees understand their roles in building sales and profits. An Australian public transportation company used the inverted pyramid organization chart in Figure 3-8 to emphasize this new approach. This structure places the customer on top followed by the front-line staff. Man-

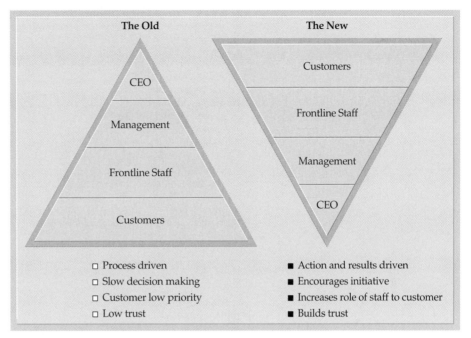

FIGURE 3-8 Customer Focused Marketing
(From Peter Daw, "Empowering Employees Drives Australian Transportation Customer Service," *Services Marketing Today,* American Marketing Association, July/August, 1992, p. 4.)

agement and the CEO are at the bottom. By empowering front-line staff to make decisions, marketing managers were free to concentrate on strategy development and implementation. This plan also focused everyone in the company on satisfying customers. After the new program was initiated at the transportation company, the number of customer complaint letters dropped by 30 percent.

Customer Checklist

After the president of the controls firm pointed out the need to work together, the managers concluded that they needed more information about present and potential customers. They also prepared a checklist to monitor how well they were doing in their drive to be more customer oriented (Table 3-3). The most common way to gather data for the items on this checklist is through the use of customer surveys. Questionnaires can be prepared, distributed to representative samples of customers, and the results summarized in reports. Useful information can be obtained from surveys, but success often depends on asking the right questions. This means you must know a great deal about customers before you can conduct a survey. Also surveys take time to complete and there is always doubt that the people who return them may not represent all customers.

A faster and more personal way to gather customer information is through some form of direct contact. One of the simplest is to listen in on your toll-free 800 customer call-in number. In some firms cassette recordings of customer calls are routinely distributed to a wide range of executives. If managers are adventuresome, they might even try to answer a few customer calls. An extension of this method is to use the phone to make regular calls on customers. For example, executives at Castle Company find a 5 × 7 inch sheet of paper with the name and phone number of a customer who has purchased a new piece of equipment on their desk three mornings a week. The executives are expected to call these people to see if

TABLE 3-3   Customer Orientation Checklist

1. *Are we easy to do business with?*
   - Easy to contact?
   - Fast to provide information?
   - Easy to order from?
   - Make reasonable promises?
2. *Do we keep our promises?*
   - On product performance?
   - Delivery?
   - Installation?
   - Training?
   - Service?
3. *Do we meet the standards we set?*
   - Specifics?
   - General tone?
   - Do we even know the standards?
4. *Are we responsive?*
   - Do we listen?
   - Do we follow up?
   - Do we ask "why not," not "why"?
   - Do we treat customers as individual companies and
       individual people?
5. *Do we work together?*
   - Share blame?
   - Share information?
   - Make joint decisions?
   - Provide satisfaction?

Source: Benson P Shapiro. "What the Hell Is Market Oriented? *Harvard Business Review,* Vol. 88, No. 6 (November–December 1988), p. 125.

they are satisfied with the company's hospital sterilizers. This lets customers know they are important and helps uncover problems before they become serious. You can also call recently lost customers and others who have not purchased for several years. Ask them why they are not buying and what can be done to bring them back as regular customers.

Plant Tours and Customer Visits

Another good way to learn about customers is to invite them in for a tour of your facilities and some informal discussions. The idea for these "How are we doing for you" sessions is to encourage customers to talk about issues that are important to them. One electrical connector company makes it a point to have their customers outnumber company personnel so they will feel free to speak up. Customers are generally delighted to be invited and often provide many new insights on their needs. A variation of this idea is to send executives out to visit customer plants. This approach was used by the controls firm mentioned earlier. They sent out 10 executives in groups of 2 to visit 20 major customers. These visits are more informative if you can talk to operating personnel or actually work for short periods in selected customer operations. Customers can also be contacted at trade shows. Hospitality suites at trade shows are often used to get customers to discuss their problems and needs.

You must realize that it is not enough to conduct one survey or call a few customers to establish a customer orientation for your company. Learning about customers is an ongoing process that reflects the changing business environment. A knowledgeable consultant suggests that senior line managers should spend not less than 30 percent of their time with customers. He also recommends that accountants, manufacturing managers, and MIS people spend 10 percent or more of their time learning about customer needs. There is no one best way to interact with customers, and the most important issue is to make sure that customer contacts are maintained on a regular basis.

SUMMARY

Marketing managers must understand customer needs in order to recognize new product opportunities, to identify meaningful bases for market segmentation, and to improve existing marketing activities. This means you should know who your customers are and where they are located. In addition, you need to know when they buy and why. Managers who understand how customers make purchase decisions are in a better position to design products and more effective marketing programs.

NOTES

1. Neil Barnard and Andrew Ehrenberg, "Advertising: Strongly Persuasive or Nudging," *Journal of Advertising Research,* Vol. 37 (January/February 1997), pp. 21–31.

FURTHER READING

Germain, Richard and M. Bixby Cooper. "How a Customer Mission Statement Affects Company Performance," *Industrial Marketing Management,* Vol. 19, No. 1 (February 1990), pp. 47–54.

REFERENCES

Peter, J. Paul and Jerry C. Olson. *Consumer Behavior and Marketing Strategy,* 5th ed. Boston: Irwin, McGraw-Hill, 1998.
Schiffman, Leon G., and Leslie Lazar Kanuk. *Consumer Behavior.* Englewood Cliffs, NJ: Prentice-Hall, 1997.
Solomon, Michael R. *Consumer Behavior.* Englewood Cliffs, NJ: Prentice-Hall, 1998.

QUESTIONS

1. The 2000 U.S. Census allowed a person to check multiple racial categories for the first time. How will this change marketing practices?

2. Around the world, countries are seeing their populations age. The approximate percentage of people over 65 in the year 2000 were as follows: Italy (17%), Sweden (16.7%), Belgium and Japan (16.4%), Spain (15.9%), France (15.6%), United Kingdom (15.4%), United States (12.4%). These percentages will surge over the next 25 years. How will this trend affect which products and services are marketed and, more important, how they are marketed?

3. The Procter & Gamble Co. developed a new-category brand called Fit, which outperforms water in removing dirt and other residues from produce. The product reportedly caused "a steep learning curve" for consumers. Moreover, produce marketers and retailers were concerned that the brand's advertising would conjure up fears about product safety. What is the right way to sell consumers on a cleanser for fruits and vegetables? Would concentrating on the dangers of produce residues be an effective way to market the product?

4. For years homebuilders have built first, then hoped for the best. Builders fill developments with a handful of cookie-cutter designs that can be mass produced economically. If a given model doesn't sell, they simply knock down its price. Is there a better approach that builders might take? Explain.

5. The heyday of roller skates, which have a double row of wheels, lasted from the 1960s through the early 1980s. During this period, a big draw at roller rinks was the disco-theme party, with *Saturday Night Fever* soundtracks and costumes to match. At roller rinks near Hollywood, celebrities like David Hasselhoff and Cher could often be spotted. More recently, the growth of in-line skates devastated roller skates, whose sales plunged. In-line skates, with a single row of wheels or rollers on a high-rise boot, move faster and more smoothly than roller skates on bumpy streets and sidewalks. There is a downside. The number of in-line skating accidents more than tripled between 1993 and 1995, prompting the U.S. Consumer Product Safety Commission to issue an advisory that all in-line skaters should wear helmets. The Commission noted that from 1992 to 1996 there were three-dozen deaths related to in-line skating. Meanwhile roller-skate manufacturers have improved their product. Softer plastic wheels cushion the ride. A wider wheel base offers better balance and a steady platform for launching jumps and other tricks. Roller skates also have toe brakes for easier stopping. How might a manufacturer encourage skaters to migrate from in-lines to roller skates?

6. In this chapter we have emphasized that you cannot know enough about your customer. However, some firms may go too far in their zeal to gather data on customers. For example, with so much consumer information now stored on computers, it is possible to find out if customers have been convicted of crimes, if they have gone to jail, if they pay alimony, if they suffer from serious diseases, if they have been treated for alcohol or drug abuse, how often they have filed for bankruptcy, how much they weigh, and how much money they owe on credit cards or previous purchases. Is it ethical for companies to use such personal data, often obtained from questionable sources, to eliminate or target certain prospects on their consideration lists?

7. LSI Logic, a high-tech semiconductor manufacturer, conducted an activity-based costing study of its customers. It found that it was making 90 percent of its profits from 10 percent of its customers. Moreover, it discovered that it was losing money on half its customers. What should LSI Logic do to address this situation?

8. J. P. Morgan & Co. is a master at providing private-banking service to the very rich. Its advertisements historically targeted prospects with $5 million to invest. Recently, however, Morgan has sought to inform investors that it will accept their business if they have $1 million in investable assets and, in some cases, with even less. Why is Morgan doing this? Is Morgan going down-market?

9. A company's main business is selling pharmaceutical products. It acquired a new product line, containing two products—Alpha and Beta, in a recent acquisition. Alpha is sold primarily over-the-counter (OTC) while Beta is sold only by prescription. Before preparing a marketing plan for the new line, the product manager commissioned a user survey to gather some basic consumer information. The resultant data is in file OTCdat.sav. The manager wondered what cross tabulations and other analyses should be run to help design distribution and promotional strategies for the new line.

CASE 3-1 PARFUM NINEVEH*

Noureddine Naybet, proprietor of Parfum Nineveh, a Moroccan Corporation, was considering the possibilities of exporting the company's line of perfume to Canada. It seemed to him possible that the behavior of consumers in Canada might be different than in Morocco, so he hired Herkimer Enslow Associates, a well-known Canadian market research firm, to undertake a study of the consumer behavior of Canadians with respect to perfume.

At a meeting set up in Toronto in early 1998 between Naybet and Enslow, the following research objectives, research questions and hypotheses were agreed upon. It was also agreed that Herkimer Enslow Associates would start by conducting a focus group study in accordance with the agreed upon objectives, questions, and hypotheses and that the target group would be Canadian women attending Canadian universities.

RESEARCH OBJECTIVES

1. To determine, study and analyze the seven steps of the decision making process using perfume as a model product.
2. To detect the specific factors that influence the decision process when purchasing perfume.
3. To identify to which stages of the consumer decision process the given influential factors apply.
4. To examine the similarities and/or differences in the decision process when purchasing for oneself in comparison to purchasing for others.

RESEARCH QUESTIONS

Our research is based on the following key questions, applied specifically to perfume/cologne.

1. What are the steps of the decision making process?
2. What factors have the greatest influence in this process? (personal, situation, etc.)
3. At what stages of the decision making process is the consumer most likely to be influenced by these factors?
4. Does the decision making process differ when buying for oneself in comparison to buying for others?

HYPOTHESES

The following hypotheses were agreed upon at a meeting held in January of 1998.

1. The decision process of perfume purchasing follows the general consumer model stated by Engel, Blackwell, and Miniard in their book *Consumer Behavior,* 8th edition (NY: The Dryden Press), a well-known book about North American consumer behavior.
2. The most influential factor consumers take into account when purchasing perfume is the existence of some kind of personal identification with the product (feeling).
3. The pre-purchase stage is the one in which the consumer is most susceptible to many surrounding influential factors.

The steps of the decision making process and key influential factors do differ when buying for someone else compared with buying for oneself.

RESEARCH METHODS

Our research identifies the decision making process consumers observe when they purchase perfume/cologne, and what key factors lead the consumer to choose a specific perfume. The research is based on an independent qualitative study.

The qualitative research was done through focus groups. A small group of five women were interviewed concerning their attitudes, involvement, and behaviors in regards to perfume and cologne.

The sessions were conducted by a mediator who asked random questions to the group members seeking out the responses to our research questions. These sessions were recorded to provide the research group

---

* This case was prepared by Yvonne Chiu, Anna Cochard, Murielle Poulain, Ena Sabih, Gladys Tiamuh, and Professor George H. Haines Jr. of Carleton University, Ottawa, Canada.

the opportunity of completing the analysis at their own convenience (see Exhibit 1 for focus group dialogue).

Focus groups are a method from which accurate information is gathered. They provide an open and easy atmosphere for consumers to express themselves. A focus group also encourages participants to provide details and personal experiences along with their product views to support their feelings and findings. It also presents the researchers with the opportunity to clarify any ambiguous aspects of given information as the questioning is done face to face. The limitation of a focus group is that the small representation of views and opinions is not an accurate portrayal of the existing consumer market.

EXHIBIT 1   Focus Group Transcript—Women

FOCUS GROUP MEMBERS:

Moderator (Ms. Joanne De Mello)
Naomi
Pauline
Monica
Darlene
Kelly

TRANSCRIPT:

Moderator: "We're going to start off first by talking a little about the product, like, why do you think perfume is so marketable? Why is it such a big deal? Why are there all those types of ads—whatever. What makes it so attractive?"

Pauline: "The people who advertise for it, you know."

Naomi: "Ya, so when you wear a fragrance you know, it's kinda like your personality, and you can show something of you without having to say anything."

Darlene: "Others think it makes people more appealing to their boyfriends or girlfriends."

Kelly: "I think people just want to smell nice."

Naomi: "There's other things too, for instance certain fragrances make you feel good you know, for springtime, sexy…"

Pauline: "Sexual arousal."

Naomi: "…or clean, fresh and natural, that kinda thing."

Moderator: "What's your favorite perfume ad or…"

Naomi: "I don't like CK, I can tell you that."

Moderator: "Why?"

Naomi: "I just find it kinda grungy, that's not what I like. I don't like the ads. I don't like it when their pants are hanging off or when you can see that half their breast is showing, like that kinda of thing."

Moderator: "So you don't like their image?"

Naomi: "I don't know."

Moderator: "Would that make you not buy that perfume?"

Naomi: "Probably not."

Pauline: "I don't like the smell of it, ya, I don't like the smell…"

Monica: "Ya, I don't like the smell either."

Pauline: "…and look at it, they look like druggies to me."

Naomi: "Ya, they do, and it almost looks dirty, even their eye makeup, it just looks like they just rubbed their eyes."

Moderator: "So you would say that advertising has a big effect on…"

Pauline: "The advertising, who is the advertising for…"

Monica: "How, and how they advertise it."

Darlene: "Not for me really, I don't … it doesn't really affect me. If it smells good, if I like it, I'll go for it. But if I see Kate Moss or 'this guy,' I won't go…"

Naomi: "Ya, me neither, I won't buy it because who, oh, it's Cindy Crawford. Oh wow, I won't buy it because it's Cindy Crawford."

Kelly: "Ya, if it gives me a headache or makes me dizzy, I won't buy it."

Moderator: "Who here has purchased perfume recently? Within the last…"

Naomi: "Just bought perfume?"

Moderator: "Ya."

Naomi, Pauline and Monica raise their hands.

Moderator: "Who wants to start? Tell us what you bought and why."

Naomi: "Why I bought it? Why I bought it is because I like it obviously. But I found it, it was one I came across by looking for something else. It was a scent, a perfume that I haven't heard of before. It's called Ibaccio, it's from an Italian maker, which is one I don't see like the ones thrown here. So I like that, it's not something that everyone wears. I don't like the fact when someone smells and it's like, oh—CK. Like I don't like that kind of … it's something's that's different."

Moderator: "So you were just shopping around?"

Naomi: "Yup, I wasn't even looking for perfume, I was just shopping."

Moderator: "So you picked up a tester?"

Naomi: "Yes, the tester was on the counter."

Moderator: "You smelled it, you tried it?"

Naomi: "Ya, I don't think it would have advertising for it. You wouldn't find it in a magazine. I've never seen it in a magazine."

Moderator: "Did you ever buy perfume before that or was that your first purchase?"

Naomi: "I actually work in a Shoppers, I give free perfume. I don't really buy perfume, like I get stuff."

Moderator: "I don't know what your name is but that's okay."

Pauline: "I was like shopping and I wanted to smell this new perfume that just came out and then this

(continued)

EXHIBIT 1   Continued

lady who works there kinda introduced me to this new … because I was looking at the Hugo Boss for men and I like that smell right and then she just showed me that there was a Hugo Boss for women and I smelled it. I just liked it—that's why I bought it."

Monica: "I was just shopping and I actually like to go and spray all the different types of perfume and I just picked up one that I think I had heard of but I didn't think much of it; it's Fire and Ice. And I love that smell. I loved it and so I just said okay let's buy it! Plus it was cheap!"

Moderator: "How important is price do you think, when you purchase a perfume?"

Monica: "It's important but sometimes you'll pay the extra bucks if you really like the perfume, for me personally."

Naomi: "And I always get it so you always have to buy the big size anyways, because like 30ml is $40 and the 100ml is $60 which is two times as much so you end up buying the big one anyways."

Pauline: "That's what happened to me when I bought mine. I ended up paying like $85 plus tax because you end up getting like twice as much more but $15 more, so it's kinda like stupid not to buy."

Naomi: "They give you those free things like a lot of times … the knapsack, the sun visor, those types of things."

Moderator: "How many people here are loyal to one brand?"

Pauline: "When it comes to a perfume you mean?"

Moderator: "Ya"

Monica: "I used to be into Obsession. Always, everything, everything…"

Moderator: "You were obsessed by Obsession?"

Pauline: "…yes, I was obsessed by Obsession but then I explored and tried a new perfume, this is the one, Fire and Ice."

Naomi: "But I get bored easily, like I won't wear one more than a year—I can't."

Moderator: "Does it vary between day and night?"

Naomi: "It's sometimes the mood I'm in, sometimes I want something light. Like I find I wear different things in the springtime than I do in the wintertime. I wear lighter things in the spring, and at nighttime I use something more musky as opposed to light."

Moderator: "Like would you say that perfume is something you wear every day, like when you go to school, or is for something when you want to feel a certain way, or for a certain occasion?"

Darlene: "Ya, that's me. I just wear it occasionally but not all the time. I don't always like it but I like the light scents better, but generally, I don't wear it every day."

Darlene: "Only if I want to, I don't know. Because I don't buy it a lot, so when I wear it, it's more for special. Not every day, I don't wear it every day."

Naomi: "I wear it every day. It's the last thing I put on so if I didn't put it on and leave the house I think 'oh no, maybe I didn't put it on,' like I notice when I don't. Also because I sell it, so I'm always smelling it, so I feel weird when I don't."

Moderator: "Anyone a collector?"

Naomi: "I know people that do."

Moderator: "So what would you say you would evaluate a perfume on? Would you say it would be … like what are its most important features? Like the price or the fact that it's the scent or it's long lasting, I don't know, it's image or the way it makes you feel. Like what would you say is the most important feature for you?"

Kelly: "For me it's the smell but second I'd say price. I don't know why but price is important I find, maybe it's because I don't make too much so, smell and then the price."

Darlene: "Ya me, it's the smell and then the price. But for makeup, it's if I like it, I don't care what the price is, I don't know, I don't know why I'm that way but for perfume, I care about the price too."

Monica: "Scent and then the price."

Pauline: "Ya, I agree, scent and then the price."

Naomi: "I would say the same thing, I think that's the most, for me it's the most important, for example personality, you know what I mean, by the certain fragrances you wear it comes across what kind of person you are. Like strong scents, or lighter ones … like people tend to be floral something I'd never wear. Like I don't find myself being that soft person, like I can never wear, like it wouldn't suit me, my particular personality."

Moderator: "Has anyone bought perfume as a gift for someone else?"

Monica: "Ya."

Moderator: "And how would you go about buying perfume for someone else?"

Pauline: "If I like it."

Moderator: "If you like it, you would buy it for someone else?"

Pauline: "Ya, if it's for my dad, and my dad doesn't really care. Like it depends on really who you buy it for. Like if it's for your dad then you buy something you like and your dad just wears it anyway. But I guess if it's someone like your boyfriend, then you kind of think what he usually wears."

Naomi: "Also what you like too?"

Pauline: "Ya, what you like of course. What you would like to smell all the time, ya."

Moderator: "You're forcing people to wear it!"

Pauline: "Ya."

Naomi: "Ya, I think for me when it comes to men, like if I'm buying for my father or boyfriend or brother,

(continued)

EXHIBIT 1   Continued

whatever, I'd pick what I like, but I think they should wear it. But when it comes to a woman, I usually know what they like anyways so I kinda buy along that range…"

Pauline: "Yup. Buy what they want, what they wear."

Naomi: "…usually they mention something they like."

Moderator: "And when you're buying for someone else, would you say it's the same features like first the smell, then the price as it would have been for you or are there different features that are more important?"

Kelly: "If it was a gift and I knew, like I wouldn't buy, I wouldn't take a guess and guess at what they would like. I would only buy it if I knew that they wear that particular brand so if it's for a gift and I know what they like then it wouldn't be important, like the price wouldn't be important. Because it is a gift and it is what they want so I don't think it would matter as much for me."

Darlene: "That's true, ya, I think that what they like is important, I once tried to change my mother's perfume, but she didn't wear it, so I've learned, ya."

Monica: "I would say the same, once you're actually buying it for someone else, especially as a gift, price shouldn't, well, it does play a part but it wouldn't be the biggest part as for yourself you know, you could cut for yourself but you don't want to cut for somebody else."

Pauline: "Ya, I agree. But sometimes you have to pay more because it's cut like the size of the bottle like you said before, it adds up like if you buy just a bigger bottle twice the size it costs a bit more, and sometimes the bit more can collect the tax. It costs a lot but you kinda have no choice when it comes to price and buying the perfume."

Naomi: "It's the same thing but usually when I get a gift, I never buy a bottle, I always buy a gift set. Because you're only paying a dollar more and you get your shower gel, body lotion, or whatever and it always looks boxed you know. It's usually what I buy if it's for a gift, it'll always be a gift set."

Moderator: "Do you think you're influenced by the outside factors? Like would you be influenced by the packaging?"

Monica: "Like the shape of the bottle?"

Moderator: "Or, let's say you're in the store, would you be influenced by a salesperson for something like purchasing perfume?"

Monica: "I hate salespeople. I tell them to get lost, I'm like no thanks!"

Naomi: "It depends where you go, sometimes they swarm you with blotters and they try to spray you, that I don't like. But I think if something's very colorful and attractive, then it might get my attention to go pick it up and look at it. But I

don't think the shape of a bottle will make me buy it more than the shape of another bottle."

Moderator: "Does everyone agree?"

Kelly: "Ya, I don't like the salespeople either because they just want to sell…"

Naomi: "Shoppers Drug Mart."

Darlene: "Ya, the bottle for me, it's not a big factor it's mainly the scent but then again especially if I'm buying for somebody else if the bottle is really, I don't know, ugly I guess but the smell's nice, I won't buy it if it's a gift for someone else."

Moderator: "So if it's a gift for someone else then the packaging is important?"

Darlene: "Ya."

Monica: "I'm like her too, I like things that look nice too. I always think that they have to look nice even though I might be paying extra for the nice-shaped bottle. But if it doesn't look nice, I don't want it usually. It has to catch my eye and if it doesn't then I don't want it."

Pauline: "I don't know, if it's a gift for somebody and they like a particular bottle or whatever, but I don't think about the shape or whatever; it's mainly the scent. But ya the shape, the color would catch your eye to walk across the counter and maybe to look at it. But it doesn't really play a factor."

Naomi: "For me it does, just to look at it but not to buy it. It's like when something's sitting on the counter that's different from the ones talked about a lot. You would always have the interest to just go and pick it up. And if there wasn't that hype or it didn't look like that or it wasn't those colors then I wouldn't have ever looked at it in the first place. But it's not the final, it doesn't have anything to do with the final factor but I wouldn't have considered it in the first place if it wasn't nice to look at."

Moderator: "So would it matter where you bought it? Like would it matter if you were choosing between Wal-Mart, Eatons, or the Bay? Or even Holt Renfrew? Where you could buy the same perfume but at different settings, does it matter to you?"

Pauline: "Well if you could get it at Holt Renfrew compared to like Eatons, I think I'd buy it at Eatons you know. Like if they hike up the price depending on where you buy it I think that's kinda stupid."

Naomi: "I don't think they do though it's usually set by the company, the price…"

Pauline: "OK."

Naomi: "…but sometimes Eatons will have a gift set and the Bay doesn't. I know that Shoppers only have gift sets during Christmas and Mother's Day. You can't find them during any other time of the year…"

(continued)

EXHIBIT 1   Continued

Pauline: "Depends because like, I guess it depends because I work at Pharma Plus and sometimes the price is cheaper than it is at Shoppers! It's a diss! It's true, I'm so sorry."

Naomi: "I don't know what to say there."

Pauline: "It's true!"

Naomi: "But the thing is that we don't make our prices. They're set by the companies…"

Pauline: "Ya."

Naomi: "…so you get mad at the companies and don't get mad at Shoppers."

Pauline: "But if they separate the companies then it should be the same right because I've gone to my store and I've gone to your store and it's been a couple more bucks expensive than yours see so like, I can see…"

Naomi: "I went to your store and I couldn't find it, oh, don't worry…"

Pauline: "Ya, that's what I mean like our store doesn't carry all of it right, but I'm just saying pricewise. Like if, like the drugstore is cheaper than the department store."

Naomi: "I've never noticed that before so that's why…"

Pauline: "Oh really? I've noticed."

Naomi: "…we've actually called department stores to get prices for our products, like we'll get an Obsession and find the retail of it. We'll call department stores and find the retail of it. I believe you."

Pauline: "But stuff like that. I don't know if I'll shop around a lot like if there's a time constraint then I'll just buy it. With perfumes, there won't be that much of a difference sometimes."

Naomi: "I think we're also limited like if you go to a drugstore we don't carry a full range of everything like that. Depends on what you're looking for."

Moderator: "By what means would you become aware of new perfumes?"

Darlene: "Advertising I think, especially that new Happy one that came out. Ya, I heard about that, because I work at Eatons anyway so there is big in-store things. And then newspapers, TV, I think it was a TV, ya, so advertising."

Naomi: "Because they bombard you, if you go to a department store, they have this CD—you can kill it. It's on everywhere on the TV screens with the girls dancing around … that's the same one over, and over."

Moderator: "So you would say advertising but in-store."

Pauline: "TV."

Darlene: "Ya, TV, magazines, but I guess for me since I was working all the time and I'd be walking past the makeup counter and perfume. Like they'd play the music and they would have the big signs…"

Monica: "Happy, happy."

Darlene: "…they'd have the makeup people there, you know, so everybody's 'happy.' So it worked, ya."

Kelly: "Mainly magazines and I also get, I don't know if you can call them tips but … from friends. And they usually tell me that this smells nice and I just check it out, that way."

Monica: "Mostly from magazines and TV actually, I'd say."

Pauline: "Magazines, now when I buy magazines they're like this fat but half of it's advertisements."

Naomi: "I'd say magazines and friends."

Moderator: "Do you use the whole bottle? Or what do you do after you've —"

Naomi: "Never, I've never used a whole bottle. I can't finish one. I find that I'll have it for a long time then I'll like something else and then by the time I go back to use it, it'll go bad. Like after a certain while, they smell bad almost."

Moderator: "Do you throw them out?"

Naomi: "Ya, I throw them out."

Monica: "I use the whole bottle. If I pay for it, I'm going to use it."

Darlene: "Well, I throw them away but my mom, I know she likes to keep them. She's had some perfume there for years. I tell her it doesn't smell the same but she figures that she's paid the money so she wants to use it up."

Moderator: "How long would you say you'd spent on actually going through, like thinking about perfume and then buying it? How long is that process?"

Naomi: "A week."

Moderator: "Like the effort that you'd put into a search, like for a perfume."

Monica: "One day."

Pauline: "Ya."

Darlene: "Ya."

Monica: "One day."

Moderator: "You go out and find it, and you find it that day."

Monica: "Yup. I'm not into those long drawn out things, go out, go shopping, can't find something I like, find something I like, done."

Naomi: "I'd probably go through the effort to find it. Like if I go to a store and a certain something is only exclusive to the Bay or something like that and I was looking in Eatons and that mall didn't have a Bay. Yes, I'd go to a Bay at another mall. But I don't think I'd go out shopping on two different occasions or three different occasions, maybe I'd wait till a couple of months later when I happen to be out at a mall, whatever."

Moderator: "Is everyone else the same? Like you go and you find it?"

Darlene: "Ya, I'd rather just get it done so that I can move on and do something else."

Naomi: "Ya, it depends on if you know what you're looking for. If you know what you're looking for I'd probably go to different stores. If I didn't know what I was looking for I'd probably go to one store and do it, I'd pick the one I liked and then leave."

(continued)

EXHIBIT 1   Continued

Moderator: "But would you say that the shopping itself just takes one day? Like what about before that?"

Moderator: "Like the whole like … let's say you see an advertisement and wonder what it smells like or whatever, the pre … before buying it, before running in the store. How interested are you in finding out what's coming out or…?"

All agree that they are not interested.

Pauline: "It's kinda like you're looking at it, you'll think about it then it's out of your mind. And if you go shopping it then may happen to click at that time you know, you might be at the department store and the perfume section is right in front of you, you might go look at it but sometimes you usually just buy it just from looking for it, but if I'm not then I don't have the urge to buy it. If it's just instinct that I like it."

Kelly: "If I see it in a magazine I might think, oh the next time I go out I'll look for it. But I don't do it, like it won't make me go the next day. Just if I'll remember, I'll be going."

Moderator: "Would you say that there's too many perfumes?"

Pauline: "Well you need different perfumes for different people of different types."

Naomi: "And things smell different on people. The same fragrance will smell different on two different people."

Moderator: "So would you say like if you found something would you try it first? Like would you test it out for a week then buy it? Or just buy it?"

Pauline: "Just spray it in the air and see if it smells good. Maybe like I'll spray some on myself and walk around the mall, do a bit of shopping."

Naomi: "I would probably be too lazy to go back."

Pauline: "Sometimes I would. It smells different after a while. But I like it, I don't know."

Moderator: "So would you like to get other people's opinions first before you make the purchase or would you just buy it because you like it?"

Darlene: "I like other people's opinions sometimes, from friends saying what do you think? Or sometimes I wish people would have asked me, like my brother, before he bought…"

Naomi: "Before it's too late."

Darlene: "…ya, it's good to ask."

Pauline: "It's good to have opinions because I think I was shopping with someone and they said something smelled like lemons and it smelled like, ya Pine Sol, something you clean with. You got to think because the other person might think 'oh ya, it's good.' Like if I'm smelling that person they might want to know what they smell like."

Monica: "Like Pine Sol."

Naomi: "It's always nice to take complements because it's flattering when they say that you smell good with what you wear."

Moderator: "Do you relate with the image of a perfume? Or do you think it's important to relate to that image of a perfume?"

Naomi: "The image no, I think the image you see would be the advertising."

Pauline: "It's all in sex."

Naomi: "I think it gives you your own, I think you'll smell something and that smell will remind you of something and I think that it puts you in a good mood. But I don't think the advertising will, like CK after I look at it. I don't feel grungy."

Moderator: Well, thank you very much. You have been extremely helpful and nervy, ah, I appreciate your, ah, willingness to talk; it made my job easier. Thank you very much. Did everybody get as many doughnuts and coffee as they would like? Please take some with you if you would like to. Thanks very much we appreciate it. Thanks, very much.

THE HIGH MUSEUM OF ART*

SPSS

A nne Baker, Director of External Affairs at the High Museum of Art, sat back in her chair as she reflected on a flash preliminary report on Phase II of a three-phase membership survey. Professors Dave Mandell, John Houghton, and Jennifer Smith from the Goizueta Business School of Emory University were running this marketing research project. She recalled her original concern with the High's lack of current marketing research. Consequently, working with Ann Wilson, Director of Public Relations at the High, she had initiated the research effort. The project had almost come undone when a new Manager of Membership, Roanne Katcher, was hired. Roanne was unenthusiastic about the research being done to say the least. Anne wondered what the strategic implications of the Phase II pilot survey were for the High Museum. She also knew she would soon have to make a go-no go decision for Phase III.

BACKGROUND

The High, located in midtown Atlanta, Georgia, is the city's premiere art museum (Exhibit 1). The museum features contemporary art, a decorative arts collection including 19th and 20th century American furniture, 19th century American landscape paintings, European painting and sculpture from the 14th through the 19th century, African masks and ceremonial figures, folk art, and photographs. In addition to its permanent collection, the High offers frequent traveling exhibitions, guided tours, lectures, films, workshops, an extensive gift shop, and a variety of adult education classes.

Revenue Sources

The museum, a not-for-profit institution, receives funding from a variety of sources, including corporate contributions, individual donations, membership fees,

EXHIBIT 1   The High Museum of Art

Photographer: Bard Wrisley © 1993

* This case was prepared by Rob Kroenert under the supervision of Professor C. B. Bhattacharya of the School of Management at Boston University as the basis of class discussion rather than to illustrate the effective or ineffective handling of an administrative situation. Some names have been disguised. The case has been edited by Leonard J. Parsons. Copyright © 1995 by the Goizueta Business School.

gift shop sales, and revenue from admission charges. Exhibit 2 provides more detail on the High's revenue mix. Regular adult admission is priced at $6, student and senior citizen admission is $4, admission for children between the ages of five and eighteen is $2, and children under five are admitted free. In 1994, approximately 220,000 people visited the High Museum. Exhibit 3 details the High's historical attendance levels. The High has attracted significantly greater numbers of visitors when the museum displays a popular traveling exhibit. For instance, a traveling China exhibition in 1985 helped attract over 600,000 visitors to the museum that year, and a traveling Monet exhibition accounted for some of the increased attendance in 1988 and 1989.

Membership

The High maintains a tiered membership program, with individual memberships selling for $40 a year. For an additional $10, an entire family can purchase a year-long membership. Standard membership benefits include free admission to the museum, priority entrance to special exhibitions, invitations to *Members Only* openings and previews, and a 10% gift shop discount. Higher donations entitle members to progressively more exclusive benefits, such as invitations to *Patrons Only* exhibition receptions or recognition in the High's biennial newsletter. A detailed list of membership costs and benefits can be found in Exhibit 4, and a fourteen-year overview of membership levels is shown in Exhibit 5. In 1994, approximately 67 percent of the High's 18,000 members renewed their membership at the end of the year, indicating a membership churn of 33 percent. In the 93/94 Fiscal year, the High acquired 3,930 new members while losing 5,404 old

EXHIBIT 2   **Revenue Mix (Percent)**

Source	1991	1992	1993	1994
Corporate	0.02	4.10	2.90	5.50
Foundation	1.80	0.70	0.60	0.70
Government	6.80	5.20	6.00	5.80
Individual	2.60	5.80	5.20	6.30
Trust/Endowment	15.90	13.30	17.00	16.80
Membership	22.90	21.00	19.50	18.70
Members Guild	4.00	4.00	1.90	1.70
Museum Shop	7.60	8.40	10.60	10.90
Space Rentals	4.80	3.20	2.90	3.40
Woodruff Arts Center	19.30	17.90	21.70	21.60
Admissions	5.60	5.80	4.30	4.60
Other	8.68	10.60	7.40	4.00
Total	100.00	100.00	100.00	100.00

members. In the first eight months of the 94/95 Fiscal year, the High acquired 4,129 new members while losing 3,874 old members.

The High also sponsors a *Members Guild* composed of five different components of museum members: *Young Careers,* generally singles in their twenties; *Peachtree Arts,* generally professional singles and couples between the ages of 30–55 who live near the museum; *Suburban Arts,* generally professional couples who live in the Atlanta suburbs; *Art Associates,* generally a slightly older group of members; and *Volunteer Educators,* individuals who have completed a year-long training program to prepare them for leading educational tours of the High Museum. Each of the five groups pays Guild dues to the High (in addition to standard membership fees) and engages in a variety of volunteer activities, including fund-raising, auctions, and tours of private art collections. In 1994, member-

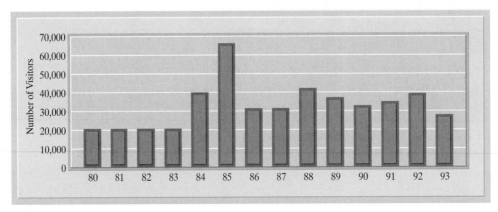

EXHIBIT 3   **Attendance History**

EXHIBIT 4   Membership Information

- Unlimited free admission to the Museum.
- Priority entrance to special exhibitions.
- Invitations to Members-Only previews and events.
- 10% member's discount in the Museum Shop.
- Subscription to the monthly Members Calendar.
- Discounts on film series, lectures, symposia, and work-shops for adults and children.
- Discounts on Atlanta College of Arts classes and select tickets to the Alliance Theater and Atlanta Symphony Orchestra.
- Discounted subscriptions to selected art magazines.
- New Member Welcome events.
- Volunteer and special-interest group opportunities.

MEMBERSHIP OPTIONS
(each level includes the benefits of all preceding levels)

Individual $40
One membership card with free admission for 1 adult.

Dual/Family $50
Two membership cards with free admission for 2 adults and all children 17 and under in the household.

Contributing $100
- Free admission for up to four guests during regular Museum hours.
- Reciprocal membership at 16 Museums in the North American Reciprocal Program.
- Travel opportunities and priority reservations on Museum-sponsored trips.
- Subscription to the quarterly newsletter, Developments.

Artists and **seniors** receive all membership privileges for a discounted rate of $25. **Students** receive a $15 membership pass for unlimited free admission for one year, the monthly calendar, plus a 10% discount in the Museum Shop.

Patron $200
- Invitations to exclusive Patrons Only receptions for selected exhibitions.
- 20% Patron discount in the Museum Shop (on most items) excluding sale items.
- Reciprocal membership at 32 additional art museums in the United States.
- Free admission to the Museum's film series.
- Invitations to Patrons Only Holiday Shopping Day.
- Recognition in the Museum's Annual Report.

Donor Patron $500
- Invitations to Behind-the-Scenes tours with Museum curators and staff.
- Selected catalogues published by the Museum.

Roundtable Patron $1,000
- Invitations to selected major donor events throughout the year.
- Reciprocal membership at 40 of the finest art museums in the country, including The Museum of Fine Arts, Boston, Philadelphia Museum of Art, The Art Institute of Chicago, and the Los Angeles County Museum of Art.
- Recognition on a special donor plaque in the Museum atrium

Your Membership—for Tax Purposes

Based on IRS guidelines and the museum's estimated fair market value of your benefits, the following amounts of your membership can be taken as a tax deduction:

Individual ($5), Family/Dual ($10), Contributing ($50), Patron ($120), Donor Patron ($400), Roundtable Patron ($850), Artists, Seniors, Students ($0).

Museum membership is a prerequisite for joining the Members Guild and any of the special-interest groups.

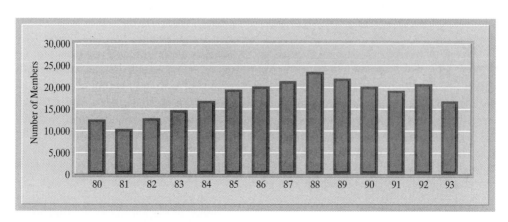

EXHIBIT 5   Membership History

ship in the Member's Guild reached 2,200, nearly half of which was in the Young Careers group.

The Need for Marketing Research

At the beginning of 1994, the High established a Board of Director's committee for the purpose of creating a long-range strategic plan for the museum. In the course of examining some of the issues involved in the development of this strategic plan, the committee realized that the High did not have access to any current marketing research about the institution. At the time, the High collected very little information from its members and visitors. The majority of the membership records were not computerized and contained only names, addresses, and, in some cases, the year the membership was purchased. In addition, almost no formal effort was made to collect data on museum visitors. This lack of information concerned the management of the High and impeded their ability to create a long-range strategic plan. According to Ann Wilson, "Anne Baker was told by the Board of Directors that one of her priorities was to do some real research to gather information about the people who visit the museum." Anne pointed out the need for the High to conduct research:

> We felt as though we weren't clear about what our membership liked, disliked, expected, didn't expect, would want more of, less of, what they knew, and what they didn't know. We felt that it was important for us to get that information in order to better meet the members' needs and decide what kind of programming and services and benefits we needed to do for them.

By conducting marketing research, Anne hoped to better understand the High's customers. This, in turn, would help the museum improve the quality of its services to better meet the needs of current members and visitors while simultaneously attracting new members and visitors to the museum.

The Relationship with Emory

When Anne first decided to investigate the possibility of commissioning a marketing research project, she contacted an Atlanta-based marketing research firm, where she was informed that the estimated cost of a project for the High would be in the vicinity of $10,000 plus actual expenses incurred. Anne, aware that the High was constrained by budget concerns, decided to look into the possibility of enlisting the help of the Goizueta Business School at Emory University. Before joining the High, she had worked at the Goizueta Business School as the Director of Development, where she built relationships with many of the business school faculty. Anne contacted Professor Mandell, who agreed to help the High by doing the project at actual expenses. Knowing that some of his other colleagues were also motivated to help cultural institutions such as the High, Mandell proceeded to enlist the help of two of his Emory colleagues, John Houghton and Jennifer Smith. The Emory professors suggested a possible course of action. Students of marketing could conduct a research project focusing on museum visitors, while the professors could concentrate on surveying museum members. Understanding that the project on museum members involved a greater commitment of both time and funds, Anne initially concentrated on working with the professors.

PROBLEM DEFINITION AND RESEARCH DESIGN

Anne and the professors decided on the following problem definition for the High:

> The High Museum does not possess an understanding of the demographic, psychographic, or behavioral profile of its membership.

According to Professor Mandell,

> The symptom, in simple terms, was that there was a lot of churn in their membership—as much as 30 percent—so the underlying problem that we came up with was they don't know who their members are, and if you don't know who your members are, what they look for in their membership, what benefits they derive from their membership, then you're not going to be able to do the kinds of things that are necessary to retain them.... The whole idea was to do a better job of catering to the needs and wants of current and potential members so the High could improve customer attraction and retention.

The professors decided to first conduct three focus groups (Phase I) where they would test draft versions of a questionnaire that they developed based on the problem definition, use the focus group findings to refine the questionnaire and subsequently mail it to a sample of current museum members. Before surveying the entire population of 18,000 members, the professors decided to conduct a pilot study by surveying a sample of approximately 1,000 members (Phase II). The professors then planned to survey a larger sample of about 3,000 members after they had analyzed the results of the initial study (Phase III).

The professors, who were volunteering their time as a service to the not-for-profit institution, estimated that out-of-pocket expenses (e.g., photocopying and mailing the surveys, data entry, data analysis, etc.) which would have to be paid by the High, would total $8,000.

PHASE I: FOCUS GROUPS

The first two focus groups progressed smoothly. The High arranged for eight to ten museum members to meet with the professors, look at the questionnaire, fill it out, then openly discuss the instrument and the museum in general. In return for their time, the participating museum members were given free pizza and a package of museum passes and discounts. As a result of these focus groups, the professors collected a great deal of qualitative information.

Enter Roanne Katcher

Unbeknownst to the professors, the High had recently hired Roanne Katcher to serve as the museum's Manager of Membership. The High's new organizational chart is shown as Exhibit 6. Ms. Katcher possessed an

extensive background working in museum membership, having worked in the field for over twenty-five years, including eleven years with The Metropolitan Museum of Art in New York.

Ms. Katcher was in the process of moving to Atlanta during the time the professors were conducting the focus groups, and she arrived in Atlanta in time to attend the third meeting. According to Professor Mandell, "We had no idea the High had hired a Manager of Membership before she showed up that night." The professors were hesitant to allow a museum employee to join the focus group, but they were also interested in gaining Ms. Katcher's acceptance of the overall project. Twenty minutes into the meeting, however, it became clear that Ms. Katcher had serious reservations about both the style of the focus group and the content of the questionnaire. The professors were surprised by Ms. Katcher's position. Jennifer Smith observed,

> Roanne took over the meeting. We would say things to Roanne like, "We're sure you know a lot about membership, but we'd really like to hear it from the members."

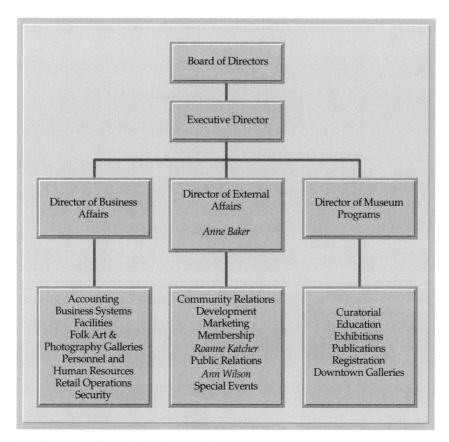

EXHIBIT 6   Organizational Chart

Roanne would reply by saying, "I know membership." The meeting had gone off in a different angle than we intended, with a lot of different agendas. The whole thing felt awkward because we felt we had a relationship with the museum. We felt we were serving their needs, and then someone with a different agenda was thrown into the mix.

Findings from Focus Groups

After all the focus groups had been conducted, the professors reviewed the major findings that emerged:

- There seemed to be a great variation in the number of times members visited the museum—some did not visit at all whereas others visited almost once a month. Similarly, different members also seemed to utilize the various benefits offered by the museum (e.g., lectures, tours, special exhibitions) to different extents.
- Members also visited the museum for different reasons; while some went to view the exhibits, others went for social purposes.
- There also seemed to be a number of reasons for joining the membership program. The benefit of unlimited free admission, the lure of gift shop discounts, and support for the arts were only a few of the ones that were mentioned.
- Members had different satisfaction levels with the various features of the museum such as the permanent collection, the travelling exhibits, calendar of events, etc.
- A large percentage of the members identified with the museum's goals and objectives, its future, and its ties to the community. Some mentioned that their membership was an investment in the future while others said that it made them feel socially responsible. Membership in the museum was also considered as a prestigious affiliation by some.

As they discussed the above findings, the professors were excited that they were onto something. Now all they had to do was to incorporate these findings into their questionnaire and then send it to the Museum for final approval. They hoped that the new Membership Manager would find the questionnaire to be a valuable tool for developing her marketing strategies.

PHASE II: PILOT SURVEY

On receiving the final draft of the questionnaire, Anne Baker asked the professors to run the survey by Roanne one more time. The professors complied, and Roanne requested some additional adjustments to the questionnaire. For instance, the survey questions about maximum education level included "elementary school" as a response possibility. Roanne argued,

> I said I think it's an insult to ask our members if they completed elementary school, but the professors insisted they had to ask all the questions in order to make the survey valid. I realized that the professors and I were basically not in agreement on what information would be useful in order to refine our program and increase member retention. I'm not into how an instrument is done; I'm into the information I need. There were some things in the questionnaire that were negative, like "The museum does not have an outstanding reputation in my community." We never ever use negatives when communicating with museum members who donate money to the institution because the High has a positive image. We encourage and plant the seeds of the positive … Also, part of the information they were looking for was information we already know. There are certain things we know about all museum members. The other information they were asking wasn't relevant to building or improving the membership program. That didn't mean the professors shouldn't do marketing research, but I wanted there not to be a misunderstanding that I was going to be able to use this information. It wasn't going to be helpful, in my opinion, in improving the membership program.

The professors made some, but not all, of the modifications requested by Ms. Katcher. Jennifer Smith remarked, "The research has to be methodologically sound. We yielded on a couple of things, but a lot of things we left. We did put in a few things she wanted."

Anne Baker faced a dilemma. Up to this point, she had been very satisfied with the progress of the marketing research project. The addition of Roanne Katcher, however, had clouded the picture. Roanne made it clear to Anne that the information gathered by the survey would not be of use to her. On the other hand, Anne knew the High needed some type of marketing research; and she did trust the judgment of the Emory professors. In addition, she felt as if she had made a commitment to the professors to proceed with the project. Despite Roanne's concerns, Anne decided not to prevent the professors from sending out the pilot questionnaire. She elaborated,

> Roanne arrived in the middle of the preparation of the questionnaire—and Roanne is the expert in membership. I am not. She pointed out some concerns about the instrument and identified that the instrument was not going to provide her with what she needed to strengthen her membership program. And I was very resistant initially. I said to Roanne, "We've made this commitment with the professors—we have to go ahead and go through this exercise and if we turn the whole instrument inside out it's just

going to take forever and drag on and on." So I was the one who pushed it with Roanne, and we went ahead. But Roanne's point of view about that original survey was very different from mine. She was able to make some changes and modifications on the original instrument that made it a little bit more useful than it was initially in its first draft.

Roanne continued to resist the survey, explaining,

At first I thought that I should refrain from offering my opinion, but I believed that the professors were approaching this the wrong way, and it was costing about $8,000. That, to me, was a significant expenditure for information that I didn't think would be helpful in improving member retention … Unless Anne would have said, "Stop the project," I could only repeat that I was very uncomfortable with this.

The professors were concerned about Ms. Katcher's resistance, but they remained confident in their approach. Professor Mandell claimed,

Our hope always was that Roanne would come around after the data analysis was complete and we'd had a chance to present the results, because by then we thought she'd see the value of what we'd done. She did not ever come out and say to us, "This is not going to be helpful to me"—in which case we might have stopped or done something different.

Sampling

In March of 1994, the professors mailed 1,043 surveys to current museum members. The population from which the sample was selected consisted of those who had been members of the museum for at least one year ($N = 14,274$) and therefore had an opportunity to renew their membership at least once, thereby indicating a base level of attachment toward the museum. A proportionate stratified random sampling technique was used where the strata consisted of different membership categories.

Respondents received a cover letter from the Museum Director explaining the purpose of the survey and a questionnaire with a postage-paid return envelope. Two free guest passes were attached to the survey as a token of appreciation and as an incentive to participate in the survey. Overall, 307 completed questionnaires were returned, indicating a response rate of 30 percent.

Data Analysis

The professors analyzed the data, and because the museum was in a rush, prepared some key tables on the basis of the 297 responses that had been coded so far, and sent them over to Ms. Baker, Ms. Wilson and Ms. Katcher. These tables are shown in Exhibits 7–14.

EXHIBIT 7   Membership Characteristics

Characteristic	Percentage
Membership Type	
Never changed since joining	72%
Changed since joining	28%
Membership Renewal	
Last year member	98%
Nonmember last year	2%
Membership Continuity	
Membership has never lapsed	86%
Membership lapsed in the past	14%
Future Membership	
Likely to renew	89%
Not likely to renew	11%
Membership Upgrade	
Likely	5%
Unlikely	95%

EXHIBIT 8   Visitation Practices

	% Ever in Last 12 Months	% At Least Once Every 3 Months
Visit Museum	88%	56%
Do not Visit Museum	12%	44%
Visit with Friends	86%	27%
Do not Visit with Friends	14%	73%
Visit with Family	72%	27%
Do not Visit with Family	28%	73%
Visit Alone	67%	25%
Do not Visit Alone	33%	75%
Visit with Business Associates	13%	2%
Do not Visit with Business Associates	87%	98%
Visit Other Art Facilities	78%	34%
Do not Visit Other Art Facilities	22%	66%
Visit Other Arts Events	97%	76%
Do not Visit Other Arts Events	3%	24%

EXHIBIT 9   Benefit Awareness and Frequency of Use

Type of Benefit	% Aware of Benefit	% Use Frequently
Free Admission to the Museum	99%	40%
Gift Shop Discount	97%	18%
Special Events (e.g., previews)	98%	22%
Monthly Calendar of Events	99%	45%
Lectures	97%	6%
Films	96%	7%
Travel Programs	91%	5%
Museum's Guided Tours	87%	6%
Guild Components	83%	n/a*
Art Support Groups	71%	n/a*
Use of All Benefits	n/a*	17%

* = Not applicable

EXHIBIT 10   Ranking of Membership Benefits

Type of Benefit	Median Rank	% Ranking Benefit* As #1 in Importance
A way of supporting the arts	1	52%
Free admission to the Museum	2	29%
A way of learning about art	3	18%
Invitations to Museum special events	4	6%
Monthly member calendar	5	4%
Gift shop discount	6	1%
A way of meeting people with similar interests	7	5%
A way of gaining prestige	8	1%

* Respondents may have selected more than one #1 benefit, thus, column total does not equal 100%

EXHIBIT 11   Satisfaction of Expectations

Aspect of Museum	Worse than Expected	Not Better or Worse	Better than Expected
Traveling Exhibits	12%	26%	63%
Monthly Calendar	6%	44%	51%
Entertaining Guests	11%	43%	46%
Special Events	10%	47%	43%
Gift Shop	7%	52%	42%
Tours	8%	55%	37%
Permanent Collection	25%	42%	33%
Social Events	16%	54%	30%
Lectures	8%	65%	27%
Discounts	9%	69%	21%
Making Friends	43%	48%	9%
Overall Satisfaction with Museum	7%	48%	45%

EXHIBIT 12   Attitudes about Membership

Commitment to the Museum (Mean = 3.10, Standard Deviation = 0.79)

Statements:
• I am very interested in what others think about the Museum
• When someone criticizes the Museum, it feels like a personal insult.
• When I talk about the Museum, I usually say "we" rather than "they."
• The Museum's successes are my successes.
• When someone praises the Museum, it feels like a personal complement.
• If a story in the media criticized the Museum, I would feel embarrassed.

Social Prestige (Mean = 3.31, Standard Deviation = 0.69)

Statements:
• People in my community think highly of membership in the Museum.
• It is considered prestigious in my community to be a member of the Museum.
• The Museum does *not* have an outstanding reputation in my community (reversed score).

Note: Using 20 statements that deal with members' attitudes toward the museum, a statistical procedure known as factor analysis was used to uncover the broader "attitudinal dimensions" underlying museum membership. Two dimensions emerged: (1) commitment to the museum and (2) social prestige associated with membership. Appropriate measures of central tendency and representative statements that comprise the dimensions are reported.

EXHIBIT 13   Demographic Characteristics

Characteristic	Percentage
Race	
Caucasian	92%
African American	6%
Other	2%
Gender	
Male	34%
Female	66%
Income	
$30,000 a year or less	4%
$30,000 to $99,999	55%
$100,000 or more	41%
Employment	
Full-time	55%
Part-time	14%
None	30%
Education	
3 years of college or less	17%
College degree	39%
Post-graduate degree	30%

EXHIBIT 14   Demographic Characteristics by Frequency of Visit

	Visit Twice a Year or Less	Visit Six Times a Year or More
Age		
50 years or less	57%	39%
51 years or more	43%	61%
Income		
Less than $100,00	52%	31%
$100,000 and more	48%	69%
Volunteer Services		
Never in the last 12 months	94%	74%
Once or more in the last 12 months	6%	26%
Fulfillment of Expectations		
HMA more than expected	37%	70%
HMA not more than expected	63%	30%
Area of Residence		
Atlanta/Decatur	53%	56%
Other GA Area	47%	44%

NEXT STEPS

As Anne Baker read over the tables, several questions came to her mind. What were the results of the pilot study trying to tell her? Were there other types of analysis that ought to be done on the pilot survey?[1]

What were the strategic implications of the results for the High Museum? How should she proceed next?

---

[1]A total of 307 responses were recorded in the file:
    highmemdat.sav.
Because of a 50 variable limit in the student version of SPSS, three files were created:
    highmemdat_Q1_Q2_Q6_Q8.sav,
    highmemdat_Q3_Q8.sav, and
    highmemdat_Q4_Q5_Q8.sav

MARKET SEGMENTATION AND PRODUCT DIFFERENTIATION

> Small opportunities are often the beginning of great enterprises.
>
> DEMOSTHENES

*I*n today's competitive environment, many companies are finding it dangerous to treat customers as a single homogeneous group. Mass markets are breaking up into dozens of minimarkets each with its own special needs. This approach to marketing is known as *segmentation* and it often is the key to developing a sustainable competitive advantage based on differentiation or a focus strategy.

Using separate marketing programs to sell to different market segments contrasts with *mass marketing* where the same marketing mix is used for all markets (Figure 4-1). Segmentation and profiling techniques (e.g., see Direct Marketing chapter) may not be worth the trouble in fast-moving consumer goods markets. The belief here is that consumer behavior is becoming more and more homogeneous.

You must decide whether to follow a mass market strategy, to focus on one segment or niche, or to compete in several segments simultaneously with different marketing mixes. Some of the issues involved here are illustrated in the detailed example for consumer appliances given in Marketing Strategies box 4-1.

MASS MARKETING

Dominant brands provide economies of scale and the efficiencies of mass media that reduce unit costs while generating greater revenues. These revenues come from not only heavy brand buyers but from the whole continuum of buyers. Popular brands are not only bought by more people, they are bought more often on average than less popular brands. Thus, brand popularity contributes to a favorable profit picture.[1]

APPLYING
*. . . to
Consumer
Grocery
Products
Marketing*

Research based on a number of grocery products in different countries has found that, within particular product category subtypes and their variants, competing brands differ little in terms of the demographic and socioeconomic characteristics of their customers.[2] This research has further discovered that even many subtypes and variants with their different physical formulations appealed to much the same kinds of consumers of their category. Thus, you don't try to find a way to appeal to different prospects than your competitors but rather you must market successfully to the same potential customers.

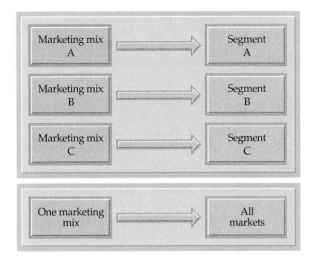

FIGURE 4-1   Segmentation versus Mass Marketing

MARKETING STRATEGIES *4-1*

Globalization of Markets

APPLYING
. . . to
Consumer
Durables
Marketing

For many manufacturers, particularly those operating out of Western Europe, the American market offers important lessons that many firms would like to replicate on a regional or global basis. In the U.S. refrigerator market, for example, a fairly standard product design and limited number of standard sizes are marketed using a small number of national brands. High volume output of a range of standard products allows for major cost savings, and efficient, low-cost production is a hallmark of the industry.

In other parts of the world, for example Europe, the market context is more complex. National markets are much smaller and significant regional differences arise because of variance in customer requirements, technical standards, and conditions of product use. In the case of washing machines, for example, national customer preferences differ in respect of two key features: method of loading and spin-speed. Clothes washers sold in northern countries like Denmark must spin-dry clothes much better than in southern Italy, where consumers often line-dry clothes in the warmer weather. Preferences for refrigerators are even more complex: Northern Europeans tend to shop once a week in supermarkets and demand large refrigerators; southern Europeans, many of whom shop at open-air markets every few days, generally prefer small ones. Northerners like their refrigerators on the bottom; southerners want just the opposite. And the English, who are big consumers of frozen foods, complicate things further by insisting on units with 60% freezer space. The impact of these national idiosyncrasies, which mainly result from differences in consumer shopping behavior, are further complicated by variation in the space available for appliances in the home, with resulting pressure for differences in product design and size.

As a consequence of the factors noted above, country segmentation has been a favored approach in the industry. Many U.S. and European manufacturers have thus traditionally focused on their home market, only venturing on a small scale into foreign markets that are not dissimilar to their home base. During the last decade, however, the pressures favoring developing world-scale operations targeted at global markets have increased, and more firms have been putting major efforts into their international business operations. The Swedish firm Electrolux has been a leader in this regard, partly because of its relatively small home market base in Sweden and the need to integrate the operations of the many foreign firms that have been acquired over the past twenty years.

Traditionally, Electrolux has structured its business around individual national markets, and management still recognizes a need to react to variation in the preferences of national customers. However the impact of globalization drivers has also been noted: "Differences are narrowing and market charac-

(continues)

MARKETING STRATEGIES *4-1*   (continued)

INTEGRATING
. . . with
Production/
Operations
Management

teristics converging. By developing the ability to transfer and leverage products, concepts, components and manufacturing techniques from one market to another, Electrolux with more new product launches and shorter development cycles can develop insurmountable advantages over others."

The recent Electrolux approach to segmenting overseas markets thus reflects both country clustering and a search for transnational consumer segments. Electrolux recognizes that some niche markets are valuable. These are typically national-based markets where output of speciality, high-end models can still be viable. Electrolux continues to market a diverse collection of national brands in different ways. At the same time, major effort has concurrently been put into developing two international brands which are used for product lines targeted at a particular regional market customer profile. In Europe, for example, Zanussi and Electrolux are international brands for relatively standard product lines with integrated international positioning and marketing. Life style and behavioral criteria are employed as key segmentation criteria. Products are manufactured in regional production centers with the aim of achieving economies of scale through the output of a product line based on standard components and efficient flexible manufacturing systems.

In summary, Electrolux operates with a mixed mode approach to segmentation. Individual national market segmentation is still undertaken in some cases, normally for premium, speciality products that are viable despite low production runs. Other product lines are targeted at a limited cluster of countries. Finally, larger area country clusters are delineated; and regional transnational customer segments, identified primarily on the basis of life style and behavioral criteria, are targeted with international brands with a key goal being to achieve significant uniformity in respect to prod-

(continued)

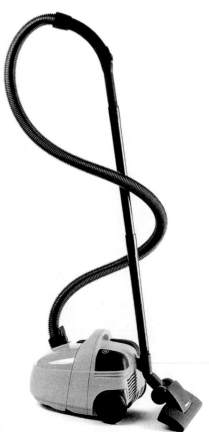

Courtesy Electrolux, Sweden

MARKETING STRATEGIES 4-1   **(continued)**

uct features and marketing policy. Electrolux has not sought to identify global demand segments on a world-wide basis. This orientation may change in the future, but segmentation practice in the industry has reflected a view in which major national markets for many household appliances have been perceived to be: "Relatively isolated from others due to differences in customer tastes and preferences, divergent technical standards, and the relatively high cost of transportation for most products of the industry."

Whirlpool holds the leading spot in the U.S. appliance market, with brand names such as Whirlpool, KitchenAid and Roper. It makes washers and dryers for Sears, Roebuck & Co.'s Kenmore brand. Whirlpool is also the No. 1 appliance maker in Latin America, partnering with a Brazilian manufacturer, Brasmotor SA, to make most of its appliances. America's largest maker of home appliances has been thwarted in its ambitious attempts to build a leading presence in Europe and Asia.

Whirlpool wasn't shy about its plans when it first went overseas. Whirlpool's cover-the-globe strategy initially came with some bold promises. After snapping up controlling interests in joint ventures in India and China, it said it would make money, or at least break even, in Asia in two years. With its purchase of Philips Electronics NV's European appliance business, it anticipated making profits in Europe even as rivals were pulling out. In an effort to convince shareholders of the wisdom of the company's Philips purchase, Chairman David Whitwam gave an interview to the *Harvard Business Review* entitled "The Right Way to Go Global." The company even decorated its annual reports to reflect its new, cosmopolitan face. Its 1990 Report featured postage stamps from around the world. The 1993 Annual Report had a gadget attached to the front cover: a tiny, working compass.

Whirlpool has retreated a bit from its global strategy, taking a $350 million charge to exit from two of its four joint ventures in China and to reorganize its European business. Now, with Whirlpool's withdrawals from joint ventures that made refrigerators and air conditioners in China, the company is expected to focus less on manufacturing its own products overseas and more on licensing. That strategy could be especially effective in Asia, where, despite deep discounting, Whirlpool has been unable to unseat General Electric Co.'s appliance business from its leading market position.

Whirlpool didn't count on the difficulty in marketing appliances—largely homogenous in the U.S.—to the fragmented cultures of Europe. Whirlpool was also caught with higher material costs, pinching margins. And the Whirlpool name, which wasn't well known in Europe, took a while to catch on with locals. Distributors were more familiar with brands like Electrolux, Whirlpool's largest European rival. When Whirlpool came on board, "It was like Whirl what?" The company recently redesigned more than half its products in Europe after a string of unprofitable quarters there. Whirlpool insists it remains committed to its foreign operations.

— *Globally integrated strategies may not always be appropriate.*

Source: The Electrolux example is from Peter G. P. Walters, "Global Market Segmentation," *Journal of Marketing Management,* Vol. 13 (1997), pp. 171–173; the Whirlpool example is from Carl Quintanilla, "Despite Setbacks Whirlpool Pursues Overseas Markets," *Wall Street Journal,* December 9, 1997, p. B4.

Mass marketing means broadening brand appeal to many different kinds of households. Mass marketers ask "how many?" not "who?"[3] You want as many category users as possible. Consequently, you want a media message that has wide appeal and a media plan that reaches most category users.

MARKET SEGMENTATION

Segmentation is the strategy of developing different marketing programs for different customer groups or segments. It recognizes heterogeneity in the market. Each customer segment has its own unique demand function based on price, physical product characteristics, and nonphysical attributes reflecting image and performance. You build volume by appealing to group preferences.

First, you need to identify the best ways to segment a market and then pin down the characteristics of each group (this second step is called *profiling*). Next, you must evaluate the attractiveness of the segments and select the most appropriate target markets. Finally, you need to position your product or service relative to competitive offerings within the chosen market segments.

Building Customer Segments

Segmentation sounds like a process of breaking large markets into smaller ones. In the extreme, segmentation involves designing a unique product and marketing program for each buyer. Examples would include designing office buildings and insurance plans to meet the needs of individual corporations. However, segmentation is really a process of aggregation. The idea is to pull together groups of customers who resemble each other on some meaningful dimensions.

Although you can consider each buying unit a segment, there are usually some economies if they are grouped into clusters. Buying units are placed into segments so there is similarity in demand within segments and differences in demand among segments. *The Farm Journal,* for example, groups its 1 million subscribers into 1,134 different segments based on location and type of farm. Content varies across editions and an issue of the magazine might have 150,000 copies for beef farmers, 7,000 copies for beef and dairy farmers, and 36 copies for top producers who raise cotton, hogs, and dairy cows. The idea of mailing out 1,134 different editions of a magazine is mind-boggling and is only possible because the firm has a computerized bindery. A more typical situation would have a company working with 2 to 12 market segments. One of your jobs as marketing manager is to decide the most appropriate number of segments for your organization.

A variety of statistical methods are available to help you with the grouping task. While a discussion of these techniques is beyond the scope of this book, you should have some notion that the choice of technique depends upon the segmentation approach employed and purpose of the analysis. Segmentation approaches can be partitioned on whether they are a priori or post hoc. An a priori approach is one in which the type and number of segments are completely specified by you without regard to the data collected, whereas a post hoc approach is one in which the type and number of segments are revealed to you as the result of your analysis of the data. An a priori approach is used when the complexity of the market can be captured by relatively few variables, you are confident about your understanding of your market, and the main focus is on segment size, and perhaps the relative importance of segmentation variables; otherwise, a post hoc approach is used. The choice of technique also depends on whether you want to identify segments (description) or test the relationship of segmentation variables with purchase behavior (prediction).

Which Characteristics Identify Segments?

The major *bases* for segmentation are geographic, demographic, psychographic, and behavioralistic. These bases, together with their typical breakdowns, are shown in Table 4-1. Some of these buyer characteristics were discussed in Chapter 3.

Geographic Basis   Markets are often segmented on the basis of nations, states, regions, counties, cities, and population density. Product usage tends to vary among buyers on these dimensions. For example, Maxwell House coffee is sold nationally in the United States but is flavored regionally. Campbell's Soup also adapts its products and promotions to local

TABLE 4-1 Alternative Bases for Segmentation

Basis	Typical Breakdown
Geographic	
Country	Canada, England, Mexico, Japan, United States
Region	New England, Metro New York, Mid-Atlantic, East Central, Metro Chicago, West Central, Southeast, Southwest, Pacific
County size	A, B, C, D
SMSA[a] population	Under 50,000; 50,000–99,999; 100,000–249,999; 250,000–499,999; 500,000–999,999; 1,000,000–3,999,999; 4,000,000 or over
Density	Urban, suburban, rural
Demographic	
Age	Under 6; 6–11, 12–17, 18–34, 35–49, 50–64, 65 and over
Sex	Male, female
Family life cycle	Young, single; young, married, no children; young, married, children; older, married, children; older, married, no children; older, single; other
Education	Grade school or less; some high school; graduated high school; some college; graduated college
Occupation	Professional and technical; managers, officials, and proprietors; clerical; sales; artisans; supervisors; operatives; farmers; armed services; retired; students; homemakers; unemployed
Race	Black, oriental, white
Manufacturer's industry	Standard Industrial Classification (SIC) Code
Psychographic	
Social class	Lower; working class; lower-middle; upper-middle; upper
Personality	Gregarious, introverted, compulsive
Lifestyle	Cosmopolitan, yuppies
Behavioralistic	
Decision-making unit	Buying committee, purchasing agent, plant or headquarters
Usage rate	Nonuser, light, medium, heavy
Readiness	Unaware, aware, interested, intending to try, trier, repeat purchaser
Benefits sought	Quality, service, value
Occasion	Regular, special
Brand loyalty	Nonloyal, loyal

[a] SMSA, standard metropolitan statistical area.

conditions. Friday's restaurant chain gives its franchisees the option of offering 30 regional items on their menu—along with 70 national items that they must serve. General Mills sells specialized Super Moist Cake Mix in specific regions. In Pittsburgh, home of the Steelers National Football League team, the mix comes with sprinkles that match the team's colors: gold and black. General Motors, Ford, and Chrysler vary their promotions and rebates by geographic regions. The use of regional marketing plans is made easier by the availability of spot TV, spot radio, local newspapers, and regional editions of magazines. Targeting for some consumer products may be as narrow as an individual neighborhood, or even a single store, thanks to the information provided by checkout scanners.

Multinational firms often segment markets on the basis of national boundaries. The attractiveness of an international market environment is a function of political stability, market opportunity, economic development and performance, cultural unity, tariff barriers, physiographic barriers, and geocultural distance. In addition, the multinational firm must take into account factors specific to the firm and its industry.

Demographic Basis Consumer markets can be segmented according to age, sex, stage in the family life cycle, income, education, occupation, and ethnicity of the customer. For instance, eye makeup usage rates tend to be higher for the young, the well-educated, and working women. Shortening usage rates tend to be higher for those who are older and have larger families. Business markets can be segmented according to the total sales, the total assets, or the number of employees of the firm.

APPLYING
... to
Consumer
Durables
Marketing

An example showing how income and age can be used to segment new car buyers is provided in Figure 4-2. The advantage of this graphical approach is that it highlights the positions of your products relative to those of your competitors. Notice that General Motors' Chevrolet, Buick, Oldsmobile, and Cadillac divisions all appeal to older drivers. The only division feeding in young customers is Pontiac. To help attract more first-time buyers, General Motors is promoting their Saturn division. Also Figure 4-2 shows that Buick and Oldsmobile appeal to the same market segment. The unpleasant result is that these cars tend to steal market share from each other rather than from competitors. General Motors is currently running some youth-oriented ads for Oldsmobile to try to differentiate these products in the minds of the customer. Another interesting finding is the hole in the middle of Figure 4-2. This suggests there is untapped potential for cars designed for 50-year-old customers with $60,000 annual incomes. When data from Figure 4-2 are combined with information on education and occupation, auto firms have precise profiles on customer segments that can be used for market programming.

Geodemographic Basis   Geodemographic segments are formed when geographic areas, say postal codes or census tracts having similar demographic characteristics, are grouped

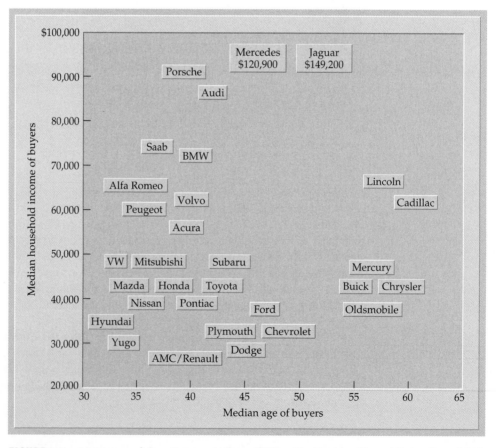

FIGURE 4-2   Income and Age Segmentation of New Car Buyers (From *Motor Trend,* July 1988, p. 44)

together. The geographic areas within a particular geodemographic segment are widely dispersed. Commercial research firms providing geodemographic offerings include Claritas (PRIZM), Donnelley (CLUSTER PLUS), and CACI (ACORN). Geodemographics allow marketers to focus their efforts on specific areas throughout the United States, and they are especially helpful in direct marketing (see Chapter 12). Geodemographics are also used for determining store locations by nationwide chains with multiple outlets.[4]

As marketing has become more targeted, demographics just do not explain enough; although demographics tell you what a customer looks like and what the customer does, they do not explain why the customer behaves as he or she does.

Psychographic Basis   Psychographics provide a useful supplement to demographics. Psychographics focus on general buyer habits, social class, lifestyles, and attitudes as they might relate to a specific product class. Lifestyle is concerned with the *activities, interests, and opinions* concerning leisure time, work, and consumption of the buyer alone or with others, with respect to both general behavior and the specific product class. Researchers find, for example, that buyers of Isuzu Motor's line of Trooper sport utility vehicles tend to be more environmentally conscious and outdoor minded than other consumers. Lifestyle research at Carnation Co. led to the creation of the Contadina line of fresh pastas targeted at two-income couples who like freshly prepared foods but have little time to cook.

Among the best-known psychographic classifications of consumers is SRI International's Values and Life Styles (VALS 2) program. Consumers are classified into eight categories as shown in Table 4-2. How can this information be used? A packager of travel tours, for example, might focus on adventure when talking to the experiencer, but emphasize luxury and service with the achiever.

Lifestyle segmentation has some limitations. Although lifestyle segmentation greatly increases survey costs, lifestyles explain only a small proportion of brand behavior. Many individuals assume multiple roles in life. How then can one lifestyle label be applied to such an individual? Even where lifestyle segments have been identified, the results frequently have not been actionable.

Behavioral Basis   A common way to segment a market is by *volume.* Marketing managers obviously distinguish between users and nonusers of their product or service. However, users consume different amounts. A small proportion of users might account for a large share of sales. Thus, the importance of a buyer is represented by the associated purchase volume. Strategies based on the heavy half are easier to implement if these users have clearly defined demographic profiles. Besides the usage rate, markets can be segmented by the decision-making unit, the end use, buyers' purchasing strategies, the degree of brand loyalty, the response to changes in our own and our competitors' marketing mixes, and the readiness stage. For industrial markets, another possibility is to group customers on the basis of similarities in *their* strategies.[5]

Rather than segment a market on the basis of descriptive factors such as the geographic, demographic, or volume, causal factors related to the reasons for purchase might be more appropriate. These causal factors are the *benefits sought* by the buyer. Once the benefit segments have been constructed, they can be characterized using conventional descriptive factors. As an example, consider the toothpaste market. Four benefit segments can be identified: (1) flavor and product appearance, (2) brightness of teeth, (3) decay prevention, and (4) price. These segments have different demographic strengths, special behavioral characteristics, brands disproportionately favored, and personality and life-cycle characteristics. This information suggests how copy directions and media choices might be tailored to reach different target segments.

The most common way of segmenting a business market is by *end use.* An industrial marketer might want to segment the pollution-control market. Some of the ways this market

TABLE 4-2   The World According to VALS 2

Actualizers
  Value personal growth
  Wide intellectual interests
  Varied leisure activities
  Well informed; concerned with social issues
  Highly social
  Politically active

Achievers
  Lives center on career and family
  Have formal social relations
  Avoid excess change or stimulation
  May emphasize work at expense of
    recreation
  Politically conservative

Believers
  Respect rules and trust authority figures
  Enjoy settled, comfortable, predictable
    existence
  Socialize within family and established
    groups
  Politically conservative
  Reasonably well informed

Makers
  Enjoy outdoors
  Prefer "hands-on" activities
  Spend leisure time with family and
    close friends
  Avoid joining organizations, except unions
  Distrust politicians, foreigners, and big
    business

Fulfilleds
  Moderately active in community and politics
  Leisure centers on the home
  Value education and travel
  Health conscious
  Politically moderate and tolerant

Experiencers
  Like the new, offbeat, and risky
  Like exercise, socializing, sports, and the
    outdoors
  Concerned about image
  Unconforming, but admire wealth, power,
    and fame
  Politically apathetic

Strivers
  Narrow interests
  Easily bored
  Somewhat isolated
  Look to peer group for motivation and
    approval
  Unconcerned about health or nutrition
  Politically apathetic

Strugglers
  Limited interests and activities
  Prime concerns are safety and security
  Burdened with health problems
  Conservative and traditional
  Rely on organized religion

Source: SRI International.

could be segmented are by the type of pollutant (e.g., odors), by the medium being polluted (e.g., water), by the source of the pollution (e.g., municipality), by the entity requiring the control products (e.g., federal), and by the type of control product (e.g., biological organisms). The attributes of a product or service must also be matched with the needs of potential customers. For example, one type of medical equipment can be used in the emergency room of a hospital, and another type in the office of a physician in private practice. Some attributes of the equipment will be more important in one market than in the other. Cost and ease of operation are more important to the individual doctor than to the hospital. The physician must collect from individual patients and use the equipment without help whereas the hospital collects from medical insurance and employs technicians.

A customer might have different reasons for selecting from a product category depending on the motivational circumstance. This gives rise to occasion-based segmentation. For example, the occasion is often a prime factor in wine selection. A wine's status is more important if the wine is served to guests than if it is to be consumed alone. The social occasion may make the buyer willing to spend more, be more sensitive to brand image, and pay more attention to label graphics.

Customer sensitivity to marketing actions is an important aspect of buying behavior. For example, Signode used sensitivity to price and service changes to help it identify buying behavior microsegments (Marketing Strategies box 4-2). Firms can shape the buying behav-

MARKETING STRATEGIES 4-2

APPLYING
. . . to
Industrial
Marketing

Fine Tuning Signode's Segmentation Strategy

The packaging division of Signode Corporation produces and markets a line of steel strappings used for packaging a diverse range of goods such as brick, steel, cotton, and many manufactured items. Signode has been the market leader for more than 25 years by bundling its strapping with other services. It provides engineering advice on customer packaging needs as well as parts and service for repair of packaging equipment at user firms. All other competitors offer only steel strapping. Despite its success, Signode's market share was being eroded by stiff price competition.

Signode traditionally segmented its customers by size—small, medium, large, and national accounts—and within each of these segments by SIC code. It did not use a buyer-behavior-based segmentation scheme. However, market pressures made customer behavior in terms of tradeoffs between price and service an important additional segmentation criterion. Since Signode could not do an in-depth analysis of the buying behavior of all its customers, it focused on its 174 national accounts whose purchases of Signode's products exceeded $100,000 annually. These national accounts generated nearly 40% of Signode's sales revenues.

(continues)

Courtesy Signode Packaging Systems

MARKETING STRATEGIES 4-2 **(continued)**

To gather information on the customer buying behavior of these key accounts, *key informants* were used because extensive surveys of multiple members of complex decision-making units have been found to be impractical. The key informants were Signode's five national account managers and 20 national account sales representatives. They provided input on 12 variables. Four buying behavior microsegments were then identified by performing cluster analysis on these variables. These segments were called programmed buyers, relationship buyers, transaction buyers, and bargain hunters. Knowledge of segment behavior helped Signode to redirect marketing resources.

— *Segmentation analysis can be used proactively to influence customers' movements to segments.*

Source: V. Kasturi Rangan, Rowland T. Moriarty, and Gordon S. Swartz, "Segmenting Customers in Mature Industrial Markets," *Journal of Marketing,* Vol. 56 (October 1992), pp. 72–82.

---

iors of potential customers by tactically altering marketing mix variables. Your next task is deciding how to balance the costs of segmentation against the potential benefits.

Evaluating Market Segments

Once you have identified some appropriate market segments, you have to evaluate whether a segmentation policy makes sense. Segmentation has a somewhat negative image as it implies brand managers deliberately abandon part of the market to the competition. However, mass markets do not have to be ignored. Usually the timing of a brand's entry determines whether a firm should segment a market or treat it as a whole. Original entrants should try to dominate the entire market, whereas latecomers might do better going after identifiable submarkets or *niches.* To determine whether segmentation is a good idea, you need a set of evaluation criteria.

Evaluation Criteria   A number of factors that have been suggested to help evaluate segmentation strategies are shown in Table 4-3. Segmentation only works when you have groups of customers with common needs or wants. If every buyer wants the product tailored to his or her own specifications, then segmentation will fail. Also you must be able to identify customers in each market segment. This is fairly easy if segments are based on demographic factors such as male/female, age, or income. These characteristics can be observed and measured with some accuracy. Segments based on lifestyles are much more difficult to use, however. For example, you might decide to focus your efforts on marketing to cosmopolitan customers. The problem with this segment is how to measure cosmopolitanism. Worldliness is made up of many traits and is not as easy to scale as age or income.

One of the key requirements for effective segmentation is that group members must respond differentially to marketing initiatives. When prospects are uneducated, illiterate, or speak foreign languages, they are not likely to understand or react to ads and other promo-

TABLE 4-3   Requirements for Effective Segmentation

1. Customers with common wants exist.
2. Segment members are identifiable/measurable.
3. Segment members are accessible.
4. The segment responds to marketing efforts differently than does the market as a whole.
5. Specialized communications media are available.
6. The seller has a competitive edge in target segment.
7. The segment is large enough to make a substantial profit.

tional communications. Encouraging segment members to buy is helped if specialized promotional media are available. This means you must have access to spot TV and regional editions of magazines and newspapers. Other special media that can be useful include ethnic and foreign language radio stations.

Direct mail is also effective with segmentation strategies. Toyota, for example, has used direct mail to build awareness when introducing its Lexus line of luxury automobiles. Since these cars sell for high prices, Toyota needed an economical way to reach a limited number of prospects without the use of mass media. Their approach was to build a mailing list from people who attended auto shows and appeared on executive referral lists and bombard them with multiple mailings about the new model. Toyota included locations of the dealers for the luxury cars so prospects would be encouraged to visit the showrooms to look at them.

Segment Size   Although a project may score well on the first six criteria in Table 4-3, segmentation will not work unless the market is big enough to make the venture profitable. Even if initially profitable, a small *niche* may soon be saturated. The main reason you have to worry about size is that segmentation strategies are more expensive than selling to everyone. Special ads, brochures, and promotions have to be created for individual groups of customers. Also segmentation leads to smaller expenditures in a wide variety of promotional media with a resulting loss in quantity discounts. You have to balance these increased costs against the profits produced by selling to relatively small groups of buyers. This issue is especially true in micromarketing and niche marketing.

Micromarketing   *Store-specific marketing,* often called micromarketing, has become possible for many consumer products because of the detailed marketing information now available. For example, one U.S. market research company, Market Metrics, collects statistics, such as store size, volume, space devoted to various departments, and shopper sociodemographic profiles on 30,000 supermarkets, which it combines with consumption pattern studies. This permits the research company to rank specific stores based on how well they should sell a specific product. Borden, for instance, used micromarketing for its Classico pasta sauce. Classico carries a premium price—40 cents more than Prego and Ragu. The Classico target market is those who earn at least $35,000, live in dual-income households in metropolitan areas, and are interested in gourmet-style pasta sauces. Because a mass market approach would have been inappropriate, a list of the best stores for the Classico consumers was generated. This permitted Borden to spend its money more efficiently. Some additional targeting examples are given in Table 4-4. Micromarketing not only helps big food companies, but it also allows retailers to allocate store shelf space correctly.

Niche Marketing   Niche marketing means serving a small market not served by competing products and of negligible interest to competitors. The real strategic use of segmentation seems to be in identifying underserved customers, then creating a new product category, subtype, or variant for them through product differentiation. You will have a temporary monopoly until the market attracts competitors.

PRODUCT DIFFERENTIATION

Our discussion of segmentation would not be complete without a consideration of product differentiation. Whereas segmentation focuses on groups of customers, differentiation emphasizes product differences to attract buyers. You must keep in mind that, when talking about a brand, what matters is not so much unique, but what is special, consistent, and

TABLE 4-4   Targeting a Product's Best Customers and the Stores Where They Shop

Brand	Heavy User Profile	Lifestyle and Media Profile	Top Three Stores in New York City Area
Peter Pan Peanut Butter	Households with children headed by 18- to 54-year-olds, in suburban and rural areas	Heavy video renters Go to theme parks Below-average TV viewers Above-average radio listeners	*Foodtown Supermarket* 3350 Hempstead Turnpike Levittown, NY *Pathmark Supermarket* 3635 Hempstead Turnpike Levittown, NY *King Kullen Market* 398 Stewart Ave. Bathgate, NY
Stouffers Red Box Frozen Entrees	Households headed by people 55 and older, and upscale suburban households headed by 35- to 54-year-olds	Go to gambling casinos Give parties Involved in public activities Travel frequently Heavy newspaper readers Above-average TV viewers	*Dan's Supreme Supermarket* 69-62 188th St. Flushing, NY *Food Emporium* Madison Ave. & 74th St. NYC *Waldbaum's Supermarket* 196-35 Horace Harding Blvd. Flushing, NY
Coors Light Beer	Head of household, 21–34, middle to upper income, suburban and urban	Belong to a health club Buy rock music Travel by plane Give parties, cookouts Rent videos Heavy TV sports viewers	*Food Emporium* 1498 York Ave., NYC *Food Emporium* First Ave. & 72 St., NYC *Gristedes Supermarket* 350 E. 86th St., NYC

Source: Spectra Marketing Systems, with data from Information Resources Inc., Simmons Market Research Bureau, Claritas Corp., and *Progressive Grocer;* appeared in Michael J. McCarthy, "Marketers Zero in on Their Customers," *The Wall Street Journal,* March 18, 1991, pp. B1, B5.

believed. This is your consistent brand promise (CBP).[6] Both segmentation and differentiation strategies are usually employed at the same time to achieve a sustainable competitive advantage. For example, see Marketing Strategies box 4-3.

Using Differentiation

The coffee market illustrates product differentiation. The first change from ground coffee was the introduction of a powdered instant for busy people. Then a way was found to remove the caffeine from coffee for those who do not want their sleep interrupted or have been told by their doctors to lower coffee consumption. The end result was a proliferation of different types of coffee to appeal to specialized customer segments. A similar explosion of product differences has occurred with Coke. Where once there was a single Coke, we now have Classic Coke, Caffeine Free Coke, Diet Coke, Caffeine Free Diet Coke, Cherry Coke, and Diet Cherry Coke.

Differentiation is more difficult when you are selling standard items like cement or metal strapping to business buyers. Decisions are often made for these commodities on the basis of lowest bid price. The Lonestar Cement people have partially overcome this problem by developing a fast-drying, superstrong cement targeted at four segments: airport construction and restoration, highway and bridge-deck building and repairs, tunnel work, and precast construction. The cement will harden in just four hours instead of the 7 to 14 days required for regular cement to set. Its niche appeal permits Lonestar to charge twice the price of regular cement. Another way to deal with commodities is to broaden the concept of the product

MARKETING STRATEGIES *4-3*

Prepaid Plans Open Cellular-Phone Market

APPLYING
. . . to
Consumer
Telecom-
munications
Marketing

Portugal's main telephone company, Portugal Telecom SA, came up with the idea of prepaid cellular service when they recognized that the existing network of automatic teller machines (ATMs) could be used as "refueling" stations. A user buys an off-the-shelf telephone, along with a card representing a certain value. Dialing a phone number and giving a personal activation number printed on the card activates the phone. When the money runs out, the card can be replenished with a fresh payment: cash at a local store, credit card charge, or ATM deduction (requires digital phone). The plan was a smashing success in Portugal (about 70% of all Portugal Telecom's mobile-phone customers are prepaid), took Europe by storm (about 25% of the European market), and is now catching on in the U.S.

A rival wireless carrier, Telecel Communicacoes Pessoais SA, markets its Vitamina prepaid telephones in brightly colored packages, each shaped in the form of a pill. One version is aimed at corporations. A company can specify exactly how much credit it wants each employee's phone to have and how often the credit can be topped off. Another product, Vitamina K (for kids), is for children ages 8 to 15. The phones look like frogs and have six colorful programmable (by a parent) buttons. The child only needs to know one is for mom, two is for dad, three is for grandma. Yet another variant, Vitamina R (for radicals), is sold to 15 to 24 year olds. Only fashionable Ericsson and Nokia models are featured. These phones provide a running display of the credit available at any one time. If one Vitamina R customer calls another Vitamina R customer, the call is 35% cheaper than a normal call.

— *You should consider marketing different product offerings to different market segments.*

Source: Gautam Naik, "Prepaid Plans Open Cellular-Phone Market," *The Wall Street Journal,* September 16, 1998, pp. B1, B4.

Courtesy Telecel Comunicacoes Pessoais, S.A.

in the eyes of the buyer. A cement company could equip its trucks with radios and advertise itself as the on-time cement company.

Costs of Differentiation

Although product differentiation can help improve sales revenues, it is expensive. Some of the added costs of differentiation include:

- *Product Modifications.* Adapting products to meet the needs of different segments requires extra payments for R&D, engineering, and special tooling.
- *Shorter Production Runs.* Product proliferation means producing items in smaller lots. Instead of producing 5,000 units of one item, you have to manufacture 1,000 units of five different products. This raises set-up times and workers have to adapt to different routines.
- *Larger Inventories.* The more products you offer customers, the larger the inventories needed to meet the demand. This occurs because the safety stock required to meet unexpected variations in demand for several products exceeds the safety stock needed for one product.

The amount of differentiation that you employ should be determined by the impact on profits. For example, not long ago customers could go into the showrooms of American auto manufacturers and order cars built to their exact specifications with regard to color, upholstery fabric, and 25 other options. However, this raised the costs of production and the more standardized Japanese cars were able to grab market share with lower prices. American car manufacturers have found that they can now make higher profits by offering less product differentiation. The use of a differentiation strategy forces managers to choose between additional revenues and the added costs of serving individual segments.

The real danger is that, while incurring higher costs of production, you might not garner enough additional sales to compensate. Even worse, you might alienate your core customers or distributors. Consider what happened to Reebok International Ltd. in the battle with Nike Inc. for the U.S. high-end sneaker market. Athletic shoe companies try to garner the cachet as a maker of performance shoes for serious athletes and thereby kindle sales in the broader consumer market. Runners, like smokers, seldom switch brands once they have settled on something they like. Reebok tried to innovate a running shoe called the Pump, which featured an inflatable bladder that wrapped around the sides. Unfortunately wearers complained of overheated and abnormally sweating feet. Runners and running specialty stores have been skeptical about Reebok ever since.

MASS CUSTOMIZATION

Technology, such as information technology and flexible manufacturing system technology, is making it economically feasible to reach the market of one. For example, Japan's National Industrial Bicycle Company sells made-to-order bicycles. Dealers fax National a set of specifications based on customers' requirements for model, color, components, and personal measurements. Computers digest the specs and print out custom blueprints. The customer's bicycle is created out of cut-to-fit and common parts. Robots do most of the welding and painting while skilled workers complete the assembly—including silk-screening the customer's name on the frame. Within a day, this bicycle is finished, packed, and ready for shipment.[7] Another example is Computer Designed Swimwear, which uses a computer and video camera to measure customers in nine ways. After buyers pick styles and fabric, the computer prints out a pattern that can be turned into a suit within an hour. Mass customization can take many forms. (See Marketing in Action box 4-1.)

MUST SEGMENTATION AND DIFFERENTIATION ALWAYS GO TOGETHER?

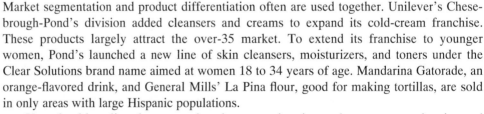

Market segmentation and product differentiation often are used together. Unilever's Chesebrough-Pond's division added cleansers and creams to expand its cold-cream franchise. These products largely attract the over-35 market. To extend its franchise to younger women, Pond's launched a new line of skin cleansers, moisturizers, and toners under the Clear Solutions brand name aimed at women 18 to 34 years of age. Mandarina Gatorade, an orange-flavored drink, and General Mills' La Pina flour, good for making tortillas, are sold in only areas with large Hispanic populations.

You should realize, however, that there are situations where segmentation is used without product differentiation and where differentiation is used without segmentation. Apple Computer, for example, sells the same basic machines to educators that they sell to businesses. Separate marketing programs are used to reach these segments and differentiation is a minor issue. Mercedes-Benz has had a great deal of success selling the same cars to different market segments in Germany and in America. In the United States, Mercedes are sold as luxury cars for the rich and famous. In Germany, the Mercedes has a more popular image and is even used as a taxicab. These examples show that advertising and promotion can be used to position products to appeal to particular buyers. Product differentiation without segmentation is shown by P&G's advertising of Charmin toilet paper as

APPLYING
... to
Consumer
Products
Marketing

MARKETING IN ACTION *4-1*

Mass Customization at Duracell

Duracell, a division of Gillette, is the world's leading alkaline battery manufacturer and has the highest U.S. market share. Its U.S. product line includes alkaline major cells, lithium photo batteries, hearing aid batteries, high-powered rechargeable pack batteries (e.g., camcorder and wireless telephone), and specialty batteries. It is a consumer packaged goods company with a component product dependent on the use of devices such as toys, flashlights, pagers and radios. Most of Duracell's batteries are sold at retail outlets. Its distribution includes grocery stores, drug stores, mass merchants, warehouse clubs, hardware stores, home centers, electronics shops, convenience stores, variety stores, and many other trade channels. As the market leader since the eighties, Duracell has close to one hundred percent distribution penetration for its product line.

Duracell's core business is alkaline major cells. These are Duracell's D, C, AA, 9 volt, and AAA batteries you find in stores. The five standard battery sizes are built into thousands of stock keeping units (skus) to ship its customers every month. Consider the more than 20 basic pack sizes such as common AA cell 2 packs, 4 packs, 8 packs, 12 packs and special 20 cell size packs for the warehouse club channel. These pack types go into various types of shipping cartons and trays creating over 80 open stock skus.

Duracell also produces more than 50 standard types of prepackaged displays, mostly to support incremental retail locations. The displays can be shipped using a variety of promotions including standard, seasonal and custom consumer marketing messages/offers. Its sales force works with retailers to optimize their return on these incremental displays using customized promotional offers and different product assortments. This creates thousands of different shipping skus each month.

Marketing and sales has effectively turned five basic batteries into thousands of skus to meet customer requirements. This has boosted Duracell's sales volume. Before this mass customization, its sales were significantly less than the current level.

— *Mass customization applies to intermediaries as well as final users and can include packaging and displays as well as product.*

Source: Rich Gordon, "A Role for the Forecasting Function," *Journal of Business Forecasting Methods & Systems*, Vol. 16, No. 4 (Winter 1997/1998), pp. 3–7.

APPLYING
... to
Consumer
Packaged
Goods
Marketing

softer than competing brands. P&G is attempting to persuade customers that there are differences in softness, but they really want to sell Charmin to everyone. The ideal combination of segmentation and/or differentiation strategies varies by products and the competitive environment.

SUMMARY

Individual customers differ widely in their individual brand choices. This does not guarantee that there are identifiable segments with consistently different reactions to similar brands. Consider the case of apparel retailing.[8] Here retailers, especially small ones, define the target market by making an initial retail mix with an intuitive notion of the kind of people to whom it will appeal, seeing who responds, then adjusting the retail mix to better serve the emergent market. In the apparel market, socio-demographic characteristics are poorly related to buying behavior. Other less easily measured variables, such as socio-cultural ones: interests, ways of life, and "mental age"—the age consumers identify with and feel and act like—are more important. Moreover, there is great variability in clothing behavior according to usage situation—"clothing moments." Thus, apparel retailers find that they appeal to every socio-demographic segment, albeit to a greater or lesser degree. The warning here is

APPLYING
... to
Apparel
Marketing

that you might not always be able to identify your target market in advance but may have to rely on your customers identifying themselves through their purchase behavior. Furthermore, you may not want to limit your market prematurely.

Advances in manufacturing technology and developments in information technologies allow for mass customization. Mass customization makes it feasible for you to reach segments of one. However, for many products, including most frequently purchased consumer packaged goods, individualized products are not justified. There is a continuum between treating the market as a whole and markets of one. You have to decide which level of aggregation yields the most efficiency and profitability.

NOTES

1. Ned Anschuetz, "Building Brand Popularity," *Journal of Advertising Research,* Vol. 37, No. 1 (January/February 1997), pp. 63–66.
2. Hammond, Kathy, A.S.C. Ehrenberg, and G. J. Goodhardt, "Market Segmentation for Competitive Brands," *European Journal of Marketing,* Vol. 30, No. 12 (1996), pp. 39–49.
3. Roger Titford and Roy Clouter, "The Case for Mass Marketing in an Increasingly Segmented World," *Admap,* Vol. 33, No. 10 (November 1998), pp. 37–39.
4. James H. Myers, *Segmentation and Positioning for Strategic Marketing Decisions* (Chicago: American Marketing Association, 1996), pp. 39–45.
5. Sudharshan, D. and Frederick Winter, "Strategic Segmentation of Industrial Markets," *Journal of Business & Industrial Marketing,* Vol. 13, No. 1 (1998), pp. 8–21.
6. Richard Jeans, "Integrating Marketing Communications," *Admap,* Vol. 33, No. 11 (December 1998), pp. 18–20.
7. Hart, Christopher W., "Made to Order," *Marketing Management,* Vol. 5, No. 2 (Summer 1996), pp. 11–16; Ali Kara and Erdener Kaynak, "Markets of a Single Customer: Exploiting Conceptual Developments in Market Segmentation," *European Journal of Marketing,* Vol. 31, No. 11/12 (1997), pp. 882–883.
8. Danneels, Erwin, "Market Segmentation: Normative Model versus Business Reality," *European Journal of Marketing,* Vol. 30, No. 6 (1996), pp. 36–51.

SUGGESTED READING

Hart, Christopher W. "Made to Order," *Marketing Management,* Vol. 5, No. 2 (Summer 1996), pp. 11–16.
Kara, Ali and Erdener Kaynak "Markets of a Single Customer: Exploiting Conceptual Developments in Market Segmentation," *European Journal of Marketing,* Vol. 31, No. 11/12 (1997), pp. 873–895.

REFERENCES

Jenkins, Mark and Malcolm McDonald. "Market Segmentation: Organizational Archtypes and Research Agendas," *European Journal of Marketing,* Vol. 31, No. 1, (1997), pp. 17–32.

McDonald, Malcolm and Ian Dunbar. *Market Segmentation: How to Do it, How to Profit from It,* 2nd ed. London: Macmillan, 1999.

Myers, James H. *Segmentation and Positioning for Strategic Marketing Decisions.* Chicago: American Marketing Association, 1996.

Sarabia, Francisco. "Model for Market Segments Evaluation and Selection," *European Journal of Marketing,* Vol. 30, No. 4, (1996), pp. 58–74.

Walters, Peter G. P. "Global Market Segmentation," *Journal of Marketing Management,* Vol. 13, (1997), pp. 165–177.

Wedel, Michel and Wagner A. Kamakura. *Market Segmentation: Conceptual and Methodological Foundations.* Boston: Kluwer Academic, 1998.

QUESTIONS

1. For years, makers of baldness remedies have made their pitches to men. Most people lose 100 to 150 hairs a day, a small percentage of the 100,000 hairs that grow on the average head. People who suffer genetic baldness problems don't replenish hair at a normal rate. Minoxidil, the generic version of Rogaine, is the only Food and Drug Administration (FDA)-approved baldness remedy. No one knows how minoxidil works on the human head. It began as a blood pressure medication with the unwelcome side effect of excessive hair growth. The drug appears to prolong the growth phase of the hair cycle. The FDA says that the drug spurs meaningful hair growth in only 25 percent of men and 20 percent of women after several months of use. The FDA has approved the drug for sale without a prescription. Most drug companies get a three-year monopoly when a product is converted to over-the-counter use. In an unusual move, the FDA decided that Rogaine failed to meet the criteria for this exclusive status and immediately approved several generic versions of the drug.

   Dermatologists estimate that about 40 million men and 20 million women suffer from hereditary hair loss. Most men eventually come to terms with hair loss. Surveys show only about half the nation's balding men are worried about their plight while nearly every woman with thinning hair is concerned. Moreover, women are more likely to endure the twice-a-day treatment and prolonged use requirements of hair-growth products. Should marketers of minoxidil pursue a risky new market: women? If so, how should Rogaine do so? A generic version?

2. People in the fashion business long held that big women—and teens—didn't want stylish, body-revealing clothes. Let them wear sweat pants and tent dresses! Designers were especially loath to court such customers for fear of losing cachet with trend-setters. Meanwhile the total number of girls ages 10 to 19 in America is rising. They are getting heavier as well as taller as a result of junk-food diets and too little exercise. Feet are growing along with waists and hips. Today's teenagers are more tolerant of body differences than previous generations. Plus-size teenagers crave more body-revealing clothes than heavy adult women tend to wear. Should fashion marketers address this niche within a niche? If so, how?

3. Private-label film accounts for about 5.5 percent of total U.S. film revenue and about 11% of total units sold. Should the Eastman Kodak Co. develop a discounted product, one that wouldn't carry Kodak's name, for the segment of the market that is price sensitive? Kodak could do so with an older-technology film emulsion than used in its branded Kodak film. The new product would have less well defined and less colorful pictures.

4. Some find it useful to classify the bases of segmentation as general (independent of products, services, or circumstances) or product specific (related to the customer and the product, service and/or particular circumstance). Further, these bases can be classified as observable (measured directly) or unobservable (inferred). Construct the corresponding four-cell classification table and put the bases in Table 4-2 into the appropriate cells.

5. In the past, many business owners or managers felt that they either did not need new insurance coverages for their business practices or that their claims would not seriously affect their business on a day-to-day basis. All that has changed as daily news of lawsuits awarding large settlements are reported. How can an individual firm in the insurance industry react quickly to emerging needs for specialized insurance coverage? How should it market these new products?

6. Many U.S. banks have shifted their policy on bounced checks so that the largest check is processed first when multiple checks are received at one time. By processing the largest check first, several small checks may bounce that day and the banks get to charge the

customer more than one $25 bounced check fee. If the small checks had been processed first, the account owner might have had to pay only one bounced check fee. Some banks have projected increases in fee income of $700,000 to $14 million from changing the order of check processing. Since it costs a bank only $.50 to $1.50 to process a bad check, banks make high profits on $25 bad check processing fees. Is it ethical for banks to target customers who bounce checks with a high to low check-processing policy and then say they have no legal requirement to inform customers of this policy?

7. There is a growing segment of up-market consumers who are willing to pay a premium to stand out. The German carmaker, Mercedes-Benz—now Daimler-Chrysler, started its car customization program called Designo in 1995. In 1998, it launched the program in the United States. About 100,000 Mercedes are sold each year in the U.S. market. While customization is needed in Germany, where taxicabs are Mercedes E-class sedans, the need in the United States is not obvious. Adding 10 percent or more to the cost of a car through custom options also runs counter to Mercedes current value theme. Should Mercedes have a customization program in the United States? What is the biggest challenge in implementing the program?

8. A telecommunications company wants to assess the attractiveness of market areas that it has yet to enter. Markets in which subscribers rack up lots of airtime minutes are preferable to those with "deadbeat" subscribers. The company has subscriber billing and demographic information for those markets that it already serves. Some markets—and the counties that comprise them—were selected at random from current service areas. To adjust for the fact that some counties are larger and more populous than others are, all demographic variables were put on a per capita, per household, or similar basis. The data are in file cellulardat.sav. The key performance measure for the telecom is average airtime usage per customer. What are the key demographic variables for predicting it?

CASE 4-1   CALAMBRA OLIVE OIL (A)*

*F*rank Lockfeld pushed his chair back from the table and surveyed the remains of the meal he had spent the afternoon preparing. After an appetizer of roasted peppers with caramelized garlic accompanied by a crisp 1982 Roederer champagne, he and his guests sat down to a main course of his own devising, designed to take advantage of the light, yet intense, flavor of Calambra olive oil. In the Chicken Breasts Calambra, he used fresh lemons, thyme, garlic, shallots, cherry tomatoes, and parsley (all from his garden), sixteen green and sixteen black olives, and five tablespoons of Calambra olive oil. (A collection of Frank's Calambra recipes is presented in Exhibit 1.) With the chicken, Frank served fresh zucchini (also

from his garden) and a shitake mushroom risotto, complemented by a superb 1986 Chalone Chardonnay Reserve. This course was followed by an endive salad with his own special vinaigrette—balsamic vinegar, fresh lime juice (from the tree in his garden), freshly ground pepper, and the 1993 vintage Calambra olive oil. Frank took another sip of the Chalone and gazed into its rich amber depths while strains of Mozart's Piano Concerto no. 20 in D Minor played in the background. Turning to his wife, B. J., and friends Marv and Linda White, he said,

> How am I supposed to decide how many gallons of olive oil to order for next year? It's only the beginning of August, and we've just begun the first selling season. It

---

* This case was prepared by Assistant Professor Dana R. Clyman and Professor Phillip E. Pfeifer of the Darden Graduate School of Business. Copyright (c) 1993 by the University of Virginia Darden School Foundation, Charlottesville, VA. Reproduced by permission.

EXHIBIT 1   A Collection of Frank's CALAMBRA Recipes

CHICKEN BREASTS CALAMBRA

4 chicken-breast halves	1 small bay leaf
5 T CALAMBRA Olive Oil	$1/2$ cup chicken broth
16 pitted black olives	$1/2$ cup dry white wine
16 green olives stuffed with pimento	2 T chopped fresh parsley
16 cherry tomatoes	$1/2$ t red-pepper flakes
2 T chopped shallots	Ground white pepper
1 T chopped garlic	Lemon juice
4 sprigs fresh thyme	

Pat chicken with lemon juice and sprinkle with ground pepper. Warm 4 T CALAMBRA Olive Oil in 12" pan. Sauté chicken, skinside down, over medium-high heat for 5 minutes. Turn, lower heat to moderate, and sauté for 15–20 minutes, turning so chicken browns evenly. Remove to heated serving dish and cover. Add olives and tomatoes to pan; turn in pan until they are warm. Place olives and tomatoes around chicken. Pour off pan contents, retaining approximately 2 T in pan. Add shallots, garlic, thyme, and bay leaf; cook for 2 minutes. Add wine and mix pan scrapings; reduce by half over high heat. Add broth, parsley, and red-pepper flakes; simmer for 10 minutes. Remove from heat and blend in remaining T CALAMBRA Olive Oil. Spoon over chicken and serve. Serves 4.

LAMB CHOPS CALAMBRA

4 lamb chops (shoulder or round bone)	3 T fresh thyme, or 1 T dried
4 T CALAMBRA Olive Oil	$3/8$ cup dry red wine
2 T chopped garlic, or to taste	2 T butter
4 T chopped fresh parsley, or 2 T dried	Lemon juice
2 T chopped fresh basil, or 1 T dried	Ground white pepper

Trim chops well. Rub with lemon juice and sprinkle lightly with pepper. Sauté garlic in CALAMBRA Olive Oil over medium-high heat for 1 minute in 12" pan. Add chops. Cover chops with $1/2$ each of the herbs. Sauté for 4 minutes. Turn, cover with remaining herbs, and sauté for 4 minutes. Turn and sauté for 2 minutes. Remove chops to heated platter and cover. Add wine to pan, stir, and reduce by half over high heat. Remove from heat, whisk in butter and juices from chops. Pour sauce over chops and serve. **Serves 4.**

SPINACH CALAMBRA

2 bunches fresh spinach, destemmed and prepared in $1/2$" chiffonade	1 T chopped garlic, or to taste
4 T CALAMBRA Olive Oil	4 T toasted pine nuts
	1 T freshly grated Parmesan cheese

Preheat broiler to 350 degrees. Blanch spinach in boiling water for 30 seconds; drain well. Sauté garlic in CALAMBRA Olive Oil in 10" pan over moderate heat for 2 minutes. Fold spinach and pine nuts into oil and garlic; mix well. Cook for 2 minutes. Sprinkle with Parmesan cheese. Place under broiler for 30 seconds. **Serves 4.**

SHITAKE AND PASTA CALAMBRA

4 T CALAMBRA Olive Oil	2 T chopped fresh chives
$1/2$ pound fresh shitake mushrooms, sliced	1 T chopped garlic, or to taste
1 pound fettucini	4 T crème fraîche
2 T finely chopped fresh tarragon	Freshly grated Parmesan cheese
1 T chopped fresh parsley	

In 10"–12" pan, sauté garlic in CALAMBRA Olive Oil for 1 minute over moderate heat. Add shitake and cook over low heat for 20 minutes. Prepare fettucini al dente; drain. Combine shitake and oil mixture with fettucini. Add and mix tarragon, parsley, and chives. Mix in crème fraîche. Serve with Parmesan cheese on the side. (Note: 3 oz. dried shitake reconstituted with water may be used if fresh shitake are not available. If fresh herbs are not available, reconstitute dried herbs in a saucer with a small amount of CALAMBRA Olive Oil. If chanterelles are used, cook for 45 minutes). **Serves 4 as an entrée, 8–10 as a pasta course.**

(continues)

EXHIBIT 1   (Continued)

GRILLED TOMATOES CALAMBRA

4 large tomatoes, halved	**2 large cloves of garlic, thinly sliced**
2 T CALAMBRA Olive Oil	**Lemon juice**
2 T finely chopped fresh oregano	**Ground white pepper**

Preheat broiler at 350 degrees. Oil baking dish just large enough to accommodate tomato halves. Sprinkle tomatoes with lemon juice and pepper lightly. Cover with sliced garlic. Sprinkle with oregano. Drizzle with CALAMBRA Olive Oil. Broil for 7 minutes with heat 4 inches from surface.

MAYONNAISE CALAMBRA

$1/4$ cup CALAMBRA Olive Oil	**1 T shallots**
1 cup plus 1 T safflower oil	**1 T lemon juice**
1 egg	**1 t prepared mustard, such as Provençale or Pommery**

In processor work bowl, place egg (white and yolk), mustard, shallots, 1 T lemon juice, and 1 T safflower oil. Process for 1 minute. Continue processing and drizzle through feed tube: $1/2$ cup of safflower oil, almost drop by drop; CALAMBRA Olive Oil; remaining safflower oil. (Garlic may be substituted for shallots.)

PESTO CALAMBRA

1 cup CALAMBRA Olive Oil	**4 oz. pine nuts**
2 cups firmly packed fresh basil	**1 T garlic, or to taste**
$1/2$ cup grated Parmesan cheese	

Place all ingredients in food processor. Process until blended and smooth. Combine with pasta al dente. Yields approximately 2 cups pesto. Unused portion can be covered with CALAMBRA Olive Oil in closed container and kept in refrigerator for up to 3 weeks.

---

was only three months ago, late last April, that we bottled the first crop of Calambra olive oil. This was supposed to be our test year. That's why we bought only 800 gallons of the 1993 vintage oil; if we can't sell that much, we probably don't have a business. Now it seems we have to make the decision about the 1994 crop before we have any real idea about how this experiment is going to turn out.

What's more, sales so far have been disappointing. But it's been only three months. We're hoping for a big jump in sales when the retail shops stock up in anticipation of holiday buying. What's more, there's the possibility we'll sign contracts with Neiman Marcus and Williams-Sonoma for inclusion in their holiday catalogs. Inclusion in either would provide a real boost to sales. But the fact remains: so far, we've shipped only 24 cases.

Sometimes, I'm very optimistic and tempted to order 3,000 gallons, as originally planned for year two. This is, after all, the best-tasting olive oil on the market. But at other times, I'm concerned that sales may never materialize. I have visions of standing in front of the warehouse filled to the brim with leftover cases of 1993 bottles just as a big truck pulls up with this huge 1994 shipment.

BACKGROUND

Shortly after Frank Lockfeld moved to California from London in 1968 to work with Wilbur Smith and Asso-

ciates, a well-known transportation-planning and -consulting firm, he planted two olive trees in the backyard of his house in Palo Alto. Several years later, after the trees began to bear fruit, Frank decided to try to make olive oil from his own olives. As Frank later explained, he was mostly "just curious" and intrigued by the idea of producing his own olive oil.

The first batch of olive oil was simply terrible, and Frank set out to determine why. The answer came in the form of one Gino Ambrano, a seventh-generation olive-oil presser of Sicilian descent. Ambrano's family had relocated to California in the early 1900s, and Ambrano, an independent businessman in Mountain View, California, continued the family tradition by maintaining a small olive-oil press, on which he would press a small quantity of oil that he sold in gallon jugs.

Ambrano explained to Frank that the olives Frank used were the wrong kind for making high-quality olive oil. Most California olives, he explained, were the wrong kind—producing oil that could only be used for such industrial purposes as making soap. The popular hand soap, Palmolive, for example, was aptly named because one of its main ingredients was olive oil.

High-quality olive oil, Ambrano explained, required olives grown in extremes of temperature—

hot, dry summers and cold, crisp winters. Palo Alto's moderate climate was neither hot enough, dry enough, nor cold enough. The only good California olives came from the Central Valley in the area surrounding the town of Oroville. There, the high volcanic-ash content of the soil coupled with the temperature extremes provided an ideal environment for growing the kind of olives needed to make high-quality olive oil.

To prove his point, Ambrano offered Frank a taste of his own hand-pressed, extra virgin,[1] olive oil. Ambrano made this oil with Oroville olives using his family's extremely gentle, traditional pressing methods. Upon tasting the latest vintage of Ambrano's olive oil, Frank knew he had met a master. The oil was light and delicate, yet intense. It had a medium-amber color, with a full, rich nose and brilliant, fruity flavor. The taste was distinctly of ripe olives, sweet and pure, with a surprisingly mild aftertaste. Frank had never tasted anything like it and thought that Ambrano's was probably the best-tasting olive oil in America.

Frank was so impressed that he arranged to purchase a small quantity of Ambrano's olive oil to give to his friends as Christmas presents. After funneling the bulk oil into wine bottles, he designed and hand-inked personalized labels for each of the bottles. These gifts were a big hit; everyone who tried the oil thought its taste was remarkable, and not a few of them suggested that Frank try to find some way to bring it to market.

THE CALAMBRA CONCEPT

Frank thought he could gain a distinctive marketing advantage by emphasizing that this oil was from California. Almost all high-quality olive oil sold in the United States was imported from Europe. Just as California wines had won market acceptance in competition with French wines, Frank was convinced that a California olive oil could do the same by winning a reputation for very high quality. He combined "California" with "Ambrano" to come up with the name of his new venture.

To encourage consumers to make the connection between olive oil and fine wine, Frank decided to sell Calambra olive oil in 750-milliliter, "dead-leaf" green wine bottles.[2] In addition, Frank decided to display the bottling year on each label. (Few people know it, but the taste and quality of olive oil vary from year to year. Furthermore, like wine, olive oil ages. If you prefer your olive oil intense, use it while it is fresh; if you prefer a mellower, more understated taste, allow it to age in the bottle.)[3] Frank believed that by dating each bottle, he could encourage consumers to pay attention to both the year-to-year differences and the effects of age, thereby differentiating Calambra from other olive oils and increasing the connection between Calambra Olive Oil and fine wine.

To complete the package, Frank designed a beautiful, high-quality label. The four-color label—a rising sun in gold foil, bicolored olive branches, and the vintage date—was so well done that it later won several design awards.[4]

In keeping with the highest-quality image, Frank saw Calambra carrying a retail price higher than any other olive oil on the market. He expected Calambra to be sold initially in specialty and gourmet-food stores. Access to such stores was provided through "fancy-food" brokers, individuals who sold an array of non-competing gourmet-food products to retail outlets in return for a fixed-percentage commission. Frank planned to start in Northern California, especially in the Bay Area, and later move on to other major metropolitan areas. Department stores and large supermarkets would follow a successful introduction in specialty stores.

Promotional plans for the introduction of Calambra were modest. Taste tests, magazine articles, and newspaper coverage were the major vehicles Frank would pursue. The primary costs of these efforts were Frank's time and whatever oil was used in marketing promotions, taste tests, and giveaways.

THE 1993 VINTAGE

In August 1992, Frank contracted with Gino Ambrano for delivery during the last week of April 1993 of 800 gallons of olive oil at $22 per gallon. Although most oils are made from olives picked in December or January, Ambrano used only handpicked, extraripe, late-

---

[1] Olive oil comes in several grades, which denote acidity level. For the highest grade, extra virgin, the acidity level must be less than 1 percent.

[2] Frank chose the expensive "dead-leaf" green bottles because they protected the oil from light. As with fine wines, exposure to light could cause olive oil to break down.

---

[3] When aging olive oil, it should be stored in a cool, dark place of constant (or, at most, slowly changing) temperature. Just as with wine, quick temperature changes could facilitate chemical reactions that cause the oil to break down.

[4] The label was so expensive relative to the alternatives that, in order to reduce unit costs, Frank purchased 100,000 labels, enough to see him through the first six years of production under even his most optimistic sales forecasts. The labels were printed without the vintage date, which was then overprinted as needed.

harvest black olives from the April crop. These extraripe fruit, which were restricted to black olives to avoid green-olive bitterness, had to be handled gently to avoid damage and quickly, from picking to pressing, to avoid mold.

As had his grandfather—and *his* grandfather before him—Ambrano, immediately upon receipt of the olives, lightly crushed the extraripe fruit. (This extremely gentle pressing avoided the bitterness of the pit because it ensured that the pit itself was never crushed.) Ambrano then took the resulting mixture of oil and skins and allowed gravity to filter it through cotton twice. This centuries-old process, using no heat, pressure, or chemicals, produced the sweetest, purest olive oil imaginable.

In preparation for delivery, Frank began exploring various ways to bottle the oil. His first surprise came when a local bottler told him that he could expect to lose about 53 of his 800 gallons during the bottling process. This loss was composed of three components. The first was a fixed loss of about 25 gallons that occurred during the setup process as target fill-levels were set, spin speeds were established, and fill apertures were chosen. The speed at which the machine filled the bottles and the apertures from which the product was poured depended on a variety of factors, including the shape, size, and mouth-width of the bottles, and the viscosity and consistency (chunkiness) of the fluid. Next, there was a variable loss of about 3 percent due to spillage during the filling process. Finally, there was a residual loss of about 5 gallons because emptying the machine fully without degrading the product was impossible.[5]

Because setup and cleaning represented major components of the bottler's activity, the cost of using the bottling plant consisted of a correspondingly high fixed cost of $3,000 and a correspondingly low variable cost of only $0.30 per bottle, plus supplies.

To avoid the loss of oil and the huge fixed costs relative to the quantity he was bottling, Frank arranged for friends and family to help him handbottle the 1993 oil over a weekend. From friends in the wine business, he borrowed a six-hole handbottling machine to fill the bottles and a foiler-spinner to put in the capsules and seal the bottles. In return for the help of his friends and the use of the machines, Frank gave away several cases of freshly bottled, first-vintage, 1993 Calambra Olive Oil. Thus, his only costs were the cost of the supplies, gifts, and the food and wine he served during his bottling extravaganza (spillage was negligible). When all was said and done, Frank had 325 cases of oil and a small cadre of friends who fully believed that Calambra was the best olive oil imaginable.[6]

Frank stored the cases of Calambra Olive Oil in space he rented from a local wine wholesaler and began the process of supporting his broker's efforts to sell the product to local specialty retailers in the San Francisco Bay Area. While the broker introduced her clients to Calambra as part of her routine calls to specialty-food stores, Frank used his spare time (mostly weekends) arranging for and conducting taste tests at specialty markets around the Bay Area and contacting editors and writers of various gourmet magazines and newspaper columns.

A case of Calambra Olive Oil was priced to retailers at $150. (See Exhibit 2 for the prices and costs of a case of 1993 Calambra Olive Oil.) The broker made 20 percent on each sale, and product was shipped directly from the warehouse to the retailer. Exhibit 3 contains Frank's projected profit-and-loss statement for the business for the years 1993 through 1999 based on actual oil purchases in 1993 and forecasted purchases of 3,000, 4,500, 6,750, and 10,000 gallons from 1994 on. Frank's origi-

EXHIBIT 2   1993 Calambra Olive Oil: Prices and Costs per Case

Calambra selling price per case		$150.00
Expenses		
Glass	$4.91	
Capsules	0.50	
Closures	0.60	
Labels	0.68	
Bottling expense[a]	0.00	
Oil[b]	$54.15	
Cost of goods		$60.84
Gross margin		89.16
Broker fee		30.00
Gross margin after brokerage		$59.16

[a] Did not use bottler—hand bottled.
[b] 800 gallons at $22 per gallon made 325 cases.

---

[5] The bottler explained that these losses were considered minor by his usual customers, who were generally bottling high-volume food products with low unit costs, like soup, vinegar, and chunky salsa. Unfortunately for Frank, this loss meant that his 800 gallons of olive oil would result in only about 314 twelve-bottle cases of 750-milliliter bottles of olive oil. (Without any loss, 800 gallons would result in about 336 cases, as there are 3.7853 liters per gallon.)

[6] Frank set aside 25 of the 325 cases for marketing purposes. Of those, five were normal 12-bottle cases. For the other 20 cases, however, Frank chose half-size (375-milliliter) clear-glass wine bottles to highlight the oil's beautiful amber color. These cases consisted of 24 bottles each.

EXHIBIT 3   Projected Profit and Loss: 1993–97

	1993	1994	1995	1996	1997
Gallons of oil	800	3,000	4,500	6,750	10,000
Net gallons[a]	773	2,881	4,336	6,518	9,671
Cases of oil produced	325	1,211	1,823	2,741	4,067
Marketing cases	25	50	50	75	100
Cases available for sale	300	1,161	1,773	2,666	3,967
Revenue	$45,000	$174,150	$265,950	$399,900	$595,050
Cost of goods					
Oil	$17,600	$62,000	$90,500	$133,250	$195,000
Bottling cost ($3.60/case)	NA	7,360	9,563	12,868	17,641
Material ($6.69/case)	$ 2,174	$ 8,102	$ 12,196	$ 18,337	$ 27,208
Selling expenses					
Freight ($4.00/case)	$ 1,200	$ 4,644	$ 7,092	$ 10,664	$ 15,868
Broker (20% of sales)	9,000	34,830	53,190	79,980	119,010
Printing ($0.12/case)	39	145	219	329	488
Warehouse ($3.50/case)	1,050	4,064	6,206	9,331	13,885
Advertising	$ 1,500	$ 2,250	$ 5,000	$ 11,000	$ 17,500
General and administrative					
Legal	$ 1,400	$ 500	$ 500	$ 500	$ 500
Accounting	850	650	650	650	650
Insurance	260	285	325	375	440
Telephone	600	900	1,500	2,400	3,000
Miscellaneous	$ 750	$ 1,000	$ 1,500	$ 2,000	$ 3,000
Total costs	$36,423	$126,729	$188,440	$281,684	$ 414,190
Profit	$ 8,577	$ 47,421	$ 77,510	$118,216	$180,860

[a] Presumes handbottling in 1993 and use of the bottling plant for years 1994 through 1997.

nal intention was to prove the market in 1993 and then roll out the business per this projection.

AUGUST 1993

The introduction of Calambra Olive Oil was an artistic success. Calambra ranked number one in a tasting of 21 Italian, French, Spanish, Greek, and California olive oils sponsored by Narsai's Market, a well-known specialty-food store in Kensington, California (see Exhibit 4 for the judging criteria and a list of the oils tested). The Narsai victory received coverage in *San Francisco Focus,* a slick, monthly magazine covering events in the Bay Area for upscale readers. It also got Frank invited back to conduct an instore tasting on July 24. On that Saturday Frank sold 20 bottles. Calambra also received a very favorable review in the article "Liquid Gold: The True Meaning of 'Extra Virgin' and Other Secrets of the Controversial Oil from the Little Black Fruit," which appeared in the "California Living" section of the *Los Angeles Herald.* A list of the selling points and accolades for Calambra Olive Oil are presented in Exhibit 5.

Unfortunately, these successes had yet to translate into shipments. As of July 30, Frank had shipped 24 cases to 17 different customers in the Bay Area, each of whom had initially ordered a single trial case and only four of whom had as yet placed a second order. This was a far cry from the 20 to 30 cases that Frank hoped the average store would sell each year. Nonetheless, Frank was hopeful that many of these stores would soon be placing orders in anticipation of holiday buying.

In addition, Frank was currently in negotiations with Neiman Marcus and Williams-Sonoma for inclusion in their Christmas catalogs. Neiman Marcus was thinking of including a bottle of Calambra Olive Oil in each of its Christmas baskets and talking about a purchase of 100 cases of oil; Williams-Sonoma was thinking of listing Calambra directly in its catalog and was considering 30 cases. Frank believed that either deal would be a great boon for Calambra, more for the enhancement of Calambra's reputation than for the sale of oil. Moreover, Frank thought it was an almost even bet that he would get at least one of the contracts. Specifically, he believed there was about a 10 percent chance that the Neiman deal would come through and about a 40 percent chance for Williams-Sonoma. Frank did not think the outcome of either negotiation would affect the other.

EXHIBIT 4   **Narsai's Taste Test, Saturday, May 29, 1993**

#1 Calambra (April 1993 Extra Virgin, Central Valley)

ITALIAN OILS

Antinori Santa Cristina (1991 Extra Virgin Chianti Classico)
I. Pozzi-Montefollonico (N.V. Extra Virgin, Tuscany)
Poggio at Sole (N.V. Extra Virgin, Val di Pesa, Firenza)
Tahoe Sardegna (N.V. Extra Virgin, Foligno)
Sasso (N.V. Pure Olive Oil, Oneglia)
Badia Coltibuono (1991 Extra Virgin, Chianti Classico)
Badia Coltibuono (December 1992 Extra Virgin, Unfiltered)
Chianti Classico-Special Bottling)
Castello di Volpaia (1991 Extra Virgin, Chianti Classico)
Il Castelluzzo (N.V. Extra Virgin, Orvieto)
Colavita (N.V. Extra Virgin, Campobasso)

FRENCH OILS

Domaine de la Gautiere (N.V. Virgin Buis les Baronnies)
James Plagniol (N.V. Pure Olive Oil, Marseille)
Old Monk (N.V. Extra Virgin, Nice)

SPANISH OIL

Siurana (N.V. Extra Virgin, Priorat, Catalonia)

Greek Oil

Arethousa (N.V. Pure Olive Oil, Calamata)

California Oils

Kimberly (1993 Extra Virgin, Northern California)
Estus Gourmet (N.V. Extra Virgin)

CRITERIA FOR EVALUATION OF HIGH-QUALITY OLIVE OIL

- Bouquet, perfume, aroma of the fresh olive
- Flavor on the tongue; fruitiness versus greasiness
- Degree of acidity and extent of burning and stinging at back of mouth; some degree of pepperiness, but not too much to override the delicate flavor
- Color—deep, rich emerald to golden green, depending on degree of filtering

---

EXHIBIT 5   **Selling Points and Accolades**

- Ranked no. 1 in tasting of 21 Italian, French, Greek, Spanish, and California olive oils at Narsai's Market, Kensington, California
- Praised as "the outstanding olive oil" at the third annual International Gourmet Food and Wine Show, San Francisco, by Harvey Steiman, *San Francisco Examiner* food critic
- Seventh-generation olive-oil master
- Full flavor and aroma of olives
- A very light oil without greasiness (does not stick to the roof of your mouth)
- Smooth, balanced taste without sharpness common to other olive oils
- Made from fully ripe black olives only; no green-olive bitterness
- Olives from selected farms in north Central Valley, where heat brings fruit to ripeness
- April harvesting when the olives are fully developed
- Very lightly cold-pressed, avoiding bitterness near pit (pit is not crushed)
- No "culls" (canned olive rejects); no heat, no chemicals
- Gravity-filtered twice through cotton; no pressure applied

THE QUANTITY DECISION

Although it was only August, Gino Ambrano was pressing Frank to decide how many gallons of oil he wanted in 1994. Although this urgency seemed premature, Frank realized that producing Calambra-quality oil required that the olives be left to ripen on the trees far longer than if the olives were to be used for any other purpose. Thus, in one sense, Frank was asking Ambrano to contract with the olive growers to "reserve" some portion of their crop for a late-April harvest so that it could be made into Calambra Olive Oil.

On the other hand, Frank also thought that Ambrano was applying pressure, in his own skillful and gentle way, simply to make Frank commit. Frank believed that, for personal reasons, Ambrano was willing to press only about 6,000 gallons of olive oil in 1994—even though he had a lot more capacity—and that the reason Ambrano wanted to know how much oil Frank wanted was so he could make plans for the rest.

As a result, Ambrano sent Frank the agreement reproduced in Exhibit 6. After several weeks of discussion, Frank came to realize that the proposed price schedule was not negotiable. Frank knew that this agreement was truly a take-it-or-leave-it offer, and that

EXHIBIT 6   Agreement

This is an agreement between Calambra Olive Oil (Calambra), a California subchapter S corporation, and Gino Ambrano, Martine Avenue, Mountain View, California.

Gino Ambrano will provide Calambra with olive oil of his own pressing from the 1994 crop according to the following price schedule:

For the first 500 gallons:	$23.00 per gallon
For any of the next 500 gallons:	$22.00 per gallon
For any of the next 500 gallons:	$21.00 per gallon
For any of the next 500 gallons:	$20.00 per gallon
For any additional oil:	$19.00 per gallon

The oil will be received by Calambra at Gino Ambrano's place of business in Mountain View, California, in 55-gallon drums, unless prior written arrangements are mutually agreed upon. Delivery will be made during the last week of April 1994.

All drums delivered to Calambra prior to April 30 will be returned not later than May 5. Calambra may, upon consent of Gino Ambrano, purchase the drums at a price of $50 per drum.

Payment for the oil shall be made by check drawn on the account of Calambra, upon receipt of delivery, excepting the first $5,000.00, which is due upon execution of this contract.

This represents the entire agreement between the parties hereto, notwithstanding any prior or verbal representations by either party. Any amendments to this agreement shall be written and signed by the parties to this agreement.

For Calambra Olive Oil

_____   _____
Frank Lockfeld   Gino Ambrano
President

date: date:

---

he would have to make up his mind by the end of the month. This situation disturbed Frank because he did not believe he was getting much of a break from Ambrano for committing to buy the oil in advance and in quantity. Nonetheless, he had no other choice. Although low-grade oil was available commercially in 55-gallon drums for about $5 per gallon, and there was some extra virgin oil available in drums for sale to restaurants at $15 to $17 per gallon, none of it tasted like Ambrano's.

In thinking about how many gallons to order, Frank was forced to project where the business might be in April 1994 when the new order would be delivered. Clearly, the events of the next few months would go a long way to help determine just how many gallons he would need next April.

As Marv and Frank began to clear the table, Marv asked Frank if he still thought he would sell all of the 1993 oil. Frank answered,

I'm not giving up hope that all 300 cases of 1993 oil will be sold before the 1994 shipment arrives, but without catalog sales, I'm afraid I'd now have to say it's a little less than an even bet. In fact, while I still think there's some chance we could sell as many as 500 cases to the retail stores if we had them, at this point if we don't get the stores to stock up for the holidays, we might sell as few as 50 cases.

The good news, though, is the catalogs. Closing either deal would be a big boon to 1993 sales in two ways. Not only would we get those extra sales from the catalog purchases, but it would easily increase our total sales to retailers by 20 cases because of the added advertising value.

"Come back to the retail market for a moment," Marv said. "If I understand you correctly—and I'm guessing that your not-quite-an-even bet means your midpoint is off by about 10 percent—what you're saying is that it's as likely that you'll sell more than 270 cases as it is that you'll sell less. Right?"

"That's about right."

"OK, let's see if we can add a little definition to this forecast. If I told you that you were definitely going to sell less than 270 cases to retailers, where do you think you'd end up? What do you think is the point between 50 and 270 that you're as likely to be over as under?"

"I don't know. I've never thought about that. Maybe 175 cases."

"And what about the similar point on the upside, assuming, of course, you had them to sell?"

"That one is easier," Frank responded. "If I knew we were going to sell more than 270 cases, that would mean the product has been at least reasonably well accepted and I'd think that if we had them to sell to the stores, we'd be as likely to sell more than 400 cases as less than 400 cases."

As Frank fired up the cappuccino machine, Linda said that she thought the question was how much oil to buy for the 1994 vintage. "Don't we need to talk about the potential for 1994 sales?" Frank agreed, but added that 1993 was the key:

> Selling out in 1993 would have an enormous positive impact on the business. Although some stores might be upset that they weren't able to reorder when they wanted to, most would realize that Calambra is like a small Sonoma Valley vineyard and that to carry the product, they would have to compete to place orders.

> In fact, if we sell out in 1993, I believe it would only lead to more, faster sales in 1994, as stores try to increase their inventories to prevent stockouts. These larger orders, plus the accompanying press, would make it very easy to move to other metropolitan areas with the 1994 crop [Los Angeles, New York, and Washington, D.C., were all on Frank's list] and truly launch this business.

> But, most importantly, selling out in 1993 provides the signal that there really are enough connoisseurs out there who appreciate the value of a fine olive oil.

As B. J. brought out her famous Linzer torte (a raspberry-and-almond torte made from her own *secret* recipe in the style and tradition of the great bakers of the city of Linz, Austria), Frank continued,

> If we sell all of the 1993 oil, whether through specialty shops or catalog sales, the experiment will have been a success and the business will be a "go." In this case, Linda, I'd say the potential for 1994 sales ranges from just matching 1993 sales of 300 cases all the way up to 1,600 cases. In this scenario, I'd be pretty optimistic about our most likely sales level; in fact, I'd stick with my original forecast of about 1,200 cases.

> On the other hand, if we don't sell out in 1993, then I'd have to conclude that Calambra is unlikely to realize the consumer acceptance it needs, and I'd have to call the experiment a failure. To me that means there aren't enough olive-oil connoisseurs in the Bay Area to support the venture. What's worse, if we can't make it happen here, it isn't likely to happen anywhere. So, if we don't sell out in 1993, we don't have a business and we don't order any more oil for 1995.

> In this depressing case, I'd have to say that the most likely outcome would be to sell about the same amount of oil in 1994 as we sold in 1993. But it could be a lot worse. If the channel is full and the product isn't selling, we might only sell a quarter as much. On the other hand, there is probably still some upside, as the business could still take off; but it's hard to imagine that we'd sell more than three times as much in 1994 as we sold in 1993. I even have a hard time thinking about this scenario.

As Frank got up to make more cappuccino, B. J. asked him what would happen should sales fail to materialize in either 1993 or 1994 and the business had to be abandoned. "What do we do with all that oil?"

"If we're not in business, we'll simply have to find a way to dispose of it," Frank answered, "but we'll probably take quite a bath. There's always Trader Joe's." (Trader Joe's was a discount chain of fancy-food stores in the Southwest that bought warehouse-sized lots of fancy-food products at distress prices, usually about 10 cents on the dollar, and then resold them in their own stores at deep discounts.) "Painful as it might be, we could always sell the oil to them."

"On the other hand, if we are in business in 1995, we could always sell leftover bottles in later years, although I don't think I'd ever want to sell more of a vintage in the out-years than sales in the year it was introduced. I'd be afraid that having too much older oil on the market could have a negative effect on sales."

"I think you're right." Marv piped in. "In fact, it seems to me you might be better off simply eating any leftover oil rather than risking the possibility of a negative market reaction. Over pasta would be nice; we'll come help."

CASE 4-2   DELTA OIL OUTLETS (B)*

IVEY

aniel and Joanne Gibson owned six Delta Oil outlets—three of them in Rosemont, Ontario. In June 1995 they had hired the Rosemont Consulting Group (RCG) to design and conduct research into the Rosemont oil change consumer. By November 1995, RCG had submitted its findings, and the Gibsons had set aside a weekend to analyze the information from the study. Their ultimate objective was to develop insights that would lead to improved marketing of Delta Oil in Rosemont.

THE COMPANY

Delta Oil was a national chain of franchised, specialty oil change outlets. The main focus of every outlet was offering to the consumer market an oil change package that included replacing a car's old crankcase oil with new oil, installing a new oil filter, lubricating automobile joints as required, and completing a 20-point check of other fluids, light bulbs, belts, etc. The 20-point oil change was sold for $26.95 or more, depending on the type of oil selected. Additional, related products and services were also offered by each outlet.

Delta's promotional efforts in Rosemont included couponing, advertisements on the exterior of city buses and community sponsorship of a charitable organization. Coupons were delivered through Rosemont's one daily newspaper, the *Rosemont Times,* approximately six times per year. The Gibson's strategy was to attract the customer with good service delivered inexpensively and quickly, then check for other car problems that could be solved with the added products and services offered by Delta.

In 1994, the Gibsons had introduced an Express Service package to the Rosemont market, offering a "no-frills" oil change for $19.99, and promising to complete the oil change in five minutes. Initially, the Express Service appeared to be responsible for a sig-

nificant increase in sales. However, by the summer of 1995, sales had fallen to the levels achieved before the new service was introduced, so Daniel and Joanne hired RCG to conduct research into the oil change consumer.

RCG'S RESEARCH APPROACH

The research questionnaire was designed through exploratory meetings with the Gibsons, a preliminary survey, a study design meeting, and a pre-test. The preliminary survey was conducted to ensure that questions on quality, service and convenience issues were appropriately addressed. The pre-test facilitated the correct wording of questions.

A total of 315 consumers were surveyed—100 Delta customers plus 215 Rosemont residents. The length and complexity of the questionnaire suggested that the survey be administered through personal interviews. A valuable coupon for future oil change services was offered as an incentive to respond.

The 100 Delta customers were interviewed at the three Delta locations, while they were receiving an oil change. The number of surveys at each location approximated that location's share of total Rosemont sales: 30 at the Fuller Drive location, 35 at both the Central Parkway and Elgin Road outlets. At all locations, $1/3$ of the questionnaires were administered on each of weekends, weeknights and weekdays. Survey dates were random, and all customers arriving during survey times were invited to respond.

The sample of 215 Rosemont residents was stratified to ensure an adequate number of responses (a) from the immediate vicinity of each Delta location and from outside those areas, (b) from areas where Delta regularly mailed coupons, occasionally mailed coupons and never mailed coupons. Areas were selected using postal codes, and included all parts of Rosemont except the city core.

* This case was prepared by Professor Ken Bowby and Sonya Head under the supervision of Elizabeth M.A. Grasby, Pre-Business Program Director, solely to provide material for class discussion. The author does not intend to illustrate either effective or ineffective handling of a managerial situation. The author may have disguised certain names and other identifying information to protect confidentiality. One time permission to reproduce granted by Ivey Management Services on February 1, 1999. Copyright (c) 1996, The University of Western Ontario. The University prohibits any form of reproduction, storage, or transmittal without written permission from the Richard Ivey School of Business. This material is not covered under authorization from CanCopy or any other reproduction rights organization.

EXHIBIT 1   Delta Research Results–Summary of Findings

		Delta Clients (n=100)		Random Rosemont (n=215)		Total (n=315)	
		#	%	#	%	#	%
1 HOW OFTEN DO YOU CHANGE THE OIL IN YOUR PERSONAL VEHICLE?							
A Under 5,000 Kilometres		6	6.4	30	15.1	36	12.3
B Every 5,000 Kilometres		40	42.6	55	27.6	95	32.4
C Over 5,000 Kilometres		16	17.0	22	11.1	38	13.0
D Every 1–3 Months		16	17.0	44	22.1	60	20.5
E Every 4–5 Months		10	10.6	23	11.6	33	11.3
F Every 6 Months		6	6.4	23	11.6	29	9.9
G Over 6 Months		—	0.0	2	1.0	2	0.7
	Totals	94	100.0	199	100.0	293	100.0
Average Kilometres		5,637		5,313		5,428	
Average Months		3.8		4.1		4.0	
2b PRIMARY PURPOSE OF THE OUTLET WHERE YOU PURCHASED YOUR LAST OIL CHANGE?							
1. An outlet that specializes in oil changes		76	78.4	64	30.3	140	45.5
2. A car dealership		11	11.3	57	27.0	68	22.1
3. A service station		4	4.1	35	16.6	39	12.7
4. A department store chain (i.e., Wal-Mart)		2	2.1	21	10.0	23	7.5
5. An automotive chain (i.e., Canadian Tire)		3	3.1	18	8.5	21	6.8
6. No outlet—I changed the oil myself		1	1.0	16	7.6	7	5.5
	Totals	97	100.0	211	100.0	308	100.0
2c LAST 4 OIL CHANGES AT SAME PLACE?							
1. Same place		39	41.5	123	61.2	162	54.9
2. Different places		55	58.5	78	38.8	133	45.1
	Totals	94	100.0	201	100.0	295	100.0
2d WHICH BEST DESCRIBES YOUR BEHAVIOUR?							
Often change oil with no other work at same time.		71	75.5	131	64.9	202	68.2
Often combine oil change and other service work.		18	19.1	45	22.3	63	21.3
Plan work together, so as few trips as possible.		5	5.3	26	12.9	31	10.5
	Totals	94	100.0	202	100.0	296	100.0
3 See Exhibit 2							
4a PREFER A SPECIFIC BRAND OF OIL?							
1. No		81	81.0	174	80.9	255	81.0
2. Yes		19	19.0	41	19.1	79	19.0
	Totals	100	100.0	215	100.0	315	100.0
4b PREFER SPECIFIC OIL TYPE (ADDITIVES, ETC)?							
1. No		83	83.0	147	73.9	230	76.9
2. Yes		17	17.0	52	26.1	86	28.8
	Totals	100	100.0	199	100.0	299	100.0
5a EXPECT TO PAY FOR OIL CHANGE & FILTER?							
A $20 and under		36	36.7	75	36.1	111	36.3
B $21–$25		28	28.6	66	31.7	94	30.7
C $26–$30		26	26.5	43	20.7	69	22.5
D $30 and above		8	8.2	24	11.5	32	10.5
	Totals	98	100.0	208	100.0	306	100.0
Average Price		$24.80		$24.64		$24.69	
5b LIKE A COMPREHENSIVE VISUAL CHECK?							
1. No		11	11.2	26	12.3	37	12.0
2. Yes		87	88.8	185	87.7	272	88.0
	Totals	98	100.0	211	100.0	309	100.0
5c WILLING TO PAY MORE FOR VISUAL CHECK?							
1. No		73	73.7	156	73.9	229	73.9
2. Yes		26	26.3	55	26.1	81	26.1
	Totals	99	100.0	211	100.0	310	100.0

(continues)

EXHIBIT 1   (Continued)

	Delta Clients (n=100)		Random Rosemont (n=215)		Total (n=315)	
	#	%	#	%	#	%
6 See Exhibit 3						
7 EXPECT HOW MUCH TIME FOR OIL CHANGE?						
A Under 15 minutes	19	19.4	11	5.3	30	9.8
B 15 minutes	36	36.7	26	12.4	62	20.2
C 16–20 minutes	28	28.6	56	26.8	84	27.4
D 21–30 minutes	14	14.3	81	38.8	95	30.9
E 31 minutes and Above	1	1.0	35	16.7	36	11.7
Totals	98	100.0	209	100.0	307	100.0
Average Expected Wait (Minutes)	18		28		25	
8 PHRASE THAT BEST SUITS YOU?						
I will pay a premium for fast service	19	19.4	19	9.4	38	12.6
I will not shop around for the lowest cost	39	39.8	89	43.8	128	42.5
I will shop around for the lowest price	33	33.7	75	36.9	108	35.9
I change the oil myself in order to save money	7	7.1	20	9.9	27	9.0
Totals	98	100.0	203	100.0	301	100.0
9 PREFERENCE FOR AMENITIES						
Attractive Waiting Room						
1. Would like it	5	5.3	46	22.7	51	17.1
2. Indifferent	69	72.6	115	56.7	184	61.7
3. Don't want it	21	22.1	42	20.7	63	21.1
Totals	95	100.0	203	100.0	298	100.0
Magazines						
1. Would like it	17	17.9	68	33.3	85	28.4
2. Indifferent	58	61.1	98	48.0	156	52.2
3. Don't want it	20	21.1	38	18.6	58	19.4
Totals	95	100.0	204	100.0	299	100.0
Newspapers						
1. Would like it	25	26.0	90	44.1	115	38.3
2. Indifferent	56	58.3	81	39.7	137	45.7
3. Don't want it	15	15.6	33	16.2	48	16.0
Totals	96	100.0	204	100.0	300	100.0
Free telephone for local calls						
1. Would like it	21	22.3	53	26.2	74	25.0
2. Indifferent	45	47.9	92	45.5	137	46.3
3. Don't want it	28	29.8	57	28.2	85	28.7
Totals	94	100.0	202	100.0	296	100.0
Washrooms						
1. Would like it	45	47.9	119	57.2	164	54.3
2. Indifferent	41	43.6	62	29.8	103	34.1
3. Don't want it	8	8.5	27	13.0	35	11.6
Totals	94	100.0	208	100.0	302	100.0
Free coffee						
1. Would like it	28	29.8	77	37.6	105	35.1
2. Indifferent	47	50.0	79	38.5	126	42.1
3. Don't want it	19	20.2	49	23.9	68	22.7
Totals	94	100.0	205	100.0	299	100.0
Giveaways						
1. Would like it	17	18.3	21	10.4	38	12.9
2. Indifferent	43	46.2	75	37.3	118	40.1
3. Don't want it	33	35.5	105	52.2	138	46.9
Totals	93	100.0	201	100.0	294	100.0

(continues)

EXHIBIT 1 (Continued)

		Delta Clients (n=100)		Random Rosemont (n=215)		Total (n=315)	
		#	%	#	%	#	%
Access to stores (shop while you wait)							
1. Would like it		10	10.8	45	22.2	55	18.6
2. Indifferent		53	57.0	93	45.8	146	49.3
3. Don't want it		30	32.3	65	32.0	95	32.1
	Totals	93	100.0	203	100.0	296	100.0
Other Amenities							
1. Would like it		8	30.8	19	30.2	27	30.3
2. Indifferent		12	46.2	16	25.4	28	31.5
3. Don't want it		6	23.1	28	44.4	34	38.2
	Totals	26	100.0	63	100.0	89	100.0
10 See Exhibit 4							
11 SERVICE AGENT BEHAVIOUR THAT IS MOST IMPORTANT TO YOU (PICK 1–3)?							
1. Reserved/efficient		22	7.8	33	5.5	55	6.2
2. Courteous		57	20.3	84	13.9	141	16.0
3. Friendly		22	7.8	43	7.1	65	7.4
4. Knowledgeable		55	19.6	109	18.1	164	18.6
5. Helpful		62	22.1	154	25.5	216	24.4
6. Trustworthy		45	16.0	130	21.6	175	19.8
7. Clean, neat, tidy		16	5.7	47	7.8	63	7.1
8. Other		2	0.7	3	0.5	5	0.6
	Totals	281	100.0	603	100.0	884	100.0
11b EXPECT MECHANIC FOR OIL CHANGE?							
1. No		72	73.5	131	62.7	203	66.1
2. Yes		26	26.5	78	37.3	104	33.9
	Totals	98	100.0	209	100.0	307	100.0
12a EXPECT INVOICE & WORK EXPLANATION?							
1. No		15	15.2	54	25.6	69	22.3
2. Yes		84	84.8	157	74.4	241	77.7
	Totals	99	100.0	211	100.0	310	100.0
12b SPEND MORE TIME FOR EXPLANATION?							
1. No		28	30.1	86	42.0	114	38.3
2. Yes		65	69.9	119	58.0	184	61.7
	Totals	93	100.0	205	100.0	298	100.0
12c SPEND MORE MONEY FOR EXPLANATION?							
1. No		77	85.6	183	88.8	260	87.8
2. Yes		13	14.4	23	11.2	36	12.2
	Totals	90	100.0	206	100.0	296	100.0
13b WHAT AVAILABLE SERVICES WOULD YOU CHOOSE WITH YOUR OIL CHANGE?							
1. All		23	11.8	60	16.4	83	14.8
2. None		16	8.2	33	9.0	49	8.7
3. Tire rotation		23	11.8	43	11.7	66	11.8
4. Belt (fan) replaced		11	5.6	47	12.8	58	10.3
5. Windshield fluid topped off		29	14.9	61	16.7	90	16.0
6. Light bulbs replaced		21	10.8	50	13.7	71	12.7
7. Engine flush		21	10.8	11	3.0	32	5.7
8. Radiator flush		23	11.8	21	5.7	44	7.8
9. Transmission service		13	6.7	14	3.8	27	4.8
10. Differential service		4	2.1	8	2.2	12	2.1
11. Fuel injector service		5	2.6	3	0.8	8	1.4
12. Not sure what some services involve		6	3.1	15	4.1	21	3.7
	Totals	195	100.0	366	100.0	561	100.0

(continues)

EXHIBIT 1   **(Continued)**

		Delta Clients (n=100)		Random Rosemont (n=215)		Total (n=315)	
		#	%	#	%	#	%
14 See Exhibit 5							
15a HOW OLD IS YOUR AUTOMOBILE?							
A Under 3 years		24	24.7	51	23.9	75	24.2
B 3–5 years		31	32.0	73	34.3	104	33.5
C 6–9 years		31	32.0	61	28.6	92	29.7
D 10+ years		11	11.3	28	13.1	39	12.6
	Totals	97	100.0	213	100.0	310	100.0
Average Age of Car (# Years)		5.1		5.1		5.1	
15b APPROXIMATE ODOMETER READING?							
A 1–30 thousand kilometres		15	15.5	31	14.8	46	15.0
B 31–75 thousand kilometres		23	23.7	59	28.1	82	26.7
C 76–150 thousand kilometres		37	38.1	78	37.1	115	37.5
D 151 + thousand kilometres		22	22.7	42	20.0	64	20.8
	Totals	97	100.0	210	100.0	307	100.0
Average Odometer Reading (000 kilometres)		98		101		100	
15c Number of Kilometres in Past Year?							
A 1–12 thousand kilometres		21	23.9	68	33.8	89	30.8
B 13–24 thousand kilometres		34	38.6	74	36.8	108	37.4
C 25+ thousand kilometres		33	37.5	59	29.4	92	31.8
	Totals	88	100.0	201	100.0	289	100.0
Average Kilometres (000) in Past Year		23.0		20.3		21.1	
16a IS YOUR CAR UNDER WARRANTY?							
1. No		63	64.9	141	66.2	204	65.8
2. Yes		34	35.1	72	33.8	106	34.2
	Totals	97	100.0	213	100.0	310	100.0
16a2 IF YES, ARE YOU REQUIRED TO TAKE CAR TO THE DEALERSHIP FOR OIL CHANGES?							
1. No		25	86.2	40	74.1	65	78.3
2. Yes		4	13.8	14	25.9	18	21.7
	Totals	29	100.0	54	100.0	83	100.0
16b FAMILIAR WITH WARRANTY REQUIREMENTS?							
1. Very familiar		13	43.3	37	56.1	50	52.1
2. Understand only some warranty aspects		17	56.7	23	34.8	40	41.7
3. Do not understand the warranty		—	0.0	6	9.1	6	6.3
	Totals	30	100.0	66	100.0	96	100.0
17 PURPOSE OF YOUR AUTOMOBILE?							
1. Used mostly for travel to & at work		24	27.9	43	22.8	67	24.4
2. Used primarily for leisure & family travel		18	20.9	51	27.0	69	25.1
3. Used (almost) equally for work and for leisure		44	51.2	95	50.3	139	50.5
	Totals	86	100.0	189	100.0	275	100.0
18a TIMES MOST OFTEN PREFER OIL CHANGE?							
A Morning		29	48.3	113	59.8	142	57.0
B Afternoon		12	20.0	40	21.2	52	20.9
C Evening		19	31.7	36	19.0	55	22.1
	Totals	60	100.0	189	100.0	249	100.0
18b WEEK VS WEEKEND?							
A Monday to Friday		58	59.8	172	80.4	230	74.0
B Weekend		39	40.2	42	19.6	81	26.0
	Totals	97	100.0	214	100.0	311	100.0

(continues)

EXHIBIT 1   **(Continued)**

		Delta Clients (n=100)		Random Rosemont (n=215)		Total (n=315)	
		#	%	#	%	#	%
19a HOW DID YOU HEAR ABOUT OUTLET WHERE							
YOU PURCHASED YOUR LAST OIL CHANGE?							
1. Media advertising		2	2.0	14	6.5	16	5.1
2. From friends		3	3.0	15	7.0	18	5.8
3. Saw sign or billboard while passing by		28	28.3	37	17.3	65	20.8
4. Coupons		9	9.1	7	3.3	16	5.1
5. Repeat customer		38	38.4	70	32.7	108	34.5
6. Other		19	19.2	71	33.2	90	28.8
	Totals	99	100.0	214	100.0	313	100.0
19b LOCATIONS AWARE OF BEFORE TODAY?							
1. Delta Oil		86	43.2	175	39.2	261	40.5
2. The Lube Master		65	32.7	154	34.5	219	34.0
3. Lube & Drive		15	7.5	26	5.8	41	6.4
4. Lube Doctor		1	0.5		0.0	1	0.2
5. Esso Quick Lube		24	12.1	68	15.2	92	14.3
6. Lube n' Go		1	0.5	1	0.2	2	0.3
7. More than two of the above		7	3.5	22	4.9	29	4.5
	Totals	199	100.0	446	100.0	645	100.0
20a FAMILIAR WITH EXPRESS SERVICE?							
1. No		46	51.7	68	68.0	114	60.3
2. Yes		3	48.3	32	32.0	75	39.7
	Totals	89	100.0	100	100.0	189	100.0
20b ATTITUDE RE: EXPRESS SERVICE SPEED?							
1. Like it		48	96.0	51	72.9	99	82.5
2. Dislike it		2	4.0	19	27.1	21	17.5
	Totals	50	100.0	70	100.0	120	100.0
20c ATTITUDE RE: EXPRESS SERVICE PRICE?							
1. Like it		50	94.3	60	84.5	110	88.7
2. Dislike it		43	5.7	11	15.5	14	11.3
	Totals	53	100.0	71	100.0	124	100.0
20d ATTITUDE RE: BASIC SERVICE (No Frills)?							
1. Like it		30	78.9	42	61.8	72	67.9
2. Dislike it		8	21.1	26	38.2	34	32.1
	Totals	38	100.0	68	100.0	106	100.0
21 PARTS OF ROSEMONT DAILY EXPRESS READ?							
1. All of the paper		39	39.8	87	41.4	126	40.9
2. None of the paper		15	15.3	25	11.9	40	13.0
3. Front page only		1	1.0	8	3.8	9	2.9
4. Front section (national and world news)		16	16.3	35	16.7	51	16.6
5. Local news section		10	10.2	21	10.0	31	10.1
6. Sports		13	13.3	18	8.6	31	10.1
7. Business			0.0	6	2.9	6	1.9
8. Entertainment & Comics		3	3.1	5	2.4	8	2.6
9. Editorials			0.0	2	1.0	2	0.6
10. Classified		1	0.0	3	1.4	4	1.3
	Totals	98	100.0	210	100.0	308	100.0
22 DO YOU USE COUPONS WHEN YOU PURCHASE							
GOODS OR SERVICES?							
1. No		29	29.3	64	30.0	93	29.8
2. Yes		27	27.3	58	27.2	85	27.2
3. Sometimes		43	43.4	91	42.7	134	42.9
	Totals	99	100.0	213	100.0	312	100.0

(continues)

EXHIBIT 1   (Continued)

	Delta Clients (n=100)		Random Rosemont (n=215)		Total (n=315)	
	#	%	#	%	#	%
23b AGE GROUP:						
1. Under 25	12	12.1	18	8.4	30	9.6
2. 26–35	31	31.3	36	16.8	67	21.4
3. 36–50	40	40.4	86	40.2	126	40.3
4. 51–56	14	14.1	55	25.7	69	22.0
5. over 65	2	2.0	19	8.9	21	6.7
Totals	99	100.0	214	100.0	313	100.0
Average Age of Respondent	40		46		44	
23c REGARDING YOUR HOME:						
1. House	83	86.5	179	88.6	262	87.9
2. Apartment	10	10.4	5	2.5	15	5.0
3. Other	3	3.1	18	8.9	21	7.0
Totals	96	100.0	202	100.0	298	100.0
23d GENDER:						
1. Male	78	79.6	144	68.9	222	72.3
2. Female	20	20.4	65	31.1	85	27.7
Totals	98	100.0	209	100.0	307	100.0

Apartments were excluded from the sample due to the difficulty in obtaining access and the resulting potential for fostering a negative image of Delta. Streets in each postal code area were randomly selected by RCG, in a manner that ensured a representative mix of housing.

Through door-to-door interviews, 101 questionnaires were completed. The remaining 114 questionnaires were received by delivering them door-to-door with an accompanying letter that asked the resident to complete the survey and return it in a postage-paid return envelope. A total of 700 questionnaires were delivered in this manner, with a response rate of 18% (14 completed questionnaires were received after the cutoff date).

The Express Service question, which identified Delta Oil, was located near the end of the questionnaire in order that responses to earlier questions not be biased by knowledge of the company name. For the same reason, the Express Service question was omitted from the questionnaires RCG delivered door-to-door for return mail.

RESEARCH RESULTS

Exhibit 1 presents the research questions and the frequency distribution of responses. Results from Delta customers (Delta) and Rosemont residents (Rosemont), are listed separately. All but four of the 23 questions are reported in Exhibit 1.

Questions 3, 6, 10 and 14 are reported separately in Exhibits 2–5, respectively. These four questions addressed concepts that were more challenging to describe:

3 = Quality   10 = Service
6 = Convenience   14 = Overall Preferences

Respondents were asked to describe their preferences or attitudes for these concepts by selecting up to three features from a list, then allocating 10 "points" to their choices so that the more important feature(s) received more points. They could allocate the points in any manner they chose (3, 3, 4 or 5, 3, 2 or 10, 0, 0 or 6, 3, 1 or…), but the total points allocated had to equal ten. This approach provided two different "scores" to consider:

An **"F-Score",** which reports how **Frequently** each feature was mentioned.

An **"I-Score",** reporting the average **Importance Points** assigned to the feature.

Exhibit 6 presents the results of selected questions cross-tabulated by gender.

Price sensitivity (survey question 8) and buying behaviour (survey question 2d) are cross-tabulated with a number of other results in Exhibits 7 and 8, respectively.

SUMMARY

Daniel and Joanne had a heavy workload for the weekend! They wondered what marketing decisions might be suggested by their analysis.

EXHIBIT 2   Selected Components of a <u>Good</u> Quality Oil Change: Summary of Points Awarded

Component	Points	Delta	Rosemont	All
3.1 – Broad choice of oil	1 to 2	7	13	20
	3 to 4	5	11	16
	5 to 10	5	6	11
	Avg. Score	**3.1**	**3.2**	**3.2**
3.2 – Improved car performance	1 to 2	8	18	26
	3 to 4	12	24	36
	5 to 10	8	19	27
	Avg. Score	**3.6**	**3.6**	**3.6**
3.3 – Job done fast	1 to 2	22	33	55
	3 to 4	33	46	79
	5 to 10	12	21	33
	Avg. Score	**3.3**	**3.2**	**3.2**
3.4 – Error free	1 to 2	12	22	34
	3 to 4	23	53	76
	5 to 10	30	54	84
	Avg. Score	**4.2**	**4.1**	**4.1**
3.5 – Cleanliness	1 to 2	7	30	37
	3 to 4	8	10	18
	5 to 10	1	2	3
	Avg. Score	**2.7**	**2.3**	**2.4**
3.6 – Visual inspection	1 to 2	21	28	49
	3 to 4	34	61	96
	5 to 10	11	50	61
	Avg. Score	**3.2**	**4.0**	**3.7**
3.7 – No pressure to purchase additional services	1 to 2	18	27	45
	3 to 4	10	22	32
	5 to 10	3	12	15
	Avg. Score	**2.6**	**3.1**	**3.0**
3.8 – Other	1 to 2	0	1	1
	3 to 4	2	4	6
	5 to 10	1	7	8
	Avg. Score	**5.7**	**5.0**	**5.2**

EXHIBIT 3   Selected Components of a <u>Convenient</u> Oil Change: Summary of Points Awarded

Component	Points	Delta	Rosemont	All
6.1 – Close to home— convenience	1 to 2	15	24	39
	3 to 4	26	53	79
	5 to 10	16	32	48
	Avg. Score	**3.5**	**3.7**	**3.6**
6.2 – Close to work— convenience	1 to 2	3	4	7
	3 to 4	4	13	17
	5 to 10	0	4	4
	Avg. Score	**2.7**	**3.3**	**3.2**
6.3 – On travel route— convenience	1 to 2	9	7	16
	3 to 4	8	14	22
	5 to 10	0	3	3
	Avg. Score	**2.6**	**3.2**	**3.0**
6.4 – Fast service	1 to 2	8	22	30
	3 to 4	41	67	108
	5 to 10	27	25	52
	Avg. Score	**4.0**	**3.6**	**3.8**
6.5 – One-stop shopping	1 to 2	3	16	19
	3 to 4	12	30	42
	5 to 10	5	29	34
	Avg. Score	**2.2**	**4.0**	**4.0**
6.6 – Can shop while waiting	1 to 2	0	2	2
	3 to 4	0	3	3
	5 to 10	0	3	3
	Avg. Score	**0**	**3.6**	**3.6**
6.7 – Free phone	1 to 2	3	2	5
	3 to 4	1	3	4
	5 to 10	1	1	2
	Avg. Score	**2.4**	**3.3**	**2.9**
6.8 – Stay in car	1 to 2	16	2	18
	3 to 4	4	3	7
	5 to 10	0	5	5
	Avg. Score	**2.0**	**3.8**	**2.6**
6.9 – No appointment necessary	1 to 2	12	28	40
	3 to 4	44	49	93
	5 to 10	18	32	50
	Avg. Score	**3.6**	**3.7**	**3.7**
6.10 – Waiting room	1 to 2	3	16	19
	3 to 4	1	10	11
	5 to 10	1	3	4
	Avg. Score	**2.6**	**2.4**	**2.5**
6.11 – Courtesy ride	1 to 2	0	16	16
	3 to 4	1	22	23
	5 to 10	0	9	9
	Avg. Score	**3.0**	**3.3**	**3.2**
6.12 – Other	1 to 2	0	1	1
	3 to 4	1	7	8
	5 to 10	1	10	11
	Avg. Score	**7.0**	**5.9**	**6.5**

EXHIBIT 4   Selected Components of Good Service: Summary of Points Awarded

Component	Points	Delta	Rosemont	All
10.1 – Added amenities	1 to 2	1	7	8
	3 to 4	4	2	6
	5 to 10	0	2	2
	Avg. Score	**3.0**	**2.6**	**2.8**
10.2 – No frills	1 to 2	9	14	23
	3 to 4	14	22	36
	5 to 10	11	17	28
	Avg.Score	**4.0**	**3.8**	**3.9**
10.3 – Helpfulness	1 to 2	9	24	33
	3 to 4	41	85	126
	5 to 10	18	37	55
	Avg. Score	**3.6**	**3.6**	**3.6**
10.4 – Thorough inspection	1 to 2	8	14	22
	3 to 4	35	74	109
	5 to 10	11	49	60
	Avg. Score	**3.5**	**4.2**	**3.9**
10.5 – Speed	1 to 2	15	26	41
	3 to 4	32	50	82
	5 to 10	18	37	55
	Avg. Score	**3.7**	**3.7**	**3.7**
10.6 – Courteous staff	1 to 2	16	48	64
	3 to 4	26	40	66
	5 to 10	6	23	29
	Avg. Score	**3.0**	**3.1**	**3.1**
10.7 – Other	1 to 2	0	0	0
	3 to 4	0	2	2
	5 to 10	1	7	8
	Avg. Score	**10.0**	**6.2**	**8.1**

EXHIBIT 5   Selected Components of Important Criteria: Summary of Points Awarded

Component	Points	Delta	Rosemont	All
14.1 – Service	1 to 2	14	37	51
	3 to 4	45	74	119
	5 to 10	11	35	46
	Avg. Score	**3.4**	**3.4**	**3.4**
14.2 – Quality	1 to 2	7	24	31
	3 to 4	55	84	139
	5 to 10	7	57	64
	Avg. Score	**4.1**	**4.0**	**4.0**
14.3 – Speed	1 to 2	23	35	58
	3 to 4	30	49	79
	5 to 10	10	11	21
	Avg. Score	**3.2**	**3.0**	**3.0**
14.4 – Convenience	1 to 2	10	39	49
	3 to 4	12	25	37
	5 to 10	2	12	14
	Avg. Score	**2.7**	**2.8**	**2.8**
14.5 – Price	1 to 2	16	36	52
	3 to 4	29	59	88
	5 to 10	11	33	44
	Avg. Score	**3.4**	**3.4**	**3.4**
14.6 – Amenities	1 to 2	0	3	3
	3 to 4	0	0	0
	5 to 10	0	1	1
	Avg. Score	**0**	**2.0**	**2.0**

EXHIBIT 6 (A)   Gender X Price Sensitivity (Q8)

Count Row Percentage Column Percentage		Will Pay Premium for Fast Service	Will not Shop for Low Price	Shop for Lowest Price	Change Own Oil to Save Money	TOTALS
Delta		16[a]	32	23	7	78
Males		20.5[b]	41.0	29.5	9.0	—
		84.2[c]	82.1	71.9	100.0	80.4[c]
Delta		3	7	9		19
Females		15.8	36.8	47.4		—
		15.8	17.9	28.1		19.6
TOTALS	#	19	39	32	7	97
	%	19.6	40.2	33.0	7.2	100.0
		—	—	—	—	100.0
Rosemont		14	59	47	19	139
Males		10.1	42.4	33.8	13.7	—
		77.8	66.3	67.1	82.6	69.5
Rosemont		4	30	23	4	61
Females		6.6	49.2	37.7	6.6	—
		22.2	33.7	32.9	17.4	30.5
TOTALS	#	18	89	70	23	200
	%	9.0	44.5	35.0	11.5	100.0
		—	—	—	—	100.0

[a]Count   [b]Row percentage   [c]Column percentage.

EXHIBIT 6 (B)   Gender X Oil Change Frequency (Q1)

Count Row Percentage Column Percentage		Under 5,000 Kilometres	At 5,000 Kilometres	Over 5,000 Kilometres	TOTALS
All		20	48	15	83
Males		24.1	57.8	18.1	—
		71.4	88.9	71.4	80.6
All		8	6	6	20
Females		40.0	30.0	30.0	—
		28.6	11.1	28.6	19.4
	#	28	54	21	103
TOTALS	%	27.2	52.4	20.4	100.0
		—	—	—	100.0

		Every 1–3 Months	Every 4–5 Months	Every 6+ Months	
All		22	15	16	53
Males		41.5	28.3	30.2	—
		52.4	65.2	64.0	58.9
All		20	8	9	37
Females		54.1	21.6	24.3	—
		47.6	34.8	36.0	41.1
	#	42	23	25	90
TOTALS	%	46.7	25.6	27.8	100.0
		—	—	—	100.0

EXHIBIT 6 (C)   Gender X Type of Outlet Last Used (Q2b)

Count Row Percentage Column Percentage		Oil Change Specialty	Auto Dealer	Service Station	Department Store	Auto Chain	Self	TOTALS
All		113	37	25	17	13	13	218
Males		51.8	17.0	11.5	7.8	6.0	6.0	—
		83.7	55.2	64.1	77.3	65.0	76.5	72.7
All		22	30	14	5	7	4	82
Females		26.8	36.6	17.1	6.1	8.5	4.9	—
		16.3	44.8	35.9	22.7	35.0	23.5	27.3
	#	135	67	39	22	20	17	300
TOTAL	%	45.0	22.3	13.0	7.3	6.7	5.7	100.0
		—	—	—	—	—	—	100.0

EXHIBIT 6 (D)   Gender X Buying Behaviour (Q2d)

Count Row Percentage Column Percentage		Buy Oil Change Only	Often Combine Service Purchases	Plan Purchases For Fewest Trips	TOTALS
All		143	44	22	209
Males		68.4	21.1	10.5	—
		73.3	71.0	71.0	72.6
All		52	18	9	79
Females		65.8	22.8	11.4	—
		26.7	29.0	29.0	27.4
	#	195	62	31	288
TOTAL	%	67.7	21.5	10.8	100.0
		—	—	—	100.0

EXHIBIT 6 (E)   Gender X Preference for Other Services Offered (Q13)

Count / Row Percentage / Column Percentage	None	Some	All	TOTALS
Delta	12	45	17	74
Males	16.2	60.8	23.0	—
	80.0	83.3	77.3	81.3
Delta	3	9	5	17
Females	17.6	52.9	29.4	—
	20.0	16.7	22.7	18.7
Delta#	15	54	22	91
Total%	16.5	59.3	24.2	100.0
	—	—	—	100.0
Rosemont	27	68	41	136
Males	19.9	50.0	30.1	—
	84.4	63.0	70.7	68.7
Rosemont	5	40	17	62
Females	8.1	64.5	27.4	—
	15.6	37.0	29.3	31.3
Rosemont #	32	108	58	198
Totals %	16.2	54.5	29.3	100.0
	—	—	—	100.0

EXHIBIT 6 (F)   Gender X Score Awarded "Fast Service" (Q6.4)

Count / Row Percentage / Column Percentage	Low Score (1–2)	Medium Score (3–4)	High Score (5–10)	TOTALS
All	20	85	40	145
Males	13.8	58.6	27.6	—
	71.4	81.7	76.9	78.8
All	8	19	12	39
Females	20.5	48.7	30.8	—
	28.6	18.3	23.1	21.1
#	28	104	52	184
TOTALS %	15.2	56.5	28.3	100.0
	—	—	—	100.0

EXHIBIT 6 (G)   Gender X Score Awarded to No "Appointment Needed"

Count / Row Percentage / Column Percentage	Low Score (1–2)	Medium Score (3–4)	High Score (5–10)	TOTALS
All	31	75	34	140
Males	22.1	53.6	24.3	—
	77.5	85.2	69.4	79.1
All	9	13	15	37
Females	24.3	35.1	40.5	—
	22.5	14.8	30.6	20.9
#	40	88	49	177
TOTALS %	22.6	49.7	27.7	100.0
	—	—	—	100.0

EXHIBIT 7 (A)   Price Sensitivity X Outlet Loyalty

Count / Row Percentage / Column Percentage	Last Four Changes at Same Outlet	Last Four Changes at Different Outlets	TOTALS
Delta Sample: Will Pay Premium for Speed	5	13	18
	27.8	72.2	—
	12.8	24.5	19.6
Delta Sample: Will Not Shop for Low Price	16	21	37
	43.2	56.8	—
	41.0	39.6	40.2
Delta Sample: Will Shop for Low Price	15	16	31
	48.4	51.6	—
	38.5	30.2	33.7
Delta Sample: Change Own Oil to Save Money	3	3	6
	50.0	50.0	—
	7.7	5.7	6.5
DELTA #	39.0	53.0	92
TOTALS %	42.4	57.6	100
	—	—	100
Rosemont Sample: Will Pay Premium for Speed	17	2	19
	89.5	10.5	—
	14.3	2.7	9.8
Rosemont Sample: Will Not Shop for Low Price	60	39	89
	67.4	32.6	—
	50.4	39.2	46.1
Rosemont Sample: Will Shop for Low Price	36	39	75
	48.0	52.0	—
	30.3	52.7	38.9
Rosemont Sample: Change Own Oil to Save Money	6	4	10
	60.0	40.0	—
	5.0	5.4	5.2
ROSEMONT #	119	74	193
TOTALS %	61.7	38.3	100
	—	—	100

EXHIBIT 7 (B)
Price Sensitivity X Combined Work Preferences (Q2d)

Count Row Percentage Column Percentage	Often Buy Oil Change Only	Often Combine with Other Service Work	Plan for Fewest Trips Possible	TOTALS
Delta Sample: Will Pay Premium for Speed	15 83.3 21.7	2 11.1 11.1	1 5.6 20.0	18 — 19.6
Delta Sample: Will Not Shop for Low Price	29 78.4 42.0	7 18.9 38.9	1 2.7 20.0	37 — 40.2
Delta Sample: Will Shop for Low Price	21 65.6 30.4	8 25.0 44.4	3 9.4 60.0	32 — 34.8
Delta Sample: Change Own Oil to Save Money	4 80.0 5.8	1 20.0 5.6		5 — 5.4
DELTA # **TOTALS** %	69.0 75.0 —	18.0 19.6 —	5.0 5.4 —	92 100.0 100.0
Rosemont Sample: Will Pay Premium for Speed	11 57.9 8.6	5 26.3 11.9	3 15.8 12.0	19 — 9.7
Rosemont Sample: Will Not Shop for Low Price	51 58.6 39.8	23 26.4 54.8	13 14.9 52.0	87 — 44.6
Rosemont Sample: Will Shop for Low Price	56 75.7 43.8	11 14.9 26.2	7 9.5 28.0	74 — 37.9
Rosement Sample: Change Own Oil to Save Money	10 66.7 7.9	3 20.0 7.2	2 13.3 8.0	15 — 7.7
ROSEMONT # **TOTALS** %	128 65.6 —	42 21.5 —	25 12.8 —	195 100.0 100.0

EXHIBIT 7 (C)   **Price Sensitivity X Last Outlet Patronized (Q2b)**

Count Row Percentage Column Percentage	Specialty Oil Change Outlet	Auto Dealer	Service Station	Department Store	Auto Chain	D.I.Y[a]	TOTALS
Will Pay Premium for Speed	11 57.9 17.2	5 26.3 10.0	3 15.8 8.8				19 — 9.4
Will Not Shop for Low Price	25 28.7 39.1	34 39.1 68.0	18 20.7 52.9	4 4.6 19.0	6 6.9 33.3		87 — 43.1
Will Shop for Low Price	26 35.1 40.6	10 13.5 20.0	11 14.9 32.4	15 20.3 71.4	12 16.2 66.7		74 — 36.6
Change Own Oil to Save Money	2 9.1 3.1	1 4.5 2.0	2 9.1 5.8	2 9.1 9.6		15 68.2 100.0	22 — 10.9
TOTALS # %	64 31.7 —	50 24.8 —	34 16.8 —	21 10.4 —	18 8.9 —	15 7.4 —	202 100.0 100.0

[a] D.I.Y. = Do-It-Yourself

EXHIBIT 7 (D)   **Price Sensitivity X Age (Q23b) (Rosemont only)**

Count Row Percentage Column Percentage	Under 25	26–35	36–50	51–65	Over 65	TOTALS
Will Pay Premium for Speed	3	3	6	6	1	19
	15.8	15.8	31.6	31.6	5.3	—
	16.7	8.3	7.5	11.3	5.6	9.3
Will Not Shop for Low Price	3	18	29	30	9	89
	3.4	20.2	32.6	33.7	10.1	—
	16.7	50.0	14.1	56.6	50.0	43.4
Will Shop for Low Price	10	13	33	12	6	74
	13.5	17.6	44.6	16.2	8.1	—
	55.6	36.1	41.3	22.6	33.3	36.1
Change Own Oil to Save Money	2	2	12	5	2	23
	8.7	8.7	52.2	21.7	8.7	—
	11.1	5.6	15.0	9.5	11.1	11.3
TOTALS	18	36	80	53	18	205
	8.8	17.6	39.0	25.9	8.8	100.0
	—	—	—	—	—	100.0

EXHIBIT 8 (A)   **Buying Behaviour X Outlet Last Patronized (Q2b) (All Respondents)**

Count Row Percentage Column Percentage		Oil Change Specialty	Auto Dealer	Service Station	Department Store	Auto Chain	D.I.Y[1]	TOTALS
Often Buy Oil		107	31	24	20	12	7	201
Change Only		53.2	15.4	11.9	10.0	6.0	3.5	—
		79.3	47.0	61.5	87.0	60.0	77.8	68.8
Often Combine Oil		20	23	10	1	6	1	61
Change & Other Work		32.8	37.7	16.4	1.6	9.8	1.6	—
		14.8	34.8	25.6	4.3	30.0	11.1	20.9
Plan Service Work for Fewest Trips		8	12	5	2	2	1	30
		26.7	40.0	16.7	6.7	6.7	3.3	—
		5.9	18.2	12.8	8.7	10.0	11.1	10.3
TOTALS	#	135	66	39	23	20	9	292
	%	46.2	22.6	13.4	7.9	6.8	3.1	100.0
		—	—	—	—	—	—	100.0

EXHIBIT 8 (B)   **Warranty Conditions X Last Outlet Patronized (All Respondents)**

Count Row Percentage Column Percentage		Oil Change Specialty	Auto Dealer	Service Station	Department Store	Auto Chain	D.I.Y[1]	TOTALS
Car Under Warranty		37	45	7	7	6	2	104
		35.6	43.3	6.7	6.7	5.8	1.9	—
		26.6	69.2	17.9	30.4	28.6	12.5	34.3
Car Not Under Warranty		102	20	32	16	15	14	199
		51.3	10.1	16.1	8.0	7.5	7.0	—
		73.4	30.8	82.1	69.6	71.4	87.5	65.7
TOTALS	#	139	65	39	23	21	16	303
	%	45.9	21.5	12.9	7.6	6.9	5.3	100.0
		—	—	—	—	—	—	100.0

EXHIBIT 8 (C)   Buying Behaviour X Outlet Loyalty (Q2c) (All Respondents)

Count Row Percentage Column Percentage		Last Four Purchases at Same Outlet	Last Four Purchases at Different Outlets	TOTALS
Often Buy Oil		97	101	198
Change Only		49.0	51.0	—
		61.8	75.9	68.3
Often Combine Oil Change & Other Work		37	24	61
		60.7	39.3	—
		23.6	18.0	21.0
Plan Service Work for Fewest Trips		23	8	31
		74.2	25.8	—
		14.6	6.0	10.7
	#	157	133	290
TOTALS	%	54.1	45.9	100.0
		—	—	100.0

EXHIBIT 8 (D)   Buying Behaviour X Score Awarded to "No Appointment Necessary" (Q6.9) (All Respondents)

Count Row Percentage Column Percentage		Low Score (1–2)	Medium Score (3–4)	High Score (5–10)	TOTALS
Often Buy Oil		31	72	36	139
Change Only		22.3	51.8	25.9	—
		83.8	80.9	81.8	81.8
Often Combine Oil Change & Other Work		4	10	6	20
		20.0	50.0	30.0	—
		10.8	11.2	13.6	11.8
Plan Service Work for Fewest Trips		2	7	2	11
		18.2	63.6	18.2	—
		5.4	7.9	4.5	6.5
	#	37	89	44	170
TOTALS	%	21.8	52.4	25.9	100.0
		—	—	—	100.0

EXHIBIT 8 (E)   Buying Behaviour X Score Awarded to Fast Service (Q6.4) (All Respondents)

Count Row Percentage Column Percentage		Low Score (1–2)	Medium Score (3–4)	High Score (5–10)	TOTALS
Often Buy Oil		16	81	41	138
Change Only		11.6	58.7	29.7	—
		53.3	81.0	82.0	76.7
Often Combine Oil Change & Other Work		9	13	5	27
		33.3	48.1	18.5	—
		30.0	13.0	10.0	15.0
Plan Service Work for Fewest Trips		5	6	4	15
		33.3	40.0	26.7	—
		16.7	6.0	8.0	8.3
	#	30	100	50	180
TOTALS	%	16.7	55.6	27.8	100.0
		—	—	—	100.0

EXHIBIT 8 (F) **Buying Behavior X Score Awarded to "One-Stop Shopping" (Q6.5) (All Respondents)**

Count Row Percentage Column Percentage		Low Score (1–2)	Medium Score (3–4)	High Score (5–10)	TOTALS
Often Buy Oil		9	14	14	37
Change Only		24.3	37.8	37.8	—
		47.4	35.0	42.4	40.2
Often Combine Oil Change & Other Work		6	19	13	38
		15.8	50.0	34.2	—
		31.6	47.5	39.4	41.3
Plan Service Work for Fewest Trips		4	7	6	17
		23.5	41.2	35.3	—
		21.1	17.5	18.2	18.5
	#	19	40	33	92
TOTALS	%	20.7	43.5	35.9	100.0
		—	—	—	100.0

CHAPTER 5

COMPETITIVE ANALYSIS AND PRODUCT POSITIONING

> A common problem is the assumption that competitors do things "the same way we do."
>
> ALAN ZAKON

*I*n business environments, domestic and international competitors are constantly attacking existing market positions. Firms that fail to respond to these challenges are destined for the scrap heap. Companies have come to realize that they must focus on global market share, not just domestic share. Toyota's "Global 10" strategy was based on their belief that they need at least 10 percent of the world market to remain strong. Gillette, the American consumer goods company, is the world leader in razor blades and razors. Its Papermate, Waterman, and Parker lines have a 15 percent revenue share of the world pen market—the next-biggest competitor is Societe BIC with 8 percent. Gillette's Oral-B toothbrush is the leading seller in the United States and several international markets and its Braun electric shaver is the top seller in Germany. Gillette sells in 200 countries. A key benefit of big market share is that it gives a company strong bargaining power with suppliers and distributors. Low costs mean that profits can grow faster than revenue.

Competitive analysis flows out of customer analysis. To truly know how you stack up against your competitors, you first need to understand your customers' wants and needs. Then you must identify both current and potential competitors in both your served and unserved markets. Industry analysis is also important. You need to know about the suppliers to your industry as well as channel members who serve as intermediaries between you and your competitors and the end users. These actors impact your competitive position. Once you have identified your competitors, it may be possible to group them by factors, such as degree of specialization or degree of globalization, to make it easier to discern patterns of competitive behavior. Now you should be in a position to do an in-depth analysis of competitors' strategies. You must be careful not to simply focus on what your competitors are doing now. You must consider where your competitors are going.

This chapter focuses on six issues:

1. Who are your competitors?
2. What are your relations with your competitors?
3. Where do you compete?
4. When do you compete?
5. How do you compete?
6. How do you position your product?

In addressing these issues a firm is examining its strengths and weaknesses, its opportunities and threats. This is known as *SWOT* analysis.

WHO ARE YOUR COMPETITORS?

You must know which of the many companies in the marketplace you are really competing with for your served market. You should respond most vigorously to those in direct competition. You also must be aware of those potential competitors who are not now in your market, but who may be in the future.

Current

One way of identifying who your competitors are is through *market structure analysis* using perceptual mapping. Products or brands that are perceived to be close together in perceptual space are more in competition with each other than those far apart.

Perceptual Mapping   Every market has a structure based on the strengths of brand attributes. The positioning of products in a market can be illustrated by a perceptual map such as the one shown in Figure 5-1 for automobiles. Perceptual maps are derived from customer

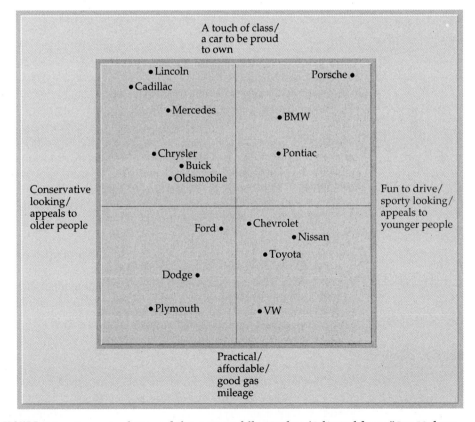

FIGURE 5-1   Perceptual Map of the Automobile Market (Adapted from "Car Makers Use 'Image' Map as Tool to Position Products," *The Wall Street Journal,* **March 22, 1984, p. 33. Reprinted with permission of** *The Wall Street Journal,* **© Dow Jones & Company, Inc. 1984. All rights reserved.)**

data measuring similarities among brands. Customers are asked to rate each pair of brands (e.g., Buick-Porsche) on a scale from very similar to very dissimilar. These ratings are fed into a computer program for doing multidimensional scaling. The program determines the relative positions of the brands and prints out a perceptual map.

APPLYING
. . . to
Consumer
Durables
Marketing

The location of the automobiles in Figure 5-1 is a direct measure of similarity across brands. Since Porsche and Plymouth are the farthest apart, customers view them as least similar. Notice that Buick and Oldsmobile are seen as the most similar. This result agrees with the findings of Figure 4-2 that showed these two brands were close in terms of customer age and income. General Motors has a serious problem with Buick and Oldsmobile since you do not want to compete with yourself. Better positioning has been achieved for Cadillac which is near Lincoln and Chevrolet which is near Ford. GM executives are sure to be ecstatic that the high-priced BMW is the closest car to Pontiac. This shows that Pontiac's marketing program has been effective in moving it into a desirable market position.

Map Dimensions   Dimensions for perceptual maps are not named by multidimensional scaling programs. Additional information must be gathered from customers to find the critical dimensions and locate them on the maps. Labeling dimensions of perceptual maps and interpreting these diagrams is rather subjective. This does not lessen the value of perceptual maps, but it does mean you have to evaluate them carefully.

Dimensions for perceptual maps are often obtained by asking customers to describe the benefits (e.g., economy, durability, ease of service) they associate with each of the brands. These ratings are then fitted to the perceptual space as shown in Figure 5-1. In this diagram the vertical axis has been named "a touch of class" at the top and "practical/affordable" at the bottom. The horizontal axis has a "conservative/older dimension" to the left and a "sporty/younger" dimension to the right. You may note that these dimensions are similar to the age and income axes of Figure 4-2. Although Figure 5-1 has two labeled dimensions, some perceptual maps have more and some less.

Perceptual map dimensions are vital in the preparation of marketing plans. Once you understand the dimensions that customers use to evaluate products, you are better able to design products to fill their needs. This applies both to modifications to strengthen the positions of existing products and in the design of new items to fill gaps in perceptual maps. In addition, map dimensions are useful when you want to reposition products through the use of advertising. For example, General Motors has been successful using advertising to give Pontiac a stronger sporty/youth image. In addition, Oldsmobile has run an ad campaign with the slogan "It's not your father's Oldsmobile" in an effort to attract younger buyers.

Ideal Points   Once you have labeled the dimensions of your perceptual map, the next step is to add in some information on personal preferences. Each customer can be represented on your map by a point showing that individual's ideal product. Ideal points are person points. Clusters of ideal points indicate where there are sufficient prospects to justify current and new products.

Potential Entrants

While focusing on your current competitors, you must be alert for the emergence of new competitors. The possibility of newcomers to an industry depends on two things: the barriers to entry that exist and expectations about competitive reactions. The barriers to entry include economies of scale, product differentiation, capital requirements, buyer switching costs, access to distribution channels, other cost disadvantages, and government policy. These factors are often interrelated. The need for economies of scale requires capital for plant construction, whereas overcoming existing brand identification and customer loyalty through product differentiation requires capital for advertising. The costs of a buyer switching to your product from that of your competitor may be formidable. For example, although many new software products are better than those already in use, they fail. The problem is not awareness of the product or the price of the product, but the cost of retraining personnel to use the new software. A new entrant may find the best distributors already under contract and retailers demanding compensation to provide scarce space. Existing firms may also have proprietary product technology, favorable access to raw materials, favorable locations, government subsidies, or other cost advantages. Governments can limit or prevent entry with regulations such as licensing. For example, foreign distillers find it hard to sell vodka to the Russians. One reason is that the Russian government imposed high taxes and import duties to protect the "strategic" vodka industry.

Potential entrants may be deterred if they expect forceful competitive reaction. Conditions under which the likelihood of reaction is high include a past history of vigorous retaliation, established firms with significant resources to fight back, established firms with commitment to the industry, and slow industry growth.

WHAT ARE YOUR RELATIONS WITH YOUR COMPETITORS?

While the primary relationship with your competitors will be a competitive one, your relationship with them may take some other form. The relationship between competitors is a continuum from conflict to collusion, passing through competition, coexistence, and cooperation along the way.[1]

Conflict

APPLYING
. . . to
Consumer
Energy
Marketing

The focus of conflict is your opponent. Confrontation is likely to occur, for example, when you have a market share growth objective in a stagnant market. You can only gain share by wresting it from competitors. More generally conflict may occur when competitors have mutually incompatible objectives. Consider the Georgia natural gas service market. For decades Atlanta Gas Light Co. had a monopoly. Then the state Public Service Commission decided to deregulate the industry, restricting Atlanta Gas Light to the natural gas transportation business only. Nineteen companies jumped in to sell natural gas. Many gave their expected market shares: EnergyOne 20–30 percent, Columbia Energy 10–20 percent, Energy America 15 percent, Shell Energy Services 10–15 percent, Scana Energy 10 percent, United Gas Management 10 percent, and so on. Atlanta Gas Light's new separate gas marketing subsidiary, Georgia Natural Gas Services, simply said that it expected to be one of the leaders.[2] The expected market shares of these gas marketers add up to much more than 100 percent. These market share objectives are mutually inconsistent, and they must lead to a fight. Threats to a company's position may elicit a harsh reaction.

Competition

Competition is object centered. Competitors strive to win the same prize—the customer. The degree of competition will depend mainly on market attractiveness (market size and growth rate, economic climate, possibilities for economies of scale, technological innovation, differentiation, and segmentation) and industry structure (number of competitors, diversity of competitors and their commitment to industry, ease of entry and barriers to exit). The competition among brands in an industry is often called "The Battle of the Brands." An example of the battle of the brands is given in Marketing in Action box 5-1. Much of the remainder of the chapter will focus on these battles.

APPLYING
. . . *to*
Consumer
Packaged
Goods
Marketing

MARKETING IN ACTION 5-1

Bathroom Brawl

Kimberly-Clark is a relative newcomer in the $3.5 billion-a-year U.S. toilet paper business. Its original Kleenex toilet-tissue brand struggled after its introduction in 1990. The company merged with Scott Paper, maker of the Scott and Cottonelle brands, in 1995 and created Kleenex Cottonelle, which helped Kimberly-Clark gain a 23% share of the market. But it trails rival Procter & Gamble's Charmin, which has 30%. Among premium tissues, Kleenex Cottonelle still ranks a distant fourth behind Charmin, Fort James's Northern and Georgia-Pacific's Angel Soft.

Overall, bath-tissue sales are flat and premium brands are losing share to economy-priced tissue. Many toilet-paper consumers treat the brands as interchangeable and simply shop for the best deal. Even the industry's most recent innovation—the triple-sized roll from Charmin is about value, rather than improved performance. Marketers of bathroom tissue have used everything from puffy clouds to cuddly babies to advertise their products. Now Kimberly-Clark wants to talk about the real reason that people use toilet paper.

Testing the limits of how much consumers want to hear about what goes on in the bathroom, the maker of Kleenex Cottonelle spent $100 million to promote the brand as the toilet paper that wipes better than regular tissue, thanks to a new "rippled texture." In conjunction with new advertisements, ten million free samples were hung on doorknobs in the Eastern United States, where the product was first introduced.

The rippled texture is the result of a patented technology that dries the tissue during manufacturing without crushing it flat and later embossing it. This method also allows the tissue to hold its rippled shape when wet, allowing it to clean better. Thanks to a $170 million investment in a manufacturing operation, the process uses less fiber while improving the bulk and strength of the tissue. As a result, the company's manufacturing costs per roll are 20% less than those for other premium tissues. With the price to consumers remaining the same, the extra margin will help Kleenex Cottonelle better withstand the price wars plaguing the tissue category and let the company spend more on marketing and advertising to grab market share.

Kimberly-Clark hosted focus groups to talk to consumers about toilet paper, and asked them to compare leading brands with the new Kleenex Cottonelle textured tissue. They discovered that even though tissue advertising doesn't talk about how well a toilet paper wipes, that is what customers are thinking about. Nonetheless, Kimberly-Clark marketing executives quickly discovered there were limits to what they could say.

Talking about the way a toilet paper performs is a major departure for a category that for years has focused on squeezable softness, quilted softness and cottony softness. Are consumers who are used to seeing Mr. Whipple squeeze the Charmin ready to hear even a hint of what he does with the product? Kimberly-Clark is convinced that they are. "It's a very delicate thing, but it has the potential, if it's done right, of taking a major share of the toilet paper market."

The $100 million launch budget was more than double what Kimberly-Clark spent on the brand the previous year. About $20 million to $30 million went toward national television advertising, including 18 weeks of primetime TV. In addition to the door-to-door sampling, another million single rolls were made available in stores for 50 cents each in the Eastern U.S.

— *Meeting consumer needs better than your competitors is important in the "battle of the brands."*

Courtesy Kimberly-Clark

Source: Tar Parker-Pope, "The Tricky Business of Rolling Out a New Toilet Paper," *The Wall Street Journal,* January 12, 1998, pp. B1, B8.

Coexistence

Coexistence is working toward a goal independent of others. Coexistence occurs when competitors define different niches of a market to dominate. For example, this happens in distribution where retail outlets have local monopolies in their core geographic areas.

Cooperation

Cooperation involves working together toward a common goal. A typology of formal forms of cooperation is shown in Figure 5-2. The main types are dyadic, joint activity, and investment in a third party. In the seed business, some major technology developers have acquired distribution networks outright, while others have formed marketing agreements to sell the products of their research. One of the industry's alliances, an illustration of joint activity, is between Novartis and Beck's Superior Hybrids. The companies signed an agreement to bring NK Bt corn hybrids to the eastern corn belt. The partnership benefits Beck's by enabling it to get a Bt product to the market fast, and Novartis gets its Bt technology planted on more acres, which in turn will help it recoup some R&D money. Another illustration of joint activity cooperation is given in Marketing in Action box 5-2. An example of an investment in a third-party alliance is Agri Tech Inc., a joint venture formed by StarSeed Inc. and DeLange Seed Inc. Agri Tech has been licensed to produce and distribute Roundup Ready soybeans. It markets the consolidated soybean line-up of each of its partners.[3] These examples show the business reasons for cooperation: speed to marketplace, new market potential, technology access, and market share protection.

APPLYING *. . . to Agribusiness Marketing*

Collusion

Collusion is cooperative behavior designed to injure third parties—customers, suppliers, noncolluding competitors, or the general public. Oftentimes collusive behavior is illegal. Collusion may be explicit involving direct communication among the parties. Such communication may take place at trade association meetings or industry conventions. Sometimes the government is a party to collusion. The intent is to protect existing domestic firms, especially from foreign firms.

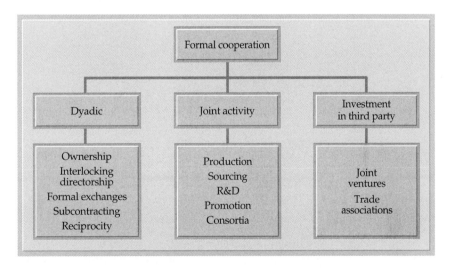

FIGURE 5-2 Typology of Forms of Formal Intercompetitor Cooperation (*Source: Geoffrey Easton, "Relationships Among Competitors" in The Interface of Marketing and Strategy,* in George Day, Barton Weitz, and Robin Wensley, eds. [Greenwich, CT: 1990], p. 73.)

APPLYING
. . . to
Pharma-
ceutical
Marketing

MARKETING IN ACTION 5-2

Building Alliances with Competitors

Not so long ago, the American pharmaceutical behemoth Warner-Lambert was regarded with contempt on Wall Street. Its number one prescription drug, the cholesterol medication Lopid, was about to come off patent, imperiling its only bright spot. Regulatory problems and a product recall, which cost it an estimated $1 billion, had brought the company to the edge of disaster. Its product lines were a ho-hum hodgepodge of everything from Listerine to prescription drugs. No new products appeared even close to being market-ready. Things had become so bleak that everybody told the company to sell out while it still could. Or at least get rid of the pharmaceutical division and stick to mouthwash.

Warner-Lambert chose radical surgery, selling two lackluster divisions—Pro toothbrush and Warner Chilcott—and ordering across-the-board cost-cutting to save 10% a year. Warner-Lambert had one promising new product, a cholesterol drug, Lipitor. It threw out the rulebook by striking a deal with rival Pfizer to co-market the new drug. Admitting it couldn't market the product on its own got Lipitor on the shelf two years ahead of schedule. It became the first drug to produce sales of over $1 billion in its first year. Released a few months after Lipitor, Rezulin, a diabetes drug, became a billion dollar drug too. Warner-Lambert's market cap increased an astonishing 750% over four years.

— *You and your competitor may both benefit from working together.*

Source: Stephan Herrara, "Health Care Products: Sow's-Ear-Into-Silk-Purse Tale," *Forbes,* January 11, 1999, pp. 180–181.

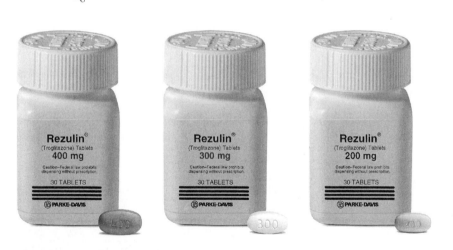

Courtesy Warner-Lambert Company

Collusion is sometimes indirect, which would involve signaling. A firm can make an announcement to test competitor sentiments. Competitive firms then can reply by making announcements communicating their pleasure or displeasure with competitive developments in the industry. If the industry responds negatively, the firm need not follow through with its intended action. Signaling occurs frequently in the airline industry. You must be able to discern between market signals that are truthful indications of a competitor's intentions and those that are bluffs.

HOW DO YOU LEARN ABOUT YOUR COMPETITORS?

The more and better the competitive information available to you, the sounder will be your marketing decisions. For competitive information to be helpful, you must process it in a methodical manner. This involves five steps.[4]

1. Set up an information-gathering system for competitive analysis.
2. Identify your competitors.
3. Gather information through a competitive audit.
4. Evaluate competitive information.
5. Integrate this information into your planning process on a regular basis.

This process forces you to consider competitive actions and reactions in formulating and executing your marketing strategies and tactics.

The *competitive audit* can generate a lot of information about your competitors. You must decide what is worth keeping. Each piece of information has to be evaluated on source reliability and information accuracy. An example of a competitor profile that could come out of a competitive analysis is given in Table 5-1. This profile is for competitors of an Internet service provider.

TABLE 5-1 Competitor Profiling

Company	America Online, Inc./Netscape Communications Corp.	At Home Corp./Excite Inc.
Strengths	• 16 million AOL service members • 31 million viewers of AOL's Web sites, or 54.% of total audience • 17.5 million viewers of Netscape's Web sites, or 30.9% of total audience • Ease of use thanks to AOL's proprietary software which guides users to selected content • Netscape's browser, loaded with features that tie in to Netscape Web site	• 331,000 At Home subscribers • 16.6 million viewers of Excite sites, or 29.2% of total audience • Distribution—thanks to 60 million homes served by At Home's cable partners • Cable operators locked into exclusive deals • On At Home service, users are connected full-time—they don't need to dial up • Extensive personalization features that deliver local news and weather
Weaknesses	• Encroachment upon its core home-user market from high-speed cable services	• Cable partners have been slow to market At Home's services • AOL and competitors are lobbying for access to cable systems, potentially negating At Home's advantages
General information	• Typical users: families looking for an easy way to get online • Acquiring Netscape to reach business customers • The biggest just keeps getting bigger	• Typical users: Power Web users who lust after At Home's high-speed connections; experienced users who prefer Excite to Yahoo • Not the biggest, but at the forefront of redefining portals from Web sites to next-generation telecommunication providers

Source: Thomas E. Weber, "The Emerging Armies of the Web," *The Wall Street Journal,* February 11, 1999, p. B1.

You are now in a position to formulate your marketing strategy by considering three key issues: where to compete, when to compete, and how to compete. We conclude with a discussion of product positioning.

WHERE DO YOU COMPETE?

Choosing market arenas to seek competitive advantage depends on market attractiveness and organization strengths. Your job as marketing manager is to pick the best of a variety of strategic options. Most firms compete somewhere on a continuum from "avoid competition" to "attack market leader." Market leaders go after the core market. Unless the leader experiences marketing inertia or encounters some disruption in the marketplace, you may want to resegment the market and target a niche. You want to establish a niche that is defensible against its imitators. This can be successful, at least in the short run. The danger is that the niche may grow and attract other larger firms.

To the extent that competing companies focus on matching and beating their rivals, their strategies tend to converge along the same basic lines of competition. They share a conventional wisdom about their industry. The companies end up competing on marginal differences. To break free from the competitive pack, you must *create new market space.* A systematic approach to value innovation requires that you "think outside the box" by looking (1) across substitute industries with whom you implicitly compete, (2) across strategic groups within your industry, (3) along the chain of "players" who are directly or indirectly involved in the buying decision, (4) across complementary product and service offerings, (5) beyond the current functional-emotional orientation taken by your industry in making appeals to customers, and (6) ahead to how emerging trends will change value to customers.[5]

WHEN DO YOU COMPETE?

The ability to compete often depends on *strategic windows* of opportunity. Strategic windows are openings in the competitive map that can be exploited at a point in time. Remember that windows that are open one moment can be closed another. To take advantage of strategic windows, you first have to be able to see them, then you have to be ready to make a move before they close. This requires insight and flexibility.

Table 5-2 provides several examples of strategic windows and shows how four firms reacted. The rapid penetration of microwave ovens into American homes opened a large strategic window for cookware. Metal pans could not be used in these ovens and everyone buying a microwave oven was an immediate customer for new pots and pans. Corning was in an excellent position to take advantage of this technology change, because they were experts at making ceramic and glass dishes for conventional ovens. However, they did not read this opportunity correctly and failed to push existing items or develop new ones until competitors had grabbed strong market positions. This lack of attention to market conditions for mature product lines is all too common and may explain why Corning spun off their housewares division to a Mexican firm.

In the case of home-delivered pizza (Table 5-2), Pizza Hut and other national chains had strong national positions in restaurant-served pizza long before Domino's came along. However, Domino's was the first to see the open window of the home-delivered pizza customer and they moved rapidly to capture many of these markets. Domino's strategy put Pizza Hut on the defensive and forced them to play an expensive game of catch-up.

APPLYING *...to Consumer Household Products Marketing*

APPLYING *...to Food Home Delivery Retailing*

TABLE 5-2 Examples of Strategic Windows

Company	Window Opportunity	Opportunity Seized	Marketing Strategy
Corning Glass Works (microwave cookware)	The microwave oven boom created a major need for "safe" cookware. Corning could immediately meet the needs of this emerging market	No	Delayed aggressively marketing existing products and developing new products until after competitors had gained important market positions
Domino's Pizza (home-delivered pizza)	Recognition of consumers' needs for rapid and reliable home delivery of pizza. No major competitive force was present at the time Domino's entered the market.	Yes	Responsive home delivery of pizza from a network of retail outlets. The company emphasizes quality, speed of delivery, courteous employees, and hot pizza
Lens Crafters (eyewear chain)	Opportunity to develop customer-responsive services in an industry dominated by optometrists.	Yes	Launched a chain of retail shops conveniently located in malls, offering eye exams and one-hour glasses
United Airlines (air travel)	Deregulation, restructuring, and an opportunity for marketing leadership due to dominant position in U.S. market. Held strong market position at the time of deregulation	No	Did not expand services and marketing capabilities to strengthen position and gain advantage. United lost market position to more aggressive competitors.

Source: David W. Cravens, "Gaining Strategic Marketing Advantage," *Business Horizons*, Vol. 31, No. 4 (September–October 1988), p. 53.

Vulnerability of Market Leaders

APPLYING
. . . *to*
OTC
Drugs
Marketing

Market leaders can be vulnerable to external forces beyond their control. These forces include government or environmental challenge, a random catastrophe, a change in industry technology, and a new "personality" in the industry. A government or environmental challenge can distract a market leader and weaken brand loyalty. When concerns mounted about phenolphthalein, the main ingredient in Correctol, Ex-Lax, and Phillips' Gelcaps laxatives, as a potential cancer risk, Correctol reformulated its product. Ex-Lax ran television ads showing two sisters discussing the fact that Correctol officials had "changed their medicine," and suggesting that it didn't work as well. Correctol ran newspaper ads pointing out that a government panel has determined that some laxatives "may cause cancer," and suggesting that Ex-Lax might need to be recalled. It also provided a toll-free number for concerned consumers. Then the U.S. Food and Drug Administration proposed banning phenolphthalein. Ex-Lax's manufacturer immediately announced a voluntary recall and plans to reformulate the product with a different ingredient. Correctol began running ads reminding consumers that Ex-Lax was being withdrawn.[6] A new "personality"—a successful firm in a related, or even different, industry—may be able to transfer its marketing expertise into the market leader's industry.

The technology used in an industry may change because of the expiration of patents or the emergence of new technologies. The expiration of patents is less a problem than would first appear. This is because a firm usually builds substantial brand equity during its period of patent protection. This raises a barrier of high marketing costs that any new entrant must overcome. Perhaps the most common challenge to market leaders is the introduction by competitors of new products for market niches. Two market leaders that handled this confrontation differently are Gillette and Schwinn.

APPLYING
. . . to
Health and
Beauty Aids
Marketing

Gillette invented the safety razor and has long dominated the U.S. wet shaving market. In 1962, a relatively small company, Wilkinson Sword Ltd., introduced the first coated stainless steel blade, cutting sharply into Gillette's market share. Gillette swallowed its pride and brought out its own stainless steel blade. This humbling experience taught Gillette several important lessons: (1) Never take a rival for granted, no matter how small; (2) don't concede market niches to competitors because market niches have a way of growing; (3) don't delay bringing out new products for fear of cannibalizing old ones-if you don't introduce, competitors will. Gillette's obsession with defending its core market has led to the expenditure of hundreds of millions of dollars on new shaving products. These efforts resulted in the innovative twin-blade Track II in 1972, the pivoting head Atra in 1977, the hugely successful Sensor, with independently suspended blades in 1989, and the MACH3 in 1998. The company also rushed out a disposable razor in 1976 to fend off French rival Bic, even though the cheap throwaways cut into sales of higher profit Gillette products. The net result of Gillette's attention to its core shaving business is that it has 64 percent of the U.S, market, 70 of the European market, and 80 percent of the Latin American market.

APPLYING
. . . to
Consumer
Semi-
Durables
Marketing

Schwinn, on the other hand, failed to implement strategies to protect its strong position in the U.S. bicycle market. Schwinn started selling bikes in 1895 and for years was the dominant U.S. brand. Their market share peaked in the 1960s with more than 25 percent of the market. Schwinn's market position was based on a reputation for quality and a powerful distribution system of exclusive dealers. In the 1980s, however, the company made a series of strategic blunders. Customer interest shifted to mountain bikes and exotic frames made of aluminum and carbon fiber. Schwinn refused to spend money to develop new products for these niche markets, and became a follower instead of a product innovator. Unfortunately for Schwinn, the mountain bike niche grew to command 60 percent of the market. Then, in 1981, workers at its main plant in Chicago went on strike. Instead of settling, Schwinn closed the plant and shipped its engineers and equipment to a plant in Taiwan that they did not own. This move cut production costs, but led to quality problems and overdependence on foreign suppliers. Schwinn's delays in developing new products and its shift to overseas production resulted in its sale in bankruptcy court in 1993. The lesson to be learned from Gillette and Schwinn is that firms that fail to protect markets from competitors often regret it.

When there is no strong number-two firm in a market, a competitor seeking to "fill the vacuum" often damages the leader in the process. Ragu held 70 percent of the U.S. spaghetti sauce market to Chef Boy-R-Dee's 11 percent. The lack of a strong number-two brand attracted Hunt's Prima Salsa and Campbell's Prego into the market. Prego emerged as the new number-two brand at the expense of Ragu.

Market leaders may be leery of cutting prices because they will lose the most from a price cut. Even in mature markets, new positioning opportunities arise. A market leader from a small firm with limited resources is very vulnerable. Finally, a strong number two company may not have as much distribution as the leader. The temptation for the number-two firm is to expand its coverage into new markets.

A market leader has only itself to blame if it is lethargic, has a significant strategic weakness, or has alienated a key distribution channel. Lethargy may arise because the leader is "conservative" and fails to make a commitment to "raise the stakes" for competitors, favors financial goals over marketing goals, is in a market that makes up only a small part of the firm's overall business, fears cannibalism, or is preoccupied elsewhere. Family-owned businesses such as Wrigley's gum are often slow to introduce new products, opening themselves up to competitive initiatives. Vlasic was able to attack and become number one in pickles because pickles were a relatively inconsequential market to Heinz and Borden. Coca-Cola was very slow to take advantage of Coke's tremendous market identification because the company did not want to dilute the Coke name. John Deere was able to wrest the farm equipment leadership away from International Harvester because IR was focusing its attention on trucks. A leader may have a significant weakness in its strategy. Hershey's long-standing policy against national media advertising made it vulnerable to a challenge by Mars. Finally, the leader may alienate key distributors which may result in the competition's using the betrayed channel to gain ground or even the channel itself emerging as a competitor. For example, Lee jeans took advantage of the opportunity that arose when Levi Strauss stopped using jeans stores exclusively to add new mass merchandising outlets. These examples suggest that followers must be sensitive to market leaders' problems so they can be exploited to gain share.

HOW DO YOU COMPETE?

In the battle with competitors, organizations must decide on what dimensions to attack or defend. This decision is based, in part, on the size of the firm relative to its competitors. It will also depend on the strategies that are viable in a particular industry.

Offensive Strategies

The guiding principle for attack is to concentrate strength against the competitors' relative weakness. Attack strategies include (1) frontal attack, (2) flanking attack, (3) encirclement attack, (4) bypass attack, and (5) guerrilla warfare. A frontal attack means taking on a competitor head-on. This is one of the most difficult and dangerous of all marketing strategies. To be successful, the firm must have a substantial marketing advantage or deep pockets. For instance, the firm might have a similar product, but be able to sell it at a lower price. A flanking attack is appropriate for segments of the market where customer needs are not being fully met. This may simply mean fighting in geographical regions of a country or the world, where the competition is weak. More likely, it means bringing out new products for emerging segments of the market. Flanking addresses gaps in existing market coverage of the competition. An encirclement attack, known also as an envelopment attack, involves forcing the competitor to spread its resources thin by probing on many fronts at once. Again, superior resources are required. The intent is to break the competitor's will. A bypass attack is one of nonconfrontation. The firm diversifies into unrelated products or diversifies into new markets for existing products. Guerrilla warfare entails small, intermittent attacks on a competitor. One goal might be to slice off small amounts of share while evoking minimal competitive reaction.

Defense Strategies

Defense strategies exist to counter each offensive strategy. The six main defense strategies are (1) position defense, (2) mobile defense, (3) preemptive defense, (4) flank-positioning defense, (5) counteroffensive defense, and (6) strategic withdrawal. The position defense requires that the firm fortify its existing position. The main risk in this strategy is marketing myopia. Redesigning or reformulating your product can keep you one step ahead of the competition. An example is given in Marketing Strategies box 5-1. A mobile defense is a defense in depth. The firm engages in market broadening. Unattacked markets can subsidize the firm's activities in more competitive markets. A preemptive defense is attacking first. This first-strike strategy could use any of the attack strategies previously mentioned. The flank-positioning defense extends the firm's offerings into new segments to protect the positioning of the firm's existing products. The counteroffensive defense involves amassing resources and counterattacking whenever threatened. Sometimes a strategic withdrawal is necessary. With this approach firms consolidate their positions by competing only where they have competitive advantages.

APPLYING
. . . to
*Consumer
Packaged
Goods
Marketing*

MARKETING STRATEGIES *5-1*

New and Improved

Procter & Gamble Co.'s Downy has a commanding 65% of the $750 million liquid fabric conditioner category. However, Lever recently boosted marketing support for No. 2 brand, Snuggle. And USA Detergents grabbed about a 6% share of the category in the past year with its new Nice & Fluffy value brand.

P&G is protecting its position by rolling out an improved Downy that uses a new technology to protect fabric colors. Procter & Gamble Co. is backing the rollout with an estimated $15 million to $20 million campaign, hoping that color protection technology can do for a fabric softener what it did for laundry detergent. The TV and print campaign is tagged "Come on in to Downy care," and in the advertising P&G claims that "new Downy" can prevent fading.

Downy's color protection differs from the carenzyme technology introduced in recent years in P&G's Tide and Cheer detergent brands to prevent fading and fuzzing of cotton fabrics. Downy's color ingredient is designed to work in the rinse cycle rather than the wash cycle and to prevent hard-water deposits and other impurities from damaging clothes. Though competitors Lever Bros. and Dial Corp. have since added color protection ingredients to their brands, carenzyme helped P&G's Tide and Cheer add several share points earlier in the decade. Combined, the two brands held 45% of the $4.3 billion laundry detergent category.

One observer cautioned that P&G might be stretching color protection too thin. "They may be solving a real consumer problem but is it a fabric softener problem?"

— *You cannot rest on your laurels.*

Source: Jack Neff, "P&G Promotes Downy as 'New' and Improved," *Advertising Age,* September 29, 1997, p. 18.

Defensive Tactics   Most defensive strategies are built around three classes of defensive tactics: raising structural barriers, increasing expected retaliation, and lowering inducement for attack. The emphasis is on deterring a competitor from taking action against you. Market leaders can raise structural barriers by filling product or positioning gaps, blocking channel access, raising buyer switching costs, raising the cost of gaining trial, increasing scale and capital requirements, or encouraging government policies that create barriers. Flanking brands and fighting brands can fill product or positioning gaps. Channel access can be blocked through the use of exclusive dealerships; the proliferation of products, brands, varieties, and sizes; and aggressive trade promotions. Providing special services can raise buyer-switching costs. The cost of gaining trial can be raised by customer sales promotions. Scale economies and capital requirements can be increased by increasing advertising expenditures, introducing new products, extending warranty coverage, and providing below market credit financing.

A market leader must let its competitors know that there will be retaliation for any attacks on it. A firm can signal its intentions through public statements at trade meetings and in the business press. In particular, the firm can resolve to match or beat any competitive move. Disrupting market tests or introductory markets can blunt actual attacks. A market leader can lower the inducement for attack by reducing its own profit targets or by manipulating competitor assumptions about the future of the industry.

A number of promotional tactics can be used to protect the market positions of established brands from new product introductions. The idea is to attack new brands when they are vulnerable to forgo short-run profits to retard or block the entry of competitive items. A classic approach is to introduce additional brands in the same product class to preempt shelf space and to deprive actual or potential competitors of profits or resources needed to compete in a market.

APPLYING
. . . to
*Consumer
Beverages
Marketing*

The ability of market leaders to fend off new entrants with defensive tactics is illustrated by events in the orange juice market. Minute Maid, owned by Coca-Cola, and Tropicana, owned by PepsiCo, are the dominant deep-pocket players in this business. Procter & Gamble launched a frontal attack on the two market leaders with its Citrus Hill brand.

P&G advertised heavily, used cents-off coupons, added calcium to its juice, and tried a screw-top spout. Minute Maid and Tropicana fought P&G's every move and prevented it from establishing needed brand loyalty. Citrus Hill never gained more than 8 percent of the orange juice market, and P&G finally abandoned it after an investment of $200 million. Defensive strategies can work for established brands, but when they don't, withdrawal may be necessary.

Withdrawal   The proper use of withdrawal is one of the more delicate maneuvers you may have to make as a marketing manager. Your objective is to cut your losses so resources can be moved to businesses with better prospects for growth. However, many managers are reluctant to give up on a business for fear the finger-pointing will hurt their careers. An example of a typical scenario occurred at Pet Inc. when the Whitman's Chocolates unit they purchased did not live up to expectations. Pet responded by firing the manager and selling the business. Johnson & Johnson has done a better job of strategic withdrawal. They continuously review their businesses to make sure they are fit and performing up to company standards. J&J takes the attitude that pruning the business tree of unhealthy units is just a natural activity when following a growth strategy. One J&J manager closed down a kidney-dialysis equipment business and a heart surgery equipment business before he became the manager of a successful disposable contact lens business.

HOW DO YOU POSITION YOUR PRODUCT?

You have been introduced to the concepts of segmentation and differentiation, so we now shift our attention to finding out how customers view our products relative to the competition. Product positioning focuses on buyers' perceptions about the location of brands within specific market segments. These positions are based on how well perceived product characteristics match up with the needs of the buyer.

The Majority Fallacy

Marketing managers are often concerned with positioning new products in established markets. Companies that are the first in a market can position themselves to appeal to the majority of customers, but this has less attraction for firms that enter late. Some of the factors influencing this decision can be shown by using the preference distribution shown in Figure 5-3. The distribution shows the proportion of customers that prefers each of three different levels of chocolate flavoring for ice cream. Preferences are displayed both as a histogram and as the smooth distribution that would result if a great many flavors of ice cream had been evaluated by buyers.

This diagram suggests that if three levels of chocolate flavoring were available, 60 percent of the customers would choose medium, 20 percent would select light, and 20 percent would choose heavy. With these preferences known, the first company to enter the market would maximize revenue by selling ice cream with a medium level of chocolate flavoring. However, if three companies divide the medium chocolate-flavored market equally, then the optimum position for succeeding entries is not immediately clear. If a new firm compared customer preferences for a light level of flavoring with the medium level brands already on the market, the medium chocolate ice cream would be preferred by most customers. Unfortunately, the firm might interpret these results to mean that the best way to enter the market would be with a medium chocolate-flavored ice cream. A new medium flavor might be expected to capture one-fourth of the 60 percent in the middle or only about 15 percent of the total market. The potential for a new light flavor, by comparison, is a full 20 percent of the customers. This example shows how the *majority fallacy* can lead an unwary firm into

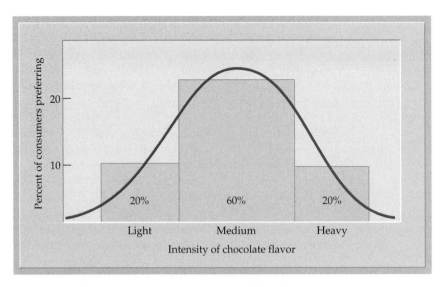

FIGURE 5-3   Customer Preferences for Chocolate Flavoring of Ice Cream

merely duplicating existing characteristics. The "fallacy" is that competition is ignored. Obviously, the "majority" of consumers do not have to prefer a particular product for it to be successful.

APPLYING
. . . to
Consumer
Food
Products
Marketing

One product category that illustrates the majority fallacy is spaghetti sauce. A few years ago relatively little product variation existed and most brands imitated the dominant brand Ragu. Ragu occupied a position near the center of a continuum from heavy, rich, spicy sauces on one end to light, thin, and sweet sauces on the other. Hunt tried to exploit differences for spaghetti sauce by introducing its Prima Salsa brand, which was much thicker and zestier than Ragu sauce. Hunt compared its new thick sauce directly with Ragu, using personal testimonials and a heavy schedule of TV and print ads. Prima Salsa's initial success attracted Campbell Soup, which introduced more spaghetti sauce variations under its Prego label. Prego was helped by a *Consumer Reports* article that rated its salt-free flavor as the best sauce available. As a result, Ragu was forced to add a variety of new products of its own. Today Ragu and Prego are continuing to bring out new flavors of spaghetti sauce to appeal to special segments of the market.

Repositioning Strategies

Perceptual maps with dimensions and clusters of customer ideal points are valuable for the management of new and existing products. A frequent problem is deciding whether to reposition a product and in what direction to move. This issue is usually a trade-off between maintaining the benefits of the existing position and possible sales gains associated with new positions. When your current position is weak, it is easier to make a case for repositioning.

APPLYING
. . . to
Consumer
Beverages
Marketing

For example, Miller beer was once sold as the "Champagne of bottled beers" to the high-income, lighter-beer-drinking segment. When Philip Morris bought the brand it had only 3.4 percent of the market and they decided to reposition Miller to appeal to heavier drinking blue-collar buyers. The "Miller Time" campaign featuring working men enjoying a Miller at day's end successfully moved the brand up to 22 percent of the market.

Creating Gaps   Repositioning decisions are more difficult when there is something to lose. For example, Chrysler, now Daimler-Chrysler, interpreted the perceptual map shown in Figure 4-5 to suggest that their cars needed a more youthful image. They also concluded that

Plymouth and Dodge needed to move up on the luxury scale. If Chrysler is successful in its efforts to appeal to a more youthful market, then they will give up the conservative older market to Buick and Oldsmobile. Further if Plymouth and Dodge are repositioned as luxury cars, what will Chrysler have to sell to buyers interested in practical low-priced cars? These examples suggest that you have to be sure that repositioning does not create new markets to be exploited by your competition.

In addition, you should realize that a gap in a perceptual map does not necessarily mean that there is an attractive market waiting to be exploited. Customer preferences change over time and a gap may mean that few buyers are currently interested in that combination of product attributes. This suggests that you need to know the number of potential buyers involved before you rush in to fill a "gap" in a perceptual map.

Serving Multiple Segments Another problem is how to keep one group of customers happy while attracting new segments needed to build future sales. Levi-Strauss's line of casual and dress pants, Dockers and Slates, have sold well, but its blue jeans hit a rough patch. Blue jeans are bought largely by men and Levi's share of men's jeans market dropped from 48 percent to 21 percent in less than a decade. The number of teen boys who cited Levi's as one of their favorite jeans brands dropped from 31 percent to 21 percent in five years. Teens drive fashion trends but that only belatedly seemed to dawn on Levi-Strauss. The company then launched an aggressive series of ads aimed at 15- to 19-year-olds. But Levi's seemed to overcorrect. Its TV commercials were far less mainstream than those of its competitors. Any firm that expects to survive in the long run must find a way to capture a share of the entry-level buyers.

Cannibalism A common reason for repositioning is a discovery that you have two brands occupying the same location on a perceptual map. This generally leads to an unacceptable level of cannibalism. For example, Procter & Gamble found that customers perceived two of their detergents as being identical. In this particular case, Procter & Gamble dropped one brand rather than attempt repositioning. However, merging Buick and Oldsmobile is not an attractive alternative to General Motors. They have spent millions of dollars establishing name recognition and dealer networks for each of these brands. General Motors is naturally reluctant to throw this money away and they are trying to separate these two cars in the minds of the customer with styling changes and some youth-oriented advertising for Oldsmobile.

SUMMARY

Successful marketing strategies are often based on differentiation, market focus, and lower costs. Firms must identify windows of opportunity and select appropriate attack and defense strategies if they expect to reach organization goals. Measure performance against your corporate mission; this will prevent you from overreacting to competitors.

Strategic marketing involves selecting a target market and positioning one's product relative to competitive products. Various elements of the marketing mix are selected to be consistent with the chosen strategy. This is one of the most fundamental concepts of marketing.

NOTES

1. This section borrows heavily from Geoffrey Easton, "Relationships Among Competitors" in *The Interface of Marketing and Strategy,* in George Day, Barton Weitz, and Robin Wensley, eds. (Greenwich, CT: JAI Press 1990), pp. 57–100.

2. "Who's Who Among Natural Gas Marketers," *The Atlanta Journal-Constitution,* October 4, 1998, p. G2.

3. Michael Kawleski, "Strategic Alliances Can Benefit Many," *Agri Marketing,* Vol. 35, No. 3 (March 1997), p. 14, and Lynn Grooms, "Seed Company Alliances Provide Access Route Genetic Super-highway," *Agri Marketing,* Vol. 35, No. 7 (July/August 1997), pp. 52–55.

4. These steps are from K. Michael Haywood, "Scouting the Competition for Survival and Success," in *Marketing,* A. Dale Timpe, ed. (New York: Facts On File, 1989), pp. 129–141. The many kinds of information you should consider collecting are listed in his Figure 1.

5. W. Chan Kim and Renee Mauborne, "Creating New Market Space, *Harvard Business Review,* Vol. 77, No. 1 (January-February 1999), pp. 83–92.

6. Laurie McGinley, "How Ex-Lax, Trusted for Nearly a Century, Became a Cancer Risk," *Wall Street Journal,* September 26, 1997, pp. A1, A8.

FURTHER READING

Day, George S., and Robin Wensley. "Assessing Advantage: A Framework for Diagnosing Competitive Superiority," *Journal of Marketing,* Vol. 52 (April 1988), pp. 1–20.

Hunt, Shelby D., and Robert M. Morgan. "The Comparative Advantage Theory of Competition," *Journal of Marketing,* Vol. 59, No. 2 (April 1995), pp. 1–15.

REFERENCES

Easton, Geoffrey. "Relationships Among Competitors," in *The Interface of Marketing and Strategy,* George Day, Barton Weitz, and Robin Wensley, eds. Greenwich, CT: JAI Press 1990, pp. 57–100.

Myers, James H. *Segmentation and Positioning for Strategic Marketing Decisions.* Chicago: American Marketing Association, 1996.

Oster, Sharon M. *Competitive Analysis.* New York: Oxford University Press, 1994.

Ramaswamy, Venkatram, Hubert Gatignon, and David Reibstein. "Competitive Marketing Behavior in Industrial Markets," *Journal of Marketing,* Vol. 58, No. 2 (April 1994), pp. 45–55.

Vandenbosch, Mark B. "Confirmatory Compositional Approaches to the Development of Product Spaces," *European Journal of Marketing,* Vol. 30, No. 3, (1996), pp. 23–46.

QUESTIONS

1. The key to dominating the Web is controlling the front door through which users connect to the Internet. The early leaders among the Internet portals were Yahoo! and aol.com. Originally most of the top destinations simply performed search functions but became portal destinations as they added features such as news clips, shopping channels, and travel and financial information. Portals tend to inspire customer loyalty fast because they usually allow their users to tailor site content. The portal strategy is popular because offering a number of features attracts sizable audiences that, in turn, attract large advertising dollars. Portals are potentially a way to make money on the Web. How can General Electric's NBC build Snap.com or Walt Disney build Infoseek into a dominant brand? How can a site without the established awareness of a Yahoo! or without the financial backing of a Disney hope to grab users?

2. W. A. Schmidt is a major manufacturer of custom-built mezzanines and other material handling equipment. A mezzanine creates new floor space in a factory or warehouse by adding a low story of structural steel within an existing higher story. They are engineered for maximum span with minimum obstruction. An example of W. A. Schmidt's material handling equipment is its HF stacking cradle that stores up to four coils of some material on the same floor footprint. The racks adjust to coil diameter when

loaded. The coils are loaded and retrieved from the rack system by overhead cranes with C-hooks. W. A. Schmidt clients include Duracell, Koons Steel, Saks Fifth Avenue, and Volvo. A situation analysis was done to determine what Schmidt's strengths were compared to their competition. The situation analysis revealed that Schmidt is widely recognized as a leader in quality. However, potential customers see Schmidt as a high-priced vendor. Some assume that Schmidt is out of reach. This perception is costing Schmidt the opportunity to even bid on some business. In addition, although Schmidt has a large following of independent, nonexclusive distributors, it wants to boost loyalty among its core distributors. Sketch out a total marketing program to address Schmidt's problems.

3. Software giant SAP AG, maker of the popular R/3 enterprise resource planning (ERP) system, is preparing stand-alone applications that will compete directly with specialty or niche products such as warehousing software. Why is SAP taking on a host of vendors of products ranging from sales force automation applications to advanced planning and optimization systems to business-to-business electronic commerce applications to applications for the management of product data, warehouses, and transportation? How will customers react? How will the niche players react?

4. Comparative advertising is a fact of life in the automobile industry. Nissan Motor Corp. USA ran a commercial that compared its Altima sedan to a Mercedes-Benz. The Altima spot touted Altima's roominess over the Mercedes. It shows the small sedan crashing through a glass display window over a Mercedes, with the words "Mercedes has just been topped." What are the advantages and disadvantages of comparative ads? Assess the Altima commercial.

5. Rob de Zwart, marketing director of Croky Chips, a subsidiary in The Netherlands of United Biscuits, was confronted with a drop in market share of Croky chips from 32 percent in March to 18.5 percent in the fall of the same year. The major cause of this dramatic decrease was the very successful Flippo campaign, launched by competitor Smith Chips in the spring. Flippos are small round plastic discs with Warner Bros. cartoons on them, that are put into the bags with the chips. There are all kinds of different Flippos—for example, Regular, Game, Flying, Chester, and Techno Flippos (335 different types in all)—and collecting and exchanging Flippos became a craze among children as well as teenagers and young adults. At the start of the Flippo campaign, Croky did not pay much attention. Flippos were thought to be too "childish" and Croky launched an "infotainment" campaign (trendy texts on chips bags) combined with discounts on CDs. When Croky realized that, against their expectations, the Flippos had actually touched a nerve with teenagers, they had to react. What should Rob de Zwart do?

6. In a survey conducted a month after the 1996 Olympics in Atlanta, consumers were asked to name the official sponsors of the Summer Games. For credit cards, 72 percent named Visa whereas only 54 percent named American Express. Those results were almost identical to a similar survey conducted after the 1994 Winter Olympics, in which 68 percent named Visa and 52 percent named American Express. One might conclude from these surveys that Visa does a better job than American Express in promoting its association with the Olympic Games—except Visa paid $40 million for the exclusive rights to be an official sponsor in the credit card category, while American Express was not an official sponsor of the Olympic Games. How could American Express achieve such a high level of recognition as an official sponsor without being one? Is it fair for companies to associate themselves with the Olympics without being an official sponsor?

7. Airline yield management programs continually change the number and price of seats on future flights so airlines can increase the number of seats sold for each flight and maximize their profits. Some observers suggest that by making their prices instantly available to their competitors, airline yield management programs allow airlines to

engage in a form of price collusion with their competitors. The argument suggests that making prices instantly available to competitors is a form of signaling that discourages price competition and independent price setting. At what point does the exchange of price information among competitors become illegal collusive behavior?

8. The global wholesale vitamin market is dominated by Roche Holdings AG, with about 40 percent of the market, BASF AG, with about 20 percent, and Rhone-Poulenc SA, with about 15 percent. Recently, Swiss vitamin maker Lonza AG plus U.S.-based executives of the Canadian Chinook Group Ltd. and the U.S. firm DuCoa LP pleaded guilty to government charges that they conspired to fix prices in the international sale of vitamins B3, also known as niacin, and B4. Both vitamins are used as nutritional supplements in human and animal products, including livestock feed, baby formula, and daily-vitamin tablets. Lonza agreed to pay a fine of $10.5 million for its role in the price fixing scheme. The U.S. Justice Department is also investigating the pricing activities of the three largest vitamin manufacturers plus at least two Japanese vitamin makers. Why would Lonza Inc. and DuCoa's president, division president, and division vice president and Chinook's vice president of sales and marketing and its U.S. sales manager employ an illegal price-fixing strategy for their vitamins? What are the upsides and downsides of collusion: to the individual? to the firm?

9. Megamergers are creating global oligopolies. What are the advantages and disadvantages of oligopolistic competition from the perspective of business? Consumers? When should government regulators intervene?

10. A national corporation purchased a small Midwestern regional producer of industrial and consumer paper products. The regional producer sold paper towels under the Countess label. As a possible prelude to taking the brand national, 500 Fort Wayne, Indiana, consumers were asked to fill out a questionnaire and to record their purchases for the duration of an 18-week study. The questionnaire, which was completed at the beginning of the study, collected information on: (1) the first brand of paper towels the person could mention, (2) the person's favorite brand, (3) recall of the brand most recently purchased, (4) an evaluation of each brand—with the highest evaluation having an index value of 100, and (5) eleven demographic variables. By the end of the longitudinal panel study, 132 participants had made one or more towel purchases. Persons who claimed to be paper towel users but who did not purchase during this time were dropped from the study. The data are given in file papertoweldat.sav. How does Countess stack up in the marketplace? Is it a strong candidate for being taken national?

CASE 5-1 ROYAL AUTOMOBILE CLUB (A)*

MEMO

TO: David Livermore, CEO
FROM: Jan Smith, Group Strategic Director
DATE: September 1, 1995

"David,

After three months in my role, I have had the opportunity to see and discuss most areas of the business, and to understand key issues:

- We lack a long-term cohesive business direction that delivers competitive advantage.
- We do not know what business we should be in for the future.
- We have an internal focus on Divisional issues and lack an appreciation of the wider marketplace and changes taking place.
- We do not have a clear brand positioning for the RAC, nor do we have a distinct customer proposition.
- We do not know what we spend across the business on marketing/sales by discipline…
- We lack 'commercial' bite.

I could continue with this list (it's not all bad) but won't bore you further…."

The fact that the Royal Automobile Club (RAC) had been steadily losing market share in breakdown and recovery services, its main business, to its rivals the Automobile Association (AA) and Green Flag; that its membership had remained virtually static at 5.8 million since 1992, and that its profitability had been eroding on an annual basis, was one concern to Smith, RAC Group Strategic Director since May of that year. But even more important was the long-term sustainability of the company: if the RAC were to see it through and prosper into the next millennium, she was convinced that it would have to seriously relook its future business direction and strategic positioning. (See Exhibit 1 for financials.)

By the 1990s motoring was being confronted by two major trends which would have a dramatic impact on the RAC's "core" breakdown and repair business:

(1) *Advanced vehicle technologies:* automobile manufacturers were increasingly embedding engine management and diagnostic electronics into their vehicles—especially in the more expensive models—which could alert automobilists to impending engine or other mechanical failure, and in the process reduced the overall car breakdown rate. Such technological improvements were becoming the norm and, as the cost of chips and other technologies continued to plummet, even the less expensive, standard cars were beginning to have such features built in.

(2) *Increasing public and legislative concern about urban traffic congestion and related pollution:* ironically, despite the impressive technological advances in automobiles, traffic speeds in major urban areas in the late 20th century had returned to late 19th century levels, leaving travelers delayed, frustrated and exhausted. Municipalities everywhere were examining a variety of options to deal with this worsening situation: taxing or even banning automobile use in city centers, and encouraging the development of mass transportation. Notwithstanding these efforts, public transport was also increasingly prone to delays, congestion and cancellations. Because of this situation, which seemed to be worsening, many drivers still preferred the "private" hassle of driving to the public hassle of mass transportation.

MOTORING IN BRITAIN AND THE DEVELOPMENT OF THE RAC

The motoring revolution in the UK began in the 1890s, when the first custom built vehicles began appearing on the roads. Few then would have predicted that, 100

---

* This case was prepared by Professor Sandra Vandermerwe and Dr. Marika Taishoff of Imperial College Management School, London. Copyright (c) 1998 by Sandra Vandermerwe. Reproduced by permission.

EXHIBIT 1   Consolidated Financials (in millions £)[a]

	1992	1993	1994	1995
Subscriptions from members	160.3	175.6	180.4	187.3
Other operating income	51.3	58.7	62.1	64.9
Investment and similar income	8.0	10.2	11.3	10.5
Total Income	219.6	244.5	253.8	262.7
Staff costs	79.1	86.3	93.1	100.1
Operating charges[b]	113.7	126.1	73.7	73.4
Administrative expenses			75.9	83.1
Bank interest payable			0.9	0.7
Share of losses of associate undertakings			–	0.1
Exceptional items	(14.3)	(17.7)	(3.6)	(16.7)
Surplus (deficit) before tax	12.6	14.5	8.2	(11.4)
Taxation	1.8	1.3	(0.4)	(1.0)
Surplus (Deficit) for Year	10.8	13.2	7.8	(12.4)

[a] Consolidated figures representing RAC Motoring Services (including RAC insurance and other companies), RAC Clubhouse, and RAC Woodcote Park Clubhouse.

[b] For 1992 and 1993, operating charges, administrative expenses and other expenses combined.

years later, the automobile would have become such an integral and necessary part of life. In its early days, the vehicle was primarily used as a sporting activity and "motoring," as it was called, was the new sport of kings and others who could afford the luxury of the "horseless buggy." The fact that the average motorist in those days drove no more than 13 miles a year did not diminish the fact that motoring was considered an important and significant activity, reserved for the privileged few. Notwithstanding this prestige however, the early cars were notorious for breaking down. The focus of early drivers was more on the mechanicals of the vehicle—oil, water, maintenance, etc.—than it was on the look, feel or style.

As with most sporting activities, soon a few motoring aficionados began meeting regularly, and it was thus that the Automobile Club was established in 1897. Within a few years practically all British motorists at that time were members of the Club. It encouraged the development of motoring in Great Britain, and strove to manage all the activities of the early motorists' journeying needs. It arranged trials, fostered touring, taught driving, issued road maps, distributed information, approved garages and hotels, organized insurance and legal assistance, and eventually established "Road Patrols" to help its members when their cars broke down. It was also actively involved in sponsoring and organizing various motor rallies, some of which have continued into the 1990s.

As motoring continued to progress in the UK, so too did the legal efforts designed to ensure that speed limits were respected and that motorists obeyed the "rules of the road" which were then being put in place. This angered many motorists who felt that the police, in enforcing speed controls and other surveillance methods, were infringing on their rights. In 1905, a group of Club members, unhappy with what they perceived to be the Club's acquiescence to the authorities on this issue, left to form an alternative, more radical organization whose sole purpose was to combat the enactment of traffic and speed controls and to uphold the rights of motorists. This group called itself the Automobile Association (AA) and within the space of five years it would have more members than the Automobile Club, and would maintain its number one market position in the decades to come.

The Club became known as the Royal Automobile Club after King Edward VII bestowed the "royal" title upon it in 1907, a source, especially in those days, of prestige and a sign of having been admitted into the "elite" class of organizations and associations.

In 1910, the RAC established its headquarters by building an Edwardian palace on Pall Mall, nestled between Buckingham Palace and Trafalgar Square in central London. Its ornate premises, in addition to being an administrative headquarters, also housed a Club with all the amenities of the finest London gentlemens' clubs: restaurant, bar, and bedroom suites open to the exclusively male members of the Club. Other RAC clubhouse activities included Pall Mall Bridge, Chess, Sub-Aqua, Snooker, Squash and Rackets and Golf. The association of the RAC with the palatial Club premises would henceforth give the group a "premium" image in the marketplace. The key activity of the RAC, however, was the providing of emergency repair services to fee paying members whose cars had broken down.

JAN SMITH ENTERS AS RAC GROUP STRATEGIC DIRECTOR

Jan Smith joined the RAC as Group Strategic director in May 1995; her mandate had been to "define the RAC for the 21st century." After taking on the job, she told her staff internally that she never stayed in a job longer than two or three years.

> "Treat me as if I am on loan, and you will get the best out of me." As Smith recalled, they were astonished at her statement. How could an executive come into an organization with this point of view? But I had already learned that if you stay on any longer than three years, you become "internal" and when that happened you lose the big picture: organizations do things—they don't spend a lot of time thinking."

Prior to joining the RAC, she had been involved between 1989 and 1991 in setting up and commercializing First Direct, the UK's first, 24-hour phone banking operation. As the marketing director for that brand-new initiative which had reshaped the insurance industry, she had taken a new and untested concept and, together with a group of highly creative communications, branding and advertising executives, helped turn it into a huge and unexpected marketplace success. Smith, born 50 years ago in the UK, had also been marketing director of Mazda Cars UK for three years. During her tenure at Mazda she had successfully posi-

tioned and built the brand, having increased customer awareness by over 18%. According to press reports written during that time, she had clashed with some dealers who had complained that the advertising she had commissioned was too "brand based" and not designed to "shift the metal."

Her reputation as an innovative and strategic thinker, combined with her familiarity with the automobile industry were the key criteria used by the RAC in appointing her to the newly created position at RAC as strategic director. She would sometimes joke that, notwithstanding her title and senior position at the RAC, as a woman she had initially not been allowed membership in the RAC club! (This rule has now been changed after 100 years.)

BREAKDOWN SERVICES MARKET IN GREAT BRITAIN

Services for members stranded on the roads when their cars broke down had long been the principal activity of the RAC as well as of its two key competitors, the Automobile Association and Green Flag, and membership fees for the service comprised the main source of income for these firms. In terms of customer base, the AA's customers tended to be slightly older than the RAC's, and Green Flag's tended to be the youngest of all.

The market size for breakdown services for individuals, and the three main players' penetration of the total market for breakdown services, and share of the actual breakdowns which occurred (only 75% of the total market has a breakdown services policy), from 1992 to 1995 are shown in Exhibit 2.

Already in the mid-1980s, the fast growing Green Flag (which had changed its name from the National Breakdown Recovery Club in early 1995) was beginning to cut into the customer base of both the RAC and the AA. It had entered the market as a quick and

EXHIBIT 2   Market for Breakdown Services

	1992	1993	1994	1995
Market Size	11238	11474	12089	12243
RAC Penetration	15.1%	15.4%	15.2%	15.1%
RAC Share	24.6	24.2	23.5	23.5
AA Penetration	34.5	34.8	34.8	34.8
AA Share	56.0	54.6	54.0	54.0
Green Flag Penetration	10.3	11.8	12.8	12.9
Green Flag Share	16.7	18.5	19.8	19.9

flexible player, priced considerably lower than the AA or the RAC (RAC prices tended to be the highest of the three). Instead of the uniformed patrolmen used by the RAC and the AA, Green Flag relied on a network of garages to perform its services. Green Flag also did less roadside repair work and offered fewer subsidiary services. It relied on sponsorship of the all England football team to create awareness of its brand name.

Smith recalled that "Green Flag has always been on our heels, and really began taking our members back in 1990. Market research done then showed that Green Flag was our biggest threat, but no one here seemed to react because they felt it was a niche price market, whereas the RAC differentiated itself on its exclusive image. Also they simply were not in tune with the new marketplace—there was a recession and people were more price sensitive." Because of its predatory pricing methods, Green Flag also ate into the market share of the AA which, with 8 million members, was the largest and most visible of the three players. The AA responded by massively updating its information technology (IT) system to make its breakdown services more responsive and cost efficient. It also created a new ad campaign—spending £14.5 million every year; launched a new slogan, "To our members we are the fourth emergency service" and began investing in insurance and financial services, and in other "home emergency services" like plumbing and electricity. It also offered insurance services by finding deals for members from a group of 30 leading insurance companies.

In addition to individual customers, another significant market sector for the RAC were contract hire, leasing and fleet management companies. Twenty-five of the top 40 of such customers were RAC clients. The RAC had the highest fleet market share of the three competitors.

RAC PRODUCT MARKET

Historically the RAC had marketed a modular range of breakdown products and sub-brands, for example Reflex and Reflex Europe. The communication campaigns for these products focused on price but also presented the RAC as a "premium" organisation. The premium fees were the same for everyone: drivers of expensive, technologically sophisticated vehicles paid the same price as those with older, more standard cars. Typically, this latter group of customers increasingly relied upon the RAC as a substitute for what should have been routine maintenance. The cost of an average breakdown was £60. Some of the RAC's major products, a brief description of each, the contribution to RAC sales, and the average fee are shown in Exhibit 3.

As the breakdown industry moved, in the eyes of the market, toward being an insurance provider there was increased pressure from the existing customer base for a no call-out discount. This no call-out discount

---

EXHIBIT 3   **Examples of Key RAC Products, Their Contributions, and Average Fees**

Product	Description	1995 contribution (%)	1996 contribution (%)	Average Fee to Customer over Two Years
Roadside	RAC comes out to fix the car; if unable, will bring driver to nearest RAC approved garage	2.8%	12.0%	£42
Roadside Recovery	RAC comes out to fix the car; if unable, will bring driver to the destination of choice	19.7%	36.1%	£75
Roadside Recovery at Home	RAC comes out to fix a breakdown within $1/4$ mile of the customer's home; if unable, will bring driver to the destination of choice	2.8%	19.2%	£100
Reflex	If breakdown can't be fixed, same as Recovery but also includes three days' free car hire	17.8%	16.7%	£120
Reflex Europe	Same as Reflex, but valid also across Europe	2.9%	1.8%	£190

had been one of the customers' top ten wishes since 1988, although the company had not responded to this request.

The roadside services were performed by the RAC Road Patrols, with their white and blue colored vans—with the royal insignia—and similarly discretely attired patrolmen. These patrolmen featured strongly in the company's main advertising theme—the "New Knights of the Road" (for total RAC advertising expenditures from 1992–1996, see Exhibit 4).

Of its 5.5 million individual customers by 1996, more than 3 million had joined because of a third party (i.e., generally as part of the purchase of a new or used vehicle). The RAC had an information service for potential customers. If someone phoned in for more information on the RAC's products, prices etc., all the data would be written down manually by RAC staff, and an information pack sent out to the prospect. No systematic file or database of these prospective customers existed.

All the breakdown service providers offered a similar set of products. The RAC had believed that a critical differentiator was the speed of response to emergency calls and rate of fix. In 1995 the RAC handled 2.9 million rescue jobs, 85% within one hour and 82% of these breakdowns were repaired at roadside. Since speed of response depended on the quality and sophistication of the IT linkups between the station headquarters and the patrol cars, the RAC invested heavily in building the infrastructure for this, and technology was considered a core competence of the company.

In addition to its core breakdown and recovery activities, the RAC also offered a wide range of motoring related services. These included insurance, holiday and hotel reservations, travel publications, legal services, traffic information, and more technically geared services such as "Battery Assist," designed to help members whose cars wouldn't start because of a flat battery. These incremental businesses were structured as profit centres in their own right. By the time Jan

Smith had joined, many of these small areas of business had been losing money.

The RAC Insurance group (RACIS), for example, had almost always been a drain on the bottom line. As she put it, "We understand our core business very well, and for the RAC that core business has always been breakdown services; insurance is seen as an add-on. For the AA, it was different: they see insurance as a key part of their core business, and they're plowing lots of money into it". On average, 5% of RAC insurance customers were breakdown customers as well. Smith was concerned that the entry of new players like Direct Line in insurance with their huge critical mass and low operating costs, intensified competition and the continuing drop in premiums, would push RAC's insurance business ever deeper into the red.

The RAC had separate divisions for Marketing, Sales and Customer Service. Marketing's role was to communicate the image of the company and to oversee memberships renewals. Sales focused on new prospects, whether individual, corporate, fleet or third party, and Customer Service was responsible for responding to customer queries and emergency breakdown calls.

UNDERSTANDING THE PRESENT MARKET

In recalling her arrival at the RAC, Jan Smith said:

> I came into a company that was dramatically losing market share. Some of the problems were well known. For instance, research had been done in the early 90s and the findings should have worried us—our image was weakening, we weren't growing, *and* we weren't keeping our existing customers.

Smith was convinced early in her appointment that the company had to update its market research if it was going to find out why it was losing market share, and in November of 1995, she commissioned a major project.

EXHIBIT 4   Advertising Expenditure

RAC Total	TV (£)	Press (£)	Radio (£)	Cinema (£)	Outdoor (£)	Total Spend (£)
1992	2,859,788	620,721	1900	0	137,883	3,620,292
1993	441,737	2,089,177	0	0	287,114	2,818,028
1994	1,008,712	5,422,169	130,172	0	1753	6,562,806
1995	1,480,156	4,013,687	8,006	0	0	5,501,849
1996	419,266	1,862,912	63,946	0	0	2,346,124

Market Research

Two jump-start groups were commissioned to get a feeling of what people thought about the different breakdown brands. The reason for these jump-start groups was that she and her team wanted to test and structure their methodology. These two groups were asked questions about how they felt about breakdown services, what they thought of the various brands, pricing, insurance, etc. The object was to get feedback on how far brands could stretch, overall direction for the research and some specific questions with which to work.

The methodology was then taken to 16 qualitative groups to assess what people (users and non-users) "felt" when it came to roadside breakdown services, and how these feelings translated into purchase criteria and decision making. Increasingly, key consumer motivations were "about *me,* not my car," for instance:

– freedom from worry;
– sense of security;
– vulnerability when stranded;
– need an ally.

Brands were tested in this research to see how far they could stretch. A brand like Virgin, they found, could be extended into banking and insurance. How far could the RAC brand be stretched? Could the RAC be attached to an airline, or to a cure for AIDS? For example, because the RAC was strongly associated with "integrity," and financial services generally were not seen as illustrative of "integrity," the RAC brand did not really stretch into financial services.

Finally a list of words or phrases, which the participants associated as positive or negative attributes of the main breakdown brands, was generated. (See Exhibits 5, 6, and 7 for the findings from the research.)

Another facet of the research was to compare the "visibility" of all the players in the breakdown services market. Here, the results were as follows:

- The RAC suffered from poor visibility, especially relative to the AA
- The AA was visible, out there, unambiguous, "busy doing it," of and for the people ... and much more than just breakdown (Roadwatch, High Street stores, inspections, road signage, etc)
- The RAC had much less presence: "another white liveried van"—could be the Police, Fire, Security Firm, Mobile Plumber ... not noticed, little sense of beavering away, getting it done

For Smith, the market research results were clear: the RAC had to play on its positives, and get rid of the negatives (see Exhibit 5). With visibility such a strong asset for the AA, the RAC would have to try to take that away from them in their strategy. Achieving both of these imperatives, and quickly, would be her chief concern in the new year.

MOVING INTO A NEW GEAR

In November 1995 Neil Johnson, the dynamic General Secretary of the Clubhouse, was appointed CEO of the RAC Motoring Services. Johnson, committed to dramatic change, was a vigorous and energetic person very supportive of the work then undertaken. One month later, almost immediately after the results of the market research study, he asked Smith to take over all of Customer Services, Marketing and Sales. A new Managing Director of Operations was brought in. Previously Marketing and Operations had been in one section under one person. The objective now was to link the strategic and day-to-day business activities. Johnson also created and chaired an Executive Committee comprised of Smith, the Group Legal Director, the Group Finance Director, the Managing Director of Operations, and the Managing Director of Technical Services.

Once Smith had decided on the actions she would take, she needed to communicate to people what was

EXHIBIT 5   RAC Market Research Results

+Integrity	−Old fashioned
+Considerable experience	−Elitist, stately and aloof
+Independent and objective	−Unapproachable
+An organization of the highest standards	−Patronizing: an adult/child relationship
+Premium	−Expensive
+Dependable	−Muddled
+Traditional values	−Obsessed with heritage

EXHIBIT 6   AA Market Research Results

+Modern	−Voraciously commercial
+Dynamic	−Short-term expediency
+Urgent	−Motives often suspect
+Competitive	−Impersonal
+Efficient	
+Visible	
+Everywhere	

EXHIBIT 7   Green Flag Market Research Results

+Cheap (or, arguably, good value)	−Minimum cover-no "safety net"
+No frills	−Contractor service experience variable
+Clarity: what you see is what you get	
+Good service, exceed expectations	

wrong, what she was doing about it and why. She knew that the changes would entail considerable upheaval for people. Videos were put together to show the reasons for the repositioning and the elements of the strategy. Every member of the Executive Committee appeared in these videos, endorsing the strategy and the commitment to the way forward. Staff were concerned and said, "we never realized it was like this!" She recalled:

> There had been an element of complacency in the company, people thinking we've always been here. They just did not know what was happening; they didn't know the reason why it was necessary to change. The video was a tangible way of communicating that there was a problem and what would be done about it.

The research results and the video woke people up. Smith went into an accelerated gear. She was adamant that, under these circumstances, the group did not have the luxury of working according to the old rules. It had to radically, and quickly rethink what it stood for, what its role was today—and would be in the future-and communicate and demonstrate this to its customers. Otherwise, she felt, the RAC's centenary year, 1997, might mark the beginning of the venerable institution's end.

Setting Up the Virtual Team

Smith formed a group to address the RAC's positioning and brand strategy. She wanted some people who

had been involved with her in designing the marketing strategy for First Direct as well as key people from key parts of the RAC to be in this team.

Rather than accept a complete team from an established agency, she engaged the skills of certain freelance marketing professionals as well as individuals from major advertising agencies with whom she had worked in the past. As she put it, "I wanted to capitalize on the brain power of just one or two people in an agency, and not the complete company." Together they began brainstorming and approaching the issue of repositioning the RAC and examining options for the way forward.

> We sat down to look at everything: the brand, the world in which we were competing, what was happening to consumers and the way in which they were living their lives. In trying to determine how to deal with the competition, how to respond to customer perceptions of the brand, and how to position the RAC as a leader for the future, we recognized we had to redefine the company's business. We also had to redefine what was meant by "premium," "leadership" and "club.

> We had always been a premium brand, leadership had always been central to our positioning. We genuinely were a club when we started out, but what did all that mean today? How would we not only respond to the changing environment, but help re-create the RAC to become the first-choice service brand of the future?

CASE 5-2   ARCTIC POWER*

"We've got some important decisions to make on Arctic Power for 1988," said Linda Barton, Senior Product Manager for the brand. "As I see it, we can continue to develop our strong markets in Québec, the Maritimes, and British Columbia or we can try to build market share in the rest of Canada." Barton was discussing the future of Arctic Power, one of Colgate-Palmolive Canada's leading laundry detergents, with Gary Parsons, the Assistant Product Manager on the brand.

"Not only do we have to consider our strategic direction," replied Parsons, "but we also have to think about our positioning strategy for Arctic Power. I'm for running the Québec approach in all our markets." Parsons was referring to the Québec advertising campaign, which positioned Arctic Power as the superior detergent for cold water cleaning.

"I'm not sure, given the mixed results achieved with our 1986 Western campaign," said Linda. "However, we are making great progress with our current advertising in British Columbia. It might be more effective outside of Québec. Remember, cold water washing is a newer concept for the western provinces. We have to overcome that obstacle before we can get people to buy Arctic Power. Let's go over the data again, then make our decisions."

THE COMPANY

Colgate-Palmolive Canada is a wholly owned subsidiary of Colgate-Palmolive, a large multinational with divisions in 58 countries. Worldwide company sales in 1986 were $4.9 billion, with profits of $178 million. The Canadian subsidiary's sales exceeded $250 million annually. Colgate-Palmolive Canada (CPC) manufactures a range of household, health, and personal care products. Among CPC's major brands are ABC, Arctic Power, and Fab (laundry detergents), Palmolive (dishwashing liquid), Ajax (cleanser), Irish Spring (bar soap), Ultra Brite and Colgate (toothpastes), Halo (shampoo), and Baggies (food wrap).

Under the product management system at CPC, product managers are assigned responsibility for specific brands, like Arctic Power. Their overall goals are to increase the sales and profitability of their brand. To meet these goals, the product manager supervises all marketing functions including planning, advertising, selling, promotion, and market research. In planning and executing programs for a brand, the product manager usually is assigned an assistant product manager, and they work closely together to accomplish the brand goals.

Prior to the late 1970s, CPC essentially followed the strategy of nationally supporting most of its brands. The result was that CPC was spread too thin with too many brands. There were insufficient resources to properly promote and develop all of the CPC line, and profits and market share were less than satisfactory. Beginning in the late 1970s and continuing into the early 1980s, the Canadian division altered its strategy. An extensive review of the entire product line was conducted, and CPC moved to what was referred to as a *regional brand strategy*. Where a brand had regional strength, resources were focused on that area, with the objective of building a strong and profitable brand in that region. For example, Arctic Power had a relatively strong market share in Québec and the Maritimes, where the proportion of consumers using cold water to wash clothes was considerably higher than the national average. Promotional support was withdrawn from the rest of Canada, and those resources were focused on Québec and the Maritimes.[1] Arctic Power was still distributed nationally but by the end of 1981, national market share was 4%, consisting of an 11% share in Québec, a 5% share in the Maritimes, and a 2% share in the rest of Canada. Over the next four years, marketing efforts were concentrated primarily on Québec, and to a lesser extent in the Maritimes. This approach worked well for Arctic Power. By the end of 1985, Arctic Power's national share had increased to 6.4%;

---

[1] The Maritimes contained the four Eastern provinces: Newfoundland, Nova Scotia, Prince Edward Island, and New Brunswick. In 1988, the population of Canada was estimated at 25.8 million people: Maritimes (2.3 million), Quebec (6.6 million), Ontario (9.4 million), Manitoba and Saskatchewan (2.1 million), Alberta (2.4 million), and British Columbia (3.0 million).

---

* This case was prepared by Gordon H. G. McDougall of Wilfrid Laurier University in Waterloo, Ontario, and Douglas Snetsinger of the University of Toronto. Copyright © 1989 by the North American Case Research Association. Reproduced by permission.

share in Québec had risen to 18%, share in the Maritimes was 6%, and less than 2% in the rest of Canada. With the increase in sales and profitability, the decision was made to target Alberta and British Columbia for 1986. The results of these efforts exceeded expectations in British Columbia but were less than satisfactory in Alberta.

THE LAUNDRY DETERGENT MARKET

The laundry detergent market was mature, with unit sales increasing by approximately 1% annually and dollar sales increasing by about 5% each year between 1983 and 1986 (Exhibit 1). Three large consumer packaged goods companies—Procter and Gamble, Lever Detergents, and CPC—dominated the market. All three were subsidiaries of multinational firms, and sold a wide range of household and personal care products in Canada. Procter and Gamble Canada had annual sales exceeding $1 billion, and some of its major brands included Crest (toothpaste), Ivory and Zest (bar soaps), Secret (deodorant), Pampers and Luvs (disposable diapers) and Head & Shoulders

(shampoo). P&G held a 44% share of the laundry detergent market in 1986, due primarily to the large share (34%) held by Tide, the leading brand in Canada.

Lever Detergents, with annual Canadian sales in excess of $400 million, operated primarily in the detergent, soap, and toiletry categories. Major brands included Close-up (toothpaste) and Dove and Lux (bar soaps). Lever held a 24% share of the laundry detergent market and its leading brand was Sunlight, with a 13% share.

CPC was the only one of the three companies to gain market share in the laundry detergent market between 1983 and 1986. In 1986, CPC's total share was 23%, up from 16% in 1983. ABC, a value brand, positioned to attract consumers interested in "value for less money," more than doubled its share between 1983 and 1986 and was the second leading brand, with a 14% share.

COMPETITIVE RIVALRY

Intense competitive activity was a way of life in the laundry detergent business. Not only did the three

EXHIBIT 1   Laundry Detergent Market

	1983	1984	1985	1986
Colgate				
ABC	6.0	9.8	11.8	13.9
Arctic Power	4.7	5.6	6.4	6.5
Fab	2.1	1.3	1.6	1.4
Punch	2.0	.7	.4	.3
Dynamo	1.0	.8	.6	.5
Total Colgate	15.8	18.2	20.8	22.6
Procter and Gamble				
Tide	34.1	35.1	32.6	34.1
Oxydol	4.9	4.2	4.0	3.3
Bold	4.8	4.2	3.2	2.3
Other P&G brands	4.7	4.8	4.4	4.3
Total P&G	48.5	48.3	44.2	44.0
Lever				
Sunlight	13.9	12.2	14.2	13.4
All	4.1	3.7	3.8	3.2
Surf	2.6	2.6	2.7	2.2
Wisk	3.8	4.1	4.1	4.4
Other Lever brands	.9	.8	.6	.4
Total Lever	25.3	23.4	25.4	23.6
All other brands	10.4	10.1	9.6	9.8
Grand total	100.0	100.0	100.0	100.0
Total Market				
Metric tonnes ('000)	171.9	171.9	173.6	175.3
(% change)	2.0	0.0	1.0	1.0
Factory sales ('000,000)	$265.8	$279.1	$288.5	$304.7
(% change)	6.2	5.0	3.0	6.0

Source: Company records.

major firms had talented and experienced marketers, but they competed in a low-growth market where increased sales could be achieved only by taking share from competitive brands. A difficult task facing any product manager in this business was to identify the marketing mix that would maximize share while maintaining or increasing brand profitability, a task that had both long- and short-term implications. In the long term, competitors strove for permanent share gains by building a solid franchise of loyal users based on a quality product and a strong brand image or position. These positioning strategies were primarily executed through product formulation and advertising campaigns. However, companies also competed through consumer and trade promotions (e.g., coupons, feature specials in newspaper ads), tactics that were more short-term in nature. Trade and consumer promotions were critical to maintain prominent shelf display and to attract competitors' customers. Virtually every week of the year, at least one brand of detergent would be "on special" in any given supermarket. The product manager's task was to find the best balance between these elements in making brand decisions.

Reformulating brands, changing the brand ingredients, was a frequent activity in the laundry detergent business. Reformulating a brand involved altering the amount and kind of active chemical ingredients in the detergents. These active ingredients cleaned the clothes. Each of these cleaning ingredients was efficacious for particular cleaning tasks. Some of these ingredients were good for cleaning clay and mud from cotton and other natural fibers, while others would clean oily soils from polyesters, and still others were good for other cleaning problems. Most detergents were formulated with a variety of active ingredients to clean in a wide range of conditions. As well, bleaches, fabric softeners, and fragrances could be included.

Thus, laundry detergents contained different *levels* and *mixes* of active ingredients. The major decision was the *amount* of active ingredients that would be used in a particular brand. In simple terms, the greater the proportion of active ingredients, the better the detergent was at cleaning clothes. However, all detergents would get clothes clean. For example, in a recent test of 42 laundry detergents, *Consumer Reports* concluded: "Yes, some detergents get clothes whiter and brighter than others, but the scale is clean to cleanest, not dirty to clean."

The Canadian brands of laundry detergent contained various amounts of active ingredients. As shown in the following table, Tide and Arctic Power had more active ingredients than any other brand.

Level of Active Ingredients of Laundry Detergents

1	2	3	4	5
Some private labels	Bold III Oxydol Surf All	ABC Fab Cheer 2 Sunlight	–	Arctic Power Tide

Source: Company records.
Note: The scale of active ingredients increases from (1) to (5).

In fact, Tide and Arctic Power were equivalent brands in terms of the level of active ingredients. These two brands, referred to as the "Cadillacs" of detergents, had considerably higher levels of active ingredients than all other detergents. While the actual mix of active ingredients differed between the two brands (with Arctic Power having a greater mix of ingredients that were more suited to cold water washing), the cleaning power of Tide and Arctic Power was equal.

As the amount of active ingredients in a brand increased, so did the cost. Manufacturers were constantly facing the trade-off between cost and level of active ingredients. At times they had the opportunity to reduce unit costs by switching one type of active ingredient (a basic chemical) for another, depending on the relative costs of the ingredients. In this way, the level of ingredients remained the same; only the mixture changed. Manufacturers changed the physical ingredients of a brand to achieve an efficient per unit cost, to provide a basis for repositioning or restaging the brand; and to continue to deliver better consumer value.

Maintaining or increasing share through repositioning or other means was critical because of the profits involved. One share point was worth approximately $3 million in factory sales, and the cost and profit structures of the leading brands were believed to be similar. While some economies of scale accrued to the largest brands, the average cost of goods sold was estimated at 54% of sales, leaving a gross profit of 46%. Marketing expenditures included trade promotions (16%), consumer promotions (5%), and advertising expenditures (7%), leaving a contribution margin of 18%. Not included in these estimates were management overheads and expenses (e.g., product management salaries, market research expenses, sales salaries, and factory overheads), which were primarily fixed. In some instances, lower share brands were likely to spend higher amounts on trade promotions to achieve their marketing objectives.

One indication of competitive activity was reflected in advertising expenditures between 1982 and 1986.

Total category media advertising increased by 12% to $14.4 million (Exhibit 2). As well, substantial increases in trade promotions had occurred during that period. While actual expenditure data were not available, some managers felt that twice as much was being spent on trade promotions versus advertising. As one example in Montréal, in a nine-month period in 1986, Tide was featured in weekly supermarket advertisements 80 times and Arctic Power was featured 60 times. Typically, the advertisement cost for a feature was shared by the manufacturer and the retailer. At times during 1986, consumers could have purchased six liters of Arctic Power or Tide for $3.49 (regular price of $5.79). There was also a strong indication that the frequency and size of price specials on detergents were increasing. The average retail price of laundry detergents (based on the volume sold of all detergents at regular and special prices) had increased by only 4% in the last three years, whereas the cost of goods sold had increased by 15% during the same period.

One final observation was warranted. Between 1983 and 1986, the four leading brands—Tide, ABC, Sunlight, and Arctic Power—had increased their share from 58.7% to 67.9% of the total market. The three manufacturers appeared to be focusing their efforts primarily on their leading brands and letting the lesser brands decline in share.

POSITIONING STRATEGIES

While positioning strategies were executed through all aspects of the marketing mix, the strategy was most clearly seen in the advertising execution.

Tide was the dominant brand in terms of share of market and share of media expenditures. Tide's strategy was to sustain this dominance through positioning the brand as superior to any other brand on generic cleaning benefits. In 1986, four national and four regional commercials were aired to support this strategy. These commercials conveyed that Tide provided the benefits of being the most effective detergent for "tough" situations such as for ground-in dirt, stains and bad odors. Tide also aired copy in Québec claiming effectiveness in all temperatures. Most of Tide's copy was usually developed around a "slice of life" or testimonial format.

Other brands in the market faced the situation of going head-to-head with Tide's position or competing on a benefit Tide did not claim. Most had chosen the latter route. CPC's ABC brand had made strong gains in the past four years, moving from sixth to second place in market share based on its value position. ABC was positioned as the low-priced, good-quality cleaning detergent. Recent copy for ABC utilized a demonstration format whereby the shirts for twins were as clean when washed in ABC versus a leading higher-priced detergent with the statement "Why pay more? I can't see the difference." Sunlight, a Lever's brand, had for several years attempted to compete directly with Tide and build its consumer franchise based on efficacy and lemon-scent freshness. Advertising execution had been of the upbeat, up-scale lifestyle approach and less of the straightforward problem solution or straight-talking approaches seen in other detergent advertising. More recently, Sunlight had been moving toward ABC's value position while retaining the

EXHIBIT 2   Share of National Media Expenditures (1982–1986)

	Percentages				
	1982	1983	1984	1985	1986
ABC	6.4	8.9	12.3	14.0	13.6
Arctic Power	6.1	6.1	6.7	7.2	9.3
Tide	21.0	17.8	19.1	16.4	29.7
Oxydol	5.1	4.5	5.9	6.6	6.4
Sunlight	14.1	10.8	10.5	9.1	11.3
All	10.3	5.5	6.9	7.7	4.0
Wisk	9.9	12.8	10.3	10.4	14.6
All other brands	27.1	33.6	28.3	28.6	12.1
Total	100.0	100.0	100.0	100.0	100.0
Total spending (000)	$12,909	$13,338	$14,420	$13,718	$14,429
% Change	N/A	3.3	8.1	−4.9	5.2

Source: Company records.

lemon freshness heritage. Sunlight was positioned in 1986 as the detergent which gave a very clean, fresh wash at a sensible price. The final brand which attempted to compete for the value position was All. The advertising for All also claimed that the brand particularly whitened white clothes and had a pleasant fragrance.

Arctic Power had been positioned as the superior cleaning laundry detergent especially formulated for cold water washing. For the Eastern market, Arctic Power advertising had utilized a humorous background to communicate brand superiority and its efficacy in cold water. For the Western market, a nontraditional, upbeat execution was used to develop the cold water market.

Wisk, which had received much attention for its "ring around the collar" advertising, competed directly with Tide on generic cleaning qualities and provided the additional benefit of a liquid formulation. Tide Liquid was introduced in 1985 but received little advertising support in 1986.

Fab and Bold 3 competed for the "softergents" market. Both products, which had fabric softeners in the formulation, were positioned to clean effectively while softening clothes and reducing static cling. Another detergent with laundry product additives was Oxydol, which was formulated with a mild bleach. Oxydol was positioned as the detergent which kept colors bright while whitening whites.

The other two nationally advertised brands were Cheer 2 and Ivory Snow. Cheer 2 was positioned as the detergent which got clothes clean and fresh. Ivory Snow, which was a soap and not a detergent, was positioned as the laundry cleaning product for infants' clothes which provided superior softness and comfort.

The positioning strategies of these brands reflected the benefit segmentation approach used to market laundry detergents. Most brands attempted to appeal to a wide target (primarily women in the 18 to 49 age group) based on benefits rather than specific demographic segments.

THE COLD WATER MARKET

Every February, CPC commissioned an extensive market research study to identify trends in the laundry detergent market. Referred to as the *tracking study,* approximately 1800 personal interviews were conducted with female heads of households across Canada each year. Among the wealth of data provided by the tracking study was information on cold water usage in Canada. Regular cold water usage was growing in Canada and, by 1986, 29% of households were classified as regular (five or more times out of ten) cold water users (Exhibit 3). Due to cultural and marketing differences, Québec (55%) and the Maritimes (33%) had more cold water users than the national average.[2] A further 25% of all Canadian households occasionally (one to four times out of ten) used cold water for washing.

For households that washed regularly or occasionally with cold water, the most important benefits of using cold water fell into two broad categories (Exhibit 4). First, it was easier on or better for clothes in that cold water stopped shrinkage, prevented colors from running, and colors stayed bright. Second, it was more economical in that it saved energy, was cheaper, saved hot water, and saved on electricity. Households in Québec, the Maritimes and British Columbia mentioned the "economy" benefit more frequently, whereas households in the rest of Canada mentioned the "easier/better" benefit more often.

---

[2] Canada has two major cultural groups, the English (who emigrated primarily from the British Isles) and the French (who emigrated from France). Of the 6.2 million French-speaking Canadians, most reside in Québec (5.3 million) and the Maritimes (264,000). Historically, many French-speaking Canadians had washed clothes in cold water.

EXHIBIT 3   Proportion of Households Washing with Cold Water (1981–1986)

	1981	1982	1983	1984	1985	1986
National	20[a]	22	26	26	26	29
Maritimes	23	25	32	40	32	33
Québec	35	41	49	48	53	55
Ontario	14	13	18	16	11	17
Prairies	12	12	13	11	10	17
B.C.	13	19	20	17	22	21

Source: Tracking study.
[a] 20% of respondents did 5 or more out of 10 washloads in cool or cold water.
N = 1800.

EXHIBIT 4   Most Important Benefit of Cold Water Washing (1986)

Reason	National	Maritimes	Québec	Ontario	Man/Sask	Alba.	B.C.
Stops shrinkage	22.7[a]	19.4	5.2	32.7	35.4	35.4	30.2
Saves energy	16.5	12.5	32.1	8.2	2.1	9.9	12.9
Prevents colors from running	11.6	17.4	0.0	21.8	21.3	9.9	2.9
Cheaper	11.1	19.4	10.4	10.2	2.8	9.3	16.5
Saves hot water	9.7	9.7	15.5	6.8	11.3	3.1	3.6
Colors stay bright	8.8	4.2	7.8	11.6	9.2	6.8	7.9
Saves on electricity	8.7	19.4	0.5	8.2	5.7	16.1	25.9
Easier on clothes	8.5	11.1	6.7	8.8	10.6	13.7	5.0

Source: Tracking study.

[a] When asked what they felt was the most important benefit of cold water washing, 22.7% of all respondents said "stops shrinking." Sample includes all households that washed one or more times out of last 10 washes in cold water.
N = 956.
Only the eight most frequent responses are reported.

ARCTIC POWER

Having achieved reasonable success in Eastern Canada and returned the brand to profitability, Linda Barton decided to increase the brand's share in Alberta and British Columbia for 1986. That brand plan is reported below.

The 1986 Brand Plan for Arctic Power

Objectives   Arctic Power's overall objective is to continue profit development by maintaining modest unit volume growth in Québec and the Maritimes while developing the Alberta and B.C. regions.

Long Term (by 1996)   The long-term objective is to become the number three brand in the category, with market share of 12%. Arctic Power will continue to deliver a minimum 18% contribution margin. This will require (1) maintenance of effective creative/media support; (2) superior display prominence, particularly in the key Québec market; (3) continued investigation of development opportunities; and (4) cost of goods savings programs where possible.

Short Term   The short-term objective is to sustain unit growth while building cold water washing dominance. This will require current user reinforcement and continued conversion of warm water washing users. Specifically, in fiscal 1986, Arctic Power will achieve a market share of 6.5% on factory sales of $22.0 million and a contribution margin of 18%. Regional share objectives are: Maritimes—6.3%; Québec—17.2%; Alberta—5%; and B.C.—5%.

Marketing Strategy   Arctic Power will be positioned as the most effective laundry detergent espe-cially formulated for cold water washing. The primary target for Arctic Power is women 18 to 49 and skewed towards the 25 to 34 segment. The secondary market is all adults.

Arctic Power will defend its franchise by allocating regional effort commensurate with brand development in order to maintain current users. In line with the Western expansion strategy, support will be directed to Alberta and B.C. to enhance the acceptance of cold water washing and thereby broaden the appeal among occasional users and nonusers of Arctic Power.

Media Strategy   The media strategy objective is to achieve high levels of message registration against the target group through high message continuity and frequency/reach. Media spending behind regional television will be allocated 75% to brand maintenance and 25% to investment spending for brand and cold water market development. Arctic Power will have the number five share of media expenditure position nationally while being the number three detergent advertiser in Québec.

	TV Spending	GRPs per Week[a]
1985 plan	$1,010,000	92
Actual	$990,000	88
1986 plan	$1,350,000	95

[a] GRP (Gross Rating Points) is a measurement of advertising impact derived by multiplying the percentage of the target population exposed to an advertisement by the average number of exposures per person.

Arctic Power's 1986 media spending of $1.35 million is a 36% increase over 1985. This returns Arctic Power to its reach objective of 90% in Québec, five points ahead of a year ago. In addition, two new television markets have been added, with enhanced support in B.C. and Alberta. Reach objectives will be achieved by skewing more of Arctic Power's spending into efficient daytime spots, which cost less than night network and are more flexible in light of regional reach objectives.

Scheduling will maintain continuous flighting established in 1985, with concentrations at peak dealing time representing 40 weeks on air in the East and 32 weeks in the West.

Copy Strategy: Québec/Maritimes   The creative objective is to convince consumers that Arctic Power is the superior detergent for cold water washing. The consumers' benefit is that when they are washing in cold water, Arctic Power will clean clothes and remove stains more effectively than other detergents. The support for this claim is based on the special formulation of Arctic Power. The executional tone will be humorous but with a clear, rational explanation.

Copy Strategy: B.C./Alberta   The creative objective is to convince consumers that cold water washing is better than hot and, when washing in cold water, to use Arctic Power. The consumer benefit is that cold water washing reduces shrinkage, color run, and energy costs. The executional tone needs to be distinct from other detergent advertising to break through traditional washing attitudes and will be young-adult oriented, light, "cool" and upbeat.

Consumer Promotions   The objective of consumer promotions in Québec/Maritimes is to increase the rate of usage by building frequency of purchase among existing users. The objective in B.C./Alberta is to increase the rate of trial of Arctic Power. In total $856,000 will be spent on consumer promotions.

1. **Jan.:** $.50 In-pack Coupon—To support trade inventory increases and retain current customers in the face of strong competitive activity 400,000 coupons will be placed in all sizes in the Québec/Maritimes distribution region. The coupon is for 6-liter (6L) or 12L sizes, and expected redemption is 18% at a cost of $50,000.
2. **April:** To generate a 17% recent trial of regular-sized boxes of Arctic Power in B.C. and Alberta, a 500-ml saleable sample prepriced at $.49 will be distributed through food and drug stores. In addition, a $.50 coupon for the 6L or 12L size will be placed on the pack of all samples. The offer will penetrate 44% of households in the region at a total cost of $382,000.

3. **June:** $.40 Coupon through Free-Standing Insert—To sustain interest and foster trial, a $.40 coupon will be delivered to 30% of homes in Alberta/B.C. The coupon is redeemable on the 3L size, and expected redemption is 4.5%, at a cost of $28,000.
4. **April/July:** Game (Cool-by-the-Pool)—Five in-ground pools and patio accessories will be given away through spelling POWER by letters dropped in boxes of Arctic Power. Two letters will be placed in each box through national distribution, and will coincide with high trade activity and the period in which the desirability of the prizes is highest, at a cost of $184,000.
5. **Sept.:** $.75 Direct Mail National Coupon Pack (excluding Ontario)—To maximize swing buyer volume (from competition) in Québec and encourage trial in the West, a $.75 coupon for the 6L or 12L size will be mailed to 70% of households in the primary market areas, generating a 3% redemption rate at a cost of $212,000.

Trade Promotions   The objective of the trade promotions is to maintain regular and feature pricing equal to Tide and encourage prominent shelf facing. An advertising feature is expected from each key account during every promotion event run in Québec and the Maritimes. Distribution for any size is expected to increase to 95%. In the West, maximum effort will be directed at establishing display for the 6L size, and four feature events will be expected from each key account. Distribution should be developed to 71% in B.C. and 56% in Alberta. Average deal size will be 14% off the regular price or $5.00 per 6L case. In addition, most trade events will include a $1.00 per case allowance for coop advertising and merchandising support. The total trade budget is $3.46 million, which includes $1 million investment spending in the West. The promotion schedule is presented below.

Arctic Power 1986 Promotional Schedule

Trade Promotions	J	F	M	A	M	J	J	A	S	O	N	D
Maritimes	X		X		X		X		X			
Québec	X	X		X		X	X		X		X	X
Alberta/B.C.	X			X			X		X	X		
Consumer Promotions												
East $.50 coupon	X	X										
West sample/coupon				X								
West $.40 coupon						X						
National game				X	X	X	X					
National $.75 coupon									X			

Results of the Western Campaign

In August 1986, during the middle of the Western campaign, a "minitracking" study was conducted in the two provinces to monitor the program. The results of the August study were compared with the February study and reported in Exhibit 5. Market share for Arctic Power was also measured on a bimonthly basis, and the figures are shown below.

The campaign clearly had an impact, as brand and advertising awareness had increased, particularly in Alberta (Exhibit 5). Brand trial within the last six months had more than doubled in Alberta and was up over 25% in B.C. However, market share had peaked at 2.8% in Alberta and by the end of the year had declined to 1.9%. Market share in B.C. had reached a high of 7.3% and averaged 5.5% for the year.

In attempting to explain the different results in the two provinces, Linda Barton and Gary Parsons isolated two factors. First, B.C. had always been a "good" market for Arctic Power with share figures around 4%, whereas Alberta was less than half that amount. Second, there had been a considerable amount of competitive activity in Alberta during the year. Each of the three major firms had increased trade and consumer promotions to maintain existing brand shares.

ARCTIC POWER—1987

The 1987 brand plan for Arctic Power was similar in thrust and expenditure levels to the 1986 plan. Expenditure levels in Alberta were reduced until the full impli-

Arctic Power Market Share

				1986						
	1983	1984	1985	D/J	F/M	A/M	J/J	A/S	O/N	Total 1986
Alberta	0.7	2.3	1.7	1.4	1.1	2.8	2.8	2.4	1.9	2.1
B.C.	3.2	4.0	3.9	4.0	4.0	6.1	6.1	7.3	5.4	5.5

EXHIBIT 5   Results of Western Campaign

	Prelaunch (February, 1986)		Postlaunch (August, 1986)	
	Alberta	B.C.	Alberta	B.C.
Unaided Brand Awareness[a]				
Brand mentioned total (%)	13.3	20.3	18.1	24.2
Advertising Awareness				
1. Advertising mentioned (unaided)[b] (%)	1.9	7.9	20.3	11.5
2. Advertising mentioned (aided)[c] (%)	18.5	27.9	31.4	34.6
Brand Trial				
1. Ever tried[d] (%)	25.0	43.0	36.3	48.0
2. Used (last six months)[e] (%)	6.8	15.1	17.1	19.4
Image Measure[f]				
• Cleaning and removing dirt	1.0	1.2	1.2	1.5
• Removing tough stains	.7	.9	.9	1.4
• Being good value for the price	.5	.9	1.0	1.4
• Cleaning well in cold water	1.2	1.3	1.7	1.8
Conversion to Cold Water				
• Average number of loads out of 10 washed in cold water	1.8	2.2	2.0	2.3

Source: Tracking study.

[a] Question: *When you think of laundry detergents, what three brands first come to mind? Can you name three more for me?* Brand mentioned total is if the brand was mentioned at all. On average, respondents mentioned 4.5 brands.

[b] Question: *What brand or brands of laundry detergent have you seen or heard advertised?* Advertising mentioned (unaided) is of brand advertising mentioned.

[c] Question: *Have you recently seen or heard any advertising for brand?* Advertising mentioned (aided) is if respondent said yes when asked.

[d] Question: *Have you ever tried brand?*

[e] Question: *Have you used brand in the past six months?*

[f] Respondents rated the brand on the four image measures. The rating scale ranged from –5 (doesn't perform well) to +5 (performs well).

cations of the 1986 campaign could be examined. Market share in 1987 was expected to be 6.7%, up marginally from the 6.5% share achieved in 1986 (Exhibit 6).

Each year, every product manager at CPC conducted an extensive brand review. The review for Arctic Power included a detailed competitive analysis of the four leading brands on a regional basis and was based primarily on the tracking study. In July 1987, Linda Barton and Gary Parsons were examining the tracking information which summarized regional information on four critical aspects of the market—brand image (Exhibit 7), brand

and advertising awareness (Exhibit 8), brand trial and usage in the last six months (Exhibit 9), and market share and share of media expenditures (Exhibit 10). Future decisions for Arctic Power would be based, in large part, on this information.

THE DECISION

Prior to deciding on the strategic direction for Arctic Power, Barton and Parsons met to discuss the situation. It was a hot Toronto day in early July 1987. Bar-

EXHIBIT 6   Arctic Power: Market Share and Total Volume by Region (1983–1987E)

Region	Market Share					1986 Total Volume[a] ('000 liters)
	1983	1984	1985	1986	1987E	
National	4.7	5.6	6.4	6.5	6.7	406,512
Maritimes	5.3	5.7	6.3	6.3	6.3	32,616
Québec	12.3	13.8	17.7	17.5	18.0	113,796
Ontario	.9	1.1	1.1	.8	1.0	158,508
Manitoba/Saskatchewan	.2	.2	.1	.1	.1	28,440
Alberta	.7	2.3	1.7	2.1	2.0	40,644
British Columbia	3.2	4.0	3.9	5.5	6.0	32,508

Source: Company records.
[a] All laundry detergent.
1987E = estimated.

EXHIBIT 7   Brand Images by Region (1986)

Image Measure[a]	National	Maritimes	Québec	Ontario	Man/Sask	Alberta	B.C.
Arctic Power							
• Cleaning and removing dirt	1.4	2.0	2.5	.8	.4	1.0	1.2
• Removing tough stains	1.1	1.6	1.9	.7	3.0	.7	.9
• Being good value for the price	1.1	1.4	2.6	.3	.2	.5	.9
• Cleaning well in cold water	1.6	2.1	2.8	1.0	.4	1.2	1.3
ABC							
• Cleaning…dirt	1.0	1.9	.5	.9	1.1	1.2	1.6
• Removing…stains	.5	1.1	.0	.6	.8	.7	.9
• Being…price	1.5	2.4	.8	1.5	1.3	1.7	2.1
• Cleaning…cold water	.6	1.0	.1	.7	.7	.7	.7
Sunlight							
• Cleaning…dirt	2.0	1.9	1.8	2.4	1.9	1.6	1.6
• Removing…stains	1.6	1.6	1.5	1.9	1.4	1.2	1.2
• Being…price	2.0	1.7	1.9	2.4	1.8	1.7	1.5
• Cleaning…cold water	1.4	1.1	1.5	1.7	1.2	1.1	.7
Tide							
• Cleaning…dirt	3.4	3.7	3.2	3.6	3.5	3.3	3.2
• Removing…stains	3.0	3.1	2.8	3.3	3.0	2.7	2.7
• Being…price	3.1	3.1	3.3	3.1	2.8	3.0	2.4
• Cleaning…cold water	2.4	2.3	2.6	2.5	2.4	2.3	1.9

Source: Tracking study.
[a] Respondents rated each brand on the four image measures. The rating scale ranged from –5 (doesn't perform well) to +5 (performs well).
N = 1816.
A difference of .2 is likely to be significant in statistical terms.

EXHIBIT 8 **Brand and Advertising Awareness by Region (1986)**

	Percentages						
	National	*Maritimes*	*Québec*	*Ontario*	*Man/Sask*	*Alberta*	*B.C.*
Unaided Brand Awareness[a]							
1. *Brand Mentioned First*							
Arctic Power	4.4	7.0	12.5	.0	.0	1.0	2.6
ABC	8.1	18.4	4.6	7.3	4.7	8.4	12.8
Sunlight	9.3	8.4	9.6	9.3	12.0	9.1	7.9
Tide	57.9	55.5	41.9	69.7	63.1	59.7	54.4
2. *Brand Mentioned Total*							
Arctic Power	23.0	43.5	49.8	5.0	3.0	13.3	20.3
ABC	61.3	82.6	47.9	64.0	56.1	67.5	64.9
Sunlight	58.1	60.2	50.8	65.0	58.5	62.0	46.6
Tide	94.8	95.7	88.8	98.0	97.3	97.4	94.4
Advertising Awareness							
1. *Advertising Mentioned (Unaided)*[b]							
Arctic Power	7.0	10.7	17.5	.7	.0	1.9	7.9
ABC	25.2	32.8	20.8	27.0	17.3	30.5	24.9
Sunlight	8.6	4.7	5.9	13.0	5.0	6.8	8.2
Tide	44.0	40.1	32.7	55.0	46.2	48.4	35.4
2. *Advertising Mentioned (Aided)*[c]							
Arctic Power	29.2	38.8	55.1	15.3	5.6	18.5	27.9
ABC	56.1	61.5	55.1	56.0	51.5	60.4	53.4
Sunlight	29.9	20.1	26.4	40.3	21.3	21.1	24.9
Tide	65.3	60.9	54.8	78.0	68.1	65.3	48.4

Source: Tracking study.

[a] Question: *When you think of laundry detergents, what three brands first come to mind? Can you name three more for me?* Brand mentioned first is the first brand mentioned. Brand mentioned total is if the brand was mentioned at all. On average, respondents mentioned 4.5 brands.

[b] Question: *What brand or brands of laundry detergent have you seen or heard advertised?* Advertising mentioned (unaided) is of brand advertising mentioned.

[c] Question: *Have you recently seen or heard any advertising for brand?* Advertising mentioned (unaided) is if respondent said yes when asked.

N = 1816.

EXHIBIT 9 **Brand Trial in Last Six Months by Region (1986)**

Brand Trial	*National*	*Maritimes*	*Québec*	*Ontario*	*Man/Sask*	*Alberta*	*B.C.*
1. *Ever Tried*[a]							
Arctic Power	42.4	67.9	75.6	19.7	20.3	25.0	43.0
ABC	60.4	83.9	50.8	60.0	53.5	62.7	67.9
Sunlight	66.3	65.6	59.4	75.0	67.1	58.1	58.7
Tide	93.6	91.0	90.1	97.3	95.0	91.9	92.1
2. *Used (Last Six Months)*[b]							
Arctic Power	19.4	29.8	46.5	4.3	2.3	6.8	15.1
ABC	37.2	56.2	34.7	32.3	29.2	39.3	47.5
Sunlight	38.3	29.8	38.0	44.3	36.2	36.7	28.5
Tide	68.1	66.6	66.0	73.3	67.8	69.5	54.8

Source: Tracking study.

[a] Question: *Have you ever tried brand?*

[b] Question: *Have you used brand in the past six months?*

Note: On average, respondents had 1.3 brands of laundry detergents in the home.

N = 1816.

EXHIBIT 10   Market Share and Share of Media Expenditures by Region (1986)

	National	Maritimes	Québec	Ontario	Man/Sask	Alberta	B.C.
			Percentages				
Market Share							
Arctic Power	6.5	6.3	17.5	.8	.1	2.1	5.5
ABC	13.9	27.8	8.6	13.8	11.6	16.1	21.5
Sunlight	13.4	7.7	12.1	16.4	14.2	10.4	11.3
Tide	34.1	24.5	28.3	39.3	40.0	36.9	28.5
All other brands	32.1	33.7	33.5	29.7	34.1	34.5	33.2
Total	100.0	100.0	100.0	100.0	100.0	100.0	100.0
Share of Media Expenditures[a]							
Arctic Power	9.3	13.1	16.1	.5	1.4	16.0	13.1
ABC	13.6	14.7	9.1	18.4	17.3	12.1	12.1
Sunlight	11.3	11.1	11.1	12.6	10.2	10.1	9.8
Tide	29.7	27.8	25.1	33.1	38.1	30.2	28.7
All other brands	36.1	33.3	38.6	35.4	33.0	31.6	36.3
Total	100.0	100.0	100.0	100.0	100.0	100.0	100.0
Total $ ('000)	14,429	695	4,915	4,758	928	1,646	1,487

Source: Company records.

[a] The total amount of advertising spent by all brands was determined. The amount spent by each brand as a percentage of total spending was calculated.

ton began the discussion. "I've got some estimates on what our shares are likely to be for 1987. It looks like we'll have a national share of 6.7%, broken down as follows: Maritimes (6.3%), Québec (18%), Ontario (1%), Manitoba/Saskatchewan (0.1%), Alberta (2%), B.C. (6%)."

Parsons responded, "I think our problem in Alberta was all the competitive activity. Under normal conditions we'd have achieved 5% of that market. But the Alberta objective is small when you think about what we could do in our other undeveloped markets. I've been giving it a lot of thought, and we should go national with Arctic Power. We've got a brand that is equal to Tide, and we've got to stop keeping it a secret from the rest of Canada. If we can duplicate the success we had in B.C., we'll turn this market on its ear."

"Wait a minute, Gary," said Linda, "in 1986 we spent almost $2,000,000 on advertising, consumer and trade promotions in the West. Even though spending returned to normal levels this year, that was a big investment to get the business going, and it will be at least four years before we get that money back. If we go after the national market, you can well expect Tide to fight back with trade spending which will make your share or margin objectives even harder to achieve. On a per capita basis, we'd have to spend at least as much in our underdeveloped markets as we spent in the West. We've got a real problem here. Our brand may be as good as Tide, but I don't think we can change a lot of consumers' minds, particularly the loyal Tide users. I hate to say it, but for many Canadians, when

they think about washing clothes, Tide is the brand they think will clean their clothes better than any other brand. I agree that the size of the undeveloped market warrants another look. But remember, any decision will have to be backed up with a solid analysis and a plan that senior management will buy."

Gary replied, "I know that even if I am right, it will be a tough sell. I haven't got it completed yet, but I'm working out the share level we would need to break even if we expanded nationally."

Linda responded, "Well, when you get that done, we will talk about national expansion again. For the moment, we have to resolve this positioning dilemma. I don't like a two-country approach but it does seem to make sense in this case. I think we might still want to focus on the brand in the East and continue to develop the cold water washing market in the West."

Gary would have preferred to continue the discussion of national expansion but realized he would have to do some work and at least produce the share estimate before he raised the subject again, so replied, "I agree that Canada is not one homogeneous market but that perspective can be taken to extremes. I worry that all of this data we get on the regional markets is getting in the way of good marketing judgment. I prefer a unified strategy, and the Québec campaign has a proven track record."

Linda concluded, "Let's go over the data again, then start making our decisions. Remember, our goal is to develop a solid brand name for 1988 for Arctic Power."

CASE 5-3 STATION KGEN*

*T*he following marketing plan has been prepared for a new radio station in Phoenix, Arizona. KGEN is targeted at an underserved Spanish language market segment. Your job is to evaluate this marketing plan and the feasibility of the entire project.

EXECUTIVE SUMMARY

This report develops a marketing plan for KGEN(FM), Phoenix. As of July 1992, the station signed on the air, broadcasting a Spanish language format to the currently underserved demographic group of Hispanic listeners aged 25–54. The station is forecasted to generate a local commercial audience share of 2.1% and a market revenue share of 2.2%. KGEN revenues are forecast at $239,000 for the last half of 1992 and $1.7 million the next year. Operating losses of $312,000 for 1992 are expected to grow to profits of $239,000 in 1993. The types of businesses that will be targeted to buy air time include food stores and car dealerships. These two types of businesses account for over one-half of the market's retail sales. Spots on the station will be priced at $605/30 seconds and $302/15 seconds for morning drive time. Prices are graduated downward as the level of listening declines. The station will maintain an upscale bilingual image and focus its promotions on community service-oriented activities. The project's estimated return on invested capital is 6.5% per year.

INTRODUCTION

This marketing plan proposes the development of radio station KGEN(FM) as a Spanish language competitor in the Phoenix, Arizona, radio market. KGEN(FM) will broadcast on a frequency of 105.9 mHz and will be licensed to Paradise Valley, located in the city of Phoenix. The station, as a Class A facility, will have a signal strength of 3 kW from an antenna height of 328 feet—the maximum operating parameters for a Class A license. Presently, the Federal Communications Commission (FCC) has an open allocation registered for such a station.

EXHIBIT 1 **Hispanic Population and Audience Shares for Selected Radio Markets**

Market Rank	Market	Hispanic Population	Local Commercial Share Points
22	Phoenix	13.9%	3.0%
187	Amarillo	9.1	1.7
3	Chicago	9.5	5.4
8	Dallas	9.7	4.6
24	Denver	9.9	1.2
194	Naples-Marcos Island	10.4	2.6
30	Sacramento	10.8	2.5
10	Houston	12.7	9.5
4	San Francisco	14.0	4.3
1	New York	14.3	6.9
188	Yakima	15.1	2.0
118	Modesto	16.5	7.1
16	Anaheim	18.6	20.9
28	Riverside	19.6	7.4
59	Austin	19.6	3.2
31	San Jose	19.8	13.7
173	Santa Barbara	20.5	4.8
169	Odessa-Midland	21.2	8.1
163	Lubbock	21.3	7.4
88	Stockton	21.7	12.9
65	Tucson	22.9	6.6
248	San Angelo	23.8	7.3
76	Monterey-Salinas	25.0	19.4
92	Bakersfield, CA	27.3	11.3
157	Palm Springs	27.6	13.7
11	Miami	29.5	22.7
2	Los Angeles	29.9	17.4
114	Oxnard-Ventura	32.1	33.4
69	Fresno	32.5	11.9
229	Pueblo	33.2	7.5
259	Victoria	33.6	16.3
79	Albuquerque	39.8	5.5
35	San Antonio	48.7	17.6
230	Santa Fe	49.7	7.2
131	Corpus Christi	54.5	15.7
78	El Paso	67.3	15.4
71	McAllen-Brownsville	83.0	37.8

Source: 1992 Investing in Radio, 2nd ed. (BIA Publications, 1992).

Facilities for KGEN will cost $450,000 for technical, studio, and office facilities. An additional $35,000 will be needed for the legal and engineering services required to obtain the FCC license.

---

* This case was prepared by Hale N. Tongren of George Mason University.

ENVIRONMENT

Spanish language radio stations tend to be found in radio markets with Hispanic populations of 9% or greater. Generally, as the Hispanic population increases, so does the audience share generated by stations serving this niche. Exhibit 1 presents all radio markets with at least a 9% Hispanic population and the total local commercial audience share points[1] earned by all Spanish language stations in the market.

Phoenix's Hispanic population measures 13.9%. By focusing on markets with similar-sized Hispanic populations—10% to 20%—it is clear that there is a wide variation in the degree to which this group is served. Among the 16 markets, 5 have no Spanish language stations at all. However, the audience shares earned by Spanish stations in such markets as Houston (9.5%), New York (6.9%), Modesto (7.1%), Anaheim (20.9%), Riverside (7.4%), and San Jose (13.7%), indicate the potential for such stations in a market such as Phoenix. Presently, Phoenix Spanish stations generate a 3% local commercial share, which is below their potential.

The development of the radio industry witnessed the growth of FM to a point where it ultimately dominated the AM spectrum. Formats that have remained successful on AM radio include news and talk-oriented formats that do not require the higher-quality sound available on FM radio. Also included are certain music formats catering to the market's older listeners who grew up with AM and have remained comfortable with it. Presently, many Spanish stations fall into this category—AM stations appealing to the older segment of the Hispanic population. Exhibit 2 breaks out Spanish radio audience shares earned by AM and FM stations. Phoenix is typical of many markets in that 100% of the market's Spanish listening occurs on AM stations.

The sign-on of KGEN(FM) will take advantage of what is predicted to be the migration of Spanish radio to the FM band. Given the prominent place music holds in Latin culture and the quality sound of FM, the development of Spanish FM radio makes sense. The disparity between markets in the degree to which FM is utilized for the Spanish-speaking population, shown in Exhibit 2, is indicative of the substantial potential for a station such as KGEN(FM).

---

[1] A local commercial audience share is calculated by dividing a station's Arbitron reported share (Exhibit 3) by the Total Local Commercial Share. This provides a more accurate indicator of the station's expected market revenue share.

EXHIBIT 2   Ratio of AM to FM Radio Stations in Selected Markets

Market	AM Stations	FM Stations
Phoenix	100%	0%
Amarillo	100	0
Chicago	58	42
Dallas	93	7
Denver	100	0
Naples-Marcos Island	100	0
Sacramento	100	0
Houston	73	27
San Francisco	44	56
New York	61	39
Yakima	100	0
Modesto	89	11
Anaheim	100	0
Riverside	100	0
Austin	100	0
San Jose	48	52
Santa Barbara	100	0
Odessa-Midland	100	0
Lubbock	79	21
Stockton	38	62
Tucson	100	0
San Angelo	0	100
Monterey-Salinas	70	30
Bakersfield, CA	91	9
Palm Springs	100	0
Miami	62	38
Los Angeles	69	31
Oxnard-Ventura	53	47
Fresno	71	29
Pueblo	100	0
Victoria	20	80
Albuquerque	63	37
San Antonio	52	48
Santa Fe	100	0
Corpus Christi	70	30
El Paso	45	55
McAllen-Brownsville	54	46

The Phoenix radio market (defined by Arbitron as Maricopa County) is home to 40 radio stations. Profiles of the Phoenix radio market, including some demographic and competitive information, are presented in Exhibits 3 and 4. Currently, the market is led in audience shares by country-formatted KNIX(FM), Phoenix; news/talk-formatted KTAR(AM) in Phoenix is a strong contender as well. A variety of formats are offered by FM stations in the market, such as contemporary hit radio (CHR), album-oriented-rock (AOR), oldies, adult contemporary (AC), and classical. There is one Spanish FM station, KVVA(FM), licensed to Apache Junction, serving Phoenix. This station often does not earn measurable shares, which may be attributable to its less powerful Class C2 facilities, and its community of license is roughly 25 miles from

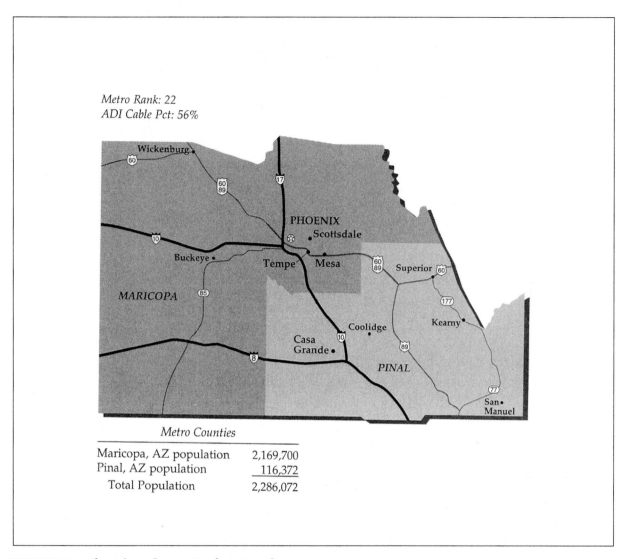

Metro Rank: 22
ADI Cable Pct: 56%

Metro Counties	
Maricopa, AZ population	2,169,700
Pinal, AZ population	116,372
Total Population	2,286,072

EXHIBIT 3   Phoenix, Arizona, Market Overview

EXHIBIT 3   (Continued)

Market Radio Financials
(all figures in 000s, except percentages and ratios)

	1985	1986	1987	1988	1989	1990	Δ 85–90
Estimated Gross	$56,000	60,800	65,700	67,300	72,400	74,300	5.8%
Revenues	Δ 90–91	1991	1992	1993	1994	1995	Δ 91–95
	0.0%	$74,300	75,800	78,100	81,200	85,200	3.5%

	1985	1990	1995
Revenue/retail sales	$4.78/1,000	$4.46/1,000	$3.68/1,000
Revenue/capita	$30.43	$34.24	$34.72

Demographic and Economic Overview
(000s, except Retail Sales and EBI in 000,000s)

	1985	1990	Growth Rate	1990	1995	Growth Rate
MSA population	1,841.1	2,169.7	3.3%	2,169.7	2,455.2	2.5%
MSA Households	719.1	826.0	2.8%	826.0	945.1	2.7%
MSA Retail sales	11,710.9	16,652.4	7.3%	16,652.4	23,168.7	6.8%
MSA EBI	21,989.7	30,177.8	6.5%	30,177.8	45,434.9	8.5%

Demographic Breakdown

	Total	Under 12	12–17	18–24	25–34	35–44	45–54	Over 55
Men (000)	1,069.0	206.1	86.6	118.4	201.8	161.0	105.2	189.8
Women (000)	1,100.7	196.6	83.0	110.5	194.8	161.5	109.7	244.5
Total	2,169.7	402.7	169.6	228.9	396.7	322.5	215.0	434.4
Percentage	100.0%	18.6%	7.8%	10.5%	18.3%	14.9%	9.9%	20.0%

Per capita $13,909   Median household $28,778   Avg household $36,535
Ethnic population: Black 2.8%   Hispanic 13.9%

Market Summary

	Class A	Class B	Class C	Viable FMs	All FMs	All AMs	Total
No. of stations	2		16	13	18	22	40
Tot 12+	2.4		66.4	64.3	68.8	23.6	92.4
Avg 12+	1.2		4.2	4.9	3.8	1.1	2.3
Tot LCS	2.6		71.9	69.6	74.5	25.5	100.0
Avg LCS	1.3		4.5	5.4	4.1	1.2	2.5

EXHIBIT 3 (Continued) **Competitive Overview**

Market: Phoenix, AZ   *Metro Rank: 22*
AM Stations   *Some stations also rated in Tucson (65).*

City of Calls	License	FCC Class	Freq	Day Power (kW)	Night Power (kW)	Owner	Date Std	Date Acq	Sales Price (000)
KOY	Phoenix	III	550	5.0	1.00	Edens Bcstg	21	8412	
KTAR	Phoenix	III	620	5.0	5.00	Pulitzer Bcstg Co	22	7904	
KMEO	Phoenix	II	740	1.0	0.29	Bonneville Intl	58	9104	
KVVA	Phoenix	II	860	1.0	1.00	Amer Bcstg Systems	49	9107	
KFYI	Phoenix	III	910	5.0	5.00	Broadcast Group	40	8201	
KOOL	Phoenix	III	960	5.0	5.00	Adams Communications	47	8610	
KUKQ	Tempe	II	1060	5.0	0.50	Grimm & Clifford	60	9105	
KRDS	Tolleson	II	1190	5.0	0.25	Interstate Bcstg	61	8112	
KISP	Phoenix	IV	1230	1.0	1.00	EZ Communications	49	8610	
KXAM	Mesa	III	1310	5.0	0.50	Gerson, B., D. & M.	46	8912	975
KNNS	Glendale[a]	III	1360	5.0	1.00	Resource Media Inc	46	8909	
KSUN	Phoenix	IV	1400	1.0	1.00	Fiesta Radio Inc	54	8612	600
KOPA	Scottsdale[a]	III	1440	5.0	0.05	Great American Bcstg	56	9201	
KPHX	Phoenix	III	1480	5.0	0.50	Continental Bcstg	58	8002	650
KCWW	Tempe	II	1580	50.0 cp	50.00	Buck Owens Bcstg	60	6705	
	No. of AM stations—15				# Combos—11				

Other AM stations: KXEG, KCKY, KTIM, KHEP, KIKO, KFNN, KASA
Stations Profiled—33

[a] Indicates a change since the last edition.
Source: Investing in Radio 1992, 2nd ed. Copyright ©1992 BIA Publications, Inc. All rights reserved.

EXHIBIT 3 (Continued)

Format	Fall 1991	Summer 1991	Spring 1991	Winter 1991	Fall 1990	Summer 1990	Spring 1990	Winter 1990	Fall 1989
AOR	3.1	2.8	4.3	3.5	2.1	2.8	3.1	3.2	3.3
News/Talk	9.6	8.6	6.7	10.6	8.8	7.6	8.6	8.3	7.9
Easy	1.6	1.6	0.9	0.8	2.1	1.7	0.7	0.6	1.2
Spanish	0.7	0.0	0.5	1.2	0.9	0.7	1.4	0.7	0.8
News/Talk	4.3	4.0	4.5	4.5	3.2	3.8	2.9	2.1	3.7
Oldies	2.0	1.7	1.5	1.4	1.5	1.5	2.1	1.4	1.4
Rock	1.4	1.4	1.5	1.3	1.0	2.0	1.7	1.2	1.1
Chrs Contemp	0.4	0.5	0.0	0.0	0.5	0.0	0.5	0.4	0.5
Urban AC	0.7	0.0	0.0	0.3	0.0	0.3	0.0	0.0	0.0
Nostalgia	0.9	1.6	1.4	0.5	0.6	0.8	0.6	0.0	0.1
News/Sports	0.6	1.9	1.5	2.2	2.4	2.3	1.5	1.8	2.8
Spanish	0.9	1.0	0.0	0.9	0.6	1.2	1.0	0.7	1.2
Clsc Hits	0.0	0.0	0.0	0.0	0.0	0.1	0.0	0.0	0.0
Spanish	1.2	1.5	0.4	0.8	1.4	1.5	1.2	0.5	1.6
Country	0.4	0.8	0.4	1.5	1.4	0.9	1.2	1.5	0.8
AM TOTALS	27.8	27.4	23.6	29.5	26.5	27.2	26.5	22.4	26.4
Combined share	0.0	0.0	0.0	0.0	0.0	0.4	0.0	0.0	0.3
Total local commercial share	92.0	93.8	92.4	93.7	93.4	93.0	93.5	93.2	92.8

EXHIBIT 4   Phoenix Market Information

1991 ARB rank: 22
1991 MSA rank: 19
1991 ADI rank: 20
FM base value: $9,300,000
Base value %: 13.2%

1991 revenue: $70,500,000
Rev per share point: $762,987
Population per station: 68,692 (26)
1991 revenue change: −2.5%
Station turnover: 20.5%

Manager's market ranking (current): 3.5
Manager's market ranking (future): 4.0
Duncan's Radio market grade: 1 Average
Mathematical market grade: 1 above avg.

Revenue History and Projections

	86	87	88	89	90	91	92	93	94	95	96
Duncan revenue est:	60.1	65.5	68.5	72.6	72.3	70.5					
Yearly growth rate (86–91): 3.3% (4.3% assigned)											
Projected revenue estimates:							72.6	75.7	79.0	82.4	85.9
Revenue per capita:	31.30	32.91	33.25	34.40	33.32	32.05					
Yearly growth rate (86–91): 0.5% (2.1% assigned)											
Projected revenue per capita:							32.72	33.41	34.11	34.83	35.56
Resulting revenue estimate:							73.3	76.8	81.2	85.7	89.2
Revenue as % of retail sales:	.0047	.0047	.0044	.0046	.0043	.0040					
Mean % (86–91): .00445% (.00040% assigned)											
Resulting revenue estimate:							73.6	79.2	86.0	92.8	99.2
Mean Revenue Estimate:							73.2	77.2	82.0	87.0	91.4

Population and Demographic Estimates

	86	87	88	89	90	91	92	93	94	95	96
Total population (millions):	1.92	1.99	2.06	2.11	2.17	2.20	2.24	2.30	2.38	2.46	2.51
Retail sales (billions):	12.7	13.9	15.4	15.9	16.7	17.5	18.4	19.8	21.5	23.2	24.8

Below-the-line listening shares: 0.0
Unlisted station listening: 7.6%
Total lost listening: 7.6%
Available share points: 92.4
Number of viable stations: 19.5
Mean share points per station: 4.7
Median share points per station: 4.2

Confidence Levels
1991 Revenue estimates: Normal
1992–1996 revenue projections: Normal

Comments
Market reports to Miller, Kaplan ... All viable stations cooperate except KFYI, and KKFR-F .... Managers predict 0% to 2% revenue change in 1992...

EXHIBIT 4 (Continued)

	Ethnic Breakdowns (%)		Income Breakdowns (%)		Age Breakdowns (%)		Education Leveles	
Rev. per available share point: $762,987	White	83.3	<15	22.8	12–24	21.9	Non high school grad:	25.0
Estimated rev. for mean station: $3,586,039	Black	2.8	15–30	28.8	25–54	51.9	High school grad:	34.9
Household income: $32,545	Hispanic	13.9	30–50	26.7	55+	26.2	College 1–3 years:	21.8
Median age: 32.2 years	Other	—	50–75	15.2			College 4+ years:	18.3
Median education: 12.7 years			75+	6.5				
Median home value: $60,700								
Population change (1990–1995): 13.2%								
Retail sales change (1990–1995): 39.1%								
Number of class B or C FM's: 13 + 1 = 14								
Revenue per AQH: $26,178								
Cable penetration: 47%								

The above information is provided through the courtesy of Market Statistics, a division of Bill Communications.

Commerce and Industry

Important Business and Industries	Fortune 500 Companies	Forbes 500 Companies	Forbes Largest Private Companies
Aerospace	Phelps Dodge (168)	Circle K	Basha's (338)
Electronics		Greyhound Dial	Abco Markets (256)
Agribusiness		Pinnacle West	
Military		Valley National	
High tech			

Inc 500 Companies

EMS (24)
Arrowhead Landscaping & Maintenance (254)
Acoustic Imaging Technologies (295)
Arizona Freight System (439)
Quality "S" Manufacturing (488)

Employment Breakdowns

By Industry (SIC)			By Occupation		
1. Eating and Drinking Places	61,811	(8.0%)	Manag/Prof.	166,520	(25.1%)
2. Health Services	58,097	(7.5%)	Tech/Sales/Admin.	219,706	(33.1%)
3. Business Services	49,755	(6.5%)	Service	82,698	(12.5%)
4. Special Trade Contractors	44,270	(5.8%)	Farm/Forest/Fish	14,450	(2.1%)
5. Wholesale Trade-Durable Goods	33,180	(4.3%)	Precision Prod.	88,366	(13.4%)
6. Electric & Electronic Equip	28,222	(3.7%)	Oper/Fabri/Labor	91,884	(13.8%)
7. Engineering & Management Serv	28,062	(3.6%)			
8. Food Stores	27,428	(3.6%)			
9. Hotels and Other Lodging Plcs	25,065	(3.3%)			
10. Miscellaneous Retail	22,289	(2.9%)			
Total metro employees:	769,570				
Top 10 total employees:	378,179	(49.1%)			

EXHIBIT 4 (Continued)

Largest Local Banks	Colleges and Universities	Military Bases	Unemployment	
First Interstate (6.7 Bil)	Arizona State (42,952)	Luke AFB (6,186)	Jun 79:	5.2%
Citibank (2.7 Bil)	Grand Canyon Univ. (1,846)	Williams AFB (3,318)	Dec 82:	8.5%
Security Pacific (4.2 Bil)	Western International (1,569)		Sep 83:	7.1%
Valley National (9.4 Bil)			Sep 84:	3.3%
Chase (854 Mil)	Total Full-Time Students: 52,378		Aug 85:	5.1%
Bank of America (5.5 Bil)			Aug 86:	5.4%
			Aug 87:	4.8%
			Aug 88:	5.4%
			Jul 89:	4.8%
			Jul 90:	4.7%
			Jul 91:	4.6%

Radio Business Information

Highest Billing Stations

1. KNIX AF	$10,900,000
2. KTAR	9,000,000
3. KUPD-F	5,900,000
4. KMLE-F	4,900,000
5. KOOL AF	4,400,000
6. KSLX AF	4,200,000
7. KKLT-F	4,100,000
8. KPSN AF	3,800,000
9. KESZ-F	3,400,000
10. KDKB-F	3,300,000
11. KFYI	$2,600,000
12. KMXX AF	2,500,000
13. KOY-F	2,000,000
14. KKFR-F	1,900,000
15. KVRY-F	1,800,000
16. KONC-F	1,200,000
17. KOY	1,100,000
18. KGRX-F	900,000
19. KLFF	500,000
20. KXAM	400,000

Heavy Agency Radio Users	Largest Local Radio Accounts	Source of Regional Dollars
Western Int.	Mervyn's	
Evans Motta	First Interstate	
EB Lane	Grubb Chevy	
Creative Advertising	Smitty's	
Moses Anshell	Safeway	
Phillips Ramsey	Continental Homes	
Media Planning		

EXHIBIT 4 (Continued)

Major Daily Newspapers	AM	PM	SUN	Owner
Phoenix Republic	339,000		531,000	Central
Phoenix Gazette		98,911		Central

Competitive Media

Major Over the Air Television

			%
KAET	Phoenix	8	PBS	
KNXV	Phoenix	15	Fox	Scripps-Howard
KPHO	Phoenix	5		Meredith
KPNX	Phoenix	12	NBC	Gannett
KTSP	Phoenix	10	CBS	Great American
KTVK	Phoenix	3	ABC	Lewis
KTVW	Phoenix	33		Hallmark
KUTP	Phoenix	45		Chris-Craft

Media Revenue Estimates

	Revenue	%	% of Retail Sales
Television	$162,800,000	39.7	.0093
Radio	70,500,000	17.2	.0040
Newspaper	161,900,000	39.5	.0093
Outdoor	14,500,000	3.5	.0008
	$409,700,000		.0234

Note: Use newspaper and outdoor estimates with caution.

Best Restaurants

Avanti's (Italian)
Stockyards (Steak)
Rustler's Roost (Steak)
Palm Court
Don & Charles
Vincents

Best Hotels

Arizona Biltmore
Camelback Inn
Princess
Boulders
Hyatt Gainey Ranch
Ritz Carlton
Pointe
Phoenician

Best Golf Courses

Desert Mountain
Boulders
Desert Highlands
Desert Forest
TPC Stadium
Troon
Troon North

Weather Data

Elevation:	1112	
Annual precipitation:	7.4 in.	
Annual snowfall:	0	
Average windspeed:	6.1 (E)	

	Jan	Jul	Total Year
Avg. max. temp:	64.8	104.8	85.1
Avg. min. temp:	37.6	77.5	55.4
Average temp:	51.2	91.2	70.3

EXHIBIT 4   (Continued)

Radio Revenue Breakdown

Local	70.8% (+0.1%)
National	29.0% (−5.0%)
Network	0.2% (+26.6%)
Trade equals	7.7% of local—up 24% in 1991

Major Radio Station Sales since 1987

1987	KLFF, KONC-F (Sun City)		$ 6,500,000
1988	KSLX A/F	From First Media to Cook Inlet	15,000,000 (E) + tax cert.
1988	KGRX-F (Globe)	Sold to Daytona	2,250,000
1988	KMLE-F (Chandler)	From Ostrander-Wilson to Shamrock	8,000,000
1989	KLFF, KONC-F (Glendale)		2,300,000
1989	KZZP	Sold by Nationwide	975,000
1990	KGRX-F (Globe)	Sold by First City	2,000,000
1990	KESZ-F	Sold by Duffy	10,400,000
1991	KVVA AF		6,000,000 (E)
1991	KPSN AF	From Westinghouse to Bonneville	12,000,000
1991	KGRX-F (Globe)		750,000
1991	KFNN		399,000
1991	KOPA, KSLX-F	From Cook Inlet to Great American	11,400,000

Note: Some of these sales may not have been consummated.

Source: Duncan's Radio Market Guide, Copyright 1992.

Phoenix. KVVA(FM)'s weakness would allow KGEN(FM) to step in easily and become the market's Spanish FM station of choice.

Among the AMs in Phoenix are three Spanish stations: KVVA, KSUN, and KPHX. These three stations currently earn a 3.0% local commercial audience share. As yet, none of the three is a solidly entrenched competitor. Although more successful than the market's single Spanish FM, these Spanish AMs do not earn shares consistently. With the higher-quality sound of FM, KGEN(FM) will prove an attractive option to persons presently tuning in to these AMs.

Demographically, the Phoenix area is very attractive. As shown in Exhibit 3, the market's population is forecast to increase at an average annual rate of 2.5% through 1995. Nationwide population growth is forecast at the much lower rate of 1%. Retail sales are closely tied to radio market revenue growth and are projected to increase at a rate of 6.8% annually over the next three years in Phoenix. This compares favorably with retail sales growth nationwide, projected at 5.9%.

Income distribution in the Phoenix radio market is presented in Exhibit 5. Overall, the market is relatively affluent, as shown by the preponderance of homes that are in the upper income brackets.

TARGET MARKETS

The market to be served by KGEN(FM) is a relatively broad segment of Phoenix's Hispanic population. The demographic information in Exhibit 6 indicates that the majority of this group, 78.7%, is below the age of 45. Approximately 54.6% of the Hispanic population falls

EXHIBIT 5   Household Income Distribution in the Phoenix Radio Market

			Level of Income				
Under $5,000	$5,000 to $9,999	$10,000 to $14,999	$15,000 to $19,999	$20,000 to $24,999	$25,000 to $34,999	$35,000 to $49,999	$50,000 to More
46,295	64,671	79,090	86,415	81,257	139,331	153,804	175,137
			Percentage of Households in Each Group				
6%	8%	10%	10%	10%	17%	19%	21%

EXHIBIT 6 Demographic Breakdown of the Hispanic Population in the Phoenix Radio Market

Persons 12 + Teens (12–17)	264,500 40,600	Percentage of 12 + Population
Men		
18–24	25,600	10%
25–34	37,400	14%
35–44	25,000	9%
45–49	7,500	3%
50–54	5,400	2%
55–64	7,500	3%
65+	6,400	2%
Women		
18–24	23,200	9%
25–34	33,300	13%
35–44	23,100	9%
45–49	7,400	3%
50–54	5,500	2%
55–64	8,200	3%
65+	8,400	3%

Source: Arbitron Radio Audience Estimate, Phoenix, Fall 1991.

between the ages of 25 and 54—the single most highly sought-after group of consumers. For this reason, and because these listeners are the least served by Phoenix's existing Spanish stations, KGEN(FM) will target this group with its programming.

Exhibit 7 presents the audience composition of the three Spanish AMs, broken out by age group and sex. Hispanic women listen to more Spanish radio than Hispanic men. However, when the listening patterns are combined, it is clear that the market's existing

EXHIBIT 7 Specific Audience Shares Earned by Phoenix Spanish Language Stations

	Age Group				
	18–24	25–34	35–44	45–54	55–64
		Men			
KPHX(AM)	1.0	0.7	—	1.0	6.5
KSUN(AM)	0.5	0.5	—	0.5	—
KVVA(AM)	2.4	0.2	0.4	0.5	—
KVVA(FM)	—	—	—	—	—
Total men	3.9	1.4	0.4	2	6.5
		Women			
KPHX(AM)	—	1.6	3.1	0.9	1.5
KSUN(AM)	1.6	0.8	2.0	0.5	5.2
KVVA(AM)	2.6	1.1	—	1.4	—
KVVA(FM)	—	—	—	—	—
Total women	4.2	3.5	5.1	2.8	6.7
Total persons	8.1	4.9	5.5	4.8	13.2

Source: Arbitron's Radio Market Report, Phoenix, Fall 1991.

Spanish stations serve persons aged 18–24 and 55–64, which generate audience shares of 8.1% and 13.2%, respectively. This is far better than the intervening groups, which generate audience shares ranging from 3.9% to 5.5%. KGEN(FM) will serve this group with a Spanish/adult contemporary music format. The music selections will include Latin artists, as well as carefully selected crossover artists with appeal to both Latin and Anglo music tastes.

Radio stations also target advertisers. Information on spending patterns in the Phoenix radio market is presented in Exhibit 8. With this information, the sales staff of KGEN(FM) can pursue those businesses that garner substantial portions of the market's overall sales. Accordingly, KGEN(FM) will target food stores/grocery stores/supermarkets, which account for 37.3% of the market's retail sales. However, those stores that cater to the tastes of the Hispanic population should receive the greatest selling effort. Automotive dealers should also be actively pursued by KGEN's sales staff, as well as restaurants, general merchandise stores, and department stores.

Because market radio listening patterns vary widely over the course of the day as well as over the week,

EXHIBIT 8 Retail Sales in Phoenix by Store Group (000s)

Merchandise Line	Dollars Spent in 1990	Percent of Total
Food stores	$3,700	13.9%
Supermarkets	3,581	13.4
Eating & drinking places	1,724	6.5
General merchandise stores	1,841	6.9
Department stores	1,426	5.4
Apparel & accessories	729	2.7
Furniture/appliances	967	3.6
Furniture & home furnishings	549	2.1
Automotive dealers	3,874	14.5
Gasoline service stations	889	3.3
Building & hardware dealers	673	2.5
Drugstores	618	2.3
Groceries & other foods	2,667	10.0
Drugs/health/beauty aids	724	2.7
Major household appliances	229	0.9
Televisions, video recorders, & tape	117	0.4
Audio equipment, musical instruments & supplies	171	0.6
Home computers & calculators	119	0.4
Furniture & sleep equipment	411	1.5
Men's & boys' clothing	418	1.6
Women's & girls' clothing	982	3.7
Footwear	246	0.9
Total Retail Sales	$26,657	

advertising spots must be priced accordingly. The initial pricing scheme to be used by KGEN(FM) for the second half of 1992 is presented in Exhibit 9. Roughly 35% of KGEN(FM)'s revenue will be generated during the four-hour "morning drive" period, weekdays from 6 A.M. to 10 A.M. Slightly over 50% will be generated in subsequent hours through 7 P.M., and only 9% will be generated during the evenings and a negligible 2% will be earned on the weekends. Based on the projected amount of station revenue and the projected commercial load scheduled for the differing time periods, KGEN(FM)'s spot prices are determined. As would be expected, morning drive spots will sell for a premium, with evening drive (weekdays from 3 P.M. to 7 P.M.) spots following in price.

OBJECTIVES

The objectives of KGEN(FM) are to generate a local commercial audience share of 2.1% by 1993 and a market revenue share of 2.2%, which will translate into gross revenues of $1.7 million. By 1997, station revenues are projected at $2 million. Market revenues have been estimated as the average of estimates contained in Exhibits 3 and 4 for the Phoenix market.

The station is projected to earn its local commercial audience share from two sources: people presently listening to the market's existing Spanish stations and those uninterested in either the younger or older fare

currently offered (Exhibit 7). However, even if KGEN(FM) took no audience from the existing Spanish stations, Phoenix's total local commercial audience share for Spanish-formatted stations would rise to only 5.1%. This is conservative in comparison with several of the markets with similar-sized Hispanic populations.

KGEN(FM)'s ability to convert its local commercial audience share into market revenue share, or its power ratio, is projected at 1.03. This is based on the estimated power ratios of operating Spanish stations in a number of the radio markets discussed previously. This information is presented in Exhibit 10.

STRATEGY

The strategy of KGEN(FM) will be to differentiate itself from the market's other Spanish stations by virtue of its quality FM sound and its appealing programming. The programming will be designed to attract the somewhat younger bicultural Hispanic adults. With respect to its advertisers, KGEN(FM) will differentiate itself by the attractive demographics of its target audience. Listeners between the ages of 25 and 54 typically have the greatest amount of disposable income and, consequently, are highly prized by radio advertisers.

An additional strategy with respect to KGEN(FM)'s advertisers will be to hire a bilingual staff, with particular attention to the members of the

---

EXHIBIT 9   Spot Pricing Scheme for KGEN(FM) in 1992

	Monday–Friday 6 A.M.–10 A.M.	Monday–Friday 10 A.M.–3 P.M.	Monday–Friday 3 P.M.–7 P.M.	Monday–Friday 7 P.M.–Midnight	Weekends 6 A.M.–Midnight
Hours per period	4	5	4	5	36
Number of persons surveyed per period[a]	4,510	4,221	3,400	1,487	2,292
Persons surveyed per hour	1,128	844	850	297	64
Percentage of total station listening per period	35%	27%	27%	9%	2%
KGEN(FM) revenues to be generated during period[b]	$84,666	$63,393	$63,828	$22,332	$4,781
Revenues per hour	$21,167	$12,679	$15,957	$4,466	$133
Spot load per hour					
30 seconds	20	20	20	10	5
15 seconds	30	30	30	15	15
Price per spot					
30 seconds	$605	$362	$456	$255	$11
15 seconds	$302	$181	$228	$128	$5

[a] Arbitron's Radio Market Report, Phoenix, Fall 1991.
[b] Based on projected 1992 revenues of $239,000 from July through December multiplied by the percentage of total station listening per hour.

EXHIBIT 10 **Relationship between Hispanic Radio Audience and Revenue Shares**

Station	Market	90 Rev	Rev. Share	90 Aud. Share	Adj. Aud. Share	Rev. Rank	12+ Rank	25–54 Rank	Rev. Share as % of Aud. Share
KWAC	Bakersfield	1.2	8.2	6.5	7.9	4	5	4	103.8
KAFY	Bakersfield	0.6	4.1	5.1	6.2	8	4	3	67.2
WIND/WOJO	Chicago	7.4	3.2	2.8	3.1	15	13	13	103.2
KUNO	Corpus Christi	1.0	12.0	7.4	8.3	4	4	6	144.6
KBNA A/F	El Paso	1.4	10.8	6.5	7.3	3	5	5	147.9
KAMA	El Paso	1.1	8.5	5.2	5.8	5	11	12	146.6
KGST	Fresno	1.0	5.0	2.9	3.5	10	11	9	142.9
KLAT	Houston	2.5	2.0	1.6	1.8	16	19	21	111.1
KXYZ	Houston	1.6	1.8	1.4	1.6	17	17	19	112.5
KTNQ/KLVE	Los Angeles	19.0	4.5	5.6	6.3	9	2	2	71.4
KWKW	Los Angeles	8.0	1.9	3.4	3.8	19	6	6	50.0
KALI	Los Angeles	3.0	0.7	1.1	1.2	27	31	30	58.3
KGBT	McAllen	1.7	13.3	14.1	15.8	2	3	3	84.2
KIWW	McAllen	1.2	9.4	7.7	8.7	4	4	4	108.0
KQXX	McAllen	0.8	6.9	5.3	6.0	6	7	7	115.0
KBOR A/F	McAllen	0.5	3.9	3.2	3.6	9	9	8	108.3
WQBA	Miami	8.0	7.5	3.9	4.3	3	11	18	174.4
WCMQ A/F	Miami	4.5	4.2	4.6	5.1	12	7	5	82.4
WAQI	Miami	4.4	4.2	5.0	5.5	13	5	16	76.4
WQBA-F	Miami	2.5	2.4	2.2	2.4	18	22	20	100.0
KLOC	Modesto	0.5	4.6	6.5	8.9	8	5	5	51.7
WADO	New York	5.5	1.6	1.8	2.0	22	20	17	80.0
KTRO	Oxnard	1.3	12.9	4.9	10.6	4	5	4	121.7
KOXR	Oxnard	1.1	10.9	4.0	8.7	6	6	6	125.3
KRCX	Sacramento	1.1	1.9	1.0	1.3	13	22	27	146.2
KCTY/KRAY	Salinas-SC	0.9	7.1	5.3	8.9	6	4	5	79.8
KCOR	San Antonio	2.8	7.0	5.5	6.0	3	9	9	116.7
KXTN/KZVE	San Antonio	2.0	5.0	3.9	4.3	10	14	8	116.3
KIQI	San Francisco	2.2	1.2	1.1	1.2	20	30	24	100.0
KBRG	San Francisco	1.3	0.7	1.2	1.3	24	25	31	53.8
	30 stations		1990 mean: 103.3					1988 mean: 107.4	
			1990 median: 105.9					1987 mean: 110.1	
								1986 mean: 103.0	
	Mean 12+ rank:	10.5							
	Mean 25–54 rank:	11.6							
	Mean revenue rank:	8.9							

Source: James H. Duncan, *The Relationship Between Radio Audience Shares and Revenue Shares (1991).*

sales and on-air staffs. These two groups of individuals, as the station's most visible representatives in the community, should move easily between the Hispanic culture and the larger Anglo culture of the business community. Spanish radio stations often face an uphill battle with local advertisers in their attempts to convince the advertisers that Hispanic listeners are potential customers and worth pursuing. With an upscale, educated appearance, KGEN(FM) will make notable progress in fighting those perceptions.

ACTION PROGRAMS

KGEN(FM) will attempt to keep a high profile within the community by engaging in promotional events on a regular basis. The events will have a community service orientation, which will increase the station's ties to the Hispanic community. Potential events might include such activities as blood donation drives, fundraising events for issues of concern within the Hispanic community, and sporting events to raise the level of health consciousness.

KGEN(FM) will also engage in cosponsored promotional/community events with non-Hispanic organizations. These will present the station and its listeners as members of the community of Phoenix, not just as members of the Hispanic community. These types of events might be conducted with such public service organizations as the police and fire departments.

With respect to its own advertising campaign, KGEN(FM) "Que Tal?" ("What's Going On?") will create an image of itself and its listeners as friendly and easygoing, yet confident. The image of the station as inquisitive will be bolstered by informal on-air surveys of its listeners to gauge the moods and opinions of the Hispanic community in regard to issues in the public eye.

KGEN(FM)'s programming, promotions, and sales efforts will be given six months to establish the station as a new presence in the market. By 1993, these efforts are forecast to pay off in terms of a 2.1% local commercial audience share and a 2.2% revenue share.

ANTICIPATED RESULTS

KGEN(FM) is projected to generate operating losses of $312,000 during the last six months of 1992. The following year, it is anticipated that operating profits will reach $239,000 and, by 1999, $286,000. This information, along with operating expenses, is presented in Exhibits 11 and 12.

Operating expenses for KGEN(FM) have been estimated based on operating norms data collected by the National Association of Broadcasters (NAB) for FM stations earning revenues comparable to those forecast for KGEN(FM). Specifically, we have relied on expenses incurred by stations operating within the 25th percentile, as this group generated gross revenues most similar to those projected for KGEN(FM). Because the NAB's operating data were dated 1990, KGEN(FM)'s expenses have been adjusted by an appropriate inflationary factor. Exhibit 13 presents the calculation of KGEN(FM)'s operating cash flows after depreciation, amortization, taxes, and capital expenditures are considered. Operating cash flows peak at $242,000 in 1994. They decline thereafter due to the onset of state and federal tax liabilities. Operating norms data are presented in Exhibit 14.

The development of KGEN(FM) has been evaluated in terms of its return on investment (ROI). The time period over which the station has been evaluated is seven and a half years. This is a typical time period because standard broadcast loans have this term. We assume that the property is then sold. KGEN's ROI over this period is 6.5%. However, this is low given that the station is a start-up property with a large initial investment combined with early operating losses.

EXHIBIT 11 **Historical and Projected Phoenix, Arizona Radio Market and KGEN(FM) Revenues (000s)**

Year	Gross Market Revenues	KGEN(FM) Local Commercial Share	Power Ratio	KGEN(FM) Revenue Share	KGEN(FM) Gross Revenues
1988	$67,900	—	—	—	—
1989	72,500	—	—	—	—
1990	73,300	—	—	—	—
1991	75,000	—	—	—	—
1992[a]	37,100	—	—	—	—
Projections					
1992[b]	$37,100	1.1%	0.60	0.6%	$239
1993	77,650	2.1	1.03	2.2	1,702
1994	81,600	2.1	1.03	2.2	1,788
1995	86,100	2.1	1.03	2.2	1,887
1996	89,791	2.1	1.03	2.2	1,968
1997	92,934	2.1	1.03	2.2	2,037
1998	96,186	2.1	1.03	2.2	2,108
1999	99,553	2.1	1.03	2.2	2,182
Average compound Annual growth					
1988–1992	2.2%				N/A
1992–1995	5.1				58.0
1995–1999	3.7				3.7
1992–1999	4.3				24.2

[a] First six months.
[b] Last six months.

EXHIBIT 12 Estimated and Projected Operating Profits KGEN(FM) (000s)

Year	KGEN(FM) Gross Revs.[a]	A/R Comms.[b]	Tech.[b]	Program/ Prod.[b]	News[b]	Ad/ Promo[b]	Sales[b]	G&A[b]	Total Expenses	Operating Profits	Operating Profit Margin[c]
				Operating Expenses							
1992[d]	$239	$21	$20	$125	$9	$54	$41	$282	$531	($312)	−130.4%
1993	1,702	148	43	261	19	112	291	589	1,315	239	14.0%
1994	1,788	156	44	273	20	117	306	615	1,375	257	14.4%
1995	1,887	164	46	285	21	122	323	643	1,440	282	15.0%
1996	1,968	171	49	298	21	128	336	672	1,505	292	14.8%
1997	2,037	177	51	312	22	134	348	702	1,569	290	14.3%
1998	2,108	183	53	326	23	140	360	734	1,636	288	13.7%
1999	2,182	190	55	340	25	146	373	767	1,706	286	13.1%
				Average compound Annual growth							
1992–1995	58.0%	5.80%	4.5%	4.5%	4.5%	4.5%	58.0%	4.5%	10.7%	N/A	
1995–1999	3.7	3.7	4.5	4.5	4.5	4.5	3.7	4.5	4.3	0.3	
1992–1999	24.2	24.2	4.5	4.5	4.5	4.5	24.2	4.5	7.0	N/A	

[a] From Exhibit 11.
[b] Based on the 25th percentile in Exhibit 14, adjusted for inflation.
[c] As a percentage of gross revenues.
[d] Station signs on the air July 1.

CONTINGENCY PLANS

The greatest danger to KGEN(FM) is that the station will not generate its projected audience shares. Should the station earn far less than its projected share, a one-year time period will be allowed to pass in order to determine whether the scheduling was inappropriate. After a period of one year, the station will cut back operating expenses to a level appropriate for its revenues, if that is feasible. A worst-case scenario would project KGEN(FM)'s audience share at approximately half of the projected level. The reevaluation of KGEN(FM)'s expected results under this scenario is presented in Exhibits 15–17. Revised operating expense norms are presented in Exhibit 18.

EXHIBIT 13 Calculation of Operating Cash Flows for KGEN(FM) (000s)

Year	Operating Profits[a]	Deprec.[b]	Amort.[c]	Taxable Income State	Taxable Income Federal	Income Taxes[d] State	Income Taxes[d] Federal	Net Income	Cap Exp	Operating Cash Flows[e]
1992	($312)	$55	$13	($380)	($380)	$0	$0	($380)	$8	($320)
1993	239	90	13	136	136	0	0	136	15	224
1994	257	64	13	180	180	0	0	180	15	242
1995	282	49	13	220	206	14	48	158	15	205
1996	292	51	13	228	207	21	70	136	20	181
1997	290	42	13	236	214	22	73	141	20	176
1998	288	31	13	245	222	23	75	147	20	170
1999	286	30	8	248	225	23	76	148	20	166

[a] From Exhibit 12.
[b] Depreciation of fixed assets and future capital expenditures.
[c] Amortization of FCC license valued at $200,000 over 25 years and acquisition fees of $35,000 over 7 years.
[d] State tax at 9.3% and federal tax at 34% less adjustments, with tax loss carryforwards.
[e] Net income less capital expenditures plus depreciation and amortization.

EXHIBIT 14 **Operating Norms Data for FM Stations Generating Revenue from $1.5 Million to $2.0 Million**

		Percentile		
	Average	*25th*	*50th*	*75th*
Network compensation	$35,380	$0	$0	$60,000
Natl/regional advertising	342,286	240,809	302,000	432,989
Local advertising	1,575,062	1,341,646	1,587,100	1,815,994
Total time sales	$1,952,728	$1,750,000[b]	$1,899,996	$2,202,614
Agency & rep commissions	218,440	152,674	225,434	284,501
Other revenue	30,514	470	19,905	50,000
Total net revenue	$1,764,802	$1,604,448	$1,725,623	$1,947,975
Departmental expenses[a]				
Engineering	$59,743	$37,340	$61,083	$73,998
Program & production	322,705	229,151	298,271	365,963
News	33,705	16,485	32,000	45,207
Sales	367,658	299,000	336,726	434,522
Advertising & promotion	152,981	98,161	118,333	198,350
General & administrative	384,921	517,110	422,485	556,047
Total expenses	$1,321,713	$1,320,008	$1,315,507	$1,478,167
Operating profits	$443,089	$284,440	$410,116	$469,808

[a] Departmental expense data and total expenses are averages of all stations comprising group.
[b] For percentile data, total is not equal to sum of component categories.

Source: NAB/BCFM Radio Financial Report (1991).

EXHIBIT 15 **Projected Phoenix Radio Market and KGEN(FM) Revenues (000s): Worst Case Scenario**

Year	Gross Market Revenues	KGEN(FM) Local Commercial Share	Power Ratio	KGEN(FM) Revenue Share	KGEN(FM) Gross Revenues
1988	$67,900	–	–	–	–
1989	72,500	–	–	–	–
1990	73,300	–	–	–	–
1991	75,000	–	–	–	–
1992[a]	37,100	–	–	–	–
Projections					
1992[b]	$37,100	0.5%	0.60	0.3%	$111
1993	77,650	1.1%	1.03	1.1%	880
1994	81,600	1.1%	1.03	1.1%	925
1995	86,100	1.1%	1.03	1.1%	976
1996	89,791	1.1%	1.03	1.1%	1,017
1997	92,934	1.1%	1.03	1.1%	1,053
1998	96,186	1.1%	1.03	1.1%	1,090
1999	99,553	1.1%	1.03	1.1%	1,128
Average compound Annual growth					
1988–1992	2.2%				N/A
1992–1995	5.1				63.6
1995–1999	3.7				3.7
1992–1999	4.3				26.1

[a] First six months.
[b] Last six months.

EXHIBIT 16   **Estimated and Projected Operating Profits for KGEN(FM) (000s): Worst Case Scenario**

				Operating Expenses							
Year	KGEN(FM) Gross Revs.[a]	A/R Comms.[b]	Tech.[b]	Program/ Prod. [b]	News[b]	Ad/ Promo[b]	Sales[b]	G&A[b]	Total Expenses	Operating Profits	Operating Profit Margin[c]
1992[d]	$111	$8	$20	$125	$9	$54	$19	$282	$509	($406)	−364.3%
1993	880	63	36	219	14	80	138	425	912	(96)	−10.9%
1994	925	67	31	185	9	50	132	273	680	178	19.2%
1995	976	70	32	194	9	52	139	286	712	193	19.8%
1996	1,017	73	34	202	9	55	145	299	744	200	19.7%
1997	1,053	76	35	211	10	57	151	312	776	201	19.1%
1998	1,090	78	37	221	10	60	156	326	809	202	18.5%
1999	1,128	81	38	231	11	62	161	341	844	202	17.9%
				Average compound Annual growth							
1992–95	63.6%	63.6%	−7.5%	−8.2%	−20.7%	−21.3%	54.2%	−20.3%	−11.2%	N/A	
1995–99	3.7	3.7	4.5	4.5	4.5	4.5	3.7	4.5	4.3	1.2	
1992–99	26.1	26.1	−0.8	−1.1	−7.2	−7.5	22.9	−6.9	−2.6	N/A	

[a] From Exhibit 15.
[b] Based on the 25th percentile in Exhibit 18, adjusted for inflation.
[c] As a percentage of gross revenues.
[d] Station signs on the air July 1.

EXHIBIT 17   **Calculation of Operating Cash Flows for KGEN(FM) (000s): Worst Case Scenario**

				Taxable Income		*Income Taxes*[d]				
Year	Operating Profits[a]	Deprec.[b]	Amort.[c]	State	Federal	State	Federal	Net Income	Cap Exp	Operating Cash Flows[e]
1992	($406)	$55	$13	($474)	($474)	$0	$0	($474)	$8	($413)
1993	(96)	90	13	(199)	(199)	0	0	(199)	14	(109)
1994	178	63	13	101	101	0	0	101	12	166
1995	193	48	13	132	132	0	0	132	12	181
1996	200	49	13	138	138	0	0	138	15	185
1997	201	38	13	150	150	0	0	150	15	186
1998	202	26	13	162	161	1	4	158	15	182
1999	202	26	8	169	153	16	52	101	15	120

[a] From Exhibit 16.
[b] Depreciation of fixed assets and future capital expenditures.
[c] Amortization of FCC license valued at $200,000 over 25 years and acquisition costs of $35,000 over 7 years.
[d] State tax at 9.3% and federal tax at 34% less adjustments, with tax loss carryforwards.
[e] Net income less capital expenditures plus depreciation and amortization.

EXHIBIT 18 **Operating Norms Data for FM Stations Generating Revenue from $800,000 to $1,000,000**

		Percentile		
	Average	*25th*	*50th*	*75th*
Network compensation	$11,746	$0	$0	$20,610
Natl/regional advertising	159,205	88,956	103,700	201,438
Local advertising	780,815	721,000	809,868	862,841
Total time sales	$951,766	$915,351[b]	$931,300	$961,285
Agency & rep commissions	92,228	65,517	79,087	101,706
Other revenue	11,342	131	2,225	17,000
Total net revenue	$870,880	$841,750	$855,000	$916,492
Departmental expenses[a]				
Engineering	$47,028	$25,903	$43,000	$64,091
Program & production	206,780	155,325	165,657	257,514
News	27,251	7,204	20,853	40,000
Sales	200,335	130,808	163,508	226,906
Advertising & promotion	87,221	41,889	55,620	114,000
General & administrative	264,231	229,302	279,769	498,390
Total expenses	$832,846	$776,316	$748,681	$1,065,979
Operating profits	$38,034	$65,434	$106,319	($149,487)

[a] Departmental expense data and total expenses are averages of all stations comprising the group.
[b] For percentile data, total is not equal to sum of component categories.

Source: NAB/BCFM Radio Financial Report (1991).

PRODUCT DEVELOPMENT AND TESTING

> No war, no panic, no bank failure, no strike or fire can so completely and irrevocably destroy a business as a new and better product in the hands of a competitor.
>
> F. RUSSELL BICHOWSKY

INTEGRATING
. . . with Cross-Functional Teams

APPLYING
. . . to Consumer Durable Goods Marketing

New product development (NPD) is the process of finding ideas for new goods and services and converting them into commercially successful product line additions. In the early 1990s when General Motors was in trouble, they asked a young engineer to design a new car that was bigger on the inside than the Toyota Camry but based on the chassis of the much smaller Chevy Cavalier. The team was given only $1 billion for the project and told the car had to make a healthy profit. The NPD team—including an engineer, an interior designer, and an assistant brand manager—began by dissecting rival cars to set benchmarks for 250 attributes. Then they ran focus groups with customers and hung out in dealerships selling competitive cars. Next they built mockups of the new car's interior and shipped them to focus groups in California. Some Chevy people said that bench seats were preferred over bucket seats by people working out of their cars. However, bench seats flunked with potential buyers and they were dropped. To keep costs down, only two versions of the new car equipped with options they expected customers to order were offered along with one suspension choice and two engines. A name was suggested by the Chevrolet general manager who proposed resurrecting the classic Malibu marque that had been used on 6.5 million cars. The end result of the Malibu NPD project was a car that had the same or more interior space than its competitors, weighed less, got higher gas mileage, was priced hundreds of dollars lower, generated unit profits of $1,000 and was named the *Motor Trend* car of the year in 1997.[1] The Malibu example shows that careful new product development can make companies more successful in the marketplace. The objective of this chapter is to explain each step of the development process from the search for new ideas to the introduction of new products to customers.

WHY DEVELOP NEW PRODUCTS?

The basic reason organizations develop new products is to replace items that have lost favor with customers. Product obsolescence is real and firms need new products to stay alive and prosper. We define new products as goods and services that are basically different from those already marketed by the organization.

219

New Products Boost Sales and Profits

The introduction of new items helps increase revenues and profits for organizations. A study of the best NPD practices used to introduce more than 11,000 items over a five-year period provides the striking results shown in Figure 6-1. Companies were divided into those with the "best" practices and "the rest." Best companies derived 39 percent of their revenue from new products compared to only 23 percent from the rest. Also best companies had twice the profits from new products as the rest and twice as many of these items were still on the market. The poorer performing firms spent more than 40 percent of their efforts improving old products and tended to ignore cost reductions that could boost profits. Other studies have shown strong positive correlations between research and development (R&D) spending and profits for 24 industries. All of these results demonstrate that NPD is a key factor in the survival and growth of business organizations.

The Product Life Cycle

APPLYING
. . . to
Consumer
Marketing
Business-to-
Business
Marketing

The most important concept supporting NPD activities is the idea that products follow a cycle of birth, growth, and decline. A diagram showing the new product life cycle at Hewlett-Packard Co. is described in Figure 6-2. This chart reveals that new products produce 20 percent of their total revenue the first year they are introduced and 34 percent the second year. In years three through eight, new product sales at Hewlett-Packard drop sharply. Figure 6-2 demonstrates that Hewlett-Packard must continually introduce new items to replace products in decline if they expect to maintain sales and profits. Hewlett-Packard spends about 10 percent of revenues on R&D each year and for the period from 1990–1993 created $13 of new product revenue for each dollar invested in R&D.[2] These results confirm that NPD is a powerful engine for growth at Hewlett-Packard.

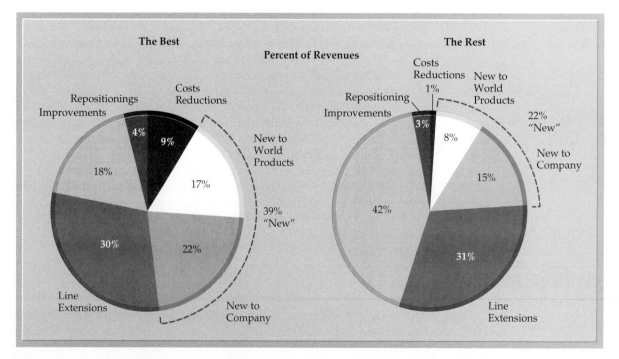

FIGURE 6-1 Innovation Pays Off (From Barton G. Tretheway, "Everything New Is Old Again," *Marketing Management,* **Vol. 7 [Spring 1998], p. 7.)**

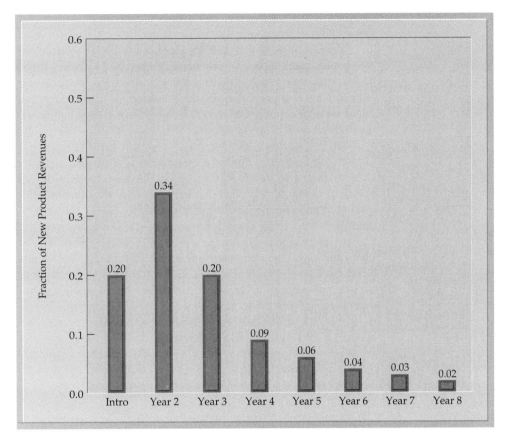

FIGURE 6-2   The Product Life Cycle at Hewlett-Packard (From Marvin L. Patterson, "From Experience: Linking Product Innovation to Business Growth," *Journal of Product Innovation Management,* **Vol. 15 [1998], p. 393.)**

APPLYING
. . . *to*
Business-to-
Business
Marketing,
Healthcare
Marketing

Competitive Obsolescence.   Product life cycles, like those shown in Figure 6-2, are becoming shorter in some lines of trade. Competitors have been increasingly quick to copy new items and introduce their own brands at low prices. This can lead to rapid declines in profit margins and market shares for innovators. For example, Johnson & Johnson invented the cardiovascular stent used to open blocked arteries in the heart. A stent is a tiny metal-mesh tube wrapped around a small balloon that is threaded into the heart arteries. At a blockage site, the balloon is inflated to deploy the stent, which is left in place after the balloon is removed. Johnson & Johnson worked for seven years to gain FDA approval and patents for their revolutionary device. Once approved, the new stent racked up sales of $1 billion in 37 months. However, Johnson & Johnson refused to give discounts off the $1,595 price of the stent to catheterization labs purchasing $1 million in stents a year, and they failed to develop longer and more flexible stents requested by doctors. The huge market for stents and the high 80 percent gross margins available, encouraged competitors to develop new designs. Doctors were so upset at Johnson & Johnson's inability to deliver new stents that they lobbied the Food and Drug Administration to expedite approval of competitive designs. When the approval was received, doctors immediately switched to new stents from Guidant Corp and in 45 days Johnson & Johnson's 91 percent market share dropped to only 21 percent. By the end of 1998 Johnson & Johnson estimated stent market share had slipped to only 8 percent.[3] Although Johnson & Johnson has started to bring out new stent designs and offer volume discounts, they will never be able to return to their former position of complete market dominance. This example shows that product life cycles are real and firms that fail to continually innovate can be ruined.

Competition is also shortening product life cycles for calculators, electronic character recognition devices, copiers, and small computers. The model life for fax machines is down to less than four months and for audio components less than six months. Each of these industries has become almost a fashion industry. If the life expectancy of new products continues to decline, firms will need to develop even greater numbers of new items to maintain their market positions.

Chances for Success.   Product development is expensive and you need to understand the chances that new items will succeed. The best product development practices study described in Figure 6-1 found that the most effective firms had 65 percent of new products meet their success criteria compared to only 47 percent in weaker companies.[4] Many new products are lost in the screening stages, and these help account for higher new product failure rates often reported in the trade press. Overall, about one new *idea* in seven is converted into a successful new product. This means that a great deal of money is spent developing products that never reach the marketplace. Research has shown that strength in R&D, engineering, and production helps increase the number of new products. In addition, the average success rate of new products is related to strength in marketing, sales force/distribution, and promotion. These data suggest that most new products succeed and that careful attention to marketing activities can make a difference.

> **INTEGRATING**
> *. . . with*
> *R&D,*
> *Engineering,*
> *Production*

SEARCH AND SCREENING

The management of product development has been described as a sequential process that converts ideas into commercially successful product line additions. The procedure is essentially a series of go, no-go decisions in which the best ideas emerge as finished products. Six steps of the product development process are highlighted in Figure 6-3. Product development begins with the search for new product ideas and then moves on to screening, revenue, and cost analysis, followed by development and market testing, and concludes with commercialization. Large numbers of new product ideas are passed into the system at one end, and months or years later, a few successful items reach the market. Ideas that fail to meet development criteria along the way are either dropped or sent back for more testing. The developmental process demands a steady stream of new ideas from which a few choice projects can be selected for more intensive development.

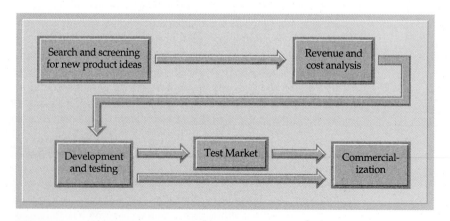

FIGURE 6-3   The Product Development Cycle

Sources of Product Ideas

The most common source of ideas for new products lies within the company itself. A survey revealed that 60 percent of industrial and 46 percent of consumer new product ideas came from the research staff, engineers, salespeople, marketing research personnel, and executives of the firm. Another 26 percent of industrial new product ideas and 30 percent of consumer new product ideas came from users.[5] In addition, consumers are often studied by using depth and focus group interviews to find opportunities for new items in individual product categories. An example showing how a focus group led to new pickle products at Vlasic Foods is described in Marketing in Action box 6-1. Market structure maps such as those discussed in Chapter 4 can reveal gaps that suggest ideas for new products.

Dependence on internally contributed ideas indicates that many firms do not pay enough attention to external sources for new projects. Company-generated ideas seem to gain acceptance easily, and there is a widespread suspicion about products that are "not invented here." An inventor developed a new type of mercury vapor lightbulb that uses much less electricity and lasts considerably longer than incandescent lightbulbs. The inventor took this attractive new product to several lighting companies, but they all turned him away. Apparently, the companies wished to protect their investments in regular lightbulbs and were not interested in gaining access to new technology. Firms that carelessly reject new product ideas that appear promising are likely to suffer in the long run in terms of lost opportunities and reduced market shares.

Good sources of new product ideas also include the U.S. Patent Office, private labs, independent inventors, and university researchers. Some firms have had success by talking to advertising agencies and attending trade shows. For example, U.S. food companies spend less than 1 percent of sales on research and development and they are continually looking outside their own offices for new product ideas. They routinely send teams to the New Products Showcase and Learning Center in Ithaca, New York, to look over an inventory of 60,000 extinct grocery products. Companies pay $750 an hour to search for product ideas that can be revived.[6] American firms also send teams to European trade shows to look at new processes such as one the French have developed to give 30-day shelf life to precooked packaged entrees. Another new idea from Europe vacuums oxygen out of packages to keep baked goods fresher longer. When looking for new products it is best to cast a wide net if you expect to catch any big fish.

Imitation

Rather than create an innovation, a firm may find it expedient to imitate competitive offerings. In the survey mentioned earlier, 27 percent of industrial new product ideas and 38 percent of consumer ideas came from the analysis of competitors. Adapting an existing product created elsewhere is less expensive and time-consuming than creating an innovation.

Even the most innovative firm will not come up with all the new products generated in its industry. Every firm should have a policy to guide its responses to the innovations of competitors. This gives you the advantage of observing the market performance of the innovative new item before launching your own product. Some people believe it is worth spending money on "reverse engineering" to tear apart your competitors' products to gain insights for your copies. Research with automobiles and computers found that reverse engineering of competitors' products tends to reduce the performance benefits to the firm from product development.[7] This suggests that although it is often useful to copy new product ideas from other firms, it may not be productive to spend a lot of time and money on reverse engineering.

MARKETING IN ACTION *6-1*

Vlasic's Hamburger Stackers

Pickle consumption in the United States has been falling 2 percent a year. This has put pressure on the number one pickle packer, Vlasic Foods International, to come up with new products to increase revenues. An idea for a new items surfaced when consumers in focus groups said they hate it when pickles slip out of their hamburgers and sandwiches. A Vlasic product development manager started slicing pickles horizontally into strips and created pickle planks that stayed in sandwiches better than the traditional small round chips. Although Vlasic sold $60 million of these pickle planks the first year, they were not perfect because they contained too much of the soft center seed cavity.

The manager then came up with the idea of creating a new giant pickle chip that would cover the whole surface of the sandwich. These giant chips would need to be cut from bigger pickles than were currently available in America. The manager scoured the world for bigger pickles and found some seeds at a small company in the Netherlands. These seeds produced poorly shaped pickles and it was not until their supplier crossbred them with another variety that Vlasic got a pickle that could be sliced into the desired 3 inch chip. The first year these were planted, hurricanes and insects destroyed all 10 acres of the new plants. Finally in 1998, Vlasic managed to harvest 2,000 bushels of giant pickles despite problems with mildew and the need to hand pick the heavy pickles.

Vlasic introduced the new 3-inch pickles chips as Hamburger Stackers and packed them 12 to a jar. The company is counting on the jumbo pickle chips to deliver at least $20 million in new sales.

— *Firms that push product development come up with new items to expand their markets.*

Source: Vanessa O'Connell, "After Years of Trial and Error, A Pickle Slice That Stays Put," *The Wall Street Journal,* October 6, 1998, p.p. B1, B4.

Courtesy Vlasic Foods International

Acquisition

One of the quickest ways of acquiring new products is to buy other companies that have developed new items. This has the advantages of eliminating all the costs of search, screening, testing, and commercialization, and it involves fewer risks because someone else has

APPLYING
*. . . to
Consumer
Health and
Beauty Aids
Marketing*

already built up a satisfied group of customers and dealers. Acquisition is common in the drug and consumer products industries. For example, Johnson & Johnson bought the Playtex tampon brand to strengthen its position in the tampon business. Before this acquisition, it was a minor player in the market, with its O.B. tampon holding 9.5 percent of the U.S. market. Despite considerable effort, Johnson & Johnson has been unable to increase the market share of the O.B. brand. Although such tampons are big sellers in Europe, U.S. women prefer tampons with applicators. By purchasing the Playtex brand, Johnson & Johnson grabbed an additional 30 percent of the market and is now second to the market leader, Tambrands.

The main problems with this approach to product development are finding available brands to acquire and paying the sometimes high asking prices. Johnson & Johnson paid $726 million for Playtex tampons, and had to take Playtex nursers, gloves, and Tek toothbrushes as well. Some analysts believe that today it is much easier to buy into a market than to try to create your own brands.

Licensing of New Products

Obtaining new product ideas through licensing offers several advantages for firms that wish to avoid the high cost of product development yet lack enthusiasm for acquiring going concerns. Probably the most important attraction is that there are more firms willing to license their ideas than there are firms willing to sell successful new products. Also, most license agreements involve the payment of royalties on a unit or percentage of sales basis so that initial costs are low and subsequent payments are due only when the product is actually sold. Furthermore, it is unusual for royalties paid on products obtained by licenses to exceed the savings achieved in R&D expenses. Licensing can also reduce lead time compared with the months or years that may be required to develop similar products in the company's own laboratories.

Screening Procedures

Surveys have shown that 76 percent of firms screen new product concepts, an activity that takes about three months (Table 6-1). The objective of screening is to eliminate new product ideas that are inconsistent with the goals or resources of the firm. Screening can be viewed as a filtering process. First, a quick judgment is made on whether the idea is compatible with the company's plans, technical skills, and financial capabilities. This evaluation is made by knowledgeable managers and staff specialists who weed out the obviously unsuitable ideas so that valuable resources will not be wasted reviewing impractical proposals. The second phase of the new product screening process is more detailed and is designed to establish a ranking for the remaining ideas. Rankings are based on an evaluation of factors relevant for product development in a particular firm. A checklist shows the relative importance of the criteria and combines the factor evaluations into a single index number for each product. The main value of a new product index is its ability to separate quickly the best proposals so that priorities can be established for succeeding stages of development. The main problem with such scoring models is that they rely on the subjective ratings of managers; hence, data input may not be very reliable.

A better scoring model would take into account the information available in the success or failure of a large number of past new product launches. One such model is *New-Prod*, a software-based new product screening, evaluation, and diagnostic tool. NewProd was developed from a statistical analysis of 200 projects from 100 companies. Managers were asked to rate their own project on 50 screening criteria. A regression was run relating these dimensions to degree of commercial success. Eight factors linked to product outcomes included product superiority, compatibility, market need, economic advantage,

TABLE 6-1 NPD Activities and Time Spent

Activity	Percent Using	Months Spent
Concept search Includes brainstorming and other creativity-stimulating techniques, preliminary discussions about the product's design, and identifying new product opportunities.	89.9	3.5
Concept screening May include scoring and ranking concepts according to some criteria and eliminating unsuitable concepts.	76.2	3.0
Concept testing Covers preliminary market research to determine market need, niche, and attractiveness.	80.4	3.6
Business analysis An evaluation of the product concept in financial terms as a business proposition.	89.4	2.6
Product development Technical work to convert a concept into a working model.	98.9	14.4
Product use testing, field testing, market testing Offering the product to a preselected group of potential buyers to determine its suitability and/or marketability.	86.8	6.0
Commercialization Launching the new product into full-scale product and sales.	96.3	6.5

Source: Alan L. Page, "Assessing New Product Development Practices and Performance: Establishing Crucial Norms," *Journal of Product Innovation Management,* Vol. 10, No. 4 (September 1993), p. 281.

newness to the firm (negative), technical compatibility, market competitiveness (negative), and size of market. The model is used to predict project ratings from new product screening questions.

NewProd studies in North America, the Netherlands, and Scandinavia have shown correct predictions for 75 to 85 percent of the new product studied.[8] For example, Procter & Gamble used a version of NewProd to assess 60 projects. Of the projects that NewProd predicted to be successes, 80 percent succeeded in test market and 60 percent were rated as financial successes when expanded nationally. On the other hand, of those it predicted to be failures, 25 percent were successful in test market but only 5 percent were financially successful when expanded nationally. NewProd predicts success and failure before development even begins.

REVENUE AND COST ANALYSIS

The business analysis phase of the product development cycle includes a detailed study of the potential profitability of new product ideas. The objective is to eliminate marginal ventures before extensive development and market testing expenses are incurred. An important first step is to measure market potential.

Market Potential

Market potential represents the maximum sales in dollars or units that can be obtained by an industry for a new product with a specified marketing effort. A simple way to estimate potential is as follows:

$$MP = N \times P \times Q \tag{6.1}$$

where

MP = market potential
N = number of possible buyers
P = average selling price
Q = average number purchased by each buyer

APPLYING
. . . to
Consumer
Semi-Durable
Goods
Marketing

For example, digital video disk (DVD) players were first introduced in March of 1997 and by the end of 1998, one million Americans owned a player. Each DVD holds a recording of one movie and sells for about $20. Since each player owner purchases seven disks a year, the total DVD market potential in 1999 would be $140 million (1,000,000 × $20 × 7). Each film studio could then estimate their market share and multiply it times market potential to get their own revenue projection for DVDs. The success of this approach depends on the accuracy of your data and your assumptions. For example, the purchase rate *(Q)* for DVDs will change with disposable income, popularity of films released for DVDs in a season, and the availability of alternative video formats. Also the number of potential buyers *(N)* is often hard to determine. Although there were one million DVD players in homes at the beginning of 1999, more would be sold during the year and the estimate for DVDs would have to be adjusted upward to reflect this expected increase in the number of players.

Chain ratio procedures provide another way to measure market potential. This approach calculates potential by applying a series of ratios to an aggregate measure of demand. A firm could start with population figures and multiply by ratios that discard nonusing segments of the market. For example, a firm estimated demand for a new replacement thermostat by noting there were 32.5 million year-round housing units in populated colder areas of the country. This number was then adjusted by the proportion of units that were owner occupied (62 percent) and the number of homeowners in the relevant age group (78 percent). Next they adjusted for buyers with sufficient income (55 percent) and for units that had central thermostats (67 percent). The final calculation (32.5 × .62 × .78 × .55 × .67) gave a total market potential of 5.7 million units. If the company was able to sell 4 percent of these homeowners their new $40 thermostat, they would generate revenues of $9.1 million (5,700,000 × .04 × $40).

Market potentials for new business products can be estimated using data made available through the U.S. Census of Manufacturers. The government surveys all manufacturers every five years and collects information on the number of firms in Standard Industrial Classifications (SIC), value of shipments, number of production workers, and other data. With the SIC buildup method, market potentials are derived by adding up the number of firms or workers in relevant SIC categories and then converting them to dollar forecasts. If a firm knows how many machines a typical firm uses, market potentials for new items can be derived by multiplying usage rates times the number of firms reported in the Census of Manufacturers. Estimates of potential sales for an individual company would be obtained by multiplying by the firm's current market share and the expected unit price of the item.

Estimating Costs and Profits

INTEGRATING
. . . with
Accounting,
Production

Predicting the costs to build products before they are introduced is a difficult but essential part of the developmental process. Sometimes firms can get an idea on costs from similar products they already make or items sold by competitors. For example, when Johnson & Johnson was developing their coronary stent mentioned earlier, they knew that standard balloon catheters used to open clogged heart arteries in a procedure called an angioplasty were selling for a few hundred dollars each. This meant that they would be able to wrap their metal-mesh stent around a standard balloon catheter for variable costs of about $100. Since they planned to sell their stents for $1,595, they would have $1,495 per unit to cover development costs, new production facilities, advertising and selling expenses, overhead, and profits. Total profits would depend, of course, on the number of units they would be able to sell. J&J knew that 400,000 angioplasties were performed in the United States each year and that 30 percent failed within six months, leading to further treatment. In addition, in five percent of angioplasties, the vessel snaps shut abruptly within minutes or a few days, prompting a life-threatening emergency coronary artery bypass operation costing $40,000 or more. Given that 120,000 angioplasties fail each year, that J&J's stent lasted longer than an angioplasty, was safer, and was less expensive than bypass surgery, J&J might be able to sell 100,000 stents the first year they were introduced. With an anticipated gross margin of $1,495 per unit, J&J could generate a gross profit of $149,500,000 on their new product. Thus J&J's revenue and cost analysis for stents was very encouraging and explains why J&J labored for seven years to show that they worked properly and gain regulatory approval for their sale. As it turned out stents were used in 80 percent of angioplasty procedures, J&J's estimates of sales were low, and stents were much more profitable than they expected.

DEVELOPMENT AND TESTING

Development and testing are concerned with establishing physical characteristics for new goods and services that are acceptable to customers. The objective is to convert ideas into actual products that are safe, provide customer benefits, and can be manufactured economically by the firm. Usually, development includes concept testing, consumer preference tests, laboratory evaluations, use tests, and pilot plant operations.

Concept Testing

The first step in the development process often includes measuring customers' reactions to descriptions of new products. Promising ideas are converted into concept statements, which are printed on cards and shown to small focus groups of customers. Sometimes pictures or preliminary models of the product are included, together with the written descriptions. Participants are asked if they would buy the item and to give reasons for their decisions. Modifications are then made in the product concept, and the revised statement is tested with another group of customers. When the product concept appears well defined in terms of customer acceptance, a real product is developed to go along with the concept. An example of how Ford and General Motors suffered when concept test data were poorly interpreted is described in Marketing in Action box 6-2.

Product Design

The success of new products is often related to how well they are designed. Attractive products catch the attention of customers, and good design makes items easier to use. In addition, products should be designed so that they are easy to manufacture. Gillette's design of its new triple-blade MACH3 razor shows the importance of careful attention to product features. The company wanted to improve on its excellent double-blade razor the Sensor Excel. First, Gillette's designers positioned three blades so that each one was progressively nearer the face. This allowed each blade to shave closer than the one before and reduced skin irritation. The designers also moved the pivot point to increase the cartridge's stability. In addition, the blue lubricating strip was designed to fade over time to indicate wear. Another design change involved coating the blades with a microscopic layer of carbon to make the edge thinner and stronger. As many as 18 percent of Sensor Excel users clip on new razor cartridges upside down. To prevent this problem, Gillette designed the MACH3 with a new single point docking system. These design improvements were expensive and required

APPLYING
. . . to
Consumer
Packaged
Goods
Marketing

INTEGRATING
. . . with
R&D

APPLYING
...to
Consumer
Durable
Goods
Marketing

MARKETING IN ACTION 6-2

How Many Doors Are Enough?

Chrysler introduced the first minivan equipped with two front doors and one sliding door on the right side to simplify loading. When Ford brought out its new Windstar van in 1995 to compete with Chrysler, it also had three doors as only a third of potential minivan buyers wanted a fourth door. Chrysler saw this one third as a market opportunity and introduced a new van in 1996 with a sliding door on the driver's side. Chrysler's minivan sales boomed and Windstar's sales were badly hurt by the absence of a second sliding door. It took Ford four years and $560 million to add a fourth door to the Windstar. Meanwhile Chrysler sold 90 percent of its minivans with two sliding doors and solidified its hold on the number one position in this market.

Also early in 1998, Chrysler was first to offer four doors on hot selling extended cab pickup trucks. The new Dodge Ram Quad Cab was a runaway hit. Ford was not far behind this time and was the first to offer four doors on its entire line of extended cab pickup trucks in 1998. By the fall of 1998, 70 percent of large pickup trucks were delivered with four doors. General Motors, however, was late to the four-door party. They introduced major revisions to their 11-year-old Silverado and Sierra full-sized pickup trucks in the fall of 1998 with only three doors available for its extended cab trucks. Full-sized pickup trucks account for $14 billion of its annual sales and a huge chunk of GM's North American profits. Since GM loses money on many of the cars it sells, the new Silverado and its cousins needed to be hits for GM to deliver on promises to restless shareholders. GM did not introduce four-door extended cab pickups until the 2000 models were introduced in the fall of 1999. This inability to see the allure of four doors in extended cab trucks was a major blunder in its new product development efforts.

— *Failure to see major changes in consumer preferences can lead to serious NPD problems.*

Source: Donald W. Nauss, "Extra Door Proved Van Marketing Marvel," *Herald Times,* August 9, 1998, p. D1, and Joseph B. White, "GM Set to Launch New Silverado Pickup, Taking Aim at Ford's Top-Selling F-Series," *The Wall Street Journal,* October 8, 1998, p. B12.

Courtesy DaimlerChrysler Corporation

Gillette to devise new continuous-assembly machinery to build the cartridges at a rate of 600 a minute. The total cost of the design innovations to bring the MACH3 to market was $750 million.[9] This example shows that creative product design is essential if you want to gain competitive advantages in the marketplace.

Preference Tests

Preference tests are employed to compare reactions to different product attributes or quality levels. Consumers usually are given two samples of the product with different characteristics to taste or use, and are then asked which they prefer and why. The idea is to isolate the most desirable characteristics and quality levels so that they can be built into the new product.

A variety of methods has been developed to identify product features that are important to consumers. Perhaps the simplest approach is to interview potential customers and ask them to rate product features on a scale from 1 (unimportant) to 5 (very important). This makes it possible to compare the relative values of product attributes and to construct distributions of customer preferences. Another method submits a full range of sample products to groups of consumers, using a forced-choice, paired-comparison technique. Whatever the method employed, marketing managers need accurate preference data so that they can set product specifications to achieve the best possible market positions.

When Gillette ran consumer preference tests between its old Sensor Excel and prototypes of its new MACH3 razors, men preferred MACH3 by nearly 2 to 1 over Sensor Excel. However, when *Consumer Reports* magazine tested the two products in homes with its own panel of men after the product had been introduced, preferences were decidedly different.[10] Although MACH3 received high marks for closeness of shave, ease of cleaning, lack of drag, and preventing cuts, so did the Sensor Excel. Some *Consumer Reports* panel members found it difficult or impossible to shave under their noses with the MACH3 because of its big head. Others found it tricky to trim sideburns or a beard because it is hard to tell where the blades meet the face. These deficiencies may explain why the Sensor Excel was voted the best overall razor in the *Consumer Reports* preference test. This raises the question of why the Gillette preference test failed to uncover MACH3's inability to shave under the nose and trim sideburns. Was their preference test poorly designed or did they just ignore these problems in their haste to get the new three-blade razor to market? The MACH3 example shows that careful product testing can be critical to new product success.

Use Tests

Once you have a viable product concept and a set of specifications, the next step in the development process is to use test samples of the product to see if they meet the needs of the customer. Usually, this is done through a combination of laboratory and field testing. Lab tests offer the advantage of controlled conditions, and they can often simulate usage of the product and obtain results faster than field trials can. Car doors, for example, can be slammed thousands of times in the lab to see if they are designed to last the lifetime of the automobile. Despite these advantages, laboratory tests are artificial, and most new products are also subjected to lengthy testing by potential customers.

Customer-use tests are designed to determine how a product performs under the realistic conditions encountered in the home or factory. General Electric, for example, tested its electric slicing knife among 800 persons in 26 different cities before introducing it to the marketplace. In another case, a food manufacturer offered 738 women from four cities sample bottles of a new pourable mayonnaise. After 10 days, personal interviews were conducted to gauge customer reactions and to give the women a chance to purchase some of the product at the regular price. Women who bought samples of the new pourable mayonnaise were contacted three additional times to see whether they wanted more of the item. In addition, the respondents were asked to keep a diary to show how they used the product. This research indicated that although consumers liked pourable mayonnaise, they tended to use it as a liquid salad dressing rather than as a mayonnaise. Thus, the use test suggested that some changes were needed in packaging and promotional appeals if the firm expected the item to compete with more traditional mayonnaise products.

Selecting a Name

New products and services are named so that they can be easily identified and promoted to consumer and industrial buyers. The best names tend to be short, distinctive, and easy to pronounce and remember. Also, desirable names often suggest action (i.e., Drano, Sinex, U-Haul).

Suggestions for names are frequently provided by advertising agencies that write promotional material for the product and by computers programmed to make up nonsense words. Sometimes consumers are interviewed to find out what images are associated with prospective brand names and to measure preferences for alternative names. Words that are made up, such as the Exxon name adopted by Standard Oil of New Jersey, are likely to have fewer negative connotations than words that are already in use. Moreover, fanciful words with no preexisting meaning but created for a specific product have the most legal protection. Some examples of the selection of car names are presented in Marketing in Action box 6-3.

A growing problem with naming new products is that it seems that most of the good names have already been trademarked by other firms. For example, a California automobile security firm challenged Chrysler Corporation over the name Viper. Directed Electronics, Inc. owned a trademark for a line of automobile security alarm systems before Dodge claimed it for its muscle car. The two companies reached an out-of-court settlement, agreeing to coexist peacefully.

Names you select do not have to be spelled the same way to cause problems. Toyota coined the word *Lexus* as a play on the word *luxurious* for a new line of high-priced sedans. However, Mead Corporation thought the name had infringed its trademarked Lexis name for computer database systems. Mead won the first round by getting an injunction that prevented Toyota from advertising its new cars. This action hurt Toyota and slowed down the introduction of the vehicle. Toyota appealed and had the initial ruling reversed. These examples show that you have to be careful with names to avoid lawsuits and delays in getting products to market.

Sometimes brand names become so popular they are used by the public to describe a whole class of products (e.g., Scotch Tape). When this occurs, the manufacturer can lose the rights to the name, as happened in the case of *aspirin* and *escalator.* One way to avoid this problem is to insert the word *brand* after the name, as in Scotch Brand Cellophane Tape, to show that the word Scotch is not a generic term.

Packaging

The main concern in designing packages for new products is to protect the merchandise on its journey from the factory to the customer. This is particularly true for industrial goods and appliances whose sales are made from display models. When consumers select products from store shelves, however, packaging becomes an important information and promotional tool. Sales are enhanced by packages that are visible, informative, emotionally appealing, and workable.

An example of how user-friendly packaging can help a new product succeed is provided by Procter & Gamble's Helidac ulcer treatment. Ulcers are caused by bacteria and are treated with a combination of antacids and antibiotics. P&G's treatment program requires patients to take 224 tablets representing three types of drugs over a two-week period. Helidac users have to take four pills every six hours. Missing even a few pills can sharply reduce the cocktail's success rate. P&G needed a package that would remind patients to take their pills at the right time. They came up with a blister pack design that held one day's pills and could be easily slipped into a pocket or purse (Figure 6-4). The blister card was divided into four perforated squares, one for each six-hour period labeled "breakfast," "lunch," "dinner," and "bedtime." The blister cards are packed in a box that is printed with a simple 14-word set of instructions accompanied by three drawings. Compliance instructions become symbols such as a wineglass in a red circle with a line through them in a glossy 20-page booklet that was placed in the box. To remind people to take their pills, P&G gave patients a sheet

APPLYING
. . . *to*
Consumer
Durable
Goods
Marketing

MARKETING IN ACTION *6-3*

What's in a Name?

What's in a name? is a time-consuming and costly question. Selecting, researching, and legally claiming a name, called a *marque*, for a new automobile can cost as much as $200,000. Here is how some cars got their names:

- *Acura:* A computer-generated name, or neologism, that doesn't mean anything but connotes precision. Created with the understanding that one of Honda's desired hallmarks for the brand was precise engineering.

Courtesy American Honda Motor Co., Inc.

- *Altima:* A neologism that hints at ultimate or best. Replaced the Stanza, a name that never caught on with the public in a decade of use.
- *Geo:* A morpheme—the smallest meaningful language unit—that means world in many languages. Used for a lineup of small vehicles sold in Chevrolet dealerships.
- *Mitsubishi:* Means three pebbles in Japanese, but the company portrayed it as three diamonds, which is Mitsubishi's logo.
- *Mondeo:* Means world in Italian. Ford's "world car" designed and engineered in North America and Europe for sale on both continents.
- *Taurus:* The vice president of Ford car product development and one of his top engineers determined that both their wives were born under the Taurus sign of the Zodiac. It was the project code name and eventually became the name of the car.
- *Windstar:* Ford's successor to its Aerostar minivan. The goal was to keep a family relationship with the Aerostar while being different enough to persuade buyers that it was a new vehicle.

Before Villager was picked as the name for Mercury's minivan, the name Columbia was a finalist. Mercury liked the name because of the symbolism of the space shuttle. It was scrapped when consumer research suggested a link with drugs, as in Colombia's cocaine trade.

— *It is very difficult to find a name that is crisp, appropriate, inoffensive, and not owned by someone else.*

Source: Alan L. Adler, "Marque of a Winner," *Atlanta Constitution,* May 7, 1993, pp. S1, S6.

of four stickers decorated with balloons to affix to a visible spot wherever they happened to be when it's time to take their pills. To provide extra motivation, P&G included a set of daily affirmation cards in the box of pills. The cards carry pithy slogans that can be peeled off to mark the passage of each treatment day; day 1 says "let's get started." P&G's creative use of packaging not only helped patients to take their pills correctly, but it also encouraged doctors to prescribe Helidac because the packaging made ulcer cures more likely.[11]

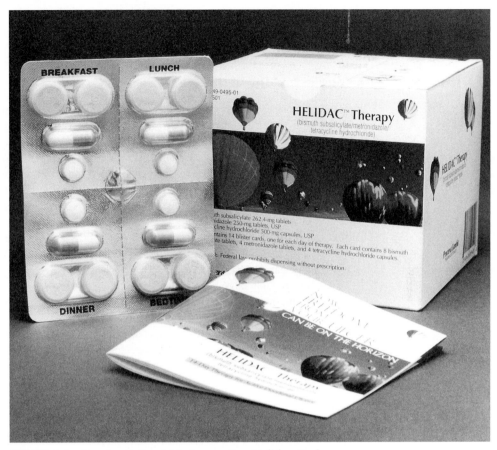

FIGURE 6-4 Procter & Gamble's Innovative Helidac Package.

Good packaging helps move consumer products off store shelves because items with high *visibility* are easier to see. Designs with good informational value tell the consumer at a glance what the package contains. In addition, packages are required by U.S. law to provide information on food additives, flammable materials, net weight, name of the manufacturer or distributor, and other factors. In the United States, the Fair Packaging and Labeling Act also has provisions designed to help standardize package sizes and make comparative shopping easier for the consumer.

Workability in packaging means that the container not only protects the product but is also easy to open and reclose, is readily stored, and has utility for secondary uses once the product is used up. Examples of package designs that have these characteristics include tear-top pudding cups, reclosable pop bottles, and the drinking mugs used to hold margarine. The pump dispenser, aseptic packaging, squeezable and recappable bottles, ultralight plastic, and plastic pouches are consumer packaging approaches that have combined convenience with cost effectiveness. The global marketplace is a good source of innovative designs.

Simulation Tests

Once the basic dimensions of a new product have been established, marketing executives often forecast future sales levels to see whether a project should be continued. The idea is to obtain some customer reactions to the new item without incurring the cost and publicity associated with a full market test. These projections are usually based on concept and product tests, historical data regressions, laboratory test markets, controlled store tests, and sales wave experiments.

Projecting Sales with Concept and Use Tests

With this approach, customers are presented with the idea or physical product, and sales are estimated from purchase intentions. An estimate of first-year trials is obtained by multiplying the percentage of prospective buyers who say that they "definitely will buy" by the percentage incidence of prospective buyers in the population. General Foods, in testing a frozen vegetable line, found that 21 percent of its sample of prepared-vegetable users would definitely buy. The prepared-vegetable segment was thought to represent 50 percent of the total population. The estimate of first-year trials was then calculated as 10.5 ($0.21 \times 0.50 \times 100\%$) percent.[12] This score was compared with data for previous vegetable products. Repeat purchases were estimated using concept fulfillment scores and posttrial attitude scores. This method does a fairly good job of predicting trials for product extensions, but it is not as accurate for repeat purchases of more innovative items.

APPLYING ... to Consumer Food Marketing

Computer models have been developed to integrate information from concept tests and other custom marketing research with information from secondary source materials, related product experiences, and informed judgments to make new product forecasts. One such model, called NEWS/Planner, forecasts consumer awareness, trial, repeat purchase, usage, sales, and market share. The model was developed for the clients of a leading advertising agency, BBDO. A more widely available model is Burke's BASES.

Projecting Sales from Historical Data

Market response can also be simulated using *historical data regressions.* Equations are constructed that relate the success of past new products to such factors as category penetration, promotional spending, relative price, and distribution. Once an equation is derived based on past experience, values are estimated for the predictor variables for the new item and plugged into the regression equation. The regression procedure works well in predicting trial but is not as accurate for items that fail to fit existing product categories. Some marketers believe that even a small amount of consumer research data collected for the new brand will lead to more insight and thus better new product decisions than will data collected on other brands.

Laboratory Test Markets

Laboratory test markets expose consumers to commercials for new and existing products and then allow them to make purchases from the product category in a simulated store. The new item is then taken home and used, and a follow-up interview measures satisfaction and repurchase intent. Frequently, repeat purchases are measured by offering consumers a chance to buy the product again after initial home placement. Although the exposure to ads and the store purchases are somewhat artificial, the method has proved to be a quick, inexpensive, and fairly accurate predictor of future sales levels. The method might not work well for highly seasonal products, emerging ill-defined categories, or therapeutic products for infrequent symptoms. Even so, Johnson & Johnson ran a test market simulation of Sundown Sunscreen that proved to be within 5 percent of its equilibrium market share in a concurrent test market.

A computer model called ASSESSOR combines executive judgments on marketing strategy with laboratory data using preference and trial and repeat purchase models of behavior. Although this model has proved to be an accurate predictor of market shares, the method can be used only when new brands seek to enter well-defined product categories. Situations in which innovative products create product categories, or in which products require long periods of usage before benefits are realized, are best evaluated by using extended sales wave tests or regular test markets.

Sales Wave Tests

Product adoption and purchase frequency can also be estimated by using *sales wave* experiments. This approach measures repeat purchase behavior by observing a sample of consumers who receive the new product through a home placement and then are offered a series of opportunities to purchase it at a special price. Forcing the consumer to pay for repeat purchases on several occasions (four to six) simulates the wear-out and adoption process that normally occurs in the marketplace. An advantage of sales wave experiments is that they can be used to forecast performance of category-creating new products. The main problem with these experiments is that they take more time and are more expensive than the other methods that have been discussed. Also, the continual recontact with the customer cannot be duplicated in the marketplace with normal advertising programs.

The market simulation procedures that we have discussed share several advantages that have made them widely used by marketing managers. First, they allow you keep the existence and the special features of new products secret from your competitors. This provides an element of surprise and often allows you to grab and keep a larger share of the market. Second, these simulations take less time to run than traditional test markets, and thus you can get products to the market faster. Third, market simulations are cheaper, and they allow you to develop more new product ideas.

TEST MARKETING

Test marketing is an optional phase of the product development process (Figure 6-2) that involves placing products in selected stores and measuring customer purchase rates in response to promotional activities. It is most often used when new products are radically different and companies do not know how to promote them or whether customers will buy them. The mock fat olestra, one of most controversial food additives ever, provides a good example (Marketing in Action box 6-4). The main drawbacks of test marketing are high costs, delayed introductions, and field tests, which give competitors a chance to steal your ideas. Gillette, for example, did not test market its new MACH3 three-bladed razor because it did not want to reveal the design to its competitors. Also high tooling costs make it impractical to test market appliances, automobiles, and many industrial products. Industrial manufacturers work closely with their customers and rely on feedback from use tests to determine when a new product is ready for national distribution.

Test Procedures

A first step in designing a test market is selecting a representative group of test cities. One rule of thumb is that two or more test areas with a minimum of three percent of all households are needed for national projectability. The objective is to find stable communities in which key demographic statistics are typical of the anticipated buyers of the product. Test cities must also have cooperative merchants and good media coverage to facilitate promotional activities. In addition, test cities should be isolated from each other so that promotional campaigns run in one city do not influence sales in other test areas. The three best-matched markets in terms of demographic profiles, media coverage, and market isolation are reputed to be Erie, Pennsylvania; Fort Wayne, Indiana; and Tucson, Arizona.

MARKETING IN ACTION 6-4

Assessing Olestra's High Price and Side Effects

APPLYING

*. . . to
Business-to-Business
Marketing,
Consumer
Food
Marketing*

Marion, Indiana, is best known as the birthplace of actor James Dean. However, it temporarily has become the world's fake-fat capital. Every product made with Procter & Gamble's mock fat, olestra, is for sale. In addition to P&G, Frito-Lay and Nabisco are test marketing chips and crackers made with the fat substitute. Almost every grocer in Marion carries the chips and crackers. Purchases are recorded by scanners so marketers can track virtually every bag sold. Even Marion General Hospital hasn't been overlooked. Frito-Lay's olestra chips are sold in its cafeteria. How this community of 32,000 and other test cities react could determine the additive's fate.

The residents of Marion closely reflect the nation. The median household income in North Marion is $37,396 versus $38,783 nationally. The town's workforce is almost evenly split between white and blue collar. Some 42 ethnic nationalities are said to live in the area.

Consumers have been given every reason to "just say no" to olestra. First, products made with olestra are pricey. Chips with it cost about 40 percent more than regular chips—in part because P&G believes that consumers will pay a premium to keep pounds off. Chips and crackers made with olestra contain virtually no fat and about half the calories of regular salty snacks. Second, olestra is saddled with an ugly image problem. Products made from it must display the Food and Drug Administration warning: "Olestra may cause abdominal cramping and loose stools." P&G, however, has worked hard to convince consumers that olestra will not make them sick.

P&G is promoting olestra's benefits and touting it in test markets. P&G spent about $5 million in these markets to create an image for olestra that makes it sound as natural as the soybeans from which it often comes. P&G is going door to door to distribute thousands of cans of Fat Free Pringles. Nearly one-quarter of the population of central Indiana soon will have tried Fat Free Pringles. Convinced that women make up the key market, Nabisco purchased regional ads for Fat-Free Ritz in most major women's magazines sold in Marion. P&G estimates that more than 15 million one-ounce servings of olestra-containing chips and crackers were sold in the past 15 months in test cities. It appears nothing can stop olestra.

— *Test markets can show if consumers are willing to pay for a product's perceived benefits.*

Source: Bruce Horovitz, "Fake Fat's Big Test: Olestra," *USA Today,* June 19, 1997, pp. B1, B2.

Limitations of Test Markets

The most serious drawbacks of test marketing are that it is expensive and potential sales are lost because of delays in getting the product to the marketplace. In addition, it is difficult to interpret sales results because the products are new, and there are no standards of performance that can be used for comparison. Except for situations where sales are unusually high or low, test results may simply reflect the basic uncertainty that prevailed when the study was initiated. In addition, the small number of test cities used and the artificial nature of the testing process make it risky to project results into national sales figures. A compounding factor is the realization that some products succeed in test markets and then fail when introduced nationally, and vice versa.

APPLYING

*. . . to
Consumer
Food
Marketing*

For example, Holly Farms developed a roasted chicken to appeal to busy customers. This convenient precooked product scored well in a year of test marketing. Holly Farms found that 22 percent of Atlanta women had tried the roasted chicken and 90 percent said they would buy it again. Based on these enthusiastic results, Holly Farms built a $20 million plant to produce the chickens and spent $14 million in advertising to gain national distribution. Despite strong customer acceptance, the national rollout did not do well and the roasted chickens gained distribution in only 50 percent of U.S. stores. Holly Farms found that poor sales were due to the short (14-day) shelf life of the product and to the fact that it took up to nine days to get the chickens to the stores. Although grocery buyers described the product as outstanding, they were not reordering because of the limited time they had to sell it.

An even more insidious problem is the response that competitors can make to test market activity. One possibility is a direct attempt to sabotage the test by introducing price cuts or coupons that upset normal sales patterns. A more likely reaction is that competitors will audit your test markets and use the results to develop their own product. For example, a health and beauty aids firm developed a deodorant containing baking soda. A competitor observed the product in the test market and was able to create and roll out its own version of the deodorant nationally before the first firm completed its testing. To add insult to injury, the second firm successfully sued the product's originator for copyright infringement when it launched its deodorant nationally! The moral of the story is that firms that allow easily copied items to languish in test markets may find that competitors have stolen their ideas, their advertising copy, and their markets.

Test markets are also inappropriate for most industrial products and for items that require extensive tooling and unique production equipment. It is simply too expensive to test-market lift trucks, automobiles, and large appliances; alternative measures of customer acceptance must be developed for these items. One possibility is to prepare some test models and introduce them at trade shows. Chrysler's Viper, Prowler and Volkswagen's revitalized Beetle all started out as show cars and were later successfully introduced as the result of enthusiastic consumer responses from trade shows. Another approach is to try out new products with regional introductions. This involves promoting and selling the product in a few markets and then expanding distribution if the product is successful. Although regional introductions are more expensive than test markets, this method is less expensive than introducing a product nationally. Also, if successful items are moved quickly from regional to national distribution, competitive responses are likely to be weak and ineffectual.

Remember that test marketing is not a cure-all for product development problems. It is simply one of many ways to gather data on new items.

COMMERCIALIZATION

The last step in the product development process is the introduction of new items to the dealers and then to the ultimate buyers of the product. The objective of *commercialization* is to get the dealers to stock the item and persuade the ultimate consumer to purchase it for the first time. Previous stages have eliminated undesirable projects and have established the specifications, prices, and promotional arrangements most desirable for the new venture. Now you must weld these elements into a new product introduction plan that will achieve your objectives. Commercialization is concerned with implementing this plan.

The Importance of Timing

The success or failure of many products depends on when the product is introduced. Conventional wisdom suggests you should be first with new products to get the early adopters and establish a dominant market position. For example, Chrysler was first to sell minivans and they are still number one in this market. However, research has shown that sometimes the first to enter a market is the most successful and on other occasions late entrants dominate. A diagram showing the relationship between time of introduction and product performance of personal digital assistants (PDA) is provided in Figure 6-5. Personal digital assistants are small hand-held electronic devices that allow users to record notes and memos, organize appointments, and communicate with others. Most PDAs weigh about a pound and measure 5 by 7 inches. The three earliest entries to the market were the PenPad manufactured by Armstrad, the Newton made by Apple/Sharp, and the Zoomer produced by Tandy/Casio. These three PDAs were the smallest, cheapest ($700), and were targeted at a broad consumer market. The three late entrants included

APPLYING
. . . *to*
Durable
Goods
Marketing

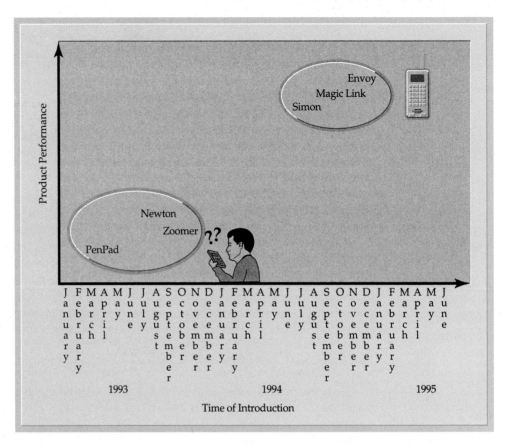

**FIGURE 6-5   Relationship Between Time of Introduction and Product Performance
(From Barry L. Bayus, Sanjay Jain, and Ambar G. Rao, "Too Little, Too Early:
Introduction Timing and New Product Performance in the Personal Digital Assistant
Industry,"** *Journal of Marketing Research,* **Vol. 34 [February 1997], p. 54.)**

the Simon developed by BellSouth, Magic Link designed by Sony, and Motorola's Envoy. These products were larger, heavier, and had some attractive additional features. They allowed the use of spreadsheets, word processing, pocket Quicken, and were equipped with fax/modems, fax receive, and two-way wireless. The late entrants cost a little more ($1,000) and were targeted at businesspeople. The data in Figure 6-5 show that PDAs like the Newton offered too little and reached the market too early to be successful. Products that came on the market later and offered more useful software and communications features like the Motorola Envoy prospered.

Although a few *market pioneers,* such as Coca-Cola, are long-lived market-share leaders, the first firm to sell in a new product category usually does not maintain this leadership very long—about five years. The firm known as the *early leader* (that is, the market share leader during the early growth phase of the product's life) is generally still the market leader today. For example, Trommer's Red Letter was the first light beer, but Miller Lite, introduced 14 years later, quickly became the dominant brand. Researchers believe that early leaders are successful because of their ability to spot a market opportunity and their willingness to commit large resources to develop the market.

One explanation of the *market development problem* may be found by revisiting the bell-shaped adopter category (Figure 3-4). Rather than the process being continuous, there may be gaps between the adopter categories as shown in Figure 6-6, especially for high-technology products. The gap between innovators and early adopters can occur when the

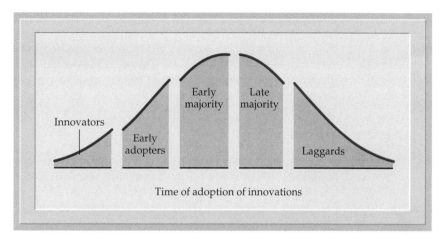

FIGURE 6-6 **Discontinuities Between Adopter Segments (From Geoffrey A. Moore,** *Crossing the Chasm* **[New York: Harper Business, 1995], p. 17.)**

excitement of the enthusiast cannot be translated into a compelling application, which would cause visionary early adopters to switch from established products. More critically, a very large gap or *chasm* can occur between early adopters and the early majority. Early adopters are willing to radically change how they do things in order to gain a major advantage over the competition. They are willing to accept some temporary minor defects or malfunctions of a breakthrough new product to gain major new benefits. On the other hand, the early majority wants properly working products that can be integrated into their organizations with minimal disruption. To be sure that they will get promised productivity benefits, they rely on good references and strong supplier support. The source of good references is typically other members of the early majority rather than early adopters. You must be careful not to mistake the early market for the desired emerging mainstream market. There can also be a gap between the early majority and the late majority. Whereas the early majority is willing and able to become technologically competent, the late majority is much less so. Consequently, a product must become even more user friendly at this point of market development or risk having the market stall prematurely.[13]

Cannibalization

Firms also have to be careful when introducing new items not to merely replace (cannibalize) sales of existing company products sold at the same prices. To avoid this problem, some firms develop new product ideas and then keep them in "cold storage" until they are needed.[14] This allows new items to be released at higher prices as interest in current products declines (product saturation) or when competitors come out with an innovation. Gillette faced this issue when they brought out their new MACH3 razor mentioned earlier. To make sure that the higher-priced MACH3 attracted enough buyers from their own and other companies' products, Gillette spent $300 million on introductory advertising the first year. Gillette also packaged the MACH3 blades in 4 and 8 packs compared with 5 and 10 packs for Sensor Excel to lessen the perception of high MACH3 blade prices. Commercialization of the MACH3 razor went well for Gillette. In the first week after introduction in July of 1998, the MACH3 became the largest selling razor in America. Also 25 percent of buyers switched from brands sold by other companies. By October of 1998, the MACH3 share of the blade market was 10.5 percent, only slightly behind Sensor Excel at 10.8 percent. This was remarkable given that stores were selling 10 Sensor Excel blades for $9.14 compared with $12.39 for 8 MACH3 blades. Con-

*APPLYING
. . . to
Consumer
Packaged
Goods
Marketing*

sumers were paying $1.55 per blade for MACH3, a 70 percent premium over the $.91 Sensor Excel blade. Although 75 percent of MACH3 sales were cannibalized from other Gillette razors, profits were expected to increase because the gross margin on the new blades was three times as high. The MACH3 introduction managed to raise Gillette's share of the U.S. shaver and blade market from 65 percent in September of 1997 to 70 percent in 1998.[15]

Coordinating Product Introductions

INTEGRATING
... with
Production

Product availability is crucial during commercialization because goodwill and sales can be lost if the product fails to reach the market on schedule. The introduction of General Motors' Cavalier compact car provides a classic example of the problems that can occur. GM announced a spring availability date for the new car with a lavish advertising campaign. Customers were told to go to their dealers and test-drive it. When they arrived, however, there were no cars because last-minute production delays had greatly reduced the supply of engines. When the cars finally arrived months later, customers found them to be underpowered and first-year sales were far below expectations. In this case, failure to coordinate production and advertising cost GM millions in lost revenues.

MANAGING NPD

INTEGRATING
... with
Cross-
Functional
Teams,
Information
Technology

Surveys have shown that firms that use formal NPD processes and do not skip steps are more successful with new product introductions. The success rate for the Best firms in one study was 80 percent compared to only 52 percent for the Rest.[16] Best companies had lower mortality rates for new product ideas across all stages of the product development process. Higher success rates and fewer losses of product ideas gives the Best firms faster revenue growth and greater profits. Also best practice organizations expect 45 percent of their sales to come from products commercialized in the previous three years and were able to deliver 49 percent over a five-year period. This is twice the rate of the rest of the firms. In addition, best firms use multi-function development teams more extensively with less innovative new product ideas. Multi-functional NPD teams are made up of people from marketing, production, R&D, and finance. Having people from several business functions work together on a new product simplifies communications and coordination. Multi-functional teams use advanced stage gate evaluations in 69 percent of best firms compared with only 52 percent usage by the rest. The most common new product team reward for best firms is a project completion dinner followed by newsletter recognition. Best practice firms do not use financial rewards for NPD.

Careful management of NPD can create a number of advantages. A telecommunications company reorganized NPD and time to market plunged, products were better aligned with customer needs, and market share and revenue improved. Quality also rose and manufacturing costs decreased, substantially improving product margins. With the same resources, the company now has significantly more development projects under way. A study of 184 auto and computer firms in four countries revealed that the use of cross-functional teams and advanced design tools in NPD led to higher returns on assets, profit to sales ratios and sales growth.[17] These advanced design tools employ sophisticated computers and digital-imaging software to speed up the creation of new items. At General Motors all the various design and manufacturing activities use the same Unigraphics software package which turns every aspect of a vehicle into digital and mathematical models. Cars and trucks are designed on a computer screen, tested on screen, and then data are forwarded to manufacturing and suppliers. This saves money by eliminating the need for physical models, cutting down engineering changes, reduces lead times for ordering production tooling by 50 percent, and makes it possible to solve manufacturing problems in "virtual" factories instead of real ones. Computerized product design is expected to save GM $200 million on each new global car and truck program. Also the advanced designed tools improved engineering productivity 13 percent in one year and helped GM cut the time from project design approval to the start of production from 42 months to 24 months.[18]

SUMMARY

Product development is an exciting, creative process that converts ideas into commercially viable goods and services. Product development is also expensive. The likelihood of increasing sales and profits from new items is enhanced by careful attention to the organization and control of this activity. A key ingredient is a full-time director of product development to expedite and coordinate the many jobs and individuals necessary to produce new merchandise. In addition, the firm must foster a climate that is receptive to new ideas and develop screening criteria that are appropriate to its own objectives and resources. Also, new products need to be carefully tested so that they reflect the attributes and quality levels actually desired by the ultimate customer. This means concept tests to gauge customer reactions to product ideas, preference tests to select product attributes, and use tests to evaluate packaging and long-run customer acceptance. Where new products are radically different, sales tests may be needed to measure repurchase rates and alternative promotional appeals. Finally, products must be introduced to the marketplace so that dealers and customers will become aware of the new items and begin to purchase them on a regular basis.

NOTES

1. Rebecca Blumenstein, "Tough Driving: Struggle to Remake the Malibu Says a Lot About Remaking GM," *The Wall Street Journal* (March 27, 1997), pp. A1, A8.
2. Marvin L. Patterson, "From Experience: Linking Product Innovation to Business Growth," *Journal of Product Innovation Management* Vol. 15 (1998), p. 394.
3. Ron Winslow, "Missing a Beat: How a Breakthrough Quickly Broke Down for Johnson & Johnson," *The Wall Street Journal* (September 18, 1998), pp. A1, A5.
4. Barton G. Tretheway, "Everything New Is Old Again," *Marketing Management* Vol. 7 (Spring 1998), p. 8.
5. Cornelius Herstatt and Eric von Hippel, "Developing New Product Concepts Via the Lead User Method: A Case Study in a 'Low-Tech' Field," *Journal of Product Innovation Management,* Vol. 9, No. 3 (September 1992), pp. 213–221.
6. Michael J. McCarthy, "Slim Pickings: Food Companies Hunt for a 'Next Big Thing' But Few Can Find One," *The Wall Street Journal* (May 12, 1997), pp. A1, A6.
7. Christopher D. Ittner and David F. Larcker, "Product Development Cycle Time and Organizational Performance," *Journal of Marketing Research,* Vol. 34 (February 1997), p. 21.
8. Robert G. Cooper, "The NewProd System: The Industry Experience," *Journal of Product Innovation Management,* Vol. 9, No. 2 (June 1992), pp 113–127.
9. Mark Maremont, "How Gillette Brought Its MACH3 to Market," *The Wall Street Journal* (April 15, 1998), pp. B1, B8.
10. The MACH3 "Razor vs. the Rest," *Consumer Reports* (October 1998), p. 9.
11. Raju Narisette, "P&G Uses Packaging Savvy on Rx Drug," *The Wall Street Journal* (January 30, 1998), pp. B1, B11.
12. General Foods' Americana Recipe Vegetables (B) case written by Lawrence J. Ring, University of Virginia.
13. Geoffrey A. Moore, *Crossing the Chasm* (New York: Harper Business, 1995).
14. For some examples, see William P. Putsis, Jr., "Why Put Off Until Tomorrow What You Can Do Today?" *Journal of Product Innovation Management,* Vol. 10, No. 3 (June 1993), pp. 194–203.
15. Mark Maremont, "Gillette's Earnings Plummeted 99% in Third Quarter," *The Wall Street Journal* (October 16, 1998), p. B12.

16. Abbie Griffin, "PDMA Research on New Product Development Practices: Updating Trends and Benchmarking Best Practices," *Journal of Product Innovation Management,* Vol. 14 (1997) pp. 429–458.
17. Christopher D. Ittner and David F. Larcker, "Product Development Cycle Time and Organizational Performance," *Journal of Marketing Research* Vol. 34 (February 1997), p. 21.
18. Robert L. Simison, "GM Turns to Computers to Cut Development Costs," *The Wall Street Journal* (October 12, 1998), p. B4.

SUGGESTED READING

Cohen, Morris A., Jehoshua Eliashberg, and Teck H. Ho. "An Anatomy of a Decision-Support System for Developing and Launching Line Extension," *Journal of Marketing Research,* Vol. 34 (February 1997), pp. 117–129.

Mukhopadhyay, Samar K. and Anil V. Gupta, "Interfaces for Resolving Marketing, Manufacturing, and Design Conflicts," *European Journal of Marketing,* Vol. 32, No. 1/2 (1998), pp. 101–124.

Shankar, Venkatesh, Gregory S. Carpenter, and Lakshman Krishnamurthi. "Late Mover Advantage: How Innovative Late Entrants Outsell Pioneers," *Journal of Marketing Research,* Vol. 35 (February 1998), pp. 54–70.

Song, X. Michael, and Mitzi M. Montoya-Weiss. "Critical Development Activities for Really New Versus Incremental Products," *Journal of Product Innovation Management,* Vol. 15 (1998), pp. 124–135.

Urban, Glen L., John R. Hauser, William J. Qualls, Bruce D. Weinberg, Jonathan D. Bohlmann, and Roberta A. Chicos. "Information Acceleration: Validation and Lessons from the Field," *Journal of Marketing Research,* Vol. 34 (February 1997), pp. 143–153.

REFERENCES

Bacon, Frank R. and Thomas W. Butler. *Achieving Planned Innovation: A Proven System for Creating Successful New Products and Services.* New York: Simon & Schuster, 1998.

Clark, Kim B. and Steven C. Wheelwright. *The Product Development Challenge: Competing Through Speed, Quality and Creativity.* Cambridge, MA: Harvard Business School, 1995.

Crawford, C. Merle. *New Products Management.* Homewood, IL: Richard D. Irwin, 1996.

McMath, Robert M. and Thomas Forbes. *What Were They Thinking: Marketing Lessons I've Learned from Over 80,000 New Product Innovations and Idiocies.* New York: Time Books, 1998.

Meyer, Mark H. and Alvin Lehnerd. *The Power of Product Platforms.* New York: Free Press, 1997.

Smith, Preston G. and Donald G. Reinertsen. *Developing Products in Half the Time: New Rules, New Tools,* 2nd ed. New York: John Wiley & Sons, 1997.

Ulrich, Karl T., and Steven D. Eppinger. *Product Design and Development.* New York: McGraw-Hill, 1995.

QUESTIONS

1. For third quarter of 1998, Revlon reported profits of 7 cents a share instead of the 73 cents that analysts had been expecting, and the stock price dropped 44 percent. Low profits were partially due to Revlon's failure to launch its new ColorStay Compact in September. The new version of easy-to-apply foundation in a mirrored compact did not fare well in consumer tests and it was sent back to the lab for reformulation. What steps could Revlon have taken to make sure its new compact reached the market on time?

2. Chuck Mellon fell off a motorbike, tore a hole in his sweatshirt, and accidentally stuck his thumb through the hole. This suggested a new product where each cuff would be fingertip length and have a thumbhole, in effect a fingerless glove on the end of each sleeve. Pop your thumb out and the "glove" could be rolled up into a regular wristlength cuff. After some false starts at selling this innovation, he managed to get a 20,000-unit order for JC Penney's catalog. The item sold out three days after the catalog was mailed. What does the product life cycle say about the need for product development activities at this firm in the future?

3. Suppose that you have a private firm recruit subjects for your new product focus groups at a central downtown facility. When you arrive for a session on cereals, you notice that your chief competitor has accidentaly left a box of a new cereal on the table in the room assigned for your use. Should you immediately return the box of the new cereal to your competitor or should you take it back to the lab and have it analyzed to see if it can be copied?

4. Panasonic introduced a $3,000, 36-inch, high-definition, cinema-style wide screen digital TV in the fall of 1998. The entire TV industry expected to sell only 10,000 digital sets in 1998 out of a total annual TV market of 23 million sets. Why did Panasonic introduce a digital TV before digital television signals and digital programming were available at a price four times the price of a similar analog TV set?

5. Philips Electronics, a Dutch firm, invented the audio cassette and co-launched the compact disk player. In 1991, they introduced a compact-disk interactive player that offered digital sound, picture, and graphics for games and education. The product was years ahead of its competition and easily attached to the back of a TV set. Operated by a hand-held remote control, the system plays easy-to-load standard music compact disks, photo compact disks, and interactive games. The machine was priced at $799 and had a limited number of game disks when it was introduced. Although Sony sold more than a million of its PlayStation game machines in less than a year, Philips sold only 400,000 of its CDi machines over five years. Philips is reported to have lost $1 billion on the CDi in the United States. What went wrong with Philips's CDi introduction? Could Philips have avoided the problems by conducting more focus groups and use tests? What changes should Philips make to its new product development process?

6. Four companies introduced electronic book reader to the consumer market in 1999. These devices store text downloaded from the Internet and reproduce it on screens for viewing by readers. Everybook comes in a two-screen color reader for $1,500. Softbook offered a device the size of a thick $8^{1}/_{2}$ by 11 inch notebook for $299 plus $19.95 a month, Nuvomedia has a paperback-sized device for $500, and Librius has a Millenium Reader in a paperback size for only $199. Liberius plans to target romance novels and best-sellers. One firm estimated electronic books will be a $2.5 billion market by 2002. The manufacturers of electronic books believe that book publishers will save so much money on paper, printing, shipping, inventory, and returns that they will offer substantial discounts for readers buying an electronic version of a book. Which of the electronic books has the best prospects for success? Is there room in this new market for four competitors? Is the success of this new product dependent on the cooperation of book publishers? If so, what should the manufacturers do to obtain this cooperation?

7. Japanese high school girls have been very useful to firms planning to introduce new products to the Japanese market. New items are shown to the girls in focus groups and they are asked for their opinions. Coca-Cola Co. asked a group of girls about a new fermented milk drink and they suggested a lighter smoother consistency than rival products, and a short stubby bottle with a pink label instead of a tall, skinny, blue-labeled bottle that Coke was considering. Shiseido asked some girls about a new line of cosmetics called Chopi. The girls told them to change the name to Neuve and change the color of the bottles from the usual black, white, or silver to beige. The high school girls also helped Dentsu Eye to talk up a previously unknown product at their schools. As a result, brand awareness increased to 10 percent of the target market, a result that would have cost $1.5 million in advertising expenditures. Why are focus groups so important in the development of new products? Why are teenage girls so helpful to companies marketing new products in Japan?

8. The development of a new low-cost microchip to act as the light gathering sensor in cameras has allowed Nintendo Co. to introduce a new accessory for its popular Game

Boy toy. The new filmless toy camera was priced at $49.95 and sold 800,000 units in six months. Does this mean that technology drives product development? How was Nintendo able to get their new digital toy camera to market seven months before Mattel Inc. introduced its Barbie digital camera for $69?

9. In 1998, Volkswagen introduced a new version of its original Beetle model that was designed in the 1930s. The New Beetle has front-wheel drive, a water-cooled engine, and was priced for about $16,000. Customer acceptance has been very good in the United States and Volkswagen expected to sell 50,000 Beetles in the first year on the market. What accounts for the success of this small cramped new model? Is it nostalgia or is it just clever marketing?

10. Campbell Soup Co. developed a new line of nutrient-fortified meals that research showed could actually reduce high levels of cholesterol, blood sugar, and blood pressure. The meals were called Intelligent Quisine and were test marketed in Ohio. After 15 months in the test market, sales were slow and Campbell dropped the new line at a cost of $55 million. Does the failure with IQ meals suggest that Campbell should reduce its expenditures on R&D? Do you think the problem was a lack of variety in meal options or was it a more basic problem that Americans resist long-term eating programs to improve their health?

11. Digital videodiscs (DVDs) were first introduced to the consumer market in 1997. DVDs offer sharper pictures than videocassette players but they cannot record movies or TV shows. DVDs sold slowly their first year on the market, because Hollywood studios released only a few films for DVDs and video rental stores did not promote them for fear they would hurt videocassette rentals. Sales picked up in the second year as video stores started to offer to rent DVD machines for five nights for $14.95 and the studios started to offer more films on disk. Why was it so important for the video stores to offer DVD rentals? Explain why new electronic devices catch on slowly.

CASE 6-1 CAPITAL (A)*

*I*t is the end of July 1991 and most Parisians are preparing to leave on holiday. But not Dr. Andreas Wiele. He, as project and executive manager, and the other members of the Prisma Presse team developing a new business magazine called *Capital,* have other things on their mind. The zero issue of *Capital* went down well with the focus group they have just been watching over closed-circuit TV. The problem is the market itself. The economic situation is bad—advertising in business magazines has dropped by about 20% since the beginning of the year and circulation is still stagnant. Should they go ahead with the planned launch in September, or postpone until the economic situation improves? If they do launch, key marketing decisions still remain to be taken: the magazine's price, its distribution and communication policies.

PRISMA PRESSE: GRUNER+JAHR'S FRENCH SUBSIDIARY

Prisma Presse, with offices in the center of Paris close to the Champs-Elysées, was founded in 1978 by the then 41-year-old Axel Ganz (Exhibit 1), the German publishing company headquartered in Hamburg, itself a subsidiary of the multimedia Bertelsmann group. Trained as a journalist, Axel Ganz had already held various

* This case was prepared by Reinhard Angelmar, Professor of Marketing, INSEAD, with the assistance of Wolfgang Munk (MBA 1992) and Thierry Azalbert (MBA 1992). Copyright (c) 1994 INSEAD, Fontainebleau, France. Reproduced by permission.

GERMANY

Magazines: Art, Brigitte, Capital, Decoration, Elterns, Essen&Trinken, FF, Flora, Frau im Spiegel, Frau im Spiegel Rätsel, Geo, Geo Special, Geo Wissen, Häuser, Impulse, Marie-Claire*, Max*, Mein Kind und ich, Neues Wohnen, PM. Magazin, P.M. Logik Trainer, Schöner Wohnen, Prima, Saison, Sandra, Schöner Essen, Sonntagspost, Sports, Stern, Wochenpost, Yps.

Newspapers: Berliner Kurier, Berliner Zeitung, Dresdner Morgenpost, Chemnitzer Morgenpost, Hamburger Morgenpost, Mecklenburger Morgenpost, Leipziger Morgenpost, Sächsische Zeitung.

SPAIN

Dunia, Geo, Mia, Muy Interessante, Natura, Ser Padres Hoy, Estar Viva, Cosmopolitan*.

UNITED KINGDOM

Best, Prima, Focus.

UNITED STATES OF AMERICA

Parents, YM.

ITALY

Vera*, Focus*.

* Joint Venture

EXHIBIT 1   Gruner+Jahr: Publications Outside France

GEO
**Travel / Discovery of the Beauty
of Nature and Civilization
upper middle class
Monthly circulation: 580 OOO
Nr. 1 travel magazine
Launch: 1979**

ÇA M'INTERESSE
**Scientific Popularization
adolescents/young adults
Monthly circulation: 350 000
Nr. 1 in segment
Launch: 1981**

PRIMA
**Women's Magazine
good housekeepers and wives
Monthly circulation: 1 220 000
Nr. 1 women's monthly
Launch: 1982**

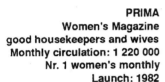

FEMME ACTUELLE
**Women's Magazine
Weekly circulation: 1 800 000
Nr. 1 women's weekly
Launch: 1984**

TELE LOISIRS
**TV Magazine
Weekly circulation: 1 220 000
Nr. 4 TV magazine
Launch: 1986**

VOICI
**The Celebrities' Private Life
Weekly circulation: 600 000
Nr. 1 women's
picture magazine
Launch: 1987**

CUISINE ACTUELLE
**Gourmet Magazine
Monthly circulation: 350 000
Nr. 1 food magazine
Acquired in 1989**

GUIDE CUISINE
**Family food magazine
Monthly circulation: 230 000
Nr. 2 food magazine
Acquired in 1989**

Monthly Business Magazine

**Planned launch date:
September 1991**

EXHIBIT 2   Prisma Presse: Product Portfolio, 1991

senior positions with leading magazine publishing companies.

During its 13 years, Prisma Presse has launched six magazines and acquired two more, increasing the circulation of the latter by a factor of three since taking them over in 1989. All Prisma Presse magazines are among the leaders in their segments (Exhibit 2). This compares favorably with the industry average: of a total 173 new consumer magazines launched between 1987 and 1990 in France, only 119 (69%) were still going at the end of 1990. This enviable track record has earned Axel Ganz such sobriquets as "magazine alchemist" and "man with the Midas touch."

With a 1990/91 sales of F2 billion (Exhibit 3), Prisma Presse has become the second biggest magazine publisher in France. It concentrates effort on text and layout in its magazines, and outsources such activities as documentation, photography, printing and distribution. Prisma Presse is structured around the individual magazine (Exhibit 4). Each is headed by a duo consisting of an executive editor and an editor-in-chief, jointly responsible for editorial policies, staffing,

circulation and revenues of the magazine. The executive editor, often working on two magazines, is specifically responsible for financial results, while the editor-in-chief, usually assigned to one magazine only, is specifically responsible for execution of editorial policy. Each magazine has its own staff of journalists, art team, and advertising department. The advertising departments of the different magazines compete vigorously for business, sometimes against other Prisma Presse magazines. Coordination of advertising policy is one of the tasks of the corporate advertising business manager.

The staff of a successful magazine is regarded by management as a pool of talent from which inside members of future magazines are recruited. For example, *Prima* was the breeding ground for subsequent women's magazines. These insiders usually account for about half of the staff of a new magazine. They are used especially on the art team, because the visual concept across the range is basically the same. Outside recruitment brings in journalists with knowledge in content areas like economics, business, fashion, cooking, and travel.

EXHIBIT 3 Key Data: Prisma Presse, Gruner+Jahr, Bertelsmann

	1987/1988	*1988/1989*	*1989/1990*	*1990/1991*
Prisma Presse				
(in million FF)[a]				
Total Revenues[b]	1,621	1,762	1,865	2,057
Growth		*9%*	*6%*	*10%*
• Circulation Revenues	1,253	1,335	1,433	1,606
• Advertising Revenues	347	401	405	424
Profits	83	104	119	159
% of Revenues	*5%*	*6%*	*6%*	*8%*
Nr. of employees	414	448	481	527
Revenues/Employee	*4*	*4*	*4*	*4*
Gruner+Jahr				
(in million DM)				
Total Revenues	2,773	2,987	3,099	3,284
Growth		*8%*	*4%*	*6%*
Profits	223	255	272	200
% of Revenues	*8%*	*9%*	*9%*	*6%*
Nr. of employees	8,745	9,170	9,286	9,613
Bertelsmann Group				
(in million DM)				
Total Revenues	11,299	12,483	13,313	14,483
Growth		*10%*	*7%*	*9%*
Profits	362	402	510	540
% of Revenues	*3%*	*3%*	*4%*	*4%*

[a] Average 1991 exchange rates were: 3.3FF for 1 DM; 5.6FF for 1$; 1.7DM for 1$.
[b] The financial year ends on 30 June

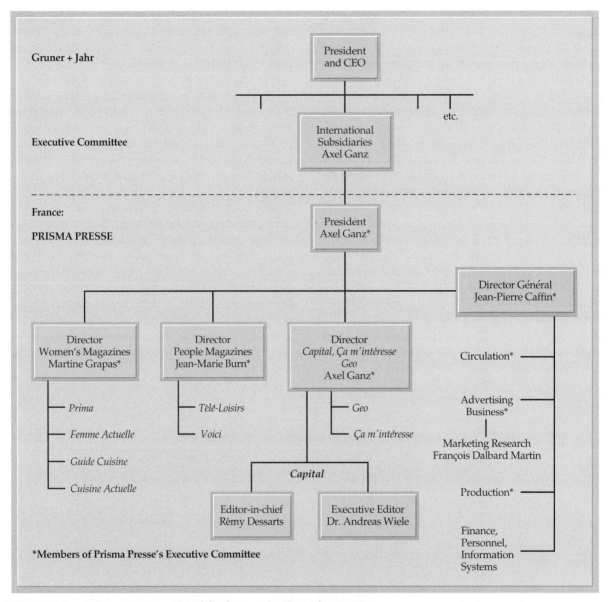

EXHIBIT 4   Prisma Presse: Simplified Organization Chart, 1991

Market research, production and distribution management, and some other functions are taken care of by specialized departments covering all Prisma Presse magazines. Tight cost controls create a sense of leanness throughout the organization.

EDITORIAL PRINCIPLES AT PRISMA PRESSE

Axel Ganz has strong convictions regarding the basic editorial principles which he imprints on all Prisma Presse magazines, regardless of their content area.

Reader/Circulation Focus

Magazines derive revenue both from readers (circulation) and advertising. In contrast to some publishers who are more advertiser- than reader-oriented, Axel Ganz's priority is clearly the reader: "Circulation is where the business is. You can act on it—and we must do everything we can to maximize it—whereas advertising also depends on factors beyond our control, like the overall economic situation." A Prisma Presse executive confirms: "Ganz is obsessed with circulation;

when a magazine's circulation starts declining, he sounds the alarm." Circulation determines the major part of bonus payments, which range from 60% of the annual salary for the managing duo to two months' additional salary for some of the regular staff. "When circulation objectives are not met, Axel Ganz puts on enormous pressure," comments one editor-in-chief. Managers who repeatedly fail to achieve objectives are asked to leave: "In this company, we get rid of teams that don't win," explains one executive.

Because the bulk of Prisma Presse circulation comes from volatile newsstand sales rather than from more stable subscriptions, reader appeal shows up quickly in circulation figures. Days when circulation figures come out have everyone in a state of feverish excitement. Outstanding results are celebrated, whereas disappointing circulation calls for quick remedial action, which may escalate from minor changes to a major overhaul. For example, *Voici*'s circulation increased from 240,000 at launch to 600,000 three years later, thanks to a series of changes resulting in the complete repositioning of *Voici* from a family magazine to one concentrating on the "celebrities' private lives."

A constant stream of market research data provides each magazine with information about its readers, and many team members are usually present to watch the focus groups which are organized regularly throughout France. This close attention to the reader is rather unusual in the French press. According to one Prisma Presse executive, "competitors are managed by Parisian journalists who only think of their egos and their connections, and who impose the dictate of their good taste. This is intellectual terrorism. As for us, we can put ourselves in the shoes of the reader from the Creuse (a backward rural area in France)." One observer put it like this: "Prisma is to the French press what Disney is to the French cinema."

A Clear Concept and Consistent Implementation

Each magazine must have a clear concept (for example, "to discover and show the beautiful things on earth, which need to be preserved" *Geo*), and every aspect of the magazine (topics, style of presentation, visuals, layout, cover, etc.) must be consistent with this concept. To Axel Ganz, a successful magazine is like any other successful brand which acquires a distinctive identity: "Why does a reader prefer one magazine to another, although often both cover the same subjects? Because each title projects a specific image and creates a special kind of relationship with the reader." The managing team must ensure that every issue fits the concept: "There may be doubts and discussions, but the manag-

ing team must identify enough with the concept of their magazine to sense immediately, nine times out of ten, whether a topic is right or not," Axel Ganz comments.

Precise, Well-Researched Information

Prisma Presse has a strict policy of not allowing advertisers to interfere in editorial content, unlike some other publishers, where advertisers sometimes influence articles which they judge detrimental to their own interests, or where journalists use company press releases as main sources for their articles.

Attractive Presentation

Presentation in all Prisma Presse magazines is geared for maximum readability: short articles ("right length for a ride in the Metro"), short words ("no more than three syllables"), short sentences, and comprehensible titles. "You have to understand the conditions in which people read—poor lighting, ill-fitting glasses, etc.— it's these kinds of details that make the difference," explains one executive. The marrying of text and visuals is vital: the editorial policy of most Prisma Presse magazines stipulates that "topics are chosen only if it is possible to produce a matching visual representation."

The art directors are the guardians of the Prisma Presse formula for attractive presentation. They train the journalists in the magic formula, follow each issue through until the final check, and are always on the lookout for changes that would enhance appeal. Together with the editors-in-chief they comprise the main bottleneck and constraint for the launch of new magazines by Prisma Presse.

SEARCHING FOR A NEW IDEA

To sustain Prisma Presse's growth, Axel Ganz has set as an objective the launching of a new magazine every 18 months. The new products should have high circulation potential, be innovative rather than imitative, and use primarily newsstand distribution, Prisma Presse's main channel. The only segments specifically excluded are newspapers and news magazines. "There are sensibilities which should not be hurt," Axel Ganz explains. "Newspapers and news magazines deal with politics, and even if we took an objective stand on an issue, we would probably be accused of taking a German view. The time isn't right. In two generations, possibly…"

Axel Ganz, together with Martine Grapas and Jean-Marie Burn, directors for the women's and people magazines respectively, are responsible formally for coming up with ideas for magazines. Ideas may float around for many years, and only a few ever make it into development. In his own search for new product ideas, Axel Ganz monitors market trends in all segments and different countries, until, "one day, out of this observation emerges a hunch that a particular area might be promising." Axel Ganz may see promise where others see only desolation. For example, he launched *Prima* and *Femme Actuelle* in a segment which, despite being crowded with fifteen magazines, had been declining for ten years. He reasoned that the decline was due not to a lack of demand, but because the offering was unsatisfactory.

Axel Ganz had a hunch that the business magazine market in France might be promising. Business magazines provide readers with business and economic news and analyses across all industries. The leading title in France was *L'Expansion* (a bi-weekly), which created the market in 1967, followed in 1975 by *Le Nouvel Economiste* (a weekly). In 1984, the Mitterand presidency's sudden shift from anti- to pro-business gave rise to an increased interest in business information and triggered a rash of product launches, not all of which survived.

Fortune France, the most recent business magazine launched in February 1988, was an intriguing case. The intention was clear: take advantage of *Fortune*'s awareness and image among international advertisers and top executives, while overcoming the language barrier which resulted, for the English language edition, in a circulation of a mere 5,000 in France. *Fortune France* was published by a 50–50 joint venture between *Fortune*'s US publisher Time-Warner and its French partner Hachette, the leading publisher in France. They shared the launch investment of F40 million and expected to reach payback within three years. The circulation goal was 50,000 initially, rising to 80,000 after 3 to 4 years.

Fortune France's editorial team consisted of eight full-time French journalists plus a network of correspondents. Changes in content, layout and paper quality resulted in a glamorous, lifestyle oriented magazine which had little in common with its American counterpart. "This magazine does not appear to be willing to upset the business establishment. One finds in it neither the bite nor the impertinence which account for the appeal of the US magazine," commented one observer. *Fortune France* cost F30, sold mainly through newsstands, and was launched with a F2.5 million advertising campaign on radio and in the national press, as well as by a direct mail campaign. Advertising business took off briskly despite high rates, but circulation remained

low. Paid circulation reached 37,000 when *Fortune France* was eventually discontinued in June 1990.

Axel Ganz felt that the French business magazines suffered from two weaknesses. First, the older magazines had not changed much and looked somewhat old-fashioned. Second, all titles appeared light on editorial quality, and most seemed to believe more in attracting subscribers through expensive direct mail campaigns than through a high-quality product.

RECRUITMENT OF A MANAGEMENT TEAM TO FILL A BLANK SHEET OF PAPER

In Fall 1989 Axel Ganz transformed his hunch into a formal development project codenamed *Hermès,* due for launch in 1991. Funds for development were budgeted in the three-year 1990–1993 plan approved by Gruner+Jahr.

Gruner+Jahr was already familiar with the business magazine market as the publisher of *Capital,* the leading business magazine in Germany. But Axel Ganz decided to start from a blank sheet of paper, without any a priori ideas about the concept or name. "I don't believe in a Euro-magazine which would be completely identical in all countries. You can't simply export and translate magazines, which are cultural products. You can transpose to another country a concept which has proven its worth elsewhere, but you have to reshape and modify it to adapt it to the local context. Up-market magazines like *Geo* can be internationalized more easily, because these consumers become more similar, whereas mass market magazines like *Prima* address a more popular audience, for which local peculiarities—eating and leisure habits, for example—are very important."

In Spring 1990, Axel Ganz set out to recruit the management team for the new magazine. He found a project and executive manager in 28-year-old Dr. Andreas Wiele, an assistant to the president and CEO of Gruner+Jahr in Hamburg, who had previously worked for one year as a journalist for a Hamburg newspaper after studying law. Dr. Wiele joined Prisma Presse in Paris in July 1990.

Finding an appropriate editor-in-chief took much longer, despite the large number of candidates attracted by Prisma Presse's reputation. Ganz was looking for somebody with experience in the French business press, not a star journalist, but someone willing to apply Prisma Presse's editorial principles to business magazines. The choice finally went to 36-year-old Rémy Dessarts, a graduate of a Paris business school who had spent eight years at *L'Expansion* before becoming associate editor of the business magazine *A pour Affaires*. Rémy Dessarts joined in September.

Forty-eight-year-old Thierry Rouxel, assigned as art director for *Hermès,* was the third key member of the team. An old hand with Prisma Presse, Thierry Rouxel brought with him the all-important Prisma Presse presentation know-how to the project.

Through the recruitment process, word got out about Prisma Presse's intentions. But competitors did not take the project seriously, doubting that a company publishing mainly for women could successfully enter the business magazine market.

ANALYZING THE MARKET FOR BUSINESS MAGAZINES

Dr. Wiele's major task during the initial months consisted of gathering and analyzing information on business magazines and other relevant publications (Exhibit 5). He found that circulation stagnation was hitting not only business magazines (Exhibit 6), but all segments of the economic press, with the exception of personal finance magazines like *Le Revenu Français* (170,000 circulation) and *Mieux Vivre* (139,000 circulation), which had enjoyed a compound annual growth of 8% over the last 10 years. The number of advertising pages in business magazines had been declining since 1988, with advertising revenues dipping slightly for the first time during 1990 (Exhibit 7).

Dr. Wiele noticed some striking differences between the French and German business magazine markets:

- total circulation was higher in France, yet supply was much more fragmented: France had many more titles, each with a relatively small circulation; e.g., *L'Expansion,* with 150,000 was the leading title in France, compared to 250,000 for *Capital,* the leader in Germany;

- French magazines invested less in editorial content: they employed fewer journalists, every one of whom had to produce more editorial pages than their counterparts in Germany;

- subscription discounts and sales were both much higher in France than in Germany; e.g., 84% of *L'Expansion*'s circulation came from subscriptions (see Exhibit 8) compared to 59% for *Capital;*

- German business magazines featured many more "personal service" topics—e.g., how to reduce taxes, manage one's career, invest money—than French business magazines, which left these subjects to spe-

cialized magazines such as *Le Revenu Français* and *Mieux Vivre.*

To obtain a broader perspective on the topics that could be covered by *Hermès,* Dr. Wiele analyzed the leading business magazines in Europe and the United States. This survey provided the basis for a detailed content analysis of the French business magazines (see Exhibit 9).

The total reader potential for business magazines in France was estimated at 4.8 million, comprising 1.5 million senior and middle managers in business firms ("chefs d'entreprise et cadres supérieurs en entreprise"), 1.2 million top non-business professionals such as lawyers, doctors and senior civil servants, and 2.1 million entry-level managers ("cadres moyens"). François Dalbard-Martin, Prisma Presse's market research specialist, pointed out that only 45% of the 4.8 million potential readers had actually read a business magazine during the preceding 12 months. The main reader target for *Hermès* would be the 1.5 million senior and middle managers in business firms. Only 59% of these were readers of business magazines.

Advertisers in French business magazines were also interested in reaching the top non-business professionals, in addition to senior and middle managers in business. The combined 2.7 million person advertising target group was called the "executives" ("affaires et cadres supérieurs"). The price which a business magazine could charge for advertising space depended mainly on: (1) its absolute number (or, equivalently, its penetration) of "executive" readers; (2) the share of "executives" among its readers; (3) the total number of buyers (paid circulation). Exhibit 10 shows the readership profile of the main competitors, and the desired profile of *Hermès* readers.

Two focus groups were held with members from the *Hermès* target group in Fall 1990 to understand their perceptions and attitudes toward existing magazines, as well as their expectations. Exhibit 11 summarizes the results.

THE DECISIVE WEEKEND: A NEW CONCEPT IS CONCEIVED

At the end of October 1990, Axel Ganz, Dr. Andreas Wiele, Rémy Dessarts, Thierry Rouxel and François Dalbard-Martin met for a weekend to decide on the future course of the project. Most importantly, they decided to develop a prototype of *Hermès*. Prisma Presse develops products one at a time and, until now,

L'EXPANSION
general business magazine
twice a month
circulation: 149 000
Launch: 1967

LE NOUVEL ECONOMISTE
general business magazine
weekly
circulation: 89 000
Launch: 1975

SCIENCE & VIE ECONOMIE
general business magazine
monthly
circulation: 106 000
Launch: 1984

DYNASTEURS
general business magazine
monthly
circulation: 95 000
Launch: 1985

L'ENTREPRISE
business magazine for owners
of small businesses
monthly
circulation: 64 000
Launch: 1985

A POUR AFFAIRES
general business magazine
monthly
circulation: 42 000
Launch: 1985

CHALLENGES
general business magazine
monthly
circulation: 72 000
Launch: 1986

LE REVENU FRANÇAIS
personal finance magazine
monthly
circulation: 170 000
Launch: 1968

MIEUX VIVRE
personal finance magazine
monthly
circulation: 138 000
Launch: 1979

Note:
all circulation figures refer to the average
1990 paid domestic circulation per issue

EXHIBIT 5   Main Economic Magazines in France, 1991

EXHIBIT 6   Circulation of Main Business Magazines in France

	Launch Year	Frequency	Paid Domestic Circulation per Issue (in thousand copies)				Circulation Growth 1990/1987	Share of Monthly Paid Circulation 1990	Gross Annual Circulation Revenue[c] in million F (estimate) 1990	Share of Annual Gross Circulation Revenue (estimate) 1990
			1987	1988	1989	1990				
L'Expansion	1967	bi-weekly	160	175	159	150	−6%	29%	74	31%
Le Nouvel Economiste	1975	weekly	93	80	84	90	−3%	34%	56	24%
Science & Vie Economie	1984	monthly	111	116	117	107	−4%	10%	25	10%
Dynasteurs[a]	1985	monthly	100	100	100	95	−5%	9%	31	13%
L'Entreprise	1985	monthly	61	62	65	65	7%	6%	20	8%
Tertel/A pour Affaires[b]	1985	monthly	33	34	35	47	42%	4%	11	5%
Challenges	1986	monthly	45	67	73	74	64%	7%	22	9%
Total Monthly Paid Domestic Circulation		thousand copies	1042	1049	1044	1048	1%	100%	239	100%
Gross Annual Circulation Revenue		million F	217	233	240	239	10%			

[a] Circulation as Indicated by publisher. Circulation data of all other magazines are audited.

[b] *Tertiel* relaunched as *A pour Affaires* in September 1989.

[c] Gross Circulation Revenue = Average Price per Copy (=Retail price − Subscription Discount) × Total Paid Circulation (Domestic and Export).

EXHIBIT 7   Advertising in Main Business Magazines in France

	Number of Advertising Pages per Year				Growth Nr Adv Pages 1990/1987	Share of Adv Pages 1990	Gross Advertising Revenue[b] 1990 (million F)	Share of Gross Adv Revenue 1990
	1987	1988	1989	1990				
L'Expansion	2875	2845	2575	2366	−18%	31%	274	42%
Le Nouvel Economiste	2940	3047	2770	2259	−23%	30%	184	28%
Science & Vie Economie	242	231	225	224	−7%	3%	17	3%
Dynasteurs	341	623	649	627	84%	8%	52	8%
L'Entreprise	954	1257	1225	1082	13%	14%	72	11%
Tertiel/A pour Affaires[a]	451	550	706	703	56%	9%	40	6%
Challenges	222	223	352	343	55%	5%	19	3%
Number of Adv Pages per Year	8025	8776	8502	7604	−5%	100%		
Gross Advertising Revenue per Year (millions of F)	516	652	668	659	28%		659	100%

[a] Tertiel relaunched as A pour Affaires in September 1989.
[b] Gross Advertising Revenue: List Price per Advertising Page × Number of Advertising Pages.
The net revenue amounts to approximately 60% of the gross revenue, the difference including the commission for media wholesalers and the advertising agency.

	L'Expansion	Le Nouvel Economiste	Science et Vie Economie	Dynasteurs	L'Entreprise	A Pour Affaires Economiques	Challenges
MARKETING MIX: CIRCULATION MARKET							
Product							
Avg. Nr. Pages/Issue	189	112	107	140	190	162	109
Editorial/Total Nr. of Pages	46%	60%	81%	59%	52%	57%	74%
Nr. Issues/Year	23	50	11	11	12	10	12
Total Nr. of Editorial Pages/Year	1,998	3,349	956	906	1,200	923	963
Avg. Nr. of Staff Members	38	40	12	15	21	19	13
Nr. Edit. Pages/Staff Member/Year	53	84	80	60	57	49	74
Price							
Newsstand Price per Copy	25 F	15 F	22 F	30 F	30 F	27 F	25 F
Subscription Discount[a]	48%	24%	18%	33%	41%	20%	23%
Distribution: Newsstand Unit Sales							
% of Total Domestic Paid Circ.	16%	23%	34%	16%	32%	35%	22%
1990 Media Adv (million F)	F8.8	F5.9	F2.8	N.A.	F2.5	F5.4	2.4
per paid domestic copy (in F)	2.60 F	1.30 F	2.40 F	N.A.	3.20 F	11.40 F	2.70 F
% of Gross Newsstand Revenue	68%	38%	31%	N.A.	33%	131%	55%
MARKETING MIX: ADVERTISING MARKET							
Price							
List Price per 4 Color Page (in F)	117,600 F	70,000 F	65,000 F	80,900 F	61,900 F	59,000 F	59,500 F
Cost per 1,000 Paid Domestic Circul	784 F	778 F	607 F	852 F	952 F	1,255 F	804 F
Cost per 1,000 Dom. Exec. Readers	162 F	232 F	230 F	234	141 F	N.A.	342 F
Advertising Department (Nr. Persons)	7	8	4	4	7	4	5
REVENUE STRUCTURE							
1990 Gross Revenue (Estimate)							
Gross Circulation Revenue	74	56	25	31	20	11	22
Gross Advertising Revenue	274	184	17	52	72	40	19
Total Gross Revenue	348	240	42	83	92	51	41
Adv Rev as a % of Total Gross Rev	79%	77%	40%	63%	79%	78%	47%
% of publisher's total revenue	35%	2%	N.A.	15%	9%	2.5%	10%
Name of publisher	L'Expansion	Hachette/Fillpacchi	Excelsior	Pearson France	L'Expansion	C.E.P.	Le Nouvel Observateur

[a] In calculating the subscription discount the retail price of special issues (e.g., travel guides) made available free of charge to subscribers is included.

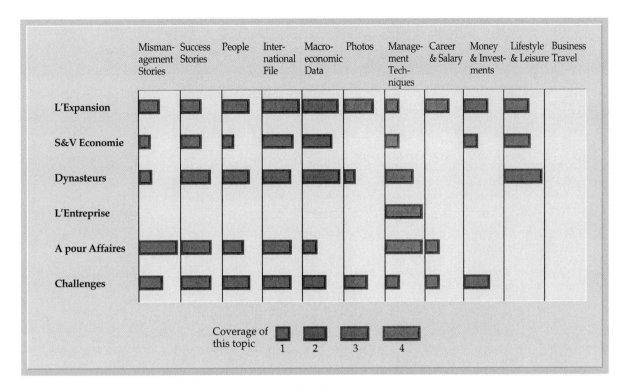

EXHIBIT 9   Content Analysis of Business Magazines in France, 1990–1991

every Prisma Presse project ever prototyped was sub-sequently launched.

The next major decision concerned the concept of the magazine. They decided that, compared to its competitors, the new magazine should be:

- **broader in scope:** in addition to the classic business coverage provided by French magazines, the new magazine should cover new trends, management techniques, and business philosophies (similar to the German *Manager Magazin*);
- **more entertaining:** the crucial role of individuals, with all their strengths and weaknesses, should be brought out more strongly; this required well researched, thrilling success and failure stories, the description of interesting personalities, including those working outside Paris, an understanding of how they operated, and a coverage of lifestyle/leisure trends relevant to managers (similar to what the U.S. magazine *Forbes* offered);
- **more useful:** more coverage of personal interest topics like career management, continuing education, salaries, insurance, personal investments, etc. (similar to the German magazines *Capital* and *DM* and to what *Le Revenu Français* and *Mieux Vivre* covered);

- **more informative:** all articles should be well researched and objective;
- **more international:** international aspects should be covered systematically and be based on facts rather than national stereotypes;
- **more visual:** the layout should be more attractive, reading should be facilitated, and the photographic material should be original, rather than relying on easily available photos of a small number of business celebrities.

This concept was immediately translated into a "flat plan." Such a plan allocates pages to the various content areas, defines specific articles in each content area and, finally, describes the order of appearance of the articles. Development of the flat plan drew on everybody's industry knowledge, and many features were inspired by other magazines, both French and foreign. Two questions were asked throughout: (1) are the choices consistent with the product concept? and (2) do they lead to a clear competitive advantage?

The next immediate step was to produce a first prototype of the magazine by January 1991 and to test it with a group of potential readers. A second, revised prototype would be produced by April 1991 and a third

EXHIBIT 10   1991 Readership Profile of Business Magazines in France

	L'Expansion	Le Nouvel Economiste	Science et Vie Economie	Dynasteurs	L'Entreprise	A pour Affaires Economiques	Challenges	Total (in million)	Hermès Target Profile
ALL TARGET GROUPS: Magazine Penetration (in %)									
a. Senior and Middle Managers in Business Firms	21[a]	10	6	14	16	7	5	1.5	
b. Highly Educated Professionals	8	4	5	2	3	0	2	1.2	
c. Entry-Level Managers	12	7	4	6	9	2	3	2.1	
Total (a+b+c)	14	7	5	7	10	3	4	4.8	
ADVERTISING TARGET GROUP: "Executives" (a+b)									
Magazine Penetration (in %)	15	7	5	8	10	4	4	2.7	
Share of "Executives" among Readers (in %)	62	56	60	63	57	66	58		
HERMÈS READER TARGET GROUP									
Number of Readers: Senior & Middle Mgrs in Bus Firms	300,068	136,466	79,535	202,546	231,562	96,924	73,080	1.5	
Reader Profile: Senior & Middle Mgrs in Bus Firms									
Sex (in %)								(in %)	(in %)
male	80	88	85	83	77	69	79	82	80
female	20	12	15	17	23	31	21	18	20
Region (in %)									
Paris Metropolitan Region	42	47	39	50	39	42	46	45	40
Rest of France	58	53	61	50	61	58	54	55	60
Age (in %)									
<35	23	20	29	21	22	23	24	24	35
35–45	34	37	41	38	39	40	42	38	45
>45	42	44	30	41	39	37	34	38	20
Annual Income (1,000 F) (in %)									
< 180	15	11	16	7	10	15	12	16	17
180–240	23	19	24	17	20	12	20	23	22
240–360	37	37	32	38	38	44	35	34	39
> 360	19	27	21	31	25	23	27	20	22
Firm Size (Nr. employed) (in %)									
< 10	22	17	18	18	18	21	18	21	15
10–50	20	17	20	16	26	27	20	18	15
50–200	14	16	22	20	17	18	11	18	20
200–500	13	14	11	10	11	8	13	8	20
> 500	31	37	29	36	29	27	37	35	30
Type of Business (in %)									
Manufacturing	32	41	31	36	45	41	40	41	40
Trade	17	17	12	21	14	12	10	14	15
Services	51	42	57	44	42	47	50	45	45

[a] Percentage of all French senior and middle managers in business firms who read the magazine during the week (*Nouvel Economiste*) or month (all other magazines) preceding the interview.

Source: IPSOS Cadres Aclifs 1991. Copyright © 1994 INSEAD. Fontainebleau, France.

EXHIBIT 11   Perceptions, Attitudes and Expectations Toward Business Magazines

1. The Existing Magazines

• repetitive in content and style, from one issue to another, between one magazine and the others
• no title with a clear profile; no originality
• the journalists are not credible: they are either too ideologically dogmatic, or mere spokesmen for the firms, or they provide inaccurate information
• the readers feel trapped, because
   – they are obliged to read this press to be informed;
   – the magazines make no effort to seduce them; reading is a real chore
• readers notice a timid change, but this concerns more the presentation (more color, more illustrations) than the content and basic philosophy of the magazines

2. Reader's Expectations

• useful information, instead of nebulous and pedantic discourse
• articles should be credible:
   – the author's point of view should be clear
   – the article should be rigorous, well-written, and well-summarized
   – the issues should be put in perspective (comparisons over time, etc.)
• more controversy:
   – stop bootlicking well-known business figures and companies
   – present conflicting theories and points of view
   – show some detachment through humor and irony
   – put issues in historical and geopolitical context
• a wider angle:
   – greater international perspective, less French-oriented
   – coverage of cultural topics
   – one or two humorous pages
• a more attractive presentation
   – clear table of contents
   – facilitate reading through titles, sub-titles, a clear visual code
   – many illustrations and schemas
   – the articles should be more "airy"
   – one or two very incisive and conclusive articles on specific topics (a double page maximum)

Source: Report on 2 focus groups with senior and middle managers. Eliane Mikowski; Paris, Fall 1990.

by July 1991. The market launch was scheduled for September 1991.

PROTOTYPING THE NEW CONCEPT

As Prisma Presse had no previous experience in the business market, five external journalists were recruited to work exclusively on the *Hermès* project. Some had extensive experience in the French business press, others were younger journalists. Just as for the editor-in-chief, it turned out to be difficult to find journalists having excellent business/economic knowledge, and willing to adapt to the editorial principles and culture of Prisma Presse. Recruitment remained a problem throughout, and several journalists were eventually asked to leave.

The team was given a separate, closed off open-plan office in the Prisma Presse building. Access was highly restricted and, apart from the management duo, the art group, and Prisma Presse's senior management, the team had no contact with any other Prisma Presse staff, nor with other parts of the Gruner+Jahr organization, including the journalists working for Gruner+Jahr's *Capital* in Germany.

Organized around the main content areas of the magazine, the journalists immediately started to implement the flat plan. The important role of initiating them in the "Prisma Presse formula" fell to art director Thierry Rouxel, who discussed with each journalist at the outset the concept of the projected article, as well as the number and types of illustrations, and the layout on the page. Constant attention was paid to the integration of text, visuals, and layout as the articles progressed. At other magazines, the journalists' role was usually limited to writing articles, with editorial secretaries and visual staff adding their contributions afterwards. The tight schedule led to a very heavy workload, sometimes forcing journalists to work around the clock.

The first prototype was ready in January 1991. Kept under tight security control, the 50-page dummy had no cover page and no name. The articles chosen were deliberately sensational to find out how far one could go in the direction of entertainment and still be considered a serious business magazine. Many focused on power struggles (e.g., "1 seat for 3 pretenders"; "The barons' conspiracy") or demolished well-known business figures (e.g., "Tapie doesn't have what it takes"). The dummy also included a psychological test ("Are you a real boss?"), an analysis of managers' difficulties with their children ("Daddy, I never see you!"), and a map of a fashionable Champs-Elysées restaurant indicating celebrities' preferred tables.

The dummy was immediately tested with two focus groups composed of target group members. After a first quick flick through they expressed pleasant surprise with the numerous photos, the big headlines, and the clear layout which made for easy reading. But as they read the articles in greater depth, their mood turned negative and even angry. The magazine was too sensational, too negative ("vitriolic") and too superficial for them, only good "to be read at the hairdresser's."

Undaunted, the team proceeded to produce a second prototype. They made small modifications in layout, headlines and sub-headings of articles already tested (see Exhibit 12), and concentrated on producing other articles that would demonstrate the seriousness of the magazine. A 16-page article on the battle between European and Japanese automobile manufacturers was the longest and most intensively researched article.

The second, 100-page prototype still without cover page or name, was tested with two focus groups in April 1991. The magazine's presentation was again very well received. But this time, the content was also praised for its diversity, factual grounding and good summarizing of important information. The managers liked the editorial style, which was "the opposite of the bland, insipid style" of the habitual business journalism and reflected a desire to "see things the way they really are." Most of them felt like buying the magazine, reading it from cover to cover and keeping it for future reference.

As always, Axel Ganz was watching the focus groups over closed-circuit TV. Before the second group drew to an end, he fetched some champagne, popped the corks and declared, "we will launch this magazine!"

Up to this point, the project had cost about F6 million. Funding for further development including a test launch was available through the development budget already approved by Gruner+Jahr. A test launch would require some more recruitment, but the team of journalists would receive no guarantee of continuing beyond the test phase. A full-blown launch like the one Axel Ganz had in mind, however, involved a more massive and longer-term commitment and required the formal approval of Gruner+Jahr and Bertelsmann. Dr. Wiele prepared a 10-page (plus exhibits) report, which summarized the market situation, explained the product and marketing concept for *Hermès,* and specified the main assumptions underlying the 8-year projected income. If circulation after 6 months failed to exceed 50,000, the magazine would be discontinued. It was estimated that cumulative investment would have reached F60 million at this point. As expected, the Gruner+Jahr and Bertelsmann boards gave the green light in May and June respectively.

THE ZERO ISSUE: *HERMÈS* BECOMES *CAPITAL*

The third prototype was the magazine's "zero" issue. Identical to a real magazine in presentation and editorial content, its main purposes were to test readers' response to the real product, to scale up and test the production process and, last but not least, to draw advertising.

To produce the zero issue, the magazine's staff was increased to 32, mostly by hiring from the outside. Almost all articles were new. The main editorial response to April's market research results was yet another increase in the number of pages devoted to "service" topics (management techniques, career and salary, personal finance), to 26 out of 110 editorial pages in total (see Exhibit 13). A separate macroeconomic section printed on pink paper (the same color as the *Financial Times* and the economic supplement of a leading French newspaper) was added in the center of the magazine, and a tongue in cheek page at the end.

What should the magazine be called? Because it was originally thought that the name *Capital* had negative connotations in France, other names had been considered, including the once more available *Fortune,* which might open doors with advertisers and information sources. Negotiations failed, however, and in the end the name *Capital* was chosen, with the subtitle "The Essence of the Economy."

Capital was the first Prisma Presse magazine created with a completely integrated PC-based publishing system. This permitted several iterations before the final version was transmitted electronically to the Bertelsmann printing plant in Gütersloh, Germany.

January '91

April '91

July '91

EXHIBIT 12   **The Evolution of Capital**

EXHIBIT 13   Number of Editorial Pages per Content Category

	CAPITAL		L'EXPANSION
Content Categories	Flat Plan January 1991	Zero Issue July 1991	July 4/17 1991
People	14	12	3
Business	16	16	14
success stories			
mismanagement stories			
International File & Macroeconomy	21	22	21
The Economy in Pictures & Special Topics	21	18	18
Service Topics	15	26	1
management techniques			
career & salary			
money & investments			
Life Style, Leisure, Business Travel	21	16	5
Total Number of Editorial Pages	108	110	62

Virtually everybody participated in the discussions of each version, including Axel Ganz. "He intervenes less in the content of articles than in the presentation, and occasionally shows a layouter how to solve a problem," commented Rémy Dessarts. In the end, all remaining issues were solved by hierarchy and, as always, Axel Ganz gave the green light after having gone through the final version page by page, line by line.

TO LAUNCH OR NOT TO LAUNCH...

Hot off the press, the zero issue of *Capital* was tested with two focus groups on July 23 and 24, with positive results (see Exhibit 14). Normally, this would be a good basis for drawing advertising, for which Constance Benqué, former head of *L'Expansion's* advertising department, has just been recruited.

EXHIBIT 14   Zero Number of Capital: Perceptions and Attitudes

The main attitude is one of surprise in front of an object which is new in the context of the economic press.
This is backed up by the following perceptions:
• great richness and variety
   "this is life, this is the world"
• great density and true information
• great ease of reading
   "freedom of reading, depending on the circumstances, how much time I have, and on how I feel"
   "one can read over lightly, for entertainment, or go for a detailed reading"
• a style
   "sharp," "the journalists take position," "interrogative"
• professional
   "well researched," "the journalists have good access," "the magazine is pleasant ... good pictures ... attractive colors"

Overall, Capital will create an event in the market. It has great competitive potential both in the business magazine market and in the news magazine market.

But readers hesitate regarding the magazine's identity and personality:
• a business or a news magazine?
• a "people" or a business information magazine?
• superficial or dense?
• structured or muddled?
• judicious advice or consumerism?
• specialisation or popularisation?

Source: Report on 2 focus groups with senior and middle managers. Eliane Mikowski; Paris, July 23–24, 1991.

EXHIBIT 15   Key Economic Assumptions for Capital

Product	1991/1992	1998/1999
number of editorial pages/issue	110	120
number of issues/year	10 (Oct 1991–July 1992)	12 (August–July)
editorial costs/editorial page	F 20,000	increase: 3% p.a.
mechanical costs/printed page	F 0.05	increase: 3% p.a.
department costs (management, advertising department)/year	F 6 million	increase: 5% p.a.

Newsstand Distribution		
distribution margin (% of newsstand price)	55%	55%
% unsold rate (% of copies delivered to newsstands which are not sold)	50%	30%

Subscription Distribution		
avg cost of a new subscriber		
• via direct mail (mailing list purchase, direct mail)	between F 300 and F 1000 per subscription[a]	between F 300 and F 1000 per subscription[a]
• via self-promotion (subscription appeals included in Capital)	F 20 per subscription	increase: 3%
self-promotion yield (share of newsstand copies for which subscription forms are sent)	1%	1%
subscription renewal rate (%)	between 50% and 60%[a]	between 50% and 60%[a]
avg. cost of renewing a subscription	between F 20 and F 80[a]	between F 20 and F 80[a]
cost of serving a subscription (administration, postage, etc.)	F 4 per copy	increase: 3% p.a.

[a] The greater the number of subscriptions, the higher the average cost of acquiring and renewing a subscription, and the lower the subscription renewal rate.

Advertising Market		
4 color ad page cost/1000 circulation	F 755	increase: 4% p.a.
avg. net adv revenue/adv page	57%	57%
Advertising Promotion/adv page	F 3200	increase: 4% p.a.

Circulation Marketing Mix

	"Subscription" Strategy			"Newsstand" Strategy		
Year	Newsstand Price (Subscr. Disct: 30%)	Media Adv per Copy	Subscription Share (% of Total Circul)	Newsstand Price (Subscr. Disc: 17.5%)	Media Adv per Copy	Subscription Share (% of Total Circul)
1991/1992	25F	11F	70%	15F	21F	9%
1992/1993	28F	5F	70%	18F	10F	17%
1993/1994	30F	3F	70%	20F	5F	24%
1994/1995	33F	3F	70%	22F	5F	30%
1995/1996	35F	3F	70%	22F	5F	34%
1996/1997	38F	3F	70%	25F	5F	36%
1997/1998	40F	3F	70%	25F	5F	37%
1998/1999	43F	3F	70%	28F	5F	38%

But is this the right time to launch a new business magazine? Since the beginning of the year, advertising volume in business magazines has declined by about 20%, and there are no signs of recovery, despite the end of the Gulf War. The entire economic press is suffering. The *L'Expansion* group, all of whose titles are in the economic press, is rumored to be in the red and reducing staff. *A pour Affaires* merged with *L'Entreprise* in June. *Science & Vie Economie* cut short its relaunch advertising campaign prematurely. The Reader's Digest group has just withdrawn its new personal finance magazine *Budgets famille,* only six months after launch.

Dr. Wiele is wondering whether he should recommend that the planned September launch of *Capital* be postponed. If they do go ahead with the launch, they have to decide on its price, distribution and communication policies. Dr. Wiele sees two main alternatives: a "subscription," and a "newsstand" strategy.

The *"subscription"* strategy would be in line with the other business magazines: a high newsstand price (e.g., F25) combined with a high subscription discount and massive direct mail investments, resulting in subscription sales mainly.

The *"newsstand"* strategy would be a new approach for the business magazine market: an F15 newsstand price, identical to that of the weekly news magazines, combined with a low subscription discount and high mass media advertising. If *Capital* were published on the same day as these news magazines (Thursday or Friday) and displayed prominently, a significant share of the 600,000 buyers of weekly news magazines at the newsstands might pick up *Capital* once a month in addition to, or instead of, a news magazine. About 20% of news magazine readers fall into *Capital*'s reader target group.

Exhibit 15 summarizes the key assumptions necessary to evaluate these alternative strategies. At Gruner+Jahr, magazines are expected to reach breakeven within 3 to 4 years, pay back within 5 to 8 years, and return 15% on investment in the long term.

CASE 6-2 GTE TELEMESSAGER SERVICE*

*I*n February 1984 Bill Bradford, manager of New Business Development, GTE Corporation, submitted a recommendation to the company's top management. The recommendation, in the form of a 150-page business plan, proposed that GTE launch TeleMessager, a new communications service that Bradford had been working to develop over the past two years.

The business plan was based in large part on the results of a year-long market test of the TeleMessager service. While Bradford interpreted the results as supporting a "go" decision, he was aware that several members of management had been, and would probably remain, less than enthusiastic about the new venture. Bradford was confident that the proposal represented his best shot at selling the new project. On the other hand, he couldn't help but wonder what, if anything, he might have done to make an even stronger case for a "go" decision.

COMPANY BACKGROUND

In 1980, GTE Corporation had sales of $9.7 billion (Exhibit 1), ranking it second on *Fortune's* list of the top 50 U.S. utilities. GTE was second only to AT&T in providing telephone service to residences and business. The Telephone Operating Group (Telops), which was also involved in data processing and satellite communications, accounted for roughly 60 percent of company sales. The remaining 40 percent was derived from the Diversified Products Group, GTE's manufacturing arm; key products included communications and telephone equipment and consumer products marketed under the Sylvania name.

GTE began in 1918 when three men—John F. O'Connell, Sigmund L. Odegard, and J. A. Pratt—invested $33,500 to purchase the Richland Center Telephone Company, serving a dairy and farming area in Wisconsin. This was a relatively new industry they entered, that of the independent telephone company.

* This case was prepared by Robert J. Kopp of Babson College and Arvind Jadhav of GTE Corporation.

EXHIBIT 1   GTE Sales: 1970, 1975, and 1980

	1970	1975	1980
Telephone operations	$1.7	$3.2	$5.9
Diversified products	1.8	2.7	3.8
Communication services	–	–	–
Total	$3.5	$5.9	$9.7

Not quite 25 years earlier, in 1894, the last of the telephone patents granted to Alexander Graham Bell had expired. It was only then that telephone companies, independent of the Bell System, were formed. They sprang up throughout the country, many in areas not served by Bell, and others were in direct competition with Bell and with other independents in the same city.

By the early 1930s the company, then called Associated Telephone Utilities, was servicing 300,000 telephones in portions of 25 states. The Great Depression brought bankruptcy, but the company was reorganized in 1935 as General Telephone Corporation. In 1951, when Donald C. Power took over as president, General Telephone consisted of 15 telephone companies serving 1.4 million phones in 20 states. Also part of the corporation was Leich Electric Company of Genoa, Illinois. Acquired in 1950, Leich was General Telephone's first venture into manufacturing.

In 1955, Power sought to boost General Telephone's manufacturing capabilities by merging with Theodore Gary and Company. In 1954, 94 percent of General Telephone's consolidated net income came from telephone operations and only 6 percent from manufacturing. Gary had the opposite mix, as manufacturing produced 81 percent of its income.

Gary's Automatic Electric Company established General Telephone as a major manufacturer of telecommunications equipment. This company had been formed to manufacture the world's first dial telephone equipment. Automatic Electric's success was built on the Strowger switch, which permitted the automatic connection of telephone calls without the use of operators. It was invented in 1889 by Almon Strowger, then a Kansas City undertaker, who was convinced that he had lost customers because operators failed to complete calls to him. He vowed to devise a telephone system which would complete calls without an operator. During the succeeding decades many telephone companies, including the Bell System, purchased large quantities of Strowger equipment from Automatic Electric, which for some time was the only manufacturer of dial equipment and thrived during the succeeding decades. In 1981, the company, now GTE Automatic Electric Incorpo-

rated, opened a 200,000-square-foot development laboratory in Phoenix, Arizona, to develop digital telephone switching systems and software. In 1983, GTE Automatic Electric became part of GTE Network Systems, a unit of GTE Communications Products.

In 1959, General Telephone moved to diversify beyond communication by merging with Sylvania Electric Products, a leader in the fields of electronics, lighting, television and radio, chemistry, and metallurgy. At that time, the company was renamed General Telephone & Electronics Corporation (shortened in 1982 to GTE Corporation) to reflect the diverse operations of Sylvania.

BIRTH OF A NEW SERVICE

In 1981, Telephone Operations management decided that new products were needed to meet the group's long-run growth objectives. To carry out this strategy, a New Business Development (NBD) team was formed and was charged with identifying and developing new product ideas. Also at this time, a New Business Task Force (NBTF) was formed to oversee NBD's new product development efforts.

William Bradford was transferred from Corporate Marketing Research to become manager of NBD. Bradford had joined GTE 10 years earlier as a senior economist and had worked in several other areas, including engineering, forecasting, and planning. Bill Bradford's charter was to identify and develop ideas for new businesses which would be profitable, and the operation of which would leverage off GTE's existing capabilities.

As the search process proceeded in late 1981, several factors converged to bring about the birth of the idea for a new communications service. In 1979, GTE had acquired Telenet, a network that transmitted text via desktop data terminals. The problem with such a system is that the sender must have access to a data terminal and must, ideally, possess some typing ability. Also, Bradford was aware of the personal touch created by telephone answering machines because messages were transmitted in the sender's own voice. Finally, he was aware of an emerging technology through which sound waves could be converted to digital form, to be stored in and processed by a computer. The technology, which was dubbed *voice store-and-forward (VSF),* would make possible a communications system which would not require users to have a special data terminal or typing ability (Exhibit 2).

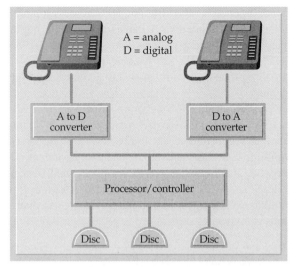

A = analog
D = digital

EXHIBIT 2 **Diagram of Voice Store-and-Forward (VSF) System**

At first glance, the VSF product appears to be very similar to a telephone answering machine. When the caller reaches a VSF, the voice of the person being called instructs the caller to leave a message. The person called then retrieves this message at a later time. Unlike the telephone answering machine, which uses an ordinary tape cassette as the recording medium, the VSF transfers the voice impulse into a digital code which can be stored on a computer disk. This *digital sound,* as it is called, can be easily saved, retrieved, and modified and can be easily sent simultaneously to any number of receivers. For example, a sales manager who wants to deposit a message in the voice mailboxes of 15 field sales reps can do so with one call on a VSF. To accomplish the same task with a normal telephone answering machine would require 15 separate phone calls.

ASSESSING MARKET POTENTIAL

As he researched the new idea more carefully, Bradford began compiling a list of the key user benefits of a VSF system. In short, VSF accomplishes the following:

1. Reduces time in call-backs; 70 percent of all business calls are *not* completed on the first try. This problem is particularly acute for communications between offices in different time zones.
2. Saves time by reducing "small talk." The average person-to-person business call is 7–10 minutes, most of which is occupied by small talk. The average VSF message is roughly one minute.

3. Reduces missed messages.
4. Provides the personal touch of voice communications.
5. Enables a single message to be transmitted to hundreds of mailboxes/telephones simultaneously.
6. Allows the user to reply to, save, delete, or reroute a message readily.

In Bradford's view, the need to exchange messages within business organizations was currently being filled by telephone answering services; answering machines like the PhoneMate; electronic beepers or pagers; and computer mail like GTE's own TeleMail service. Bradford saw in the voice digitizing technology the ability of VSF to fill the messaging need better and at lower cost than provided by existing products. For example, the VSF outperformed the answering machine in that messages could be saved, deleted, or redirected to one or several destinations with the touch of a button.

To assess the business potential for VSF, Bradford utilized studies conducted by three consulting organizations (Exhibit 3). It was estimated that VSF systems provided by service bureaus would generate revenues of $630 million in 1985, growing to almost $2.5 billion by 1990.

In addition, Bradford viewed the voice mailbox as having a good fit with GTE's corporate image as a leader in the communications industry. Down the road, he envisioned the possible integration of a voice mailbox system with other GTE services such as telephone operations, TeleMail, and SPRINT. In addition, because a VSF system could run on currently available computers—customized software was required—entrance into the new business required a rather modest capital outlay.

IN-HOUSE PRODUCT TEST

In early 1981 the voice mailbox idea was presented to the NBTF, and an agreement was reached to test a VSF

EXHIBIT 3 **VSF Market: U.S. Market Annual Revenues (000,000)**

	1981	*1985*	*1990*
Private systems	$65	$390	$800
Service bureaus	–	630	2,420
Tel. ans. services	500	700	800
Total	$565	$1720	$4020

Source: A. D. Little, IRD, SRI studies, 1981.

system in GTE's Stamford headquarters. A hardware manufacturer, who also had developed a basic VSF software package, was located and the system, tentatively named Voicemail, was introduced in April 1981 for a six-month trial run. Sixty-five GTE executives, who were judged to comprise a "close communications group," were chosen to participate in the trial. Participants were given a Voicemail manual, a "quick dial card" summarizing the manual, a template containing dialing instructions to be placed over the telephone face plate, and a directory of other Voicemail users. Training sessions were held with small groups of users, and a system help hotline was established.

In a cover memo to the test group, R.J. Cryder outlined the objectives of the trial as follows: to provide feedback on system features design; to measure productivity gains, if any; and to collect statistics on system use.

The results of the in-house test produced several findings which would guide the development and marketing of the new service. In a memo to Cryder in December 1981, Bradford summarized the conclusions of the test as follows:

1. The VSF concept is most useful to customers where there exists a close user group, members of which do not come into frequent face-to-face contact.

2. Usage of VSF increases where one member of the user group acts as a "champion" of the service.

3. System capacity does *not* appear to be a constraint.

4. Two additional features appear to be particularly desirable to customers: (a) a message waiting indication and (b) permitting outsiders (nonsubscribers) to have open access to the system.

In addition, the in-house test revealed implications for system development with respect to features such as length of message storage, message sequencing, mailbox labeling, formatting of pushbutton commands, and the like.

PROPOSAL TO TEST-MARKET VOICEMAIL

In Bradford's view, the in-house test had been a success, both in terms of fine-tuning the service concept and in terms of the VSF system's overall favorable reception by business users. At the same time, the six-month test did *not* provide data on which customer segments—that is, company size, location, and industry group—would represent the most productive target markets for the VSF service. And the test provided little guidance on how the new service should be priced or promoted. Nevertheless, Bill Bradford was anxious to test the service under real market conditions, and in October 1982 he went to the NBTF with a proposal to run a test market of Voicemail for a year beginning in January 1983. In order to save money and to simplify the operational aspects of the test, a single city, Dallas, Texas, was selected as the test market. In his proposal, Bradford outlined five objectives of the test: (1) to identify target customer segments; (2) to pretest and fine-tune product offerings; (3) to test alternative pricing levels; (4) to develop technical and operating expertise; and (5) to forecast demand. Exhibit 4 presents an overview of the Marketing Plan contained in the proposal.

Bradford's proposal recommended that a business unit be established reporting to a general manager. Initially, the Voicemail group would consist of two departments, marketing and sales, which would also handle in-field customer support; and operations, consisting of installation, maintenance, customer support, and training. Later, two more functional areas would be added: finance and product development, which would develop the system software.

The test market proposal met with a mixed reaction from the NBTF. Some members were impressed with the progress made to date on what would be one of the company's first internally originated new products developed for an unregulated market. In addition, the potential synergy between Voicemail and other GTE services was seen as a positive point. On the other hand, certain NBTF members questioned whether the move to test-market was premature, given the lack of

EXHIBIT 4   Summary of Marketing Plan for Dallas Test Market

Target customers (business users)
   Small (2–9 employees)
   Medium (10–99 employees)
   Large (100+ employees)
Product
   Single product—messagebox for subscribers only
Price
   $30 per month
   $0.50 per minute (for use of the long-distance network)
Promotion
   Direct mail
     "Improve productivity"
     "Save time, save money"
   Personal selling
   Advertising
   Sales promotion: "30-day free trial"

research on defining target segments and their specific needs. In this group's view, further marketing of Voicemail should be put on hold until Bradford and his group had in hand a thorough market study which described market segments and recommended specific marketing programs to meet their needs. While some members of the NBTF were encouraged by the absence of major competition in the VSF market, others took the apparent lack of interest by AT&T and IBM as a sign that GTE might be overestimating the potential size of the market. Finally, some NBTF members saw the revenue potential for VSF to be relatively small by GTE standards, and they reacted unfavorably to the fact that the breakeven period for the new business might be as long as 24 months.

Bill Bradford responded: "The objection that we needed more up-front marketing research really made me pause. I began to wonder whether we were, in our enthusiasm, moving too quickly. At the same time, everything we knew about VSF told us that the concept itself would be very difficult to describe to respondents in a survey/market study format. In an early concept test that we did, most people came away thinking that the product was just an elaborate answering machine. Therefore, I had serious doubts as to whether paper-and-pencil research could accurately forecast customer reactions to the actual service. I came to the conclusion that the only accurate way of gauging customer response was to observe real behavior under market conditions."

After much debate, Bradford was given the go-ahead to test VSF in Dallas during 1983. Initially, he was elated at having secured the right to further develop a new market in which he saw GTE as establishing a leadership position. However, he was sobered by the fact that he had only three months to find a location, to recruit and hire personnel, and to plan and execute promotional programs.

SEARCH FOR TRADEMARK

In preparation for the market test, GTE's advertising agency, Doyle Dane Bernbach (DDB), was asked to suggest a new brand name for the voice messaging service. Responding quickly, the agency submitted a long list of possible names including Phonemail, Phonememo, Phone-A-Gram, Telememo, Voice Mail Box, Autovoice, Messagephone, and MaxiMail. DDB recommended that Phonemail be chosen, and Bill Bradford agreed. However, in late December 1982, a press release announced the launching of a new VSF service named PhoneMail by the Rolm Corporation. A few

days later GTE's next choice, Voicemail, was trademarked by another competitor. In frustration, Bradford asked the advice of the department secretary, Jan Bouchet, who immediately suggested the name Telemessage. Shortly thereafter, an "r" was added, the "m" was capitalized, and TeleMessager (TM) was born.

THE DALLAS TEST

By December, Bill Bradford had obtained office space in Dallas, and he needed to put together a staff. First, Jon Potts was brought over as marketing manager from GTE's Southwest Telephone division, where he was a sales manager. Potts recalls: "They couldn't tell me exactly what I'd do or how much I'd be paid—little things like that. But I'd have the opportunity to help set up a new enterprise." Potts then interviewed 35 people from within GTE and hired 5; by April 1983 the new TM group had seven people. Bradford comments: "Since I didn't have the financial resources to offer pay raises, the initial TM group was clearly motivated by the challenge of starting a new venture. Later, when we expanded to new locations, I found that the extraordinary level of commitment exhibited by this founding group was very difficult to duplicate."

A particularly fortuitous personnel move was the recruiting of Bob Wilson as director of product development. Wilson, 25, had worked a six-month stint with the then Voice Messaging division as part of GTE's Associate Development Program for college graduates. Bradford recalls: "During this first assignment, I gave him a six-month project which he completed in four months! As the head of Product Development, he managed to keep up with marketing's demands to add new features on virtually a continuous basis."

With the TM organization in place in Dallas, marketing of the new service began in earnest in February 1983. To kick off the new business, a press release was issued and was picked up by key newspapers in Texas and New Orleans. The release said in part:

> New Orleans, Jan. 31—GTE TeleMessager Service, a public voice messaging system that offers convenience and increased productivity to the business customer by putting an end to telephone "tag," is being marketed in the Dallas–Ft. Worth area, GTE Corp. announced today.
>
> "This new method of voice communications offers a number of important advantages over written correspondence, telephone calls and telephone answering machines," said William E. Starkey, group vice president—headquarters staff of the GTE Telephone Operating Group. "It provides business people with a fast, reliable

message service that can be accessed at any time and from anywhere in the world without the need for special equipment."

Next, a direct mail piece describing the service and offering a 30-day free trial was sent to roughly 60,000 businesses, equalling the entire census of companies in the Dallas–Ft. Worth area. The brochure invited potential customers to learn more about TM by calling telemarketing reps located at the Dallas office. These reps were to explain the TeleMessager concept further and to qualify the customer as a prime prospect. Qualified sales leads would then be followed up by a TM salesperson.

On April 14 and 15 a meeting to review the status of the TM test was held in Dallas. At this meeting M. McDonough, GTE marketing researcher, presented the following information:

1. The response rate has remained consistent for all mailings at about 1 percent. Of the responses, 30–35 percent were classified as "positive" leads by the telemarketing agency. The sales staff reports that many of these positive leads expressed no interest in the service when contacted.

2. The telemarketing agency contacted 210 randomly selected, medium-sized establishments from mailing wave 3. This resulted in about 20 leads, but the TeleMessager staff regarded them, for the most part, as unproductive.

3. A survey of 33 nonsubscribers and 50 nonrespondents was conducted as of April 6. Results include:

   a. The nonsubscribers have little or no interest in the service. It is perceived by many of the small and medium-sized establishments as a service for bigger businesses. My guess is that this perception is a result of the service itself and the way we are promoting it.

   b. Little pricing information was obtained, so we don't know if price is an important barrier to purchase.

   c. The mailing was regarded as high in quality and well laid out. It was regarded as lacking in specificity in terms of service description and money-saving benefits.

   d. A very small percentage (8 percent) of the nonrespondents remembered receiving and sending the material or were aware of the service. Thus the general level of market awareness in the Dallas area is low.

The direct mail program, put together by a consultant, assumed that a mailing of 60,000 would yield 1125 qualified leads, 340 trial customers, and 200 who would adopt the service. Each customer would average 10 messageboxes at a revenue of $42 per box. "The first three months were a disaster," Bradford recalls. "The phones were quiet. As of June 1, we mailed to 42,000 businesses; we got 60 qualified leads and sold *six* boxes. That was a very frustrating period." There was considerable pressure from GTE headquarters to discontinue the test market. Bradford recalls:

> I became known around Stamford as a dog holding the bone. I wouldn't let go. I made a few enemies in the process, because I was so persistent.
>
> We were subjected to ridicule, actually. At meetings I'd be asked, "Have you got one more user now?" Or "Have you lost any more money?" While some of this was good humor, a lot of people sincerely felt the project should be scrapped.
>
> Some people in the company began saying that TeleMessager had no future. I argued that you don't plant a bulb during October and expect it to come up in mid-January. You have to give it time. They told me I had 15 days to make TeleMessager work. I said not enough. Give us two months to show signs of progress.

Arguing that the opportunity was too good to give up, Bradford got approval to continue the test in Dallas, with the proviso that he would show improved performance within two months. At this low point, Bradford and his team shifted into high gear to implement changes based on their experience over the first three months of marketing TM. The direct mail piece, which looked too commercial and impersonal, was rewritten and personalized with the recipient's name. Telemarketing personnel, who had not been able to respond adequately to customers' questions, were given additional training. The original TM product, which consisted of a single service—Universal Messagebox—was reconfigured into a five-product line, thus offering the customer more options (Exhibit 5). Pricing was revised to include quantity discounts at the 50-, 100-, and 200-unit levels.

Finally, Bradford and his sales team realized that the TM product had considerable benefits for companies which operate multiple locations around the country. In this case, the product needed to be marketed nationally as well as locally. They identified as a prime target medium-sized companies which have sales reps, customers, or executives scattered across different time zones. Two of the TM sales reps spent many long hours in the Dallas Public Library identifying such prospects. One mailing to 335 "prime prospects" resulted in 34 qualified leads—a return rate of 10 percent—and sales of 460 messageboxes.

EXHIBIT 5   GTE TeleMessager: Customer Features in Five-Tiered Service

	Service Level[a]				
	1	2	3	4	5
Personalized greeting	×	×	×	×	×
Save message	×	×	×	×	×
Delete message	×	×	×	×	×
Exchange messages		×	×	×	×
Send to a group		×	×	×	×
Reply w/o caller address		×	×	×	×
International service			×	×	×
Receive from any messagebox			×	×	×
Send to any messagebox			×	×	×
Redirect messages			×	×	×
Message delivery indication			×	×	×
Nonsubscribers can access				×	×
User can select nonsubscriber					×
Nonsubscriber can select user					×

[a] 1: telephone answering service; 2: private messagebox service; 3: universal messagebox; 4: public messagebox; 5, message desk service.

At this time, John Potts, TM's marketing director, proposed and received approval to offer a special sales incentive to TM's four sales reps. The program, dubbed "Reach for the Beach," offered a vacation trip to Hawaii as the top prize if the quota for signing up new customers was achieved. Also at this time, one of the sales reps, Nancy Peterson, made the kind of sale that signals a business turnaround. The Dallas office of a large multinational oil company was spending $120,000 a year on Mailgrams to announce frequent price changes to salespeople and customers. Peterson presented the company with the TM feature known as *group calling*, which enables a single message to be transmitted to many people. John Potts recalls: "They reached for their calculators, concluded we'd cut their communications cost 40 percent, and suddenly we sold 200 messageboxes!"

With a sharper definition of the target customer, and with new programs in place in the areas of product, pricing, and promotion, TM's sales volume improved dramatically during the July–December 1983 period. For example, one mailing targeted to a more well-defined group of prospects yielded a response rate of 10 percent. Final results for the 10-month test are given in Exhibit 6.

All things considered, Bradford was satisfied with TM's performance. Despite the slow start, total sales of messageboxes had come in at (1910 ÷ 2000) = 96 percent of target. While only 50 percent of the target number of customers was achieved, each customer on average purchased *twice* the target number of message-

EXHIBIT 6   Dallas Test Market Results, 1983

	Target	Actual
Number of customers	200	98
Messageboxes/customer	10	19.5
Total messageboxes	2000	1910
Revenue/messagebox	$42.00	$31.20
Total revenue (000)	$465	$313
Total expense (000)	$965	$938

Source: Company records. Data have been disguised.

boxes. Revenue per messagebox came in at 75 percent of the goal, largely, Bradford thought, because of the quantity discount program implemented at mid-year. On the positive side, total expenses came in somewhat below the original target.

The results of the test confirmed the TM group's suspicion that the service would need to be sold nationally. While Dallas accounted for 30 percent of sales and Texas 45 percent, a full 55 percent of sales were to businesses in 16 cities from Boston to Los Angeles.

Feedback from customers revealed their preference for being located close to the VSF supplier. The motivation behind this response was reduced transmission costs and the psychological satisfaction of having a supplier nearby to respond to urgent needs.

Further breakdowns of sales revealed that demand came from a wide spectrum of business types (Exhibit 7); that sales were skewed to large customers (Exhibit 8); and that the decision to offer a multiproduct line was a good one (Exhibit 9).

EXHIBIT 7   Customer Distribution by Industry

Industry	Number of Messageboxes
Aerospace	191
Air freight	2
Banking	371
Communications	319
Consulting	124
Electronic mfg.	88
Industrial supplies	43
Lodging	23
Oil and gas	219
Packaging mfg.	5
Pharmaceutical	89
Publishing	16
Restaurants	6
Securities	1
Software	52
Steel	57
Transportation	63
Utility	78
Wholesale auto.	22
Misc.-sml. Bus. & Res.	141
Total	1910

EXHIBIT 8   Dallas Test Customer Size Distribution

Messagebox Group	Companies	Messageboxes
1–25	76[a]	225
26–50	3	114
51–75	3	160
76–100	3	254
Over 100	4[b]	1157
Total	89	1910

[a] Includes residential customers.
[b] Includes GTE.

A PROPOSAL TO ROLL OUT THE NEW SERVICE

Overall, the results of the Dallas test convinced Bradford that TM represented a major business opportunity for GTE. In late 1983, he put together a 150-page business plan, containing marketing and operating plans, and proforma income statements for the 1984–93 period. Excerpts from this business plan are provided in Appendix A. In his cover memo to the NBTF, Bradford listed five major conclusions based on the Dallas test market: "(1) there is widespread demand for TeleMessager; (2) current product is acceptable, but ongoing enhancement is necessary; (3) pricing is acceptable, but further experimentation is recommended; (4) a cost-effective advertising program to increase customer awareness should be developed; and (5) the break-even period is short." The memo concluded that "a phased roll-out program should be undertaken to establish GTE leadership in the voice store-and-forward market."

The business plan recommended that the number of message centers be expanded to 7 in 1984, to 9 in 1985, and to 12 in 1986 and beyond. GTE's long-run market share of VSF was projected to be 50 percent. At this level, TM would break even in 1985. An alternative income statement showed that even at a 35 percent market share, TM would operate profitably in 1985.

Like the original proposal to open the Dallas test market, the proposal to roll out TM met with a mixed reaction from the NBTF. Task Force members were,

EXHIBIT 9   Dallas Test Sales by Product Category

Category	Number
Telephone answering service	162
Private messagebox service	241
Universal messagebox service	861
Public messagebox service	637
Message desk service	9
Total	1910

for the most part, dubious about the market share and financial projections. This skepticism was reinforced when Steve Washington, a marketing consultant to GTE, stated at a meeting between Bradford and the NBTF that there was a "zero chance" that the TM group would deliver the exact numbers contained in the roll-out plan. Nevertheless, some NBTF members shared Bradford's optimism for TM, agreeing with him that the new venture had a good fit with GTE's existing businesses and that it offered acceptable returns. Further, they saw that the risk level was kept low by the fact that the new business did not require a heavy capital outlay or the establishment of manufacturing facilities.

Other NBTF members remained skeptical of the TM roll-out proposal. In their view, a key weakness of the plan was the fact that the TM group still did not have a clear picture of the target customer. Marketing, therefore, would continue to follow a "shotgun" as opposed to a "rifle" approach. Some NBTF members holding this view recommended that more marketing research be undertaken immediately. Still others on the NBTF, Bradford thought, would be content to see the TM project scrapped without further delay.

Against these objections, Bradford countered that despite problems, the TM business had shown steady progress throughout the Dallas test. And while the test had not been a clear success from a numbers standpoint, a great deal had been learned about how to run the business. Bradford maintained that this was a business opportunity which GTE could not afford to walk away from because of its financial promise, its potential for synergy with other GTE offerings, and its symbolic role as one of GTE's first internally developed new products under the aegis of the New Business Development organization.

APPENDIX A

GTE Corporation/Telemessager Excerpts from Business Plan February 1984

RECOMMENDATION

This business plan recommends a roll-out of the TeleMessager service from a single location (Dallas) to a total of 12 regional centers in 1984 (Exhibit A-1).

At the targeted 50 percent market share, Telemessager will lose $1 million in 1984, will pay out by the end of 1985, and will generate substantial earnings in

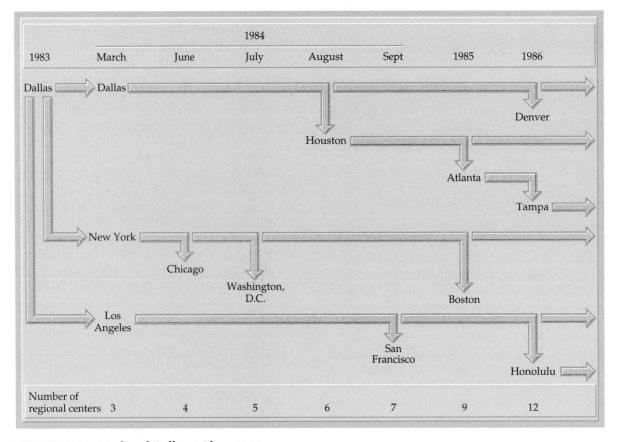

EXHIBIT A-1   Regional Roll-out Plan, 1984

1986 and beyond (Exhibit A-2). At a 35 percent market share, losses will be $1 million in 1984 and payout will be achieved in mid-1986 (Exhibit A-3).

RESULTS OF TEST MARKET

A full discussion of the Dallas test was included here. The relevant details of this test have been summarized in the body of the case.

SERVICE EVOLUTION

Clearly, the VSF market is in the introductory/early growth of the life cycle. Over the next five years the market will undergo rapid changes. The projected shape of this service evolution is discussed here and summarized in the next chart.

The value of this service will increase with the increase of its rate of adoption by consumers. The ini-

EXHIBIT A-2   Financial Projections Assuming a 50 Percent Market Share

	1984	1985	1986	1987	1988	1989	1990	1991	1992	1993
Market share (%)	51	51	50	50	50	50	50	50	50	50
Messageboxes (000)	15	48	81	147	233	302	379	473	584	709
Revenues ($ mil)	3	11	23	41	70	100	129	164	207	258
Expenses ($ mil)	4	10	19	34	57	79	102	130	165	206
Net income ($ mil)	(1)	1	4	7	13	21	27	34	42	52
Return on sales (%)	(34)	6	16	17	19	21	21	21	20	20
NPV at 20% ($ mil)										42
Working capital requirements ($ mil)	0.4	0.4	0.5	1.0	1.4	1.2	1.4	1.8	2.2	2.6

EXHIBIT A-3   Financial Projections Assuming a 35 Percent Market Share

	1984	1985	1986	1987	1988	1989	1990	1991	1992	1993
Market share (%)	35	35	35	35	35	35	35	35	35	35
Messageboxes (000)	10	33	58	103	163	212	265	331	409	496
Revenues ($ mil)	2	8	16	29	49	70	91	115	145	181
Expenses ($ mil)	3	8	14	24	40	56	72	92	116	145
Net income ($ mil)	(1)	—	2	5	9	14	19	23	29	36
Return on sales (%)	(51)	—	15	17	18	20	21	20	20	20
NPV at 20% ($ mil)										28
Working capital requirements ($ mil)	0.4	0.3	0.3	0.7	1.0	0.9	0.9	1.3	1.6	1.9

tial adopters are the business customers who can easily recognize and capture the benefits of the service. Among the business community, acceptance has started with large firms and will gradually permeate to small firms. Government customers are expected to follow the large firms. Residence customers will be the last customer segment to subscribe to this service.

The geographical locations of the majority of customers will initially be limited to major metropolitan centers but are expected to spread to the rest of the United States by the end of 1985. Acceptance of this service by industrial nations has already begun, and the process will be accelerated after 1985. By 1986, international applications of this service will start playing a significant role in service and equipment configuration as a solution to international time zone problems in communications.

The equipment used in providing the service is already undergoing a change from closed systems, which only allowed messaging among the subscribers, to open systems that allow message receipt from nonsubscribers and message delivery to nonsubscribers. A limited capability of networking on an analog basis between systems manufactured by the same manufacturer is available. International standards for network interfaces will be developed in the 1985–1986 time frame. User friendliness of the systems will also increase, although uniformity of message processing commands may not be accomplished until legal issues relating to the Sudbury and VMX patents are resolved. By 1985, voice messaging systems will be integrated with text messaging systems for text-to-speech conversion. Speech-to-text conversion and automatic language translation capabilities do not appear feasible over the next five-year horizon. Store-and-forward service of images is possible now, but its integration with the voice and text combined systems will lag, depending upon its economic viability.

MARKET SIZE AND COMPETITION

As a result of revisions to consultants' forecasts and TeleMessager experience over the past 11 months, the estimates of market size for voice store-and-forward service bureaus are as follows:

Service Evolution Patterns			
Customer Segments	Large and Medium-Sized Business, Government	Small Business	Residence
	|	|	|
	1984	1985	1986
Geographic Coverage	Metropolitan areas	National within U.S. Industrial nations	International
	|	|	|
	1984	1985	1986
Equipment	Partially open systems	Integration with text network interface	
	|	|	|
	1984	1985	1986

	1984	1985	1986	1990	1993
U.S. employment (mil)	93.6	96.2	97.3	104.9	108.3
Business users (000)	30	94	161	534	955
Residential users (000)	—	—	4	223	465
Total users (000)	30	94	165	757	1420
Penetration (%)	0.03%	0.10%	0.17%	0.53%	0.930%

With only one location, GTE Telemessager was the leader among VSF service bureaus in 1983 (Exhibit A-4). Strengths and weaknesses of major players in the industry are given in Exhibit A-5. It is expected that a number of these competitors will not be able to survive the year 1984, and the industry will undergo a shake-out. A new generation of competitors will emerge, among which the notable are a few Bell Operating Companies (BOCs) like NYNEX and BellSouth. IBM is testing its service bureau potential in the Canadian market. If this experiment succeeds, IBM is expected to make its appearance in the U.S. market. It should be noted that current IBM equipment is not suited for service bureau operation.

The degree of rivalry among the competitors is currently low. This has been mainly due to the fact that competitors are gaining customers through growth of market rather than at each other's expense. Rivalry will intensify beyond 1984.

At this stage, there do not appear to be any barriers to entry in the voice messaging business. Barriers like brand identification, customer loyalty, preemptive distribution channels, proprietary products, and regulatory limitations (with the exception of major BOCs) have not developed significantly in the introductory phase of this service.

TECHNOLOGY

Current systems providing voice store-and-forward service have the following characteristics:

- Voice digitization for efficient reproduction of stored messages.
- Voice compression to reduce storage requirements without significant distortion.
- Software control for flexibility to change and add features.
- High-density disk storage for less expensive mass storage capability.

Next-generation voice store-and-forward systems are expected to incorporate the following features:

- Multimedia integration and voice synthesis for text and voice store-and-forward capability with text to voice translation (1985).
- Intersystem digital transmission and networking (1986).
- Voice recognition for receiving verbal commands (1987).

EXHIBIT A-4   Market Share Estimates, December 1983

Competitors	Equipment	Estimates Mailboxes	Percent Share
American Express	VMX	300	5.6
GTE TeleMessager	VMX	1910	35.6
Information Network Exchange	VMX	—	—
Interstate Communications	VMX	450	8.4
Mobilcom	VMX	50	1.0
Republic Steel	VMX	150	2.8
SBS Realcom	VMX?	—	—
United Telecom	VMX	50	1.0
Voice Express	VMX	400	7.5
Voice Memo	VMX	—	—
Voice Message Centers	COMMTERM	250	4.6
VoiceMail International	VMI	1100	20.5
Western Union	VMI	700	13.0
		5360	100.00

EXHIBIT A-5   Voice Store-and-Forward Service Bureaus

Vendor	Strengths	Weaknesses
GTE TeleMessager	Name recognition Experience Market presence Trained personnel	Uncertain commitment to business
Voice Mail International	Reputation Service experience International capability	Focus split between domestic and international markets Possible financial problems
VMX, Inc.	Market leadership in stand-alone systems Reputation/image Service experience System quality/reliability Patent for VMX technology awarded	Not committed to service bureau business as an operator Interested in selling systems
Interstate Communications	Parent with telephone operations Possible tie-in with resale business	Not widely known Weak image
Western Union	Nationwide marketing capability Familiar name Enhancement of existing business Financial resources of parent Offers international messaging Potential joint operations with other business	Commitment to financial objectives rather than marketing goals
Voice Message Center, Inc.	VSF experience of founder	Untried hardware/software added to Comm Term EVX 1000 Lack of capital resources
IBM Canada Data Center Services Division	Timesharing service experience Proprietary IBM-ADS equipment	Limitations of IBM equipment
Information Network Exchange	Founded by former experienced VMX officer, Bob Nacon	No name recognition Questionable financial resources
Voice Express	Founded by Bob David, former VMX president, with Mike Fanin, former VMX vice-president	Recent entry in market No name recognition

System hardware consists of readily available off-the-shelf type components. The software is the major distinguishing characteristic among the current generation of systems. Several manufacturers are currently producing voice store-and-forward systems. VMX, Inc., and IBM appear to have established an early lead.

MARKETING PLAN

Product

The five-tiered product developed in the Dallas test will be continued. In order to maintain product differentiation and to keep ahead of competitors, a program of ongoing product enhancements will be undertaken. Specific enhancements and expected date of availability are presented in Exhibit A-6.

Pricing

Pricing will be similar to that developed in Dallas. Pricing innovations being strongly considered include:

- Pricing contracts requiring a customer to subscribe to the service for a minimum period of 180 days should be encouraged for all customers subscribing to 50 or more messageboxes. The inducement to sign the contract should come in the form of a 10 percent discount on the monthly basic charge.

- Bulk pricing will be explored. This option consists of offering a large customer part ownership in a specific system from which he is served. Although this will amount to charging the lowest possible price for service, it also means that a customer makes a long-range commitment to subscribing to the service, thereby reducing TeleMessager risk.

EXHIBIT A-6   Expected Product Improvements, 1983–1984

Feature	Description	Due Date
Message-waiting indicator	The indication that a user has a message in the messagebox can be given either through a simple attachment to a telephone or through a radio pager.	March 1984
Personal identification	Will enable a user to provide a name response in user's own voice for confirming an address entered by either a subscriber or a nonsubscriber.	March 1984
Message outcall	Outcalling by TeleMessager on behalf of a user opens a new medium for delivering one-way voice messages to one or more telephones simultaneously.	April 1984
Audio services integration	Services such as financial news, stock quotes, and jokes can be deposited in messageboxes.	May 1984
User-changeable group codes	Will facilitate the addressing of messages to different calling groups.	July 1984
Intracompany two- to three-digit addressing capability	Will give the customer the sense of an internal network and facilitate use of TeleMessager.	August 1984
Text-to-speech integration	This product will enable integration of optical display (on radio pager or CRT) and printed text (on TeleMail) with TeleMessager. This development will make TeleMessager a unique messaging service.	October 1984

Promotion

Based on Dallas, direct mail, personal selling, and telemarketing will be used as the primary promotional tools. To add impetus to the opening of each regional center, a sales force contest will be employed.

A general media campaign covering the TeleMessager roll-out markets would cost up to $2 million. Instead of a broad general campaign, our plan calls for testing several direct response general media alternatives.

Experimentation with alternative media, frequency of exposure, and copy approaches are intended to provide direction regarding which is the most efficient and effective response vehicle for Telemessager Service as a supplement to direct mail.

Test schedules are planned in trade and in-flight airline magazines, as well as newspapers (Exhibit A-7). Testing is scheduled through September 1984, leaving the fourth quarter open to schedule the media which prove to be most effective and efficient in lead responsiveness.

CONTINGENCY PLANS

Although the operating plan has a built-in go, no-go decision to prevent overallocation of resources, we have set forth a few generic measures for outcomes that are not expected in the plan. These are given in detail in Exhibit A-8. The precise extent of contingency action will depend upon the extent of deviations from the anticipated scenario in the plan.

CONCLUSIONS

Based on the above, we conclude the following:

- There is widespread interindustry demand for the service.

EXHIBIT A-7   1984 Media Flow Chart

	March	April	May	June	July	August	Sept.	Oct.	Nov.	Dec.
Direct mail	×	×	×	×	×	×	×	×	×	×
Sales and Marketing Management			×		×					
American Way		×		×						
United		×		×						
Los Angeles Times							×	a		
Chicago Tribune							×	a		

[a] With positive results in September, the advertising should be continued into October.

EXHIBIT A-8   TeleMessager Contingency Plans

Scenario	Contingency Plan
Market growth higher than expected	Use available capacity in other centers via satellite links
	Order a stock item like VMXIII/32 for immediate relief
	Recruit and train personnel faster than scheduled
Market growth lower than expected	Delay opening of centers
	Serve new customers through existing centers
	Carry out operations with existing personnel
Market share lower than expected	Refocus the service on appropriate target market segment
	Determine why competitors are doing better and TeleMessager's shortcomings
	Repackage product line, reprice products, and retain personnel if necessary
New-generation equipment available	Attempt to bring compatibility with existing equipment through networking and standardization
	Analyze revenue potential and competitive advantage of equipment changeout
Personnel turnover excessive	Develop better incentive programs in line with competition
	Conduct frequent training sessions for new personnel
	Have backup for key positions identified and trained
Profitability lower than expected	Close uneconomic centers
	Eliminate excess equipment
	Relocate personnel to other GTE units

- Current product categories meet customers' needs, but constant enhancement of the product is necessary.
- Pricing is proper from the company and customer point of view, but further experimentation is required.
- A cost effective advertisement program to increase customer awareness needs to be designed.
- A phased rollout program should be undertaken to establish market leadership.
- GTE can enter and capitalize on a new nonregulated market opportunity.
- The breakeven period for the service is short.

CASE 6-3   TIMOTEI (A)*

COMPANY BACKGROUND

Timotei shampoo is a Scandinavian concept. The product was developed locally by a Unilever subsidiary in Scandinavia. However, the first introduction in Finland was a big flop. In 1975 the concept was improved and Timotei was subsequently introduced in Sweden. This was a big success: Timotei had a market share of approximately 11–12%, which was stable over the years. Early in 1983, because the product was such a big hit in Sweden, Lever-Sunlight BV was considering introducing Timotei in the Netherlands.

Unilever came into existence as a result of a merger between the "Margarine Unie" and Lever Brothers. How did this come about? Towards the end of the last century, in 1869, the new product margarine was developed as a replacement for butter. Two traders in butter, Anton Jurgens and Simon van den Bergh, both obtained the rights to this product. Independently of each other, they built two small margarine factories and they established a network of purchasing offices—

---

* This case was prepared by the Marketing and Marketing Research Team, Department of Economics, University of Groningen, The Netherlands. Edited by Leonard J. Parsons. Copyright © 1990 by the University of Groningen.

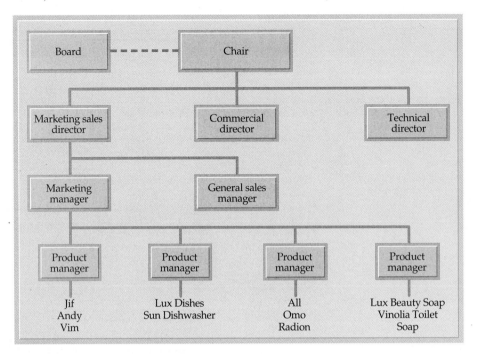

EXHIBIT 1   Lever Organization

in order to obtain the necessary raw materials—all over Europe. The result was a strong competition between the two of them, until they realized that this struggle was disadvantageous to both of them. In 1927 they decided to cooperate under the name Margarine Unie.

However, Margarine Unie experienced a great deal of competition on the market for raw materials from a British enterprise named Lever Brothers. Lever Brothers produced soap products and also needed large amounts of fat. The competition between the two companies made the prices of raw materials rise, and this motivated the bundling of the purchase of raw materials. In 1930 Margarine Unie and Lever Brothers merged and established a new company: Unilever. Over the years the activities of Unilever have expanded on the basis of oils, fats, and soaps—first, from soaps in the direction of washing powders and, later on, in the direction of personal products.

Lever Sunlight began in England in 1875, when a grocer, William Hesketh Lever, sold bars of Sunlight soap. His sales increased so quickly that 14 years later a new, big soap factory was built; this complex, Port Sunlight, is still one of the biggest soap factories in the world. At the beginning of this century, a great amount of Sunlight soap was exported to the European continent. In support of this export, companies and factories were established locally. Consequently, Lever's Soap

Company was founded in the Netherlands in 1901. In 1914 a Dutch factory was built for the production of Sunlight soap in Vlaardingen. In 1930, when the Unilever concern came into existence after the merger of Margarine Unie and Lever Brothers, Lever's Soap Company, as a part of the English Lever Sunlight, became one of the pillars of Unilever.

At the beginning of the 1950s, the first synthetic washing powder entered the market: Omo. Thereafter, other washing powders followed quickly, such as, for example, Sunil, Radion, and All. Over the years the number of products kept expanding. In 1976 the name of the factory, Lever's Soap Factory, was changed to Sunlight BV.

Until 1958, personal products were part of the detergents company Lever-Sunlight BV, after which they were transferred to Vinolia Gibbs NV, an operating company established especially for personal products. In 1980 Vinolia Gibbs NV was liquidated. Since personal products were no longer of such great importance to Unilever, the existence of a special operating company—with all the overheads involved—was no longer justified. The products were divided among three companies: the operating companies Lever-Sunlight BV, Unilever Export, and the agent Intertrade. The current production of Lever-Sunlight BV breaks down as follows: washing powder 50%, detergents 40%, and personal products 10%.

Lever-Sunlight BV uses a product management organization. Its organization chart is shown in Exhibit 1. The Marketing Sales Director directly supervises the Marketing Manager and the General Sales Manager. The Marketing Manager supervises four Product Managers, who are responsible for the following products:

• Product Manager and assistant: the detergents Jif, Andy, and Vim
• Product Manager and assistant: the detergents Lux Dishes and Sun Dish Washer
• Product Manager and assistant: the personal products Lux Beauty Soap and Vinolia Toilet-soap
• Product Manager and assistant: the washing powders All, Omo, and Radion

The General Sales Manager is responsible for the sale of all the products mentioned above, which initially resulted in little extra attention for the personal products.

THE MARKET

Cosmetics, or personal products, are products having a number of technical characteristics which are relatively easy to copy. However, they do have a high expressive value, which means a strong image to the consumer. They also give a good margin to the distributive trade. A user segmentation for cosmetics is shown in Exhibit 2.

An overview of 1983 sales, in volume and money, of the various personal products (primary demand) in the Netherlands is given in Exhibit 3. The figures in the third column are based on out-of-factory prices. This price equals the consumer price minus the trade margin and the value-added tax (VAT) and amounts to approximately 63% of the consumer price. The cost structure of a typical personal product is found in Exhibit 4.

The channels of distribution which are relevant for personal products in the Netherlands can be divided in two groups: the food sector, on the one hand, and the drug/perfumery sector, on the other. The distribution shares for the two channels for various personal products are found in Exhibit 5.

In 1983 the total shampoo market in the Netherlands amounted to 8,400,000 kilograms and 78 million guilders (out-of-factory price). Possible segmentation

EXHIBIT 3 Total Cosmetic Sales in the Netherlands

Cosmetic	Volume (1000 kg)	Revenue (out of factory, in millions of guilders)
Toilet soap	8700[a]	46[b]
Shampoo	8400	78
Toothpaste	4800	53
Bath foam	5000	30
Deodorant	1400	37

Source: A. C. Nielsen
[a] 2.2 lb = 1 kg.
[b] Exchange rate *f*/$: app. *f*1.95/$.

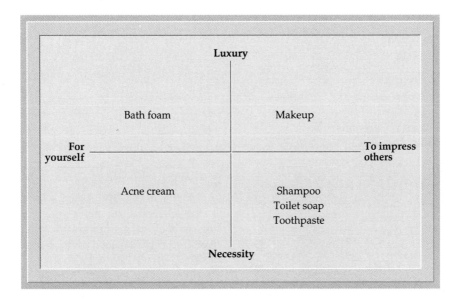

EXHIBIT 2 User Segmentation

EXHIBIT 4 Cost Structure of a Typical Personal Product

Consumer price	100	
VAT	16	19%
Trade margin[a]	21	
Price out of factory	63	
Direct costs[b]	32	
Gross profit	31	50% price out of factory
Advertising[c]	9	15% price out of factory
Promotions/merchandising[c]	6	10% price out of factory
Profit before indirect costs	16	25% price out of factory
Indirect costs	9	
Profit before taxes	7	
Taxes	4	
Net profit	3	

[a] The average trade margin of shampoos is approximately 25%. Depending on the purchasing and price policies, differences among the various channels of trade are conceivable. However, producers may count on an average trade margin of 25%.

[b] The direct costs can easily be estimated based on the price of, in particular, raw materials.

[c] Competitive analysis shows the advertising/promotion expenditures within a certain market. In the case of shampoos, these expenses amount to, on average, 15% of the consumer price.

criteria for the shampoo market are price and whether or not it is a specialty and/or medical shampoo. A shampoo is specialty if it is positioned with a clear and more or less unique claim. A shampoo is called medical if it refers to a hair problem: for example, antidandruff shampoo. The positioning of a specialty, nonmedical shampoo is usually based on a use situation and often has an emotional character, such as, for instance, mild shampoos and baby shampoos.

The various market segments mentioned above have the following characteristics:

- The specialty medical segment:
  Small submarkets
  Relatively few competitors
  Large price premium
- The general segment

EXHIBIT 5 Distribution Channels

	Food (%)	Drug (%)
By Volume		
Toilet soap	98	2
Shampoo	76	24
Toothpaste	81	19
Conditioner	61	39
By Revenue		
Toilet soap	93	7
Shampoo	65	35
Toothpaste	76	24
Conditioner	52	48

Source: A. C. Nielsen.

Many competitors
Price competition
Great deal of advertising
- The specialty, nonmedical segment
  Price premium
  Many "me-too" introductions
  Increasing competition

From 1981 until mid-1983 the following introductions and reintroductions took place on the shampoo market:

	Company	Product
1981		
QT 2	Intradal	7-Days (four types)
QT 3	Nordtend	Minirisk (hypoallergenic)
QT 4	P&G	Head & Shoulders
1982		
QT 1	Andrélon	Andrélon (anti-dandruff)
QT 3	Gillette	Silkience
QT 4	Andrélon	Anti-Oily Hair Special
1983		
QT 1	P&G	Head & Shoulders (oily hair)
QT 2	L'Oréal	Frequence (2 types)
	Schwarzkopf	Baby Mild

Exhibit 6 describes the situation in the shampoo market in 1983. The market shares based on the volume of the various brands are given. The table also shows in which segment of the market the brands operate. See Exhibit 7 for details.

In terms of usage, 75% of men and 57% of women wash their hair more than once a week. In terms of purchases, women are the gatekeepers, mak-

EXHIBIT 6   1983 Shampoo Market Shares Based on Volume

	Specialty Nonmedical	*General*	*Specialty Medical*
Premium price	Zwitsal 13%	Elsève 5%	Head & Shoulders 5%
Medium price		Andrélon 14%	
		Schwarzkopf 11%	
Low price		Palmolive 18%	

Source: A. C. Nielsen.

ing 98% of all purchases. Purchases are made in one of two channels: (1) food, including chain stores (C.S. I and C.S. II) and voluntary branch stores; and (2) drug, including drug discount stores, chemists, perfumeries, and hairdressers. See Exhibit 8 for a list of organizations belonging to the food and drug channels.

THE PRODUCT

The name Timotei is taken from a Swedish type of grass to emphasize the fact that Timotei products are mild and natural. Because of Timotei shampoo's pH value of 6.5, Timotei shampoo is mild and soft to hair and scalp. To achieve this effect, it contains extracts from specially selected herbs, such as camomile, rosemary, and thyme. These herbs also give Timotei its characteristic fresh scent.

Timotei shampoo was developed for people with normal hair who wish to wash their hair frequently without having it become too dry or damaged. Timotei shampoo washes hair carefully and gives it softness and shine.

Timotei has a fresh, pure, and young image. The brand is linked to unspoiled nature, country air, spring, and summer. These aspects are emphasized in print and TV advertising. The Timotei girl embodies them. These aspects are also reflected by the package, in which the colors green and white are essential. This package is clear, not exaggerated, and reflects the integrity of the product. Key words with regard to the intended target group of Timotei are *young, fresh,* and *uncomplicated.* Timotei has a wonderful, fresh perfume and can be bought in an eye-catching, beautiful, and handy bottle.

Timotei was the first shampoo in the medium-priced segment of the mild shampoos, which constitutes approximately two-thirds of the total market. The standard unit of Timotei shampoo is 200 ml or 208 g. The boxes used for retailers contain three trays of 10 bottles.

MARKET RESEARCH

In order to establish whether or not there would be a market for Timotei, two market research studies were conducted. The purpose of the first study was to

EXHIBIT 7   Overview of the Shampoo Market

Brand	Unit (ml)	Market Share (%) Volume	Value	Trend[b]
Zwitsal	200	13	14	–
Elsève	250	5	6	– –
H & S	150	5	10	+ +
Andrélon[a]	300	14	15	–
Schwarzkopf[a]	200	11	8	0
Palmolive[a]	400	18	11	– –
On average in food	225			
On average in drug	225			
Other brands (F + D)	200	29	33	0
Private labels	225	5	3	+ +

[a] More than one type/size.
[b] *Legend:* 0 = neutral, – = mildly negative, – – = strongly negative, + + = strongly positive.

Source: A. C. Nielsen.

EXHIBIT 8   Organizations within the Food and Drug Channels

Food
C.S. I
  Albert Heijn
  Edah
  Albrecht
  Jac Hermans
  Etos
C.S. II
  Superunie
    de Jong, Linders
    Hoogvliet, Nettorama
    Witte Prijzenhal
    Maxis
  Ziko
    de Boer, Groenwoudt
    Dekamarkt
    Trekpleister
    Kruidvat
  Intergro
    Konmar/Vomar
    Nieuwe Weme
  Koopconsult
    Dirk van de Broek
    Bas van der Heijden
    Dirks Discount

Drug
Drug discount
  Etos
  Kruidvat
  Trekpleister

answer two questions: (1) Is the product concept successful? and (2) What is the market potential? This is the so-called Frevert test. When the results of this test proved to be encouraging, another type of product test was carried out: the so-called Sensor marketing-mix test.

Frevert Test

In February 1983, Inter/View BV conducted a study, commissioned by Lever-Sunlight BV, regarding the possibility of the introduction of Timotei in the Dutch market. The goal of this study was twofold:

- To determine to what degree the product concept of Timotei was successful.
- To estimate the market potential by means of the Frevert test.

The Frevert test measures the trial purchases as well as the repeat purchases. The trial purchases are measured after showing the respondent the concept or the advertisement/commercial. The repeat purchases are measured after actual use of the product. The total sample consisted of 823 people who were divided into three groups:

Group 1: This group was shown a commercial (298 people).
Group 2: This group was shown the print advertisement (264 people).
Group 3: This group was shown the bottle (261 people).

After exposure to the three stimuli mentioned above, the respondents were asked to answer several questions of a qualitative nature. Thereafter they could make a trial purchase of the product at a price of ƒ4.25. After three weeks those people who had indeed made a trial purchase were visited again and were offered the opportunity of a repeat purchase. Exhibit 9 gives an overview of the most important tables and results of the Frevert test.

Sensor Marketing-Mix Test

Based on the results of the Frevert test, it was decided to conduct further market research. The price was lowered to somewhere between ƒ2.45 and ƒ3.45. The Sensor marketing-mix test of Socmar, which is quantitative market research that simulates a test market, was chosen. Based on this study, various estimates can be made.

The Sensor marketing-mix test of Socmar is a method used to predict the future market share of a new product. This method avoids some of the disadvantages of conducting a test market. In addition to a market share prediction, Sensor also supplies information regarding price sensitivity, penetration, and substitution of other brands. The respondents are interviewed twice when the Sensor method is used.

First Contact   A group of selected consumers is invited to a test center. The procedure is as follows:

1. The respondents are asked which brands of a particular product group (in this case, shampoos) are known to them. The brands mentioned are the so-called salient set of the consumer. The new brand is not yet known and therefore cannot belong to the salient set.

EXHIBIT 9   Results of the Frevert Test

A. People who made a trial purchase

	Total Sample N = 823	Group 1[a] N = 298	Group 2[b] N = 264	Group 3[c] N = 261
People who made trial purchase	235	48	99	88
(%)	(29%)	(16%)	(38%)	(33%)

[a] This group was shown a commercial.
[b] This group was shown a print advertisement.
[c] This group was shown the bottle.

Remark: When there are no differences between the three groups or between those who did or did not make a trial purchase, these groups are not mentioned separately in the tables. In some cases, Group 1 (commercial) is used, in which case this group is representative of the total sample.

B. What did they think of Timotei?

Percent Who Thought:	Commercial	Print Ad
Is appealing	16	33
Nature is appealing	19	1
Fun	32	23
Nothing special	43	30
Exaggerated	18	0

Remark: It is striking that Groups 1 and 2 thought that the fact that Timotei has an herbal basis was a strong point (16% and 24%, respectively). Many favorable characteristics were attributed to the herbal basis.

C. Question: What do you think this shampoo will do for you?

	Percent of:		
Remarks	Group 1	Group 2	Group 3
Soft shampoo for hair	37	22	43
Refreshing	20	0	23
Wholesome	15	1	13
Like all the others	7	38	7
Don't know	9	35	11

Remark: Spontaneous remarks after the bottle of Timotei was shown to the three groups: 63% of the sample thought that the fact that Timotei was an "every-day" shampoo was a good quality. Other "every-day" shampoos mentioned by the respondents were Head & Shoulders (46%) and Zwitsal (43%).

D. What type of hair does one have?

	Percent of Total Sample
Oily hair	40
Normal hair	40
Dry hair	19

Remark: People who made a trial purchase had more problems with regard to their hair than those who did not make a trial purchase. Of the people who made a trial purchase, 8% had many problems with their hair, compared to 1% of those who did not make a trial purchase.

E. How often do you wash your hair?

	Group 1
At least twice a week	57%
About once a week	34%
Less often	5%

Remark: Group 1 is representative of the total sample.

(continues)

EXHIBIT 9   (Continued)

F. Which brand do you use at the moment?

Mentioned Most Frequently	Group 1
Schwarzkopf/7 herbs	15
Andrélon	11
Zwitsal	15
Elsève/L'Oréal	14

Remark: Is there more than one shampoo within your household? Of the households in the sample, 43% used more than one shampoo.

G. Do you use other products for oily hair?

	Percent Always or Regularly Use
Conditioner	27
Blow-dry lotion	17
Coloring	7
Hair spray	10

H. Do you often change shampoos?

	Group 1	Trial Purchase	No Trial Purchase
No, I'm very satisfied and stick to my brand	66	47	69
Considering a change/has not yet decided on a brand	27	47	23

I. What do you think of Timotei after having used it?

	Percent of Group Who Made Trial Purchase (N = 235)
Good	55
Makes hair soft	24
Nice scent	24
No difference	17
Hair immediately oily	8

J. Reasons why Timotei is thought to be better or worse than own shampoo.

	Percent of Total Sample
Makes hair soft	22
Cleans well	19
Hair immediately oily	10
Not very mild	8

Remark: Of the total sample, 69% did indeed think that you can wash your hair frequently with Timotei.

K. How many people made a repeat purchase after three weeks?

	Percent of Those Who Made Trial Purchase			
	Group 1	Group 2	Group 3	Total
Yes	27	36	34	33

L. Reasons for no repeat purchase

	Percent of Those Who Made No Trial Purchase
Prefer own brand	20
Own brand cheaper	28
Have enough left	35

2. Within the salient set, the respondents are asked to rank the brands in order of preference.

3. After this exercise, the respondents are asked to look at or listen to commercials or ads of brands belonging to the product group (the new product is included).

4. Subsequently, the respondents are given money to buy a product from the product group studied in a simulated supermarket. In this "store" the new product is also available. Depending on the price of the chosen product, the customer either receives change or has to pay the difference.

5. Since it is the intention to have all the respondents try the product, those who have not bought it also receive the product.

Second Contact After a period of one to four weeks (depending on the nature of the product), all the respondents are visited by an interviewer of Socmar. This interview entails the following:

1. A new salient set is determined, in which the new product can also be included, and a new preference ranking is composed.

2. The respondent is now offered the opportunity to buy the product at a predetermined price.

3. Subsequently, the prices of the various brands are changed a number of times, and it is determined which product the consumer would buy at the various prices.

4. Finally, the attitude of the consumer regarding the new product is determined (advantages/disadvantages of the new product, etc.).

The collected data are the input for three consumer behavior models, which the Sensor method uses to predict, among other things, a market share.

The three consumer behavior models were for trial/repeat, brand preference, and brand price trade-off. The trial/repeat model uses the data concerning the purchasing behavior of the respondents (in the "store" as well as at home) to forecast the eventual market share of the new product. The brand preference model uses the changes in the salient set to assess substitution effects. The brand price trade-off model makes use of the influence of the different

EXHIBIT 10   Outcomes/Results of Sensor Test

A. *Market share with minimum consumer price (MCP) of $f3.45$ (%)*

	Weighted Distribution (%)		
Recall (%)	*80*	*70*	*60*
60	5.0	4.0[a]	3.5
50			3.0

Ceteris paribus: competition, other environmental factors.
[a] In case of an MCP of $f3.45$, a recall of 60%, and a weighted distribution of 70%, the expected market share is 4%.

B. *Market share with MCP of $f2.95$ (%)*

	Weighted Distribution (%)		
Recall (%)	*80*	*70*	*60*
60	6.0	5.0	4.5
50			3.5

Ceteris paribus: competition, other environmental factors.

C. *Market share with MCP of $f2.45$ (%)*

	Weighted Distribution (%)		
Recall (%)	*80*	*70*	*60*
60	7.0	6.0	5.5
50			4.5

Ceteris paribus: competition, other environmental factors.

price scenarios on brand choice to determine price sensitivity. The results of the Sensor test are found in Exhibit 10.

DECISION

Lever-Sunlight had reached a decision point. Should it launch Timotei shampoo in the Netherlands, and if so, how? It knew that if the decision was made to launch, the characteristics (and costs) of the various media for advertising personal products would need to be considered. Exhibit 11 contains some of the relevant information.

EXHIBIT 11   Data Regarding Advertising Policy

A. Characteristics of the various media

	TV	*Radio*	*Magazines*	*Newspapers*
Feasible media reach	+ +	+ +	+ +	+ +
Selectivity	– –	– –	+ +	+
Structure reach	– –	– –	+	+ +
Availability	– –	– –	+	+
Possibilities of use	– –	– –	+	+

Legend: — = very poor, += good, + + = very good

B. Costs of the media (with exception of introduction)

	Unit	*App. in Guilders*
TV	Second	500
Radio	Second	75
Women's magazine	1/1 full color	35,000
Newspaper	1/1 national	40,000
Movie theater	National	68,000
Outdoor advertising	A piece	30

Source: Ad Media.

7

BRAND MANAGEMENT

> Nothing is more profitable than adding a few share points to an existing brand.
>
> WILLIAM TRAGOS

Brand management is concerned with the supervision of brands of products and services from the time they are introduced until they are removed from the marketplace. Our focus is on the specific plans and strategies needed during each phase of the product life cycle to improve the competitive position of the firm. The objective is to show how marketing executives work to control the destinies of brands on a day-to-day basis.

You must first understand what brands are and how they fit into the offerings of your organization. In addition, you need to know the advantages of identifying products by national and store brand names. Finally, it is your job to decide when to rescue declining brands and when to bury them.

WHAT IS A BRAND?

A brand is a name, term, sign, symbol, or design intended to distinguish the goods and services of one seller from another. The idea with brands is to select a unique term for a product so that customers will be able to identify the item and find it in the marketplace. However, brands are more than just a product. The usual definition of a product is anything that can be offered to a market to satisfy buyer needs. This means products can be physical goods (cars), services (bank), retail stores, a person (member of Congress), place (Hawaii), or an idea (pollution control). A brand is a name attached to any of these product classes to help sell them to customers. In addition, a brand includes a summation of consumers' perceptions and feelings about a product's attributes. Marketers attempt to create appealing images around their products based on quality, shape, color, and lifestyle compatibility. These tangible and intangible image associations help marketing managers differentiate their brands from their competitors. Everyone knows the differences between Coke and Pepsi and many people have developed strong brand loyalty to each of these sodas. Brand loyalty means that a certain portion of buyers come back and buy your product again and again. When brands create repeat buyers, managers build value that can be turned into profits for the firm.

Brand Functions

Brands are found everywhere. Virtually all consumer products in America are identified by brands. In addition, many industrial products carry brand designations. For example, the "Intel

Inside" brand label we see on PCs identifies the Intel microprocessor chip that is built into Dell, Compaq, and IBM brands of personal computers. This suggests you need to understand the functions that brands perform that make them so valuable to buyers and sellers.

For buyers, a key attraction of brands is they simplify product decisions (Figure 7-1). Brands help buyers identify products, thereby reducing search costs and assuring a buyer of a desired level of quality. As a result the buyer's perceived risk of buying the product is reduced. In addition, buyers receive psychological rewards by purchasing brands that symbolize status and prestige. This reduces the psychological risks associated with owning and using the "wrong" product. Brands can be effective in signaling product characteristics and value to consumers for complex machines, insurance, and drugs. An example showing how effective brands can be is described in Marketing in Action box 7-1.

For sellers, brands make it easier for firms to promote repeat purchases and to introduce new products (Figure 7-1). Brands also facilitate promotional efforts and encourage brand loyalty across product categories. Brands make it easier to use premium pricing by creating a basic level of differentiation that should prevent the product from becoming a commodity. Brands facilitate market segmentation by allowing the seller to communicate a consistent message to a target customer group. Brands are useful in building brand loyalty in categories where repeat purchasing is common.

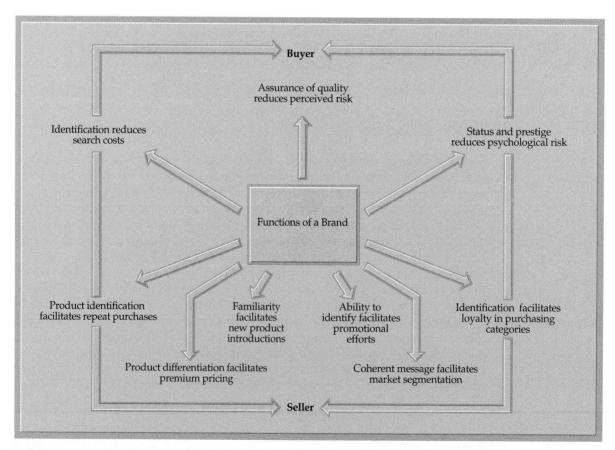

FIGURE 7-1   Functions of a Brand for the Buyer and Seller (From Pierre Berthon, James M. Hulbert and Leyland F. Pitt, "Brand Management Prognostications," *Sloan Management Review,* Vol. 40, No. 2 [Winter 1999], p. 54.)

APPLYING
*. . . to
Pharmaceutical
Marketing*

MARKETING IN ACTION *7-1*

Why Do Brands Outsell Generic Drugs?

Generic drugs are copies of national brands that are sold at lower prices. Brand name drugs are patented and when the patents expire, generic drug firms introduce imitations to try to steal market share from the original developer of the product. Although generic drugs are chemically similar to branded drugs and are sold at lower prices, they have not been able to grab a significant portion of the market. In 1997, brand name drugs had 92 percent of the dollar sales of pharmaceuticals in the U.S. Consumer preferences for brand name drugs is based in part on customer satisfaction and a concern that generic clones may not be manufactured with the same consistent high quality as the original. Also the larger pharmaceutical companies have done a better job of marketing their branded products. Name brand drug companies send out armies of sales reps to introduce new brands to doctors and provide them with free samples to give to patients. Once the samples run out, patients often end up on long term or lifelong prescriptions for the branded drug. They also advertise in journals directed at doctors, host medical seminars and pay marquee professors to laud their brands. In addition, brand companies spend heavily on direct consumer advertising to increase consumer awareness of their branded drugs. For example, the innovative Viagra brand male impotence drug received substantial direct consumer advertising and a great deal of news commentary because of its ability to improve the sex lives of older men. Generic drug companies are generally smaller than the brand drug firms and do not have the resources to build brand recognition with similar marketing programs.

— *Branded products can outsell generic copies.*

Source: Thomas M. Burton, "Bested Interests: Why Generic Drugs Often Can't Compete Against Brand Names," *The Wall Street Journal,* November 18, 1998, p. A1.

Other advantages of brands include the legal protection they offer for unique features. A brand can retain intellectual property rights, giving legal title to the brand owner. This allows the firm to protect its brands with trademarks and patents. Firms can then invest in a brand with the assurance they alone will benefit from its success. In addition, brands build goodwill that creates barriers of entry to keep competitive firms from entering the market. Further, companies can use brands to signal quality levels to satisfied customers.

Brand Personality

Many marketers believe that brands have human-type personalities that allow consumers to express themselves through the purchase of particular products. A brand personality framework is shown in Figure 7-2. The five dimensions in Figure 7-2 are based on consumer ratings of similarities between 114 personality traits and 37 brands of consumer products. The first brand personality dimension, sincerity, is described as wholesome, down-to-earth, and is typified by Hallmark cards. An excitement dimension is more daring, imaginative, and is associated with the MTV channel. Competence, the third brand personality dimension, is reliable, intelligent, and is represented by *The Wall Street Journal*. A fourth dimension, sophistication, is charming, upper class, and would be characterized by Guess brand jeans. The last brand personality dimension in Figure 7-2, ruggedness, is tough, outdoorsy, and is represented by Nike athletic shoes. Once a manager knows the dimensions of brand personality, they can be used to mold brand images to match desirable customer groupings. It is no accident that Nike advertising shows people climbing mountains and that ads for Mountain Dew focus on young sky divers and in-line skate daredevils.

BRAND EQUITY

Having described what brands are and why they are used in marketing, we now turn to an important concept called brand equity. Although brand equity has been defined in a variety

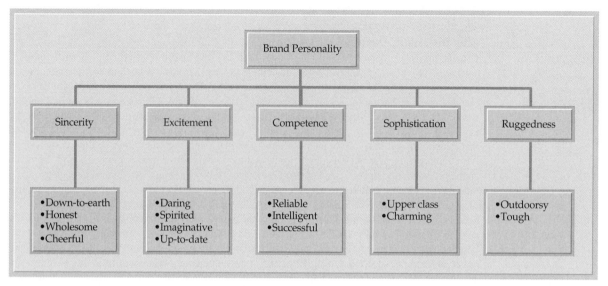

FIGURE 7-2   A Brand Personality Framework (*Source:* Jennifer L. Aaker, "Dimensions of Brand Personality," *Journal of Marketing Research,* Vol. 34 [August 1997], p. 352.)

of ways, we will focus our attention first on the word *equity.* When something has equity, it has value. This means that when firms invest in a brand they create added value or equity much like the cash prices assigned to stocks and bonds. If brands have value, then they can be bought and sold just like other financial instruments. For example, when Cadbury Schweppes bought Hires and Crush soft drinks from Procter & Gamble for $220 million, only $20 million went for the physical assets of the brands. This means Cadbury Schweppes paid $200 million for the brand equity associated with Hires Root Beer and Orange Crush soda. Similarly, when Newell Co. bought the floundering Rubbermaid Inc., they paid an astounding 49 percent premium over the closing price of Rubbermaid stock. Rubbermaid is the leading American manufacturer of consumer and commercial plastic products, and Newell paid billions to acquire Rubbermaid's brand equity.[1] In another case, when Volkswagen paid more than $700 million to acquire Rolls-Royce and Bentley cars from Vickers PLC, they were surprised when BMW paid $60 million to grab the rights to the Rolls-Royce brand name from Rolls-Royce PLC.[2] In this case, BMW paid $60 million for Rolls-Royce's car brand equity and Volkswagen was left with only the Bentley brand name and the Rolls-Royce car plants. All of these examples show that brand equity has value that can be measured in dollars and cents.

Customer-Based Brand Equity

Although the value dimension of brand equity is important, you should understand that there is a critical customer dimension as well. One definition of customer-based brand equity is the differential effect that brand knowledge has on consumer response to the marketing of the brand.[3] This suggests that brand equity arises when customers react more positively to one brand than to another. Second, differences in reactions are directly related to customer's knowledge of the brand. The more consumers know about a brand, the more lasting the brand's impression on a customer's memory and the stronger the resulting brand equity. Third, differential response is based on all elements of the marketing mix (advertising, pricing, promotional coupons, retail displays, etc.). Thus the source of brand equity is customer reactions in the marketplace and the result is added dollar value for the brand.

Brand Awareness

Brand equity occurs when customers have a high level of awareness of a brand and hold strong, favorable brand associations in memory. Knowing about a brand may be enough to trigger a positive purchase response for low involvement decisions where customers base choices on familiar brands. In more complex situations, brand associations can play a critical role in the differential responses needed to build brand equity. Brand awareness is developed by repeated exposure to advertising and promotion to build brand recognition. Brand recall is enhanced by strengthening associations with the right product category or consumption situations.

Brand awareness is amplified when marketers visually and verbally reinforce the brand name. One approach is to develop a slogan or jingle that matches the brand with the desired product category and consumption scenario. Other elements that can build awareness include logos, symbols, characters (the Energizer bunny), and unique packaging. Another way to intensify brand awareness is through careful matching of the brand with desired usage in a variety of communications alternatives. These may include featuring the brand or logo on race cars or sports teams, endorsements by celebrities on television, placement of favorable stories in magazines and newspapers, or prominent displays of the brand in movies or television shows. Anything that causes the consumer to experience the brand can magnify brand awareness.

Brand Image

Brand equity is reinforced when consumers have a positive image of a brand in memory. Brand images can be strengthened by marketing programs that link strong, favorable, and unique associations to the brand. Brand associations can be enhanced by direct experience (free samples and test drives for cars) and by word-of-mouth communications with friends. Another source of brand image information is nonpartisan data published by consumer testing groups such as *Consumer Reports.* These organizations describe product features of individual brands and list Web sites and telephone numbers so consumers can call in to get additional information on products they are thinking of buying.

Brand images are also influenced by the strength of brand associations. The more a person thinks about product information and ties it to existing knowledge, the stronger the ensuing brand affiliations. The key to building strong affiliations is to make sure the data are relevant to the individual and are consistent over time. In addition, brand images are intensified by presenting the brand in a context that is both familiar and provides cues for action. This means the models in the ads must match the ages of the target audience, the background scenery used for the ad should be familiar, and the text should build on such powerful motivators as better health, safety, or financial security.

BRAND STRATEGY

Brand strategy focuses on deciding which products should be branded and whether they should be sold under one's own label or under labels controlled by other firms. *Brands* include all names, terms, symbols, or designs that are used to identify and differentiate the goods of one seller from those of the competitors. Brands allow the customer to recognize products and increase the chances for repeat sales. Brands also encourage the use of preselling and reduce the need for personal contact at the retail level. In addition, brands facilitate the development of permanent price-quality images for products. Brands also simplify the introduction of new products and allow the manufacturer some control over the channel of distribution. Branding is easiest where identifying tags or symbols can be attached directly to the product and where the customer is willing to use brand designations to differ-entiate among products.

Umbrella Brands

Umbrella brands are groups of products sold under one label by a single firm. Heinz, Del Monte, and General Electric are companies that endorse a wide array of products with their own corporate name. Other firms, such as Procter & Gamble, prefer to use separate brand names for each product. Research has shown strong support for the idea that consumers transfer quality perceptions from one product to others sharing the same brand name. Consumer experience with one umbrella brand provides signals on quality and helps them reduce risks associated with the purchase of new items. These results suggest that providing free samples can help umbrella brands when the sample is perceived to be of high quality.

Umbrella brands have the advantage that advertising for one brand promotes the sales of all items carrying that particular label. Umbrella brands also make it easier to introduce new products to distribution channels and the customer. On the other hand, it is more diffi-cult to create and maintain an identity for each item using an umbrella brand strategy. One possible compromise is to use separate brand names for each product and then tie them together with a unifying trade name. This is the strategy used by General Motors; cars are promoted under their own names, and the GM symbol is used as a common point of refer-ence.

National versus Store Brands

There are basically two types of brands available to American consumers. National brands typically receive national advertising support, enjoy wide distribution, are sold at higher prices than other brands, and are frequently stocked by competing retailers. Store brands or private labels have more limited distribution, are often sold at lower prices than national brands, and are available only in stores that share a common wholesaler. The marketing of national brands is controlled by manufacturers that *pull* products through the channel of dis-tribution with direct consumer advertising that emphasizes product quality. Store brands are managed by retailers that use shelf positions and low prices to attract customers to their brands.

Historically, national brands have outsold store brands because manufacturers have spent more money on advertising and product development. Store brands typically gain mar-ket share during economic slowdowns when customers are more price sensitive and are attracted to the less expensive store brands. However, the recent growth of mass merchan-disers and the trend toward more mergers among grocery and drug retailers have strength-ened the position of store brands.

Store Brands.   Store brand market shares vary widely across product categories. For exam-ple, store brands represent 65 percent of the sales of frozen green and wax beans and 25 per-cent of liquid bleach but only 1.1 percent of personal deodorants. One explanation for these differences is that the risks consumers accept when they buy private labels also varies widely across product categories. For example, if a consumer buys a $.98 package of private label frozen beans and is dissatisfied with its quality, the buyer is out only a small amount of money and there is little personal risk of embarrassment. However, when the consumer pur-chases a $6 private label deodorant and it is not effective in a social context, there is a higher dollar cost and a greater chance of humiliation in front of people that are important to the customer. Thus when perceived risk is high, buyers may prefer prestigious national brands with their strong reputations for performance. Store brands tend to do better in categories where they offer high quality comparable to that of national brands. They do much worse in

categories where multiple national manufacturers are investing a lot of money in national advertising.[4] Where store brands were once positioned solely on the basis of price, many firms are having success using a "quality" focus. This is especially evident in Europe where retailers such as J. Sainsbury have achieved dominance over national brands in many product categories.[5] Indeed, researchers have noted that the price gap between national and store brands has no predictive power in determining store brand market share.[6] This means that the issue is really consumer perceptions of product quality.

Retailers have a number of advantages in their private label war with national brands. First they decide which national brands to carry in their stores, how much shelf space to devote to each brand, and the prices at which they will be sold. In addition, retailers can dilute the effects of manufacturers' promotions by not allowing full pass-through of trade discounts, promotional allowances, and slotting allowances to customers. Retailers also manipulate price gaps between store and national brands and shelf space elasticities of demand across product categories to earn higher margins on their own store brands. This means that store brands generate 10 to 15 percent higher margins than national brands and retailers can sell them for lower prices. For example, chain drugstores have been very successful selling store brand over-the-counter cold remedies alongside national brands. Store brands are also umbrella brands that help build store loyalty and help introduce new items.

National Brands.   Although store brands have had success in some product categories, national brands have their own advantages. The key weapons for manufacturers are investments in high-quality production facilities, large advertising budgets, and the clever use of coupons and mail-in rebates to help strengthen brand equity. They also have more money for product development and packaging innovations. National brands have an enormous storehouse of brand preference with consumers. When *Consumer Reports* polled their subscribers, they found that 80 percent preferred national brands because they were perceived to be of higher quality. Thus national brands should not try to narrow the gap with store brands using trade promotions, but would be better off spending the money on brand advertising and new product development.[7] Sometimes national brands lose market share to store brands because the product category is losing favor with consumers. For example, the typical American breakfast is moving away from the traditional cold cereal and milk toward bagels and fruit that can be eaten on the run. This shift in preferences has had serious and long-term effects on national brand manufacturers of cold cereal. Kellogg has lost market share to store brands and has had to lay off employees to maintain profitability. Consumers who still eat cold cereal see fewer quality differences and are quick to pick up store brand cereals that sell for $2 a box less.

APPLYING
. . . to
Retailing

Mass merchandisers such as Wal-Mart and Target love to feature national brands in the weekly newspaper inserts to draw people to their stores. Once there, the retailers try to sell customers the higher-margin store brands. Even Sears has cut back on the number of its own Kenmore appliances and now features many popular national brands such as GE, Whirlpool, Kitchen Aid, and Sony. Sears purchases its Kenmore refrigerators from GE and Whirlpool and places them alongside of each other to promote the lower-priced Kenmore models. You should be aware that if the Worldwide Web becomes a significant channel of distribution, national brands will become more important as beacons to attract buyers to the Internet and as a way to assure consumers they are getting high-quality products.

New Brands versus Brand Extensions

When a new item is added to the firm's product line, you must decide whether to create a new brand name or use an existing name. For instance, when Coca-Cola first developed a diet cola drink, it chose to use a new name, Tab, rather than capitalize on its existing con-

APPLYING
... to
Consumer
Beverages
Marketing

sumer franchise by using the name Diet Coke. However, when PepsiCo came out with Diet Pepsi, Coca-Cola countered with Diet Coke and phased out the Tab brand. Sometimes a firm will want to draw on its investment in a brand name and consequently will direct its product development to products that fit its existing image.

The various possibilities for products and brands are shown in Figure 7-3. When the firm simply adds another variant to an existing brand in an existing product category, the firm has a *line extension*. An example would be the addition of baking soda to Crest toothpaste. The new brand, "Crest with Baking Soda" is an extension of regular Crest toothpaste with the standard fluoride antidecay ingredient. The idea with line extensions is to use the customer's familiarity with a flagship brand, Crest, to gain acceptance of new brands that broaden a firm's product line by appealing to niche market segments. In this case "Crest with Baking Soda" joins other brands such as "Crest with Tarter Control" and "Crest Gel" to boost shelf facings for Procter & Gamble and increase total toothpaste sales. The use of a line extension by Duracell to fight the Energizer bunny is described in Marketing Strategies box 7-1.

APPLYING
... to
Consumer
Packaged
Goods
Marketing

Brand Extension.   Using an existing brand name to enter a new product category is called brand extension or brand leveraging. For example, the brand name Healthy Choice was first used with a line of frozen dinners with reduced levels of fat and salt. The success of these items encouraged the manufacturer to leverage the Healthy Choice brand into a number of other food categories. Now we have Healthy Choice Soups and Healthy Choice Ice Cream.

Brand extension is potentially very attractive. It makes use of existing customer awareness and goodwill. As a result, the advertising expenditures needed to introduce the product to the market are minimized. Although the introduction of Always sanitary napkins, an entirely new brand name, cost Procter & Gamble about $100 million, the introduction of Liquid Tide cost a relatively modest $30 to $40 million because of existing name recognition.

APPLYING
... to
Consumer
Packaged
Goods
Marketing

Flanker Brands.   When a firm markets a new brand in a category in which it already had a presence, the firm is protecting its market position and the product is said to be a flanker brand (Figure 7-3). A special case of a flanker brand is a fighting brand. When a firm has a

	Product category	
	Existing	**New**
Existing	Line extension	Brand extension
New	Flanker brand	New Product

(Brand name — rows: Existing, New)

FIGURE 7-3   Types of Brands

APPLYING
. . . to
Consumer
Packaged
Goods
Marketing

MARKETING STRATEGIES 7-1

Duracell Versus the Energizer

Duracell Inc., owned by Gillette, introduced a new line extension called Duracell Ultra in its increasingly bitter marketing war with Energizer brand batteries sold by Eveready Battery Co. Duracell says the Ultra batteries last up to 50 percent longer than its ordinary alkaline batteries in so-called high drain products such as flash cameras and compact disk players. These devices use up batteries far more quickly than low drain products such as wall clocks. The company says consumers can continue to use regular Duracell batteries for these applications. Duracell sells the new line extension alongside its existing range of alkaline batteries. The new Duracell Ultra batteries are priced 20 percent higher than its regular batteries and represent a first attempt to segment the alkaline battery market into distinct categories. When Energizer introduced its reformulated batteries, they simply replaced the old AA and AAA batteries with the new version. Duracell expects that the Ultra will eventually comprise about 20 percent of Duracell's AA and AAA alkaline battery sales. They also expect that one-fourth of Ultra's sales will be incremental, not just replacements for sales of other Duracell products. Thus the Ultra line extension should increase both Duracell's margins and their share of the alkaline battery market. In a direct challenge to the Energizer bunny, Duracell's head of sales and marketing says the Ultra batteries "give superior performance to any other alkaline battery on the market." When *Consumer Reports* magazine tested the new Ultra alkaline batteries, they found they performed as advertised. The strong brand awareness created by Energizer and Duracell ads claiming superior performance has allowed these two national brands to continue to dominate the alkaline battery market.

— *Line extensions can lead to increased sales and profits for the firm.*

Source: Mark Maremont, "Duracell Tactic Could Charge Battery Wars," *The Wall Street Journal*, February 18, 1998, p. B1.

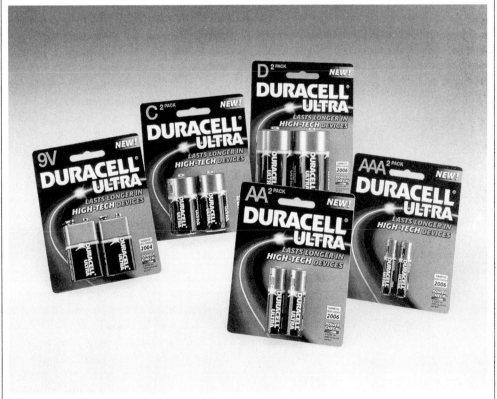

Courtesy Duracell

high relative market share, it is usually not in its best interest to cut price because it will be hurt most by the price cut if primary demand does not expand to offset the cut. This makes a dominant brand susceptible to having share sliced away by aggressive pricing by smaller firms. To discipline such firms, a fighting brand is created for which no money is invested in advertising, and the product is sold on price. Fighting brands are expendable and are sometimes discontinued after they have served their purpose of warning competitors to avoid predatory price competition.

APPLYING
. . . to
Financial
Services
Marketing

American Express sells premium-priced products in the form of its green, gold, and platinum charge cards. Facing new entrants in the credit card business, such as AT&T, and intensified competition from veterans, including Visa and MasterCard, American Express brought out a credit card called Optima as a fighting brand.

You have to decide whether to bring out a new item as a line extension or as a new brand. Generally it is better to employ a line extension strategy when parent brand penetration is high and a new brand strategy when parent brand penetration is low. This is true even though a line extension will cannibalize parent brand sales much more than a new brand will. To maintain profit margins, a rule of thumb is that a new product must gain two share points for each point lost by the original company brand. Usually, half of the gain will come from users of competitors' products and half from new users being drawn into the market.

New Product Brands.   The most risky and expensive brand strategy is the creation of a new brand name for an item to be sold in a new product category (Figure 7-3). New product brands have no parent or flagship brands to help introduce them to customers and reduce consumers' anxiety about purchasing a new product. We mentioned earlier that it cost Procter & Gamble $100 million to introduce the new product brand Always. This was more than three times what it cost P&G to bring out a brand extension in the detergent market. New product brands are best used when the item is truly revolutionary and unique to the market. In this case the attributes of the new product are so powerful they overcome customer's unfamiliarity with the new brand name. An example of a successful new product brand is the PrimeStar direct satellite TV reception system. The PrimeStar system offered consumers in rural areas better TV reception, 150 channel alternatives, and the option to rent movies directly using their remote controls. Direct satellite TV offered so many advantages over regular cable or over-the-air reception that customers stampeded to sign up for the new service despite the fact that PrimeStar was an unknown brand.

APPLYING
. . . to
Consumer
Services
Marketing

The Limits of Brand Proliferation

There are risks to using one brand name on many different products. The image conveyed by the brand name may become too diffuse as the specific customer benefit the brand name stands for is lost. Care must be taken not to extend the brand name to categories where it cannot provide its inherent customer benefit. The basic idea is that new brand extensions should be complementary. This means that a fresh use of a brand name should enhance the sales and reputation of existing brands. For example, the publishers of the U.S. auto magazine *Car and Driver* have licensed the use of the *Car and Driver* brand name to manufacturers of motor oil and antifreeze. While some brand loyal *Car and Driver* readers will buy the new brands of motor oil and antifreeze, these brand extensions clearly fail the complementary test. Although Car and Driver motor oil and antifreeze generates extra revenue for the publisher, the sale of these products damages the editorial independence of the magazine. The problem is that readers rely on the objectivity of articles in the magazine to help them select cars and products to purchase. Now that *Car and Driver* is selling motor oil and antifreeze, readers will no longer be able to believe the magazine's recommendations concerning these two critical automotive products.

An additional problem is that as the number of linked brands increases, the ability to reposition an individual item decreases. Finally, a bad product can tarnish the other products sharing a common brand name. Research has shown that inconsistent extension brands can dilute important consumer beliefs about individual products that carry the parent brand name.[8] This dilution of beliefs is more serious for line extensions where there are more company brands to be affected than with brand extensions where the firm is entering a new product category.

At some point, the number of brands and products in a category becomes greater than customers' need for variety and creates duplication. Too many sizes and too many me-too products simply add to distribution costs. Consumers feel that they don't require 16 barbe-cue potato chip products to satisfy their need for variety. A Food Marketing Institute study found that retailers can reduce stock-keeping units (skus) by 5 to 25 percent without hurting sales or consumers' perception of variety offered by the store. As a result of the concern over brand proliferation, the prediction is that only the No. 1 and No. 2 brands will be assured of distribution. The No. 3 brand will probably need to go to value positioning to remain viable. Lesser-ranked brands will likely disappear. Even the leaders will need to rationalize the lines and reduce the number of skus. The U.S. leader in salty snacks, Frito-Lay, has dropped about 100 sizes and flavors.

APPLYING *. . . to Consumer Packaged Goods Marketing*

Procter & Gamble has employed several strategies to accommodate retailers that want to consolidate the number of products. In detergents, P&G is continuing product innovation and differentiation even for secondary brands, reducing skus—mainly package sizes—rather than eliminating brands and strengthening secondary brands in regional markets. On the other hand, P&G has put Puritan cooking oil under the Crisco label and has discontinued the White Cloud toilet tissue brand by turning it into a Charmin extension called Charmin Ultra. The new tissue is 30 percent thicker than White Cloud and 50 percent thicker than regular Charmin, P&G's leading brand.

BRAND QUALITY

The ability of a firm or a country to compete is often influenced by the quality of the brands it offers for sale. Some American firms have been complacent about product quality deterio-ration, and their share of some markets has declined sharply. These changes are related to the ability of foreign firms to produce higher-quality products and sell them at lower prices in the United States.

INTEGRATING *. . . with Engineering Production/ Operations Management*

Research has shown that most quality problems are a result of poor design (40 percent), errors in the manufacturing process (30 percent), and defective supplier goods (30 percent). Thus careful monitoring of customers' complaints and tough standards for suppliers can lead to improved quality. Moreover, high quality does not necessarily mean higher costs. The potential impact of higher quality on the performance of the firm has been shown by the Strategic Planning Institute. They examined 525 American business units and found that those with low relative product quality earned 17 percent; medium quality, 20 percent; and high quality, 27 percent. This suggests that continuous improvements in product quality can raise profits.

Quality is important, but how do you go about raising it? Many firms focus on *total quality management* (TQM). TQM calls for a comprehensive master plan for continuously improving quality in an organization. Concepts stressed in TQM are "continuous improve-ments," "zero defects," "do it right the first time," "faster is better," and "empowerment—employees closest to the situation know best how to improve it." Going further, a good approach is to adhere to a set of quality standards endorsed by more than 50 countries, including those of the European Community and the United States. The International Orga-nization for Standardization has created a set of five standards, known collectively as *ISO*

9000, to offer a uniform way of determining whether manufacturing plants and service organizations implement and document sound quality procedures. To register, a company must undergo a third-party audit of its manufacturing and customer service processes, covering everything from how it designs, produces, and installs its goods to how it inspects, packages, and markets them. This is not cheap—it may cost $250,000 and take nine months to certify a plant. Nonetheless, ISO registration is rapidly becoming the passport to success in the international marketplace.[9]

APPLYING
. . . to
Consumer
Durable
Goods
Marketing

Our discussion of brand quality concludes with a story. Regina Company grabbed 11 percent of the U.S. vacuum cleaner market by heavy use of rebates, low prices, and an allocation of 20 percent of revenues for TV advertising. Unfortunately, it neglected product quality, and up to 20 percent of its vacuums were returned by customers for broken belts, handles, and beater bars. Meanwhile, their competitors (Hoover and Eureka) kept their returns at less than 1 percent of sales and remained profitable. Regina's profits plummeted, and the company was almost destroyed by the low-quality reputation of its vacuum cleaner brands.

BRAND WARRANTIES AND SERVICE

When customers are concerned about brand quality, warranties are often used to help reduce anxiety. Warranties represent commitments on the part of the seller to repair and adjust products that fail to perform after purchase. The main objectives of brand warranties and services are to encourage sales by reducing customers' worries about postpurchase problems and to build repeat business from satisfied customers. The linkages between consumers' attitudes about product performance and subsequent buying behavior were described earlier in Chapter 3.

Warranties Can Sell

Historically, warranties have been written statements that tell the buyer what steps the seller will take if the brand fails within a specific period of time. They were usually designed to limit the liability of the seller in case damage claims were filed by the buyer. In recent years, however, the courts have ruled that warranties do not have to be written and that they do not limit the liability of the seller. As a result, marketing managers have become more concerned with the promotional aspects of brand warranties. For example, a warranty that offers "double your money back" is clearly designed to boost sales by having the buyer try the product at little or no risk. Under these conditions, a warranty becomes a competitive tool designed to build customer confidence and to woo customers away from firms with weaker warranty policies.

After high-quality Japanese brands stole a significant portion of the U.S. car market, American manufacturers responded by offering longer warranties. When the standard Japanese warranty was 36 months or 36,000 miles, GM offered 60 months or 60,000 miles and Chrysler offered 70 months or 70,000 miles. The objective was to show buyers that American automakers had improved auto quality and stood behind their products. The evidence suggests that longer warranties helped Chrysler but did not increase GM's market share.

Service Strategies

Service strategies are concerned with establishing procedures for repairing merchandise after the brand has been sold to the customer. Over the years, product complexity and high wages for service personnel created service problems for many manufacturers. Consumers have found that it is difficult to get products repaired, and the cost is often out of proportion to the value of the product. As a result, consumers are now demanding and receiving better repair service from manufacturers. Many firms have expanded their regional repair centers and have installed "cool lines" so that customers can call directly when they encounter repair problems.

In the past, some manufacturers considered service a necessary evil and attempted to keep expenditures as low as possible. This raised profits in the short run, but eventually consumers began to rebel at the absence of local repair facilities. The failure of Fiat and Renault to penetrate U.S. auto markets is often attributed to the lack of adequate service facilities.

An alternative service strategy is to consider repair work as a profit-making opportunity. If most of the products owned by customers are out of warranty and require periodic repair, then the active solicitation of service work can be a lucrative business. Automobile manufacturers, for example, profit from the sales of fenders and other parts to their dealers and independent service facilities. However, too great a reliance on service profits may stifle product improvements and allow competitors to grow by introducing new items.

A more desirable market-oriented strategy for service emphasizes fast, economical repairs, with the objective of building long-run sales. Although a liberal factory service policy may cost more than other strategies, it can help protect the brand names owned by manufacturers and reduce problems caused by poor dealer service. Implementation of this strategy often requires extensive training of dealer repair personnel and the establishment of regional service centers run by the company. In recent years, the appliance industry has adopted a factory service policy of this type.

APPLYING
. . . to
Consumer
Durable
Goods
Marketing

Manufacturers have used product service in a variety of ways to help promote the sales of merchandise. Sears, for example, emphasizes the nationwide availability of its service, so that even if customers move to another area, repair service will be available. Maytag, on the other hand, takes a more whimsical approach and shows its repair personnel with nothing to do, suggesting that Maytag appliances rarely break down. One of the most aggressive manufacturer service policies offers a lifetime of free service repairs. At the other extreme, service costs can be minimized by making the product disposable—for example, cigarette lighters that can be simply thrown away when they break or run out of fuel. These examples suggest that the choice of an optimum service strategy depends on the cost, complexity, and life expectancy of the brand; the importance of repairs to the customer; and the manufacturer's concern for maintaining a satisfied group of repeat buyers.

EXPLOITING THE BRAND LIFE CYCLE

Most successful brands follow a life cycle that includes introduction, growth, maturity, and decline stages (Figure 7-4). At the start, brands are unknown, so the emphasis in the marketing mix is on promotion to acquaint customers with the brand and gain product trial. As sales increase during the growth phase, emphasis shifts to opening new distribution channels and retail outlets. When a brand reaches maturity, competition increases and marketing managers emphasize price, deals, coupons, and special promotions to draw attention to their merchandise.

The main danger during the growth and maturity stages of the brand life cycle is marketing inertia. If a firm becomes too complacent with its success, it may lose touch with its customers and ignore competition. Thus, when the market changes, the firm may fail to react quickly enough—or perhaps not at all—to the changed circumstances. An example of mature brand complacency is described for Campbell Soup in Marketing Strategies box 7-2.

One way of increasing customer interest during the growth and maturity phases of the brand life cycle is to expand product lines and offer greater variety. Another possibility is to follow a strategy of market segmentation and sell the product under a variety of brands owned by distributors or other manufacturers. A third alternative is to engage in clever promotional campaigns devised to catch the eye of selected groups of customers.

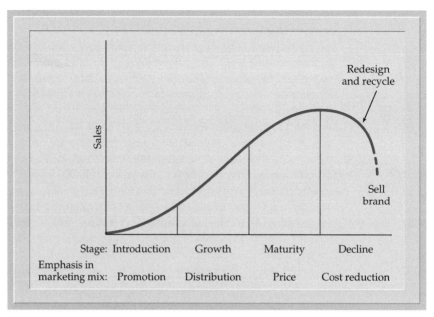

FIGURE 7-4   Brand Life Cycle and Marketing Mix

Brands in decline often need to be redesigned or reduced in cost so that they can continue to make a contribution to the company. When items become unprofitable, the company must decide whether the brand should be carried at a loss or sold to make room for more profitable lines. The effect of the brand life cycle on the marketing strategies of a toothpaste that periodically reenters the market with a "new and improved" version is illustrated in Figure 7-5.

Brand life cycles vary in length from a few weeks for fashion merchandise to up to 100 years for soaps, appliances, and food items. The amount of time a product stays in any one stage of the life cycle depends on customer adoption rates and the amount of new brand competition. Because businesses invest a great deal of money to gain consumer acceptance, it makes sense to extend the life of their brands as long as possible. Three methods that can be employed to stretch brand markets are (1) promoting of more frequent and varied usage among current users, (2) finding new uses for the basic material, and (3) creating new users for the brand by expanding the market.

APPLYING
. . . to
*Pharmaceutical
Marketing*

Ciba-Geigy AG has extended the life cycle of its aging antiarthritis drug, Voltaren, by formulating a spate of new versions. To hold off the inevitable erosion caused by generic competition as its patents expire on the original tablet form of Voltaren, Ciba-Geigy now sells it in the form of eyedrops, as intravenous solutions, as time-release pills, and as emulgel—a cross between a cream and an ointment. The last product is so novel that it earned Ciba-Geigy a new 20-year cycle of patent coverage. As a result of these actions, Voltaren continues to be a blockbuster pharmaceutical.

BRANDS IN DECLINE

The brand life cycle suggests that brands are born, grow to maturity, and then enter a period of decline. The length of the decline phase is determined by changes in consumer preferences, activities of competitors, and the brand elimination policies of the firm. Although usually little can be done about basic shifts in consumer preferences and the entry of competitive items, the firm has a wide range of alternatives that can be exercised for brands with falling sales.

MARKETING STRATEGIES 7-2

Campbell Counters Declining Soup Sales

APPLYING
... to
Consumer
Food
Marketing

The Campbell Soup Co. derives 62 percent of its revenue from the sale of soups and sauces. Over the four years from 1994 through 1997, total canned soup sales in the United States declined every year and Campbell's sales decreased more than the category as a whole. In 1997, Campbell's soup sales dropped 3.5 percent compared to 2.4 percent for other soups. Sales of condensed soups fell another 2 percent in the fall of 1998. Campbell's market share for canned soups has fallen from 80 percent in 1992 to 74 percent in 1997. Shrinking soup sales led to lower profits in 1997 and 1998. In January of 1999, Campbell's stock price dropped 13 percent to reach a 52-week low as a result of the company's failure to reach profit goals. Most of the market share losses have been to lower priced store brand soups produced by H.J. Heinz Co. Consumers are also buying more ready-to-serve soup instead of the condensed soup primarily sold by Campbell. Progresso is a strong competitor in the ready-to-serve segment where Campbell's market share is only 55 percent. Reversing the decline in soup sales will not be easy because of changes in America's shopping and cooking habits. People are buying fewer canned foods of any kind. To counter this trend, Campbell has begun switching to glass jars for its ready-to-serve soup and aseptic boxes for its broth. Also the demand for "cooking soups" has declined. In the early 1980s Campbell sold as much as 40 percent of its tomato and other condensed soups to shoppers who used them as a cooking ingredient. However, today fewer people are preparing meat loaf and tuna-noodle casserole recipes that call for canned soup.

To help stem the declining sales of its Campbell brand soups, the company has made a number of changes in its marketing programs. In 1998, they did not take their usual 3 to 7 percent spring price increase. Customers were paying 20 percent more for Campbell brand soup compared to the prices of store brand soups and Campbell's battered brand equity would no longer allow them to raise prices every year to improve revenues. Campbell also planned to increase its soup advertising budget from 3.5 percent of sales to 8 percent of sales. Some of the new ads tout Campbell's soups as cooking ingredients and others will be run on children's shows. Also, hundreds of new recipes will be made available on Campbell's Web site. To cut costs, Campbell plans to end its long time practice of offering retailers rebates and steep discounts at quarter's end to entice stores to stock up on soup so Campbell can meet its sales targets. Basil Anderson, chief financial officer of Campbell Soup Co., blames the lack of enough new products for market share losses. He indicated that "Without significant innovation, any name brand tends to lose share to private label." The company is working on a number of new products.

— *Managers who fail to adjust mature brands to meet changing market conditions and consumer preferences can expect to lose volume to competitive brands.*

Source: Vanessa O'Connell, "Changing Tastes Dent Campbell's Canned Soup Sales," *The Wall Street Journal*, April 28, 1998, p. B1. Vanessa O'Connell, "Campbell Sees Profit Shortfall and Stock Gets Creamed," *The Wall Street Journal*, January 12, 1999.

Courtesy Campbell Soup Company

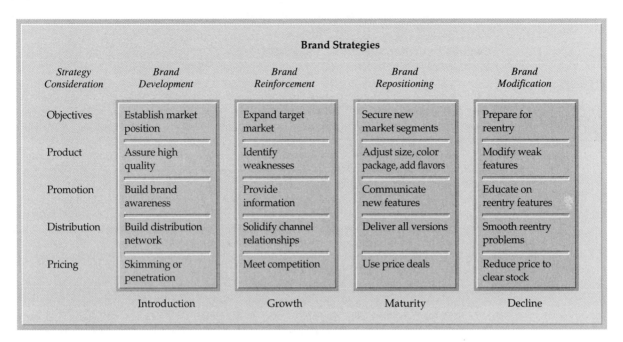

FIGURE 7-5   Life-Cycle Strategies for a Toothpaste Brand

Strategies for Reviving Brands

Perhaps the most important task of brand review procedures is to separate the items that can benefit from a redesign of the package or promotional plans from those that are on an irreversible downhill slide toward extinction. Often large sums of money are wasted in trying to save brands that have no future.

What Is the Problem?   The job of identifying candidates for rescue operations is not easy, and specific reasons for sales declines must be identified. The first step is to determine the contribution to the sales loss due to changes in the number of buyers versus the amount they buy. When customers are purchasing less of a brand and the number of buyers is holding up, the brand may be salvageable. The next step is to assess the underlying causes of such losses. If the quality is found to be inferior and customers are shifting to improved versions, there may be little hope for the brand. The best rescue situation occurs when most people have positive memories of the brand and the product still has a loyal group of fans.

The easiest solution to declining sales is to move the product into new foreign or domestic markets. This may require the addition of new distributors or the enlargement of the existing sales force. An alternative to greater breadth of market coverage is finding and promoting new uses among existing customers. Manufacturers of consumer products are particularly skilled at devising new uses for baking soda or bleach and coming up with new recipes that help extend the life of old brands. Since it costs millions to introduce a new brand, it can be cheaper to reformulate an existing product.

What Can Be Done?   A classic turnaround occurred with Kraft's Cheez Whiz. The processed cheese had been on the market for 36 years and was losing 3 to 4 percent of its sales each year. The marketing manager suggested repositioning Cheez Whiz as a sauce for the microwave oven. New ads were created emphasizing its use in microwave ovens, and the ad budget was tripled. Cheez Whiz was also repackaged in multipacks of 4-ounce cups designed for microwave heating. As a result of these activities, sales increased 35 percent.

APPLYING
. . . to
Consumer
Food
Marketing

Frito-Lay nearly dropped its Tostitos tortilla chip after sales slumped 50 percent from a peak. Instead, hoping to latch onto the Tex-Mex food craze, it reformulated Tostitos into a restaurant-style chip—doubling its size, changing its shape from circular to triangular, and substituting white corn for yellow. Packaged in a new clear bag with big, bolder graphics, Tostitos Restaurant Style Chips set new revenue records. This proves that consumers crave what's old and familiar. You just have to freshen it up. Another example of a brand revival is shown in Marketing Strategies box 7-3.

Despite the successful revivals that we have mentioned, however, not every aging brand can be saved. Also, spending money on weak products often takes energy and resources away from your leading brands. This suggests that fading brands such as Carnation powdered milk, Serutan laxative, and Del Monte canned peas do not warrant expensive new promotional programs. Marketing expenditures on declining products are risky and are justified only when there is good reason to believe that the item can be saved.

Strategies for Fading Brands

Perhaps the best strategy for poor performing brands is to sell them while they are still profitable so you can recoup some of the brand equity that remains. If you wait too long, no one will want the brand and you may be faced with paying significant costs to drop the brand from the product line. In 1998, Procter & Gamble reviewed its smaller and low-performing brands and sold off its Duncan Hines cake mix business which accounted for about 10 percent of its food sales. P&G also announced plans to sell the North American portion of its Attends incontinence-care business and Hawaiian Punch juice. Hawaiian Punch was profitable, but P&G wanted to focus its resources on brands with better growth prospects.[10] Hershey Foods also decided to sell its Ronzoni, Skinner, and San Giorgio brands of pastas.[11] Although these brands made Hershey the number-one pasta marketer in the United States with revenues of $400 million, sales declined 2 percent in 1998. Another reason Hershey wanted to sell the pasta brands is they produced operating margins of only 10 percent compared to 20 percent for candy. Hershey believed that by focusing resources on other brands they could generate a better return for their shareholders. Smaller firms that buy Hawaiian Punch and the pasta brands can make money because they require little promotion and no fixed investment in facilities. Sometimes a new buyer can expand a business through more aggressive marketing. Marketing Strategies box 7-4 describes what happened when IBM sold off its small printer division.

MARKETING STRATEGIES 7-3

Clairol Rescues Herbal Essences

APPLYING . . . to Health and Beauty Aid Marketing

Herbal Essences shampoo went from a moribund relic of the 1970s to the second largest shampoo brand in the U.S. thanks to a radical overhaul and a frisky ad campaign. The 1995 relaunch positioned the shampoo as an indulgence in the time pressed 90s, with a soothing scent and an ad campaign that touted it as a "totally organic experience." The campaign played on the "organic" tagline by showing women going delirious with pleasure while using the shampoo. One TV spot for the shampoo featured the well known sex therapist Dr. Ruth. The positioning and tagline continued into the launch of an Herbal Essences body wash in 1997. Clairol backed the Herbal Essences hair care brand with $34 million in ad support during 1998. As a result, Herbal Essences went from a market share of 2.1 percent in 1995 to 10.1 percent of the $1.68 billion market in 1998. Four percent of this growth was stolen from Procter & Gamble's market leading Pantene shampoo brand.

— *Creative positioning and great ads can revive lethargic products.*

Source: Mercedes M. Cardona, "Brands: In Trouble—In Demand," *Advertising Age*, February 22, 1999, p. 20.

APPLYING
. . . to
Industrial
Marketing

MARKETING STRATEGIES 7-4

IBM Sells Off Its Printer Business

As IBM struggled with its core computer businesses, they decided to focus on mid- to high-end printers and sold off their low-end desktop printer unit in 1991. Once free of IBM's bureaucracy, that business became Lexmark International Inc., a flourishing printer company based in Lexington, Kentucky. This left IBM with a niche role for its line of medium and large printers in the global printer industry. IBM's printer sales reached a peak of $935 million in 1994 and declined to $757 million by 1997. These declines were mainly due to new designs and aggressive marketing by rival printer manufacturers such as Xerox. Sales in the U.S. were particularly hard hit, declining by 27 percent. Since the printer unit produced only modest profits, IBM decided to sell out and buy any printers they needed from other firms.

— *Sometimes it pays to sell noncore business orphans.*

Source: Raju Narisetti, "IBM Is Seeking to Sell Its Printer Business," *The Wall Street Journal,* June 17, 1998, p. B6.

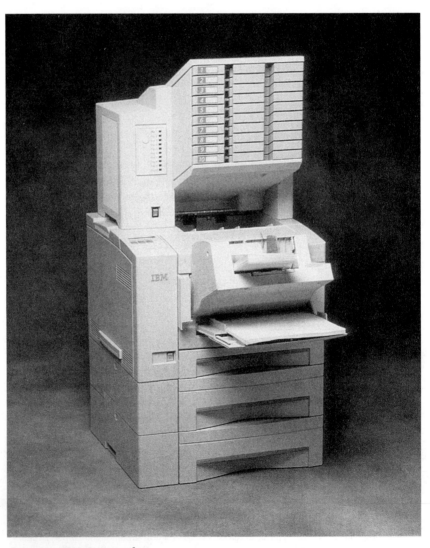

Courtesy IBM Corporation

Another successful strategy for fading brands is to drop all promotional activities and rely solely on repeated purchases from current customers. Where promotional expenditures have been substantial, sales are likely to decline slowly, and the savings from discontinued advertising can make the brand quite profitable in the short run. For example, when Chrysler introduced its new Jeep Grand Cherokee sport utility vehicle, they kept the outdated Jeep Cherokee model as a low-priced fighting brand. The boxy old model did not have air bags, a modern 4-wheel drive, or enough interior room, but Chrysler had written off all developments' costs for the brand so they could make money selling the Cherokees at low prices. This strategy was so successful that Chrysler sold enough Cherokees to pay for adding air bags and some other improvements.

APPLYING
. . . to
Consumer
Durable
Goods
Marketing

Sharing the Risks. Another useful strategy for declining products is to continue to sell the item but to contract with another company for manufacturing. An alternative is to continue to make the product but license others to sell it. A third possibility is to begin exporting the brand to foreign markets where it might be viewed as new and exciting. Sometimes brands that have worn out their welcome in one country can find new life when marketed in another. While cigarettes are viewed as unhealthy in the United States, American cigarette brands are still quite popular in Eastern Europe and China.

Helping the Dealers. In situations in which nothing can save a declining brand, the firm should dispose of it with a minimum of inconvenience to the interested parties. This means notifying dealers in advance and helping them clear out old stock. Frequently, special discounts are offered to dealers to stimulate the sale of discontinued brands. It may even be necessary for the manufacturer to buy back the unsold merchandise. Dealers should also be informed about replacement brands that are being promoted to take the place of the discontinued items, which can help maintain consumer goodwill, and arrange to provide service and parts for recent buyers.

SUMMARY

In this chapter we have explained what brands are and the important concept of brand equity. We have also described the strategies used to manage brands over their life cycle. Brands are vulnerable to competitive pressures and you must know how to manipulate line extensions, brand extensions, umbrella brands, quality, promotions, prices, warranties, and repair services to optimize profits. Finally, a variety of strategies for brands with stagnant or declining sales have been explained.

NOTES

1. Steven Lipin, "Newell to Buy Rubbermaid for $5.8 Billion," *The Wall Street Journal*, October 21, 1998, pp. A3, A8.
2. Michelle W. Fellman, "Just the Name, Thanks: Why Beemer Bought Rolls," *Marketing News*, September 14, 1998, p. 6.
3. Kevin L. Keller, *Strategic Brand Management: Building, Measuring, and Managing Brand Equity* (Upper Saddle River, NJ: Prentice-Hall, 1998), p. 45.
4. Stephen J. Hoch, "Private Label a Threat? Don't Believe It," *Advertising Age*, May 24, 1993, p. 19.
5. P. Fitzell, *Private Label Marketing in the 1990s* (New York: Global Book Productions, 1992).
6. Stephen Hoch, "How Should National Brands Think About Private Labels?" *Sloan Management Review* (Winter 1996), pp. 89–102.
7. Steven J. Hoch, "Private Label a Threat? Don't Believe It," p. 19.

8. Deborah Roedder John, Barbara Loken, and Christopher Joiner, "The Negative Impact of Extensions: Can Flagship Products Be Diluted?" *Journal of Marketing Research,* Vol. 62 (January 1998), pp. 19–32.

9. Cyndee Miller, "U.S. Firms Lag in Meeting Global Quality Standards," *Marketing News,* Vol. 27, No. 4 (February 15, 1993), pp. 1, 6.

10. Tara Parker-Pope, "Procter & Gamble Mulls Selling Off Hawaiian Punch," *The Wall Street Journal*, November 12, 1998, p. B8.

11. Vanessa O'Connell, "Hershey, Faced with Limp Pasta Sales, Announces Plans to Sell Eight Brands," *The Wall Street Journal*, November 10, 1998, p. A4.

SUGGESTED READING

Aaker, Jennifer L. "Dimensions of Brand Personality," *Journal of Marketing Research,* Vol. 34 (August 1997), pp. 347–356.

Keller, Kevin L. *Strategic Brand Management: Building, Measuring, and Managing Brand Equity* (Upper Saddle River, NJ: Prentice-Hall, 1998).

REFERENCES

Aaker, David A. *Building Strong Brands* (New York: Free Press, 1995).

Aaker, David A. *Managing Brand Equity* (New York: Free Press, 1991).

Cortada, James W. *TQM for Sales and Marketing Management* (New York, McGraw-Hill, 1993).

Kapferer, Jean-Noel. *Strategic Brand Management: Creating and Sustaining Brand Equity Long Term* (London: Kogan Page Ltd, 1998).

Ries, Laura and Al Ries. *22 Immutable Laws of Branding: How to Build a Product or Service into a World-Class Brand* (New York: HarperCollins, 1998).

Shocker, Allen D., Rajendra K. Srivastava, and Robert W. Ruekert, Eds. "Special Issue on Brand Management," *Journal of Marketing Research,* Vol. 31 (May 1994), pp. 149–304.

QUESTIONS

1. Bausch & Lomb is the leader in the market for premium sunglasses costing more than $75, with an estimated 35 percent market share. Yet in 1997, the sunglass division lost $59 million on revenue of $492 million. In 1998, the company expected to make a small profit. Bausch & Lomb has hired an investment banker to help it decide whether to sell the sunglass division, enter a joint venture, or spin it off to shareholders. Why is a market leader considering getting rid of a business that provides 25 percent of its revenue?

2. Nabisco introduced a brand extension reduced fat cookie called SnackWell's at a premium price and they were an instant hit. In a few years sales mushroomed to more than $400 million per year. However, competitors rushed to bring out competitive brands and by 1998 sales had declined to only $150 million a year. In addition, Nabisco's total dollar sales fell 1.7 percent in 1997 while sales at rival Keebler Foods rose 7 percent. Nabisco responded by replacing the head of its biscuit unit with an executive from Pillsbury. What caused Nabisco to go from a successful SnackWell's marketer to an also-ran in the quest for cookie customers?

3. Dr Pepper/Seven-Up Inc. changed the formula of its 7-Up soft drink to be less sweet with a crisper lemon-line taste like its fast-growing competitor Sprite marketed by Coca-Cola Co. In 1997, Sprite was the fastest-growing soft drink in the United States with a market share of 5.8 percent. Meanwhile 7-Up's market share had declined from 3.2 percent in 1987 to 2.4 percent in 1996. In addition to changing the flavor of 7-Up,

the company is planning to increase promotion and advertising activities to try to revive the brand. Do you think 7-Up's sweeter flavor caused it to lose market share to Sprite? What marketing advantages does Coca-Cola have that helped it steal the lemon-lime soda market from 7-Up?

4. The Driscoll Strawberry Associates, Inc., of Watsonville, California, has been growing and shipping strawberries and raspberries since 1940. Given the success of Dole and Del Monte in branding fresh produce, should Driscoll launch branded berries for consumers? If so, how can they nurture the perception among consumers that their strawberries and raspberries are something different, something better? That is, suggest a positioning statement for them.

5. Several automobile manufacturers have had success with brand extensions into a new breed of vehicle that combines features from sedans and truck-based sport utilities. These light sport utilities are built on platforms from cars instead of truck platforms used for large sport utilities. The end result is a smaller, lighter, cheaper, and more easily handling vehicle such as Honda's CR-V, Toyota's RAV4, and Subaru's Forester. These small sport utilities are especially popular among women and young buyers. Why do manufacturers offer brands that attract single and young married customers? How can brand loyalty to these entry level products help them in the long run?

6. Are warranties primarily designed to protect consumers and manufacturers against loss or to boost sales of goods and services?

7. Parker Brothers introduced a new toy brand called Riviton that outsold any other toy the company had ever introduced. Children could use the plastic parts, rubber rivets, and riveting tool to assemble anything from a truck to a house. A total of 450,000 kits retailing for $15 to $25 were sold the first year, and sales were expected to reach $10 million in the second year. However, two children choked to death on the rubber rivets in the kits. Parker, which is a division of General Mills, decided to stop selling Riviton and ordered a recall. These steps were taken even though the product met all safety standards and was not under investigation by the Consumer Product Safety Commission. After three months, 370,000 kits had been returned at a cost exceeding $8.3 million. Do you agree with Parker's decision to recall the kits? Why or why not? Why did Parker move so quickly on the recall?

8. Research has shown that 91 percent of American women ages 18 to 39 advocate specific brands. Also women believe the brands they choose reflect their personality. Women also tend to advocate brands from a wide range of product categories. However, men advocate brands for only three product categories: cars, technology, and sports equipment. Do you believe this information would be useful to brand managers and if so, how?

9. Hughes Electronics Corp. introduced the first satellite-TV system in the United States carrying the brand name DirecTV. The digital system offered excellent reception, 150 channels, and employed a small 18-inch receiver dish. By 1998, DirecTV had 4 million subscribers and revenue rose 8 percent from the year earlier. However, Hughes lost $61 million on DirecTV due to costs of expanding coverage to Japan, the growth of digital cable alternatives, and competition from other satellite providers. Hughes hopes to break even in 1999. Should Hughes sell its DirecTV brand or try to find a way to rescue the brand? If they keep DirecTV, what steps do you recommend to make the brand profitable?

10. The Victoria's Secret chain is best known for flooding malls with provocative lingerie. It is now selling is own Victoria Secret's Cosmetics line through its stores. Assess this line extension.

11. The American Lung Association was launched almost a century ago to combat tubercu-

losis. The battle has largely been won. TB now kills about 1,000 people a year in the United States, compared with 150,000 in 1900. Lung cancer was a natural successor cause for the Lung Association, but other health-oriented charities had already adopted it. Meantime, the Lung Association's revenue machine, the annual Christmas Seal campaign, was losing its fund-raising wallop by failing to connect with a new generation of donors. The Lung Association decided to focus on asthma. Though a growing problem, among children and the urban poor, asthma has been a financial and public-relations flop for the Lung Association. Asthma has failed to excite the critical big-money donors. Simply put, the Lung Association does have a big scary disease anymore. What should the Lung Association do about its acute identity crisis?

CASE 7-1 MCILHENNY COMPANY: JAPAN*

*I*n January 1988, Carlos Malespin, vice-president, International, of the McIlhenny Company, was reviewing all the market and product studies for a new line of Tabasco brand spaghetti sauces to be introduced in Japan later that year. While reassured by the findings, Malespin realized that this product was an important "first" for this old-line company, and he was anxious that each detail should withstand careful analysis and scrutiny. He was also a firm believer in action, however; as he said, "Any idea can be killed by hypothesizing it to death." Therefore, he was prepared to proceed with the next step, which was to introduce the product at FoodEx (Harumi), a major trade show, in March. Now he needed the go-ahead from his boss, Ned Simmons, a fourth-generation McIlhenny and president of the company.

COMPANY BACKGROUND[1]

McIlhenny Company was a closely held family business located on Avery Island, Louisiana. Although the company name was relatively unknown, its major product, Tabasco pepper sauce, was marketed in at least 103 countries, with labels in 20 different languages. The brand was over 120 years old, but its recipe had changed little since Edmund McIlhenny

first invented and refined it at the close of the Civil War. He had been given the seeds of a pepper (*Capsicum frutescens*) by a friend who had brought them from Mexico; he experimented extensively with both the plants and the sauce he made from the peppers. Finally, because of the product's distinctive flavor and uncompromising quality, his friends and family had recommended that he bottle it for the retail market.

In 1907 McIlhenny Company was formally incorporated with the ownership and rights to all the titles, copyrights, formulas, and trademarks for Tabasco sauce. In 1949 Walter S. McIlhenny was elected president, and under his leadership, McIlhenny Company was launched on an impressive period of growth; in addition, the company introduced the Tabasco brand Bloody Mary mix and Tabasco brand picante sauce. As the demand for Tabasco sauce increased, its quality was never compromised, and continual improvements were made to the growing, bottling, and other aspects of its manufacture.

In 1982 Ned Simmons, great grandson of the founder, assumed the presidency. Simmons began an aggressive marketing and sales program, and he was also extremely concerned with improving productivity, streamlining operations, and reducing overhead to improve bottom-line profit. As a closely controlled organization, McIlhenny's financial data were not available, but industry experts estimated that 1988 sales would be $50 million, up over 1987. The com-

---

[1] Parts of this section come from the case study, "McIlhenny Company," UVA-OM-0653.

---

* This case was prepared by Professor Christopher Gale of the Darden Graduate School of Business with the cooperation of the McIlhenny Company and is intended as the basis for classroom use only. Some figures have been disguised. "Tabasco®" is a registered trademark of the McIlhenny Company. Copyright (c) 1989 by the Darden Graduate Business School Foundation, Charlottesville, VA. Reproduced by permission.

pany's excellent trade relations indicated that the company was well managed and had the resources necessary to finance new-product introductions. U.S. sales of 40 million 2-ounce bottles were growing about 5 percent a year (representing about one-third of the pepper-sauce market), but overseas growth was about 8 percent annually. Simmons said that the U.S. business, divided about equally between home use and use in restaurants, had the highest market saturation, but that

> the potential even here for added penetration is tremendous. Our penetration is far less in foreign markets, but growth in those areas will require a slow build. We can take advantage of the interest in "international cuisine"—such as, for example, the popularity of western food in Japan—to increase usage.

His goal was to double corporate sales over the next five years.

TABASCO SAUCE IN JAPAN

Tabasco was introduced in Japan at the end of World War II by the U.S. occupation forces. By 1988 Japan was McIlhenny's largest international market, followed by West Germany, Canada, and Mexico. The product was handled in Japan by the company's sales agent, PBI Japan, which received a 5 percent sales commission; in return, the agent recommended and worked with the five exclusive importers, formulated an annual sales and marketing plan, searched out new markets, commissioned market research, supervised the work of the advertising agency (Dentsu), kept alert for new opportunities, and in every other respect acted as Malespin's alter ego in Japan. Recent annual sales growth in Japan was about 8 percent.

Five exclusive importers carried the line; they included some of the largest trading companies in Japan (Sumitomo, Marubeni, Meidi-ya, Toyota, and Nippon coffee). These importers distributed to "primary wholesalers," who in turn sold to "secondary wholesalers," who then sold to tertiary wholesalers or small neighborhood grocery shops and restaurants. About 80 percent of Tabasco sales were to restaurants and coffee shops, and the little red bottle was a familiar sight to all Japanese. The product was not used on traditional Japanese foods, which were typically mild dishes, but on "western food," particularly pizza and spaghetti.[2]

Surveys indicated that Tabasco enjoyed 95 percent unaided awareness, that it could be found in about 60 percent of all homes, and that it was on the tables of

practically all restaurants serving western food. Consumer research indicated that it enjoyed a reputation as "a U.S. product of very high quality." The company had worked with local chefs and cooking schools to develop new recipes using Tabasco sauce that would appeal to the new "hot taste"; these recipes were promulgated via package inserts, quarterly news letters distributed through the Cajun Cooking Club, and at the company's booth at FoodEx, which annually attracted over 100,000 distributors, retailers, and sales agents. There was no direct competitor to Tabasco.

JAPAN: THE SPAGHETTI-SAUCE OPPORTUNITY

Malespin was the company's first manager for international marketing. Prior to his arrival, the company used a New York-based export-management company for sales overseas and had licensing agreements with a few foreign firms for manufacturing and/or marketing Tabasco. Malespin had obtained an MA in economics and an MA in international trade from the Catholic University of Louvain in Belgium. After graduation, he spent eight years in various international assignments, including working on tariff and trade matters in the Nicaraguan Central Bank and as an export sales manager for a trading company in New Orleans.

Upon joining McIlhenny in 1985, Malespin spent a great deal of time studying the company's various international markets and preparing a handbook on "how to do business abroad." He took a long tour of the company's major international markets to meet licensees, importers, and major retail accounts.[3] From these studies, he concluded that the Tabasco name had built up as much equity abroad as it had in the United States and that attractive opportunities existed to offer other products under this ample umbrella.

He decided to make his first move in Japan, where the size of the market, the trend toward western foods, and the rapid growth of U.S. fast-food chains (especially Kentucky Fried Chicken and McDonald's) seemed to offer McIlhenny a platform for new growth. For example, a growing interest in Cajun food was a felicitous opportunity to popularize jambalaya and gumbo (Cajun specialties based on rice, vegetables, and seafood), because these dishes used basic Japanese culinary ingredients and cooking systems. Through the services of Paul Prudhomme (a gifted U.S. chef spe-

---

[2] More information on Japan and its people is given in Appendix A.

[3] "Too long!" he said. "I spent 5 weeks on that trip, and increasingly found that my clients were far more refreshed than I was! Most practitioners would say that 15–18 days abroad is max, before you lose your acuity in cutting deals."

cializing in Cajun delights), these recipes were introduced at the 1986 Matsuo Food Fair; they received
national attention, and over time, jambalaya became
part of the repertoire of modern Japanese cooks and
housewives.

By 1987, however, Malespin could not envision
any further accelerated growth for Tabasco through
recipe programs. He therefore explored other avenues
by asking such questions as, "What is Tabasco Sauce?
What does it mean to Japanese consumers? How do
they use it?" In the process of answering these questions, he and the managers of PBI Japan concluded that
the spaghetti-sauce market offered a promising opportunity. PBI agreed to undertake research on this market
and on consumer attitudes toward and use of spaghetti
sauce.

MARKET RESEARCH

PBI's research indicated that wholesale *canned*
spaghetti sauce accounted for $86 million of the total
estimated market of $110 million (the balance of sales
was in retort pouches). The meat-sauce portion had
sales of $73 million.[4] Of the approximately 35 brands
of canned sauce currently on the market, none was
dominant. The top four brands controlled 62 percent of
market share; they were Kewpi ($15 million), Mama
($13.5 million), Kagome ($12.5 million), and Oh-My
($11.8). Five other brands had sales of $30 million
altogether, and the remaining brands controlled $2.5
million. All were Japanese companies with the exception of a Heinz joint venture ($6.8 million).

The industry spent $4.2 million annually in 1986
for advertising (based on data for five of the top seven
brands). Malespin observed that 10 feet of gondola
space was devoted to this product in grocery stores ("a
tremendous amount of shelf space!") and that spaghetti
was perceived in Japan to be a western dish.

Malespin believed that the market was ready for a
new entry that (1) built on the excellent reputation
and distribution of the Tabasco name, especially
given its powerful association in Japan with spaghetti
and pizza products and (2) offered a better product
but priced the same as competition. The new product
was to offer more beef, yet be formulated to appeal to
Japanese tastes.

For the past 20 years, the company had retained a
food consultant, Ms. Ichikawa, to create recipes using
Tabasco sauce. Now she was asked to develop a new

spaghetti-sauce recipe using not only Tabasco sauce
but other ingredients that she believed would improve
on the major brands and still appeal to Japanese
palates. At this point, the decision on sourcing the
product was deliberately held open.

In her lab, Ichikawa analyzed the current brands
with respect to flavors, size of cans, texture, appearance, etc., based on both taste tests and ingredient
analysis. From this analysis, she elicited complaints
ranging from "thin, color drab" and "smells too spicy,
bad can smell" to "good but doesn't go with spaghetti
well," and so on.

Ichikawa then experimented with different ingredients, including red wines, beef, pork and mutton,
cheeses, olive and sunflower oils, and such different
vegetables as carrots, onions, potatoes, celery, and
many more. These recipes were tested among small
consumer groups and, once refined, were subjected to
production in larger quantities in order to see if the
"homemade" characteristics were preserved.

By December 1987, the product formulation was
complete: compared with U.S. brands, the product was
darker (a "meaty-brown"), thicker, and sweeter. Containing 12 percent meat solids, it could be imported into
Japan under current beef tariff restrictions (20 percent
maximum) yet still be called "meat sauce" under U.S.
standards. (By now the company had determined that
the high price of beef in Japan made production in the
United States more profitable than in Japan). Ichikawa
reported that, based on the taste tests, "Texture, aroma,
freshness, and can smell all got highest marks."

Based on an assumed first-year sales level of 1
percent of the market, Malespin estimated the production and marketing costs (see Exhibit 1). The proposed retail price of ¥300 for a 300-gram can would
yield a factory price of $1.09 and a unit profit of
$0.24.

For the typical three layers of distribution between
the retailer and the factory, the margins (over the
buyer's cost) were as follows: importer, 12 percent;
primary wholesaler, 6 percent; secondary wholesaler,
6 percent; and the retailer, 38 percent. For companies
importing into Japan, the sales agent received a fixed
commission, usually 5 percent. In addition, promotional allowances were frequently given to the
importer, which were in turn passed down the chain
in the form of price discounts; these allowances could
include "1 free case in 10" or discounts off invoice.
Thus a 300-gram can of spaghetti sauce with a list
price of ¥300 normally sold for ¥220 to ¥240. (See
Exhibit 2 for a projection of distribution costs and
trade pricing.)

---

[4] At this time, the exchange rate was $1.00 = ¥128.

EXHIBIT 1 Spaghetti-Sauce Estimated Product and Selling Costs, 1988 (300-gram can)

	$	¥	%
Gross Sales[a]	$1.09	¥139.5	100.0%
Cost of Goods Sold	.64	81.9	58.7
Gross Profit	.45	57.6	41.3%
Selling Expenses			
Advertising and Promotion	.07	9.0	7.8
Returns and Allowances	.025	3.2	3.3
Interest	.005	0.6	0.5
Containerization[b]	.02	2.5	1.8
Freight to Japan	.024	3.1	2.2
Commission	.06	7.7	5.5
Miscellaneous	.01	1.3	0.9
Total Selling Expenses	.21	26.9	19.3
Net Profit	$0.24	¥30.7	22.0%

[a] C&F Japan. That is, all McIlhenny prices were quoted in U.S. dollars.
[b] Including inland cartage (U.S.).

Source: Company records.

CONSUMER SURVEYS

In July 1987, the sales agent, PBI, had conducted an initial written survey involving 110 respondents (basic conclusions are in Exhibit 3). In October PBI commissioned two focus groups (selected results from this research are in Appendix B). Two more focus-group sessions were conducted in December to test the actual Tabasco formulation, packages, and "catch phrases"; selected results from these sessions are found in Appendix C.

THE PROPOSAL

In its review of the situation, PBI stated,

There is currently no clear, overall leader in the canned meat sauce market. Tabasco brand spaghetti sauces will interface well with the Tabasco pepper sauce principal market position as *the* pasta/pizza condiment. Tabasco spaghetti sauce offers an opportunity to capitalize on consumer brand awareness. The sauce will expand McIlhenny's product base and its distribution channels can carry the product along with the pepper sauce. Tabasco brand spaghetti sauce products would increase tabasco pepper sauce sales by 1) creating more Tabasco brand merchandising space at the retail level, 2) standardizing Tabasco brand merchandising locations in retail outlets, 3) creating Tabasco pepper sauce impulse-buy opportunities, and 4) broadening the entire Tabasco brand base of consumers in Japan.

Malespin proposed offering the spaghetti sauce in Japan in three 300-gram versions: a mild version (suitable for children), a regular, and a "spicy" version. Because even the spicy version was relatively mild by American standards, there was still opportunity for

EXHIBIT 2 Distribution Costs and Trade Pricing (300-gram can)

A. Importer's Cost

McIlhenny Price	¥139.5[a]
Insurance	0.5
Duty Charges	13.5
Landed Cost	¥153.5
Customs	2.5
Warehouse (90 days)	5.0
Delivery	5.0
Interest (150 days)	5.4
Total Cost	¥171.4

B. Typical Trade Selling Prices

	¥	Percentage of Retail Price	Profit Margin[b]
Retail Price	300	100.0	38%
Secondary Wholesaler Price	216	72.0	6%
Primary Wholesaler Price	204	68.0	6%
Importer Selling Price	192	64.0	12%

[a] Based on $1.00 =¥128.
[b] The gross margin is based on the buyer's cost.

Source: Company records.

**EXHIBIT 3   Findings from Initial Written
Questionnaire, July 1987 (*N* = 110 respondents)**

- 64% were between 25–40 years old; 40% had children, mostly ages 1–17; dinner meals were probably eaten at home.
- 72% prepared spaghetti at least every 2 weeks; 65% prepared it for family consumption, 22% for themselves; 74% prepared 2–4 servings.
- 66% bought spaghetti in a supermarket; the frequency of purchase was at least every 2 months.
- 62% prepared meat sauce or Japanese-style sauce–could be soy-based, sukiyaki type, fermented soy bean sauce, fish egg, ground white radish and barbecue meat slices, Japanese mushrooms, or even seaweed.
- Spice was the most popular additive (38%), then meat (30%), mushrooms (14%), tomato or onion (11%), and Tabasco (7–11%).
- 65% had no regular brand; those who were loyal cited "taste" and "price" as the reason for their loyalty.
- 76% would try new brands.

Source: Company records.

consumers to use Tabasco on the product. In order to offer a fuller product line, McIlhenny would also produce a chili con carne sauce (in mild and regular flavors), which was similar to spaghetti sauce but had pinto beans. This product had been as thoroughly tested by Ichikawa as had the spaghetti sauce.

By this time, about ¥6.5 million had been spent on the consumer research, product development, and product/consumer tests. The next step was to introduce the product to the trade in the company's booth at the March FoodEx show. In addition to this chance for the 100,000 distributor/retailer representatives to taste the product, Malespin planned a private showing to the five trading companies that imported Tabasco pepper sauce into Japan.

Malespin believed there was no point in conducting a regional test market, because Japan was so concentrated: a regional test would be tantamount to a national introduction. As he pointed out, 45 percent of the country's population lived within 100 miles of Tokyo.

Thus, given no surprises at the show, Malespin anticipated a national introduction in November 1988. He would give one of the usual trade allowances to spur trial, which in this case would be "one case free with ten." Advertising for the product would be piggybacked by taking the top third of the one-page newspaper and magazine ads normally used for advertising Tabasco sauce; two ads were scheduled for November and two for December in the three major national Japanese newspapers. The copy points were:

Tabasco made it—it must be delicious! There are a number of sauces with meat, but Tabasco has made a real meat sauce as it should be: 1) High volume of meat; 2) only high quality, 100% beef; 3) best-quality ingredients carefully selected to complement nutrition and taste.

These production criteria have guided Tabasco's recipe development. We hope that you and your family will enjoy this sauce soon.

Malespin's target was to get the product on the shelves by November 20 and to attain a 1 percent share by the end of the first year. While he believed that the Tabasco brand could be the market leader in five years, he knew the project had some risks. The greatest was the possible loss of goodwill among the many levels of distribution should the product fail. Malespin was aware that few of the 80,000 new products introduced into the market each year survived. A major contributor to this worry was the fact that the Japanese government could ban the product if it did not live up to the inspectors' very high quality standards, including the prohibition of food additives. So far, only samples of the imported Tabasco sauce had been submitted for government inspection, and any question about the company's standards could lead to more rigorous inspection of that product as well. Not only would such an eventuality cloud the company's name, it could substantially increase the difficulty and costs of working in this most important market.

APPENDIX *A*

Selected Facts on Japan and the Japanese[1]

PART I. SELECTED DATA FROM STUDENT REPORT, DECEMBER 1987

Population   Japan was one of the most densely populated nations in the world. The total Japanese population approximated 120 million densely settled, highly literate, and homogeneous inhabitants. The total population was estimated to peak at 130 million soon after the coming century, at that time reaching a zero population growth rate. The land area of Japan was about 146,000 square miles (378,000 square kilometers), approximately the size of the state of Montana.

---

[1] Part I of the material in this appendix was taken from parts of "Tabasco in Japan," a study performed by students at the American Graduate School of International Management in the fall of 1987. Part II is taken from a presentation made by PBI in its yearly presentation to McIlhenny executives at Avery Island.

Over half the population was concentrated within the Tokyo/Osaka urban belt. The population continued to grow at a .6 percent rate annually, but the average age was increasing. It was estimated that, by the year 2000, the elderly (those over age 65) would account for over 15 percent of the total population. Japan currently had the highest life expectancy in the world for both males and females, at 72.2 and 77.4 years, respectively. The total labor force was over 60 million. Japanese women were becoming increasingly significant in Japanese industry. Currently, women were over one third of the total work force.

Language and education Japanese was the language of Japan and was understood throughout the land. There were regional dialects, but on the whole the language was the same. The writing system consisted of the three alphabets of Hiragana, Katakana, and Kanji (Chinese characters). Japan had a literacy rate of 99.7 percent, which was one of the highest in the world. There was compulsory and free education up to the age of 15. English was a required subject from junior high through college. About 41 percent of men and 33 percent of women went on to higher education.

Religion The basic religions of Japan were Buddhism and the Japanese religion of Shinto. However, some Japanese (0.8 percent) practiced Christianity and other religions. Most Japanese actively practiced Buddhism only when honoring the dead. Shintoism, on the other hand, was associated with happy occasions such as weddings, purification of buildings, ground-breaking ceremonies, etc. Many national holidays were closely related to significant religious events.

Psychographics Traditionally, housewives held the purse strings in the Japanese family. Except for very large purchases, the housewife made most shopping decisions. Typically, the Japanese housewife made several trips a week to the neighborhood grocery store.

The Japanese consumer was one of the most demanding in the world. She was brand conscious and expected high quality regardless of price. Because of the immeasurable number of consumer goods available (both foreign and domestic), the Japanese consumer placed great emphasis on the reputation of the producer. When it came to consumer goods, the Japanese were obsessed not only with product quality, but also with the way the product was packaged. The market almost seemed to require "over-packaging."

The *Shinjinrui* (new humankind) was a new breed of image-conscious Japanese consumer who was the driving force behind the current restructuring of the Japanese retail industry. The young adults' affluence and changing personal value system had forced mom-and-pop corner store retailers to specialize or be left behind. Specialty stores carrying a single line of merchandise continued to gain share in the Japanese market. In many cases, their success was a result of their ability to market a slice of American life. The young Japanese generation was very attuned to American culture.

Fish, vegetables, rice, or noodles were the main fare of most Japanese, but such food as pizza, hamburgers, steak, etc., had been receiving attention among younger Japanese consumers. The Japanese tended to distinguish types of food depending on the occasion and location. For example, pizza, hamburgers, or fried chicken could replace Chinese or Japanese food for lunch. These types of food were usually consumed for lunch or a snack rather than as a main dish at dinner. Traditional Japanese cooking was often time consuming and required the preparation of many kinds of food; as many as 30 dishes might be served at one meal.

The Japanese did not invite guests into their homes as frequently as Americans did. This was partially because Japanese homes were not large enough to accommodate guests. Seventy-six percent of the population were urban dwellers, and Japanese urbanites often lived in very small apartments, or "rabbit hutches," as some foreigners called them.

Legal environment By far the most common problem experienced by exporters of food to Japan was the prohibition of food additives. There were several hundred inadvertent violations per year. Consumer co-ops existed that viewed additives as one of the key trade issues, ranking them more important than market access or pricing and distribution of goods. Japan allowed 347 synthetic chemical compounds to be used as food additives, fewer than in many western countries.

Japan's customs tariff was administered by the Ministry of Finance through its Customs Bureau. All imported food products had to be labeled in Japanese. Any artificial coloring or preservatives, the name and address of the importer, and the date of manufacture had to be stated on the outside label.

There were few legal restrictions on advertising in Japan. Commercials for liquor and cigarettes flourished, and sexy images were not uncommon. One of the few restraints placed on advertising concerned the amount of time allotted to commercials during each broadcasting hour: the limit was set at six minutes. However, networks had colluded with advertisers in finding a loophole: by rearranging program scheduling, they stretched hourly advertising to eight minutes.

Income distribution and expenditure Japan's gross national product was the second largest in the Free World, amounting to approximately half of U.S. GNP. The average family income was between ¥4 and ¥6 million, which at an exchange rate of ¥142.41 to the dollar (as of September 11, 1987) equaled $28,000 to $42,000. Japan had one of the highest savings rates in the world, at slightly under 20 percent of total net income. Real disposable income had stagnated since 1978, resulting in more women entering or remaining in the work force. Because of the contribution of working women to the family budget, two-income families were able to save and consume more.

Communication Japan was ideally suited for much mass-media advertising because of its literate, highly concentrated, and homogeneous population. There were over 4,000 advertising agencies servicing the country through newspapers, television, magazines, radio, and outdoor advertising. Traditionally, Japanese advertising agencies had assumed the role of "space broker," buying media space or time and reselling it to clients. The top 5 advertising agencies in Japan did over 50 percent of the total business, with the largest, Dentsu, accounting for 26.5 percent of the total. There were 102 commercial television broadcasters across Japan, 5 in the Greater Tokyo area alone. The largest national daily newspapers were the *Yomiuri* and the *Asahi.* Each printed roughly 13 million copies (morning and evening editions) and carried 37 percent of all newspaper advertising.

Distribution For a foreign company looking to establish a presence in Japan, the most common approach to market entry was the use of the existing distribution channels of the large trading companies (sogo shosha). They could handle up to 25,000 different products and provide a range of services that included financing, warehousing, transporting, wholesaling, and servicing. However, many foreign companies believed that the sogo shoshas were too large and would not aggressively market their products. Of the 2,300 U.S. companies operating in Japan, the majority chose subsidiaries or joint ventures.

The traditional distribution system was changing, albeit gradually, to the advantage of the foreign manufacturer. This was partially a result of the formation and growth of specialty, chain, and convenience stores. Recently, supermarkets and department stores had been moving toward selling their own brands.

PART II. EXCERPTS FROM A PBI PRESENTATION TO MCILHENNY, 1988

A. Macroenvironment Overview

1. Japan's population is about 122 million. Its GNP is the second largest in the free world at $2.5 trillion. In consumer spending and capital investment, Japan's domestic market is the world's second largest.

2. The typical Japanese household consists of 4 persons living on an average monthly income of about $3,600, nearly 85 percent of which is disposable. Purchasing power in dollars has doubled since 1981.

3. Japanese consumers can afford to be selective and choose products that meet strict standards of quality. Ownership of consumer durables is high, with over 98 percent of households owning refrigerators, washing machines, and color televisions. Central heating is uncommon, and space heaters remain the most prevalent way to heat residences.

4. Standards of education are high—compulsory through 9th grade, but 95 percent of all students go on to senior high school and 35 percent on to higher education. The five leading newspapers have a combined morning circulation of more than 25 million.

5. Medical and health facilities are good, with life expectancy among the highest in the world, and nearly the entire population is covered by national or company health insurance provided at a cost that varies according to income.

6. Crime-related injury is low. In 1985 there were 15 murders per million population in Japan (compared with 79 in the U.S. and 37 in the U.K.). Property crime is low, while arrest and conviction rates are very high.

7. Housing standards are lower than western industrialized countries, since both land and construction are expensive in Japan. About 60 percent of Japanese households own their homes.

8. Japanese consumers spend less time at home than people in other industrialized countries. The number of workers having only a five-day workweek is

increasing but is still far lower than in the U.S. The number of national holidays is greater than in the U.S. or Germany, but companies give fewer individual paid holidays to employees. The working year in Japan in recent years has been 253 days (compared with 233 in the U.S. and 230 in the U.K.). The Japanese take 10 days paid vacation yearly (compared with 19 in the U.S. and 31 in Germany).

B. Japanese Consumers

1. Consumer spending in Japan is highly influenced by the compensation used by most companies. Although changing, the features of the current system show that wages are tied to seniority and that lifetime employment provides security for significant portions of the population and their families. Also, the practice of paying semiannual bonuses coincides with the two gift-giving seasons. The bonuses are paid in mid-summer and in December, the best times for purchases of high-quality foods, accessories, and other gifts as well as for major consumer durables such as color televisions, VCRs, etc. These bonus seasons are prime marketing targets for both domestic producers and imported goods manufacturers.

2. The largest expenditures in the typical family's budget are for food, transportation, communication, reading and recreation, and apparel. The Japanese have a reputation for demanding quality at reasonable cost and place emphasis on product appearance and packaging as well as superior functions.

3. The Japanese sense of taste for color is affected by a long heritage and differs from that of most other nations. For consumer items other than clothing, there has been a trend toward individuality, leading to a wider variety of colors in appliances and interior furnishings.

4. The Japanese diet has become greatly influenced by other cuisines, and families eat a wide range of foods.

5. The Japanese market is highly segmentable by income, region, age, sex, and lifestyle. Mass media and compulsory education have had substantial influence on growing homogeneity, but climate, food, and consumer preferences nevertheless vary from region to region.

6. Different age groups in Japan have very different tastes and lifestyles. While a majority of men go on to university, more women attend shorter programs at junior colleges. Single working women have high discretionary incomes. After marriage, women leave their jobs to take care of the household and budget, while men concentrate on career advancement within the company.

C. Dietary Habits and Trends

1. The Japanese diet has been strongly influenced by other countries' cuisines over the past 15 years and has become more westernized and diversified. It is characterized by a high consumption of cereals and fish, and by a low consumption of dairy products.

2. As a proportion of food expenditures, rice has declined since 1970, and bread has taken up the slack. Fish and meat expenditures have increased, while spending on dairy products has declined slightly.

3. The proportion of frozen foods consumed has risen with the increase in ownership of home freezers, and a rise in the ownership of microwave ovens has laid the groundwork for an increasing use of prepared frozen foods and oven-cooked foods:

							Prepared
Year	Rice	Bread	Fish	Meat	Vegetables	Dairy	Foods
1970	¥41,890	5,814	44,670	33,189	44,830	24,791	12,044
	(20.2)*	(2.8)	(21.6)	(16.0)	(21.6)	(12.0)	(5.8)
1986	¥74,397	24,059	130,191	96,567	112,663	42,657	61,972
	(13.7)	(4.4)	(24.0)	(17.8)	(20.8)	(7.9)	(11.4)

Annual Household Expenditures—Major Food Items

* Figures in parentheses indicate percentage of food expenditures.

4. The predominant flavors in Japan tend to remain the traditional ones, such as soy sauce and miso, but the Japanese diet has diversified to a great extent. Many products in the growing category of prepared foods are sauces and bases for Chinese and other types of cuisine.

5. Although the Japanese welcome an increasing variety of foods, they still generally tend to prefer the milder flavors. In addition, foods are presented in a pleasing manner—attractive to the eye with subtle combinations of color and design.

6. Salt intake, most of which comes from the traditional flavorings, has been high in the past but has dropped as consumers have become more concerned with salt-related health problems. Growing concern with health has also created a growing demand for low-calorie foods.

D. Summaries of Market Research Surveys

1. Sumitomo Bank: *Eating Habits in the Gourmet Age.* 800 wives of salaried workers in Tokyo and Osaka (multiple answers).
   - 73% often watch TV programs featuring eating and cooking.
   - 64% try to choose foods without additives.
   - 59% like to read books and articles on dining out.
   - 22% think they are "gourmet"; 44% definitely do not.
   - 55% of families dine out once a month or more.

2. Ministry of Health and Welfare: *National Nutrition Survey.* 7,000 households throughout the country.
   - Intake of animal fat continues to decrease.
   - Intake of salt continues to decrease.
   - Levels of calcium considered inadequate by Ministry of Health.
   - Intake of green vegetables continues to increase.

3. Ajinomoto: *Food Preferences.* 5,000 men and women aged 12 and up in 16 cities around the country.
   - Those below the age of 30 prefer a variety of western foods.
   - Those aged 50 and up prefer traditional Japanese foods.
   - Those in their 30s and 40s have no strong likes or dislikes.
   - Men generally tend to prefer protein foods.
   - Women seem to prefer carbohydrates.

Source: Company records.

APPENDIX *B*

McIlhenny Company: Japan
Selected Findings from Focus-Group Study (conducted October 12, 1987)

I. OBJECTIVE:

To evaluate the concept of a Tabasco brand canned spaghetti meat sauce and to estimate future potential for this product in Japan.

II. RESEARCH SCHEME:

1. Focus Group Participants—Users of canned spaghetti meat sauce. Half of the participants use it 2–3 times per month, and the rest use it less often (no habitual usage).

2. Region—Tokyo and suburban areas.

3. Sampling—Two groups of eight participants.
   Group No. 1   Housewives from 23–46 years old with annual income of ¥4 million or more.
   Group No. 2   Single women 21–30 years old with annual income of ¥2.5 million or more.

III. FINDINGS:

Conditions of Usage and Purchase

Housewives' group Demographics of participants' family members are widely dispersed. The largest family is seven members of three generations. Children vary from kindergarten to adult ages. Eating habits include Japanese, western, and Chinese dishes, but there is an inclination toward western-style foods. Spaghetti is one dish favored by children and appears on the family's dinner menu frequently.

Although participants make small efforts at consuming lots of vegetables and maintaining a low-sodium diet, they are not very strict about it, and the desire for tasty food seems to be somewhat stronger.

Dining-out frequency is two-to-three times per month, and spaghetti is one of the meals ordered most often. On these occasions, they tend to order Tarako (cod eggs), Natto (soy beans), Wafu (soy sauce), and other flavors that they don't usually prepare at home.

Single women's group All but one live with their parents and all but one bring their lunch to work. All claim their cooking repertoire is very limited. They eat out two or three times per week and often frequent spaghetti restaurants, where they order sauces not usually home prepared such as Tarako (cod eggs), white sauce, etc.

Household usage About 70 percent of the participants use canned spaghetti meat sauce 1–3 times per month, and the other 30 percent, most of whom are housewives, use it once per week. Usage by housewives varies from normal meals to lunch with children, late-night snacks, sudden visitors, and Sunday lunch. When they have time, they add meat or vegetables that are on hand such as green peppers, carrots, onions, tomatoes, and mushrooms. Spices added are usually oregano, cinnamon, black pepper, Tabasco, basil, or flavorings such as broth, Worcestershire sauce, and wine according to taste. If time does not allow for additional ingredients, they use it as is.

Compared with the housewives, single women tend to use canned spaghetti meat sauce for breakfast or lunch on days when the mothers are away, or when supper has not been made for them. Most of them simply heat the sauce and put Tabasco on it.

In most cases, usage of the sauce is for two or more people—especially housewives who eat with their children.

Utilization of canned meat sauce varies from such dishes as gratin and lasagna to potato casseroles and stews for housewives. Single women say they use it for cheese casseroles with noodles or broccoli and often simply use it as stuffing for hot-dog buns.

The majority of housewives use 2–3 300-gram cans at once, whereas single women use only 1 can.

Reasons for usage The major attraction for canned spaghetti meat sauce is that it is "very handy and easy to use," and some participants think the flavor is close to sauce in restaurants. Also, it's difficult to make from scratch.

The reasons housewives add things to canned meat sauce are to: (1) eliminate the can smell, (2) increase the meat content, and (3) insure enough flavoring to suit everyone's taste. A psychological element is that they don't want to appear lazy by using sauce "as is." Historically, most housewives started using canned sauce when they got married, while single women began usage five to six years ago in high school home economics classes.

The most common reason for use is "Mother used it." Other reasons given include TV commercials, noted products on store shelves, and heard about it from others.

Although retort pouch and packaged sauces from hotels or restaurants are sometimes used by participants, canned meat sauce is by far the main vehicle. Single women think the retort pouch is convenient because of its one-serving size, but housewives say the pouch is uneconomical and show little intent to purchase.

Canned-sauce and retort-pouch comparisons Advantages of the can include long storage time, easy to store, restaurant flavor, and easy to prepare. Advantages of the retort pouch are convenient for one, easy to prepare, no can smell; disadvantages are insufficient amount and hands get dirty.

Purchasing conditions Within the single-women's group, two claim they buy the product themselves, while others eat the brand their mother buys. Hardly any participants recognize any taste difference between one brand and another.

Housewives claim they buy canned meat sauce when supermarkets are having a sale or when they don't have much other shopping to do. They buy from two to four cans at each purchase.

Most participants show no brand loyalty and are only concerned that the brand name is a well-known one or that they have seen the product advertised on TV. Taste is thought to be standard among most brands.

Brands Purchased		
Kewpi	9	• Kewpi is purchased by both groups, but housewives buy mostly Heinz.
Heinz	5	
Kagome	5	• Reasons for purchasing Kewpi are: commercials, packaging (red and white), used to taste, and usage of other Kewpi products.
Mama	3	
Oh-My	2	
Meidi-Ya	1	
		• Reasons for purchasing Heinz are: used to taste, safe product, and children seem to like it. No real brand loyalty noted among participants.

Other brand images and reasons are: Mama: often discounted and same brand as spaghetti noodles. Meidi-Ya: high quality, reliable, can be used as a gift. Kagome: same brand as famous ketchup.

Housewives said that average prices for the 300-gram can were ¥250, but they said it could be bought for ¥200 on sale. Single women had very little idea on prices but thought that ¥300 sounded reasonable.

Flavor Evaluations

Canned meat sauce General complaints about flavor and contents of canned meat sauce are made concerning its sweetness and lack of spice, but are for the most part focused on the scarcity of meat. Both housewives and single women, however, think that's all they can expect from canned sauces and seem to value convenience above any other factors.

Housewives Flavor suits everyone, but too sweet/not enough spice; too thin/watery; insufficient amount; tomato too strong; flavor unsatisfying; strong can smell; gets lumpy. Therefore: add Tabasco and more spices, more base ingredients, and more parmesan cheese.

Single women   School lunch flavor, children like it, but not enough meat; too sour or too sweet; too much for single serving; too rich, can't finish. Therefore: add sugar, put Tabasco for more flavor, add spices for distinct taste.

Evaluation of Overall Concept

Brand not shown to participants   Housewives' group said the concept photo had "lots of ingredients and seems thick enough not to soak through the noodles ... actually looks very tasty." On the other hand, single women showed very little interest in the photo, saying "all products look alike."

Both groups, nevertheless, felt a difference between the concept brand and the ordinary types. Housewives felt the concept brand is one that can be served to family or visitors without having to add anything. All of them wanted to try it and thought it was a "real meat sauce." The single women split into two factions: One saying they had no interest in it, since "all canned meat sauces taste the same," and if they want a special dish, they could go to a restaurant. The other half of single women wanted to try the concept brand because they could make it and "it really looks thick and complete."

Standard and mild types   Single women thought the brand was aimed at those who were unsatisfied with conventional products and those who like spicy and hot tastes. The housewives think the concept is attractive because it seems to have an adult taste and uses many spices. Both groups felt the concept sauce would be difficult to make at home by themselves with any success.

Pricing of ¥500   Housewives accept this price if the product is tasty, since it would still be cheaper than going out to eat. Also, most said the price should be in accord with the taste.

Some of the single women felt it would be acceptable if tasty and if ¥500 is for two servings, but others said it was expensive for a canned meat sauce and showed surprise and hesitation. Most said they would go to a special restaurant if the price difference was trivial.

100% lean beef   Participants felt that the secret in making an ideal sauce is to use 100% beef. Many do not know what kind of meat is in the canned sauces they currently use, a fact especially true with the single women's group. It was pointed out that it would be better to use ground beef than shredded beef or chunks of beef.

Some felt that the phrase "Beef—40 percent of the contents" was somewhat ambiguous and desired a clearer, easily understood explanation of all ingredients in the product.

Tabasco brand shown to participants   The initial response from both groups upon hearing the brand "Tabasco" was similar: "It sounds hot and spicy." The housewives said they welcomed the concept of a Tabasco brand as a flavor for adults, while the single women showed surprise, having a strong image of "Tabasco" as a spice manufacturer.

Although all the participants thought about a spicy type for adults and a mild type, it was a common opinion that the "Tabasco" name gives a direct impression that it is too hot and spicy for children, regardless of the two different types. Therefore, it was felt that a phrase which emphasizes its mild flavor be used to convey the idea that it would suit anyone's taste.

Some housewives thought Tabasco originated from the U.S.A. or Mexico. Most, however, thought it came from Italy, where pasta has its origins, since Tabasco is used on pizza and spaghetti in Japan. Single women had an impression that Tabasco came from some area in Latin America.

Even after the brand name "Tabasco" was opened to the participants, there was no change in response to the ¥500 price inquiry put to them earlier regarding the 300-gram can. The housewives were still positive, and the single women were split into two groups.

Evaluation of Current Packaging

Both groups showed amazingly similar tastes in packaging. Favorable responses came forth on all the existing brands except for extremely negative comments on Mama and Showa.

Type of packaging   About half the participants prefer litho cans, claiming paper labels (1) are easily torn, (2) fade quickly, and (3) get dirty if stored a long time. Some showed a strong rejection of paper labels and said they project an "image of pineapple cans." The other half say they receive a high-class image from paper labeling.

Colors   Both groups shared the common opinion that a combination of red, white, and green colors give an Italian image. However, nearly every manufacturer uses them in some way, and group participants suggested a unique design and color pattern to create a high-class image.

Tabasco logo   Housewives think the Tabasco logo is quite fashionable and feel it should be on the label, using its quality image to assist in advertising and promotions. The single women split again; half saying the logo should be used, and half insisting it will confuse the consumer by implying the product is a type of spicy flavoring and not a meat sauce.

Source: Company records.

APPENDIX *C*

McIlhenny Company: Japan
Second Focus Group, Conducted with Actual Product

PARTICIPANT PROFILES

Housewives

Twelve housewives aged between 25 and 45 who reside in the suburbs of Tokyo. Four participants have no children. The others all have two children each from kindergarten to high-school ages. In terms of eating habits, most of them make home meals where children's tastes get first consideration since husbands arrive home late. The trend, therefore, is to light and sweet flavors. Those with no children cook easy-to-prepare foods when husbands come home late and tend to favor hot and spicy tastes.

Single Working Women

Four single working women participated. Two of them work full time, and the two others work part time. One lives with her parents, two live by themselves, and one lives with a grandfather. All but the one who lives with her parents prepare meals regularly. Most of them claim they dine out almost half of the time. The three who cook regularly make simple meals at home.

EATING AND PURCHASING HABITS

Almost half the participants claim they eat spaghetti two or three times a month, and the other half claim they eat it at least once a week. Housewives with children use it largely for lunch or snacks on holidays, when schools do not serve lunches, or when the husband comes home late. Housewives with no children and single women don't specify times of use.

Housewives with children normally add some ingredients like onions, carrots, mushrooms, and meat for nutritional purposes, and tend to adjust flavors by adding spices and some condiments such as ketchup or tomato puree. Housewives with no children and single women use salt, pepper, Tabasco, and often spices and Worcestershire sauce or soy sauce. They take more advantage of convenience factors.

Housewives with children also tend to make other dishes—such as eggplant gratin, omelets, and lasagna—with canned spaghetti meat sauce.

TASTE TESTING

Mild Meat Sauce

Close to conventional meat sauce; weak tomato taste, seems thin, lacks spices, lacks richness.

Regular Meat Sauce

Plus points: conventional flavor, flexible usage; minus points: instant taste, ordinary. Because of its light flavor and admitted flexibility, nearly half felt that it would be suitable for children. [*Note:* The focus group moderator cautions that panel members feel a psychological need to be critical of the product.]

Spicy Meat Sauce

Nearly all of the participants in this, the second, focus group felt that the spicy variation of sauce offers a unique alternative to what is currently on the market in Japan. The level of spiciness is judged to be stimulating and with a flavor that differs from other products.

Those who prefer a spicy product (about one-third of the group participants) are usually in their 20s and feel the spicy product has both flavor and character. The rest of the participants feel it is too spicy and kills the flavor of the meat sauce itself, leaving a lingering taste which is unsuitable to them.

Most housewives feel it is too strong and spicy for children to eat, and the overall impression is that the product is one for young adults and grown men.

The smell of red peppers in the sauce is believed to be attractive to men, and it was felt that the sauce would go well with beer in the evening.

Plus points: elaborate taste, good overall aroma; minus points: too spicy for children.

RELATIVE EVALUATION

Almost 40 percent of the participants picked the mild meat sauce as the best among the flavors, and if we consider the number of second-place votes mild meat sauce received, that flavor gets a 60 percent vote of confidence.

Family considerations: Housewives with younger children chose the mild meat sauce and the regular meat sauce because of their relatively sweeter flavors. The choices by single women were spread across the mild, regular, and spicy meat sauces in near-equal sectors. The spicy meat sauce was least popular due to its high spice level.

CATCH-PHRASE EVALUATION

Ten "catch phrases" were shown to respondents: (1) Beefy sauce made by Tabasco, the spaghetti specialist; (2) A supreme sauce with supreme beef—dedicated to spaghetti lovers; (3) Pasta luxury—supreme beef and secret flavors; (4) Ungrudging amount of supreme beef—ungrudgingly real; (5) Thick and profound—finished with supreme beef and ripe spices; (6) Starting today, learn the taste of a real sauce full of selected beef; (7) Real sauce with simmered beef—the epitome of a luxurious pasta; (8) Supreme beef meets supreme spices; (9) Full of the tasty flavor of excellent beef. The true sauce of luxury; (10) Finally—a sauce that's too tasty for words.

General comments: Participants in this focus group chose each of the ten proposed catch phrases except "Starting today, learn the taste of a real sauce full of selected beef."

Fully 40 percent of the participants liked the last copy best of all. Reasons for this particular selection were: simple and unpretentious; concise and clear; sounds nice; easy to imagine.

The phrase that was thought to be second by the group was: "Supreme beef meets supreme spices."

Reasons given were: easy to understand; simple and clean.

The third-place phrase was: "A supreme sauce with supreme beef—dedicated to spaghetti lovers." This phrase was chosen based on the idea that it sounds as though people would like to hear it in commercials on TV or read it in magazine and newspaper advertisements.

PURCHASING INTENTIONS

(Prior to being told the price): Judging from the average existing price of canned sauces, which is felt to be between ¥250–¥260 at most supermarkets, housewives showed an intent to purchase if it is below ¥350. They claim they would definitely buy if it were ¥300 or less.

On the other hand, single women showed intent to purchase if the price is ¥340–¥350 or up to ¥400 at most; reflecting a wider range than housewives.

(After being told the price): When a target price of ¥350 was shown, most participants showed intent to purchase once on a trial basis, and if it doesn't taste any different from the others, they will go back to their old brands.

The image of canned meat sauce is that they all taste about the same, and the focus-group participants felt that the ¥300 price will be lowered to the mid-¥200 range on sale eventually.

A couple of participants admit that their decision on purchasing is affected greatly by the image they get from packaging.

Source: Company records.

CASE 7-2 OHMEDA MONITORING SYSTEMS*

ooking out his office window at the magnificent Front Range of the Colorado Rockies, Joseph W. Pepper, General Manager of Ohmeda Monitoring Systems, was deep in thought concerning the future of Finapres, a relatively new Ohmeda product. Introduced in 1987, the product had not lived up to its expectations. Now, in mid-June 1990, Pepper was considering a number of options. His choice, he knew, would have a significant impact on Ohmeda Monitoring Systems.

BACKGROUND

Finapres (the name was derived from its use of finger arterial pressure) was the only product on the market providing continuous noninvasive blood pressure monitoring (CNIBP). As such it was the only unique product that Ohmeda could offer in 1990.

Originally introduced to the market in 1987, initial results had been disappointing. Its introduction in the United States had been generally unsuccessful. Results in Europe, and internationally, had been somewhat better but still had failed to meet the firm's expectations. Concerns about the product had led Ohmeda to stop shipments on May 1, 1990, pending a review of product problems and the overall situation.

At an all-day meeting on May 23, 1990, marketing research, field sales, and R&D had presented information on the status of Finapres. In particular, R&D had given its assessment as to the likelihood that proposed product changes and improvements would solve some of the product's shortcomings.

The specter of the disappointing initial introduction, and the uncertainty that R&D could improve the product sufficiently to satisfy all the concerns, hung over the decision to commit more funds to the product. An unsuccessful reintroduction would further hurt Ohmeda's credibility, both with customers and with the field sales force. On the other hand, successful reintroduction of Finapres would ensure a strong, and possibly dominant, position in the noninvasive blood pressure monitoring market, plus the possibility of increased sales of other monitoring products as Finapres was combined with other Ohmeda products into packaged systems.

Subsequently, Pepper had many discussions with his key managers regarding their views of Finapres. In early June he visited a number of Ohmeda customers and distributors in Japan, many of whom were very interested in Finapres. Although there were several unanswered questions, it was up to Pepper to make the key decisions concerning Finapres.

BOC/OHMEDA

Ohmeda Monitoring Systems was a business unit of The BOC Group, a multinational firm headquartered in Windlesham, England. The Group had an international portfolio described as "world-competitive" businesses, principally industrial gases, health care products and services, and high-vacuum technology. The Group operated in some 60 countries and employed nearly 40,000 people. Group sales in 1989 were £2,821.5[1] million, up 10% from 1988. Group profits, after tax, were £225.1 million, up 24% from 1989. For the Group as a whole, the Americas and Asia/Pacific contributed the largest volume. Europe, however, contributed as much profit, before tax, as the Americas and Asia/Pacific combined. Exhibit 1 shows a partial organization chart of The BOC Group.

BOC Health Care

BOC Health Care provided products and services for critical care in hospitals and the home. Their equipment, therapies and pharmaceuticals were used in operating rooms (OR), recovery rooms (PACU), and intensive care (ICU) and cardiac care (CCU) units throughout the world. Worldwide revenue in 1989 was £668.2 million, up 25% from 1988, which contributed

---

[1] On December 28, 1989, £1 = $1.605. Group results were stated in £. Ohmeda Monitoring Systems' results were calculated in $ and then were translated to £ for inclusion in Group results.

---

* This case was prepared by Professor H. Michael Hayes and Brice Henderson of the University of Colorado at Denver. Copyright © 1990 by the University of Colorado at Denver. Reproduced by permission.

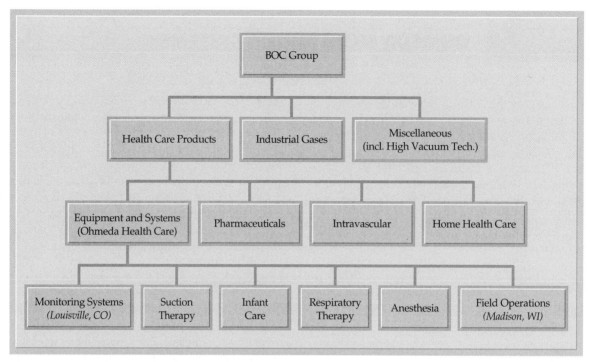

EXHIBIT 1   Partial Organization Chart, BOC Group

£106.5 million in operating profit, up 17% from 1988. Revenue in Europe was £166.6 million. In the Americas it was £403.1 million, of which something over 90% came from the United States. Divisions of BOC Health Care were organized around pharmaceuticals, home health care, intravascular devices, and equipment and systems.

Ohmeda Health Care

Ohmeda Health Care (the equipment and systems component) was an autonomous division of BOC Health Care. It was made up of five major business units, plus a field operations unit. The five business units manufactured products for suction therapy, infant care, respiratory therapy, anesthesia, and monitoring systems. Field operations provided field sales and sales support worldwide on a pooled basis to all the business units. Exhibit 2 shows a partial organization chart of Field Operations. A 1985 reorganization had put all business decisions in the hands of the business general managers and established profit of the business unit as a major performance measure. In 1990, the managers of the business units and the manager of field operations reported to the President of Ohmeda Health Care, Richard Leazer, who, in turn,

reported to the Managing Director of BOC Health Care, W. Dekle Rountree.

Ohmeda Monitoring Systems

Ohmeda Monitoring Systems (headquartered in Louisville, Colorado) designed, manufactured and sold monitoring equipment for a number of segments of the health care industry. It focused its business activities on three classes of products:

• Oximetry products, used to measure oxygen content in arterial blood.

• Gas analysis products, used to measure a patient's respiratory gas levels.

• Noninvasive blood pressure measurement products.

Applications for these products were found in a wide variety of departments within hospitals and other health care facilities. Products were usually sold to the health care facility, either directly by the field sales force or by a distributor. Some products, however, were also sold to equipment manufacturers (OEMs) for incorporation in a larger measurement package.

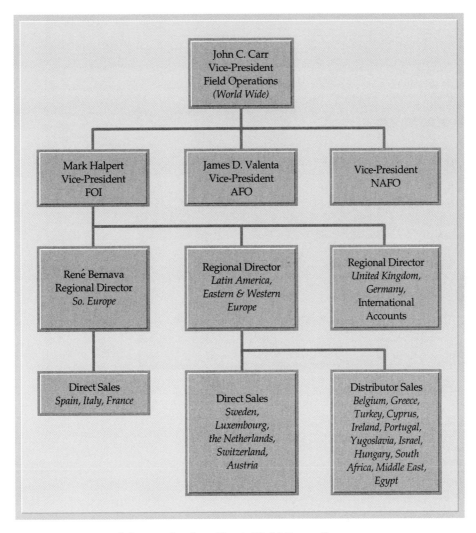

EXHIBIT 2 Partial Organization Chart, Field Operations

Most Ohmeda oximetry and Finapres products consisted of a "box" containing the hardware, software and a display unit, and a probe, or cuff, to allow a noninvasive way to measure the parameter of interest. These were of two types, disposable or reusable, and were designed to be attached to the patient's toe, foot, finger, hand, or ear, depending on the application. Exhibit 3 provides a catalog listing of probes.

Ohmeda had access to Finapres technology by virtue of a worldwide exclusive license obtained from Research Unit Biomedical Instrumentation TNO (Amsterdam, the Netherlands). Many other technologies had also been acquired, either by license or outright purchase.

Ohmeda estimated that the noninvasive monitoring market was $1.2 billion worldwide, with 60% of the market in the United States. Overall, its market share was 15% of those segments it served. In selected categories, however, its market share was considerably higher. With considerable variation by country and specific product, Ohmeda estimated the growth rate of its served market at 5–10% per year.

The competitive picture for Ohmeda was complex. Its main competitors were U.S.-based firms. Many of its products, however, faced strong competition from European firms. In oximetry there were an estimated 25 competitors, although only 4 had significant shares. Major competitors and estimated market shares were:

Ohmeda gives you the right probe to monitor every patient, conveniently and easily.

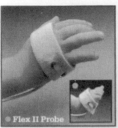

● Flex II Probe

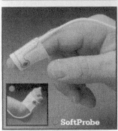

SoftProbe

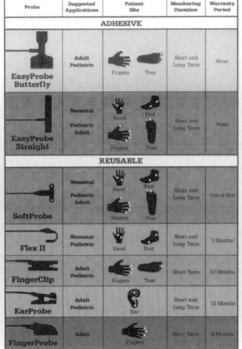

Probe	Suggested Applications	Patient Site	Monitoring Duration	Warranty Period
ADHESIVE				
EasyProbe Butterfly	Adult Pediatric	Fingers Toes	Short and Long Term	None
EasyProbe Straight	Neonatal Pediatric Adult	Hand Foot / Fingers Toes	Short and Long Term	None
REUSABLE				
SoftProbe	Neonatal Pediatric Adult	Hand Foot / Fingers Toes	Short and Long Term	Out-of-Box
Flex II	Neonatal Pediatric	Hand Foot	Short and Long Term	3 Months
FingerClip	Adult Pediatric	Fingers Toes	Short Term	12 Months
EarProbe	Adult Pediatric	Ear	Short and Long Term	12 Months
FingerProbe	Adult	Fingers	Short Term	6 Months

FingerClip

● FingerProbe

● EarProbe

Probe	Part Number
EasyProbe-Butterfly (8 ft.) (6-pack)	0380-1000-095
EasyProbe-Straight (8 ft.) (6-pack)	0380-1000-098
EasyProbe-Butterfly (12 ft.) (6-pack)	0380-1000-112
EasyProbe-Straight (12 ft.) (6-pack)	0380-1000-111
SoftProbe (6-pack)	0380-1000-051
Flex II Probe (8 ft.)	0380-1000-080
Flex II Probe (12 ft.)	0380-1000-081
FingerClip Probe (8 ft.)	0380-1000-043
FingerClip Probe (12 ft.)	0380-1000-042
EarProbe	0380-1000-021
FingerProbe (8 ft.)	0380-1000-019
FingerProbe (12 ft.)	0380-1000-023

Probe Accessories	Part Number
SoftProbe Tape-Narrow (100/pkg.)	0380-1000-084
SoftProbe Tape-Wide (100/pkg.)	0380-1000-097
Posey Wrap Accessory Kit for Flex II (24/pkg.)	0380-0800-104
Adhesive Disks (10 sheets of 12 disks)	0380-1500-082
EarProbe Stabilizers (10/pkg.)	0380-1500-003
Headband	0380-1500-002
Probe Cable Clips (2/pkg.)	0380-0100-001

Ohmeda
We monitor life.

1315 West Century Drive
Louisville CO 80027 USA
To Order: 1 800 345 2700
Telephone: 303 666 7001

A Division of The BOC Group Inc

A BOC Health Care
Company
Critical Care
Worldwide

©1989 The BOC Group Inc
Form #E041A Printed in USA
2 91 5

Source: © 1989 by The BOC Group, Inc.

EXHIBIT 3   Ohmeda Monitoring Systems

Nellcor (U.S.)	50%		Datex (Finland)	16%
Ohmeda (U.S.)	30%		Ohmeda	15%
Criticare (U.S.)	10%		Siemens (Germany)	14%
Novametrix (U.S.)	8%		Hewlett-Packard (U.S.)	12%

In respiratory gases there were an estimated 12 competitors. Major competitors and estimated market shares were:

In blood pressure measurement only five companies competed. With an 80% share, Critikon (U.S.) dominated the noninvasive market with its oscillometric, or noncontinuous, product. Ohmeda's sales of its noninvasive products represented just 2% of this market.[2]

Based on pretax operating profits in 1989, Ohmeda's financial situation appeared to be healthy. There were concerns, however. As Pepper observed:

> We tend to be more financially driven than market driven. Also, we have not been investing heavily in R&D. As a result, our product line is relatively mature, and I don't know how much longer we can count on present products for high contribution margins.
>
> Finapres is the only major new product that is close to ready to go. Perfecting Finapres, and successfully reintroducing it, would not only produce direct sales, but its uniqueness could also benefit our other monitoring businesses through integrated packages that included a technology available nowhere else. The sales force in Europe, and also in Asia, is very excited about the product, even with its present deficiencies, and believes that with reasonable improvement it could become a major contributor to sales and profits. In the United States there is not the same excitement. There is agreement that if all the product deficiencies could be corrected we would have a real winner, but R&D can't give us any guarantees.

Field Operations

Following the 1985 reorganization of Ohmeda Health Care from a functional organization to the five therapy units, the firm had considered how to organize its field sales operations. Given the complexity of the five product lines, and some desire on the part of the therapy unit managers to have more direct control over the sales forces that represented them, there was considerable support to establish specialized sales forces. There was also support for direct sales, as opposed to extensive use of distributors or dealers. Selling anesthesia equipment, it was argued, was very different from selling patient monitors and other Ohmeda products, both because of product differences and customer buying procedures. Many of Ohmeda's competitors (e.g., Siemens and Hewlett-Packard) relied heavily on direct sales, feeling that distributors or dealers could not provide the required level of technical knowledge and service. Arguing against specialized selling was the belief that it was far more efficient, in terms of time, travel expense, and customer knowledge, to have one salesperson calling on a hospital, rather than three, as was contemplated in one proposed form of organization. Further, there was great concern about the consequences of terminating distributors or dealers, some of whom had been associated with Ohmeda (or its prede-

cessor companies) for over 70 years. Finally, Ohmeda was aware that Baxter-Travenol, the largest medical supplies and equipment company in the world, had specialized its sales force in 1981 but had subsequently gone back to a general sales organization.

After extensive study, it was decided to continue with a pooled form of sales organization, together with pooled product service, customer service, and finance, all reporting to the vice president of Field Operations. As of early 1990 Field Operations had three principal regional components: NAFO, responsible for sales and service in North America (the United States and Canada); FOI, responsible for sales and service in Europe, the Middle East, and Latin America; and AFO, responsible for sales and service in Asia, including Japan. Depending on the particular country, sales were all direct, a combination of direct and dealer, or totally through dealers.

Ohmeda recognized the need for making specialized product knowledge, beyond the expertise of the local salesperson, available quickly to the customer. In NAFO it was assumed that such specialized knowledge could be provided by specialists from manufacturing locations. In FOI and AFO it was deemed impractical for specialists to travel from the United States, and product champions were appointed in the major countries. Paid principally by salary, the product champions supported the sales force for their assigned products in a variety of ways. They were available to call on customers with the salespeople. They held product seminars, either for salespeople or for customer groups. In some instances they acted as missionary salespeople, soliciting orders from new customers. In all instances, they provided a focused communication channel between the field and headquarters marketing. Ohmeda believed that the product champions had played a major role in assisting the introduction of Finapres in Europe. There was also some concern that not enough manpower was available from headquarters to provide similar support to the field sales force in the United States and Canada.

HEALTH CARE MARKETS

The health care industry was one of the largest and most rapidly growing segments of the world economy. While growth was occurring worldwide, the potential for Ohmeda products was greatest in the United States, Europe, Japan, and generally in the developed countries of the world. With certain exceptions, the United States tended to lead the world in the development and use of technologically sophisticated health care prod-

---

[2] Market shares were for the U.S. market.

EXHIBIT 4   U.S. Market Sales Potential in Units, 1990–92

Segment	Potential Sites[a]	Oximetry	Gas Analysis	Blood Pressure	Saturation
OR/PACU	60,000	26,000	31,000	15,000	High
ICU/NICU/CCU	78,000	20,000	15,500	9,750	High
L&D	57,000	10,000	0	4,000	Medium
FLOORS	800,000	15,000	0	2,000	Low
NONHOSP.	65,000	10,500	0	200	Medium

[a] Number of physical locations.

ucts. U.S. manufacturers of such products generally felt that the rest of the world followed the U.S. lead in acceptance and use, with countries in Europe following in as little as six months but with longer delays in other parts of the world.

Hospitals were the principal buyers of Ohmeda products. With some variation, due mainly to government regulations, purchasing practices were similar in the developed countries of the world. All purchases of medical equipment required budgetary approval of the hospital administration. Their purchasing influence, however, was generally inversely related to the complexity of the item. Purchase decisions of disposable supplies and gases, for instance, were generally made solely by the hospital purchasing agent, based on the lowest price. By contrast, capital equipment was invariably selected by the hospital's medical specialists and clinical area end users. Because any machine malfunction was potentially life-threatening, medical specialists were especially concerned with precision, reliability, and safety. In addition, both the sophistication of clinical procedures and the technical expertise and interest of medical specialists were increasing. As a result, the product and clinical knowledge required to sell medical equipment was also increasing.

Ohmeda segmented its market by hospital department or application, as follows:

OR/PACU (Operating Room/Post Anesthetic Care
    Unit or Recovery Room)
ICU/NICU/CCU (Intensive Care Unit/Neonatal Intensive Care Unit/Coronary Care Unit)
L&D (Labor and Delivery)
FLOORS (Basically patients' rooms in hospital wards)
NONHOSPITAL (The growing nonhospital segment, which included ambulances, surgicenters, physicians' offices, dental and home care, for oximetry and blood pressure products)

Sales potential varied substantially, depending on the particular segment and the product, as shown in

Exhibit 4. Segments outside the United States generally had lower saturation levels than in the United States. As was pointed out, however, saturation levels were not always the best indicator of sales potential. In many instances the replacement markets offered high potential as well.

In the operating room, the physician (generally the anesthetist) was the key buying influence for all products. In all other segments decision making was a shared responsibility, as indicated in Exhibit 5. Key buying influencers were thought to be influenced by different factors, in order of importance as indicated below:

Physician	Nurse
Technology	Ergonomics
Ergonomics	Relationship
Relationship	In-service
Price/value	Technology

Technician	Administrator
Serviceability	Company reputation
Technology	Price/value
	Revenue generation

Financial Officer	Material (Purchasing)
Leasing options	Price/value
Total package cost	Total package cost
Reimbursement	Serviceability

Personal contact with key buying influences, by direct sales representatives or distributors, was an essential ingredient to securing an order. Key to success, however, were favorable results from experimental trials, particularly of new products, as reported in medical journals. Manufacturers worked closely with the medical community worldwide to identify opinion leaders interested in equipment who were willing to experiment with it and then publish their results in scholarly journals. Most such experiments were reported in English language journals, but these were widely read in non-English-speaking countries.

EXHIBIT 5 Buying Influencers

	OR	ICU	NICU	PACU	CCU	FLOORS	L&D
Probes	P	NTM	NT	NT	NTM	NTM	NT
Blood pressure	P	PNM	PN	PN	PNM	PNM	PN
Gas analysis	P	PTM	PT	PT	—	—	PT
Oximetry	P	NTM	NT	NT	NTM	PNTM	NT

Abbreviations: P = physician; N = nurse; T = technician; A = administrator; F = financial officer; M = materials (purchasing); OR = operating room; ICU = intensive care unit; NICU = neonatal intensive care unit; PACU = postanesthetic care unit; CCU = coronary care unit; L&D = labor and delivery.

FINAPRES

Modern medicine viewed measurement of arterial blood pressure as essential in the monitoring of patients, both during and after surgery. Traditional monitoring techniques have included both invasive and noninvasive methods. Arterial line monitoring provided continuous measurement but invasion (meaning surgical insertion of a long, small-bore catheter into the radial or femoral arteries) involved the risks of thrombosis, embolism, infections, and nerve injuries. These risks were acceptable when arterial blood samples had to be taken regularly but otherwise were to be avoided.

An oscillometric monitor, such as Critikon's Dinamap, was noninvasive. As commonly used, such a device provided readings automatically every 3–5 minutes or on demand. Dinamap could provide readings more frequently, but this involved considerable patient pain or discomfort. As normally used, therefore, it could miss vital data due to the time lag of the readings. Ohmeda sold a noninvasive blood pressure monitor of this type, manufactured for them, but had not promoted it heavily. Manual methods were noninvasive but were dependent on the skill of the clinician and the application of the correct-size arm cuff and involved even more time lag.

Finapres Technology

In 1967 a Czech physiologist, Dr. Jan Peñaz, patented a method with which it was possible to measure finger arterial pressure noninvasively. Exhibit 6 provides a detailed description of the method. In 1973 the device was demonstrated at the 10th International Conference on Medical and Biological Engineering at Dresden. Subsequently, a group of engineers at the Research Unit Biomedical Instrumentation, TNO in the Netherlands became interested in the technology and constructed a laboratory model and then a model which they felt was clinically and experimentally useful and commercially viable. In 1983 Ohmeda acquired an exclusive license for the Finapres technology.

Finapres and Ohmeda

Although TNO had produced a working model of Finapres, Ohmeda had invested between $2 and $3 million in R&D in order to develop a manufacturable box and cuff and to recode the software to conform to Ohmeda protocols. The resultant design could be built largely on existing equipment, although some $100,000 was required for tooling for the cuff. Prior to commercial introduction, extensive work was done with opinion leaders to establish the credibility of the product. Favorable test results of clinical studies of Finapres were reported in medical journals and were widely distributed to the medical profession. The cost of this work, and other market development expenditures, was roughly equivalent to the cost of R&D.

Ohmeda introduced a commercial design of Finapres in 1987 in the United States and in 1988 in Europe and other world markets. The initial offering consisted of a box, a patient interface module which attached to the patient's hand, and three reusable cuffs (Exhibit 7). It was positioned to compete against invasive measuring products. Although it was expected that it would ultimately be offered to the OEM market, it was originally introduced directly to the OR market. Priced at approximately $9500, it was expected to return a contribution margin in excess of 70% typical for new and unique products in the health equipment industry. Some price resistance was experienced, and the U.S. price was reduced to $8500 six months after introduction. Disappointingly, U.S. sales through 1989 totaled only 200 units.

In 1988 the product was introduced internationally at a U.S. equivalent price of $9600. In contrast to the U.S. introduction, the product was targeted for direct sale at a number of segments in hospitals. As in the United States, price resistance was encountered, and by 1989 the price had been reduced to approximately the U.S. equivalent of $5000.

To some extent, low sales in the United States were blamed on tactical marketing errors, such as the posi-

EXHIBIT 6   Finapres Operating Principles

Arteries transport blood under high pressure to the tissues. The artery walls are strong and elastic; that is, they stretch during systole (when blood is forced onward by contraction of the heart) and recoil during diastole (dilation of the heart when its chambers are filling with blood). This prevent arterial pressure from rising or falling to extremes during the cardiac cycle, thus maintaining a continuous, uninterrupted flow of blood to the tissues. The volume of blood inside the artery increases when it expands and decreases when it contracts. This change in volume is the key phenomenon on which the Peñaz/Finapres technology was based.

In the Finapres system, a cuff with an inflatable bladder was wrapped around the finger (see diagram below). A light source (LED) was directed through the finger and monitored by a detector on the other side. This light was absorbed by the internal structures according to their various densities. The emitted light was an indication of blood volume in the artery. Through a complex servo-mechanism system, the cuff was inflated or deflated to maintain the artery size at a constant level. Thus, cuff pressure constantly equaled arterial pressure and was displayed on the monitor both as an arterial waveform and digitally.

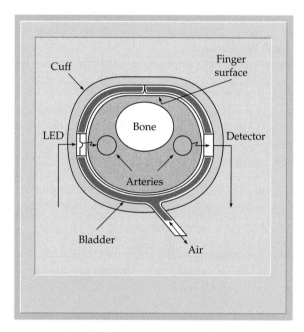

tioning and price of the product at introduction. There were also some technical problems with the system. Some were cosmetic in nature and easily fixed. Others were more serious, both for the clinicians using the equipment and for Ohmeda. Major problems were the difficulty in applying the cuff properly in order to get an accurate reading and drift in readings that occurred after several hours of continuous use, a particularly serious problem in the OR. Another problem was the inability of the equipment to accurately monitor patients with poor blood circulation.

Results were more promising in Europe. The European medical community had been anxious to get access to Finapres. Much had been written about the Peñaz methodology and the system developed by TNO

in the European medical press. The noninvasive aspect of Finapres was particularly attractive. European doctors were less comfortable with arterial line methodology than were their American counterparts. In addition, they tended to be more willing to invest time and effort to learn new technologies, and there was less preoccupation with patient throughput than in the United States.

News of the problems experienced in the ORs in the United States had made penetration of the OR segment in Europe difficult. With its broader contacts, the sales force was able to introduce the product to other segments, particularly in CCU and physiology in teaching hospitals, where stability over long periods of time was either not as critical as in OR or where con-

Ohmeda

**With the Finapres™ Continuous NIBP Monitor,
the pressure is always on.**

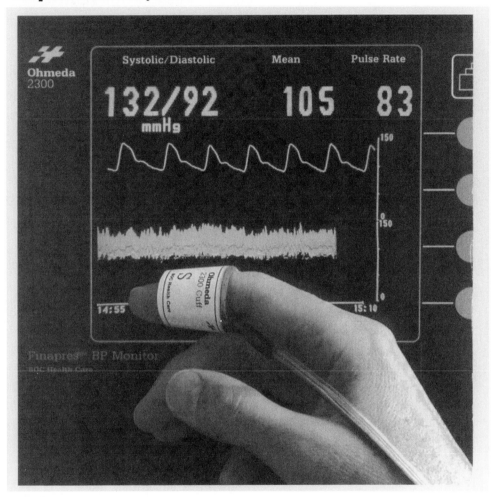

EXHIBIT 7   Finapres Monitoring System

tinuous blood pressure monitoring was of paramount importance. With this approach, supported by the willingness of the sales force to train medical personnel in application of the cuff, the company experienced much greater success, selling a total of 700 units in these markets through 1989.

Commenting on results through 1989, Melvyn Dickinson, International Marketing Manager, observed:

> There are significant differences between the hospital markets in the United States and Europe, and in how our

sales forces sell to them. In the United States, for example, anesthetic machines, made by one of our sister therapy units, are sold by the same field sales force that sells our monitoring equipment. The U.S. machines are made to more stringent requirements and are much more expensive than those sold in Europe. In addition, they tend to be replaced on a 5-year cycle, compared to 10–15 years in, say, Italy. As a result, our sales force in the United States tends to really concentrate on the OR market, whereas in Europe the sales force takes a broader approach.

It's also important to recognize that the key influence for OR purchases is an anesthesiologist, for whom blood pressure is just one of many concerns. In other segments of the hospital, the situation is very different. In the CCU, or the cardiac operating theater, blood pressure is of paramount importance. Not all procedures are lengthy, and even where they are, many cardiologists saw value in CNIBP, even though there was drift. For physiological measurements in research hospitals or in hypertension units, there were even fewer drawbacks, and the clinicians in these situations were much more inclined to take extra care with application of the cuff.

Beyond these differences, we misread the market in general. It had been our assumption that arterial lines [the term for invasive systems] were the major competitors for Finapres. We priced and positioned Finapres accordingly. Unfortunately, our promotion didn't get this position established in the minds of our customers. As it turned out, many customers viewed the oscillometric machines as our major competitor. For these customers, our original price involved too large a premium, versus the less expensive oscillometric machines. Now there is some real question about going back to the original positioning strategy.

The two years following the introduction of Finapres were characterized by indecision about its future and lack of significant support for the product. Once introduced, Ohmeda required it to be self-supporting, with product improvements made on an ongoing basis, financed out of current revenues. When the sales force began to report complaints from the clinicians in the field, it was felt that the major problems were cosmetic, concerning the size of the box and the readability of the screen. Complaints regarding inaccurate readings were thought to result from misapplication of the cuff. Despite some modifications, complaints continued and sales declined. As 1990 began, it was apparent that decisions as to the future of Finapres needed to be made.

Reassessment

Reassessment of Finapres had started with the development of the 5-year plan for Ohmeda Monitoring Systems. Subsequently, concerns on the part of the sales force about the commitment to Finapres indicated the desirability of a meeting involving sales force management, product management, and R&D. On May 23, 1990, Joe Pepper convened a meeting of representatives of all three groups, as well as headquarters marketing. The main points that emerged from the meeting were as follows:

- There was general agreement that the market potential for CNIBP was large. There was, however, considerable disagreement as to its exact size. Some estimates of the U.S. market were as large as 7740

units per year. International estimates were considerably lower. There was general agreement that the largest market segments for Fiñapres were OR and ICU/CCU. It was the view of Ohmeda's product managers, however, that the focus of the NAFO sales force on the OR market made selling to the ICU/CCU segment difficult.

- It was emphasized that the diffusion of innovation in many instances took a long time. Acceptance of some currently standard medical equipment came only after a number of years. Oximetry, for example, took 14 years, echocardiography took 10 years, and, as it was emphasized, capnometry (CO_2 gas analysis) took 40 years to become accepted. However, if Finapres was to ultimately succeed, investment was necessary not only in technological development, but in market development as well.

- The following reasons for lack of success to date were identified:

  Drift in readings over time

  Not accurate for the average clinician

  Not easy to use

  Inadequate alert for misapplied cuff

  No alerts for problems with poor circulation

  No toe/pediatric/neonatal/thumb cuffs

- Concerns were expressed about:

  Lack of a research culture

  Bottom line/short-term focus

  R&D research shortage

- R&D gave its assessment of the time and cost to develop fixes and their likelihood of success:

  The cause of drift was not certain, but there was a high probability that the problem could be fixed with changes in software, probably in 1990. If this fix worked, the cost would be relatively modest.

  Assessing the present cuff as offering 30% of ideal requirements, currently contemplated modifications could be expected to improve performance to 40% by January 1991, again with relatively modest cost. With a more substantial effort, it was expected that performance could be improved to 80% in 2 years.

- Noninvasive oscillometric blood pressure machines were not likely to be thrown out in favor of Finapres. It was more likely they would be replaced on a normal schedule.

- On the positive side, a number of strengths were identified:

  Patents lasting past the year 2000 (except in the

United Kingdom and Germany)

Strong distribution, particularly in the OR

Technical expertise

Head start over competition

Following extensive discussion, four options were presented:

1. Stay on the present course. Make sufficient modifications to make it possible to carefully reintroduce the product in selected markets. This approach was estimated to cost $307,000 in R&D expense, generate sales of 820 units through 1994, and have a net present value of $30,000.

2. Stop the project. Taking into account writing off current inventory costs and possible return costs, this approach was estimated to have a negative net present value of $160,000.

3. Make a significant investment in R&D and marketing (including going forward with a mini-Fini, a much smaller version of Finapres that would be targeted at the OEM market). This contemplated a 50% penetration of the OR market by 1995, a 50% penetration of the ICU market by 1998, and significant penetration of the OEM market. Cumulative sales estimates for this approach were 7700 units in the United States and 4000 internationally (through 1995). With projected revenues of $40 million, investment in R&D of $2 million, and investment in marketing of $1.2 million, the net present value of this approach through 1995 was estimated to be $2,200,000.

4. Sell the business. There was considerable discussion of this option, but the general view was that it was not likely that Ohmeda could find a buyer willing to pay any significant amount for the business. In any event, it was unlikely that top management at BOC would approve such a step.

Management Views

Subsequent to the May 23 meeting, a number of views were expressed by Ohmeda managers. As John Carr, Vice President of Field Operations, saw it:

The international experience with Finapres was more successful for a variety of reasons. The original technology was developed by a European company (TNO), so the European medical community was familiar with the concept. The sales force is more balanced in its approach to the market. Hence, it was able to exploit niche markets where the device worked very well. The initial sales built confidence. The real key was the use of product champi-

ons. The product was given support and attention that it did not receive in the states.

Finapres represented a once in 5 to 10 years type of opportunity. It was a significant new technology which didn't seem to fit Ohmeda's culture or annual financial cycle. If the initial effort had been followed by product enhancements, Finapres would have been successful. From here, the only two decisions I see are sell or go.

Similar views were expressed by James Valenta, Vice President for Asia (AFO):

Finapres is a great product which, from my view in the Asian markets, has significant customer appeal. It seems that things were stacked against the product from the beginning. Very soon after Finapres was purchased, Ohmeda reorganized. The individual who had pushed to buy the technology moved on to other assignments, which resulted in some lost momentum. Finapres never really had a home, which compounded the problems with the system itself. (See Exhibit 8 for Ohmeda's marketing organization in 1990.) Had there been a quicker response to feedback from the international sales force, most of what was discussed at the meeting today—the drift issue and the cuff—could have been resolved some time ago. Ohmeda had trouble accepting the fact that there was a problem. The feedback domestically was focused more on cosmetic rather than substantive issues. Changes were made without knowledge of the impact to other parts of the system.

Japan is more technologically oriented; they grasped the idea of the system quickly and easily. Maybe it's just that invasive technology isn't as advanced overseas as in the United States. The doctors in Japan seem more interested in learning about new technology than in the States.

If Ohmeda doesn't want to continue with Finapres, I'll buy it and produce it. I believe in the product that much.

A somewhat different perspective was given by René Bernava, Regional Director for Southern Europe:

Europe was ready for Finapres. The medical community, especially in Germany, was excited about the studies and papers written about the product. As a whole, European doctors were much less comfortable with arterial monitoring than their American counterparts. Finapres should have been a dazzling success in Europe but there were problems, both with the product and the way it was marketed.

The technology for Finapres was purchased but not improved. The early version did not work. The project had software problems and lacked leadership. The original plan was to make an inexpensive disposable cuff. With this focus, a cuff that really worked, regardless of cost, was never developed. Also, the product was introduced at a premium price. That philosophy did not work.

The international sales force felt we had the top technology and wanted to go ahead. The meeting today

DIRECTOR OF MARKETING
Lloyd Fishman

Administrative Assistant
Elaine Luttrell

Marketing Manager Product Development
J. Stochert

- Group Prod. Mgr. Resp. Gas (RGM) M. Stevenson
- Product Mgr. OxiCap / Agent J. Tinagila
- Clin. Spec. M. Patterson
- Group Prod. Mgr. Vital Signs D. Dickerson
- Sr. Product Mgr. Finapres B. Belew
- Product Mgr. CardiacPlus J. Robin
- Group Prod. Mgr. Oximetry (3700, 3740, 3760) B. Shriver
- Product Mgr. Probes A. Howard
- Product Mgr. New Oximeters K. Dekem
- Clin. Spec. J. Simpson

Marketing Manager International
M. Dickinson

- Product Mgr. *S. Europe* Open
- Product Mgr. *N./W. Europe* R. McCue
- Sr. Product Mgr. *Asia* S. Helm
- Sr. Product Mgr. *Canada/L. America* P. Perredin
- Secretary D. Hammond

Sales Manager Non-Hospital
S. Vierke

- Mktg./Sales Assistant M. Davis

Director OEM
B. Bednarski

- Clin. Spec. J. Ocken

Communications Manager
M. Crandall

- Comm. Coordinator S. Dunahay
- Secretary K. O'Reilly

Customer Support Manager
L. Rice

- Cust. Support Rep. P. Sperle
- Int'l Export Coord. C. Perryman
- Int'l Export Coord. S. Evans
- Int'l Export Coord Trudi Tompek-Guarriere
- Order Systems Asst. R. McCauley
- Order Systems Asst. R. Cellus

EXHIBIT 8   Ohmeda, Colorado, Marketing Department, July 17, 1990

occurred because we were the most vocal. I went to Dekle [Dekle Rountree] some time ago and asked him to investigate the product, renew agreements and TNO, and put some money into the project. Some money was forthcoming, but it wasn't a continuing process.

As Mark Halpert, Vice President for FOI, saw the situation:

There are several reasons Finapres was more successful in Europe and overseas than in the United States. The sales force in Europe sells many products whereas in the U.S. the sales force only sells Ohmeda products. With the large product line, we developed customer expertise. We know what the customer wants, and we use technical support to help conclude the transactions.

The organization of the medical community in Europe is different also. Anesthesia and monitoring are the same customer. In the United States there are more specialists. The sales force, with its broader coverage and experience, went after other niches rather than anesthesia, where the product had failed in the United States.

The key difference internationally was the product champions. Internationally, the product champion was part of the sales force, thus closer to the customers. In the United States, management served this role. Europe is still enthusiastic about the product. In Germany, just with the 1991 cuff, the product will be a success.

Bonnie Queram was Manager, Sales Programs and Administration in NAFO, and reported to the Vice President of Sales. As she recalled:

Everyone was enthusiastic when Finapres was introduced. It looked easy to sell, although the box was big and clunky. Initially there was a high level of sales activity and orders. Unfortunately, when problems surfaced, we tended to focus on cosmetic fixes, and sales tapered off in the United States. In contrast, sales held up well in Europe. I developed a questionnaire to find out why. The responses indicated that there is a major difference in clinical practice between the United States and Europe. The physicians, for instance, are more down to earth there. In contrast to the United States, they are very patient and want to work with the manufacturer, particularly on a new product. The anesthesiologists will spend lots of time in pre-op making sure that things like the cuff are OK, whereas in the United States they are very impatient. For these reasons, and a number of others, I concluded that the European experience wouldn't transfer to the United States. Our normal assumption is that we can develop our products for the U.S. market, and then go abroad with the same strategy. This is the one case in a hundred where this assumption doesn't apply.

Bill Belew, a Senior Product Manager in Louisville, had a somewhat different view. According to Belew:

The product problems in Europe and the United States are

identical. The only difference is the sales approach. What we need is a complete fix. That will cost in the neighborhood of $2 million, but once we have it, we can go after the OR/ICU markets anywhere in the world.

He went on to say:

The May 23 meeting was both good and bad. The potential for the product was reiterated, and we heard that the product would not be killed. On the other hand, it didn't sound as if we were going to make the kind of commitment the potential justified. And this was despite information that Nellcor might introduce a CNIBP product in September.

The enthusiasm for Finapres was shared by Lloyd Fishman, Director of Marketing. He had a number of concerns, however:

I've been watching Finapres evolve since joining Ohmeda $2\frac{1}{2}$ years ago. I think the product has potential to represent as much as 10% of our sales, but I was concerned that there was no sense of purpose, no vision, about the product. We were doing lots of little "fixits" without any real sense of our markets or what the product should be. I called the May 23 meeting to see if we couldn't develop such a sense of purpose or vision.

There's no question that we face a complex situation. The markets in the United States and internationally are very different. The financial orientation of the doctors in the United States rubs off on our sales force, and they're much less inclined to sell concept products than in Europe, where the doctors like to work with us on new developments.

Ray Jones had recently joined Ohmeda as R&D Group Manager and was responsible for the Finapres R&D effort. As he put it:

I think Finapres has lots of potential, but we need to resolve a number of critical issues. For instance, we use finger pressure as a measure of central blood pressure, but we're not sure how closely finger pressure simulates central pressure or how accurately we're measuring finger pressure.

Management would like us to give some performance guarantees, but that's not the nature of R&D. We can, however, identify the key technical and physiological issues and identify milestones with the expectation that we can get data to indicate if the issue is resolvable.

One of the things that would really help would be for marketing to give us some better performance criteria.

Finally, Joe Pepper reflected on his thoughts subsequent to the May 23 meeting, his various discussions with his managers, and his visit to Japan:

I know the people in the organization feel we don't spend enough on R&D. But it's a question of balance. We have been spending over 6% of sales on R&D, and the corporation has a major research facility at Murray Hill, New Jersey, where we do the riskier, blue sky R&D. In the past our competitors have spent a higher percentage of sales on R&D. We estimate that Nellcor, for instance, spent over 10% during the last 4 years. However, we also estimate that they will reduce this in the next 4 years.

The May 23 meeting was valuable, and we got a lot of opinions on the table. One option that was not looked at, however, was to go exclusively with OEMs.

In Japan the product is selling well. The physicians appear more willing to fiddle with the product to make it work. Based on what's going on in Japan and what is going on in Europe, I wonder if we might not be able to bootstrap their experience to back into the U.S. market.

Part of our problem is our whole development process. We've hired some new people, Ray Jones as Product Development Manager and Nick Jensen as a research scientist, but it's going to take them some time to sort out the problems and establish better procedures.

I know John Carr wants us to go with a product that will sell in the United States. Part of the question, though, is, how much faith do I put in the numbers?

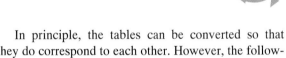

CASE 7-3   TIMOTEI (B)*

*T*he year 1987 was potentially a pivotal year for Timotei. There was a strong-felt need to assess Timotei's brand equity position, as reflected in its market share and share-of-mind positions; to evaluate the contributions of the marketing mix instruments in achieving these positions; and, most importantly, to decide how to increase customer interest during the growth phase of the product life cycle. Attention focused on how to expand product lines and offer greater variety. In this regard, Timotei Balsam had been introduced in the first quarter of 1986. Other possibilities such as Timotei Extra Mild needed to be explored.

THE PERSONAL PRODUCTS MARKET, 1983–1986

The development of the various personal products, both in volume and in money, is described in Exhibits 1 and 2. However, the figures for 1986 cannot be compared to the figures given for the years prior to 1986 because different units were used for measurement. In 1986 the following changes took place:

1. Volume is now measured in units (bottles); until 1986 weight was used.

2. Money value is now measured in consumer price; until 1986 the price "out of factory" was used, which equals the consumer price minus the value-added tax (VAT) and minus the trade margin.

In principle, the tables can be converted so that they do correspond to each other. However, the following problems present themselves:

1. A bottle of Timotei contains 200 ml, which corresponds to 208 grams. However, there are several shampoos sold in different volumes, and therefore different weights. In order to adapt the tables, one has to know exactly how much has been sold of a particular shampoo.

2. As stated, the "out of factory" price equals the consumer price minus VAT (18.5%) and trade margin. If the trade margin is assumed to be approximately 25%, the consumer price equals the "out of the factory" price plus 40–45%. This holds true only for the shampoo market. The other personal products have different margins and should therefore be converted in a different way.

Nevertheless, it is possible to make a few statements concerning the development of the personal products market. The sales fell a bit in 1984, and after 1984 they started to grow again. Exceptions are the sales of shampoos, which continued to increase, and the sales of toilet soap, which continued to decrease. Revenue (units × price) continued to increase for all products in the personal products market.

The distribution relations for the years 1983–1986 can be found in Exhibit 3. These relations indicate

* This case was prepared by the Marketing and Marketing Research Team, Department of Economics, University of Groningen, the Netherlands. Edited by Leonard Parsons. Copyright © 1990 by the University of Groningen.

EXHIBIT 1   The Personal Products Market, 1983–1985

A. Volume

In Thousands of Kilograms	1983	1984	1985
Toilet soap	8,700	8,500	8,500
Shampoo	8,400	8,800	10,000
Toothpaste	4,800	4,400	4,900
Bath foam	5,000	4,600	5,300
Deodorant	1,400	1,180	1,450

B. Revenue[a]

In Millions of Guilders	1983	1984	1985
Toilet soap	46	46	47
Shampoo	78	80	83
Toothpaste	53	55	59
Bath foam	30	36	41
Deodorant	37	39	41

Source: A.C. Nielsen.

[a] "Out of factory" price.

EXHIBIT 2   The Personal Products Market, 1986

A. Volume

In Millions	1986
Toilet soap (units)	70
Shampoo (bottles)	37
Toothpaste (liters)	33
Bath foam (bottles)	18
Deodorant (bottles)	16

B. Revenue[a]

In Millions of Guilders	1986
Toilet soap	97
Shampoo	128
Toothpaste	90
Bath foam	81
Deodorant	78

Source: A.C. Nielsen.

[a] Consumer price.

which percentage of the sales of each product take place through which channel.

THE SHAMPOO MARKET, 1983–1986

A description of the shampoo market in 1985 can be found in Exhibit 4. When compared to the shampoo market in 1983 (see Exhibit 6, Part A), that is, before the introduction of Timotei, a number of differences can be noticed. The market shares of the brands Zwitsal, Elsève, and Palmolive went down, as measured both in volume and in value. The market share of Schwarzkopf went down in value only, whereas the market share of Andrélon decreased only with regard to volume. Head & Shoulders was the only brand which managed to increase market share. The market share of Timotei reached 4.9%, based on volume, and 4.4% based on value, while selling for an average consumer price of ƒ2.99.

The shampoo market has seen a number of product introductions and reintroductions:

EXHIBIT 3   Distribution of Personal Products

	Food (%)				Drug (%)			
	83	84	85	86	83	84	85	86
Volume								
Toilet soap	98	97	96	95	2	3	4	5
Shampoo	76	74	73	72	24	26	28	28
Toothpaste	81	80	77	75	19	20	23	23
Conditioner	61	61	61	61	39	39	39	39
Revenue								
Toilet soap	93	92	91	90	7	8	9	10
Shampoo	65	63	61	61	35	37	39	39
Toothpaste	76	73	70	67	24	27	30	31
Conditioner	52	52	51	51	48	48	49	49

Source: A.C. Nielsen and estimates of Elida Gibbs.

1984		
QT 1	Akzo	Zwitsal Baby Shampoo 300 ml
QT 2	Tendo-Haco	Dr. Schupp (2 types)
	L'Oréal	Ultra Mild (4 types)
QT 4	Gillette	Silkience Extra Mild
	L'Oréal	Elsève Proteine
	Indola	Natural Silk (4 types)
1985		
QT 1	Beiersdorf	Nivea Mild Shampoo
	Schwarzkopf	Every Day Shampoo
QT2	Andrélon	Swimmers' Shampoo
1986		
QT1	Wella	Introduction Lavona Line
	Lever	Timotei Balsam

Some of these offerings were direct competitors of Timotei in the mild shampoo segment.

In the first quarter of 1986 Lever BV introduced Timotei Balsam (conditioner), which is complementary to Timotei shampoo. Other marketing actions for Timotei, initiated by Lever BV, are given below:

1984		
QT 1:	wk2–	ƒ3–refund for two bottles of shampoo
QT 2:	wk 18–	win a hair dryer
QT 3:	wk	free comb
QT 4:	wk 42–48	win a free visit to a hairdresser
1985		
QT 1:	wk 1–5	ƒ3–refund for one bottle of shampoo
QT 2:	wk 13–	display + free folding brush
QT 3:	wk 25–	ƒ3–refund for two bottles of shampoo
QT 4:	wk 38–	25% (50 ml) free (shampoo)
1986		
QT 1:	wk	ƒ3–refund for two bottles of shampoo

		ƒ4.50 refund for one bottle of conditioner
QT 2:	wk 19–26	free sample of 25 ml conditioner
QT 3:	wk 29–34	25% free (shampoo)
		50% discount on conditioner by means of refund
QT 4:	wk 43–47	ƒ2.50 refund by means of trading stamps

The effectiveness of these activities, in part, was examined by conducting recall studies.

Starting in the last quarter of 1983, Burke-Inter/View conducted a recall study. This study measured, among other things, total recall, unaided and aided recall; frequency of use; and intention to buy. The results of this study for the years 1983–1986 can be found in Exhibit 5. Some of the findings of this study were:

1. Recall increased enormously until 1986, after which it stabilized. The unaided recall increased from 0% to 20%; aided recall increased from 9% to approximately 60%. Total recall therefore increased from 9% to approximately 80%.

2. The percentage of respondents who actually bought Timotei continued to increase slowly.

3. The percentage of respondents who usually use Timotei was approximately 5% in 1985 and 6–7% in 1986.

At first, the results of Timotei fell short of expectations. Sales slowly increased, and it took two years to really get them going. The strong increase in sales between 1984 and 1986 (see Exhibit 6) clearly shows this, although the advertising and promotion expenditures were lowered in this period.

EXHIBIT 4   Shampoo Market, 1985

			Market Share (%)		
	Ml	Consumer Price	Volume	Value	Trend
Zwitsal	200	3.79	9.6	11.5	– –
Elsève[a]	200	3.98	3.9	5.2	– –
Head & Shoulders	150	4.45	6.6	10.2	+ +
Andrélon[a]	200	3.98	11.8	14.8	–
Schwarzkopf[a]	200	1.98	11.1	7.0	–
Palmolive[a]	400	1.98	16.0	9.5	+
Timotei	200	2.99	4.9	4.4	+ +
Other brands	200	3.50	29.5	34.0	+ –
Private labels		1.95	6.6	3.4	+ +

Source: A. C. Nielsen.

[a] More than one type/size.

EXHIBIT 5   **Recall of Timotei**

A. 1983

Week	44	50
(% of total)		
Total recall	9.4	24.5
Unaided recall	0.3	1.3
Aided recall	9.1	23.3
Uses sometimes	—	—
Uses most of the time	—	—
Uses at the moment	—	—
Has already bought	1.3	2.8
Positive intention to buy	3.5	7.9
Received sample	—	—

B. 1984

Week	4	9	14	20	25	30	37	43	49
(% of total)									
Total recall	41.0	39.0	51.0	61.0	64.5	61.6	62.5	60.7	64.7
Unaided recall	5.0	6.0	7.2	7.6	10.0	9.1	8.8	7.9	11.9
Aided recall	36.0	32.6	43.8	43.3	54.5	52.5	53.8	52.8	52.8
Uses sometimes	—	—	—	—	—	—	—	—	—
Uses most of the time	—	—	—	—	—	—	—	—	4.1
Uses at the moment	—	—	—	—	—	—	—	—	—
Has already bought	6.0	5.3	10.6	8.4	9.7	12.9	13.2	14.4	17.6
Positive intention to buy	13.5	13.2	15.0	20.0	29.0	23.5	24.4	19.4	26.3
Received sample	—	—	—	—	—	—	—	—	—

C. 1985

Week	6	12	18	24	30	36	42	48
(% of total)								
Total recall	69.8	66.9	66.0	67.4	66.9	73.0	70.1	63.1
Unaided recall	13.7	12.2	7.8	16.5	13.2	15.6	15.4	9.4
Aided recall	56.1	54.7	58.3	51.0	53.8	57.4	54.7	53.8
Uses sometimes	—	3.1	3.1	9.7	6.7	7.5	6.3	6.3
Uses most of the time	5.4	2.9	5.3	5.6	2.9	5.9	5.3	4.4
Uses at the moment	5.6	3.2	5.0	7.2	6.0	6.9	6.6	5.3
Has already bought	16.9	14.7	21.2	24.6	18.5	30.0	24.4	22.2
Positive intention to buy	28.1	26.6	20.0	20.5	26.0	21.8	22.6	20.4
Received sample	—	6.3	5.6	5.0	4.4	6.0	8.2	6.0

D. 1986

Week	2	8	17	23	29	36	45	52
(% of total)								
Total recall	70.0	79.8	78.5	82.3	75.7	80.7	80.2	82.3
Unaided recall	10.9	15.1	14.7	17.7	17.8	18.9	20.2	18.4
Aided recall	59.2	64.5	63.8	64.6	58.0	61.8	60.0	63.9
Uses sometimes	7.8	9.7	7.5	8.7	6.9	4.9	6.9	8.8
Uses most of the time	6.1	6.6	6.0	7.5	8.4	9.8	6.9	6.6
Uses at the moment	6.8	6.6	—	—	8.7	10.1	6.6	5.9
Has already bought	27.3	31.5	27.9	32.6	30.9	33.2	33.9	23.4
Positive intention to buy	21.4	23.1	—	—	20.9	28.5	21.7	40.0
Received sample	5.6	4.1	—	—	—	—	—	—

Source: Burke Inter/View.

EXHIBIT 6   Timotei Results, 1984–1986

A. Financial

	1984	1985	1986
Sales (1000 kilogram)	290	450	675
Advertising expenditures[a] (1000 guilders)	1,500	1,400	1,000
Sales promotion (1000 guilders)	750	350	600

B. Other

	1984	1985	1986
Weighted distribution			
Food	57	80	95
Drug	72	78	83
Food/drug	63	75	91
Total consumer recall	63	65	80

Source: Elida Gibbs.

[a] Print advertisements + TV.

TIMOTEI EXTRA MILD SHAMPOO

In November 1987 Lever BV commissioned Research International Nederland BV to conduct a study regarding the effects of a possible introduction of Timotei Extra Mild on total sales. Timotei Extra Mild is an answer to the specific needs of people with *fine hair*. Research showed that 50% of Dutch women think they have fine hair. This is, among other things, a result of the increased use of blow dryers and curling irons, perms and coloring, etc. These consumers have no particular problems with their hair, but they are nevertheless looking for another, extra mild shampoo. With this shampoo, they can even wash fine hair as often as they want.

Timotei Extra Mild gives fine hair softness and shine, and adds a bit more volume and bounce. This is a result of the addition of a special conditioner. When using Timotei Extra Mild, you do not have to be afraid of limp hair.

The study revealed that in the case of a sample which consisted of 50% of users of Timotei, a growth of market share of 4.7% to 7.0% could be expected. One percent of the present Timotei users are responsible for this growth, which means that if the number of Timotei users in the sample had been cut in half, the estimated growth would have been 0.5% less: i.e., an estimated market share of 6.5% instead of 7.0%.

The study also made clear that because of the introduction of Timotei Extra Mild, the total expected

EXHIBIT 7   Price Study

	Prices of Timotei Extra Mild (*f*)					
	2.70	2.85	2.98	3.15	3.30	3.45
Trial %						
Users of Timotei	90	93	90	61	44	36
Users of other brands	43	39	40	23	23	18
Total	65	64	64	41	33	26
Market share						
Timotei	4.7	4.7	4.7	4.7	4.7	4.7
Timotei Extra Mild	3.4	3.0	2.3	1.0	0.8	0.5
Total	8.1	7.7	7.0	5.7	5.5	5.2

market share of 7% would have the following structure: 3.1% Timotei shampoo and 3.9% Timotei Extra
Mild. Since the market share of Timotei amounted to
4.7% at that time, this implied a cannibalization of
1.6%. The market share of Timotei Extra Mild would
therefore consist of 1.6% cannibalization at the
expense of Timotei and 2.3% from enlarging the market. It was estimated that the future relation between
Timotei and Timotei Extra Mild would be 40/60 to
50/50. The best price of Timotei Extra Mild was also
researched. The results can be found in Exhibit 7.

The time had come to make a decision on what to
do to remain competitive in the shampoo market. Any
action taken had to take into account the current status
of the Timotei brand franchise, as well as environmental conditions.

SERVICES MARKETING

> If you can sell green toothpaste in this country, you can sell opera.
>
> SARAH CALDWELL

*O*ne of the most important marketing developments in your lifetime has been the explosive growth of services in the U.S. economy. Today more than 75 percent of all businesses and personal consumption in the United States goes to purchase services. This growth is related to a decline in the manufacturing sector, additional wealth, an expansion in leisure time, and increases in the number of dual-career families. With their extra money, people are surfing the Internet, renting cellular phones, paying bills electronically, traveling more, and turning to a host of special cleaning and child-care services. Growth in services is not limited to the United States; many firms are finding new markets overseas. An example of the vast opportunities for growth in communication services is described in Marketing in Action box 8-1.

Now that the world is becoming more service oriented, it is essential for you to know how to sell these items. This chapter will acquaint you with the nature of services, their special characteristics, and show you how to manage service marketing activities.

NATURE OF SERVICES

Most physical products include some service elements as part of the offering. For example, a common service is the warranty to replace or repair durables such as compact discs, computer programs, or books that are defective. Goods with a low service component are positioned in Sectors 3 and 6 of Figure 8-1. Goods with a higher service component are shown in Sectors 2 and 5. Hotels are a classic example because, while rooms are a service, customers also consume food and take advantage of flower and gift shops that sell goods. Pure services such as mail delivery, medicine, and engineering are shown in Sectors 1 and 4 of Figure 8-1. Thus the service component of a product can range from very low to very high, and marketing programs vary for each type of product.

Recent Trends

A number of changes in the economic environment in the last few years have increased the importance of marketing in service industries.

Less Regulation. Service industries have traditionally been highly regulated. Government agencies often mandated price levels, constrained distribution areas, and even regulated pos-

MARKETING IN ACTION 8-1

Season's Greetings Using E-mail and Web Sites

INTEGRATING
... with
Information
Technology,
Production/
Operations
Management

An increasing number of Americans are now sending out greetings using e-mail and their own Web sites. Some people register their sites with a Web hosting service and use personal software to design it. This allows them to include an unlimited amount of pictures, family news, and musical accompaniment in their holiday message. Once they design their greeting, they tell their friends the location of the Web site using e-mail. Others buy a holiday letter, Web site, and e-mail package from companies such as Verio Inc. and Network Solutions Inc. After an initial payment, the quarterly fee is $59.95. Consumers who use e-mail and Web sites to send messages to their friends save enough on postage and the cost of cards to more than pay the costs of the electronic letters. The Internet division of Hallmark Cards Inc. offers a free service allowing people to go to Hallmark's site and design their own newsletter using preset formats and art. Another online card company, Blue Mountain Arts Inc. of Boulder, Colorado, offers a site that allows you to create and send personal greeting cards. Blue Mountain is now the 14th most visited site on the Web.

— *Creative marketing of new services can boost company sales.*

Source: Rebecca Buckman,"Season's Greetings From Our Web Site!" *The Wall Street Journal,* December 21, 1998, p. B1.

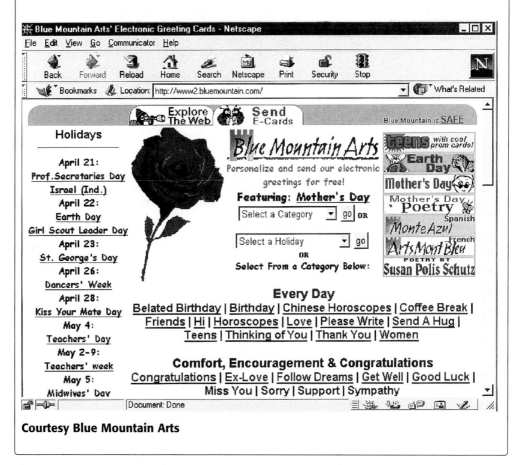

Courtesy Blue Mountain Arts

sible product features. However, the trend in the United States and throughout the world is toward deregulation of major services. This means that there are fewer constraints on competitive activity in airlines, energy, railroads, trucking, banking, securities, insurance, and telecommunications. Barriers to entry by new firms have been dropped, geographical restrictions on service delivery have been reduced, and there is more freedom to adjust

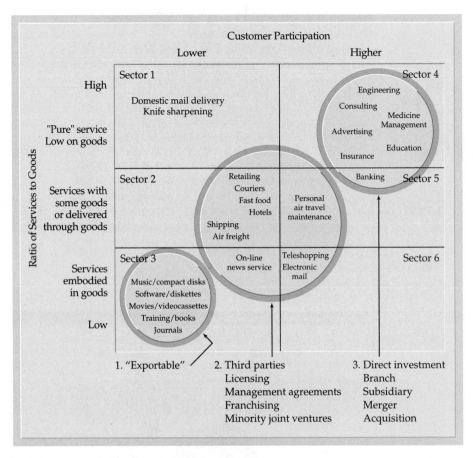

FIGURE 8-1   Service to Goods Ratios and Customer Participation (From Sandra Vandermerwe and Michael Chadwick, "The Internationalization of Services," *The Services Industry Journal* [January 1989], pp. 79–93.)

APPLYING
. . . to
Tele-
communications
Services
Marketing

prices. Substantial relaxation of trade regulation of services is occurring in the European Union, and rules are being eased in Japan as well. The impact of deregulation on pricing of phone services in Germany has been dramatic. Viag Interkom, partially owned by British Telecommunications, cut some phone prices 60 percent. Deutsche Telekom responded by saying it would cut prices further to match the cuts by Viag, O.tel.O, and other German phone companies.[1]

A related trend has been a move to force professional associations to remove bans on advertising and promotional activities. Professions that now allow more competitive activity include accounting, architecture, medicine, law, and optometry. This has led to more use of informational advertising and more price competition.

Privatization.   With the growth of government deficits, there has been a trend to return government-owned service industries to private investors. In England, France, Italy, and Japan there is a move to convert telecommunications, national airlines, and utilities to private ownership. Municipal governments are also selling airports and contracting with private firms to haul trash. The new result is more emphasis on cost cutting and more interest by new owners in meeting customers' service needs.

Customer Participation

Services can also be classified by the amount of customer participation that is required. High-participation services shown in Figure 8-1 include banking and education; low-participation services include shipping and couriers. When you are having a couch reupholstered, you do not have to be present. This means that the upholstery firm can be located in an old building without a waiting room, while a dentist needs to offer a convenient location, comfortable seating, pleasant views, and soothing music. Marketing In Action box 8-2 shows how buyers work with an auction company to find new suppliers.

The degree of customer participation and the ratio of services to goods have an impact on international marketing strategies. Figure 8-1 groups products into three strategy clusters. Cluster 1 includes low-participation, low-service products that are best exported. Products with intermediate values in cluster 2 should be handled by third-party arrangements with overseas businesspeople through licensing or franchising. For pure services with high customer participation, you need to consider direct international investment in sales branches or subsidiaries.

Major Service Industries

A good way to understand the breadth of the service industry is to look at how the government classifies services for the Census of Business. Table 8-1 lists the major categories of service industries and gives examples. These include communications, consulting, educational, financial, health, household operations, housing, insurance, personal, and transportation. Note that retailing and restaurants are not considered to be major service industries even though they provide a service element in their product offerings.

Services Are All Around

One of the most striking things about Table 8-1 is how many services are routinely used by consumers and businesses. Consider a day in the life of Paula, an assistant product manager.

MARKETING IN ACTION 8-2

Bidding for Nuts and Bolts on the Net

APPLYING ... to Industrial Services Marketing

A new Web company called FreeMarkets On Line Inc. helps firms get bids for parts from present and prospective suppliers over the Internet. FreeMarkets structures the auctions to maximize the psychological pressure on suppliers to offer their best possible price. First it prescreens the bidders to those acceptable to the buyer and arranges to have at least six to eight bids on each lot to assure brisk competition. Then it arranges for the first lots to have the most bidders. No bids of just a few dollars less than the last bid are allowed. Bidding is conducted on a secure computer network and the bidders are not told who they are bidding against. They also don't know the price the buyer paid for similar items in the past. FreeMarkets sends each bidder thick packages detailing the parts being sought and the buyer's quality requirements. In this type of online auction, the low bidder does not necessarily win. Sometimes buyers stay with incumbent suppliers even if their prices are higher because they have a good sense of their abilities. At an online auction session, United Technologies was hoping to identify potential savings of 15 percent on $7.3 million of simple machined parts. At the end of the day they saved 25 percent.

— *Internet auction services can help firms find low cost suppliers.*

Source: Timothy Aeppel, "Bidding for E-Nuts and E-Bolts on the Net," *The Wall Street Journal*, March 12, 1999, pp. B1, B4.

TABLE 8-1   Major Service Industries

SIC Code	Industry	SIC Code	Industry
48	*Communications*	49	*Household Operations*
	Telephone		Electrical companies
	Radio broadcasting		Sewer companies
	TV broadcasting		Laundries
73	*Consulting*		Cleaning
	Advertising agencies	65	*Housing*
	Outdoor advertising		Apartment buildings
	Direct mail		Rental agents
	Employment agencies		Hotels
	Testing laboratories		Trailer parks
	Temporary help	63	*Insurance*
	Auditing		Insurance agents
82	*Educational*		Life insurance
	Colleges & professional schools		Health insurance
	Libraries		Fire & casualty
	Technical institutes	72	*Personal*
60	*Financial*		Beauty & barber shops
	Banks		Motion picture theaters
	Savings & loans		Bowling alleys
	Credit unions		Skating rinks
	Commodity dealers	4	*Transportation*
	Security exchanges		Suburban transit
80	*Health*		Airlines
	Hospitals		Motor freight
	Medical laboratories		Automobile rental
	Physicians & surgeons		

When she wakes up in her rented apartment, one of the first things she does is switch on the lights to get ready for work. Soon she jumps in her leased BMW and turns on the radio to catch the traffic report. Parking the car in the pay lot at the subway station, she notices an outdoor ad for a movie she wants to see at a local theater. When she arrives at the office, she checks her e-mail and picks up the phone to talk with the advertising agency that handles one of her brands. Later that day, she calls her insurance agent about the liability coverage on her sailboat. On the way home, she stops at a teller machine to pick up some cash and then spends some of it on repairs for her watch. Back home, she flips on the TV to catch the evening news. As Paula prepares dinner, she checks a Web site, pays some bills, and arranges a vacation trip to Hawaii. After dinner she heads out to her marketing class at the local university.

All of this businesswoman's daily activities have involved contact with service organizations. But why did Paula select certain companies? The implication is clear. For service companies to succeed, they must understand how to market their benefits to customers. Marketing Strategies box 8-1 describes the ongoing battle to be the bill payer for American consumers.

SERVICE MARKETING CHARACTERISTICS

Services have special characteristics that affect how marketing programs are created and executed. These features include intangibility, perishability, inseparability, variability, and client relationships.

> **MARKETING STRATEGIES 8-1**
>
> ### Paperless Bill Paying
>
> APPLYING ... to Financial Services Marketing
>
> The time is coming when most U.S. citizens will be able to pay their bills online with a click of a mouse. With current electronic bill payment systems, consumers get paper bills in the mail and pay them by typing out checks on their home computer that are then sent by a bank or outside processor such as CheckFree Holdings Corp. In the future, consumers will log on to a Web site and see a message telling them "You have bills." They would be able to scan the bills or pay them immediately with a click of their mouse. Paperless bill delivery is currently in limited use by a few American banks. However, with the potential for a multibillion dollar market up for grabs, a variety of financial, utility and technology firms are jockeying for position. Banks have a huge role to play if they are willing to capture it and a great deal to lose if they don't. As the trusted keepers of consumers' checking accounts, banks could become hubs of online financial activity. Also paper checks are expensive for banks to process, costing the nation $181 billion a year. Converting to electronic checks could save consumers 90 billion dollars. However, banks have been slow to cash in on this new online service and only 16 of the 35 largest banks offer even the old style electronic bill payment over the Web. Everyone is trying to figure out who is going to pay the start-up costs to convert to paperless bill paying even though savings for the country would be immense. Banks who have charged consumers extra for the new system have run into customer resistance. This has opened the door to firms like Intuit Inc. that allows its customers to view and pay bills online through its popular Quicken personal finance software. If banks fail to see the opportunity in paperless bill paying, brokers and Web outfits like Yahoo!, Inc. and America Online, Inc. could start delivering bills to consumers and steal away a huge market.
>
> — *Banks stand to lose when the Web pays the bills.*
>
> *Sources*: Rebecca Buckman, "Bills, Bills (Click), More Bills … A Race Is On for Best Paperless Payment System," *The Wall Street Journal*, November 19, 1998 p. C1; Lucinda Harper, "Americans Won't Stop Writing Checks," *The Wall Street Journal*, November 24, 1998, p. A2.

Intangibility

The most obvious problem with marketing services is that they are intangible. Buyers cannot touch, smell, see, taste, or hear services before they are purchased. When they buy goods, customers get something to take home. When they buy services, they receive only a ticket stub or a piece of paper. With services, consumers buy a performance rather than a physical product. As a result, intangibility of services raises the perceived risk of purchase compared with buying goods. Service buyers cannot effectively evaluate services prior to purchase and there is usually no way to try out services before purchase. The implication for marketers is that it is important to build and maintain high brand loyalty to make buyers feel secure about the higher risks they are taking with service purchases. For example, when customers purchase a home the cost of insurance is built into the monthly payment and stored in an accrual account at the financial institution making the loan. This is paid once a year by the financial institution directly to the insurance company. This means that customers may not know what they are paying for homeowners' insurance, so it is critical that brand loyalty is strong enough to overcome homeowner's fear that their insurance company may overcharge them.

Also the abstract nature of services means that marketers must find a way to dramatize the concept for the customer. Several clever solutions to this problem are offered in Figure 8-2. To overcome the lack of a physical product, marketers need to develop a tangible representation of the service. One of the best examples is the use of plastic cards to symbolize bank credit. Ads can then be created showing customers using their bank cards to pay for real products such as meals or souvenirs of exotic locations.

Another dilemma with intangibles is that it can be hard for buyers to grasp the idea of service concepts. One solution is to use physical symbols in the advertising that are more easily understood by the customers (Figure 8-2). For example, Travelers Insurance is well known for its umbrella. Insurance companies convey security by association with familiar rocks, hands, umbrellas, and blankets.

A third approach focuses on the service provider (actor, lawyer, professor), who is more tangible than the actual service (screen role, courtroom appearance, education). In this case, advertising emphasizes the skills and technical competence of the person who is in contact with the buyer. Insurance agents are shown as family counselors and loan officers as friendly neighbors; the Maytag repairman is depicted as someone with little to do. Thus, the service being offered becomes more tangible because of the fellowship with the provider.

Perishability

Services cannot be stored or carried in inventory. If they are not used when offered, they go to waste. The empty classroom or hospital bed represents revenue that is lost forever. Most of the problems with perishability are related to inaccurate forecasts of demand. When

FIGURE 8-2   Marketing Intangible Services

demand is steady, service organizations are able to provide staff and equipment to meet customers' requests. However, unpredictable demand can lead to serious difficulties. For example, on a cold December day one of the author's cars broke down. He called AAA on his car phone to get a tow truck and was put on hold for 10 minutes. Then he was cut off and had to call back and was put on hold again. When he finally reached AAA, he was told it would take three to four hours to get a tow truck. Since it was 10 degrees outside, he flagged down an independent tow truck. In this case, AAA did not have enough people answering the phone and they did not have enough tow trucks under contract to provide the emergency services customers expected.

The best way to avoid service problems is to do a better job of matching supply with demand. This can be done by adjusting supply or by smoothing out demand. Some suggestions for supply-side management include the following:

- Perform maintenance at night when services are not in demand. Examples include airplanes and transit buses.
- Encourage customers to perform part of the service, such as filling out forms in doctors' offices or at the car rental counter.
- Hire temporary help to meet peak demands. An example is the use of Manpower and Kelly Services in offices.

Demand can be managed by the following methods:

- Differential pricing to shift demand from peak to off-peak periods. An example is low weekend rates at urban hotels.
- Advertising campaigns that focus on the solitude of island beaches during off-season periods.
- Offering complementary services to those who are waiting. Theaters sell popcorn and candy and rent videotapes to people waiting to see a movie.
- Reservation systems guarantee services to customers who cannot be handled during peak periods. These extra customers can be told of available service times and kept from going to competitors.

Inseparability

A tangible product is first manufactured by a firm; next, it is distributed to dealers who sell it; and finally, the product is consumed. With services, however, the sale comes first. Then the service is produced and consumed at the same time. For example, a customer buys an opera ticket; then, on the night of the performance, the opera is presented and viewed by the audience. Simultaneous production and consumption forces services to be delivered directly to the customer. This close relationship with buyers makes the image of the service provider more important in the purchase decision. In addition, services must be easily accessible to customers.

Outlet Accessibility. Because services cannot be stored or transported, they have to be delivered to customers by local sales agents. This means that the revenue of service marketers is often limited by the number of service outlets they maintain. Although customers may be willing to drive 50 miles to an airport, they will travel only a few miles to go to a bank, dry cleaner, financial advisor, insurance agent, or bowling alley. Service marketers have to balance the revenues produced by additional outlets against the costs of maintaining the facilities. Service marketers have tried various strategies to reduce the costs of getting close to customers. H&R Block opens hundreds of temporary offices during the tax season

INTEGRATING
. . . with
Information
Technology

and then closes them. Century 21 uses a system of franchising local offices to expand its coverage and enhance revenues. One of the best ways to expand coverage is through the use of technology. Many firms now make airline and theater tickets available on the Internet. Also online service providers such as America Online and retailers like Amazon.com have agreed to share their revenues with computer manufacturers Compaq and Hewlett-Packard Co. In exchange, the PC makers have redesigned their keyboards to add "quick access" keys and to give prominent placement to the Web sites and services of their partners.[2] Ticketmaster has machines that dispense theater and sports tickets at locations accessible to customers. Banks have been very successful at providing low-cost services by placing teller machines in convenient sites that would not support a full-service outlet.

Image Is Important.   Since the buyer must be present to obtain certain services, marketers should be aware of the image projected by their facility. Doctors' and lawyers' offices are often luxuriously decorated to instill a feeling of confidence in the client. Attractive furnishings imply that the business is doing well and suggest professional competence.

APPLYING
. . . to
Professional
Services
Marketing

The same concept applies to auto repairs. If you visit a shop and find the floor strewn with broken parts, tools, and pools of grease, you are likely to question the mechanic's ability to fix your car. Successful service suppliers maintain the quality of their customer contact facilities to attract repeat buyers.

Variability

INTEGRATING
. . . with
Production/
Operations
Management

Because most services are produced by people, service quality tends to vary considerably from one transaction to the next. Products, on the other hand, are produced in factories where inspectors can ensure uniformity from item to item. The lack of standardization by service providers means that you may be satisfied with your haircut, your dry cleaner, or your dentist on one visit and be dissatisfied on your next visit. Service buyers face greater uncertainty in the marketplace and try to reduce that risk. One result is that customers are more likely to seek a friend's recommendation when selecting a doctor than when buying a microwave oven.

A good way to reduce service variation risk is to provide warranties such as those used for physical products. One warranty program for auto repairs claims that if Ford doesn't fix the car correctly, the customer does not have to pay. Customers will be more willing to take their cars to Ford service departments if they know that the company stands behind its repair work.

One of the best ways to reduce variability in service delivery is through the increased utilization of technology. The expanded use of computers has led to greater standardization of services and less variation in the quality of service delivery. For example, ATMs and personal computer banking programs now allow consumers to transact their banking business without the use of tellers. CPAs now prepare tax returns using a sophisticated $1,000 computer program that reduces calculation and preparation errors. Other programs allow investors to trade stocks without a broker and gather instant information on securities they are considering buying.

Another way to reduce variability in services is to hire and train employees very carefully. For example, Disney World's success is clearly related to the enthusiasm and courtesy of its employees. Disney is selective in hiring and spends a great deal of time training its employees to deal with the public. If Disney can build a loyal and dedicated team of customer contact people, so can other service organizations.

Firms that expect to reduce service variability need to monitor service production to detect when problems exist. Information on customer satisfaction can be obtained through suggestion boxes, phone surveys, and mail questionnaires. Once a firm identifies rude, discourteous, and uninformed personnel, these employees can either be retrained or terminated.

Client Relationships

Relationships between service organizations and customers are often close and long-lasting. Under these conditions, service providers should work to develop client rapport. When you are dealing with clients, try to associate on a first-name basis and include customers in social activities (assuming this is appropriate to the culture). Clients are willing to deal on a first-name basis with the person who cuts their hair, buys stock for them, and creates their advertising. This means that service providers who are attempting to steal clients from competitors need to have a clearly superior product. Also, existing service customers need to be rewarded with extra perks and benefits. For example, it is not uncommon for stockbrokers to host cocktail parties and intimate dinner parties for clients. Even airlines have had success with "presidential lounges" for preferred groups of customers.

The objective of creating a client relationship is to make it easier to sell new services. The longer you provide a service to customers, the more confidence they will have in your recommendations. After all, it is easier for most people to consider new hairstyles, new investments, and new vacation ideas from those we like and respect. The task for the service company is to build an ongoing relationship so that customers will resist the blandishments of competitors and come back to buy again and again.

MANAGING THE SERVICE MARKETING SYSTEM

> **INTEGRATING**
> . . . *with*
> *Production/*
> *Operations*
> *Management*

Services marketing is complicated because services are created and consumed simultaneously. This also means that you must produce services and sell them at the same time.

Service organizations usually have an operations person in charge of facilities, hiring, and customer contact personnel. As a result, marketing activities do not always get the attention they deserve. When marketing managers are employed, they usually advise staff on services development, pricing, promotion, and delivery. Thus service organizations often lack a strong marketing orientation that focuses on determining and filling customers' needs.

Systems for Service Marketing

A better structure for services marketing integrates the activities of the operations and marketing supervisors. The relationships between these two managers are highlighted in Figure 8-3. A service marketing system should consist of three interrelated parts: services operations, services delivery, and marketing support.

Services operations is responsible for facilities, equipment, and personnel. In a hotel, the operations manager runs the building and hires, trains, and supervises the employees. Only half of the services operations are visible to the customer. Hotel guests see the rooms and talk to the desk clerk and dining room personnel, but they do not come in contact with the kitchens, laundries, garage, and office areas behind the scenes.

Services delivery is concerned with the interface between the provider and the customer (Figure 8-3). The goal is to promote pleasant exchanges with customers so that they will return. Companies can encourage this trend by giving the marketing manager some control over service delivery. In a hotel, for example, marketing can oversee the reservation service, convention scheduling, and the information booth in the lobby. These activities solicit future business and take care of special needs of customers. If these tasks are handled efficiently, the flow of new business will be enhanced. Successful service delivery systems demand the coordinated efforts of marketing and operations personnel to make sure that customers are satisfied. A good marketing manager will handle inquiries and complaints to make sure that the quality of the services offered is maintained.

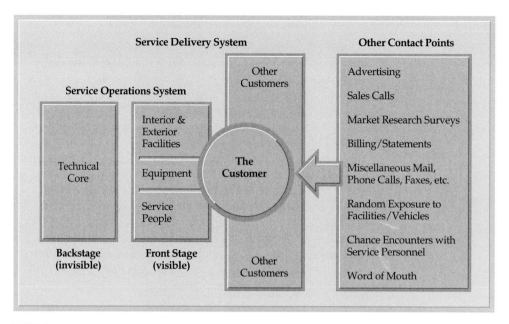

FIGURE 8-3   Services Marketing System (From Christopher H. Lovelock, *Services Marketing*, 3rd ed. [Englewood Cliffs, NJ: Prentice-Hall, 1996], p. 55.)

Customer Compatibility

Services frequently require that customers be present for service delivery (doctors, lawyers, dentists, cruises, concerts). This means that services are delivered in an environment where the customers interact with other clients. Note that Figure 8-3 highlights this relationship by showing one customer surrounded by other customers. There often is a direct connection between how a customer fits in with other clients and overall customer satisfaction. Successful service firms recognize this problem and are careful to segment their markets and group customers accordingly. For example, it would be foolish for a law firm to offer estate planning services and criminal law representation out of the same office. This would force wealthy customers interested in preserving their assets to sit in the same waiting room as clients seeking representation for robbery and theft. These two groups are incompatible and need to be serviced by offices located in separate buildings. The cruise ship industry is very good at ensuring customer compatibility by offering theme cruises targeted to bridge players, ballroom dancing enthusiasts, singles, and other groups.

APPLYING
. . . *to*
Professional
Services
Marketing

Managing Service Quality

Firms that consistently deliver high-quality services can expect higher returns than organizations with poor customer relations. Table 8-2 shows how the top third of a sample of business units outperformed the bottom third in terms of service quality. These data reveal that high-service businesses were able to charge higher prices, grow faster, and make more profits on sales than their low-service competitors. Other research has shown that service quality is an antecedent of customer satisfaction. These results suggest that service organizations must pay attention to quality.

While it is easy to talk about delivering quality services, there are a number of problems that must be overcome. First, service quality is much more difficult to measure than product quality. Good service from a doctor is clearly a more subjective evaluation than whether a

TABLE 8-2 Service Quality and Performance

	Top Third in Service Quality	Bottom Third in Service Quality
Prices relative to competitors	7%	−2%
Change in market share per year	6%	−2%
Sales growth	17%	8%
Return on sales	12%	1%

Source: Phillip Thompson, Glenn Desoursa, and Bradley T. Gale, "The Strategic Management of Service and Quality," *Quality Progress,* (June 1985), p. 24.

INTEGRATING
. . . *with*
Production/
Operations
Management

dishwasher detergent cleans the spots off your drinking glasses. Remember, services are delivered by highly variable humans, whereas products are produced on assembly lines that are more easily checked and monitored.

Another problem is that customers often blame themselves for poor service delivery because they did not play their role correctly. If a garage fails to fix your car or a haircut is not right, customers often think they were unable to explain the malfunction or hairstyle adequately. In these situations, the customer does not complain about poor service quality, but simply goes to another shop in the future. Sophisticated service providers understand the presence of self blame and make a special effort to follow up by phone or mail to check on customer satisfaction.

To manage service quality successfully, you have to know what level of service customers expect. When clients call a securities firm, they do not expect to be put on hold for five minutes and bombarded with recorded excuses and Musak. Thus part of your job is to run surveys, analyze complaints, and review customer comment cards to determine exactly what buyers expect from service companies. Southwest Airlines is doing better than other airlines because customers know that Southwest planes are on time and offer low fares. Marketing Strategies box 8-2 shows how Southwest is moving its quality operation East.

Once you know what customers expect from a service company, you are in a better position to deliver. Frequently the easiest way to improve service quality is by providing front-line people with more training. This gives customer contact representatives a more solid background in solving problems and completing transactions more quickly. Another technique that can reduce human errors and improve quality is to provide additional automated equipment. Some firms have boosted their quality by adding Web sites and more toll-free phone lines, switching to 24-hour automated access to account data, and using computers to schedule doctors' appointments. Web sites are particularly attractive because of their ability to reduce customer errors and allow greater customization of services.[3]

INTEGRATING
. . . *with*
Information
Technology

The use of technology to improve service quality is demonstrated by Alaska Airlines, a Seattle-based carrier that serves the West Coast. Alaska was one of the first U.S. airlines to sell tickets on the Internet and to offer electronic ticketing. However, the company saw little consumer benefit if the traveler still had to queue for 20 minutes at the gate to obtain a boarding pass. So in 1996 it was the first U.S. airline to install self-service check-in computer kiosks for its e-ticket fliers. The machines verify the traveler's itinerary, pose security questions, sell upgrades, and dole out boarding passes, all in little more than a minute.

APPLYING
. . . *to*
Transportation
Services
Marketing

Alaska plans to have 310 kiosks in place in 1999 and is starting to put them in remote sites such as airport parking garages and hotels. The company is also working on machines to automatically identify frequent fliers as they approach the counter and allow self-service baggage checking in an effort to make it easier for passengers to avoid lines and delays at airports. By offering better service than its competitors, Alaska expects to attract more customers.[4]

APPLYING
... to
Transportation
Services
Marketing

MARKETING STRATEGIES 8-2

Southwest Moves East

Southwest Airlines, which began operations in Texas in 1981, has now expanded its high quality service to the Washington, Boston, and New York metropolitan areas. In each case, Southwest has chosen to land at small uncontested airports. To serve Washington, Southwest operates from Baltimore and the Boston market is handled by departures from Manchester, New Hampshire, and Providence, Rhode Island. These airports have lower landing fees and Southwest's planes do not have to enter the crowded Washington and Boston airspace. For New York, Southwest plans to operate out of Long Island's MacArthur Airport near Islip, New York. The addition of Islip will allow Southwest to compete in the lucrative market for direct flights to Orlando, Florida, Chicago, Illinois and Los Angeles, California. The secret of Southwest's success is to offer high departure frequencies, the best on-time record in the industry and low fares. The expected fare from Islip to Orlando is $160 compared to a standard fare of $259 and the fare to Los Angeles is only $302 while competitors charge $900. Southwest cuts its costs by operating only one type of airplane and skips amenities such as fancy meals. This allows Southwest to turn its flights around quickly at the small airports it uses and maximizes utilization of its fleet. At each of the secondary Eastern airports it has entered, average fares have declined sharply and passengers per day have risen dramatically.

— *Providing high quality services at economical prices improves sales and profits.*

Source: Scott McCartney, "Southwest Puts New York on Map," *The Wall Street Journal*, November 4, 1998, p. B1.

Courtesy Southwest Airlines

Managing Service Demand

Most services cannot be stored in inventory. When demand is high, there is usually no backup stock to help fill orders, and potential business is lost. When demand is low, service capacity is wasted. With manufactured goods, it is much easier to match production with demand and to draw down inventories when demand is unusually high. Service organizations need extra help to manage demand.

The first step is to list the major factors that affect sales. Does demand vary by the hour, day, week, or month? What are the underlying causes of demand changes? In some situations, service demand is affected by work schedules, pay dates, climate, and school schedules. Once managers know why customers use services, adjustments can be made to smooth fluctuations over time.

An example of the impact of demand variation on services is shown in Figure 8-4. In sector 1 of the diagram, demand exceeds maximum service capacity and customers are lost. When demand is greater than optimum capacity (sector 2), the quality of service deteriorates. This is undesirable because customers who wait in line for service may never return. With low demand (sector 3), service capacity is wasted and investors and customers may get the impression that the business is poorly run.

Inventorying Demand.   Although most services cannot be carried in inventory, astute marketers can inventory demand. The idea is to get customers to wait in line for services or to make appointments for a future slack period. Both of these approaches can help shift peak demand (Figure 8-4, sector 1) to periods with excess capacity.

The use of queues to manage demand is simplified if you know how long customers will wait. Amusement parks understand customer time constraints and sometimes use clocks to show how long it will take to get on a particular ride. They also provide covered ramps to provide shade and refreshment stands to make waiting easier. Other ways to make queues more enjoyable include providing seating, reading material, and numbered tags to show people their positions in line.

Inventorying Supply.   Although we have emphasized that many services cannot be carried in inventory, firms can carry inventories of required equipment. Thus car and truck rental

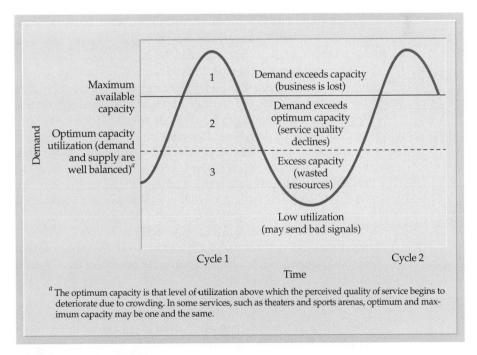

FIGURE 8-4   **Impact of Demand Variation on Service Utilization (From Christopher H. Lovelock, *Services Marketing*, 3rd ed. [Englewood Cliffs, NJ: Prentice-Hall, 1996], p. 210.**

INTEGRATING
... with
Production/
Operations
Management

firms can have storage lots of vehicles that can be quickly dispatched to areas of high demand. Also transportation companies maintain fleets of backup equipment that can be called in as needed. FedEx, for example, keeps 17 unused DC-10 aircraft stored on a desert field in Arizona so they can be phased into their fleet when demand is strong.[5]

Using Price.   A common method for balancing a limited service supply with varying levels of demand is through the use of pricing. The best approach is to set regular prices for high-demand periods and then offer special low prices to attract budget-minded customers to off-peak times. This procedure is used by ski resorts where special reduced-price lift tickets are offered for early and late season periods when snow conditions are less favorable. The advantage is that customers prefer paying lower prices during slow periods rather than paying higher prices when facilities are crowded. High regular prices help allocate demand and can increase profits at the same time. Also, special low prices attract customers during periods of low demand (Figure 8-4, sector 3). Because many service costs are fixed, special low prices can improve profits if demand is sufficiently elastic.

A good example of using pricing to manage demand is provided by the airlines. They charge high rates for inflexible business travelers and much lower rates for vacationers and people with limited resources. This successful strategy of pricing to shift air travel usage is based on a thorough understanding of the price elasticity of demand for each market segment. Service providers also have to ensure that the low-priced off-peak services do not attract too many peak customers. Airlines solve this problem by attaching enough restrictions to their excursion fares so that they cannot be used by full-fare business travelers.

Using Advertising.   Another effective technique to shift peak demand to slack periods is through advertising. Appropriate signs and advertising messages can encourage prospective customers to buy services during slack periods. Off-season promotions by resorts have been effective because some customers prefer vacationing when beaches are less crowded and there are no lines at the tennis courts. Suggestions to avoid the rush are also successful when aimed at movie theater and transit customers. When intermediaries such as travel agents are used, they can tell customers when the best slack-demand periods occur.

APPLYING
... to
Home
Entertainment
Services
Marketing

Overcoming Regulations with Technology.   When satellite TV service companies began to offer hundreds of channels and high-quality digital images for subscribers, Congress passed laws to protect broadcast and cable companies by limiting satellite access to local TV stations. Consumers could get hundreds of wonderful channels, but they could not get local news and weather. This blatant example of protective lobbying by the established TV industry slowed the growth of satellite TV in America and made it more difficult for satellite firms to manage demand. To avoid this regulatory problem, satellite TV firms have been signing marketing agreements with regional phone companies. This has allowed them to add a powerful new antennae to their satellite dishes to get local channels along with a package of phone, video, and high-speed data services. Many satellite customers are now enjoying more channels, better reception, and lower monthly costs than they were paying for cable. By using technology to overcome the restrictions on local TV access, satellite firms have now gained access to a much broader range of market segments for their direct satellite services.[6]

Managing the Mix of Service Customers

The selection of customers is much more important for service organizations than for manufacturers. While many manufactured goods are consumed in the privacy of customers' homes, service clients are often part of the product. In addition, service providers face fixed capacity constraints, whereas factories can easily schedule overtime to meet surges in demand. As a result, service managers must choose their customers with care.

Customer Profitability.   Service organizations have a high ratio of fixed to variable costs because of expensive facilities, equipment, and a cadre of full-time personnel. As a result, most of the costs of service organizations continue on and are not dependent on whether the hotel rooms are rented or the theater tickets are sold. Under these conditions, the firm does better by setting prices low enough to fill all available seats in a plane or sports arena. Generally the higher the usage rate, the greater the profit.

A common measure of performance in service firms is the percentage of capacity sold. Airlines talk of their "load factor" and hotels of their "occupancy rate." Although these percentages tell us something about how a company is run, they say very little about profits because the customers may have been obtained by aggressive price cutting. This suggests that success depends on knowing how much each customer segment will pay for services at different points in time.

In pricing services, one measure of success compares the average price obtained per unit with the maximum price that might have been charged.[7] When this ratio, called the *yield percentage,* is multiplied by *capacity utilization,* the result is an index of *asset revenue-generating efficiency* (ARGE). Suppose that a hotel has 200 rooms with a posted price of $100. On a particular night, 80 rooms are sold for $100 and 40 for $70. The yield percentage would be:

*INTEGRATING
. . . with
Accounting
Production/
Operations
Management*

$$\frac{\dfrac{(80 \times \$100) + (40 \times \$70)}{120}}{100} = \frac{\$90}{\$100} = 0.90$$

When this ratio is multiplied by the utilization factor of $120 \div 200 = 0.60$, an ARGE value of 0.54 is obtained ($0.90 \times 0.60 = 0.54$). ARGE can also be calculated by looking at the actual revenues relative to the maximum revenues that could be obtained:

$$\text{ARGE} = \frac{(80 \times \$100) + (40 \times \$70)}{(200 \times \$100)} = 0.54$$

These results show that the simple utilization ratio of 0.60 was lowered to a more meaningful *ARGE* of 0.54 by some price cutting. The ARGE ratio is a handy yardstick for evaluating how well a firm manages the desired customer mix.

Planning the Customer Mix.   One of the tricks of service marketing is recognizing the opportunity costs associated with accepting business from different groups of customers. For example, should a hotel book a block of rooms at a low price or hold them in case some transient guests show up to pay full rates? The answer might be that it depends on the probability of transient customers arriving. In reality, the solution is much more complicated. The reason is that customer demand is also influenced by personal selling and advertising. Since both of these factors are under the control of management, marketing managers must carefully plan how to allocate service capacity among different customer segments at particular times.

*APPLYING
. . . to
Transportation
Services
Marketing*

Perhaps the most successful *revenue management systems* are employed by airlines to allocate seats to different classes of passengers. American Airlines was the first to use a sophisticated computerized reservation system that allowed them to change seat allotments and prices as the flight time approached. For example, American might allocate 50 super-saver seats for a flight to Florida leaving in 60 days and 100 seats to higher-paying tourist customers. If they sold 30 super-saver seats in 20 days, they might cut the allocation to 40 seats with the idea of selling the other 10 seats to higher-paying tourist passengers as the departure time of the flight approaches. Airlines change the capacity allocations and prices of airline seats on an hourly basis to make sure that their planes are as full as possible and revenues are maximized. The system is so refined that it automatically sends last-minute e-mail announcements of seat availability to people who have expressed interest in traveling certain routes.

Managing Productivity

Because service organizations are highly labor-intensive, many tasks are difficult to automate. This means that when wages increase, prices have to be raised and service growth tends to slow down. As a result, service managers are continually looking for ways to make operations more efficient.

The types of problems managers face are illustrated by employees answering customer-service calls at mutual fund companies. Phone reps are in relatively low-paid, low-glamour, high-turnover positions. A few years ago, a phone rep at Fidelity took 3 minutes and 188 keystrokes to complete a transaction. Now an advanced software package allows the transaction to be completed with 33 keystrokes in just 1 minute and 9 seconds. This allows Fidelity to handle more calls with fewer people and reduces customer waiting times. An even more advanced program is in the works that will allow phone reps to call up short bulletins on taxes, IRAs, and optimum fund allocations. These programs make it easier to train personnel, and phone reps will soon carry out most of the services offered by full-service brokers.

Another way to increase productivity in service industries is to move the work to lower-wage offshore locations. Recent advances in telecommunications technology and improved educational systems have made it easier to move backroom operations abroad. In Jamaica, 3,500 people work at office parks connected to the United States by satellite dishes. There they make airline reservations, process tickets, handle calls to toll-free numbers, and do data entry work. More than 25,000 documents a day are scanned electronically in the United States, and copies are transmitted to Montego Bay for processing. In Ireland, multilingual workers answer questions on computer software programs for customers in the United States and Europe. Metropolitan Life has 150 workers in Ireland analyzing U.S. medical insurance claims. Offshore service workers tend to be more productive and cost 35 percent less than U.S. workers do. In addition, foreign governments often grant tax concessions, and workforce turnover is usually very low.[8]

SUMMARY

Consumption of services is growing rapidly, so you need to understand how to market these intangible products. Marketing of services is tricky because services are perishable and often require the presence of a buyer. Since services are created and consumed at the same time, the delivery channel can be vital to your success. Other special characteristics of services include greater variability and stronger client relationships than for durables. Services have a high ratio of fixed to variable costs and require careful management to avoid losses during slack times. Successful managers know how to use reservation systems, pricing, and promotion to shift demand from peak to off-peak periods. Those who master the subtleties of service marketing are likely to satisfy customers, improve bottom-line performance, and reap financial rewards.

NOTES

1. "German Tele-Wars, Episode Umpteen," *The Wall Street Journal,* December 30, 1998, p. A6.

2. Evan Ramstad, "PC Makers Hunt for Gold in Internet Hookups," *The Wall Street Journal,* August

12, 1998, pp. B1, B4.

3. Leyland Pitt, Pierre Berthon, and Richard T. Watson, "Cyberservice: Taming Service Marketing Problems with the World Wide Web," *Business Horizons,* January–February 1999, pp. 11–17.

4. Susan Carey. "New Gizmos May Zip Travelers Through Airport Lines," *The Wall Street Journal,* January 4, 1999, pp. A13, A15.

5. Douglas A. Blackmon, "Will FedEx Shift from Moving Boxes to Bytes?" *The Wall Street Journal,* November 20, 1998, pp. B1, B8.

6. Leslie Cauley, "Antennae Attract Viewers to Satellite TV," *The Wall Street Journal,* December 3, 1998, pp. B1, B4.

7. Christopher H. Lovelock, *Services Marketing,* 3rd ed. (Englewood Cliffs, NJ: Prentice-Hall, 1996), p. 191.

8. Brian O'Reilly, "Your New Global Work Force," *Fortune,* December 14, 1992, p. 62.

SUGGESTED READING

Cross, Robert G. "Launching the Revenue Rocket," *Cornell Hotel and Restaurant Administration Quarterly,* April 1997, pp. 32–42.

REFERENCES

Fitzsimons, James A. and Mona J. Fitzsimons. *Service Management* (Boston: Irwin/McGraw-Hill, 1998).

Goncalves, Karen P. *Services Marketing* (Upper Saddle River, NJ: Prentice-Hall, 1997).

Kurtz, David L., and Kenneth E. Clow. *Services Marketing* (New York: John Wiley & Sons, 1997).

Lovelock, Christopher H. *Services Marketing,* 3rd ed. (Upper Saddle River, NJ: Prentice-Hall, 1996).

Payne, Adrian, and Malcolm B. McDonald. *Marketing Planning for Services* (Butterworth-Heinemann, 1993).

Zeithaml, Valarie A. and Mary Jo Bitner. *Services Marketing* (New York: McGraw-Hill, 1996).

Zimmerman, Jan, Michael Mathiesen, and Jerry Yanj. *Marketing on the Internet: A 7 Step Plan for Selling Your Products, Services, and Image to Millions over the Internet,* 3rd ed. (Gulf Breeze, FL: Maximum Press, 1998).

QUESTIONS

1. Alaska Air Group Inc. announced plans to enter a marketing arrangement with American Airlines and American Eagle commuter carrier. Why would Alaska, the nation's tenth largest airline, want a closer relationship with a giant service provider like American?

2. A marketing consultant to the legal profession has said: "Law firms are finding that the most effective way to get new business is to hire lawyers who already have it." Does this mean that the $45 million a year that lawyers spend on TV advertising is wasted? Should lawyers spend money on Yellow Pages advertising, entertainment, brochures, seminars, and newsletters?

3. Alltell Corporation Inc., a Little Rock, Arkansas, provider of local, long-distance, wireless and Internet access services has agreed to acquire Aliant Communications of Lincoln, Nebraska, for $1.4 billion. Why are we seeing so many mergers between local, long-distance, wireless, and Internet communications providers? What advantages do the combined companies gain?

4. An automatic teller machine (ATM) costs an average of $50,000 a year to service and maintain. This is twice the cost of a human teller. Why are banks and savings and loans installing ATMs, and how do they make them pay? Why do people use ATMs for withdrawals but not for deposits? How could this behavior be changed?

5. AT&T, historically America's largest long-distance phone carrier, has bought the largest U.S. cable TV company, TCI of Denver. They plan to use TCI cables to offer local telephone and high-speed Internet service circumventing the Bell company lines that AT&T must rely upon. Why is AT&T so eager to spend billions to get into local phone service?

6. Video rental is one of the fastest-growing departments in supermarkets. Sales are increasing 11 percent per year. Should supermarkets devote more space to the sale of other services?

7. Today 91 percent of U.S. hospitals have marketing programs costing more than $1.6 billion; about $500 million of which is spent each year on advertising. A survey of customers revealed that hospital advertising is considered boring, unclear, and uninformative. Respondents were turned off by "mushy" image-enhancing advertising slogans. Does this mean that hospitals should spend less on advertising? What would you recommend?

8. The cruise industry is attracting more passengers by adding exercise equipment, conference centers, small TVs in cabins, movie theaters, Las Vegas-style shows, financial seminars, shopping arcades, and casinos. They have also had great success with "theme" cruises that appeal to jazz enthusiasts, stamp collectors, bridge players, and pastry chefs. Does this mean that segmentation is the salvation of all service businesses?

9. The Canadian government has proposed legislation that would prohibit American magazine publishers from selling advertising space to Canadian firms. The intent of the law is to protect Canadian culture by reserving Canadian advertising dollars to Canadian publications. The United States objects to the law and says it will retaliate with tariffs on millions of dollars of trade with Canada. Since Canada has a free-trade agreement with the United States, it is fair for Canada to restrict U.S. sales of advertising services to Canadian firms?

10. You work for Media, Inc., which specializes in buying and selling airtime from radio and TV stations. Media, Inc., pays for airtime with travel, recorded jingles, and equipment and then resells the airtime to advertisers. You notice that Media, Inc., also routinely provides clients and prospects with cars, prostitutes, and envelopes filled with cash. Should you report these activities to your boss? the president of the company? the Securities and Exchange Commission? the police? Or should you remain silent?

11. Andrew Jackson Cooper was recently promoted to Vice-President of Marketing of an Atlanta region bank. When he moved into his new office, he found a very dated bank segmentation survey among the files there. Before throwing the survey away, he decided to have his summer intern reanalyze the data. If important relationships could be found, a new survey to update the information might be justified. The data is in the file bankdat.sav. It contains mainly categorical variables: reasons for choosing one's current bank, bank services used, media habits—especially radio listening—and sociodemographic characteristics.

CASE 8-1 SINGAPORE AIRLINES*

As Robert Ang left the marketing executives' meeting and walked through the open air gallery back to his office in Airline House, he remembered what J. Y. Pillay, Singapore Airlines' Chairman, had said four years earlier at the company's 40th anniversary celebrations in 1987. "At 40 the symptoms of middle age begin and that's when complacency sets in," he had warned. Ang thought to himself, "And now that we are 44, this risk is even greater if we don't do something to hold onto our customer-oriented image." The discussion at the meeting on this fine May morning had centered on the role of technology in achieving this goal.

Ang paused to watch a Boeing 747-400 coming in to land. Dubbed the "Megatop" because of its extended upper deck, the aircraft was the most recent addition to the company's ultra-modern fleet. Singapore Airlines' blue, white, and yellow colors shone brightly in the steamy midday heat.

As Ang entered the office complex that housed his marketing systems team, he imagined the passengers starting to disembark after a 12- to 13-hour nonstop trip from Europe. What sort of flight had they had? Had the long journey gone well, reinforcing Singapore Airlines' reputation as one of the world's best airlines? The cabin crew would now be saying goodbye, and the passengers would soon be welcomed into the spacious elegance of Terminal 2 at Changi Airport, one of the largest and most modern in the world.

Ang knew that the company's achievements were already considerable; it had become one of the world's 10 biggest international airlines. But now, on the threshold of a new decade, the question was: could Singapore Airlines continue to attract increasing numbers of international customers?

"We are leaders in service, in comfort and luxury. Our customers tell us they fall in love when they fly with us. Where do we go from here?" were some of the remarks voiced at the meeting. For Robert Ang, there was only one logical answer: they had to satisfy the needs of contemporary travelers, which meant being able to bring the sophisticated technology found in people's homes and offices into the air. "Very little

attention has been given to adapting technology strategically for our business," he had declared to his colleagues that morning. "For instance, home audio systems are fantastic. But in the air, they're terrible. We have to close this technology gap and provide modern customers with interesting and useful technology-based services."

Ang's views had been received with interest. His boss, the director of marketing planning, had closed the meeting by asking him to come up with some specific suggestions. "But," he had cautioned, "don't suggest anything that might conflict with the romance and superb personal service we're rightly famous for!"

BACKGROUND

"How did it all begin?" was a question that people encountering Singapore Airlines for the first time often asked. Many were surprised that a small island republic, measuring only 38 km long by 22 km wide (16 × 24 miles), and with a population of 2.7 million, could have one of the world's largest and most profitable airlines. Even more remarkable were the accolades bestowed by air travel organizations. In 1990, *Air Transport World* magazine named SIA "airline of the year"; *Conde Nast's Traveler* termed it the "world's best airline"; and *Business Traveler International* called SIA the "best international airline."

Republic of Singapore

Just north of the equator, with a command of the straits between Malaysia and Indonesia, Singapore was ideally located for both shipping and airline routes. Being at the intersection of East and West, it saw itself at the heart of trade and business between the two.

In the 26 years since its independence in 1965, the nation had made what most observers considered to be astonishing economic progress. Per capita national income had reached US$10,450, representing 37% that of Switzerland, which Singaporean planners often cited as their economic model. It boasted not only one of the world's largest and most modern port facilities, but an airport, opened in 1981 and expanded in 1990,

* This case was prepared by Sandra Vandermerwe and Christopher H. Lovelock. Copyright (c) by the International Institute for Management Development (IMD), Lausanne, Switzerland. Reproduced by permission.

of equal caliber. Other accomplishments included a state-of-the-art telecommunications system, well-engineered highways, and the new Mass Rapid Transit rail system. Heavy investments in education and a strong work ethic had created a well-trained and motivated workforce. By 1991, Singapore was one of the world's largest shipbuilding and ship-repairing centers, the third largest oil refining and distribution complex, and had also become an important banking and financial center.

Singapore had made a particular effort to attract high technology firms, and many international companies had set up offices and plants on the island. Government planners saw technology as a driving force in the economy. As advances in telecommunications proceeded, and Singapore Telecom continued to push toward a fully digitalized system, planners spoke about creating an "intelligent island."

History of Singapore Airlines

Who would have believed that a country only one-quarter the size of Rhode Island, the smallest state in the United States, would produce one of the most profitable airlines in the world? The story of Singapore Airlines officially started on May 1, 1947, when the first scheduled flight of Malaysian Airlines from Singapore landed in Penang. When both Malaysia and Singapore became independent in the mid-1960s, the name of the carrier was changed to Malaysia-Singapore Airlines. However it soon became obvious that the two nations had different priorities. Malaysia's main interest was having a flag carrier that would provide domestic and regional routes. But, being a small island, Singapore did not need domestic services; instead, its goal was to have long-distance international routes. It was agreed that the assets should be divided and two separate airlines created.

Singapore Airlines first flew under its own colors in October 1972. When it was announced that Malaysia and Singapore had agreed to establish two separate flag carriers, optimism was tempered by uncertainty and disbelief. Could an airline from such a small country compete in the international big league? Nevertheless, the 1970s seemed to be a good time for an airline to take off and succeed. Not only did the remarkable passenger growth of the 1960s—when traffic was doubling every five years—promise to continue, but ever increasing numbers of people worldwide were traveling to more places. In addition, exciting new high performance jets were being introduced.

Although Singapore Airlines (SIA) was state owned, the government's role in policy making and day to day management was minimal; senior executives were told not to expect any subsidy or preferential treatment. What the government did do, however, was to offer foreign carriers the opportunity to operate out of Singapore, under the condition that SIA would receive similar rights, even if they were not exercised immediately. The new airline pushed relentlessly for growth and innovation. Three months before operations began, it signed a contract with Boeing for the delivery of two B747-200s, with an option on two more. It was the first airline in Southeast Asia to order jumbo jets.

Singapore Airlines also concentrated on marketing: the airline's name and its logo—a stylized yellow bird—decorating the aircraft's dark blue tail fin soon became well known on the routes it operated. The goal was to create a distinctly different airline that would be international but retain its Asian personality. Most importantly, top management insisted that it emphasize service to passengers who, they constantly reminded staff, were the unique reason for the airline's existence. In a world where one carrier resembled another, they realized that the cabin crew was the prime link between the passenger and the airline. The idea was to use the island's only real resource—the natural hospitality of its people—as a competitive advantage. In this way, it seemed certain that Singapore's national carrier would be remembered—and remembered favorably.

Research had shown that, when all other things were equal, passengers responded most to the appeal of high quality in-flight services. SIA was the first airline to put "snoozers" (fully reclining seats) in its aircraft. Since the company did not belong to IATA (International Air Transport Association), SIA's management went against the rules by serving free drinks, offering free movie headsets and other extras. The intent was to firmly establish an image of SIA in customers' minds as *the* airline for fine service.

The "Singapore Girl"—the personification of charm and friendliness—became a reality after painstaking recruiting, training and retraining. The best-looking and most helpful young women were selected as stewardesses. They were given a maximum of three contract terms of five years each, above average wages, and high status in the company. Better staff were given the possibility of promotion to senior jobs within SIA after the 15 year period. An extensive and distinctive advertising campaign promoted these stewardesses dressed in multi-colored, ankle-length dresses made from beautiful batik fabric designed by the Paris couturier, Balmain. Male flight attendants were more conventionally dressed in light blue blazers and black trousers.

These sarong-sebaya clad women became the symbol of the airline's mission to deliver high quality personalized service. Research showed that they had the most lasting impact on passengers. Travelers reported that their distinctive uniform and charm were, in reality, all that the advertising had promised, and that in-flight service was better than anything they had experienced in a long time.

Top management was equally concerned with services on the ground. In 1973 a subsidiary company, Singapore Airport Terminal Services (SATS), was formed to perform ground handling, catering, and related tasks. Later, it started offering its services on a contract basis to other carriers that had operations in Singapore. In 1985, SATS was restructured into a holding company with four subsidiaries—SATS Passenger Services, SATS Catering, SATS Cargo, and SATS Apron Services.

Singapore Airlines survived the two oil shocks of the 1970s and continued to grow, creating headlines with such innovations as supersonic Concorde service between London and Singapore, operated jointly with British Airways, featuring BA colors on one side of the aircraft and SIA colors on the other. It also expanded its route structure. Huge aircraft orders, including what was then the largest in civil aviation history, were made. Thanks to strong profits, the airline was able to invest in new equipment without incurring significant debt. These enormous purchases were not all incremental additions to the fleet, for the company resold used aircraft after only a few years. Because they had been so well maintained, the "old" aircraft found ready buyers at good prices in the second-hand market.

THE SITUATION IN 1991

As one industry observer remarked, "1990 was a year that most airlines would sooner forget!" Battered by recession, a hike in oil prices, high interest rates on heavy debt loads, and the tensions arising from the Iraqi invasion of Kuwait, most major airlines suffered heavy financial losses. The outbreak of hostilities in the Gulf intensified problems; fear of terrorist attacks sharply reduced passenger loads on most international routes. But, at a time when many other airlines were retrenching, Singapore Airlines actually increased its advertising budget.

SIA's consolidated financial results for the fiscal year ending 31 March 1991 showed only a slight decline in revenues, from S\$5.09 billion to S\$4.95 billion.[1] The number of passengers carried climbed from 6.8 million to 7.1 million, even though the load factor dropped from 78.3% to 75.1% as a result of a jump in fleet size. In 1990, SIA had the highest operating profit of any airline in the world: US\$775 million. Apart from its marketing appeal, Singapore Airlines had another point in its favor—the higher margins obtained on airline services in Asia. The Asian carriers did not compete on price among themselves. They preferred non-price forms of competition such as better service, more destinations, more frequent schedules, and newer fleets. With the entry of American players into the region, however, price became a more important feature.

The airline's fleet of 29 Boeing 747s and 14 Airbus 310s was the youngest fleet of all international carriers, with an average aircraft age of 4.75 years, compared to an industry average of around 10 years. The company had 36 new aircraft on order (of which 28 were the new B747-400s) and another 34 on option. Management was convinced that newer planes were not only more attractive to passengers and helped staff provide better service, but also offered other advantages such as greater reliability and lower fuel consumption. (Exhibit 1 compares Singapore Airlines' performance measures with those of other major international airlines.)

By 1991 Singapore Airlines was among the ten biggest airlines in the world, as measured in terms of international tonne-kilometers of load carried. Its network linked 63 cities in 37 countries, and soon it would fulfill a long-held ambition to serve the East Coast of the United States with transatlantic service from Frankfurt to New York. Singapore Changi Airport had become one of the world's largest and busiest terminals.

Government holdings had been reduced through stock sales to 54% of the company's assets. The airline had joined in a trilateral alliance with Swissair and the American carrier, Delta Airlines, to cooperate on customer servicing, interchangeable tour packages, through check-in, joint baggage handling, sharing of airport lounges, and joint promotions. It had also become a member of IATA in order to give the airline a voice in key industry forums, and greater access to their technical expertise and accredited sales agents. However, SIA did not want to participate in delibera-

---

[1] At the end of March 1991, the exchange rate for the Singapore dollar was: SF1.25 = S\$1.00; US\$1.00 = S\$1.70; £1.00 = S\$3.10.

EXHIBIT 1   Key Performance Measures 1990

1990 Scheduled Passengers Carried (International)		1990 Scheduled Passenger-Kilometers Performed (International)		1990 Operating Profits of the Top Ten of these Airlines	
Rank:	Numbers (in thousands)	Rank:	Numbers (in millions)	Rank:	US Dollars (millions)
1 British Airways	19,684	1 British Airways	62,834	1 Singapore Airlines	774
2 Lufthansa	13,326	2 Japan Airlines	42,690	2 Cathay Pacific	468
3 Air France	12,417	3 Lufthansa	38,744	3 Japan Airlines	464
4 Pan American	10,096	4 Pan American	38,241	4 British Airways	345
5 Japan Airlines	8,354	5 United	35,334	5 SAS	264
6 American Airlines	8,343	6 Singapore Airlines	31,544	6 American Airlines	67.9
7 SAS	8,335	7 Air France	29,023	7 Lufthansa	0
8 Cathay Pacific	7,378	8 Qantas	27,687	8 KLM	(19.3)
9 Alitalia	7,105	9 KLM	26,382	9 Alitalia	(75.7)
10 Singapore Airlines	7,093	10 American Airlines	24,086	10 Air France	(286)

tions on tariff coordination where fare issues were discussed.

Despite the airline's achievements, there were some disquieting signs on the horizon. Competition was intensifying and service quality improving among a number of both Western and Asian airlines, including Hong Kong-based Cathay Pacific, Japan Airlines, a new strongly financed Taiwanese start-up called Eva Air, Thai International, and Malaysia Airlines. The latter two both featured stewardesses in eye-catching uniforms based on traditional costumes.

With rising living standards in Singapore came higher expectations among its more than 13,000 employees, of whom some 4,200 were cabin crew. The company was finding it increasingly difficult to attract younger people, motivate existing employees and maintain its policy of employing the best staff for customer contact roles.

MAINTAINING THE CUSTOMER SERVICE PHILOSOPHY

Recognizing that the most exciting years were now over, top management continued to stress the importance of SIA's customer philosophy and service culture. The underlying principle that the customer came first was carried through at all levels of the organization. How customers were handled at each point of contact was considered of paramount importance. Company policy stated that if a trade-off had to be made, it should be made in favor of the customer. For example, contrary to the practice at other airlines, no customer was allowed to be downgraded for a Singapore Airlines senior executive who wanted a special seat.

Ground had recently been broken for a new US$50 million training center, designed to drill all employees in the fine art of serving customers. As reported in the *Straits Times,* Singapore's leading newspaper, everyone—from the floor sweeper to the deputy managing director—would receive this training. The underlying philosophy was to enable staff to place themselves in the customer's position. A lot of the training time was thus experientially based. Key people were sent on special missions to see what other airlines were doing and how customers were handled. Special delay simulation games groomed staff on ways to cope with delay situations, one of the major complaints received from passengers.

One principle remained constant: staff had to be as flexible as possible in their dealings with customers, even if it took more time and effort. Management constantly reiterated that customers could not be told what to do simply because it suited the company. Some passengers wanted to eat as soon as they boarded, others preferred to wait. Customers could not be pigeonholed; they often changed their minds. They might come on board intending to sleep and then decide to watch a movie after all. On long hauls, flexibility was especially important. Most passengers had individual habits that corresponded to their travel agendas, which could include sleeping at the beginning and working later, or vice versa.

Staff had learned that customers were happier when given a choice. Offering more meal variations automatically reduced the number of unhappy people. Menus, typically changed by other airlines no more than four times a year, were altered every week on SIA's high frequency flights. Information technology enabled the chefs to fine-tune menus and immediately withdraw any dishes that were poorly received. Although there were marginal costs associated with such tactics, management firmly believed that these efforts distinguished Singapore Airlines from its competitors. Staff were instructed to find other ways to save money. For instance, the chefs prepared meals only from ingredients in season. Crew members were briefed by the kitchen on how to prepare and serve anything new.

Complaints were encouraged as they provided insight about problems. Once they were received, something could be done to rectify the situation; all complaints were tracked down and followed up. Travelers were invited to submit these complaints in writing. While some customers—typically Americans, Germans and Australians—readily complied, others were less willing to do so in writing. These customers were specifically questioned in follow-up surveys.

A Service Productivity Index (SPI) was computed each quarter in order to assess service quality standards. Multilingual in-flight surveys were used to itemize customers' impressions on key issues; then this information was compiled along with data on punctuality, baggage mishandled/recovered per 1000 passengers, and the ratio of complaints to compliments addressed to management.

As soon as a complaint relating directly to a specific in-flight experience was received, crew members could be temporarily taken out of the system and given training. Cabin crew members were released from their flight schedules three or four times a year to meet with training experts. Senior cabin crew members met every Monday morning for feedback and exchange sessions with service support personnel. One "ritual" practiced was to address the crew from the control center just before takeoff about topical issues, special promotions and other issues relevant to services.

At the airport in Singapore, staff were encouraged to do everything possible to deal with legitimate customer problems. One story—now part of company folklore—was about a supervisor who found a tailor at midnight and paid a deposit from his own funds to have a suit made for a customer whose luggage had been lost so that the customer could attend an important meeting at noon the next day.

CUSTOMER PROFILE AND THE PRODUCT LINE

The product line was divided into three classes of travel—First, Raffles (business), and Economy. First Class accounted for 5% of passengers, Raffles Class for 10%, and Economy Class for 85%. About one million of the seven million seats sold annually were to Singaporeans. Revenues from non-Singaporeans were proportionately higher since they tended to fly longer distances. Of the airline's passengers, 75% were from outside the country and 25% were from home base.

Flights varied in length—from less than one hour to over 13 hours for nonstop flights to Europe. Flights under four hours were all non-smoking, reflecting Singapore's strong national commitment to curtailing tobacco use. (Exhibit 2 gives the airline's daily flights by number of hours and amount of overnight travel.)

On average, the load factor was somewhat higher in Economy Class (close to 80%) than in Raffles or First. Passengers who flew Raffles Class on a daytime flight might travel First Class on an overnight flight for the extra comfort.

Top management believed that the business passenger market held the future for the airline—both in numbers and yield. At the marketing executive meeting Robert Ang had just attended, everyone had concurred that technology was the key to improving service to this segment of the market. The expectations of these particular customers, the executives knew, were constantly rising and their needs had changed greatly since the previous decade. Research revealed that business travelers:

- preferred to eat small amounts and less often;
- wanted more nutrition in their diet;
- tended to be impatient and resented having to wait;
- wanted to have the facilities found in airport lounges—such as showers and fax machines—also available in the sky;
- disliked wasting time on board and wanted to be occupied throughout the flight.

At the start of the meeting, Robert Ang had pointed out that the only way for the company to genuinely cater to travelers' increasingly sophisticated needs was

EXHIBIT 2　Details on Duration of Flights

	Duration of Flights		
	up to 3 hrs	4–8 hrs	9 hrs+
Flights	60%	18%	22%
Revenues	25%	25%	50%
Mainly during day[a]	all	60%	25%
Mainly during night		40%	75%

[a] Depending on whether it goes through midnight of the originating point.

to use technology more strategically for enhancing the quality of service. It was not enough to simply pick easily replicated innovations on an *ad hoc* basis. He had declared:

> Just going out and looking for technology-based solutions will give the market the impression that we are gimmicky and arbitrary in our approach. If we want to protect our competitive position, we've got to find ways to move faster than our competitors and create an enduring advantage for the company. There will be a million problems but, once we agree on the principle of "technology in the sky" as a competitive tool, we can solve the technical hassles. We have to use technology in the future as we used people in the past to serve customers. If we can match our high-tech services with our soft services, we will be irresistible to customers and will be distinguished from the rest.

Several technological innovations were already planned for introduction later that year. One was the installation of small TV screens at each First and Business Class seat, offering passengers video entertainment. Since other airlines were also doing this, ensuring variety would be pivotal. Another was satellite-linked air-to-ground telephone service which, unlike previously, allowed passengers to make calls even when the aircraft was above the ocean. Although these innovations were important, Ang felt it was not enough. He knew that there would be innumerable possibilities for adding value to the customers' total flying experience—but only if the know-how and technology could be applied correctly.

Almost 80,000 travelers were registered in the Priority Passenger Service (PPS) program. To become a member, a passenger had to fly at least 60,000 km (37,500 miles) a year in First or Raffles Class. Benefits included extra baggage allowance, automatic flight reconfirmation, priority wait listing, a complimentary magazine subscription, and discounts on car rentals, hotels, and shopping. Information about each PPS member—such as seat and meal preferences—was stored in a computer and could be automatically implemented when reservations were made. Ang considered this kind of service to be only the beginning; there was no end to what information technology could do to improve customer service. There was also no reason to confine the system to only 80,000 people simply because the company's technology capacity was limited.

ADVERTISING CAMPAIGNS

Around 2% of Singapore Airlines' gross income was devoted to advertising and promotion. All expenditures were carefully controlled by the head office, and strategic advertising decisions were all centralized. Tactical advertising that focused on specific routes, schedules, or promotions were handled locally, but were strictly monitored in Singapore to guarantee consistency.

The "Singapore Girl" theme had remained a key element in the company's advertising strategy since day one. Initially, the aim of this strategy was to impart a feeling of romance and luxury service, and so it was dominated by images of sarong-clad women against exotically romantic backdrops. The modern fleet campaign which followed featured aircraft exteriors or interiors with just a small cameo inset of a stewardess at one side.

The purpose of the fleet modernization campaign was to give another strong message to the market: that Singapore Airlines was a leader in aircraft technology. The object was to show that the "steel" did not overpower the "silk." The photographs gave the advertising a deliberately dream-like quality, a theme carried through in the 1990 Raffles campaign—SIA's first attempt to aim specifically at business class travelers.

Research revealed that two out of every three Europeans, Americans and Australians preferred the romantic ads to the technical ones. These passengers were spellbound by the beauty of the stewardesses and impressed by their competence and caring. Japanese and other Asian clients, on the other hand, seemed to prefer the high-tech ads which denoted modernity, reliability, and new experiences. The Singapore Girl did not seem so exotic, unusual or appealing to this group.

Sales and Distribution System

Like most fleets, Singapore Airlines depended heavily on independent agents to sell its service. In 1973, the airline initiated its own computer reservation and check-in system, KRISCOM. By 1991 this had been replaced by Abacus, a computer reservation system which provided travel agents with an extended array of services including airline and hotel reservations, ground arrangements, and regional travel news. Originally created by Singapore Airlines and two other Asian carriers, Abacus was now owned and operated by SIA and nine other carriers, including three American firms. More than 100 carriers, 80 hotel chains, and many other travel services had signed up with Abacus to distribute their services through the system.

When reservations were made on Singapore Airlines by travel agents, the recorded preferences of Priority Passenger Service (PPS) travelers would automatically be retrieved from the computer. A wide variety of special meal options, reflecting travelers' many different health and religious needs, were offered. Special meal requests were forwarded to the catering department which received a print-out of all such requests for each flight. The special meal request was linked to the seat allocated to the passenger. (Exhibit 3 shows a simplified flowchart of the linkages between the different databases and the departure control system.)

TECHNOLOGY AND ON-THE-GROUND SERVICES

The Ground Services Department was responsible for the ground handling of passengers, baggage, cargo, and mail at all 63 airports in the Singapore Airlines' network. At Changi, SATS were in charge, but at other airports the airline had to rely on subcontractors. Even though some Singapore Airlines' employees were allocated to these stations, most staff members were host country nationals and frequently had a different way of thinking.

Since what people really wanted most was to get in and out of airports as quickly and easily as possible, Ang believed that interventions with staff should be kept to a minimum. Specific problems had to be dealt with and overcome:

> It's easier to control the quality of service in the air than on the ground. Key decisions are made at the head office and implemented on board. Airports, on the other hand, are difficult to control. Technology is the key. The airports themselves are too crowded, with too few gates, too few counters and long lines. While in-flight service staff typically give customers something—free headsets, free newspapers, free drinks, free meals, free movies—ground service staff take—tickets, excess baggage fees, or they say you can't have the seat you want. Thirty percent of all complaints relate to seat assignments, another 20% to aircraft delays. How these delays are handled has a big impact on customer opinion. Passengers become really unhappy when staff can't provide information, find them seats on alternative airlines, or obtain hotel rooms when they are delayed overnight. Lost baggage also accounts for about 20% of total complaints. With better technology and information, not only can we give the same kind of service on the ground as in the air, but we can minimize our risk by providing everyone around the world with a system we know works.

An Outstanding Service On the Ground Program (OSG) had been started for all passengers and complemented the lounges, equipped with every possible luxury and convenience, instituted earlier for First and Business Class travelers. When Terminal 2 opened at Changi, a new Departure Control System (DCS90) was phased in. A key component was an improved simplified format for the screens used at check-in. It had become increasingly difficult to recruit and retain staff for check-in positions, and the complex software led to delays for passengers. A new user-friendly program, with menu-driven, on-screen commands was introduced, which simplified both the task and the training.

The benefits for passengers included a simplified and speedier check-in process, with boarding passes and baggage tags being automatically encoded and printed at the check-in. The boarding pass included seat allocation and gate information, and confirmed special requests such as vegetarian meals. At the boarding gate, passengers would simply slip their boarding passes through a reader at the gate and the DCS90 software would verify check-in details against boarding passengers. An important security benefit was the automatic matching up of checked baggage with passengers going on board (refer to Exhibit 3).

A Telecar system was introduced to take baggage from one terminal to another within three minutes. It was then manually sorted and handled. If an urgent flight connection had to be made, this fact was communicated to the staff in advance so that baggage could be taken by trolley to the awaiting aircraft. Unlike the situation at most other airports, the Skytrain not only took passengers to and from terminals, but staff directed and accompanied passengers to flights with short connecting times, thus minimizing confusion and delays.

TECHNOLOGY AND IN-FLIGHT SERVICES

By realizing such innovations as video screens at each seat and better air-to-ground telecommunications, Ang wanted to transform the cabin into an "office and leisure center in the sky" which would enhance entertainment as well as business services. Surely almost anything could be possible in the future thanks to technology. But, what did customers value? What was feasible? What would distinguish Singapore Airlines from the competition? What were the real issues? At the meeting, he had told the others:

> We have to be able to provide passengers with as much distraction—be it entertainment or professional—as possible during their flight. It's just the opposite from the situation on the ground. Customers must be able to do whatever they need to do throughout their time with us. And, the choice must be theirs, not ours. They shouldn't have to encounter any problems in dealing with our staff and should, in fact, be encouraged to interact with them as much as possible, since we're very good at that. If tech-

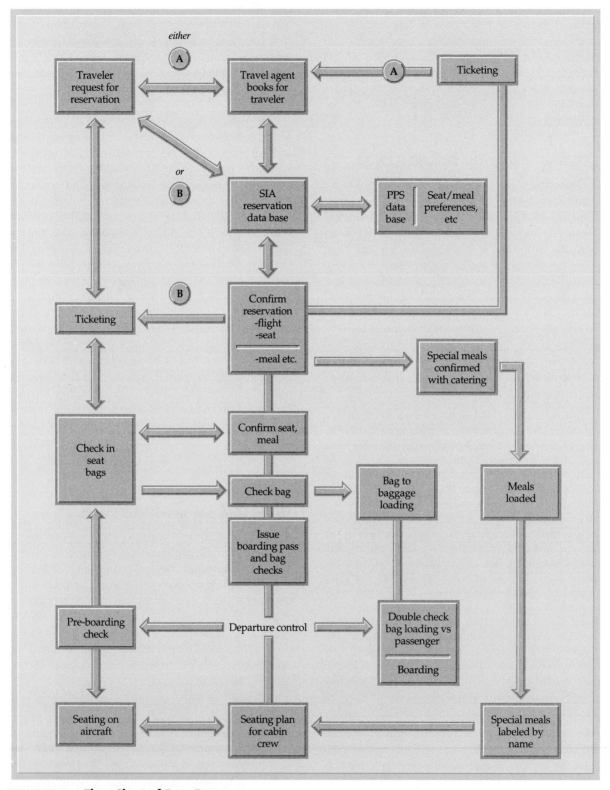

EXHIBIT 3   **Flow Chart of Data Bases**

nology is used properly and creatively, we can personalize our services still more and make people feel that we really care. For instance, hand-held computers can tell on-board crews everything they need to know about each customer so that services can be customized.

After the meeting, Ang's boss, the director of marketing planning, commented on the suggestions Ang had made. Although the ideas were interesting, he said, there should be nothing to disturb other passengers, reduce valuable seating space, or adversely affect the company's high level of personal service. Ang, who had anticipated this reaction, responded by saying that the location of the technology on board would be the determining factor. He could think of several options: centering the technology at each passenger's seat; demarcating work and leisure centers at a given spot inside the aircraft; or, alternatively, using crew members to handle the bulk of passenger requests, for instance sending faxes.

ANG SETS TO WORK

Back in his office, with a good feeling about the meeting that morning, Robert Ang thought about the three pillars which provided the quality experience the company insisted on for its customers: first, modern aircraft (where it was already well ahead); second, on-the-ground services (where much remained to be done, despite the accomplishments at Changi Airport). In particular, technology had to be developed so that the company's worldwide network of sales and air staff, agents and subcontractors could function in unison.

The third pillar was in-flight services. What technology-based services should be developed to improve the customers' experience in the air? Could an "office in the air" actually work? To what extent could more comfort and entertainment be provided, and how could the first and business class facilities be differentiated from the ones in economy? Most important, how could all these ideas be consolidated and effected so that Singapore Airlines would be the technological leader in civil aviation?

Ang knew that the *how* questions needed a lot of thought before a formal presentation could be made to his boss. But, it was even more crucial to find a cohesive concept that would be appreciated and bought company-wide. Perhaps it would be best to set out the various customer activities in a framework. He began to sketch out a rough flowchart showing the sequence of a typical journey. Before long, he had segmented the chart into three sections: preflight activities, flight activities, and postflight activities (refer to Exhibit 4).

EXHIBIT 4　Customer Experience Preflight

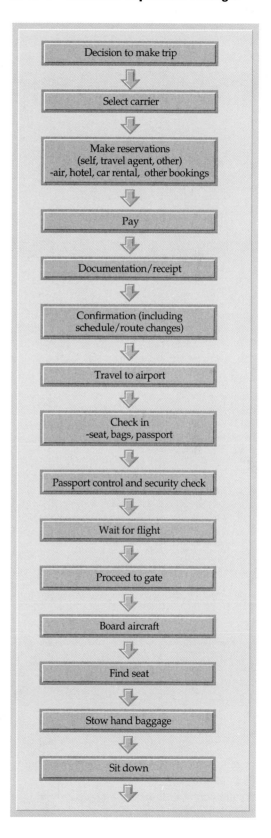

EXHIBIT 4 (CONT.)   Customer Experience
Inflight

EXHIBIT 4 (CONT.)   Customer Experience
Postflight

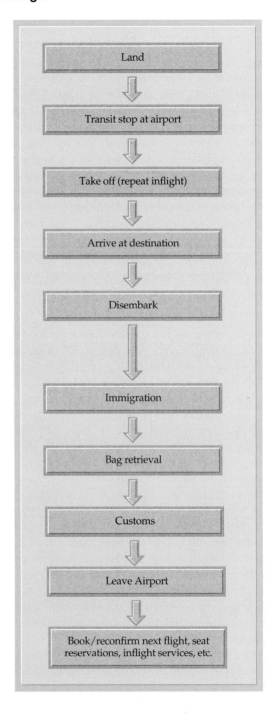

Inflight
Fasten seat belt
↓
Safety demonstration and other mandatory announcements
↓
Basic inflight amenities -Audio/video system -Seats -Overnight kits -Pillows, blankets -Toilets
↓
Informational announcements
↓
Inflight diversions -Newspapers, magazines -News updates -Games for kids/adults -Food/beverages -Movies -Audio channels entertainment -Audio/video for business and other purposes -Medical help -Assistance with work -Physical exercise
↓
Shopping
↓
Prearrival connection/transfer activities
↓

Postflight
Land
↓
Transit stop at airport
↓
Take off (repeat inflight)
↓
Arrive at destination
↓
Disembark
↓
Immigration
↓
Bag retrieval
↓
Customs
↓
Leave Airport
↓
Book/reconfirm next flight, seat reservations, inflight services, etc.

He began to fill in his ideas for using technology at each key point.

When he finally stopped for a coffee break, the sun had already begun to touch the horizon, creating a pale pink haze in the tropical sky. As he rose and stretched, he heard the soft hum of a plane above. "Must be the flight leaving for Frankfurt," he said aloud.

CASE 8-2   JOE DIMAGGIO CHILDREN'S HOSPITAL*

The Joe DiMaggio Children's Hospital is a 144 bed children's hospital located in Hollywood, Florida. It is owned and operated by the South Broward Hospital District and is located under the same roof as the District's Memorial Hospital. The mission of the South Broward Hospital District is to "provide quality, cost effective, customer focused healthcare services to its patients regardless of their ability to pay, with the goal of improving the health status of the community it serves."

In the late 1980s, the South Broward Hospital District Board of Commissioners, hospital administrators and staff began to examine the healthcare needs of children in the area. At the time, what became the Joe DiMaggio Children's Hospital was a pediatric department known as Memorial Hospital Children's Center. The Center was not able to fulfill the Hospital District's mission to the children in their service area. A decision was made to expand the Children's Center so that it could be designated a separate children's hospital. The Hospital District then designed and implemented a marketing plan that would increase awareness of the Children's Center and its services. In September 1992, the Children's Center was renamed and dedicated as the Joe DiMaggio Children's Hospital. By 1998, the Board of Commissioners decided it was time to hire a consultant to review marketing activities at their Children's Hospital. After interviewing several candidates the board hired David Lawrence.

JOE DIMAGGIO

Joe DiMaggio was one of the greatest American baseball players, and became a legend in his time. He played for the New York Yankees for 13 seasons, played in 10 world series, and retired in 1951 with a lifetime batting average of .325, 361 home runs and several baseball records. Joltin' Joe, and Mr. Coffee (based on a coffee advertisement in which he starred) were some of his affectionate nicknames. He was inducted into the Baseball Hall of Fame in 1955. He was generally regarded as a man of style and grace, and a role model for children and adults alike.

Morris Engelberg, his long-time friend, insists that only Queen Elizabeth II of England has a more valuable autograph than Joe DiMaggio. DiMaggio earned several million dollars in endorsements and other fees. He was paid $9 million in a two-year deal with Scoreboard, a memorabilia firm, and millions more for signing 1,941 baseball bats in honor of the year in which he had his 56 game hitting streak.

He did a few baseball card shows, at a reported $150,000 each, appeared in some charity golf tournaments, flew to Japan to oversee baseball clinics, and tossed out the first ball at the Yankee Stadium on Opening Day. He walked away from a $3 million deal to write his autobiography. He refused to discuss his late, former wife, Marilyn Monroe whom he married in January of 1954. They were divorced less than a year later.

Joe DiMaggio Children's Hospital hopes that the hospital will gain greater acceptance because it is named after a respected figure—much like the Arnold Palmer Hospital for women and children in Orlando, Florida, named after the famous golfer.

HOSPITAL HISTORY

The South Broward Hospital District was created by the Florida Legislature in 1947, at the request of voters. The municipalities within the Hospital District include Hollywood, Pembroke Pines, Pembroke Park, Miramar, West Hollywood, Dania, Hallandale, and Davie. The Hospital District is operated by a seven member Board of Commissioners appointed by the Governor of Florida. The Commission has taxing powers to assist in the operation of the Hospital District. Exhibit 1 provides a brief history of the South Broward Hospital District.

Memorial Hospital, owned and operated by the South Broward Hospital District, was built to provide hospital services for the residents of this area and opened in 1953 with 100 beds. The demand continued to exceed the available beds and services, so a multimillion dollar addition was constructed in 1961 to increase capacity to 360 beds. Continued expansion and the addition of the Ester L. Rosenthal Memorial

---

* This case was prepared by Jonathan N. Goodrich of Florida International University. Joe DiMaggio passed away in 1999 (after this case was written).

EXHIBIT 1   South Broward Hospital District History

1947	The South Broward Hospital District was created by the Florida Legislature.
1953	Memorial Hospital opened as a 100 bed hospital in Hollywood.
1961	Eight story addition was constructed bringing Memorial's capacity to 360 beds.
1976	Addition of the Esther L. Rosenthal Memorial Pavilion and neuro-psychiatric unit, increased number of beds to 530
1976	Walk-In Medical Center, a 24-hour facility, opened on Douglas Road.
1977	Completion of the S.S. Holland Wing, bringing capacity to 730 beds
1987	S.A. Mudano Tower opened at Memorial Hospital.
Late 1980s	Memorial Hospital Children's Center was established to help meet pediatric healthcare needs.
1988	MRI Center, Memorial Oncology Center, opened.
1989	Memorial Manor Nursing Home opened with 85 beds.
1990	Surgery Center, Radiation Therapy Center, South Broward Outpatient Diagnostic Center, and the Memorial Health & Fitness Center opened.
1992	Memorial Hospital West and adjacent Medical Office Park opened in Pembroke Pines Memorial's Psychiatric Center expanded to 102 beds.
1992	The Joe DiMaggio Children's Hospital was dedicated.

Pavilion in 1976, and neuro-psychiatric unit atop the structure, increased the number of available beds to 530. Construction of the S.S. Holland Wing began in the fall of 1973. This new section increased the total number of available hospital beds to approximately 725.

In 1976, construction was completed at the Walk-In Medical Center located on Douglas Road. This facility provided 24-hour healthcare services and offered complete cardiology, laboratory, and radiology services. Other areas of expansion included the S.A. Mudano Tower, which opened in 1987, the Magnetic Resonance Imaging Center (MRI), which opened in December of 1988, Memorial Oncology Center which opened in January 1988, Same Day Surgery center, Radiation Therapy Center, South Broward Outpatient Diagnostic Center, and the Health and Fitness Center, all of which were opened in the late 1980s and early 1990s.

The Hospital District expanded by adding Memorial Manor Nursing Home, an 85-bed skilled nursing facility, in July 1989. Memorial Hospital West, a 100-bed full service hospital with an adjacent medical office Park, opened in May 1992 in Pembroke Pines. Memorial Hospital expanded psychiatric services to 102 beds when the Psychiatric Center opened in July 1992. In August 1992 the Memorial Home Health Services program was implemented. This program consists of in-home visits of medical staff to treat patients.

In the late 1980s, Memorial Hospital Children's Center was established to help meet pediatric healthcare needs. It included a specially-designated treatment area in Memorial's Emergency Department. A renewed focus was placed on pediatric care. The Children's Center was then renamed the Joe DiMaggio Children's Hospital in July 1992. The baseball legend loved children, and agreed to the use of his name to rename the hospital.

SERVICE

The Joe DiMaggio Children's Hospital (JDCH) is a state-of-the-art facility staffed by pediatricians, pediatric specialists, specialty-trained nurses, and ancillary support staff. To meet the complex medical needs of children, the Children's Hospital offers a comprehensive range of inpatient and outpatient pediatric programs that are supervised by the largest diversity of board-certified pediatric specialists in Broward County. Exhibit 2 lists the pediatric specialty services offered by JDCH during different periods of growth. Note that the number of specialty services grew from ten in 1989 to twenty-nine in 1995.

Ambulatory Service

The Ambulatory Service staff is specially trained to treat children on a "short term" basis. For example, some children go to JDCH for minor surgery in the morning and go home the same night. The same goes for some kids who need chemotherapy, blood transfusions, cardiac catheterization and other diagnostic procedures.

Cancer Program

JDCH has three board certified pediatric hematology/oncology specialists. They work in conjunction with the Florida Community Clinical Oncology Program and the National Pediatric Oncology Group to provide the latest in investigational and therapeutic medicine to children.

EXHIBIT 2 **Pediatric Specialty Services at Joe DiMaggio Children's Hospital During Different Periods of Growth**

Memorial Hospital Children's Center	Dedication as Joe DiMaggio Children's Hospital (1992)	Joe DiMaggio Children's Hospital
Allergy	Allergy/Immunology	Allergy/Immunology
Anesthesia	Anesthesia	Anesthesia
Cardiology	Behavioral Development	Cardiac Catheterization
Gastroenterology	Cardiology	Cardiac Surgery
General Pediatrics	Gastroenterology	Cardiology
Neonatology	General Pediatrics	Critical Care
Nephrology	Hematology/Oncology	Emergency
Neurosurgery	Infectious Disease	Hematology/Immunology
Pulmonology	Intensive Care	Gastroenterology
Surgery	Neonatology	General Pediatrics
	Nephrology	Hematology/Oncology
	Neurosurgery	Infectious Disease
	Otolaryngology	Intensive Care
	Pulmonary Medicine	Neonatology
	Surgery	Nephrology
	Urology	Neurology
		Neurosurgery
		Ophthalmology
		Orthopedic Surgery
		Otolaryngology
		Perinatology
		Plastic Surgery
		Psychiatry
		Pulmonary Medicine
		Radiology
		Rehabilitation
		Surgery
		Trauma Services
		Urology

Cardiac Catheterization and Cardiac Surgery Program

JDCH's heart specialists perform diagnostic cardiac procedures and open heart surgery on even the smallest infants.

Diabetes Center for Children

An average of 1 in 600 children develop childhood diabetes. JDCH's Diabetes Center for children focuses on patient education, diet programs and stress-relieving techniques to contain diabetes.

Endoscopy Suite

The Endoscopy Suite at JDCH is equipped with state-of-the-art, computerized video equipment and special scopes to aid in the diagnosis of problems in the gastrointestinal tract. The pediatric gastroenterologist can perform a biopsy, remove polyps or any other anomaly, and treat problems such as infections and hernias. Many of these procedures can be performed on an outpatient basis.

Home Health Care

Sometimes the best place for kids to recover is back home in their own beds. A team of pediatric specialists at JDCH visit in-home sick children and administer a variety of care, such as IV antibiotic therapy, post surgical care, and respiratory therapy.

Neuro-Oncology Center

The Neuro-Oncology Center was opened in 1994. It offers medical care to children with brain tumors, both pre-and post-surgery.

Pediatric Primary Care Center

This center at JDCH provides basic medical care for children such as vaccinations, physicals, or treatment for the pesky flu. More than 14,000 children were treated at the Pediatric Primary Care Center in 1997.

Pediatric Trauma Center

Some 130 kids were trauma patients in JDCH in 1997. Many of them were car accident victims with broken bones, skull fractures, deep lacerations, and damage to internal organs; and victims of playground accidents, and severe burns.

Perinatal Intensive Care Center

Infants born of high risk pregnancies receive state-of-the-art treatment, therapy, and support services in JDCH's neonatal services and treatments include surgery, medicines, special diets, and therapy.

Exhibit 2 shows the growth of medical services at JDCH from 1989 to 1995 and Exhibit 3 shows a breakdown of the major medical and support services at JDCH. Support services include home health, humor therapy, educational services and nutritional services, pharmacy and volunteer services. Humor therapy, for instance, includes clowns and magicians who visit JDCH and entertain the kids. Humor helps to bring joy and laughter to the kids, and can have a positive impact on their recovery from illnesses.

Educational services, as another example of support services, include literature, videos, and talks by professionals on prevention, and treatment of various illnesses and accidents. For instance, JDCH trauma professionals talk to school children and organizations about how to avoid trauma. "Don't drink wine and drive." "Wear your seat belt." "Wear your bike helmet." Or these professionals may discuss the appropriate topics such as "Poison Prevention," "The ABCs of CPR," "Attention Deficit Disorder," "Toilet Training," "Infant Nutrition," and "First Aid" with children or patients.

Exhibit 4 shows JDCH's "Kid's Bill of Rights." It is informative, humorous, and is posted around the hospital.

MEDICAL PERSONNEL

There are some 60 medical doctors who work at JDCH. They cover a wide range of medical specialties

---

EXHIBIT 3   Fast Facts on Services at JDCH

Pediatric Medical Services	**Pediatric Support Services**
Allergy/Immunology	Ambulatory Services Unit
Cardiac Catheterization	Bereavement Team
Cardiology	Child Life Specialists
Child and Adolescent Psychiatry	Endoscopy
Emergency Medicine	Extra Corporeal Membrane Oxygenation
Endocrinology	(ECMO)
Gastroenterology	Home Health
General Medicine	Humor Therapy
Hematology/Oncology	Nutritional Services
Infectious Disease	Nursing
Intensive Care	Pharmacy
Neonatology	Rehabilitation/Early Intervention Program
Nephrology	(includes occupational, physical, speech and
Neurology	audiological therapy)
Perinatology	Respiratory
Pulmonary Medicine	Social Services
Radiology	Support Groups
	Teddy Bear Tours
Pediatric Surgical Services	Transport Teams:
Anesthesiology	Neonatal
Cardiac Surgery	Pediatric
General Surgery	Art Therapy
Neurosurgery	Foster Grandparent Program
Ophthalmologic Surgery	Music Therapy
Orthopedic Surgery	Pet-A-Pet Program
Otolaryngologic Surgery	
Trauma Surgery	**Educational Services**
Urologic Surgery	**Ambulatory/Outpatient Services**
	Cystic Fibrosis Center
	Diabetes Center
	Neuro-Oncology Center
	Oncology Center
	Primary Care Center

EXHIBIT 4   Kid's Bill of Rights

Please:
Look at me and talk to me in a way I can understand.
Knock on my door before entering and please introduce
  yourself.
Be honest with me … always.
Offer me a choice whenever possible.
Communicate with my parents … If they feel less anx-
  ious it will help me a lot.
Tell me what you are going to do … please try to make
  time.
Please don't:
Tell me it won't "hurt" if it will.
Tell me "don't cry."
Forget to listen when I have something to say.
Forget I want my favorite toy to go along with me to dif-
  ferent places in the hospital
Please remember:
To respect me by letting me show my feelings. They are
  part of me and I need to be allowed to express
  them.
Hugs often help me feel better.

Source: JDCH's 1993 Annual Report

EXHIBIT 5

Accreditation, Licenses

Florida State Board of Health
Florida State Department of Family Services
Health Care Finance Administration
Joint Commission on Accreditation of Healthcare
  Organizations
Medicaid Program
Regional Perinatal Intensive Care Center
State Approved Pediatric Trauma Referral Center
The American Association of Blood Banks

Memberships

American Health Care Association
American Hospital Association
Association of Voluntary Hospitals
Coalition for America's Children
Florida Center for Children and Youth
Florida Health Care Association
Local Interagency Coordinating Council
National Association of Children's Hospitals and Related
  Institutions
National Association of Public Hospitals
Pediatric Oncology Group
The Children's Consortium, Inc.
Wellness Council of South Florida

such as those represented in Exhibits 2 and 3. Exhibit 5 provides a list of JDCH's accreditation, licenses, and memberships in professional associations.

DELIVERY SYSTEM

The distribution of JDCH services occurs through three levels: 1) JDCH and its programs, physical units and centers (see Exhibit 3); 2) its medical staff; and 3) the educational literature distributed by JDCH to patients, nurses, doctors, and the community. All three levels of distribution are interrelated.

JDCH receives tax assistance, government funding in return for providing care to the children in Broward County. The total population of Broward County is about 1.5 million people. Of this the total number of children under the age of 18 is about 285,000 (19 percent). JDCH was established to meet the healthcare needs of this segment of the population, i.e., children up to 18 years old. However, JDCH often treats children over 18 years old. Since JDCH is a tax assisted hospital it also has a responsibility to provide care to the 36,687 of these children who lived below the poverty level. In addition, since there is no children's hospital in Palm Beach County, JDCH serves the children from this area as well.

ADVERTISING AND PROMOTION

JDCH is promoted in many ways. These include word-of-mouth, the media, billboards and other outdoor signs, and publicity. Also, television advertisements about JDCH and its medical facilities for children occasionally appear on local television stations in Dade and Broward Counties in Florida. Television advertisements are not emphasized because they are expensive. Sometimes, radio announcers mention new medical procedures (e.g., cancer treatments) at JDCH, or accident victims (children) air-lifted to JDCH for treatment. Local newspapers occasionally run stories about JDCH and the various celebrities who visit. These local newspapers include the *Ft. Lauderdale Sun Sentinel* and the *Miami Herald.*

Muhammad Ali is one of the most popular visitors to JDCH. He loves magic, does magic tricks for the children, teases them, signs autographs for them (and adults too), and poses with them for photographs. He has also contributed money to JDCH.

A billboard, located nearby on Highway I-95 South, shows a picture of Joe DiMaggio holding a baby with copy reading "DiMaggio and the Babe." I-95 South and I-95 North are two of the most heavily traveled highways in Florida, with over one million people using those two highways every day. "DiMaggio and the Babe" billboard attracts a great deal of attention from southbound traffic on I-95, and helps to maintain visibility for JDCH.

JDCH receives a lot of media publicity for medical events and conferences, fundraising functions, and the Memorial Classic, its annual charity baseball event for the old timers. It is estimated that each year the memorial Classic baseball game raises over $250,000 for JDCH.

Prices are regulated by federal, state, and local governments and insurance companies. Therefore, competition between hospitals cannot really be based on pricing. In addition, the South Broward Hospital District is a public, not-for-profit hospital. As such, all Hospital District facilities, including JDCH's, receive state funding from tax revenues.

In return for this tax assistance, the South Broward Hospital District has agreed to provide care to everyone, regardless of their ability to pay. This is a key part of the Hospital District's mission. Hospitals define uncompensated care as charity care to indigent patients, write offs of balances not paid by insurance, and bad and uncollected debt. The total amount of uncompensated care given by the South Broward Hospital District is more than three times its tax revenue (Exhibit 6). However, through cost shifting, good management, wise investment, and increased private philanthropy, the South Broward Hospital District has not increased its tax rate in the last 6 years. Exhibit 6 shows a comparison of tax revenues versus uncompensated care for the South Broward Hospital District from 1990 to 1997.

COMPETITION

In a broad sense, nearby hospitals, clinics, and doctors offices can be thought of as competitors to JDCH. However, most medical practitioners at JDCH believe that JDCH's main competitor is Miami Children's Hospital (MCH), some 60 miles south of JDCH in Dade County. MCH is a private 208 bed hospital specializing in full service pediatric medicine, surgery, and dentistry. It has about 600 pediatricians on staff (against 70 at JDCH). Other competitors include the pediatric units at Jackson Memorial Hospital, Columbia Hospital, and Baptist Hospital—all some 60 miles south of JDCH.

From the viewpoint of consumers, the concept of competition in hospitals is different from many other industries. Patients cannot usually choose which hospital to use, as this is determined by their physician. In some cases, if a patient has heard of a hospital and is impressed by its reputation, he/she can attempt to find a doctor who practices at that particular hospital.

Another form of competition among hospitals pertains to fundraising events, and soliciting financial contributions from wealthy philanthropists. That is, many hospitals often seek donations from the same philanthropic individuals and organizations and put on similar kinds of fundraising events, such as banquets.

ALL-STAR IMAGE

Joe DiMaggio was a baseball legend. His name has been mentioned by artists such as Ernest Hemingway, Simon & Garfunkel, Billy Joel, Madonna, and Jerry Seinfeld. To his generation Joe DiMaggio evoked feelings of nostalgia, class, and greatness. The Joe DiMaggio Children's Hospital thus gains the same reputation and is perceived as a top quality hospital for children. Also, the hospital gets public attention simply because of the name Joe DiMaggio. For example, news clippings about Joe DiMaggio and his association with the children's hospital have appeared in newspapers all over the USA. These newspapers include *USA Today, The New York Times,* the *Miami Herald,* the *Orlando Sun-Sentinel,* and the *Fort Lauderdale Sun-Sentinel.*

FUNDRAISING SUCCESSES

Since the change in the name of the Memorial Hospital Children's Center to the Joe DiMaggio Children's Hospital, charitable contributions to the Memorial Foundation have increased. Much of this success can be attributed to the association with Joe DiMaggio. A few months after the renaming of the hospital, Comic Relief held an event in South Florida and donated $100,000 to the hospital. Gifts have been received from many people and companies in the New York area, including the New York Yankees.

EXHIBIT 6   Tax Revenue vs Uncompensated Care

Year	Tax Revenue	Uncompensated Care[a]
1990	$15 million	$40.25 million
1991	$15 million	$50 million
1992	$15 million	$50 million
1993	$15 million	$61 million
1994	$15 million	$80 million
1995	$17 million	$80 million
1996	$18 million	$82 million
1997	$20 million	$80 million

[a] Figures are estimates

Several national celebrities, including Muhammad Ali, Tom Selleck, and Michael Bolton have either visited the hospital and/or made donations. Former Florida Marlins' all-star left fielder, Jeff Conine, staged a golf tournament to benefit the hospital. Over the years, many wealthy people have donated a few million dollars to JDCH.

Exhibit 7 shows the growth of philanthropic dollars raised for JDCH from 1991, when it was still the Memorial Hospital Children's Center, to 1997. In 1991, for example the Memorial Hospital Children's Center raised about $150,000. In 1993, the year after it was named after Joe DiMaggio, philanthropic contributions to JDCH more than tripled to $500,000. In 1997, JDCH raised over $1 million in donations. Exhibit 7 shows that contributions to JDCH are increasing steadily year after year.

GALLUP SURVEY

In 1992 and 1993 Gallup surveys of people in Broward County were conducted on awareness of JDCH ads and the image of JDCH. Overall, 82% of the respondents had a positive and favorable reaction to JDCH ads. Recall of JDCH ads was higher in 1993 than in 1992 due largely to the Joe DiMaggio name change (affiliation). JDCH's image was also enhanced since the name change. See Exhibit 8 for more details.

JDCH ADMISSIONS

The number of children admitted to the Joe DiMaggio Children's Hospital are shown for the years 1991 through 1998 in Exhibit 9. Admission grew at a slow and steady pace throughout the period. This growth in admissions was due in part to the increased visibility and fame of the hospital and to the growing population of Broward County.

EXHIBIT 8   JDCH Gallup Survey Results

Awareness of Ads:
  Eighty-two percent of the respondents had a positive reaction to JDCH ads
  Respondents who recall JDCH ads increased from less than 1% in 1992 to 6% in 1993
  Thirty-two percent of the respondents recalled content of ads regarding the grand opening of JDCH
  Twenty percent of the respondents regarded the JDCH ads favorably

Image:
  The image of the comprehensive pediatric care at Memorial increased by 12%, following the name change and marketing campaign in fiscal year 1993
  JDCH was listed as being the first hospital that people thought of for specialized pediatric care by 23% of the respondents in 1993 (compared to 0% in 1992)
  JDCH was chosen as having the most comprehensive pediatric care by 44% of the respondents
  Twenty-six percent of the respondents expressed preference for JDCH for specialized pediatric care

MARKETING PLAN

In 1997, the marketing staff developed a marketing plan for JDCH. A synopsis of the plan is shown in Exhibit 10 and covers areas such as objectives, target market positioning, selling messages, media, and the budget. After reading the marketing plan and the other exhibits, David Lawrence started to write his report for the South Broward Hospital District Board of Commissioners.

EXHIBIT 7   Philanthropic Contributions to JDCH, 1991–1997

Year	Contributions
1991	$150,000
1992	$425,000
1993	$500,000
1994	$600,000
1995	$1,000,000
1996	$1,200,000
1997	$1,200,000

EXHIBIT 9   Inpatient Admissions,[a] JDCH, 1991–1998

Year	Admissions
1991	2933
1992	3015
1993	3041
1994	3100
1995	3182
1996	3225
1997	3314
1998	3421

[a] About 40 to 50 children are admitted as outpatients each day for x-rays, injections, and other treatment.

EXHIBIT 10   JDCH's Marketing Plan & Budget

Objectives:
  To increase awareness and establish a positive image for the new children's hospital
Method of Measurement:
  Gallup Survey
  Timing of campaign: May 1992 through April 1993 (done every year)
  Target Market: Women and children under the age of 16
Positioning:
  Current Perception—Memorial is seen as a leading hospital in the area for a range of medical care, although pediatric ser-
    vices are not fully understood relative to the competition.
  Desired Target Perception—Leading children's hospital throughout the primary service area.
  Key Promise—Your child's health is safe in our hands
  Desired Action—Use JDCH for your child's health care needs
Selling Messages:
  Depth of Service—Assurance that any medical problems your child might experience can be handled at one convenient
    location.
  Quality of Staff—Assurance that your child will be cared for by a knowledgeable and caring staff.
  Commitment to Pediatric Care—Assurance that your child will receive the most up-to-date care available due to JDCH's
    leadership on ongoing investment in pediatric.
  Desired Personality:
    Trustworthy
    Approachable
    Family-centered
    User-friendly
  Required Elements:
    Logo
    800 number
  Restrictions: Sensitivity to the Joe DiMaggio name
  Newspaper:
    Advertisements
    "DiMaggio and the Babe" and "Joe DiMaggio Fan Club"
    Magazine/Newsletter
    Home Plate insert in local newspapers
  Other:
    New Logo, stationery, employee name badges, internal communications (such as directories, handbooks, etc.)
  Outdoor:
    Signage
    Vertical rotary signs with 3 panels (with different versions of the "Fan Club" theme)
  Billboard:
    "DiMaggio and the Babe" on I-95
Television:
  Channel selection based on demographics (Lifetime, USA)
Radio:
  Station selection based on demographics (Coast, WQAM)
  Content—"New Generation" kids talking
Tapes:
  Mini ad on cassettes
  Targeting at managed care providers and physicians
  Focus on depth, commitment, quality, and cost services

BUDGET

Media:	
TV/Cable	$ 60,000
Print	$ 50,000
Radio	$ 40,000
Production:	
Logo, stationery, materials	$ 1,500
Billboard	$ 40,000
Ceremony, programs, pins	$ 12,000
Agency Fees:	$ 30,000
TOTAL	$233,500

PRICING

> The art of pricing is to have the price be an equate to the value of the product to the customer—anything less than that represents a sacrifice in potential profits.
>
> E. RAYMOND COREY

*P*ricing is a critical job in the successful operation of for-profit and not-for-profit organizations. Price is the primary element of the marketing mix that generates revenue. Many marketing executives are under great pressure to increase prices to boost short-term profits. Stock markets in the United States, for example, are sensitive to quarterly earnings reports, and managers often raise the prices of cash cows to maintain earnings growth. However, high earnings tend to attract competitors—and even investigations from government agencies. We discussed earlier how Campbell Soup once raised the prices of its condensed soups every spring until competitors began to steal the market with lower-priced private label soups and ready-to-eat soup.

Low prices can be used as a weapon to build market share. Prices that undercut competitors attract new customers and allow for greater utilization of facilities. However, low prices can squeeze contribution margins and may reduce net profits. Thus your challenge as a marketing manager is to find a pricing strategy that balances your need for sales growth against your demand for profits.

This chapter will answer three basic pricing questions: What are the basic ingredients for a successful pricing strategy? What pricing methods should be chosen? How and when should prices be changed?

FINDING THE RIGHT PRICE

Setting prices for new and existing products appears simple enough. All you apparently have to do is estimate your costs, add a margin for overhead and profit, and you have your selling price. However, this approach raises several important issues.

A first issue is that the amount you can sell varies with the price you set. Moreover, costs change with volume, so profits also depend on price.

A second issue is that some customers are value oriented and want to pay low prices for acceptable quality. At the other extreme are buyers who want high quality and are willing to pay more to get it. Thus your price must be congruent with the prospective buyers you choose to target.

A third issue involves competitors. The prices they set often limit what you can charge. Furthermore, when you sell several items, you have to consider how the price of one product affects the sales of others in your line.

Setting Pricing Goals

Your first pricing task is to select an overall pricing goal for the firm and then determine objectives for individual product lines. If your company is the first to enter a particular market with a patented product, you are in a good position to follow a premium pricing strategy. On the other hand, firms that enter later often use low prices to buy market share.

Profit Maximization.   Many organizations need profits to satisfy stockholders and provide funds for expansion and product development. To maximize profits, you need data on the number of units that can be sold at different prices plus estimates of fixed and variable costs. If these data are available, then it is fairly easy to calculate the combination of price and revenue that generates the highest profits. Unfortunately, many firms do not know enough about the shape of their demand curves to pursue a profit maximization strategy.

A variation of profit maximization occurs when a company starts with a high price to "skim" the market. This profit goal is often used with new products that cannot be easily copied. The idea is to charge high prices to early buyers and then slide down the demand curve with lower prices to capture successive layers of more price-sensitive buyers. The price-skimming goal tries to maximize profits and sometimes revenue by extracting the highest possible price from each market segment. For example, in 1999 television manufacturers were selling their new high definition TV sets for $6,000 each, while regular sets of the same screen size were selling for $600. These skimming prices will decline as more HDTV programming becomes available and unit costs decline with increased volume. The major problem with any profit maximizing goal is that high profits attract competitors, who try to steal away your customers with similar products offered at lower prices.

> **APPLYING**
> . . . to
> *Consumer*
> *Durable*
> *Goods*
> *Marketing*

Revenue and Market Share Maximization.   An alternative pricing objective is to maximize revenue or market share. The usual approach is to lower prices to boost revenue while temporarily ignoring the impact on profits. Some managers who are looking for sales growth are willing to trade a little profit for higher volume. The lower prices associated with revenue or market share maximization are often employed to break into new markets or keep competitors out of a market. Some retailers demand that you obtain and keep a certain market share before they will stock your products. Revenue and market share maximization strategies are risky because the low prices required to achieve these goals typically lead to lower profit margins. This means that these strategies are usually employed for short periods or when firms have cash cows in other lines of trade.

An illustration of a firm pursuing a market share goal occurred when General Motors tried to improve labor efficiency at a key stamping plant in 1998. The United Auto Workers union saw this as a threat to their membership and the resulting strike shut down almost all of GM's North American assembly plants. Due to the shortage of cars and trucks, GM's market share dropped below 29 percent compared with the 31.2 percent share they obtained in 1997. After the strike was settled, GM offered consumers and fleet buyers generous rebates and price cuts in an effort to regain lost market share. By the end of 1998, GM had pushed its market share back up to 29.3 percent, but its profit margins suffered.[1] While Ford reported more than 5 percent profit on its sales in 1998, GM's drive to restore market share reduced profits to only 3 percent of sales.[2]

> **INTEGRATING**
> . . . *with*
> *Human*
> *Resource*
> *Management*
> *Production/*
> *Operations*
> *Management*

Quality Leadership.   Another pricing goal is to support an image as the quality leader in a market. Some customers seeking superior products use price as an indicator of quality. Buyers often prefer higher-priced products when price is the only information available, when they believe that the quality of available brands differs significantly, and when the price difference among brands is large. If customers believe that the quality is high, you can often charge a premium price. For example, Maytag builds very durable washing machines and advertises their lonely repairman. A survey by *Consumer Reports* showed that Maytag is the second-best company for repairs. The magazine also reported that Maytag washers are only average on washing performance, yet cost $140 more than the top-rated Sears washers. Maytag buyers are willing to pay more to get a repair-free washer.

Measuring Demand

Each price you charge for your goods or services is associated with a different level of sales. Assume that in the process of making price adjustments you have learned the general shape of the demand curve for battery-powered vacuum cleaners. This tells you how many units you can expect to sell at alternative prices (Figure 9-1). The basic relationship is negative: the quantity purchased increases as the price declines, and vice versa. When the price is set at $60, demand is 1,600 units and profits are maximized. If the price is cut to $25 per unit, demand expands to 3,000 units. When you know the shape of your demand schedules, you can set prices to reach any of a variety of goals. Today many firms have estimates of their demand schedules. The usual way to obtain these data is to vary prices in a laboratory or in the store over a short period of time and measure how much customers purchase.

Price Elasticity of Demand

The preferred way to express customer sensitivity to price is with a ratio known as the *price elasticity of demand.* This is obtained by dividing percentage changes in the quantity sold by associated percentage changes in price. The formula for price elasticity is

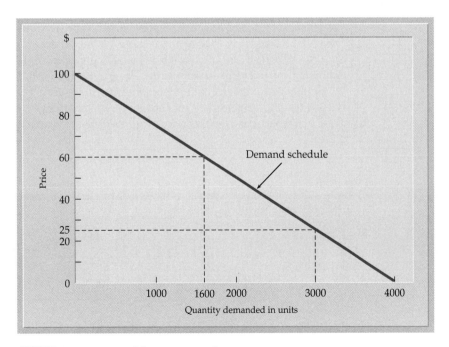

FIGURE 9-1   Demand for Vacuum Cleaners

$$\text{Price elasticity of demand} = \frac{\text{\% change in quantity demanded}}{\text{\% change in price}} \qquad (9.1)$$

The usual relationship between demand and price is inverse. When a relative change in volume is more than the relative change in price, demand is described as *elastic.* If the price is cut by 1 percent and demand increases by 5 percent, the elasticity is –5 (Figure 9-2). When demand is this sensitive to price, it almost always pays to cut prices. You will more than make up in volume what you lose in margin per unit. This, of course, should be verified by break-even analysis.

When a relative change in the quantity sold is less than the relative change in price, demand is said to be *inelastic.* Thus, if a price increase of 10 percent results in a 3 percent reduction in sales, price elasticity will be –0.3. In situations where elasticity is between 0 and –1, revenues increase as prices are raised (Figure 9-2). This suggests that when demand is inelastic, profits can be improved by raising prices. Demand is most likely to be inelastic when the product is infrequently purchased or it has few substitutes or competitors. Positive values for elasticity are unusual and signal that prices should be raised.

PRICING EXERCISE

A manufacturer observes that when the price of a $200 TV in the California market is cut $10, volume increases by 21,000 units. If the original volume was 300,000 units, what is the price elasticity of demand? What does the calculated value of price elasticity suggest should be done with the pricing for the TV set? Why?

You should understand that although an industry's price elasticity may be inelastic, an individual brand's elasticity is usually elastic. Thus, while the industry elasticity for gasoline is –0.3, the demand for Shell and Texaco brands across the street from one another is much more elastic. Brand studies have shown that the price elasticity of cars is –1.5; that of coffee, –5.3; and that of confectionery, –2.0.[3]

Price elasticities tend to vary over the product life cycle. Prices for brands often decline over time—even in the face of improvements to product quality. Products that are inelastic when introduced may become more elastic as they mature.[4]

An important part of your job as marketing manager is to make your brands less elastic, allowing you to charge higher prices. This can be done with advertising or by bundling your basic product or service with other products or services. For example, Technimetrics markets financial databases. It commands premium prices by bundling free consultations, research reports, and other services with its database products.

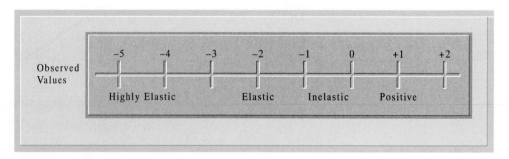

FIGURE 9-2   **Range of Likely Values for Price Elasticity**

Estimating Costs

Our discussion of demand provides a ceiling price that the organization can charge for goods and service. At the other extreme, costs determine the price floor. Organizations must charge enough to cover their total costs in the long run and have enough left over to reward the stockholders or buy replacement animals for the zoo.

Types of Costs.   Costs come in two basic forms, fixed or variable. *Fixed costs* include expenditures for overhead such as plant, equipment, and executive salaries. These costs do not vary with the level of output. In the case of the battery-powered vacuum cleaner manufacturer, the fixed costs of tooling and other overhead amounted to $15,000 (Figure 9-3). These costs are the same at all output levels.

Variable costs represent the direct labor, materials, and commissions needed to produce and sell each unit of merchandise. The unit variable costs for the vacuum cleaner are $20. Variable costs are so named because their total varies with production levels (Figure 9-3). When you look at per unit costs, you notice that variable costs for this product are constant across different levels of production (Figure 9-4).

Total costs are the sum of the fixed and variable costs at various levels of output. Note that total unit costs for the vacuum cleaner decline sharply as the fixed costs are spread over more units of production (Figure 9-4). Most of the economies of scale that occur when plants are run at capacity are due to a decline in allocated fixed costs per unit. Although the unit variable costs in Figure 9-4 are shown as constant, they also may decline if volume purchases lead to quantity discounts on raw materials. Managers who have a decreasing unit-cost curve are in a strong position to lower prices to expand market shares.

Historically, American firms have looked at the product characteristics important to customers, estimated engineering and component costs, and added in a profit margin to give a selling price. The Japanese have taught us how to do it differently. They look at what the customer wants, check competitive prices, and come up with a planned selling price. Next,

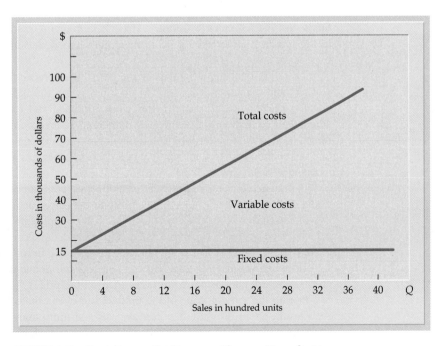

FIGURE 9-3   **Cost Curves for Vacuum Cleaner Manufacturer**

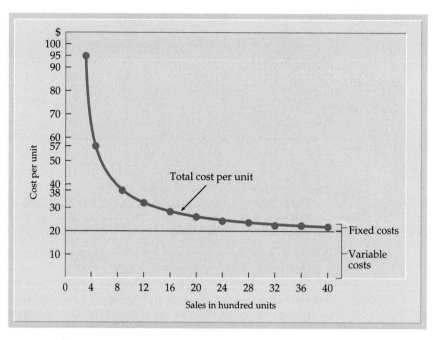

FIGURE 9-4   Vacuum Cleaner Costs per Unit

APPLYING

. . . *to*
Consumer
Durable
Goods
Marketing

they subtract the desired profit to give a target cost. Then the product is designed and engineered to achieve the target cost. This system focuses on getting costs out during the planning and design stages. Careful attention to costs allowed Daimler Chrysler to cut the cost of their redesigned 1999 Jeep Grand Cherokee sport-utility vehicle by $250 even though it has an improved engine, a better climate control system, more interior space, and other luxury features.[5]

Costs and the Experience Curve.   There is convincing evidence that the cost of manufacturing products also declines as workers gain experience in their jobs. An example of an experience curve is shown in Figure 9-5.

INTEGRATING

. . . *with*
Production/
Operations
Management

There are two major sources of the cost reductions shown in experience curves. First, workers and managers learn how to do a better job through repetition. Assembly workers develop greater dexterity and better work routines, and machine operators learn how to adjust their equipment for the greatest output. Also, marketing managers learn through experience how to do a better job of introducing and promoting new products. A second source of cost reductions is technology. New production processes are introduced, and products are redesigned to save money.

Experience curves suggest that costs decline continuously over the entire product life cycle. This means that you have the ability to cut prices on a regular basis to meet competitive threats and to achieve sales objectives. For example, the learning curve allowed Ford to cut the price of its 1999 Taurus sedan $1,000 and the Taurus station wagon $1,800 in an effort to boost sales of this aging model.[6] Also, during introductory periods, it is common to set prices below current actual costs to help expand demand for the product. Firms expect profits to return later as costs fall faster than selling prices.

During the growth stage of the product life cycle, there is little incentive to cut prices. As a result, prices do not fall as fast as costs and profit margins grow fat (Figure 9-5). This price umbrella attracts new entrants who are able to make money despite high initial costs. The new firms survive by stealing market share from the market leader. Dominant organiza-

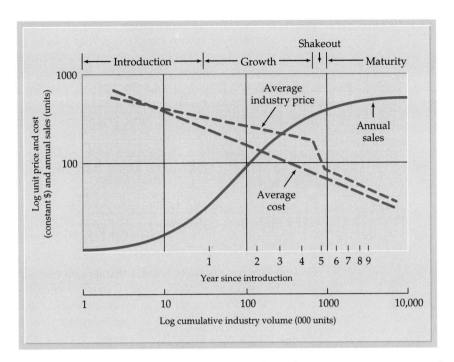

FIGURE 9-5 **Experience Curves and the Product Life Cycle (From George S. Day and David B. Montgomery, "Diagnosing the Experience Curve,"** *Journal of Marketing,* **Vol. 47 [Spring 1983], p. 51. Reproduced by permission of the American Marketing Association.)**

tions that allow a price umbrella during the growth stage are actually trading long-run market share for current profits.

At the end of the growth stage of the life cycle, a shakeout occurs and prices drop sharply (Figure 9-5). This may happen because the market leader is attempting to stop the loss of market position or regain previous share levels. During the maturity phase of the life cycle, the margin between costs and prices erodes continuously, and cost savings are harder to find.

CHOOSING A PRICING METHOD

Now that you understand demand and costs, you are ready to select a price. Remember, prices should be high enough to produce some profit but not so high that customers refuse to buy. The primary external constraint on your prices is the actions of competitors. Any pricing procedure that you select must be in line with the prices set by competitors. Your task is to find a method that balances demand, costs, and competitive factors for an individual product.

Markup Pricing

Many organizations prefer pricing procedures that are easy to administer and require only limited assumptions about demand. Perhaps the simplest and most popular one is known as *markup pricing.*

With markup pricing, you add an amount to the cost of the item to yield a selling price. This amount is the markup designed to cover overhead expenses and produce a profit for the firm. Markups are stated as a percentage of the cost or selling price of the item. Setting prices with cost markups involves multiplying the markup percentage (expressed as a fraction) by the cost of the item and then adding the result to the cost. For example, if an item cost $5 to manufacture and the firm wanted a 300 percent markup on the cost, the markup would be $3 \times \$5$ or $15 plus the cost of $5, giving a selling price of $20. This may be simplified by adding 1 to the markup percentage to create a cost multiplier.

Markups on selling price are more complicated because they cannot be multiplied directly by the cost to give a price. With these markups, costs are divided by 1 minus the markup percentage (expressed as a fraction) to yield the selling price. Thus, if a dealer wanted a 30 percent margin on the selling price and an item cost $7, the selling price would be

$$\text{Selling price} = \frac{\text{cost}}{(1 - \text{markup on selling price})} = \frac{\$7}{1 - 0.3} = \$10 \qquad (9.2)$$

Cost markups are always larger than markups on the selling price because of the smaller base. Note that markups on cost can be any amount, whereas markups on selling price range between zero and 100 percent. Traditionally, firms use *markup* (on cost) in internal operations and report *margin* (markup on selling price) in finanacial communications.

Markup pricing does not adequately handle demand when the same markup percentage is applied to different classes of goods. If you select this method, you should vary markup percentages according to customers' price sensitivities. For example, supermarkets use markups of 9 percent on baby food and 50 percent on the more inelastic greeting cards. This strategy of varying margins by price elasticities leads to greater profits.

APPLYING
. . . to
Retailing

Markup pricing was the most common technique reported in a study of small and medium-sized firms in England.[7] The method is easy to understand and the size of the markups can be set to accomplish a variety of objectives.

PRICING EXERCISE

If a retailer buys a dress for $40 and plans to use a 60 percent markup on the selling price, what will be the final purchase price for the customer? What is the dollar markup? A manufacturer calculates the cost of producing a lamp to be $25. To obtain a 400 percent markup on cost, what selling price should be set for the lamp?

Break-Even Pricing

Break-even pricing shows how many units must be sold at selected prices to regain the funds invested in a product. Suppose that the fixed selling, advertising, R&D, and tooling costs for a barbecue grill are $200,000 and the variable costs $6 per unit. At a factory selling price of $8, the break-even volume is

$$\text{Break-even volume} = \frac{\text{fixed costs}}{\text{price} - \text{variable costs}} = \frac{\$200,000}{\$8 - \$6} = 100,000 \text{ units} \qquad (9.3)$$

Profits are generated when volume exceeds the break-even point, and losses occur when volume fails to reach the break-even point. Break-even volumes for factory selling prices of $8, $10, and $12 are shown in Figure 9-6.

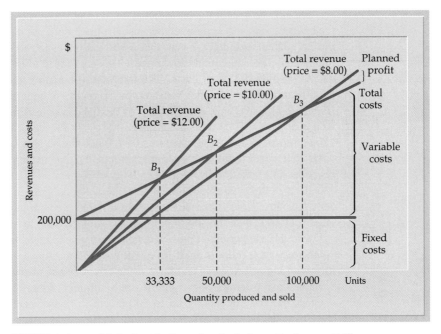

FIGURE 9-6   Multiple Break-Even Analysis for a Barbecue Grill

Although break-even pricing shows the volume needed to cover your costs, it makes some simplifying assumptions about demand. The total revenue lines in Figure 9-6 are straight, implying that larger volumes can be sold without lowering prices. This is unrealistic, and executives must be able to estimate the number of units that will be sold at each tentative price. Remember the prices shown in Figure 9-6 are factory prices and you have to add in margins for retailers to get accurate estimates of how many can be sold to consumers.

PRICING EXERCISE

The total fixed costs of producing a DVD player are $2.1 million and the variable costs are $80. If the manufacturer is considering factory selling prices of $150 and $200, what are the break-even volumes? What factory selling price do you recommend? Why?

Variable-Cost Pricing

Variable-cost pricing is based on the idea that the recovery of full costs is not always realistic or necessary for organizations. Instead of using full costs as the lowest possible price, this system suggests that variable costs represent the minimum price that can be charged. For example, assume that you have been able to sell 100,000 barbecue grills at $8.50 through your regular discount store channels. A supermarket chain offers to purchase 20,000 barbecue grills at $7 each. The buyer suggests that the grills carry the supermarket's label without the wheels found on the regular model. If the design changes reduce variable costs to $5.75, the order represents a potential profit of $25,000.

Should you accept the offer and price the modified grills at $7.00? Some would say that the order can *never* be approved because the price does not cover the full cost of $7.42 (Figure 9-7). Others would point out that if you cut prices to the supermarket, your regular customers may demand equally low prices. This could lead to losses, because it would be difficult to recover the fixed costs. The important point to remember is that the full cost to manufacture the grills is not constant, but in reality is quite sensitive to changes in volume (Figure 9-7), where unit costs decline as the fixed expenses are spread over a large volume. At a volume of 20,000 units the grills cost $16, but this cost declines to $7.42 at a volume of 120,000 units and to $7 at a volume of 200,000 units. This shows that very low prices can cover full costs if volume expands sufficiently. An example of variable cost pricing is described in Marketing in Action box 9-1.

Perhaps the most important issue in variable-cost pricing is whether the markets can be kept separate. If the supermarkets are in different geographic locations or service different income classes, then the additional business looks attractive.

Variable-cost pricing that focuses on *revenue management* is common where fixed costs comprise a large proportion of total unit costs. The airlines, hotels, and railroads are industries with high fixed costs that have made effective use of the volume-generating aspects of variable-cost pricing. For example, one summer American Airlines slashed fares on advance-purchase tickets by up to 50 percent to boost vacation business. These low fares were matched by other airlines, and within a few days, all the excursion seats on the major U.S. airlines allocated to these programs had been sold. This illustration shows that the demand for summer travel is very elastic and that low prices will fill seats on airplanes. However, the airlines had trouble keeping the special low fares out of the hands of their regular customers. Many people were able to exchange higher-priced tickets for the excursion fares, and others who had planned to pay regular fares rushed to take advantage of the low rates. Because of the size of the price cuts and their inability to restrict the low fares to new customers, all the major U.S. airlines lost money with variable-cost pricing that summer.

APPLYING
. . . to
Transportation
Services
Marketing

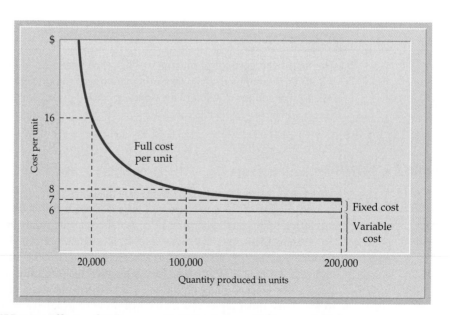

FIGURE 9-7   Effects of Volume on Unit Costs for a Barbecue Grill

MARKETING IN ACTION *9-1*

Lunch by the Minute

During a recession in Japan, a number of restaurants started charging by the minute for all-you-can-eat buffet lunches as a way to improve business. At the 43 Tohtenkoh restaurants the first 30 lunch customers get to pay by the minute. Customers are asked to punch in on a time clock so there is no haggling over the time spent in the restaurant. The price is 30 cents per minute and one customer was charged $5.70 for a 19 minute lunch. At Tohtenkoh the regular luncheon buffet cost $15.95. At a price of 30 cents per minute, the restaurant does not make a profit on the 30 lunches, but they do cover the variable cost of the food served. However, minute pricing has drawn more customers paying the regular price so total revenue has increased. The manager claims minute pricing is good publicity.

— *Innovative use of variable cost pricing can boost revenue.*

Source: Yumiko Ono, "We're Eating Out Tonight, So Please Bring a Stopwatch," *The Wall Street Journal*, December 23, 1998, pp. A1, A4.

Courtesy Tohtenkoh Company Ltd.

Since this fiasco, airlines have refined their computer programs that help them manipulate prices to maximize profits. Marketing Strategies box 9-1 explains how the new revenue management programs work at American Airlines.

PRICING EXERCISE

A golf course has a regular greens fee of $15 for play during the week and $25 on the weekend. Sixty women golfers ask for a special rate of $10 per person to play on a Thursday afternoon. The variable cost of handling this special group is estimated at $4 each. Should the golf course accept the proposal of the 60 women golfers? What other factors would influence your decision?

MARKETING STRATEGIES *9-1*

Using Computers to Optimize Airline Prices

Airline travel is a high fixed cost industry and the demand for leisure travel is very elastic. Under these conditions, profits can be increased by cutting ticket prices for tourists to fill empty seats. American Airlines computers combine historical data bases on ridership with up-to-the-minute bookings to predict how many business customers will want seats on a particular flight. Business clients typically buy unrestricted tickets at the last minute and are charged higher fares than tourists who must book weeks ahead and stay over a Saturday night. For example, American's Flight 2015 from Chicago to Phoenix has its 125 coach seats divided into seven classes with prices ranging from $238 for the lowest priced tourist fare to $1404 for a last-minute unrestricted fare. In the weeks before each Chicago to Phoenix flight, American's revenue management programs constantly adjust the number of seats available in each price class, taking into account tickets sold, historical ridership patterns, and the number of connecting passengers likely to use the route as one leg of a longer trip. If advance bookings are slim, American adds more low-fare seats. If business customers buy unrestricted fares earlier than expected, the computer takes seats out of the discount class and preserves them for last-minute bookings. With 69 of 125 coach seats already sold four weeks before one recent departure of Flight 2015, American began to limit the number of low priced seats. A week later, it totally shut off sales for the bottom three tiers. One day before departure, with 130 passengers booked for the 125 seat flight, American still offered five seats at full fare because its computer indicated 10 passengers were likely not to show up or take other flights. Flight 2015 departed full and no one was bumped. Also American's computers make price changes instantly available to other airlines and this tends to dampen price cutting by competitors. Computerized pricing of tickets has allowed airlines to raise their percentage of seats filled to over 70 percent and increase profits.

— *Revenue management programs can set prices to correspond with elasticities of different buyers.*

Source: Scott McCartney, "Ticket Shock: Business Fares Increase Even as Leisure Travel Keeps Getting Cheaper," *The Wall Street Journal,* November 3, 1997, pp. A1, A6.

Sidebar labels:

APPLYING *. . . to Transportation Services Marketing*

INTEGRATING *. . . with Accounting, Information Technology Management*

Courtesy American Airlines

Nonlinear Pricing

APPLYING
. . . to
*Entertainment
Services
Marketing*

Nonlinear pricing is based on the observation that the second, third, and additional units of a product or service have a lower value to the customer than the first purchase. An illustration is provided by a movie theater that offered discounts for successive visits within a month. The number of visits is monitored by a free card that is issued at the first visit. The plan requires that the theater owners know how much different customer groups are willing to pay for successive visits. Revenue generated by offering a uniform price can then be compared with sales produced by offering lower prices for second, third, and more visits. Since virtually all costs of a movie theater are fixed, revenue projections provide a good estimate of the profit impact of nonlinear pricing. Profit improvements from nonlinear pricing can range up to 50 percent because marketing managers are reaching more segments of a demand curve (see Figure 9-1) than they would get with a uniform price.

Price Bundling

APPLYING
. . . to
*Consumer
Durable
Goods
Marketing*

Bundling involves selling two or more products at a price that is less than the sum of their individual prices. With pure bundling, only the package of products is offered. In a mixed bundling strategy, the individual products are sold separately as well. Bundling is widely used in the sale of fast food, automobile option packages, tourism, and telecommunications. An example of a successful mixed bundling strategy for automobile options is shown in Figure 9-8. The manufacturer was considering offering comfort, sports, and safety packages. A study revealed that buyers were quite sensitive to the discounts for the option bundles as compared to the price of options if purchased individually. Bundling was attractive to the

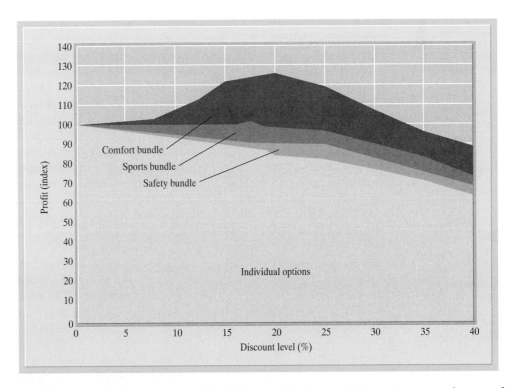

FIGURE 9-8   Profits Associated with Option Bundle Discounts (From Hermann Simon and Robert J. Dolan, "Price Customization," *Marketing Management* [Fall 1998], p. 16.)

manufacturer because it lowered the cost of the purchased components and reduced complexity in logistics and auto assembly. Figure 9-8 shows the relation between profits and the discount level to be offered on the three discount packages. As the discount on the packages increases, the profit generated on individual options declines as customers switch to the bundles. However, overall profit increased because of the growth in the total number of options sold. In this example, the maximum profit was reached with a bundle discount of 21 percent.

The key to successful bundling is to find combinations where willingness to buy varies across products. For example, in America the popular $1,000 air-conditioning option is often bundled with less popular options such as cruise control, power door locks, and power windows. Customers who want air conditioning have a choice of buying it as a separate option for $1,000 or in a package where they pay $800 and get 20 percent off the price of cruise control and the other options in the price bundle. Enough buyers who want air conditioning are attracted by the discounts offered in the package to make a mixed bundling strategy the most profitable for the manufacturer. Typically price bundling increases profits by 14 to 25 percent.[8]

New-Product Pricing

One of the more complex pricing issues that you must resolve is setting prices for new products. These decisions are complicated by the frequent lack of information on demand and costs. Because new products have not been sold before, price elasticity cannot be estimated from an analysis of historical data. Asking consumers if they are interested in buying a new product at a particular price is not very helpful. Also, the desire to prevent competitors from learning about new products may prevent the firm from using test markets to obtain elasticity data. Even the simple expedient of copying a competitor's price is not a practical alternative for new products. Despite these problems, marketing managers must find a price that will sell the product and still contribute to the profits of the firm.

Value-in-Use Pricing.   This approach stresses understanding price from the customer's point of view. Business buyers are often more interested in the total value of the product or service than they are in the initial price. These buyers are concerned with how long products last, availability of repair parts, length of warranties, timeliness of delivery, and other operational or financial benefits. In addition, you have to know what costs customers incur beyond the price of the product. These costs may include order handling, freight, installation, and training. Customers also have other costs, such as the fear of late delivery, the need for custom modification of the delivered product, or the impact of product failure on organizational productivity. Thus, you must understand the customer's possible applications of the product. Once a firm assesses customers' benefits and costs in terms of the complete usage system, it is in a position to set the price.

The importance of value-in-use-pricing was made clear to one of the authors who had to replace a national brand PC due to early hard drive failure. When I took the American brand PC to the shop, I was surprised to find that the machine was assembled overseas from components manufactured by offshore companies. When the shop owner offered to configure a computer with an American hard drive and a full two-year warranty on all new parts, I accepted even though I could have bought a name brand PC at a lower price. In this case, doubling the length of the warranty and access to local repair service provided more value over the expected life of the product than the seductive allure of a low initial price.

APPLYING
. . . to
Consumer
Durable
Goods
Marketing

Skimming Prices.   Research has shown that the more innovative a new product is, the less sensitive customers are to price.[9] This suggests that high skimming prices should be used for new products and then gradually reduced over time. This situation is described by the downward-sloping curve DD in Figure 9-9. The high initial price (P^1) is designed to skim off the

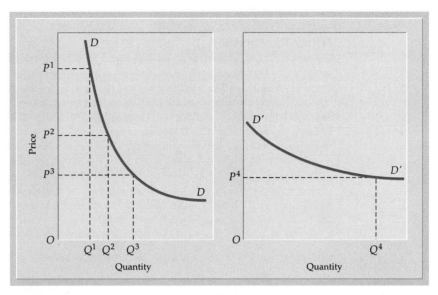

FIGURE 9-9   Demand Curves Assumed by Skimming and Penetration Price Strategies

segment of the market that is insensitive to price, and subsequent reductions (P^2, P^3) broaden the market by tapping more elastic sectors of the market. The logic of the skimming price strategy is supported by the observation that many new products have few technical substitutes and that the price is not as important as it is for more established products.

APPLYING
... to
Industrial
Marketing

A successful application of a skimming price strategy occurred with the microprocessor chips that control personal computers. Intel is the leading supplier to this market and it regularly introduces new more powerful microprocessors at high initial prices of $500 or $600. Over time, these prices are periodically reduced to expand sales to lower prices segments of the PC market. Older versions of its Pentium processor are now sold under the Celeron label with prices as low as $71.[10]

The main disadvantage of a skimming price policy is that high margins attract competitors into the field. This suggests that a skimming price is best used when the product has strong patent protection or when there are other barriers to entry, such as technical know-how or high capital requirements. Although skimming prices can increase short-term profits, they may not be sustainable in the long run. An example of price skimming in the toothbrush market is described in Marketing Strategies box 9-2.

Penetration Prices.   A penetration price is set below current costs and is designed to open mass markets quickly. This pricing strategy is based on the assumptions that (1) there is little prospect of creating or maintaining product superiority, (2) there are few barriers to entry by competitors, and (3) demand is highly elastic (curve $D'D'$ in Figure 9-9) and low prices will significantly expand the market. In addition, penetration pricing assumes that the high volume associated with a low introductory price (P^4 in Figure 9-9) will reduce costs, so that a profit can be made during the growth phase of the product life cycle. Penetration prices are encouraged by the experience curve and declines in unit costs over the product life cycle (Figure 9-5). One of the most successful examples of penetration pricing in recent years was Chrysler's introduction of its small Neon cars.

Why do managers set high prices on new products when it is often in their long-run interests to set the price low to keep competition out? The answer seems to be that current profits are needed to fund growth in production capacity, R&D, and market development activity. Also, the reward system for managers often emphasizes immediate profits. Remem-

APPLYING
. . . to
Consumer
Packaged
Goods
Marketing

MARKETING STRATEGIES 9-2

Pricing Toothbrushes

Gillette Co.'s Oral-B Laboratories has introduced the most expensive mass market toothbrush ever at a list price of $4.99. The new CrossAction brush will cost the consumer 50 percent more than any of its high end rivals. Oral-B has the largest share of the U.S. toothbrush market and their new brush is designed to strengthen this position. Bristles on the CrossAction don't stand up straight, but are set in three rows of bristles of varying sizes angled in opposite directions. This allows the new brush to remove 25 percent more plaque than competitive brushes. Also the CrossAction has a fat ergonomic rubberized handle and denser bristles at the tip to clean behind back teeth. Gillette test marketed the new brushes at $3.99 and $4.99 and found no significant difference in sales. Since many customers are willing to pay $7 to $12 for replacement heads for electric toothbrushes, Oral-B decided that a skimming price of $4.99 for the new CrossAction brush was feasible. One of the authors bought a CrossAction brush to see if it worked as claimed. The fat grippy handle made the brush easier to maneuver and the dense tip bristles did clean better behind back teeth. Also, the angled bristles seemed to scrub adeptly at the gum line. Looks like Gillette has a winner at $4.99.

— *Skimming prices for innovative products can raise profits.*

Source: Mark Maremont, "New Toothbrush Is Big-Ticket Item," *The Wall Street Journal*, October 27, 1998, pp. B1, B6.

Courtesy The Gillette Company

ber that if you are or can become the low-cost producer, low initial prices are often the best way to build market share and long-run profits.

PRICING EXERCISE

Extensive research has led to the development of an innovative new digital phone with longer battery life and greater range than its competitors. The manufacturer is considering either a skimming price of $190 or a low penetration price of $99. The variable cost of producing the new phone is $70. First-year sales at the $190 price are estimated to be 500,000 units and 2,069,000 units at the $99 price. Which price should the firm use? Why?

Multidimensional Pricing

With multidimensional pricing, firms break up prices into two or more components. When companies buy steel, sulfuric acid, and industrial gases, they pay a flat rate per pound or gallon. Each customer pays the same price. One supplier in the industrial gas market introduced a multidimensional price program that charged customers a daily rental fee for the steel cylinder and a reduced price per pound for the gas. With the new system, customers who use the gas quickly pay a lower total price than those who use it slowly do. Success with multi-dimensional pricing requires that the seller take a great deal of care to make sure the two prices are set correctly.

An example of effective multidimensional pricing is shown by German Railroad Corp.'s introduction of a two-dimensional scheme for passenger travel. In the past, the company set prices for passenger tickets as a simple multiple of a rate times the distance traveled. Unfortunately, this scheme led to prices that were higher than the cost of driving for many potential riders. To attract more business, the company introduced a new BahnCard at a cost of $300 per year for first class and $150 per year for second class. Travelers with these cards could buy tickets at 50 percent off the standard per kilometer price. Once purchased, the BahnCard is a sunk cost and the car or train decision depends on the marginal price per kilometer. With the marginal cost of train travel now below the cost of driving for many customers, German Rail was able to attract 3.5 million loyal card holders. The net result of multidimensional pricing in this case was an increase in profits of $200 million per year for the German Railroad Corp.[11]

APPLYING
*. . . to
Transportation
Services
Marketing*

WHEN SHOULD PRICES BE CHANGED?

Once you have selected a basic price for your goods and services, there are a number of situations in which adjustments have to be made to account for unique market conditions.

Responding to Competitive Cuts

One of the most difficult challenges you will face as a marketing manager is responding to price cuts by competitors. This situation is fraught with danger no matter what you do. If you play it safe and maintain your prices to keep short-run profits up, you risk losing market share and long-run profitability. If you match competitive price cuts to maintain market share, short-term profits and the price of your company's stock will plummet. Price wars with competitors appear to be a no-win situation. An example of a price war in the mature beer market is described in Marketing in Action box 9-2.

Brand loyalty does not last forever when competitors cut prices. If you expect to survive a price war, you must keep your costs under control so that you can continue to make money when prices are pushed down. Some firms are able to avoid price wars by differentiating their products and focusing on customers in niche markets. It is also desirable to have some "fighting brands" available to do battle when price competition heats up. Another approach is to develop computer models to help predict what will happen when competitors cut prices. For example, Research International offers its PriceSolve model to help you plan pricing strategies for the future.

Geographic Pricing

There is often money to be made by charging different prices to customers located in separate geographical areas. These adjustments reflect variation in transportation costs and price elasticities. The most common geographic pricing system is known as *FOB pricing*.

FOB Pricing. With FOB pricing, the manufacturer places goods *free on board* a carrier, and the buyer pays the freight to the destination. The system is fair because customers near the plant pay the lowest freight charges and those farthest away pay the highest charges. With FOB pricing, buyers tend to purchase from the closest supplier. The main problem with FOB pricing is that it is difficult to build market share by selling in distant markets.

MARKETING IN ACTION 9-2

Beer Price Wars

APPLYING
. . . to
Consumer
Beverages
Marketing

Per capita consumption of beer has been declining in America. Under these conditions, the best way to increase revenue is to take market share from competitors. Miller, a distant No. 2 to Anheuser-Busch, started a price war in 1997 and was initially successful. Anheuser-Busch didn't immediately follow, and Miller was able to increase their market share from 20.6 percent to 22.4 percent while Anheuser-Busch's share dropped from 46.6 percent to 43.8 percent. When Anheuser-Busch found out the size of its market share decline, it started to cut prices and by the end of the fourth quarter of 1997 its share had soared back to 47.5 percent and Miller's dropped back to 20.9 percent. The heavy discounting hurt beer profits and Miller's revenue per barrel fell $2.60 from 1996 and Anheuser-Busch's fell $0.54. As a result of the price war, the combined market share of Miller and Anheuser-Busch rose 1.2 percent at the expense of smaller brewers. Coors Brewery and Stroh Brewery stayed out of the price war and managed to increase revenues. Stroh decided to give up some market share to maintain profits. As it turned out, Anheuser-Busch's 1 percent price cuts led to a 4 percent increase in sales while Miller's 2 percent price cuts actually led to a 1 percent decline in revenue.

— *Those who start price wars do not always win them.*

Source: Rekha Balu, "Big Brewers Find Price War Seems to Have No End," *The Wall Street Journal*, July 2, 1998, p. B6.

Courtesy Anheuser-Busch Companies

Delivered Pricing. Firms that want to expand into other markets often set prices on a delivered basis. Under this plan, an average freight charge is added to the factory price, and everyone pays the same delivered price. This is the system used by American automobile manufacturers to set retail selling prices for their vehicles. A delivered price strategy favors distant customers and allows the use of a single nationally advertised price. However, customers close to the factory pay higher prices, and they may buy from local competitors who use FOB pricing. Delivered pricing tends to sacrifice sales nearby to gain business from more distant buyers.

Zone Pricing. Under a zone pricing system, markets are divided so that all customers within a zone pay the same price. Zone pricing is often used to take advantage of differences in price elasticity across markets. In the United States, the most common example of zone pricing is the sale of national brands of gasoline. Large manufacturers divide states and even cities into pricing zones so they can charge different prices in each area. This makes it easier

APPLYING
. . . to
Consumer
Non-Durable
Goods
Marketing

for them to prevent damage from the spread of gasoline *price wars.* When low prices hurt profits in one area, manufacturers can charge higher prices in other higher income areas where demand is more inelastic. Zone pricing works for gasoline because the franchised independent dealers are obligated to buy from their national brand supplier and it is not practical to pump out the gasoline from the tanks of one dealer and haul it to higher-priced markets for resale. Also consumers are not likely to drive 50 miles to buy gas and take advantage of lower prices in other pricing zones.

Zone pricing has the disadvantage that price disparities across zones may become large enough to catch the attention of dealers and customers. In Indiana, for example, gasoline prices may vary as much as $.15 a gallon over a distance of only 50 miles. Clearly a differential this large is not related to the cost of hauling gasoline to the dealers. Rather it reflects an effort on the part of manufacturers to maximize profits. Some independent Indiana franchised Shell dealers have sued their supplier claiming that Shell's zone pricing is discriminatory. Independent dealers usually own stations in one town and often feel they are treated unfairly when other dealers in nearby zones are able to buy gasoline at lower prices. Although zone pricing may appear to be discriminatory in some situations, courts of law have ruled that zone pricing for competitive products like gasoline is perfectly legal.

A more serious problem occurs when zone pricing is used for high-value products that are easily shipped. When price differentials become large enough to pay for shipping, independent dealers will start buying products in low-priced zones and haul them to high-priced markets for resale. These parallel importers, as they are called, can quickly destroy the profit maximizing appeal of zone pricing. *Parallel importing* is common with cameras, watches, liquor, and cigarettes. This suggests that zone prices must be set carefully if border disruptions are to be kept to a minimum.

Discounts and Allowances

To help field representatives close sales, many firms offer special discounts and allowances.

Cash Discounts. The most common incentive is a cash discount for paying bills early. For example, an organization might offer terms of "2/10, net 30," which means that the buyer can deduct 2 percent of the price if the bill is paid by the tenth of the month; otherwise, the

INTEGRATING
. . . with
Finance

whole amount is due on the thirtieth. A 2 percent discount may not seem like much incentive, but it encourages buyers to pay 20 days early, and this amounts to 36 percent on an annual basis. Cash discounts improve the cash flow for the seller and reduce collection costs.

Seasonal Discounts. Consumer purchases in industries such as toys and swimwear are highly concentrated, leading to underutilization of labor and factories in the off-season. To help control this problem, many firms in these industries offer seasonal discounts to encourage buyers to place orders early. Seasonal discounts are often substantial and can be thought of as an example of variable-cost pricing.

Allowances.   Allowances for price reductions are designed to compensate buyers for certain activities. Promotional allowances, for example, include cash or free merchandise designed to get dealers to advertise or build in-store displays to promote products. Trade-in allowances are another incentive offered on durable goods to help reduce down payments and get customers to buy. To be legal, discounts and allowances must be made available to all competing channel members.

Product-Line Pricing

When there are several items in your product line, prices must be set to maximize profits for a whole array of products. This may be difficult because margins vary and some items have interrelated costs. A further complication is that the sales of one product may be influenced by the price charged for a second product. This can be measured by calculating values for *cross-price elasticity.* Suppose that when you raise the price of Bayer Aspirin 5 percent in your store, sales of Tylenol increase 10 percent. In mathematical terms,

$$\text{Cross-price elasticity} = \frac{\%\ \text{change in sales of Tylenol}}{\%\ \text{change in price of Bayer Aspirin}} = \frac{+10\%}{+5\%} = +2 \quad (9.4)$$

The positive cross-price elasticity of +2 indicates that consumers considered the two items to be substitutes. A negative cross-price elasticity would indicate that the products were complementary and typically were sold together.

A study of egg pricing revealed that the price elasticity for large eggs was a very elastic −3.3. This means if you raise the price of large eggs, customers will start to buy medium or private label eggs. Cross-price elasticities among the three types of eggs were all positive, indicating consumers considered them to be substitutes. Thus, a consideration of price elasticities and cost data can lead to the most profitable price level for each brand sold by the company. The results suggest that total profits would increase if you consider cross-price elasticities when you set prices for different sizes and brands of eggs. When price elasticities can be measured, marketing managers no longer have to rely on rules of thumb for product-line pricing.

Price Discrimination

Price discrimination is an attractive pricing strategy that can boost volume and profits by taking advantage of differences in customers' price sensitivities. For example, you can segment your market on age and offer lower-priced admission tickets to children. Another approach is to vary price by time. Customers who want to play golf on weekdays are offered low prices, whereas weekend players are charged high prices. A third way to segment customers is by location. Theater managers and sporting events promoters charge higher prices for front-row seats than for seats in the balcony.

Price discrimination works best when customer segments have different elasticities. Also, a low-price customer must not be able to resell the product to the high-price segment. Moreover, the cost of segmenting and policing the market should not exceed the benefits of price discrimination. You must make sure that the form of discrimination employed is not illegal.

SUMMARY

Pricing is a key component of the marketing mix, and it is essential that you understand the different pricing options that are available. Prices must be set that are consistent with your product's positioning and appropriate for your target market segment. Effective pricing is impossible without a keen awareness of price elasticities. When demand is inelastic, you can increase profits by raising prices. When demand is elastic, lower prices increase revenues. You also need to understand markup procedures to help set prices for wholesalers and retailers. No pricing analysis is complete without a review of the fixed and variable costs associated with different product alternatives. Sometimes prices should be set below current full costs to expand markets and keep out the competition. At other times multidimensional and bundle pricing should be used. The ideal pricing system combines estimates of costs and price elasticity to maximize the discounted stream of profits of the firm. Finally, no pricing scheme can last unless it considers the actions of competitors and is within the law.

NOTES

1. Gregory L. White, "Sales of Cars, Light Trucks Rose 7% in December," *The Wall Street Journal,* January 7, 1999, pp. A3, A4.
2. Fara Warner and Joseph B. White, "Ford Plans to Reduce Costs by Another $1 Billion," *The Wall Street Journal,* January 8, 1999, pp. A3, A6.
3. Dominique M. Hanssens, Leonard J. Parsons, and Randall L. Schultz, *Marketing Response Models: Econometric and Time Series Analysis* (Boston: Kluwer, 1990), pp. 187–191.
4. Philip Parker, "Price Elasticity Dynamics over the Adoption Cycle," *Journal of Marketing Research,* Vol. 20 (August 1992), pp. 359–367.
5. Gregory L. White, Fara Warner, and Joseph B. White, "Bumper Crop, Competition Rises, Car Prices Drop: A New Golden Age?" *The Wall Street Journal,* January 8, 1999, pp. A1, A8.
6. Ibid., p. A1.
7. David Carson, Audrey Gilmore, Darryl Cummins, Aodheen O'Donnell, and Ken Grant, "Price Setting in SMEs: Some Empirical Findings," *Journal of Product & Brand Management,* Vol. 7, No. 1 (1998), p. 78.
8. Hermann Simon and Robert J. Dolan, "Price Customization," *Marketing Management,* (Fall 1998), p. 16.
9. Ronald E. Goldsmith and Stephen J. Newell, "Innovativeness and Price Sensitivity: Managerial, Theoretical and Methodological Issues," *Journal of Product & Brand Management,* Vol. 6, No. 3 (1997), p. 168.
10. Dean Takahashi, "Intel Introduces 2 Low-End Chips, Cuts Some Prices," *The Wall Street Journal,* January 5, 1999, p. B5.
11. Simon and Dolan, "Price Customization," p. 13.

SUGGESTED READING

Hamilton, Will, Robert East, and Stavros Kkalafatis, "The Measurement and Utility of Brand Price Elasticities," *Journal of Marketing Management,* Vol. 13, No. 4 (May 1997), pp. 285–298.

Simon, Hermann, and Martin Fasfnacht. "Price Bundling," *European Management Journal,* Vol. 11 (December 1993), pp. 403–411.

REFERENCES

Cross, Robert G. *Revenue Management* (New York: Broadway Books, 1997).

Dolan, Robert J. and Hermann Simon. *Power Pricing: How Managing Price Transforms the Bottom Line* (New York: Free Press, 1997).

Holtz, Herman. *Priced to Sell: The Complete Guide to More Profitable Pricing* (Upstart Publishing Company, 1996).

Monroe, Kent B. *Pricing: Making Profitable Decisions* (New York: McGraw-Hill, 1990).

Nagle, Thomas T. and Reed K. Holden. *The Strategy and Tactics of Pricing: A Guide to Profitable Decision Making* (Upper Saddle River, NJ: Prentice-Hall, 1994).

Wilson, Robert B. *Nonlinear Pricing* (London: Oxford University Press, 1997).

QUESTIONS

1. Since 1997, Fuji Photo Film Co. of Japan and Eastman Kodak Co. have been engaged in a furious price war for the U.S. consumer photographic film market. In 1998, Fuji stunned Kodak by offering a four-pack of 24-exposure rolls for $4.99 through Wal-Mart and other mass merchants. Kodak responded with a rebate promotion at Sam's Club stores with a six-pack for $5.99, a new low of 4 cents a snapshot. The average price per roll has fallen 9.6 percent for Fuji and 7.3 percent for Kodak, hurting profits for both firms. Why is Fuji with 15 percent of the market going after Kodak which holds 73 percent of the market? How should Kodak respond?

2. If a retailer has product costs of $42 and plans to make a 40 percent margin on its selling price, what price would it charge?

3. Some stores are selling replacement blades for Gillette's new MACH3 razor for 70 percent more than the cost of blades for the Sensor Excel razor that it displaced. Should Gillette allow this price gap to continue? Why are consumers willing to pay a premium to get the new blades?

4. A retailer notes that a line of woks is selling at a rate of 100 per week. When the price is cut from $40 to $35, sales increase to 106 per week. What is the price elasticity of demand? What happens to revenue? What price should the retailer place on the woks?

5. Florida's attorney general has charged 10 large paper companies with conspiring to fix the prices of toilet paper sold to schools, hospitals, prisons, hotels, and other commercial customers. The suit notes that while the price of wood pulp (which is used to make toilet tissue) has dropped 18 percent, the price of tissue has risen 41 percent. Why do large firms conspire to fix the selling prices of toilet paper, citric acid, and other basic commodities?

6. Matsushita announced an introductory price of $1,000 for a digital compact cassette deck. DCC machines boost quality by storing sound digitally instead of in the analog format used in conventional cassettes. The new players will also play conventional cassettes, but without enhanced sound quality. Why has Matsushita set the DCC price so high?

7. A shortage has developed for a popular model of automobile, and customers must now wait two months for delivery. A dealer has been selling these cars at list price. Now the dealer prices this model at $500 above list price. Is this acceptable behavior or is it unfair?

8. Advanced Micro Devices was able to grab a large piece of the microprocessor market for PCs selling at under $1,000 by offering chips for $100 or less. Intel, the high-priced market leader, responded by offering similar chips for as low as $71, causing AMD to lose money in 1998. What should AMD do to start making profits?

9. A grocery store has several months' supply of peanut butter in stock which it has on the shelves and in the storeroom. The owner hears that the wholesale price of peanut butter has increased and immediately raises the price on the current stock of peanut butter. Is this acceptable or is the grocer unfairly taking advantage of his customers?

10. The manager for a brand of margarine wondered how sensitive the total market was to changes in margarine and butter prices. Using the data in the file margarinedat.sav, cal-

culate margarine's own-price elasticity and butter's cross-price elasticity. Hint: If you first compute the natural logarithm (LN) of each variable and then run a linear multiple regression on the transformed variables, the regression coefficients of the variables can be interpreted as elasticities.

CASE 9-1   BAXTER (A)*

*P*eter Leyland, newly appointed UK Business Unit Director for Baxter Renal Division early in January 1997, was with his top team discussing the following week's presentation to senior management in Belgium. A decision had to be made. His greatest task would be to convince the board to give him the go ahead without all of the data they would have demanded in the past. He wasn't too worried though—the global giant had learned to accept the need for taking risks in the new competitive environment and, furthermore, a customer-focused approach was becoming more integral to their culture.

But what Leyland needed so badly from the board, if he was to genuinely put Baxter Renal back onto a growth track, was time.

He would never forget the year-end Sales and Marketing Meeting he had attended a month before having taken up the new appointment. The mood was one of low morale and even despondency. Having worked with the company in the UK years previously (he had been in global marketing and strategy positions in the US for three years, the UK for six years and three years in Europe), he was now taken aback by what he saw and heard at that meeting.

> I was used to them being a bit more uppish, bullish, confident that what they were doing was making a positive contribution to the outside and to themselves. But listening to the tone of their discussions, I was amazed: it wasn't the sort of bouncy optimism that I had experienced in the past.

Despite the Renal Division's still close to 80% market share in the UK peritoneal dialysis (PD) market, equal to about 20,000 bags a day sold to 5000 patients with kidney ailments, events in 1996 had marked what could be an irreversible turning point for Baxter, Leyland believed, unless something was done (Exhibit 1).

The company had lost a significant amount of business with one of its major accounts—the Queen Elisabeth II Hospital in Birmingham—to its key competitor, Fresenius, who had the other 20% of the PD market. Four other key accounts, from the "Black County" consortium of hospitals, were lost to a brand new competitor, Gambro, who had tried before to make inroads into the UK and failed but now not only had entered the market but had actually been invited in by the customer.

As Leyland thought back to that December meeting, he remembered a genuine sense of bewilderment on the part of the 50 sales and marketing executives as to:

> What the hell was going on—never before in the history of the renal division had five accounts been lost in one go. … Having been a successful unit you carry a lot of baggage with you: lots of expectations, budgets expected to always be growing and your performance next year is always supposed to be greater than last year's. But it was clear 1997 would be different. The key drivers in the business—the number of patients treated, the kind of treatment they received, the number of bags sold, and the proportion or market share of those cared for with a given treatment—were going down, and going down fast. Also, the balance of power from doctors and other users to so called "economic buyers" had swung dramatically, the market was destined therefore to become increasingly demanding and price sensitive.

BAXTER INTERNATIONAL

Baxter International was the world's largest supplier of medical products and services, and ranked among the 200 largest companies in the world. The company employed 60,000 people world-wide, with 7000 in Europe, and offered more than 200,000 products to healthcare providers in over 100 countries. Although

* This case was prepared by Professor Sandra Vandermerwe and Dr. Marika Taishoff of The Management School, Imperial College. Copyright © 1997 by The Management School, Imperial College of Science, Technology and Medicine, London, England. Reproduced by permission.

EXHIBIT 1   **Market Data**[a]

	1994	1995	1996
Baxter PD Market Share (number of patients)	78.5%	78%	77.5%
Competition in PD Market			
• **Fresenius**	21%	21%	21.5%
• **Gambro/Other**	0.5%	1%	1%
PD Penetration	49%	45%	42.2%
UK Take-on rates	69 people per million	72 people per million	73 people per million
UK Treatment Rates	456 people per million	490 people per million	507 people per million
PD & HD Patient Numbers in UK	11661	12855	13314
Transplant Patient Numbers in UK	14140	14983	15608

[a] Figures averaged to represent annual period.

American, the company's focal point for R&D had always been in Europe, where it had three of its key research centers in Belgium, Sweden, and Germany.

The company was a leader in technologies related to the blood and circulatory system, and had market-leading positions in four businesses:

1. *biotechnology:* therapies and products in transfusion medicine
2. *cardio-vascular medicine:* products and services to treat late stage cardio-vascular disease
3. *renal:* products and services to improve therapies to fight kidney disease.
4. *intravenous systems/medical products:* technologies and systems to improve intravenous medication delivery.

Over the years, some of Baxter's key innovations included:

- the first sterile intravenous solutions
- the first flexible sterile blood pack
- the first control serum
- the first prosthetic heart valve
- the first artificial kidney

The company was also a leader in research on xeno transplants (which used organs from other species, especially porcine transplants) to help patients whose organs needed replacement. Across Europe, waiting lists for human organs had been growing every year, and there had been an urgent need for substitutes to fill this gap and save lives. Many patients died each year because of the inadequate number of donors to fill the need.

RENAL FAILURE

The most critical and ultimately fatal implication of renal failure, which was how the sufferers' problem was referred to, was the kidneys' inability to dialyze and eliminate toxins from the blood system. When this happened, waste products accumulated, the fluid and electrolyte balance of the body became disturbed, and ultimately life was put at risk. If the disease had been diagnosed early enough, and properly monitored and treated, a chronic sufferer's life expectancy could be normal.

As of 1997, there were about 132,000 people across Europe suffering from renal failure. In the UK, there were over 13,000 patients being treated for this ailment, and over 16,000 who had received a kidney transplant because of it. Some experts suggested that this total figure of around 30,000 was equivalent to only one eighth of the people who really needed treatment, and that the UK under-recognized the extent of the disease. They pointed to the fact that there was a large discrepancy between the take-on rate in the UK—80 people per million and, in the UK ethnic population, 240 people per million—and other European countries.

One of the problems with treating the disease was that it was frequently unrecognized by general practitioners (GPs). GPs tended to be unfamiliar with the disease as they were rarely exposed to it firsthand. This had to do with the fact that the 25,000 GPs, who worked in groups with roughly 10,000 patients, each typically only saw one or two new patients a year so new renal sufferers didn't often come into contact with them.

Symptoms of the Disease

The symptoms of the disease were fairly constant and easy to misdiagnose. Typically a patient would begin to feel tired as toxins started to build up in the body. As the disease advanced patients started to experience fluid overload due to the kidneys' inability to remove the excess fluid. As the fluid built up in the lungs, chest pains and wheezing could result. Itching was also a symptom as excess salt began to be excreted through the skin. The skin could also become slightly discolored as the toxins accumulated in the patient's body.

Since these symptoms were very akin to those of cardiac failure and other diseases, when sufferers went to their GPs with these ailments, they could frequently be sent on to a cardiac or other specialist who either may or may not have recognized that it was renal and not cardiac or another failure. Also, if the patient was over 60 (as was frequently the case since age was strongly correlated with incidence of the disease) many GPs simply ascribed the symptoms to old age. The chance of being non-diagnosed was so frequent that a Baxter executive commented that if urine sticks—which could identify potential renal insufficiency—were placed in every GP's office and all patients were obliged to take the test, the UK health service would go bankrupt in days since so many cases of renal insufficiency would finally be recognized!

It was estimated that about 50% of UK renal failure sufferers entered the hospital system at the very last minute as emergency patients, known as "acute chronic" cases. At this last stage of the disease the survival rates were reduced dramatically and patient managed costs increased substantially. If patients could be detected and referred early on, however, they could be treated, their life expectancies could be extended, as well as their lifestyles improved. Also their costs could be managed more effectively. These patients, estimated to be the other 50% of the UK renal market, were known as "planned chronic" cases.

Predispositions to the Disease

There were several recognized factors which predisposed people to renal insufficiency:

- Having other diseases, in particular (50%) diabetes, or hypertension (high blood pressure) and still another percentage from cardio-vascular ailments. In these cases, renal insufficiency was a consequence of the primary illness and, if detected early enough, could indicate the presence of these other diseases which also required treatment. Many patients on renal treatment would die from heart failure.
- Certain UK minority ethnic groups were also more likely to get the illness than others. This was espe-

cially the case as these ethnic groups crossed boundaries and radically changed their dietary habits, which accelerated and increased the latent predisposition to get the disease. For instance, Mexicans in Mexico did not have the same rate of renal problems as Mexicans in the US did.

- Age was also a major factor in the likelihood of getting the disease. The older the population, the greater the risk of more widespread renal disease. In countries such as the UK, where there was the combination of a rapidly aging population together with a large ethnic community (in particular Bengalis who had a naturally high predisposition to the illness) some spoke of a "time bomb" that was waiting to go off when it came to treating renal failure.
- Inheritance was another factor—in some cases renal insufficiency could be transmitted from generation to generation.

Treating the Disease

There were two ways of treating renal failure: *dialysis* and *kidney transplants*.

The fundamental treatment (not cure) for renal failure was to dialyse the bloodstream. This meant that the toxins which were not being eliminated in the urine by the kidneys would have to be taken out of the body by means of a form of dialysis. As the disease progressed, the amount of dialysis had to be increased. Dialysis therapy placed higher demands on patients than most other forms of medical care.

There were two forms of dialysis treatment which could be applied: hemodialysis (HD), and peritoneal dialysis (PD). Peritoneal dialysis could be continuous (CAPD) or automated, known as automated peritoneal dialysis (APD). The fundamental difference between HD and CAPD and APD was that with the former the dialysis was done outside of the body by an "artificial kidney," whereas with the latter the filtering process was performed internally with the input of fluid into the abdomen's peritoneum membrane.

The decision as to which one to use depended on the nature of the patient's illness and lifestyle. Such a decision was typically a joint one between the renal doctors, nurses, and the patients when the disease was detected. Here are some details of these treatments:

- **Hemodialysis (HD):** basically involved taking blood, via bloodlines and needles, from the body, purifying it of toxins through an external filter called an "artificial kidney," and then returning this purified blood back into the body. In order to do this, a small, one-off vascular (vein) operation was necessary. The treatment had to be done in a specialized hospital's dialysis unit, three times a week for a four-hour session each time. Throughout this period the patient would have to lie down to be connected to the purification and filtration machine. Special renal nurses administered the treatment. The patient would have to be monitored in a hospital three times a week. This system had been first introduced and marketed commercially by Baxter in 1956.

- **Continuous Ambulatory Peritoneal Dialysis (CAPD):** this procedure used the peritoneum (the semi-permeable membrane which lines the abdominal organs) instead of an external filter for dialysis. Access to the peritoneum was gained via a tube a few inches long (which would remain permanently fixed to the patient's abdomen) which was inserted during one minor operation. Waste products would be removed and the blood filtered into a special dialysis solution, and then returned to the peritoneum. To achieve this a twin bag, one a full compartment which held the dialysis solution, and the other an empty compartment for the waste, was connected to the abdominal tube. Baxter had developed and introduced this system in 1979.

Patients did this CAPD procedure themselves, at home or at work, without having to go to a hospital (although they would go once every six weeks for monitoring). The fluid would have to be changed four or five times a day, depending on a person's size or weight (on average two liters of fluid would be injected each time), and each fluid exchange needed about 20 to 30 minutes, during which time a patient could read, watch television, or spend time with the family. The patient could do the fluid exchange procedure in any safe, clean environment (it could even be done in the back of a car if necessary). Once the fluid had been injected, the patient could walk around and do whatever else he or she did during the day. The patient had to follow an aseptic technique to avoid the risk of peritonitis, an infection of the peritoneum, and had to have all necessary supplies and keep track of them. Patients also had to monitor their dry and wet body weights on a daily basis. Blood tests had to be taken at a hospital when they went for a checkup to monitor toxin clearance levels which were crucial to the outcome for the patient. Research and experience had shown that the more accurate the prescription on the solution needed for an individual patient the better the outcome that could be obtained. For example, for a 12 liter fluid patient an incorrect

solution prescription could get a 33 clearance of toxin in the bloodstream whereas for a correct prescription the figure could go up to 70.

In contrast to HD, which was an intermittent treatment, CAPD was a continuous dialysis which took place every few hours on a daily basis. One contra-effect of the CAPD procedure was that since real membranes—the peritoneum—were being used, there was a limitation as to how long this form of treatment could be used. Once the membranes succumbed, generally after about two years of CAPD treatment, the patient would typically be put onto the HD treatment.

One patient who had been on HD and on CAPD treatments said that, with CAPD, "I dictate the time and the place, and I make the decisions." Another patient said that despite the time it took to get to and from the hospital for HD, and the time spent in the dialysis unit, he liked it because he enjoyed the social contact with the other dialysis patients and chatting with the nurses. He also liked the fact that the nurses were responsible for the entire procedure, so that not only did he not have to do anything, but the risk of infection was minimized. One patient who was told that she would have to go on HD because of the membrane problem said she had been devastated: "I wanted to die I was so unhappy. Even the thought of a spontaneous weekend away was impossible now because I was so constrained by my treatments. And vacations away from home were out of the question."

Both HD and PD treatments were considered equally effective for clinical purposes of dialysis and in any population both forms of treatment were necessary. About 50/50, Baxter believed, was a reasonable balance to expect from buyers. However it appeared that some sufferers were better off on one treatment than the other. For instance, very large or big patients required more fluid than small or average size patients; they would probably therefore be uncomfortable using PD, since so much liquid would have to be circulating in their systems while they were walking around or working. Such patients would probably prefer the HD treatment. Also many patients who started out on PD would eventually have to go on HD if no transplant was available.

In the UK, in the four-year period from 1992 to 1996, the utilization of PD as a treatment had been coming down. Whereas in 1992 PD accounted for just over 50% of all dialysis treatments, by the end of 1996, when Peter Leyland had arrived, it accounted for about 42%. The main reason for this, according to the renal team, was that the base line economics had shifted towards HD as the marginal cost, on a fluid bag-for-bag basis (consumables including bloodlines, needles, dialyzers and solutions), was cheaper with the HD treatment than the PD.

Research in Scandinavia had shown that early referral was essential. If the patient was diagnosed early on—and therefore "planned chronic"—then having been given the correct information at the pre-dialysis stage and the transition made easy, 70% of the sufferers would choose the PD home treatment, while 30% would opt for HD. This would then level out at 50/50 since, given the membrane problems, patients had to move onto the HD treatment. If sufferers were late referrals, and therefore "acute chronic"—for whatever reason, depending on area, clinic and doctor—almost all would have to go onto HD immediately. Between zero and 55% of these "acute chronic" patients would survive and, at a 20% survival rate, each cost £342,595 at which point those who survived would go onto a systematic regime incurring the planned chronic cost of dialysis. The higher the survival rate the lower the cost per patient (see Exhibit 2 for a breakdown of the Scandinavian research results).

• **Automated Peritoneal Dialysis (APD):** This procedure also used the peritoneum as the internal filter but the fluid exchanges were fully automated by the use of a compact machine about the size of a PC printer. This meant that the treatment, which required eight to nine hours to fully dialyze the fluid, could be carried out at night while the patient was asleep. If the patient was very heavy, it might also require a daytime exchange. Because it was not used continuously, the peritoneum membrane under APD was less affected by the procedure so using the machine prolonged a patient's use of peritoneal dialysis. Similarly, because the patient was lying down while the exchange was taking place, the membrane was less affected by the treatment.

The APD method was not applied over a 24 hour time period, so for each liter of solution used, less toxins were drawn away but since more liters were used more toxins overall were eliminated overnight. The APD procedure used up to 50% more solution however and so was considered less efficient than traditional PD. One common use of APD was on small children, where efficiency was greater because they tended to sleep uninterruptedly for ten hours or so, enabling the osmosis process to proceed smoothly. One patient who switched to APD was happy that it gave her "total freedom to do whatever I want during the day. It used to be whenever I went for a walk in the park or shopping or whatever, I'd always to have to think when I had to stop for my treatment; I'd always be checking my watch and always nervous that I would be late and get sick. Now I don't even think about it." Another patient, who had switched to APD because the CAPD had caused an eruption in his stomach lining, said that "I had always wanted to keep my

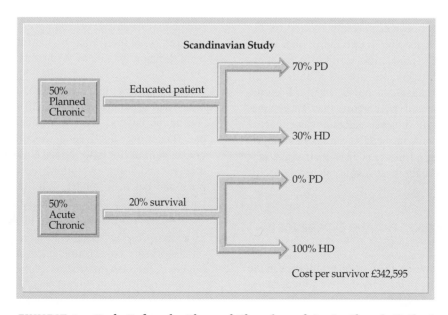

EXHIBIT 2   Early Referrals: Planned Chronic and Acute Chronic Patients

renal problems away from my family. With the APD machine in the bedroom though, my renal problems have been brought right in front of them what with this puffing, creaking, cranking machine. But even my wife has now gotten used to it. And what's good is that it is portable, so I can take it with me when I go away on business trips or on holidays."

APD was an alternate to CAPD but cost Baxter more and the machine was thus priced higher. Also the APD needed larger and more expensive bags which Baxter believed should be offset by lifestyle benefits. Once a patient's abdominal membranes had become weakened by use of CAPD, APD became a viable clinical alternative because there was less damage to the abdominal membrane. Ultimately, the patient had to go on HD which involved hospitalization. Baxter had developed the first system for APD in 1989, and it had since become the fastest growing dialysis modality in the world, growing at a rate of 50% a year in Europe. More than 14% of peritoneal dialysis patients in the UK were treated with APD, currently with about 20% of Baxter's UK patients on it.

- **Kidney Transplants:** In addition to the HD and PD dialysis treatments, the most radical treatment, and also the most curative, was a kidney transplant. The transplant offered total freedom from dialysis. On the downside, because of the massive doses of steroids needed before and immediately after the transplant, patients frequently complained of excessive facial hair growth and excessive weight gain due to an increased appetite.

This option was however severely limited by the need to find a close match between the tissues of the organ donor and the patient who required the kidney. Even with a match, there was always a high risk of graft rejection and transplants never lasted a lifetime, although patients could have more than one transplant. The quantity of kidneys available was expected to continue to diminish in the UK as a result of legislation requiring that all motorcyclists wear crash helmets, together with more stringent punishment for drunk drivers.

THE CHANGING MARKET FOR AND ECONOMICS OF HEALTH CARE

Similar to other countries, the cost of health care in the UK had been steadily rising over the past few decades, while government budgets for health services had remained fairly flat. In particular, the increase had come from a dramatic rise in emergency services, where a week in acute care could cost between £18,000 and £20,000.

The management and overseeing of the UK health scheme had been the responsibility of several authorities. Their mandate was to determine how to best allocate resources under a flat budget to meet the health and treatment needs of the UK population.

These authorities or the "economic buyer" community were comprised of the following:

- **Health commissioners** for specific regions. The commissioner purchased the healthcare needs of the population on behalf of the UK health authority and was advised by public health physicians who assessed the medical requirements of the population and informed the commission as to how many people required certain kinds of health services. Generally commissions served populations of between 5 and 15 million, and so had more than one hospital under their jurisdiction. It seemed that up to about 1996 these commissions were the decision makers and thus the "economic buyers" of the treatments and health services to be offered in their regions, and the concomitant allocation of resources.

- **Trustees:** looked after the needs of the health trust in the different regions. These needs could include several services, including managing hospitals and their ambulance facilities for example. Some trusts managed just one or two very large hospitals, as was the case in London. By the 90s, many of these trusts had highly professional top management, many recruited from large multinational companies with highly competitive salaries. Beginning in 1996, the CEOs, together with their finance managers, became the main decision makers of the healthcare services purchased. Given the large deficits which most UK hospitals—including the Queen Elisabeth II in Birmingham—had accumulated, the chief mandate for these "economic buyers" was "to balance the books." As one Baxter Renal Division executive put it, "their golden rule in life is to reduce everything to a commodity, and bring everything down to the lowest price and put it on tender. With this logic, the less people that have to be treated the better, whereas what we want to achieve is the opposite."

- In addition to the "economic buyers" who actually purchased services, an influencer on and part of the buying decision came from the "clinical buyer" who, in the case of chronic renal insufficiency treatment, included hospitals' renal consultants and/or senior sisters in hospitals' nephrology departments. Unlike the "economic buyers," they were more concerned with their day to day contact with the customers and getting the "best" therapy for sick patients.

Baxter had long considered these "clinical buyers" to be its end users, and its salespeople had concentrated their efforts primarily on them in the past. By 1996, however, it was clear to Baxter that the decision makers had moved rapidly from these "users" to economic purchasers, i.e., the commissioners, public health physicians, and the CEOs of the trusts. And the loss of the QEII hospital account to the competition demonstrated for the first time the gaping difference between these purchasers and end user needs and priorities. Despite the apparent suddenness of the change in decision making power, Baxter's marketing people had anticipated that the switch would happen. Nonetheless, they acknowledged in retrospect, so focused had they been on selling products and achieving budgets that they had been too slow to react—nor had they really known how to react. Although many people in the division had ideas, these had been dispersed all over the place and had not really been pulled together in one cohesive strategy. A marketing executive for Baxter UK put it this way:

> We had always had a high market share and we were very comfortable in the market. We felt that we could dictate to the market instead of respond to it because we had been doing that for a long time. It's not that we were complacent, we offered value and customers did perceive the value we offered. It's just that we had missed the change. We should've anticipated the flip to the economic buyer and the shift in the economic argument—been more aware of what was going to happen and when, and been more prepared, but we weren't.

BAXTER RENAL DIVISION

Baxter Renal Division had long been at the forefront of developing and marketing products for renal patients. In 1956 the division created the first commercially available disposable dialyzer for hemodialysis treatment. The unit's company, Travenol, in fact became well known for the HD treatment. By the mid-1970s, when HD had become commoditized, Baxter Renal began researching peritoneal dialysis, which it first marketed in 1979 and with which it soon become synonymous, having discontinued making and commercializing products for the HD market. In 1989 it launched APD.

The fluid bag (i.e., consumable) was the main source of revenue and profits for Baxter Renal, and each patient undergoing CAPD treatment required four to five bags a day—the glucose solutions in the bags—which was the critical element to perform the dialysis—could be modified according to different patient needs and requirements. According to numerous independent clinical studies, infection rates with Baxter bags and solutions were significantly lower on a monthly basis than competitors' systems because of better connectology and procedures. This lower infection rate meant that the peritoneum for Baxter patients using one of the two Baxter PD systems lasted longer than for patients using competitive Fresenius or Gambro PD products.

In addition to the fluid bags, Baxter Renal had a full product portfolio for Peritoneal Dialysis therapy through the patients renal experience (see Exhibit 3). It also had the facilities to provide a complete range of systems, solutions and volumes necessary to tailor individual prescriptions to patients—each patient needing that solution inside the bag that was relevant for them and would change over time.

EXHIBIT 3 Baxter Peritoneal Dialysis (PD) Therapy Range

- **CAPD and Solo Spectrum:** a fully integrated system to minimize risk of contamination (and thus peritonitis) during the fluid exchange process. The system was based on a small connector placed between the abdominal tube and the fluid bags. It operated by inactivating organisms if touch contamination had occurred.
- **Quantum PD Night Exchange System:** had been developed to assist those patients requiring a fifth CAPD exchange. This was achieved by automatically draining solution from the patient, then filling with the prescribed amount of new solution while the patient was asleep.
- **APD and Home Choice:** the Home Choice technology was promoted as a revolutionary system in APD treatment since it was smaller, easier to use and more portable than the standard APD.
- **Solution Development and Nutrineal:** Nutrineal was designed to improve the nutritional status of PD patients by providing the patient with a wide range of amino acids, including those that were lacking as a direct result of renal failure, while at the same time providing the necessary dialysis.
- **PD Adequest:** PD Adequest was a PC-based prescription model designed to help hospital renal units develop PD prescriptions and identify the optimal therapy and regimen for every individual patient. It was the only program clinically validated against actual patient results. It was provided by Baxter to support Baxter PD programs and was being used in over 50 hospitals in the UK.

New Extraneal Innovation

A recent introduction in the Baxter product portfolio was the extraneal solution. Since the peritoneum is a membrane, it acts as a sieve and over time the "holes" in that sieve get larger and larger, thus accelerating the deterioration of the membrane. Because the PD solution had glucose molecules in it, these molecules were able to pass right through into the body, with especially serious consequences for patients with diabetes. The extraneal solution mitigated that problem by having molecules which were much larger than in the traditional solutions, and which were thus able to draw the toxins into the bag. The end effect was that the peritoneum membrane could function more efficiently for a much longer period of time. This meant that, in theory, patients could survive happily and longer. On the other hand the solution cost more for Baxter to produce than the old one.

Educational Services

Baxter Renal Division also produced a series of educational services for patients and healthcare professionals. For patients, a series of "self-help" products were designed. These included books, leaflets, interactive computer programs and audio-visual materials to help them through their treatments. For prescribers, the company established the "Best Demonstrated Practice" program, designed to keep them up to date on new advances. They had also teamed up with the Academic Medical Centre of the University of Amsterdam to form the Peritoneal Dialysis University which provided intensive training in all aspects of peritoneal dialysis. By 1997, more than 100 doctors and nurses from 14 countries had graduated.

The responsibility for organizing many of these programs was given to a team of Clinical Coordinators who acted as consultants and educators to healthcare workers at all levels.

Sales and Distribution

When Leyland had arrived, the Renal Division's sales force was organized according to four territories across the UK (see Exhibit 4). Their relationship was primarily with the clinical customer (i.e., the nurses and doctors) and they excelled at selling products through this clinical system. Contracts were typically for three years.

Unicare, a separate profit center consisting of 120 people reporting to the Renal Division, handled all home deliveries and logistics warehousing and transport. Four small vans (carrying about 12 ton each) would go up and down the motorways distributing the necessary bags and solution mixtures to patients' homes. Typically these trucks would load the material from the warehouse in Harlow and from there take them to required local platforms. Depending on distances and number of homes to visit, drivers could sometimes spend two nights a week away from home and up to four days in transit. For emergency orders Baxter used courier companies which in their experience had proved expensive and not always 100% reliable.

A CHANGING COMPETITIVE PICTURE

The combination of more competitors and a shift in decision making from the clinical to the "economic buyers" posed, Leyland knew, a profound threat to Baxter Renal Division's predominance in the market. More importantly, market share could no longer be assumed to remain stable as it had for so many years, and the unit's profitability would inevitably be affected.

Moreover, one of the major hurdles Leyland and his team faced in the new competitive environment of the UK health system was customer costing—now the key concern for economic purchasers. Although every hospital had their own system, all "economic buyers" looked at marginal costing and made decisions based on the cost of the consumable items i.e., bags with solution (fluid bags) to them. And these Baxter bags were more expensive which, Leyland believed, is why they lost the Queen Elisabeth II account as well as the four accounts in the Black County Consortium.

Peter Leyland and his top team had to make a choice:

- They could either cut prices and margins in order to be competitive in their fluid bags, which meant Leyland's business unit's profitability—upon which he was judged—would suffer. This would have to be to the tune of a 20% discount equivalent to about 4% per fluid bag (a fluid bag includes all consumables) across the board—if the erosion to market share was to be halted. If so, how would the shortfall be made up?
- Or they could keep prices as they were and find a way to persuade the market to accept this.
- Or alternatively they needed to find some other way to approach the problem.

Despite his newness to the job Leyland intuitively knew that they could never win if they continued to

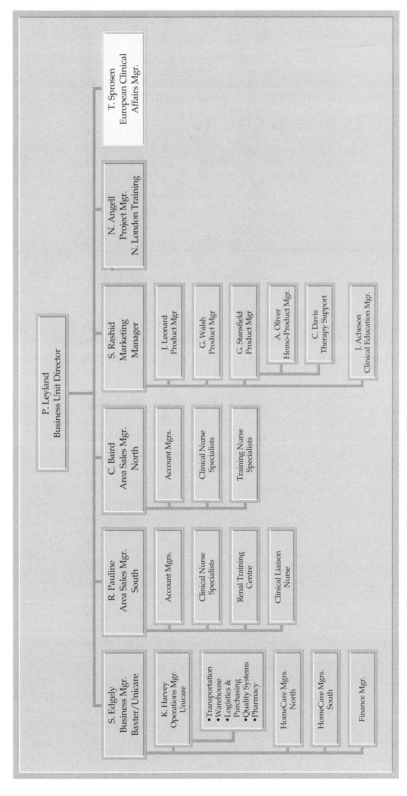

EXHIBIT 4   Organization Chart: UK Renal Division (simplified)

play the same old game as they had in the past, or if they tried to beat the competition at that same old game. He was convinced that what the division, with a turnover of US$ 100 million, needed to do was take the lead to change the game. That was the message he intended to take to Baxter's European top management the following month.

CASE 9-2 ALIAS RESEARCH, INC.*

"*I* can't believe they did it again!" exclaimed Isaac Babbs, district sales manager for the south-western United States for Alias Research, Inc. For the fourth time in 1990 he had lost a sale to Wavefront, his major competitor in the animation software market. He had worked on this sale for a month, and he felt confident that the prospective customer was ready to buy Alias's $100,000 software. But Wavefront had stepped in at the last moment, cut their price from $55,000 to $25,000, and obtained the sale. Wavefront, a California-based company, seemed determined to dominate the region, while Alias, based in Toronto, was at least equally determined to make further inroads into the California market. "How does Toronto expect me to compete if they won't give me some flexibility on pricing?" Babbs lamented as he thought about Alias's rigidly enforced policy of not permitting any price discounting on its products. With a sigh of resignation, he reached for the phone to call Toronto and let them know that another sale was lost to a price-cutting competitor.

THE HIGH-END GRAPHICS MARKET

Alias Research, Inc., a software company located in Toronto, was a recognized market leader in high-end, three-dimensional (3D) computer graphics. Its product, ALIAS, was used in film animation, industrial design, architecture, education, medical and scientific visualization, packaging and product design, flight or space simulation, and a number of other applications. Seventy percent of the world's automobile manufacturers used ALIAS in their design processes. Some of its customers in other industries included Goodyear, Timex, Kraft, Motorola, Northern Telecom, Johnson & Johnson, and Industrial Light and Magic. Alias had sales offices in Boston, Princeton, Los Angeles, Chicago,

and Detroit, as well as in France and Germany. The corporate officers for Alias are listed in Exhibit 1.

The total size of the market served by Alias was estimated at $81 million (U.S.) in 1990, of which Alias held a 15% share. Industry experts had forecast that the market would increase to $300 million by 1992. Virtually all of the growth was in the field of industrial design, which currently accounted for 40% of the market. The remaining 60% was in the animation field, which was growing at a rate of only 1% each year. The animation market was saturated with a variety of competing products.

Alias's three main competitors were Wavefront Technologies, Thompson Digital Image (TDI), and Evans and Sutherland Computer Corporation (E&S). Originally a private custom software builder, Wavefront entered the video animation market in 1985 at approximately the same time as Alias. It had recently modified its package to provide some industrial design capability. However, Wavefront's product did not easily translate into manufacturable designs, and it required extensive training before any of its advanced tools could be properly used. Wavefront's major advantage was that its product could be run on many different types of computers, as opposed to Alias's, which could only be run on Silicon Graphics hardware or IBM workstations.

Based in Paris, France, Thompson Digital Image (TDI) was Alias' principal competitor in the European market. TDI was a subsidiary of the Thompson Group, though 56% of TDI was owned by the French government. TDI's primary market, accounting for 80% of sales, was the video animation market. It was estimated that TDI had approximately 20 clients in the video post-production industry. TDI was also pursuing industrial design customers and had been successful with some leading French firms including Renault, the

---

* This case was prepared by Douglas Snetsinger and Susan Spencer of the University of Toronto. Copyright © 1990 by Douglas Snetsinger. Reproduced by permission.

EXHIBIT 1   Alias Research, Inc.—Executive Officers and Directors

Name	Age*	Position
Stephen R. B. Bingham	40	President, Chief Executive Officer and Chairman of the Board of Directors
Susan I. McKenna	31	Executive Vice-President and Director
William J. McClintock	38	Vice-President Finance, Secretary, Treasurer, and Chief Financial Officer
Arthur W. Bell	34	Vice-President Marketing
Martin I. Tuori	38	Vice-President Research and Development
Gregory S. Hill	35	Vice-President Business Development
David N. Macrae	34	Vice-President Sales
Brian J. Conway	31	Director
William S. Kaiser	34	Director
Barry L. Stephens	50	Director

* Ages are as of July 1990.

automobile manufacturer. TDI was currently overhauling its design software based on a similar technology to the Alias product.

Evans and Sutherland (E&S) was a large, multidivisional computer hardware and software company with total sales, of $129 million (U.S.). Based in Salt Lake City, they were engaged in the development of interactive super-computers for large-scale scientific and technical computations, modeling, and simulations. The Graphics Products Group designed and built high-performance three-dimensional graphics hardware and specialized software. E&S's closest product to ALIAS was the Conceptual Design and Rendering System, a turnkey, computer-aided design system that was introduced in 1988. The system was developed in partnership with Ford and Chrysler. It was based on Alias-type technology and was priced at $200,000 (U.S.) to $250,000 (U.S.) and ran only on proprietary hardware manufactured by E&S.

ALIAS HISTORY

The Beginning

Alias Research, Inc., was founded in 1983 by Stephen Bingham, Nigel McGrath, Susan McKenna, and David Springer. With few resources, they borrowed $500,000 of computer graphic equipment from McGrath's company and rented an office in an old elevator shaft for $150 per month. Though starting small in scope, the owners of this fledgling company had a big dream: to create an easy-to-use software package that would produce realistic 3D video animation for the advertising industry post-production houses.

Many companies in this industry had difficulty raising start-up funds, and Alias was no exception. The problem was that it required substantial time and effort to develop software to the point where it was "debugged" and ready to be sold to customers. As much as 150 person-years of research and development effort might go into making the first working piece of software. Thus, investors were reluctant to provide funds on promises, as opposed to finished products.

However, Alias was able to obtain a $61,000 grant from the National Research Council, which, when combined with the limited funds of the founders, allowed work to begin. Other financial support was gained from the federal government through Scientific Research Tax Credits (SRTCs). A SRTC was actually a contract that allowed an investor to hire Alias to do a specified amount of research, in return for which the investor would get a tax credit for his or her own company. This sort of arrangement yielded two benefits for Alias. It provided much needed start-up funding and it allowed the four founders to maintain control of the company. It also allowed Alias to earn money by doing the research that was required for its own project.

Development of the software continued until mid-1985. One of the early decisions made was building the software based on a relatively new form of modeling technique which used cardinal splines rather than traditional polygonal lines.[1] Silicon Graphics, a small hardware firm based in California, produced a workstation that was specifically designed to work with spline technology. Silicon Graphics soon became a

---

[1] A cardinal spline is based on the first derivative of the modeling equation, while polygonal lines are based on the actual equation. The results that were achieved from cardinal splines, in terms of computer graphics, were a much smoother, more realistic line or surface than had been possible from a polygonal line.

staunch supporter of Alias as they saw the opportunity for enhanced applications for their workstation.

The product, ALIAS, was unveiled at the Special Interest Group on Graphics (SIGGRAPH) show in July 1985. The annual SIGGRAPH show was attended by many people who were involved in design (for example, designing products, labels, packages) and by many people who could help the designers (for example, software companies like Alias). For a company like Alias, the SIGGRAPH show provided an important opportunity to introduce and market new products. Many of the Alias group would attend the show and work long hours to generate leads for the ALIAS system. In fact, sales of ALIAS could often be traced to an initial meeting at the SIGGRAPH show.

The first sale, to a post-production house, came on July 15th. Then the unexpected occurred; General Motors Inc. (GM) expressed an interest in buying a system. GM was looking for a system that was compatible with their spline-based computer-aided-design (CAD) systems, and ALIAS was the only spline-based system available. Initially, the Alias group were reluctant to enter this new market; industrial design applications had not been part of the corporate objective and seemed too distant from their animation market. Further, GM wanted the package to run on basis-splines (b-splines),[2] which would require yet another significant investment by Alias in research and development (R&D). However, when GM kept dropping broad hints about 20 systems, potentially representing millions of dollars of revenue, Alias decided to go ahead and, in November 1985, the deal with GM was signed.

Once again, money was required to finance the research. However, Alias now had a major customer, more or less in hand, which reduced the risk of the venture in the eyes of potential investors. Early in 1986, Crownx, a venture capital company associated with Crown Life, invested $1.2 million for a 20% stake in Alias.

By early 1986, the company had sold ALIAS to a number of firms. Most of the sales were to small production houses in the video animation market, but sales were also made to Kraft, Motorola, and NASA. By the middle of 1986, there were 70 people working for the company, of whom 40 were programmers, morale was high and the employees were beginning to see the fruits of their labors in print and on video. The work environment was flexible and relaxed—purposely

designed to facilitate and stimulate creativity. Improvements and upgrades to the original package were constantly being developed, and a new release of the software (with a b-spline base) was planned for mid-1986. Staff increased to 80 in April 1987, with the opening of three sales offices in the United States. In the same year, almost $3 million in new venture capital was received from two American companies. Everything was moving quickly and the people at Alias were looking forward to a promising future.

The Downturn

The development of ALIAS/2 (using b-splines) took much longer than had been expected and the product was not released until late in 1986. Initial sales were strong, but a problem was discovered with the new system. The final rendered picture was not matched to the original design on a consistent or reliable basis. While Alias could fix the bug on the installed systems on a patchwork basis, the sales force would find it next to impossible to sell new installations of ALIAS/2 until the problem was solved. The company immediately pulled members of the marketing and R&D staff together with a product management group to fix the software.

The first half of 1987 saw the beginnings of what was to become a major downturn in the animation industry as a whole. Premium, high-end systems, like those of Alias, were particularly affected by the slump. At the same time, personnel changes and budget cuts at GM had reduced the number of systems purchased from the expected number of 20 to only 4. Some of the new investors in Alias were dissatisfied with the company's performance and were demanding cuts in investment, particularly on R&D spending and personnel. Bingham and the other original owners still retained control and resisted the pressure. However, by late summer 1987, Alias was forced to lay off 12 employees from marketing and administration.

The Recovery

Following the layoffs, quarterly company meetings were instituted in which the status of the company as a whole, plans for the future, and the past quarter's performance were reviewed with all employees. Day-long meetings of the management team (vice-president level and above) were held monthly. Efforts at clearing the lines of communication between departments were made to build a more cohesive team atmosphere than had existed previously. Although the culture of the company remained informal, the methods of control and the way of doing business became more formal-

---

[2] B-splines are based on the second derivative of the modeling equation and were generally regarded as producing the smoothest lines and surfaces available in computer graphics.

ized, with more attention being paid to earnings and profit. Although Alias experienced an operating loss in fiscal 1989, it was considerably less than in fiscal 1988 (the corporate year end is January 31).

In the summer of 1989, for the first time in two years, the company began to hire people for new positions. A new vice-president of finance, Bill McClintock, took over the financial aspects of the company and tightened the purse strings on all expenditures. Staff were added to R&D, customer support, and marketing. For over two years, marketing of ALIAS had been handled primarily by the vice-president of marketing and communications, Arthur Bell. People were now hired to fill the positions of product manager, CAD marketing manager, distributor marketing manager, and communications manager. These people came from a variety of different backgrounds, not necessarily in computer-related industries. Bell, who was very enthusiastic about his new recruits, commented:

So often, people who market software come directly out of R&D, or they are engineers. They are way too "techi" for most of our customers, who are designers. I wanted people who understood marketing, but who did not necessarily know computers. Peter Goldie [formerly senior brand manager for Crisco at Procter & Gamble] understands shelf space and everything that leads up to getting that shelf space. No one knows it better. He knows how to market, no matter what, and he can do that for us.

Perhaps most important of all were the changes made to the software itself. Because of all the "bugs" in ALIAS/2, R&D immediately went to work on a "bug-fix" version, known as ALIAS/2.1. Other versions followed, which in some cases included only bug-fix material and in other cases included new applications or improved processes. By the summer of 1989, Version 2.4.2 was being used by most Alias customers. At that time, Alias had $3 million in the bank. The income statements for 1988 to 1990 are provided in Exhibit 2.

Alias Culture

The culture at Alias was by design relaxed and informal. Everyone, from the programmer in the R&D department to the president, appeared in jeans most of the time. Suits were worn only when people were expected from outside the company. In the words of Bill McClintock: "There are very few `ties' around here, never mind `suits,' and that is the way it should be." Friday was known as "shorts day," and throughout the summer, anyone not wearing shorts on a Friday had better have been expecting company.

Employees referred to themselves as "Alians," and the term was expressed with affection and pride. A friendly rivalry existed between the R&D and administrative sides of the company, each housed in a separate section of the office. Employee birthdays were celebrated by all, with cake, drinks, and the occasional

EXHIBIT 2   Alias Research, Inc.–Consolidated Statement of Operations ($000 U.S.)

	1988	1989	1990	First Three Months of Fiscal 1991
Revenue:				
Products	5,709	6,466	10,962	3,106
Maintenance and services	451	744	1,044	271
Total revenue	6,160	7,240	12,006	3,377
Costs and expenses:				
Direct cost of products*	2,861	2,131	1,810	336
Direct cost of maintenance and services	448	509	615	198
General and administration	842	910	1,956	533
Sales and marketing	1,716	2,172	3,527	1,100
Research and development	1,150	954	973	525
Depreciation and amortization	480	500	560	145
Total costs and expenses	7,497	7,176	9,441	2,837
Operating income (loss)	(1,337)	64	2,565	540
Interest income (expense)	(39)	(20)	134	73
Other income (expense)	13	(9)	163	13
Income (loss) before income taxes	(1,363)	35	2,862	626
Provision for (recovery) income taxes	(43)	0	1,229	258
Net income (loss)	(1,320)	35	1,633	368

* Hardware purchased for resale.

Elvis impersonator supplied by the company. Team spirit abounded, and everyone regarded it as a great place to work. This was reflected in an article that appeared in the August 1990 *Report on Business Magazine* which described the company, its culture, and the software industry (Exhibit 3).

ALIAS MARKETING

In many ways, marketing software is unlike marketing any other product. For example, security is a serious problem. Once the product has been sold, it is always possible that the product will be copied or even copied and resold. Once the product has been purchased, cus-

EXHIBIT 3   Excerpts of an Article in *Report on Business Magazine*, August 1990

- Unlike cars or clothes or bread, no raw material is required to manufacture software. It is purely a creation of the mind, which is why it [Alias] attracts people that include a former comedian, a French horn player, and a former cabinetmaker.

- When the Honda Accord became the first car made by a foreign manufacturer to head the U.S. best-seller list last year, it was more than just another triumph for Japanese industry. Only a few insiders knew that it was also a triumph for Alias. All of Honda's cars, like those of BMW and Volvo, are designed on three-dimensional graphics software created at Alias.

- Canada produces almost no original industrial design—there is no such thing as a Canadian-designed car—but the eccentrics at Alias have created a wonderful tool for industrial designers. Until their software was developed in 1985, these designers did their work the old-fashioned way—with pencil and paper and clay models. Now the designers for such Alias customers as Timex, Motorola, Mitsubishi, British Telecom, and Goodyear can create moving, three-dimensional designs on their computer screens. The models are so realistic that a designer can see how light will reflect off a watch face or a car body long before the actual objects exist. Using Alias software can shave precious months, even years, off the time it takes to create a product.

- Good software is a living thing, constantly growing and adapting to meet its users' needs. That means long nights in front of computer screens. The Alias office contains two eating areas because software developers don't have time to go out for lunch or dinner. On a typical evening, the company will order in large quantities of chicken or pizza. Then the denizens of the factory might amuse themselves for a while playing the latest computer games or reading. A favorite writer at Alias is Vancouverite William Gibson, who writes science fiction novels about "cyberpunks" with computer chips embedded in their brains.

- In the software industry, tiny companies can grow into billion-dollar giants like Lotus and Microsoft almost overnight. That's exactly the sort of future the president, Stephen Bingham, has in mind for Alias, and he is off to an impressive start. Sales were just $12 million last year, but more than a third of those sales were to the Japanese—not known to deal with bantam-weights unless they have very good reasons to do so. The company even managed to forge a strategic alliance with mighty IBM. But for all its successes, there is no guarantee that Alias will make it. In fact, the odds are stacked against it. Software companies in Canada are starved for capital. Without money they can't grow, and in this business if you don't grow fast, you're dead.

- The sale is only part of the story. After you sell someone a $150,000 hardware and software package, you don't just wander off in search of the next customer. Software must be continually enhanced, and most of the enhancements are suggested by the users. Alias personnel meets regularly with their biggest customers. Investing in software is a commitment, and customers are anxious to know where the company is going long term. Several have visited Alias's offices. "The Japanese were impressed that we can turn out so much new technology so quickly," Mr. Bingham says. "A visitor from Honda said we had 20 people doing the work of 200."

- Alias got early support from Montreal "angel" Jim Muir, a friend of one of the partners, and Crownx Inc. of Toronto. Two Boston-based venture capitalists who specialize in high-tech also chipped in. But the company's growth has been largely financed through its own sales. Banks have so far refused to offer more than a small line of credit, saying they do not wish to finance foreign receivables which are the only kind Alias has. Banks also like to have collateral in case a loan goes sour—and by collateral they mean some real estate or a yard full of steel ingots. They don't mean a numeric code on a computer disc—software—which is where the wealth of a company like Alias resides.

- It's not hard to understand why lenders shy away from technology companies. Just look at the record of those high-tech darlings of the '70s—companies like Mitel and Lumonics. More recently, Canada's biggest software firm, Cognos, lost $17 million in fiscal 1990 after several years of good earnings. From an investor's viewpoint, the problem is the rapid rate of change. One banker notes: "In a traditional borrowing relationship, you might analyze the company's record over the last five years. With high-tech companies, I look at the last five quarters. They go through the same cycles as a traditional firm but they do it at an accelerated pace. The products they were selling two years ago are now all obsolete and they've got new products."

Source: Daniel Stoffman, "Big Dreams, No Backers," *Report on Business Magazine,* August 1990, pp. 47–51.

tomers have to be kept up-to-date on new developments. When new versions and developments occur,
the decision needs to be made whether current customers should be given free upgrades or not. Selling
expenses are very high in the industry. Customers are
geographically dispersed, and sales are often achieved
over an extended period and with the support of a
number of individuals. As was the case with the Isaac
Babbs sale that fell through or the GM installations
that were slow in coming, significant resources were
invested in a potential sale which might evaporate at
the most inopportune time.

Having a professional marketing and sales team
was critical. As well, knowing how much to spend on
marketing and in what areas was a perplexing task.
Another difficult task was deciding how much R&D
should be spent and on what projects. The company
needed to determine how much customer service and
support to provide and what price, if any, to charge for
that support and service. The potentially crippling
problem of bugs needed to be considered and what
actions were to be taken if, and when, they occurred.
How should the product be priced in the first place?
Should all the R&D, marketing, and overhead be factored into the price? How flexible should the company
be with its pricing strategy?

The ALIAS Product

When a data tape containing the ALIAS product left
Toronto, it contained a "hole" or a missing line of code
which must be filled in before the software would
operate. This line of code, called an *encryption string*,
was twelve digits long and could contain numbers,
punctuation marks, and upper- or lowercase letters.
The string was unique to one tape of software and to
the one piece of hardware upon which it would run. In
other words, the same data tape could not be used to
start up several different machines.

When customers purchased the software, they purchased customer support for that software. Phone support was provided 12 hours a day, as well as free
upgrades and bug fixes for a period of one year. The
support contract had to be renewed each year by the
customer if continuing support was to be received. No
services were provided until the contract was renewed
and payment was received.

A major advantage with the ALIAS system over
other software was that ALIAS was easy to learn and
easy to use. See Exhibit 4 for a comparison of Alias and
Wavefront products. Those who were not computer literate, and even those who regarded computers with suspicion, were able to make use of most of the system's
tools after only a few days of training. Like Apple products, ALIAS was menu-driven, and most "drawing" was
done with the aid of a mouse. Once the design, or "modeling" process was finished, the information could be
sent to a variety of media. The information could be fed
to a plotter, which gives a flat wireframe picture of the
object, or it could be directly linked to a CAD machine,
which was then used to construct the object from the
computerized data. Other options included creating a
surface and background for the object and outputting the
picture or pictures to slides or videotapes, or even to a
stereolithography vat[3] where a plastic prototype is cre-

---

[3] A stereolithography vat is a vat filled with molten plastic and
equipped with a pinpoint laser. The path that the laser takes is determined by the instructions in ALIAS. The result is a perfectly propor-
tioned, solid, three-dimensional plastic model of the original computerized design.

EXHIBIT 4   A Comparison of Wavefront and Alias

Dimension	Wavefront	Alias

Ease of use	Not easy
	Requires substantial training to
	  use advanced functions
		Pioneer in the development and improvement
		  of making the product easy to use

Price	Negotiable Approximately U.S. $55,000 Discounts as much as 50% to make a sale	Fixed Base price is approximately U.S. $65,000 Discounts to educators and co-developers only
Primary market	Animation Some industrial features recently added	Industrial design but also has found wide application in animation
Basic technology	Polygonal lines	Basis splines
Hardware	Runs on many different kinds of hardware	Dedicated to Silicon Graphics and IBM workstations (industry standards)

Source: Company records.

ated. In any case, ALIAS shortened the time between the conception of an idea and its appearance on the market, be that idea a car, a building, a piece of jewelry, or a special effect for a movie.

Customers, in general, had responded favorably to the flexibility and ease of use of ALIAS and its convenient access to a wide range of powerful options. Designers had liked the way ALIAS reduced the time between the conception of their ideas and having prototypes built, as well as having the capability of examining more iterations, improvements, and changes at the early stage of product development. Engineers had found that ALIAS provided a precise reading and measurement of designers' concepts and took advantage of its ability to directly link into CAD/CAM systems.

The fundamental source of ALIAS's strength had been as a communication tool. It had given designers and engineers a common language to speak and, in the process, sped up the design-to-market cycle. The enthusiastic response of designers and engineers had led to the steady shift of Alias' revenue from animation into industrial design markets (Exhibit 5). While this trend was expected to continue, there are no plans to abandon the animation market.

MARKETING AND SALES

Alias promoted its products through participation in trade shows like SIGGRAPH, an annual world demonstration tour, articles and advertisements in industry publications, live demonstrations, television advertising, and sponsorship of cultural events. These activities were augmented by print and videotape sales support materials. A direct sales force was employed in North America and Europe. This group, which also managed Alias' distributor and dealer network, consisted of 19 people. There were sales offices in five cities in the United States, as well as in France and Germany. Alias's network of 16 dealers and distributors represented the product in 11 countries. This network gener-

ally specialized in design and engineering hardware and software complementary to the ALIAS product.

PRICING THE PRODUCT

As is shown in the consolidated income statement for 1990 (Exhibit 2), the direct costs of sales amounted to only 20% of revenue. Almost all of the direct costs were for hardware purchased for resale, for maintenance, and for other services. The direct cost of the software was negligible. Using a cost-based approach to pricing would give Alias substantial room to maneuver on price; however, that was not their approach.

The approach used was to price the software at parity to the hardware upon which it was mounted. For example, a Silicon Graphics Personal IRIS Workstation cost the customer approximately $100,000 (U.S.). The ALIAS tape installed on that workstation would cost another $100,000 (U.S.). This method of pricing put ALIAS at or near the top of what the market would bear. A stripped-down version of ALIAS could sell for as little as $65,000 (U.S.), while the version with every option could run as high as $150,000 (U.S.). Once a system was installed, further options could be added at a cost of $10,000 (U.S.) to $30,000 (U.S.) per option. Customer support was provided on a two-tier pricing schedule. The first tier, which included software release updates and installation only, was provided for an annual fee equal to 10% of the then current software price. A second tier, in addition to incorporating the services of the first tier, provided hotline support and could be purchased for an annual fee of 15% of the then current software price. Training and consultant services were provided on a per day or per task rate (usually about U.S. $500 per person per day).

BACK TO THE FIELD

As Isaac Babbs drove down Highway 1 on the California coast to meet a new prospect at Boeing, his

EXHIBIT 5   Alias Research, Inc.—Sales History by Line of Business ($000 U.S.)

	1987	1988	1989	1990
Industrial design market				
Sales	790	3,374	5,320	10,186
Percent of revenue	17%	55%	73%	85%
Animation market				
Sales	3,970	2,786	1,920	1,820
Percent of revenue	83%	45%	27%	15%
Total sales	4,760	6,160	7,240	12,006

thoughts wandered back to his telephone call with Arthur Bell. Arthur had expressed his disappointment over the lost sale but had refused to make any changes in the pricing policy.

Isaac Babbs had a lot of confidence in the company. Alias's management had made some tough calls over the history of the company and been proven right. However, Toronto was a long way from California, and he felt he knew his customers better than anyone did. He disliked losing any sale, and he was still smarting from this last one. He understood why Alias had not engaged in price-cutting in the past, but he was unsure if he could continue to compete against aggressive price-cutters like Wavefront. Maybe it was time for a change. How many times had he heard about what a flexible company Alias was, he thought. Perhaps the pricing policy was the correct one, but he could not help worrying over the long-term implications of this rigid policy.

Arthur Bell had been disappointed to have received the news from Babbs. Babbs was one of his best field representatives and had been very successful in cultivating the lucrative southwestern market. Arthur Bell respected Babbs's opinions and was not pleased to hear about his concern over the lost sales and the inflexible pricing policy. The morale and commitment of any member of the sales force could not be treated lightly. Bell wondered if he came across as too intransigent on the issue of pricing. Perhaps it was time to review the pricing policy and bring it forward at the next management meeting. As he began preparing the memo, Stephen Bingham, the president, walked by. Arthur told him about the California incident and his interest in putting the pricing policy on the agenda. "Sure, let's take a look at the issue," said Stephen. "I think our current pricing policy is just fine, but I am prepared to listen. However, I don't think we can look at price in isolation from the other marketing policies. It would be more useful if it was in the context of a review of the entire marketing program."

CASE 9-3 COOK, INC.*

Cook, Inc. is the world leader in cardiovascular catheters and is the largest subsidiary of the Cook Group, Inc., a holding company with 30 diversified companies. Cook recently received preliminary Food and Drug Administration (FDA) approval for a new coronary product. The device, called a *stent*, is used in the treatment of heart disease. Brian Bates, Vice President of Product Development, had the job of developing a marketing plan to introduce the new stent.

PRODUCT LINE

Cook sold a broad assortment of 4000 different medical devices. Most of its volume came from diagnostic catheters used to inject radiopaque dye into the heart so that x-ray pictures can illuminate blocked arteries. In 1978 Cook and its competitors started making and selling catheters with tiny balloons on their tips. These catheters were used to reopen vessels obstructed by fatty plaque. With this *angioplasty* procedure, the balloon is inflated inside an obstructed artery to open it. Then the balloon is deflated and the catheter removed. There are two areas of medicine that use this type of device—radiology and cardiology. Because of its marketing strength in radiology, Cook opted to concentrate its development and marketing efforts in radiology. Both market segments grew rapidly, but although Cook gained a reasonable market presence for balloon catheters in radiology, it lacked exposure in cardiology. Brian estimated that three firms had most of the cardiac balloon angioplasty market (Exhibit 1).

STENT DEVELOPMENT

Although angioplasty is popular, it often does not provide a permanent cure for the problem of partially

---
* This case was prepared by Douglas J. Dalrymple of Indiana University.

EXHIBIT 1   Estimated Balloon Catheter Market Shares

Firm	1992 Market Share
ACS	40%
SciMed	30%
Bard Schneider	20%
Others (including Cook)	10%

Source: Estimated by Brian Bates.

blocked coronary arteries. In about 30 percent of these procedures, a second angioplasty has to be performed in less than a year to reopen the clogged arteries. Sometimes the vessel closes abruptly during these balloon procedures. When this happens, the patient must often undergo emergency open-heart bypass surgery.

The idea of placing a stent in an artery to prevent it from collapsing was first conceived by Dr. Cesare Gianturco in 1980. Dr. Gianturco was a retired radiologist associated with the Carle Clinic in Champaign, Illinois. He had been a consultant for Cook, Inc., for many years and helped Cook with the development of its diagnostic x-ray catheters. Gianturco was 74 years old at the time he came up with the idea of the coronary stent, and development work was passed on to Dr. Andreas Gruntzig, a cardiologist located at Emory University. Dr. Gruntzig, a pioneer in the development of balloon catheters, was killed in a plane crash soon after he began working on the stent. Responsibility for animal testing and clinical trials was then given to Dr. Gary Roubin, who was also at Emory University. Animal tests were completed in 1985 and clinical trials began in September 1987.

The coronary stent developed by Cook, Inc., is a small piece of coiled stainless steel wire that forms a series of U and inverted-U shapes. The stent is wrapped around a balloon catheter and inserted into a coronary vessel using a wire guide. Once the balloon and stent are in the right position, the balloon is inflated and the stent expands to widen the clogged artery. Then the balloon is deflated and removed, leaving the metal stent in place. The inner lining of the vessel begins covering the stent within a few days. By the end of 2–3 weeks endothelial cells completely cover the stent. The wires themselves become embedded within neointima produced by the proliferation of smooth muscle cells.

Developing the stainless steel stent was an expensive, time-consuming process. The metal wire had to be soft enough to be expanded into position with a tiny plastic balloon. Once the stent was expanded, it had to

be strong enough to keep the vessel open without the threat of collapsing. An example showing a preloaded and balloon-expanded Cook stent is given in Exhibit 2. A wire guide used to direct the catheter to the coronary artery is seen extending from the tip of the balloon catheter. The catheter and balloon-expanded stent are shown in their actual size. The separate expanded-wire stent pictured in Exhibit 2 is somewhat larger than actual size.

Inserting a coronary stent closely resembles balloon angioplasty in difficulty. The procedure is performed with a local anesthetic, and circulation within the vessel is usually restored quickly. The cost of a balloon angioplasty plus a stent is about one-third the cost of balloon angioplasty followed by bypass surgery. During clinical tests with over 1000 patients, 97 percent of the stents were successfully placed. Also, the immediate success rate measured by the absence of in-hospital heart attack, bypass surgery, or death was 99.3 percent. On the basis of successful clinical trials in 13 hospitals around the country, Cook gained approval from the FDA Circulatory System Device Panel in May 1992.

Phyllis McCullough, president of Cook, Inc., was very pleased to get unanimous recommended approval for the coronary stent. She said, "This is a significant lifesaving device. There definitely is a niche for this. Stents may be the hottest thing in medical devices today." Although Cook was the first company to gain FDA approval, competitive firms including Medtronics, Johnson & Johnson, and others were working on stent products.

STENT MARKETING PLANS

Once FDA approval had been obtained, Brian Bates had to prepare a marketing plan that would ensure successful commercialization of the new item. The first decision Brian made was to name the new product the "Gianturco-Roubin Coronary Flex-Stent." This name emphasized the two doctors who were instrumental in the development of the stent, as well as the stent's flexibility, which is a very important characteristic. Both doctors were well known in the field, and the inclusion of their names would help gain acceptance by cardiovascular surgeons.

An important consideration in creating a marketing plan for the coronary stent was the estimate of potential sales. Although 30,000[1] angioplasties are done each year, only a small proportion resulted in collapsed

---

[1] All figures shown in this case have been disguised.

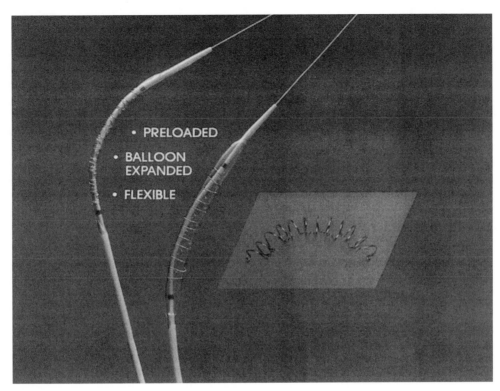

EXHIBIT 2   Gianturco-Roubin Coronary Flex-Stent

vessels where coronary stents can be used. Cook's approval for stents applied to emergency situations in which bypass surgery was under consideration. The 10,000 operations per year in which angioplasty was repeated to reopen an artery were not eligible for stent use at the present time. Brian projected that about 600–700 coronary stents would be sold during the first year the product was on the market.

Brian also knew that cardiologists would expect the stents to be available in a variety of sizes to accommodate patients with different-sized vessels. The coronary stent was currently produced in 2-, 2.5-, 3-, 3.5-, and 4-mm diameters and would be available in 4.5- and 5-mm sizes in a few months. Only one length, 20 mm, was available at the present time, but 12-, 30-, 40-, and 50-mm lengths were under development.

Cook used a sales force of 35 people to sell its diagnostic catheters to radiologists and hospitals. These salespeople were paid average salaries plus expenses of $45,000 per year. Since the new Gianturco-Roubin Flex-Stent was similar to existing products, one choice was to use the regular sales force to promote the new stent. An alternative approach that Brian was considering was to set up a separate sales force of six to eight reps to focus exclusively on car-

diovascular devices from the current line and the new coronary stent. This would ensure that the stents got the attention they needed. A separate sales force would also emphasize Cook's commitment to building volume in the cardiovascular treatment market, an area it had not had much success with in recent years.

Brian knew that once decisions had been made on the sales force and introductory activities, he would be in a better position to set a price for the coronary stent. At the present time, the most popular Cook diagnostic catheters sold for between $8 and $10 each. Balloon catheters were more difficult to make and were priced at around $80. To date, out-of-pocket development expenses for the coronary stent had amounted to $450,000. This included the costs of laboratory and clinical trials but not the salaries of executives who devoted part of their time to the new product. Estimated variable costs to the manufacturer of the balloon/stent catheter were $55 per unit.

There were 9000 cardiologists in the United States who could use the new coronary stent. To train these doctors with the Gianturco-Roubin Coronary Flex-Stent, Cook planned a series of regional symposiums. Brian estimated that between one and three seminars per month would be needed for a year, depending on the speed of the introductory process. In addition to this initial training, Cook would be expected to run in-service training classes after the first year to keep hospital personnel up-to-date on stent procedures. Each initial seminar would cost $6,000 to $8,000 or more for travel, lodging, meals, equipment, supplies, and honoraria.

Since Cook was not a big player in the market for balloon catheters and other devices used to treat coronary disease, the argument had been made that Cook should price the new coronary stent low to gain a larger market share. Most cardiologists thought of Cook as a manufacturer of diagnostic catheters, not as a supplier of devices to correct coronary problems. Aggressive pricing of the new catheter line would show the physician that Cook was a leader in the field.

On the other hand, Cook and its competitors were working on coronary stents with medicinal coatings. These coatings were designed to reduce the proliferation of smooth muscle tissue associated with balloon angioplasty. If competitive coated stents received FDA approval for use in reducing this problem, then the market for Cook's uncoated stents could disappear. Thus Cook did not know how soon competitive stents and new technology would begin to eat into anticipated sales.

Phyllis McCullough was eager to get the new line on the market, and she had told Brian that he had 10 days to complete the marketing plan for the coronary stents. Brian realized that he would need a careful financial analysis to support his decisions on pricing and promotional activities.

SELECTING DISTRIBUTION CHANNELS

> The art of getting rich consists not in industry, but in a better order, in timeliness, in being at the right spot.
>
> RALPH WALDO EMERSON

A critical task for marketers in the new millennium is the efficient movement of goods and services from the point of production to the points of consumption. Distribution costs between 25 to 35 percent of the value of most products and it is your job to get products to customers quickly and at the lowest possible expenditure. Your job is complicated by the vast array of distribution alternatives available. Some firms sell directly to customers through the use of the Internet, telephone, mail order, or calls by company salespeople. Others use marketing intermediaries such as wholesalers, distributors, and retailers to get their goods and services to buyers. Another approach is to use agents who search for customers and negotiate sales but do not take title to the goods they handle. Each approach has its advantages and disadvantages. In this chapter, we explain how distribution networks are created and adapted to changing market conditions. The key tasks are selecting the best channels for each firm and finding ways to operate them efficiently.

DISTRIBUTION ALTERNATIVES

There are hundreds of ways goods and services can be distributed to customers. No one distribution system can satisfy the needs of every firm, and many organizations use several distribution channels to reach different market segments. A paper mill, for example, may contact large users directly and service small customers through independent wholesalers.

When Should Intermediaries Be Used?

Industrial firms sell to relatively few customers and usually contact these buyers directly. Intel, for example, set up a Web site in July to take orders and by November of that year was booking $1 billion in orders a month over the Internet. This amounted to about half of the company's total revenue. It has been estimated that by the year 2007, 100 percent of business-to-business sales will be over the Internet.[1] However, consumer products need wider distribution than industrial goods and have traditionally been sold using channel intermediaries such as wholesalers and retailers.

**APPLYING
. . . to
Consumer
Durable
Goods
Marketing**

For many firms, the cost of owning a consumer channel of distribution can be prohibitive. Ford has a network of 5,300 dealers who sell its cars in the United States. To own this channel, Ford would have to spend billions of dollars. Rather than invest this huge amount, Ford initially used franchising so that the cost of setting up its distribution network was borne by the local independent dealers. More recently, Ford has been buying up dealerships in local markets and creating networks of superstores under the brand Auto Collection. By 2003 Ford expects to have expanded its ownership to 25 percent of its dealers.[2]

Another distribution problem occurs when your product is part of an assortment. Mars M&M candies are sold along with other brands of candy in supermarkets, drugstores, theaters, vending machines, and convenience stores all over the world. Instead of owning all these businesses, Mars has decided to work with established wholesalers and retailers.

Selling Through the Internet

The newest and most rapidly growing channel of distribution is the sale of goods and services using Web sites on the Internet (Figure 10-1a & b). Customers log on to the Internet using their computers and then call up Web sites for products in which they are interested. The sites function as electronic catalogs that provide pictures, information, and prices on merchandise that is available for sale. Interested customers complete a purchase by typing in a credit card number and then have the goods shipped to an address by mail or UPS delivery services. Web shopping allows customers to easily compare an unlimited breadth of offerings from a wide variety of suppliers and quickly order items they want. Web selling is attractive because it offers a fast way to reach customers without paper record-keeping, bricks and mortar shops, and piled-up inventories.

You must understand that some Web sites are owned and operated by manufacturers or service providers (Figure 10-1). Merchandise sold on these sites represents *direct* sales from the producer to the final consumer. Other Web sites are owned by intermediaries that buy products from a number of manufacturers and resell to final users. These Web sites function as electronic retailers (Figure 10-1a). An example showing how the largest Web retailer of

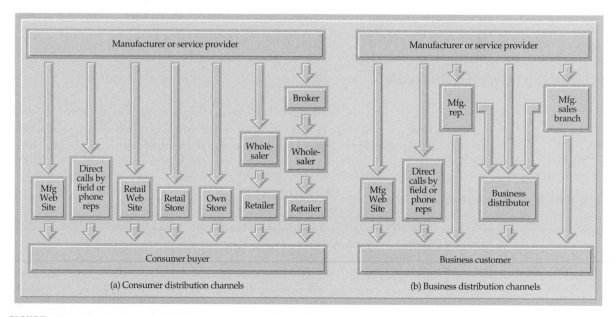

FIGURE 10-1   Consumer and Business Channel Alternatives

consumer items, Amazon.com, operates on the Internet is described in Marketing in Action box 10-1.

What Sells on the Internet?   If you define Internet commerce broadly to include all business-to-business purchasing, all Web site advertising, and all consumer on-line shopping, the total has been estimated to be $200 billion in 1998 and could rise to a trillion by 2002.[3] Consumer on-line shopping alone was $13 billion in 1998 and is expected to rise to $60 billion by 2002 (Table 10-1). The most popular items are travel and computer hardware with more than half of all Web sales. In third place is the sale of securities with 11 percent of Web business. Given the huge sales of computers and related hardware on the Web, it is not surprising that software provides 8 percent of Web sales. Clothing ranks seventh on the Internet with 4.6 percent of the business. This can probably be explained by the problems buyers sometimes encounter with fit, colors, and fabrics when they order electronically. Also it is understandable that groceries account for only 2 percent of Web sales given consumers' preferences to select food to meet their nutritional and freshness needs.

APPLYING
. . . to
Industrial
Marketing

One of the most successful and profitable Web site direct sellers is Cisco Systems. Cisco sells routers that shuffle data from one computer to another over the Internet and the software to go along with these machines. Customers can easily download their software purchases direct from the company Web site. In 1998, Cisco's web sales were $14.9 million a day or 64 percent of the company's total revenue of $8.5 billion. Part of Cisco's Internet success is due to its policy of paying its field sales representatives commissions on Web-driven sales. Reps make money on Web sales and they encourage their customers to gather information and check orders at the Cisco Web site.[4]

MARKETING IN ACTION *10-1*

Selling on the Internet

INTEGRATING
. . . with
Information
Technology
Management,
Production/
Operations
Management,
Logistics

Amazon.com Inc. has become one of the largest retailers of consumer products over the Internet. The company began selling books over the Internet and has now expanded into music and videos. In the third quarter of 1998, Amazon.com reported revenues of $153 million and its music sales of $14 million surpassed those of its two rivals N2K Inc. and CDnow Inc. Amazon.com's success is due to its convenience (open 24 hour a day, 365 days a year) and its huge assortment of titles. Where a Barnes & Noble bookstore and a Tower Records store offer a combined 275,000 titles, Amazon.com had 3 million titles. However, Amazon.com keeps very few of these titles in stock. When Amazon.com receives an order, a computer determines if the book is on hand or must be ordered. Amazon.com relies on quick delivery of books, CDs, and videos from publishers or wholesalers to fill most of its orders. The company maintains one distribution center in Seattle and another in Delaware. These centers are run 24 hours a day and most of the items received in the morning are sent out by the end of the day. While Amazon.com is growing rapidly, its two major competitors, Barnes & Noble and Borders, both reported net losses in profits in the third quarter of 1998 on their combined Internet and retail store book sales. However, the higher combined sales of Borders and Barnes & Noble may enable them to undercut Amazon's prices in the long run.

— *Distribution channels are constantly tested by new networks and only the strong and the innovative survive.*

Sources: Paula L. Stepankowsky, "Amazon.com Gets Real at Distribution Site," *The Wall Street Journal*, November 16, 1998, p. B7G. Kara Swisher, "Amazon.com Posts Wider Period Loss, But Tops Forecasts," *The Wall Street Journal*, October 19, 1998, p. B8.

TABLE 10-1   **Internet Sales in the United States in 1998**

Product Categories	Percentage of Sales
Travel	30.5%
Computer Hardware	20.3
Stocks	11.3
Software	8.2
Books	7.1
Content (pay-per-use sites such as stock quotes)	4.7
Clothing	4.6
Groceries	2.0
Music	1.2
Other	5.2
	100.0%
Estimated total revenue	$13.0 billion

Source: Adapted from material presented in Rebecca Quick, "Internet Retailing May Drum Up $13 Billion in Revenue This Year," *The Wall Street Journal*, November 18, 1998, p. B6 and Christina Lourosa, "Change in Store," *The Wall Street Journal*, November 18, 1998, p. R28.

APPLYING
... to
Consumer
Financial
Services
Marketing

Another product that seems to be made for distribution over the Internet is the buying and selling of securities. More than 80 brokers now offer Web site trading and online business now accounts for over 30 percent of all trades by individuals. High-speed transactions are important to investors, and the Internet offers almost instant execution of buy and sell orders. Also the transactions are recorded electronically and there are only a few pieces of paper to deliver to the customer. The main problem with online trading is the conflict between expenditures needed to build brand strength and relentless price-cutting by competitors. The number-one and number-two online brokerage firms (Charles Schwab and E*Trade) have lost market share to firms that charge as low as $7 to $10 a trade. Thus E*Trade, which was able to make a profit in 1998 on revenues of $215 million by charging $14.95 a trade compared to Schwab's $29.95 fee, had to spend heavily to keep its number-two position. E*Trade spent $150 million on advertising in the latter part of 1998 and 1999 to maintain its market share in the online trading market. These massive expenditures were expected to produce losses for several quarters and the firm projected marketing costs would eventually decline to 25 to 35 percent of revenues.[5]

APPLYING
... to
Consumer
Durable
Goods
Marketing

Although not reflected in the numbers shown in Table 10-1, the Internet is becoming quite popular with automobile buyers. Surveys have shown that 25 percent of new car buyers shop on the Internet and this number is expected to increase to 50 percent by the year 2000. A popular site is Autobytel.com Inc. which offers dealer cost data for cars and helps match buyers with dealers that are willing to negotiate prices online. Autobytel.com's success has prompted General Motors, Ford, and Chrysler to upgrade their Web sites.[6] GM's BuyPower program at www.gm.com will eventually make it possible for customers to get a price for the specific vehicle they want (with optional equipment), find the vehicle in dealer inventories, and arrange for a test drive. Where Autobytel.com charges dealers for customers referrals, GM's BuyPower program will be initially offered to dealers free of charge.

Is the Web Profitable?   Although many firms are jumping on the Web site selling bandwagon, only a few are making good profits. Amazon.com Inc., for example, has been selling millions of dollars' worth of books, CDs, and videos over the Internet for years, yet profits are elusive. In the third quarter of 1998, Amazon.com reported record sales of $153 million compared with $37 million in the year earlier period and loss of $45 million.[7] The problem is that it is expensive to set up Web sites and it takes low prices (30 to 40 percent off list for best-sellers) and high advertising expenditures to grow a Web site business. Amazon.com spends 23 percent of sales on marketing expenses alone, and analysts project it will not be profitable until 2001. If Internet retailers require margins of 25 to 30 percent of sales to operate, they are not going to drive supermarkets and Wal-Mart out of business on the basis of lower prices. These conventional retailers can make a profit on gross margins of 22 percent of sales.

In addition, Internet buyers have powerful search engines available to find the lowest price available anywhere on the Net. This makes it difficult for Internet retailers to raise prices. Thus while the two larger chain bookstore retailers, Barnes & Noble and Borders, have opened Web sites to compete with Amazon.com, they do not know when the sites will break even. A further problem for Web buyers is that although advertised prices may appear to be low, customers are often charged a "handling fee" of several dollars plus postage to ship the merchandise to their homes. This means that many consumers would save money by stopping by their local Borders' stores to pick up a book on the way home from work. Despite all the problems we have mentioned, Internet shopping is growing rapidly because it is so "convenient." Buyers can shop the Internet from their homes or offices and avoid the driving, parking, walking, and standing in line at check-out counters at conventional retail stores. Innovations in the sale of postage stamps over the Internet are described in Marketing in Action box 10-2.

MARKETING IN ACTION *10-2*

Selling Stamps on the Internet

APPLYING
. . . to
Consumer
Services
Marketing

The U.S. Postal Service began testing the sale of postage over the Internet in 1998 and expected the business to expand rapidly starting in 1999. To buy stamps, customers link up to their Internet postage vendor and establish electronic links to their bank accounts to draw on when needed to buy digital postage. Stamps are printed on envelopes when customers type in a recipient's address and the required postage. Software then generates an intricate checkerboard of coded data that contains the letter's source, its destination and the current date. This information can be read by a scanner and appears below a more traditional postage mark. Electronic postage appeals to small businesses who want the convenience of printing postage on demand. The new delivery system is expected to steal business from traditional postage meters sold by Pitney Bowes Inc.

— *Internet distribution can threaten traditional channels.*

Source: George Anders, "It's Digital, It's Encrypted—It's Postage," *The Wall Street Journal*, September 21, 1998, p. B1.

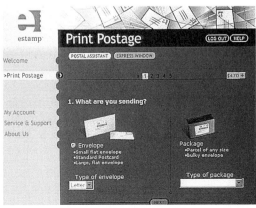

Courtesy E-Stamp Corp.

Selling by Phone, Catalogs or Sales Reps

Direct channels of distribution also include phone contacts by telemarketers and sales calls by field representatives (Figure 10-1). Sales reps are widely used to sell insurance and complex industrial products where buyers need tailored presentations and personal attention. Field sales calls are also used to sell Electrolux vacuum cleaners direct to consumer buyers. Because of the high cost of field calls ($400 to get a sale) and because phone sales cost considerably less than field calls, many firms are hiring telemarketers to contact consumer and industrial buyers over the phone. An amazing amount of business is conducted by telemarketing. Many people trade securities, buy flowers, books, seeds, CDs, and clothing using toll-free phone numbers offered in catalogs and direct mail advertising. Fifty-four percent of Americans buy from catalogs they receive in the mail, spending about $90 billion each year.[8]

In the past, marketers believed that only simple, standard items such as tickets and tapes could be sold direct. Today, however, cars and even complex computer equipment are being sold over the phone. For example, one of the authors responded to a newspaper ad and bought a Honda Civic over the phone with a credit card. Many firms are running print and television ads featuring toll-free 800 phone numbers to encourage customers to buy direct over the phone.

Customers are offered money-back guarantees and toll-free service lines to encourage sales. The result has been an explosion in the amount of business conducted over the phone. Michael Dell was the first to see that computers had become a commodity that could be sold direct using phone reps. Now Dell is a $20 billion company and a leading player in the U.S. computer market. Marketing Strategies box 10-1 describes how Michael Dell revolutionized the mail-order sale of computers with toll-free numbers. Direct marketing is discussed in more detail in Chapter 12.

Adding Retailers

Retailers have been a part of distribution channels for hundreds of years (Figure 10-1). They provide shopping convenience, local inventories, exchange services, and repairs. The use of retailers has proved effective and efficient for both consumers and manufacturers of food, clothing, tires, video rentals, hardware, dry cleaning, pharmaceuticals, furniture, office supplies, and auto sales.

The most exciting recent changes in retailing have been the growth of chain stores in the sale of pharmaceuticals, video rentals, hardware, and office supplies. Small family-run pharmacies, hardware stores, video rental stores, and stationers are vanishing under the onslaught from giants like CVS, Home Depot, Blockbuster, and Office Depot. The new larger pharmacy chain stores sign contracts with big health care providers for exclusive pharmaceutical coverage and patients buy liquor, paper goods, aspirin, and other items while they are waiting for their prescriptions to be filled. Hardware superstores like Builder's Square and Home Depot offer huge selections, low prices, and seven-day-a-week access.

The Blockbuster chain has become the number-one video rental store by offering broad selections of titles and multiple copies of new movies. Blockbuster signed new agreements with Hollywood studios that allows them to get movies for $6.50 each plus a 40 percent share of rental income instead of the usual $65-purchase price. This arrangement allows them to stock up to 400 copies of hits such as *Titanic* and helped slow the growth of the independent competitors. Within a year Blockbuster's revenue was up 16 percent and the greater availability of titles made it easier for them to compete with direct-to-home satellite services that allow customers to choose from an assortment of movies from menus on their TV screens.[9]

MARKETING STRATEGIES *10-1*

Dell Sells Direct

One of the most successful direct sales organizations in the history of American business is Dell Computer. In the past, complex, high-priced items that required after-sale service were thought to be inappropriate for mail-order distribution. Virtually all major PC manufacturers elected to sell through storefront dealers that allowed customers to touch and feel the machines and provided repair service. Michael Dell was the first to realize that PCs were a commodity business. Dell's strategy was to cut out the middleman and sell his computers directly to consumers via heavy advertising in the computer press, toll-free numbers, and Internet purchasing. He eliminated the uncertainties of mail-order purchasing by offering next-day, on-site service as well as phone and online technical support. Dell also offers factory integration of proprietary hardware and software, leasing and installation, warranty coverage, and an online superstore with 30,000 complementary items from industry leading companies.

Some people assume that Dell's success is simply due to its low prices. While Dell's prices are lower than those of its major competitors, they are not the lowest in the industry. Dell succeeds because it builds a quality machine and backs it with the best service in the country. In addition, Dell builds its computers to meet the needs of individual customer orders. This allows Dell to stay abreast of changing market conditions and greatly reduces inventory carrying costs.

Dell is a very efficient manufacturer and distributor of computers. Its selling and administrative costs are dramatically lower than those at Compaq, Apple, and IBM. Dell's sales organization includes thousands of telephone sales representatives. About 30 percent of Dell's sales are now made over the Internet.

The highest praise of Michael Dell's genius is that *all* of his major competitors (IBM, Apple, and Compaq) have instituted direct sales operations. Dell will be remembered as the greatest computer marketer of the twentieth century.

— Technical products can be sold successfully over the phone and Internet.

Source: Dell Publications, 1999.

APPLYING
. . . to Durable Goods Marketing, Business-to-Business Marketing

INTEGRATING
. . . with Information Technology Management, Production/Operations Management, Logistics

Courtesy Dell Computer Corporation, 7/99

Selling to Business Buyers. Many medium-sized and smaller firms buy computers and office supplies from large chain retailers. Currently the 1,940 office superstores run by Staples, OfficeMax, and Office Depot dominate the office supply business in the United States. These stores were initially in large towns, but now they are opening units in towns as small as Lebanon, New Hampshire, with only 12,000 people.[10] These stores succeed because their long hours of operation, broad assortments of supplies and computer equipment, and low prices can blow away their small independent competitors.

Another recent trend is for some of the giant direct selling PC manufacturers to strengthen their relationships with retail dealers. Dell gets 75 percent of its revenue from large corporate buyers, and about 15 percent of these orders are configured and installed by computer dealers. Gateway 2000 Inc., the number-two direct seller of personal computers, gets only 30 percent of its sales from corporate buyers and has begun opening retail stores to give them better access to this market segment. Gateway uses dealers as order and installation points and does not let them carry inventories of finished units.[11]

What Is Retailing's Future?   Some people believe that the rapid growth of telephone and Web site selling will lead to declines in the business done by traditional retailers. Although this may be true for some categories of merchandise, there are clear limits to what can be bought over the phone and Internet. Some consumers will always buy their food from supermarkets because they want to inspect the meat, produce, and packaged goods to see that they are fresh and meet their needs. Also, large grocery chains such as Kroger now offer bigger stores with one-stop shopping for food, banking, liquor, pharmaceuticals, video rentals, books, and take-out prepared foods.

Another service advantage of local dealers is highlighted by a mail-order purchase of some tires by one of the authors. I bought a set of tires over the phone from a low-priced magazine ad and they were delivered in two days. I had them mounted and threw away the old tires. The new tires were fine around town, but when I took the car out on the freeway I noticed an annoying vibration in the steering wheel at 65 miles per hour. When I called the phone tire dealer, I was told I would have to drive 250 miles to their office to have the tires checked with no assurance the tires could be exchanged unless they found them defective. My dilemma was that since I dumped the old tires, I could not mail the new tires back, I did not want to drive 500 miles to have them checked, and I did not like the vibration in the steering wheel. After having the tires rebalanced several times to no avail, I replaced them with another brand from a local dealer. My substantial loss on this phone purchase suggests that for products that require service, local retailers are unlikely to vanish from the channel of distribution anytime soon.

Using Wholesalers

When products are sold in many different types of retail stores scattered throughout the country, wholesalers may be needed to help transfer the merchandise from manufacturers to retailers (Figure 10-1*a*). Wholesalers are dealers that buy in volume and resell to retailers in small lots. They provide retailers with assortments of merchandise, backup stocks, credit, delivery, promotional assistance, and may stock the shelves. Organizations use wholesalers to get maximum exposure when direct contact with retailers is not justified because of low volume or lack of resources. For example, magazines and paperback books are stocked on display racks in newsstands, drugstores, discount stores, and supermarkets by specialized wholesalers. A few years ago there were 180 of these wholesalers in the United States. However, large supermarkets and discount stores have reduced the number of wholesalers they deal with to improve efficiency, and now there are fewer than 60.[12] The new larger wholesalers have better information systems and can help retailers fine-tune their displays and cut unprofitable titles. Ralph's Grocery, a West Coast supermarket chain, found that when it cut the number of titles from 1,100 to fewer than 500, overall magazine sales increased.

While wholesalers are a standard component of many distribution systems, they are currently losing market share to factory outlets, mail-order catalogs, warehouse clubs, and mass merchandisers that buy directly from manufacturers. Research suggests that wholesalers'

INTEGRATING
. . . with
Information
Technology
Management,
Production/
Operations
Management,
Logistics

share of producer shipments will fall to 36 percent by the year 2000.[13] Mergers have increased sharply among food and pharmaceutical wholesalers as more and more retailers and hospital chains are buying direct. If the 300,000 mostly small wholesalers in the United States expect to survive in the future, they will have to find ways to cut costs and improve customer benefits.

Agents and Brokers

Some manufacturers use brokers and independent representatives to sell goods in a channel of distribution (Figure 10-1). Reps are specialized agents who neither own nor take possession of the merchandise they sell to wholesale, distributor, business, or retail customers. They operate on commission in specified territories and sell where manufacturers cannot handle the job. For example, small food packers with a limited product line often lack the resources to hire their own sales force. By using a rep, the manufacturer avoids the high fixed costs associated with salespeople and branch facilities and gains the benefits of the contacts the rep has already established with the wholesale and retail trade.

Although reps are a common element in distribution channels, they have begun to lose clout in many markets. Large retail chains like Wal-Mart, the cataloger Fingerhut, and K-Mart's Builder's Square no longer deal with reps in favor of direct negotiations with executives of supplier organizations. If this trend continues, reps may be relegated to special situations and employment by small manufacturers. This change suggests that distribution channels are rarely permanent and that you must continually search for new ways to lower costs and improve service to customers.

Channel Ownership

Some organizations can sell their goods and services through their own retail outlets. When an organization extends its activities to the wholesale and retail levels, it has a *vertically integrated channel.* This method of distribution can improve efficiency by eliminating promotion and selling expenses that normally occur between the organization and the wholesaler and between the wholesaler and the retailer. With a completely integrated channel, the main job for marketing executives is to increase demand among the final buyers and to coordinate the activities of different units in the channel. The primary advantage of this system is that it gives maximum control over the selection of products sold in the channel, their prices, and the promotional activities designed to sell them to the final consumer. Examples of completely integrated distribution channels are provided by Sherwin-Williams, which operates 2,000 paint stores; Hart Schaffner Marx, which owns more than 200 clothing stores; and Japan's Bridgestone which owns 1,500 Expert and Firestone tire stores in the United States. Although the completely integrated channel offers manufacturers the most control over the distribution of their products, it also requires the greatest financial investment and good managers to operate the facilities efficiently.

Franchise Distribution

Franchising is a system of distribution whereby independent business managers are given the right to sell products or services in exchange for a fee or agreements on buying and merchandising policies. The main advantage of franchising is that it offers the parent organization a low-cost way to expand rapidly. For example, when Prudential Insurance Company opened a chain of real estate agencies, the franchisees put up most of the money and the business was profitable from the start. Prudential estimates that it would have cost more than 10 times as much to open its own outlets. Ashland Oil chose franchising to expand its quick-lube business. Ashland wanted to grow from 178 outlets to over 2,000. Since each unit cost more than $500,000, growth by franchising saved Ashland over $1 billion.

In the case of franchised ice cream stores, franchisees pay an initial fee ranging from $10,000 to $30,000 and then put up between $80,000 and $675,000 to get the business started. Local outlets also pay a royalty and advertising fee of 2 to 9 percent of sales. This shows how franchisees pay to expand a distribution network for you and then subsidize the advertising needed to make it successful.

APPLYING
. . . to
Consumer
Durable
Goods
Marketing,
Retailing

A revolution in the ownership of some franchised outlets is shifting power away from manufacturers and service providers to corporations that own large numbers of franchised outlets. Historically franchisees were family owned, but today they are often controlled by big business. The most conspicuous example is Republic Industries, which owns 350 car and truck franchises in 18 states. The company is operated by former Blockbuster video executive Wayne Huizenga. Republic also owns Alamo Rent-A-Car, National Car Rental, and 39 AutoNation USA used car superstores. By grouping car franchisees together, Republic expects to cut costs 30 percent on such things as advertising, insurance, and the costs of borrowing money. Dealers in the same area can share ad campaigns instead of running separate promotions. Republic has become America's largest car dealer with sales in 1997 of $6.1 billion and an operating loss of $68.4 million. Critics point out that although the average auto dealer made a profit of 1.7 percent of sales in 1997, Republic reported losses of 1.1 percent of revenue. While General Motors, Ford, and Chrysler have supported Republic's growth, Toyota and Honda have gone to court to try and stop Huizenga from buying up their dealers. These maneuvers have not deterred Republic, and it seems determined to continue expanding and eventually break even.[14]

CHANNEL CHOICE

Distribution channels are designed to give customers ready access to goods and services at a minimum cost. Thus you have to balance the costs of employing different types of channels against the revenues generated. Using a wholesaler, for example, reduces the manufacturer's sales and communication costs and can increase profits. Some customers, however, may want to buy direct. A model of the channel selection process is shown in Figure 10-2. The choice of distribution method begins with a decision on planned market coverage. Depending on the product and the number of customers, the organization must decide whether it wants broad distribution or more selective coverage with a few dealers.

Intensive Distribution

The intensive distribution approach is used for convenience goods when the firm wants the product available in as many retail outlets as possible. Intensive distribution can be achieved by recruiting large numbers of jobbers and wholesalers to cover every market area. Candy, photographic film, and cigarettes are made available in thousands of stores for easy access and more impulse sales.

Selective Distribution

With selective distribution, several dealers in each area are designated to handle the product, but the merchandise is not made available to every retailer. The idea is that restricted availability will increase the volume per dealer and make the brand more important to them. Also, selective distribution is used when dealers require extensive training and carry large stocks and parts inventories. Selective distribution is common with automobiles and branded

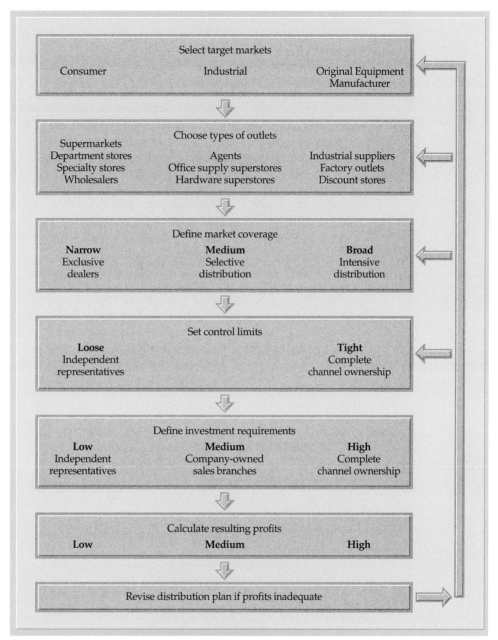

FIGURE 10-2 Choosing Distribution Channels

clothing. For example, designer jeans and Liz Claiborne-dresses are available in department and specialty stores but are kept out of K-Mart.

Exclusive Distribution

With exclusive distribution, the organization appoints a single dealer in each local market area to handle branded goods or services. Exclusive distribution has been used in the sales of luxury automobiles, Schwinn bicycles, Midas mufflers, and soft drink concentrate. By granting dealers local monopolies, the firm expects to gain cooperation on price maintenance, promotion, and inventory levels. Exclusive distribution helps dealers build customer loyalty and allows the dealers to charge higher markups. In addition, the use of exclusive territories allows dealers that invest in marketing activities to capture all the customers who want to buy the firm's goods and services.

Multiple-Channel Distribution

When an organization is new, it is common to concentrate its efforts on a single channel of distribution. As the firm grows, however, there are strong incentives to add channels to reach new market segments and to accommodate changes in customer shopping preferences. As a result, many companies distribute goods and services through several channels at the same time. Sometimes the addition of new channels creates morale problems with existing dealer networks. Firms face the terrible dilemma of choosing between the slow growth offered by traditional distribution channels and faster growth via new channels, which in turn, may cause regular dealers to drop the product.

APPLYING
. . . to
Business-to-
Business
Marketing

One solution pursued by Pella, a manufacturer of premium windows and doors, was to introduce a special ProLine of lower-priced items for sale in home supply stores such as Payless, Cashways, and Home Depot. To keep its regular distributors happy, Pella designated them as quality assurance representatives for all ProLine products sold in their territory. Distributors now train local retailers and help with installation and customer service. Pella distributors also earn a commission on every ProLine window the chain outlets sell. As a result, Pella's stagnant sales and profits have improved.

International Distribution

Once the firm has established distribution channels for domestic markets, emphasis often shifts to finding ways to sell in foreign countries. Because of the high costs and risks associated with international distribution, most firms start by making arrangements with foreign dealers to handle their products. For example, joint ventures have helped a number of American firms to enter the Japanese market. Black & Decker, the leading U.S. manufacturer of power tools, has been losing market share in the domestic market to Mikita Electric. Its response has been to sign an agreement with Shin-Daiwa Kogyo to market Black & Decker's tools in Japan. The idea is to take advantage of Shin-Daiwa's extensive sales force, distribution network, and service operations.

APPLYING
. . . to
Consumer
Durable
Goods
Marketing

Careful attention to building strong distribution networks is often the key to successful foreign sales. The Germans, for instance, have grabbed 76 percent of the imported car market in Japan due to their strong local dealers. Volkswagen sells its cars in Japan through Yanase & Company, the largest group of foreign car dealers in the country. BMW purchased its own dealer network in Japan and then expanded it. BMW has also set up a service and parts system so that Japanese buyers do not have to worry about repair problems. The lesson from these examples is that you cannot ignore distribution problems if you expect to win overseas sales.

MANAGING THE CHANNEL

Once you have a distribution network, the emphasis shifts to finding ways to improve performance. This is an ongoing process of evaluating results, modifying dealers' incentives, and replacing weak players.

Dealer Incentives

Independent wholesalers and retailers are in business to make money and are interested in stocking and promoting items that will increase *their* profits. Organizations that sell through these dealers must design products and marketing programs that are equal to or better than competitive offerings if they expect to gain support of these entrepreneurs. The most common dealer incentives are price concessions granted for volume purchases, advertising support, and seasonal orders. Other, more indirect methods for building dealer excitement include display materials, training programs, sales literature, and the hiring of in-store demonstrators. Perhaps the most enduring technique used to gain dealer cooperation involves the extension of credit. This may take the form of loans to finance inventories of display merchandise, loans for fixtures and equipment, or cash to finance customer purchases.

Another way to encourage dealers' cooperation is to give them exclusive rights to sell particular brands or models. Although Michelin sells a few lines of tires through K-Mart discount stores, its premium tires are available only through its traditional independent dealers. Dell has expanded its distribution channels to include retail outlets and has tailored its Precision line of computers for warehouse stores such as Sam's Club and Price Club. In a similar fashion, Hallmark sells Ambassador cards through supermarkets and reserves its own name cards for sale through its franchised independent outlets.

Disincentives that damage dealer relations include delayed delivery, shipment of unwanted products, slow warranty claims, and high prices. Firms that discuss their strategies with dealers and those that make simple requests are able to gain dealer agreements on inventory levels, participation in special programs, number of salespeople, and advertising expenditures. On the other hand, companies that make threats, promises, legalistic pleas, or specific recommendations have a negative impact on dealer cooperation.

Channel Power

Power in a distribution channel is the ability to get people to do things they might not otherwise want to do. Manufacturers and service providers who own their distribution channels have the power to set price, inventory, and promotion levels as they see fit. However, many firms distribute their products through independent dealers, so there are limits to what they can be forced to do. Firms that exercise too much channel power are likely to lose shelf space and dealers, be sued, or face additional legislation designed to protect channel members.

An example of a power struggle between food manufacturers and grocery stores developed over slotting allowances. In the old days, large manufacturers could bully grocers into carrying their products, and the manufacturer could dictate prices. However, supermarket chains consolidated into regional giants with immense distribution clout. Supermarkets used their control over shelf space to ask for slotting allowances of $15 to $1,000 per store to place new items on their shelves. Manufacturers were told that they had to pay cash to gain retail distribution they once purchased with consumer advertising. Manufacturers grew tired of this game and began to push food sales in discount stores, warehouse clubs, and superstores that were not so greedy. As a result, the share of the food business handled by traditional supermarkets has declined. This example suggests that firms that abuse their power in distribution channels may lose in the long run.

Gray Market Distribution

One of the most difficult distribution control problems facing multinational firms is the so-called gray market issue. The *gray market* is a system in which retailers import branded goods from foreign countries without approval of the product's manufacturer. These importers purchase branded goods from wholesalers in countries with low taxes and markups and then resell them in countries where markups are high. Gray market goods typically sell for 25 to 40 percent less than imports handled through regular distribution channels. Common gray market merchandise includes cameras, watches, fragrances, cosmetics, electronics goods, liquor, and tires made overseas.

Gray market (or parallel) importation develops when multinational firms sell products at higher prices in one country than in another. Firms often use larger markups in new markets to help attract wholesalers and pay for advertising and sales promotion activities. Although high markups help build a strong distribution network, they also attract gray market importers. The problem with gray markets is that the regular distribution network supplies inventory backup, spare parts, repairs, and promotional support that are not provided to customers who buy through gray markets. Thus, the gray market grows under an umbrella of services provided by the regular channel. Parallel importation can seriously damage authorized dealers by siphoning off sales.

The best way to eliminate gray markets is to reduce price differentials across countries that allow parallel importation to exist. Another solution is to buy up the merchandise brought in by gray marketers to protect your regular dealers. This approach could become expensive if it encouraged dealers to bring in even more merchandise. The U.S. Supreme Court has ruled that gray market importation is legal, so the problem is likely to exist for many years.

ORGANIZING DISTRIBUTION

For many products, distribution costs can be 30 percent of a product's cost. Firms that learn how to cut these costs can sell at lower prices and steal market share from their competitors. Amazing changes are taking place in physical distribution systems, and this area may be a key profit area for marketing in the twenty-first century.

Using Scanner Data

The engine fueling the revolution in distribution efficiency is improved information on customer purchases. These data are gathered by optical scanners in retail stores that read bar codes on product packaging. Whenever a customer buys anything, data on the purchase goes directly—in real time—to the retailer's central computer and on to the manufacturer's plant.

INTEGRATING
...with Information Technology Management, Production/ Operations Management, Logistics

Computers prepare a manufacturing schedule and instructions on when, how, and where to ship. This type of system is used by the largest retailer in the United States—Wal-Mart. By tying point-of-sale terminals to suppliers' factories, Wal-Mart has made several cost savings. Most of the cost of distribution involves keeping inventory in three warehouses: the manufacturer's, the wholesaler's and the retailer's. With Wal-Mart's system there is no need for factory buffer stock, because the goods are made to order and shipped immediately. Also, some of the orders go directly to the stores, reducing the need for wholesale inventories. Since store shipments replace stock already sold, Wal-Mart needs less safety stock at the store level. Wal-Mart allocates only 10 percent of its square footage for inventory compared to 25 percent at other stores. Another area for savings is reduced order cycle time. Because of direct computer linkages, communication delays are eliminated and it takes less time to get merchandise into Wal-Mart stores. This means that fewer people are needed to process the orders, and quick delivery cuts out-of-stock conditions and boosts sales.

INTEGRATING
...with Suppliers

Wal-Mart's direct information ties with suppliers has allowed it to reduce its expense ratio to only 15 percent of sales. This compares with expense ratios of 23.8 percent at J.C. Penney Co., 21.6 percent at Sears, Roebuck & Co. and explains how Wal-Mart is able to use low prices to become the world's largest retailer.[15] No traditional retailer, no supermarket, and no catalog store can compete with Wal-Mart on price. Wal-Mart has successfully employed advanced information technology to achieve a sustainable competitive advantage in distribution costs.

Although the use of scanner data to automatically reorder merchandise has lowered distribution costs, the systems are not perfect. This was shown by the experience of one of the authors who went to a Target discount store to get some cat food and cat litter on a Sunday afternoon. Target was out of one flavor of cat food that I wanted and did not have my preferred brand of cat litter in stock. I went to a K-Mart store and found the chicken-flavored cat food, but they were out of the Arm & Hammer cat litter. Walking through the store I noticed that many of the shelves were depleted of merchandise. I asked the service person at the front of the store when they would have more cat litter. She indicated that the store received merchandise Monday through Friday. This meant that the reorder system did not provide enough inventory to get the store through the weekend. Thus while Target's and K-Mart's automated reorder systems improve distribution efficiency, they do not always take care of Sunday afternoon shoppers. In my case, I found Arm & Hammer cat litter at a Kroger supermarket that was open 24 hours a day, 7 days a week, suggesting the system was better able to keep products in stock. The cat litter was priced 10 percent higher at Kroger, however, suggesting I could save money by adapting my shopping trips to coincide with Target and K-Mart's restocking cycle.

Are Warehouses Necessary?

> **INTEGRATING**
> *. . . with Information Technology Management, Production/ Operations Management, Logistics*

In the past, inventories were carried at factory warehouses, wholesale warehouses, and retail warehouses. Today the question is whether they are needed at all. Firms that produce to customers' orders and sell directly do not have to operate any warehouses. Dell Computer, for example, takes orders over the phone, builds machines to these specs, and then ships directly to customers via UPS. Inventories and warehouses are not required in this distribution system. Any storage in the channel is maintained by the shipping company.

Other firms are also finding ways to reduce the need for warehouses. In one medium-sized supermarket chain, half of the merchandise goes directly from manufacturers to stores. The other half still goes through company warehouses, but it is not held there: the merchandise is shipped to stores within three hours. These warehouses are *switching yards* instead of storage bins. Any retailer that stores only half of its goods for three hours in a warehouse is saving a great deal on inventory carrying costs.

Firms that serve many small customers requiring warehouse distribution have found ways to operate their remaining warehouses more efficiently. Helene Curtis, for example, has built a highly automated and computerized warehouse that can handle twice the volume of the six older warehouses it replaced. The new system helped Helene Curtis cut distribution costs by 40 percent. These savings allowed the company to cut prices to the consumer by 10 percent and increased market share. Mervyn's has built four new automated distribution centers to serve its 247 department stores. These centers cut the average time merchandise spends moving from vendor to store from 14 days to less than 9 days. The results have been spectacular. Mervyn's sales have grown 50 percent, but inventory carrying costs have remained the same as they were five years ago. Manufacturers and retailers that refuse to buy into computerized information systems will have trouble competing in the future.

SUMMARY

This chapter has discussed selecting channels of distribution and designing systems to move goods and services efficiently to the point of final consumption. You have to decide whether to sell direct over the Internet or to organize a channel made up of independent brokers, wholesalers, or retailers. This choice is influenced by customer preferences, the supply of independent distributors, and by the amount of money and sales volume the firm has to support its own distribution network. If independent dealers are selected, you must find ways to care for and nourish channel members to ensure their continued cooperation and survival. A common problem today is finding ways to keep your regular dealers happy as you add new distribution channels to build market share.

The last frontier of marketing efficiency is finding ways to reduce the costs of distribution. Some of the most spectacular savings have been achieved by linking optical scanners in retail stores to factories. Others have had success by automating field warehouses and using intermodal transportation systems. American distribution systems are undergoing radical changes, and firms that do not pay attention may not survive.

NOTES

1. William M. Bulkeley, "Peering Ahead," *The Wall Street Journal* (November 16, 1998), p. R4.
2. Fara Warner, "Ford Motor Files for 'Shelf' Stock to Buy Dealers," *The Wall Street Journal*, (November 16, 1998) p.B2.
3. Ken Auletta, "The Last Sure Thing," *The New Yorker* (November 9, 1998), p. 41.
4. Julie Schmit, "Cisco Embraces 'Internet Economy,'" *USA Today* (September 23, 1998), p. 3B. Melanie Berger, "New Sales," *Sales & Marketing Management* (April 1998), p. 90.
5. Michael Schroeder, "SEC Is Stuck Refereeing Big Board, Web-Trade Spat," *The Wall Street Journal* (September 24, 1998), pp. C1, C17. Rebecca Buckman, "Brokerages Spend Big on Web-Site Ads," *The Wall Street Journal* (September 11, 1998), p. C22.
6. Gregory L. White, "General Motors to Take Nationwide Test Drive on Web," *The Wall Street Journal* (September 28, 1998), p. B4.
7. Kara Swisher, "Amazon.com Posts Wider Period Loss, But Tops Forecasts," *The Wall Street Journal* (October 29, 1998), p. B8.
8. *Newsweek* (October 19, 1998), p. 8.
9. Eben Shapiro, "Blockbuster Seeks a New Deal with Hollywood," *The Wall Street Journal* (March 25, 1998), p. B1. David Segal, "Blockbuster Thrives on Deals with Studios," *Herald-Times*, September 20, 1998, p. G2.
10. William M. Bulkeley, "Office Supply Superstores Find Bounty in the Boonies," *The Wall Street Journal* (September 1, 1998), p. B1.
11. Evan Ramstad, "Gateway Unit to Bolster Ties to PC Dealers," *The Wall Street Journal* (April 20, 1998), p. B1.
12. G. Bruce Knecht, "Rack or Ruin," *The Wall Street Journal* (May 26, 1998), p. A1.
13. Michael Selz, "Firms Innovate to Get It for You Wholesale," *The Wall Street Journal* (July 24, 1993), p. B1.
14. Fara Warner, "Republic Extending Auto Nation Brand to New Car Sales in Bid to Build Chain," *The Wall Street Journal* (September 24, 1998), p. A4. Kerry Pipes, "Used-Car 'Superstores' Fail to Dominate Market," *Car and Driver*, (November 1998), p. 36. Oscar Suris, "Honda Sues Republic Industries in an Effort to Limit Franchises," *The Wall Street Journal* (May 12, 1997), p. B1.
15. Robert Berner, "Moving the Goods," *The Wall Street Journal* (July 16, 1996), pp. A1, A6.

SUGGESTED READING

Dant, Rejiu P., and Patrick L. Schul. "Conflict Resolution Processes in Contractual Channels of Distribution," *Journal of Marketing*, Vol. 56 (January 1992), pp. 38–54.

Frazier, Gary, and Raymond C. Rody. "The Use of Influence Strategies in Interfirm Relationships in Industrial Product Channels," *Journal of Marketing*, Vol. 55 (January 1991), pp. 52–69.

Keep, William W., Stanley C. Hollander, and Roger Dickinson. "Forces Impinging on Long-Term Business-to-Business Relationships in the United States: A Historical Perspective, *Journal of Marketing*, Vol. 62, No. 2 (April 1998), pp. 31–45.

Siguaw, Judy A., Penn M. Simpson, and Thomas L. Baker. "Effects of Supplier Market Orientation on Distributor Market Orientation and the Channel Relationship: The Distributor Perspective," *Journal of Marketing*, Vol. 62, No. 3 (July 1998), pp. 99–111.

REFERENCES

Coyle, John J., Edward J. Bardi, and C. John Langley, *The Management of Business Logistics,* 6th ed. (St. Paul, MN: West, 1996).

Rosenbloom, Bert, *Marketing Channels,* 5th ed. (Chicago, IL: Dryden Press, 1994).

Stern, Louis W., Anne T. Coughlan, and Adel El-Ansary, *Marketing Channels,* 5th ed. (Englewood Cliffs, NJ: Prentice-Hall, 1996).

QUESTIONS

1. Twenty-five automobile dealerships in the Northwest settled Federal Trade Commission charges in 1998 that they threatened to boycott Chrysler Corp. unless it restricted the number of vehicles allocated to Dave Smith Motors of Kellogg, Idaho. Smith Motors offers lower preset prices over the Internet to attract buyers. Why did the 25 dealers try to boycott Chrysler and how should they respond to Dave Smith's Internet program?

2. PepsiCo has announced plans to acquire one of its largest independent franchised bottlers for an estimated cost of $275 million. Independent bottlers buy syrups from PepsiCo, package beverages in cans and bottles, and deliver the products to retail stores. Why would PepsiCo want to buy up its bottlers and how will they justify the $275 million purchase to their stockholders?

3. SuperValu, Inc., of Minneapolis, Minnesota, has purchased Wetterau, Inc., of Hazelton, Missouri, for $643 million. The combined firm is the nation's largest food wholesaler. Before the merger, SuperValu serviced 2,600 independent grocery stores in 31 states plus 105 of its own stores, including its deep-discount Cub Foods stores. Wetterau owned 160 retail stores and distributed to 2,800 independent grocers. Why are mergers taking place among America's wholesalers?

4. Avon Products Inc. is one of the largest direct sellers of cosmetics and other products in the world. It has a corps of over 400,000 sales representatives who sell to customers in their homes and workplaces. The company has announced plans to open its first ever retail outlet in the United States. Why is Avon making this move? Won't the stores steal sales from the field sales reps?

5. The media giant Time-Warner is planning to become a Web retailer, selling an array of products such Madonna compact disks, Batman videos, books, and Tweety Bird socks on the Net. Why is Time-Warner opening a Web store that is likely to cannibalize sales from its 185 Warner Brothers Studio Stores and its current direct-mail businesses?

6. The Jones Company was trying to decide whether to continue using independent sales reps or to replace them with company salespeople. The firm produced a line of ceramic dinnerware that was sold by 15 rep organizations employing 55 salespeople to contact 12,100 retail stores. Management felt that the reps were not giving Jones's dinnerware enough attention, particularly in the large department stores. Annual sales of the Jones Company were $5.2 million. The company liked to have its retail accounts contacted every six weeks. The reps were paid 10 percent of sales, although 12 percent was typical for this type of merchandise in other firms. Compare the advantages of reps over company salespeople for making personal contacts. How many company salespeople would be needed to call on the retail accounts? Should Jones switch to company sales-

people? If not, what should it do to improve the performance of the present reps?

7. General Motors has announced plans to open 75 regional distribution centers across the United States with large inventories of cars and light trucks. Some of the centers will carry as many as 2,000 vehicles. This plan will move some of the dealer's inventory, which GM subsidizes to the new regional centers. With 75 new regional distribution centers, GM's inventory interest charges will increase. How will the new centers help the retail dealers and how will they help GM?

8. Hewlett-Packard and Motorola have traditionally sold their high-powered workstations directly to engineers and technicians or to value-added resellers that market complex packages of computer equipment, software, and service. They recently agreed to sell workstations through mass market dealers MicroAge and Intelligent Electronics, which sell PCs to businesses. Explain why they are making this change in their distribution channels.

9. A manager of a large cola bottling company in the United States was charged with paying bribes to an employee of a U.S. military installation to gain sites for soda vending machines on the base. Why was the bottler trying to gain distribution of its products on the base? What can manufacturers do to prevent managers from paying bribes and kickbacks to customers who ask for them?

10. The German pudding-with-topping market is dominated by four national competitors: Gervais-Danone (a subsidiary of the French BSN group), Dr. Oetker (part of a highly diversified firm), Chambourcy (a subsidiary of the German Nestle group), and Elite (belonging to the German Unilever concern). The remainder of the market is shared by approximately 30 locally or regionally operated competitors. One of these regional companies, Ehrmann, is attempting to broaden its geographic reach. Annual data on sales (1000 tons), advertising (1000 DM), price (DM), and distribution penetration (%) are available for four years. In addition, a dummy variable for distinguishing between national (1) and regional/local brands (0) has been created. Pooling the data, i.e., combining cross-sectional and time-series data, from the file puddingdat.sav, assess the marketing mix of a prototypical brand. Use the $\alpha = 0.10$ level of significance. *Hint:* If you first compute the natural logarithm (LN) of each variable and then run a linear multiple regression on the transformed variables, the regression coefficients of the variables can be interpreted as elasticities. Because regional brands do not advertise and the natural logarithm of zero is minus infinity, you must add one to ALL advertising values before taking the logarithm, i.e., ladv = LN[adv+1]. Also, do not take the natural logarithm of the dummy variable.

CASE 10-1   THE COCA-COLA COMPANY: VENEZUELA*

*A*tlanta, March 1996. Inside the chairman's office on the 25th floor of The Coca-Cola Company's stately headquarters, located across from the campus of Georgia Institute of Technology, Roberto Goizueta ponders the distribution situation in Venezuela. Venezuela is one of the few markets dominated by archrival PepsiCo despite the millions in new investment that he had approved. The average Venezuelan drinks about 17 servings of Coca-Cola products annually, compared with 248 in Chile and 122 in Brazil. To improve the situation, Coca-Cola bought six bottling plants in Venezuela just this past October. These bottlers already produced and distributed Coca-Cola but Roberto wanted to put in place a more aggressive management team. At the time of the acquisition, Coca-Cola and its bottlers vowed to spend $200 million over the next two years to boost Coca-Cola's market share in Venezuela. These actions serve to provide a cover for secret negotiations going on with the leading Venezuelan bottler and to provide insurance in case the negotiations fail.

Pepsi's success has been due largely to the efforts of Oswaldo Cisneros' Embotelladora Hit de Venezuela, the premier bottler of Venezuela. It is a $400-million-a-year Pepsi bottler. Cisneros has maintained a close relationship with Pepsi for many years and has renewed its Pepsi franchise agreement through 2003. Indeed, Cineros is a personal friend of PepsiCo's Roger Enrico. Despite these legal and personal relationships with PepsiCo, Roberto had received a call from Cisneros in 1994 asking for a meeting. As a result, Oswaldo along with his cousins Gustavo and Ricardo traveled to Atlanta for a furtive meeting with Roberto and Coca-Cola president Douglas Ivester.

Roberto assigned Ivester to negotiate the deal. Roberto warned Ivester not to talk about the negotiations even with Weldon Johnson, president of Coca-Cola's Latin American operations, to avoid a security breach. Ivester met with Oswaldo Cisneros at least ten times.

Several issues came up in the negotiations. Price was one. Another was the nature of the partnership. Cisneros wanted to sell as much of the company as possible. Roberto did not want an outright buyout. His experience with eight anchors around the world had

proven that a 25 percent stake was enough to gain significant voting control while limiting the size of Coca-Cola's investment. Balking at the size of this stake, Cisneros had walked out of the most recent meeting saying "Goodbye. It's over." Roberto had to decide whether a better offer was justified and, if so, what should go into the offer.

THE COCA-COLA COMPANY

The Coca-Cola Company is the world's leading soft drink producer. Established in 1906, it has become by most estimates not only the largest producer of beverages in the world, but also the most recognized trademark on earth. A 1990 survey by Interbrand, a consultancy that specializes in branding, named Coca-Cola as the world's leading brand. Coke is the epitome of a global power brand (Exhibit 1). The annual *Financial World* magazine survey finds the Coca-Cola brand the most valuable in the world. Coca-Cola derives 70 percent of its sales and 80 percent of its profits internationally.

Coca-Cola has focused on soft drinks—and, to a lesser extent, other beverages. In the top left-hand drawer of his desk, Roberto has for many years kept a chart describing Coca-Cola's fundamental business: selling the concentrate that transforms fizzy (carbonated) water into Coke. The diagram plots the four reasons that explain why he adores the business: (1) Selling concentrate requires little capital; (2) it produces superb returns; (3) it demands minimal reinvestment; (4) it spills an ocean of cash.

Key executives of The Coca-Cola Company involved in Venezuela are Roberto and Doug Ivester. Other executives, who have been involved or would become involved, are Weldon Johnson, president of Latin American operations, and Sergio Zyman, senior vice-president for global marketing.

Roberto C. Goizueta, Coca-Cola Chairman and CEO

Roberto C. Goizueta, 64, was born in Cuba. Roberto was greatly influenced in his childhood by his maternal grandfather, Marcelo Cantera. Cantera was a hard-working, thrifty man who made sure he could take care

* Research by Kerry Annel and others. Edited by Leonard Parsons. Original sources cited in Case Note in *Instructor's Manual*.

EXHIBIT 1   **How Strong a Brand is Coca-Cola?**

	Market Leader	*Leadership Margin[a]*	*Second Place*
Australia	Coca-Cola	3.9:1	Diet Coke
Belgium	Coca-Cola	7.7:1	Coca-Cola Light
Brazil	Coca-Cola	3.3:1	Brazilian brand (Guarana)
Chile	Coca-Cola	4.6:1	Fanta
France	Coca-Cola	4.3:1	French brand (Orangina)
Germany	Coca-Cola	3.1:1	Fanta
Great Britain	Coca-Cola	1.9:1	Diet Coke
Greece	Coca-Cola	3.8:1	Fanta
Italy	Coca-Cola	3.1:1	Fanta
Japan	Coca-Cola	2.3:1	Fanta
Korea	Coca-Cola	2.1:1	Korean brand (Chilsung Cydar)
Norway	Coca-Cola	3.3:1	Coca-Cola Light
South Africa	Coca-Cola	4.1:1	Sparletta
Spain	Coca-Cola	3.0:1	Fanta
Sweden	Coca-Cola	3.8:1	Fanta

[a] Over second-place brand.

Source: Coca-Cola Company records and store audit data.

of his family, a sometimes difficult task during the depression years of the 1930s. During those years Cantera had saved enough money to acquire a sugar refinery, some real estate, a mansion, and enough to make his extended family secure.

When Roberto was in his teens, he was sent to Cheshire Academy in Connecticut, where he learned to speak English and prepared for college. He attended Yale University, majoring in chemical engineering. When he finished, he returned to Cuba to help run the family business. But being an ambitious youth, he wanted to strike out on his own. He applied for an entry-level job at Coca-Cola in Havana, and began his work there on July 4, 1954. He advanced rapidly at the firm, and by 1960 was top technical director for five Coca-Cola bottling plants in Cuba.

Fidel Castro took over the island in 1959, and Roberto realized that the family business and assets would soon be confiscated as well. In August of 1960 he and his wife, Olguita, took a two-week vacation to Miami, and, while there, decided not to return to Cuba. The government seized the Coca-Cola bottling plants in Cuba, leaving Roberto without a business, but still with an affiliation with Coca-Cola.

Roberto began work with Coca-Cola in Miami. He wound up based in Nassau, The Bahamas, commuting to work from Miami. He became staff assistant to the senior vice president for Latin America. He was responsible for coordinating technical operations not just in soft drinks, but in Coca-Cola's citrus, coffee and tea operations. He found himself working for Bob Broadwater, a freewheeling executive and a survivor of the Bataan death march as a Japanese prisoner during World War II. Broadwater took Roberto along on three-week jaunts through Latin America, focusing attention on the Venezuela market where Roberto would become acquainted with Gustavo Cisneros, a scion of one of the county's wealthiest families.

In 1964 Roberto moved to Atlanta. At age 35, he was promoted to vice president in charge of technical research and organizational development. Five years later Roberto and his wife became American citizens. In 1974, Roberto's boss suffered a massive heart attack while in London. Roberto moved into his office and job as head of Coca-Cola's technical operations. By 1979 Roberto was one of six top executives named to Coca-Cola's new "office of the chairman." As head of technical operations, Roberto spearheaded the development of Diet Coke to make a name for himself. Coca-Cola's chairman and chief executive, however, killed the promising project.

In May 1980 Roberto was named president of The Coca-Cola Company. One of his first acts was to greenlight the Diet Coke project. A year later he became chairman and CEO. When he assumed this position, there was a major identity crisis within the firm. The company had been slowly losing market share for nearly two decades, and was reticent to take risks that might tarnish its beloved trademark. In 1982, Coca-Cola introduced Diet Coke. It has been a huge success, becoming the leading low-cal soft drink and the number three soft drink overall.

Before taking charge of Coca-Cola, Roberto put together a document with a vision and mission statement to set a direction for the company and to imbue it with a distinctive culture that would mesh with his leadership style. Roberto's leadership style is formal and aristocratic, but reserved and polite. He does not like open confrontation, and tends to prefer a predictable schedule. He loves the traditions of the company.

Roberto believes "the name of the game is creation of wealth for the shareholders, and the key is efficient allocation of capital. It is the essence of banking. You borrow money at a certain rate and then invest it at a higher rate and pocket the profit." His business philosophy has served the company well. In 1981 the net annual income of the company was $482 million; by 1995 it had grown to almost $3 billion. The firm's share of the worldwide soft drink market grew from 37 percent to 45 percent. The price of the company's stock grew at a compound annual rate of 26 percent, creating almost $89 billion in share-holder wealth. In 1981, Coca-Cola's market value was $4.3 billion; in 1995, it had grown to $115 billion. Recent results are displayed in Exhibit 2. Coca-Cola ranks as one of the most successful corporations in the world.

M. Douglas Ivester, Coca-Cola President and COO

Doug Ivester, 48, is a product of his Southern Baptist, rural Georgia upbringing. He worked his way through the University of Georgia as a Kroger bag boy. He climbed the Coke ranks on the financial side of the business. Having spent 10 years with the accounting firm of Ernst & Whinney, where he eventually headed Coca-Cola's audit team, he joined Coca-Cola as assistant controller and director of corporate auditing in 1979, working his way up to chief financial officer in 1985. He was the main force behind Coke's $150 million investment in information technology, driven by his frustration in trying to get faster financial information. He acted as president of Coca-Cola's European Community Group from June 1989 to August 1990, when he assumed the Coca-Cola USA presidency. In Europe he backed Coke's rapid—and high risk—deployment into the former East Germany, which set the company's pace in Eastern Europe. In the United States, he was central to working out strategic alliances with huge customers like Wal-Mart and McDonald's. In early 1993 Ivester became corporate executive vice president and principal operating officer/North America, with responsibility for Coca-Cola Foods and global marketing for The Coca-Cola Company. He succeeded Donald Keogh as the president and chief operating officer in the summer of 1994.

Ivester earned his promotion by successfully rejuvenating brand Coke. He noted that his job was to break through the clutter by focusing on what makes Coke "special, different, and better." He made two bold moves. First, he rocked Madison Avenue by giving Hollywood's Creative Artists Agency (CAA) carte blanche to revitalize the soft drink's advertising. CAA shattered Coke's longtime, "one sight, one sound, one agency" approach—typified by the "Always Coca-Cola" campaign. CAA's campaign featured images as

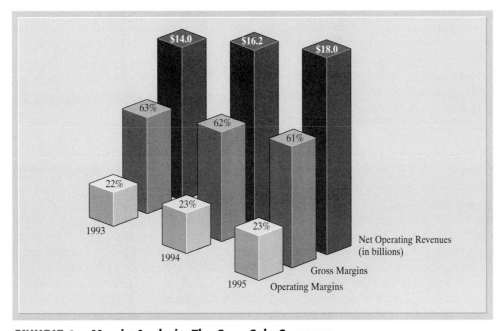

EXHIBIT 2   **Margin Analysis: The Coca-Cola Company**

diverse as Coke-chugging polar bears and punk rockers. CAA calculatedly jam packed its messages with the brand's traditional symbols—the trademark red disk, the contour bottle, and the classic Coca-Cola script—reinforcing to consumers the symbols that say Coke. Second, he fired Peter Sealy, senior vice-president for global marketing, and rehired Sergio Zyman, a native of Mexico who left the company under a cloud after spearheading the New Coke reformulation. Zyman has clashed with Coca-Cola's tradition managers. He has made some stubborn managers wear a shirt bearing the words, "I'm not the target audience." Ivester brought Zyman in on the planning of the Cisneros Group negotiations. In particular, Zyman assessed Pepsi's marketing programs in Venezuela.

Ivester, who speaks no foreign languages, has been described as tenacious, intense, and unequivocal, if uncharismatic. He urges managers to play by the rule of Ray Kroc, the founder of McDonald's quick service restaurants: "What do you do when a competitor is drowning? Get a live hose and stick it in his mouth."

At a more strategic level, Ivester knows that consumers get thirsty every two hours. He, consequently, focuses beyond Coca-Cola's 50 percent share of the world carbonated soft drink business to the 98 percent of "share of throat" now held by coffee, tea, milk, juice, and water. Data on the consumption of Coca-Cola beverages in selected markets around the world is given in Exhibit 3.

THE CISNEROS GROUP

The Cisneros family emigrated from Cuba to Venezuela in 1928. Today the Cisneros Group, based in Caracas, runs a multinational communications and consumer products conglomerate, controlling more than 50 companies in Latin America, the United States, and Europe with revenues estimated at $3.5 billion. Its interests, among others, include Venezuela's largest television network, a beer company, mining interests as far away as Africa, Burger King and Pizza Hut franchises, the largest chain of grocery stores in Puerto Rico, a Blockbuster video franchise, and a retail franchise for Apple Computer, Inc.

The business is co-owned by Oswaldo Cisneros and two of his cousins, Gustavo Cisneros and his younger brother Ricardo. Oswaldo, 55, heads Pepsi's largest and oldest foreign bottling franchises, Embotelladora Hit de Venezuela. In addition to Pepsi products, Hit produces and distributes its own flavored soft drinks. Gustavo is a dapper, high-profile billionaire who is one of Latin America's leading media magnates. The Cisneros fam-

ily media and telecommunication investments are shown in Exhibit 4. Ricardo is a former director of Venezuela's Banco Latino. Although he says that he was uninvolved, Ricardo is one of scores of executives charged in the country's largest ever bank collapse. He lives in self-imposed exile in London.

PEPSICO

The Coca-Cola Company is not alone among producers of soft drinks. Pepsi stands as Coca-Cola's chief rival, and in recent years has come to occupy a strong number two position in the United States and in many markets around the world (Exhibit 5). Pepsi has been able to edge out Coke in some markets, and in at least one, Venezuela, it has achieved total dominance.

PepsiCo has had an altogether different strategy than Coca-Cola, one in which it has poured billions of dollars into capital-intensive businesses like restaurants. PepsiCo was formed after the merger of Pepsi and Frito-Lay in 1965. Donald Kendall led it for the next 21 years. The Pepsi-Cola Company spans more than 190 countries and accounts for about one quarter of the world's soft drinks. Frito-Lay is the largest and most profitable snack-food company in the United States, with a 53 percent share of market. Pepsi generates 70 percent of its beverage profits in the United States. PepsiCo with almost 500,000 employees, is the world's third largest employer after General Motors and WalMart. Wayne Calloway succeeded Don Kendall.

Key Pepsi executives, in addition to Calloway, who have played or would play a role in Venezuela, include Roger Enrico, Christopher Sinclair, and Craig Weatherup. Also involved is Alberto Uribe, vice president for the Andrean region.

Wayne Calloway, PepsiCo Chairman and CEO

Wayne Calloway, 60, was born in Winston-Salem, North Carolina. He attended Wake Forest University and received a B.B.A. in accounting. In 1995, Wake Forest University named its school of business and accountancy in his honor.

After holding accounting positions with a local chemical company and later at ITT, Calloway began his career at Pepsi-Cola as director of planning and profit control. He served as president and chief operating officer of PepsiCo's Frito-Lay snack division starting in 1976 and as its chief executive officer beginning in 1978. During his tenure at Frito-Lay, Inc., its operating profits tripled. He became executive vice president and chief financial officer of PepsiCo in 1983, Pep-

EXHIBIT 3 **Coca-Cola Company's Estimated 1995 Volume: Selected Markets**

	Unit Case[a] Growth				Soft Drinks	Total Beverages[b]	
	10-Year Annual Growth		1995 Annual Growth		1995 Share	1995 Share	1995 Per Capita Consumption
	Company[c]	Industry[d]	Company[c]	Industry[d]	Company[d]	Company[e]	Company[f]
Worldwide	7%	5%	8%	5%	47%	2%	54
North America Group[g]	5	3	6	3	42	11	326
United States	5	3	7	3	42	12	343
Greater Europe Group	9	4	8	6	45	3	76
East Central Europe	17	6	25	8	40	1	42
France	13	7	8	7	46	2	71
Germany	6	5	4	1	56	7	201
Great Britain	12	6	11	5	32	4	114
Italy	5	4	(10)	(4)	52	3	87
Nordic & Northern Eurasia	12	(2)	13	9	30	1	19
Spain	8	4	5	3	53	6	179
Middle and Far East Group	9	7	10	7	39	1	16
Australia	8	4	4	2	65	10	292
China	49	21	38	12	23	0	4
Japan[h]	6	0	2	(7)	34	5	136
Korea	5	4	3	(5)	56	2	71
Middle East	9	7	15	9	23	1	18
Philippines	7	5	10	9	75	4	105
Africa Group	6	4	9	8	80	1	24
Northern Africa	6	2	16	10	77	0	13
Southern Africa	6	5	4	6	83	2	73
Latin America Group	7	5	8	6	55	5	157
Argentina	5	4	(7)	(15)	62	6	179
Brazil	10	10	34	45	51	4	122
Chile	16	13	16	9	68	8	248
Colombia	3	1	4	10	42	4	107
Mexico	6	4	(1)	(8)	61	11	322

[a] Unit case equals 24 8-ounce servings.

[b] Consists of all beverages, including tap water.

[c] Consists of all Coca-Cola Company beverages (excluding those distributed by Coca-Cola Foods).

[d] Includes soft drinks only.

[e] Derived by dividing Coca-Cola Company's unit case sales in ounces in a given market (excluding products distributed by Coca-Cola Foods) by the product of the market's population multiplied by the commonly accepted norm for daily fluid intake, 64 ounces, multiplied by the number of days in a year.

[f] 8-ounce servings of Coca-Cola Company beverages per person per year (excludes products distributed by Coca-Cola Foods).

[g] Consists of the United States and Canada.

[h] Coca-Cola Company's share of soft drinks includes its noncarbonated beverages in Japan; conforms with Japanese industry standards.

siCo's president and chief operating officer in 1985, and chairman and chief executive officer in 1987.

Calloway has been a key figure in tightening PepsiCo's strategic focus to three core lines of business—restaurants, soft drinks, and snack foods—while molding it into a global growth vehicle. With brands such as Kentucky Fried Chicken, Pizza Hut, and Taco Bell, Pepsi under Calloway has become the largest restaurant operator in the world. Calloway is not identified primarily as a soft drink man.

Calloway focuses on building a strong management team, empowering employees, and achieving excellent results for shareholders. During his tenure as chairman and chief executive officer, PepsiCo's sales have more than tripled and its market value has grown by more than $35 billion. In a survey of business executives and securities analysts published in *Fortune* magazine in 1993, Calloway was ranked the sixth most admired chief executive officer in the United States.

Calloway is currently believed to be seriously ill with prostate cancer. He has announced that he will step down as chief executive April 1st and as chairman next February. Roger Enrico has been tapped to succeed him.

EXHIBIT 4　Cisneros Media and Telecommunications Investments

Investment	Business	Percent Owned
Cablevision	Venezuelan cable provider	100
Chilevision	Chilean television station	100
Carribean Communications Network	Television station in Trinidad	20
DirecTV channels	Twelve new channels to be broadcast by DirecTV in Latin America (partner in one channel: Hearst Corp.)	50
DirecTV International Iberia	Direct-to-home satellite broadcast (joint venture with Hughes Communications and Spanish partners)	10
DirecTV local	Local operations in two dozen Latin American countries	20
Galaxy Latin America	Direct-to-home satellite broadcast (joint venture with Hughes Communications, Brazil's TV Abril, and Mexico's Multivision)	20
Univision	Leading Hispanic television network in the United States (partners with Mexico's Grupo Televisa SA, and Perenchio Communications Inc.)	25
Sprintel	Development of a long distance carrier in Latin America telephone markets (joint venture with Sprint)	50
Telcel Cellular	Venezuelan cell phone company (partners with Bell South)	40
Viel and Americatel	Development of wireless communications services and sale of Motorola products (joint venture with Motorola Corp.)	50
Rodven	Events promotions, manufacturer and retailer of recorded music	100

Source: Cisneros Group

Roger Enrico, PepsiCo Vice Chairman and PepsiCo Restaurants International Chairman and CEO

Roger Enrico, 51, grew up in Chism, Minnesota. He went to Babson College. He knew that he was people-oriented, and figured "Why not personnel?" An opening at General Mills took him back to Minnesota. But he decided the personnel department was boring; he wanted to be in the action. He thought about getting an MBA, but enlisted instead. He served in Vietnam as a naval supply officer. He returned to General Mills for a position in brand management.

Enrico joined PepsiCo's Frito-Lay in 1971 as an associate product manager for a tiny brand of onion-flavored snacks, Funyuns. He began to travel the globe on behalf of the salty snacks division. At age 31 he was president of Frito-Lay/Japan. He gained experience in the other—the soft drink—side of the business serving as area vice president of Pepsi-Cola International's Southern Latin America Division. In Brazil, he was boss to Sergio Zyman, now Coca-Cola's top marketing executive. By 1980, Enrico was full-time in beverages as senior vice president of sales and marketing of the Pepsi-Cola Bottling Group. Two years later, he was executive vice president of Pepsi-Cola USA, en route to succeeding John Scully as head of Pepsi USA when Scully departed to head Apple Computer in 1983. Enrico became president and chief executive officer of Pepsi Worldwide Beverages in 1986. In this position, he became one of the most visible soft drink executives of all time when he took the lead in fighting

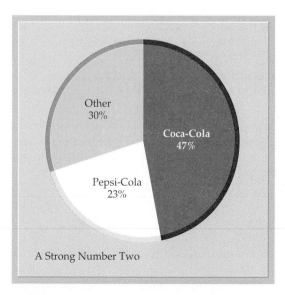

A Strong Number Two

EXHIBIT 5　Worldwide Market Shares

the infamous "Cola Wars" against Coca-Cola in the mid-80s. He signed a then record $5 million contract with Michael Jackson to launch the "Choice of a New Generation Campaign."

In explaining his actions, Enrico told *Beverage World* magazine that "The soft drink industry is first and foremost a marketing industry. No one has to drink a soft drink. Water is a lot cheaper. Booze gives you a better kick. The reason people drink soft drinks is that we offer simple refreshment and good taste. Through marketing we make that part of people's lifestyles."

In April 1985, Pepsi realized that Coca-Cola was going to announce a reformulation of Coke as "New Coke" in reaction to the Pepsi Challenge, which emphasized that consumers preferred Pepsi to Coke in blind taste tests. In what started out as a letter to the Pepsi system and franchiser employees, Enrico took out an ad in America's major newspapers, including the *Atlanta Journal-Constitution,* with one of the most in-your-face pronouncements anyone could remember in business (Exhibit 6). This would be the start of what would become a major public relations disaster for Coca-Cola. Millions of Americans decided that they hated New Coke without trying it. Within three months, Coca-Cola had to bring the original formula back as Coke Classic to placate faithful Coke drinkers. Enrico's take on the "Cola Wars" is given in his autobiography, *The Other Guy Blinked: How Pepsi Won with Cola Wars.* In the book, he tweaked Roberto for his failure to establish New Coke.

Roger Enrico and his wife, Rosemary, are close personal friends of Ozzie Cisneros and his wife, Ella. While Enrico headed Pepsi-Cola Worldwide Beverages, the two couples often traveled together. Indeed, Enrico was dancing with Ella when stricken by a heart attack in Istanbul in 1990. Some think this heart attack mellowed Enrico. He seemed to turn his sights from competition to cooperation. For a while he dropped out of the marketing game altogether to coach young managers.

Enrico became chairman and chief executive of PepsiCo Worldwide Foods (Frito-Lay) in 1992. During a casual lunch with his friend Ozzie Cisneros in 1993 on Grand Cayman Island, Enrico allowed as how he was tempted to leave PepsiCo. Enrico explained that he was being considered for the CEO position at American Express, whose board had just eased out James Robinson III. Cisernos advised, "You're a beverage man, not a banker." Enrico ultimately stayed loyal to Pepsi. A year later he switched to chairman and chief executive officer of PepsiCo Worldwide

EXHIBIT 6   Pepsi Newspaper Advertisement

It gives me great pleasure to offer each of you my heartiest congratulations. After 87 years of going at it eyeball to eyeball, the other guy just blinked.

Coca-Cola is withdrawing their product from the marketplace, and is reformulating brand Coke to be 'more like Pepsi.' Too bad Ripley's not around ... he could have had a field day with this one.

There is no question the long-term market success of Pepsi has forced this move.

Everybody knows when something is right it doesn't need changing. Maybe they finally realized what most of us have known for years ... Pepsi tastes better than Coke.

Well people in trouble tend to do desperate things ... and we'll have to keep our eye on them.

But for now, I say victory is sweet, and we have earned a celebration. We're going to declare a holiday on Friday.

Enjoy!

Best regards,
Roger Enrico
President, Chief Executive Officer
Pepsi-Cola USA

Restaurants. As such, Enrico has changed the restaurants from operating as autonomous businesses with fractured, highly competitive cultures into something resembling a system.

Christopher Sinclair, PepsiCo Foods and Beverages International President and CEO

Chris Sinclair, 45, is Pepsi's much admired, go-for-growth chief of international operations. He was born in Hong Kong and raised in India. Sinclair comes across as quiet and reserved but he is an inspiring leader and fearless marketer. The secret of success, Sinclair tells his managers, is to follow the advice of a race car driver: "Press the accelerator to the floor and keep turning left."

Sinclair is the architect of a 1989 aggressive push into Brazil by Argentina bottler Buenos Aires Embotelladora SA (Baesa) backed by Pepsi investment. Pepsi has a 25 percent stake in Baesa. Baesa is to be Pepsi's model "superbottler." Baesa is to buy up small operators across Latin America, crank up their marketing and distribution, and assault Coca-Cola.

Sinclair has only visited Caracas once since Enrico left soft drinks in 1990 to run Pepsi's snack food business and that was in 1993—Calloway never has.

Craig Weatherup, Pepsi-Cola North America President and CEO

Craig Weatherup, 50, joined Pepsi-Cola in 1974. He was named senior vice president, sales and marketing of the Pepsi-Cola Group in 1982, president of the division in 1986, president of Pepsi-Cola Company in 1988, and president and CEO of Pepsi-Cola North America in 1991. He is a meticulous, pragmatic, profit-conscious manager. Some say that he reacted slowly to private label competition. Calloway, however, has said of him: "The success Weatherup's achieved in his very nice, very determined way has been beyond almost any business person in America over the last 10 years." Weatherup hasn't worked abroad in 14 years.

COCA-COLA'S INTERNATIONAL DISTRIBUTION STRATEGY

Roberto understood well that politics, economies, and weather are inevitable factors in running a global business. He knew, for example, that with operations in nearly 200 countries and in about 100 different currencies, Coca-Cola constantly faced currency fluctuations—and that fewer revenue dollars are generated when local currencies are weak compared to the U.S. dollar. What he could not stomach was the fact that The Coca-Cola Company, despite the power of its global brand, had so little to say in how its product was bottled, shipped, and marketed around the world. Something had to be done to shore up international bottling operations. The model for doing so was born in 1980.

In the Philippines, Coke had dominated Pepsi since American armed forces had popularized the drink during World War II. However, Coca-Cola's bottler, the San Miguel Brewery, neglected soft drinks in building its beer business. This allowed Pepsi to take a commanding market share lead by the 1970s. John Hunter, whom Roberto had put in charge of the Far East region, proposed that Coca-Cola buy 30 percent of the bottler and run the San Miguel bottling operation under a joint operating agreement. Although Roberto initially had reservations, he ended up championing the proposal over the objections of Coca-Cola financial executives, winning board approval for the investment. The "anchor bottler" concept was born.

Over time Roberto built Coca-Cola's entire international bottling effort around the concept of taking minority ownership positions in underperforming but high-potential bottlers, then working with local management to improve the bottling and marketing of its product while at the same time keeping the demand for Coca-Cola's own capital outlays as small as possible. Roberto requires anchor bottlers to be substantial international businesses with capital to invest in their existing markets and expansion abroad. Currently, Roberto approves capital outlays for anchor bottler investments only if they promise a 20 percent return on Coca-Cola's capital. Coca-Cola's average borrowing cost is 11 percent. In the first decade of the anchor bottler program, Roberto had designated only eight companies as anchor bottlers. They operate in 40 countries and comprise nearly 70 percent of Coca-Cola's international volume.

Pan American Beverage Company (Panamco), based in Mexico City, is currently Coca-Cola's only anchor bottler in South America. Panamco operates in Brazil, Colombia, Costa Rica, and parts of Mexico. Coca-Cola invested $75 million in Panamco in November to raise its stake from 7 to 13 percent. Its other bottler in Mexico, Coca-Cola Femsa S.A., is in the process of building its 14th plant. Bottlers can be very profitable as indicated in Exhibit 7. Coca-Cola is also considering buying stakes in two Chilean bottlers: a 15 percent stake in Embotellas Polar S.A., based in Santiago, for $32 million and a 6 percent stake in Embotelladora Andina S.A., Chile's largest bottler. Polar operates in Argentina as well as Chile.

LATIN AMERICAN MARKETS

Coca-Cola's Latin America Group stretches from Tijuana, Mexico in the north to Tierra del Fuego in the south and includes all of Coca-Cola's operations in Central and South America. Latin America accounts for about 24 percent of Coca-Cola's worldwide volume of 1.9 billion unit cases. A breakdown of the Latin America Group's unit case sales is given in Exhibit 8. Annual per capita consumption of Coca-Cola products ranges from a low of 7 to a high of 522.

Latin America is a seen as a prime opportunity for Coca-Cola for at least two reasons. Its population is very large, and it is essentially an untouched market. The per capita consumption of soft drinks is very low compared with the U.S. average, which is over 300 eight-ounce servings of beverage per year. Although the Mexican market is fairly well developed, with the consumption of beverages per capita being just about the same as that in North America, most of the other South American countries have yet to be sold on the

EXHIBIT 7 *Beverage World's* **Most Profitable Nonalcoholic Beverage Companies**

Company	1995 Net Income (billions)	Comment
The Coca-Cola Company Atlanta, Georgia	$2.986	Coca-Cola USA Coca-Cola International Coca-Cola Foods
Coca-Cola FEMSA Piso, Mexico	2.434	Bottling companies representing an estimated 25 percent of Mexican Coca-Cola volume
PepsiCo Purchase, New York	1.606	Pepsi-Cola Company Pepsi-Cola International Pepsi COBO system representing an estimated 55.9 percent of Pepsi volume in the United States
Quaker Oats Company Chicago, Illinois	0.802	Quaker Beverages
Cadbury Schweppes Stamford, Connecticut	0.466	DrPepper/Cadbury Beverages Cadbury Beverages International Mott's
Whitman Corporation Rolling Meadows, Illinois	0.134	Pepsi-Cola general bottlers representing an estimated 12.1 percent of Pepsi volume in the United States
Coca-Cola Enterprises Atlanta, Georgia	0.080	Coca-Cola bottling companies representing an estimated 57.4 percent of Coca-Cola volume in the United States
Buenos Aires Embotellado Buenos Aires, Argentina	0.043	Pepsi-Cola general bottlers
Coca-Cola Bottling Company Consolidated Charlotte, North Carolina	0.011	Coca-Cola bottling companies representing an estimated 7.6 percent of American Coca-Cola volume
Coca-Cola Beverages Toronto, Canada	0.004	Bottling companies representing an estimated 95 percent of Canadian Coca-Cola volume

Source: TopBiz.com

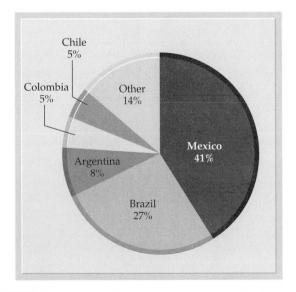

EXHIBIT 8 **Coca-Cola Company's Estimated 1995 Volume: Latin America**

idea of Coke. Coca-Cola made early successes in Brazil and Chile, achieving a better than 3 to 1 margin over its nearest rivals. Expansion into neighboring countries proceeded with varying degrees of success, but, all in all, Coca-Cola was able to establish a share of each country's market and to establish itself as a legitimate competitor in the beverage market.

In none of the South American markets is Pepsi in second place or even a close competitor of Coke. That is, in none of these countries except one, that being Venezuela, as indicated in Exhibit 9. Pepsi also has a lead in the Central American country of Guatemala.

VENEZUELA

Venezuela is located in northern South America, bordering the Caribbean Sea and the North Atlantic Ocean, between Colombia and Guyana (Exhibits 9 and 10). Its longest border is with Brazil. Its land area is slightly more than twice the size of California. Its cli-

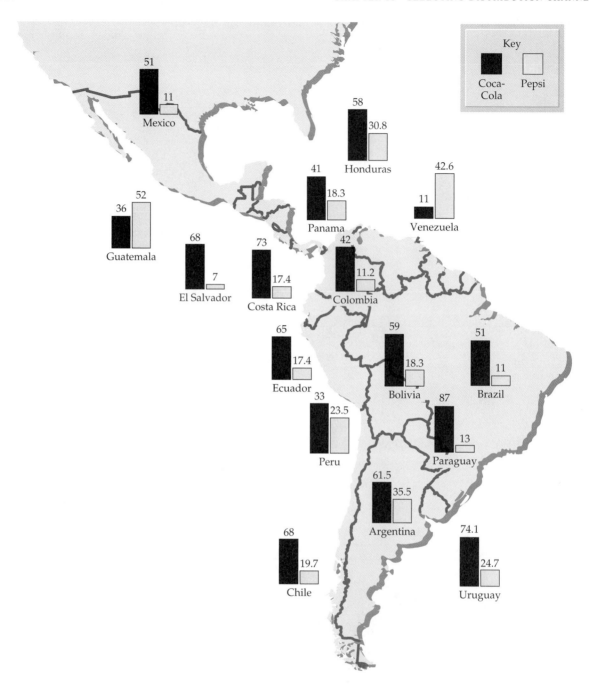

EXHIBIT 9   Latin America: Coca-Cola versus Pepsi

Source: Beverage Digest.

mate is hot and humid in its tropical zone and more moderate in its highlands.

Venezuela has a population of over 20 million, which is growing at 2.1 percent annually. About 35 percent of the population is under 15 years old, 60 percent is between 15 and 64 years old, and 5 percent is over 65 years old.

THE VENEZUELAN SOFT DRINK MARKET

The carbonated beverage industry in Venezuela had humble beginnings. In 1922, a forward-looking businessman imported from New York 25 cases of Coca-Cola to satisfy workers in the country's oil fields. This event marked the entrance of transnational soft

EXHIBIT 10 **Venezuela**

drink companies into Venezuela. Three different groups throughout the years held the Coca-Cola franchise, but they did not have enough financial strength or an effective marketing plan to ensure the product's widespread acceptance by consumers. They neglected their distribution channels and limited their investment to what was needed to cover the closest operating markets.

Antonio Cisneros saw how vulnerable existing bottlers were and, along with his brother Diego, obtained the Pepsi Cola franchise for Venezuela in 1940—Pepsi's first independent bottler outside the United States. The key to success was a large-scale promotion campaign involving free distribution of the product to all restaurants. Pepsi was also sold door to door as a way of informing the consuming public of the product's existence. These measures facilitated the market's expansion and gradually put the company in its current dominant position. But it was Oswaldo Cisneros who made Pepsi the most popular dark cola

drink in Venezuela, dominating that portion of the market by over 80 percent, while Coca-Cola held most of the remainder. Venezuela became the only major consuming country in the world where Pepsi outranked Coke. Today there are several small markets in the Far East, such as the Philippines, where Pepsi is first, but none of them provides the dollar profits that Venezuela has over the years.

Pepsi became solidly entrenched in the Venezuelan market, dominating all other brands of carbonated beverages. The Cisneros family, now three generations strong, continued to groom its relationship with Pepsi, and developed a powerful distribution system that was able to reach every part of the country. Cisneros operates 18 plants with over 4000 delivery trucks, decorated with both cola and Pepsi logos. As a result, the Pepsi name became synonymous with cola in Venezuela. Cisneros concentrated on developing publicity around the drink, and his success was apparent.

Pepsi has been the undisputed leader among Venezuelan soft drinks, chiefly as a result of Oswaldo Cisneros' marketing strategies and policies. These had allowed it to maintain, and at times, even increase, its sales volume. Neither economic crisis nor the constant decline of consumer purchasing power had affected its permanence as the country's strongest soft drink company. Venezuela generates annually about $10 million in Pepsi profits. Pepsi assured itself of a continuing alliance when Oswaldo Cisneros, as President of Embotelladora Hit de Venezuela, in 1988 renewed the franchise contract through 2003.

While Pepsi is the leading brand, Coke is not even second. Two of Cisneros' own brands, Hit and Chinotto, are second and third, and another, Frescolita, is fifth. A market share breakdown is given in Exhibit 11.

To improve its position, Coca-Cola purchased six bottling plants in Venezuela in early October 1995. They included two in Caracas, and one each in Valencia, Maracaibo, Cumaná, and El Vigia (near Mérida), and are indicated in Exhibit 10. Coca-Cola had no financial interest in the bottlers before the acquisition.

THE CURRENT SITUATION

Roberto went over in his mind key aspects of the situation. He also thought about various contingencies for which planning is needed.

First, this is an historic strategic opportunity to radically improve Coca-Cola's situation in Venezuela.

EXHIBIT 11   Venezuela Soft Drink Market Shares

Soft Drink	Market Share
Pepsi-Cola (P)*	40.0
Hit (C)	22.5
Chinotto (C)*	8.7
Coca-Cola (CC)*	8.5
Frescolita (C)	7.1
Golden Cup (G)	2.7
Fanta (CC)	1.3
Grapette (C)	1.1
Sprite (CC)	1.0
Brown Cola (G)	0.9
Laim (G)	0.4
Seven-Up (C)	0.2
Orange Crush (C)	0.2
Others	5.4
Total	100.0%

Note: (C) Cisneros, (P) Pepsi, (CC) Coca-Cola *Includes Pepsi-Cola Light, Chinotto Light, Coca-Cola Light

Source: Roger Prunhuber León, *The Monthly Report,* which is an affiliate of the *Venezuelan Economic Review.*

The bottling alternatives were few. The only other alternative is powerful Venezuelan brewing group Empresas Polar SA. Polar beer not only has bottling plants but a strong distribution network. The latter was the principal factor in their driving Cervececía Caracas practically out of the market.

Second, because of health problems, Oswaldo Cisneros, 55, wants to sell 50 to 100 percent of his business. All his life he has had enormously high cholesterol, between 400 and 650. Moreover, none of his three daughters wants to run the business. A $300 million Coca-Cola investment, however, would be required to acquire 50 percent stake in the Cisneros bottling business, plus its home-grown beverage brands.

Third, for the past five years Cisneros has wanted to improve and expand his plants in Venezuela. Cisneros also wants new additional brands for Venezuela. Modernization will require an additional $200 million Coca-Cola investment over the next four years—bringing Coca-Cola's total in new Venezuela investments to $500 million.

Fourth, the Cisneros Group wants to expand its export opportunities and grow outside of Venezuela. Cisneros Group wants a partner to distribute overseas Hit and other Cisneros brands. The Cisneros Group certainly desires to be an anchor bottler. They were astounded to see Pepsi back Baesa's assault on their neighbor to the south, Brazil—the world's third-largest soft-drink market after the United States and Mexico. Oswaldo Cisneros, nonetheless, had dangled the prospect of Pepsi buying into the Cisneros Group before Enrico in 1990. Enrico indicated that Pepsi would only be interested in a 10 percent stake and, furthermore, it wanted only the Cisneros' flavor concentrate business, not the entire bottling business.

Fifth, Oswaldo Cisneros, at a gut level, seemed to be having a hard time betraying Pepsi. He earned the nickname "Casper the Ghost" because he disappeared at times during the negotiations. Roberto knew Cisneros had flirted with leaving Pepsi for Coca-Cola before. Coca-Cola and the Cisneroses discussed a possible partnership in the late 1980s but the Cisneros Group renewed their Pepsi franchise. The raising of Enrico to the head of PepsiCo could change the dynamics of the negotiations.

Roberto thought about what might happen if Coca-Cola did make the investment. What could Pepsi do? At a minimum, he had to take into account the legal ramifications. Pepsi has a contract with the Cisneros Group through 2003. The penalty for early withdrawal could be more than $100 million.

The Venezuelan government, furthermore, would be likely to examine any deal to see if the agreement would create a soft drink monopoly. A key agency would be the Superintendency for the Promotion and Protection of Free Enterprise. Roberto had to consider what actions Coca-Cola might take to assuage the regulators.

Perhaps most importantly, Roberto had to be careful not to create a distraction from the upcoming Atlanta Olympics. Coca-Cola had years of planning and $350 million invested in the 1996 Olympics.

As he got up from his desk to go to a meeting in Coca-Cola's pecan-paneled boardroom, Roberto knew it was time for a decision.

CASE 10-2 JEFFERSON PILOT CORPORATION*

On February 28, 1993, Roger Soles, Jefferson-Pilot's (J-P) President, Chairman of the Board, and Chief Executive Officer for the last 25 years, retired. J-P Corporation had 1992 revenues of $1.2 billion from its four business segments (individual, group, casualty and title insurance; and a communications group) and from investment income.

Soles had used a strong leadership style to guide J-P during his tenure. Decision-making and management had a top-down focus, and Soles exercised a high level of control. Despite J-P's success under Soles' leadership, however, revenues had been basically flat for the last five years (1988–92). Low interest rates, which affected investment earnings, and declining life insurance sales contributed to the sluggish revenues and earnings. The corporate culture also seemed resistant to change and fixed on retaining the status quo—the traditional way of doing things.

J-P's Board of Directors felt the company needed aggressive new leadership if the company were to be a market leader. In order to provide for a smooth transition following Soles' retirement, the Board selected David A. Stonecipher to become President-elect and brought him on board in September 1992. Stonecipher had been the president and CEO of Life of Georgia, an Atlanta-based insurance company. He also served as President of Southland Life Insurance Company and had recently become President of Georgia US Corporation, the parent company of both Life of Georgia and Southland Life.

Stonecipher had a reputation as an aggressive, outgoing leader who was willing to change and try new things. He realized that increased sales would be the key to J-P's revenue growth and that he needed a strong management team if he were going to make the necessary changes. With that in mind, one of his first acts was to appoint Kenneth Mlekush as Executive Vice President of Individual Insurance. Mlekush, who had previously served as President and CEO of Southland Life, brought over 30 years of experience to the position and specialized in marketing individual life and annuity products. Mlekush later asked Ron Ridlehuber, who had worked with him at Southland, to join J-P as Senior Vice President for Independent Marketing. Ridlehuber had 18 years of experience in marketing and field sales management. Stonecipher also promoted Bill Seawell from his position as an agency manager in J-P's career sales force to serve as Senior Vice President for Ordinary Marketing. Seawell had been with J-P since 1976 and had managed the Greensboro agency since 1981. During that time, the Greensboro agency had consistently been among J-P's leading agencies.

A STRATEGIC REVIEW

After assembling his management team, Stonecipher asked a major consulting firm that specialized in working with life insurance companies to conduct a strategic marketing review of the firm. Now, in early 1993, Stonecipher had assembled the new team in a conference room in the firm's corporate offices in Greensboro, North Carolina, to hear the consultant's report. He knew this report would provide a basis for the

*This case was prepared by Dr. Lew G. Brown, Associate Professor, and Michael Cook, MBA, of the University of North Carolina at Greensboro. The authors express their appreciation to Jefferson-Pilot Corporation for its cooperation in development of this case. Copyright © by Lew G. Brown and the North American Case Research Association. Reproduced by permission.

strategic decisions the group would have to make if the company were going to meet the Board's and the shareholders' expectations. The managers knew that a key focus of the report and of the decisions facing them would be how J-P should structure and manage its sales force because life and annuity sales would need to grow dramatically in order to increase revenues significantly.

J-P'S SALES FORCE

J-P distributed its individual insurance products through three separate systems: career agents, independent producing general agents, and financial institutions. J-P hired career agents and provided them with extensive training, an office, and full staff support. The company paid the agents a salary subsidy during their training year and then changed them to a commission-only basis. The agents earned a commission on the premiums each policy generated. The agent earned a higher commission rate on the first-year premium and then earned a lower commission rate on renewal premiums thereafter as the policyholder renewed the policy year after year. The career agents were very loyal. In fact, the company was very selective in choosing career agents. Becoming one was difficult, and those who were successful were very proud of their position. But growth based on a career system was slow, and the costs of maintaining the sales force were high.

In early 1993, J-P had approximately 800 career agents. They sold about 90 percent of its life insurance policies. Agents on average during 1992 wrote about 30 policies and earned about $26,000 in first-year commissions (the commissions paid on the policy's first-year premium). The first-year commission rate averaged 50 percent of the first-year's premium. The average career agent earned total income, including commissions on renewal policies, in the high $40,000 range. Bill Seawell was responsible for managing the career sales force.

At the beginning of 1993, there were approximately 1,400 independent producing general agents (PGAs) distributing J-P's life and annuity products. Twelve salaried regional directors recruited about 15 to 20 PGAs each year, seeking agents who were already established in the insurance business. Although the independent agents did not work directly for J-P, the company provided extensive training and support. The PGAs allowed J-P to extend its marketing operations (in a limited way) beyond its core geographic distribution areas. Although there were more PGAs than career agents, many of them sold few J-P policies each year.

They had contracts with J-P as well as with other insurance companies and could sell policies offered by any company they represented. First-year commission rates on policies PGAs sold were in the 80–85 percent range. These rates were higher than those for career agents because J-P did not pay any of the PGAs' expenses, as it did for career agents. Ron Ridlehuber was responsible for managing the independent sales force.

J-P also used an additional distribution channel consisting of 19 relatively small community banks and savings institutions that contracted to distribute life and annuity products. J-P designed the annuity products for these institutions and controlled pricing. Jefferson-Pilot financial data are presented in Exhibits 1 and 2.

THE CONSULTANTS' PRESENTATION

David Stonecipher glanced around the conference room to make sure everyone was ready. "Well, gentlemen, let's begin." Aaron Sherman and Larry Richardson, who directed the project for the consulting firm, began the presentation.

"Gentlemen, I have given each of you a detailed report summarizing our findings. We wanted to meet with you today to present an overview of the key points and to answer any questions you have," Aaron Sherman began. "As you are aware, we began this process by holding a workshop with J-P's executives at which we asked them to rate issues the company faces. The number one issue they identified was that your total annualized premium income has declined during the past five years while most of your major competitors' revenues have grown. Although J-P has an excellent core of field and home-office people and is in excellent financial condition, our analysis highlights areas where you need to take action.

Target and Managerial Peer Companies

"In conducting our analysis, we looked at a group of 13 companies, 7 of which we call 'managerial peers' and 6 of which we call 'target companies.' The target companies are those you face on a day-to-day basis in competing for policyholders and new agents. Some of these operate using a 'general agent,' that is, an independent agent who is not a company employee. The managerial peer companies are those you compete with when you sell policies or recruit agents, but all of them use a career system like J-P, with agency managers who are responsible for the agents who work out of their offices. J-P has the highest rating in terms of claims-paying ability from both A.M. Best and Stan-

EXHIBIT 1   Consolidated Statements of Income

(Dollar Amounts in Thousands Except Per Share Information)	*Year Ended December 31*		
	1990	*1991*	*1992*
REVENUE			
Life premiums and other considerations	$238,326	$230,369	$230,034
Accident and health premiums	375,872	382,624	383,552
Casualty and title premiums earned	$47,078	45,270	44,815
Total premiums and other considerations	661,276	658,263	$658,401
Net Investment income	342,053	352,772	360,882
Realized investment gains	28,201	33,963	48,170
Communications operations	127,330	125,045	129,734
Other	3,753	3,433	5,142
Total Revenue	1,162,613	1,173,476	1,202,329
BENEFITS AND EXPENSES			
Death benefits	111,444	104,131	105,013
Matured endowments	5,223	4,455	4,576
Annuity benefits	13,903	14,912	15,054
Disability benefits	1,224	1,151	1,185
Surrender benefits	59,297	47,174	38,485
Accident and health benefits	322,922	318,876	317,350
Casualty benefits	34,605	36,657	30,025
Interest on policy or contrast funds	89,651	93,995	94,106
Supplementary contracts with life contingencies	4,997	5,346	5,637
(Decrease) in benefit liabilities	(10,050)	(764)	(1,292)
Total benefits	633,216	625,933	610,139
Dividends to policyholders	16,950	16,598	16,997
Insurance commissions	63,396	57,237	54,382
General and administrative	125,101	124,470	128,501
Net (deferral) of policy acquisition costs	(15,745)	(12,214)	(11,536)
Insurance taxes, licenses and fees	22,750	24,351	24,660
Communications operations	95,356	92,334	93,560
Total Benefits and Expenses	941,024	928,709	916,703
Income before income taxes	221,589	244,767	285,626
Income taxes (benefits):			
Current	68,031	77,839	88,889
Deferred	(4,079)	(8,759)	(6,501)
Total Taxes	63,952	69,080	83,388
Net Income	$157,637	$175,687	$203,238
Net Income per Share of Common Stock	$2.94	$3.42	$3.99

Source: Jefferson-Pilot 1992 Annual Report.

dard and Poor's rating services. Only 5 of the 13 peer companies have similar ratings. Some of your agents see the company's financial strength as a competitive weapon, while some others question whether the company has been too conservative.

Performance Analysis

"This overhead (Exhibit 3) presents a summary of your operating performance over the 1987–91 period as compared with the 13 target and managerial peer companies. As you can see, premium income and net gain before dividends have grown more slowly than the tar-

get group's average but faster than the managerial peers' average. Over this same period, the number of J-P's career-ordinary life agents has shrunk from 1,186 to 546. As a result, you have seen a decline in the percentage of your total premium income coming from life insurance. This results also from a decline in the number of policies written and in the face amount per policy. It also appears that the productivity of your agents has lagged behind competitors. You also rely heavily on the business you develop in North and South Carolina and Virginia, as this over-head indicates (Exhibit 4).

EXHIBIT 2   Jefferson-Pilot Segment Information

	(Dollars in Thousands)		
	1990	*1991*	*1992*
REVENUE			
Life insurance	$946,262	$956,426	$965,862
Other insurance	55,164	53,472	53,907
Communications	127,330	125,045	129,734
Other, net	33,857	38,533	52,826
Consolidated	$1,162,613	$1,173,476	$1,202,329
INCOME BEFORE INCOME TAXES			
Life insurance	$179,725	$202,349	$217,635
Other insurance	6,575	919	7,820
Communications	16,902	18,023	24,262
Other, net	18,387	23,476	35,909
Consolidated	$221,589	$244,767	$285,626
IDENTIFIABLE ASSETS AT DECEMBER 31			
Life insurance	$4,132,811	$4,535,398	$4,817,482
Other insurance	136,449	147,309	158,741
Communications	111,130	102,836	99,938
Other, net	74,518	139,677	159,676
Consolidated	$4,454,908	$4,925,220	$5,235,837
DEPRECIATION AND AMORTIZATION			
Life insurance	$5,031	$5,741	$6,055
Other insurance	155	209	194
Communications	9,980	10,013	8,425
Other, net	324	327	172
Consolidated	$15,490	$16,290	$14,846

Source: Jefferson-Pilot 1992 Annual Report.

EXHIBIT 3   Jefferson-Pilot's Summary of Operations, 1987–1991 (Dollar Amounts in Millions)

	1987	*1988*	*1989*	*1990*	*1991*
Premiums & annuity considerations	$648.1	$718.0	$716.3	$727.2	$768.9
Net investment income	250.1	295.3	313.0	326.6	338.7
Other income	32.0	25.8	24.1	28.0	26.8
Total income	930.2	1,039.1	1,053.4	1,081.8	1,134.4
Total expenses	802.3	916.8	890.0	896.9	930.6
Net gain before dividends	127.9	122.3	163.4	184.9	203.8
Dividends to policyholders	18.8	25.3	24.7	23.8	22.5
Net gain after dividends	109.1	96.9	138.7	161.1	181.3

	Change from 1987–1991			*Average Annual Percent Change*		
	JP	*Target Group Average*	*Managerial Peers Average*	*JP*	*Target Group Average*	*Managerial Peers Average*
Premiums & annuity considerations	$120.8	$850.9	$3,182.0	4.4%	7.5%	11.7%
Net investment income	88.6	371.7	723.4	7.9%	9.1%	6.2%
Total income	204.2	796.5	3,590.1	5.1%	4.7%	8.6%
Deductions	(128.3)	(528.9)	(3,337.8)	(3.8)%	(3.5)%	(8.8)%
Net gain before dividends	75.9	267.6	252.3	12.4%	14.4%	6.3%

Source: Jefferson-Pilot.

EXHIBIT 4   Jefferson-Pilot 1991 Market Share for Selected States

	JP Share of Ordinary Life Insurance			JP's Ordinary Life Premiums (000)
	% Premium	% Issues	% In-Force	
Core Southeastern states:				
North Carolina	3.97%	2.86%	3.57%	$63,794
South Carolina	2.08	1.62	1.86	15,884
Virginia	0.94	0.54	0.88	13,017
Other major Southern states:				
Texas	0.58	0.36	0.50	19,368
Florida	0.37	0.19	0.35	10,268
Georgia	0.59	0.39	0.55	8,785
Tennessee	0.57	0.30	0.52	5,865
Louisiana	0.51	0.52	0.55	4,352
Alabama	0.36	0.07	0.28	3,108
Mississippi	0.63	0.29	0.68	2,794
Kentucky	0.33	0.35	0.31	2,181
Outside the South:				
Virgin Islands	3.73	0.60	3.28	433
Puerto Rico	2.58	1.15	1.89	3,853
California	0.07	0.03	0.05	3,738
U.S. total	0.32%	0.20%	0.29%	$175,446

Source: Jefferson-Pilot.

Customer Analysis

"Next, we looked at your customers. This overhead (Exhibit 5) first compares J-P and the peer groups on the basis of premium per policy and average size per policy. Then, we break down your customers into male, female, and juvenile groups. As you can see, J-P has a lower premium per policy, average size policy, and a lower premium per $1,000 coverage than do the peer companies. Like the peers, however, your typical customer is a male, under 35 years old who is employed in a professional or executive position. Your career

EXHIBIT 5   Comparison of Premiums and Average Size Per Policy

Premium/Policy Size	Jefferson-Pilot	Target Group	Managerial Peers
Premium per policy	$889	$1,211	$966
Average size policy	$101,470	$126,940	$91,580
Premium per $1,000	$8.76	$9.54	$10.55

PERCENT OF POLICIES
(PREMIUM PER POLICY)

Customer Demographics	Jefferson-Pilot	Target Group	Managerial Peers
Male	51%	57%	53%
	($1,213)	($1,567)	($1,257)
Female	38%	33%	36%
	($639)	($879)	($744)
Juvenile	11%	10%	11%
	($233)	($255)	($303)

By Whom Sold	Full-Time Agents	PGAs
Percent of policies	91%	9%
Premium of policy	$837	$1,439
Average size policy	$100,920	$127,580
Premium per $1,000	$8.29	$11.28

Source: Jefferson-Pilot.

agents sell 91 percent of your policies, but the policies they sell are smaller in terms of size and premium than those sold by your PGAs.

"Because adult males account for a little over half of your policies and 70 percent of your premiums, we wanted to look more closely at this group. This overhead (Exhibit 6) shows the occupation, age, and income distribution for your male customers and those of the peer companies. Although we saw earlier that your typical customer is under-35 years old, you will note that the peer companies have larger percentages of their customers in this group and that you have a higher percentage of your customers over 45 years old. This would suggest that you should have higher premiums per policy, yet your premiums per policy are lower in both the younger and older groups and overall. Our analysis indicates that your typical male customer has a median income of $37,500."

"Why do you think our premiums are typically lower than those of the peer companies?" Ken Mlekush asked.

"That's a good question, Ken," Larry Richardson responded. "Our feeling is that the lower premiums are the result of your company's concentration in the Southeast, where incomes are generally lower than in

the Northeast. A number of the peer companies have a major presence in the Northeast. Also, some of your agents may not be capitalizing on the opportunities in their markets, but we believe the regional difference is the key factor."

Product Comparison

"If that answers your question, Ken, we'll move on to our discussion of your products," Aaron Sherman resumed. "Our next overhead (Exhibit 7) presents an analysis of J-P's product mix, based on first-year commissions, as compared with the peer companies. As the exhibit shows, J-P has been steadily selling less life insurance, down from 76 percent of first-year commissions to 63 percent, just since 1989. The other companies' life insurance shares have held relatively constant over this time. Your salespeople are selling considerably more disability income and health insurance and annuities than are the other companies."

"Why do you think our agents are selling more annuities and disability income policies?" David Stonecipher asked.

"Our experience indicates that agents find it easier to sell disability income and annuities as compared to life insurance," Aaron Sherman answered. "Consumers

EXHIBIT 6 **Analysis of Adult Male Consumer by Occupation, Income, and Age**

	PERCENT OF POLICIES (PREMIUM PER POLICY)		
Occupation	Jefferson-Pilot	Target Group	Managerial Peers
Executive	37%	36%	28%
	($1,756)	($2,003)	($1,728)
Professional	33	41	28
	($1,234)	($1,651)	($1,492)
Blue Collar	21	18	38
	($710)	($884)	($772)
Clerical	9	5	6
	($866)	($1,664)	($734)
Income			
Under $25K	26%	14%	24%
	($625)	($582)	($603)
$25K–49.9K	45	41	51
	($841)	($811)	($956)
$50K or over	29	45	25
	($2,421)	($2,400)	($2,541)
Age			
Under 35	39%	47%	47%
	($561)	($671)	($688)
35–44	31	32	27
	($1,169)	($1,647)	($1,034)
45 or over	30	21	26
	($2,056)	($3,536)	($2,494)

Source: Jefferson-Pilot.

EXHIBIT 7 Product Mix Trends (Percent of First-Year Commission)

	1989	1990	1991
JEFFERSON-PILOT			
Life	76%	70%	63%
DI/health	9	12	12
Annuities	11	13	17
Investment Products	4	5	7
Group	0	0	0
Total	100%	100%	100%
TARGET GROUP			
Life	78%	75%	75%
DI/health	7	6	6
Annuities	4	6	7
Investment Products	5	6	8
Group	7	7	5
Total	100%	100%	100%
MANAGERIAL AGENCY PEERS			
Life	76%	78%	77%
DI/health	5	5	5
Annuities	8	9	9
Investment Products	3	3	4
Group	7	6	4
Total	100%	100%	100%

Source: Jefferson-Pilot.

EXHIBIT 8 Sales Force's Ratings of JP's Products (Percent of Agents Agreeing)

Agents' Overall Assessment of Companies' Products	Jefferson-Pilot	Norm
I am pleased with the variety of products our company offers.	66%	78%
I am satisfied with our company's development of new products.	33	65
Our company is market driven, responding to the needs of its target market with appropriate products and services.	25	66

Source: Jefferson-Pilot.

can understand these policies better and salespeople find them easier to explain. Thus, the salespeople go for the easy sale. What is more important to understand, however, is that it is unusual for a company with a large career sales force to stress universal life. Whole life policies provide more support for the field sales force because consumers tend to keep the policies in force longer and the renewal premiums are higher."

Sales Force Comparison

"How do our salespeople feel about the products we give them to sell?" Bill Seawell asked.

Larry Richardson responded by presenting an overhead (Exhibit 8). "This overhead summarizes our findings on that question. As you can see, relative to the norm for other companies we have surveyed, your agents were less pleased with the variety of products and were significantly less pleased with new product development. They also seemed to feel that the company is not as market driven as it should be."

"Larry, while we are on the subject of how the salespeople feel, how did we stack up relative to recruitment and retention of the sales force?" Ron Ridlehuber wondered.

"That's an important question, Ron. Our study shows that only 35 percent of J-P's new agents made it

through the first year, 15 percentage points below the industry average, and only 24 percent made it through the first two years. Moreover, only 7 percent stay more than four years.

"This overhead (Exhibit 9) summarizes your situation pretty well. The first part of the overhead shows that in 1991, recruits represented 48 percent of your base sales force, as compared with 29 percent and 38 percent for the two peer groups. Further, as we've noted, your base sales force has been declining while your peers' sales groups have been stable or increasing. Likewise, your turnover rates have been consistently higher than your peers. Finally, the overhead shows that only 35 percent of your sales force has been with you more than 5 years as compared with 40 percent and 46 percent for the two comparison groups. And after five years, we expect agents to be in their most productive period."

"Larry, what did you determine about our agents' productivity versus the peer groups?" David Stonecipher asked.

"We looked closely at the issue of productivity. We found that J-P agents earned on average lower first-year commissions (not including renewal commissions) in each year as compared with the peers. Your base sales force had average first-year commissions of about $22,000 versus $31,000 for the target group and almost $25,000 for the managerial peer group. When we looked at number of policies sold, we also found that your agents sold fewer individual life policies."

"Do you have any ideas as to why our productivity is lower, Larry?"

"Yes, David. Although there are many factors that affect productivity, it seems to the project team that J-P's production standards are low compared to the peers' standards. This may cause more experienced agents to place less business with J-P. They may meet

EXHIBIT 9　Sales Force Recruitment and Retention

RECRUITS AS A PERCENT OF BASE FORCE

| | Jefferson-Pilot | | | |
	Rate	No. of Recruits	Target Group	Managerial Peers
1991	48%	280	29%	38%
1990	58	378	31	41
1989	34	316	30	40
1988	40	459	30	45
1987	42	501	33	41

PERCENT CHANGE IN BASE FORCE

	Jefferson-Pilot[a]	Target Group	Managerial Peers
1991	−6%	−1%	−1%
1990	−11	b	2
1989	−31	b	1
1988	−2	b	9
1987	−2	1	6
TURNOVER RATE			
1991	36%	24%	28%
1990	44	24	28
1989	48	23	28
1988	30	23	25
1987	31	24	25
DISTRIBUTION OF SALES AGENTS BY YEARS OF SERVICE			
Years of Service			
1	35%	24%	29%
2	15	14	15
3	10	9	9
4	5	7	7
5+	35	46	40

[a] The field force has declined from 1,161 to 546 full-time agents.
[b] Less than $1/2$ of 1 percent.

Source: Jefferson-Pilot.

their performance goals with you and then place other business with other firms in order to meet goals there.

"There is also evidence that the agents feel that the production levels are too low. As this overhead (Exhibit 10) shows, your managers believe that they help agents set high but attainable goals, yet slightly less than half of the agents feel that way. In looking at the validation requirements, the performance standards that first-year agents must meet, 69 percent of the agents believed they were modest or too low. Finally, your agents had considerably less activities in direct mail, telephone prospecting, etc., than did agents from the peer companies. Many salespeople don't like to perform these activities, but experience shows that the activities are a key part of building a clientele.

"Your managers and agents also seem to have different perspectives on what is required of new agents. This overhead (Exhibit 11) indicates that over 90 per-

cent of your managers felt they give a realistic picture of an agent's career to an agent they are recruiting, yet only 32 percent of the agents felt that way. Moreover, when we asked the managers which activities they required of a new agent prior to signing a contract with them, we got a very different set of responses than we got when we asked the new agents the same question. Seventy-three percent of your new hires have not been full-time life agents previously, so it is not hard to understand that they might not fully understand what being a career agent requires."

Marketing Costs

"How did we compare as far as marketing costs, Aaron?"

"Ken, our analysis indicates that your marketing costs are generally in line with the managerial peer group. As you know, because of the one-time cost of

EXHIBIT 10 Results of Agent Survey—Production Goals

IN OUR AGENCY, A GOOD JOB IS DONE OF HELPING AGENTS SET CHALLENGING BUT ATTAINABLE PRODUCTION OBJECTIVES:

	Percent Agreement
Agency Manager	88%
Sales Manager	73
Agent	49
Norm for FT agent	52%

IF VALIDATION REQUIREMENTS WERE A PRODUCTION LEVEL GOAL TOWARD WHICH I WAS WORKING, I WOULD SEE IT AS:

	Jefferson-Pilot	Target Group	Managerial Peers
Challenging	30%	40%	48%
Modest	51	35	33
Too low	18	23	14
Too high	1	2	5

IN THE PAST MONTH, HOW MANY:

	Jefferson-Pilot	Target Group	Managerial Peers
Prospects have you mailed to	99	231	278
Prospects have you phoned	113	211	147
Cold calls have you made	41	74	63
Appointments have you had	29	49	41
Fact-finders have you completed	22	17	17
Closing interviews have you done	17	18	18

Source: Jefferson-Pilot.

EXHIBIT 11 Results of Agent Survey—Precontract

IN OUR AGENCY, NEW AGENTS ARE GIVEN A REALISTIC PICTURE OF THE AGENT'S CAREER:

	Percent Agreement
Agency Manager	100%
Sales Manager	93
Agent	32
Norm for FT agent	39%

MANAGERS: WHICH ACTIVITIES DO YOU TYPICALLY REQUIRE OF PRODUCERS PRIOR TO CONTRACT?

	Jefferson-Pilot	Target Group	Managerial Peers
Learn a sales talk	100%	63%	83%
Make joint calls	93	57	60
Market opinion surveys	93	74	78
Complete sales	81	57	53
Basic insurance knowledge	70	79	77
Become licensed	59	82	93

AGENTS: WHICH OF THE FOLLOWING ACTIVITIES WERE YOU REQUIRED TO COMPLETE PRIOR TO BEING CONTRACTED?

	Jefferson-Pilot	Target Group	Managerial Peers
Market opinion surveys	64%	24%	39%
Basic insurance knowledge	51	54	51
Become licensed	49	62	66
Complete sales	47	28	27
Learn a sales talk	39	36	40
Make joint calls	30	19	18
None	8	17	12

Source: Jefferson-Pilot.

issuing a policy and the high first-year sales commission, it costs J-P about $1.65 for each $1.00 of premium income in the first year. In other words, you lose $.65 for every dollar of premium income in the first year. That's why it is so important to keep policies on the books. It takes into the second or third year before the company makes any money on the policy.

"Your $1.65 figure compares with $1.66 for the managerial group, but it is higher than the target group's average of $1.45. We think that comes from your having more smaller offices. When we controlled for office size, your costs seemed to be in line. This overhead (Exhibit 12) shows the elements of your costs as compared with the peer companies. Your costs are higher for both producer (agent) compensation and management compensation due to your competitive bonus structure and your agent financing plan. Your home office expenses are probably higher simply because you are a smaller company than some of the peers, and there are certain fixed costs you have to bear. You should be able to grow and spread those fixed costs. To help you compare your agencies' costs with the peer group's, I prepared this overhead (Exhibit 13). It shows that your agencies are on average about one-third the size of the average peer agency."

"How do our agents feel about their compensation, Larry?"

"Bill, I prepared this overhead to summarize our findings on that point (Exhibit 14). As you can see, your full-time agents are below the norm in every category for all agents in our survey. On the other hand, your managers are above the norm in each category except for how secure they feel about their income.

"David, I think that about covers the points we wanted to present at this time. We will, of course, be available to answer additional questions you have as you proceed with your planning," Larry concluded.

"Thank you, Larry and Aaron. Your work will be very helpful. We'll let you go now while we continue our discussion."

OPTIONS

"Well, I don't know that any of the consultants' findings surprised us, but hearing them all together is certainly sobering," David began. "We've got our work cut out for us if we are going to achieve the growth and profitability goals the Board has set. It wants us to grow earnings per share by 10 percent per year and achieve above average returns on capital. Ken, what do you think our options are?"

"David, even if we choose the option of continuing to have the same kind of company we've had, that is one focused primarily on using the career agent to sell our products, we've got to make a number of changes to address the issues in the report. We seem to be in a cycle of declining performance. Fewer agents lead to less new business. This causes an expense problem. Due to that problem, we don't do the things we need to do to develop competitive products. It's a vicious cycle. Don't you agree, Bill?"

"Yes, Ken. But I think it is important for us to remember that our career-agent system is our key strength. We are known as a company because of that system. We have many long-term, loyal agents. As you know, my father worked here and was in charge of our career agents. We need to improve the quality of our recruits, train them better, and keep them with us. If we can do those things, we will grow faster and be more profitable."

"That's true, Bill," Ron joined in, "but it seems to me that we need to look more closely at complementing the career system by increasing our emphasis on the independent agent. We have many independent

EXHIBIT 12   Components of Marketing Costs: 1991 (Per $100 of Weighted New Premiums)

	Jefferson-Pilot	Target Group	Peer Group
Producer Compensation[a]	$61	$55	$62
Management Compensation[b]	26	23	19
Field Expenses Paid by Company[c]	37	36	43
Field Benefits	17	17	24
Sub-Total	141	131	148
Home Office Marketing Expenses	24	14	18
Total	$165	$145	$166

[a] Includes all compensation other than renewal commissions; includes first-year commissions on management personal production.

[b] Includes compensation paid to agency managers and second-line supervisors.

[c] Includes all operating expenses paid by company (e.g., clerical salary, rent, postage, telephone, etc.).

Source: Jefferson-Pilot.

EXHIBIT 13   1991 Average Agency Characteristics

	Jefferson-Pilot	Peers
Manager income[a]	$100,913	$150,145
Agency first-year commission revenue	$247,941	$778,431
Managers' years of service	9.9	6.1
Number of agents	11.1	32.9
Number of recruits	5.7	11.2
Number of 2nd-line managers	1.5	2.2
2nd-line manager income[a]	$23,489	$52,075
Number of agencies	35	473

[a] Excludes personal production

Source: Jefferson-Pilot.

agents now, and the report shows that they are very productive. But they have never been the focus of our system. Under a new system we would contract with existing insurance agents, allowing them to offer our products. This avoids the problem of having to hire and train new recruits, and it would allow us to expand our geographic coverage more quickly. Further, we would not have to pay the office costs and associated salaries. We could pay these independent agents on a commission-only basis. Instead of using our 12 regional directors to recruit, we could license independent marketing organizations to recruit for us, with them earning an override commission on sales their agents made."

"Ron, I know you used this kind of system at Southland, but it would be such a radical change for J-P," Bill responded. "If you increased the size of our sales force substantially by using independent agents,

I'm not sure how our career force would react. I'm afraid they'd be terribly threatened. And the folks in the home office are used to working with career agents. The independents would not be loyal to the company. We would have less control over what they sell and over the quality of their work with policyholders. And can you imagine what will happen the first time one of our career agents runs into an independent agent trying to sell the same product to the same customer!"

"David, you asked about options," Ken continued. "I guess this exchange points out that we could continue with a predominantly career-based system, move to a predominantly independent system, or have a combination of the two approaches. We're going to have to make significant changes under any of the options, and I'm sure there will be problems we'll have to address. A final growth option, of course, is to

EXHIBIT 14   Attitudes Toward Compensation

FULL-TIME AGENT RESPONSES (PERCENT AGREEMENT)		
	Jefferson-Pilot	Norm
I have a secure income.	39%	46%
I have a good compensation plan.	46	58
My compensation plan is competitive.	38	49
My compensation plan is clear and understandable.	51	53
I have good fringe benefits.	51	64
MANAGERS' RESPONSES		
	Jefferson-Pilot	Norm
I have a secure income.	33%	58%
I have a good compensation plan.	67	65
My compensation plan is competitive.	56	55
My compensation plan is clear and understandable.	66	57
I have good fringe benefits.	44	73

Source: Jefferson-Pilot.

acquire other insurance companies. We certainly have the financial strength to do that, but even then we are going to have to address the issue of how we distribute, how we sell, our products to our policyholders."

"Yes, Ken, distribution is a key issue. I can see that there are many issues we need to think carefully about before we make a decision. Here's what I'd like for you to do. I'd like for each of you independently to consider our situation and develop recommendations as to how we should proceed. I'd like to meet again in two weeks to hear your presentations. I'll call you to set up a specific time once I check my calender."

PERSONAL SELLING AND SALES FORCE MANAGEMENT

> In the world of business, it is useless to be creative unless you can sell what you create. Customers cannot be expected to recognize a good idea unless it is presented by a good salesperson.
>
> ANONYMOUS

Marketing communications encourage customers to buy goods or services. The three principal means of communications, in order of the strength of their relationship with the customer, are the sales force, direct marketing, and advertising. Supporting activities include sales promotion and public relations. These communication methods interact to build sales. They must be carefully coordinated so that they conform with the brand platform and reinforce brand values—giving rise to the term *integrated marketing communications* (IMC). While the basic concept of IMC is not new, the information age has made its implementation feasible.

Marketing depends on personal contacts made by sales representatives, and these calls represent a key channel of communication for the firm. Personal selling accounts for more than 50 percent of the marketing budget, and it costs more than $456 to close each sale.[1] Thus you need to manage sales resources effectively if you expect to have a successful marketing program.

Your first job is to come up with a selling strategy and a plan of action. Then you have to locate target customers and recruit, train, motivate, compensate, and organize a field sales force. You also have to manage the interactions between customers and salespeople very carefully. This dialogue is influenced by the buyer's needs and the salesperson's skills. The results of successful salesperson–customer interactions are orders, profits, and repeat customers. An example of an effective sales manager at work is shown in Marketing in Action box 11-1.

THE ROLE OF PERSONAL SELLING

Sales managers help define the role that personal selling plays in marketing programs. In some door-to-door companies, such as Avon, personal selling dominates the marketing program almost to the exclusion of other forms of promotion. At the other extreme, book clubs and mail-order firms rely entirely on advertising and employ no field salespeople at all.

APPLYING
...to
Business-to-
Business
Marketing

MARKETING IN ACTION *11-1*

Turning It Around in Cleveland

When Frank Pacetta took over the Cleveland district sales office for Xerox, turnover was high, and revenue was the lowest in the region. Customers were complaining about erratic service and slipshod billing. Pacetta knew he had to build relations with customers, so he hired seven more sales reps. This reduced the number of large customers per rep so important customers got more attention. Pacetta spent lavishly on promotional campaigns and customer parties.

In the office he created a fraternity atmosphere with parties and pep rallies and recognition for birthdays and anniversaries. He showered reps with plaques and praise for jobs well done. He created elaborate sales contests with some winners getting $2,500 to $3,000 extra per year. Pacetta also weeded out employees who failed to meet his pumped up sales targets.

Pacetta believes sales reps should be well groomed. He hands out shoe polish, asks overweight reps to slim down, and requires that shirt collars be heavily starched. He even demands clean-shaven faces. His dress code and management style did not appeal to everyone, but in his first year the Cleveland district soared to No. 1 in the region and No. 4 among Xerox's 65 districts.

Source: James Hirsch, "To One Xerox Man, Selling Photocopiers Is a Gambler's Game," *The Wall Street Journal,* September 24, 1991, p. 1.

> **Pacetta's Selling Tips**
> - Prepare customer proposals at night and on weekends.
> - Never say no to a customer—everything is negotiable.
> - Make customers feel good by sending cards for birthdays, etc., take them to lunch and ball games.
> - Meet customers' requirements even if you must fight your own bureaucracy.
> - Do things for customers you don't get paid for, like solving billing problems.
> - Know competitive products better than they do.

THE DOCUMENT COMPANY

XEROX

Courtesy Xerox Corporation

Thus, you must decide how to balance personal selling with direct marketing, advertising, and sales promotion to achieve the goals of your organization. Next, you have to determine the source of field sales help.

Reps Versus Own Sales Force

Your first decision as sales manager is whether to hire your own sales force or to hire salespeople from independent rep organizations. Some firms adopt a strategy of spending all available cash on product development and promotion, so field sales work is left to independent representatives. Because reps are paid a percentage of sales, the companies pay only when sales are made, thereby avoiding the fixed costs of hiring, training, and supervising their own sales force. Furthermore, the firm can capitalize on the reps' already established relationships with the trade. The advantages and disadvantages of independent sales reps are summarized in Table 11-1.

TABLE 11-1   Comparing Company Salespeople with Reps

	Advantages	*Disadvantages*
Company Salespeople	1. Sell only your products 2. Can be directed to specific accounts 3. Can train them to sell by company guidelines 4. Sell full product line 5. Can be paid lower wages	1. High fixed costs 2. Takes time to hire them 3. Takes time to train them 4. Costs more initially 5. Sales grow more slowly
Independent Reps	1. Paid straight commissions so fixed costs are low 2. No need to hire or train reps 3. Produce sales quickly 4. Have established relationships with customers	1. Sell for several firms 2. Cost more as sales grow 3. Tend to push popular items 4. Only call on best accounts 5. More difficult to control

The use of a company sales force offers several advantages. For example, firms can exert more control over the activities of their own field personnel and can train them to sell according to fixed guidelines. In addition, inexperienced people can be hired and paid relatively low salaries, and these fixed costs help to keep expenses down as sales increase over time. A company's own salespeople spend all their time selling the firm's products rather than dividing their efforts among the products of several firms.

The choice between a rep strategy and a hire strategy is made on the basis of costs and benefits. When a firm is small, with limited financial and personnel resources, it may make more sense to hire independent reps. This approach conserves cash and provides more flexibility for growth. As your product line grows, however, the firm eventually reaches a point where it is more cost-effective to hire and train your own salespeople. Thus sales managers must choose between the variable costs, flexibility, and special services offered by reps and the fixed costs and greater control offered by a company sales force.

The Selling Job

Personal selling is a sequence of eight tasks (Figure 11-1). Most organizations do not have enough customers, and it is the responsibility of the field sales force to go out and discover who may need your products so as to identify new prospects. Once they are located, they must be qualified to make sure that they can use what you are selling and have the financial resources to pay for it. Then salespeople have to prepare what they will say to the prospect during the sales call. Next, the salesperson must overcome the obstacles erected by receptionists, secretaries, and assistants to gain an audience with the person with buying authority. At this point, the salesperson should try to find out something about the customer's needs. Sometimes information can be gleaned from trade gossip or talks with shop personnel. The salesperson should deliver a sales presentation tailored to fit the special needs of the prospect. This is called *adaptive selling*.

Because every sales presentation encounters objections from the prospect, the salesperson must be prepared with counterarguments. Salespeople frequently fail to try to close a sale after they have made their presentation. Salespeople do not want to be turned down, and customers can't be expected to volunteer orders. This means that sales managers must train salespeople to ask for the order. The average number of calls needed to close a sale is four, so managers need to encourage salespeople to go back again and again to get the order.

After-sale service is important in cementing relations with customers. Service work is designed to help customers solve problems related to the goods and services sold by the firm. This includes such activities as expediting orders, obtaining repair parts, setting up displays, stocking shelves, taking inventories, and training dealer personnel. Equipment salespeople, for example, often help customers rearrange machinery and personnel to improve

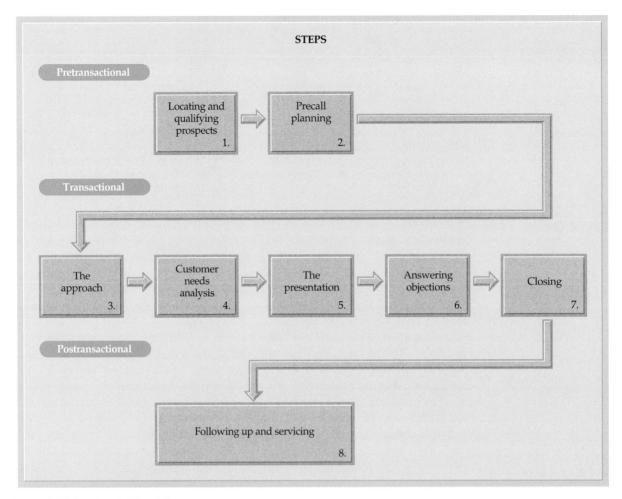

FIGURE 11-1   The Selling Job

efficiency. After the role of personal selling has been determined, managers must decide on how many salespeople to hire.

HOW MANY SALESPEOPLE?

Finding the right size for a sales force is complicated by variations in salespeople and customer needs. However, a rough idea of the personnel needed can be obtained by looking at costs and the number of customers.

What Can I Afford?

The size of the sales force is often a compromise between what the firm can afford and the total number of people needed to call on all existing and potential customers. An example of the "What can I afford?" approach suggests that a firm with $20 million in annual volume might be able to allocate 10 percent for field sales, or about $2 million a year. If supervisory expenses amounted to about 15 percent of selling costs, the firm would have $1,700,000 to hire salespeople. Assuming that salespeople cost $70,000 a year each for salary, commissions, bonus, benefits, and expenses, the company could afford to acquire 24 field salespeople. The size of the sales force is thus a direct function of the amount budgeted for field selling. The main problem with this approach is that it does not consider market potential or customers' needs.

The Workload Approach

The workload method of determining the size of the sales force is based on decisions regarding the frequency and length of calls needed to sell to existing and potential customers. An estimate of the total number of salespeople required using this approach can be made with this formula:

$$\text{Number of salespeople} = \frac{\left(\substack{\text{number of} \\ \text{existing} \\ \text{customers}} + \substack{\text{number of} \\ \text{potential} \\ \text{customers}}\right) \times \substack{\text{ideal} \\ \text{calling} \\ \text{frequency}} \times \substack{\text{length} \\ \text{of call}}}{\text{selling time available one salesperson}} \quad (11.1)$$

For example, if you had 3,000 existing customers and 2,250 potential clients to be called on five times a year for two hours (including travel time) and available selling time per salesperson was 1,500 hours, the size of the sales force would be

$$\text{Number of salespeople} = \frac{(3,000 + 2,250) \times 5 \times 2}{1,500} = 35 \quad (11.2)$$

Note that the number of salespeople based on workload estimates is larger than the number derived using the percentage of sales method. This points out the biggest weakness of the workload approach: its failure to consider the costs and profits associated with different levels of customer service. Because ideal call frequencies are based on executive judgment, you never really know if you have set the number of calls to maximize profits.

Setting Sales Force Size at Loctite

APPLYING
. . . to
Industrial
Marketing

An example showing how one firm set the size of its sales force is shown by Loctite, an industrial adhesives firm. In a push to improve profits, Loctite allowed its sales force to decline through attrition, and hired telemarketing people to fill in the gaps. Although profits increased, Loctite's reps were unable to provide adequate service to existing customers and sales growth stalled. Adhesives require a lot of technical support that could not be provided over the phone by telemarketers. The solution in this case was to hire 30 new salespeople over a one-year period; soon afterward sales began to grow. The moral of this story is that sales growth is often tied to the number of salespeople operating in the field.

Sales Force Turnover

The size of the sales force is also influenced by the problem of personnel turnover. If salespeople are constantly leaving, then unfilled territories make sales goals hard to reach. Turnover is calculated by dividing the number of separations during a year by the average size of the sales force. Thus, if 15 people leave or are fired each year and the size of the sales force is 150, then the turnover rate is

$$\text{Turnover rate} = \frac{\text{separations per year}}{\text{average size of sales force}} = \frac{15}{150} = 10\% \qquad (11.3)$$

Turnover is important because customers prefer to establish long-term relationships with suppliers. When they have to deal with a new salesperson on every contact, they are less likely to continue working with these organizations. In addition, a constant turnover of salespeople may indicate poor management supervision and cause buyers to lose confidence in a supplier. Also empty territories mean lost sales, and high turnover raises hiring and training costs. For example, assume that it costs $25,000 to recruit and train each sales force replacement. This means that a turnover of 30 percent in a sales force of 150 people would cost the firm $1,125,000 (0.30 × 150 × $25,000 = $1,125,000).

INTEGRATING
. . . with
Human
Resource
Management

When turnover costs $1 million a year, sales managers seek ways to reduce separations. Turnover can be cut by balancing territories and by improving the financial rewards paid to salespeople. Another way to lower turnover is to offer a variety of nonfinancial rewards such as trips, prizes for sales contests, plaques, trophies, and recognition awards. All these techniques are designed to make salespeople feel better about their jobs and to reduce the attractiveness of outside offers.

We have discussed the problems of high turnover, but turnover can be too low as well. For instance, when a sales force has no turnover, it could mean the salespeople are happy with their job. There is immediate suspicion, however, that the salespeople may be resting on their laurels, overpaid, or both. A lack of turnover may also signal that salespeople are all of the same age. The situation can be serious because they are likely to retire at the same time, and the firm will have to recruit and train an entirely new sales force. The ideal situation is to have salespeople of various ages so that a few retire each year and new recruits can be added on a regular basis. For example, if the average sales career spans 20 years, then 5 percent of the sales force would retire each year. Because some salespeople leave before they retire—because of promotions, resignations, or dismissals—a turnover rate of 10 to 15 percent a year can be considered normal. Beyond the issues of size is the problem of how to build an efficient sales organization.

ORGANIZING THE SALES FORCE

In small firms with only a few employees, the sales force usually reports directly to the president of the company. However, when firms grow larger, there is often an opportunity to raise productivity by adding sales managers. An example of a line sales organization employing two regional and six district sales managers is shown in Figure 11-2. In this case, 12 salespeople report to each district sales manager. This span of control can vary from 6 to 1 to 14 to 1 or more, depending on the type of product. Narrow spans of control are used for expensive technical products and wider spans of control are used for simpler consumer products.

As sales organizations grow larger, it is often necessary to hire additional staff personnel. For example, Figure 11-3 shows staff recruiters, trainers, and sales analysts reporting to a national sales manager. These staff specialists act as advisers to the general sales manager and interface with the regional and district sales managers.

Field salespeople are usually organized around geographic control units. Each salesperson is given an area, and these areas are grouped into districts and regions headed by sales managers. In a straight geographic orientation, salespeople sell all products to all customers in their territories (Figure 11-3, Western Region). Geographic organization produces the smallest territories and is the most economical way to structure a sales force. Only one person calls on each customer, and there is no cross-travel.

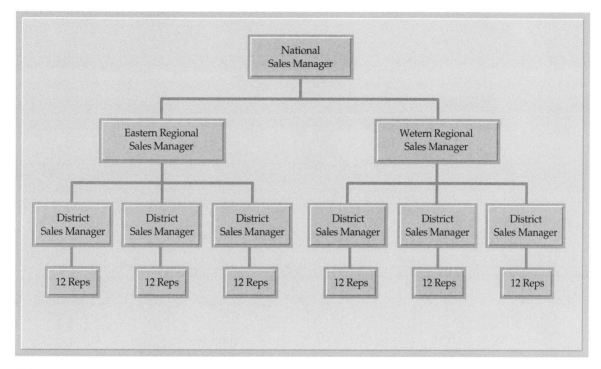

FIGURE 11-2   A Line Sales Organization

Organizing salespeople around customers makes sense when customers have unique purchasing requirements (Figure 11-3, Central Region). For example, one computer company uses a customer approach, with one sales team selling data entry systems to banks and a second group selling to other retailers. When companies have a diverse, highly technical product line, it may be desirable to hire salespeople to sell groups of products (Figure 11-3, Eastern Region). Under this plan, salespeople are product specialists, so it is unlikely that buyers will become bored during sales presentations. Salespeople who focus on groups of customers or products tend to work larger territories, and the resulting cross-travel increases selling expenses. To help control costs, customer and product salespeople often operate out of district sales offices that are organized on a geographic basis. Geographic-, product-, and customer-oriented sales forces have all been used successfully, and some firms switch back and forth, depending on the needs of the times.

RECRUITING AND SELECTING SALESPEOPLE

After you have decided on the dimensions of the sales force, you have to hire salespeople. Basically, two recruiting strategies are available. You can recruit experienced salespeople who can be placed in the field immediately, or you can hire inexperienced people and teach them product knowledge and sales skills. Although experienced salespeople must be paid higher wages, they begin producing orders sooner and in larger amounts than new trainees. Small firms selling technical products often hire experienced people because they lack the time, personnel, or facilities to train new employees. Larger companies, on the other hand,

APPLYING
. . . to
Business-to-
Business
Marketing

have the resources to train new salespeople to follow directions and act in a prescribed manner with customers. One of the risks of hiring experienced sales personnel is that they have changed jobs in the past and are more likely to be hired away by competitors. The advantages of hiring experienced reps is shown by Information Systems of America, which sells

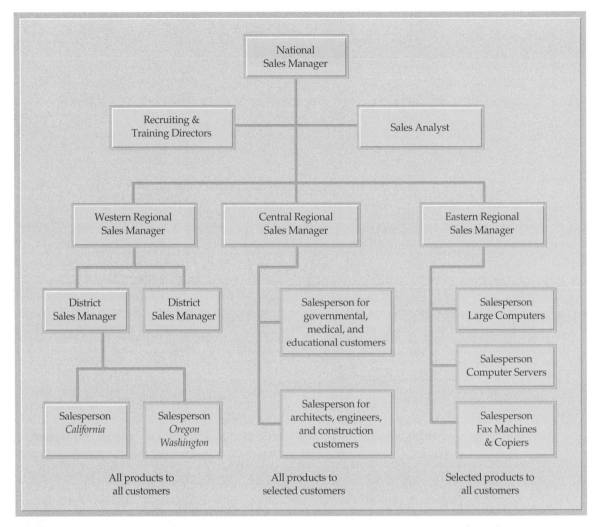

FIGURE 11-3   A Line and Staff Sales Organization Using Geographic, Customer, and Product Specialization

financial applications software. People with related selling experience are able to master the product line quickly and training costs have been slashed to $3,000 per person.

Screening Procedures

INTEGRATING
. . . with
Human
Resource
Management

Once you have accumulated a pool of candidates from Web site announcements or searches, newspaper ads, visits to schools and colleges, and employment agencies, the next step is to select and hire the best salespersons (Figure 11-4). This job is complicated by a need to fill open territories quickly and by the fear that poorly selected salespeople may damage your firm's relations with important customers.

As a result, companies spend more time screening applicants for sensitive industrial sales positions than they do for more routine selling jobs. In the case of retail delivery people, door-to-door salespeople, and insurance agents, turnover is high, and it doesn't pay to spend a lot of time searching for the perfect candidate. With these jobs, the best policy is to place recruits on the job as quickly as possible and let the "sink or swim" policy identify those with the most potential.

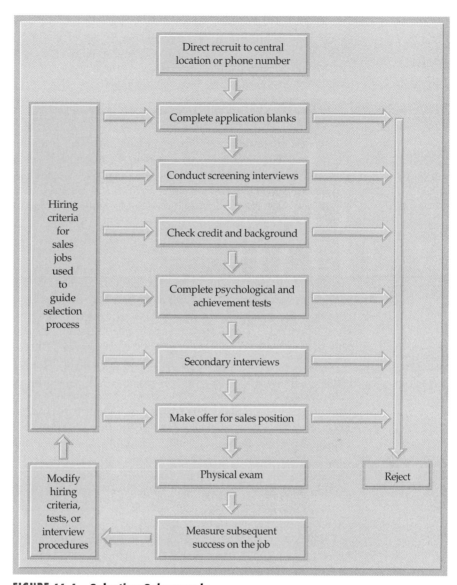

FIGURE 11-4   Selecting Salespeople

There are no hard-and-fast rules guaranteed to match job requirements with the best candidates. You have to weigh the job qualifications against the background of the applicants and make a decision. The best approach is to have candidates fill out application blanks, go through a series of interviews, have references checked, and complete aptitude and psychological tests (Figure 11-4).

Application blanks are a standard screening device for sales positions because it is essential that salespeople be able to read and write. They also provide useful background information on educational level and experience that can be explored during personal interviews. However, federal regulations prohibit questions related to age, sex, race, marital status, financial position, national origin, and other subjects. As a result, sales managers tend to place more emphasis on testing and personal interviews to screen sales candidates. Hiring tests are widely used, but they have to be validated to show a correlation between test scores and job performance.

Another way to evaluate sales candidates is to send out candidates with a regular sales-person to see how they react to actual field selling conditions. In one insurance company, candidates selected after exposure to conditions in the field were much more successful than salespeople selected by other methods.

MOTIVATING AND COMPENSATING SALESPEOPLE

Salespeople are rewarded with compensation and other incentives to help inspire them to do a better job. The ideal compensation plan motivates salespeople to achieve both their own goals and the company's objectives at the same time. Sometimes the desire of salespeople to make money for themselves conflicts with the firm's need to control sales expenses. Thus you have the difficult task of designing compensation programs that motivate the sales force without financially ruining the company.

Straight Salary

Perhaps the simplest reward system for salespeople involves paying a fixed amount each pay period. *Straight salary* rewards people for time spent on job responsibilities and was used by 7 percent of the firms reported in Table 11-2. The major benefits of salary are more control over wage levels and generally lower compensation for field salespeople. For example, senior sales reps on salary make an average of $64,900 compared with $122,900 for those on straight commission.[2] With a salary plan, wages are a fixed cost to the firm, and the proportion of wage expense tends to decrease as sales increase. Another advantage of salary is that it allows maximum control over salespeople's activities. Salaried employees can be directed to sell particular products, call on certain customers, and perform a variety of nonselling jobs for customers. Because a salesperson's income is not tied to the volume of business done with specific customers, it is easier for the sales manager to divide territories and reassign salespeople to new areas. Further, salaried salespeople exhibit higher loyalty to the firm than employees under

other plans. Salary plans are common in industrial selling, where service and engineering skills are important. Salary is also effective when salespersons spend their time calling on retailers to set up displays, take inventory, and arrange shelves. Pharmaceutical detail people, for example, are not expected to make direct sales and are paid a salary to strengthen relations with doctors and pharmacists. Because pay is not tied directly to performance, salary systems are often criticized for failing to provide incentives for extra effort.

Commission Plans

Ten percent of firms pay salespeople a percentage of the sales or gross profits that they generate (Table 11-2). The straight commission plan rewards people for their accomplishments

TABLE 11-2   Use of Compensation Plans

Method	Percentage of Companies Using
Straight Salary	7
Straight Commission	10
Salary Plus Bonus	34
Salary Plus Commission	21
Salary Plus Bonus Plus Commission	24
Commission Plus Bonus	4
Total	100%

Source: Donald W. Jackson, John L. Schlacter, and William G. Wolfe, "Examining the Bases Utilized for Evaluating Salespeoples' Performance," *Journal of Personal Selling & Sales Management,* Vol. 15, No. 4 (Fall 1995), p. 59.

rather than for their time. Also, salespeople who are paid commissions typically make more money than with other wage programs. Higher wages tend to attract better-qualified applicants and provide a strong incentive to work hard. For example, most new car salespeople in the United States are paid a 20 to 25 percent commission on the gross profit produced on each car sold. This plan encourages salespeople to sell cars at prices as high as possible to maximize returns to the dealer and the salesperson.

The advantages of a commission plan are shown in Figure 11-5. Notice that when sales per person are low, the costs of the commission plan are low. In contrast, the fixed-cost salary plan ($32,000) gives higher costs when sales are low. Companies that want to minimize their financial risk can choose variable-cost commission plans. Firms that want to minimize compensation costs as sales grow use fixed-cost salary programs. Thus, in Figure 11-5, when sales are less than $400,000 per year, the commission plan results in lower total costs for the company. But when sales exceed $400,000 a year, the straight salary plan costs less. Thus small firms use the commission plan to get started and then tend to shift to the salary plan as they grow larger.

Despite some obvious advantages, straight commission has a number of drawbacks. The major problem is that sales managers have little control over commission salespeople, and nonselling activities are likely to be neglected. Commission salespeople are tempted to sell themselves rather than the company, as well as to service only the best accounts in their territories. Because salespeople's wages are directly related to sales to particular accounts, salespeople are often reluctant to have their territories changed in any way.

Combination Plans

The most common compensation plan, used by 79 percent of firms, combines a base salary with a commission and/or bonus (Table 11-2). The base salary provides salespeople with

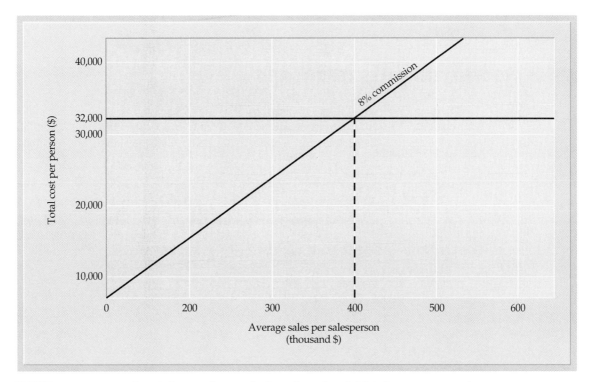

FIGURE 11-5 Comparing Salary and Commission Plans for Field Sales Representatives

income security and the commission and/or bonus give added incentives to meet the company's objectives.

These plans allow wages to be tailored to the needs of a particular firm. If an organization wanted a modest incentive, the plan could be designed so that 80 percent of the compensation was salary and 20 percent was earned by commissions or bonuses. Firms that needed more *push* to move their products could raise the incentive portion to 40 percent or more.

Some firms start paying commissions on the first dollar of sales; others establish base points or quotas that must be reached before commissions or bonuses are paid. Many organizations vary commission rates by sales volume or by the profitability of groups of products. For example, one industrial fastener company pays a base salary of about $30,000 a year, plus a commission that varies from 0.3 to 1 percent of sales and a discretionary bonus for reps who show good sales increases.

When products are largely presold by advertising, like many consumer items, it does not make sense to pay a salary plus a commission to push for added volume. Procter & Gamble spends more money on advertising and promotion to *pull* its detergents, diapers, and tissues through the channel of distribution than any other packaged goods company in the United States. Under these conditions, a salary plus a bonus is enough to get the job done.

Sales managers can obtain guidelines about current pay levels by reviewing surveys published by the Dartnell Corporation, the Conference Board, and trade and industry associations. For example, Table 11-3 shows typical pay levels for combination plans in sales organizations in 1996. Note that the highest pay goes to top sales executives followed by regional sales managers. First-level field sales managers ($83,700) earn more than the key account reps ($71,200). However, sales managers may earn less than the top rep in their district. Also other studies suggest that the relatively low pay of telesales reps ($33,900) can lead to morale problems and high turnover. On the other hand, having positions such as key account rep in the middle of the compensation range provides incentives for trainees and telesales reps to move up the promotion ladder. Although sales trainees start with a base salary of $28,800, they usually get a car, an expense account, and an opportunity to earn a bonus.

DESIGNING EFFICIENT SALES TERRITORIES

Dividing customers into geographic territories improves both market coverage and customer relations. Territories encourage salespeople to get to know their customers' needs and allow managers to evaluate sales performance more easily. Sales territories are constructed from

TABLE 11-3 **Compensation Levels for Firms Using Salary Plus Incentives, 1998**

Position	Salary ($000)	Incentive ($000)	Total Compensation ($000)
Top Sales Executive	$91.0	$29.0	$119.9
Regional Sales Manager	74.5	21.9	96.4
National Account Manager	72.2	26.0	98.2
District Sales Manager	64.5	20.3	84.8
Key Account Rep	57.4	22.3	80.3
Senior Sales Rep	47.5	26.0	73.5
Intermediate Rep	36.1	15.3	51.4
Entry Level Rep	29.7	13.4	43.1

Source: Sales Force Compensation Survey (Chicago: Dartnell Corporation, 1999), p. 28.

groups of present and potential customers and assigned to individual salespeople to help ensure adequate customer contact, minimize selling costs, and simplify control. Territory design is a never-ending task because customers, products, and salespeople change regularly and territorial boundaries must be adjusted to meet the new conditions.

The Buildup Method

The most popular technique used to create sales territories is the *buildup* method. This approach follows a five-part decision process:

1. Select a geographic control unit.
2. Decide on allocation criteria.
3. Choose starting points.
4. Combine adjacent control units.
5. Compare territories on allocation criteria.

Geographic control units usually are counties, but they can be states, zip code areas, or census tracts. Control units must be small enough to allow flexibility in setting boundaries, yet not so small that the areas lose their identity. States, for example, are often too large for effective combination into sales territories, and census tracts may be unnecessarily small. The selection of appropriate control units for individual companies depends on the availability of data on population, sales, and prospective customers in each of the areas.

Allocation Criteria: An equitable way to group control units into territories would be to divide the market to minimize differences in the number of present customers and the amount of sales potential per territory. Equal opportunity territories can lead to better morale and greater incentive to earn a better living. In addition, similar territories make it easier for the sales manager to identify and reward outstanding performance. If territories are essentially the same, differences in productivity can be attributed to individual effort.

Combining Control Units: Suppose that you have the problem of dividing a territory that has become too large for one person to handle. A map of the territory is shown in Figure 11-6a, with the numbers of present accounts in each county labeled. The salesperson currently assigned to the territory lives in Brockton. A logical home base for the second salesperson is Hillsdale, located in the west center of the territory. If these cities are used as starting points, new territories can be constructed by adding and subtracting adjacent counties until all the counties are assigned and the number of customers is the same for both territories.

One solution to this problem is shown in Figure 11-6b. Note that the heavy concentration of customers in the Brockton area has produced one small territory in the eastern region and one very large territory in the west. Although the two new territories have the same number of customers (225), the western territory requires considerably more travel because the customers are more scattered. In addition, the western territory is likely to have greater sales potential than the small eastern territory.

Designing Territories by Computer

Computer are now routinely used to help design sales territories. Sales managers can save a great deal of time by building territories with computer programs. The simplest computer programs display territory data on computer screens and allow the manager to use the buildup method to create improved sales territories. More sophisticated design programs are also available that allow managers to balance territories optimally using several factors and minimize drive time. MapInfo advertises a ProAlign program that automatically optimizes sales territories and shows the results on a computer screen. The heart of this program is a TerrAlign algo-

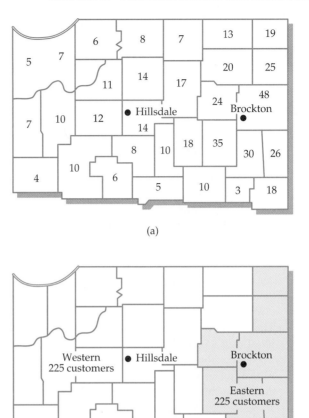

(a)

FIGURE 11-6   Dividing a Large Territory

rithm that searches out the optimum realignment solution.[3] Computer programs have been successfully used to build territories for pharmaceutical reps and for salespeople who call on supermarkets. Sales managers are generally pleased with the computer territories; they feel the solutions are imaginative, realistic, and relieve them of a major clerical burden.

ALLOCATING SELLING EFFORT

Careful scheduling of sales calls can minimize travel time and expenses. One firm has reported that an analysis of driving patterns reduced the travel of salespeople by 15,000 miles a year and allowed each salesperson to make eight more calls a week. Techniques used to schedule and route salespeople have received considerable attention from management scientists, and the issue has become known as the *traveling salesman problem.* The dilemma is usually stated as a search for a route through the territory that visits each customer and returns to the starting point with a minimum expenditure of time or money.

A variety of techniques can be employed to search for the best routes for salespeople, including linear programming, nonlinear programming, heuristic programming, and branch-and-bound methods. They all appear to provide good solutions. One disadvantage of these methods is that they require complicated manipulations of travel costs between cities to find the optimal route. A simpler way to find the best sequence of calls is based on a consideration of the location of points in two-dimensional space.

Four basic rules should be followed when designing routes through a sales territory:

1. Tours should be circular.
2. Sales tours should never cross.
3. The same route should not be used to go to and from a customer.
4. Customers in neighboring areas should be visited in sequence.

The idea of circular tours is reasonable because salespeople usually start at a home base and then return at the end of the sales trip. Also, if sales tours cross, the salesperson knows that a shorter route was overlooked.

EVALUATING SALES PERFORMANCE

Evaluation is a complex task because salespeople and territories are all different, and field reps spend most of their time away from their supervisors. In addition, salespeople perform a vast array of jobs, and there are a host of control measures that can be used to monitor their activities. Traditionally, managers have relied on qualitative measures such as product knowledge, selling skills, communication skills, number of calls, and number of days worked to evaluate salespeople. Research has suggested that there is a trend away from input based measures and an increase in output factors such as sales to quota, sales growth, orders secured, size of order, and gross margin per sale.[4] It is your job to design a performance evaluation system that looks at all the dimensions of the salesperson's job and helps the firm achieve its objectives. A computer program that can help managers monitor salespeople is described in Marketing in Action box 11-2.

Sales by Territory

Territorial sales at Bear Computer are shown in Table 11-4. At first glance, things look good because dollar sales are up in all four territories. Also, overall growth is 8.3 percent in the current year, which compares favorably with the performance achieved in 1999. The largest dollar increases in sales were achieved in territories 1 and 3, and the weakest performance was in territory 4. However, these results take on a different meaning if you look at the sales potential of the four territories.

If actual sales in territory 1 of $825,000 are divided by planned sales of $943,000, the sales manager finds that this territory is running about 13 percent below expectations. Territory 3 has not achieved planned sales even though it has the largest potential of all (32 percent). Territory 4, which had the lowest dollar increase, was still able to sell 102 percent of the sales plan. Thus, the two territories with large dollar increases in computer sales actually were the two weakest territories when sales are related to potential. The best performance

TABLE 11-4 Analyzing Territorial Sales in the Eastern Division of the Bear Computer Company, 1999–2000

Territory	Sales 1999 Jan–Sept ($000)	Sales 2000 Jan–Sept ($000)	Dollar Change ($000)	Market Potential Index (%)	Planned Sales ($000)	Percentage of Plan Achieved	Sales Variance ($000)
1	$750	$825	+$75	26%	$943	87%	–$118
2	500	570	+70	15	543	105	+27
3	1025	1110	+85	32	1160	96	–50
4	960	1000	+40	27	977	102	+23
Total	$3235	$3505	+$270	100%	$3623		

MARKETING IN ACTION *11-2*

Using Computers to Eliminate Paperwork

Sales departments are often the last area in an organization to take advantage of computers. After reviewing sales statistics at RealWorld Corporation, the national sales manager realized that the sales force was becoming stagnant. Further research revealed that salespeople were buried in mountains of paper, with lists and tickler files everywhere. The company decided it was time to introduce a computer system for field sales reps. The objective was to make the salespeople more efficient so that they could make more calls and keep better track of existing proposals and accounts. They also wanted the sales managers to have more control over the field reps.

RealWorld looked for a computer program that included tickler reports, lists, a calendar, personal notepad, word processing, calculator, activity reports, proposals, and the ability to generate orders. Existing packages were unable to fill the bill, so RealWorld developed its own system. Next, it ran a field test and found that reps using the new program increased sales 16 percent compared to salespeople operating with the old manual system. This success prompted RealWorld to equip all 35 reps with laptop computers.

Since the new computer system was installed at RealWorld, the volume of contracts, number of proposals, and dollar sales have increased 10 to 20 percent due to better organization. Leads are handled more rapidly and are no longer lost in the shuffle. Also, sales managers are better able to track the productivity of each rep and to print reports and graphs to monitor results.

— *Giving salespeople laptop computers can increase efficiency.*

Source: Sam Licciardi, "Paper-Pushing Sales Reps Are Less Productive," *Marketing News,* Vol. 24, No. 23, November 12, 1990, p. 15.

Courtesy RealWorld Corporation

was achieved in territory 2, which had the smallest potential in the division and was third in terms of dollar sales growth. These results suggest that you should consider cutting the size of territory 3 and giving some of this potential to the salesperson who is currently handling territory 2. This change should increase total sales of the division, for the salesperson in territory 3 is not covering this large market adequately.

TABLE 11-5   Analyzing Sales by Product Line, Bear Computer Company

Product Line	Industry Sales Ratio (%)	Actual Sales ($000)	Bear Sales Ratio (%)	Forecast ($000)	Variance ($000)
Computers	60%	$18,200	70%	$18,816	–$616
Accessories	20	5,200	20	5,000	+200
Software	20	2,600	10	3,064	–464
Total	100%	$26,000	100%	$26,880	–880

Sales by Products

Breakdowns by products are also useful in evaluating sales performance (Table 11-5). Industry figures suggest that Bear Computer should sell 60 percent of its volume in basic computers, 20 percent in accessory equipment, and 20 percent in computer software. Actual sales figures in 2000 show that Bear is selling 70 percent computers, 20 percent accessories, and only 10 percent in the software category. This heavy emphasis on machine sales can lead to long-run problems, because customers will not have enough programs to use their computers effectively. Perhaps existing commission rates encourage salespeople to push the sales of higher-priced machines rather than lower-priced software.

Another breakdown that provides valuable information for the sales manager is based on the number of units sold (Table 11-6). Unit sales are useful when inflation and other price changes distort dollar sales figures. For example, dollar sales of Bear computers went from $16.8 million in 1999 to $18.2 million in 2000. However, unit sales actually declined from 560 to 520 over the same period, meaning that the average price of a Bear computer went from $30,000 in 1999 to $35,000 in 2000. Although some of the 17 percent increase in computer prices was due to inflation, some other factor is contributing to this change. The data suggest that the sales force is trading customers up to the most expensive computers in the line. Another breakdown of unit sales by individual models of Bear computers would tell you what items are being ignored. Unit sales growth is desirable because it keeps production lines and employees busy.

A somewhat different situation exists with Bear's line of accessory equipment (Table 11-6). Note that dollar and unit sales both increased between 1999 and 2000. Unit sales grew much more rapidly than dollar sales, however, and the average unit price dropped from $1,200 in 1999 to $1,100 in 2000. These results suggest that the sales force is cutting prices to boost unit volume. This push for market share is to be applauded as long as profit margins are not completely destroyed.

Cost Analysis

Although a sales analysis provides useful data on the operation of a field sales force, it does not tell the whole story. Sales figures show general trends, but they do not reveal the effects

TABLE 11-6   Sales by Products and Units for Bear Computer Company, 2000 versus 1999

Product Line	1999 Sales			2000 Sales		
	Thousands of Dollars	Units	Average Price per Unit	Thousands of Dollars	Units	Average Price per Unit
Computers	$16,800	560	$30,000	$18,200	520	$35,000
Accessories	4,800	4000	1,200	5,200	4727	1,100
Software	2,400	1200	2,000	2,600	1280	2,031
Total	$24,000	5760		$26,000	6527	

of price cutting or the differences in selling costs, potential, and saturation that exist across products or territories.

INTEGRATING
. . . with Accounting

An example of a territorial cost review is shown in Table 11-7 for the Bear Computer Company. The analysis begins with net sales for each territory, from which the cost of goods sold and sales commissions are then subtracted. The resulting contribution margin is greatest in territory 4, even though territory 3 had the highest sales. Note that territories 1 and 4 had high contribution percentages compared with territories 2 and 3. Salespeople in territories 2 and 3 are apparently pushing low-margin products and are cutting prices to gain volume.

Another selling cost issue is raised by the activities of the salesperson in territory 1. This territory produced almost as much contribution margin as territory 3 and had an outstanding contribution percentage, but the resulting profit contribution in territory 1 was $7,700 less than that generated in territory 3. The explanation for this difference lies in the various expense categories. Although the salary of the salesperson ($42,000) seems reasonable, the amounts spent on travel, food and lodging, and entertainment appear to be high. Although salespeople in the other three territories averaged $9,700 for these expenses, the person in territory 1 spent $17,400. The typical response of a sales manager to expenditures of this size would be to pressure the salesperson to cut back so that the profit contribution will increase. These above-average expenditures might explain why territory 1 was generating a 40 percent contribution margin on sales. The salesperson is apparently entertaining customers so effectively that they are buying high-margin computers at list price, although it is possible that the salesperson is using the expense account to offer customers under-the-table discounts on the computers. If these travel, food, and entertainment expenditures are legitimate, the manager might consider asking the other salespeople to increase their spending on these items.

Jones Versus Smith

An example comparing the performance of two sales reps is presented in Table 11-8. The data show that although Pete Jones had high sales, Ann Smith worked more days, made more calls, had lower expenses, and landed more orders. As a result, Smith made one more call per day and had a 50 percent batting average (orders per calls). Although Jones closed the sale on only 40 percent of his calls, he had a high average-order size. Thus, despite lower values for days worked, calls per day, and batting average, Jones obtained larger orders and the highest total sales volume.

TABLE 11-7   Analyzing Costs and Profits of the Southern District of the Bear Computer Company

	Territory Performance ($000)			
	1	*2*	*3*	*4*
Net Sales	$825	$570	$1110	$1000
Less: CGS and commissions	495	428	777	660
Contribution margin	330	142	333	340
Contribution margin as a percentage of sales	40%	25%	30%	34%
Less: Direct selling costs				
Sales force salaries	42.0	25.0	45.0	55.0
Travel	8.5	4.1	5.5	5.0
Food and lodging	6.5	4.0	4.2	4.5
Entertainment	2.4	0.3	0.5	1.0
Home sales office expense	4.5	2.0	4.0	4.5
	$63.9	$35.4	$59.2	$70.0
Profit contribution	$266.1	$106.6	$273.8	$270.0
Profit contribution as a percentage of sales	32%	19%	25%	27%

TABLE 11-8   Evaluating Individual Performance

Performance Factors	Peter Jones	Ann Smith
Sales	$1,000,000	$650,000
Days worked	210	225
Calls	1,200	1,500
Orders	480	750
Expenses	$22,000	$14,300
Calls per day	5.7	6.7
Batting average (orders per calls)	40%	50%
Average order	$2,083	$866
Expenses per call	$18.33	$9.53
Expenses per sales	2.2%	2.2%

In this case, you might be tempted to encourage Ann Smith to increase the size of her average order. Larger orders should increase total sales but would probably result in fewer and longer sales calls and a reduction in her batting average. Fewer calls per day produced larger orders in Jones's territory, but it is not clear that this strategy would work as well for Smith. The differences in performance may be due to the presence of many large firms in Jones's territory and mostly small companies in Smith's area. The data in Table 11-8 suggest that managers need to understand differences in selling styles and character of each territory when evaluating performance data.

Performance Rankings

One way to simplify sales force comparisons is to convert performance results into rankings. The rankings can then be added up to give an overall measure of efficiency. For example, Table 11-9 shows how five salespeople ranked on 10 different control factors. Sales per person is a good overall measure, but it can be deceiving. Note that Ford had the highest total sales but was last on sales-to-potential, suggesting that his volume was due to a large territory. Gold, on the other hand, had low volume and high sales-to-potential, indicating good coverage of a limited market. Sales-to-quota is also popular, showing primarily a salesperson's ability to increase revenue. Sometimes attainment of quotas qualifies salespeople for special commissions or bonuses.

Sales per order is important because many firms have found that small orders are unprofitable. Thus, salespeople who sell large quantities to each customer are viewed as the most efficient. Ford, for example, achieves a high sales volume by making a large number of calls and selling small amounts to each customer (Table 11-9). The ratio of orders to calls

INTEGRATING . . . *with Human Resource Management*

TABLE 11-9   Ranking Salespeople on 10 Input/Output Factors

Ranking Factors	Ford	Bell	Shaw	Mann	Gold
Dollar sales	❶	2	3	4	5
Sales to potential	5	3	4	2	❶
Sales to quota	5	4	2	❶	3
Sales per order	5	❶	4	3	2
Number of calls	2	5	❶	3	4
Orders per call	4	2	5	3	❶
Gross margin percent	5	❶	3	4	2
Direct selling costs	4	3	5	❶	2
New accounts	❶	4	2	5	3
Number of reports turned in	4	3	❶	5	2
Total of ranks	36	28	30	31	25

measures the ability of the salesperson to convert prospects into buyers. Sometimes called the *batting average,* this ratio shows how successful salespeople are at closing sales presentations.

The gross margin percentage achieved by salespeople shows how good they are at controlling prices and selling the right mix of products. Table 11-9 suggests that Ford's low margins are the result of price cutting to open new accounts and boost sales. Direct selling costs usually vary with the size of a territory, and salespeople have only limited control over these costs.

The performance of the five salespeople in Table 11-9 varied widely across the 10 factors, and each person ranked first on two criteria and last on at least one factor. If all of the criteria are considered equal in importance, then the ranks can be added down to give a measure of overall performance.

This procedure shows that Bell, Shaw, and Mann had total performance scores close to the expected value of 30 points, whereas the scores of Ford and Gold were different enough to warrant special attention. Note that although Ford had the highest sales volume, he actually had the worst overall record, whereas Gold was doing an excellent job despite low sales volume. The most obvious change suggested is to shift some of Ford's territory to Gold, giving Gold more to do and providing better coverage for some of Ford's customers. Also, Ford should be encouraged to work for larger orders and told to stop cutting prices.

SUMMARY

Selling is a personal encounter between the salesperson and customers, and the firm must understand how this relationship works. If salespeople with certain characteristics are more successful than others, it may pay to select or train field representatives to fill these needs. The optimum size of the sales force is obtained by hiring salespeople until the marginal profit from an additional salesperson is equal to the marginal cost of adding another person. In the absence of sales response data, the firm can set the size of the sales force on the basis of what it can afford or the actual workload. The creation of equitable territories for salespeople is important for building morale and improving the efficiency of the sales organization. Sales territories are usually created by combining geographic areas, and the computer has proved to be a great help in speeding up this tedious, recurring task. Once sales territories have been created, you must decide how to deploy the sales force to cover different customers and product lines. In addition, the careful scheduling and routing of salespeople through their territories can reduce expenses and increase the number of calls that can be made. Salespeople also must be rewarded for their services, and the design of compensation plans is one of the most creative jobs performed by sales managers. The idea is to provide a blend of salary, bonuses, commissions, and noncash incentives that stimulates the salespeople to work hard, maximizing the profits of the firm at the same time. This requires decisions on what factors measure success and the subsequent inclusion of these criteria in a sales reporting system that is both easy to use and economical to operate.

NOTES

1. The average intermediate salesperson on salary plus incentives costs $75,014 in wages, benefits, and expenses per year. Since they make about 660 calls per year and it takes 4 calls to close a sale, the cost is ($75,014)/(660) = $114 × 4 = $456 cost to close. (*Sales Force Compensation Survey* [Chicago: Dartnell Corp., 1999], pp. 20, 50.)

2. Christen P. Heide, *Sales Force Compensation Survey* (Chicago: Dartnell Corporation, 1999), p. 49.

3. *Sales & Marketing Management* (May 1998), p. 23.

4. Jackson, Donald W., John L. Schlacter, and William G. Wolf, "Examining the Bases Utilized for Evaluating Salespeoples' Performance," *Journal of Personal Selling & Sales Management,* Vol. 115, No. 4 (Fall 1995), p. 64.

SUGGESTED READING

"The 25 Best Sales Forces," *Sales & Marketing Management* (July 1998), pp. 32–50.

Bollinger, Caroline. "Building a Sales Force from Scratch," *Sales & Marketing Management* (February 1998), pp. 26–28.

REFERENCES

Brooks, William T. *Niche Selling: How to Find Your Customer in a Crowded Market* (Homewood, IL: Business One Irwin, 1992).

Churchill, Gilbert A., Neil M. Ford, and Orville C. Walker, Jr. *Sales Force Management,* 4th ed. (Homewood, IL: Irwin, 1990).

Dalrymple, Douglas J., and William L. Cron. *Sales Management: Concepts and Cases,* 6th ed. (New York: John Wiley & Sons, 1998).

Stanton, William J., and Rosann L. Spiro. *Management of a Sales Force,* 10th ed. (Chicago: Irwin, 1999).

QUESTIONS

1. Precision Cutting Tools manufactures industrial products for a national market. Until recently, they employed 12 salespeople to call on accounts. Dissatisfied with the results, the sales manager discharged all 12 in favor of 9 independent manufacturer's representatives. (Manufacturer's reps are not employed by the company; usually they sell for a number of companies.) The rep in this case sold other industrial products along with the Precision line to the same customers. Immediately, sales began to increase, old business was retrieved, and new accounts were acquired. What possible reasons might explain this? What are the advantages and disadvantages of manufacturer's reps compared to an in-house sales force?

2. Phil Tumminia, director of the Glassboro State College Development Fund in southern New Jersey, made a cold call on a local industrialist in 1990, and asked for and received a gift of $1,500. On succeeding calls, he got $3 million for the library, $20 million for the business school, and finally $100 million for a new engineering school. Why did personal sales calls work better than direct mail, phone calls, or media advertising for this tiny college's development program?

3. A district sales manager said, "I have a rule I never break. I only hire salespeople who are in their thirties, married, with three or more kids, and carrying mortgages as big as the Ritz. That way, they'll need me more than I'll need them, and I know they'll be back on the job each and every morning." Comment on this statement. Are there other ways to minimize turnover of the sales force?

4. Suppose an office supplies dealer has 750 large customers that need to be called on each month, 1,500 medium-size firms that should be called on every six weeks, and 3,000 small organizations that need to be serviced once every quarter. Given that salespeople make 10 calls per week, how many salespeople are needed?

5. Although insurance agents rarely have exclusive territories, insurance companies are finding that mapping programs are quite useful. Sales managers load demographic data, policies in force, and agent locations on computerized area maps. How would a manager use this information?

6. You are the district manager and have all the accountability that comes with the job. You have the feeling that your salespeople are not following many of your instructions. Are you becoming paranoid? John seems to be the informal leader of the salespeople in his district. Deliberately or not, he seems to have become very influential. Although John is also one of your top salespeople, district sales overall are dropping. Is there a connection? You must correct the situation soon, and you do not want to lose John because he is a valuable salesperson. Why did an informal leader emerge? How do you handle John? What can you do to prevent a recurrence?

7. A car salesperson spent three hours selling a new Nissan Maxima for $800 over cost. The dealer kept the first $600 of the gross profit and split the remaining $200 with the salesperson on a 75 percent/25 percent basis. This left the salesperson with only $50 for three hours' work, which he had to divide with another salesperson who talked with the customer over the phone. Is this system beneficial for the dealer? For the salesperson? What changes would you recommend?

8. Merck & Company, one of the largest pharmaceutical companies in the United States, uses a forced distribution of a bell curve to reward its employees. This means that the high-performing reps are paid considerably more than average or below-average reps. The strong emphasis on individual quantitative performance measures has met some resistance from those who believe in promoting group cooperation. Merck has responded to these concerns by offering a 100-share stock option grant to all employees. Staff turnover is running at a low 5 percent per year. How should Merck measure the performance of reps who call on doctors but rarely take orders? Should Merck's plan be used by other firms? Why or why not?

9. Sears has cut the base hourly pay of its salespeople who sell big-ticket items and increased their commission rates. Why has Sears made this change, and how well do you think the new plan has been received by the salespeople?

10. Julie has the talent and experience to greatly improve sales in her territory. A veteran salesperson, 15 years with the company, Julie has been a top performer in the past, but just gets by now. Her husband is a doctor and their children are on their own, so Julie's financial needs are fully met. Julie's sales volume is third in the district of five people, so it's not that she doesn't sell; it's just that her sales volume has not increased much in the past three years and you believe there is opportunity for greater sales out of her territory. Your company has recently downsized and budgets are tight. It's time to do something about Julie. How would you address this situation without losing a strong salesperson?

11. The CEO of Vanstar Corporation found that one of his top sales reps came to the office early every morning and called customers' voice mail and left messages with her opening ideas for them for the day. When she called later, the customers always took her calls personally to respond to the ideas she had left on their machines. Should the CEO incorporate this activity in the company's sales performance evaluation system? How would you measure performance on this activity?

12. You are a sales manager for an industrial manufacturer. The performance of one of your salespeople, James Weber, has slipped; he has achieved only 75 percent of his quota for the past six months. The average sales quota achievement in your district is 90 percent. Weber has worked for your firm for six years and has a bachelor's degree in business administration. Jim's territory is above average in potential but requires considerable travel. At the recent company picnic, Weber seemed depressed and spent his time drinking rather than interacting with the other salespeople. Weber is divorced, and his ex-wife lives in another city with their three children. You have decided that it is time to call in Weber for a conference. Develop a script for a meeting with Weber that will motivate him to work up to his potential.

13. A United Technologies employee has charged that the company's Sikorsky Division offered two Saudi princes a "bonus" of 3 to 5 percent of a $130 million portion of a $6 billion potential Blackhawk helicopter order. The employee is seeking $100 million in damages from United Technologies. What seems to be the motive of the employee in reporting the attempted bribe? Why are such "commissions" so common in foreign sales agreements? How should the company handle these demands for special favors?

14. The product manager for industrial cleaning products in the inorganic products division of a large German chemical company is concerned about the performance of the company's sales force. Information is available for 19 sales territories on the sales revenue, number of calls made, and number of inhabitants (a measure of potential). To properly appraise the performance of field representatives, the sales of giant buyers were eliminated because they dealt directly with territorial managers. Using the data in the file indchemdat.sav, assess salesforce performance. *Hint:* If you first compute the natural logarithm (LN) of each variable and then run a linear multiple regression on the transformed variables, the regression coefficients of the variables can be interpreted as elasticities.

CASE *11-1*   ARAPAHOE PHARMACEUTICAL COMPANY*   SPSS

As he reread the annual report that he had prepared for Phil Jackson, his regional sales manager, John Ziegler, shook his head and kept repeating to himself, "What a year!"

He could not forget the surge of pride he felt when his district sales manager asked him to call Phil Jackson to let him know whether or not he wanted to accept a promotion to district sales manager for the Dallas area. As he remembered, he couldn't get to the telephone quickly enough, and it was only after Phil had asked him how his wife had taken the news, that he realized that he had forgotten to ask her. He immediately telephoned Lynn and found that she was thrilled both with his promotion and the move to Dallas even though neither one of them had been there before. Lynn was particularly pleased that her company had a sales opening in Dallas and she felt that she could obtain a transfer to that city. John once again expressed his appreciation to his sales manager, Betsy Warner, for all of the help that she had given him so that he could qualify for the promotion.

John had joined Arapahoe Pharmaceutical as a sales rep immediately after graduating from San Fran-

cisco State University. While he had been interested in science in high school, and he had taken one course in chemistry and another course in biology at San Francisco State, he was more interested in marketing communications. When Arapahoe Pharmaceuticals recruited at the college in his junior year and again in the spring of his senior year, John decided that he might combine the interests in science and marketing communications as a sales representative. He was interviewed, hired, and assigned to a territory near Omaha in Betsy Warner's district. John's willingness, personality, and communications skills, plus Betsy's encouragement and guidance, helped him in quickly achieving above average productivity and allowed him to win a transfer to a territory in the greater metropolitan Denver area. The new territory offered him additional experience in working with food and drug chain headquarters, large hospitals, and drug wholesalers. John reviewed these experiences with considerable pleasure as he recalled the events of the past year. Betsy worked regularly with him, and delegated to him some of the training of new sales reps, which he found both challenging and rewarding, especially when the

* This case was prepared by Professor Richard C. Leventhal of Regis University in Denver, Colorado. Reproduced by permission.

new sales trainee did well. His selling skills flourished as did his income and the recognition of his achievements by Betsy and the regional sales manager. A year later he was selected to attend his company's leadership training program, which was a milestone in his career.

Even before his first trip to Dallas, John was asked by Tom Boyle, the general sales manager, to spend a couple of days at the corporate headquarters in Philadelphia with him and various department heads in marketing, legal and human resources. They were all very complimentary about his past performance and how much he deserved his promotion. However, each of them in a different way seemed to repeat the same message: "Managing people is different from selling products." How well the events of the past year were to bear that out. The thrust of Boyle's message was a bit different. He wanted John to realize that he had full confidence in his ability, that John had earned his promotion, and that although John was a sales rep one day, and a district sales manager the next, the company recognized the change wouldn't take place overnight and it would provide him with further training. In the meantime, Boyle advised John that the Dallas district was productive, operating efficiently, and staffed with well-trained sales reps, and that he was not expecting John to "Sweep the district clean" and make radical changes. He also emphasized that (1) John should give the sales reps in Dallas time to get to know him and he them; (2) he would be surprised and disappointed to discover that all the reps didn't operate with the same level of efficiency that he did nor use the same methods he used when he was a rep; (3) he shouldn't try to correct too many deficiencies at one time; (4) telling someone to do something doesn't necessarily get it done; (5) everyone doesn't remember hearing something the same way; and (6) it's better to have three sales reps working with you than ten working for you.

One year later, John realized that at the time he and Boyle talked, he didn't understand or appreciate the full meaning of that advice. The legal department wanted him to be aware of his increased responsibilities as a manager in speaking or acting for the company. The various departments in sales, marketing and human resources emphasized the importance of his new role and his support in administering the company's promotional programs and gaining the compliance of his sales reps. Increasingly, he realized the duality of his role as a member of management and of the field sales force. The sales management training programs he attended during the succeeding months

reinforced these points and helped prepare him for the types of problems he was to encounter.

His introduction to the ten sales reps in the Dallas district went quite well. His predecessor, Chuck Morgan, who was retiring after 30 years with Arapahoe, fully reviewed all of the sales statistics for the district and the human resource records of the sales reps. He also gave him the benefit of his thoughts for the future and what John's immediate concerns should be. John had inherited a district that was operating on target both for sales and expenses, and appeared to have no major personnel problems other than one territory that had been open for four weeks. Chuck even had two resumes on promising candidates who needed processing.

John telephoned both applicants and scheduled interviews for the following week, along with trips of two days each with two of his sales reps. The interviews seemed to go well, but they took almost a full day. On his first day at his office the following week, John called the references and previous employers of both applicants, scheduled a second interview several days later with Larry Palmer, the most promising applicant, and, in accordance with the company's interviewing procedure, set up an information session with Larry and his wife for the following evening. Since this was John's first session of this type, he was pleased that it went well. Jean Palmer, Larry's wife, had numerous questions about transferring, the amount of travel, and how much extra time that her husband would have to spend responding to e-mail and other computer-type reports. John was glad that he was able to address her concerns. The telephone conversations with the other applicant's references and previous employers had been an interesting experience and tended to confirm what the applicant had said, except in two instances. A previous employer and one reference were guardedly enthusiastic about the applicant. When John pressed the issue, the reference refused to say more, while the previous employer provided specifics which confirmed an earlier impression John had noted at the initial interview. Comments about Larry Palmer all emphasized the great personality he had and what a terrific job they thought he would do in sales. Following the second interview with Larry Palmer and the spouse information session, John completed the company's applicant appraisal reports on both applicants and decided that Larry was the better of the two. He telephoned his regional sales manager, Phil Jackson, to set up a final interview for Larry. Then he faxed Phil his applicant appraisal reports and wrote the other applicant a polite turndown letter.

The day following Larry's interview, Phil Jackson called to say that while he had some misgivings, he had hired Larry to begin training in a class at the regional office the first of the month. John's reaction was a sigh of relief because of all of the time he had put into the screening and the hope that he wouldn't have to do that too often. The reports that he completed on his first field trips with his reps took longer to prepare than he anticipated. Coupled with the correspondence and appraisal reports on the applicants, John realized that communications were going to be a bigger part of the job than he had realized. He would have to learn how to use the computerized information system in a more effective and efficient manner if he were to have the necessary time for his other responsibilities.

John's relationship with his sales reps seemed to go well during the first few months on the job, with the exception of Dick McClure, an above average producer, aged 50, with 12 years experience, and the senior man in the district. Dick had been described by Chuck Morgan as a friendly, outgoing individual with a good sense of humor and a highly individualistic style of selling. As John worked with Dick, he was able to confirm in Dick's interaction with his customers, the general description Chuck had given him. However, Dick was curt with John, relatively subdued, and at other times almost hostile. For the next several working trips, John tried to ignore Dick's conduct and concentrated on the calls that they were making and the objectives that they were trying to achieve. At a recent sales meeting, Dick seemed to take delight in being argumentative and disruptive until John jokingly asked him if he would like to take over the sales meeting. After that, Dick settled down but made almost no contribution to the discussions for the rest of the meeting.

The situation came to a head immediately following a physician call, during which Dick introduced John without indicating who he was or his purpose for being there. The physician's reaction was: "Oh a new rep, eh?" and to Dick, "Are you being promoted?" This forced Dick, somewhat embarrassed, to indicate that John was his new district sales manager. As they left the office, it was clear that Dick was furious, as he muttered in a sarcastic manner, "Are you being promoted?" John decided that it was time to take action, whereupon he said emphatically, "Dick, I don't know what is eating you, but I think that it's time that we get it out in the open. You've been complaining from the day that I arrived. You're sarcastic, uncooperative, and just as cool as ice. If you and I are going to continue to

work together, things had better change. I don't know what I have done that has upset you, but whatever it is or whatever I've said, it certainly wasn't intentional and I'm sorry. You're too good a person to go around perpetually angry. What the heck is bothering you?"

Dick's reaction was an angry, somewhat subdued and embarrassed, "I just guess it's not really your fault or anything that you did. I've been here 12 years and I'm the best rep in this district. Chuck even told me so. And bam—you get promoted and I'm left hung out to dry. Man, that's gratitude for you!"

Now that the problem was out in the open, John realized how long Dick had been carrying his anger locked up inside himself, and felt sorry for him. With that, he said, "Dick, I've sure been blind. Let's knock off and sit down somewhere to talk this thing out." Three hours later they shook hands and parted on a much better understanding. Their relationship improved steadily, and now as John reflected on the district's productivity for the past year, he realized that Dick's support had been of paramount importance in terms of the district's overall success.

Thinking about the successful year reminded him of Peggy Doyle, the sales trainee who was doing such a terrific job. She was the one who had taken Larry Palmer's place. When he thought of Larry Palmer, he winced thinking about the mistake that he had made. Larry was the first sales rep that he had recruited. He had completed the basic sales training class, but just barely. The report from the sales training manager was anything but encouraging. Larry had difficulty acquiring the necessary product knowledge and his scientific communication skills were marginal at best. The qualities that saved him from being dropped from the sales training class were his desire, his willingness to work, and the fact that he was such a great guy—everybody loved him! Notwithstanding Larry's short-comings, John was convinced he could turn Larry around. He worked with him every opportunity he had, quizzed him, coached him, and drilled him in an effort to improve his knowledge and skills so that Larry could be able to capitalize on his sincerity and personality.

As the months wore on, John became increasingly aware that while Larry's customers liked him, he couldn't sell and his sales showed it. It was a tough decision John had to make to let Larry go, and an even tougher decision to implement, but John realized it really was in everyone's best interests. As he looked back on all the time and effort he had put into Larry's ultimate failure, John realized that it was at the expense of the time and effort he should have spent with his more productive sales reps. He also realized that in spite of the overwhelming evidence, he had carried Larry much longer than he probably should have, and was thankful that Phil Jackson did not remind him of it. Sometimes, however, events have a bright side. As much as John regretted the amount of time that it took to recruit Larry's replacement, he felt that he had lucked out with Peggy Doyle. She seemed to do everything right. In the four months since she'd been in the territory, sales had taken a noticeable increase and her enthusiasm was infecting the other sales reps in the district. John hoped her progress and productivity would continue on in this manner for a long time to come. Some performance data for Peggy and the other reps are shown in Exhibits 1 and 2.

Peggy's performance, however, did not eliminate the logjam that recruiting her had created in John's other activities. Her interviews, reference checking, early sales orientation and training, plus the extra time he had spent over the last few months helping Larry try to succeed, extended the intervals since he last worked in the field with his above average sales reps, to the extent that several were beginning to make humorously sarcastic comments about being "orphans." John tried to explain that they were practically self-sufficient, while others needed his help more urgently. While they were willing to listen, John could see that they weren't buying into his excuse.

To further compound the problem, he received an e-mail that his semiannual appraisal interviews were to begin within 30 days. This would be the second time he would be holding these performance reviews, but it would be the first time alone since Phil Jackson had helped him. As John began to review the trip reports and correspondence in each sales rep's file, along with sales performance data generated from the company's computerized database (Exhibits 1 and 2),[1] he realized the files of the above average producers were relatively thin. If it hadn't been for performance data, John would have been at a serious loss to justify his appraisal of their productivity.

Preparing for and conducting the performance reviews took a lot of time and this was when he really earned his salary. When the reps and John had different evaluations, the differences were resolved and then it became a matter of jointly agreeing on a plan of action to close the gap between actual and desired performance. As difficult as it was to achieve the agreement at times, and harder still to implement the agreed upon plan, John felt that it was at this point that he was making a significant contribution to the success of the company and the growth and development of the individual sales rep in the district.

The second appraisal and counseling session of the year had its peaks and valleys. It had been a pleasure to provide several with the recognition their performances merited, and to help them to further define the goals they would achieve for the forthcoming year. The case of Jared Murphy was another matter. Jared had been in the training class at the time John was hired. He had done reasonably well, but hadn't really lived up to his potential. Lately, Jared seemed to have lost interest. When John challenged Jared's own evaluation of his performance Jared sheepishly commented that he "wondered whether you'd let it pass." When John pressed him for an explanation of his performance in view of the potential in his terri-

---

[1] Data on sales, number of calls, and physicians in territory are in file arapahoedat.sav. Peggy's data has been annualized.

EXHIBIT 1   **Performance Data for Sales Reps in the Dallas/Ft. Worth District**

Sales Rep	Last Year's Sales	This Year's Sales	Sales Quota Current Year
Larry Palmer[a]	$180,000	$181,000	$275,000
Dick McClure	450,000	583,000	535,000
Peggy Doyle[b]	—	120,000	150,000
Tom Jones	445,000	555,000	550,000
Bill Morrison	465,000	560,000	550,000
Sam Hanna	435,000	535,000	525,000
Jared Murphy	365,000	370,000	420,000
Marty Nakai	475,000	625,000	575,000
TOTALS	$2,815,000	$3,529,000	$3,580,000

[a] Sales and quota figures are for eight months.

[b] Peggy Doyle has been in her territory for only four months, there is no sales figure for the previous year. This year's sales and quota are for four months.

EXHIBIT 2 Input Factors Affecting Territory Coverage in the Dallas/Ft. Worth District

Sales Rep	Number of Sales Calls	Annual Expenses ($)	Physicians in Territory
Larry Palmer[a]	800	$6,300	1,600
Dick McClure	1,500	9,300	2,100
Peggy Boyle[b]	400	2,500	1,650
Tom Jones	1,300	8,000	1,850
Bill Morrison	1,350	8,300	1,800
Sam Hanna	1,350	8,500	1,900
Jared Murphy	1,050	7,800	2,000
Marty Nakai	1,550	9,800	2,200
TOTALS	9,300	$60,500	15,100

[a] Number of sales calls and expenses are for an eight-month period.
[b] Number of sales calls and expenses are for a four-month period.

tory, Jared quickly replied: "I didn't know you cared that much."

John also stated he felt that Jared had sufficient experience and intelligence to exert the necessary self-discipline to do what was required without a lot of personal attention from him. At this point, John said: "Jared, I think that it's time to decide whether or not you really have a future with Arapahoe. You definitely have the capabilities to be an above average performer. If you really want to do a better job, I'll make every effort to help you to do a better job, but you will have to help me and really want to work at it. So what I want you to do is to go home, think about what I said, talk it over with your wife, and we will get together next Wednesday and make a plan for your future."

The problem John faced with Marty Nakai was almost the opposite. Marty was a young, single sales rep who had three years' experience in a territory that required quite a bit of travel in the Texas panhandle. He had about every good quality anyone could want in a salesperson, except maturity and self-control. He was smart, eager, highly motivated, and extremely ambitious. His favorite question of John was: "What else do I have to do to get promoted?" and he posed that question on every field trip and frequently at sales meetings. In addition, John could count on Marty calling him at home on weekends. In a way, John wished he had more sales reps who were as productive and as eagerly cooperative, but he also wished that Marty would develop more patience and self-discipline.

While John certainly didn't want to do anything to dampen Marty's enthusiasm, he was running out of ways to help Marty grow up.

As he thought about the challenges he had with his reps and the logjam he had created as a result of his recruiting activities, he realized that he had to formalize a set of objectives and specific plans for the coming year to discuss with Phil Jackson during his own coming appraisal session. Although the year had been a successful one, their performance on a couple of major products could have been at a higher level and he would have to figure out some kind of action plan to correct that situation. And then there were the territory revisions to be done to take advantage of the growth potential in the Ft. Worth area. Not the least important or urgent matter he needed to address was to evaluate his own performance during the past year and to set some personal objectives.

In addition, John had to prepare some written comments on the performance of each of his reps for the past year to put in their personal files. He thought he should calculate some ratios from the data in Exhibits 1 and 2 such as sales growth, sales to quota, sales per call, sales per physician, expenses per call, and selling expenses as a percent of sales to include in his report on each rep. Also he had to decide what to do about Jared and Marty. Overall, John saw his problems were really people problems and people opportunities, and their interaction and interdependence were what made his job both challenging and fun.

CASE 11-2   PRACTICAL PARTIES*

George Thomson is employed by the Howard Hills Holding Company, a conglomerate with its headquarters in the UK, but operating worldwide. He has a reputation as a trouble shooter, and has been given a number of assignments in the group where Thompson has successfully carried out turn-round operations on subsidiary companies. Some of these have been acquisitions purchased very cheaply as the companies have been in a state of near insolvency.

Arnold Newby, the group's managing director has invited you to his office to discuss a new assignment. "You are aware of our takeover of Practical Parties about two years ago. We are very unhappy with its performance and would like you to sort it out." This strikes Thompson as surprising, as he knew that the subsidiary concerned is profitable, but Newby goes on to explain further. "We paid a good price for Practical Parties on the basis of its prospects for growth, but to be frank, the growth has not happened. To make matters worse, the executive we put in charge has left suddenly after a major disagreement with us. We thought we had made a major coup in being able to recruit him

from another party plan company. All he seems to have done is upset some of our consultants by changing procedures to those of his previous company, and now he says that the growth we looked for is not possible. I would like you to take over from him, produce a plan for growth, and get it started before moving on to a new challenge. It will not be easy, but I know you won't let us down."

Newby explains that if a case can be made for it the group can make investment funds available. He does not expect you to agree to the assignment immediately, but would like your thoughts on how or whether sales and profits growth could be established in the next three years. This is expected in the form of an interim report to be delivered and discussed in only a week's time. To help, Thompson is given a folder prepared by Jane Fraser, a recent Business School Graduate who has worked for Practical Parties for the last year. The folder contains comments and material written by Jane, in addition to photocopies of material she thinks might be useful. On the basis of this material, which follows, Thompson is expected to complete his report.

EXHIBIT 1   Comments from Jane Fraser

1. Background

Practical Parties is a successful and profitable company. Its founder worked for another party plan company bringing with him some of the best staff. Unfortunately, sales have been nearly static for the last three years. In fact, after allowing for inflation, sales have declined somewhat.

Party Plan is a method of selling where a hostess (almost all party plan activities are female oriented) invites friends to her house, light refreshments are provided, and there is the opportunity to buy goods. In the case of Practical Parties, orders are taken and the goods delivered and billed later. This avoids problems of hostesses getting involved with the collection of money and storing goods. The hostess is rewarded with a relatively modest cash payment and a gift from the Practical Parties product range, which can broadly be described as giftware, but has a strong bias to glass and china goods. The hostesses are recruited by Practical Parties consultants, who are paid on commission, and classed as self-employed.

Hostesses are seen as key factors in the success of the company's operations. If a hostess has a wide network of friends and acquaintances then a suitable mix of guests can be found which enables the party to be an enjoyable social and buying occasion. Prior to the arrival of the previous executive of Practical Parties, hostesses received incentives not only on sales made, but also on the number of guests

(continues)

---

* This case was prepared by Mark Adams, Mike Easey, and Harry Robinson of the University of Northumbria at Newcastle, England. Copyright © 1991 by the University of Northumbria at Newcastle. Reproduced by permission.

EXHIBIT 1 (Continued)

attending and the number of further parties arranged. A dynamic and expanding network of hostesses, with parties held at regular and appropriate intervals, is the cornerstone of a consultant's success.

In all there are 2500 consultants, of whom about one in twenty are supervisors responsible for a group of consultants under them. These supervisors receive commission on the sales of the consultants under them. They are expected to recruit consultants, and they conduct usually fewer parties themselves than the average for the people under them.

The consultants' role is to demonstrate the product, actively sell gift items, collect orders, and make deliveries. A minimum requirement is that at least one guest at the party agrees to host another party. The consultant is also responsible for recruiting all the hostesses and briefing them on such matters as invitations, refreshments, and the creation of a friendly atmosphere.

The quality of consultants varies considerably. Some consultants produce their own special invitation cards and follow-up brochures to encourage repeat orders independent of the parties. A number of consultants are also agents for other party plan companies and it is suspected that products for these other companies may be sold at functions organized in the name of Practical Parties. Training of consultants is the responsibility of the senior consultants who have themselves often been selected primarily for their sales performance. Training is not standardized, aside from the sales conferences.

Turnover of consultants has recently increased. Some of those with the most successful records have moved to recently started party plan companies undergoing rapid growth. Methods of recruiting more consultants are being considered. With more consultants, there will be more hostesses having more parties, thus giving more sales. Direct payments to consultants to recruit more consultants has been rejected for the time being, as that might be construed as pyramid selling (a form of selling that involves payment for recruiting people who would have to pay fees to join or for stock). This was considered illegal and unethical. Practical Parties was a member of the Direct Selling Association, and adhered to a code of practice which would make sure that it remained a respectable company which did not become involved in dubious practices.

In addition to commission, the company tried to motivate consultants through lavish sales conferences, competitions, and merit awards.

A full-time buyer scours the world for interesting giftware. If we are in the giftware business, perhaps we could consider opening a chain of gift shops using our economies of scale and sourcing knowledge as a distinctive competence. This could perhaps be turned into a franchising operation. On the orders of the recently departed managing director, slightly poorer quality products were being sold in order to at least increase margins if volume could not be increased. This had partly backfired, as it had led to experienced consultants moving on. In the past they had always been able to claim that the company sold reasonable products.

Administration is efficient, with deliveries being accurate and on time. This is made possible with a highly advanced computer operation. The computer manager boasted that the company had records of all the parties indicating who purchased what product, when the product was purchased, and where the purchaser lived. Not much use has been made of this data, but preliminary analysis reveals disappointment with performance in the South-East of England, where it was considered the most purchasing power lay.

Very little advertising is used, as it is deemed inappropriate for this type of operation.

2. The Market

It is very difficult to define the market for Practical Parties. If the market means any product that might be given as a gift, then it means almost any product. However, most of the products are in the china and glass category, and a fair amount of secondary data exist for that.

During the early 1990's retail sales of tableware and kitchenware were valued at approximately £400m, and glassware at around £220m, giving a total of £620m. Both sectors have grown in real terms with tableware growing faster than glassware.

Growth has been attributed to increasing interest in the house and home entertaining, as well as increases in income. The market was affected by cheap imports in the mid-1980s, but made a recovery. Since 1990 there have been signs of a downturn due to lower rates of new house formation because of demographic factors, and a reduction in disposable income resulting from higher interest rates for mortgages. As a company we are not sure what the effects will be of the increasing trend to single person and single parent households.

China and porcelain are losing market share to stoneware and earthenware which are cheaper. The glassware market is divided into two categories, hand gathered glass and machine gathered glass.

(continues)

EXHIBIT 1   (Continued)

Hand gathered glass can be either hand made crystal, with a high lead oxide content, or less elaborately cut glass with a lower lead content. Much of the better quality glassware is bought by tourists, especially Americans, and is therefore affected by fluctuations in the number of visitors caused by such things as the variations in exchange rates. Machine made glass is produced for the mass market and everyday use. It is hit at the cheaper end from time to time by petrol retailers using free glassware as promotions. Practical parties tends to sell either lower quality hand made products, or glassware at the higher end of the machine made market.

3. The Competition

If the competition is thought to be organizations selling similar goods, then department stores and gift shops would be considered the main competition. If the "product" is more of the party as a social occasion, then the competition would be other party plan operations, or perhaps other organizations engaged in direct selling.

Direct selling could include such things as direct mail selling and selling insurance door to door. For this reason, statistics from different sources never seem to tally on the total market for goods sold direct.

Overall the direct selling sector is characterized by being very fragmented, with several hundred individual enterprises. The majority of these are very small, and the sector is dominated by a relatively small number of larger organizations. Most of the organizations which sell consumer goods direct, involving personal contact, use party plans. One notable exception is Avon Cosmetics, possibly the largest in personal selling terms, which uses individual to individual contact rather than the groups involved in parties.

The UK market for direct selling of consumer goods involving face to face contact was worth approximately £600m in 1990. The 1980s were characterized by slow growth rates, much of which came from new, smaller companies. Indeed, it appears that all the companies eventually become victims of the product life cycles of the goods they sell, with the company growth slowing as the product category growth slows. An alternative hypothesis is that as well as the advantage of the social occasion, parties need novelty to interest those attending, and once the novelty of a new organization wears off, then the attractiveness of the party also declines.

Brief profiles of some of the chief competitors in various forms of direct selling follow.

EXHIBIT 2   Profiles of the Major Competitors

Avon

Avon Cosmetics is still the largest direct selling company in the UK. The company is a subsidiary of Avon Products Inc, the US conglomerate of New York. It is primarily involved in selling cosmetics and toiletries, and holds significant market share in many product sectors. Avon mainly sells by means of a small catalogue which is regularly changed and updated, although the customer can still sample the products if they wish. The catalogues also feature other products such as jewelry items and personal goods.

Rosgill

The Rosgill Group comprises a number of wholly owned subsidiaries which are listed below. It is the largest party plan company in the UK, with a current turnover somewhere in the region of £45m. The company has been quoted as holding 42,000 parties each year, by some 6000 demonstrators. Significantly they appear to be the only party plan company to encourage children to attend their parties, which may well be used as an added pressure to buy.

Rosgill Holdings (Pippa Dee Parties, Dee Minor Limied	**Merchandises clothing by direct sales**
Pippa Dee International	**Jewelry by direct sales**
Wanderkurst	**Clothing manufacture**
Melrose Marketing	**Consumer goods by direct sales**
Matchmaker Parties Ltd.	**Housewares by direct sales**

(continues)

EXHIBIT 2   **Profiles of the Major Competitors (Continued)**

Tupperware

Tupperware effectively established the party plan selling method in the UK. However, recent years have shown a loss of presence and turnover has fallen slightly. This probably is because plastic housewares are now much more widely available through retail outlets and have lost some of the individual appeal they once had. In response to this, the company has widened its product range to merchandise plastic toys and general household goods.

The company started in the UK in 1960, although it originated in the USA in the 1950s. Internationally in 1996 Tupperware claimed a sales force of 800,000, worldwide net sales of US $1.4 billion, and 97 million attendances at parties worldwide.

The mode of operation remains predominantly Party Plan although it is now far less rigid and "kitchen consultants" are being used for house demonstrations. This is mainly a response to more women working and, as such, attempts have been made to sell the products at places of work. The Tupperware image which launched their initial success is now possibly proving more of a hindrance than a help, for although the company has a huge range of products, it is still strongly identified with its base products.

Amway

The company is a wholly owned subsidiary of the Amway Corporation and is most strongly identified with the sponsorship and multi-level approach to party plan. The Amway Corporation had worldwide sales of US $6.3 billion in 1995, which marked 11 years of consecutive growth for the organization.

They offer a wide range of merchandise, including household cleaning products, cosmetics, skincare, dietary aids, and jewelry.

EXHIBIT 3   **Practical Parties Consultants**

Average number of parties per week per consultant

0–1	1	2	3	4	5	6+
45%	26%	16%	9%	2%	1%	1%

Interpretation: The table should be read as percentage of consultants arranging a given number of parties, e.g. 45% of consultants arrange on average less than one party a week.

Performance of consultants by length of service

Length of Service	% of Consultants	% of Sales
0–12 weeks	4	1
13–18 weeks	8	6
19–24 weeks	12	7
25–30 weeks	12	10
31–52 weeks	15	16
1–2 years	18	25
2–3 years	16	20
3+ years	13	15

Twenty-five percent of consultants leave each year.

EXHIBIT 4   Results of Survey of 948 Respondents on Party Plan Attendance

Consumer reaction to Party Plans is difficult to express with any degree of accuracy, given the wide variability in quality of product offerings. Some secondary research, although dated, did indicate that roughly 80% of consumers thought the products were expensive at Party Plan schemes, but over 60% thought they were good value for money. Approximately 90% did feel under some pressure to buy something. The extent to which these finding apply to Practical Parties is unknown.

Percentage Yes response from the survey question "Have you ever been to a party or consultant where goods are sold?"

Base: 948 responses   %Yes response overall = 75%

Age Groups	%	Social Class %		%UK Adults
15–24	69	AB	64	22.3
25–34	75	C1	75	27.1
35–44	92	C2	82	22.5
45–54	81	DE	67	28.1
55–64	74			
65+	58			

Social Class Definitions
A Upper Middle Class: Higher Managerial, administrative or professional.
B Middle Class: Intermediate managerial, administrative or professional.
C1 Lower Middle Class: Supervisory or clerical, and professional, junior managerial or administrative.
C2 Skilled Working Class: Skilled Manual Workers
D Working Class: Semi and Unskilled Manual Worker
E Those at the lowest level of subsistence: State pensioners or widows unemployed, casual or lowest grade workers.

Television Regions
The main Commercial Television Contracts in the UK are awarded on a regional basis

TV Area	Contractor	% Attending Party Plan
London	Carlton/LWT	60
South & South East	Meridian	64
Wales & West	HTV	75
South West	West Country TV	73
Midlands	Central TV	78
East	Anglia	71
North West	Granada TV	75
North East	Channel 3	74
Yorkshire	Channel 3	78
Border	Border TV	72

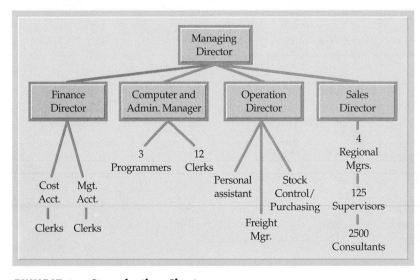

EXHIBIT 5   Organization Chart

EXHIBIT 6 **Summary Accounts for Practical Parties Ltd (Thousands of Pounds)**

	1996	1995	1994	1993
Sales	19379	19808	17629	15395
Commission	6775	6716	6522	6003
Net Sales	12604	13092	11107	9392
Interest paid	50	50	46	38
Sales Expenses	660	587	426	309
Manufacturing and Dist. Exp.	73	81	68	52
Other Expenses	197	183	126	102
Depreciation	420	381	261	222
Advertising	7	11	3	3
Variable Cost	8879	9133	7659	6545
Bad Debt	0	0	0	0
Admin. remuneration	1193	1040	999	943
Total Expenses	11479	11466	9588	8214
Non-trading income	58	50	48	35
Net profit before tax	1183	1676	1567	1213
Exports	0	0	0	0
Fixed assets	1974	2138	1836	1756
Stocks	1892	2004	2403	2399
Trade debtors	0	0	0	0
Other current assets	182	263	192	176
Total current assets	2074	2267	2595	2575
Total assets	4048	4405	4431	4331
Creditors	1653	1923	1836	1820
Short term loans	96	83	81	69
Other current liabilities	5	0	1	1
Total current liabilities	1754	2006	1918	1890
Net assets	2294	2399	2513	2441
Shareholders funds	1823	2017	2131	2109
Long term loans	471	382	382	378
Capital employed	2294	2399	2513	2487
Ratio Analysis				
Return on Net Assets	51.57	69.86	62.36	48.77
Return on Total Assets	29.22	38.05	35.36	28.01
Operating Margin	6.10	8.46	8.89	7.88
Asset turnover	4.79	4.50	3.98	3.55
Current ratio	1.18	1.13	1.35	1.36
Quick ratio	0.10	0.13	0.10	0.09
Interest cover	23.66	33.52	34.07	31.92
Debt/Equity	0.26	0.15	0.19	0.18
Stock turnover	10.24	9.88	7.44	6.42

CASE 11-3   YORK ELECTRONICS*

Y ork is a medium-sized electronics company that specializes in the manufacture of circuit boards, customized computer chips, and test equipment. The electronic components are sold by company salespeople directly to original equipment manufacturers (OEMs), and test equipment is handled by a second group of independent reps. Bill Hicks was recently appointed national sales manager at York to supervise the company's salespeople and the independent reps.

Company sales for the Electronic and Test Equipment divisions amounted to $135 million in 1998. Test equipment sold for relatively high prices and made up the major portion of sales revenue. Independent reps were paid straight 6 percent commissions on all York equipment sales in their territories. The volume of test equipment shipments had increased 15 percent the previous year, and Bill was satisfied with the performance of the reps. Also, the reps' compensation plan made it difficult for York managers to direct their day-to-day activities. About all Bill could do with the independent reps was to replace them if they failed to push York's equipment. York's testing products were only one of several lines of equipment carried by these reps.

Bill Hicks was convinced, on the other hand, that a review of the Electronics Division's sales force would be quite useful. York currently covered the U.S. electronics market with 18 company salespeople. The assignments of individuals and descriptions of their territories are given in Exhibit 1. Electronics salespeople acted as consultants to OEMs and helped them solve product design problems using York boards and customized chips. They were paid a base salary plus a commission and an annual discretionary bonus. Since electronics salespeople did a great deal of developmental work, their base wage amounted to about 60 percent of their total compensation. Commission rates varied from 0.3 to 1.0 percent of sales, depending on the products sold. The highest commissions were paid on items with the largest gross margins. In the past, bonuses had been based on sales increases, with some attention to profitability. Each salesperson was also given a company car and an expense account to cover travel and entertainment costs.

York's sales of electronic components increased in 1998, but profits were relatively flat. Price competition was intense, and Hicks had been brought in to improve

EXHIBIT 1   Descriptions of Sales Territories

Territory Number	Salesperson Assigned	Area Included
1	Mary Holmes	Vermont, New Hampshire, Rhode Island, Massachusetts, Maine
2	James Potter	Connecticut, upstate New York (Rochester and east; includes Westchester County)
3	Harvey Stewart	Long Island (Nassau and Suffolk counties), western Pennsylvania (Altoona and west)
4	Jane Thomas	New York City (New York, Kings, Queens, Richmond, and Bronx counties), north Jersey, western New York from Buffalo to Rochester
5	Chad Hunter	Eastern Pennsylvania to Altoona, south Jersey, Maryland, Delaware
6	Harvey Phillips	Ohio, West Virginia, Kentucky
7	Greg Lewis	Indiana, Michigan
8	Anne Forbes	Missouri, Nebraska, Kansas, Iowa
9	Bill Fredericks	Illinois, Wisconsin, Minnesota, North and South Dakota
10	Sally Smith	California north of Santa Barbara, Oregon, Washington, Idaho
11	Fred Reilly	Los Angeles north to Santa Barbara (includes Santa Barbara, Ventura, and the western part of Los Angeles County)
12	Marilyn Reed	California south of Los Angeles (includes Orange, Riverside, San Diego, and Imperial counties)
13	George Pardo	Los Angeles (most of Los Angeles County and part of San Bernadino County)
14	Henry Dodds	Colorado, Arizona, New Mexico, Utah, Wyoming, Montana
15	Todd Young	Texas, Oklahoma, Arkansas, Louisiana
16	David Wood	Mississippi, Alabama, Tennessee
17	Tammy Cook	Virginia, North Carolina, South Carolina
18	Brad Wolf	Georgia, Florida

* This case was prepared by Douglas J. Dalrymple of Indiana University.

sales force productivity and profits. Bill began his analysis by collecting some performance data on his electronics sales force (Exhibit 2). After reviewing these numbers, he thought it might be useful to calculate some additional control factors such as sales per call, expenses to sales, sales growth, dollars of gross margin, and sales to potential. York measured potential by the number of manufacturers who used electronic components in each sales territory and the value of their finished product shipments. These numbers were derived from U.S. Census of Business data using SIC codes and territory boundaries. Bill decided to calculate penetration by dividing territory sales by the total value of electronics shipments in each area.

To help with his analysis, Hicks called up the new SPSS software that he had recently installed on his computer. He then retrieved the yorkdat.sav file. The next step in Hicks' sales force analysis was to calculate simple correlation coefficients among his control factors. The correlations that came up on the screen varied from 0.0 to ±1.0, and they showed the direction and intensity of associations among the performance variables. For example, a strong positive correlation observed between sales and dollars of gross margin (+0.806) was expected because gross margin dollars is simply sales minus the cost of goods sold (Exhibit 3).

Once his sales analysis was complete, Hicks had a number of decisions to make. The annual sales meeting was scheduled in two weeks, and he needed to identify the best salespeople in each district and nationwide so that "Salesperson of the Year" awards could be made. He wondered whether these choices should be made on the basis of sales alone or whether he should use some combination of performance variables. He also had to identify salespeople for retraining and for possible termination. If the data showed evidence of plateauing among his middle-aged salespeople, then changes would be needed to correct this problem. Hicks would have to specify the topics needed to be covered for those picked for retraining. In addition, Bill had $55,000 in annual bonus money that he had to allocate among the electronics salespeople. He was also concerned about whether changes were needed in basic wage levels and commission rates. Another strategic question was whether York had enough electronics salespeople. If extra salespeople were hired, Bill had to decide how old they should be when hired and how much experience was necessary. In addition, he had to decide if the present sales territories needed to be redesigned. A reallocation of the territories would have to consider where to place any new salespeople. The more Bill thought about these problems, the more he was convinced that he needed one of those new computerized territory design programs he had seen advertised. Without a computer program, he would have to draw some maps to analyze the existing territories and plan for possible added salespeople.

Beyond these decisions, Hicks had to make decisions concerning the factors he wanted to emphasize to motivate his electronics salespeople to reach corporate objectives. Bill knew that his goals were unlikely to be reached if he asked his salespeople to improve on 10 different control factors all at the same time. Besides, improving some of the factors conflicted with the achievement of others. What he needed was a short list of prioritized factors to highlight at the upcoming sales meeting.

EXHIBIT 2 Sales Force Performance Data[a]

Territory Number	Sales, 1997 (millions)	Sales, 1998 (millions)	Gross Margin (%)	Calls, 1998	Years of Service	Age	Potential			Salary, 1998	Commissions, 1998	Expenses, 1998	District
							Territory Size in Miles^2 (000)	Total Number of Firms	Total Value of Shipments (millions)				
1	$1.839	$2.214	40%	770	2	32	58.4	1965	$9959	$34,100	$16,500	$ 4269	1
2	2.398	2.411	38	660	6	40	44.2	1461	10190	40,150	17,710	7096	1
3	2.497	2.640	33	1250	25	50	16.7	1023	4719	35,860	21,450	9510	1
4	1.509	1.739	36	900	7	34	8.7	2601	10360	37,950	11,440	15628	1
5	2.167	2.686	31	678	20	49	46.7	2264	16287	33,330	22,330	13027	1
6	1.183	1.190	44	610	3	40	104.8	2286	21195	33,000	10,450	9785	2
7	2.232	2.431	37	870	12	38	92.9	2465	23010	33,000	16,610	11797	2
8	1.561	1.632	45	580	16	46	283.3	1601	14240	33,000	11,660	22425	2
9	2.147	2.032	42	630	14	48	334.9	3306	25600	31,900	18,370	12014	2
10	2.012	2.621	40	492	3	32	356.3	3329	17980	39,600	17,380	12523	3
11	.831	.885	52	600	2	26	4.6	136	540	27,500	8,470	4741	3
12	1.658	2.251	28	1030	6	39	16.4	994	4047	33,000	12,100	4938	3
13	1.377	1.146	39	540	5	38	4.0	2127	10590	46,200	6,600	3477	3
14	1.058	1.081	49	480	2	26	662.9	1407	6407	33,000	10,560	14165	3
15	1.898	3.083	37	460	2	29	427.3	3130	26280	33,000	12,100	19431	4
16	1.856	2.578	25	820	5	36	139.1	1603	12303	33,000	14,520	18747	4
17	2.090	2.317	23	820	20	50	118.7	2167	18840	38,500	16,280	9602	4
18	1.224	1.565	39	830	5	28	112.2	2479	13232	28,050	10,340	25394	4

[a] Data are in file yorkdat.sav.

EXHIBIT 3 Correlations Among Sales Force Control Factors

	1998 Sales	1998 Calls	Sales/ Calls	Expenses	Exp/ Sales	Exp/ Calls	Years Service	Age	GM (%)	GM ($)	Terr. Size	No. of Firms	Value Ship.	Penetration	Sales Growth	Commissions
Sales	1.000	.285ª	.718	.140	-.435	.115	.346	.332	-.666	.806	.000	.353	.389	.279	.637	.738
Calls	.285	1.000	-.430	-.112	-.221	-.492	.499	.371	-.562	-.047	-.583	-.318	-.343	.725	.071	.358
Sales/call	.718	-.430	1.000	.254	-.204	.517	-.079	-.035	-.174	.810	.447	.576	.587	-.203	.611	.355
Expenses	.140	-.112	.254	1.000	.807	.875	.061	-.124	-.021	.174	.428	.369	.359	-.337	.436	-.060
Exp/sales	-.435	-.221	-.204	.807	1.000	.714	-.121	-.302	.379	-.282	.445	.082	.048	-.386	.026	-.412
Exp/call	.115	-.492	.517	.875	.714	1.000	-.120	-.241	.207	.301	.718	.425	.450	-.452	.440	-.147
Years of service	.346	.499	-.079	.061	-.121	-.120	1.000	.874	-.429	.120	-.216	-.030	.117	.249	-.211	.640
Age	.332	.371	-.035	-.124	-.302	-.241	.874	1.000	-.478	.098	-.284	.057	.244	.180	-.297	.599
GM (%)	-.666	-.562	-.174	-.021	.379	.207	-.429	-.478	1.000	-.117	.356	-.111	-.125	-.354	-.420	-.430
GM ($)	.806	-.047	.810	.174	-.282	.301	.120	.098	-.117	1.000	.248	.486	.472	.064	.478	.631
Territory size	.000	-.583	.447	.428	.445	.718	-.216	-.284	.356	.248	1.000	.333	.331	-.326	.174	-.075
No. of mfg.	.353	-.318	.576	.369	.082	.425	-.030	.057	-.111	.486	.333	1.000	.846	-.570	.238	.192
Value ship.	.389	-.343	.587	.359	.048	.450	.117	.244	-.125	.472	.331	.846	1.000	-.630	.203	.236
Penetration	.279	.725	-.203	-.337	-.386	-.452	.249	.180	-.354	.064	-.326	-.570	-.630	1.000	.116	.271
Sales growth	.637	.071	.611	.436	.026	.440	-.211	-.297	-.420	.478	.174	.238	.203	.116	1.000	.131
Commissions	.738	.358	.355	-.060	-.412	-.147	.640	.599	-.430	.631	-.075	.192	.236	.271	.131	1.000

ª Correlations of .320 and larger are significant, with a probability of error of <.10.

CHAPTER 12

DIRECT MARKETING

*D*irect marketing allows you to speak directly to the people who are most likely to buy your product.[1] You ask them to take an immediate action in the form of an order, a donation, an inquiry, or a store visit. You want to establish an ongoing customer relationship. You focus on the profit generated *over the life of the customer.*

Direct marketing usually involves building a database of respondents. Hence the term *database marketing* is often used. A survey of packaged goods marketers found that two-thirds were compiling and using consumer databases. Among those building databases, mail-in premium offers and sweepstakes are the most commonly used methods of information collection, followed by trackable coupons and rebates. More than two-thirds of those using database marketing enhance their data with outside demographic and lifestyle information. Sophisticated database methodologies identify high-potential prospects. Marketing resources are concentrated on these select-list segments.

Strategic decisions in direct marketing include program scope (test versus rollout or full program), the basic offer (product, incentives, and premiums), the concept and theme, versioning and/or personalization, and media selection. We begin by addressing targeting.

TARGETING

Your starting point must be "Who is my customer?" One way to answer this question is to collect your own data. HoneyBaked Ham Co. of Georgia has been collecting the telephone numbers of its customers for $3^{1}/_{2}$ years. The resulting database, with addresses and buying habits of those customers, now numbers about 1.5 million people in the Southeast. The database is the foundation of HoneyBaked Ham's catalog and its business-to-business line as well as being a critical tool for its retail side. The database represents about 25 percent of its marketing budget. HoneyBaked Ham, which doesn't share its customer list with other marketers, focuses on its customers' buying patterns, showing what times of the year they make purchases, what they buy, and how much they spend. It can do targeted mailings, whether going to formerly faithful customers or to frequent buyers. Customers are sent coupons and other offers. HoneyBaked Ham has had 25 percent of volume from a sales promotion driven completely by direct mail where three to four percent is usually considered successful.[2]

Custom data providers are another source of data. For example, National Decision Systems segments the population into 50 subgroups based on demographic factors weighed against national averages. Some examples of these subgroups are given in Table 12-1. One

TABLE 12-1   Selected National Decision Systems U.S. Segments

A Good Step Forward

Typically 22- to 34-year-olds living in non-family households with one or two people. Two-thirds are renters, with very high per capita income. Only 14 percent of households have children. Twice as likely as U.S. average to have a bachelor's or graduate degree; almost 80 percent have white-collar occupations. Second most likely to listen to classic rock radio.

City Ties

Adults who tend to be between 50 and 59 years, with children in the 10- to 17-year-old range. More likely than average to be a single-parent household, very often with five or more residents. More than 75 percent of households are African-American. Per capita income is 25 percent below average. They are 24 percent more likely than average to not have a high school diploma. Six percent more likely than average to own their home, with a property value 14 percent lower than average. Twice as likely to take public transportation to work. Most likely to have call waiting, call forwarding, and automatic call return. Listen to urban contemporary radio stations.

Country Home Families

Typically married adults, between 40 and 54, with children between 10 and 17. Average median household income 12 percent below average. Nineteen times more likely than average to work in blue-collar occupations, and rank first in precision production and crafts. Among most likely to have only a high school diploma. More than 80 percent own their homes, and almost 15 percent live in mobile homes. Almost 50 percent more likely than average to live in relatively new homes. Tend to own motor homes, boats, rifles, and fishing equipment.

Family Ties

Families with children, living in suburbs. Adults typically between 35 and 44, children between 5 and 17. Forty percent more likely than average to have three to six people in the household. Median household income 19 percent above average, but large number of household members drops per capita income 6 percent below average. Rank third in having attended some college and having received an associate degree. Like to go boating, camping, bowling, or golfing. Most likely to have unsecured line of credit and to use the phone to transfer funds.

Great Beginnings

Younger adults, typically between 22 and 34 years old. Thirty-one percent of these households have children, with most younger than 4. Median household income is 8 percent above average, and they are 56 percent more likely to be renters. Tend to drive alone to work in a sub-compact car, play pool, drink Coors beer, have overdraft protection, and listen to album-oriented rock stations.

Home Sweet Home

Typically married couples between 50 and 69, with one or no children at home. Rank in the top 15 nationwide in household income, and eighth in the percentage that receive retirement income. Almost 80 percent own their homes, with property value 60 percent above average. Typically have two or more vehicles, drive alone to work, and have an average commute time of just under 22 minutes. They get their carpets professionally cleaned and are likely to have recently had a home energy audit. A relatively high percentage finance home improvements with a home equity line of credit.

Mid-Life Success

Typically between 40 and 54 years old, with a median income 68 percent above average. Thirty-six percent have children. A majority own their home, which has an average value three times the norm. Primarily work in white-collar occupations such as sales, executive, and managerial positions. Very likely to own a PC and access online services. Typically save more than $5,000 a year and buy stock from discount brokers.

Movers and Shakers

Typically, households include two working adults between 35 and 49, with no children. Median household income is 46 percent above average. Twice as likely to have a bachelor's or postgraduate degree, and rank fourth in working in white-collar occupations. One-third are renters, who pay almost 50 percent more in rent costs than average. Twice as likely to dine at upscale restaurants, own a PC, and use a full-service stockbroker.

Upper Crust

Highest income of the 50 subgroups, with a median household income almost three times the average. Adults primarily between 45 and 59 years old, and 38 percent have children at home. Three-fourths are married, and almost 80 percent live in the suburbs. Rank first and second in bachelor's and post-graduate degrees. Highest percentage of children enrolled in private schools. More than 40 percent more likely to own their home, with property values four times the national average. Most active in using financial services. Large contributors to PBS (Public Broadcasting System), most likely to own a notebook computer, and home fax machine.

service it provides is a market profile report, which shows what type of consumers live where.[3] An example is given in Figure 12-1 for the five-mile radius around Lenox Square, Atlanta's largest mall.

MEDIA SELECTION

Our focus is cost-effective media selection for the product and situation. Telemarketing and direct mail are two media that traditionally have been used for direct marketing, although

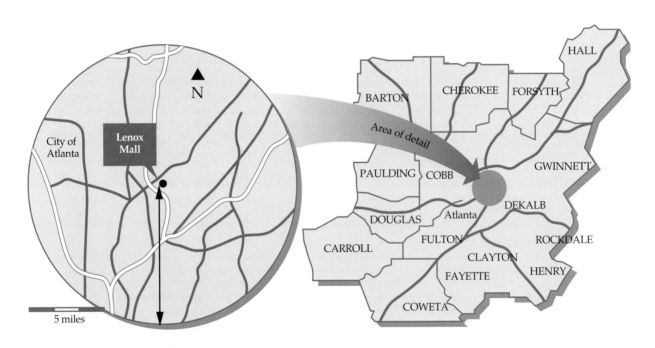

Lenox Square 5-mile radius

Total households: 113,124

16-county metro Atlanta area

Total households: 1,357,472

The five top profiles for this area comprised more than 80% of all residents.

profile	households
A Good Step Forward	41,612
Movers and Shakers	19,896
Great Beginnings	15,853
Upper Crust	8,624
Midlife Success	5,343

The six top profiles for this area comprise more than 44% of all residents.

profile	households
Country Home Families	148,992
A Good Step Forward	116,233
Great Beginnings	104,634
City Ties	99,389
Family ties	66,942
Home Sweet Home	66,740

FIGURE 12-1   Lenox Square Mall Market Profile (From "Here's What Companies Know about Your Habits," *Atlanta Journal-Constitution.* **[October 12, 1998], p. E6)**

general mass media can be used as well. The Internet is the newest medium and opens up the possibility of *interactive marketing.*

Telephone

The telephone is the third largest medium in the United States with more than 18 million calls being made each day. Telephone marketing uses communication technology as part of a marketing program that prominently features the use of personal selling. Telemarketing works because it is personal, urgent and deadline-driven, interactive, and flexible, generates immediate response, allows for constant improvement through testing, and is cost-effective. You can take the initiative in contacting your customer (outbound operations) or you can let your customer contact you (inbound operations).

Outbound Operations With the average cost of business-to-business sales call costing more than $300, many firms are turning to telephone marketing where the average cost per contact is only $7. A major advantage of telephone marketing over other direct marketing approaches is *flexibility.* Scripts can be changed as events unfold in real time (see, for example, Marketing Strategies box 12-3).

The acceptability of telephone marketing varies by type of product or service being offered. A recent survey shows customer reactions to telephone marketing: 62 percent terminate call before or during presentation, 32 percent listen to the entire presentation, and 6 percent comply with request. When asked what was the impression of your last phone call: 42 percent said it was an unpleasant experience; 39 percent a pleasant experience; and 19 percent said neither or don't know. Another survey followed up calls placed 30 days earlier and found: 72 percent didn't mind the call while 2.8 percent objected to all calls. Overall, 95 percent said relationship was unchanged or better. Reasons for a call being unpleasant are poorly trained caller, computer message, inconvenient timing, and poor targeting/no need.

Inbound Operations The telephone can be used to take customer-initiated orders, requests for information, and complaints. You have to decide whether you want a lot of calls that are free to the caller (800 numbers) or fewer, but more qualified calls, for which the caller has to pay (900 numbers). The telephone is one way to listen to your customers, what they like about you, what they don't like. The Buick Division of General Motors handles 30,000 calls monthly through an 800 number for customer assistance.

Telecommunications technology lets you know the telephone number of a caller before actually picking up the phone. With Automatic Number Identification (ANI), the caller's telephone number is sent along with the call. When ANI is coupled on a real-time basis with reverse directory match, customers can be given more personalized service. With the help of some software, you can have displayed on a computer screen not only the customer's name and address, but also the record of past purchases, credit history, and other information.

Direct Mail

More than 60 billion pieces of mail, from fashion catalogs to ads offering pizza coupons, arrive at American homes each year. About 68 percent of all magazine subscription are sold through the mail and 25 percent of all charitable contributions are raised in the same fashion.

Direct mail involves sending a sales proposition to targeted respondents through the mail. The aim is to create a direct response to the mailing, whether it be by mail, phone, or personal contact. This response can be measured. A 2 percent response rate represents success if the target market is enormous and undifferentiated. One key to improving upon this rate is the targeted mailing list. The targeted list makes it possible to establish relatively personal relationships with potential and existing customers.

Mailing Lists   Target marketing depends on qualified list choices. If you are selling a product for children, the most significant qualifier in a list selection process would be the presence of children on the list. On the other hand, if your product is geared to the agricultural market, you would want lists of farmers and suppliers to the agricultural community. 3Com, a maker of computer network adapters, targeted LAN coordinators and MIS managers for its Etherlink II adapter (Marketing Strategies box 12-1). In any case, be sure to test your assumptions about who your customer is. One conservative organization was convinced that medical doctors would contribute to its cause. An order was put in for a 5,000-name test list. The prospect package cost 55 cents to mail out, but only raised 10 cents per name mailed!

Lists may be classified as internal or external. An internal list, called a *house file,* is an organization's own file which may include buyers, former buyers, subscribers, lapsed sub-

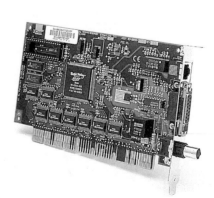

> **APPLYING**
> *. . . to*
> *Not-for-Profit*
> *Marketing*

> **APPLYING**
> *. . . to*
> *Business-to-*
> *Business*
> *Marketing*

MARKETING STRATEGIES *12-1*

Business-To-Business Direct Mail

3Com, a leader in computer network solutions, launched a new adapter board, EtherLink III. The company's biggest challenge was the commoditylike nature of the network adapter market. Adapters from competing manufacturers often offer price as their only distinguishing feature. In addition, the network adapter market is traditionally a low-involvement category in which purchases are not based on brand name. The value-added reseller (VAR), who installs the board and tests it for hardware and software compatibility, recommends adapters. 3Com's objectives were to persuade VARs to recommend 3Com network adapters over the competition and to encourage end users to try 3Com boards.

EtherLink III used direct mail and sales tools featuring bright, colorful visuals and headlines that focused on the benefits of the product rather than technical features. In this marketing effort, EtherLink III adapters were christened "SuperBoards." The initial direct mailing to resellers used short copy, bright colors, and sophisticated illustrations to make the point that EtherLink III network adapters are faster than the competition, yet competitively priced. The resellers were asked to fill out a business reply card or call an 800 number to receive a free sales kit. A direct mail piece sent to LAN coordinators and MIS managers at Fortune 2000 companies used a series of humorous cartoon vignettes to drive home key points about the product and the technology, and to grab the prospect's attention.

This product launch elevated EtherLink III above other entries in the crowded 16-bit board market. End users began requesting the board by name.

— *Creative, nontechnical approaches can be developed to market even the most technical products.*

Source: Marcia Kadanoff, "Nontechnical Approach to Marketing High Tech Has Benefits," *Marketing News,* April 26, 1993, p. 10.

Courtesy 3com

scribers, donors and former donors, prospects, inquiries, employees, salesperson contacts, warranty card respondents, stockholders, and so on. External lists include compiled and direct response lists. *Compiled lists* do not necessarily represent people who have bought by direct mail, but who do have common relevant characteristics. There are compiled lists that cover most of the households and businesses in the United States. Households can be selected by demographic, geographic, or other identifiers. Businesses can be selected by Standard Industrial Classification code, number of employees, net worth, and many other factors. Some sample records from one list company are shown in Figure 12-2. In addition, there are compiled business lists of executives by names—including chairmen, presidents, and treasurers—which can be selected by line of business and other important characteristics. *Direct response lists* contain the names of past direct mail purchasers. These lists are possible because many firms make the internal mailing lists available to noncompeting firms. Obviously, the most responsive list is the house file. Maximum financial return comes

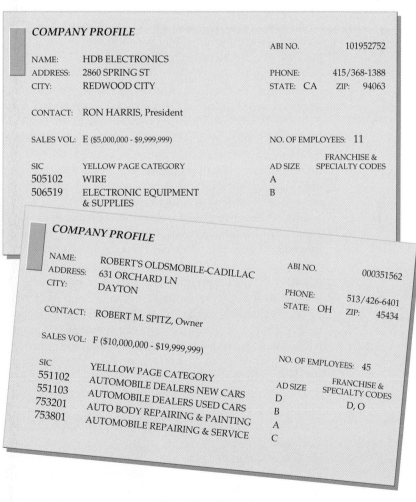

Key: Ad size   Key: Franchise code
       A - Regular listing   D - Cadillac
       B - Boldface listing   O - Oldsmobile
       C - In-column ad
       D - Display ad

FIGURE 12-2   Sample List Records (from American Business Information)

from taking into account the recency, frequency, and dollar amount of past purchases or gifts.

The use of *overlays* has surfaced as a value-added marketing technique. This involves matching the house file against the 85 million households, which are classified by key demographic, socioeconomic, housing, and ethnic characteristics. The measurement units are then clustered into groups with similar demographic and lifestyle characteristics and applied against the internal file. The result is a profile of customers and products. When you need an external list, you could do your own list research, which may involve some creativity. The Sierra Club gathers the names of environmentally aware young people with tabletop displays at rock concerts, setting up voter registration booths on college campuses, and marketing an affinity credit card to college students. Such diverse direct marketing activities attracted 45,000 members at a cost per thousand (CPM) of $9.70 and these members had a net dollar value to the Sierra Club of $18.80. In contrast, while direct mailings yielded more members, 105,000, the CPM was $27.60 and the net dollar value only 40 cents.

APPLYING
. . . to
Not-for-Profit
Marketing

Getting names yourself is time consuming and expensive, so why do it when there are thousands of lists available? Within each list, there are segments that can be selected based on interest categories, geographics, and other elements. Thus, you will probably want the services of a list broker to help you. The list broker serves both parties—the list owner and the user. The list owner pays the broker's commission (usually 20 percent of the list rental price).

Because not everyone on an external compiled list is a prospect, you want to reach your prospects economically. You will need to develop a model or *overlay* to identify your prospects from a larger list. To do so, enough offers or appeals must be mailed to an nth of a large compiled list with appended data to assure a statistically viable response group. This means doing systematic sampling with perhaps 100,000 pieces. Respondents are compared to the file at large by their appended data—information on spending or giving, lifestyle, and any other data available. Once a model for your organization is determined, you can mail sections of compiled lists using your overlay.

Most list transactions are on a onetime rental basis. List rental transactions are priced on a per M (per thousand basis). List rental prices are biased toward mailers that mail entire lists and penalize those that need more narrow selects of lists. The rental of lists involves certain important conditions. First, the names are rented for onetime use only. No copy of the list is to be retained for any purpose. The only names that can be retained are those that respond to the specific mailings. Second, usage must be cleared in advance with the list owner. The mailing piece approved by the list owner is the only one that can be used. Third, no reference to the list being used can appear in the promotional package. And finally, the mailing must be made on the mail date approved by the list owner.

Catalogs   Catalog sales have been increasing rapidly in the United States in recent years and now exceed $50 billion. The very large catalogers, such as JC Penney and Spiegel, continue to perform well, and niche marketers have uncovered audiences for catalogs devoted to everything from African violets to barbecue sauce. See, for example, Marketing Strategies box 12-2.

Catalog marketing has some characteristics of both direct mail and retail selling. However, unlike most direct mail, customers rarely make an immediate decision based on impulse; rather they wait until something triggers a buying impulse. Response to many solo mailings comes in just three weeks, whereas response to a typical catalog comes in over many weeks, perhaps up to six months later. Unlike retail selling, a catalog does not provide an opportunity to touch and feel the merchandise or ask questions of a salesperson (although this last issue can be addressed by an inbound telephone operation).

Catalogers often have multiple catalogs as a way to reach another market segment without compromising their image. Spiegel entered a partnership with Johnson Publishing's

MARKETING STRATEGIES 12-2

Limited Too: A Catalog for the Preteen Girl Segment

Preteen girls are a lucrative market these days. The over-300-store Limited Too chain sells clothes mostly to 10- and 11-year-old girls, though some of its customers are as young as seven. While households receive over 100 catalogs a year on average, very few are addressed to preteen girls. The Limited Too is launching a catalog to pitch its products, such as trendy embroidered jeans and shimmering body lotion. The catalog is to be mailed directly to preteen girls, not their parents. Catalogs aimed at teens already exist but most 10-year-old girls would find themselves too small for what is offered in the Delia's, Wet Seal, Alloy Designs, and Just Nikki catalogs. The Limited Too's target audience will top out at age 14, an age when girls start getting interested in teen catalogs.

Targeting such a narrow age range means a lot of shuffling of catalog-mailing lists, for preteen girls grow quickly into teenagers. The company hopes that the girls who get initial catalogs will show them off to friends at school, quickly boosting the mailing list.

Moreover, while many girls aspire to wear the same cutting-edge fashions as older teens, the clothes must appeal to parents, who typically do the buying. Thus, a crew of in-house designers has been trying to adapt the latest teen fads for younger girls, while running elaborate reality checks to see if parents will object. For example, the Limited Too carries white cardigans, with matching tank tops cut close to the neck and arm—made with thick material so they aren't see-through.

One challenge for the Limited Too catalog is to replicate the superstimulating atmosphere in its stores. In addition to loud pop music and flower-shaped tables spilling with sample makeup bottles, the retailer has been adding things to try to get girls to linger in stores. One example is an instant-photograph machine that prints your picture onto 16 tiny stickers for $3.00.

— *You have to explore alternate ways of reaching your customer.*

Source: Yumiko Ono, "Limited Plans a Preteen Cataloging Blitz," *The Wall Street Journal*, August 25, 1998, p. B8.

APPLYING
. . . to
Ethnic
Marketing

Ebony magazine to create a new catalog targeting black women. Market research indicated that, on average, black women have distinct fit and proportion needs and prefer better tailored clothing. The new catalog, called E Style, contained 64 pages showing a complete line of apparel and accessories along with selected merchandise for the home. To promote E Style, Spiegel ran a print ad in an issue of *Ebony* that resulted in the largest response to a single print ad in its history. E Style is also promoted through ads for Speigel's big book and with cards inserted in the company's other catalogs.

Interactive Media

APPLYING
. . . to
Personal
Computers
Marketing

The Internet is not just changing where people buy (see Chapter 10, "Selecting Distribution Channels") but how they buy. The customer is in charge of the sale. What the customer wants to buy is what counts. Dell Computers and Micron Computers have been highly successful selling computers by direct mail. The Internet only serves to enhance this type of buying experience. Dell, Micro, and others provide the buyer with detailed information at their Web sites. This makes it possible for customers to build computers to suit their needs without talking to anyone. Live customer service representatives are available, if necessary. But they are facilitators, not salespeople; their role is to assist and answer questions. Dell consistently receives top honors for its record of high-quality customer satisfaction.

The real power of marketing over the Internet comes when an organization offers meaningful interactive services that create a relationship with the customer. Amazon.com, the poster child of Internet commerce, built a "community" around the product. Amazon publishes customer reviews as well as those by staffers and outside reviewers. You can build an online community to sell almost anything—for example, seeds and garden tools (Garden Escape). Developing a Web presence that engages the customer with individually tailored content and services is what differentiates the Internet from other direct marketing media. Amazon maintains records of customer preferences (books, authors, and genres) and tells you what new books have come out since you last logged on that might be of interest to you. Amazon's collaborative filtering software program tells you what other people of similar tastes liked.

You have to do everything possible to draw prospects into your "web-net" until they decide that it is a place to do business. You may have to spend heavily on traditional advertising to establish your brand. Effective banner advertising on the Internet asks questions. For example, one dry cleaner seeking off-season clothing storage business used a banner that asked, "Need more closet space?" You want to make alliances and exclusive agreements with related sites to do "syndicated selling." Amazon has arrangements with approximately 30,000 sites. When consumers visit StarChefs.com to check out recipes from celebrity chefs, for example, they can click a button to let them order a cookbook from Amazon. Don't simply: sell, sell, sell. Be an information source. Useful, helpful information establishes confidence.[4]

Mass Media

Direct response marketing makes use of mass media—print and broadcast—to make initial contact with customers, especially for single product appeals, and to support other media approaches. Cable shopping channels and infomercials demonstrate mass media's important role as a primary direct response medium.

Print   Print, or space, media include magazine ads and free-standing inserts (FSIs). Magazines help you efficiently reach groups of people with special interests, such as tennis players or gardeners. See Marketing in Action box 12-1. Newspaper costs-per-thousand CPMs are often a fraction of the cost of magazines or direct mail. Direct response print ads provide a way for your customer to respond by incorporating a clip-out coupon, coming with a bind-in reply card, or giving an 800 number.

Broadcast   Broadcast media include radio, cable, and broadcast television. A key feature of broadcast is speed. When coupled with a toll-free telephone number, results can be known in a matter of hours rather than having to wait several weeks as in the case of direct mail. This provides you with an opportunity to adjust, fine-tune, and improve a broadcast campaign while it is being conducted.

Although the price of a direct mailing is relatively stable, broadcast time fluctuates widely market by market and even day-to-day. Because broadcast time is a perishable commodity, a station will frequently reduce prices on unsold inventory. This means you must continually assess the cost of the broadcast.

You can use broadcast as support for another medium or as the primary sales medium. A radio or television spot commercial can tell your prospect to "Watch for your mailing," or "Look for your ad." In this supporting role, broadcast works more efficiently with print media, with their more predictable delivery dates, than with direct mail. With direct mail you have to run announcements over an extended period of time to bracket anticipated delivery dates. Cable shopping channels and infomercials are two specialized ways of using broadcast as a primary direct response medium.

Cable Shopping Channels   The home shopping industry has annual sales of more than $2 billion in the United States. It is drawing name retailers, including Saks Fifth Avenue, which sells merchandise on the home shopping network QVC.

APPLYING
...to
Publishing,
Healthcare
Products
Marketing

MARKETING IN ACTION *12-1*

Reader's Digest Targets Patients by Their Ailments

Health data was long considered off-limits to direct marketers because it was so private and difficult to get. Then *Reader's Digest* mailed out a survey to its 15 million U.S. subscribers asking them to disclose medical information about their families. The cover letter accompanying the survey said, "In every issue of *Reader's Digest,* we give you medical information to help you stay healthy. Now we'd like to give you information and product news that specifically addresses those medical conditions that directly affect your household. But to do that we need your help." *Reader's Digest* asked about specific illnesses:

1. I or someone in my household:

	Suffers from	Wants more information on
Arthritis	○	○
Asthma	○	○
Bladder Control Problem	○	○
⋮	⋮	⋮

The survey also asked respondents to tick off prescription medicines in use in the home. The letter said, "some of the information in this survey may be shared with healthcare companies." The survey came with a sweepstakes offer, with prizes of $45,000 or a new Cadillac Coupe de Ville.

Reader's Digest sorted the responses and created mailing lists of sufferers of diseases and medical conditions. The magazine in 1998 had about nine million names on file, about 800,000 arthritis sufferers, 700,000 people with high blood pressure, 600,000 with high cholesterol, 400,000 with frequent heartburn, 200,000 with osteoporosis, and 500,000 smokers. Now the magazine could send these people something extra with their magazine: a booklet filled with articles and prescription drug ads, all about the very ailment each subscriber has. Each booklet carries four pages of ads from a single drug-company sponsor. For example, SmithKline Beecham, maker of Tagamet acid blocker and Nicorette gum, initially sponsored two booklets.

— *You can collect and use even sensitive personal data to target customers.*

Source: Sally Beatty, "*Reader's Digest* Targets Patients by Their Ailments," *The Wall Street Journal,* April 17, 1998, pp. B1, B3.

Who shops by TV? Deloitte & Touche conducted a national survey of home TV shoppers. People who shop regularly by television are younger than previously thought. Almost half of home shoppers are in the 25 to 44 age range. Their household income was lower than the market average, the number of children living in their households higher. They are more likely to watch sporting events but less likely to exercise. These shoppers are more interested in fashion than in value or comfort.

Infomercials   An infomercial is a 30-minute (typically) TV commercial that incorporates an 800 number for viewer response. The emphasis is on reality-based commercials with real, live people. Originally associated with kitchen gadgets, beauty products, and "get-rich" schemes on late-night TV, most products and services can be sold in the format and at virtually any time thanks to cable and independent networks. Infomercials are typically run in off-hours because the rates are lower. Even though H.U.T. (households using television) rates are lower at off-hours, the return on investment is greater. From a marketing perspective, an infomercial is long-form, direct response advertising that pays for itself.

APPLYING
. . . to
Tele-
communications
Marketing

GTE, a leading-edge telecommunications company, launched a new package of services with an infomercial. The services included Personal Secretary, a person's own voice-messaging system for important reminders, and Smart Ring, a service for distinguishing rings on different lines into the same place so that you always know for whom the call is intended. The 30-minute length gave GTE an opportunity to educate and inform its customers on what these services were all about. The day after the first program ran, GTE knew it had a winner.

INTEGRATED DIRECT MARKETING

Adding media to a marketing program will raise total response more effectively than simply increasing the level of activity in a single medium because different people are inclined to respond to different stimuli. When a mailing piece that might generate a 2 percent response on its own is supplemented by a toll-free 800-number ordering channel, response typically rises by 50 percent. A skillfully integrated outbound telemarketing effort can add another 50 percent lift in response. Integrated direct marketing builds synergies.

APPLYING
. . . to
Financial
Products
Marketing

For example, one of Citicorp's primary goals is to break down the traditional geographic restrictions on financial institutions to expand its business and consumer customer bases. The keystone product of one campaign was a fixed-rate home equity loan. Bank research indicated that the same target market segment would also be interested in a flexible revolving credit line vehicle. Thus, more than the immediate sale of a financial instrument was at stake. Each completed transaction produces a new, geographically remote customer for continued solicitation in an ongoing banking relationship. To assess how to market the home equity loan product to territories outside the area where the corporation maintains a branch banking presence, Citicorp tried four test packages involving increasing levels of integration starting from a common direct mail package. The impact of each was carefully tracked with the results shown in Table 12-2. Based on these figures, Citicorp decided to roll out the fourth package—the combination of all media tested. At a 1 percent higher cost than the third test package, the fourth package produced a 15 percent higher market share. An illustration of integrated direct marketing for a nonprofit organization is given in Marketing Strategies box 12-3.

TABLE 12-2   Citicorp Integrated Marketing Test

Test Packages	*Accounts Opened*	*Revenue per Account*	*Cost Decrease per $1000 Loaned*
Basic *control* package: a direct-mail piece with a lengthy application to be filled out and mailed to the bank.	Baseline	Baseline	Baseline
The same mail piece with the addition of an 800 number inviting the customer to call, ask questions, and have the application completed by phone.	+7%	+30%	−63%
The same mail package with 800 service plus a business reply card for requesting further information. People who returned the card received a follow-up telephone call.	+13%	+19%	−72%
Newspaper ads featuring an 800 number were run in the test market. These ads were timed to coincide with the mail drop.	+15%	+23%	−71%

Source: Ernan Roman, "Integrated Direct Marketing," in *Resource Report* 506.03A, New York: Direct Marketing Association, July 1989, p. 3.

APPLYING
. . . to
Sports
Marketing,
Not-for-Profit
Marketing

MARKETING STRATEGIES *12-3*

Financing the America³ Team

For the Defender Selection Trials for America's Cup, the financing of the America³ Team, the American challenger skippered by Bill Koch, depended largely on individual donations. This was in contrast to competitor Dennis Connor, who relied on major corporate funding to compete. To encourage current members of the America³ Foundation to upgrade their memberships to higher levels of giving, selected members were invited to become charter members of the Foundation's newly created Masthead Society. As part of the overall marketing strategy, an integrated direct marketing program was executed. Direct mail, a video, and a personal call as a follow-up were used.

Each person first received a letter telling them to watch for a 10-minute, fast-action videotape—featuring live footage of the America³ yacht entries, *Jayhawk* and *Defiant*—in their mail within the next week. They were also given an 800 number to call in case the tape was never delivered. Enclosed with the video was a four-page letter, introducing the Masthead Society, and inviting the member to be a guest at the Defender Trials by joining at one of three levels. Each level or "club" offered various benefits based on its value. The highest level, the Skipper's Club, entitled the member to two, four-day Defender Selection Trial passes, deluxe double accommodations for four nights, two invitations to a formal Masthead Society Reception, and a personalized commemorative America³ yacht identification flag. Approximately one week after the member received the video, a telephone marketing firm called on behalf of the Foundation to personally invite them to the Defender Trials. The script was straightforward and benefit driven. The member was offered the option of paying by credit card or invoice. If they chose to be billed, they were sent an invoice accompanied by a personalized letter, acknowledging the phone conversation, thanking them for becoming members, and restating the many benefits of their membership. Even when members were unable to attend the Defender Trials, they were extremely impressed with the video and that the Foundation would personally call with an invitation. The success of the program went beyond dollars and cents to reinforce the loyalty of the members to the organization.

Subsequently the Foundation decided to take advantage of the enthusiasm of the races by launching an emergency, last-minute fund-raising campaign during the week of the America's Cup. Members were telephoned starting the day of the first race. Throughout the scripted presentation, communicators referenced the race, specific happenings, and the outcome, adding timeliness, excitement and authenticity to the appeal. In fact, during the days when the race was actually taking place, a supervisor monitored the race on the cable television sports channel, ESPN, and made up-to-the-minute script changes as events transpired. As a result of this flexible scripting, the Foundation was able to convey its own enthusiasm and engage in a knowledgeable interaction with the member over the phone. [The America³ Team won the America's Cup, four races to one against the Italians.]

— *Integrated direct marketing is a powerful marketing approach.*

Source: TransAmerica Marketing Services, Inc.

Courtesy America3 Foundation

SUMMARY

As lifestyle changes have created the need for convenient, time-sensitive, and reliable ways for people to shop and as increased competition segments the market into every more-distinct niches, traditional mass marketing has become less efficient. Marketing funds are being shifted to database-driven direct marketing. Direct marketing creates a dialogue between you and your customer. The key to exploiting this relationship is the use of a customer database to maintain up-to-date information on your customers and your exchanges with them.

Integrated direct marketing emphasizes the coupling of diverse marketing media to create powerful media interrelationships. Although integrated direct marketing increases your upfront investment, more customers are contacted and more orders per thousand contacts are produced.

NOTES

1. Major portions of this chapter have been taken from materials provided by the Direct Marketing Educational Foundation at their Direct Marketing Institute for Professors.
2. Mickey H. Gramig, "Mailbox Marketing Mania," *The Atlanta Journal-Constitution* (October 12, 1998), p. E6.
3. Check out the specifics of the demographic profile for your ZIP code at National Decision Systems Web site. Go to *http://www.natdecsys.com/* and then click on "Lifestyle Game."
4. Clint Willis, "Does Amazon.com Really Matter?" *Forbes* (April 6, 1998), pp. 55–58; Steve Ditto and Briggs Pille, "Marketing on the Internet," *Healthcare Executive* (September/October 1998), pp. 54–55; John R. Graham, "Capturing the Cyber Customer," *American Salesman* (November 1998), pp. 9–15.

SUGGESTED READING

Blattberg, Robert C., and John Deighton. "Interactive Marketing: Exploiting the Age of Addressability," *Sloan Management Review,* Vol. 33, No. 1 (Fall 1991), pp. 5–14.

FURTHER READING

Berry, Michael J. A. and Gordon Linoff. *Data Mining Techniques: For Marketing, Sales, and Customer Support* (New York: John Wiley, 1997).
Direct Marketing Educational Foundation Inc. *Resource Reports* (New York: Direct Marketing Association, 1989).
Hughes, Arthur M. *The Complete Database Marketer* (Chicago: Probus Publishing, 1996).
Magliozzi, T. L., and P. D. Berger. "List Segmentation Strategies in Direct Marketing," *OMEGA,* Vol. 21, No. 1 (January 1993), pp. 61–72.
Muldoon, Katie, and Anne Knudsen (Eds.). *How to Profit Through Catalog Marketing* (Lincolnwood, IL: NTC Business Books, 1996).
David Shepard Associates, Inc. *The New Direct Marketing* (New York: Irwin, 1995).
Stone, Bob. *Successful Direct Marketing Methods* (Lincolnwood, IL: NTC Business Books, 1997).

QUESTIONS

1. Federated Department Stores, parent of stores such as Bloomingdales, Macy's, and Stern's, announced that it was buying Fingerhut, a big direct marketer. Federated's core customer base is middle- to upper-middle-income households. Fingerhut, which sells everything from cookware to gift baskets through its core catalog business, caters mainly to low-income customers who usually can't get credit elsewhere. Federated has about 60 million credit card accounts. Fingerhut has a database of more than 30 million current and former customer names. Fingerhut has developed its own Web sites and and has bought stakes in a number of other Internet retailers. Traditional retailers have circled warily around Web sites and electronic malls fearful that online sales would cannibalize those in their own stores. Why do you think Federated bought Fingerhut? Would you have?

2. CVS Corp., America's second-largest drugstore chain, uses prescription information to send mailings to its own customers. Drug makers fund some of these mailings. For exam-

ple, a diabetes sufferer received a letter from a CVS pharmacy. The letter, paid for by Warner-Lambert Co., touted the company's new diabetes drug, Rezulin, as a "breakthrough option" that could eliminate their injections completely. What is your opinion of CVS's practice of doing these mailings?

3. A "cookie" is a file that Web sites install on your computer's hard drive when you visit a site that offers cookies. They are very small files. Cookies are used for Web-site tracking, delivering targeted advertisements, storing IDs, personalization, and target marketing. For example, online vendors, such as Amazon.com, can read the user's cookie and match it with a stored profile that would contain credit card information, so that the user won't have to enter the information each time. Cookies enhance the Web experience for the user by limiting the repetitiveness of advertising and increasing the level of relevant content on the Web. There is the possibility that unscrupulous Web sites might take your information and sell it to offline marketers. Should a Web site be allowed to use cookies?

4. Most healthcare organizations recognize the importance of bonding with the people they serve. How could a hospital use the power of the Internet for deepening consumer relationships? Focus on the case of consumers expecting their first baby.

5. Magazine subscription businesses use frequent and repeated mailings to promote sweepstakes to encourage the purchase of merchandise. Their marketing practices are sometimes borderline. For example, customers of the Publishers Clearing House have received letters from contest representatives urging them to make purchases to "avoid embarrassment" when the PCH shows up at their door with the big money prize. Whose responsibility is it to protect the elderly, disabled, retired, and homebound from suffering major financial losses by spending heavily on merchandise?

6. Why is getting someone to buy something via telemarketing, through the mail, from a catalog, or over the Internet considered the ultimate test of branding?

7. Some direct marketing organizations collect names of prospects from obituaries published in newspapers. Family members are called by phone and asked to buy burial urns and artificial flower arrangements to place in cemeteries for deceased relatives. Other firms clip out obituaries from newspapers and mount them in plastic. These mementos are mailed to family members with a request for contributions to a charity. Are these direct marketing activities ethical? Why or why not?

8. The credit card division of a large western bank wants to forecast applications received (and eventually new accounts opened). Three factors drive applications: marketing spend, annual maintenance fee (AMF), and annual percentage rate (APR). Accounts opened is subject to a lag effect, in as much as two to three weeks pass from the time an application is received. Therefore, applications received is considered to more accurately reflect the effects of marketing spend and pricing options offered, assuming the bank's credit policies remained unchanged throughout the period. Marketing spend used the cost accumulated in the functional area "Credit Processing and Account Acquisition Expense." Costs that appeared related to processing of incoming applications and to ongoing department operations have been removed. The bank's prices are not considered in a vacuum but are considered relative to competing products. Market prices were estimated from data in *American Bank Management* magazine. Information is available for 12 months (July-June) and is given in the file creditcarddat.sav. Estimate the response function (assuming that there is no substantial temporary promotion during the period by major card issuers). Does marketing spend have an effect? Which is more important, annual maintenance fee or annual percentage rate? *Hint:* First compute relative AMF and relative APR by dividing bank prices by market prices. As always, if you compute the natural logarithm (LN) of each variable and then run a linear multiple regression on the transformed variables, the regression coefficients of the variables can be interpreted as elasticities.

CASE *12-1* **FIRST DIRECT: BRANCHLESS BANKING**

*I*n October 1996, seven years after it first opened outside Leeds, England, First Direct was still attracting attention as an innovator that operated a bank with no branches. Intrigued by its success, financial service providers wanted to understand how unseen customers conducted business around the clock over the telephone. An article in the *New York Times* [*September 3, 1996*] reported:

> Representatives from banks around the world are making the pilgrimage to this industrial city in the north of England for a glimpse of what might be their stagnant industry's equivalent of a miraculous cure. For not only is First Direct the world's leading telephone-only bank, it is the fastest growing bank in Britain. In just six years, it has signed up 2% of Britain's notoriously set-in-their-ways banking subjects, who call its rows of bankers 24 hours a day, seven days a week to pay bills, buy stock, and arrange mortgages.

Success not only put First Direct in the media limelight but it also helped to maintain high levels of enthusiasm, pride, and motivation internally. Fearful that complacency might hinder the bank's ability to uphold growth and success, CEO Kevin Newman never lost sight of the bank's challenges in an increasingly competitive and deregulated environment:

> I believe that in going forward three things need to be developed. We have to be utterly low cost. We must be able to individualize the manufacturing process and recognize that all our customers are individuals. Thirdly, we must build a strong brand as people need to identify with institutions they can trust.

"Kevin", as everyone called the chief executive, sat among the telephone sales staff in First Direct's headquarters on the outskirts of Leeds, 190 miles (300 km) north of London. Newman had installed the information systems that were instrumental in getting the new bank off the ground in 1989. Subsequently, he was promoted to operations director in 1990 and CEO in October 1991. Newman came to the bank from the mass-market retailer, Woolworth's, after having worked at Mars, the candy and consumer goods manufacturer. Although Kevin Newman did not start his

career as a banker he was, at 35 years of age, undoubtedly the youngest banking CEO in Britain.

THE BIRTH OF THE FIRST DIRECT CONCEPT

In the mid-eighties, Midland Bank, the fourth largest bank in the UK with 2,000 branches, began looking at ways of attracting more affluent and up-market customers. As Peter Simpson, subsequently First Direct's commercial director, remarked:

> If you are losing market share you can do two things: you can grow organically or inorganically. Midland Bank had limited capital, so there was nowhere to go inorganically; its reserves had been spent on the over-priced Crocker National Bank acquisition in North America and with Latin American debt. Organically, the retail banks in the United Kingdom were giving away current accounts for free, and sacrificing their profits in terms of customer value.

Consequently, in June 1988 Midland drafted a team of executives on a project code-named "Raincloud". Mike Harris, a former Midland executive, returned as a consultant to lead the top-secret investigation. An examination of consumers' banking habits highlighted that there was a substantial niche of people whose banking transactions were not branch-based. According to a national market research study of British bank customers by MORI in 1988:

- 20% of account holders had not visited their branch in the last month
- 51% said they would rather visit their branch as little as possible
- 48% had never met their branch manager
- 38% said banking hours were inconvenient
- 27% wished they were able to conduct more business with the bank over the phone

This was the beginning of an idea. Rather than reposition the branch network, the taskforce wondered what it would be like to have a bank with no branches. The team discovered that as early as 1981 a Dutch

* This case was prepared by Delphine Parmenter, Research Associate, under the supervision of Jean-Claude Larréché, Alfred H. Heineken Professor of Marketing and Christopher Lovelock, Visiting Professor at INSEAD. Copyright (c) 1997 INSEAD, Fontainebleau, France. Reproduced by permission.

bank, Nederlanse Credietbank, had set up Direktbank with a small telephone staff to cater to the needs of an upscale segment. Since 1986, Bank of America offered an additional service that enabled branch customers to process transactions by pressing buttons on touch tone telephones in response to a voice-activated computer. And in France, several banks allowed customers to make account inquiries via the videotext Minitel screens linked to their home phones.

The Midland team envisioned an entirely new type of bank that would operate from one center, 24 hours a day, 365 days a year. Employing the UK's 47 million telephones as a low cost delivery system, it would use human operators rather than a machine to perform all the functions of a traditional bank. Next, Harris' team faced the difficult task of presenting to the Midland board of directors a proposal for a new concept that might compete with its own branch network. Although Midland Bank had successfully retained its customer base with a long list of innovative banking products, it had to acquire additional business to stay afloat. Working with experts in marketing, operations, human resources, and technology, Harris was named chief executive of the proposed stand-alone telephone bank. He was given one year to design and launch it.

DEVELOPING OPERATIONAL SYSTEMS AND INITIAL JOB DESIGN

Rather than incur the delay and expense of obtaining its own bank charter, First Direct was set up as a division of Midland Bank. Short on time—Midland anticipated another bank would introduce a similar telephone service—the team proceeded secretly, working 18-hour days. After much brainstorming, the team baptized the new bank "First Direct" to reflect its pioneering concept of working directly with customers. As far as Midland was concerned, First Direct was a completely new brand and a completely new business. A black and white corporate identity symbolized the simple, economical nature of the new bank.

The start-up staff of about 50 worked initially out of London while the operations team evaluated a variety of potential sites for First Direct's one and only office. They were attracted to Leeds as the city offered moderate rental rates and a regional labor pool accustomed to lower salaries than in southern England. Additionally, the Yorkshire accent was recognized as easy to understand, warm, and friendly. First Direct leased a modern building in an industrial park outside Leeds that could be modified to suit the bank's needs.

Procedures had to be built from scratch so that any traditional branch transaction could be handled in one telephone call. The planners decided that customers could obtain cash through the Midland automatic teller machines (ATM) network and make deposits electronically, while transactions would be cleared and statements processed at one of Midland's regional processing centers. First Direct would benefit from its parent's massive technology investments of the late eighties; otherwise Midland played no managerial role.

Next, the team turned to new technology to deliver a portfolio of payment, savings, and lending instruments over the phone. A survey of the best call centers in the United States and Canada provided guidance in setting up the systems. First Direct improved upon existing technology to make all customer information accessible by any telephone operator. Furthermore, they integrated the screen and telephone systems so a call could be passed along without the customer having to repeat the entire conversation.

Another group designed job descriptions to meet service standards and the use of high-tech work tools. It was obvious that the new bank's telephone-based staff would have an assignment very different from a traditional bank teller who counted cash, filled out deposit slips, and looked for forged signatures. A visit to Federal Express's Memphis hub provided insight as to how to recruit, train and motivate staff. Kevin Gavaghan, then marketing director of Midland Bank, remembered how the hiring criteria were determined:

> In hiring, First Direct were looking for people that were fast and efficient but more importantly people with warm and engaging personalities. The first flood of applicants showed the way; the first six months proved it. The qualities required were more often than not found in the social profession—teachers, nurses, even firefighters—frequently people working difficult hours under difficult circumstances. Empathy and responsiveness under pressure marked these types out from the traditional bank clerk whose reserve and process-orientation proved at times impossible to reverse.

Initial recruitment advertising gave only sketchy details of employment opportunities in the financial services sector; there was no mention of Midland Bank. As early as May of 1989, First Direct began hiring telephone advisors who were called Banking Representatives (BRs). Training sought to improve the candidate's communication and listening skills so that they sounded friendly, mature, and well informed over the phone. By the time of launch, 200 BRs were prepared to answer inquiries and process customer transactions.

GETTING OFF TO A SLOW START

First Direct inaugurated its service at midnight on Sunday, October 1, 1989, in a pointed reference to its seven days a week, 24-hour operation. Although for legal reasons its advertising had to mention that First Direct was a division of Midland Bank, it sought to distance itself from Midland to bring in new customers. First Direct selected a British agency known as a creative "hot shop", Howell Henry Chaldecott Lury (HHCL), to orchestrate an aggressive £6 million advertising campaign that kicked off one hour before the bank opened for business.

Traditional banks did not see First Direct as a threat. Skeptics doubted that the concept of telephone banking would ever catch on, or that it would ever be profitable. The competitive spirit within Midland was such that no one anticipated a great deal of cannibalization. Furthermore, as First Direct targeted individuals with relatively high disposable incomes, existing banks never feared it would gain significant market share. Although First Direct was from the outset overwhelmed with telephone inquiries, acquiring new customers proved difficult. Soon the media reported it to be a flop.

Despite its slow start, First Direct began winning a growing number of customers after its first full year of business. By December of 1992, it had almost 250,000 account holders, about 70% of whom had reportedly been attracted from competitors. A year later, Gene Lockhart, CEO of UK Banking at Midland, declared that First Direct had acquired over 350,000 customers, only 20% of whom were formerly Midland customers. The bank lost very few customers, approximately 2 to 3% per year, the majority as a result of "natural causes". In 1996, the bank had 640,000 customers and was acquiring about 125,000 new customers a year—the equivalent of opening one new branch each week (Exhibit 1).

During the first six years of operations, First Direct's offices adapted to accommodate this phenomenal growth. With the 75,000 square foot (7,000m²) building in the Arlington Business Center fully utilized, First Direct unveiled a second purpose-built facility three miles away at Stourton in November 1994. The Arlington location accommodated both back-office operations (foreign investments section, lending services, and mortgage underwriters) and the front-office call center (customer service and new customer department) on a single floor without walls. Besides a second call center, the 150,000 square foot (14,000m²) Stourton site housed credit and risk services, investments, new mortgage inquiries, the insurance division, and customer inquiries (Visa, direct debits, standing orders, customer relations). The operations and information technology (IT) staff occupied part of the same trading floor at the center of the business. The different teams mapped their areas by the signs that hung from the ceiling (Exhibit 2).

Telephone advisors did not have their own desks but transferred mobile units containing stationery and personal belongings to any desk available during their shift. This "hot desking" approach enabled full capacity utilization over the non-stop work shift. Kevin Newman was based in Arlington and all the directors sat with their departments at their respective sites—no one had a private office. Richard Rushton, customer services director, had a desk at each site. A mini-van made the ten-minute connection between the two sites every hour.

By early 1996, it was estimated that First Direct served a customer base equivalent to 200 branches. However, the telephone bank employed only 2,400 individuals where a branch network would require a staff of almost 4,000. Its staffing costs were about half those of a typical retail-oriented commercial branch. The construction of a third building adjacent to Stourton was scheduled for completion by June 1997.

EXHIBIT 1   First Direct: Estimated Account Data

Date	Total Number of Customers	Total Number of Accounts	Calls/day	Staff
April 1996	641,000	1,100,000	32,000	2,400
December 1995	586,000	800,000	26,000	2,300
December 1994	476,000	700,000	21,000	1,900
December 1993	361,000	500,000	16,000	1,500
December 1992	241,000	350,000	11,000	1,000
December 1991	136,000	200,000	7,000	500
December 1990	66,000	105,000	3,000	300
December 1989	11,000	N/A	N/A	250

Source: Estimates based on Midland Bank Annual Reports and Internal Sources First Direct, 1996.

Arlington Main Floor

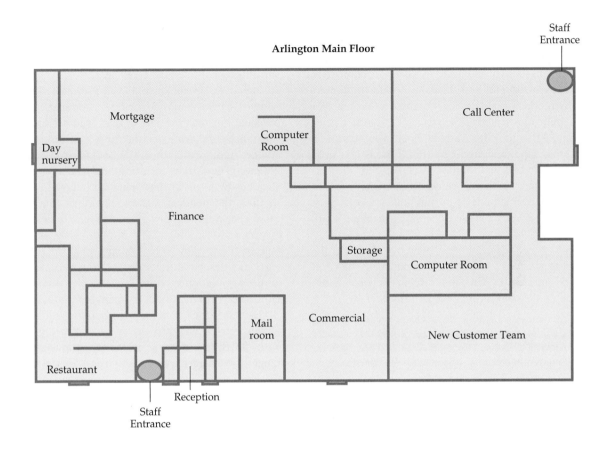

Stourton Trading Floor

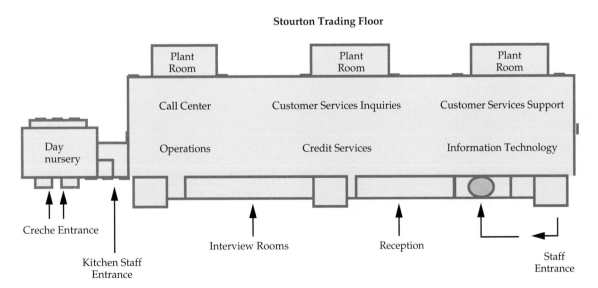

EXHIBIT 2   **Simplified Floor Plan Arlington and Stourton**

Efficient information systems were instrumental in keeping costs down. The business required non-stop processing power to perform on-line transactions and to access the bank's mainframe computers. The hub of First Direct's operations, the on-line customer database, used two Sequoia UNIX-based computers at Arlington and Stourton. It also supported and interfaced with the 1,800 personal computers that ran various applications across the two sites. Third parties provided IT support for transaction clearing, card service processing, and credit scoring. First Direct used an automatic call distribution (ACD) system to manage one of the largest call centers in the UK. It routed calls to unoccupied operators and bounced calls back and forth between the two centers to balance work loads.

First Direct achieved break-even by the end of the 1994 financial year and in 1995 reported its first full year of profitability. In 1996, Kevin Newman commented on the bank's financial performance:

> As you know, we have been circumspect about releasing this information for commercial competitive reasons and I do not wish to change this policy. I can, however, indicate that our return on equity is extremely attractive (i.e, 25% plus). Our return on investment is equally attractive, at least as good as that currently being achieved by the UK clearing banks.

RETAIL BANKING IN THE UNITED KINGDOM

Until the seventies, the so-called Big Four British clearing banks, namely Lloyds, Midland, Barclays, and National Westminster (NatWest) dominated retail banking in the United Kingdom while building societies controlled the mortgage market. Much like the U.S. savings and loan institutions, building societies provided funds for the purchase of homes from a pool of members' savings. No new bank charters had been issued by Britain's central bank, the Bank of England, since the end of the nineteenth century.

However, in the seventies the Bank of England allowed banks to provide a more complete range of personal financial services, from share dealing and insurance brokering to the provision of financial advice. Additionally, the 1979 Banking Act opened up the mortgage market to institutions other than building societies by formally dissolving the interest rate cartel. In turn, the building societies obtained the right to offer checking accounts and unsecured loans. Abbey National was one of the first institutions to take advantage of this shake-up, becoming a bank in 1989. The early eighties saw further deregulation, tax incentives, and an economic boom in the UK that greatly enhanced personal wealth for many individuals.

By 1993, four of the top ten building societies had obtained bank charters and were competing directly with the Big Four banks in the provision of a broad range of consumer banking services. Consequently, by the early nineties Britain had an excessive number of banks and branches, difficult to sustain in the face of economic recession and increased automation. Inevitably, several much-publicized mergers followed. The Hongkong & Shanghai Banking Corporation (HSBC) bought Midland Bank in July 1992. Three years later, Britain's biggest building society, Halifax, planned a merger with Leeds Permanent, the country's fifth biggest. The consolidation process accelerated markedly in 1995 (Exhibit 3).

EXHIBIT 3 UK Retail Banks—Statistics 1989 & 1995

Retail Banks	Assets (£ millions) 1989	1995	Pre-tax Profits (% of total assets) 1989	1995	Number of Branches 1989	1995	Number of Employees 1989	1995
National Westminster Bank	116,189	166,347	0.3	1.1	2,997	2,215	86,600	61,000
Barclays Bank	127,616	164,184	0.5	1.3	2,645	2,050	85,900	61,200
Lloyds Bank TSB[a]	83,023	131,750	−0.7	1.3	3,722	2,858	87,500	66,400
Abbey National[b]	37,201	97,614	1.3	1.1	678	678	13,600	16,300
Midland Bank[c]	62,619	92,093	−0.4	1.1	2,042	1,701	47,500	43,400
Royal Bank of Scotland	27,436	50,497	0.8	1.2	842	687	20,500	19,500
Bank of Scotland	14,073	34,104	1.3	1.3	527	411	12,100	11,300

[a] Lloyds Bank merged with TSB in October 1995 and acquired Cheltenham & Gloucester in 1995.
[b] Abbey National acquired National & Provincial in 1995.
[c] Midland Bank was acquired by HSBC Holdings plc in July 1992.

Source: Annual Abstract of Banking Statistics, British Bankers Association, 1996, volume 13

Parallel to this industry-wide reshaping, individual banks and building societies embarked on their own downsizing programs by closing branches and centralizing transaction processing. The total number of branches fell by 15% between 1980 and 1992, with a loss of over 100,000 jobs. More qualified or senior staff were often replaced by lower-paid, less-qualified workers. The banks and building societies soon attracted unfavorable media attention and criticism for their long queues, high level of errors, and exorbitant customer charges. In response to these attacks, Midland Bank was the first to introduce charge-free banking and personal loans. In the late eighties, the Henley Center for Forecasting found that customer dissatisfaction remained higher in banking than in any other retail sector in Britain. However, only one in thirty British consumers switched banks in a given year. Despite increased competition, only one person in five could distinguish between the services offered by the various banks.

Many financial institutions saw automation and new technology as ways to replace some expensive branch transactions. Customers responded enthusiastically and automated teller machines proliferated. Banks made ATM network share agreements and also installed cash machines in non-branch locations like supermarkets. With new technology, telephone-based banking now offered person-to-person, person-to-computer, or even computer-to-computer based transactions at an estimated cost as low as one-sixth that of conventional branch-based transactions (Exhibit 4).

As early as 1983, the Nottingham Building Society offered Britain's first subscription telephone banking service, known as Homelink. However, the service attracted only 5,000 subscribers. Another pioneer, The Royal Bank of Scotland launched its Home and Office Banking System in 1984 and Direct Line insurance in 1985. By 1996, the use of telephone banking in one form or another was widespread throughout the industry (Exhibit 5).

The introduction of debit cards and smart cards also favored the advent of electronic banking. As an alternative to cash, NatWest and Midland Bank piloted the Mondex smart card in July 1995. Positioned as an electronic wallet, it allowed customers to store cash, debit purchases electronically, and replenish the card from their accounts at an ATM or through specially equipped telephones. In 1995, Barclays, the largest retail bank in the UK, launched a home banking service accessed through the customer's personal computer.

EXHIBIT 4   Alternative Home Banking Technology

- **Automatic Call Distribution—ACD**
  Systems that manage a high volume of incoming calls by routing and placing each call in a queue to the next available operator so that the caller never hears a busy signal.
- **Computer Integrated Telephone—CIT**
  Computer databases are linked to the incoming call, allowing call handlers to quickly access customer files.
- **Calling Line Identification**
  An additional CIT service which shows the number at the source of the call.
- **Interactive Voice Recognition and Response**
  CIT systems can react to the tones entered by telephone, or even recognize certain predetermined voice inputs.
- **Teletext and Videotext-based Access**
  Videotext terminals, with screens and keyboards, provide an interactive access to a bank's computer. The national French Minitel system is the most developed network in Europe; British Telecom offers a similar Prestel network.
- **Multi-Media Kiosks**
  Stand-alone multi-media kiosks may communicate with the customer using powerful interactive digital text, audio, video and animation.
- **PC-based Access**
  A personal computer may access a bank's computer via a modem and telephone network.
- **Internet World Wide Web Site**
  Home banking customers may connect to their bank's proprietary Web site via private dial-up networks and tap into their personal accounts.

Source: Data gathered from various publications.

ACQUIRING NEW CUSTOMERS AT FIRST DIRECT

The majority of First Direct's new prospects called the bank on a toll-free line. Direct mail activity produced high call volume and brought in nearly one-half of new customers. More importantly, word-of-mouth recommendations generated about one-third of customer acquisitions. Customer polls showed that 87% of the customer base was either extremely or very satisfied with First Direct, compared with an average of 51% for conventional banks; 85% of its consumers actively recommended the bank to friends, relatives, or colleagues (Exhibit 6). In both 1994 and 1995, First Direct achieved the largest net gain of all UK banks and building societies in customers transferring their checking account.

The new customer team answered inquiries, opened accounts, explained the mechanics of telephone banking, and carried out the initial processing

EXHIBIT 5   Sample of Direct Financial Services in the United Kingdom

Institution	Service	Launched	Description
Bank of Scotland	CardCall	October 1993	add-on telephone inquiry service using interactive voice response
	HOBS	1985	add-on teletext banking service
	Phoneline		add-on operator-based home banking
Royal Bank of Scotland	Direct Line	1985	direct insurance services via telephone operators
	Direct Banking	April 1994	full service 24-hr telephone banking by touch tone phone or operator
TSB	Speedlink	1987	add-on mass-market telephone banking service via voice recognition
	PhoneBank	October 1994	operator-based home banking
National Westminster Bank	Actionline	September 1988	add-on automated 24-hr touch-tone inquiry service later with operators
	Primeline	September 1991	up-market fee-based telephone service via personal account managers
NatWest in partnership with Thomas Cook	Touch	1995	add-on banking and travel services via stand-alone videotext kiosks
Nottingham Building Society	Homelink	1983	add-on home banking service offered via BT Prestel videotext network
Midland Bank	Customer Service Center	May 1993	add-on customer service inquiry via operators
Co-operative Bank	Armchair Banking	1992	add-on telephone banking service with operator
Barclays Bank	Barclaycall	July 1993	add-on mass-market telephone banking service via operators
		1995	electronic computer to computer banking
Alliance & Leicester Giro	Telecare	1995	integrated telephone banking via operator
	Swiftcheck		automated telephone inquiry
Nationwide	Home Banking	1995	computer-based home banking
Clydesdale	Telebank	1995	computer-based home banking
Lloyds Bank	Lloydsline	1994	add-on up-market telephone banking service manned by operators
Marks & Spencer		April 1995	insurance services by telephone
Virgin Group	Virgin Direct	March 1995	financial services via telephone

Source: Data gathered from various publications.

and assessing of the 17,000 prospects that applied every month. They obtained basic customer details (name, address, date of birth) before taking the caller through the application process over the telephone. Then, the computer system automatically generated a preprinted application form for customers to sign and return. Next, First Direct formally processed the application and made various fraud and credit checks. Credit scoring requirements were strict because new customers were instantly issued 25 checks and a £100 check guarantee card that potentially gave access to £2,500 credit. The bank rejected about 50% of applicants.

New customers received a "Welcome" pack and established security procedures to ensure proper identification and confidentiality. Ninety-seven percent of new customers opened a checking account; about 70% also transferred their direct salary deposits, 60% opened a savings account, and 40% a credit card account. Although First Direct did not require a minimum balance, the average checking account balance was about £1,000. After the first three months of activity, First Direct made several mailings and telephone calls to take customers through the "Education" phase in order to build awareness of the range of investment and lending services provided.

EXHIBIT 6   Customer Satisfaction Survey for UK Retail Bank Customers Year-end 1995

Bank	Very or Extremely Satisfied		Have Recommended at Least Once in Last 12 Months
	Q4 1995	Q4 1994	Q4 1995
First Direct	87%	86%	85%
Big 5 Main Banks (avg.)	51%	44%	16%
Building Societies	66%	65%	27%
Other Banks (avg.)	69%	65%	42%
Midland	54%	46%	14%
Lloyds	55%	46%	18%
NatWest	44%	41%	16%
Barclays	47%	37%	15%
TSB	59%	56%	15%

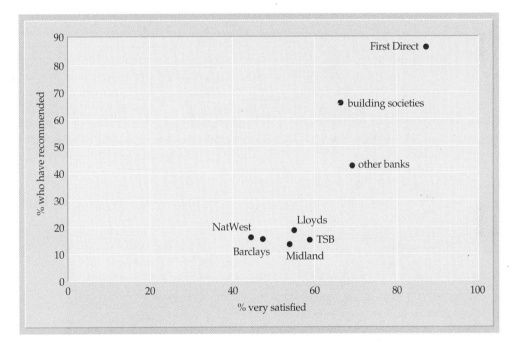

Source: First Direct Survey conducted between November 20, 1995 and January 21, 1996.

CUSTOMER SERVICE

The heart of First Direct was the call center. Regular customers could call at any time of the day or night on a special Lo-call telephone number charged at local rates, regardless of where the call originated in the UK, or contact the bank from overseas via a special number. First Direct received over half of all calls outside traditional banking hours, many on public holidays. The average customer called First Direct once a month. During peak hours, from 10 a.m. to 12 noon and 6 p.m. to 9 p.m., nearly 800 people worked the phones. That number dropped in the middle of the night to about 40 operators.

Banking Reps verified the customer's identity and retrieved the account information on the computer screen. The Customer Information System recorded each customer contact and gave BRs access to all the customer's accounts and business history. Day-to-day transactions such as balance inquiries, electronic payment of bills, or a transfer of funds between accounts could all be completed by the same representative, without the customer being transferred. In fact, BRs could handle 85% of the inquiries. Some BRs were accredited to deal with more complicated Visa card or foreign currency requests.

For more specialized information regarding loans, personal insurance, mortgages, or investments, BRs transferred customers to telephone advisors within the respective business units. For example, mortgage counselors were available from 7 a.m. to 12 midnight, seven days a week, for advice on a new mortgage, remortgage, or a home improvement loan. A mortgage application could be completed over the phone. Additionally, an experienced group of BRs manned what was called an overnight "mushroom squad" to answer any type of customer inquiry in any business area.

Telecaster screens suspended from the ceilings in each department signaled the number of calls waiting, the average length of the wait, and the current service level expressed as a percentage. To meet minimum service objectives, 75% of all calls had to be answered within 20 seconds or less. If callers were put on hold for more than two minutes, BRs apologized and arranged a call-back. The bank recorded customer calls to safeguard against transaction errors. As much as possible was done via the phone, but for legal reasons it was sometimes necessary to complete written documents after the phone had been put down.

Although no one at First Direct dealt with customers face-to-face, the employees elected to wear business dress to convey a sense of professionalism. The 1,200 Banking Representatives (50% of the total staff) formed the customer's overall impression of the company. Bringing with them their own experience as bank customers, BRs strove to be flexible enough to accommodate those customers who complained that the bank's rigid systems did not always meet their needs. When things went wrong, BRs tried to go overboard to recover customers.

At First Direct there was no such thing as a normal workday. Workweeks varied between 16 and 36 hours and there was no premium paid for night or weekend shifts. Full-time BRs worked a 36-hour week with a 10-minute break every two hours and a half-hour lunch break. The 1996 television advertising campaign put pressure on the call center not only from increased inquiries but also by increasing the average call length of existing customers from three to three and a half minutes. Some telephone advisors were more than willing to work overtime, often putting in 14-hour shifts and taking over 200 calls in a day. (Overtime was paid at one and a quarter times the hourly rate.) Although the staffing was based on sophisticated forecasts, an additional 30 seconds spent with each of First Direct's 26,000 daily callers was likely to jam the call center. Newman recognized that working in the call center was a tough job:

> Calls come in incessantly, one after another. So, after having answered 150 calls it is difficult to keep the momentum going and to be sincerely friendly on the phone especially when handling tedious transactions. But our business is built on how the next call is answered. The biggest part of my leadership role is to enable a culture which allows people to feel very positive about their contribution to our business so that they may deliver genuine smiles over the phone. This cannot be obtained by *telling* people to do so; they can only do it because they believe it.

The commercial department's principal function was data management geared at building a one-to-one customer relationship. Database specialists fed information to the new product development team and the communications team to jointly determine and optimize marketing strategies. The Management Information Database (MIND) software combined transactional information with behavioral data to predict the next product a customer was likely to purchase. This database prompted BRs to cross-sell other financial services when clients called with routine requests and also helped personalize their conversations with customers:

Sylvia (BR):	Hello, First Direct. How may I help you?
Mr. Scott (Customer):	Good evening, I would like to order some US dollars please.
Sylvia:	Your account number please?
Mr. Scott:	58-395-123
Sylvia:	Thank you. Please bear with me while I verify some information for security reasons. Could you please give me the third digit of your password?
Mr. Scott:	Five.
Sylvia:	And the date of your wedding anniversary?
Mr. Scott:	February 14th.
Sylvia:	Thank you, Mr. Scott. How many US dollars would you like to order?
Mr. Scott:	It depends, I'm going skiing in the States. Can you tell me if there is a cash machine in Vail, Colorado, please?
Sylvia:	I'll need to ask you to hold the line for a minute while I find that information for you sir.
Mr. Scott:	Thank you.
Sylvia:	Hello, yes in fact there is a Cirrus ATM machine at the First Interstate Bank at 38 Redbird Drive in Vail.
Mr. Scott:	In that case, I'll only take $500 in cash with me and use the cash machine at the resort.

Sylvia:	Right. I'll put in an order for $500. Shall I debit your checking account and have the currency delivered by registered mail to your home address?
Mr. Scott:	Yes, please.
Sylvia:	Thank you sir. You should receive it within three days. We'll include a confirmation of the amount deducted. Have a nice trip!

A few weeks later:

Peter (BR):	Hello, First Direct. How may I help you?
Mr. Scott:	Good evening, I would like to make a payment to British Gas please. My account number with First Direct is 58-395-123.
Peter:	Thank you. Please bear with me while I verify some information for security reasons. Could you please give me the first digit of your password please?
Mr. Scott:	Three.
Peter:	And your mother's maiden name?
Mr. Scott:	Bradford
Peter:	Thank you, Mr. Scott. I'll be glad to arrange your payment to British Gas. By the way, were you able to find the First Interstate cash machine in Vail when you were on your skiing holiday in Colorado? I hope everything went well.

PEOPLE AND DEVELOPMENT

First Direct was the largest private employer in Leeds with over 2,400 employees by early 1996; it projected to add an extra 550 by year-end. On average the staff were between 20 and 40 years of age; nearly 69% were women and 24% part-timers (Exhibit 7). Recruitment was carried out continually via a 24-hour phone answering service that provided application information. Two meeting rooms adjacent to the lobby in Arlington were reserved exclusively for interviewing. It was becoming more difficult to recruit telephone advisors because Leeds had become a hub for call centers. (By 1996, there were over 350 24-hour call centers within the United Kingdom in the retailing, banking, and utility sectors.) The team leaders who interviewed the 60 BRs hired each month looked for people with a positive attitude who were enthusiastic about joining a first-class organization. First Direct also had a reputation for providing comprehensive training and a benefits package that included a mortgage subsidy, a pension scheme, and 27 vacation days.

Recruited from a non-banking background, BRs did not come into contact with customers until they had successfully completed a seven-week training course conducted by twenty in-house trainers. Four weeks were devoted to understanding the bank's products and communication systems. They also practiced telephone techniques such as voice projection skills to regulate the pitch and volume vital to create trust and confidence. The last three weeks concentrated on role-playing to build excellent listening skills and the ability to access and input data accurately and efficiently. Only a small part of the customer interaction was scripted for the beginning and end of conversations. Banking Representatives were encouraged to use what they thought were the right phrases, given the nature of the rapport. To become a full-fledged BR required passing a total of 54 internal accreditation tests over the first nine months of employment (Exhibit 8).

All the BRs were assigned to teams of individuals working the same shift pattern. A team leader acted as a coach and watched the customer service screens to make sure that everything ran smoothly and to identify any members who might need assistance. A lengthy call was a clear signal of a customer problem or complaint. There were over 100 teams in the two call centers with names like "Vernon's Vikings", "JJ and the Dinos", and "Hard Time Lovers". Sales competitions, product awareness sessions, and theme days were organized regularly between the teams to bond people together.

The level of basic pay related to the market and to individual acquisition and development of skills rather than to the pay and grading structures of traditional

EXHIBIT 7 First Direct Workforce Profile

Sex	%	Status	%	Age	%	Service Length	%
Male	31%	Full-time	76%	<20	1%	<1 yr	22%
Female	69%	Part-time	24%	20–25	29%	1 yr	22%
				26–30	26%	2 yr	16%
				31–35	20%	3 yr	14%
				36–40	14%	4 yr	7%
				41–45	6%	>5 yr	19%
				46–50	3%		
				>50	1%		

Source: First Direct Workforce Profile, May 1996.

EXHIBIT 8   **First Direct Training Programs**

Customer Service	Duration
Account Operating	7 weeks
Back Office	1 day
Customer Development	1 day
Team Leader Development Program	**Duration**
Coaching and Feedback	2 days
Motivation	2 days
Effective Team Leading	3 days
Time and Priority Management	2 days
Formal Training for Managers	**Duration**
Counseling Skills	2 days
Developing Your Team	2 days
Influencing and Assertion	2 days
Miscellaneous Formal Training Courses	**Duration**
Presentation Skills	1 day
Written Communication Skills	1 day
Interview Skills	2 days
Appraisal Skills	2 days

Source: First Direct, Training & Development Guide, May 1996.

banks. Annual appraisal ratings determined the level of performance bonuses that could go as high as 5% of annual salary. Each year, nearly 30% of the BR staff moved to other departments such as lending services or mortgages. It took about 18 months to learn the job and

to get to know the company before applying for other jobs. Such career opportunities helped keep turnover low at 11%. In 1996, 40% of the employees had been with the firm for at least three years.

First Direct's facilities reflected the needs of a 24-hour workforce. A private security firm manned the entrance to the car parks and reception areas throughout the night. The company restaurant served breakfast, lunch, and dinner from 7 a.m. to 9 p.m. seven days a week while vending machines made hot and cold drinks available free of charge around the clock. Day-care centers at both Arlington and Stourton looked after 150 small children.

MARKETING STRATEGY

Management did not foresee telephone-only banking as having universal appeal. In fact, First Direct estimated that telephone banking would ultimately attract up to 10 million of the UK's 36 million bank customers. Most First Direct customers were between 25 and 44 years of age, living in metropolitan areas and working as professionals, managers, or in high-grade clerical positions (Exhibit 9). Research also showed that about 50% of its customers owned personal computers—twice the market average. These busy profes-

EXHIBIT 9   **Comparative Customer Profiles: First Direct vs All British Banks**

			First Direct Customers	*British Bank Customers*
Age:		15–19	1%	9%
		20–24	3%	6%
		25–34	33%	20%
		35–44	32%	17%
		45–54	22%	16%
		55–64	9%	13%
		65+	0%	19%
Sex:		male	50%	49%
		female	50%	51%
Socio-economic group:		AB	46%	19%
		C1	36%	29%
		C2	12%	23%
		DE	6%	29%

British socio-economic group definitions

Grade	Social status	Occupation
A	Upper middle class	Higher managerial, administrative or professional
B	Middle class	Intermediate managerial, administrative or professional
C1	Lower middle class	Supervisory or clerical, and junior managerial administrative or professional
C2	Skilled working class	Skilled manual workers
D	Working class	Semi and unskilled manual workers
E	Lowest level of subsistence	State pensioners or widows, casual or lowest-grade workers

Sources: First Direct NOP Survey January 1996 Fieldwork Nov 95–Jan 96; The Financial Research Survey NOP April–Sept 1996.

sionals were attracted by the offer of speed and convenience; their extensive use of the bank's services also generated higher profitability. A *New York Times* (September 3, 1995) journalist estimated:

> The average balance is ten times higher at First Direct than at Midland, while the overall costs are 61% less. Overall, First Direct makes money on 60% of its customers, compared to 40% at the average British bank.

First Direct rated several times among the "Best Buys" of *Which?* magazine's consumer reports on retail banking (Exhibit 10). It also won the 1995 *Unisys/Sunday Times* "Customer Champion Awards" for outstanding customer service in financial services and as overall winner. The First Direct brand seemed to create a service halo; research showed that First Direct customers had a satisfaction level with the ATM system double that of Midland Bank customers, even though they shared the identical network.

Among its full range of traditional banking services (Exhibit 11), First Direct featured its interest bearing checking account that offered an automatic fee-free overdraft facility of £250 and daily cash withdrawals of £500 a day subject to sufficient funds. However, fees accumulated rapidly if customers exceeded the agreed overdraft. First Direct encouraged customers to maximize short-term returns by frequently transferring money between their checking accounts and multiple savings accounts. There were no transaction charges for any of First Direct's basic services. Advertising claimed that the lack of branches enabled it to pass on savings to customers. Even the Visa card was free of annual charges, offering up to 56 days interest-free credit as well as free travel accident insurance. First Direct was also known to offer better interest rates on mortgages, personal loans, and Visa cards (Exhibit 12).

While most UK banks marketed mortgages in the spring or car loans in July, First Direct's approach was to mail customers information only when they needed it. When First Direct added car insurance in March 1995 to complement the life and household insurance products already offered, it adopted a soft-sell approach. BRs were prompted to collect car insurance renewal dates from customers and to record this information on the customer database. As renewal dates approached, customers either received a quotation in the mail or by phone.

COMMUNICATIONS STRATEGY

The First Direct brand tried to communicate a no-frills, hassle-free approach to banking more in tune with customers' lifestyles. Matthew Higgins, market planning manager, explained:

> People do not see banks as a fundamental part of their lives. We are trying to market First Direct as a background activity. No bank should be at the top of customers' minds. The whole idea with First Direct is that it is efficient, easy, and available when you want it. You simply tap into it and then you go away and do something more interesting.

The purpose of First Direct's initial offbeat ad campaign was to break into a sluggish market by getting people to switch banks. This was a challenging task as it was an industry joke that the British were more likely to change their partners than their bankers. The launch advertising helped First Direct stand out in the crowded financial services market. In 1991, First Direct entrusted Chiat Day, a creative American agency, to invest £3 million in television commercials underlining its customers' extraordinary satisfaction with the new telephone bank. Unfortunately, the resulting campaign did not build the brand and First Direct stayed off the air for three years in search of new solutions. The 1995 television campaign also failed to develop the theme of banking and living in harmony.

Between 1991 and 1995, the press was used almost continuously to attract new customers through offers of high-quality service and no fees. As competition intensified, Chiat Day came out in 1993 with a press campaign to differentiate the pioneer from the new players. Simultaneously, First Direct mailed out brochures explaining the mechanics of telephone banking to a broad upscale audience. The mailing combined with the press ads generated an overwhelming number of customer inquiries. Unable to keep up with the demand, First Direct cut short the campaign so as not to compromise service quality.

Finally, in 1996, First Direct turned to WCRS, a major international advertising network, part of the EURO-RSCG group. Their brief revolved around the necessity of developing a more disciplined approach to building the First Direct brand. WCRS had a solid reputation for image development with clients like BMW cars and Orange mobile phones. Not until 1996 did television advertising demonstrate what it meant to bank with First Direct. Back on the air with two six-week bursts between January and April of 1996, the "Tell me one good thing about your bank" campaign underlined the advantages of First Direct to attract dissatisfied customers from competitors. The £7 million television, radio, press, and direct mail campaign raised meaningful brand awareness among the target audience from 30% to 45% (Exhibit 13).

EXHIBIT 10 Home Banking Systems Compared by *Which* Consumers Association

	Name of service	Cleared balance	Recent transactions	Standing orders	Bill payment	Customer transfer	Transfer to third party	Order statement	Order cheque book	Availability	Service charge	low user (£)	medium user (£)	frequent user (£)	heavy user (£)	Other information
Tone-based and voice-based																
Abbey National	Switchcheck	✓			13	✓		✓	✓	24 hours		0.59	5.17	14.13	20.33	
Alliance & Leicester Giro	Cytel	✓	12							24 hours	£10 a year	11.58	21.37	40.64	56.59	Tone only
Bank of Cyprus		✓				✓		✓	✓	24 hours		1.58	13.75	36.89	59.22	Tonepad £12
Clydesdale	TeleBank Telephone Service	✓			11	✓		✓		24 hours		0.59	5.17	14.13	20.33	Tone only
Co-operative	Routine Information Line	✓						✓		24 hours		0.59	5.17	14.13	20.33	Tonepad £5
NatWest	Actionline	✓	25	✓	44	✓	✓	✓	✓	24 hours		1.58	13.75	36.89	59.22	Tone only
National & Provincial	Tele Banking	✓	5		10	✓	✓	✓	✓	24 hours		1.58	13.75	36.89	59.22	Tone only, Tonepad £7.99
Nationwide	Home Banking	✓	6		21	✓	✓	✓	✓	24 hours		1.58	13.75	36.89	59.22	Tone only
Northern Rock	Telephone Banking	✓	5			✓		✓	✓	24 hours		1.58	13.75	36.89	59.22	Tone only
The Royal Bank of Scotland	Direct Banking 'Push Button'	✓	No limit		No limit	✓	✓	✓		24 hours		0.59	5.17	14.13	20.33	
Save & Prosper	Serviceline	✓	5					✓		24 hours		0.59	5.17	14.13	20.33	
Operator-based																
Abbey National	Telephone Banking	✓	No limit	✓	13	✓		✓	✓	Mon-Fri 8am to 9pm / Saturday 8am to 4pm		0.59	5.17	14.13	20.33	
Alliance & Leicester	Telecare	✓	3 months	✓	No limit	✓	✓	✓	✓	24 hours		0.59	5.17	14.13	20.33	
Alliance & Leicester		✓	3 months	✓	No limit	✓	✓	✓	✓	24 hours		0.59	5.17	14.13	20.33	
Bank of Scotland Centrebank	Banking Direct	✓	3 months	✓	No limit	✓		✓	✓	24 hours		0.59	5.17	14.13	20.33	
Bank of Scotland	Phoneline	✓	3 months	✓	No limit	✓		✓	✓	Mon-Fri 7am to 11pm / Sat-Sun 9am to 5pm		0.59	5.17	14.13	20.33	
Barclays	Barclaycall	✓	3 months	✓	No limit	✓	✓	✓	✓			0.59	5.17	14.13	20.33	
Clydesdale	Telephone Centre	✓	4 months	✓	No limit	✓	✓	✓	✓	Mon-Fri 8am to 8pm		0.59	5.17	14.13	20.33	
Co-operative	Armchair Banking	✓	No limit	✓	No limit	✓	✓	✓	✓	6am to 12am		0.59	5.17	14.13	20.33	
First Direct		✓	No limit	✓	No limit	✓	✓	✓	✓	24 hours		0.59	5.17	14.13	20.33	
Lloyds	LloydsLine	✓	No limit	✓	No limit	✓	✓	✓	✓	8am to 10pm		0.59	5.17	14.13	20.33	
NatWest	Primeline	✓	No limit	✓	No limit	✓	✓	✓	✓	24 hours		0.59	5.17	14.13	20.33	
The Royal Bank of Scotland	Direct Banking	✓	6 months	✓	No limit	✓	✓	✓	✓	24 hours		0.59	5.17	14.13	20.33	
Save & Prosper	Premlor 24 Hour Banking Service	✓	2 years	✓	No limit	✓	✓	✓	✓	24 hours		1.58	13.75	36.89	59.22	
TSB	PhoneBank	✓		✓	99	✓	✓	✓	✓	24 hours		0.59	5.17	14.13	20.33	
Computer-based																
Bank of Scotland and Bank of Scotland Centrebank	HOBS	✓	3 months	✓	No limit	✓	✓	✓	✓	Mon-Fri 6am to 1am / Sat-Sun 6am to 12pm	£4 per month	48.59	53.17	62.13	68.33	Screenphone £99 or use your own PC
Clydesdale	TeleBank	✓	250/6 mths	✓	No limit	✓	✓	✓	✓	24 hours	£4 per month	48.59	57.97	76.53	80.33	
Nationwide	PC Home Banking	✓	12	✓	21	✓	✓	✓	✓	24 hours		0.59	5.17	14.13	20.33	

Source: Which? (May 1996, p. 53) an independent monthly consumer magazine published by Consumers' Association, 2 Marylebone Road, London NW1 4DF.

EXHIBIT 11   First Direct Products and Services

Type	Product	Features
Checking	Interest bearing checking account	- interest bearing, no fees - £250 automatic fee-free overdraft - automatic bill payment
Debit/Credit Cards	First Direct Debit Card	- £100 check guarantee card - £500 daily cash withdrawals from 7,000 ATMs - access to Switch[a] network - access to Cirrus and Maestro ATM network
	VISA Card	- no annual fee - 56 day interest free credit - £500 daily cash withdrawals - membership Visa points program
Savings & Investments	High Interest Savings Account (HISA) 60-day accounts	- unlimited withdrawals - minimum deposit £2,500 - 60 day notice for withdrawals
	Fixed Interest Savings Account Money Market Account Tax Exempt Savings Account (TESSA) Personal Equity Plan (PEP) Share Dealing Direct Interest Savings Account	- - £5,000 minimum deposit - - medium to long term tax-free investment - buying or selling on London stock exchange - high interest rates paid on balances over £1,000 - one free withdrawal or transfer per quarter
	Financial Planning	- personal financial planning advice
Mortgages	Variable Rate Mortgages Home Improvement Loans Equity Release Loan	- 25 year financing of 80% of purchase price - - financing from £3,000 of 95% of home value
Loans	Flexiloan	- rolling loan plan between £500–£10,000 - variable interest rate
	Personal Loan	-
Insurance	Car Insurance Life Insurance Home Insurance	- - -
Travel	Foreign Currency/Travelers Checks	- home delivery within 24 hours
Services	Travel Insurance	- 12 month individual coverage

[a] Switch electronic debit card was launched in October 1988 by a consortium of three banks: Midland Bank, National Westminster Bank, and Royal Bank of Scotland. It enabled purchases to be paid in supermarkets, gas stations, and shops using the Switch network in the UK.

Source: First Direct Brochures, March 1996.

EXHIBIT 12   Comparative Interest Rates: First Direct and Other British Banks

VISA Card					
	NatWest	*Lloyds*	*Royal Bank of Scotland*	*Barclays*	*First Direct*
Card	Access/Visa	Access	Visa	Barclaycard	Visa
APR[a]	22.9%	22%	21.7%	21.6%	19.5%
Annual Fee	£12	£12	£10	£10	none

[a] APR = Annual Percentage Rate
Source: First Direct, February 1996.

Variable Rate Mortgages					
	NatWest	*Alliance & Leicester*	*Halifax*	*Abbey National*	*Barclays*	*First Direct*
Interest Rate	6.99%	6.99%	6.99%	7.04%	6.99%	6.69%
APR[a]	7.20%	7.20%	7.20%	7.30%	7.20%	6.90%

[a] APR = Annual Percentage Rate
Source: First Direct, March 1996.

EXHIBIT 13   First Direct Television Advertising Slogans 1996 Campaign

> **Tell me one good thing about your bank:**
>
> You don't get passed around from person-to-person when you want to open a new account
>
> I like the way they are on call 24 hours a day.
>
> I was their first customer, they've got a half a million now.
>
> I can settle my bills over the phone.
>
> They always treat you like a grown up.
>
> There's no standing in queues.
>
> I can get cash wherever I go.
>
> There are no walls.
>
> I don't have to get dressed to go to my bank.
>
> It's easy.
>
> They never sleep.
>
> Freedom.

Source: First Direct 1996 Television Campaign—Each spot (from 10 to 20 seconds) featured one of the above slogans as a response to "Tell me one good thing about your bank".

MANAGEMENT STYLE, ORGANIZATION, AND CULTURE

In February 1996, Newman restructured the business into five units that operated as profit centers: banking, savings and investments, lending, insurance, and mortgages. Product management moved out of the commercial department into integrated operational units at the heart of the business. With this structure each business could eventually acquire customers directly. All the business unit heads reported to Richard Rushton who also managed the banking unit directly—including the call center, the new customer team, customer service relations and inquiries, customer service support, and business planning. All the central support functions such as IT, finance, operations, commercial, credit services, and personnel and training were outside this structure.

Known for its leading edge management practices, First Direct attracted top quality managers. Only 50% came from a banking background. Six directors reported to Newman: commercial, customer and financial services, information technology, personnel, finance, and credit services (Exhibit 14). Their principal task was to develop strategy and people through coaching, while Newman dealt directly with their sub-ordinates on business issues. Thirty distinct roles were key within the organization, where individual accountability and competence were far more important than titles or functions. Although First Direct ran a business around the clock, most managers kept traditional 8 a.m. to 6 p.m. schedules, spending a great deal of time on the floor where they could get first-hand feedback from employees and a feel for service levels. Unlike traditional British banks, everyone was on a first name basis and ate in the same cafeteria. Newman firmly believed in leading by example; the only perk he enjoyed was a company car.

The corporate mission statement greeted all employees as they entered the lobby at each site:

Our mission: to be the best in the world of personal banking
Pioneering: the first 24-hour person-to-person telephone bank
Successful: UK's fastest growing bank with 640,000 customers
Responsive: the most satisfied bank customers in the UK

First Direct had earlier identified five core business values—responsiveness, openness, right first time, respect, and contribution—which were a fundamental part of the training program and widely shared by employees. This mindset made employees feel part of something special and it was reflected in the image projected to customers over the phone. In 1996 a sixth core value, "*kaizen*", or continuous improvement, was added following the suggestion of a new management hire. To get the entire organization focused on continuous innovation, the internal communications specialist launched a theme day during which the building was decorated in "*kaizen* yellow" and everyone wore T-shirts that they had decorated with colored pens to express their own creativity.

THE CHALLENGES AHEAD

In only seven years, First Direct had made a significant impact on the industry and had become a worldwide reference for telephone banking. By 1996, most banks and building societies offered their customers some form of direct access. Direct Line insurance had broadened its offering to include lending, mortgages, and savings products to its two million policy holders. Furthermore, competition was now by no means restricted to banks, building societies, or insurance companies. Richard Branson's Virgin Direct, launched in March 1995, subsequently introduced savings plans and low-cost life insurance via the telephone. Even the retailing chain Marks & Spencer offered life insurance from early 1995 (Exhibit 15).

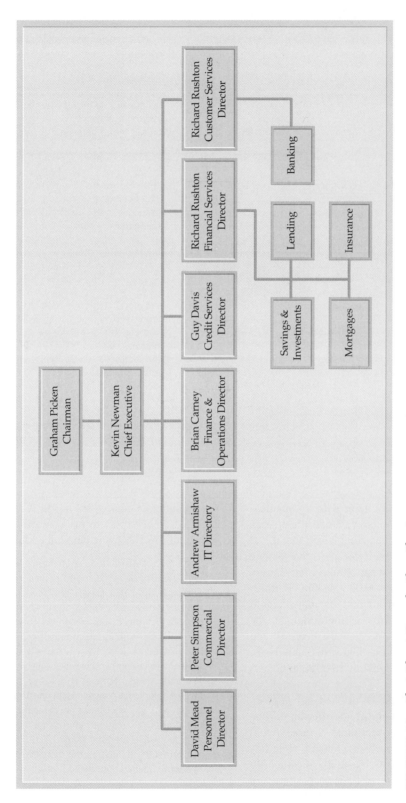

EXHIBIT 14   First Direct Organization Chart

Source: First Direct, May 1996.

EXHIBIT 15   Sample of Direct Financial Services Across the Globe

Country	Bank	Service	Launched	Description
France	Paribas	Banque Directe	March 1994	full service telephone banking with 30 operators
	Credit Commercial de France	Videocompte	1983	originally add-on Videotext service, eventually offered phone-based vocal access, customer advisors, and PCs
	Compagnie Bancaire	Cortal	1984	stand-alone home banking offering videotext access, phone-based vocal system, and customer advisors
	Credit Mutuel Bretagne	Citelis	1995	Web site home banking
Germany	Commerzbank	Comdirect	February 1995	add-on full service telephone banking via operators and interactive voice response
	Citibank	CitiDirect	September 1995	add-on full service telephone banking via 100 operators
Holland	Nederlanse Credietbank	DirektBank	1981	stand-alone telephone bank with small telemarketing staff
Portugal	Banco Commercial Portugues	Banco 7	1994	stand-alone full service telephone banking via telephone operators
Spain	Banco Santander Argenteria Group	Open Bank Bex Banco Directo	April 1995	Spain's first stand-alone telephone bank
Sweden	Skandia	Skandia Bank	October 1994	stand-alone telephone bank using an interactive voice recognition system and a few agents
Middle East	National Bank of Kuwait	Watani National Phone Bank	August 1990	add-on telephone service via interactive voice response system
Brazil	Banco 1	Unibanco		stand-alone full service telephone banking service answered by managers
USA	Wells Fargo	Person-to-Person	1988	add-on 24-hour customer service with operators
	Chase Manhattan	Chase Direct		add-on service
	First Chicago Bank	First Direct		add-on service
	Huntington Bancshares	Huntington Direct		stand-alone full service telephone banking via operators and interactive video kiosks

Source: Data gathered from various publications.

First Direct was constantly faced with the predicament of not compromising on service and price so as not to lose those customers who complained that it had grown too quickly. Yet to meet the objective of one million customers by the year 2000, First Direct needed to sign on another 400,000 people. Furthermore, First Direct recognized that its management methods might not necessarily be appropriate in the future. Management wondered how to keep all the strengths of the business and its innovative culture as, over the next five years, it grew to 10,000 employees located at four or five sites.

Critics charged that First Direct had not kept up with banking technology as it did not offer an on-line home banking service. This additional channel would provide increased convenience to customers while further reducing transaction costs. A significant minority of First Direct customers had spontaneously requested PC access to their accounts. Although the HSBC

Group signed a deal with Microsoft in late 1995, First Direct did not expect to offer an on-line banking service until 1997. Newman explained his perspective:

The mode of distribution is changing—at the moment we definitely see it as person-to-person over the telephone. Do we believe that people will bank electronically over the next ten years? We are not fussed about how quickly or by which means our customers choose to access all or part of their banking electronically. The elements for us are: when they do so what is the role of a bank, and how do we deliver competitive advantage in this environment? We must always remember that our "moments of truth" are the telephone contacts with the Banking Representatives. With PC access this disappears, thus limiting our opportunities. Creating value in an electronic world will be a key issue for First Direct. We like to think that we are not really in banking but distribution. We just happen to supply financial products.

CASE 12-2 NASHUA PHOTO*

*I*n the summer of 1993, Bob Barton had a lot on his plate. As the new director of New-Customer Acquisitions for Nashua Photo, the country's largest mail-order photofinishing firm, his immediate task was to plan the firm's promotion activities for the remainder of the year. His long-term goal was to revisit the entire new-customer-acquisition process at Nashua. Last year Nashua spent several millions of dollars to distribute hundreds of millions of promotional mailers to the 94 million households in the United States. Although the company was quite profitable, he wondered whether they were spending too much (or too little) on acquiring new customers.

THE U.S. PHOTOFINISHING INDUSTRY

Americans love to take photos. In 1990, 92 percent of U.S. households owned at least one camera and purchased slightly over 600 million rolls of 35 millimeter film. On average, 62 percent of households either bought or processed film during that year. Involvement with photography increased with household income (43 percent of households with income less than $12 thousand purchased film in 1990 compared with 74 percent of households with income greater than $50 thousand) and with the presence of young

children (81 percent of households with at least one child aged two or under bought film compared to 55 percent of households with no children). It was estimated that about 15 billion color photos were taken in 1990.

Amateur photographers tended to buy their film at a discount/department store and get it developed at the drug store (see Exhibit 1). Drug stores usually sent the exposed film to one of a few large wholesale photofinishing laboratories for processing. These wholesale labs were huge photofinishing factories, built to process large amounts of film quickly, professionally, and at low cost. Until the early 1980s, almost all film processing was accomplished by large labs. At that time, the minilab was introduced. Minilabs were small, stand-alone film-processing machines that, when placed in a photofinishing store or inside a large discount store, offered the consumer "one-hour" photofinishing. The on-site minilabs eliminated the delays associated with mailing film to and from the wholesale labs, but had two drawbacks: prices were higher and customers perceived them as producing lower quality photos. See Exhibit 2 for a perceptual map of the various photofinishing outlets. Minilab retail revenues had been growing steadily in recent years, while wholesale lab revenue had been stagnant.

EXHIBIT 1 Percentage of Volume by Distribution Outlet

	Film Purchased	Film Processed	
Outlet	1990	1990	1989
Discount/Department stores	35%	18%	18%
Drug stores	25	25	23
Grocery stores	15	13	13
Camera stores	10	11	11
Minilabs	5	19	19
Mail order	4	9	11
Other	6	5	5
	100%	100%	100%
Total rolls (in millions)	759	698	690

Source: AGFA 1990 Research Report.

* This case was prepared by Professor Phillip E. Pfeifer as a basis for class discussion rather than to illustrate either effective or ineffective handling of an administrative situation. Some elements of the case have been disguised. Copyright © 1994 by the University of Virginia Darden School Foundation, Charlottesville, VA. Reproduced by permission.

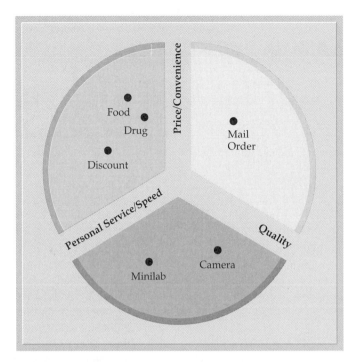

EXHIBIT 2   Perceptual Map of Photofinishing Outlets

Source: AGFA Photofinishing Research

The growth of minilabs led to a consolidation of the many independent wholesale photofinishing labs. Industry giants Qualex (49 percent owned by Kodak), Fuji, and Konica bought most of the smaller independents and, in the face of an overall decline in the market, began aggressively pursuing volume. The three big wholesale labs began to lower prices and expanded into new channels such as grocery stores and wholesale clubs.

The other major outlet for photofinishing was mail order. Customers would place their exposed rolls of film in a preprinted mailing envelope, or "mailer," add the requisite amount of postage, stick it in the mail, and wait four to fourteen days for their developed photos to arrive by return mail. Approximately 7 percent of all rolls were developed via mail order in 1992. Mail order's share of total rolls processed had been declining steadily over the past few years, from 8.0 percent in 1988 to 6.8 percent in 1992.

A recent AGFA[1] survey of U.S. amateur photographers explored their attitudes toward photofinishing outlets, with particular emphasis on mail order. A full 45 percent of the sample had never used mail order,

citing fear of loss (34 percent), slow speed (29 percent), and satisfaction with their current finisher (11 percent) as the top three reasons why they had not. Other survey results appear in Exhibit 3.

COMPANY BACKGROUND

Nashua Photo was a wholly owned subsidiary of the Nashua Corporation, one of the oldest companies in North America. The Nashua Corporation provided a diverse mix of products and services reflected in their four business groups: Coated Products (duct tape, labels, fax paper), Computer Products (disks, diskettes, toner cartridges), Office Supplies (toner supplies for photcopying machines, copy paper), and Photofinishing. See Exhibits 4 and 5 for selected financial information.

Located in Nashua, New Hampshire, the company was recognized as one of the first Fortune 500 companies to implement the principles of total quality management. In the late 1970s, the company hired Dr. W. Edwards Deming to help bring continual quality improvements to the company's manufacturing and customer-service processes.

Nashua Photo had the largest share of the mail-order photofinishing market in the three countries where it operated (United States, the United Kingdom,

---

[1] AGFA, a division of Miles Laboratory, manufactured film and photographic paper in Germany.

EXHIBIT 3   AGFA Survey Results (1,236 respondents)

Factor Used in Deciding Photo Outlet	Number of Mentions	Rating[a] Minilab	Camera Store	Mail Order
Picture quality	1,119	3.74	4.17	3.69
Good value for the price	897	3.05	3.24	4.06
Convenient to home and work	716	3.90	3.82	3.79
Speed of processing	667	4.47	3.93	2.61
Good customer service	623	3.85	4.28	3.32
Security that film is not lost	524	4.10	4.28	3.16
Added incentives (free film, prints, etc.)	378	N.A.	N.A.	3.26
Ease of ordering	372	N.A.	N.A.	3.91
Photo experts	340	N.A.	N.A.	3.17
Variety of services	288	N.A.	N.A.	3.52

[a] Rating by outlet: 1 = poor, 5 = excellent. N.A. = not available.

Source: Company records.

EXHIBIT 4   Condensed Consolidated Statement of Operations (All figures in thousands)

	Year Ended Dec. 31, 1992	Dec. 31, 1991
Net Sales	$552,479	$526,112
Cost of Products Sold	421,440	409,016
Research, Selling, Distribution, and Administrative Expenses	118,850	112,551
Interest Expense	2,690	1,744
Interest Income	(953)	(650)
Income Before Income Taxes and Cumulative Effect of Accounting Principle Changes	$ 10,452	$ 3,451

EXHIBIT 5   Sales and Income by Business Group (All figures in thousands)

	Year Ended Dec. 31, 1992	Dec. 31, 1991
Net Sales		
Coated-Products Group	$175,383	$171,833
Computer-Products Group	107,211	85,652
Office-Supplies Group	107,975	106,007
Photofinishing Group (Worldwide)	161,910	162,620
Total	$552,479	$526,112
Operating Income		
Coated-Products Group	$ 4,390	$5,739
Computer-Products Group	(7,523)	(23,079)
Office-Supplies Group	4,836	6,720
Photofinishing Group	17,793	19,490
Corporate Expenses Including Interest	($9,044)	($5,419)
Total	$10,452	$3,451

and Canada). With 4.2 million households sending film to them in 1992, its share of the U.S. mail-order market was 44 percent. Of these 4.2 million households, close to 2 million were new customers trying Nashua mail order for the first time. About 40 percent of those who tried Nashua came back to try them again as repeat customers, 80 percent of the repeat customers came back to use Nashua a third time, and about 90 percent survived with each subsequent order.[2] Nashua customers sent in 14.4 million rolls of film in 1992. Exhibit 6 shows a five-year history of Nashua's U.S. sales volumes.

Nashua Photo operated photofinishing plants in Canada, the United Kingdom, and the United States. Its Parkersburg, West Virginia, plant was one of the largest photofinishing labs in the world. This modern, efficient facility, with an annual capacity of 30 million rolls, kept Nashua's processing costs as low as any in the photofinishing industry.

In the United States, Nashua Photo primarily used the brand name York. In the United Kingdom, its brand names were York and Truprint. And in Canada, its brand names were York, Filmposte, and Scot. Nashua's multiple brand names were more a result of a series of past acquisitions than any conscious marketing strategy. For example, the Downeast brand, a 1988 acquisition, was kept because its accompanying higher price made it a profitable piece of their business. Nashua did not promote this brand heavily, choosing instead to serve mostly existing Downeast customers.

NEW-CUSTOMER ACQUISITION

Bob Barton had been hired away from his position as director of Marketing at Colombo Yogurt to become director of New-Customer Acquisition in November of 1992. Bob liked to describe the marketing strategy at Nashua Photo as consisting of three parts: Get 'em, Keep 'em, and Grow 'em. Because the company had

[2] Tests had shown that the repeat rate of newly acquired customers did *not* depend on the type of promotion to which the new customer responded.

been spending the bulk of its marketing budget on the Get 'em function, Bob took as his first challenge improving the efficiency of this phase.

Get 'em

Nashua acquired new customers by putting a film-processing mailer in the hands of potential new customers and hoping they would use the mailer the next time they had film to develop. The company had several different mailers and several different means of getting them in the hands of potential customers. Some of the most used mailers in 1992 were the following:

- Free: featured an introductory offer of free processing of a 24-exposure roll of film.
- 59 cent: featured a 59 cent price to develop 35-millimeter color film up to 24 exposures.
- 89 cent: was the same as the 59 cent mailer except the featured price was 89 cents.
- Take One: was used in racks in hotel lobbies and at tourist attractions. Because customers could take as many as they wanted, pricing was not always discounted. The mailer featured a discounted-film offer.
- Military: featured a one cent upgrade to super glossy prints and first class postage "for U.S. Military & Civilian Personnel Overseas" on the envelope .

These promotional mailers were distributed to potential customers in the following ways:

- Co-op mailings: bulk-rate mailings to individual households consisting of a large envelope filled with coupons and promotional materials from a variety of marketers. Perhaps the best known of these co-op marketers was "Carol Wright."
- Newspaper inserts: mailers inserted in a newspaper.
- Magazine inserts: mailers inserted in a magazine.
- Package inserts: mailers included in the package of merchandise ordered from another company.
- Sampling packs: bundles of free sample goods and coupons. A good example was the take-home pack given to a family taking a newborn home from the

EXHIBIT 6   Nashua U.S. Photofinishing Sales History

	1988	1989	1990	1991	1992
Number of orders processed (millions)	10.8	11	11.1	10.6	10.4
Number of rolls processed (millions)	15.1	15.4	15.5	14.9	14.4
Total revenue ($ millions)	$60.5	$65.9	$68.9	$69.0	$67.7

Source: Company records.

hospital. These packs usually included sample formula, disposable diapers, baby toys, and plenty of coupons appropriate to families with babies.

- Take One displays: displays, frequently in the lobbies of hotels or tourist attractions.

All told, Nashua spent $6 million in 1992 on distributing several hundred million promotional mailers.

These promotions were tailored to match the seasonality of photo taking (more in June, fewer in February). Nashua devoted the remainder of its marketing budget to mailings to existing customers.

As might be expected, not all promotional mailers met with equal success. Exhibit 7 is an example of the "Efficiency Report" that had been used prior to Barton's arrival to rank promotions based on cost per cus-

EXHIBIT 7   1993 First Quarter Efficiency Report

Promotion Number	Media Type[a]	Mailer Type	%59	Circ[b]	CPM[c]	Total Resp.	New Cust.	Total Cost[d]	% Resp.	Cost per Resp.
Agfa-Showtime	p	FREE		336	$0.00	14196	6678	$3,286	4.23%	$0.23
AMA Free Dev Offer	t	FREE		5	$0.00	211	99	$49	4.22%	$0.23
Corpus Christi Caller	n	59		81	$20.78	3044	852	$2,475	3.76%	$0.81
Camden Courier-Post	n	59		318	$12.36	8030	2248	$7,042	2.53%	$0.88
Action Arena	t	TO		6	$38.50	315	123	$290	5.25%	$0.92
The Times Herald	n	59		72	$34.96	3157	990	$3,221	4.38%	$1.02
Coachman Deluxe	t	59		10	$0.00	93	52	$98	0.93%	$1.05
Parents	m	59/89	88.89%	315	$16.50	7518	4042	$8,278	2.39%	$1.10
Freedom Press	n	59		40	$19.64	1017	399	$1,177	2.54%	$1.16
Advantage Promotions	c	59/89	88.51%	435	$16.50	9861	5301	$11,432	2.27%	$1.16
Bonnie Walton	t	89		6	$0.00	47	22	$59	0.78%	$1.25
Baby's first foto	p	59/89	66.67%	132	$37.40	4972	2784	$6,228	3.77%	$1.25
Lansing Journal	n	59		20	$16.50	401	189	$526	2.01%	$1.31
Pittstown Press	n	59		72	$21.98	1702	705	$2,287	2.36%	$1.34
Wheeling Reader	n	59		390	$34.50	12498	3079	$17,268	3.20%	$1.38
Christian Books	p	59		100	$24.20	2418	1083	$3,398	2.42%	$1.41
Winn Dixie	n	59		1,624	$28.05	42752	20110	$61,436	2.63%	$1.44
Specialized Products	p	59/89	63.88%	526	$22.00	11228	5030	$16,716	2.13%	$1.49
New Haven Journal	n	59		158	$21.98	3369	1509	$5,018	2.13%	$1.49
Bangor News	n	59		40	$18.98	767	301	$1,150	1.92%	$1.50
New Baby Basket	s	59/89	66.67%	3,552	$14.30	57010	29371	$85,532	1.61%	$1.50
Cold River Herald News	n	59		120	$21.98	2537	994	$3,811	2.11%	$1.50
Rotland Planet	n	59		56	$21.98	1164	587	$1,778	2.08%	$1.53
Hartford Courant	n	59		80	$21.98	1634	769	$2,541	2.04%	$1.55
Beaumont Enterprise	n	59		84	$34.98	2361	926	$3,760	2.81%	$1.59
Lowell Patriot	n	59		58	$10.99	749	311	$1,205	1.29%	$1.61
Allentown Morning Call	n	59		60	$22.00	1151	541	$1,907	1.92%	$1.66
Fort Meyers News	n	59		23	$22.00	441	163	$731	1.92%	$1.66
Superworks	c	59		120	$16.50	1893	891	$3,154	1.58%	$1.67
Marlboro Sales	p	59		140	$18.26	2347	1104	$3,926	1.68%	$1.67
Winchester Telegram	n	59		396	$25.16	8230	3042	$13,835	2.08%	$1.68
Value Coups	c	59		1,070	$6.60	10189	4793	$17,527	0.95%	$1.72
Dixie Shopper	c	59/89	72.75%	2,477	$14.55	34966	17623	$60,273	1.41%	$1.72
Fiarbridge Times	n	59		52	$36.30	1378	386	$2,396	2.65%	$1.74
Mail Network	c	59		400	$16.50	5954	3001	$10,512	1.49%	$1.77
World Book	p	59/89	45.45%	220	$30.80	4959	1389	$8,928	2.25%	$1.80
Grolier Intros	p	59/89	56.64%	3,955	$13.20	49798	22310	$90,886	1.26%	$1.83
Just for Mothers	s	59/89	66.67%	3,000	$27.50	61020	30754	$111,840	2.03%	$1.83
Pick N' Save	n	59/89	64.29%	28,000	$11.55	322616	151759	$597,240	1.15%	$1.85
Wal Mart Shared Mail	n	59/89	74.17%	6,040	$20.50	98761	48669	$182,915	1.64%	$1.85
Greatlakes Mail	c	59/89	66.67%	432	$38.50	11210	5022	$20,857	2.59%	$1.86
Artistic Success	p	59/89	55.99%	8,467	$19.25	130910	65978	$245,797	1.55%	$1.88

(continues)

EXHIBIT 7   (Continued)

Promotion Number	Media Type[a]	Mailer Type	%59	Circ[b]	CPM[c]	Total Resp.	New Cust.	Total Cost[d]	% Resp.	Cost per Resp.
Southern Values	c	59/89	75.37%	3,715	$13.75	46518	18235	$87,414	1.25%	$1.88
Family Value Pack	c	59/89	70.65%	44,290	$8.80	436752	215232	$822,908	0.99%	$1.88
Lubbock Avalanche	n	59		328	$19.64	5117	2178	$9,648	1.56%	$1.89
JC Whitney Catalog	p	59		100	$11.00	1095	564	$2,078	1.10%	$1.90
Family Mail Coupons	c	59/89	71.91%	17,080	$6.53	146390	68862	$278,643	0.86%	$1.90
Petersburg Virginian	n	59		382	$21.98	6369	3638	$12,132	1.67%	$1.90
JC Penney Shared Mail	n	59/89	73.21%	10,450	$13.43	126744	42586	$242,555	1.21%	$1.91
Macon Telegraph	n	59		130	$21.98	2144	961	$4,129	1.65%	$1.93
Carol Wright Toys	p	59/89	84.36%	3,516	$16.50	47417	19650	$92,400	1.35%	$1.95
Hanes Multis	p	59/89	66.67%	1,200	$26.40	22032	10364	$43,416	1.84%	$1.97
Canton Repository	n	59		130	$23.38	2144	961	$4,310	1.65%	$2.01
Dollar Bill	n	59		100	$25.30	1739	974	$3,508	1.74%	$2.02
Wonderful Visions	s	59/89	60.00%	500	$35.20	11136	5238	$22,490	2.23%	$2.02
Good Housekpng US	m	MIL		4,140	$9.06	38295	18014	$78,014	0.93%	$2.04
Outdoors	m	59		200	$5.50	1497	704	$3,056	0.75%	$2.04
National Network	c	59/89	85.53%	760	$13.20	8440	4537	$17,465	1.11%	$2.07
Gift-Pax -prenatal	s	59/89	66.67%	3,840	$16.50	48456	22794	$100,915	1.26%	$2.08
Keltar Records and Tapes	p	59/89	74.12%	4,250	$22.00	63769	28568	$135,065	1.50%	$2.12
Adtel	c	59/89	79.32%	46,682	$8.80	404237	203735	$867,352	0.87%	$2.15
Columbia House	p	59/89	65.71%	875	$44.00	21644	9212	$47,058	2.47%	$2.17
New Parenting	p	59/89	88.89%	378	$19.24	5021	2531	$10,969	1.33%	$2.18
Baby Moments	p	59		2,536	$20.61	35029	19616	$77,079	1.38%	$2.20
Holden Tucker	c	59		250	$0.00	1085	729	$2,445	0.43%	$2.25
Blacksburg Hoakie	n	59		164	$21.98	2295	1208	$5,208	1.40%	$2.27
MT Hispanic	c	59		73,000	$12.11	696150	325442	$1,598,043	0.95%	$2.30
Baby Bunting	s	59		25	$22.00	345	162	$795	1.38%	$2.30
Nostalgia Thoughts	c	59/89	80.00%	1,000	$33.00	18461	9304	$42,780	1.85%	$2.32
Middlebury News	n	59		194	$21.98	2645	1244	$6,161	1.36%	$2.33
Safari Coupons	c	59		50	$14.10	512	241	$1,194	1.02%	$2.33
Good Housekpng Overseas	m	MIL		628	$9.06	5032	2818	$11,834	0.80%	$2.35
Military Life	m	MIL		300	$14.30	3064	1887	$7,224	1.02%	$2.36
Miles Kimball	p	59/89	57.14%	525	$19.80	6534	3367	$15,530	1.24%	$2.38
Family Coupons	c	59/89	50.00%	564	$41.25	12064	6215	$28,781	2.14%	$2.39
Newsweek	p	59/89	73.31%	19,670	$18.15	22526	121101	$549,383	1.15%	$2.44
Carol Wright PIP	p	59/89	85.71%	3,500	$16.50	37675	14347	$91,980	1.08%	$2.44
Daily Mason	n	59		36	$21.98	465	182	$1,143	1.29%	$2.46
Lowell Patriot	n	59		228	$21.98	2945	1221	$7,241	1.29%	$2.46
Dollar Bill Store	n	59		100	$33.00	1739	974	$4,278	1.74%	$2.46
Frank's Discount Store	n	59		50	$33.00	869	438	$2,139	1.74%	$2.46
World Kid Clubs	p	59/89	42.86%	70	$30.80	1144	384	$2,841	1.63%	$2.48
Home Shopping Network	p	59		200	$24.20	2734	1286	$6,796	1.37%	$2.49
Family Savings	c	59/89	50.00%	220	$17.09	2340	917	$5,912	1.06%	$2.53
Family Records	p	59/89	64.46%	2,195	$30.80	35036	12949	$89,073	1.60%	$2.54
Cosmetics Exchange	p	59/89	48.84%	430	$16.50	4425	1982	$11,300	1.03%	$2.55
Mailshare	c	59		50	$16.50	512	241	$1,314	1.02%	$2.57
Mr. Media PIP	p	59		125	$16.50	1280	602	$3,285	1.02%	$2.57
Telstar Mail Network	c	59		818	$16.50	8374	3939	$21,497	1.02%	$2.57
Coupon Express	c	59/89	63.01%	73,000	$14.85	698004	304888	$1,797,990	0.96%	$2.58
Durham News	n	59		204	$21.98	2453	1374	$6,479	1.20%	$2.64
Country Living	m	59		280	$10.00	2096	986	$5,538	0.75%	$2.64
Norwalk Bulletin	n	59		58	$21.98	697	391	$1,842	1.20%	$2.64
Scranton Times	n	59		58	$21.98	697	266	$1,842	1.20%	$2.64
Book of the Month	p	59/89	81.48%	10,800	$26.40	142800	71971	$390,744	1.32%	$2.74
Judy Anderson	t	MIL		3,000	$26.61	39094	24082	$109,167	1.30%	$2.79
Cosmetics Plus	p	89		500	$16.50	4488	2010	$13,140	0.90%	$2.93

(continues)

EXHIBIT 7   (Continued)

Promotion Number	Media Type[a]	Mailer Type	%59	Circ[b]	CPM[c]	Total Resp.	New Cust.	Total Cost[d]	% Resp.	Cost per Resp.
Great American Savings	c	59/89	43.48%	11,500	$14.58	95225	57933	$280,083	0.83%	$2.94
Winston-Salem News	n	59		182	$21.98	1961	1054	$5,780	1.08%	$2.95
Money	m	59		400	$12.94	2994	1408	$9,086	0.75%	$3.03
Weedham News	n	59		98	$21.95	1003	506	$3,109	1.02%	$3.10
Neighborhood Weeklies	n	59		60	$21.95	614	289	$1,904	1.02%	$3.10
Danville News	n	59		46	$21.98	471	222	$1,461	1.02%	$3.10
Buffalo News	n	59		276	$21.98	2826	1424	$8,765	1.02%	$3.10
Canterbury Republican	n	59		80	$21.98	819	413	$2,541	1.02%	$3.10
Sun Group Papers	n	59		34	$21.98	348	175	$1,080	1.02%	$3.10
Home Shopping News	n	59		50	$22.00	512	241	$1,589	1.02%	$3.10
Consumer Reports	m	59		1,395	$13.62	10442	4912	$32,640	0.75%	$3.13
Wichita Eagle	n	59		236	$22.21	2363	1112	$7,549	1.00%	$3.19
Middlesex Times	n	59		110	$23.05	1126	530	$3,611	1.02%	$3.21
Overseas	m	MIL		330	$43.01	5049	3110	$17,421	1.53%	$3.45
Welcome Package	c	59		100	$30.80	1024	482	$4,058	1.02%	$3.96
Value Portraits	p	59		25	$33.00	256	120	$1,070	1.02%	$4.18
Motown Records & Tapes	p	59/89	30.23%	86	$19.80	584	360	$2,544	0.68%	$4.36
Gift Pack—new moms	s	89		25	$27.50	203	96	$932	0.81%	$4.59
True Grit	m	89		50	$27.50	394	185	$1,864	0.79%	$4.73
No Nonsense Direct	p	89		54	$27.50	425	181	$2,013	0.79%	$4.74
First Foto	p	89		300	$41.25	3188	1785	$15,309	1.06%	$4.80
RCA Compack Discs	p	89		500	$44.00	5381	2531	$26,890	1.08%	$5.00
Newborn Magazine	m	89		50	$32.73	394	185	$2,125	0.79%	$5.39
MPR Cable Program	p	89		1,000	$37.77	7875	3704	$47,554	0.79%	$6.04
Hertz Gift	p	89		25	$27.50	144	68	$932	0.58%	$6.47
Jen-Aire Gift	p	89		25	$27.50	144	68	$932	0.58%	$6.47
Camp Fire Girls	n	59		48	$68.75	551	124	$3,769	1.15%	$6.84

[a] Legend:

Co-op mailings	c	Sampling packs	s
Newspaper inserts	n	Take-one displays	t
Package inserts	p	Magazine inserts	m

[b] Circ is the total number of mailers, in thousands.

[c] CPM is the cost per thousand for using this medium.

[d] Total cost = ($9.78 + CPM) × Circ., where $9.78 is the variable printing and production cost per thousand.

tomer. Barton's primary concern was to evaluate the relative profitability of the past promotions, in order to decide which deserved to be used in future months.

At first Barton had thought that returning to a previous promotion could only lead to less success and lower profitability. But a recent test, known within the company as the frequency test, convinced him otherwise. In the frequency test, the same promotion (same mailer and same newspaper, in this case) was used every three months over a two year period—eight times in total. Contrary to expectations, response rates to the promotion did not decline with repeated use. Barton took this result to mean that it would be appropriate and profitable to return to previously successful promotions.

Keep 'em

Once a customer ordered from Nashua, every effort was made to encourage that customer to reorder from Nashua the next time he or she had a roll of film that needed processing. Every new customer (someone who had never before ordered) received their finished photos in a "Welcome to York" package, which included a welcome letter, some coupons from other companies, and a couple of "bounce-back" mailers. Bounce-back mailers were the standard, nonpromotional, regular-price ($1.99 for a roll of 24-exposure 35-millimeter film) mailers sent along with every return mailing of finished photos.

Newly acquired customers who had not responded to the "Welcome to York" package were sent up to four more mailings over the course of two years. These mailings (at a cost of $350 per thousand) were in plain-manila envelopes and contained a label set (a package of peel-and-stick labels printed with the customer's name and address for use when placing future orders), two or three bounce-back mailers, and inserts from other companies. Customers who had not ordered after receiving four of these additional mailing were considered "lost."

Mailings of finished photos to existing customers included two bounce-back mailers and some inserts. If the customer had not ordered for a certain length of time, the four-mailing sequence would commence for them.

A recent survey of 400 customers who last used Nashua 13 months previously suggested that many customers were "lost" simply because they took photos infrequently. Of the 400 customers, only 17 said they purposely left Nashua because of a bad experience or a mistake made by Nashua. About half said they simply had not finished a roll of film in the last year.

About three-quarters of all orders received by Nashua were in a bounce-back mailer. The remaining one-quarter were received in one of the various types of promotional mailers. There appeared to be quite a "desk drawer" phenomenon, as many orders were received in very old promotional mailers. On average, 53 percent of redeemed promotional mailers were from existing customers.

The average gross margin for an order received in a bounce-back mailer was $2.27. This number reflected

EXHIBIT 8 Gross Margins by Type of Mailer

Type of Promotional Mailer Used	Average Gross Margin per Order
Free	$(1.75)
59 cent	0.97
89 cent	1.32
Take One	1.97
Military	1.87

the fact that most orders contained more than one roll of film (1.38 on average), as well as other sources of revenue (double prints and a 25-cent-rush option, for example). Average gross margins for each type of promotional mailer are listed in Exhibit 8.

Grow 'em

Grow 'em refered to promotional activities designed to increase sales per customer. Along these lines the company mailed a catalog of photo-related merchandise, sold its own private label film, and offered an extensive array of reprint, enlargement and personalized apparel (shirts, aprons, etc. with the customer's photo on them). Once Barton improved Get 'em and Keep 'em, he planned to turn his attention to Grow 'em.

THE COMPETITION

Nashua's biggest competitor in mail-order photofinishing was Clark. With a share of 34 percent, Clark's

EXHIBIT 9 Mail-Order Photofinishing 1993 Competitive Overview

Market Segment	Major Brands	Brand Position	Rolls (MM)	Market Share	Product	Average Price
Return Film	Seattle	Special-Film Retention: The serious amateur's brand	2.7	8.2%	Processing price includes replacement film. Premium packaging. Credit cards. Prepaid postage. All-in-one pricing.	$10.10
	Skrudland	Special Film	0.6	2.0%		
Premium	Mystic	Highest level of quality and convenience	2.0	6.0%	Premium packaging. Credit cards. Prepaid postage. All-in-one pricing.	$7.69
	Vermont	High quality and fast service	.2	0.4%		
No Frills	York	Lowest Prices	14.4	44.0%	Basic packaging. Breakout pricing. No credit cards. Requires postage.	$3.83
	Clark	Lowest Prices	11.1	34.0%		

strategy was one virtually identical to York's—no frills and low price. Exhibit 9 presents a competitive overview of the mail-order market.

NASHUA CUSTOMERS

Nashua commissioned a PRIZM[3] study of its customer base in 1992. The study showed that customers spanned a wide array of demographic categories. The single highest PRIZM cluster for Nashua customers was "Shotguns and Pickups," with a score of 120. The incidence of Nashua customers in the PRIZM cluster of "Shotguns and Pickups" was 20 percent higher than average.

---

[3] PRIZM, a product of Claritas, L. P., stands for Potential Ratings in Zoned Markets. PRIZM uses cluster analysis to classify neighborhoods based on census data, market geography, and media databases. PRIZM allows marketers to assign customers and prospects to neighborhood types based solely on their addresses.

CHAPTER 13

DESIGNING ADVERTISING PROGRAMS

> Associating meanings with products in order to turn products into brands is the real value of effective advertising.
>
> CHARLES YOUNG
> MICHAEL ROBISON

Advertising communication expenditures have a variety of purposes: enhance the image of the organization, build brand preferences, promote the sale of particular items, announce a special promotion or sale, and encourage participation in causes. Advertising is employed around the world because it is a very cost-effective method of communicating ideas to mass audiences. It works for promoting disease prevention as well as for selling soap.

In your role as marketing manager, you will need to identify the appropriate target market segments and uncover the relevant buying motives. You then must make a series of decisions that establish the scope and direction of your advertising program. These include

- Select advertising objectives.
- Develop advertising budget.
- Develop campaign themes.
- Pick appropriate media.
- Monitor results.

These decisions are shown in Figure 13-1 and are explained in more detail in the following sections. These decisions are part of an ongoing process and the market results feed back into the next round's decisions. In making these decisions, you must have an appreciation of when and how advertising works. Thus, this chapter begins with a discussion of the foundations of advertising.

THE FOUNDATIONS FOR ADVERTISING

To avoid wasting advertising expenditure on ineffective campaigns, you should understand when advertising works and the predominant theories of how it might work.

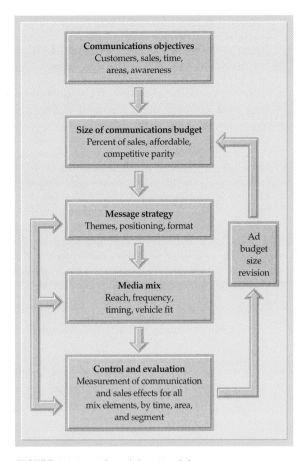

FIGURE 13-1 Advertising Decisions

When Advertising Works

Before setting budgets and other advertising planning, you must decide whether you should do any advertising. The Hershey chocolate bar, for example, became a leading product in the United States on the basis of extensive distribution gained through the use of salespeople, and not as the result of consumer advertising. Even so, Hershey now spends heavily on advertising. A product's brand equity may suffer if there is a long hiatus in its advertising. This happened to Heinz ketchup as discussed in Marketing in Action box 13-1.

An appraisal of the opportunity for advertising begins with an assessment of potential for stimulation of demand. The ability to increase demand with advertising varies across product categories. To assess opportunities for advertising, you must understand the factors that account for these differences. Four of the more important factors are that

- The trend in primary demand is favorable.
- Product differentiation is marked.
- Hidden qualities of the product are important to customers.
- Funds for advertising are available.

The social and environmental factors that underlie the basic trends in product demand are often more important than the amount of advertising expenditures. Advertising can accelerate an expansion in demand that would have occurred without advertising or, correspond-

APPLYING
. . . *to*
Consumer
Food
Marketing

MARKETING IN ACTION *13-1*

Heinz Seeks to Reestablish Dominant Ketchup Position With Heavy Ad Spending

For five years in the mid-1990s, H. J. Heinz did not advertise ketchup on television. During this period, Heinz ketchup maintained its position as market leader, with more than double the sales and volume of its nearest competitor, ConAgra's Hunt's ketchup. However, Heinz saw its market share erode from more than 50% to about 47%. Price competition was stiff due to private-label brands. Meanwhile the ketchup category also suffered from a change in consumers' eating habits. Consumers were snacking more on munchies, especially chips with salsa. Salsa has a healthy, veggie image.

Ketchup is present in 97 percent of U.S. households. Unfortunately, it has a problem that many staples have: people don't use it as often as they might. For example, about 60 percent of ketchup is eaten on hamburgers, hot dogs, and french fries. Although these three food dishes are the most-eaten for kids and adults, they are eaten with ketchup less than 40 percent of the time. Children consume more ketchup per capita then adults. In particular, children three to 11 account for 5.4 percent of the U.S. population but 24 percent of the ketchup-eating occasions.

Heinz responded with a $20 million advertising campaign timed for the barbecue season. The new ads began by showing a gaggle of healthy looking tomatoes squeezing themselves into a ketchup bottle. Next came a shot of someone pouring ketchup onto a hamburger and a child biting into it with glee. The tag line was "Mine's Gotta Have Heinz."

— *No matter how powerful a brand is, if you stop advertising, there will be erosion of brand equity.*

Source: Rekha Balu, "Heinz Ketchup Readies Super Bowl Blitz," *The Wall Street Journal*, January 5, 1998, p. B6.

Heinz trademark and tag line are owned by The H. J. Heinz Company and used with permission.

ingly, might retard an adverse trend. A reversal of a trend by advertising alone, however, is most unlikely. You are better off repositioning your product through advertising than fighting the tide as illustrated in Marketing Strategies box 13-1. You should also realize that the elasticity of advertising is believed to decline over the product life cycle.

When demand is expanding, there are frequent opportunities for selective advertising appeals. These selective appeals are more effective if the product has "special" attributes. Product differentiation facilitates the establishment of brand preference, and this preference enables the product to have a larger gross margin than might have been possible with an undifferentiated product. In turn, a larger gross margin provides more funds for advertising. The firm must have sufficient resources to make an impression on the customer, however, and high advertising costs are a barrier to entry in some markets.

How Advertising Works

You need to understand how advertising affects consumers in order to formulate more effective advertising strategies. Two views of what takes place when a person receives an advertisement have been put forth: accumulation and replacement.

Accumulation   Desirable response tendencies increase with advertising exposure and compete with undesirable or incorrect response tendencies, such as positive attitudes toward competing products or misinformation. New information is combined with existing concepts. From an information processing perspective, then, product positioning and message consistency are critical. This model implies it is necessary to measure the strength of both desirable and competing responses.

Replacement   Existing concepts are replaced in memory by new concepts with increasing exposure to advertising. This theory implies that you can capture your product category by

---

APPLYING
. . . *to*
Consumer
Food
Marketing

MARKETING STRATEGIES *13-1*

Special K Changes Advertising Strategy

Kellogg's launched Special K in 1955 as a weight-control product targeted at women. Advertising messages emphasized "thinness is everything." For example, some commercials showed women trying to "pinch an inch" on their waists. In the process, Special K became one of the top ten global cereal brands. However, this strategy began to wear thin in the United States as "baby boomers" started to reject the emphasis on perfection—and Special K's market share slid.

A Kellogg survey found that more than two-thirds of women believed TV ads and fashion magazines influenced society's image of ideal height and weight, which few felt that they had attained. For baby boomers, careers and sports had much more relevance to how they viewed themselves than did having a perfect body. Indeed, a 1995 poll by *USA Today*/AdTrack found that nearly 30 percent of women ages 25–54 actually disliked Special K's advertising campaigns.

Kellogg decided to change its long-time advertising strategy accordingly. Kellogg felt a self-esteem message would resonate more strongly with contemporary women. Its advertising agency, Leo Burnett, created a new campaign centered on the theme "Reshape your attitude." In one TV commercial, a fellow on a barstool asks an unseen interviewer, "Do I look fat?" Another man wonders aloud if his posterior is too big. A third sighs and says, "I have my mother's thighs. I have to accept that." The commercial's parting shot was "Men don't obsess about these things. Why should we?"

— *You must recognize when market changes require that your consistent-theme advertising have a new theme.*

Source: Rekha Balu, "Special K Ads Flip-Flop on Body Attitude," *The Wall Street Journal*, August 12, 1998, p. B7.

delivering more messages than your competitors. You would want to have the highest "share of voice."

With this backdrop, various theories of how advertising works have been suggested. Psychological *learning* theory states that a *new* stimulus first has to be grasped then seen to be relevant before it is accepted or rejected. This reasoning fostered the notion that advertising can be strongly persuasive and play a key role in brand building. The learning theory approach to advertising is known as the hierarchy-of-effects theory.

The Hierarchy of Effects   The hierarchy-of-effects hypothesis states that advertising guides the consumer through a sequence of steps which culminates in purchase. Consumers can be classified into seven groups. The first group contains potential purchasers who are *unaware* of the existence of the product. The second group contains consumers who are merely *aware* of the product's existence. The third group contains consumers who *possess* knowledge of the product and its benefits. The fourth group contains customers who *like* the product. The fifth group is those who have developed a *preference* for the product over all other possibilities. The sixth group contains consumers who are *convinced* that they should buy the product. The final group contains consumers who *purchase* the product. Variants of this hierarchy-of-effects theory include AIDA and ATR.

Awareness-Interest-Desire-Action   The *AIDA* theory asserts that advertising is a *strong* market force that propels the prospect through a sequence of steps which culminates in purchase. Advertising works by changing consumer attitudes about brands. The emphasis is on brand image. The theory focuses on *new* buyers of a brand and does not say much about former buyers of the brand. Your job would be to develop a brand position that was appealing and unique. A different view of advertising is given by *ATR* theory—one that does not require an attitude shift prior to purchase.

Awareness-Trial-Reinforcement   The *ATR* theory contends that advertising is a *weak* market force that is suggestive rather than strongly persuasive. ATR says that advertising can only exert influence at each stage of the process. First purchase for a frequently purchased consumer good is viewed as a trial purchase. Consequently, advertising plays a role in reducing cognitive dissonance and reinforcing satisfaction. Given brand switching, advertising rekindles brand awareness and retrial by lapsed users. You want to reassure heavy users and remind light buyers. Thus, the *R* in ATR theory stands for *reminder, reassurance,* and *retrial* as well as *reinforcement.* The process is diagrammed in Figure 13-2. The emphasis is on *brand salience* (or presence). Brand salience refers to which brands consumers think about rather than what they think about the brands. The order in which brands come to mind, for example, top-of-mind awareness, is crucial. Your job would be to register your brand name with the public.

Advertising spending could be directed toward improving both brand salience and brand image. The reality is that many businesses do not have adequate advertising budgets to have a large impact on brand image; it is easier to change brand awareness. Moreover, most advertising is not about learning but about reminding. Most consumers are already *familiar* about what is being presented in ads for established products.

APPLYING
. . . to
Consumer
Services
Marketing

Consider the U.S rent-a-car market. Car rental is an established service category with companies that spend "moderately" on advertising—typically $50 million or less per year. Tracking research has shown a strong relation between the amount of money a car rental company spends on advertising and its share of market. A further analysis showed that awareness measures (brand salience) accounted for approximately 70 percent of advertising's effect and content-related measures (brand imagery) about 30 percent. Finally, highly recalled themes and slogans, such as "We try harder," were most likely to be supported by not only well-funded campaigns but also long-standing ones.[1]

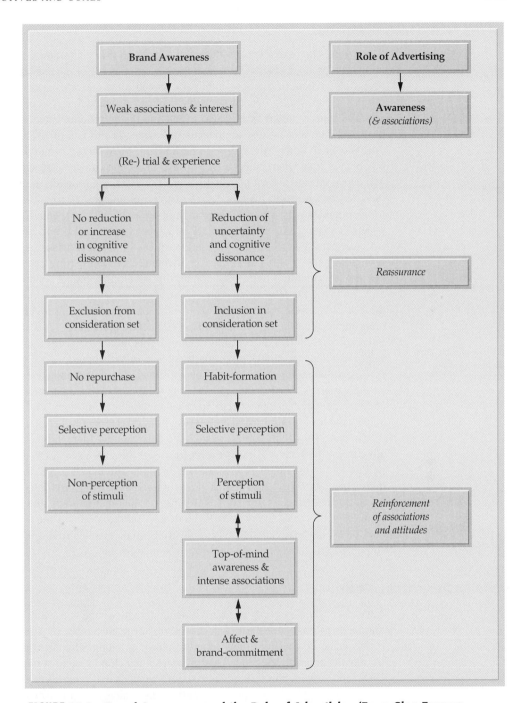

FIGURE 13-2 **Brand Awareness and the Role of Advertising (From Giep Franzen,** *Advertising Effectiveness,* **[Henley-on-Thames: Admap Publications, 1994], p. 214.)**

ADVERTISING OBJECTIVES AND GOALS

Under most conditions the primary objective of a firm is shareholder value. This usually means that you should select the advertising alternative that generates the highest present value for long-term profits. Nonprofit organizations focus on net benefits rather than on profits.

Setting Advertising Objectives

Advertising objectives for a product will depend on the stage of the life cycle that the product is in. New product advertising makes the customer aware of the existence of the new product, forces distribution of the new brand, and provides the customer with a reason for buying the product. Established product advertising is aimed at maintaining the product's market position.

The task of advertising is also a function of the product category. For more expensive products such as cars and appliances, the decision process of the buyer is deliberate and occurs over a comparatively long time horizon. Most buyers would be able to identify various brands even when labels are removed. In contrast, many packaged goods such as soaps and detergents are almost physically identical, and these products are often of low interest to buyers. Consequently, manufacturers of these products seek to achieve top-of-mind awareness among buyers. Ideally, they attempt to associate their brand name with the generic product category. An example would be Kleenex and facial tissue.

Advertising can increase the number of customers or increase the usage rate among current customers or both. More customers come from converting customers from competing brands, from holding current customers by developing brand loyalty, and from expanding the total market for the product class. Greater usage comes from reminding customers to use the brand and from telling them about new uses. Encouraging loyal customers to use your brand more often is sometimes called "frequency marketing." Advertising is also aimed at intermediaries in the distribution channel. This advertising seeks to encourage the wholesaler and retailer to stock and promote the advertiser's brand.

Advertising objectives should be coordinated with the objectives set for the other marketing variables. For instance, advertising can be used to solicit sales leads, and salespeople can then contact these prospects. In cases in which the product is too complex to explain in an ad, advertising might be used to presell the salesperson rather than the product.

In sum, advertising objectives can be described as "demand pull" or as "demand push" advertising. Pull advertising is designed to sell the final user of the product so that the user will go to the distributor and ask for the product, and in effect pull the merchandise through the channel of distribution. Most brand name advertising falls into this category (Timken bearings, Hagger slacks). Push advertising, on the other hand, is directed at brokers and distributors and is intended to presell the dealers on the merits of the product. It is more common to use push advertising with industrial products and stress direct mail, trade journals, and display materials rather than broadcast media.

Defining Advertising Goals

Advertisers should specify their advertising objectives and subsequently measure the results. The idea is to measure performance in terms of achievement of a quantitative statement of performance. A goal for a new brand might be to attain 80 percent brand awareness within six months after introduction. This provides a benchmark against which to measure accomplishment. Advertising performance should be measured in terms of sales whenever possible because of the simple accounting equation that relates sales to profits.

Under the AIDA model, the consumer moves through a sequence of steps from awareness of a brand to action. The role of advertising in moving consumers from one group to another in this process tends to vary. A panel survey can provide the data necessary to assess the economic value of causing consumers to change groups. This means that immediate sales results might not be the major criterion for measuring advertising effectiveness. Simply measuring the consumer's progress through the intermediate steps may provide a better indicator of the long-term effects of advertising.

The danger with defining advertising goals for measured results (*DAGMAR*) is that rather than defining your goals first and then determining how to measure the results, you might be tempted to decide what can be easily measured first and then set your goal. More-over, if you select some intermediate measure of performance, you have to assume that your measure ultimately drives sales—and it may not.

THE BUDGET

Various procedures are used to determine the size of advertising expenditures. The efficiency of these procedures often depends on a firm's ability to measure the effectiveness of advertising. Judgment-oriented techniques include the subjective approach, the affordable approach, and the fixed guidelines approach, while data-oriented techniques include the competitive parity approach, the objective and task approach, the experimentation and testing approach, and the modeling and simulation approach. Selection among these methods depends on the extent to which returns from advertising can be identified.

The Subjective Approach

The subjective method sets budgets on the basis of executive judgment and experience. The executive generally has the task of allocating a fixed budget between advertising and other marketing costs. When direct customer contact is viewed as the most important element in the marketing mix, advertising needs are often subordinated.

The Fixed Guidelines Approach

A fixed guidelines approach involves setting the advertising budget in terms of a percentage of sales, a fixed sum per unit, or competitively with other firms. Many companies determine their budgets as a percentage of the sales volume forecasted or anticipated for the period that the advertising budget will cover. A variant of the percentage of sales method sets the budget as a fixed sum per unit. In this approach, the appropriation for advertising is determined by multiplying the projected unit sales volume by a certain number of dollars, euros, or yen per unit. The method is used primarily for consumer durables. When applied to convenience goods, the method is called the case-rate method. One problem with the judgment-oriented approaches is that when a firm is under pressure to lower costs, advertising is usually cut because of the absence of hard data to support the need for promotion.

Competitive Parity Approach

The competitive parity approach sets spending in line with major competitors. To some degree it reflects a belief in collective industry wisdom. The focus is on share of voice. Information on competitive spending comes from sources such as Nielsen Ad Tracker. This system automatically monitors the commercial content of network, national cable, spot TV, and national syndicated programs by recognizing the unique programs signal of each commercial broadcast. Local cable spending is estimated.

The Objective and Task Approach

The task approach involves setting objectives, translating these objectives into a series of communication-specific tasks, then determining the necessary appropriation. Firms using this approach begin by setting specific and measurable objectives for their advertising. The Texasgulf Company provides a useful case history.

Texasgulf supplies phosphoric acid to fertilizer manufacturers. Before advertising began, Texasgulf had a market share of about 5 percent, and about six large customers

APPLYING
. . . *to*
Industrial
Marketing

accounted for most of the sales. A short-term advertising goal was set to increase the awareness of Texasgulf's superior phosphoric acids by 10 percent in a one-year period. The campaign that was employed emphasized that Texasgulf acid products had fewer impurities than
those of the competition, and had a distinctive green color. The acid products were always
referred to as being "clean and green," and the overall campaign theme was "Texasgulf has
changed things."

A before-and-after research study found the following: (1) an increase from 15.3 to 35.1
percent in the number of respondents who recognized that Texasgulf made a clear, green
acid; (2) an increase from 3.6 to 16.3 percent in the number of respondents who associated
Texasgulf with the theme "(Blank) has changed Things"; (3) an increase from 9.4 to 24.3
percent in the number of respondents who thought that Texasgulf made an "above-average"
acid. The results indicate that the advertising campaign met the objectives that were set.

Experimentation and Testing

APPLYING
. . . *to*
Consumer
Marketing,
Business-to-
Business
Marketing

The experimentation and testing approach involves controlled field experiments. The impact
of spending and weight variations in test markets is compared to baseline results from controlled markets.

An example of a controlled field experiment is Du Pont's evaluation of its advertising
for Teflon coatings for cookware. Du Pont was following a pull strategy in which it hoped
that advertising could create sufficient consumer demand so that cookware manufacturers
would be forced to coat the inside of their utensils with Teflon. Advertising was varied in
selected markets to determine the best level of Teflon advertising expenditures between zero
and $1 million. There appeared to be a threshold effect at which $500,000 had little impact,
but $1 million gave significantly greater sales. The million-dollar expenditure was known to
be profitable, but not necessarily the most profitable level. Another experiment was conducted in which much higher levels were tested. This second experiment permitted Du Pont
to set the advertising level so that the marginal profit from the sale of Teflon was just greater
than zero.

INTEGRATING
. . . *with*
Information
Technology

Today controlled market testing often involves split-cable markets or electronic test
markets and scanning data. This process is illustrated in Figure 13-3. Traditional split-cable
heavy up tests often fail to show a significant sales response to large increases in advertising
spending. The reason may well be that heavily exposed groups are already beyond their saturation limits. Once customers decide that they have enough information to make a purchase, they will tend to ignore more information.

Modeling and Simulation

Econometric methods can be used to estimate the unknown parameters of an advertising
sales response function from historical data. Once estimation is complete, the estimated
sales response function can be used to answer "what if" questions.

A simulation is the representation of the behavior of one system (in our case, the "real
world") through the use of another system (i.e., a computer program designed for that purpose). Typically a planner can input alternative advertising levels to assess their impact.

In conclusion, research has shown a significant movement by medium- and large-size
companies toward more professional approaches to advertising budgeting. The objective and
task approach, and to a lesser extent experimentation and testing, are being adopted by
advertising managers. If you use a data-oriented technique, remember it generates only suggestions and must be tempered by your judgment. "What you can afford" seems to play an
important role in determining the degree to which the prescriptions of these more sophisticated techniques can be implemented. The budget-setting process in many organizations is a
political process.

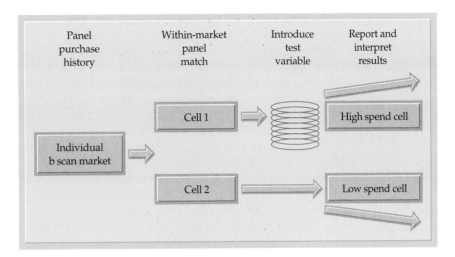

FIGURE 13-3   Split-Cable TV Market Test

MESSAGE CONTENT

The message content of a marketing communications strategy typically falls into one of three broad categories. The first approach stresses product features and customer benefits. The focus is on "demonstrable differences" or the "unique selling proposition." For instance, Mrs. Butterworth's Lite Syrup advertises itself as "The only Lite syrup made with Grade A Butter." A brand personality is developed in the second approach. The focus is on "image," "goodwill," "brand franchise," and "brand equity." An example would be Pillsbury's use of the "doughboy." The third approach positions the product through the great idea. The focus is on "strategy." For instance, 7-Up positions itself as the "Un-Cola."

Advertising Strategies

Under the assumption that advertising works by changing brand attitudes, as in AIDA theory, you have several advertising strategy options:

1. Influence the choice criteria that govern product class selection.
2. Change the relevance of a product attribute (create a salient attribute).
3. Change the ideal amount of an attribute that a brand should possess.
4. Change the perceived amount of an attribute held by the firm's brand.
5. Change the perceived amount of an attribute held by a competitor's brand.

Note that these advertising strategies are substrategies of the more general marketing strategy of positioning.

> **APPLYING**
> . . . to
> *Consumer*
> *Durable*
> *Goods*
> *Marketing*

Strategy 1 attempts to stimulate primary demand by modifying the individual's motivation and choice criteria. Usually, this involves accelerating an environmental trend, such as the use of margarine instead of butter. Compaq encouraged demand for multimedia personal computers using a print advertisement having the headline "Just because you learned the hard way doesn't mean your kid has to." Strategy 2 can take several forms. Sometimes an existing attribute can be made more prominent. At one time, all appliance manufacturers had wheels as an optional feature for their refrigerators so the homemaker could move the appliance in order to clean under it, but none of the firms advertised this feature. One company with a history of noninnovation decided to advertise this attribute. After the campaign, image studies revealed that the consumer viewed the firm as innovative! Sometimes a new attribute is added to extend the life of a mature product. The low-suds detergent market in Great Britain is dominated by Procter & Gamble with its Ariel, Bold, Fairy, and Daz brands and Lever Brother with its Persil, Surf, and Wisk brands. During the 1980s, Lever lost share to P&G. To reverse this trend, Lever launched Radion in late 1989. Advertising introduced the concept of odor removal as the ultimate test of a detergent's cleaning power and conferred ownership of this property on Radion. This odor-removal proposition was based on a Unilever patented technology, a unique deo-perfume system that deodorizes clothes rather than merely masking odor. Advertising worked to position Radion to complement other Lever brands. The impact of Radion's launch upon brand images in the low-suds sector is shown in an image map by Millward Brown (Figure 13-4). The communication of odor removal placed Radion in the modern/efficient quadrant of the map. Moreover, Radion was differentiated from the Lever portfolio, market leader Persil in particular.

The remaining three strategies involve positioning the firm's brand in relation to ideal and competing brands by moving the ideal toward its own brand position (strategy 3), by moving its brand toward the ideal (strategy 4), or by moving competitive brands away from the ideal (strategy 5). Croft Original pale cream Spanish sherry employed strategy 3. When Croft Original was launched, all sweet or cream sherries, including market leader Harveys Bristol Cream, were dark in color. Croft Original's advertising presented paleness as a positive product attribute while also establishing Croft Original as the superior pale cream sherry. Creative executions were based on P. G. Wodehouse's characters, Jeeves and Wooster. The relationship between the likable but basically inept Wooster and his butler Jeeves, the arbiter of good taste and discernment, provided the platform for projecting the quality of Croft Original and the stylish sophistication of its drinkers. Jeeves leaves no doubt as to the discerning quality of Croft Original: "One can tell a great deal, sir, just by looking at things. Your Croft Original, for example, with its light delicate color. One glance at the sherry tells one all one needs to know about the quality." The concept of paleness was later expanded, associating it with modernity (and dark with old-fashioned). The success of this

APPLYING
. . . to
Consumer
Packaged
Goods
Marketing

APPLYING
. . . to
Consumer
Beverages
Marketing

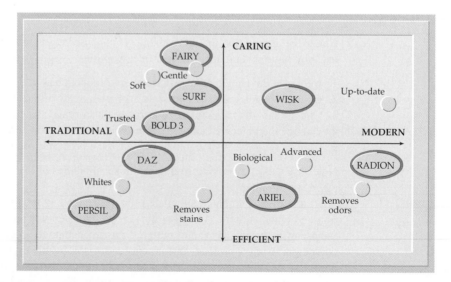

FIGURE 13-4 **Detergent Brand Image Map (From "The Case for Radion Automatic: A New Brand in the Lever Portfolio," in *Advertising Works 6,* Paul Feldwick, ed. [Henley-on-Thames: NTC Publications, 1991], p. 220.)**

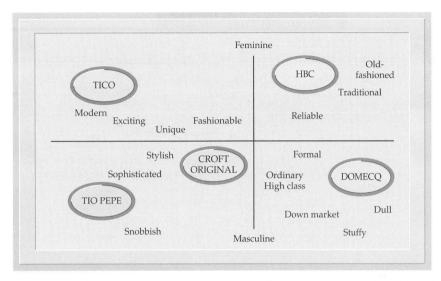

FIGURE 13-5 Spanish Sherry Market Brand Personality Map (From "Croft Original `One Instinctively Knows When Something Is Right'," in *Advertising Works 6*, Paul Feldwick, ed. [Henley-on-Thames: NTC Publications, 1991], p. 41.)

communication strategy is evidenced by the correspondence map by MAS shown in Figure 13-5.

Strategy 4 can be illustrated by L&M cigarettes. Liggett & Myers decided that their L&M brand of cigarettes was not properly positioned and that it must be repositioned into the full-flavor category. Although L&M was reformulated so that it had a new tobacco blend and a new cork filter, the primary repositioning effort was a massive advertising campaign. The first print advertisements showed a rugged, powerfully built man clearing an area and building a cabin in the wilderness. Liggett & Myers was trying to move its brand closer to Marlboro, which was already in the full-flavor category. Rather than repositioning toward a competitor, it is more likely that you would want to differentiate yourself from your close competitors as illustrated by Marketing in Action box 13-2. An example of the strategy 5 is a china ad that reads "Royal Doulton, the china of Stratford-on-Trent, England versus Lenox, the china of Pomona, N.J." Thus, Royal Doulton is repositioning Lenox china, a brand that many consumers believed was imported. This advertisement resulted in a 6 percent gain in market share for Royal Doulton.

APPLYING
. . . *to*
Consumer
Tobacco
Marketing

APPLYING
. . . *to*
Consumer
Housewares
Marketing

Product Line Positioning

APPLYING
. . . *to*
Consumer
Food
Marketing

Creative strategy plays a crucial role in product line positioning. Kraft was interested in a multibranded, segmented positioning approach that would maximize its opportunity within the ice cream category. Kraft had been marketing an ice cream called Breyers in the northeastern region of the United States. Breyers ice cream does not contain any kind of artificial flavoring, added coloring, stabilizers, or emulsifiers. Kraft wanted to take this premium ice cream national by capitalizing on its all-natural positioning through an advertising claim that Breyers was "*The* All-Natural Ice Cream." The only problem was that Kraft already had premium quality ice cream, Sealtest, on the market. Blind product testing showed that Sealtest compared favorably on taste with ice cream parlors' ice cream. Given that Sealtest cost only half, or less, of what these hand-packed ice creams cost, Sealtest offered the consumer real value. Sealtest was positioned as "The Supermarket Ice Cream with That Ice Cream

APPLYING
. . . *to*
Consumer
Beverages
Marketing

MARKETING IN ACTION *13-2*

Repositioning Kronenbourg 1664

Les Brasseries Kronenbourg is a unit of the French DANONE Group. City sophistication is at the core of Kronenbourg's new British campaign with its humorous take on famous French sayings. Premium lager Kronenbourg 1664 has gone for Parisian sophistication in its new television campaign, abandoning the rustic image the brand used to share with arch-rival Stella Artois. Three 30-second executions feature vignettes of city life, with a humorous twist on French expressions. "C'est la Vie" shows a young clubber failing to pick up a girl by buying her a Kronenbourg 1664, when she makes off with both their drinks and joins her female lover. In "Déjà Vu" a young woman poses as a lost tourist to get men to buy her a beer in the local cafe. And "Savoir-Faire" features a young man jumping the queue at a crowded bar by using his mobile to place a telephone call to himself. "The proposition is to bring Kronenbourg 1664 to life as the best-loved premium beer in France."

The shift to the city is intended to put a bit of distance between the brand and Stella Artois, which projects a rural image in its long-running TV campaign, originally based on the film *Jean de Florette.* Kronenbourg commercials last year also featured the French countryside, with two old men in a vineyard bemoaning people's growing preference for beer. Kronenbourg is one of Scottish Courage's three core brands, with Foster's and John Smith's, all supported by substantial advertising campaigns. Its Frenchness is belied by the German-sounding name: it actually originated in the 17th century in Strasbourg, straddling the French-German border.

Premium lager is the fastest growing sector of the beer market, as younger consumers seek out quality. Kronenbourg 1664 is the second largest premium draught brew with 18% market share compared to Stella's 28%, and Carlsberg Export and Heineken Export each with under 10%.

Kronenbourg has enjoyed year-on-year growth of around 20%, and the current TV and cinema push is part of a 10 million spend aimed at keeping the momentum going. It benefited from a press campaign during the World Cup in France, including a guide to areas where matches were being played. "We are trying to increase brand saliency on a national basis. Premium lager is biased toward the south of the country where it continues to do well, but northern sales are growing faster from a smaller base."

The focus on women in two of the three commercials has been viewed as a conscious attempt to win over female drinkers to what has traditionally been seen as a male product. The company says that while this was not an active part of its strategy, it recognizes female purchasers are a growing sector of the market. That applies especially to the off-trade, as women often do the buying for their partners or for parties, and can be influenced to purchase a familiar brand even if they are not themselves regular beer drinkers.

— *You can use advertising to differentiate your product.*

Source: Robert McLuhan, "Kronenbourg's Urbane Tales," *Marketing*, December 17, 1998, p. 17.

Parlor Taste." This appeal was not in conflict with Breyers' natural ingredient appeal. In the first five years after the start of the new advertising campaigns, total sales of packaged ice cream only rose about 5 percent, but Sealtest sales increased 23 percent and Breyer's sales jumped 50 percent. Each brand established its own niche in the marketplace.

Appeals by Target Segment

Where a product's image is important, psychographics are critical. Cosmetic firms, for example, use psychographics to make sure that the image of their products and ads is in sync with their customers' self-image. Marketers tend to reflect their own lifestyle in marketing communications without adequate attention being paid to the lifestyle target group. You have to make sure it's your customers, not yourself, to whom you are talking.

Many firms make different appeals to different segments. AT&T Long Lines segmented its residential long-distance market and found a group of prospects with reasons to call long distance, but who didn't because of a perceived price barrier. As a result, AT&T augmented its successful emotional appeal, its "Reach Out and Touch Someone" campaign, with a pragmatic appeal, a "Cost of Visit" campaign.

Message Creativity

Message creativity often is a deciding factor in the success of an advertising campaign. For example, one year California raisins had the most popular ads on television despite a budget of only $6.8 million. McDonald's spent a total of $385 million on TV ads in the same year and only ranked third in popularity. The difference was the appeal of the animated dancing raisins dreamed up by the agency Foote, Cone, and Belding. This campaign was so successful that the California Raisin Board received millions of dollars in licensing fees from the sales of toy raisin figures.

Copy Pretesting

Focus groups are frequently used to evaluate rough commercials. The purpose is to ensure communication objectives are met—that the message you want to send is the same one being received. This screening procedure prevents spending money on flawed commercials.

A variety of commercial copy-testing services test finished commercials. They differ in whether they conduct on-air or off-air tests, use a pre/posttest design or posttest-only (matched-group) design, provide a single exposure or multiple exposures (reexposure), and other details. A major concern you should have in using one of these services is whether their audience corresponds to your target market.

Copy-testing measures fall into six general categories: measures of persuasion, brand salience, recall, communications (playback), overall commercial reaction (liking), and commercial diagnostics. Representative examples are given in Table 13-1.

The ARF Copy Research Validity Project studied five pairs of commercials for established packaged goods that had produced significant sales differences in split-cable copy tests. The pairs were commercials that had not previously aired from advertisers making minimal use of print in the test markets. The commercials were the only ones in use during the tests. At least six months of sales data were available. The Validity Project found that copy testing is helpful in identifying commercials known to be generating incremental sales. The most surprising finding is a strong relationship between likability of the copy and its effects on sales. On the other hand, the IRI "How Advertising Works" study found that the relationship between standard recall and persuasion scores and the sales impact for established brands is tenuous, at best.

TABLE 13-1 Copy-Testing Measures

Measure	Example
Persuasion	Overall brand rating
Brand salience	Top-of-mind awareness
Recall	Recall brand from category cue
Communications (playback)	Main point communication
Commercial reaction (liking)	Impression of commercial (average)
Commercial diagnostics	Told me something new about the product that I did not know before

MEDIA SELECTION

The objective in media planning is to select the set of TV and radio programs, magazines, newspapers, and other media vehicles, including online Web (i.e., banner ads), that will maximize profits within a given budget. Your problem is that the optimum allocation tends to vary for each individual organization. Computer models have been developed to help evaluate media and audience data. The success of these models depends on understanding the appropriateness of media vehicles and on knowledge of how media are matched with markets.

Reach Versus Frequency

The total impact of an advertising campaign can be measured by counting the number of exposures that result from *reaching* different people and multiplying by the average *frequency* of ad exposure per person. Thus, we have

$$\text{Total exposures} = \text{Reach} \times \text{Frequency}$$

This implies that high total exposure can be obtained by reaching a large number of people with a few ads or by exposing a small number of potential buyers to many ads. Your problem is to decide which combination of advertising reach and frequency is best for a particular product at a point in time.

When an advertiser has a message that has to be heard only once, a media schedule that maximizes reach is used. The idea is to have every exposure appeal to a different potential buyer. Most of the retail advertising that emphasizes special sales and prices falls into this category. Also, many of the direct-mail promotions used for book and record clubs are designed to make a sale on the first impression and reach is crucial to their success. In addition, reach can be important when introducing new products to the marketplace. This is especially true when cents-off coupons are offered to encourage trial use and the firm wants each potential buyer to get only one coupon. When emphasizing reach, duplication is an issue. *Duplication* in advertising occurs because some of the individuals exposed to an ad in one vehicle will also see the ad in a second vehicle. This suggests that the more media vehicles you buy, the greater the chance for duplication and the more likely you are to have diminishing returns to advertising.

Continuity in advertising is used to keep the name of the product in the buyer's mind so that when a purchase is planned, the company's brand will be remembered. *Recency* is particularly important for frequently purchased consumer goods for which brand loyalty is low. Reminder ads can also be used to promote the sale of products and services that are bought infrequently. Funeral homes, insurance agents, and car dealers all employ continuity in their advertising so they will be considered when the buyer is ready to make a purchase. Given budget constraints that most firms face, continuity requires that reach be stressed.

Alternatively, some advertisers must repeat ads frequently to get the buyer's attention and bring about attitude changes that precede purchase. In these situations, the emphasis is on the number of exposures per person rather than the reach of the campaign. This approach is based on research, which shows that recall of ads and purchase intentions increase with the number of exposures per person. For many consumer products, the best exposure frequency, called the "effective frequency," seems to be at least two, and perhaps three, exposures within a purchase cycle. Given budget constraints that most firms face, effective frequency requires that advertising be pulsed.

Because of differences in products and market conditions, it is probably foolish to generalize about the optimum combination of reach and frequency for an advertising campaign. However, managers usually have better data on the reach of media vehicles than they have on duplication and the effects of repetition on sales. This suggests that media selection will often emphasize reach, with a more subjective adjustment made for frequency.

Media Vehicle Appropriateness

Media vehicles are not passive conductors of messages and can often influence the effectiveness of the message. Factors that determine the appropriateness of media vehicles include editorial climate, product fit, technical capabilities, comparative advertising strategy, target population receptiveness, and the product distribution system.

A vehicle has an image and personality that can add to or detract from a message. *Sunset* is regarded as an expert source and *Vogue* as a prestige source. The relative value will depend on the campaign objectives (awareness versus attitude change versus image creation), the target segment, the campaign tactics (image versus reason-why advertising), and the product.

Media are believed to work in different ways. At each state in the purchase process, one medium may be superior to another. In relation to TV commercials, print advertisements are less able to command attention, are more able to arouse personal involvement, and are more likely to cause conscious, discrete attitude change.

Consumers can pay *no* attention to a print advertisement or deliberately expose themselves to one. They do the latter when they are seeking information for decision making. Consumers can concentrate longer on an advertising theme and thereby make more personal connections with it. This means they can become more personally involved in print advertisements for products that possess intrinsic interest. Because attention is voluntary, the consumer is more likely to be consciously influenced. Attitude change under conditions of high involvement occurs through the process of dissonance resolution.

Even when customers do not watch a TV commercial, they usually listen to it. Their involvement is low and they are unaware that their attitudes are slowly being modified by the onslaught of repeated exposure to the message. Their attitudes may change more rapidly later when the source of the message is forgotten. This phenomenon is called the *sleeper effect.* When the consumer ultimately faces a purchasing situation, these shifts in attitude move to a more conscious level.

These differences suggest that print and TV advertising may be used most effectively in combination. One may be more suitable than the other for a particular step in the intermediate process. Thus, you need to match the media with company goals. Next, the manager must match the media with the target audience.

Matching Media with Markets

Advertisers prefer media whose audience characteristics are closest to the profile of market characteristics of their customers. Characteristics by which the target population may be identified include demographic, psychographic, and purchase behavior variables. Matching takes two forms: direct matching, in which media are matched to product usage variables from syndicated product-media research services, and indirect matching, in which media are matched to demographics or psychographic profiles. The latter is useful when target markets are defined using a company's market research survey, and media usage is obtained from a syndicated research service. Managers also need methods to help them select media that show the best combination of cost and exposure value.

MEASURING ADVERTISING EFFECTIVENESS

A firm's ability to measure the effectiveness of its advertising is crucial to developing more efficient advertisements, to determining the level of expenditures, and to allocating available funds to media. As soon as the relationship between advertising pressure and effectiveness is known, a firm can calculate the advertising budget size, compare various media, and select vehicles within the same medium.

The four most commonly used measures of advertising effectiveness are changes in sales, number of inquiries received, increases in knowledge of the product, and attitude changes. In the case of online advertising, the measure is click-throughs, the number of times a banner ad was actually clicked on by a guest. Although the intermediate measures of effectiveness can provide helpful insights, sales is the best criterion to evaluate advertising results.

The analysis of the influence of advertising on the sales of a product or service is a complex undertaking. The methods available for measuring advertising elasticity include controlled experiments and econometric procedures. Controlled field experiments can provide good data, but they are expensive. Econometric methods are more popular for studying the impact of advertising on the sales of existing products. We begin with a discussion of the effects of advertising on demand.

Effects of Advertising on Demand

Advertising can increase the demand for a particular brand within a product category or raise per capita consumption—that is, encourage customers "to choose" or "to use." The competitive activity generated when brands attempt to increase their own sales may result in an increase in total demand.

At an operational level, advertising is measured in monetary units and we talk of advertising expenditures or *adspend.* After all, you need this number to budget and to calculate your profits. But this is an internal measure. You also need an external measure that expresses advertising *delivery* to prospects. Here we speak of opportunity-to-see (OTS), television rating points (TVR), or gross rating points (GRP). GRP is calculated by multiplying a program's audience share by the number of times an ad is run. If an ad is shown 14 times a week on two programs, you will get

$$\begin{array}{lr} \text{4 showings in a time slot with a 12 rating} = & \text{48 GRPs} \\ \text{10 showings in a time slot with a 9 rating} = & \underline{\text{90}}\text{ GRPs} \\ \text{Total for the week} & \text{138 GRPs} \end{array}$$

Since ratings are expressed as percentages, the average person will be exposed 1.38 times. Of course, some people will not see the ad at all and others could be exposed 14 times. Depending on the media mix employed, the same adspend could generate quite different GRPs. A further refinement comes when we do household-level measurement of the actual number of advertising *exposures* received by each household.

The impact of advertising is often spread over several periods. Not everyone who sees an advertisement in a particular week will buy in the same week. Consequently, we allocate advertising delivery in part to when it actually happens and distribute the rest in decreasing amounts to subsequent periods. This new advertising variable is called *adstock.* An example of this process is shown in Figure 13-6.

The sales response function for advertising may be S-shaped. At low levels of advertising, sales response may be negligible. The advertising does not have sufficient weight to break through the clutter of advertisements. At some *threshold,* sales response begins to increase at an increasing rate. Finally, additional advertising produces further sales, but at a decreasing rate. This is the region of *diminishing returns to scale.* Empirical evidence shows that this is the region in which most major brands operate.

The sales response functions for two brands in the same product category are shown in Figure 13-7. These are important brands in a very large package-goods category. Data are from the 20 largest U.S. markets covering 1.5 years of weekly scanning and media data. The horizontal axis shows television gross rating points (GRPs or TVRs) that have been adjusted for adstock. The vertical axis is a sales index scaled so that 1.0 corresponds to no advertising. For example, a continuous delivery of 100 GRP stock for Brand A corresponds to about

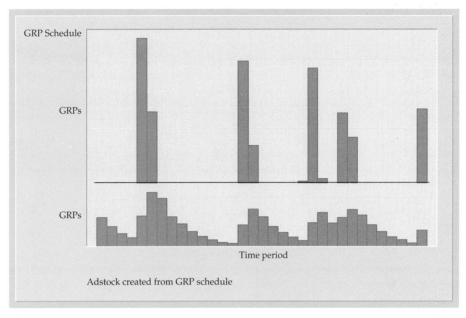

FIGURE 13-6 Adstock

an index of 1.15. This level of stock will increase sales 15 percent over what sales would have been with no advertising. Brand A shows diminishing returns to advertising.

One way to measure the impact of advertising is by calculating advertising elasticities. The formula is

$$E_{adv} = \frac{\%\ \text{change in sales}}{\%\ \text{change in advertising}}$$

A representative advertising elasticity for a fast-moving consumer good is probably on the order of 0.10. This means that doubling the advertising spending will only increase sales volume by 10 percent. Research has shown that advertising elasticities typically range in value from 0.03 to 0.25.

Tracking

Consistent theme advertising maintains the saliency of the mental connections that constitute the brand. You should then track the advertising memories that people associate with brands. One company that does this is Millward Brown.

Andrex toilet paper is closely associated with the benefits of being "soft, strong, and long." These associations were developed, maintained, and enhanced from advertising. Andrex has used a series of "puppy" ads. One specific advertisement was known as "little boy" and featured a young boy sitting on the toilet and watching a puppy run off with the toilet roll. Millward Brown tracked this advertisement in Great Britain as the ad consolidated the traditional associations and added some more emotional strands. One question they ask consumers is, "when you think of all the advertising you've seen for Andrex, what if anything, do you particularly remember from it?" The results are shown in Figure 13-8. Notice how heavy media weight gradually brings images from the "little boy" ad into people's minds in connection with Andrex. This approach gives us information about when the communications job is done. Often measures of brand loyalty and brand equity are included

APPLYING
. . . *to*
Consumer
Packaged
Goods
Marketing

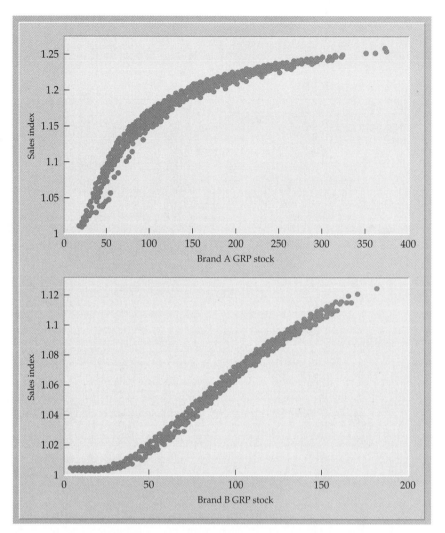

FIGURE 13-7   Sales Response Functions (From Laurence N. Gold, "Let's Heavy Up in St. Louis and See What Happens," *Journal of Advertising Research,* **Vol. 33, No. 6 [November/December 1992], pp. 34–35.)**

in tracking studies and improvements in these measures are taken as indicators of advertising's success.

Qualitative research in the form of before-and-after brand image maps can indicate whether or not your advertising is working as desired. Silentnight launched a new bed in the United Kingdom. Unfortunately, a serious industrial dispute that hampered production mired the launch down. After the industrial dispute was ended, Silentnight needed to relaunch an improved version of the product. The ultimate Sleep System was a unique combination of mattress and base that offered individual support for two sleepers no matter what the differential in weight, support right up to the edge of the bed to eliminate roll off, and a posturized zone of extra springs in the central third to provide extra support where the body weight was the greatest. The creative advertising solution for communicating these features was a unique product demonstration that was sufficiently novel to overcome customer apathy and to convincingly communicate the product's principal benefits. The stars of this demonstration were a hippo and a duck! Consumers reacted enthusi-

APPLYING
. . . to
Consumer
Semi-
Durable
Marketing

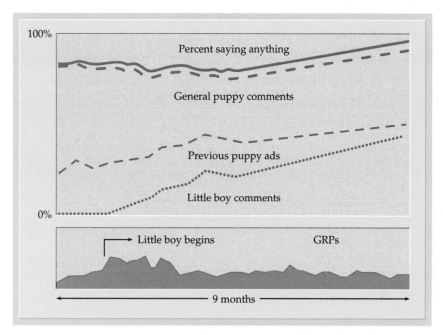

FIGURE 13-8   Andrex Long-Term Ad Awareness (From Jeremy Green, "How Repetition and Consistency Build Mental Connections," in *People, Brands & Advertising* [Millward Brown, 1992], p. 48.)

astically. The establishment of Silentnight's differential positioning is tracked over 18 months in Figure 13-9*a,* while the improvement in perception of the brand is tracked over 24 months in Figure 13-9*b.*

Experimental Methods

APPLYING
. . . *to*
Consumer
Services
Marketing

Successful users of field experiments include AT&T, Nabisco, and Campbell Soup. AT&T used a dual-cable television system in conjunction with its own long-distance usage tracking system to test the impact of a new "Cost of Visit" campaign against the existing "Reach Out" campaign. Households in test markets are connected to either an "A" or "B" cable in checkerboard fashion. This allows different ads to be sent to each group. The experimental design executed by AT&T is shown in Table 13-2. The test results indicated that, over a five-year period, the "Cost of Visit" campaign would generate some $100 million more than the "Reach Out" campaign.

RJR Nabisco was resigned to slow growth from its biscuit division because it was in a mature industry. Nabisco experimented with saturation advertising aimed at small population segments and found that the whole cookie and cracker business was underpromoted. Nabisco advertised heavily for its 40-year-old Ritz crackers, in six different geographical markets, representing 3.2 percent of the adult population in America. The buying behavior of this group in the face of heavy TV and store promotions was monitored for one year. The purchases of a control group were also recorded. The experimental group had a 16 percent increase in sales. Nabisco modified its promotional strategy in light of its experimental findings.

APPLYING
. . . *to*
Consumer
Food
Marketing

Campbell Soup has conducted a series of experiments and subsequent analyses that have shown that budget levels generally had little or no impact on sales of well-established brands. Changes in copy strategy, media selection, media mix, and targeting had a substantial payout. Products studied included Campbell's Condensed Soup, Chunky Soups, Franco-American, V-8, and Swanson.

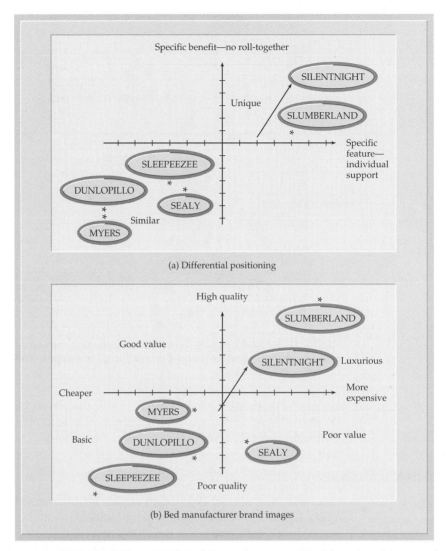

FIGURE 13-9   Brand Maps (From "The Ultimate Success Story," in *Advertising Works 6,* Paul Feldwick, ed. [Henley-on-Thames: NTC Publications, 1991], pp. 59–60.)

ADVERTISING VERSUS DIRECT MARKETING

While general mass media advertising allows you to target your audience somewhat, ultimately your customers self select themselves while remaining anonymous. Direct marketing, on the other hand, sells to identifiable customers at their location. As discussed in Chapter 10, direct marketing has the added benefit of delivering your product directly to the customer's door. Advertising is often used as part of direct marketing to generate

TABLE 13-2   AT&T Field Experiment

Study Phase	5-Month Preassessment	15-Month Test	6-Month Reassessment
Cable A	"Feelings"	"Reach Out"	"Reach Out"/local company
Cable B	↓	"Cost of Visit"	↓

TABLE 13-3 **Comparison of Direct Marketing and General Mass-Marketing Advertising**

Direct Marketing	General Mass-Marketing Advertising
Selling to individuals, with customers identifiable by name, address, and purchase behavior (personal, targetable, ability to vary the message by segment, measurable, ability to capture data).	Mass selling, with buyers identified as broad groups and sharing common demographic and psychographic characteristics (cost efficient where identity of customers is unknown).
Products have the added value of distribution to the customer's door as an important product benefit.	Product benefits do not typically include distribution to the customer's door.
The medium is the marketplace.	The retail outlet is the marketplace.
Marketing controls product all the way through delivery.	The marketer typically loses control as the product enters the distribution stream.
Uses targeted media.	Uses mass media.
Is hard for competitors to monitor—the stealth factor.	Can be monitored by competitors using syndicated services.
Advertising is used to generate an immediate inquiry or order, with a specific order.	Advertising is used for its cumulative effect over time in building awareness, image, loyalty, and benefit recall. Purchase action is deferred.
Repetition is used within an ad or mailing.	Repetition is used over a period of time.
Consumer feels a high perceived risk—product bought unseen, distant recourse.	Consumer feels less risk—has direct contact with product and direct recourse.

Source: Adapted from DMA's Direct Marketing Institute; and Jim Kobs, *Profitable Direct Marketing* (Lincolnwood. IL: NTC Business Books, 1991), p. 13.

inquiries and orders. A comparison between direct marketing and general mass marketing advertising is laid out in Table 13-3. The main distinction between direct marketing—and especially interactive marketing—and general mass marketing is that of a dialogue versus a monologue.

SUMMARY

Advertising can assume an important role in building awareness and providing information about goods and services. Advertising begins with the determination of objectives and goals. Next you need to set the size of the advertising budget. This can be done using percentage-of-sales methods, the task procedure, or normative approaches. Given a budget, you need to develop appropriate themes and campaign materials. The next step is to pick an appropriate set of media vehicles. Advertising agencies are often employed to help with this work. Finally, you need to measure the effects of advertising expenditures.

NOTE

1. Stephen Miller and Lisette Berry, "Brand Salience versus Brand Image: Two Theories of Advertising Effectiveness," *Journal of Advertising Research*, Vol. 38, No. 5 (October 1998), pp. 77–82.

SUGGESTED READING

Achenbaum, Alvin A. "Reversing the Advertising Productivity Crisis," *Marketing Management,* Vol. 1, No. 3 (1992), pp. 22–27.

Gold, Laurence N. "Let's Heavy Up in St. Louis and See What Happens," *Journal of Advertising Research,* Vol. 33, No. 6 (November/December 1992), pp. 31–38.

REFERENCES

Broadbent, Simon. *Accountable Advertising* (Henley-on-Thames: Admap Publications, 1997).

Duckworth, Gary. *Advertising Works* 9 (Henley-on-Thames: NTC Publications, 1997).

Forker, Olan D., and Ronald W. Ward. *Commodity Advertising: The Economics and Measurement of Generic Programs* (New York: Lexington Books, 1993).

Franzen, Giep. *Advertising Effectiveness* (Henley-on-Thames: Admap Publications, 1994).

Jones, John Philip. *When Ads Work* (New York: Lexington Books, 1995).

McDonald, Colin. *How Advertising Works* (Henley-on-Thames, NTC Publications, 1992).

Millward Brown International Plc. *People, Brands & Advertising* (London: 1992).

Randazzo, Sal. *Mythmaking on Madison Avenue* (Chicago: Probus Publishing, 1993).

Vakratsas, Demetrios, and Tim Amber. "How Advertising Works," *Journal of Marketing,* Vol. 63, No. 1 (January 1999), pp. 26–43.

QUESTIONS

1. The Gillette Company fosters a unified strategic position for its men's shaving products by advertising that it's the "Best a man can get." Develop an advertising theme for positioning its women's shaving products—one that would position Gillette's products as an essential part of a woman's beauty regime and as the key to being physically and psychologically ready for anything.

2. The Internet is the most-hyped and fastest growing medium yet invented. Ironically, Internet Service Providers (ISPs) must use traditional media to attract more customers. Construct a media strategy to help an ISP gain customers.

3. The network television business is built around the belief that advertisers covet youth. Programming emphasizes sassy sitcoms and steamy soap operas that appeal to 18- to 49-year-olds, and especially adults under 35. The premise is that this group is free spending, impressionable, and trendsetting. Meanwhile, the growing number of older viewers is more affluent than ever. They are the best customers for luxury cars, cold and allergy medicines, food, toothpaste, detergents, computers, travel, medical services, financial services, and entertainment. Can the networks and advertisers continue to justify their devotion to youth?

4. Off-price shopping is not unlike a treasure hunt. Shoppers can find designer and name-brand clothes, shoes, crystal, and jewelry for 20 to 60 percent below some department store prices. When off-price retailer TJX Cos., known for its TJ Maxx chain, bought its rival Marshalls, Marshalls' sales were falling and profits were nonexistent. TJX's solution was to slash Marshalls' ad spending from 2.5 percent of sales to 1.5 percent of sales—this when many retailers spend 5 to 10 percent of sales. What do you think of TJX's turnaround strategy? Marshalls' ads had frequently featured new shipments of clothes or highlighted the price of a number of products, noting how much of a discount

they represented. Do you think TJX should change Marshalls' advertising message appeals? If so, why and how?

5. September is always a blockbuster month for women's fashion magazines. One study found readers of *Harper's Bazaar* would have to slog through 127 pages before they got to the first feature article; for *Elle* it was 140 pages, and for *Vogue* it was 128 pages. Indeed, 77 percent of the pages in *Vogue,* America's top-selling women's fashion magazine, were advertisements; and *Elle* ran 32 ad pages before its table of contents page! Why would advertisers continue flock to these magazines? How does an advertiser stand out?

6. With the threat of an AIDS epidemic, public health organizations ran massive media campaigns to stress the seriousness of AIDS and that everyone was at risk. These campaigns created a high level of awareness and generated anxiety. However, for health organizations to maintain publicity at a high intensity was impossible. When the publicity died down, people believed the threat of AIDS had lessened. The swing from alarm to complacency needs to be addressed. Construct a media campaign for preventing HIV/AIDS slipping off the public agenda and for encouraging sexually active heterosexuals (demographically 16 to 34-year-olds with two or more sexual partners in the last 12 months) to use condoms. This target group has already forsaken the sensible advice of abstinence outside of marriage.

7. Consumers discovered that boxes of Dassant's New England Pumpkin Spice Bread & Muffin Mix were not made in New England and did not contain any pumpkin. Is this an example of deceptive advertising?

8. The economic turmoil in Asia generated a new experience—recession—for most professionals in that region. What is the primary role of advertising during an economic downturn? To what extent should the advertising budget be adjusted?

9. What responsibility does an advertiser have to ensure that advertisements meet the mores of society? To ensure that the editorial contents of media vehicles in which advertisements are placed meet these mores? Who determines the mores of society? Are marketers contributing to the decline of moral values in society?

10. The brand manager for a salad dressing would like to assess the impact of advertising versus price on the brand's sales. She first removed the impact of temporary promotions. She wants to focus on the impact of base price and brand awareness on base sales. These data can be found in file dressingdat.sav. To be able to do "what if" simulations, she decides a linear regression should be estimated. What would be the incremental base sales volume from a $0.10 base price decrease? an awareness increase of 200?

CASE *13-1*   AIR MILES™ (A) IVEY

*T*he big day comes in two weeks' time," said Craig Underwood, President of Loyalty Management Group Canada Inc. It was mid-March 1992, and the 'big day' that he was referring to was the scheduled launch of the Canadian AIR MILES™ program. "We think we have put together an advertising strategy that will be very effective in getting enrollments off the ground quickly," continued Craig, "but you are always nervous until you have the program up and going."

THE CONCEPT AND ITS ORIGIN

The AIR MILES™ program was a customer loyalty program which offered consumers the opportunity to collect AIR MILES™ travel miles and redeem them for air travel on selected airlines. Consumers purchased goods and services from specific program sponsors to earn travel miles. These program sponsors were in a wide variety of retail and service categories and were not necessarily travel-related.

The AIR MILES™ program was the brainchild of Keith Mills and originated in the U.K. in November 1988. Its development in the U.K. occurred for a number of reasons. First were the challenges facing the airline industry. The airlines were experiencing high fixed costs and excess capacity and were always looking for ways to fill this excess capacity.

Second, the U.K. airline industry had seen the success of the U.S. frequent flyer programs during the previous six years. The U.S. airlines were creating customer loyalty by giving business travellers the opportunity to earn free trips for their loyalty to that airline. The frequent flyer programs, while successful, did not allow the infrequent traveller to earn enough points for free trips.

Third, U.K. businesses, as well as businesses throughout the world, were looking for unique marketing opportunities. Finally, the advertising agency of Nadler, Larimer and its chairman, Keith Mills, were looking for their next big idea.

As a result, the U.K. AIR MILES™ program was born. The U.K. program was structured so that collectors would receive AIR MILES™ vouchers for purchases made from sponsor organizations. These vouchers differed from the points collection systems of frequent flyer programs in that purchases for everyday items such as gasoline would provide collectors with AIR MILES™, rather than points. The goal of the AIR MILES™ program was to give the average consumer, the non-frequent business traveller, the opportunity to earn free travel. One AIR MILE was worth one mile of air travel and collectors could redeem AIR MILES™ vouchers for flights on British Airways.

THE START IN CANADA

The development of the Canadian AIR MILES™ program began in April 1991 with the efforts of three business planning and sales executives. They began Loyalty Management Group Canada Inc. (Loyalty Management), which administered the AIR MILES™ program. The Canadian market was chosen because it had many national retail chains and the majority of its population was in a few large urban centers. The Canadian program was modelled after the U.K. program with some differences.

The plan for the Canadian AIR MILES™ program was to target sponsors in eight critical customer categories: Credit Cards, Retail Banking, Department Stores, Retail Grocery, Automobile Repair, Home Improvement, Car Rental and Hotels. AIR MILES™ Canada started by focusing its efforts on gaining contracts with the Bank of Montreal and Sears Canada. By the launch of the program, on March 30, 1992, AIR MILES™ Canada had signed contracts with 10 sponsors (see Exhibit 1).

In order to create a long-term sustainable advantage for its sponsors, the AIR MILES™ program was committed to having only one sponsor in each consumer

* This case was prepared by Carol Steer under the supervision of Professor John Kennedy solely to provide material for class discussion. The author does not intend to illustrate either effective or ineffective handling of a managerial situation. The author may have disguised certain names and other identifying information to protect confidentiality. One-time permission to reproduce granted by Ivey Management Services on February 1, 1999. Copyright © 1994. The University of Western Ontario. The University prohibits any form of reproduction, storage, or transmittal without written permission from the Richard Ivey School of Business. This material is not covered under authorization from CanCopy or any other reproduction rights organization.

EXHIBIT 1   Launch Sponsors

Sponsor	Products/ Services	Canadian Geographic Area Of Operations	Air Miles™ Awards
Bank of Montreal Master Card	Credit Card	National	1 AM™ for every $20
Bank of Montreal	Financial services	All 10 provinces	Variable award levels
Bell Mobility Cellular	Cellular telephone equipment and air time	Ontario and Quebec	1 AM™ for every $15
Goodyear Tires & Auto Service	Tires and automobile service	All 10 provinces	1 AM™ for every $4
Holt Renfrew	Fashion retailer	Major cities across Canada	1 AM™ for every $20
LensCrafters	Eyeglasses	Ontario, Manitoba, Saskatchewan, Alberta, British Columbia	75 AM™ for every pair of glasses
Le Groupe Ro-Na Dismat	Building hardware, home improvement	Quebec	1 AM™ for: – first $15 of purchase – each additional $10
Safeway	Grocery retailer	Thunder Bay, Manitoba, Saskatchewan, Alberta, British Columbia	1 AM™ for: – first $20 of purchase – each additional $15
Sears	Department store	All 10 provinces	Tiered offer depending on volume. Starts at 1 for $20 up to 1 for $10.
Tilden Interrent	Car and truck rentals	All 10 provinces	25 AM™ for each
United Van Lines	Moving and storage	All 10 provinces	Tiered offer depending on volume moved. Starts at 100 AM™ for <5,000 lbs., up to 200 AM™ for >10,000 lbs.

category. As well, sponsors were required to be committed to the program for a minimum of two years.

While the U.K. program provided collectors with AIR MILES™ redeemed for airline tickets, the Canadian program tracked collectors' AIR MILES™ on a database by using a personalized collector card.

AIR MILES™ Marketing Information System (AMMIS) was developed and managed by an outside organization, Rapp Collins Marcoa. Individual collector accounts were set up on AMMIS and Rapp Collins updated travel miles by posting transactions when information was received from sponsors. Collectors received regular statements indicating the number of AIR MILES™ collected during the period, where the AIR MILES™ were collected, and the total number of AIR MILES™ collected to date. The periodic statement mailings included a newsletter and also provided an opportunity for sponsors to market to collectors and the opportunity for cross marketing between sponsors.

The planned process for enrolling consumers into the AIR MILES™ program was to encourage consumers to visit sponsoring organizations where take-

one application forms were displayed. The consumer would complete the application and send it to AIR MILES™. The demographic information in the application form would provide an opportunity to enrich the database capabilities.

At the program launch, customer service for the Canadian program was handled by a shared U.S./Canadian facility in Orlando, Florida. AIR MILES™ Canada planned to open its own customer service facility in Toronto.

THE LAUNCH

The AIR MILES™ Canada launch strategy was greatly influenced by the increasing number of competitors in collection-based loyalty programs in Canada. Competitors included Club Multipoints in Quebec, a cross-category points collection program, and Zellers Club Z. Zellers had its own points collection loyalty program with over two million participating households. Before the AIR MILES™ program in Canada was developed, Zellers had begun discussions with other businesses in Canada to offer Club Z points to their customers. Because of this, Loyalty Management realized that it was necessary to launch the AIR MILES™ Canada program with a major marketing effort to brand AIR MILES™ as the first national cross-category shopping reward program offering consumers the opportunity to earn free travel.

The AIR MILES™ program was to be positioned as "the best travel reward program for me". The purpose of the launch advertising was to make the target audience aware of what the AIR MILES™ travel reward program was and how it worked. This information would motivate potential consumers to join the program and actively start collecting AIR MILES™.

The target audience for the AIR MILES™ program was the top 50% of Canadian households by income. This consisted of adults between the ages of 25 and 49, who were married with one to two children and had household incomes above $40,000 per year ($45,000 in Toronto). The target audience had a female skew, as the member of the household doing most of the family shopping was generally female.

Loyalty Management's launch advertising plan included a major press conference, newspaper advertising, radio advertising in Western Canada, and television advertising that prominently featured all sponsors. Television advertising was planned because of the goal to reach as many people as possible as quickly as possible. The reach and frequency capabilities of television advertising would satisfy these requirements.

Newspaper advertising would allow Loyalty Management to provide potential consumers with the necessary information and to reach many potential consumers. A two-page newspaper spread would be used at the time of the launch with a follow-up one-page spread one week later.

Loyalty Management conducted two phases of copy testing for the launch advertising campaign. Copy testing was conducted during the agency search, with focus group testing of the various agency ideas. Focus group testing was also conducted using the concepts of the agency selected, DDB Needham.

Two television advertisements were developed for the program launch. The advertisements were designed to provide the general message of "a new way to shop and fly free—JOIN NOW!". The script for the first advertisement, "Flying People," appears in Exhibit 2, and the script for the second, "Conveyor Belt," appears in Exhibit 3.

Loyalty Management's media budget for the first year of the program was $3.4 million. Included in this figure was an amount of $500,000 for advertising pro-

EXHIBIT 2   Script for "Flying People" 30-second TV Commercial

ANNCR:	To fly.
	To fly free.
	Long the dream of people everywhere.
	Now, thanks to a program called AIR MILES™, the dream of free air travel is a possibility for anyone who shops.
	Buy goods and services you buy every day, collect the AIR MILES™ travel miles that come with them, and before you know it...
	You're flying, free.
	So wherever you see this symbol, *shop like always.™ Fly like never before.™*
LOGO & SUPER:	AIR MILES™
SUPER:	*Shop like always. Fly like never before.*
	1-800-854-8965
LEGAL SUPER:	Collector must pay taxes and other non-ticket costs.
	Sponsor offers and participating locations may vary. See Collector Guide for conditions.

Logo: Abbreviation for logo type, the name for the special design of the advertiser's (or product) name that appears in all advertisements.
Super: Words superimposed on the picture in a television commercial.

duction costs. Exhibit 4 is a media scheduling chart, known in the trade as a blocking chart.

LAUNCH IMPLEMENTATION ACTIVITIES BY SPONSORS

Approximately 75% of launch sponsors planned to participate in their own launch advertising. The media used by each sponsor varied but were generally consistent with the sponsor's current advertising media. Most sponsors had take-one displays in their store/branch.

Bank of Montreal not only had take-one displays in its branches, but also displayed posters in the branches and sent direct mail pieces to selected customers. Sears and Safeway both developed their own television advertising for the launch of AIR MILES™, emphasizing their involvement in the program.

Sears also sent a direct mail brochure to its current Sears Club members introducing the AIR MILES™ program. The brochure provided customers with information on the program and its sponsors, and introduced a contest to win extra AIR MILES™ by joining the program at that time.

EXHIBIT 3   Script for "Conveyor Belt" 30-second TV Commercial

Video	Audio
1. This commercial opens on a baggage handler standing beside a conveyor belt. He turns it on and walks off.	(Appropriate SFX throughout) ANNCR V/O: We'd like to tell you about the Air Miles™ travel reward program…
2. A large Bank of Montreal logo goes by.	when you use selected services at Bank of Montreal…
3. A refrigerator with a Sears Club logo goes by. A young child sits against it. His trike is nearby.	shop as a Sears Club member…
4. A Tilden Interrent counter with a smiling attendant goes by.	rent a car or truck from Tilden Interrent…
5. Legal Super: Collector must pay taxes and other non-ticket costs. Sponsor offers and participating locations may vary. See collector guide for conditions.	
6. Two movers holding a United Van Lines sign go by.	or move with United Van Lines,
7. A family—mom, dad, grandma and daughter goes past. A tag on their luggage says "Vancouver."	companies like these thank you with travel miles. Collect enough, and you're flying free. It's that simple.
8. The baggage handler reappears. The Air Miles™ logo and slogan comes up.	Air Miles™. Shop like always. Fly like never before.
Air Miles™. Shop Like Always. Fly Like Never Before.	

SFX: Sound effects
V/O: Voice over

EXHIBIT 4   1992 Media Launch Schedule

Medium	Specifications	Mar 30	Apr 6	Apr 13	Apr 20	Apr 27	May 4	May 11	May 18	May 25	Jun 1
English											
Television	30 seconds weekly A25–54 group	300 GRP	300 GRP	225 GRP	225 GRP	130 GRP	130 GRP	130 GRP	100 GRP	100 GRP	100 GRP
Newspaper	double page spread (27 markets)	IX									
	1200 lines-top 7 mkts	IX									
	full page-top 7 mkts		IX								
	1200 lines-20 mkts		IX								
Radio (West)	Western Canada: 30 seconds weekly A25–54 group	160 GRP	150 GRP	150 GRP							
French											
Television	30 seconds	300 GRP	300 GRP	200 GRP	200 GRP		150 GRP	150 GRP	150 GRP	150 GRP	150 GRP
Newspaper	full page-1 color	IX	IX	IX							

Line: A unit for measuring space. There are fourteen lines in a space one-inch high and one column wide.
GRP: GRP is the abbreviated form of gross rating point. One gross rating point means that one percent of the target population is expected to have media exposure. Gross rating points are measured over a time period, which is often a week. Further, they are composed of two parts. Reach is the proportion of the target audience with an expected exposure of at least once. This number is divided into total GRP's to give the average frequency of expected media exposure.

Safeway set up in-store enrollment booths to enroll its customers into the program at the store. Safeway also used its weekly newspaper supplement to announce the launch of the AIR MILES™ program.

It was anticipated that approximately $10 million would be spent on advertising by Loyalty Management and its sponsors in the first year of the program.

PROGRAM GOALS

"Our goals are to achieve 75% aided awareness nationally by the end of the first year of our program," said

Craig Underwood, "and to have 1.5 million households enrolled in the program during the same period. We are expecting that the majority of these enrollments will come during the program launch, since the launch advertising weights will be much higher than the rest of the year."

CASE 13-2 PEPSI-COLA SPAIN*

At the end of March 1994, senior executives at Pepsi-Cola Spain decided to review the events of the previous three years, possibly the period of fiercest competition in the soft drinks market in Spain. They planned to evaluate the marketing actions taken during this period, particularly the new product launches and the advertising strategy.

On the other side of the table sat the Spanish team of the company's worldwide advertising agency, Tiempo BBDO. They entered the meeting with the aim of convincing their client to continue the approach begun just over a year earlier, when Pepsi Spain had decided to abandon the creative line dictated by the home office and develop a specific campaign that would take into account both the peculiarities of the Spanish market and Pepsi's position in that market.

In early 1992, Pepsi's strategy in Spain had undergone major changes. Management believed that, at last, they had found an approach that would allow them to grow significantly and even take away some of Coca-Cola's business. The reasons for this growth were to be found in a greater control of the distribution channels, more focus on product development, and a new advertising positioning that was much more aggressive and focused almost exclusively on the younger segment of the market.

However, some executives of the Spanish subsidiary wondered whether such hard-hitting advertising should be continued. The image being projected in Spain by the brand was different from the desired corporate image, and recently almost all the managers of the European office and the New York office—who had been in Madrid for a short time—had mentioned the need to begin to return to the standardized advertising campaign.

SPANISH SOFT DRINKS MARKET

In volume, the Spanish soft drinks market was the seventh largest in the world, with total sales in 1993 of 2.8 billion liters and projected growth for 1994 of almost 10%. Taking this growth into account, average annual growth over the period 1991–94 would come to 1.75%. However, growth had been very unevenly distributed; in 1993, volume had actually declined by 2.3%. The industry employed more than 12,000 people. There had been some downsizing of manufacturing/bottling plants in 1994 on account of the poor sales results the previous year.

Exhibit 1 provides some basic figures for the industry for recent years. Per capita soft drink consumption had grown from 70.5 liters per year in 1990 to 73.7 liters in 1993. The share of colas had been

* This case was prepared by Professors José M. Pons and Francisco Iniesta of IESE, International Graduate School of Management, University of Navarra, Barcelona-Madrid, Spain. Copyright © 1997, IESE. Reproduced by permission.

EXHIBIT 1 The Spanish Soft Drinks Market

	1990	1991	1992	1993	1994[a]
Volume (million liters)	—	2,821	2,824.5	2,755.8	3,050
Food Channel	—	—	—	1,913.9	2,070
Coca-Cola	1,363	1,437	1,488.6	1,435	1,550
Pepsi[b]	150	157	400	413	460
Kas	175	173	—	—	—
Schweppes	214	265	238.9	216	—
La Casera	526.5	504	455	385.9	—
Consumption by categories (percent)					
Colas	—	45.9	48.2	49.9	50.7
Citrus	—	29.1	28.0	27.6	28.0
Carbonated	—	15.2	14.2	13.6	13.0

[a] Estimate made in February 1994.
[b] After 1992, numbers include Kas and Seven-Up.

increasing faster, and Pepsi management thought this was due to larger advertising expenditures and wider product lines, including sugar-free and low-calorie versions, which had grown to 8% of the market in 1994.

The market was traditionally divided into two large segments: the Food channel and the Hotel, Bar and Restaurant segment—also known as the "immediate consumption" segment. In 1993, the Food channel sold 1.9 billion liters, according to AC Nielsen estimates. This channel was expected to grow slightly less than the market as a whole in 1994. Within the Food channel, hypermarkets accounted for 24% of the volume, small supermarkets for 21.1%, and traditional stores for 10%; large supermarkets accounted for only 6.7%.

Vending machines were growing very fast and were receiving greater attention; the vending channel was seen as an opportunity to have greater control over distribution and to reap bigger margins. Of the 55,000 vending machines in operation in early 1994, Coca-Cola controlled 65%.

The breakdown of sales volume per package type in recent years had been as follows:

	1993	1994[a]
Returnable glass	28.7	23.1
Non-returnable glass	4.3	3.8
Plastic	43.9	48.9
Cans	19.2	20.4
Vending machines	3.9	3.8

[a] Forecast.

In the Food channel, the most popular format was the two-liter plastic bottle, which accounted for 33.6% of the soft drinks volume in that channel.

The most important trends in the Spanish market were not very different from what was happening in the rest of the world. Soft drinks had long been a global business and the main players tried to standardize their marketing approaches across different countries. The industry had experienced substantial concentration in recent years, and acquisitions of local companies, such as Kas or Trinaranjus in Spain, had reinforced the position of the multinationals.

Management at Pepsi was most concerned about the apparent decline in brand franchise. Consumers across Europe and the US were showing increased sensitivity toward price promotions offered by the large retail channels. Additionally, private label share had increased to almost 10% of total soft drink volume, although there were large differences between countries.

COMPETITION

Coca-Cola

The Atlanta-based company had been established in Spain since the late 1920s, although it was only in 1953 that the first bottling plant started operations.

In the '90s, Spain was the second most important European country—behind Germany—and the sixth in the world in terms of absolute sales of Coca-Cola products. The Spanish market represented around 5% of worldwide revenues. Coca-Cola dominated the soft drinks market to such an extent that of the ten soft drinks most popular in the country, five were marketed by Coke.

Apart from its traditional soft drinks—Coca-Cola (Regular, Caffeine-free, Diet), Fanta, Sprite, Finley Tonic—the company had been very successful in developing new segments of the market, such as isotonic drinks (12.5 million liters of Aquarius sold in 1993) and tea drinks (42 million liters of Nestea sold also in 1993).

In Spain the structure of the company included Coca-Cola Spain, a services division which advised the 13 independent bottlers distributed around the country in all aspects of management (merchandising, promotions and distribution). In early 1994, Cola-Cola Gestión was set up jointly with the bottlers in order to strengthen the negotiation position of the brand with large hypermarket and supermarket chains as well as other large chain buyers.

Schweppes

With forecasted revenues of 51 billion pesetas in 1994 and a 7% market share, Schweppes had been losing sales in the last few years. The company had started downsizing its operations in 1993. Some years earlier—in 1990—it had acquired Trinaranjus, a local company strongly positioned in the orange soft drink segment. The need for a restructuring of Schweppes in Spain was also due to the termination of some bottling agreements the company had had with Pepsi for certain geographic areas, notably Catalonia in the Northeast of the country.

In January 1994, Schweppes accepted the manufacturing contract for a private label cola for the hypermarket chain Continente—one of the largest in the country—in an agreement which also included the Canadian group Cott. Cott was the most important bottler of private label soft drinks in the world and had played a key role in the development of strong distributor brands in its home market, Canada.

La Casera

La Casera was the largest Spanish-owned company in the ranking of soft drink companies in Spain. With a dominant presence in the carbonated drink segment (of which it held 63% in 1993), its sales had been falling slowly but steadily in recent years due to the inroads of private label soft drinks, whose penetration was, for the moment, much greater in carbonated drinks than in other types of soft drinks such as colas.

Private Label Bottlers

This group of companies was clearly dominated by Refrescos del Sur de Europa, which supplied some of the country's most important large hypermarket and supermarket chains, such as Alcampo, Día, IFA and Pryca. The rest of the bottlers—mostly small and medium-sized bottling companies—were growing by more than 25% per year.

THE PROBLEMS OF PEPSI IN SPAIN

For many years the Achilles heel for Pepsi in Spain had been the quality of its distribution network. Different formulas of going to market were used in different geographic areas. In many cases the company relied on third-party networks through a complicated system of franchises that had evolved since 1955, the year of Pepsi's introduction in Spain. As part of this complicated arrangement, Schweppes was responsible for bottling and distribution in Catalonia, Andalusia, and part of the North (excepting Galicia); Kas dominated the business in Madrid and the Balearic Islands; and in Valencia the franchise was held by a local company, Valencian Bottling. As a consequence, the brand had very little leverage when it came to trade sell-in and so could only aim for a very limited share of shelf space, especially with the large-volume channels of distribution. During the last three years, a substantial number of chain stores had grown to national coverage and required a more homogeneous selling approach.

If distribution had made penetration of the Food channel difficult, the situation in the Hotel, Bar and Restaurant segment was even worse. Pepsi's lack of brand image strength meant that most of the points of immediate consumption could very easily do without the product, simply because the consumer did not ask for it.

In 1987, management at Pepsi Spain set about tackling its distribution problem. The decision was made to reduce the network of franchisees and rebuild distribution through Kas, a local company with strong roots in the Northern area and good market share in orange and lemon-flavored drinks. Later—in 1989—Pepsi acquired 30% of Kas at a cost of 2.5 billion pesetas. By 1992, the changes in distribution were beginning to pay off, with volume increases higher than overall growth in the market.

The company's distribution problems were clearly related to Pepsi's lack of a strong brand image. One of the executives of the Pepsi account in the Spanish advertising agency summed the situation up:

> In Spain, Pepsi was not even an alternative to Coca-Cola; our studies showed that the brand did not enter into the set of brands evoked before purchase. Almost 50% chose Coca-Cola as their preferred brand, and only about 2% preferred Pepsi.

Coca-Cola's advertising, in the meantime, was attempting to connect the brand to a great variety of aspects of life: love, friendship, music, sports, film … Coca-Cola was "sensación de vivir," or simply "it"; a complete lifestyle.

Pepsi's thematic brand-building advertising was decided in the United States; the central message of its positioning had been, for a good number of years, "the choice of a new generation". Although the campaign had produced a number of highly creative executions, they seemed to have little—if any—impact on the Spanish market, where Pepsi had no image at all. The company had considered, as an alternative, the comparative advertising approach—which had given such excellent results in the United States in the '70s and '80s—under the "Pepsi Challenge" banner. The message, however, was felt to have little credibility given the huge distribution advantage that Coca-Cola enjoyed in Spain.

A clear example of the problems associated with the market situation of Pepsi in Spain were the campaigns featuring rock stars and pop musicians such as Michael Jackson, Brian Ferry and Tina Turner. Performing at different locations around the world, the campaigns were run in the second half of the '80s and combined ads with sponsored concerts. Pepsi aimed to give the brand a youthful, modern and attractive image while departing from the creative efforts of traditional industry advertising.

In the Spanish market, however, Coca-Cola benefited most from the noise generated by these events. When it came to actually organizing the concerts, the company realized it was impossible to find locations—soccer stadiums, indoor arenas, bullrings—where the exclusive rights for the sale of soft drinks had not already been given to Coca-Cola. Coke's advertising took advantage of this fact and completely "contaminated" the events; Pepsi's market research indicated that a great majority of attendees associated the events with Coca-Cola.

Advertising expenditures for Pepsi in these years were around 200 to 300 million pesetas, distributed over the whole country. Although advertising reach was reasonable, the required level of frequency could not be achieved, and bottlers in areas where the brand had better coverage—such as Andalusia—complained loudly about the apparent lack of support.

Not surprisingly, the delicate situation of the Spanish subsidiary had become a source of worry for Pepsi headquarters. In 1990, Pepsi Spain had losses of 278 million pesetas, and in the following year it showed a profit of only 48 million pesetas, after accounting for the sale of assets such as a plant in Torrejón de Ardoz, near Madrid. Results from the soft drinks division were particularly negative when compared with the growth of Matutano, the snack division of Pepsi in Spain, which enjoyed a market share above 60% for potato chips and other snacks.

Faced with an almost stagnant soft drinks market in the American home market (especially the cola market), Pepsi decided to focus on Europe to help the category grow and further develop its presence. Growth in the US soft drinks industry was down from an average of 6.7% per year in 1975–80 to 4% in 1985–90 and 1.5% in 1991–92. After almost 20 years of intense competitive rivalry, the market shares of Pepsi and Coca-Cola in the US were 33% and 41% respectively, while Pepsi Europe was lagging way behind Coca-Cola. Moreover, the US market had recently seen the aggressive launch of distribution-controlled brands—such as Wal Mart's—which were stealing share from the most important brands.

Coke seemed to have the upper hand in the forthcoming European battle. "With a 75% share in the cola market, it could even dismiss its rival as insignificant in the international market. We have the number 1, 2 and 3 soft drinks in Europe. We outsell Pepsi 6 to 1," said Ralph Cooper, president of Coke's European Community Group. "This is not a Pepsi-Coke head-to-head. It's Coke, way ahead."[1]

John Derkash, general manager of Pepsi Spain, was convinced that importing thematic advertising from the US—whether the "choice of the new generation" or the sponsoring of rock stars—would never break Coke's domination. He felt that the Spanish market ought to be used to experiment with new advertising and creative copy as a sort of pilot test for other European markets where Pepsi faced a similar situation vis-à-vis Coca-Cola.

NEW MARKETING AND ADVERTISING STRATEGIES

Around the middle of 1992, Wayne Calloway, President and CEO of Pepsi-Cola worldwide, announced while on a trip through Spain:

> We see Spain as one of the most significant investment opportunities in the entire world. Given its base of solid consumption and stability and the continuing economic growth, we have made a long-term commitment to this market.

The starting point of the commitment was a further step towards building an adequate distribution network. The company announced this change as part of a total investment package of some 100 billion pesetas over five years.

---

[1] Quoted from *Newsweek*, June 21, 1993. "Opening Up a French Front. New PepsiCo ads bring the cola wars to Europe".

In September 1992, Pepsi Spain announced that it was entering negotiations with BBV,[2] one of the country's largest banks, and the Knorr family with a view to acquiring 100% of the KESA group, owner of all KAS bottlers. The investment was necessary to guarantee access to distribution throughout the country. It was also thought that the two companies had complementary product lines. Local management at Pepsi Spain saw the acquisition as the only way to avoid the brand's exit from the Spanish market. In a few months, an agreement was reached. Pepsi paid some 30 billion pesetas for KESA and became the second largest Spanish soft drinks and fruit juice group.

As part of the repositioning effort, Pepsi Spain went to its advertising agency—Tiempo BBDO—to analyze a possible change in the creative copy of its advertising. The agency, after a thorough analysis of the market, proposed that the following elements should be pursued for an effective communication of the brand:

– Realistic, in line with Pepsi's market situation and presence in Spain.
– Aggressive.
– Directed exclusively at the young (Coca-Cola targets all age groups).
– Should reflect a real world (not idyllic like Coke's).
– Unique; it should not be an imitation of Coca-Cola.
– Give the brand an element of pride.

Further efforts to find a message culminated in the proposal of the "Are you crazy? ... drink Pepsi" campaign.[3] The connotations of the proposed copy, in the opinion of one of its creative authors, were:

– Seize the moment.
– Break with routine.
– Live life to the full.
– Be a leader.
– Be admired and imitated by the rest of the group.
– Be an extroverted and spontaneous person; don't be worried about what other people might say about you.

Pepsi's first reaction to the proposal was somewhat cautious. The campaign seemed to depart too much from the image headquarters sought. Moreover, Pepsi's policies worldwide effectively prohibited country subsidiaries from creating their own thematic advertising.

After intense discussions, the decision was made to try the new positioning. In order to avoid problems with Pepsi headquarters the new concept was "camouflaged" as a tactical support campaign for a local promotion of a new product (over which local country management was given decision-making authority). The chosen product format was the large bottle of Pepsi. Initial levels of consumer recall were high.

As 1992 came to an end, the Spanish managers had reason to celebrate. Results indicated that Pepsi had grown twice as fast as Coca-Cola, while most other competitors had experienced severe difficulties: their sales volume was stagnant and Schweppe's volume even fell 12%, while Trinaranjus—part of the same group—fell 10%.

The first quarter of 1993 brought a decline in consumption that alarmed the major competitors; in the first two months the decline was 5%, as Spain entered a period of general economic recession. It was precisely for this period that Pepsi had planned the launch of its largest marketing campaign ever in Spain, with a 5 billion peseta budget. The investment was intended to improve the company's position in the food channels. At this time the company also shut down its bottling plants in Alicante and Guijón. Coca-Cola had announced a proposed marketing investment in the order of 7 billion pesetas, which represented an increase of 12% over the previous year.

Building on the apparent impact of the "Are you crazy? ... drink Pepsi" campaign, the company started to produce a larger number of spots designed specifically for the Spanish market. Coke reacted by targeting a large number of different audiences through the use of a variety of spots, with entertainment as their common element. Exhibit 2 provides information on advertising expenditures for Coca-Cola and Pepsi in recent years.

In late August '93, at the end of the peak sales season, Coke's sales had dropped 4.3% and Pepsi's sales volume had grown 3.4%, while total industry volume had decreased 2.4%. By the end of the year, the same parameters showed that Coke had declined 3.6%.

Pepsi Spain had revenues of 68 billion pesetas in 1993, an increase of 13% over the previous year. The results were received with great pleasure at Pepsi as a sign that at last a way had been found that would draw them closer to the market leader. Studies to measure advertising effectiveness confirmed the good results. (Exhibit 3 contains a summary of comparative measures.)

---

[2] BBV: Banco Bilbao-Vizcaya.

[3] " ¿Estás loco? ... bebe Pepsi" was the original message.

EXHIBIT 2 Advertising Spending: Coca-Cola and Pepsi (in million pesetas)

	1992	1993	1994[a]
Regular Pepsi			
TV	821	1,921	1,580
Events	67	1	19
Radio	2	3	20
Billboards	9	14	8
Total	899	1,939	1,627
Pepsi Max			
TV			1,874
Events			99
Radio			15
Billboards			7
Total			1,995
Regular Coke			
TV	3,369	5,027	5,039
Events	1,660	74	18
Radio	59	123	88
Billboards	177	95	75
Total	5,265	5,319	5,220
Diet Coke			
TV	883	1,515	351
Events			
Radio	4		
Billboards	120	85	
Total	1,007	1,600	351

[a] Data for 1994 are estimates.

EXHIBIT 3 Effectiveness of Pepsi's Advertising Campaign

	1992	1993
Absolute figures (in percent)		
Top of mind (first brand)	3	7
Brand name recall (unaided)	29	41
Advertising recall	40	44
Prefer Pepsi	3	7
Prefer Coca-Cola	78	74
Sample	(600)	(600)
Index of Pepsi vs. Coca-Cola (in percent)		
Attractive image	21	29
Brand more and more popular	20	29
Modern brand	20	29
Quality soft drink	21	32
My friends like it	15	23
Preference	7	8
Consumed last month	18	24
Share of voice	6	19

Source: LTD.

Entering 1994, the company planned the launch of Pepsi Max, a sugar-free cola targeted at young people. Marketing support for the launch would follow strictly the guidelines issued by the US, and a substantial advertising budget had been allocated (Exhibit 2). Some members of the Spanish management team wondered whether it made sense to divert these resources from the flagship brand just when it was beginning to pick up market share against Coke. They argued that it would be better to hold off on the launch of Pepsi Max in Spain for another year or two.

In the early months of 1994, for which only partial data and estimates were available, Pepsi seemed to be on track for a 10% volume increase, again higher than Coke's.

MARCH 1994: ADVERTISING ALTERNATIVES

At the meeting between the top management of Pepsi Spain and the executives of its advertising agency the following alternatives were discussed:

1. Continue with a specific focus on the Spanish market, with aggressive copy that would help the younger consumers identify with the brand. The agency clearly favored this alternative, as it provided them with opportunities to show their creative capacity. They tried to support their recommendations with some data on the segmentation of the cola market (Exhibit 4) and demographic data on the Spanish population (Exhibit 5).

   Pepsi HQ had indicated that only with a very thorough analysis and brief would they allow such differential positioning. Local management also feared that advertising targeted at such a narrow segment might negatively impact on the rest of the consumers. Finally, one of them voiced a somewhat different concern:

   The greatest volume of sales in our market is in hypermarkets and what sells in hypermarkets are the two-liter bottles. I don't know many 15-year-olds who do the family shopping, and the parent won't really care much for our message of craziness, own personality, and even a certain dose of "rowdiness."

2. Adopt the thematic advertising prepared by the head office, giving the product a broader appeal with greater potential reach among a wider range of demographic segments. The use of existing spots also had clear cost advantages that would permit increased media expenditure. This was considered an important factor in improving reach, frequency and,

EXHIBIT 4   Breakdown of the Cola Market by Age of Consumers (Spain, 1993)

	\ Age of the Consumers						
	6–9 years	10–13 years	14–18 years	19–24 years	25–30 years	31–40 years	Total
Pepsi	1.3	1.3	2.8	3.1	1.0	1.1	10.6
Coca-Cola	9.7	9.9	21.9	22.1	12.5	8.7	84.8
Others	2.0	1.5	0.3	0.2	0.4	0.2	4.6
Total	13.0	12.7	25.0	25.4	13.9	10.0	100.00

Sample: 1,580 interviewed.

EXHIBIT 5   Growth of the Spanish Population (thousands of people)

Year	Total	0–4	5–9	10–14	15–19	20–24	25–29	>30
1993	39,083	1,973	2,210	2,723	3,220	3,255	3,280	22,422
1995	39,188	1,903	2,090	2,480	3,085	3,261	3,270	23,097
1997	39,244	1,824	2,012	2,292	2,857	3,246	3,249	23,764
1999	39,268	1,774	1,947	2,156	2,601	3,158	3,250	24,383
2001	39,258	1,761	1,871	2,054	2,384	2,976	3,252	24,960

Source: National Statistics Institute.

eventually, impact. Managers defending this alternative argued that the more aggressive message of recent years had barely modified brand preference. Measurements were most positive on certain image-related variables, but sales results did not correlate.

As the discussion went on, an intermediate alternative was developed. Both campaigns could be run next year, and from then on, increasing weight would be given to the Spanish-specific one, but still keeping some of the classic advertising in order to retain the more conservative consumers. The proposal looked at the example of Coca-Cola, which was able to use a number of different messages in parallel, thus widening its market reach.

3. Go back to comparative advertising copy, which—to anybody at Pepsi—meant the Pepsi Challenge used in the United States in the '70s and early '80s. A similar campaign had been produced in the United Kingdom in 1993 and seemed to be working reasonably well. When this strategy was adopted in the US, the results in terms of market share shifts had been truly spectacular, even in markets where Pepsi had badly trailed Coke. Some managers of the main office still loved to exchange war stories about those days and thought the campaign had definitely contributed to breaking the market and creating a good base of profitable growth.

Legal restrictions in the Spanish market and most EU countries would make it impossible to mention Coke. Any company using comparative advertising in Europe was also forced to show sworn evidence to support anything stated in its ads.

4. The last alternative considered at the meeting was aimed at improving the acceptance of the product in the distribution channel, especially at points of sale where the drink was consumed on the spot, i.e. hotels, bars and restaurants. Managers supporting this alternative argued that recent improvements in the Pepsi image had not translated into greater penetration in this channel. Penetration had reached a plateau since 1992 at around 41%, falling to the mid-thirties in the winter months. Market share in this channel had increased only slightly, from 8.6% in February '92 to 9.4% in February '94, the latest period for which information was available.

Most of the Spanish managers remembered a campaign used by La Casera in the mid-'80s with the message "If there's no Casera ... we're leaving."[4] The campaign had reflected typical consumption situations in humorous settings and had contributed to increased acceptance of the product in bars and restaurants. A campaign like that, some thought, could reinforce the presence of Pepsi in a channel where a higher proportion of younger people buy and consume soft drinks.

---

[4] "Si no hay Casera ... nos vamos" was the original message.

CASE *13-3*   **DAEWOO MOTOR COMPANY UK (B)***

On Tuesday morning, June 10, 1997, Pat Farrell and his marketing team were finalizing the details of the simultaneous launch of three new car ranges in September. The new cars were family cars and were expected to replace the Nexia and Espero. The advertising budget for the 1997 launch had been severely cut, and it looked as though little TV advertising would be possible. But the decisions facing Farrell were not simply about advertising expenditures and the creative use of small budgets. Since 1996, the staff numbers at Daewoo had doubled as the company built its network of retail outlets and service centers. The "laidback" approach of the Daewoo sales staff, which had earned plaudits in industry and consumer magazines, was in direct conflict with the increasing pressures to sell cars. The success of the initial launch had heightened the market's expectations as well as those of head office and staff. He needed to decide how best to build on the success of the 1995 launch.

THE 1995 LAUNCH

The Daewoo Offer

Daewoo's research indicated that private individuals' experience of buying and owning a car was not ideal. Aggressive salespeople, hidden costs, poor after-sales service and advertising that focused on performance and/or fantasy portrayals of the driving experience did not appeal to a substantial portion of the car buying public. Research indicated that over a third of car buyers regarded their car primarily as a way to get from A to B, and were more concerned with the day-to-day practicalities of owning a car than with the car performance and engineering.

Daewoo decided to sell car ownership as a service, not cars as products. Farrell recalled:

> We decided car prices would be fixed, with no haggling required. We would focus on offering outstanding customer service, which meant we would need to have complete control of the interface with the customer.

Daewoo's Nexia and Espero were reworked latter-day versions of old Vauxhall designs from a decade earlier. The Nexia was based on the old model Astra, and the Espero on an obsolete Cavalier. Priced from £8,295 for the Nexia and £10,695 to £12,195 for the Espero, Daewoo's prices were roughly 10% below average in the relevant market sectors, but were not positioned at the bottom of each sector. The price included delivery to the buyer's home, tax for the first year, license plates, a full tank of petrol, a three year/60,000 miles warranty, three years' membership of the AA, including European cover, free servicing for the first three years, including labor and parts, and a 30 day money back/exchange guarantee.

Building Awareness

Daewoo began a £10 million TV, radio and print advertising campaign in October 1994 aimed at building brand awareness, credibility and conveying the company's customer focus intentions. The campaign, tagged "The biggest car company you never heard of," sought to cultivate confidence in the brand from UK car buyers by playing on Daewoo's reputation as one of the world's largest industrial companies. In order to build awareness quickly prior to launch, Daewoo ran their TV ads at twice the normal industry frequency. By Christmas 1994, prompted awareness of the Daewoo brand was 50%. Launch advertising was highly creative with four key messages: Daewoo Deal DIRECT; HASSLE FREE buying; PEACE OF MIND package; and COURTESY SERVICING.

Distribution

Daewoo decided to build a direct marketing and service structure. This gave Daewoo complete control over the selling process and after sales servicing. On launching with four showrooms on April 1, 1995 Farrell commented:

> We weren't certain that four sites would be sufficient to meet the immediate sales targets, and the quality and reliability of the cars was still an unknown.

Over the next 12 months, Daewoo rolled out the launch to include 18 retail stores and 100 smaller used car and servicing depots at a cost of £150 million. To provide the national presence it needed to service buy-

---

* This case was prepared by Research Associate Debra Riley under the supervision of Professor Sean Meehan of IMD. Copyright © 1998 by IMD—International Institute for Management Development, Lausanne, Switzerland. Reproduced by permission.

ers' cars, the company formed a joint initiative with Halfords, the automotive parts retailers and servicing chain. Two Daewoo staff and three courtesy cars were placed at each of the 136 Halfords stores involved. Daewoo worked in conjunction with Halfords to run a hassle-free servicing operation; cars were collected from and returned to any location the customer required, with a free courtesy car left if requested.

The company estimated that 400,000 people visited its showrooms in the first 12 months, representing around 20% of the two million new car buyers each year. Daewoo designed its showrooms to cater for the whole family. Showroom staff were not allowed to approach unless invited, and they earned bonuses based on customer approval of how well they were treated, not how much they spent. Each showroom had a "greeter" to welcome anyone who entered and to advise them of the facilities available. Junior showroom staff did not typically have car industry experience, and were hired based on fitting desired personality profiles. A free café, supervised creche and interactive video units enhanced the "shopping experience."

THE MARKET RESPONSE

It was the most successful marque launch since 1975, the earliest year for which data were available. Daewoo sold 1,500 cars in the first month and 18,000 cars in the first year—0.92% market share. Nine months earlier, Daewoo had been unknown in the UK, with only 4% of car buyers having ever heard of the company. The company captured 1% share of the April 1995 market and outsold a string of long-established marques (Exhibit 1). Further, this performance was sustained throughout the first 12 months. Daewoo received much media attention. Despite the cars' limitations, public response was enthusiastic.

Autocar (January 1996) rated both Daewoo's Nexia and Espero worst product in their sectors.

Top Gear (March 1996) rated Daewoo Espero 12th out of the 12 family cars it reviewed.

Daewoo's revolutionary approach to car retailing feels like a gale of fresh air blowing through the motor trade. (*Observer,* 9 April 1995)

Competitive Response

The entry of Daewoo into the market did little to upset the major car manufacturers. Ford, Vauxhall, and Rover, with their large manufacturing facilities in the UK, were not fazed by a new entrant targeting 1% market share. At the dealer level, the story was different. Daewoo's advertising portrayed car salespeople as sharks, great play was made of hidden costs, and to cap it all, Daewoo published a survey of potential customers which highlighted how many disliked the whole car buying process. Daewoo was expelled from one trade show, and newspapers were contacted by the dealer networks and asked to pull Daewoo ads. Overall, the effect was negligible. Those dealers or manufacturers in a position to respond to Daewoo's aggressive entry strategy found it difficult because of their traditional manufacturer/dealer network structure that squeezed profit margins through the distribution chain. Only Renault, which had 20 company owned sites out of 300, responded with Daewoo-type offers.

Post Launch Performance

Daewoo's strong performance continued through 1995. By December, prompted awareness was 90%, and research showed it to be the third most "customer focused" car company, after Vauxhall and Nissan. The consistent investment in brand positioning continued in 1996, with the communications strategy focused on providing more details about the cars' appearance, pricing and specification, and re-emphasizing the Daewoo offer.

In February, Daewoo was forced to issue a safety recall on all 8,000 Nexias sold to date, due to a potential fire risk with engine bay wiring. Despite this setback, by May 1996 Daewoo total sales outstripped Hyundai, Suzuki, Saab and Mitsubishi. Continuing research showed that Daewoo was perceived as the best "value for money" marque and second only to Vauxhall for customer care. Sales performance remained unaffected through two price rises, in September 1995 and March 1996. Although Daewoo was targeting the individual buyer, they did manage to secure some fleet customers, mainly rental.

In September 1996, Daewoo cut its advertising budget in order to achieve annual profit targets. The company's objective was to reach break-even within three years. This would mean maintaining sales without the heavy advertising support required in the first 18 months. Marketing efforts began focusing on achieving short term volume targets through tactical incentives. Despite the reduced support, sales performance remained strong through 1996.

1997: A CHALLENGING YEAR

The Daewoo marketing team faced increasing pressure in 1997. Sales declined 19% over 1996, as the public

EXHIBIT 1   New Car Registrations in UK by Marque: 1994–1997

	1994 Number	%	1995 Number	%	1996 Number	%	H1 1997[a] Number	%
Ford	418,657	22.2	410,722	21.4	396,988	19.7	195,793	18.9
Vauxhall	310,617	16.4	294,131	15.3	283,989	14.1	143,437	13.9
Rover	245,250	13.0	240,007	12.5	221,658	11.0	100,317	9.7
Peugeot	146,551	7.8	143,321	7.5	153,242	7.6	80,123	7.7
Renault	112,663	6.0	120,485	6.3	132,374	6.6	77,169	7.5
VW	74,548	3.9	81,656	4.3	114,084	5.7	59,711	5.8
Fiat	58,703	3.1	70,828	3.7	85,948	4.3	42,768	4.1
Citroën	84,522	4.5	80,241	4.2	76,485	3.8	41,016	4.0
Nissan	91,955	4.9	91,972	4.8	93,408	4.6	36,443	3.5
Toyota	51,939	2.8	54,384	2.8	58,491	2.9	34,402	3.3
BMW	45,574	2.4	55,034	2.9	56,840	2.8	30,426	2.9
Honda	38,187	2.0	45,772	2.4	50,075	2.5	25,978	2.5
Mercedes	29,186	1.5	32,694	1.7	35,813	1.8	20,795	2.0
Volvo	41,599	2.2	39,654	2.1	33,737	1.7	20,285	2.0
Audi	22,978	1.2	25,555	1.3	30,327	1.5	18,078	1.7
Mazda	16,741	0.9	16,291	0.8	24,273	1.2	14,957	1.4
Hyundai	12,247	0.6	13,984	0.7	18,959	0.9	11,668	1.1
Mitsubishi	9,227	0.5	10,823	0.6	16,383	0.8	10,845	1.0
SAAB	9,339	0.5	11,534	0.6	14,886	0.7	9,280	0.9
Daewoo	0	0	13,169	0.7	21,438	1.1	9,200	0.9
SEAT	12,921	0.7	11,049	0.6	13,530	0.7	7,884	0.8
Chrysler Jeep					11,624	0.6	7,870	0.8
Skoda					13,017	0.7	7,459	0.7
Suzuki	10,380	0.5	13,817	0.7	14,195	0.7	6,199	0.6
Jaguar	6,659	0.4	8,727	0.5	8,401	0.4	4,855	0.5
Proton	12,452	0.7	9,800	0.5	9,555	0.5	4,683	0.5
Subaru	4,995	0.3	4,616	0.2	5,753	0.3	3,579	0.3
Daihatsu	4,869	0.3	3,378	0.2	3,536	0.2	3,161	0.3
KIA	3,939	0.2	4,004	0.2	4,919	0.2	2,619	0.2
Lada	9,398	0.5	8,259	0.4	4,762	0.2	1,595	0.1
Isuzu	2,165	0.1	1,938	0.1	2,419	0.1	1,350	0.1
Lexus					2,012	0.1	1,132	0.1
Total	1888251	100	1917809	100	2013121	100	1035077	100

[a] These figures are for the first six months of the year.

Sources: "Motor Industry of Great Britain—World Automotive Statistics." 1997 SMMT (Society of Motor Manufacturers and Traders), Daewoo Corporation.

became less interested in cars that could not offer the performance and styling of competitive offerings. All measures for the Daewoo brand were at their lowest since summer 1995. Internal retail targets were up 77% versus the same period in 1996. Translating these goals to the retail centers was proving difficult, as they were not measured on sales targets, but customer service. Farrell had recognized the potential conflict in Daewoo's approach early on—the customer-driven, "demand-pull" strategy—was in direct conflict with the "supply-push" philosophy adopted by all car manufacturers with high fixed costs and excess capacity. Improving the conversion rate from store visit to actual sales was proving difficult, as the staff had been trained to take a very low key approach with customers. The relaxed culture at the retail centers was also damaging efforts to build its direct marketing database. Frequently, customer questionnaires were sent to the head office incomplete or had been completed by Daewoo staff rather than the customer.

In addition, concerns over the residual values of the used cars had become apparent. In 1995, Daewoo's embryonic sales network did not have much retail space for used cars. As sales to rental companies typically return to the manufacturer within six months, Daewoo found it had more used cars than could be promoted through its own retail structure. Rather than push these vehicles to other potentially hostile dealer networks, a decision was made to hold the cars. This temporary policy was extended into 1996 and resulted in insufficient used cars coming onto the market for the industry to assess an accurate residual value. By early 1997, this issue was being highlighted in the press. According to *Motor Trader,* the car trade magazine,

EXHIBIT 2   Daewoo New Model Pricing

Model	Description	Price	Rivals
Lanos	3, 4, 5 doors 1.3/1.6 liter	£8,795–£10,695	Ford Escort Peugeot 306
Nubira	4 door saloon estate (later)	£10,495–£12,995 £12,995–£13,995	Vauxhall Vectra Ford Escort
Leganza	4 door saloon 2.0 liter	£13,795–£14,995	Ford Mondeo, Toyota Carina, Hyundai Sonata VW Passat

Source: Daewoo Corporation.

80% of new and used car dealers in Britain would not take a Daewoo as part exchange for another vehicle, citing concerns over residual values. At the same time, *Glass's Guide,* one of the two "bibles" used by the trade to work out used values, slashed 10% off the prices of used Daewoo's. A Nexia worth £11,000 today was estimated to be worth no more than £4,450 after two years and 30,000 miles. Recognizing the negative impact this would have on new car sales, Farrell had promoted a change in strategy that pushed used Daewoo's onto other manufacturer's retail networks.

Despite the general downturn in the market, other Asian manufacturers were also gaining share, particularly Hyundai. The company had over 150 showrooms nation-wide, and benefited from the "Korean-ness" brand associations that had been established by Daewoo. Other manufacturers were also looking at ways of bypassing the traditional salespeople. In 1997, Daihatsu announced the launch of "virtual showrooms," where teams of mobile salespeople would deliver a new, licensed and insured vehicle to your home for a test drive.

THE NEW CAR LAUNCH

Farrell and his team hoped that the launch of the Lanos, Nubira, and Leganza would resolve the performance and price issues associated with the existing models (Exhibit 2). New car buyers would be offered the same extensive service and warranty package offered with the Nexia and Espero. Test marketing gave the new models a more favorable rating than the Nexia and Espero, but highlighted continuing issues such as the engine design (carried over from the previous models) and poor interior details. Farrell was keen to build on the success of the market entry and develop the Daewoo brand further. The impending launch was critical; he needed all the input he could get and looked forward to input from his marketing team.

14 SALES PROMOTION AND PUBLIC RELATIONS

*E*ach element in the basic marketing mix is supplemented by a group of marketing instruments whose main purpose is to induce immediate buying behavior by strengthening the basic mix elements for a short period of time. This group of instruments is called the *promotion mix.* Specific support activities are often classified as either sales promotions or public relations. *Sales promotions* have been defined as "action-focused marketing events whose purpose is to have a direct impact on the behavior of the firm's customers."[1] Sales promotions involve such activities as specialty advertising, rebates, couponing, temporary price reduction labels, bonus packs, samplings, premiums, point-of-purchase material, trade allowances, sales and dealer incentives, trade shows, exhibits, and demonstrations. *Public relations* are actions that promote goodwill between a firm and its customers. Public relations involve activities such as customer service, crisis management, consumer education, publicity, special events, and sponsorships.

Companies make considerable investments in sales promotion as a strategy for building and maintaining brand dominance. Although you might believe most of a company's promotion budget is spent on media advertising, the various sales promotion activities taken as a whole involve much larger expenditures. Product marketers in the United States spend about 25.1 percent of their promotional budgets on media advertising, 49.5 percent on trade promotions, and 25.4 percent on consumer promotions. Trade promotion passed media advertising as the leading category in the mid-1980s. The relative importance of some components of promotion is indicated in Figure 14–1. Sampling, particularly in-store, continues to grow in popularity. Companies try to weave sales promotion into their marketing strategies in a way to create a "brand experience" among consumers. We begin by discussing the elements of the sales promotion mix in more detail.

SALES PROMOTION MIX

The sales promotion mix can be described in the same terms as the marketing mix. The instruments that support each element of the marketing mix are shown in Table 14–1.

TABLE 14-1   Promotion Mix

Mix Element Supported	Instruments Used
Product	Samples, bonus product, premiums
Price	Coupons, temporary discounts, temporary price reduction labels, refunds, slotting fees, temporary favorable terms of payment and credit, end-of-season sales
Distribution	Trade promotions, point-of-purchase materials
Communications	
Personal selling	Temporary demonstrations, trade shows, exhibitions, sales force contests
Mass	Customer contests, sweepstakes
Publicity	Special events, press bulletins, press conferences, tours by journalists

Source: Based on Walter van Waterschoot and Christophe Van den Bulte. "The 4P Classification of the Marketing Mix Revisited," *Journal of Marketing.* Vol. 56, No. 4 (October 1992), pp. 83–93

Product

The main type of product promotion is the *sample.* A sample is a free trial of a product. A sample is usually smaller than the actual product and is given away at no charge. About 90 percent of sampling is for new products.

There are a variety of ways to deliver a sample: instore, direct mail, on doorknobs, and in plastic bags along with newspapers. The most effective way to get product trial is to mail or distribute free samples directly to customers' homes. This is illustrated in Marketing in Action box 14–1. Sampling efficiently requires precise target market information. Since buying Carol Wright from Donnelly Marketing in the mid-1990s, CoxDirect has revamped the mailing list to identify more promotionally responsive households. It created a 25-million-name, household mailing file from sources including retailers, manufacturers, personal

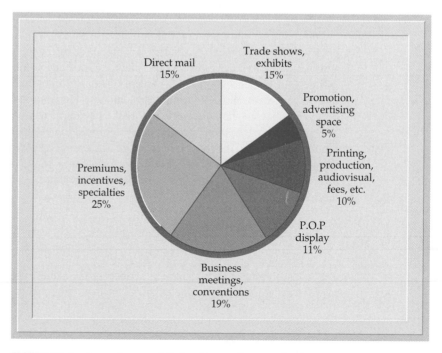

FIGURE 14-1   Importance of Sales Promotion Methods

APPLYING
. . . to
Consumer
Beverages
Marketing

Sampling with Co-Op Mailings

The best place to sample herbal tea drinkers is in a soothing setting, like their own living rooms. That was the thinking of Thomas J. Lipton Co.'s Canadian division when it looked for trial of its new Bedtime Blend flavor. "Those who drink it tend to drink a lot of it. It's very important to find those

(continues)

Courtesy Lipton, a Division of UL Canada, Inc.

people." Lipton turned to direct mailer ICOM to locate the niche target and reach them with a test offer. ICOM surveys Canadians with detailed questionnaires deriving household-level information on buying behavior. Surveys go to one out of every four households every six months, and the company receives a better than 20 percent response. "Their survey showed who the heavy users were." A Lipton sample was sent out to medium and heavy users and competitive users in co-op mailing with other offers. Lipton paid $150 per thousand to be in the co-op mailing, not including the cost of the samples. The tea sample, plus a 75 cent coupon, appeared in 255,000 of the 550,000 envelopes in the mailing. Initial response was positive based on coupon redemptions and calls through an 800 number.

"When you do a mass sampling for niche categories there is a tremendous amount of waste, even if you consider demographics," said ICOM. "Our mailing is based on purchase behavior." Lipton estimated it would have cost 15 times more to reach each 1,000 people in-store.

— *Direct mail zooms samples to select user segments.*

Source: "Pushing the Envelope," *PROMO,* September 1998, p. 51.

computer sellers, and pet shop owner lists. "We wanted this mailed to families with children who own a house with an average income of $52,000. They spend more money on everything." It then plotted neighborhoods around the top 50 food, drug, and mass merchant retailers in 160 markets.

Research has shown that 75 percent of the homes will try the free samples and 25 percent of these will buy the product. Up to 20 percent more users can be obtained by including a coupon with the free sample. Sampling should be used if the product exhibits a demonstrable superiority, if the concept is difficult to convey by advertising, if a sizable budget is available for a broad usage category, or if product class dominance is sought.

Sampling can be expensive but it does ensure that people will try the product and it has proved to be one of the most powerful promotional devices available to marketing managers. Moreover, the *cost per customer converted* is much lower than any other promotion because there is no barrier to trial.

Another product promotion is to give all persons making a purchase a free gift, known as a *premium.* For example, Frito corn chips has employed a promotion in which they attach flower seeds to packages of the product. A variation on the gift idea is the offer of merchandise at low prices to customers who send in labels from packages. These *self-liqui-dating premiums* are one of the least expensive of all promotional devices because the revenue derived from customers usually covers most of the costs of the promotion. The "self-liquidating" feature is made possible by volume purchases and the elimination of the normally high retail margins on premium-type merchandise. The most desirable premiums are showy items that inspire retailers to build off-shelf displays and encourage usage of the product by the consumer.

Price

The primary consumer price promotion is the *coupon.* Where promotional funds are limited, "cents-off" coupons can be an effective means of getting product trial. The average coupon face value in the United States is about 70 cents. In addition, retailers earn an 8-cent handling fee per coupon. U.S. manufacturers of consumer packaged goods distribute about 250 billion coupons a year. The largest coupon vehicle in the United States is the free-standing insert (FSI), the glossy coupon-in-a-print ad typically distributed in Sunday newspapers. The coupons are also sent by mail, appear in magazine and daily newspaper ads, are attached on pack, or enclosed in pack. The number of coupons returned is one measure of the impact of the promotion.

The typical coupon shopper in the United States is a middle-aged married working white woman who has a household income of $29,000 and who knocks $6 off her weekly $74 grocery bill by using coupons. Lower-income families aren't exposed to as many coupons because the vast majority of coupons are distributed through newspapers and magazines and such families spend less than average for reading materials.

A slight variation is to offer the consumer a package with a special *temporary price reduction (TPR) label.* A "cents-off" designation indicates the amount the regular retail price is supposedly reduced during the special promotion. Although the manufacturer may lower the price to the dealer, there is no assurance that the retailer will pass the savings on to the consumer. Manufacturers have encountered sharp trade resistance to "cents-off" packs because retailers resent handling problems and duplicate inventories. The inability of the manufacturer to adequately control "cents-off" promotions makes this technique less desirable than couponing. On-pack instant coupons have largely replaced it.

Because coupons suffer from misredemption problems, some manufacturers prefer cash *refunds* or *rebates.* Although these refunds carry higher values, a much lower redemption rate may be expected. Many people buy with the intention of sending in for the refund, but never get around to it.[2]

Distribution

Point-of-purchase (P-O-P) displays can increase sales markedly. Numerous studies have proved having P-O-P at retail will increase sales 5 to 15 percent above normal movements. The key is to get the retailer to use them. Stores are inundated with P-O-P, especially during certain times of the year. Stores often have no idea what to do with many of the P-O-P materials they receive, so they get left sitting in the back room. If manufacturers emphasize retail compliance—ensuring that stores and merchants put up all the P-O-P they receive, sales increases can soar as high as 40 percent.[3] See Marketing in Action box 14–2.

Communication

Manufacturers frequently try to build customer interest and sales volumes with *contests, sweepstakes,* and other games of chance. The idea is to attract consumer attention by offering substantial merchandise and cash prizes to a few lucky winners. Entry blanks and lottery tickets are dispensed at the retail level to tie the promotion to the sales of the product. The main objective of most contests is to stimulate sales with in-store displays of the product rather than produce a large number of entries. For on-line merchandisers, however, encouraging visits to their Web pages is important as discussed in Marketing in Action box 14–3.

The activities that have been discussed represent only a few of the many techniques that can be used in creating a promotional strategy for the firm. The only real limit to the variety of promotions is the depth of the imagination of the managers in charge.

TYPES OF PROMOTIONS

Promotions can be directed at intermediaries in your channels, in which case they are called trade promotions, or they can be directed at the ultimate buyer, and are called consumer promotions. These two kinds of promotions are usually used in concert, especially for new product introductions.

Trade Promotions

Trade promotions are designed to improve dealer cooperation, and they include such things as training sessions for sales personnel to familiarize them with the goods and services of a

MARKETING IN ACTION *14-2*

APPLYING
. . . to
Consumer
Automotive
Products
Marketing

Winning the P-O-P Compliance Game

Mobil used an outside merchandiser, Professional Inventory Management and Merchandising Services (PIMMS), to effect a huge retail tie-in for its "Mobil Oil Tour" concert series starring country music stars Reba McEntire and Brooks & Dunn. PIMMS asked store personnel of automotive chains and mass merchandisers to make island or endcap case displays of Mobil I motor oil and use concert-related P-O-P to recommend the product to customers. Stores were supplied with a standee promoting the tour's stars plus window posters, counter cards, and take-one pads affixed with offers to win concert tickets and CDs.

Mobil was worried about its ability to track the fate of all that P-O-P. "The number of personnel available for monitoring the campaign came down to seven. There was no way seven field reps could cover a promo of that size. We needed a special promotion force to give us information from the field." With the tour running from February through the end of the year, PIMMS sent mystery shoppers into several participating retail chains to verify and reward promotion compliance. Mobil's chief concern was to find out if stores were putting up the P-O-P displays and if sales staffers were recommending the designated products, which was part of the commitment retailers had made to the company.

Once mystery shoppers began working a particular city, store managers would call other stores to tell their peers that compliance prizes were being handed out. In addition to mass merchants, PIMMS mystery shoppers visited automotive aftermarket retailers including AutoZone, Discount Auto Parts, Grand Auto, and VIP Discount Auto. The secret merchandisers checked out a total of 1,000 stores coast to coast, hitting on an average of 25 stores per major market.

Posing as average shoppers, the PIMMS spies first determined that the proper window signage and P-O-P displays were in place. Then, working from three prepared scenarios, they asked retailer personnel several questions about choosing a motor oil. When store employees made an endorsement for Mobil, the mystery shoppers gave them vouchers for free concert tickets.

The campaign was a complete success, with a compliance rate of 100 percent scored by stores visited by the shoppers, including stores that had no advance notice of the shoppers' arrival.

— *You need to get serious about getting your displays up.*

Source: Richard Sale, "The Display Police," *Promo,* March 1999, pp. 80–81, 84.

Courtesy Mobil Oil Corporation

APPLYING
... to
Internet
Retailing

MARKETING IN ACTION 14-3

Web Promotions

CDNow Inc., a leading Internet music store, was once called by *USA Today* "the most recognized e-commerce brand." CDNow ran the first million dollar promo on the Internet and the prizes ranged from phonecards to instant cash to cruises. CDNow Million Dollar Music Mania! instant-win sweepstakes awarded more than 60,000 prizes, as well as a chance for customers to win a $1 million grand prize. The contest was offered to hundreds of thousands of participants in 26 countries. With each online purchase, the CDNow customer received an electronic "Scratch & Win" game card that showed instantly if the participant had won anything. Since chances were one-in-five, there were many repeat players. Each time a customer made a purchase, he was automatically entered in a weekly vacation sweepstakes for eight world-class destinations such as Paris, London, and Rome.

For CDNow the value of the promo lay in the way it built the CDNow brand. "Brand exposure is one of our goals and, no matter what, the repeated exposure is absolutely crucial. The aim is also to have fun, to make winning a game, and make the game part of an explicit bargain—rewarding customers for engaging in a dialog with CDNow." When visitors repeat, they feel more at home at the site, can move around better, and view more frequently the offers from CDNow and the merchants and retailers with whom CDNow partners for its marketing campaigns.

CDNow's more recent music trivia promotion, the Honorary Roadie Sweepstakes, produced the greatest outpouring of letters praising the brand. CDNow got comments saying, "We love your store," or "You give away great prizes." CDNow wanted to reinforce itself as the music authority on the Net. To do this, they needed content. By setting up a trivia game about music, CDNow could much more quickly take the customer through the store to learn about its product range, including which bios of musical figures were available or which record jackets offered vital music information. And it did all this in the guise of testing the consumer's knowledge of the field. (Did you know that the Grateful Dead was originally called Mother McCree's Uptown Jug Champions?) Ian Plimsoll, the "world's greatest roadie" character featured in CDNow radio and television ads, acted as guide for game players. Correct answers won entry in an Honorary Roadie Sweepstakes that offered top prizes of airplane tickets to any destination in the continental United States or Canada.

CDNow measures traffic and session time on their site, as well as the purchase behavior of repeat visitors. The trivia contest changes each week to ensure that players return. "We have huge customer loyalty. At least 50 percent of players are repeat customers."

CDNow is starting to partner with big, established brands. The Plimsoll roadie character was created solely to blend CDNow's offline and online branding effort. The company just completed a holiday promotion with Coca-Cola in which Coke linked its Web site with CDNow in an offer of a special Christmas CD from EMI Music. It also hooked up with Prodigy to offer new customers of the Internet service provider $10 gifts at CDNow.

— *Real promotion strategies and tactics can be applied to online marketing.*

Source: Scott Thurm, "CDNow," *Promo*, January 1999, pp. 30–32.

particular company. A related procedure is to give dealer salespeople special gifts or bonuses when they push the sale of certain products. Dealer interest can also be improved by providing attractive point-of-purchase (P-O-P) materials. As an added incentive, prizes are frequently offered to the merchants who construct the best displays utilizing the product and promotional materials. Perhaps the most popular promotional device directed at distributors is the "deal" or special reduced price offer. "Deals" are short-run discounts designed to build dealer stocks and to stimulate retail sales. They may be expressed in terms of lower prices or as "free" merchandise offered for minimum orders. Another effective promotional technique is a sales contest for distributors. Dealers who sell the most merchandise during a certain period are rewarded with vacations in Hawaii, mink coats, and cash bonuses. All promotional efforts are designed to raise sales, but most dealer programs have the goal of improving relations with those who sell the product to the final consumer. Better dealer relations can increase the number of distributors willing to carry the product, enlarge display areas, and gain acceptance of larger inventories and new items.

Trade promotions have been increasing—reflecting the increasing power of the retailer. A survey of product marketers found that 87 percent implemented account-specific promotions for key retail customers. Information Resources, Inc. analyzes a number of trade promotions annually and finds that very few of them pay out—IRI estimates it is less than 20 percent. We will return to this point shortly.

Consumer Promotions

Consumer-oriented promotional activities are designed to induce consumers to try products. A proportion of those introduced to a product will become steady customers. Moreover, brand switching is a fact of life for low-cost, frequently purchased products. You want to gain more customers than you lose in this churn. Thus, getting back former customers through encouraging retrial is very important. The relative importance of alternative consumer promotions is shown in Figure 14-2.

Price promotions may have a "mortgaging" effect as consumers purchase for inventory. When the brand returns to regular shelf price, sales may be initially slow as consumers draw down promotion-subsidized stocks. Thus, manufacturers will also often drop coupons to head off a big splash by the competition. Timed to reach consumers in an area just before a competitor launches a product or sponsors a special event such as a concert, coupons effectively knock consumers out of the market by encouraging them to stock up their home pantries.

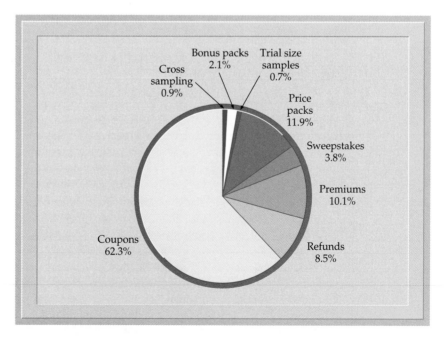

FIGURE 14-2 Consumer Promotions (From Dancer Fitzgerald Sample's "Consumer Promotion Report")

Retailers use price promotions to build traffic. Because they might not be profitable in their own right, but encourage purchases of profitable products, they are known as "loss leaders." Retailers also use price promotions to clear inventories of obsolete products.

New Product Promotions

If a new package good does not establish itself in six months, the lost momentum is hard, if not impossible, to recover. A comprehensive sales promotion plan is consequently a necessity for new product introductions. New products must first be explained to the company's own salespeople. They should be enthusiastic about the product and be convinced that it will be a winner. Second, trade awareness should be built so that when the salespeople arrive, the buyer has some favorable predisposition toward the product.

The presentation to the trade should place its emphasis on the retailer and the consumer's need for the product. The retailer is not about to drop a private label in favor of a branded item. Moreover, the retailer is not interested in simply trading profits with an existing brand. The quantity of buy-in must be decided. An *early-buy allowance* might be used to get a new product into distribution before advertising starts. Such allowances lower a distributor's risk in stocking new brands. Sometimes you have no choice. Mass merchandisers charge package-goods producers *slotting fees* to carry new products in their stores, and these fees may amount to four- or five-figure numbers per item per chain in the United States. Determination of the correct size pack for the appropriate stores and the correct size and type of display are also important. Special promotions for new products can be very expensive. The practical constraints on promotional efforts include the availability of funds and the need to find some reliable measure of sales effects.

If a manufacturer is striving to gain retail distribution, a *stocklift* or *buyback* of merchandise already in the store may be necessary. As retailers consolidate into fewer but larger chains, suppliers are working harder to get into stores and get rivals out—taking an initial hit in the hope that the buyback will pay off in the long run. Retailers say new suppliers bombard them with offers to clear out rival products, and they add that retailers don't make any money on the deals because products are usually sold off at wholesale. Still, for retailers, a stocklift can help them avoid selling remaining inventory at a discount, potentially at a loss, while letting them quickly add a product that they think may sell better. Driving the covert tactic is the emergence of product hit men, contracted to discreetly dispose of competitors' products. In many cases, the firms that do the job are barter companies or liquidators that normally help route overstocked or flawed goods to close-out stores. Their logistical expertise in disposing of merchandise cheaply has become a sophisticated, powerful tool for stocklifting. The process of stocklifting is described in Marketing in Action box 14-4.

As already noted, sampling is a good way to get consumer trial. An example of its use, along with a contest, is given in Marketing in Action box 14-5. Couponing can also play a role. Coupon users need an average increase of 40 percent in coupon face value to try products they don't normally buy. For example, if a user redeems a 50-cent coupon for a favorite product, he or she will require at least a 70-cent coupon to try a new or not normally used product.

CONFLICTS BETWEEN THE PROMOTIONAL MIX AND MARKETING MIX

While the promotional mix is supposed to support the marketing mix, some major concerns have arisen that, improperly used, the promotional mix might undermine the marketing mix. This is especially true in the case of price promotions with respect to list price and advertising.

APPLYING
*. . . to
Business-to-
Business
Marketing*

MARKETING IN ACTION *14-4*

Stocklifting a Competitor's Merchandise

At the Athens, Georgia, giant Lowe's Home Improvement Warehouse store in aisle 23 near the lawn mowers, hundreds of garden gloves recently vanished. The missing merchandise was manufactured by Wells Lamont, the nation's largest garden-glove company. And almost overnight, the empty shelves were restocked last January with gloves made by its archrival, Midwest Quality Gloves Inc. The same scene played out in 100 other Lowe's stores: Wells Lamont gloves were replaced by Midwest gloves in floral, pigskin, cowhide and other designs.

Behind the inventory switch was Midwest. It had struck a deal with Lowe's to buy 225,000 pairs of Wells Lamont gloves and clear them all out so it could fill shelf after shelf with its own product.

Lowe's, the No. 2 home-center chain after Home Depot Inc., has about 450 blue-and-white stores. For years, Lowe's had primarily sold gloves made by Wells Lamont. But last year, it decided to try out another supplier in about 100 stores in the South. Lowe's typically has two ways to get rid of inventory. The new supplier, Midwest, could have paid Lowe's a "markdown allowance" to sell off the Wells Lamont gloves gradually, at discounted prices. But with the crucial gardening season approaching, Lowe's opted for a stocklift, to clear the shelves in one sweep. "It just gives a better presentation to the customer than mixing two different vendors." Midwest declined to discuss the specific stocklift. But in general, Midwest works hard to meet retailers' requests, including hanging the gloves on metal rods attached with clips, called "clip strips," for better shelf display. "We try to make it as easy as possible for the retailer to take our product in." Midwest added that such efforts have helped the company expand aggressively into new retail chains and increase sales an average of 35% a year.

Wells Lamont, the stocklift victim, had no immediate recourse. "Of course we mind it, but that's not illegal. We sold the product to the customer," said the retailer. "It's their inventory, not ours." So, last winter, the Wells Lamont gloves were pulled off the shelves, packed up, and whisked away to a storage room. Meanwhile, Midwest arranged to sell all the gloves to a liquidator, International Purchase Systems. The Wells Lamont gloves arrived in the warehouse and, for weeks, sat in a dark cor-

(continues)

Courtesy Midwest Gloves

MARKETING IN ACTION *14-4* **(continued)**

ner. Some were stuffed into a hodgepodge of boxes that once held refrigerators and washing machines. Others still sealed in Wells Lamont boxes, bore a sign that said "Buyback" in magic marker. With rap music blaring from a radio that hung from a pillar, workers sorted out the gloves, discarding the shop-worn ones and separating them into about a hundred new cardboard boxes according to size and style—Cotton Hob-Nob, Vinyl-Coated K-Wrist, Work No Sweat and Yard & Garden with extra-long protective cuffs. Ten people working eight-hour shifts took about six weeks to sort out and count the gloves before they were resold. Time was running out. "The season is now. Spring and Fall are when people do gardening." Two weeks later, with the gardening season in full bloom, some of the Wells Lamont gloves surfaced in downtown Manhattan's National Wholesale Liquidators store, amid a jumble of photo albums, vacuum cleaners, cordless telephones and $3.97 salad spinners. In the basement of the close-out store's home-improvement department, an open box marked "Lowe's" sits next to coiled garden hoses. It is filled with Wells Lamont's purple Yard & Garden gloves. The "regular" price tag of $2.99 is crossed out. The gloves are on sale for $1.49.

International Purchase Systems believes that Midwest paid about $700,000 for the 225,000 pairs of gloves—about the wholesale price. In turn, it bought the gloves for about $280,000; the difference, about $400,000, may indicate just how eager Midwest was to get its gloves into Lowe's stores. Then, International Purchase Systems sold the gloves to an array of close-out stores, including National Wholesale Liquidators Inc. and Building 19 Inc. It took in about $70,000, before its own operating expenses. That may seem slim, but it expects to be rewarded in the long run. It has also expanded business by tapping the revenge impulse: After purchasing stocklifted products, it puts in "courtesy calls" to the victims, encouraging them to "return the favor" by working with International Purchase Systems.

— *Buybacks are a necessary evil in gaining market share. You get the market share immediately, but at a price.*

Source: Yumiko Ono, "Where Are the Gloves? They Were Stocklifted by a Rival Producer," *The Wall Street Journal*, May 15, 1998, pp. A1, A8.

Advertising Versus Price Promotion

In boosting list prices and making deep promotional price cuts, consumer goods companies have let their focus be diverted from long-run profits to short-term sales volume and market share. In the process they shifted more and more moneys from consistent theme advertising to consumer and trade promotions. Research from the Promotion Marketing Association of America (not an unbiased source) shows that senior executives believe promotion is more effective than advertising. The executives also said that consumer promotion does build brand equity, and trade promotion can build brand equity. Others believe that price promotions devalue brand image. Managers at Unilever have characterized the process as "promotion, commotion, demotion."

On the other hand, consistent theme advertising strengthens a brand's image for the long haul. The resultant brand equity offers some protection from competitive forays. Reductions in advertising expenditures in order to fund price promotions may weaken consumers' perceptions of a brand. We should note that price promotion costs are variable with volume and permit small regional brands to compete against the heavily advertised national brands.

Research has shown that FSI (free standing insert) coupons generate more penetration when distributed in weeks in which effective advertising is aired than when distributed in off-air weeks. This interaction is of an economically useful magnitude. The interaction is only present when advertising is effective in its own right.[4] Consistent theme advertising and sales promotion can work together in a synergistic manner if executed in the context of an integrated marketing communications (marcom) plan.

APPLYING
*. . . to
Consumer
Paper
Products
Marketing*

MARKETING IN ACTION *14-5*

Targeting Gatekeepers and End-Users

About five years ago, Ledesma, Argentina's largest sugar company, developed a process to make paper out of sugar cane husks. It acquired two writing paper brands—Gloria and Exito—and poised to go to market with an ecological positioning. But there was a problem. The sugar cane paper lacked resilience and tore if one tried to erase on it. Public perception said the paper was substandard. Ledesma scientists and manufacturing executives eventually perfected a viable product, but that meant little if consumer skepticism could not be counteracted.

The key market for Exito Ecologic and Gloria Ecologic writing tablets was school children. The marketing problem obviously called for a sampling solution—but how to get writing paper into the hands of kids at school? Ledesma found two ways. On five successive Sundays, spread ads ran in newspaper magazine sections reaching two million Argentineans a week. A sheet of Ecologic lined notebook paper was inserted in the middle of the spread. Copy told of the unique environmental benefits of the product and invited kids six to 18 to draw pictures of endangered species on the paper and enter them in a contest. Winners in four age groups, chosen by a judging team of internationally known philatelists, would have their drawings immortalized on an actual set of Argentine government stamps. [The government postal service, which had consumer perception problems of its own readily agreed to hitch on to a program with concern for ecology, endangered species, and education.]

The second sampling program was aimed at the primary influencers: teachers. Ledesma distributed paper and contest forms to public and private schools and encouraged teachers to make entering the promotion a class project. On the first day of school in Argentina, most teachers give students a list of the materials they will need to buy, and most times they suggest the name of a [Ledesma] competitor's notebook. "We knew that if we could get them to try our paper, they would see it was as good as the competitor's. And teachers like environment-friendly products."

Ledesma received more than 90,000 drawings from school children. Sales of Exito and Gloria brands grew a combined 11 percent, gaining Ledesma a three-point share gain. And throughout Argentina—as well as around the globe—Ledesma's lined paper could be detected behind the endearing animal drawings on the stamps. That's exposure that cannot be bought.

The four winners and their families also got a trip to the south of Argentina for a whale-spotting expedition—a fitting conclusion to a whale of a promotion.

— *Large rewards come from unearthing the proverbial Big Idea and daring to execute it.*

Source: Amie Smith and Al Urbanski, "Have a More Active Role," *Promo*, December 1998, p. 28.

Courtesy Ledesma, s.a.a.i.

List Price Versus Price Promotion

Many manufacturers believe that a high-list, high-deal policy is more profitable than offering a single price to all consumers. This is because it permits them to price-discriminate among customer segments. This is one aspect of *demand pricing.* Consider the case of a brand targeted at two segments: regular customers and deal-prone, price-sensitive customers. Suppose that you face the (linear) demand curves for each segment shown in Table 14-2 and your product has a unit variable cost of $0.80. If you never did any promotion, what price should you charge? The maximum contribution occurs at a list price of $1.60. Suppose, however, you want to price-discriminate among the segments; what prices should you charge within the ranges given? The best prices would be a $2.00 list price for regular customers and a $1.40 promotion price for deal-prone customers. Demand pricing yields higher profits. You do not want to leave money on the table!

The demand pricing approach is not without problems. Care must be taken in executing it. Two negative things can happen: leakage and slippage. *Leakage* occurs when consumers not targeted for a price promotion manage to take advantage of it. *Slippage* occurs when those who should receive a promotion do not.

Trade deals pose further complications. Distributors may not pass through the benefits of a deal to the consumer. Attractive trade deals may also lead distributors to forward buy or divert goods. *Forward buying* involves purchasing more inventory now than is needed to run a concurrent consumer promotion. The extra merchandise can then be sold at regular prices after the deal period. Enough merchandise may be bought to last until the next deal. *Diversion* involves buying goods in regions where manufacturers are offering unusually deep discounts and moving the goods to regions where the deals being offered are not so attractive. Deep-discount stores and warehouse clubs are especially adept at gaining advantage by these practices. To counteract the advantage of these low-cost retailers, competing chains have demanded that manufacturers sell everything to them at the lowest promotion price offered anywhere the chain operates. This uniform pricing policy limits a manufacturer's ability to engage in regional pricing.

INTEGRATING
*... with
Production/
Operations
Management*

Forward buying and diversion impact a manufacturer's ability to produce in an efficient manner and raise inventory costs throughout the distribution system. Forward buying plays havoc with a firm's manufacturing cycle, creating frantic overtime followed by unproductive lulls. Moreover, deep-discount stores that find these practices attractive are not long-term customers inasmuch as they carry only a few items in any product category and have no commitment to carry any brand on a regular basis.

TABLE 14-2   Segment Demand Curves

	List-price Segment		Promotion-price Segment		Total Market (Both Segments)	
Price	*Units*	*Contribution*	*Units*	*Contribution*	*Units*	*Contribution*
$2.00	*70.0*	*$84.00*	00.0	$00.00	70.0	$ 84.00
1.90	72.5	79.75	15.0	16.50	87.5	96.25
1.80	75.0	75.00	30.0	30.00	105.0	105.00
1.70	77.5	69.75	45.0	40.50	122.5	110.25
1.60	**80.0**	**64.00**	**60.0**	**48.00**	**140.0**	**112.00**
1.50	82.5	57.75	75.0	52.50	157.5	110.25
1.40	85.0	51.00	*90.0*	*54.00*	175.0	105.00

Source: Paul W. Farris and John A. Quelch, "The Defense of Price Promotions," *Sloan Management Review.* Vol. 29, No. 1 (Fall 1987), p. 67.

To try to regain the initiative some manufacturers have begun to emphasize *everyday low prices* (EDLP) or *value pricing.* Procter & Gamble has tried to implement an EDLP on most of its brands. Some retailers have opposed the plan because they were concerned that they would lose promotional flexibility as well as profits. They believed that P&G's plan favored retailers, such as Wal-Mart Stores, which were already following an "everyday low prices" approach. Competitors moved in, offered substantial deals, and stole share from P&G in the short run. The move to a more rational everyday list price system seems inevitable. The question is whether enough advertising and promotional support will be maintained to keep consumers interested in the product category.

PUBLIC RELATIONS

Today more and more customers are taking the time to phone or write companies when they encounter a problem with a purchase. Sophisticated marketers realize that prompt responses to these complaints can help correct problems and retain customers. Managers know it is a lot less expensive to maintain current customers than to find new ones.

Firms are expanding their customer relations departments because these investments pay off. Most complainers are satisfied with a personal letter and some coupons. Failure to respond to questions, however, can lead to bad word-of-mouth publicity. Inquiries are also a valuable source of information. This approach is detailed in Marketing in Action box 14-6.

MARKETING IN ACTION *14-6*

Maintaining Customer Contacts

APPLYING ... to Consumer Food Products Marketing

Two consumers who objected to the bland flavor of a new potato chip alerted Borden to a manufacturing error in one batch. People who inquire about products can be identified and used later in direct mail campaigns. For example, when Campbell decided to roll out a new line of low sodium soups, its customer relations division assembled a list of every customer who inquired about the salt content of its other soups. These customers were then sent a brochure on the new soups as well as some coupons.

APPLYING ... to Consumer Clothing Marketing

The type of response that customers like to receive can be illustrated by two examples. When a buyer wrote to Liz Claiborne to complain about buttonholes unraveling on a dress, the company replied immediately with a letter of apology. The company included instructions to have the dress repaired by any tailor, along with reassurances that reimbursement would be forthcoming. A letter sent to Health Valley Foods complaining about the lack of raisins in a box of cereal, prompted a two-page reply from the company president. In addition, the company sent a replacement box of cereal, an Oat Bran Jumbo Fruit Bar, a packet of herb seasonings, and a $1 coupon for cookies or bars. Health Valley doesn't advertise and the company is tickled when people take time to let them know about a problem.

— *It is simply good business for you to stay in touch with your customers.*

Source: Kathleen Deveny, "For Marketers: No Peeve Is Too Petty," *The Wall Street Journal*, November 14, 1990, p. B1.

By permission of Campbell Soup Company

APPLYING
. . . *to*
Sporting
Goods
Marketing

Public relations is also responsible for consumer education, publicity, special events, and sponsorships. The idea is that getting attention in a crowded marketplace doesn't have to be expensive. Franklin Sports Industries designed a baseball batting glove of Spandex and English leather to fit around a bat. Most important, the gloves sported the Franklin logo in inch-high letters on the back of the hand. Franklin handed them out by the dozen to every major-league ballplayer. Since then, Franklin's name shows up on television every time a camera focuses in on a batter. It has appeared on batters on the cover of *Sports Illustrated.* As a result Franklin sells about $65 million of all types of sporting goods, yet spends less than a million dollars a year on advertising.

APPLYING
. . . *to*
Consumer
Beverages
Marketing

Event marketing can be used to lure the customer into the retail outlet to purchase, while at the same time building awareness and impacting imagery. During the 1988 Olympics, Seagram Coolers launched a program called "Send the Families," designed to raise money to send a family member to accompany an athlete, all expenses paid to Seoul, Korea. The program involved point-of-sale displays with appropriate literature explaining how consumers could participate based on purchase and details about Seagram's contributions. The program was supported by an aggressive public relations effort involving the world's largest greeting card, transported across the country on a flatbed truck and signed by dignitaries and consumers at each stop. Tying all the pieces together was an advertising campaign that got the message out about the program and Seagram's support for American athletes.

APPLYING
. . . *to*
Pharma-
ceutical
Marketing

MARKETING IN ACTION *14-7*

Using Sports Figures in a Prescription Drug Promotion

Astra Pharmaceuticals hopes to score in the fiercely competitive arena of hypertension drugs with its sports-themed launch of Atacand (candesartan). Atacand joins Pfizer's Norvasc (amlodipine) and Procardia (nifedipine), Hoechst Marion Roussel's Cardizem CD (diltiazem), and other hypertension medications aimed at an estimated 50 million U.S. citizens with the disease. Norvasc leads in sales, with five million total prescriptions in the quarter ending September 1998.

Hall of Fame members Ernie Banks of the Chicago Cubs and football player Deacon Jones of the Los Angeles Rams joined Astra and NY-based Ketchum Public Relations at New York's All-Star Cafe recently to kick off Atacand's four-month, 19-city promotional tour. Banks, Jones, and Hall of Fame member Whitey Ford of the New York Yankees will carry the theme, "Have a Heart—Help Yourself and Someone Else," during visits to community centers and local broadcast shows throughout the United States. "This is the real World Series for people we love," Banks, who is a hypertension patient, told an unusual combination of medical and sports reporters attending the launch. Jones and Ford also suffer from hypertension.

Atacand, an angiotension receptor blocker, is a once-a-day pill that, according to clinical trials, causes few side effects. Dr. Alan Gradman, chief of the Division of Cardiovascular Diseases and director of Cardiology Fellowship Training at Western Pennsylvania Hospital, says nearly two-thirds of hypertension patients stop taking blood pressure drugs within a year of diagnosis because of unpleasant side effects such as dizziness, leg swelling, and headaches.

Gradman says using popular African-American sports figures like Banks and Jones to spread the hypertension message is an attempt to reach those who most need to hear about hypertension treatments. "Scientific findings might impress people like me," Gradman says, "but people typically at risk are interested in talking to Deacon Jones." As many as 30 percent of all deaths in hypertensive African-American men may be attributable to the disease, according to Astra's figures, with men in general showing the greatest hypertension risk up until age 55. The risk in women rises between 55 and 74 years old.

— *Celebrities may create the stir you need to call attention to your message.*

Source: Diane West, "Atacand Up at Bat," *Pharmaceutical Executive*, December 1998, p. S16.

MEASURING CAMPAIGN EFFECTIVENESS

APPLYING
. . . to
Consumer
Packaged
Goods
Marketing

You have to look at the effectiveness of any marketing activity you undertake. For example, Colgate-Palmolive applies a strict profit-and-loss formula in measuring the effectiveness of its ongoing cause-related sponsorship of the Starlight Foundation, which grants wishes to seriously ill children. Colgate's effort involves free standing insert coupons and is easily tracked. Your ability to track the impact of consumer promotions has been greatly enhanced by the availability of scanner data. The scope of information now available is indicated by a sample page from Information Resources, Inc.'s *Marketing Fact Book* shown in Table 14-3. Using supermarket scanner sales data, Colgate compares product sales in the three weeks following a coupon drop with average sales for the six months preceding it. The difference is then multiplied by the brand's net profit margin and the event's cost on a per-unit basis is subtracted to find the true incremental profit.

A common criterion used to evaluate the success of promotional activity is plus sales per dollar of company expenditure. This ratio shows how sales respond to the prizes and trips used as incentives and allows comparisons to be made among different types of promotions. Some firms break historical sales data into trend, seasonal, and irregular components so that the plus sales produced by promotional efforts can be measured. This method, called "bump analysis," adjusts sales for seasonal factors and removes the trend so the remaining irregular component reflects the impact of the promotion. Figure 14-3 shows the impact of a campaign on the sales. Note that the campaign produced losses in volume both before and after the effective dates of the promotion. The reduced volume before the promotion may have been due to the sales force holding back on deliveries to take advantage of campaign benefits. The drop after the promotion may indicate that the campaign had exhausted the available consumer demand. Total plus sales for the "sales campaign" were obtained by adding in sales for the two 10-day periods before and after the promotion. If the before-and-after losses were ignored, the estimate of plus sales in Figure 14-3 would be inflated. Once a reliable figure for plus sales has been estimated, it is divided by the costs of the promotion to get a ratio that can be used to evaluate the results of current and past campaigns.

There is an automated promotion evaluation system called PROMOTER, which incorporates concepts from expert systems and contains a knowledge base to recognize and adjust for data irregularities. The system estimates a *baseline* of what sales would have been if the promotion had not been run. This is possible because from 30 to 90 percent of the time, a consumer product is not on promotion in a particular store. Thus, using sales data from individual stores, sales from these nonpromotional weeks can be compared with those from promotional weeks. The incremental impact of the promotion can be measured. Experience with PROMOTER gave rise to a more sophisticated decision support system, PROMOTIONSCAN. Whereas PROMOTER measures total incremental volume for only one brand, PROMOTIONSCAN does so for all brands, including competitors. PROMOTIONSCAN also relates that incremental volume to retailer merchandising variables such as features, display, and price reductions.

The incremental impact of a trade promotion can be seen in the representative numbers shown in Table 14-4. As noted earlier, most trade promotions are unprofitable. The brand promotes to the trade at a 15 percent discount over a four-week period. Assume that all the stores in the market feature the brand for one week in their weekly newspaper advertising supplement. What's more, half the stores support the brand with three weeks of in-store display and consumer price reductions, whereas the other half only reduce the price but for the full four weeks. (It is unusual to get such excellent trade support.) Nevertheless, the promotion ends up costing 64 cents for each incremental dollar it generates. Unless the product's gross margin is more than 64 percent, the promotion will lose money. This is because the manufacturer has to sell a high number of cases at the discounted price to cover the normal

TABLE 14-3 Scanner Summary Data

Category—Liquid Soap Volume Is Pounds. Annual—Jan to Dec Including Only Brands Purchased by 0.5% or More of All Households	Ctgry Volume Share	Type Volume Share	— Data Reflect Grocery Store Purchases Only —						% Volume with the Specified Deal						
			% of Hshlds Buying	Volume per Purch	Purch per Buyer	Purch Cycle (days)	Share Ctgry Rqmts	Price per Volume	Any Trade Deal	Print Ad Featr	In-Store Disply	Shelf Price Reduct	Store Coupn	Man-ufactr Coupn	Avg % Off on Price Deals
Category—liquid soap	689.1*	100.0	31.9%	0.9	2.4	94	100%	2.29	24%	8%	6%	17%	1%	31%	35%
Type—liquid soap	100.0	100.0	31.9	0.9	2.4	94	100	2.29	24	8	6	17	1	31	35
Benckiser Cons Prods	9.8	9.8	5.4	0.8	1.5	97	42	1.96	8	1	2	7	0	12	26
Clean & Smooth	9.8	9.8	5.4	0.8	1.5	97	42	1.96	8	1	2	7	0	12	26
Colgate Palmolive	20.6	20.6	8.5	1.1	1.6	92	52	2.21	39	18	14	24	3	22	34
Softsoap	18.9	18.9	8.0	1.1	1.5	93	50	2.15	40	19	15	23	4	23	35
Softsoap Shower Gel	1.7	1.7	0.8	0.7	2.0	92	33	2.82	29	3	1	26	2	12	29
Koa Corp of Amer	17.1	17.1	8.2	0.9	1.7	93	48	1.86	17	4	2	13	2	35	40
Jergens	10.9	10.9	5.4	0.9	1.5	99	44	1.63	12	2	2	10	1	27	41
Jergens Antibacterial Plus	6.2	6.2	3.7	0.8	1.5	81	34	2.28	26	8	4	19	4	50	39
Minnetonka	3.6	3.6	3.2	0.6	1.3	100	30	2.13	40	10	2	35	1	23	44
Softsoap Country Designs	2.2	2.2	2.1	0.6	1.3	96	28	2.12	44	8	3	36	1	26	47
Softsoap Pastels	0.8	0.8	0.8	0.6	1.2	108	27	2.19	34	1	0	35	0	21	36
Procter & Gamble	17.7	17.7	9.5	0.8	1.6	96	45	2.19	15	4	5	10	1	34	37
Ivory Liquid	8.5	8.5	3.0	1.1	1.9	107	57	1.92	6	2	0	4	1	21	27
Ivory Liquid Accents	2.0	2.0	2.1	0.5	1.3	94	24	2.03	16	5	1	14	1	43	53
Ivory Liquid Classics	1.2	1.2	1.2	0.5	1.3	88	23	2.17	16	6	1	15	0	35	43
Safeguard	6.0	6.0	4.6	0.7	1.3	76	30	2.62	28	6	13	15	1	50	34
The Dial Corporation	22.6	22.6	9.4	0.9	1.8	102	59	2.57	25	6	3	21	1	42	29
Dial	22.5	22.5	9.3	0.9	1.8	101	59	2.56	25	6	3	21	1	42	29
Unilever	3.8	3.8	3.5	0.5	1.5	102	33	3.80	30	11	5	20	2	66	39
Dove Beauty Wash	3.8	3.8	3.5	0.5	1.5	102	33	3.80	30	11	5	20	2	66	39
Private label	1.5	1.5	0.6	1.1	1.4	99	48	1.42	17	0	0	17	0	1	13
Private label	1.5	1.5	0.6	1.1	1.4	99	48	1.42	17	0	0	17	0	1	13

* Category volume per 1000 households.

Source: The Marketing Fact Book. Chicago: Information Resources, Inc., 1992, p. 241.

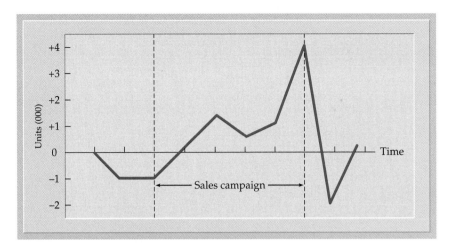

FIGURE 14-3   Measuring the Effects of a Sales Promotion

sales that would have taken place without the promotion. In addition, the manufacturer must also cover the forward buying by the retailer.

A promotion should be judged on the value of new customers attracted to it in addition to the immediate sales volume it generates. New customers may like the brand and, thus, buy it for many years. Therefore, immediate sales may not indicate the real value of a promotion; instead, it would be reflected by the number of new triers and their acceptance of a brand. It is important to distinguish between gaining triers (the job of the promotion) and gaining acceptance (the job of product development).

The value of event marketing is often measured by adding up the number of seconds of TV airtime or column inches of press clipping that feature a company's name or logo, then multiplying that by the equivalent ad cost. Some research companies make a business of doing such research. Some believe that measures such as "media equivalencies" are irrele-

TABLE 14-4   Trade Promotion Economics

	Cases	*Gross Dollars*
Baseline*		
Sales that would have occurred during a four-week promotion period even without promotion	400	$ 4,000
Incremental sales to consumers†		
Due to a one-week feature	100	$1,000
Due to 50% of stores with three weeks of displays and price reduction	250	$2,500
Due to 50% of stores with four weeks of price reduction only	80	$ 800
	430	$4,300
Ten weeks of forward buying by retailers	1,000	$10,000
Total sales during promotion	1,830	$18,300
Cost of promotion		$2,745
Cost per incremental dollar of sales		$0.64

* Assume weekly base sales of 100 cases and a list price of $10 per case.
† Based on analysis of single-source data and retailer promotion purchases.

Source: Magid M. Abraham and Leonard M. Lodish, "Getting the Most Out of Advertising and Promotion," *Harvard Business Review,* Vol. 68, No. 3 (May–June 1990), pp. 50–60.

vant, and what you should measure are favorable impressions of your brand that remain in people's minds. Thus, researchers recruit event spectators and conduct follow-up telephone interviews several days later to measure sponsor recall and consumers' intent to purchase sponsors' products.

Real-time scanner monitoring and the Internet have some marketers adjusting their promotions while they are ongoing rather than simply doing postmortems of their sales promotions. McDonald's gauges the success of a four-to six-week sales promotion by the reaction in the first five days. RealTime Media does daily promo-tracking for CDNow (Marketing in Action box 14-3). If the day-by-day information indicated that CDNow wasn't getting the traffic it wanted, it would take out additional banner headlines, buy more media support, send out e-mails, and/or seed more offers into the promotion.[5]

Rather than just evaluating each activity in isolation, you should strive to assess the synergistic effects of marketing communications (marcom) because their integration is important. Unfortunately, research methods for showing the effect of integration have not yet been developed.

SUMMARY

The promotion mix allows you to fine-tune your marketing mix. A review of the literature finds these reasons for promotions:

- Enables you to adjust to variations in supply and demand without changing list price.
- Allows you to price-discriminate among consumer segments.
- Rewards consumers.
- Secures distribution for new products.
- Induces consumer trial for new products.
- Encourages different retail formats, for example, shoppers clubs.
- Permits smaller regional brands to compete against nationally advertised brands.
- Adds excitement at point-of-sale to mature products.
- Defends shelf space against existing and anticipated competition.
- Clears inventories of obsolete products.

Thus, the promotion mix gives you flexibility to address very specific marketing situations.

You must approach the consumer with an integrated marketing communications package—sales force, direct marketing, advertising, sales promotion, and public relations all at once. As one observer puts it: "An ideal integrated marketing communications program combines media advertising to build awareness, sales promotion to generate an inquiry or response, database marketing to capture customer or prospect information, and ongoing direct marketing to specifically target customer needs and personalize, perhaps even customize, the communication to achieve measurable results."[6]

NOTES

1. Robert C. Blattberg, and Scott A. Neslin, *Sales Promotion: Concepts, Methods, and Strategies* (Englewood Cliffs, NJ: Prentice-Hall, 1990), p. 3.
2. William M. Bulkeley, "Rebates' Secret Appeal to Manufacturers: Few Consumers Actually Redeem Them," *The Wall Street Journal,* February 10, 1998, pp. B1, B6.
3. Richard Sale, "The Display Police," *Promo,* March 1999, pp. 80–81, 84.
4. Michael von Gonten, "Tracking Advertising Effects," *Admap,* Vol. 33, No. 9 (October 1998), pp. 43–45.
5. Richard Sale, "Evaluation in Evolution," *Promo,* September 1998, pp. 63, 65, 67–68.

6. Neil M. Brown, "Redefine Integrated Marketing Communications," *Marketing News,* March 29, 1993, pp. 4–5.

SUGGESTED READING

van Waterschoot, Walter, and Christophe Van den Bulte. "The 4P Classification of the Marketing Mix Revisited," *Journal of Marketing,* Vol. 56, No. 4 (October 1992), pp. 83–93.

REFERENCES

Abraham, Magid M., and Leonard M. Lodish. "Getting the Most Out of Advertising and Promotion," *Harvard Business Review,* Vol. 68, No. 3 (May–June 1990), pp. 50–60.

Abraham, Magid M., and Leonard M. Lodish. "An Implemented System for Improving Promotion Productivity Using Store Scanner Data," *Marketing Science,* Vol. 12, No. 3 (Summer 1993), pp. 248–269.

Blattberg, Robert C., and Scott A. Neslin. *Sales Promotion: Concepts, Methods, and Strategies* (Englewood Cliffs, NJ: Prentice-Hall, 1990).

Buzzell, Robert D., John A. Quelch, and Walter J. Salmon. "The Costly Bargain of Trade Promotion," *Harvard Business Review,* Vol. 68, No. 2 (March–April 1990), pp. 141–149.

Jones, John Philips. "The Double Jeopardy of Sales Promotions," *Harvard Business Review,* Vol. 68, No. 5 (September–October 1990), pp. 145–152.

Schultz, Don E., William A. Robinson, and Lisa A. Petrison. *Sales Promotion Essentials,* 3d ed. (Lincolnwood, IL: NTC Business Books), 1998.

Shapiro, Arthur. "Advertising Versus Trade Promotion: Which Is Which?" *Journal of Advertising Research,* Vol. 20, No. 3 (June/July 1990), pp. RC-13–RC-16.

QUESTIONS

1. Spain's Basque country-based bank, Caja de Burgos, wants clients for its pension plans account. Its pension plans are designed to appeal to self-employed males who already own a minimum of four of the bank's products. The bank has identified its targets—about 10,000 of them. Create a sales promotion to interest these prospects in opening new pension accounts.

2. Warner-Lambert wants to get a trial of its new anti-itch cream Benadryl. Prospects are those most likely to become victims of poison ivy, mosquito bites, and heat rash. Propose a plan for sampling this over-the-counter drug.

3. Visa USA wants customers to use its card more often. Create a sales promotion for the Christmas holiday season.

4. Bass Brewing's market share for Worthington Bitter beer has seen significant growth in the United Kingdom due to increased distribution and product superiority. Create a sales promotion that rewards pub-goers. The target audience is 25- to 40-year-old, blue-collar men who tend to reflect fondly on their laddish days, but now have family responsibilities.

5. With stocklifting, consumers don't know why some products vanish—or turn up—in a store. One critic has pointed out "You've taken away what should drive the market, which is the preferred product." How do you feel about the ethics of stocklifting? How does it fit with having a customer orientation? When might stocklifting violate the law?

6. A relaxation of rules on the marketing of professional services has led to increased interest in the use of promotions to boost sales. For example, an orthopedic surgeon who wanted to specialize in joint replacement came up with a brochure designed to appeal to older people and distributed it by direct mail to retirement communities. This appeal was so successful that the surgeon had to open two more offices and find a partner. In another case, a dentist who doubled the size of his Yellow Pages ad found that demand for his services doubled as well. How should professionals allocate their marketing budgets across different promotional alternatives to maximize sales?

7. When PepsiCo launched its "Pepsi Stuff" promotion, industry executives feared it might be too challenging for consumers. To win a denim jacket emblazoned with the Pepsi logo, for instance, people had to collect 400 award-points from peel-off strips on Pepsi or Diet Pepsi—the equivalent of 200 two-liter bottles. In fact, the contest wasn't challenging enough. Even before the last phase of media advertising in a six-month campaign was scheduled to run, bottlers reported that redemptions were running about 15 percent of total points available rather than the expected 10 percent—a burden for bottlers who have to pay half the costs of all prizes. How should Pepsi respond to redemptions running 50 percent higher than expected?

8. *Yo quiero Tylenol?* Taco Bell's advertisements featuring a Chihuahua proved surprisingly popular. To capitalize on Chihuahua fever during the holiday season, Taco Bell brought out four toy dogs that spoke lines from the chain's ads when they were squeezed: "Yo quiero Taco Bell"; "Here leezard, leezard" (with the "free-food" picket sign from the Godzilla spot); "Viva Gorditas" (with beret); and "Feliz Navidad, amigo" (with Santa hat). The Chihuahua campaign ran into an unexpected problem. The head of a chapter of the League of United Latin American Citizens, a Hispanic civil rights group, equated Taco Bell's advertising with hate crime. How should Taco Bell respond?

9. Philip Morris Co., with brands such as Marlboro, has about a 50 percent share of the U.S. cigarette market. It supports its consumer "marcom" activities with a sales-incentive program for independent retailers. The program, called Retail Masters, rewards participating retailers with payouts based on sales and display of Philip Morris brands. Under the program, displays of non-Philip Morris brands must be temporary. For agreeing to the display restrictions, the retailer earns "contract money." Moreover, the retailer also earns "Flex Funds" based on the proportion of its sales that are Philip Morris brands. Do Philip Morris's actions unfairly restrict distribution of competing brands?

10. Labor disputes in sports, such as those in Major League Baseball, the National Hockey League, and the National Basketball Association in recent years, can diminish the value of the product and the value of sponsorships of the product by alienating fans. What damage control in such situations might professional sports leagues do? their individual teams? the sponsors?

11. Based on scores of illnesses to consumers who drank Coca-Cola products, Belgium and Luxembourg banned Coca-Cola products in early June 1999. Coca-Cola traced its problems to bad carbon dioxide in its Antwerp plant and to traces of fungicide on wooden pallets used in its Dunkirk, France, canning facility—both owned by Coca-Cola Enterprises. France, and the Netherlands, then banned the sale of any products that came from those plants. Soon health ministers in Switzerland, Italy, and Spain were warning consumers about Coca-Cola products from those plants—even though Coca-Cola did not ship to those countries from the plants in question. How should The Coca-Cola Company and its anchor bottler, Coca-Cola Enterprises, respond to this crisis?

12. McDonald's restaurants and EMI Records Group North America, a unit of the London-based Thorn EMI PLC, teamed up for a purchase-with-purchase promotion. McDonald's customers were given the opportunity to purchase specially-priced 10-track compact disks (CDs) or cassettes of music by four different artists, including Garth Brooks. The $5.99 CDs and $3.99 cassettes were all compiled from previously released music. A coupon was included in the album that could be redeemed at Musicland stores that permitted consumers to purchase other titles by artists included in the promotion at a $2

discount. The promotion was run in over 9,500 McDonald's restaurants. The promotion was initially scheduled to occur from September 2 to 22, but was extended an additional week and ended September 28. The promotion was accompanied with a $20 million advertising campaign featuring Garth Brooks as a spokesperson. Sales of about 10 million units of special compilation CDs and cassettes took place. EMI is curious about the impact of the promotion on regular sales of its artists. SoundScan data are given in the file garthdat.sav on weekly sales of two older Garth Brooks' albums: *In Pieces,* released the previous summer, and *No Fences,* released 4 summers before. Because each of these albums had been available for at least a year, EMI assumed that any change in sales during the weeks of the promotion could be directly attributable to the McDonald's promotion. Total industry sales serves as a possible control for seasonality.

CASE 14-1　AMERICAN EXPRESS: MEMBERSHIP REWARDS EUROPE*

On November 10th 1995, Enrique Ortiz, head of American Express Consumer Loyalty for Europe, was thinking about the critical steps the company had to take to make a full success of the European Membership Rewards Program launched in 1993. He knew that the success of such loyalty programs depended on two elements: the "customer proposition," i.e., the type of rewards offered to the customers, and the ability to manage the program's cost base, i.e., the funds spent in securing strategic program partners and controlling administrative costs.

Enrique Ortiz considered the penetration rate the Program had achieved so far. With an average of over 20% of the cardholders enrolled in Membership Rewards in Europe, he wondered if it was time to modify the "customer proposition" in order to make the Program more attractive to a wider base.

The Membership Rewards Program had been designed for business travellers. The type of rewards offered appealed mainly to members of Airline Frequent Flyer Program, who collected miles on American Express and then transferred them to their preferred airline to collect free tickets or upgrades. Enrique Ortiz believed that a different kind of partner had to be recruited if the penetration rate was to reach the 50% target he had in mind. Partner diversification

could go various routes: car rental companies, restaurants, show ticket agencies, even household appliance companies. Additionally, he wondered how to attract customers of the alternative payment instruments to "the Card" that American Express was increasingly marketing.

At the same time, Enrique Ortiz felt the need to carefully manage the cost of the program. This could be achieved by signing low cost deals with partners and by encouraging customers to redeem points on these low cost deals. He was wondering how feasible this option was and how co-operative the partners would be.

CREDIT AND CHARGE CARDS IN EUROPE

Credit and charge cards allow the purchaser to "buy now and pay later," an idea initially introduced by Diners Club in 1956 and followed by American Express in 1957. There are two types of card: charge cards and credit cards. Charge cards such as American Express and Diners Club are sometimes also referred to as travel and entertainment cards. They differ from credit cards in that the cardholder has to pay the outstanding balance on his or her account in full at the end of each month. Credit cards or bank cards are typically issued

* This case was prepared by Paul McGilvey of the J. L. Kellogg Graduate School of Management, Sven Rose of the University of Chicago, Graduate School of Business, and Magali Spinther of the London Business School under the supervision of Professor Luis Maria Huete of IESE, International Graduate School of Management, University of Navarra, Barcelona-Madrid, Spain. Copyright © 1996, IESE. Reproduced by permission.

by specific banks under the umbrella of one of the two international credit card organizations, Visa International and MasterCard. Holders of this type of card have the option of paying their balance in full at the end of the month or rolling over any portion into the following month and thereby opting to pay interest (APR of around 22% in the UK) on the balance carried. Visa is the dominant credit card in the European Community, with some 33.4 million cardholders at the end of 1988. Eurocard/MasterCard had some 18.9 million cardholders at the same date, while American Express was a distant third, with over 4.5 million cards in 1994 (see Exhibit 1 for market shares of major companies).

The European market for credit and charge cards (referred to as credit cards from here on) has devel-

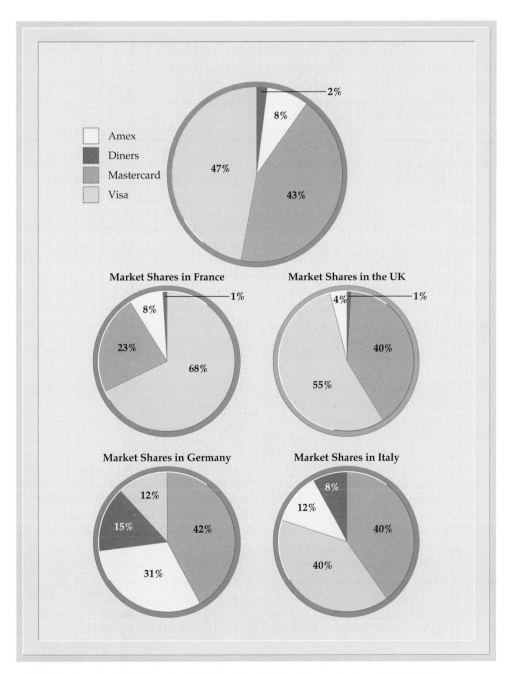

EXHIBIT 1 **Market Shares of Major Credit Card Companies, 1988–1989 World Market Shares**

oped rapidly since the 1970s. Credit card charging levels have increased in response to favorable consumer market conditions and advances in banking technology. In 1995 more than 10% of consumers' expenditures were made by credit card. This figure has been growing as the number of outlets accepting credit card payment has increased. As more banks and even corporations have entered this market as issuers, annual fees charged to consumers have come down (in many cases there are none), allowing consumers to carry multiple cards.

Merchant fees—3% as an average for American Express—and interest charged to cardholders on outstanding account balances account for the vast majority of the issuers' revenues. Thus, consumer spending is the key driver of company revenue. Card companies have recognized the importance of establishing a consumer preference for their card relative to the competition. One of the methods used in an attempt to increase market share and build a loyal customer base are rewards and loyalty programs.

AMERICAN EXPRESS

The American Express Company was born as an express freight company in 1850, when Henry Wells merged Wells & Co. with other express carriers—Livingston & Fargo, and Butterfield, Wasson & Co. American Express created the first private pension plan in the US in 1875, and in 1882 the American Express Money Order was introduced as a safer alternative to shipping sums of cash. American Express invented the Traveller's Cheque in 1891, liberating travelers from the need to obtain letters of credit. American Express freight offices in England, France and Germany entered the travel business in 1898 by selling tickets for European railroads and transatlantic ships. To accommodate international financial operations in Latin America, Europe and the Far East, the American Express Company was incorporated in 1919. The company launched the American Express charge card in the US in 1958, and five years later the American Express Sterling card was launched in the UK.

Under James D. Robinson, who served as CEO from 1977 to 1993, American Express acquired various businesses as part of a strategy to turn the company into a "financial supermarket". Acquisitions included Shearson Loeb Rhodes (brokerage, 1981), the Boston Company (banking, 1981), Balcor (real estate, 1982), Lehman Brothers Holding Company (investment banking, 1984), Investors Diversified Services

(brokerage, 1984), and E. F. Parker (brokerage, 1987). In 1982 American Express officially became a blue chip company when it was named as the first financial services company to the Dow Jones Industrial Average.

In the early 1990s, however, losses mounted in the brokerage subsidiaries, while the company's flagship charge card business was facing unprecedented competitive pressures: merchants were angry about the fees paid to American Express, which ranged from a 20% to 300% premium over fees paid to other card companies, while cardholders were questioning the annual fee for the card.

Harvey Golub was named CEO in 1993, and under his leadership the company has accelerated a process of divesting most of its financial subsidiaries, aside from Investors Diversified Services, which was reconstituted as American Express Financial Advisors. Golub has reduced and reorganized American Express' operations while defining a new mission for the corporation: "to become the world's best service brand."

Today American Express defines its businesses as travel related services, investment and financial services, and information processing services, provided throughout the world. In 1994 Travel Related Services enjoyed net revenues of over $10 billion, which represented 72% of the company's total revenue. American Express Financial Advisors was responsible for 23% of net revenues, while the remainder came from the American Express Bank. In 1994 Travel Related Services was the company's most profitable activity, with a reported income of $998 million or 66% of the company's total income in 1994 (see Exhibit 2 for selected financial information).

Travel Related Services

The flagship TRS product was the American Express Personal Card (the original card). In 1995 the product range also included the Gold Card, the Platinum Card, the Corporate Card, the General Revolving Credit Card, the Company Card, as well as Optima, a newer credit card that allowed consumers to carry interest-bearing revolving debt. In addition, TRS operated a world-wide travel agency with offices in 160 countries. It also published lifestyle and travel magazines and sold life insurance though AMEX Life Assurance.

In 1994 there were 36.3 million cardholders worldwide and more than 4.5 million in Europe. "The card," as it is often called, is issued in 32 currencies and is used for payment in 160 countries at more than 3.9 million service establishments. Customers spent $141

EXHIBIT 2 **American Express Selected Financial Information, 1994 (million dollars)**

	Travel Related Services	American Express Financial Advisors	American Express Bank
Net revenues	10,256	3,270	652
Pretax income (loss) from continuing operations	1,396	631	119
Income (loss) from continuing operations	998	428	80
Assets	42,483	40,155	13,281

billion using their American Express Cards in 1994; 80% of the expenditure was done by 20% of the cardholders. The remaining 20% of the expenditure was split equally between a group of 30% of cardholders and another group of low-spenders that accounted for 50% of the cards. Enrique Ortiz commented:

> Our approach over the past year or so has been to develop distinctly different products to meet the needs of the major market segments we want to serve—in effect, moving from a "one card fits all" approach to different products for different customer segments. Our products will increasingly include various configurations of rewards, interest rates, fees, grace periods and services.

Along these lines, the company was experimenting with "smart cards", which would perform ID, calling card, key card ATM and credit charge functions. Other options are "stored value" cards that can be pre-paid, spent and re-loaded with cash, as well as cards that can be debited directly against a checking account.

In 1994 American Express, including its Travel Related Services division, went through a major reorganization and moved from a geographically run organization to a customer focused one. Three major customer groups were created: the Customer Service Group concentrated on the needs of individual cardholders, the Travel Service Group attended to the needs of corporate customers, and the Establishment Service Group was responsible for relations with merchants accepting the American Express card.

Within the Customer Service Group, activities were organized by processes: Acquisition, Loyalty, Membership Reward, New Product Development and Lending Process, as well as Advertising and Brand Management (Exhibit 3).

THE REWARDS CONCEPT

History

American Express first launched Membership Miles in the US in June 1991. At that time it was discovered that the company was too focused on growth through acquisitions and was neglecting its existing customers. At the same time, a lot of business schools were saying that it was three times more effective to keep an existing customer than to capture a new one. Therefore, in the early 1990s American Express took a conscious decision not to concentrate on acquisition but to channel its efforts into existing card members.

Membership Rewards was a competitive response to the moves of two banks that had entered into partnership alliances with major US airlines. Citibank was the first to enter the market in 1990 with a Visa card that allowed its users to collect miles on American Airlines. A year later First Chicago signed a similar deal with United Airlines. Additionally, a consulting project commissioned by American Express underlined the profit imperative of securing customer loyalty.

American Express credits Membership Rewards with having helped stabilize market share. By 1995, the Membership Rewards concept had expanded across the globe, with nearly five million American Express card members participating in individual programs in 21 countries.

Program Conditions

Program conditions are similar in all European countries. The UK serves as a good example to illustrate the way the program works. The program is available to all cardholders. There is a £20+VAT annual program

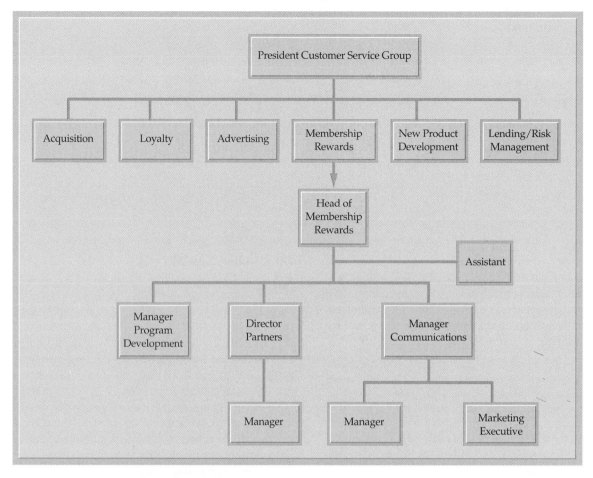

EXHIBIT 3   American Express Travel Related Services Customer Service Group

fee for card members and the fee is lost in the first year.

Each enrolled card member accrued one point for every pound charged and billed on the card. Points could only be redeemed once the member had accrued at least 3,000 Membership Rewards points and paid for eligible charges. Membership points accrued could be transferred to a number of frequent flyer programs of participating airlines or converted into vouchers for free rooms at participating hotels. Points could also be converted into other rewards from participating partners at specified conversion rates (see Exhibit 4). In contrast with many other reward schemes, Membership Rewards points did not expire within a certain time period.

Launch of Membership Rewards in Europe

In Europe Membership Rewards was first introduced in France in May 1993 due to increasing competitive

pressures (Carte Bleu) and a favorable market opportunity (Air France). Germany and the UK introduced Membership Rewards in November 1993. These programs were run independently by each country's marketing team. This local approach required each office to negotiate on an entirely independent basis with potential program partners.

The new American Express Rewards division decided to launch "one single European reward program with one single technological platform and one single customer base." This drastically changed the negotiating power of American Express vis-à-vis its partners, bringing discussion to a European, and in some cases, to a global level, as in the case of Air France, which is an American Express Partner worldwide.

However, because of the cultural differences between countries, American Express did not try to impose a uniform Membership Rewards program

Partners	Membership rewards points	Translates into X points in partner program	Reward options	Points required in partner program	Total pounds spent on Amex card to get reward
Air France	2	3	Free economy ticket London–Paris	25,000	16,667
Swissair	1	1	Free business ticket London–Madrid	45,000	45,000
Austrian	1	1	Free economy ticket London–Los Angeles	70,000	70,000
SAS	1	2	Free economy ticket London–Copenhagen	20,000	10,000
Continental	1	1	Free economy ticket London–Rome	45,000	45,000
Iberia	7	1	Free economy ticket London–Malaga	2,200	15,400
Sabena	1	1	Free economy ticket London–Brussels	16,000	16,000
Virgin	1	1	Free economy ticket London–Frankfurt	12,500	12,500
Forte Crest	300	1	1 night	10	3,000
Oberoi Hotel	6,500	1	1 night	1	5,000
Occidental Hotels	5,000	1	1 night	1	5,000

EXHIBIT 4   Membership Rewards Options

across Europe. Rather, it centralized the administrative and marketing functions in London, while continuing to conduct negotiations at the local level to align with partners that customers valued most. (Exhibit 5 lists the partners for each European country.) In some countries this strategy has been particularly successful, as in Sweden, where American Express has established a relationship with the national airline, the national cruise line and the national hotel chain. This has allowed American Express to achieve a disproportionally high spending rate among membership rewards participants. Similar to this customized approach to partner selection, the Rewards division publishes a monthly newsletter in 13 languages, in which the latest "deals" negotiated are described.

Customer Service

Enrique Ortiz reflected on the customer service imperative at American Express:

> Our service is the best in the world; if you're a Platinum card member, you can call us up from anywhere in the world to arrange a conference, deliver flowers or send a plumber to your house in the middle of the night. The ordinary cardholder doesn't see that, unless he travels abroad and loses his card and needs immediate help. As a result, we'll have only 1–2% non-renewals of Platinum and Gold cards each year, while the Green card non-renewals may range from 10–20%. In Spain, just as an example, the figure is 12%.

Service quality, then, was a key objective for the Membership Rewards Program. Enrique Ortiz described the UK's operation:

EXHIBIT 5   Membership Rewards—Program Partners May 1995

MARKET	FRANCE	UK	GERMANY	SPAIN	ITALY	HOLLAND	SWEDEN	$CARD	BELGIUM	SWITZERLAND
AIRLINE PARTNERS	Air France	Air France	Air France	Air France	Air France	Air France	Air France	Air France	Swissair	Air France
	Swissair	Swissair	Swissair	Swissair	Swissair	Swissair	SAS	Continental	Austrian	Swissair
	Austrian	Austrian	Austrian	Austrian	Austrian	Austrian	Sabena	Sabena	Sabena	Austrian
	SAS	SAS	SAS	Continental	Iberia	Sabena	Swissair			Sabena
	Continental	Continental	Continental	Iberia	Sabena		Austrian			
	Iberia	Iberia	Sabena	Sabena						
	Sabena	Sabena								
		Virgin								
NON-AIR PARTNERS	Sofitel	Forte	Steigenberger	Grupo Sol	Cogetta	Sofitel	Scandic	Steigenberger	Sofitel	Sofitel
	Lucien Barriere	Lucien Barriere	Dorint	Melia	Jolly	Steigenberger	Lucien Barriere	Lucien Barriere	Steigenberger	Steigenberger
	Oberoi	Occidental	Arabella	Occidental	Sina	Occidental	Silja Line	Sofitel	Occidental	Lucien Barriere
	Occidental	Oberoi	Romantik	Steigenberger	Star	Scandic		Oberoi	Scandic	Oberoi
	Disneyland Paris	Restaurants	Lucien Barriere	RENFE	Notturno	Dorint		Occidental	Dorint	Occidental
		Theatre tickets	Oberoi	Disneyland Paris	Steigenberger	Lucien Barriere		Wine club	Lucien Barriere	Wine Club
		Wine club	Disneyland Paris		Occidental	Camille Oostwegel			Wine Club	Möwenpick
		Disneyland Paris			Oberoi	Relais Du Silence			Möwenpick	
					Disneyland Paris	Disneyland Paris				
						Möwenpick				

We have a dedicated service center in Brighton that will transfer points to any partner, or print a voucher for a partner, at the actual time of the customer call. Of course, it may take time for the partner to then credit the member's account.

Carlos Mansilla, the service manager for Membership Rewards in Madrid, reported that 4 employees were dedicated to serving MR customers in Spain. They fielded, on average, 3,000 calls per month. The average call duration was three minutes and 40% of calls were for point transfers, 30% for information and sign up, and 30% for other inquiries. Ninety-nine percent of all customer questions did not require any follow-up and were handled right over the phone.

Competing Programs

Many credit cards use point collection schemes to stimulate use and retain customers. In Europe, American Express had to face competitive responses from a number of players. For example, in January 1994 Ford launched a Visa card in the UK in partnership with Barclays bank. Under the Ford program, card users apply 5% of each transaction to rebates from $900 a year up to a maximum of $2700 on a Ford vehicle over a five-year period. GM had a similar program with Household bank.

In the UK, the Air Miles scheme represents American Express's toughest competition. Owned 49% by British Airways, Air Miles has partnership agreements with British Telecom, Shell, National Westminster Bank, Courtyard by Mariott, Coutts & Co, and Ulster Bank. Through Air Miles, National Westminster Bank

cardholders acquire points on British Airways Executive Club. For every £20 charged on a Natwest Visa or Mastercard, the customer receives one British Airways point. Points appear automatically on the Executive Club Statement, along with any points gained by flying on British Airways. The customer can then choose to convert these points into free flights, weekend holidays, or dinners, according to the conditions of the British Airways Executive Club Program (see Exhibit 6). Similarly with other partners, customers gain points through their spending and use them in the British Airways Executive Club. Air Miles had plans to launch similar program in various European countries.

First Results

Reflecting on the program's first two years in Europe, Enrique Ortiz considered that it had been a qualified success. Since the program was first launched in France in May of 1993, over 1,000,000 American Express cardholders had joined Membership Rewards in one of the nine European countries where it was available. In 1995 membership numbers were still increasing in all countries, but were highest in Sweden (43% of all cardholders) and in those countries where the program had been established first, i.e., UK (33%) and France (23%). In other major markets the membership rewards program penetration was lower, i.e., Germany (11%), Italy (16%) and Spain (14%). "Our target is to get at least half of the cardholders in each country to join membership rewards," remarked Enrique Ortiz. He continued, "Of course, not everybody plays the rewards game and research has shown that the maxi-

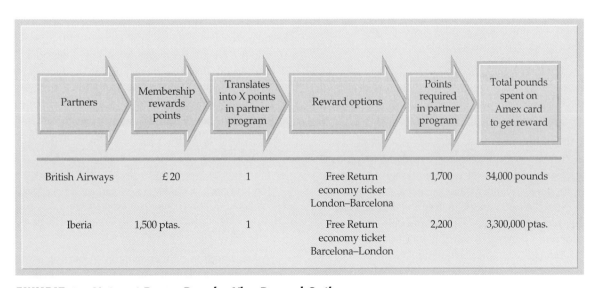

Partners	Membership rewards points	Translates into X points in partner program	Reward options	Points required in partner program	Total pounds spent on Amex card to get reward
British Airways	£ 20	1	Free Return economy ticket London–Barcelona	1,700	34,000 pounds
Iberia	1,500 ptas.	1	Free Return economy ticket Barcelona–London	2,200	3,300,000 ptas.

EXHIBIT 6 **Natwest Banco Popular Visa Reward Options**

mum achievable penetration rate varies from country to country, but eventually should reach a level between 50% and 60%."

Customer Comments

Reactions to the Membership Rewards Program are mostly positive, particularly among the cardholder base that has been enrolled for a period of over one year. Lawrence J. O'Connor, a London-based business executive, remarked:

> I have been an American Express Cardmember for about ten years now and do most of my spending between the three Amex cards I carry, the UK green card, a European $ card and the Optima card. This month alone I will run up more than £5,000. Through my participation in the Membership Rewards Program, I earn about two to three meals a month. Without this program I would have switched to another card a while ago.

In Barcelona, Rafael Torres, an American Express card member had the following to say:

> I still carry an Amex card because I have done so for a while, but they are just not competitive anymore. The annual fee is high and many places don't accept the card anyway. I prefer to use my Banco Popular Visa Card. They have a loyalty program with Iberia that allows me to earn approximately 30% more Iberia points than I would get using my Amex card in the Membership Rewards Program. Although my Visa has just let me down. Since March 1996 you earn just about the same number of Iberia points with both cards.

Jan Cron, a German university student, who has also been participating in the Membership Rewards Program since the beginning, voiced the following opinion:

> I think the program is great. I just wish more places would take the American Express card, but I guess that has more to do with Germany and not with American Express. It will just take longer earning one of these rewards. Perhaps by that time they will also include car rental rewards in the program.

Financial Results

"The Program wasn't designed expressly to produce profits," said Enrique Ortiz, "but rather to increase value to our cardholders and enhance customer loyalty." Nonetheless, American Express has developed complete marginal profit and loss models to measure the program's impact. American Express has defined more than 12 customer segments as measured by behavioral characteristics, such as travel patterns, type of purchases, etc. By comparing Membership Rewards participants with a control group of non-participants in the same customer segment, the company has observed that marginal spending per Rewards member increases on average by over 40% in the first year of membership and 5–10% annually in subsequent years. Consequently, American Express calculates that only 30% of Program revenues derive from membership fees, while 70% are attributable to increased spending. These revenues are tracked against all Program expenses, including partner fees, systems costs, and advertising and promotional expenses. On this basis alone, Membership Rewards has produced a net profit for American Express. "Moreover," says Enrique Ortiz, "the research shows that program participants are only one-half as likely to cancel their card membership as non-program participants. We are not even factoring that into the financial model." Overall, American Express believes that the benefits of the program split approximately equally between spend, new customers, retained customers, and program fees.

THE PROGRAM PARTNERS

In 1995 American Express had three kinds of partners: airline partners, lodging partners, and a third grouping of restaurants, wine clubs, fitness centers, etc. The first two categories represented approximately 75% of American Express partners.

> Selecting the right partners is important for the success of the program," says Beth Parker, Manager of Cardmember Rewards at American Express. "Members are more likely to use the card if they really want one of the rewards offered. People are more interested in a select list of key partners than a long list of second category ones.

American Express takes the process of selecting partners for the Membership Rewards Program very seriously. Testing among program members has demonstrated that the image of the partner is very important and has to match the aspirational preferences of the American Express cardholder. In most countries, airlines meet these criteria and are therefore target partners around which a country-specific rewards program can be built.

Beth Parker remarked about the process:

> The lead time in signing a new partner is very long and sometimes it takes one or two years before a new partner is included in the program. For example, it took nearly two years to sign EuroDisney as a participant.

As a condition of membership, American Express partners must participate first in their home markets (e.g., Swissair in Switzerland) and only then in any other. Additionally, partners must treat points earned with American Express in exactly the same way as those earned with their own loyalty program. "Customers certainly appreciate that," reports Beth Parker, who shared these comments from a French customer:

> I really enjoy flying and participating in the Membership Rewards Program from American Express. It allows me to accumulate points and then transfer them to any of several frequent flyer programs I belong to. No other loyalty program has this kind of flexibility. For example, I fly a lot on Air France and can now earn free trips on Air France sooner by simply calling Amex and asking them to transfer points from their program to Air France. What a great concept.

For each full participant point credited to a cardmember's airline or hotel program, American Express compensates the partner in a way that has previously been agreed upon, which is typically in the range of 0–30% of the full retail value of service. For instance, airlines tend to be compensated at a higher level, hotels at a middle level and restaurants at a lower level. Agreements are typically signed for periods of no less than three years.

In return, American Express advertises the partner's participation in the Membership Rewards Program in communication vehicles, such as the Membership Rewards Program statements, quarterly updates, and fulfillment packages. To assist in general marketing co-ordination between the parties, each partner notifies American Express of significant Participant Program promotions for inclusion in the quarterly newsletter.

Melinda Adams, Director of Marketing in the UK and Europe of an important chain of hotels in Asia, remarked:

> The country managers don't see the value in giving away the room below cost and they can't track what the customer spends at the bar or restaurant. But 40–45% of our business comes from the European business traveller and this program gets me in front of 1 million of our target customers four times a year.
>
> We are the only hotel chain participating in our geographic market and hotel category. Of course, the Program would be less attractive to us if direct competitors were participating, but American Express is a company you do business with because you know you can trust them.

Javier Alonso, a marketing manager for Iberia's *Tarjeta Plus,* the frequent flyer program for Spain's national airline, commented on Iberia's reasons for partnering with American Express:

Of the 350,000 Iberia Tarjeta Plus frequent flyers, about 20% are also participating in the Membership Rewards Program of American Express. Those customers can purchase Iberia tickets with the Amex card, earning "double" points. This makes the Iberia Plus program more attractive, thereby increasing loyalty among Iberia customers.

THE FUTURE

Enrique Ortiz reflected on the changes at American Express and their implications for Membership Rewards:

> The company is expanding beyond its traditional revenue base in merchants' and cardholders' fees into interest-bearing services and selling third party products and services to our cardholders. I now have to find ways to serve all these customer groups.

Should mass-customization be the next step for American Express? If so, how could it be implemented?

An article he had seen in the *Harvard Business Review* concluded that rewards create loyalty if a company understands how to share value. He was wondering if American Express was sharing value with its customers. Was Membership Rewards really as successful a loyalty program as it appeared? What was the cash value of the program? He knew that customers valued choice of rewards. Was the choice of rewards wide enough, or should they try to sign additional partners to increase the redemption options? What about the aspirational value of the reward options? Were MR participants really motivated by predominantly travel-related rewards? How convenient was it for MR members to claim their rewards?

In addition, he thought that it was time to measure in numbers the potential impact of Membership Rewards over the coming years. He knew what the average spending per cardholder was and by what percentage it increased when the customer joined the program. How much additional revenue would American Express generate thanks to the program within five years?

REFERENCES

American Express Company, Annual Report 1994.

American Express Company, "Product Information," internal document, 3/5/95.

Credit and Charge Cards in Europe, *Market Research Europe,* Volume XXII, June 1990, Euromonitor Publications Ltd.

"Credit & Other Finance Cards," *Market Report,* Key Note, 1995.

Grant, Linda, "Why Warren Buffett's Betting Big on American Express", *Fortune,* October 30, 1995, pp. 80–86.

Marketing Week, "A Question of Loyalty", 1 July 1994.

Marketing Week, "Keep the Customer Satisfied—American Express," 24 March 1995.

Miller, Robert, "Amex fights back in the credit card war," *The Times,* London, 20 April 1995.

Mitchell, Alan, "Amex begins battle for the big wallets. A famous charge card is broadening its appeal," *The Times,* London, 26 April 1995.

O'Brien, Louise and Charles Jones, "Do Rewards Really Create Loyalty?" *Harvard Business Review,* May–June 1995, pp. 75–82.

Walker, Jo-Anne, "Keeping the Customer Satisfied," *Marketing Week,* 24 March 1995, pp. 19–20.

Wentz, Laurel, "GM, Ford Lead Charge to Gas Up European Sales", *Advertising Age,* 17 January 1994, I27–I30.

CASE *14-2*   TESCO SUPERMARKETS*

On the 13th February 1995, grocery multiple Tesco launched Clubcard, the UK's first, national, supermarket loyalty card scheme. A spokesman for Tesco explained that the principal objective of the scheme was not to lure shoppers away from competitors' stores. Clubcard was, he claimed, "a way of saying thank you to existing customers". He went on to add that Tesco was aiming to recreate the kind of relationship that had existed between local shops and their customers 50 years ago.

In the weeks following the Clubcard launch, Tesco's leading competitors were dismissive of the whole idea of loyalty cards. None more so than David Sainsbury who regarded the Clubcard as "the Green Shield Stamp way of offering value." In his opinion the scheme would "cost at least £10 million just to administer. That's wasted money which brings no benefits at all to customers. We have no plans at all to go down that route." The 1% discount offered by Clubcard was, he believed, of insignificant value to the customer. Observers in the City were equally skeptical and the anticipated additional marketing overheads were cited by financial analysts as being partially responsible for the two pence mark-down in Tesco's share price following Clubcard's launch.

Nevertheless, speculation was rife that within a matter of weeks other leading supermarket chains would be forced to follow with their own national loyalty schemes. Market leader J Sainsbury already had its own Saver Card scheme in place in a limited number of stores, as did third placed rival, Safeway, with its Added Bonus Card (ABC). Both schemes were devised as promotional devices, offering small percentage discounts to shoppers in a bid to boost sales at poorly performing stores.

INDUSTRY BACKGROUND

Tesco's initiative had served to heighten the competition in the already fiercely competitive supermarket sector. The total value of the UK grocery sector in 1994 was £54.9 billion (EUI 1995)[1] and was dominated by larger businesses (defined as those with 1990 turnover of £4.5m or more) who generated £49.7 billion of total sector turnover, whereas small businesses had only 10% share with £5.2 billion. Several major multiples dominated the sector: Sainsbury, Tesco, Safeway [Argyll group], Asda, Somerfield [Gateway & Somerfield stores], Kwik Save and Iceland, together with the co-operative societies. Since 1990 large grocery retailers had advanced their turnover by an average of 40%, while smaller ones had grown by only 8%. By 1992 chains with 100 or more stores accounted for 68.5% of sector sales.

---

[1] Economic Intelligence Unit Report. No. 36, December 1995.

---

* This case was prepared by Helen Mitchell and Helen Peck of the Cranfield School of Management, England as a basis for class discussion, rather than to illustrate effective or ineffective handling of an administrative situation. Copyright ©1997 by Cranfield School of Management. Reproduced by permission.

The market was commonly beset by price skirmishes with each store trying to wrest the price initiative from their rivals. Growth had not come from traditional product categories and consumer expenditure on food as a percentage of total consumer expenditure had actually fallen over this period, but it was the larger supermarkets that were better equipped to sell products in other expenditure categories to achieve growth. The market was considered to be saturated apart from the discounters and the multiples were selling more or less the same things for the same prices. However, one area where there was seen to be a difference was in the demographic profile of the shoppers for each chain: J. Sainsbury was seen to have an older more up-market clientele, Tesco's profile was much younger, with a larger percentage of 25 to 45 year olds and Safeway's was very similar to Tesco. Kwik Save, with most stores situated in poorer city centers in the North, had an older, less affluent customer profile, while Asda catered for the younger family on a tight budget. Exhibit 1, showing sector performance for 1993, shows Sainsbury with a clear lead, Tesco in its familiar second place, and the remaining players fighting it out below them.

THE WAY FORWARD

In an industry where margins were slim, increasing market share was vital. Due to its position in Exhibit 1, Tesco had been battling to improve its performance; 1991 and 1992 had been bleak trading years for them and gloomy early figures for 1993 had shown that they had lost 3% of customers in the previous year. In response to this decline, research was undertaken in order to throw some light on the reasons for the fall-off in customer numbers. Results showed that customers wanted better value, service and responsiveness as well as a supermarket that was innovative. Under the charge of Terry Leahy, then Marketing Director, a strategy plan was devised on the basis of these findings which concluded that Tesco, "should aim to be positively classless, the best value, offering the best shopping trip. This will be achieved by having a contemporary business and therefore one that remains relevant by responding to changing need. We should aim to be the natural choice of the middle market by being relevant to their current needs and serving them better, i.e. customer focused."[2]

In the early 1990s the corporate strategy had been margins-focused and efforts had been directed at extracting higher returns in a nationwide cost-efficiency drive. Under the new plan, strategy was changed to the aim of delivering the best shopping trip for the customer. This covered a variety of attributes so, starting in 1993, Tesco embarked on a series of initiatives designed to offer better value, improve the stores, and give a higher level of service to their customers.

---

[2] The Best Shopping Trip? How Tesco keeps the customer satisfied. Transcript of a speech delivered to The Marketing Society on September 11, 1996 by Tim Mason.

EXHIBIT 1   UK Grocery Sector—Performance Figures 1992/1993

1992/1993	*Market Share*[a]	*Turnover*	*Pre-tax Profits*	*Profits as % of Turnover*
	% of Total Mkt.	£million	£million	%
Sainsbury[b]	17.3	9,685	732.8	7.6
Tesco	14.9	7,581	580. 9	7.6
Safeway[c]	8.6	5,196	417.3	8.0
Asda[d]	8.4	4,614	142.1	3.0
Kwik Save	5.8	2,651	126.1	4.7

[a] Please note: Market Share is assessed across 179 selected markets (Packaged Goods, Fresh Foods & Toiletries) by Taylor Nelson AGB, which is recognized by the sector as the most comprehensive measurement. It is not related to Annual Turnover but represents each retailer's share of these specific markets. Annual turnover is made up of non-grocery goods, e.g. petrol, fashion clothing and in Sainsbury's case also includes Homebase sales and as a result market share cannot be easily or fairly judged by turnover figures.

[b] Sainsbury + Savacentre

[c] Safeway + Presto + other Argyll stores

[d] Asda + Dales

Source: Taylor Nelson AGB: Retailer ShareTrack and Reuters

BETTER VALUE

The Tesco shopper was found to be a value-oriented customer and, in response to requests for cheaper prices, Tesco launched a commodity range across 110 core products. In their distinctive blue and white packaging, they were designed to communicate value for money for every-day goods and negate the need for cross shopping at discount stores. Customer response was very positive and trading improved. This was then followed by a reduction in the price of popular, key branded items, to give the Tesco shopper the cheapest prices in the market-place. In 1995 this was extended to key lines of fruit and vegetables, the most notable of these being bananas. This sparked a mini banana war in which the price fell from 49p to 19p per pound in the space of a few weeks, one of the lowest across the world. In-store bakeries were next to offer cheaper prices (a category which had only previously seen the northern supermarket chains, Morrisons and Asda, offer value lines), resulting in a significant increase in customer volume. Pricing initiatives culminated in the launch in September 1996 of the "Unbeatable Value" scheme in which the prices of over 600 core products were reduced, together with a promise that if the price can be beaten then Tesco will refund twice the difference.

IMPROVED STORES

The research had shown that shoppers found it difficult to find products in existing stores and that they perceived the shops as sterile, grey and industrial in style. As a response to that, and also to forthcoming government curbs on superstore development, new, more flexible, store formats were introduced. The first were called "Compacts," slightly smaller than superstores and more suitable for market towns while "Metro" marked a return to the high street and served the sophisticated urban shopper. Finally, development of the "Express" format saw the Tesco brand enter the petrol station/convenience store sector. Existing stores were also improved and many stores were upgraded and extended with the customer in mind. The next three years saw the introduction of many new product ranges: meat counters, pharmacies, textiles, hot chicken counters, delicatessens and fresh fish counters, all of which were very popular and well received by staff and customers alike.

CUSTOMER SERVICE

Research had also shown that service was an important component of the shopping experience. In 1993 Tesco began a series of Customer Panels in which they recruited shoppers for half-day sessions with local managers and head office staff, to ask them exactly what they wanted from their shopping trip and encourage them to suggest improvements. Issues and tasks which arose from the panels were then allocated to either corporate or local personnel, whichever was more appropriate.

In order to manage the changes, Customer Service strategy was then broken down into three areas: Facilities, Standards, and Culture. Facilities were upgraded with the launch of the "New Look" initiative in 1993, which introduced tangible innovations to improve the shopping experience. For example, hand towels were placed in the meat aisle for wiping hands that were sticky after handling meat packs; barriers were removed at the entrance to the store as a result of customer requests, despite their obvious security advantages. More checkouts and customer service desks were installed and all signage was changed to blue and white and made much easier to read. The aim was that customers would reach any point in the shopping trip and think that Tesco understood shopping from *their* viewpoint. Overall, there was a range of over 100 different improvements: for example, meat counter towels, fish display units, specialized trolleys, from which a regional director and local store manager would choose, costing from £20,000 to £500,000, to achieve the "New Look" for each individual store.

The next element of service was about standards, i.e. setting, measuring and managing them in each store. Queuing was known to be one of the things customers disliked most about shopping. However, further research showed that if there was only one person in front of them and they were busy unloading the trolley, they didn't consider that they were queueing. In response, autumn 1994 saw the introduction of "One in Front" in which £15 million was spent in ensuring that Tesco could pledge to immediately open more tills if there was more than one person in front of a customer at any time. Launched with a major advertising campaign, it was regarded by management as one of the most successful initiatives to date.

Culture was considered as the most difficult and intangible element of the service strategy. In 1992 Tesco had begun to address this issue with the launch of "First Class Service." It was a radical change and very different from the centralized "command and control" style that previously operated. Each member of the 130,000 staff was given responsibility to look after customers in the way they thought best and managers were then encouraged to recognize staff achievements and to treat them as individuals, so that they in turn treated customers as individuals too. After four years the scheme is considered by management as a remarkable success. Staff now perceive each and every customer as valuable and are aware that keeping them loyal to Tesco means that, over a lifetime, each individual has the potential to spend an average of £90,000 with the company. The initiative was developed further with the introduction of Customer Assistants in every store. Twenty million pounds was spent in hiring and developing staff to be responsible only for helping customers in each store, the idea behind this being that ultimately they would come to know them by name, seek them out and develop a one-to one relationship with them. The culture and climate created by these initiatives is seen as "pure alchemy" by the management, which they believe has allowed each individual store to develop stronger alliances with their own customers.

THE CLUBCARD LAUNCH

The Clubcard launch in 1995 was also an integral part of the move to a customer-centred strategy. Launched as a "Thank You Card," it allowed Tesco to develop one-to-one relationships on a corporate level. The cost of running the scheme is considerable. In addition to the 1% discount on sales it was estimated that start-up costs alone were £10 million, but the company was convinced that this was money well spent. During pre-launch trials at 14 stores, over 250,000 Clubcards were issued, representing an uptake at the sites involved of between 70 and 80%. During the trials, high spending customers were identified and given special treatment, including invitations to "meet the staff" cheese and wine evenings at their local stores. The customers seemed to appreciate the events and responded favorably to the Clubcard.

This success paved the way for the UK national launch. Membership of the scheme was open to all Tesco customers through any of its 519 stores. Cards were issued on application and were able to be used to accumulate points on every shopping trip. The customer presented the magnetic stripe card at the checkout, where it was swiped through existing credit card reading equipment. Details of the customer's purchases were recorded, with Clubcard points automatically awarded for every £5 spent in the store, over a minimum of £10 per visit. Points are added up quarterly and (provided that the customer has accumulated a minimum of 50 points) money off vouchers are posted directly to customers' homes to be redeemed

against future spending. In addition to the vouchers, customers also receive money-off promotional vouchers for specific branded goods.

The costs of the mailings were high. By October 1996 these were estimated to be £11 million alone, but Tesco was seeking a return from this investment. The card was an important tool for gathering individual customer data: what they purchase, how much they spend, when and how often they shop, with the information revealing a great deal about the lifestyles of the shoppers themselves. It allowed Tesco to segment its customer base according to real purchase behavior, rather than a version of purchase behavior based on demographic or socio-economic stereotypes. The intention was to use the data to build loyalty through tailored, value-based offers, mailed to the homes of specific groups of customers. Early indications were encouraging, with 300 people turning up one morning at a store for breakfast in response to a Clubcard offer.

By the end of March 1995, one month after the launch, over 5 million people had joined the Clubcard scheme and Tesco recorded a like-for-like increase in sales. Clubcard's impact on sales was confirmed by independent researcher AGB who announced that, according to their Retailer Share Track monitoring system, Tesco had surged ahead of Sainsbury (for the first time) to become Britain's leading retailer of packaged goods. Tesco now had 18.1% of the market, with a 2.1% increase in market share since Clubcard's launch. Household penetration had increased by almost 1%, meaning that an additional 200,000 households had come to shop at Tesco's stores. Over a third of the gains were reported to be at Sainsbury's expense. Tesco endeavored to play down reports of market share gains, saying it was the fact that it was pleasing its customers that really counted.

Reaction from competitors was mixed. Safeway increased the number of stores participating in its ABC scheme from 25 to 106, to fend off direct competition from Tesco at vulnerable sites. They also began to develop the ABC card data capture capabilities so, although points were redeemed in-store, they could still accumulate customer information. Sainsbury, although widening availability of the Saver card, initially resisted any further reaction. It still saw the Clubcard as a margin-slashing initiative and as having little effect on their own performance. Their results for the year ending May 1995 appeared to justify this stance: pre-tax profits were up by 10% to £808 million and yearly sales of £12 billion were the highest for any UK-based retailer. David Sainsbury, when asked about Clubcard, said that it had been launched at substantial cost, "We are still not convinced of the benefits to customers but we are not against cards *per se.* Indeed, our own scheme rewards customers at the point of sale, which is far less costly to operate than theirs."

EARLY DAYS FOR CLUBCARD

After the enormous success of the launch and as customers became used to using the card, Tesco began to realize the full implications of running a nationwide loyalty scheme. Communication was proving to be a two-way process; hundreds of letters and up to 30,000 calls being received every week from customers keen to find out more or comment on the Clubcard service. It became clear that refinements would be needed, many in direct response to customer requests. One of the first of these was the introduction of a second card to enable another family member in the same household to have their own card which proved to be more convenient for the two shoppers in the household. Another was to lower the minimum spend required for pensioners to £5 since many had complained that they were unlikely to achieve the £10 amount to qualify for points, as they were living alone and did not buy large volumes. It emerged from early Clubcard data that pensioners shopped very frequently but filled smaller baskets. This was also later applied to students through the introduction of a Student Clubcard with a lower spending threshold before which points were awarded.

The scheme also allowed Tesco to form alliances with other brands. One of the earliest was with Thompson Holidays who allowed points to be redeemed for holiday discounts and also B & Q where Clubcard holders could earn points by spending on any product within their stores and accumulate Clubcard points to be redeemed in Tesco stores.

However, one of the most successful refinements was the introduction of points for petrol purchases. At the time of its introduction many of the major petrol retailers were involved in competitive schemes to increase market share. Esso had recently introduced the "Price Watch" promotion promising the lowest prices, while Shell was developing the "Smart Card" scheme, in which they were recruiting a number of high profile organizations and brands to join forces behind their loyalty card scheme. At one point Sainsbury was rumored to be committed to joining the Smart Card retailers. For Tesco, the introduction of points for petrol, combined with a price pledge, resulted in a large increase in petrol sales for the group.

However, not everything was plain sailing. One of the earlier problems to emerge with Clubcard was in

the sheer amount of data that was being collected. As well as having one of the largest customer databases in the UK, this was also continually updated with purchase information, every time an individual customer used their card. Initially there were rumored to be problems with data overload as the system struggled to cope with the volume and complexity of the data being collected.

Another issue to tackle was exactly how to use the information collected. The database management was initially out-sourced. Meanwhile the consultants worked together with an in-house team, with the intention of Tesco developing its own expertise over time. A timely reminder of how difficult it was going to be was evident in the first mailing of money back coupons to over 5 million Clubcard holders in May 1995. The first mailout, worth over £12 million in money back vouchers, also offered money-off promotional vouchers for specific goods. Initially these were for an own-label product, PG Tips tea and Coca-Cola. The response was enthusiastically received by members but many also wrote to say that they were mystified by receiving offers for Coca-Cola, one typical complainant remarking that he had never drunk the product in his life and, as he was 85 years old, was very unlikely to start now!

This aspect of the scheme also attracted criticism by the Direct Marketing Association, for giving all customers the same reward. Tesco admitted that in the first mailing there were only slight regional variations in the offers. One commentator said, "It makes no sense to spend the same amount on all customers and the more personalized and specialized the communication with customers, the better." This proved to be an early lesson for the database team and as a result the next mailing to pensioners was an offer for biscuits, which had a more successful 25% redemption.

SUCCESS OF CLUBCARD

Six months after the launch of Clubcard, the company was able to report concrete evidence of their success. Figures showed a 16% rise in half-yearly pre-tax profits to £290 million, together with a 2.1% increase in market share. More importantly, the group also reported an increase in like-for-like sales of 10%—its best for over five years. While stressing that the Clubcard is part of its long term customer service plan, Sir Ian McLaurin, Tesco chairman, attributed a large part of the company's success to the scheme, "We were determined to be the first and now Tesco Clubcard is *the* loyalty card in retailing. There is no doubt that it has helped boost our profits." He commented that the card now had almost 7 million members who had received £25 million worth of vouchers so far, of which £24.5 million had been redeemed.

In contrast, Sainsbury's figures were now beginning to show the possible knock-on effect of Clubcard with like-for-like sales down by 2.2% over the same six months. David Sainsbury conceded that the Clubcard had eroded individual store sales by 0.6%, where a Sainsbury store was in direct competition with a nearby Tesco, which in his eyes "was not a very great one." David Simons, CEO of Somerfield (no. 5 in the industry) openly disputed this claim and calculated that it was much more likely that Tesco would be taking nearly 3% in sales from any nearby rival. Despite the insistence that the effect was of little consequence, Sainsbury widened trials of their Saver Card to 170 stores in June (although it still did not have the data capture facilities of Clubcard). Meanwhile the Marketing Director, Antony Rees, stressed that they would not be rushing into a national scheme, "Why come first and get it wrong? We would rather come second and get it right. We will continue to listen to our customers to see what they want and react to *them,* rather than our competitors."

However, they did extend the Homebase Spend and Save Card (which was one of the UK's first loyalty cards), to include all purchases at the recently acquired 214 Texas Homecare stores. The vouchers earned from expenditure on DIY (do it yourself) and gardening products in these stores could be redeemed in all of Sainsbury's UK outlets, including supermarkets. Analysts saw this as a sensible stop-gap measure to counter the impact of the Clubcard. Sainsbury did confirm that the company was looking at ideas for a loyalty card with better benefits than Tesco. David Sainsbury was quoted as saying that, "we want to find something which gives better value to the customer, which really rewards loyalty. I remain to be convinced that a card which gives just a 1% discount on all your purchases gives the customer much advantage." Another Sainsbury's spokesman said that the company's experience with Savercard had shown that interest had waned after six months, but Spend and Save was different because spending on DIY products and the margins involved meant higher discounts could be given and it was much easier for customers to accrue points. He added that Spend and Save would never become the standard loyalty card for the company's food stores.

Coinciding with the widening of the Homebase card scheme was the launch of the Sainsbury's "Customer First" campaign in June 1995, in which they pledged to offer a variety of customer services including extra packers, freephone customer hot-line, baby changing facilities, parent and child parking, and 10 different types of carts. A company spokesman said that this was a direct response to customers, "We talked to them and a demand for old-fashioned shopping came through loud and clear."

Safeway entered the arena a few months later by offering the ABC card nationally in the autumn of 1995. Many commentators saw the offer of one point for every pound spent as better value than the points system offered by Tesco. ABC cardholders could also claim money off particular products and take up special offers, such as a free car wash, dry cleaning or cinema tickets. One advantage which Safeway had over Tesco was that their points were redeemable at point of sale, so they had a greater opportunity for promotional contact with their customers than Tesco's quarterly mailouts, as well as the fact that mailing costs were not incurred. By the end of December 1995, Safeway was able to announce that they had successfully enlisted 3.5 million members to their ABC scheme (approximately half its customer base).

Other retailers were by now also rolling out their own loyalty schemes. For instance, Somerfield partnered with Argos in their Premier Points scheme and Budgen, a smaller retailer with a significant presence in the South of England, launched a VISA card. Their card gave back 5p in the pound to shoppers using it in their own stores and £10 for every £400 spent on the card elsewhere. Asda, while not launching a card of their own, insisted they would stick to price pledge initiatives, offering customers value for money. They also announced that they would meet Tesco head on by honoring any Clubcard voucher in their own stores, which caused Tesco to complain to the Advertising Standards Association. This was to little avail as the Association could only meet to review the case after Christmas and so Asda reaped the benefits of its offer during the busy pre-Christmas rush. Shortly after this time, Sainsbury quietly dropped their Saver card scheme, claiming it could not justify the £30 million cost to extend it on a nationwide basis.

In February 1996, one year after the launch of Clubcard, Tesco's market share stood at 19% (AGB Superpanel).[3] Although a part of this rise was due to the takeover of William Low supermarkets in Scotland, the card was credited with raising the average

---

[3] AGB Taylor Nelson Superpanel. Retailer Share Track—179 markets covering Packaged Groceries, Fresh Foods and Toiletries.

weekly spend to £75 and the average spend of each shopping trip from £23 to £26. Over the first year the cost of Tesco's "thank you" was estimated to be at £60 million and operating costs £8–10 million. However, it was against a background of customer-led initiatives that the full value of the Clubcard could be assessed. Tim Mason, Tesco's recently promoted Marketing Director, saw the real impact working at the local level, "I believe that the key to the future is going to be an individual response to individual customers. It is no good talking about which is the 'best shopping trip'; you have got to deliver the best shopping trip for each and every customer." He predicted that each of the 524 stores would become a marketing unit where staff would get to know their own customers individually and also confirmed that "Micro-Marketing will be at the forefront of our future strategy."

CLUBCARD MAGAZINE

By now, due to the database facilities that had been developed, segmentation of Clubcard members was also possible at the corporate level. In March 1996 the store announced the planned launch of the first Clubcard Magazine. Produced in five different versions to suit five different lifestyle bands (students, younger adults without children, younger people with families, older people with children and pensioners), each version of the magazine was tailored to suit its audience. Students would read features about overseas travel, parents would read about family issues and so on; offers in the magazine were also designed to be appropriate to each group. Each publication carried promotions, competitions and advertising from many suppliers as well as information on new product launches on branded and own-label goods. The magazine proved to be highly popular, with high redemption of money-off tokens which Tesco attributed to their value and relevance for each of their customers.

THE LAUNCH OF CLUBCARD PLUS

By late spring, it was clear that Tesco had achieved dominance in the UK food retailing industry. This was confirmed by the subsequent news that Sainsbury had reported a dramatic fall in pre-tax profits of around £100 million, its first fall in 22 years, from £802 million to £712 million. This profit shortfall was followed by an announcement that the company was set to launch a national loyalty card in June of that year. The turn-around was seen as an attempt to pacify furious shareholders and to redeem the tarnished company image. Industry analysts felt that the move merely reinforced the already-held notion in the City that Sainsbury's marketing strategy was lacking in ideas.

While not announcing a launch date (City rumors were predicting late summer), Kevin McCarten, the newly appointed marketing director, insisted that the "Reward Card" would be better value than Tesco's Clubcard and that they would "be looking at things that our competitors cannot copy; we don't want to do anything they can replicate." Brian Woolf, an international customer loyalty consultant, predicted that Sainsbury "would go for the jugular and leapfrog Tesco, not just catch them up." However, first impressions of the offer suggested that it was similar to the Tesco Clubcard. Customers were offered one point for every £1 spent above £5 and this could be redeemed for a voucher for £2.50, once they had accumulated 250 points. The card also enabled customers to collect Air Miles in a tie up with British Airways. Each voucher entitled a customer to 40 Air Miles which could also be exchanged for ferry tickets, holidays, or cinema tickets. This meant that an average family spending £60 a week could earn a free individual flight to Paris every year.

With devastating timing, Tesco announced that the launch of Clubcard Plus was to be June 17, 1996, causing Sainsbury to bring forward the launch date of the Reward card to the same week. Modeled on a scheme run by Carrefour in France, Clubcard Plus allowed shoppers to deposit money into an account by a monthly standing order, so when customers shopped at Tesco, the cost of groceries or petrol could be deducted from the account. However, the real value to customers was the 5% gross interest paid on the account (if in credit). This was up to twenty times the interest paid by some high street banks and building societies. The scheme also allowed for an overdraft facility which charged 9% APR (the cheapest agreed overdraft rate in the UK at the time of the launch) and a cash withdrawal facility was available through the ATMs of the National Westminster Bank, the retailer's partner in the scheme, as well as at Tesco checkouts. Clubcard points were accumulated in the same way as before, building up points based on the amount of money spent and converted into money-off coupons every three months.

Describing the arrangement as "own-label banking," Chairman Sir Ian McLaurin explained at the press conference that, "since we launched Clubcard last February we have been trying to find ways to make it more user friendly; many of our customers wanted to be able to pay with Clubcard. This system allows them to do so." A Nat West spokesman saw the deal as a "co-branding" opportunity and said it would quickly be followed by a number of similar deals. "We do what we are good at; they do what they are good at. What we do best is processing, administering accounts and credit management."

Some commentators saw this not only as an assault on other food retailers but on financial institutions as well. Gill South, writing in the *Daily Telegraph,* described the move as "the first time that customers are being offered accounts, overdrafts, and cash back at extremely competitive rates, by a company that they trust more than their bank." The move was reported to have sent tremors through the banking industry as well as other competitors in the grocery retailing sector. Conversely, some commentators failed to see how Tesco could afford to pay 5% on small accounts; they also predicted some cannibalization of accounts for National Westminster and were uneasy about the clash between what they saw as two intrinsically different cultures. Despite these reservations, the City reacted favorably and the Tesco share price edged ahead to 303p, up from its low in 1994 of 227p.

FROM BEANS TO BANKING

This time reaction from competitors was swift. In October 1996 Sainsbury announced that they were to launch a bank in partnership with the Bank of Scotland. Going further than the Clubcard Plus debit scheme, the move would make Sainsbury the first UK retailer to offer comprehensive banking services. Sainsbury's Bank, scheduled to open in the first quarter of 1997, would offer customers fully-fledged checking accounts via a telephone banking service, combined with in-store, multi-functional teller machines. The service would not be tied in any way to Sainsbury stores, by restricting the offer to loyalty card holders, but customers would be able to use a Sainsbury Classic or Gold Visa card in the same way as any other Visa card. One analyst saw this as an extension of Sainsbury's own-label strategy, "Bank of Scotland will manufacture the product, but it will be packaged with the Sainsbury Bank label." The joint venture, of which Sainsbury will own 55%, was seen to make sense for the Bank of Scotland as it has weak market presence in England and Wales.

As a result of this move, Dino Adriano, the new Deputy CEO of Sainsbury, signalled that the arrangement for the big four banks' ATMs, currently sited at Sainsbury stores, would be likely to be reconsidered when the contracts, usually lasting three to five years,

came up for renewal. Any move to scrap the ATMs, in favor of Sainsbury's Bank machines would be likely to be fiercely opposed by the banks. Nat West commented that they were likely to be a target because of its relationship with Tesco, "Sainsbury's will probably get rid of us which will leave us with fewer supermarket ATMs."

In the same week Sainsbury also announced an increase in the number of points that it would award Reward Card holders. The scheme, based on bulk purchases of around 200 selected products, meant that a customer purchasing three 200g jars of Nescafé could earn 300 points which previously would have required a spend of £300. This meant that, with selective buying, a family spending £75 a week could earn enough points to get four free flights to Paris in one month. Costs were split between Sainsbury and their suppliers. At the launch, Kevin McCarten said that the scheme would make all other loyalty cards seem pointless and that they were rewarding their customers "better than any other retailer in the UK."

This activity was accompanied by the announcement that the retailer would also target one million "high value, promiscuous" Reward Card customers in Sainsbury's first, large-scale, direct marketing campaign. A catalogue offering extra Reward benefits would be sent to families spending £120 per week or more in order to tempt them to the store. It was hoped that this would act as a boost to the rather flat sales growth of 3%, which was just in line with inflation. McCarten predicted that observers "will see a much greater degree of targeting within our customer base and a lot more experimentation in order to target our specific customers." He denied however that Sainsbury was to follow Tesco's route, taken in the previous Christmas period, when it switched a large proportion of its annual £30 million advertising spend into direct marketing. However, these announcements did little to soften the blow of less than encouraging interim results released that same week, showing half year profits of £393 million, below the previous year's figure of £456 million and falling far short of City expectations.

Safeway was quick to follow in Sainsbury's wake, announcing that it would be joining forces with Abbey National to offer a range of financial services to its customers. The first product of the new partnership was to be a new ABC bonus card, a similar scheme to Tesco's debit account scheme, due to be launched in March or April 1997. However, it took the debit account scheme even further by allowing card holders to use the card to pay for goods at any of the 70,000 other retail outlets that accepted the Visa Electron scheme, whose participants included WH Smith, C & A and Our Price. The card would also allow cash withdrawal from more than 1,500 Abbey link machines and give customers a free 24-hour telephone banking service although, unlike Tesco, there would be no overdraft facility.

Colin Smith, CEO of Safeway, described the card as a logical extension of Safeway's customer proposition "aimed at making shopping easier." He hinted that in the future they would hope to offer a full range of financial services, through a planned Abbey National presence in Safeway stores. Meanwhile, Ambrose McGinn, Abbey's Marketing Director, recognized mutual benefits, "There's a large degree of customer overlap; we can use behavioral data from each database to make timely and relevant offers to our customers." Safeway shares subsequently climbed to a new high for the year.

Other food retailers appeared to maintain a respectful distance from these developments. As yet Asda had only tested different types of loyalty schemes, one being a "Style card" which gave vouchers for its range of clothing and leisure goods. It had also linked up as a redemption member of the British Gas Goldfish credit card in which holders of the card could earn discounts for gas bills and also spend Goldfish points in Asda and other redemption member outlets. Asda's chairman, and his new CEO Alan Leighton preferred to stress that "simplicity is divinity," in contrast to their competitors' forays into financial services. However, rumors of discussions between Asda, Kwik Save, and Somerfield with various banking and insurance companies were common. A survey by ICL Financial Services Group gave credence to the notion that supermarkets had a strong position from which to enter this market. They found that 32% of people would be happy to buy financial services from a supermarket and that more people were likely to have a loyalty card than a credit card.

The high level of financial services activity in this sector continued. Sainsbury announced the introduction of insurance services through Homebase stores in a partnership with insurance brokers Willis Coroon. Speculation then focused on Sainsbury's rumored plans to enter the mortgage market. Many saw a natural synergy between the Homebase brand and a mortgage lending operation, although warning bells were sounded by some that mortgage lending is very different to selling groceries or even running current accounts. "Retailers have no experience of the segmentation and management of customers; they are not used to turning them away."

However, focus was to shift quickly from partnerships to performance as Sainsbury was forced to issue a dramatic profits warning, causing shares to fall sharply to 341p, their lowest for five years. The company said that profits for 1996/97 would be around £640–650 million, well below City expectations of £715 million. One large institutional shareholder said the warning was particularly surprising as it came only a month after Sainsbury's management had visited investors with an upbeat message. Others were less kind. Frank Davidson, an analyst at James Capel, was quoted as saying, "This is not the bottom. I see nothing here to say that this business has turned the corner."

A spokesman for Sainsbury blamed the fall on high costs associated with building sales through its loyalty card scheme as well as conversion costs to change Texas stores to the Homebase brand. The warning came with an announcement that sales in the eight week run up to Christmas were up by 4.4% but this offered little solace as Tesco's were said to be 7.5%. The Reward Card was said to be contributing a 2% uplift to sales which, in the words of the spokesman, "were at the bottom end of their pre-launch expectations and barely enough to cover the card's cost." Analysts believed that Tesco's performance not only eclipsed but was at the expense of Sainsbury. When asked to comment, the Sainsbury press office would only say that they "do not comment on competitors."

The problems encountered by Sainsbury were likely to influence other organizations within the sector. Asda, who since 1995 had tested various loyalty schemes and had been involved most recently in rumors of a banking partnership with the Royal Bank of Scotland, had still to decide on its strategy. Having differentiated itself as the "value-for-money store" with a low price proposition, it was considered unlikely that the management would lead the chain into banking unless it could offer a cut price account for customers and some predicted this could lead to a price war with the four high street banks. An Asda insider said that banking had long been shelved and that it was looking at a loyalty card close to the Clubcard Plus scheme. Commentators were divided about their wait-and-see stance, some believing that Asda had waited to learn from the mistakes of its rivals, others believing that it was too late in entering the market, while others pointed to the latest research commissioned by *Checkout* magazine which questioned any justification of loyalty schemes at all. In a survey of 990 adults, two-thirds professed to have a loyalty card but a further two-thirds expressed a strong preference for lower prices rather than card schemes. One of the research team pointed out that "you have high levels of holding and using, especially among the prime target of heavy grocery spenders, but it appears cards are not influencing people's behavior." Replying to its critics, an Asda source remarked that "you can pull out of a loyalty scheme and replace it with home delivery, catalogue schemes, and other devices but you can't pull out of a bank that easily. I think retailers will get out of financial services and loyalty cards in three years, by which time they will have the lists."

Tesco took the opportunity of its rivals' troubles and deliberations to call a press conference in late January 1997 to announce strong Christmas trading figures which showed like-for-like sales up by 7.5%. Total sales growth in the period was even greater at 13.1%. Only two years after analysts had so readily marked down Tesco shares after the launch of Clubcard, they were having to eat their words. Exhibit 2 shows that all performance indicators had improved dramatically, charting a scenario previously unthought of. Tesco's share price was at its highest, market share had risen sharply, and operating profits were predicted to overtake Sainsbury in Spring 1997 for the first time in their history.

Tesco's success in satisfying customers had not gone unnoticed in other quarters: *Wine* magazine voted

EXHIBIT 2   Food Retailers: Turnover and Pre-Tax Profits 1992–1997

Year ending	1992	1993	1994	1995	1996	1997
	£ millions	£ millions	£ millions	£ millions	£ millions	£ millions
Tesco						
Turnover	7,097	7,581	8,600	10,101	12,094	13,887
Pre-tax Profits	545	558	435.5	551	675	750
J. Sainsbury						
Turnover	8,695	9,685	10,583	11,357	13,499	14,312
Pre-tax Profits	628	732.8	368.8	809.2	712.2	609
Safeway						
Turnover	4,729	5,196	5,608	5,815	6,069	6,589
Pre-tax Profits	364.5	417.3	361.8	175.6	429.4	420
Asda						
Turnover	4,529	4,614	4,882	5,285	6,042	6,952
Pre-tax Profits	−364.8	142.1	−125.9	257.2	311.5	405.2
Kwik-Save						
Turnover	2,391	2,651	2,800	2,992	3,254	3,010.5
Pre-tax Profits	74.3	126.1	135.6	125.5	2.8	73.7

Source: Reuters Business Briefing.

Food Retailers: Market Share 1993–1997

	1993	1994	1995	1996	1997
	% of Total Mkt	% of Total Mkt	% of Total Mkt	% of Total Mkt	% of Total Mkt
Tesco	14.9	15.7	18.1	19	20.5
Sainsbury[a]	17.3	17.9	17.5	17.4	17.8
Safeway[b]	8.6	8.5	8.4	9	9.4
Asda[c]	8.4	8.9	9.7	10.7	11.9
Kwik Save	5.8	5.6	5.5	5.5	4.6

[a] Sainsbury + Savacentre

[b] Safeway + Presto + other Argyll stores

[c] Asda + Dales

Source: Taylor Nelson AGB: Retailer ShareTrack.

(*Please note:* Market Share is assessed across 179 selected markets (Packaged Goods, Fresh Foods, and Toiletries) by Taylor Nelson AGB, which is recognized by the sector as the most comprehensive measurement. It is not related to Annual Turnover but represents each retailer's share of these specific markets. Annual turnover is made up of non-grocery goods, e.g. petrol, fashion clothing and in Sainsbury's case also includes Homebase sales and as a result market share cannot be easily judged by turnover.)

the store as "Wine Merchant of the Year", readers of *Woman* magazine voted Tesco as "Supermarket of the Year" and directors of Britain's 10 largest companies across 26 sectors had unanimously voted it as their "Most Admired Company". These accolades culminated in the award of "Retail Brand of the Year" by *Marketing Week.*

Speculation was now mounting as to the response they would take to Sainsbury's banking launch. The company was rumored to be planning enhancements to the Clubcard Plus scheme with the introduction of a credit card and allowing customers to pay from home computers. Estimates put membership of Clubcard Plus at the 150–180,000 mark, and Tesco was thought to want to boost this to the 500,000 level but research had shown that many customers would like more facilities on the scheme before they joined it. Nat West,

their partner in the Clubcard Plus scheme, was quoted as saying that working with Tesco to create a new bank "was not high on the priority list". However, at the press conference management preferred to focus attention on their recent performance.

The recently elevated peer, Lord McLaurin, said "the figures have revealed another excellent trading period, our sales have continued to outperform the industry average in what remains a highly competitive climate." He attributed the improved performance to the "Unbeatable Value" campaign of low prices and the growing popularity of Clubcard which now had 9.5 million members. Reaction in the City was enthusiastic, the figures were far better than analysts expected and, as a result, profit forecasts for the year ending 1996/97 were raised to £750 million and Tesco's share price rose to 369p.

CASE *14-3* DEL MONTE FOODS*

Anne Hart was a sales promotion manager for Del Monte Foods. Her job involved the design and coordination of all sales promotion activities for Del Monte's canned product lines. Anne reported directly to the Vice President of Marketing at corporate headquarters. In her role as a staff person, Hart worked closely with the brand managers, the advertising director, and the field sales force who sold her promotions to the retail trade. Although the brand managers had the final profit responsibility for individual items, Anne was expected to design promotions that paid their way. Hart created most of her own promotions for canned goods, but she did rely on outside vendors for some contests, self-liquidating premium offers, and in-store display materials.

In July 1991, Hart started work on her 1992 promotional program for canned fruit. To gain a perspective on previous promotional activities, she obtained some grocery store scanner data. The figures showed weekly Del Monte canned fruit sales for a blue-collar downtown store and an upscale suburban store. In addition to unit sales by store and by product, the figures

revealed the proportion of sales when an in-store display was used and the proportion of sales with a display plus an ad feature (Exhibits 1-3). Newspaper advertising for canned fruit varied by size, and the data indicated the proportion of dollar sales when three different-sized features (A, B, C) were used by the retailer. Anne also received data on the proportion of units sold on price reduction, the price paid per unit, and the regular shelf price. The average unit cost for the retailer varied from week to week, reflecting the impact of current and past trade deals (Exhibit 1). There was considerable retailer stockpiling and forward buying of trade deals, and these activities caused store costs to change weekly. Dollar sales and dollar gross profit figures shown in the exhibits were calculated using the unit sales and cost figures.

In addition to data on Del Monte products, Hart obtained some figures on Dole and private-label mixed-fruit promotions (Exhibits 4, 5). Anne was convinced that an analysis of the store-level data could help her prepare promotions for the 1992 season. She needed to decide which items to promote in which

---

* This case was prepared by Douglas J. Dalrymple and Rockney G. Walters of Indiana University.

EXHIBIT 1 **Sales and Promotion Data for Del Monte Canned Mixed Fruit, Blue-Collar Downtown Store**[a]

Week Ending	Unit Sales	Percent of Units w/Feat. & Disp	Percent of Units Sold w/Feature Size A (lg.)	B (med)	C (sm.)	Percent of Units w/ Price Redctn	Average Price per Unit ($)	Base Price ($)	Sales ($)	Gross Profit ($)	Average Unit Cost ($)
Apr 8, 1990	213	0.0	59.6	0.0	8.9	68.5	0.90	0.97	191	13.43	0.83
Apr 15, 1990	208	38.9	0.0	0.0	11.1	72.6	0.91	0.98	189	29.25	0.76
Apr 22, 1990	91	0.0	0.0	0.0	0.0	0.0	1.09	1.10	99	27.83	0.78
Apr 29, 1990	73	0.0	0.0	0.0	0.0	0.0	1.10	1.10	80	23.07	0.79
May 6, 1990	88	0.0	0.0	0.0	0.0	28.4	1.11	1.14	98	24.82	0.84
May 13, 1990	152	0.0	50.0	0.0	30.9	90.1	0.95	1.11	145	22.35	0.81
May 20, 1990	132	0.0	0.0	0.0	0.0	19.7	1.01	1.02	133	33.37	0.76
May 27, 1990	86	0.0	0.0	0.0	0.0	19.8	1.07	1.09	92	15.47	0.88
Jun 3, 1990	83	0.0	0.0	0.0	0.0	20.5	1.00	1.01	83	12.76	0.85
Jun 10, 1990	104	0.0	0.0	0.0	0.0	15.4	1.02	1.04	106	19.23	0.84
Jun 17, 1990	79	0.0	0.0	0.0	0.0	20.3	1.15	1.17	91	17.76	0.94
Jun 24, 1990	97	0.0	0.0	0.0	0.0	0.0	0.96	0.96	93	14.50	0.81
Jul 1, 1990	76	0.0	0.0	0.0	0.0	0.0	1.07	1.07	81	15.20	0.88
Jul 8, 1990	70	0.0	0.0	0.0	0.0	0.0	1.00	1.00	70	12.07	0.83
Jul 15, 1990	65	0.0	0.0	0.0	0.0	0.0	1.12	1.12	73	14.92	0.89
Jul 22, 1990	66	0.0	0.0	0.0	0.0	0.0	1.15	1.15	76	16.12	0.92
Jul 29, 1990	86	0.0	0.0	0.0	0.0	0.0	1.05	1.05	90	22.71	0.78
Aug 5, 1990	78	0.0	0.0	0.0	33.3	33.3	1.17	1.27	91	19.75	0.93
Aug 12, 1990	77	0.0	0.0	0.0	0.0	0.0	1.09	1.08	84	23.38	0.83
Aug 19, 1990	48	0.0	0.0	0.0	0.0	0.0	1.13	1.13	54	13.02	0.85
Aug 26, 1990	75	0.0	0.0	0.0	0.0	0.0	1.09	1.09	82	18.16	0.85
Sep 2, 1990	48	0.0	0.0	0.0	0.0	0.0	1.06	1.06	51	10.13	0.83
Sep 9, 1990	79	0.0	0.0	0.0	0.0	0.0	1.00	1.00	79	14.97	0.80
Sep 16, 1990	181	64.1	0.0	0.0	23.8	87.8	0.88	1.02	159	13.62	0.80
Sep 23, 1990	85	0.0	0.0	0.0	0.0	0.0	1.07	1.07	91	22.13	0.81
Sep 30, 1990	39	0.0	0.0	0.0	0.0	0.0	1.18	1.18	46	9.97	0.90
Oct 7, 1990	79	0.0	0.0	0.0	0.0	0.0	1.16	1.16	92	21.79	0.89
Oct 14, 1990	54	0.0	0.0	0.0	0.0	0.0	1.28	1.28	69	15.51	0.95
Oct 21, 1990	53	0.0	0.0	0.0	0.0	0.0	1.09	1.09	58	12.73	0.85
Oct 28, 1990	57	0.0	0.0	0.0	0.0	0.0	1.16	1.16	66	13.57	0.90
Nov 4, 1990	73	0.0	0.0	0.0	0.0	0.0	1.23	1.23	90	22.75	0.92
Nov 11, 1990	99	0.0	0.0	0.0	0.0	0.0	1.11	1.11	110	25.24	0.85
Nov 18, 1990	76	0.0	0.0	0.0	0.0	0.0	1.08	1.08	82	14.97	0.87
Nov 25, 1990	71	0.0	0.0	0.0	0.0	0.0	1.15	1.15	82	16.00	0.94
Dec 2, 1990	54	0.0	9.3	0.0	0.0	0.0	1.24	1.24	67	13.50	0.99
Dec 9, 1990	88	0.0	0.0	0.0	0.0	0.0	1.19	1.19	105	19.22	0.96
Dec 16, 1990	68	0.0	0.0	0.0	0.0	0.0	1.03	1.03	70	11.37	0.85
Dec 23, 1990	80	0.0	0.0	0.0	0.0	0.0	1.06	1.06	85	16.84	0.84
Dec 30, 1990	54	0.0	0.0	0.0	0.0	0.0	1.13	1.13	61	13.36	0.90
Jan 6, 1991	59	0.0	0.0	0.0	0.0	0.0	1.19	1.19	70	16.37	0.88
Jan 13, 1991	144	0.0	58.3	13.2	0.0	71.5	0.94	1.07	136	23.92	0.78
Jan 20, 1991	95	0.0	0.0	0.0	0.0	0.0	1.16	1.17	110	31.03	0.83
Jan 27, 1991	77	0.0	0.0	0.0	0.0	0.0	1.05	1.05	81	18.76	0.80
Feb 3, 1991	78	0.0	0.0	0.0	0.0	0.0	1.00	1.00	78	15.43	0.79
Feb 10, 1991	78	0.0	0.0	0.0	0.0	0.0	1.10	1.10	86	20.16	0.84
Feb 17, 1991	60	0.0	0.0	0.0	0.0	0.0	1.03	1.03	62	15.25	0.78
Feb 24, 1991	49	0.0	0.0	0.0	0.0	0.0	1.04	1.04	51	11.94	0.80
Mar 3, 1991	66	0.0	0.0	0.0	0.0	0.0	1.06	1.06	70	15.02	0.80
Mar 10, 1991	78	0.0	0.0	0.0	0.0	0.0	1.10	1.10	86	21.38	0.83
Mar 17, 1991	156	69.2	11.5	6.4	0.0	87.2	0.99	1.09	154	24.39	0.84
Mar 24, 1991	73	0.0	0.0	0.0	0.0	0.0	1.10	1.09	80	22.08	0.79
Mar 31, 1991	87	0.0	0.0	0.0	0.0	0.0	1.09	1.09	95	24.34	0.80

[a] dmbluedat.sav

EXHIBIT 2   Sales and Promotion Data for Del Monte Canned Mixed Fruit, Upscale Suburban Store[a]

Week Ending	Unit Sales	Percent of Units w/Feat. & Disp	Percent of Units Sold w/Feature Size A (lg.)	B (med)	C (sm.)	Percent of Units w/ Price Redctn	Average Price per Unit ($)	Base Price ($)	Sales ($)	Gross Profit ($)	Average Unit Cost ($)
Apr 8, 1990	286	0.0	59.8	0.0	7.3	95.5	0.87	0.97	250	21.40	0.81
Apr 15, 1990	303	0.0	0.0	30.7	8.9	88.8	0.91	1.00	275	39.29	0.78
Apr 22, 1990	107	0.0	0.0	0.0	0.0	0.0	1.12	1.11	120	33.75	0.82
Apr 29, 1990	120	0.0	0.0	0.0	0.0	0.0	1.23	1.23	148	42.44	0.89
May 6, 1990	106	0.0	0.0	0.0	0.0	12.3	1.18	1.19	125	33.97	0.85
May 13, 1990	345	41.4	40.9	0.0	15.1	98.0	0.88	1.06	304	41.28	0.76
May 20, 1990	130	0.0	0.0	0.0	0.0	13.8	1.09	1.10	142	38.55	0.80
May 27, 1990	106	0.0	0.0	0.0	0.0	8.5	1.12	1.13	119	22.69	0.92
Jun 3, 1990	87	0.0	0.0	0.0	0.0	11.5	1.08	1.09	94	18.20	0.89
Jun 10, 1990	78	0.0	0.0	0.0	0.0	15.4	1.00	1.01	78	12.58	0.84
Jun 17, 1990	100	0.0	0.0	0.0	0.0	20.0	1.11	1.12	111	19.66	0.92
Jun 24, 1990	103	0.0	0.0	0.0	0.0	0.0	1.10	1.10	113	22.88	0.88
Jul 1, 1990	74	0.0	0.0	0.0	0.0	0.0	1.19	1.19	88	16.77	0.98
Jul 8, 1990	68	0.0	0.0	0.0	0.0	0.0	1.09	1.09	74	13.25	0.89
Jul 15, 1990	92	0.0	0.0	0.0	0.0	0.0	1.08	1.08	99	20.80	0.86
Jul 22, 1990	63	0.0	0.0	0.0	0.0	0.0	1.10	1.10	69	16.09	0.86
Jul 29, 1990	53	0.0	0.0	0.0	0.0	0.0	1.02	1.02	54	15.66	0.74
Aug 5, 1990	91	0.0	0.0	26.4	19.8	46.2	1.05	1.14	96	17.82	0.86
Aug 12, 1990	69	0.0	0.0	0.0	0.0	0.0	1.26	1.25	87	23.00	0.93
Aug 19, 1990	65	0.0	0.0	0.0	0.0	0.0	1.35	1.35	88	24.97	0.97
Aug 26, 1990	97	0.0	0.0	0.0	0.0	0.0	1.29	1.29	125	33.16	0.95
Sep 2, 1990	61	0.0	0.0	0.0	0.0	0.0	1.18	1.18	72	18.70	0.87
Sep 9, 1990	70	0.0	0.0	0.0	0.0	0.0	1.34	1.34	94	24.92	0.99
Sep 16, 1990	183	48.6	0.0	0.0	42.6	91.3	0.99	1.15	181	20.35	0.87
Sep 23, 1990	112	0.0	0.0	0.0	0.0	0.0	1.21	1.21	136	34.51	0.92
Sep 30, 1990	66	0.0	0.0	0.0	0.0	0.0	1.21	1.21	80	21.50	0.90
Oct 7, 1990	83	0.0	0.0	0.0	0.0	0.0	1.36	1.36	113	29.91	1.00
Oct 14, 1990	83	0.0	0.0	0.0	0.0	0.0	1.23	1.23	102	27.94	0.89
Oct 21, 1990	76	0.0	0.0	0.0	0.0	0.0	1.26	1.26	96	26.28	0.92
Oct 28, 1990	102	0.0	0.0	0.0	0.0	0.0	1.14	1.14	116	30.08	0.84
Nov 4, 1990	81	0.0	0.0	0.0	0.0	0.0	1.21	1.21	98	23.94	0.91
Nov 11, 1990	99	0.0	0.0	0.0	0.0	0.0	1.32	1.32	131	35.90	0.97
Nov 18, 1990	71	0.0	0.0	0.0	0.0	0.0	1.24	1.24	88	19.70	0.95
Nov 25, 1990	97	0.0	0.0	0.0	0.0	0.0	1.06	1.06	103	19.49	0.86
Dec 2, 1990	112	0.0	5.4	0.0	0.0	0.0	1.10	1.10	123	26.59	0.87
Dec 9, 1990	79	0.0	0.0	0.0	0.0	0.0	1.24	1.24	98	21.57	0.97
Dec 16, 1990	87	0.0	0.0	0.0	0.0	0.0	1.20	1.20	104	20.71	0.95
Dec 23, 1990	94	0.0	0.0	0.0	0.0	0.0	1.14	1.14	107	25.65	0.88
Dec 30, 1990	61	0.0	0.0	0.0	0.0	0.0	1.00	1.00	61	12.66	0.78
Jan 6, 1991	122	0.0	0.0	0.0	0.0	0.0	1.11	1.11	136	34.93	0.82
Jan 13, 1991	265	0.0	69.4	14.7	0.0	84.2	0.94	1.10	249	41.74	0.78
Jan 20, 1991	144	0.0	0.0	0.0	0.0	0.0	1.22	1.21	175	48.15	0.88
Jan 27, 1991	119	0.0	0.0	0.0	0.0	0.0	1.22	1.22	145	38.41	0.90
Feb 3, 1991	97	0.0	0.0	0.0	0.0	0.0	1.39	1.39	135	39.17	0.99
Feb 10, 1991	120	0.0	0.0	0.0	0.0	0.0	1.20	1.20	144	40.34	0.88
Feb 17, 1991	113	0.0	0.0	0.0	0.0	0.0	1.19	1.19	135	35.81	0.87
Feb 24, 1991	88	0.0	0.0	0.0	0.0	0.0	1.19	1.19	105	28.22	0.86
Mar 3, 1991	97	0.0	0.0	0.0	0.0	0.0	1.31	1.31	127	36.26	0.95
Mar 10, 1991	96	0.0	0.0	0.0	0.0	0.0	1.19	1.19	114	31.47	0.86
Mar 17, 1991	161	0.0	57.8	20.5	0.0	78.3	1.04	1.17	168	31.47	0.85
Mar 24, 1991	108	0.0	0.0	0.0	0.0	0.0	1.17	1.17	126	31.99	0.85
Mar 31, 1991	108	0.0	0.0	0.0	0.0	0.0	1.11	1.11	120	34.66	0.80

[a] dmupdat.sav

EXHIBIT 3   Sales and Promotion Data for Del Monte Lite Mixed Fruit, Blue-Collar Downtown Store[a]

| Week Ending | Unit Sales | Percent of Units w/Feat. & Disp | Percent of Units Sold w/Feature Size | | | Percent of Units w/ Price Redctn | Average Price per Unit ($) | Base Price ($) | Sales ($) | Gross Profit ($) | Average Unit Cost ($) |
			A (lg.)	B (med)	C (sm.)						
Apr 8, 1990	71	0.0	100.0	0.0	0.0	100.0	0.79	0.87	56	0.62	0.78
Apr 15, 1990	45	0.0	0.0	100.0	0.0	100.0	0.80	0.88	36	5.40	0.68
Apr 22, 1990	17	0.0	0.0	0.0	0.0	0.0	0.88	0.88	15	3.44	0.68
Apr 29, 1990	14	0.0	0.0	0.0	0.0	0.0	0.86	0.86	12	2.48	0.68
May 6, 1990	26	0.0	0.0	0.0	0.0	0.0	0.88	0.88	23	5.32	0.68
May 13, 1990	44	0.0	100.0	0.0	0.0	100.0	0.80	0.86	35	5.08	0.68
May 20, 1990	34	0.0	0.0	0.0	0.0	0.0	0.88	0.86	30	6.88	0.68
May 27, 1990	25	0.0	0.0	0.0	0.0	0.0	0.88	0.88	22	2.50	0.78
Jun 3, 1990	13	0.0	0.0	0.0	0.0	0.0	0.85	0.85	11	0.86	0.78
Jun 10, 1990	18	0.0	0.0	0.0	0.0	0.0	0.89	0.89	16	1.96	0.78
Jun 17, 1990	8	0.0	0.0	0.0	0.0	0.0	0.88	0.88	7	0.76	0.78
Jun 24, 1990	11	0.0	0.0	0.0	0.0	0.0	0.91	0.91	10	1.42	0.78
Jul 1, 1990	10	0.0	0.0	0.0	0.0	0.0	0.90	0.90	9	1.20	0.78
Jul 8, 1990	21	0.0	0.0	0.0	0.0	0.0	0.86	0.86	18	1.62	0.78
Jul 15, 1990	21	0.0	0.0	0.0	0.0	0.0	0.86	0.86	18	2.88	0.72
Jul 22, 1990	15	0.0	0.0	0.0	0.0	0.0	0.87	0.87	13	2.20	0.72
Jul 29, 1990	8	0.0	0.0	0.0	0.0	0.0	0.88	0.88	7	1.48	0.69
Aug 5, 1990	59	100.0	0.0	0.0	0.0	100.0	0.80	0.92	47	5.70	0.70
Aug 12, 1990	13	0.0	0.0	0.0	0.0	0.0	0.85	0.85	11	1.90	0.70
Aug 19, 1990	8	0.0	0.0	0.0	0.0	0.0	0.88	0.88	7	1.32	0.71
Aug 26, 1990	15	0.0	0.0	0.0	0.0	0.0	0.87	0.87	13	2.35	0.71
Sep 2, 1990	7	0.0	0.0	0.0	0.0	0.0	0.86	0.86	6	1.03	0.71
Sep 9, 1990	20	0.0	0.0	0.0	0.0	0.0	0.85	0.85	17	2.60	0.72
Sep 16, 1990	27	0.0	0.0	100.0	0.0	100.0	0.74	0.86	20	0.56	0.72
Sep 23, 1990	15	0.0	0.0	0.0	0.0	0.0	0.87	0.86	13	2.20	0.72
Sep 30, 1990	10	0.0	0.0	0.0	0.0	0.0	0.90	0.90	9	1.80	0.72
Oct 7, 1990	10	0.0	0.0	0.0	0.0	0.0	0.90	0.90	9	1.80	0.72
Oct 14, 1990	11	0.0	0.0	0.0	0.0	0.0	0.91	0.91	10	2.08	0.72
Oct 21, 1990	4	0.0	0.0	0.0	0.0	0.0	0.75	0.75	3	0.12	0.72
Oct 28, 1990	12	0.0	0.0	0.0	0.0	0.0	0.83	0.83	10	1.36	0.72
Nov 4, 1990	15	0.0	0.0	0.0	0.0	0.0	0.87	0.87	13	2.20	0.72
Nov 11, 1990	17	0.0	0.0	0.0	0.0	0.0	0.88	0.88	15	2.76	0.72
Nov 18, 1990	15	0.0	0.0	0.0	0.0	0.0	0.87	0.87	13	2.20	0.72
Nov 25, 1990	4	0.0	0.0	0.0	0.0	0.0	0.75	0.75	3	0.12	0.72
Dec 2, 1990	10	0.0	0.0	0.0	0.0	0.0	0.90	0.90	9	1.50	0.75
Dec 9, 1990	11	0.0	0.0	0.0	0.0	0.0	0.91	0.91	10	1.75	0.75
Dec 23, 1990	7	0.0	0.0	0.0	0.0	0.0	0.86	0.86	6	1.45	0.65
Dec 30, 1990	11	0.0	0.0	0.0	0.0	0.0	0.91	0.91	10	2.85	0.65
Jan 6, 1991	15	0.0	0.0	0.0	0.0	0.0	0.87	0.87	13	3.25	0.65
Jan 13, 1991	98	0.0	100.0	0.0	0.0	100.0	0.69	0.92	68	4.30	0.65
Jan 20, 1991	14	0.0	0.0	0.0	0.0	0.0	0.86	0.85	12	2.90	0.65
Jan 27, 1991	18	0.0	0.0	0.0	0.0	0.0	0.89	0.89	16	4.30	0.65
Feb 3, 1991	21	0.0	0.0	0.0	0.0	0.0	0.86	0.86	18	4.35	0.65
Feb 10, 1991	11	0.0	0.0	0.0	0.0	0.0	0.91	0.91	10	2.85	0.65
Feb 17, 1991	18	0.0	0.0	0.0	0.0	0.0	0.89	0.89	16	4.30	0.65
Feb 24, 1991	12	0.0	0.0	0.0	0.0	0.0	0.83	0.83	10	2.20	0.65
Mar 3, 1991	12	0.0	0.0	0.0	0.0	0.0	0.83	0.83	10	1.48	0.71
Mar 10, 1991	22	0.0	0.0	0.0	0.0	0.0	0.86	0.86	19	3.38	0.71
Mar 17, 1991	69	100.0	0.0	0.0	0.0	100.0	0.80	0.88	55	6.01	0.71
Mar 24, 1991	13	0.0	0.0	0.0	0.0	0.0	0.85	0.85	11	1.77	0.71
Mar 31, 1991	13	0.0	0.0	0.0	0.0	0.0	0.85	0.85	11	1.77	0.71

[a] dmliteblue.sav

EXHIBIT 4　　**Sales and Promotion Data for Dole Mixed Fruit, Upscale Suburban Store[a]**

Week Ending	Unit Sales	Percent of Units w/Feat. & Disp	Percent of Units Sold w/Feature Size A (lg.)	B (med)	C (sm.)	Percent of Units w/ Price Redctn	Average Price per Unit ($)	Base Price ($)	Sales ($)	Gross Profit ($)	Average Unit Cost ($)
Apr 8, 1990	23	0.0	0.0	0.0	0.0	0.0	0.91	0.91	21	7.33	0.70
Apr 15, 1990	125	0.0	92.8	0.0	0.0	0.0	0.90	0.90	112	25.66	0.69
Apr 22, 1990	56	0.0	0.0	0.0	0.0	0.0	0.89	0.90	50	12.27	0.69
Apr 29, 1990	61	0.0	0.0	0.0	0.0	0.0	0.90	0.90	55	12.80	0.69
May 6, 1990	41	0.0	0.0	0.0	0.0	0.0	0.90	0.90	37	11.47	0.64
May 13, 1990	30	0.0	0.0	0.0	0.0	0.0	0.90	0.90	27	8.40	0.64
May 20, 1990	46	0.0	0.0	0.0	0.0	0.0	0.91	0.91	42	11.11	0.64
May 27, 1990	46	0.0	0.0	0.0	0.0	0.0	0.91	0.91	42	11.97	0.64
Jun 3, 1990	20	0.0	0.0	0.0	0.0	0.0	0.90	0.90	18	4.16	0.69
Jun 10, 1990	41	0.0	0.0	78.0	0.0	0.0	0.90	0.91	37	8.62	0.69
Jun 17, 1990	23	0.0	0.0	91.3	0.0	0.0	0.91	0.91	21	5.11	0.69
Jun 24, 1990	28	0.0	0.0	0.0	0.0	0.0	0.89	0.89	25	6.61	0.69
Jul 1, 1990	20	0.0	0.0	0.0	0.0	0.0	0.90	0.90	18	4.12	0.69
Jul 8, 1990	12	0.0	0.0	0.0	0.0	0.0	0.92	0.92	11	2.64	0.70
Jul 15, 1990	23	0.0	0.0	0.0	0.0	0.0	0.91	0.91	21	5.87	0.64
Jul 22, 1990	24	0.0	0.0	0.0	0.0	0.0	0.92	0.92	22	6.00	0.66
Jul 29, 1990	113	0.0	91.2	0.0	0.0	91.2	0.81	0.92	91	19.21	0.63
Aug 5, 1990	21	0.0	0.0	0.0	0.0	0.0	0.90	0.89	19	5.47	0.64
Aug 12, 1990	23	0.0	0.0	0.0	0.0	0.0	0.91	0.91	21	6.21	0.64
Aug 19, 1990	17	0.0	0.0	0.0	0.0	0.0	0.88	0.88	15	4.11	0.64
Aug 26, 1990	11	0.0	0.0	0.0	0.0	0.0	0.91	0.91	10	2.95	0.65
Sep 2, 1990	29	0.0	0.0	0.0	0.0	0.0	0.90	0.90	26	8.25	0.64
Sep 9, 1990	11	0.0	0.0	0.0	0.0	0.0	0.91	0.91	10	2.95	0.65
Sep 16, 1990	11	0.0	0.0	0.0	0.0	0.0	0.91	0.91	10	2.79	0.64
Sep 23, 1990	21	0.0	0.0	0.0	0.0	0.0	0.90	0.90	19	5.28	0.64
Sep 30, 1990	15	0.0	0.0	0.0	0.0	0.0	0.93	0.93	14	4.20	0.64
Oct 7, 1990	21	0.0	0.0	0.0	0.0	0.0	0.90	0.90	19	6.07	0.63
Oct 14, 1990	20	0.0	0.0	0.0	0.0	0.0	0.90	0.90	18	5.46	0.66
Oct 21, 1990	20	0.0	0.0	0.0	0.0	0.0	0.90	0.90	18	5.40	0.67
Oct 28, 1990	11	0.0	0.0	0.0	0.0	0.0	0.91	0.91	10	2.61	0.66
Nov 4, 1990	14	0.0	0.0	0.0	0.0	0.0	0.93	0.93	13	4.06	0.64
Nov 11, 1990	33	0.0	0.0	0.0	0.0	0.0	0.91	0.91	30	9.12	0.63
Nov 18, 1990	34	0.0	0.0	0.0	100.0	50.0	0.88	0.90	30	8.07	0.64
Nov 25, 1990	17	0.0	0.0	0.0	0.0	64.7	0.88	0.91	15	3.96	0.65
Dec 2, 1990	29	0.0	0.0	0.0	0.0	0.0	0.90	0.90	26	8.49	0.64
Dec 9, 1990	15	0.0	0.0	0.0	0.0	0.0	0.93	0.93	14	4.37	0.63
Dec 16, 1990	22	0.0	0.0	0.0	0.0	0.0	0.91	0.91	20	4.94	0.65
Dec 23, 1990	55	83.6	0.0	0.0	0.0	0.0	0.89	0.86	49	14.45	0.65
Dec 30, 1990	25	0.0	0.0	0.0	0.0	0.0	0.92	0.94	23	6.75	0.65
Jan 6, 1991	87	0.0	0.0	0.0	0.0	86.2	0.54	0.95	47	11.69	0.58
Jan 13, 1991	79	0.0	0.0	0.0	0.0	87.3	0.53	0.94	42	10.17	0.50
Jan 20, 1991	48	0.0	0.0	0.0	0.0	68.7	0.60	0.91	29	7.34	0.56
Jan 27, 1991	16	0.0	0.0	0.0	0.0	0.0	0.88	0.88	14	3.92	0.59
Feb 3, 1991	19	0.0	0.0	0.0	0.0	0.0	0.89	0.89	17	5.03	0.63
Feb 10, 1991	14	0.0	92.8	0.0	0.0	0.0	0.86	0.86	12	3.18	0.61
Feb 17, 1991	15	0.0	0.0	0.0	0.0	0.0	0.87	0.87	13	3.55	0.63
Feb 24, 1991	13	0.0	0.0	0.0	0.0	0.0	0.92	0.92	12	3.81	0.63
Mar 3, 1991	33	0.0	0.0	0.0	0.0	0.0	0.88	0.88	29	8.21	0.63
Mar 10, 1991	8	0.0	0.0	0.0	0.0	0.0	0.88	0.88	7	1.96	0.63
Mar 17, 1991	22	0.0	0.0	0.0	0.0	100.0	0.77	0.86	17	3.14	0.63
Mar 24, 1991	167	100.0	0.0	0.0	0.0	100.0	0.79	0.86	132	26.79	0.63
Mar 31, 1991	27	0.0	0.0	0.0	0.0	0.0	0.89	0.86	24	6.99	0.63

[a] doleupdat.sav

EXHIBIT 5 Sales and Promotion Data for Private-Label Canned Mixed Fruit, Blue-Collar Downtown Store[a]

| Week Ending | Unit Sales | Percent of Units w/Feat. & Disp | Percent of Units Sold w/Feature Size | | | Percent of Units w/ Price Redctn | Average Price per Unit ($) | Base Price ($) | Sales ($) | Gross Profit ($) | Average Unit Cost ($) |
			A (lg.)	B (med)	C (sm.)						
Apr 8, 1990	111	0.0	0.0	0.0	0.0	0.0	0.88	0.88	98	0.00	0.00
Apr 15, 1990	105	0.0	0.0	0.0	0.0	0.0	0.90	0.90	95	0.00	0.00
Apr 22, 1990	90	0.0	0.0	0.0	0.0	0.0	0.90	0.90	81	0.00	0.00
Apr 29, 1990	112	0.0	0.0	0.0	0.0	0.0	0.96	0.96	107	0.00	0.00
May 6, 1990	105	0.0	0.0	0.0	0.0	0.0	0.90	0.90	94	0.00	0.00
May 13, 1990	78	0.0	0.0	0.0	0.0	0.0	0.91	0.91	71	0.00	0.00
May 20, 1990	84	0.0	0.0	0.0	0.0	0.0	0.82	0.82	69	0.00	0.00
May 27, 1990	86	0.0	0.0	0.0	0.0	0.0	0.92	0.92	79	0.00	0.00
Jun 3, 1990	89	0.0	0.0	0.0	0.0	0.0	0.89	0.89	79	0.00	0.00
Jun 10, 1990	103	0.0	0.0	0.0	0.0	0.0	0.94	0.94	97	0.00	0.00
Jun 17, 1990	88	0.0	0.0	0.0	0.0	0.0	0.91	0.91	80	0.00	0.00
Jun 24, 1990	92	0.0	0.0	0.0	0.0	0.0	0.87	0.87	80	0.00	0.00
Jul 1, 1990	82	0.0	0.0	0.0	0.0	0.0	0.90	0.90	74	0.00	0.00
Jul 8, 1990	97	0.0	0.0	0.0	0.0	0.0	0.96	0.96	93	0.00	0.00
Jul 15, 1990	100	0.0	0.0	0.0	0.0	0.0	0.86	0.86	86	0.00	0.00
Jul 22, 1990	219	66.7	0.0	0.0	0.0	66.7	0.76	0.85	166	0.00	0.00
Jul 29, 1990	81	0.0	0.0	0.0	0.0	0.0	0.85	0.85	69	0.00	0.00
Aug 5, 1990	85	0.0	0.0	0.0	0.0	0.0	0.88	0.88	75	0.00	0.00
Aug 12, 1990	74	0.0	0.0	0.0	0.0	0.0	0.91	0.91	67	0.00	0.00
Aug 19, 1990	83	0.0	0.0	0.0	0.0	0.0	0.89	0.89	74	0.00	0.00
Aug 26, 1990	61	0.0	0.0	0.0	0.0	0.0	0.85	0.85	52	0.00	0.00
Sep 2, 1990	60	0.0	0.0	0.0	0.0	0.0	0.87	0.87	52	0.00	0.00
Sep 9, 1990	88	0.0	0.0	0.0	0.0	0.0	0.90	0.90	79	0.00	0.00
Sep 16, 1990	66	0.0	0.0	0.0	0.0	0.0	0.92	0.92	61	0.00	0.00
Sep 23, 1990	67	0.0	0.0	0.0	0.0	0.0	0.87	0.87	58	0.00	0.00
Sep 30, 1990	72	0.0	0.0	0.0	0.0	0.0	0.83	0.83	60	0.00	0.00
Oct 7, 1990	91	0.0	0.0	44.0	0.0	44.0	0.90	0.97	82	0.00	0.00
Oct 14, 1990	90	0.0	0.0	0.0	0.0	38.9	0.89	0.96	80	0.00	0.00
Oct 21, 1990	63	0.0	0.0	0.0	0.0	0.0	0.94	0.94	59	0.00	0.00
Oct 28, 1990	96	0.0	0.0	0.0	0.0	0.0	0.94	0.94	90	0.00	0.00
Nov 4, 1990	93	0.0	0.0	0.0	0.0	0.0	0.86	0.86	80	0.00	0.00
Nov 11, 1990	112	0.0	0.0	0.0	0.0	0.0	0.95	0.95	106	0.00	0.00
Nov 18, 1990	185	57.8	0.0	0.0	0.0	57.8	0.81	0.86	149	0.00	0.00
Nov 25, 1990	157	49.7	0.0	0.0	0.0	49.7	0.83	0.88	130	0.00	0.00
Dec 2, 1990	85	0.0	0.0	0.0	0.0	0.0	0.89	0.90	76	0.00	0.00
Dec 9, 1990	94	0.0	0.0	0.0	0.0	0.0	0.90	0.90	85	0.00	0.00
Dec 16, 1990	85	0.0	0.0	0.0	0.0	0.0	0.87	0.87	74	0.00	0.00
Dec 23, 1990	164	61.0	0.0	0.0	0.0	61.0	0.80	0.86	131	0.00	0.00
Dec 30, 1990	105	0.0	0.0	0.0	0.0	0.0	0.90	0.91	95	0.00	0.00
Jan 6, 1991	77	0.0	0.0	0.0	0.0	0.0	0.88	0.88	68	0.00	0.00
Jan 13, 1991	93	0.0	0.0	0.0	0.0	0.0	0.90	0.90	84	0.00	0.00
Jan 20, 1991	86	0.0	0.0	0.0	0.0	0.0	0.87	0.87	75	0.00	0.00
Jan 27, 1991	95	0.0	0.0	0.0	0.0	0.0	0.87	0.87	83	0.00	0.00
Feb 3, 1991	108	0.0	0.0	0.0	0.0	0.0	0.85	0.85	92	0.00	0.00
Feb 10, 1991	93	0.0	0.0	0.0	0.0	0.0	0.87	0.87	81	0.00	0.00
Feb 17, 1991	88	0.0	0.0	0.0	0.0	0.0	0.90	0.90	79	0.00	0.00
Feb 24, 1991	79	0.0	0.0	0.0	0.0	0.0	0.86	0.86	68	0.00	0.00
Mar 3, 1991	78	0.0	0.0	0.0	0.0	0.0	0.87	0.87	68	0.00	0.00
Mar 10, 1991	101	0.0	0.0	0.0	0.0	0.0	0.86	0.86	87	0.00	0.00
Mar 17, 1991	88	0.0	0.0	0.0	0.0	0.0	0.86	0.86	76	0.00	0.00
Mar 24, 1991	65	0.0	0.0	0.0	0.0	0.0	0.82	0.82	53	0.00	0.00
Mar 31, 1991	165	60.6	0.0	0.0	0.0	60.6	0.77	0.84	127	0.00	0.00

[a] plbluedat.sav

markets and when the promotions should run during the year. In addition, she had to allocate her limited promotional funds across trade price deals, support for retail ad features, and retail display materials. However, just looking at the raw figures did not generate any obvious strategies. Hart decided that she would have to run some plots, correlations, and multiple regression equations to unlock the secrets of her canned fruit data. She suspected that an analysis of the data would reveal some cross-elasticities where changes in price and promotion for one item could have impacts on other brands. As a first step, Hart decided to use an optical scanner to load the numbers into her desktop computer. Then she could use some statistical programs to analyze the data. Anne knew that she had only until September 1991 to come up with her preliminary 1992 promotional plans for canned fruit.

INTERNATIONAL MARKETING

> Free trade, one of the greatest blessings which a government can confer on a people, is in almost every country unpopular.
>
> LORD MACAULAY

*N*o economies today prosper without international trade. Indeed, some of the strongest (Germany and China) regularly sell more abroad than they import. Even the United States exports 20 percent of its industrial production and sells two out of five acres of its farm produce abroad. Today one-third of U.S. corporate profits is derived from international trade, and this proportion is sure to increase in the future. When you travel, you notice signs for Coke, Pepsi, McDonald's hamburgers, Philips Electronics, Michelin tires, and Caterpillar tractors. These firms have learned how to operate in international markets.

Successful international trade is based on the *law of comparative advantage.* This principle states that countries are better off producing items where they have inherent advantages and buying from others products where they have handicaps. The United States has comparative advantages in the production of agricultural products and airplanes, which it exports, and is at a disadvantage with newsprint and oil, which it imports. Despite the tremendous benefits of trade for the U.S. economy, 58 percent of Americans agreed with the statement that trade is bad because cheap imports hurt wages and jobs.[1] Only people making more than $100,000 a year (56 percent) and college graduates (46 percent) felt that trade creates growth and jobs. Clearly more people need to know how international marketing benefits society.

Another factor supporting international marketing is opportunity. Today the United States represents less than 25 percent of the world market for goods and services. Almost all firms that have achieved national distribution in the United States must become international to continue to grow. For non-U.S. firms the potential outside the home country is even greater. Although the Japanese market is large, the potential market outside Japan is 85 percent of worldwide demand. Our discussion suggests that international markets present tremendous opportunities for growth. This chapter will analyze the special character of international trade and present some aggressive marketing strategies for operating in this arena. An example showing how Nissan made a series of crippling errors in its North American operations is described in Marketing in Action box 15-1.

APPLYING
. . . to
Consumer
Durable
Goods
Marketing

MARKETING IN ACTION *15-1*

Nissan Drops the Ball in the U.S.

Nissan was one of the first Japanese auto manufacturers to enter the U.S. market in the 1970s with sporty cars like the 240Z. In the early 1990s, they gained ground with the muscular Maxima sedan and in 1995 they sold over 800,000 cars in America. As the third largest seller of foreign cars in the U.S., Nissan was able to construct an assembly plant in Tennessee to build its small Sentra model, the intermediate Altima and small trucks. However, due to a series of blunders, Nissan's U.S. sales declined in 1996, 1997, and 1998 resulting in a loss of $513 million in 1997. Although America contributed 32 percent of Nissan's total sales revenue, the company lost track of the needs of its U.S. customers. Their first mistake was an attempt to make more profit on the imported Maxima by cutting product features and quality. They dropped the sophisticated rear suspension that made the sporty Maxima stick to the road and the American auto press was quick to point out this deficiency. Instead of manufacturing the Maxima in America to compete with Toyota's Camry and Honda's Accord, they chose to build the smaller and inferior Altima in Tennessee to compete in the important intermediate four door sedan market. Nissan was also slow to take advantage of the growing importance of trucks in the U.S. market. In 1998, Nissan's U.S. manufactured truck sales declined an amazing 30 percent at the same time Chrysler increased truck sales 13.8 percent. Indeed, for the first time ever Americans bought more trucks in 1998 than they bought cars and Nissan was unable to participate in this bonanza. Part of the problem was that Nissan did not have a big pickup to compete with Ford and General Motors. They also failed to see the importance of offering the four door option in their small extended cab pickups as was done by their more successful competitors. Also Nissan was advertising its trucks with TV ads featuring a dog who drives its sleeping owner's recliner down a steep slope to a dealer showroom. The ads were a huge hit with everyone except Nissan dealers, who quickly discovered the brand image ads didn't sell cars or trucks. To counter declining sales, Nissan began offering large rebates and low monthly leases that assumed higher end of lease residual values than was the industry norm. As a result, Nissan ended up owning over 100,000 high-priced used cars that they chose to keep rather than accept large losses on their resale. Even Nissan's Infinity luxury cars were trumped by Toyota's Lexus division.

— *Firms that fail to keep up with consumer preferences in overseas markets can expect their market shares to wilt.*

Source: Robert L. Simison, "Nissan's Crisis Was Made in the U.S.A.," *The Wall Street Journal*, November 24, 1998, pp. B1, B4.

ENVIRONMENT OF INTERNATIONAL MARKETING

International trade provides attractive opportunities for sales increases, but it also carries a number of risks. Part of your job as marketing manager is to know how to balance revenue gains from trade against the possibility of financial losses. Some of the most serious problems include fluctuations in exchange rates, trade barriers, unstable governments, and piracy of trade secrets by outsiders. Perhaps the most difficult issue is what to do about governmental trade restrictions.

Trade Barriers

Economists all agree that trade among countries increases wealth. However, politicians have found that running positive trade surpluses with other countries while maintaining regulations that protect domestic industries from outside competition are popular with the people. Production workers, for example, view international trade as a threat to their jobs. They believe imports close factories rather than provide a source of low-cost merchandise. Thus, while trade clearly helps an economy as a whole, many people see only the negative impact on high-cost local producers.

APPLYING
. . . to
Agrimarketing

An example of the politics of trade barriers is shown by Japanese restrictions on the importation of rice, citrus fruits, and beef. Japan runs a huge trade surplus with the United States and could easily afford to buy more American agricultural products. However, Japanese farmers are unusually strong politically and have long been favored with tight import rules. The result is that Japanese consumers pay exorbitant prices for rice, beef, and oranges, although their economy would be better off buying these items from abroad. Politically, it is easier to protect jobs in the short run than it is to maximize wealth.

Tariffs and Quotas   There are basically two types of restrictions that countries use to keep unwanted products out and protect domestically produced goods. The more common one is a tariff, or tax on imports. Tariffs are usually expressed as a percentage of the value of the good and are added on to get the selling price. Tariffs range in size from nuisance taxes of 2 percent to prohibitory values of 50 percent or more designed to stop the importation of certain items. For example, a few years ago, European Common Market slapped stiff tariffs on fresh chickens imported from the United States to protect their own expanding chicken business. The United States responded by slapping a 25 percent tariff on imported trucks, which at that time were primarily small Volkswagen pickup trucks coming from Germany. This high "chicken" tax continues to this day and effectively protects U.S. manufacturers from imported truck competition. The net result is that American manufacturers have been able to raise their prices on trucks to the point where they are much more profitable than automobiles, and margins run to $8,000 per vehicle. Although the 25 percent tariff has helped U.S. firms in the short run, foreign manufacturers have begun to build truck factories in the U.S. to avoid the tariff. Toyota, for example, built a plant in Indiana in 1998 to produce large pickup trucks with V8 engines to compete directly with similar trucks from Ford, General Motors, and DaimlerChrysler. Given the huge profits American firms are making on trucks, the current tariff on imported trucks cannot be justified on economic grounds. American consumers would be better off without the tariff, since they would have more makes of trucks to choose from and would pay much lower prices for pickup trucks.

APPLYING
. . . to
Agrimarketing,
Consumer
Durable
Goods
Marketing

A second type of import restriction is the quota. This is an absolute limit on the number of certain items that can be imported. Italy, for instance, had an annual quota of only a few thousand Japanese cars for a number of years. Although the low quota helped to protect Italian car manufacturers, there is some question about whether the Italian economy was better off as a result. Germany has no quotas on cars, and the Japanese have a significant share of that market. The Germans, in turn, have the largest share of imported-car sales in Japan. We argue that the absence of German and Japanese auto quotas leads to greater trade and wealth for these two countries.

Another class of trade restriction that can cause problems for export-minded firms is the nontariff barrier. This often takes the form of technical specifications or inspection procedures that make it difficult or impossible to move goods across borders. For example, at one time the French required all videocassette recorders (VCRs) coming into the country to pass a customs inspection at a small interior community. This forced the Koreans and the Japanese to route all shipments through this isolated town. In addition, not enough customs inspectors were assigned to this community to handle the work, so the number of VCRs admitted to France declined sharply.

APPLYING
. . . to
Agrimarketing

The United States has disagreed with European Union restrictions on banana imports by American firms. While the United States does not raise bananas in North America, Chiquita Brands International has extensive banana plantations in Latin America and claims to have lost 4,000 jobs and $1 billion in profit to the European banana rules. Europe's banana trade rules tend to favor imports from former colonies and have benefitted Europe's largest banana distributor, Fyffes of Dublin. The United States appealed to the World Trade Organization (WTO) about the discriminatory rules. The WTO ruled in favor of the United States but the European Union's modified rules still favored its former colonies. America countered by slapping 100 percent tariffs on a list of high-priced imported European items. This banana war is foolish and both parties would be better off settling this dispute with fewer restrictions on trade.[2]

Recent Trends   Despite the periodic imposition of tariffs, quotas, and nontariff barriers, there has been a gradual loosening of trade restrictions in the world economy in the past 60 years. The General Agreement on Tariffs and Trade (GATT) is one international agreement that has reduced the level of tariffs throughout the world on several occasions. The trend toward free trade is gathering momentum in the European Union (EU). Trade barriers among EU members have been eliminated, and nonmembers are scrambling to gain access to this huge market. However, EU protectionism is slow to die. While the Japanese automobile manufacturers were first kept out with tariffs and quotas, when they built factories in Europe they found they still faced restrictions on the number of cars they could sell. Also EU allows member countries to control pharmaceutical prices to manage their national drug budgets. To sell medicine in France, companies must sign secret agreements that stipulate prices and volume ceilings for each drug sold in the country and may include guarantees on employment levels at French factories and funding for state run research institutes.[3] These agreements stifle competition and make it difficult for outsiders to enter the French pharmaceutical market.

The North American Free Trade Agreement (NAFTA) between Canada, America, and Mexico has increased trade among the three countries and seems to be working fairly well. For example, automobiles and auto parts can move freely among the three countries to benefit all concerned. However, Mexican cattle and pork producers have not been happy with the dramatic increase in shipments of American beef and pork to their local markets. In 1998, the Mexican meat producers had a serious drought and claimed that U.S. producers were dumping beef and pork in Mexico at unfairly low prices.[4] A description of the effect of NAFTA on American producers of brussels sprouts is described in Marketing Strategies box 15-1.

When business firms encounter unfair trade restrictions, they can ask their governments to appeal to GATT to impose sanctions to stop the offending practices. In addition to sanctions such as countervailing tariffs and antidumping fines, governments threaten retaliatory

---

MARKETING STRATEGIES 15-1

Free Trade in Brussels Sprouts?

Before the North American Free Trade Agreement passed, 93 percent of the U.S. brussels sprouts were grown in foggy, oceanside fields in central California. With the passage of NAFTA, brussels sprouts are now being shipped in from Mexico. About 3,500 acres in California are devoted to producing the smelly mini-cabbages that are hated by children. The problem for U.S. growers is brussels sprouts are labor intensive and must be picked by hand. Where U.S. growers pay their workers $6 per hour, Mexican farmers pay theirs $6 day. This pay differential makes the future for U.S. growers look bleak. NAFTA has some protections against this type of economic damage, but it takes influence that the few U.S. brussels sprouts growers do not have. U.S. brussels sprouts production amounts to only $27 million a year and the average American eats only three a year. To help save their businesses, American growers are trying to persuade the Mexican growers to delay exporting until late January when the U.S. harvest slows. Of course, if the growers could get Americans to eat a few more brussels sprouts the market would let them survive. However, if Mexico continues to ship brussels sprouts in November and December, American growers will have to find something else to grow on their valuable oceanside fields.

— *The law of comparative advantage is quite willing to eat brussels sprouts.*

Source: Martha Mendoza, "Brussels Sprouts NAFTA'd," *The Denver Post*, November 25, 1998, p. 13A.

action. For example, not long ago, the EU said it would no longer accept U.S. beef that had traces of growth hormones. This would have drastically reduced the amount of U.S. beef shipped to Europe. The United States countered by saying it would impose tariffs on an equivalent amount of EU food shipped to the United States. Since neither side wanted trade to decline, there was a strong incentive to compromise on this issue.

Currency Exchange Problems

International marketing is complicated because each country or trading block has its own currency. Thus, when you sell products in Japan, you are likely to be paid in yen. Since the exchange rate between dollars and yen changes hourly, you may receive fewer dollars than you expected. The possibility of serious exchange losses is so high that some small firms avoid international trade altogether. More experienced companies have learned to hedge their financial positions in the futures markets to reduce currency exchange problems.

The impact of realignments among currencies can seriously damage a firm's sales and profits. To help control these problems, 11 European countries have formed a monetary union. The currencies of the 11 EMU nations are no longer quoted separately, but are valued only in terms of their fixed relationship to the new euro. In 2002, national currencies will be phased out and the euro will be the standard currency of Europe. The advantage to business is that they will no longer have to cover the costs of exchanging currencies. Firms outside the EMU will benefit as well since they will no longer have to hedge future exchange risks for 11 different currencies.[5] An example of the impact currency values can have on international marketers is described in Marketing Strategies box 15-2.

An even more serious problem occurs when you want to trade with a country whose currency is not readily convertible. This has been a problem in doing business with the Russians. The ruble has little value outside the country since the Russians have few products that outsiders want to buy. Thus companies that do business in Russia often have to work out complex barter arrangements to extract their profits. PepsiCo, for example, has converted rubles into Russian Stolichnaya vodka for the past 20 years and shipped the vodka to the United States, where it is sold for dollars. Recently, PepsiCo entered a joint venture with three Ukrainian companies to sell $1 billion worth of ships to foreign firms. Some of the proceeds will be reinvested in the shipbuilding venture, and some will be used to buy bottling equipment and to build five Pepsi bottling plants in the Ukraine. The rest will finance the opening of 100 PepsiCo-owned Pizza Hut restaurants in the republic. This example shows the complex financial deals that are needed to get around currency exchange problems and to help Pepsi protect its market share in the Ukraine from inroads by Coca-Cola.

One solution to the exchange problem is for the seller to accept payment only in dollars or other hard currency. However, some countries have limits on the amount of these currencies that are available to pay for imports. Thus, when you trade with countries with foreign exchange restrictions, you have to be imaginative in arranging for payment.

Unstable Governments

When the governments of trading partners change frequently, there is a greater risk of business losses. New governments often modify the rules that determine how business is conducted. The most extreme action is nationalization of the property of foreign firms. Other drastic actions that can cause trouble are restrictions on the transfer of currencies and revisions in tariffs or quotas. When you have to deal with unstable governments, there is a strong incentive to export rather than risk direct investment.

Historical examples of countries where nationalization of industry caused serious problems for foreign firms include Mexico with petroleum, England with transportation, and Italy with cars. In each of these cases, nationalization has led to monopolies for the govern-

MARKETING STRATEGIES *15-2*

Falling Peso Kills U.S. Venture

APPLYING
. . . *to*
Business-to-
Business
Marketing

INTEGRATING
. . . *with*
Finance

The U.S.'s biggest distributor of office supplies, Unisource Worldwide Inc., saw an opportunity in Mexico to modernize an industry dominated by small, inefficient family enterprises. Unisource bought up 20 Mexican distributors in 1995 and went to work. They quickly found that the warehouses of the companies they bought often had dirt floors, making it impossible to use forklifts. Also many of the existing accounts were too small to be serviced economically and the field salespeople had to be retrained on how to sell. Unisource stuck with their new venture for three years, but when the Mexican government devalued the peso in 1998 they decided to divest themselves of the Mexican unit and take a $70 million write-down against earnings. Mexico's declining currency hurt because Unisource made its investments in dollars and was earning in pesos. The company was also damaged by falling prices for paper, which accounted for two-thirds of their sales in Mexico.

— *Currency risk can make the difference between success and failure in overseas ventures.*

Source: Joel Millman, "Unisource's Exit From Mexico Is Cautionary Tale for U.S. Firms," *The Wall Street Journal*. October 23, 1998, p. A17.

Courtesy Unisource Worldwide, Inc.

ment firms and losses for foreign competition. Once governments own business firms, they routinely protect them with tariffs and quotas. Thus countries with a history of nationalization are not good environments for international investment. One way you can compete in these countries is to form joint ventures in which capital is raised locally and the outside firm provides technical and marketing expertise. While there are still risks with this arrangement, the chances for massive capital losses are reduced.

Cultural Factors

Successful international marketing demands that you pay close attention to the special needs and customs of your buyers. Overseas buyers often have different concepts of time, space, and etiquette. Thus, before you create a marketing plan for overseas business, you need to find out how these customers regard and use your products. The marketing of automobiles provides a number of examples of the impact of cultural differences.

APPLYING
. . . to
*Consumer
Durable
Goods
Marketing*

Selling Cars Internationally There are many large auto markets in the world where cars travel on the left side of the road (Japan, England, and Australia). This makes it important to have the steering wheel on the right side of the car. For many years American manufacturers ignored this factor and tried, without much success, to sell left-hand drive cars in these countries. American cars also sold poorly in Japan because U.S. automobile firms did not provide the folding side mirrors and the fit and finish demanded by Japanese buyers. On the other hand, when Toyota came to America, they sold only left-hand drive cars, they made their cars bigger, more powerful, and they added the cup holders and extra storage spaces needed by Americans for their long auto trips. Careful attention to cultural differences allowed the Japanese to grab a large piece of the U.S. market while the insensitive American firms have yet to figure out why they failed in the Japanese market.

American firms have also not done well shipping cars to Europe. Part of the problem is that American cars are too big for European roads, parking spaces, and garages. Also many American cars come equipped with automatic transmissions and air conditioning that either are not needed or do not appeal to European buyers. A further problem is that gasoline carries much lower taxes in America than it does in Europe, which means the engines in American cars tend to be larger and consume more fuel than European buyers can afford. In addition, American firms do not offer diesel engines preferred by many European buyers for their high mileage potential. Diesel engines seem underpowered, noisy, and dirty to Americans and are only used in trucks. The only success American firms have had in Europe is to design and build cars locally for the special needs of that market.

Other Social Considerations Some cultures are more protective of their citizens' privacy than in America and some European countries. Mall interviews to gather consumer data, for example, are totally unacceptable in Muslim countries. In some countries, women are not allowed to drive or to work in certain occupations. In many countries comparative advertising is taboo and sexual innuendo in ads is unacceptable. Other markets severely restrict the content and duration of television advertising. Some further examples showing the impact of cultural differences on marketing plans include the following:

- Japan's Mitsubishi Motors had to rename its Pajero model in Spanish-speaking countries because the term describes the process of masturbation.
- Germans prefer salad dressing in a tube.
- Kellogg's Pop Tart failed in Europe because many homes do not have toasters.
- PepsiCo's Mountain Dew soft drink is difficult to pronounce in Portuguese, and sales have been slow in these markets.
- Two-liter pop bottles failed in Spain because refrigerators were too small.
- Toyota Motors was forced to drop the number from its MR2 car in France because the combination sounds like a French swear-word.

APPLYING
. . . to
*Consumer
Services
Marketing*

Although these examples suggest that you should adapt products and brand names to fit local cultural norms, it is possible to go too far. Some imported products are successful *because* they are different, and drastic changes can destroy their appeal. For example, when Disney was designing a theme park for Japan, its local partners insisted that nothing be changed from what was available at Disney World in Florida. They cautioned that customers did not want an Americanized Japanese park; they wanted the "real" Disney creation. This means that you must study the needs of each country to determine what portions of the product and marketing program need to be changed and what should be left alone.

WHICH MARKETS TO ENTER

Selecting international markets for expansion resembles the process of segmentation. First, you want to be sure that there are enough people in the new market to make the project worthwhile. Also, it is important that your product or service have distinct competitive advantages. Finally, you need to consider the higher risks that accompany global marketing because of cultural differences and the possibility of government restrictions. For example, many international firms consider South Korea to be a difficult market to enter because of excessive government red tape and the problems in bringing additional capital into the country. However, disposable income there is rising rapidly, and South Korea is now the second largest consumer market in Asia after Japan. Also, the population is well educated, and the number of two-income families is rising. This makes convenience foods and higher-quality products that are popular in the West more attractive among South Koreans. Ralston Purina saw milk consumption rising—the consumption of breakfast cereal closely tracks milk consumption throughout the world—and jumped in. It built a $10 million plant to make Chex cereal, and sales are growing rapidly. Purina's success in South Korea was helped by the absence of strong local cereal manufacturers.

APPLYING
. . . to
Consumer
Packaged
Goods
Marketing

Another way to control risk is to enter markets that are nearby and that share a common cultural heritage. American businesspeople have followed this advice; Canada is our largest trading partner and an important area for investment. Not only do we share a language with English-speaking Canada, but most Canadians live near the border. This makes it easier to deliver merchandise and facilitates cross-border promotion by radio and television.

The ultimate test of international market viability involves a financial analysis to determine the potential return on investment. As a first step, you need a good measure of potential demand. Then you must estimate the costs of making your goods and services available in another country. If you are exporting, you must predict transportation costs, tariffs, and dealer margins. If you are locating production facilities in the new market, the costs of labor, raw materials, and taxes have to be considered. Sometimes the availability of raw materials is a serious problem in less developed economies. McDonald's, for example, learned a great deal about local conditions while developing its first fast-food restaurants in Russia. This market appears to be a tremendous opportunity for McDonald's. The population is large, and there is need for high-quality, quick-service restaurants. However, the limited supply of food in the grocery stores that ensures success of the restaurants also means that it is difficult to get the needed raw materials for its french.fries and burgers. Currency exchange problems limit the amount of food that can be imported, and McDonald's has had to work with local suppliers to bring them up to the required quality standards. This takes time, and it will be years before McDonald's has a significant market share in Russia.

APPLYING
. . . to
Restaurant
Marketing

The last step in your evaluation of export marketing is to calculate the profitability for each prospective country. These profits should be compared and adjusted for different levels of risk. Remember that a high profit is less attractive if there is a strong chance for property expropriation and restricted financial transfers. Obviously, the presence of a stable and friendly host government makes international marketing much more attractive.

MARKET ENTRY STRATEGIES

Once you have selected an international market for development, you have to decide on the best way to proceed. A variety of entry strategies can be employed to present your products to global customers. The main choices are exporting, licensing, joint ventures, and investing in your own facilities (Figure 15-1). These alternatives vary in commitment, risk, and profit potential. Note that these approaches are not mutually exclusive. Different entry strategies can be used at the same time in separate markets. Also, you may want to use more than one strategy to enter a single foreign country. A line of products might be licensed for local production and another line manufactured in a joint venture (country B, Figure 15-1). Each of these approaches will be discussed in the following pages.

The emphasis here is on expanding the market for a product from your home country to international markets. You could, of course, acquire brand names that already exist in global markets. To expand as a world marketer of fish products, H.J. Heinz (Star-Kist Seafood) established a beachhead in Europe with the acquisition of the Marie Elisabeth trademark from a Portuguese sardine packer. Also, Thomson, the French electronics giant, invaded the United States by snapping up the GE/RCA television brands.

Exporting

The most common way to enter international markets is through export (Figure 15-1). Extra production from the home market is simply shipped overseas using established distribution channels. This approach only requires transportation and payment of duties, so there is little financial risk. A slightly more expensive approach is to make modest adjustments in your product to adapt it to the special needs of overseas customers. These changes may include modification in the size of the product or package, a new name, local language instructions, and special colors.

INTEGRATING
. . . with
Production

Several levels of organizational arrangements can be employed to assist exporting activities. Often, the first step is to hire a special agent or trading company from your own country to help you contact international customers. These people are paid on commission and handle all the paperwork involved in overseas selling. The second step is to set up an export department in your own organization. This department is staffed with an export sales manager and clerks to handle the necessary documents. A third level of commitment involves hiring for-

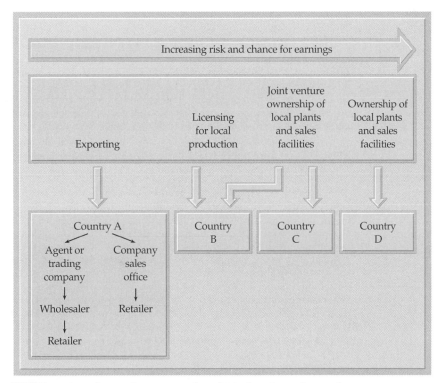

FIGURE 15-1 Alternative International Market Entry Strategies

eign-based dealers or agents. In exchange for exclusive rights to sell your products, these people provide invaluable access to local buyers. For example, in 1998 Honda announced plans to double the number of locally owned car dealers in eastern and southern Europe by the year 2000. Honda wanted to expand its dealer network ahead of the introduction of the common European currency, the euro.[6] The highest level of export investment involves setting up your own international-based sales branch. Although this requires higher fixed costs for salespeople, facilities, and inventory, it gives you more control over the global marketing effort. Your choice of export arrangements depends on the size of the opportunity and the amount of money you have to risk on this venture. A summary of key considerations in developing an international dimension to your business is given in Table 15-1.

APPLYING
... *to*
Consumer
Durable
Goods
Marketing

An example of how to make money exporting bicycles is provided by Cannondale, a U.S. manufacturer of high-priced racing and mountain bikes. Cannondale sells more than 30 percent of its $77 million bike volume in Europe and other countries. Its initial distribution channel in Japan was through Mitsubishi, a large trading company. Mitsubishi insisted that Cannondale add another layer of traditional bicycle wholesalers to sell to retailers (see Figure 15-1, country A). This raised costs, and since the wholesalers handled several manufacturers, they provided less attention to any one brand. Cannondale did not like the service it was receiving, so it terminated Mitsubishi and set up its own sales office in a small town outside Osaka. Next, it hired two Japanese-speaking American professional bicyclists who lived in Japan to promote its bikes. The two raced Cannondale bikes every weekend, gaining a lot of free publicity in the bicycle press. On weekdays they make sales calls on bike dealers. Working directly with the dealers has revealed that Japanese prefer smaller bikes in flashier colors—feedback the company never got from Mitsubishi. In the first year of the new program, Cannondale tripled the number of dealers carrying its bikes and sales quadrupled to $2 million. Despite the startup costs of opening its own sales office, Cannondale Japan earned $60,000 in profits in its first year of operation.[7] These results show that exporting can be profitable.

TABLE 15-1   Marketing Do's and Don'ts for New Exporters

- **Do develop a marketing plan before you begin.** You must have clearly defined goals and objectives and know how to reach them. Don't take this crucial first step without competent advice.
- **Do secure top management commitment for the long haul.** It takes time and money to establish yourself in any new market, particularly one with which you are unfamiliar.
- **Do select overseas representatives with care.** Evaluate personally the people who will handle your account, their facilities and resources, and how they work.
- **Do establish a base for orderly growth.** Concentrate on one or two overseas markets and build them up before expanding worldwide.
- **Modify products to comply with rules and the local culture.** Local regulations and preferences cannot be ignored. Make necessary product modifications at the factory.
- **Do print sales, service and warranty data in the local language.** Be sure to *use an experienced translator.* Don't cut corners here—the results can be disastrous.
- **Do consider using an export management company.** If you don't want or can't afford an export department right now, consider appointing an export management company.
- **Don't neglect export business when domestic sales rise.** Letting exports slide when domestic sales boom discourages your overseas agents, turns off your customers, damaging your reputation abroad, and leaves you without recourse when domestic sales fall.
- **Don't treat export business like a stepchild.** If you regularly boost domestic sales through advertising, discount offers, sales incentive campaigns, and preferential credit and warranty protection, apply these same incentives to overseas markets.
- **Don't assume that the same marketing technique works everywhere.** Cultural preferences and taboos must be respected. Your overseas representative should be able to advise on effective local marketing.

Source: U.S. Department of Commerce

Licensing

INTEGRATING
... with
Finance,
Production

Once you get some experience with export marketing, you may want to license organizations in other countries to produce goods and services to expand market coverage. With this approach, a licensor signs contracts with licensees for the use of a manufacturing process, trademarks, or trade secrets for a fixed royalty percentage. These royalties typically run 2 to 4 percent of sales but sometimes amount to 10 percent or more. The licensor gains exposure in new markets without having to risk local investments. Because very little investment is required, the profits on licensing agreements can be extremely lucrative.

APPLYING
... to
Consumer
Beverages
Marketing

Licensees gain production or management knowledge of well-known products without having to spend money on R&D. In addition, licensees benefit from advertising and promotion expenditures by the parent organization designed to build worldwide demand. Coca-Cola and Pepsi both used licensing to expand their business internationally. With the reunification of East and West Germany, Coke moved quickly to license beverage organizations in eastern Germany to bottle and distribute Coca-Cola. Coke advanced $140 million to help its licensees upgrade bottling machinery and vending machines. As a result of such aggressive moves, international sales now account for 80 percent of the company's soft drink profits. Coke and Pepsi maintain control over their international licensees by supplying them with the concentrated syrup that provides the flavor for the soft drinks.

APPLYING
... to
Industrial
Marketing

Although licensing can be very profitable and can allow you to expand rapidly, it does carry some serious risks. You have very little control over a licensee's production and marketing efforts. For example, an American company signed a licensing agreement with an Asian firm to produce trademarked fasteners for its Australian customers. After teaching the licensee how to make quality fasteners, the U.S. company was surprised when the licensee began to ship its own private brand of fasteners into the Australian market. The American firm felt betrayed by these actions so they terminated the licensing agreement and bought a plant in China to serve the local market and Australia. Another example of the perils of licensing is described in Marketing in Action box 15-2.

In addition to reducing control over marketing activities, licensing exposes you to potential losses of trade secrets and production technology. To make licensing work, you have to show outsiders how production processes work. This means that you may be training competitors to enter your market when the licensing agreement ends. For example, Quicksilver Enterprises was unable to sell its ultralight airplanes in Brazil because of steep import duties, so the U.S. firm licensed a local firm to build and sell its planes in Brazil. However, six months after Quicksilver's engineers taught the concern how to build, fly, and fix the planes, the royalties stopped. The Brazilian company claimed that it had changed the design, and Quicksilver was out $100,000 in royalties and lost all sales in Brazil for several years.

Another problem is that royalties are paid on the basis of sales reported by your licensee, which means that it is to the licensee's advantage to understate volume to reduce the size of royalty payments. Obtaining an accurate audit of sales figures may be difficult in some countries, and signing up trustworthy business partners is critical to the success of a licensing program.

Joint Ventures

INTEGRATING
... with
Finance,
Production

The objective of joint ventures is to find local partners to share the risks and profits of international market expansion. This can be done by buying an interest in an existing local business or by starting up a new venture with a resident business. Teaming up with a local partner cuts the size of your investment and allows you to gain valuable assistance in regard to customers, labor availability, raw material services, and distribution channels. The outside partner often provides the technical and production expertise, and the inside partner provides marketing connections.

APPLYING
. . . to
Consumer
Food
Marketing

MARKETING IN ACTION *15-2*

The Perils of Licensing

A number of international firms have ended long-standing partnerships with Japanese companies. These associations provided outside firms with easy entry for their products, but they often led to problems. Borden ventured into Japan in 1971 with a licensing agreement with Meiji Milk, Japan's biggest dairy company. Initially the agreement worked well, as Borden got access to Meiji's vast distribution network and local production assured prompt delivery of fresh products. Together, Borden and Meiji created a large market for premium ice cream. Their Lady Borden brand secured 60 percent of an eventual $125 million market. However, liberalization of milk product import rules allowed the entry of Häagen-Dazs and Breyer's Grand Ice Cream from the United States. Lady Borden's market share slipped from 60 to 50 percent and Meiji was slow to respond to the competitive challenge.

Borden tried to renegotiate its agreement with Meiji to gain more control over the marketing of Lady Borden. Unfortunately, a change in management at Meiji delayed the implementation of new arrangements. Borden decided to break its ties with Meiji and set up their own sales subsidiary. Meiji agreed to continue to promote Lady Borden for 14 months until its licenses expired. Since Meiji had learned a great deal from Borden about ice cream manufacture, they decided to protect their position in the market by introducing two new premium brands of their own in the interim until the licensing agreement with Borden expired. One brand, Aya, stressed Meiji's Japanese roots. A second brand, called Breuges, is similar in price and content to Lady Borden. Borden did not believe it was fair for Meiji to introduce new brands while it was committed to promote Lady Borden and threatened to sue to stop their distribution. In addition, the loss of local production capacity meant that Borden had to import ice cream all the way from Australia and New Zealand. What appeared to be an attractive deal for Borden turned out to be a public relations and financial disaster.

— *Licensing works well for entering markets quickly but often creates problems in the long run.*

Source: Yumiko Ono, "Borden's Messy Split with Firm in Japan Points Up Perils of Partnerships There," *The Wall Street Journal*, January 28, 1991, p. B1.

Joint ventures are also attractive when the outside firm does not have the financial reserves to start a wholly owned operation or wishes to limit the financial risk of market expansion. Sometimes joint ventures are the price host governments exact when they allow access to their markets. Politicians often view joint ventures as a way to generate jobs, train workers, and reward local business interests.

The main problem with joint ventures is disagreement on how to manage the business. Outside firms often prefer to be majority stockholders in joint ventures so that they can control the operation to minimize the chance of losses. After all, outside partners usually provide the technology and production support for the project and have the most to lose if the project goes bad. Local partners may be more concerned with extracting current profits rather than with long-term success. The control issue is complicated further by rules in some countries that local people must own 50 percent or more of the stock of joint ventures. This has been the case in China until recently. Six Japanese firms negotiated a joint venture for a $4 billion petrochemical plant with two Chinese firms. The plant is located in Liaoning, China, has a refining capacity of 2 million metric tons, and produces 450,000 metric tons of ethylene a year. Ethylene is in short supply in China, and the project looks promising to the Japanese. To protect themselves, the Japanese firms have negotiated a 51 percent stake in the project.

Ownership of Facilities

You can obtain the most control over international marketing activities by constructing your own factories in host countries. Local manufacturing provides significant savings on transportation costs, and resident labor is often cheaper than home market workers. Also, host governments may provide lucrative financial incentives to attract outside manufacturers.

INTEGRATING
*. . . with
Finance,
Production
Management*

Ownership also gives you a better image with customers because you are creating jobs for residents. In addition, ownership of facilities allows you to learn more about local demand so that you can tailor your products, advertising, and distribution plans to host country needs. Sometimes the operation of factories in other countries is the only way to get around tariff barriers and alleviate political pressures against imported goods.

The main problem with local manufacturing is that you expose yourself to a higher risk of serious financial loss. Overseas facilities may be damaged by war, nationalized by governments, or hamstrung by inflation or local currency exchange problems. In addition, host governments may have stiff requirements on severance pay that make it expensive to close down overseas operations.

APPLYING
*. . . to
Consumer
Durable
Goods
Marketing*

Some of the factors influencing decisions on ownership of facilities are demonstrated by DaimlerChrysler's decision to build Dakota pickup trucks in Brazil. Until the year 2000, Brazil had a 49 percent tariff on imported vehicles. This very high tariff placed an effective limit on the number of vehicles that could be imported into Brazil and forced manufacturers to build local plants if they expected to share in the large Brazilian auto market. Chrysler was late getting to Brazil, a country where 13 auto companies announced plans to invest $19 billion in new factories by the year 2000. The DaimlerChrysler plant cost a modest $315 million and was designed to limit their financial risk in this emerging market. Chrysler arranged for Dana Corporation of Toledo, Ohio, to assemble a rolling chassis consisting of a frame, axles, brakes, and wheels at a nearby plant. The Dakota truck chassis are then rolled into the Chrysler plant where engines, transmissions, and body parts are added to complete the vehicles. Dana's locally produced chassis accounts for 33 percent of the value of the vehicle. Because Dana assembles the rolling chassis in Brazil, Chrysler can count the entire value of the unit as local, allowing Chrysler big discounts on import duties on body panels, engines, transmissions, equipment, and thousands of other cars it brings into Brazil from the United States. If Chrysler made the chassis at its own plant, it could credit only the parts it actually made in Brazil as local. The rolling chassis plan allowed Chrysler to hire fewer people, made its factory smaller, reduced its upfront investment, and shortened the start-up time.[8] Since Chrysler opened its Dakota truck plant, Brazil and Argentina have agreed that the Mercosur trading block will have a common import tariff of 35 percent and eliminate tariffs on trade of cars and parts between member countries. This means that Chrysler will have free access to sell Dakota pickup trucks in Brazil, Argentina, Paraguay, and Uruguay, a market of 200 million consumers.[9]

GLOBAL VERSUS LOCALIZED MARKETING

An ongoing controversy is whether firms should pursue a global or localized strategy in their international marketing activities. Global marketing emphasizes selling the same product with the same ads all over the world. This approach implies that the world is becoming homogenized and everyone wants the same things. One reason global marketing is so effective today is that global communications networks are opening access to more markets. CNN now reaches 78 million households in 100 countries, and MTV has an audience of 310 million in 78 countries. Localized marketing, on the other hand, implies that customers' needs are different in each country, and that you should adjust your product and your ads to meet local market conditions.

Both sides in this controversy have their advocates and a rationale. Global marketing can save money and increase profits. Colgate-Palmolive, for example, introduced its tartar-control toothpaste in more than 40 countries using only two ads. For every country that used the same ad, the firm saved $1 to $2 million in production costs alone. Colgate has saved millions more by standardizing the look and packaging of certain brands and reducing the number of factories that make them. Although global marketing has worked well for some companies and product categories, there seem to be an equal number of examples where it has failed. Marketing in Action box 15-3 describes such a situation in the German PC market.

MARKETING IN ACTION *15-3*

Compaq Dumps Global and Goes Local

APPLYING
. . . to Consumer Durable Goods Marketing

Compaq is a large and successful company with 8 percent of the world consumer market for personal computers. The company's chief executive is German and it was natural for Compaq to set up its European headquarters in the biggest country, Germany. However, despite the large numbers of technology savvy consumers with money to spend, Compaq was only able to get 1.2 percent of the large German market. Sixty percent of the German consumer PC market is owned by an army of 30,000 mom-and-pop computer assemblers. Although Germany is not known for bargains, personal computers are dirt cheap. The average price of a midrange PC is $1,272 in the U.S.; it is only $1,059 in Germany. Two-thirds of German PC buyers are willing to buy inexpensive no-name brands without features considered essential for U.S. computers. Normally, Compaq uses a global approach and designs computers to sell all over the world without considering differences in local manufacturing costs or market conditions. In Germany, Compaq pinpoints an appropriate German cost and design and tells local developers to design a PC to fit. To meet their price objectives, Compaq has dispensed with expensive custom software and Compaq keyboards and Compaq mouses. This allowed its local manufacturer to swap any component that it could find cheaper elsewhere. The resulting Compaq PCs for the German market do not have the usual internal modem and speakers. They are also taller and thinner to make them easier to ship and move around the factory. As a result of Compaq's decision to go local, its German market share jumped to seventh from 10th with 3.5 percent of the market.

INTEGRATING
. . . with Production/ Operations Management

— *Local PC manufacturing can cut costs and raise market share.*

Source: Matthew Rose, "Compaq Finds German Market Tough to Crack," *The Wall Street Journal*, November 20, 1998, pp. B1, B8.

Courtesy Compaq Computer

Problems with Global Marketing

APPLYING
. . . to
Consumer
Packaged
Goods
Marketing

Procter & Gamble took a sexy soap commercial that worked well in Europe and tried to use it in Japan. The Camay soap ad was based on the premise that women want to be attractive to men. In the ad a Japanese woman is seated in a bathtub when her husband walks into the bathroom. The woman starts telling him about her new beauty soap, but the husband, stroking her shoulder, hints that suds aren't on his mind. Japanese saw this ad as rude and intrusive, and it was withdrawn. P&G concedes that it would not have made the mistake if a Japanese woman had been running the campaign there. When a woman was put in charge, a successful ad showing a beautiful European woman, alone, in a European-style bath was created for the Japanese market.

Insufficient Research   Often the failure of global marketing programs is due to insufficient research on the intended target countries. Blockbuster, the number-one video rental store in the United States, looked to attractive overseas markets and found that Germany is the fourth largest video rental market in the world. Also, preliminary research revealed that the name Blockbuster had good brand recognition among young and middle-aged Germans. In 1995, Blockbuster opened 7 stores in Munich and 10 in Berlin. Although Blockbuster paid attention to the German market, the stores languished. Subsequent research showed the Germans preferred to watch movies in theaters. Also Blockbuster placed the stores in downtown areas, whereas all competitors were in residential areas. Perhaps Blockbuster's most serious error was that initial research failed to reveal that one-third of all video rentals in Germany are for pornographic films. Even though Blockbuster did not rent pornographic films, all video stores had a negative image in Germany and children were encouraged to stay away from them. After two years, Blockbuster closed all of its stores in Germany. Blockbuster conducted extensive market research on the Japanese market and its 38 stores there have been more successful.[10] Blockbuster was allowed to keep its Japanese stores open every day from 10 A.M. until midnight, whereas store hours in Germany were restricted and Blockbuster had to close on Sundays and holidays. These examples suggest that it is essential to conduct careful research before entering overseas markets.

APPLYING
. . . to
Consumer
Services
Marketing

Overstandardization   Sometimes global marketing programs are too rigid about product specifications and the use of standard promotional activities. Ford, for example, has tried on several occasions to develop "world" cars that could be sold in Europe and North America. The company failed in the 1980s to develop a "world" Escort and again in the 1990s with its Mondeo-Contour-Mystique family of midsize cars aimed at both continents. Anyone who has driven a car in Europe realizes how difficult it is to make a car small enough to negotiate the narrow streets of Europe yet big enough to compete on the wide avenues of America. Ford's Contour/Mystique twins did not sell well in the States because they cost almost as much as larger Toyota Camrys and Honda Accords, and their backseat area was very small. Ford has developed another world car about the size of an Escort that they think will do well in Europe and the United States. The Ford executive in charge of global small car development avoided regional jealousies by installing a Briton as chief program engineer, a German as chief technical officer, an Irish woman as project manager, and an Australian as chief designer. To make the car roomier for the U.S. market, the designer made the new Focus model three inches taller so occupants sit up straighter, allowing more legroom and making it easier to enter and exit the car. They also tightened the steering, improved the ride, the crash protection, and occupant comfort. Ford contracted the manufacture of 15 major subassemblies for the Focus to outside suppliers so they could cut the cost of making the new model by $1,000. Ford expects to sell one million of the Focus cars a year worldwide.[11]

APPLYING
. . . to
Consumer
Durable
Goods
Marketing

Another standardization problem occurred when Heinz tried to expand its 9 Lives cat food and Morris the Cat logo into Moscow. They found Russians thought Morris the Cat should be fatter-looking, which they deemed healthier. Also Russian cat lovers prefer to feed their cats beef-flavored food instead of the tuna favored by Americans.[12] These cases show that excessive standardization of global marketing programs can create problems.

Think Global but Act Local

The examples we have discussed suggest that global marketing often works and can save money. Perhaps the best approach is to think global but act local. This means that you should have global objectives but should not ignore local market conditions. While Colgate toothpaste is available worldwide, for example, the company also makes a spicy toothpaste especially for the Mideastern market and sells a baby soap named Cadum only in France. Similarly, PepsiCo allows offices in other countries to edit and dub its global ads and to plan their own promotional activities. The extent of decentralization of marketing planning is shown by surveys indicating that host country marketing managers make up to 86 percent of advertising decisions, 74 percent of pricing decisions, and 61 percent of channel decisions. However, product design decisions are usually reserved for the parent organization. Global marketing is alive, but the trend seems to be to adjust plans to meet the special needs of particular customers in other countries.

Strategies for Localized Marketing

A set of strategies for adapting to local conditions is shown in Figure 15-2. Strategy 1 is a global marketing approach that sells the same product in all countries with the same promotional appeals. This strategy has the advantage of low costs and seems to work best for business products such as airlines, computers, and machine tools. Strategy 2 sells the same product in different markets but changes the message for each set of customers. An example is the motor scooter that is sold as primary transportation in less developed countries and as a recreational vehicle in the United States. Strategy 3 focuses on adapting the product to meet local conditions but uses the same advertising message in all countries. Detergents and gasoline are routinely adjusted to meet water and weather conditions in each market area and are sold with standard promotional campaigns.

Strategy 4 in Figure 15-2 adapts both products and communications for each market entered. When Nestlé tried to break into the British instant coffee market, it found that coffee preferences were more American than European. This forced Nestlé to prepare a lighter blend of instant coffee for the British market. Because coffee is not as popular as tea in England, Nestlé had to use more aggressive advertising to attract the attention of potential customers. Strategy 5 is to invent something to meet the special needs of a local market. This is likely to be an expensive and risky approach to global marketing. For example, because of the lack of electricity in many underdeveloped countries, a South African firm invented a hand-powered radio. Users turn a crank that activates a spring powered generator inside the radio. Each time the spring is tightened it powers the radio for an hour of listening. This radio can be sold anywhere in the world where consumers lack access to electricity or expensive batteries for portable radios. Although the strategies shown in Figure 15-2 do not cover all possible market situations, they do provide a useful set of approaches for many localized marketing problems.

SUMMARY

Every day the world becomes smaller because of improvements in transportation and communications. One result is that international marketing is becoming more important to the success of business organizations. Part of your job as marketing manager is to under-

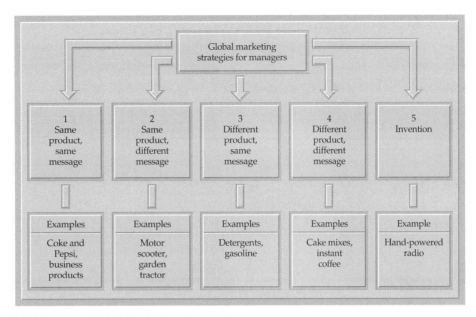

FIGURE 15-2 Global Marketing Strategies

stand the environment of international business and to select the best markets for overseas expansion. This involves calculating the expected rate of return on investment for each country and balancing it against the risk of loss. Next, you must decide on the most appropriate method for entering international markets. In some situations, exporting is the best approach; in others, you may want to use licensing, joint ventures, or direct investment.

A common problem with international marketing is deciding whether to adapt your products and advertising to the special needs of individual countries. Some organizations have been successful with a global approach where the same products and promotions are used throughout the world. Others have had more luck tailoring their products and advertising to the preferences of each market.

NOTES

1. Jackie Calmes, "Despite Buoyant Economic Times, Americans Don't Buy Free Trade," *The Wall Street Journal*, December 10, 1998, p. A10.
2. Robert S. Greenberger, "No Quick Solution Is Seen with EU in Banana Dispute," *The Wall Street Journal*, December 3, 1998, p. A14; James Cox, "The United States vs. The European Union: Two Sides of the Banana Split," *USA Today*, March 3, 1999, p. 3B.
3. Stephen D. Moore, "Hopes Dwindle that EU Will Dismantle Draconian Price Controls on Medicines," *The Wall Street Journal*, December 7, 1998, p. A26.
4. Joel Millman, "Mexican Meat Producers Take on U.S.," *The Wall Street Journal*, November 5, 1998, p. A17.
5. "Review & Outlook: Lessons from Europe," *The Wall Street Journal*, December 7, 1998, p. A30.
6. "Honda to Expand in Europe," *The Wall Street Journal*, November 6, 1998, p. A17.
7. Andrew Tanzer, "Just Get Out and Sell," *Forbes*, September 26, 1992, pp. 68–69.
8. Gregory L. White, "Chrysler Makes Manufacturing Inroads at Plant in Brazil," *The Wall Street Journal*, August 13, 1998, p. B4.
9. Peter Fritsch, "Argentina, Brazil Agree on Car Tariffs," *The Wall Street Journal*, December 11, 1998, p. A10.
10. Khanh T. L. Tran, "Blockbuster Does Boffo In Japan, A Positive Sign for U.S. Retailers," *The Wall Street Journal*, August 19, 1998, p. A14.

11. Robert L. Simison, "Ford Hopes Its New Focus Will Be a Global Bestseller," *The Wall Street Journal*, September 15, 1998, p. B10.
12. Erika Rasmusson, "Global Warning," *Sales & Marketing Management*, November 1998, p. 17.

SUGGESTED READING

Chryssochoidis, George M., and Veronica Wong. "Rolling Out New Products Across Country Markets: An Empirical Study of Causes of Delays," *Journal of Product Innovation Management,* Vol. 15 (1998), pp. 16–41.
Maruca, Regina F. "The Right Way to Go Global," *Harvard Business Review* (March–April 1994), pp. 134–145.

REFERENCES

Cateora, Philip R., and John L. Graham. *International Marketing,* 10th ed. (Homewood, IL: Irwin, 1998).
Czinkota, Michael R., and Ilkna A. Ronkainen. *International Marketing,* 5th ed. (Chicago: Dryden, 1998).
Jain, Subhash C. *International Marketing Management,* 5th ed. (Cincinnati, Ohio: South Western, 1995).

QUESTIONS

1. Dell Computer announced plans in 1998 to invest $125 million over five years to build a plant in the Brazil state of Rio Grande do Sul. International companies with local production plants dominate Latin America's personal computer market. Dell ranked ninth in 1998 with 1.2 percent of the Latin America market. Rio Grande do Sul offered Dell generous tax and financial incentives plus 140 acres of land to build its plant. Why does Dell want to make computers in Brazil rather than export them from Texas?

2. In 1998, overall imported car sales in Japan declined 26 percent while the sales of the Rover Mini rose 17 percent. The squat, boxy Mini has barely changed since the first one was produced in England in 1959. Half the Minis made in the United Kingdom are shipped to Japan despite the Mini's selling price being twice that of equivalent Japanese produced cars. The Mini is popular because it is cute, agile, different, and it looks like the car driven by the hapless Mr. Bean, a popular television character in Japan. Rover's success with the Mini in Japan is also due to their careful attention to special campaigns and fervent fans who have built up an industry that includes Mini shops, Mini races, Mini clubs, and a magazine called *Mini Freak.* Is the Mini triumph in Japan an example of global marketing or is it due to localized marketing?

3. The EU has imposed antidumping duties on 15 Japanese makers of computer printers for selling at prices below those charged in their domestic market. The growing European printer market is estimated to be $1.75 billion a year, and Japan's share has grown from 49 percent to 73 percent in three years. Is the EU really concerned with the evils of dumping, or does it have some other agenda? Are European buyers better off paying the higher prices that the new duties will require? How are the Japanese likely to respond to the new duties?

4. When the Japanese economy was in a recession in 1998, Anheuser-Busch had success selling a cheap, potent low-malt brew by emphasizing its "extra strong" alcohol content. Japanese regulations allow the sale of beverages with a dry weight content of only 25 percent of expensive malt, whereas beer must have 66.7 percent malt. Although the U.S. Bureau of Alcohol, Tobacco and Firearms prohibits brewers from using messages that hype strength on labels or ads, Japan does not have these restrictions. Is it ethical to use alcohol content to sell low malt beverages in Japan when it is illegal to use these tactics in the United States and the higher alcohol content could be detrimental to the health of Japanese consumers?

5. The Chinese have agreed to lower barriers to U.S. exports ranging from cigarettes to refrigerators. The agreement averted a trade war in which the United States threatened to impose 100 percent tariffs on $3.9 billion worth of Chinese imports. Products covered by the agreement include chemicals, computers, integrated circuits, medical equipment, autos and auto parts, telecommunications equipment, fruits, grain, and edible oil products. Why was it to the advantage of China to lower its barriers to American imports?

6. When 3M enters international markets, it typically begins by exporting products from the United States and selling them through company-owned overseas subsidiaries. As volume increases, 3M ships semifinished goods, such as huge rolls of tape, and uses local workers to cut and package the material. The next step is to move into local manufacturing. Why does 3M use this approach instead of licensing or joint ventures?

7. Canada and the United States have the world's largest bilateral trading relationship, valued at $173.4 billion. All tariff barriers between the two countries have been eliminated. Canada has a population of only 26 million compared to 271 million in the United States. Some people have speculated that certain small Canadian businesses will suffer because of the trade agreement. As a marketing person, explain how the new pact will actually help some small Canadian companies.

8. DaimlerChrysler is a manufacturer and a world leader in commercial trucks. Rather than export trucks from Germany, the company has 42 factories spread across five continents. Why has a global strategy of shipping parts among its plants helped it succeed?

CASE 15-1   GPS[1] ONE-HOUR SERVICE (C)*

As 1997 was unfolding, the GPS management team had to take a high risk, difficult decision. Would Grand Optical—the successful optics division of Groupe Photo Service (GPS)—go international? Or would trying to export a concept that was so well suited to the French market be asking for trouble?

Daniel Abittan and Michael Likierman, co-Presidents and founders of GPS, felt confident that the Grand Optical concept was strong enough to venture across the French borders into new territory. But they were not so sure which market they should enter first. Nor were they sure about the strategy to follow and the speed with which to go. Grand Optical had grown successful by adhering emphatically to its concept of customer focus, large open stores, one-hour service, quality, convenience, maximum choice,

and highly professional staff. Would the transfer of Grand Optical skills to employees in another country be possible?

International competitors had already started expansion outside their home countries and it was likely that they would advance into France as well. Additionally, in some countries, one-hour service already existed. Daniel Abittan:

> We can see the limits of our development in France. By the year 2000, Grand Optical should have covered its natural territory in France. We must be ready for the new stage. Additionally, we must preempt others from conquering markets we would like to be in.

Although there was a sense of urgency, Likierman and Abittan were not going to jump in unprepared. In

---

* This case was prepared by Research Associate Els van Weering under the supervision of Professor Jacques Horovitz of IMD. The research for this case was done by IMD MBA students Pierluigi DiTuri, Jim Hinds, Giles Houghton-Clarke, Jean-Francois LaBorde, Allan Li, and Richard White. Copyright (c) 1997 by IMD—International Institute for Management Development, Lausanne, Switzerland. Reproduced by permission.

[1] On December 22, 1997 GPS changed their name to GrandVision. "…Why GrandVision? Grand: like the world that is the future horizon of our development. Vision: only visionary enterprises do well in the long term. And also, the word belongs to our two professions, photo and optical. GrandVision: a name easily pronounced in French and English. It will be quickly adopted by all…" (GrandVision 1997 Annual Report).

1996, they had commissioned a group of IMD MBA students to research the opportunities for Grand Optical in seven countries around the globe.[2] The group had come up with descriptions of attractive markets as well as signals for caution. The management team was now ready to make decisions.

---

[2] *Sources: Retail Trade Monitor, Euromonitor, EIU, Retail Trade International,* $^{20}/_{20}$ *Europe,* $^{20}/_{20}$ *Vision Asia, Eurostat, World Bank, Company Annual reports, Yearbook of Statistics, World Competitiveness Yearbook, Press, Stock Market reports, European Optical Society, AC Nielsen Market Research, European Directory of Shopping Centers, National Associations of Opticians, OECD Economic surveys, Price Waterhouse, Healey & Baker, Internet pages, Interviews, Site visits.*

GRAND OPTICAL AND PHOTO SERVICE IN FRANCE

By 1997—16 years after GPS was born—the company had evolved from a being a pioneer in minilaboratory film development service to holding various companies in the amateur photo and optical industry (refer to Exhibits 1A and 1B). GPS had over 430 stores in France, sales (exc. VAT) of FF 2692 million and 3327 employees. All of the companies in the Group shared a drive to satisfy their clients' needs and exceed their expectations, which resulted in exceptional customer loyalty (refer to Exhibit 2). Another core competence of GPS was its ability to create and develop original retail concepts. Many of these concepts originated from constant benchmarking of new and successful concepts, both in France and abroad. GPS continually conducted both quantitative and qualitative research

EXHIBIT 1A   Representation of the GPS Group

GPS companies are divided over the optical and the photo market (horizontal) and serve customers on the service and on the price axis (vertical).

Number of stores and employees are quoted as of 12/31/96. Sales are annualized for stores open as of 12/31/1996. (The total figure for the optics market includes 16 Solaris stores. The total figure for the Photo market includes 12 Photo Points stores. The total headcount for GPS includes 25 employees at the head office.)

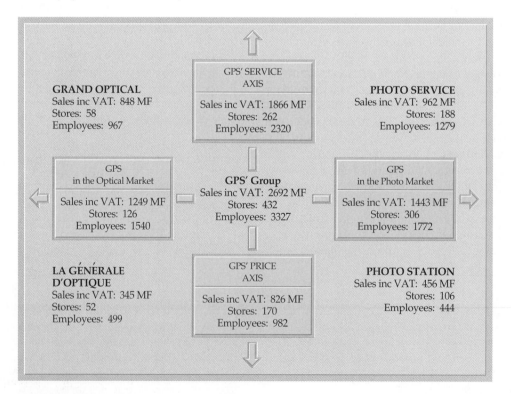

EXHIBIT 1B   GPS Consolidated Profit & Loss 1992–1996

FF Million

Year to December	1992	1993	1994	1995	1996
Net Sales Revenue	763	868	1040	1615	2012
% Growth		13.9	19.7	55.3	24.5
Gross Profit	500.9	586.6	742.3	1,210.4	1,493.0
% Gross Margin	64.9	66.8	70.3	73.9	72.2
Current Pre-tax Profit	56.4	75.4	95.7	124.8	229.6
Employee Profit Share	3.1	4.7	8.5	11.8	18.8
Net Profit After Tax	29.7	38.0	56.3	35.1	117.9
Net Profit as a % of Sales	3.8	4.3	5.3	2.1	5.8

Source: Company Report and Goldman Sachs estimates.

into customers' changing motivations, so that they could understand and respond to new client needs.

GPS in the Photo Market

GPS's first innovation was its one-hour photo film development service in shopping malls. Photo Service started in 1980 with the first development mini laboratory in France. In 1996, the company had 188 stores. It was a built with strong emphasis on one-hour service, quality and convenience. In 1995, "Photo Station" was acquired. Photo Station had 106 stores and was positioned as a budget photo developer. Photo Station offered its clients photo developing services in less than 48 hours. The different designs of the two stores emphasized the difference in positioning.

EXHIBIT 2   The Spirit of GPS

The sharing of core values by all employees is at the heart of GPS and is the means of binding the Group together. Each new employee joining the Group receives a presentation of these values supported by examples of their application, so that everyone is aware of their rights and their responsibilities.

Our Core Values	The Rights of Our Employees	The Responsibilities of Our Employees	The Rights of Our Clients
Growing People • understanding why • clarity • empowering • sharing **Performing as a Team** • professional • alert • innovating • growing **Serving** • the client first • quality • reactive • ethical	• The right to do everything necessary to satisfy a client • The right to take initiative and test ideas • The right to constructive criticism • The right to make mistakes • The right to understand • The right to be trained • The right to be clearly informed • The right to be recognized for one's achievements • The right to develop at one's own pace within the company • The right to be helped	• The responsibility to do everything possible to satisfy each client • The responsibility to contribute to the performance of one's team • The responsibility to be a trainer and a mentor • The responsibility to communicate • The responsibility to set an example • The responsibility to be honest and loyal • The responsibility to respect one's obligations and those of the company • The responsibility to answer for one's actions • The responsibility to have ideas • The responsibility to constantly improve	We aim for the total satisfaction of our customers and recognize their rights: • The right to be loved • The right to be recognized • The right to services and products adapted to their real needs • The right to freedom to choose • The right to reliable products and services • The right to understand • The right to be treated as someone of good faith at all times • The right to have their interests defended • The right to make a mistake • The right to be … amazed!

EXHIBIT 3   Quick Look at the Optical Industry

The players in the optical industry included the manufacturers of frames, glasses, and lenses, the central labs that put frames and lenses together according to a specific prescription for a customer and, of course, the different retail outlets where consumers bought glasses and contact lenses. It was a market of change in which the retail side, in particular, was going from a fragmented market with local players only, to a more organized market in which chain stores were gaining market share over independent opticians. These chain stores had begun expansion beyond their own borders, so the optical market was slowly becoming European or even global. The speed of these developments differed by country. Influential factors were legislation, consumer buying patterns in general and the development rate of shopping centers.

Manufacturing Frames

Eye wear frame manufacturers were mostly small, with the exception of some key players like Luxotica and Safilo in Italy and Ray-Ban in the US.

The design of frames was playing a more and more important role as consumers no longer considered glasses a medical device. Many brands in fashion, cosmetics, and leisure such as Armani, Dior or even Disney had created spectacle models under license. Retail prices ranged from FF 100 to FF 3,000 (not including couturier and "jewelery-like" glasses that sold for FF 20,000 or more). Selling spectacles under a brand name was a very good way for a high profile consumer brand to reinforce its image and make some money on licensing fees.

However, except for a few designs, it was very difficult for the consumer to show that he was wearing branded goods, since the logo or brand name appeared on the side pieces of the frame in very small print only.

This made it very easy to imitate the brands' models. Fielmann in Germany—Europe's largest optical retailer—had pushed this opportunity to the extreme by asking manufacturers to make look-a-like models. Fielmann would then display the look-a-like's in the shop windows side by side with the much more expensive branded models. Sometimes the Fielmann model would cost DM 20 and the brand DM 200.

Depending on the country, the manufacturers sold either directly to retailers (usually the larger retailers only) or through distributors, of whom some had exclusivity for a particular brand.

Manufacturing and Mounting Lenses

In contrast to frames, lenses for spectacles and contact lenses were manufactured by only a few international competitors: Bausch & Lomb for contact lenses, Essilor, Zeiss, and Rosenstock for spectacle lenses. These companies had plants and sales offices in different countries. In highly automated laboratories, they cut, surfaced, and mounted the lenses in frames for independent retailers.

Surfacing and mounting could also be done in independent laboratories or central labs. These labs bought lenses

from the big manufacturers and then cut., surfaced, and mounted them according to the specific shape of the spectacles. They would also add specific features chosen by the customer, such as anti-reflection coating or anti-scratch coating. Laboratories were owned by retailer chains or located in optical stores, as was the case of one-hour service outlets. Next to taking care of mounting, the labs cut the lenses and applied an anti-reflection coating or other features. Typically, in a store, an optician could do about 15 to 20 glasses a day. In a centralized and automated lab, one person could do as many as 50 glasses a day.

Retailers

There were five different kinds of retail outlets for the sale of spectacles and lenses.

Independent Opticians

Independent opticians took a traditional approach to business. They were usually located in the center of a small town or city and offered 600 frames. They catered especially to the elderly. In most European countries, a store needed to have at least one licensed (Master) optician. Studies for becoming a Master optician lasted from two years in France to eight years—including part-time study and apprenticeship—in Germany. Diplomas were not internationally recognized. The requirement of having a Master optician in the store made it difficult to start up in the optical business. As not many new competitors were opening up shop, the existing independent retailers had been profiting with gross margins on sales of more than 70%.

Buying Groups

Buying groups consisted of opticians who had formed associations or cooperations to buy in large quantities and perform other common tasks like advertising. In France, for instance, Krys and Optic 2000 comprised 500 stores under each name and did centralized buying and advertising. They had sites in shopping centers as well as in city centers.

Franchised Networks

Franchised networks were composed of stores with the same look and the same assortment. They had joint buying power, shared the same marketing policy and advertised heavily. Afflelou in France, for instance, had 500 stores under franchise and spent over FF 100 million in advertising for a turnover of FF 1,700 million.

Branch Stores

Branch stores were the true "industrialists" in the business. Whether they provided one-hour service or had a service delivery of two to three days, they had uniform stores, marketing practices, and assortments. Boots (300 stores), Dollond & Atchison (450 stores) and Vision Express (100 stores) in the UK, GPS (Grand Optical 50 stores) in France, Fielmann (350 stores) and Apollo (177 stores) in Germany represented the new players. These stores relied heavily on advertising, except for Grand Optical, which did none.

(continues)

EXHIBIT 3   (Continued)

Mail Order

Mail order was the most recent player in the optical industry. It was appearing only in Scandinavia and focused mostly on contact lenses.

Pricing Frames and Lenses

The classic independent store tended to price branded goods high. Buying groups, franchise operations, and branch networks offered promotions (typically "buy one, get one free") or a 40% discount on both brand and non-brand eyewear. They had cheap, non-brand eyewear made to their specifications by small manufacturers in Europe and the Far East. As for GPS, Grand Optical did not actively promote its branded goods, and La Generale d'Optique—another store chain started up by GPS in 1993—focused on an everyday, low price policy for its non-brand glasses. As Grand Optical did not invest in advertising, it used the stores as its main communication medium.

Costs of Setting Up Stores

The costs for setting up a store varied per country, as one of the main variables was costs for space. In some countries, one only had the costs of the rent of the building; in others, one had to pay "key money" to get in (Latin Countries). If the location kept the same value, key money could be returned after leaving. In France, for example, key money usually amounted to around FF 17,000 per m².

The Euro Consumer Myth or Reality

When Likierman and Abittan started thinking about going abroad, the question arose as to the extent of adaptation needed to fit the needs and tastes of the consumers in the new country. No comparative study was available on the subject, but some points were the same for every country in the world. The first, most common feature was that about 40 to 50% of every country's population needed glasses (20% at age 20, 35% at age 40, 45% at age 65). Wearers needed to change these glasses every three to five years, depending on vision correction factors. Wearers over 55 needed to change them every two years. Only 10 to 20% preferred contact lenses and, at least at this point in time,

surgery could not replace glasses (except maybe in 5% of the cases).

About 20 to 40% of the customers based their purchase on price, as they considered buying glasses a medical obligation. Of course, they preferred good design for a cheap price. About 20 to 25% of the buyers preferred branded goods. These people considered glasses a fashion item. In all countries, there was high loyalty to the optician that customers once started with.

Differences in consumer behavior per country were caused by many factors, including legislation. In some countries, customers could not get glasses in a retail store without a prescription from an ophthalmologist (at least if they wanted compensation from the state insurance or private insurance). This was the case in France. In other countries, the prescription from the ophthalmologist was not compulsory. Lenses could be measured in the store by a licensed optometrist or optician (Germany, UK, Spain, Luxembourg). This did not mean that all consumers actually did that. In Germany, for instance, more than half still went to their doctor; in the UK, less than 20% did.

Reimbursement systems and levels also had an effect on the price consumers were willing to pay. In general, the local insurance system did not reimburse generously for eyewear (for example, in France the maximum was FF 87.50). Sometimes, it was more generous for lenses. Consumers often had complementary insurance to compensate for the lack of state reimbursement. But to give an example from France: for a pair of branded glasses costing FF 3,000, a typical client would get around FF 150 from the state and FF 1,500 from the insurance (about 50%). For spectacles priced FF1,000, one would get FF 600.

Finally, more and more customers were alert to the dangers of ultraviolet radiation from the sun and, depending on where they lived, they increasingly wore sun glasses. Other differences in consumer behavior with regard to eyewear had to do with the level of multi-possession, average price paid, add-ons for the lenses (an anti-reflection coating, for example), preferences for plastic versus metal or organic versus plastic, tastes for shapes and colors, etc. With respect to both technical and quality factors, the most demanding customers in Europe were the Germans.

GPS in the Optical Market

Grand Optical For an overview of the Optical Industry refer to Exhibit 3. Grand Optical was launched in 1989. Likierman and Abittan made use of Photo Service's core competencies in the area of one-hour service. The new, one-hour concept for buying spectacles appealed to the French; by the end of 1996 Grand Optical had 58 outlets in France, sales were FF 848 million, and Grand Optical had a market share of 5%. Grand Optical's rapid growth was the result of its locations in regional shopping malls where customers

could do their shopping while their glasses were being prepared. Of all eye correction equipment (spectacles and lenses), 93% could be ready within an hour. Recently, Grand Optical had also appeared in city centers. It had opened a flagship store on the Champs-Élysées in Paris that posted sales of FF 45 million in 1996 (it was Grand Optical's top selling store).

The HPV (high perceived value), one-stop shopping concept had required the management to work according to a set of typical, Grand Optical principles. The stores were in the best locations; they were open, with high quality shop fittings, and with 300 m², they were large (typical, traditional optical stores were no more than 50 m^2). In contrast to its competitors, Grand Optical believed that its outlets—rather than advertisements—were the best medium for promotion, and they were treated as such (refer to Exhibit 4). In the stores, the customer was offered a large selection of frames (at least 3,500) and lenses. Purchasing was centralized, which entailed frequent deliveries and careful logistic planning. Marketing focused mostly on the stores that communicated a strong image of quality and superior—one-hour—service. Staff was selected carefully, trained extensively and motivated to provide the high, Grand Optical service levels.

La Générale d'Optique   Grand Optical was not the only optical activity of GPS. To be able to cater to the more price-conscious buyers, GPS created "La Générale d'Optique" in 1993. By the end of 1996, it had 52 stores. It targeted consumers who were primarily motivated by price when buying medical products. The store offered a relatively large selection of frames (2,200 models) and sold them under its own brand label "Selection La Generale". In order to make its offer simple, it had created three collections with three all-inclusive prices (FF 490, 690, 990). Price levels were approximately 30% under the prices of traditional outlets. This allowed the store to present models that would be almost totally reimbursed by the health system. La Générale d'Optique also offered customers the option to pay only the difference between the price of their spectacles and the reimbursement of complimen-

tary insurance. To be able to do this, La Générale d'Optique had signed numerous agreements with mutual societies and insurance companies. Spectacles were finished in a central edging and mounting laboratory, which meant that customers would usually have their spectacles within two days.

For La Générale d'Optique, GPS partly followed the same big shopping mall-location policy as for Grand Optical, but it also looked at convenience shopping centers (centers with a large hypermarket and a few stores) as rents were lower. La Générale had also started to open in city centers as rents were lower and opening hours shorter. La Générale d'Optique had a market share of 1.5% (refer to Exhibit 5).

THE GPS OPTICAL HOME MARKET

The first step in the MBA students' research into the options for introducing Grand Optical in other countries was to make a benchmark of home country France. France had provided the resources and consumer profile to realize Grand Optical's growth to 51 shops in six years. One of the main reasons for success was the French one-stop shopping culture. Around 25% of all retail sales were made in hypermarkets. The market share of these stores gave an indication of the popularity of one-stop shopping habits. France counted 100 regional shopping malls and 600 convenience shopping centers of hypermarket galleries in 1996.

France had 27 million spectacle or lens wearers (nearly 50% of the total population) and represented a market value of FF 15.7 billion. Over the last three years, the optical market had experienced slow growth in value (between 1 and 3% per year). The average French person purchased a new pair of glasses after 3.5 years, at an average price of FF 1,500. The average price that was paid for a pair of glasses at Grand Optical was FF 1,600.

The French could be regarded as brand and fashion conscious people. An indicator for this was their high rate of shoe buying. In France, people bought around six pairs of shoes a year. After Japan (8.2 pairs) and Singapore (6.8 pairs), this was the highest figure.

In contrast to many other countries, the French had to visit an ophthalmologist (outside the stores) to have their eyes tested if they were to be reimbursed, fully or partially, for their eyewear. Reimbursements in France were generally poor, although for 80% of the population, mutual society or insurance policies helped reimburse a further part of the costs.

Some 6800 opticians were divided between independents (41% of the market and 59% of the outlets),

EXHIBIT 4   Costs and Income of a Typical Grand Optical or La Générale d'Optique Store in France

	La Générale d'Optique Model	Grand Optical Model
Sales Per Store on Average in FF (ex. VAT)	6 million	12 million
Net Sales in %	100	100
Gross Margin in %	60	71
Store Costs in %:		
Staff	20	22
Space	11	12
External	3	3
Communication	4	3
Leasing m/c	–	3
Depreciation	3	5
Store Contribution %	19	23
Head Office Overhead %	10	12
Operating Result %	9	11
Financial Result %	2	2
Current Pre-tax Profit %	7	9

EXHIBIT 5 Grand Optical Facts and Figures as per December 1996

Typical Profile of a Grand Optical Store	Typical Profile of a La Générale d'Optique Store

• 300 m² of which 100 m² laboratory space
• Catchment area: 300,000 inhabitants
• Sales (inc. VAT) per store: FF 15 million
• Investment: FF 12 million
    ⇒ key money: FF 5 million
    ⇒ store design: FF 5 million
    ⇒ equipment: FF 2 million
• Frames on view: 3,500
• Stock of optical lenses: 9,000
• Stock of contact lenses: 600
• Number of staff: 14
• Sells about 8,000 equipment per year
• Average sale per equipment: FF 1,600
• Store locations: 60% out of town shopping centers, 30% town center shopping centers, 10% high street
• No advertising, the store is the medium
• Pay back period: 5 years
	• 200 m²
	• Catchment area: 150,000 inhabitants
	• Sales (inc. VAT) per store: FF 7 million
	• Investment: FF 5 million
	    ⇒ key money: FF 3 million
	    ⇒ store design FF 2 million
	    ⇒ equipment: 0
	• Frames on view: 2,200
	• Stock of optical lenses: 0
	• Stock of contact lenses: 300
	• Number of staff: 7
	• Sells about 7,000 equipment per year
	• Average sale per equipment: FF 1,000
	• Store locations: 90% out of town shopping centers, 10% town center locations
	• Advertising: 5%
	• Pay back period: 4 years

multiple and voluntary chains (45% of the market with 36% of the outlets), and mutual society opticians (14% of the market and 5% of the outlets). Grand Optical and La Générale d'Optique were the major branch networks. The other chains were co-operatives or franchisees. As in the photo market, bipolarization was developing between the higher-priced, service-and-choice segment (branded frames and lenses crafted with the latest technologies—("the best") and a low-price/low service segment based on the mutual societies ("the cheapest").

DRIVING FORCES BEHIND INTERNATIONALIZATION

Internationalization had become an opportunity as well as a need. Within a reasonable time, the Grand Optical concept would not gain much more market share. A Grand Optical store needed a catchment area of around 300,000 people to justify its investment in size and machinery. So, there was still an additional potential of only 30 to 50 stores for Grand Optical in France. A Générale d'Optique, however, needed 100,000 people in its catchment area, given its cost structure and target market, so its potential in France could still be as high as 250 new stores.

Grand Optical had inspired others to make frames accessible on the store's wall, to give the customers more choice and therefore to create larger stores (although Grand Optical still remained the biggest optical store in France). So far in France, no one had imitated the one-hour concept, but one-hour service had become common in other countries like the United

Kingdom and had recently been launched in Spain. No doubt, other optical chains would be venturing into France and other countries outside their home markets. To preempt foreign competitors. Grand Optical would have to make a decision this year on which country—or countries—to enter first, and with what strategy. Marcel Cezar, General Manager for Grand Optical:

> Going international is a necessity. Otherwise, we will have less and less growth; we will get old, and we will waste a lot of energy searching for minor locations.

Grand Optical would certainly not be the first international optical chain. The following competitors had already gone beyond their home country borders, or were planning to. Vision Express (United Kingdom) had opened in Belgium. Poland, Russia, Argentina, Malaysia and more recently in Germany and Luxembourg. Fielmann (Germany) had just bought a company in Switzerland. Dollond & Aitchison (United Kingdom) was already present in Italy and Spain (refer to Exhibits 6 and 7). In some countries, there was already a strong presence of local multiples such as Visilab (Switzerland) and Boots (United Kingdom). The independents were declining in importance, although this varied per country. In Germany, the independents retained only 23% of the market value as opposed to Italy, where they were nearly the only providers of optical services, with a 96% share of the market.

Going international had many attractions for Grand Optical: there would be scale economies in purchasing and in distribution. Grand Optical would gain access to

EXHIBIT 6   Overview of International Competitors

- **Vision Express expanding rapidly but into less competitive markets**
  - ⇒ emphasis on one-hour service and promotion
  - ⇒ started in the UK
  - ⇒ heavy advertising (10% of sales)
  - ⇒ smaller outlets, size is not essential
  - ⇒ heavy advertising, just for mass media
  - ⇒ expanding rapidly, formula easily implemented
  - ⇒ opportunistic, no clear focus
  - ⇒ present in: Philippines (1), Poland (9), Czech Republic (1), Belgium (9), Argentina (7 franchised), Latvia (6). Ireland (6), Russia (2, franchised), UK (100), Rest of the World (10)

- **Fielmann plans aggressive European expansion but no one-hour service**
  - ⇒ founded in Hamburg in 1972
  - ⇒ largest optical retailer in Europe, large selection
  - ⇒ positioned itself initially as the store for spectacles for free
  - ⇒ accepts lower margin per pair of glasses
  - ⇒ has high operating margin per square meter of shop
  - ⇒ employees sell four pairs of glasses a day (industry average: 1.8)
  - ⇒ does not believe in one-hour service
  - ⇒ quality guarantee of three years on all spectacles
  - ⇒ central labs for processing
  - ⇒ varying store sizes, up to Superoptical size
  - ⇒ consistent in merchandising to smallest detail in all stores
  - ⇒ saturation of home market in 3–4 years, then growth by acquisition abroad
  - ⇒ believe competitive advantage is price, quality, service, in that order
  - ⇒ present in: Germany (350), Austria (2), Switzerland (9; 20 planned)
  - ⇒ planned expansion in: United Kingdom, Spain, Italy, France?

- **Dollond & Aitchison are international but undifferentiated**
  - ⇒ neither LDC (Low Delivered Cost), or HPV (High Perceived Value)
  - ⇒ covers regular and superoptical outlets
  - ⇒ local management and local adaptation, not one formula across markets
  - ⇒ present in: United Kingdom (469), Spain (70), Italy (90), Switzerland (15), Ireland (6)

- **Pearle Vision has problems**
  - ⇒ sometimes one-hour service
  - ⇒ broad assortment of private label and middle market brands
  - ⇒ heavy promotions, "buy one get one free"
  - ⇒ two attempts to enter the German market failed
  - ⇒ financial problems?
  - ⇒ present in United States (822), Belgium (60), Holland (147)
  - ⇒ Grand Met is seeking to divest since 1990

cheaper supplies—in Italy for example, supplies would cost 25% less than in France. In addition to the benefits of economies of scale and international purchasing, Grand Optical acknowledged that its customers traveled and that finding Grand Optical abroad would reinforce their choice of Grand Optical as a supplier of their glasses.

SCANNING FOR OPPORTUNITIES AND PITFALLS IN SEVEN MARKETS

The MBA students studied and visited the following countries to assess Grand Optical's chances: Ger-

many, Italy, Portugal, Spain, Switzerland, Hong Kong and Singapore. This selection of countries came from a previous study that had looked into a wider selection of possible locations. Some were already regarded as too-late-destinations, as competitors had already taken the best spots in shopping centers and established themselves comfortably. In the seven prospective countries, the MBA project team made use of sources like opticians' associations and local data banks. They also went to the local stores and shopping malls to get a feel for store formats, customer approaches, prices and assortments (refer to Exhibits 8 and 9).

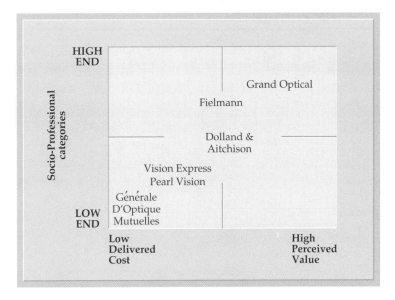

EXHIBIT 7   Positioning of the International Optical Chains

EXHIBIT 8   Quantitative Market Data

	France	Germany	Italy	Portugal	Spain	Switzerland	Hong Kong	Singapore
Wearers in millions	27	36.8	24.5	3.8	17	3.5	3.5	1.7
Market value in FF billion	15.7	18.4	10.4	0.5	6.0	2.9	1.7	0.4
Repurchase rate in years	3.5	3	3.5	N/A	3.5	4	2	5.2
Average price pair of glasses in FF	1300	1600	750	900	900–1000	1700	1,100–1,550	1,000–1,500
No. of shopping centers in 1995	614	180	300	30	326	45	est. 20 that would be suitable for Gr. Opt.	N/A
Square meters (in millions) of shopping centers	13.2	6.2	3.7	0.4	3.6	0.7		
Increase in number of hyper/ supermarkets in period '89–'93	27	21	69	187	91	N/A	N/A	N/A
Shopping hours	moderately flexible	were restrictive but were changing	flexible	flexible	flexible	moderately flexible	flexible?	flexible?
Wearers per outlet	3,978	4,300	2,400	3,040	3,272	3,700	2,040	2,667
Independent's share of market value in %	32	23	96	90	35	95		
Chain's share of market value in %	N/A	27	2	N/A	17	17	N/A	N/A

EXHIBIT 9　Competitors' Profiles per Market (as evaluated by the IMD MBA project team)

	Broad Range	1 Hour Service	Customer Service	Self Service	LDC/ HPV[a]	Fashion/ Store Brands
GRAND OPTICAL (market share 5%)	**yes**	**yes**	**yes**	**yes**	**HPV**	**both**
FRANCE						
Mutual Insurance companies (19% market share)	no	no	no	no	LDC	store
Krys (14% market share)	yes	no	no	no	HPV	both
Afflelou (11% market share)	yes/no	no	no	yes/no	LDC	both
Optique 2000 (9% market share)	yes/no	no	yes	yes/no	HPV	both
GERMANY						
Fielmann (349 stores, $657m)	yes	no	yes	yes	LDC/HPV	both
Apollo (177 stores, $165m)	yes	no	yes	yes	LDC	store
Abele (51 stores, $50m)	no	no	yes	yes	HPV	both
Krane (72 stores, $63m)	yes	no	yes	no	HPV	both
Binder (34 stores, $41m)	no	no	yes	no	HPV	fashion
Family (10 stores)	yes	no	N/A	yes	HPV	
Matt (41 stores)	no	no	yes	yes	LDC	store
Vision Express (1 store)	no	yes	yes	yes	LDC	both
ITALY						
Salmoiraghi (102 stores, $48m)	no	no	no	no	HPV	both
Poliedros (30 stores, 12 one-hour)	no	yes	yes	yes	LDC	fashion
COI (166 stores, $49m)	no	no	yes	yes	HPV	fashion
Green Vision (105 stores, $43m)	no	no	yes	no	HPV	both
PORTUGAL						
Pro Visao	no	Yes	yes	no	HPV	fashion
Multiopticas	no	yes	yes	no	LDC	store
SPAIN						
General Optica (85 stores, $114m)	no	no	yes	no	HPV	both
Opticost (78 stores, $20m)	yes	yes	yes	no	LDC	store
Vision Lab (20 stores)	yes	yes	yes	no	HPV	both
Optica 2000	no	no	yes	no	HPV	both
SWITZERLAND						
Visilab (17 stores, $55m)	no	yes	yes	yes	HPV	fashion
Fielmann	yes	no	yes?	yes	LDC/HPV	both
Delta Optik (16 stores, $15m)	no	no	yes	yes	HPV	fashion
Hong Kong and Singapore						
Optical 88[b] (HK 76 stores)	yes	yes	yes	no	HPV	fashion
The Optical shop[b] (HK 49 stores, Sin 8 stores)	yes	no	yes	some	HPV	fashion
Capitol Optique (Sin 20 stores)	yes	no	yes	no	HPV	fashion
Paris Miki (Sin 8 stores)	yes	no	yes	some	HPV	fashion

[a] LDC: Low Delivered Cost/HPV: High Perceived Value.
[b] Heavy discounts on brands.

Germany

Germany represented the largest market in Europe, with 36.8 million wearers who repurchased slightly more frequently than the French: every 3 years. In comparison to France, German shopping habits were still traditional. The Germans had many in-town shopping areas where most of the shopping took place. Until the rush of building after the reunification in 1990, Germany had relatively few purpose-built shopping centers. As of 1993, more and more of these cen-

ters had been opened. In 1996, there were 180 in the country, totaling 6.2 million square meters of space, up from 67 centers in 1980 and 93 in 1990[3].

With the increase of newly built shopping centers, there was a shift to out-of-town shopping. Shopping hours were being extended from the traditional nine-to-six to include evening shopping. Especially the inde-

[3] *Source: "Corporate Intelligence on Retailing,"* The European Retail Handbook, 1997, p. 123.

pendent shops (and 8000 independent opticians) resented the new shopping hours regulations. It was forecast that the new regulations would favor sales in malls, with a 3 to 12% increase in sales.

Shopping for Eyewear in Germany   The fashion consciousness of the Germans was on the higher end of the "shoe buying scale" (4.8 pairs a year). As for eyewear, the Germans put strong emphasis on both fashion and technical aspects; 70% of the lenses sold were anti-reflection coated (in France, only 35–40%). A drawback of anti-reflection lenses was that their preparation was more time-consuming, which made it impossible to keep the one-hour promise. The average price of eyewear was FF 1600. In addition to these fashion and technical conscious buyers, there was also a large budget-conscious group (20% of the eyewear units were priced below FF 167). In fact, the leading discounter, Fielman, had 33% of the volume and 16% of the value of spectacle sales.

Only 2% of the optical outlets were found in shopping malls; most were in the city centers. In 1996, there was only one store in Germany (a newly opened Vision Express outlet in a brand new shopping mall in Oberhausen) that offered one-hour optical service. It was too early to tell if the one-hour concept would prove successful. Chains represented 27% of the optical market value, buying groups 50%, and the independents 23%. Among the existing opticians, there was already fierce competition, which was intensified by the fact that the market volume was decreasing (4% for lenses, 8% for frames).

Fielmann: A Major Competitor   The strongest player among the chain stores was the German multiple "Fielmann." The rapidly growing world's number two in optical retailing had 33% market share in volume and 16% market share in value. Fielmann had positioned itself as the store for "null Tarif"—zero priced—glasses, which meant DM 20 (around FF 60). This was the amount the social insurance reimbursed per frame. In 1997, this reimbursement would disappear, even though the reimbursement for lenses (DM 80) would remain intact. Fielmann was the only optical chain in Europe that matched Grand Optical's large branded assortment. They had 343 stores in Germany (and six in Switzerland), including some super stores, all of which had high in-store traffic. Fielmann even had "greeters" at their doors who welcomed the customers and indicated where to go for specific needs. Daniel Abittan's opinion of Fielmann:

It is good, it is cheap, there is choice. Fielmann is a great competitor. Their DM 20 glasses are very fashionable. They are always put near more expensive branded products, so the consumer can compare. Fielmann's guarantee is also strong. If the customer finds any branded item for a lower price in another store, they will be reimbursed with the difference! When a competitor offers fashion, choice, and price, it is not easy to beat him.

Fielmann differed from Grand Optical in that it emphasized price rather than the convenience of one-hour service. Fielmann glasses took five to six days from order to delivery.

Fielmann had been enjoying continuous growth in its home market, but the question was if it would be able to maintain such growth in the years to come. It would not be able to keep on capturing an increasing proportion of the German market indefinitely. Goldman Sachs Europe research indicates that Fielmann should reach saturation in Germany at 450 to 460 stores, beyond which the company would be moving into catchment areas that were too small or would cannibalize existing stores.

Legislation   In Germany, the measurement of eye corrections could be done in the stores, but it was heavily regulated by the "Masters system". The hiring, training and managing of opticians staff was left to Masters, who ran the optics stores. Becoming a Master took five years of study and two years of apprenticeship. Each year, only 200 Masters were certified. In 1996, there was a shortage of Masters, which led to increases in their salaries. With the extension of shopping hours, the shortage of Masters would only grow; 40% of the prescriptions were made in-store, 60% were made by ophthalmologists outside the stores. The relationship between the two professional groups was tense.

Over time, Fielmann had been able to find a way around the restrictive Master practices by putting a growing number of its own employees through the training program. Fielmann master opticians received a higher remuneration by working in a Fielmann store than when they started up their own.

Pearle Came and Went   Fielmann had seen competition come and go. In 1981, Pearle had entered the German market by acquiring Bode, and a bitter fight for market share ensued. Pearle was an American optical chain with 875 stores worldwide, 183 in Europe, mainly in The Netherlands and Belgium. Fielmann was able to draw on its reserves for price competitiveness and won a price war. Pearle consequently left

Germany in 1983. But in 1990, Pearle entered the market anew with superstores and a one-hour service, but Fielmann was again able to rely on its price competitiveness to parry the threat. Pearle withdrew in 1993.

Italy

In Italy, there were no restrictions on in-store testing; 65% of the prescriptions were done in-store. It had 24.5 million wearers, a number that was expected to increase due to an aging population. The Italians had flexible shopping hours. Only 3.5% of retail sales were realized in hypermarkets, and there was a trend toward more sophisticated retailing techniques. One-stop shopping was starting up, and since 1992, more and more shopping malls were appearing. As French mall developers had a strong presence, French retailers had the lead in the foreign entrants in Italian malls.

Optical chain stores had 2% of the optics sales value. The few that there were sold 2.5 times as much as the independents. Only 1% of the optical stores were found in malls, but a sevenfold increase was expected in the next three years due to the number of new malls and their cheaper rents. Although the one-hour concept had just been introduced by others, none of the existing stores had a wide range of frames, and few shops had an area larger than 250 m². Customers considered spectacles more a fashion item than a visual aid. Well known, fashionable brands sold well. The National Health Service covered the expenses of only consumers with extreme sight deficiencies. Private insurance was gaining in importance.

One competitor—Poliedros, a small but aggressive chain—offered a one year guarantee, in addition to excellent service with self service, a fidelity card, "satisfied of reimbursed" policy, free sight tests and maintenance, and 90% of the spectacles in one hour. Poliedros could be expected to use its franchising strategy for rapid expansion.

Access to resources was difficult in Italy. Establishing relations, getting the right locations (key money and trading licenses were required in commercial centers as well as for occupied locations in city centers), and getting enough opticians were the most important issues to be tackled. Grand Optical had some talented Italian people in the company who could help make a possible move into Italy smoother.

Portugal

Portugal's retail sales had doubled to FF 150 billion in the last six years. The population was shifting from the countryside to the towns. There was an explosive growth of shopping centers over the last ten years, mostly in and around Lisbon and Porto, where 38% of the population lived but where 74% of the retail sales were realized. This was attracting many foreign retailers such as Toys R Us, Marks & Spencer and Carrefour. At least four of the new shopping centers would be attractive Grand Optical locations. One-stop shopping was still underdeveloped, although there had been a growth of 187% in the number of hypermarkets during the period of 1989–1993. In 1996, 24% of retail sales took place in super and hypermarkets. Opening hours in Portugal were flexible.

There were close to four million eyewear users. The young and urban Portuguese were highly fashion conscious and willing to pay a high price for their glasses, however, the average price for a pair of glasses in Portugal was about 30% lower than in France. Repeat purchase was once every 3.8 years on average.

Ninety percent of the market was served by independent opticians, and chains were small. By law, only ophthalmologists could prescribe corrective lenses. In practice, however, as consulting an ophthalmologist was expensive and not well reimbursed, most customers had their refraction done at optical outlets. The National Health Service reimbursed an average 10% of the costs of spectacles, depending on the type of lenses needed. Only a minority of the population had access to complementary insurance.

There was no other superoptical concept, and there were no apparent intentions of other players to enter the Portuguese market, except for Visionlab, the major, Spanish one-hour service competitor who was due to start in September 1997. Being the first in the best locations could create an advantage and keep other players out. Key money was required in the shopping centers. High street locations were more difficult to obtain due to antiquated tenure laws. Around the bigger cities, it would not be difficult to recruit qualified opticians. In the areas outside Lisbon and Porto, recruitment could become a problem as the rates of literacy and skills were much lower.

Spain

The Spanish market was fragmented, large and growing quickly. There were 17 million wearers who were used to renewing their glasses every 3.5 years. The shopping habits were shifting toward one-stop shopping in hypermarkets and shopping centers. In the period 1980 to 1992, the number of hypermarkets had grown from 15 to 110. Shopping Centers also mushroomed (680% in the period 1980–1992). By 1996, they represented 8% of the retail sales. There were seven promising and two possible regions for Grand Optical stores in Spain. The Spanish were moderately fashion conscious (3.8 pairs of shoes per year). They saw spectacles mostly as a medical device. Opening hours in Spain were flexible.

In the optics sector, the independents and groups were losing out, although independents still had 55% of the outlets. Chains had 8% of the outlets, but 25% of the turnover. They consisted of four major national chains and a number of regional players. Spanish buyers had experienced one-hour service but not self service, as all opticians kept their frames in the drawer instead of on a self-service display. Most prescriptions were delivered in-store. There was no state health insurance. The Spaniards paid an average price of around FF 1000 for a pair of glasses.

"Ferri" (Vision Lab) was a genuine competitor that offered one-hour service in its 20 big stores: each between 300 and 600 m^2. Visionlab spent heavily on advertising. Compared to Grand Optical, it was cheaper, since it offered mostly unbranded frames from the Far East.

The prime locations in malls were taken by existing optical stores that usually had a loyal customer base. Key money had to be paid. Recent legislation had severely restricted new shopping center development. However, the new centers were outcompeting the older ones. Excess demand for space in the new centers was high (a waiting list of 50 was typical). The older centers were willing to accept rent as a percentage of turnover. Getting good locations on the high street was also difficult; the waiting lists were even higher than the ones in the shopping centers. Key money was high, and much of the good space changed hands without reaching the open market. French retailers were generally well accepted in Spain, and there was a proximity to French procurement.

Switzerland

Switzerland had 3.5 million spectacle wearers, the repurchase rate was 4 years, the average price for spectacles was the highest in Europe, a little over Germany's FF 1600. Shopping cultures varied by canton. In search for lower prices, the Swiss in many areas resorted to cross-border shopping and discounting. Shopping centers thrived in the big cities only (Zurich and Geneva). There were only eleven shopping centers of more than 20,000 m^2. In contrast to other countries, key money was not always required in the Swiss shopping center locations. But the prices of real estate, especially in the prime locations, were among the highest in Europe.

Fifty percent of the retail sales was realized in city centers, 20% in villages, 15% in business quarters, 7% in suburbs and 8% in shopping malls. Superstores were just emerging. Opening hours in Switzerland were semi-flexible. Despite its still more traditional shopping habits, Switzerland was an attractive market due to the high disposable income of its inhabitants.

Most optical stores were located in main streets and city centers. Independents still had around 90% of the market. Chains had 5%, and the buying groups had 5% of the market value. Refraction was done in-store in 60% of the cases, normally in the shops that had a certified optician (Master). The other 40% of the customers had refraction done by an ophthalmologist. The one-hour concept had been established in the French-speaking part (Visilab) with a limited range of products. It was still undeveloped in the German-speaking cantons, where two thirds of the optical stores were located. Insurance reimbursed FF 840 every three years, provided the customer had a prescription; 50% of the spectacle wearers had additional insurance.

Fielmann from Germany had entered the market in 1995 by buying Pro Optic AG. They had six outlets in the German-speaking part of Switzerland and would be opening stores in three more locations in 1996. They were offering the Swiss a broad range of frames (over 3000). Despite this, Grand Optical could still distinguish itself because it had both a broad range and one-hour service, a combination that none of the competitors offered (they did offer one of the two selling points).

The biggest barrier to entry was the access to Master opticians and their very high salaries. They were the only persons to do eye tests. There was only one school for Master opticians, which was controlled by Master opticians themselves. Another barrier was a law that prohibited advertising free eye tests. Competitors like Visilab and Fielmann were not to be underestimated for their power to react to new market entrants.

Hong Kong and Singapore

The people in Hong Kong had a shoe buying rate of 5.8 pairs per year. There were 2.5 million spectacle wearers, who repurchased every 2 years. The listed prices for glasses were very high, but usually a customer could get large discounts.

Singapore had 1.6 million wearers and a repurchase rate of 1.5 to 2 years. Their indicator for fashion consciousness was high, with 6.8 pairs of shoes a year.

Both markets had a trend toward fashion buying and a focus on professional services. The young age group was growing fast; they valued professional service and high quality product features. European brands had a stylish image. The shopping mall was developing in Hong Kong (there were around 20 malls in Hong Kong that would be able to carry a Grand Optical store), but it was already well established in Singapore. Most retailers in the malls were foreign.

In Hong Kong, fewer than 50% of the optical stores were found in malls. The optical shops in the malls were usually small. The chains owned around 25% of the optical stores.

In Singapore, more than 70% of the optical stores were in a mall; 17% of all optical stores were owned by a chain. In Singapore, most optical stores were small, and one-hour service was offered by many.

In both markets, the majority of the stores were owned by independents, although due to pressure from chains that offered discounts, buying groups could develop. Even within the chain stores, the market was highly fragmented. They usually had a limited number of outlets, and often, there was no clear consistency among the outlets in shop plan, selection, service and even the names of the stores. Self-service was limited, and there was a limited assortment of frames. Open shop plans were rare. Pushy sales techniques dominated customer service. Neither market offered government reimbursement or insurance benefits for customers.

Regulation in both countries used to be focused on contact lenses. Singapore had no formal regulatory body and no regulation of normal spectacles, but new regulation was likely to come in the near future. Singapore had no formal education program in optometry.

Hong Kong's official regulation of opticians came into effect in August 1996. As of that date, all shops needed to have a licensed optometrist. Hong Kong Polytechnic University offered an optometry degree and had 25 graduates per year.

Real estate was very expensive, especially in Hong Kong, and key money was often required. In Hong Kong rents were FF 3,750-5,000 per m² per month. In Singapore, rents were FF 300-600 per m² per month and typically FF 10,000–15,000 per slot (30–50 m²). Grand Optical would have to negotiate with several retailers in a center in order to get the right space and enough of it. Competition was strong, though the other opticians were not as clearly positioned as Grand Optical. Recruiting qualified opticians could pose a problem as there were not enough of them. There was economic growth in both countries—Singapore at 10% and Hong Kong at 5%. But the uncertainty of political stability in Hong Kong was a drawback for Grand Optical, as it was for many other businesses.

Grand Optical considered moving into Singapore or Hong Kong as a longer term option. There was no quick money to be made because of the high investments that were required, but one could see other reasons for opening up in Asia fast, as Michael Likierman said:

> Asia is the future; half of the world's trade is supposed to happen there in twenty years. By being there, we can also be ready when the Chinese market opens up. We know it is going to take long, so the sooner we start, the better off we will be when China opens up.

STRATEGY

After the MBA group presented their findings to the Grand Optical Management team, GPS managers would have to make up their minds about which country or countries to enter. After that, a strategy had to be formulated.

GPS had two choices for expanding abroad: either exporting the Grand Optical concept as it was, or adapting the French Grand Optical concept to the local market. Abittan and Likierman believed strongly in the first option as the concept was proven and they knew how to do it. On the other hand, strategies from France could have a totally different impact in another country and—after major investments—prove to be unsuitable. But then again, adapting to local markets also had its attraction; it could turn out cheaper, and there was an interesting learning potential in trying out new concepts in new markets, something that appealed much to the two pioneers. Daniel Abittan:

> We must show that in three or four years, the store brand can be developed abroad. Hence we must start now; the optical business differs in each and every country, and we need time to learn.

Some voices in the team suggested that GPS had also acquired competencies in the budget segment with La Générale d'Optique. Maybe it was not Grand Optical that should be seeing the world, but La Générale d'Optique. No matter which part of GPS would travel, many aspects had to be taken into account. Would the location strategy that GPS had followed in France be as effective in the new country? What about marketing, human resources and service? How would competitors react?

CASE 15-2   J. MILLER, INC.*

Karl Krantz sat in his office in Cleveland, Ohio, and wondered what he should do about his European Division. Karl was president of J. Miller, Inc., a manufacturer of industrial fasteners. European sales were down, and management controls appeared to be weak. Although Krantz was busy gearing up for some new products for U.S. customers, it appeared that he would have to go to Europe to straighten things out.

COMPANY BACKGROUND

J. Miller was founded by a German inventor in 1948. The company's first production facility was located in Holland to serve the European market. However, the U.S. market for fasteners had grown rapidly, and a second U.S. plant was opened in Cleveland in 1960. Because sales in North America soon exceeded those in Europe, the corporate headquarters was moved from Holland to Cleveland in 1972. The Holland plant proved to be expensive to run and was moved to Spain to take advantage of lower wages and overhead costs. The company is controlled by the son of the founder,

who owns 60 percent of the stock. He makes his home in Bern, Switzerland.

Current sales of J. Miller and its international divisions are $163 million, with profits of about $8 million (Exhibit 1). A five-year summary of sales and income is presented in Exhibit 2. The asset/liability situation is shown by the balance sheet data in Exhibit 3.

EUROPEAN DIVISION

The European Division of J. Miller was run by Jose Gonzales, who had an office in Madrid. Fastener distribution in Europe was handled in the large markets of France and Germany by company-owned sales offices. Customers in England were serviced through a licensee. Hanson Limited manufactured fasteners using J. Miller designs and technology and sold them to English firms. J. Miller received a $2\frac{1}{2}$ percent royalty on all fastener sales by Hanson Limited.

An exclusive independent distributor was employed to handle the Italian market, with products shipped from Spain. The German office in Hamburg was run by Kurt Muller and Greta Klein, and the Paris sales office was managed by Jacques LeGarde.

EXHIBIT 1   Statement of Income and Expenses, 1995–97 (in thousands)

Fiscal Year Ending	08/31/97	08/31/96	08/31/95
Net sales	$162,990	$159,078	$146,437
Cost of goods	111,526	108,315	96,508
Gross profit	51,464	50,763	49,929
Sell gen & admin exp	37,374	36,974	36,789
Advertising	1,488	1,308	1,114
Distribution expenses	1,294	1,152	1,089
Market research	879	864	724
Sales promotion	1,017	943	850
Operating income	9,412	10,522	9,363
Nonoperating income	−261	−2,911	−2,904
Interest expense	136	981	1,821
Income before tax	9,015	6,630	4,638
Prov for inc taxes	903	325	373
Net income	$ 8,112	$ 6,305	$ 4,265
Outstanding shares	3,741,280	3,737,341	3,578,406

---

* This case was prepared by Douglas J. Dalrymple of Indiana University.

EXHIBIT 2   Five-Year Summary of Sales and Income (in thousands)

Date	Sales	Net Income	Earnings per Share
1997	$162,990	$8,112	$2.17
1996	159,078	6,305	1.69
1995	146,437	4,265	1.19
1994	138,561	−5,211	−1.46
1993	143,572	−13,206	−3.13
Average growth rate	+3.2%	NA	NA

Recently, the company controller, Ben Casey, had come to Karl with information concerning an unusual purchase by the French sales office. An internal audit had revealed that Jacques LeGarde had purchased a new Mercedes 300E and charged it to the firm. Since this large expenditure had not been cleared by the Cleveland office, Ben was authorized to dig further to see if this initial "smoke signal" indicated the presence of a more serious "fire."

With the help of a firm of French lawyers, Ben made a thorough review of the French operation. He found that Jacques had deceived the company six months earlier when he told Karl Krantz that the Paris sales office was too small to meet the needs of the company. Based on Jacques' comments, Karl had authorized that the office be moved to another build-

EXHIBIT 3   Balance Sheet

	Annual Assets ($000)		
Fiscal Year Ending	08/31/97	08/31/96	08/31/95
Cash	$ 9,864	$ 3,565	$ 1,945
Marketable securities	NA	NA	NA
Receivables	27,912	23,632	21,922
Inventories	15,576	21,552	18,861
Other current assets	565	726	660
Total current assets	53,917	49,475	43,389
Prop, plant & equip	98,041	94,740	88,371
Accumulated dep	62,265	60,808	57,132
Net prop & equip	35,776	33,932	31,239
Other noncur assets	NA	348	522
Deferred charges	NA	NA	NA
Intangibles	8,353	4,696	5,043
Deposits & other assets	823	1,167	501
Total assets	$98,869	$89,618	$80,694

	Annual Liabilities ($000)		
Fiscal Year Ending	08/31/97	08/31/96	08/31/95
Accounts payable	$ 9,585	$ 9,687	$ 9,421
Cur long-term debt	201	309	264
Cur port cap leases	NA	NA	NA
Accrued expenses	12,010	12,255	17,574
Income taxes	151	939	865
Total current liab	21,947	23,191	28,124
Long-term debt	1,167	1,089	NA
Noncur cap leases	385	598	720
Other long-term liab	8,478	5,383	4,540
Total liabilities	31,977	30,260	33,384
Common stock net	28,548	29,248	23,910
Capital surplus	NA	NA	NA
Retained earnings	36,873	29,325	23,400
Other liabilities	1,471	784	NA
Shareholders' equity	66,892	59,356	47,310
Total liab & net worth	$98,869	$89,618	$80,694

ing. Research showed that Jacques had moved the sales office to a building that he owned. This meant that Jacques signed the lease as the manager of J. Miller's office, but a false name was given as the building owner on the lease. Further review found that four of the nine sales office employees were relatives of Jacques LeGarde.

KARL KRANTZ'S TRIP TO EUROPE

J. Miller's top management decided that it was time Jacques was confronted with his misdeeds and fired. Since Karl Krantz was the chief operating officer and spoke French, German, and Spanish, he was dispatched to Europe to repair the damage. The meeting with Jacques LeGarde did not go well. Jacques protested that he had done nothing wrong, and he refused to move out of his office. After talking with the other employees, Bill realized that they all thought they worked for Jacques rather than J. Miller. Other conversations with the building service personnel revealed that Jacques had been seen loading what appeared to be company documents into a van and delivering them to a nearby mini-warehouse storage facility. To check this out, Bill and the company's lawyers tried to get a locksmith to open the storage facility. However, they didn't know which unit Jacques had rented, and they failed to uncover the documents.

J. Miller's French lawyers estimated that it might take two weeks to get Jacques to vacate his office. He would then be eligible for a severance package of $125,000 under French law. Karl argued that misrepresenting the lease was criminal and that Jacques should be thrown in jail.

Now that Jacques was on the way out, Karl wondered if it was time to reconsider how the French office was organized. Jacques had served as office manager and as manager of the field sales staff. The tendency with this plan was for the manager to spend most of his time in Paris on paperwork rather than in the field with customers. In the German sales office, the job was split into two parts. Greta Klein acted as office manager and took care of the paperwork and the inside sales staff. A field manager, Kurt Muller, traveled with the sales force to help solve customers' problems associated with the use of J. Miller fasteners. Karl wondered if the German plan would work in France. Having two managers in Paris would, of course, be more expensive than the current arrangement.

Another issue was what nationality of person or persons to hire as a replacement for Jacques LeGarde.

Karl had observed that the French and German managers tended to think that they were better businessmen than Jose Gonzales, the European Division manager, and should be reporting directly to corporate headquarters. While anyone hired for the Paris job or jobs would have to speak French, would this be an appropriate time to hire someone who could get along better with Jose? Perhaps Jose should do the interviewing and make the final decisions on personnel for the French sales office. While there were serious problems in Paris, Karl was also concerned about the British operation.

HANSON LIMITED

Since the early days of J. Miller's existence, it had licensed its basic technology to a British firm, Hanson Ltd. Even after the patents for the basic fastener had expired, J. Miller had continued the arrangement. Essentially Hanson had the exclusive rights to the Miller trademark in England as long as it continued to pay the royalties, which amounted to about $100,000 per year.

However, times had changed. To sell effectively now in one country in Europe often required contacts in another. In particular, Ford Europe had design centers in England, and decisions critical to sales to the German automotive plants were made in England. Recently Taiwan firms had begun to steal market share away from J. Miller brands sold in the British fastener market.

While the license agreement was not breakable, the lawyers had indicated that it would be legal to sell Miller's line of fasteners in England under a different trademark. Thus one option would be to start selling fasteners in England under a new label and import them from Spain. This would require J. Miller to appoint a new distributor for the line or open another company-owned sales office.

Another option would be to try to talk Hanson Limited into an upgrade of its licensing agreement to a joint venture. The idea behind a joint venture would be to have Hanson focus on manufacturing, whereas J. Miller could emphasize sales and distribution. However, Hanson would be unlikely to go for a joint venture unless it made more money under the new arrangement. Thus J. Miller would have to offer some special inducements to gain Hanson's cooperation. Another option would be to try to buy Hanson's fastener production facilities or to gain an ownership position in the company.

PROBLEMS IN THE ITALIAN OFFICE

While the French lawyers were trying to evict Jacques LeGarde from his own office building, Karl decided to fly to Italy to visit the J. Miller distributor. Gino Pardo had been J. Miller's exclusive independent Italian distributor for 20 years and was headquartered in Milan. Gino had complained over the years about how hard it was to sell fasteners in Italy. He grumbled that he wasn't buying at competitive prices from J. Miller and that J. Miller's fastener line was not right for the Italian market. Karl thought Gino's complaints lacked credibility, as sales were growing in other Common Market countries.

While there were no reliable figures for market size or share due to the fragmentation of the suppliers and of the market itself, Karl had managed to obtain the volume of a French competitor's sales office in Italy. These data were available from public records at the local city hall, although with some delay (Exhibit 4). In the current fiscal year, J. Miller's Italian sales were down 40 percent.

The recent declines in Italian sales were clearly unacceptable, and Karl wondered if this was the time to switch from an independent distributor to a company-owned sales office. Karl was convinced that sales would increase if he had his own personnel working full time on J. Miller products. A significant sales volume would, of course, be necessary to pay the anticipated $200,000 annual costs of a small company sales office. Gino set his own prices and typically operated on a planned margin of 25 percent of the selling price. This margin was considerably higher than J. Miller's own profit margin on the fasteners. One problem with making a change in Italy was that Gino had an exclusive contract that specified one-year notification of the intent to cancel the distributor agreement. This termination clause had been negotiated by a J. Miller sales manager who was no longer with the firm. If Karl gave Gino his one-year notification, fastener sales would probably fall off sharply for the rest of the year.

Karl wondered if there were some actions that could be taken to encourage Gino to give up his distributorship voluntarily prior to the one-year period. One possibility would be to arrange for some of Gino's orders to be delayed or packaged in the wrong assortments. Customers would blame Gino, and he might be willing to get out of the fastener market. Another approach would be to raise fastener prices in the Italian

EXHIBIT 4   Italian Sales Comparison ($000)

	J. Miller, Inc.	Lucain et Fils
1992	$4236	$3260
1993	$4876	$4672
1994	$5568	$5430
1995	$5246	$6192
1996	$5712	None available
1997	$3374	None available

market. This would make it harder for Gino to sell fasteners and could lead to an early cancellation of the Italian distribution agreement. Of course, both approaches could lead to customer dissatisfaction and make things difficult when the J. Miller sales office opened. Krantz did not consider either solution unethical, as Gino was not performing his responsibilities in a clearly one-sided distribution agreement. Karl felt that an ideal solution would be to keep Gino's company as a *nonexclusive* distributor, as he was strong in other market sectors.

Another factor to consider in the possible replacement of Gino Pardo was the widespread use of "black money" in Italy. Many of Italy's large manufacturing firms were owned by the government. As a result, there was a great deal of bureaucratic control over business transactions. For example, bureaucrats maintained lists of "approved" bidders to supply parts for many projects. This meant that sometimes gratuities, or black money, had to be paid to become an approved bidder. Gino was not particularly adept at this and had once paid $25,000 to the wrong person. Payments of black money in Italy were not a serious problem for J. Miller because Gino was an independent distributor. However, if J. Miller opened its own sales office, then there might be some question of whether black money payments violated U.S. laws on the payment of overseas gratuities. Because of the difficulties of operating in Italy, J. Miller had previously elected to continue with a local distributor even though the potential market was as large as that of France or Germany.

Before the plane landed in Milan, Karl needed a strategy to solve the Italian problem. It would also be nice if he could work out an approach to the crises in Paris and England. Karl knew that if he failed to turn things around in the European Division, he would be in for some sharp questioning at the next meeting of the board of directors.

CHAPTER 16

MARKETING PLANNING

A good plan, violently executed today, is better than a perfect plan tomorrow.

GENERAL GEORGE S. PATTON

One of your most important jobs as marketing manager is the preparation of marketing plans. Organizations that plan for the future are more likely to survive. Marketing plans are normally developed on an annual basis and often include actions that take place over several years. A marketing plan is a formal statement that explains where each product or service is today, where you want it to be at the end of the planning horizon, and how you intend to get there. Once marketing plans have been prepared, they are used to guide field marketing activities for the planning period. You must influence others—some of whom you have no formal authority over—to carry out your plans. As the planning period unfolds, you must monitor marketing performance and compare results with the goals set in the marketing plan. Not everything will go as planned; you must *act and adapt.* The objective of this chapter is to show you how to prepare and implement a marketing plan.

BRAND MANAGER AS PLANNER

The most common place for marketing planning to begin is in the offices of brand or product managers. Figure 16-1 provides an example of how product managers fit into the organizational life of a large business. The actual organizational structure used by an individual firm may, of course, be different. Note that brand/product managers are generalists who operate alongside the line field sales organization. Product managers usually report to either a category manager or a group marketing manager. Group managers have responsibility for products in more than one product category. Category marketing managers focus on items in one category, which allows for better coordination of strategic and marketing efforts.

Brand and product managers operate as independent entrepreneurs, with responsibility for generating revenues and profits on the goods and services under their supervision. They create the marketing plans that attract customers, and they function as the key decision makers in the day-to-day management of groups of products. The assignment of planning to product managers is essentially a bottom-up procedure. Plans prepared by product managers go up the organization before they are sent back down to be executed by the sales organization (Figure 16-1).

Brand managers also coordinate pricing, promotion, distribution, and research activities on a daily basis. Some of the duties assigned to product managers are listed in Table 16-1. A

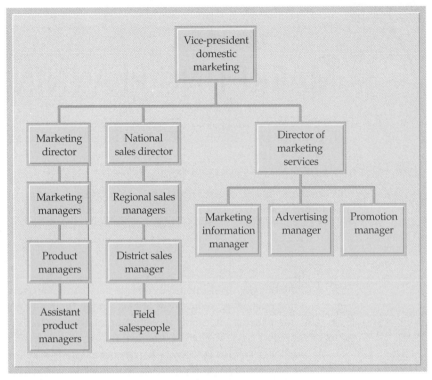

FIGURE 16-1   **Marketing Organizational Structure**

new assistant brand manager typically starts out developing coupon and promotion programs, examining costs, and getting involved with production and advertising. Brand managers must be brand stewards and assume responsibility for the environmental impact of their products, processes, and packages. The job of a product manager encompasses almost all elements of the marketing mix and is one of the most challenging occupations in the business world.

A key problem at both the product management level and the category level is keeping the same people in place so that they become experts. There is often too much churning, with the average tenure in a position only 18 months. As a result, continuity becomes lost.

TABLE 16-1   **Primary Activities of Product Managers**

Prepare marketing plans for the following year, including merchandising, advertising, and selling activities to reach sales and profit goals.
Recommend prices, discounts, and allowances.
Forecast sales and set sales quotas with the sales manager.
Analyze sales results, share of market, competitive activity, and brand profits and adjust plans where necessary.
Request market research when necessary.
Initiate product improvements in anticipation of, or in reaction to, shifts in customers' requirements, advances in technology, or actions by competitors.
Continually appraise product performance, quality, and package design.
Recommend products to be eliminated.

THE MARKETING AUDIT

A good place to start marketing planning is with a marketing audit. Audits are periodic reviews of the entire marketing efforts of the firm. They are designed to point out the strengths and weaknesses of marketing plans, objectives, organization, personnel, and operating procedures employed by the organization. The idea is to appraise the overall condition of the marketing program so that the firm can capitalize on its strengths and improve areas that are weak.

Areas to Be Audited

The marketing audit is not concerned with measuring past performance; instead, it looks to the future to see how well the firm's resources are being used to exploit market opportunities. The auditor first looks at marketing objectives to make sure that they are sufficiently broad so that the firm is not trapped with an obsolete product line. For example, an abrasives company would be advised to state its objective as improved sales of metal polishing and removal services rather than just as improved sales of grinding wheels. This approach allows the company to offer a variety of ways to solve customers' problems without restricting itself to the sale of a single product.

The audit should also include an appraisal of the structure of the marketing organization. Does the chief marketing officer have enough power to control all relevant marketing functions? Are the channels of communication open among sales, advertising, promotion, and product development executives? Do the managers of each marketing function have the skills, training, and experience needed to perform their jobs successfully? Should new-product development be handled by a committee, venture teams, or a separate department?

In addition, marketing audits must evaluate the procedures that are used by the firm to implement marketing programs. This means that the auditor must consider how well the product line meets the needs of the perceived market segment. In addition, the auditor reviews the coverage of the sales territories and checks the speed of delivery provided by the warehouse and the transportation network. Auditors should also speak with dealers and customers to find out how they view the marketing operations of the firm. One thing auditors look for in judging operating efficiency is balance across elements of the marketing program. It would be foolish, for example, to spend lavishly on trade promotion unless salespeople are available to make follow-up calls. In another case, an auditor found a large proportion of a pharmaceutical manufacturer's ad budget devoted to billboards, which is an unusual way to promote prescription drugs. The selection of billboards as an advertising medium had been made years before and had become such a sacred cow that no one in the company questioned its efficiency. Fortunately, the auditor convinced the company to drop billboard advertising in one area, and sales remained constant. Thus, in this case, a single operational change saved the manufacturer many times the cost of the marketing audit.

Implementing the Audit

A good marketing audit will turn up a number of suggestions for improving the plans and operation of marketing departments. It is the job of marketing managers to take these ideas and incorporate them into the plans being developed for specific brands and product lines. The most effective marketing audits are conducted by someone outside the marketing organization. This avoids the problems of having an audit conducted by a manager who is a weak link in the marketing department. The best audits provide a lighted pathway to the development of moneymaking marketing plans.

BUILDING THE MARKETING PLAN

Marketing plans are a comprehensive statement of what you expect from each brand or service in the future. They evolve from the firm's mission statement which defines the businesses the company wishes to pursue and the customers to be targeted. Plans are prepared on an annual basis, and include both historical data and recommendations on how to improve performance. The plan combines a set of marketing strategies with a timetable for action so that specific financial goals can be achieved. An annual plan usually includes such sections as an executive summary, current company situation, business environment, target markets, objectives, strategy, action programs, anticipated results, and contingency plans (Table 16-2).

Executive Summary

An executive summary is a one- or two-page review of the main facts and recommendations that often appears at the front of a marketing plan. The idea is to highlight the most important parts of the program for top management. This allows executives to gain a quick overview of the plan without wading through the whole report and the supporting exhibits. Managers who need more detail than is provided in the executive summary can go directly to the sections of the marketing plan that include the required information. Executive summaries are designed to make marketing plans more usable, and they are one of the last elements of the plan to be prepared.

Company Situation

The company's situation sets the stage for the rest of the report by telling the reader where the company stands. The situation analysis reviews historical data accumulated for each product. This section includes information on sales, earnings, market shares, shareholder equity, cash flow, and other variables for the past several years. Often this information is presented in chart form to make it easier for executives to grasp trends and relationships.

In addition to providing basic financial data, the company situation should describe current marketing mix variables, such as product quality standards and communication themes, to help show the way to tomorrow. You must know your strengths and weaknesses. You cannot plan for the future unless you know what is going on in the present. Marketing in Action box 16–1 describes how a weak company situation led to a buyout by a more successful firm.

TABLE 16-2   Sample Marketing Plan Headings

1. *Executive Summary:* Short review of the facts and recommendations (optional).
2. *Company Situation:* Current sales, net income, market share, strengths, weaknesses.
3. *Environment:* Competitive plans, opportunities, threats, laws, regulations.
4. *Target Markets:* Who your customers are, where they are, how they buy, and how much they will buy.
5. *Objectives:* Where the firm is going in terms of sales, market share, distribution, stockholder equity, technology, quality, and how objectives will be measured.
6. *Strategy:* Market development, cost reduction, differentiation, penetration, diversification.
7. *Action Programs:* Six-month activity plan, tactics, media plan, individual assignments, timetables, and completion dates.
8. *Anticipated Results:* Projected profit and loss statement and cash budget by month and quarter, break-even analysis.
9. *Contingency Plans:* What to do if sales, profit, and other goals are not met.
10. *Appendices:* Supporting exhibits and tables.

MARKETING IN ACTION *16-1*

First Brands Sells Out

First Brands Corp. of Danbury, Connecticut, is primarily known for its Glad plastic wraps and trash bags which account for nearly half its sales. They also sell STP motor oil and several brands of cat litter. Plastic bags and motor oil are mature markets with many competitors that use price cuts and promotional discounts to gain market share. First Brands reported disappointing profits in August of 1998 due to heavy promotional costs for a new line of Gladware plastic containers. Also, First Brands depended on weakening overseas markets for 22 percent of its revenues. First Brands' situation was bleak with aging brands and few prospects for growth. The company's stock declined from $28 in 1997 to a low of $20 in September of 1998. When Clorox Co. made an offer for the firm, an agreement was quickly reached for stock valued at $39 per share. Clorox projected $90 million in annual cost savings as a result of the merger. These savings were expected in advertising terms and costs where both firms have products such as cat litter, charcoal and fire logs. Sometimes when firms are in a weak competitive position, it pays to sell to a more diversified company. Certainly in this case the stockholders of First Brands and their executives were quite happy to receive $39 a share for stock that had been selling for $20 a few weeks earlier.

— *Sometimes a review of a company situation is grim and it pays to sell out.*

Source: George Anders, "Clorox, Still Growing, to Buy First Brands," *The Wall Street Journal*, October 20, 1998, p. A3.

APPLYING
. . . to Consumer Packaged Goods Marketing

INTEGRATING
. . . with Strategic Planning

Environment

This section describes the external environmental factors that influence business planning. These include shifting customer demands, technological change, competition, governmental regulations, and availability of labor and materials. New customer wants and needs and advances in technology open opportunities for new markets and products. Competition is a constant threat to business success, and you need to know who the major domestic and foreign rivals are. You also need data on competitive strategies, pricing, cost structure, and distribution channels. Governmental regulations and court decisions also set limits on what marketing managers can do in particular situations. Thus you must be aware of what is allowable in the areas of the environment, employee rights, and competitive practices in pricing and advertising. Sometimes marketing plans are constrained by the availability of skilled labor and raw materials or uncooperative labor unions. You must keep up with these changes so you can plan accordingly. An example of how changing customer needs altered the planning process at Mohawk Industries is described in Marketing in Action box 16-2.

Target Markets

The target market section of a marketing plan provides a detailed explanation of who your intended customers are. The plan should define your market in terms of demographics (age, income, education), geographics (location), and lifestyle. Be sure to include a discussion of the size of each intended market segment. In addition to size, you need to know how fast the target groups are growing and what product or service features customers are looking for. Knowing who your customers are, how much they buy, and when they buy makes it easier to design marketing plans to meet their needs.

Information on target markets can often be gathered over the Internet. For example, the U.S. Patent and Trademark Office now offers simple and free searches of its trademark database through its World Wide Web site. In May of 1998, Microsoft Corp. filed applications

APPLYING
... to
Industrial
Marketing

INTEGRATING
... with
Production/
Operations
Management

MARKETING IN ACTION *16-2*

Planning to Meet Customer Needs

Historically, architects and builders ordered carpet 45 days in advance allowing mills plenty of time to plan production and ship carpet to commercial customers. However, today with lean inventories, carpet manufacturers are receiving more surprise orders with shorter delivery requirements. In 1996, Mohawk Industries was only able to fill 80 percent of its order queries in the time requested. Since margins in the commercial carpet business are very high, no one wanted to turn away even a single customer. Mohawk needed a better way to predict orders so it could do a better job of planning its production schedules. A DuPont scientist who had been studying production scheduling problems came up with a remarkable solution. Instead of predicting sales for 30 days into the future, why not create a new plan every day, a kind of rolling forecast based on up-to-the-minute customer orders. He wrote a computer program that captured every order and predicted the size and timing of future orders. DuPont offered the program to their nylon customers and now Mohawk runs the program each night to decide which of their 4,000 products should be produced the next day. Now only 35 percent of work in process has actually been ordered, compared to 85 percent in the past. The new planning system allows Mohawk to fill 95 percent of customer's orders on time. This has led to significant revenue and profit gains for the company.

— *Careful planning can lead to increases in sales and profits.*

Source: Thomas Petzinger, Jr., "In This Carpet Mill, The Best Laid Plans Are Rolled Out Daily," *The Wall Street Journal*, October 30, 1998, p. B1.

Courtesy Mohawk Industries, Inc.

for trademarks for Microsoft Taxsaver and Microsoft Taxbreak. These names are to be used with computer software for tax planning and the preparation and filing of tax returns. Knowing that Microsoft is thinking of entering the tax preparation market would be valuable to Quicken, whose Turbo Tax currently dominates this segment, and to others who might want to target this market.[1]

Objectives

The objectives section of the marketing plan describes where you intend the product or business unit to go in the future. These objectives must be in agreement with the overall objectives of the firm, but they do not have to be the same for each line of trade. Thus, the objective for a question mark product might be to build market share, whereas with a cash cow you might prefer to lose market share rather than waste money trying to save a lost cause.

Company objectives, for example, might call for 20 percent sales growth, a 15 percent pretax profit margin, a 1 percent increase in market share, and a 20 percent growth in stockholder equity. Products in attractive markets would be expected to match or exceed these goals, and businesses in more competitive or mature environments would have lower expectations. The idea is to push each business to do as well as it can in the light of differences in potential.

Your marketing plan must specify how the data needed to measure the achievement of objectives will be collected and analyzed. Market share data, for example, can come from store audits, scanner data, A.C. Nielsen figures, trade associations, or from customer surveys. There are also many different ways to measure growth in stockholder equity.

Strategy

INTEGRATING
. . . with Strategic Planning

The strategy section of the marketing plan provides a statement showing how the business will achieve its objectives. The statement indicates the areas the firm will emphasize in its drive for victory. Effective strategies tell management what paths to follow for key marketing mix variables. For example, you can build a sustainable competitive advantage through brand identification, product differentiation, niche marketing, or low costs. Brand strength and product differentiation can be improved through the use of new advertising themes, increased ad expenditures, reallocation of ad dollars across media vehicles, and special promotional events.

Businesses that need to improve profitability could pursue a strategy of raising prices. This strategy, in turn, could mean selective price increases for high-demand items or across-the-board increases on all products. Cost-cutting strategies can involve a variety of areas both within the marketing department and in other parts of the firm. The most common approach is to redesign products to make them easier and cheaper to manufacture. Another effective technique is to expand the use of Web selling to lower distribution costs. One popular cost-cutting strategy is to drop low-profit items and to restrict the number of product variations offered to customers. Other cost-saving strategies might include staff cuts, reductions in corporate image-building advertising, and temporary cuts in sales training activities. An example of the use of diversification to enhance revenue growth is shown in Marketing Strategies box 16-1.

Action Programs

The next step in the planning process is to translate broad strategy statements into specific actions and tactics. This can be helped along by setting up timetables to show the starting and completion dates for each activity. In addition, it is useful to assign responsibility to one individual to ensure that each project is completed on schedule. For example, a program to identify products for elimination might be given to a group product manager. These managers oversee the work of several product managers, and they have the experience needed to pick items for divestment. The group product managers could also farm out some of the elimination decisions to subordinates who monitor the day-to-day activities of each brand.

MARKETING STRATEGIES *16-1*

Growth from Diversification

APPLYING
. . . to
Health and
Beauty Aids
Marketing

Playtex Products Inc. was launched in 1986 as a leveraged buyout from its owner Beatrice Cos. Playtex sold its bra and underwear lines to Sara Lee Corp. in 1991, leaving it with 54 percent of its business derived from the sale of tampons. In 1996, Playtex found itself mired in price and promotion wars with Tambrands, now owned by Procter & Gamble. Heavy promotion by Tambrands for its market leading Tampax tampons forced Playtex to respond with its own two-for-one offers. The resulting battle left a glut of tampons in retail warehouses and consumers' medicine cabinets. This competitive struggle convinced Playtex that it needed to reduce its dependence on tampon sales. Playtex has since bought up Binky Pacifiers, Carewell Industries, a toothbrush maker, and the Personal Care Group which owns brands including Wet Ones, Mr. Bubble, Chubs baby wipes, and Binaca breath spray. Another recent acquisition is Diaper Genie that wraps soiled diapers in plastic. As a result of these purchases, Playtex has doubled its revenue from infant care to 34 percent of sales and feminine care products now amount to only 34 percent of revenue. Playtex's strategy of diversification has given it a 42 percent share of the rapidly growing infant care market to balance its slow growth position in the tampon business.

INTEGRATING
. . . with
Strategic
Planning

— *Diversification can lead to revenue growth for narrowly focused firms.*

Source: Tara Parker-Pope, "Playtex to Add Diaper Genie to Buying Spree," *The Wall Street Journal*, January 14, 1999, pp. B1, B3.

Courtesy Playtex Products, Inc.

The steps taken by America Online to protect its number-one position in Internet access provides a good look at a real action program. AOL currently offers slow dial-up service over phone lines that may become obsolete with the very quick broadband service coming from cable companies. To counter this threat, AOL purchased NetChannel, a firm that offers the Internet over TV sets. They also have appointed a manager of broadband marketing and are exploring relationships with Time Warner and other cable providers to reach cable modem customers. Perhaps AOL's most critical action program is lobbying legislators and the Federal Communications Commission in Washington to force cable companies to give them access to broadband cables being installed to give consumers faster Internet access.[2]

Anticipated Results

Once the specific tactics have been selected, managers are in a position to forecast the results of the new marketing plan. These are usually presented in the form of break-even charts, projected profit and loss statements, and cash flow budgets. Anticipated unit sales and total revenues are shown for each model and time period. When price changes are expected to occur during the planning horizon, they are factored into the revenue calculations and are shown in the profit and loss statement as net realized price. Costs are broken into fixed and variable categories for planning and control purposes. Production and physical distribution costs are subtracted from revenues to give estimates of gross margins in dollars and percentages. Next, gross margins per unit are divided into fixed costs to give break-even volumes at different prices. Then budgets are set for the sales force, advertising, sales promotion, market research, product development, and administrative expense categories. The difference between these expenses and the gross margin available is the profit for the planning period.

After the projected marketing budget has been approved by top management, it is used to monitor results. Actual sales and expenses recorded in each period are compared with the projected figures on a monthly and a year-to-date basis. Significant differences between the planned and actual results provide signals for remedial action.

Contingency Plans

Contingency strategies are needed because real-world events such as fires, drought, war, inflation, floods, and price cutting often interfere with even the best market plans. This section asks a series of "what if" questions about possible events in the marketplace and then answers them. For example, what if the market grows faster than forecast levels? A trigger point for action might occur when new orders are 30 percent above the long-range forecast. At this point, the firm could run into capacity limitations, although excess capacity might be available elsewhere in the industry. Possible responses in this situation might be to go to a three-shift production schedule operating seven days a week, advance the timing of capacity additions, be selective in accepting orders, and provide leadership in raising prices. Other contingency plans would be formulated to combat price cutting by competitors and failures to meet sales goals.

Some examples of contingency planning are provided by the interactions between Mexico's largest brewer, Modelo, and America's giant Anheuser-Busch Cos. With the expected passage of NAFTA, Modelo sold a majority stake to Anheuser to protect it from an expected influx of American beers. This did not happen, however, and Modelo saw its share of the Mexican market expand to 55 percent and its flagship Corona brand become the number-one imported beer in America. Corona's success caused Modelo's stockholders to ask Anheuser for more money for the shares they were selling. Anheuser refused, so Modelo renewed a distribution contract with its American distributor for a 10-year period before Anheuser could gain complete control of the company. Anheuser had expected to sell Corona through its own distribution network in the United States and was forced to make contingency plans. To satisfy its U.S. distributor's need for an imported beer, Anheuser began to market three Corona clones—Azteca (made in Mexico), Tequiza (made in the United States), and Rio Cristal (brewed in Brazil) to compete with a beer it already owns.[3]

The main advantage of contingency plans is that they force management to think about a broader range of problems than might occur when strategies are designed only to meet immediate company objectives. Also, contingency plans that have been made ahead of time can be implemented quickly if the need arises. As a former chairperson of General Motors has said, "I don't like people running into my office saying, 'Jeez, this just happened. So what do we do next?' I want to have a plan for just about everything."

Appendixes

This section contains supporting documents and exhibits. Make sure that they are numbered correctly and appear in a logical order. Remember that well-designed charts with three-dimensional shading and color are easier to read and understand. Attractive graphics are also useful if you are called on to give an oral presentation of your marketing plan.

Marketing Plan Example

APPLYING
. . . to
Medical
Products
Marketing

A sample marketing plan for a product acquired by Cook Inc. is shown in the Appendix. Cook Inc. is a successful medical products manufacturer in Bloomington, Indiana. The company had an opportunity to produce a new machine designed to help remove material from blocked arteries. The new product was an endarterectomy oscillator that fit in well with Cook's current product lines of diagnostic catheters. Our sample marketing plan suggests that the prospects for success with the endarterectomy oscillator looked good. However, the oscillator sold poorly and the item was one of very few product failures at Cook Inc. In this case the product proved to be dependable, it filled a need, was priced appropriately, and distributed effectively. The product failed because surgeons were slow to switch to new approaches to clear blocked arteries. Looking back, Cook should have done more with trial placements and education in hospitals to acquaint surgeons with the product and teach them how to use it. This example shows that marketing innovative surgical machines is much more complicated than introducing new types of catheters.

TESTING THE MARKETING PLAN

To help reduce risk, many marketing managers test their marketing plans using computer simulations. This approach saves time and money compared with field test markets or regional market evaluations. The use of simulations also provides secrecy and prevents your competitors from auditing your tests, stealing your ideas, or sabotaging your plan with special advertising gimmicks.

How Do Simulations Work?

Simulation is the use of a model to replicate the operation of a real system over time. Marketing simulations, for example, feed price, promotion, advertising, and distribution values into a model to estimate the sales volumes or market shares the products might have at the end of a time period. The main advantage of marketing plan simulations is that they allow you to bring together and study the interaction of several marketing variables at the same time. In addition, you can test various combinations of marketing factors without having to spend money to take the risks associated with making changes in the real world.

An example of how simulation is used by managers might be described as follows:

INTERVIEWER: Do you make regular simulation runs for assessing the marketing mix for a new product?

ANALYST: Oh, yes.

INTERVIEWER: Do you implement the results?

ANALYST: Oh, no!

INTERVIEWER: Well, that seems odd. If you don't implement the results, perhaps you should stop making the runs.

ANALYST: No, no. We wouldn't want to do that!

INTERVIEWER: Why not?

ANALYST: Well, what happens is something like this: I make several computer runs and take them to the brand manager. He is responsible for this whole multimillion-dollar project. The brand manager looks at the runs, thinks about them for a while, and then sends me back to make a few more, with conditions changed in various ways. I do this and bring them back in. He looks at them and probably sends me back to make more runs. And so forth.

INTERVIEWER: How long does this keep up?

ANALYST: I would say it continues until finally the brand manager screws up enough courage to make a decision.

Simulation thus encourages manager-model interaction to improve understanding of the business environment and to help make better plans. When you do not agree with the simulation results, the input data can be reexamined and tests run to see how sensitive the results are to changes in parameters. This process of interacting with a model allows you to learn more about your problems without giving up control to the computer.

Simulation Examples

Simulations have been used to test marketing plans in many firms. It is common, for example, to run alternative advertising schedules through simulation models to find which media give the best customer exposure. One new product model is used to evaluate the impact of alternative package sizes, coupon schedules, and promotions on the sales of newly introduced items. This program has proved to be so valuable that it is often run more than 400 times in a single month.

Simulation can help you build better marketing plans by employing models that replicate the operation of real-world systems. Simulation is not a cure-all; it is merely one of several tools available to simplify complex marketing problems. The main problem with marketing simulations is because many variables are involved, it is often difficult to find optimum solutions. One approach is to make a series of simplifying assumptions, but this can lend an aura of unreality to the recommendations. A better approach is to restrict the number of marketing variables in each simulation project. For example, Figure 16–2 shows the results of a simulation designed to find the optimal product mix and prices for an individual firm. This simulation involved a search across 20 product alternatives and preferences of 60 consumers divided into eight market segments. The lines at the bottom of the figure represent combined utility curves for the eight segments. Note that the utility curves rise to ideal points and then decline across product alternatives. In this case, a profit-maximizing solution was found in less than a minute, using appropriate heuristics and a desktop computer. Complex simulations that take hours to run on a mainframe computer are not much help to marketing decision makers.

The solution recommended in Figure 16-2 suggests marketing the three products shown by the dark price bars. Profit maximization raised prices so that segments 1 to 3 were shut out of the market. Segment 4 chose product 4, and segments 5 to 7 chose product 10. Seg-

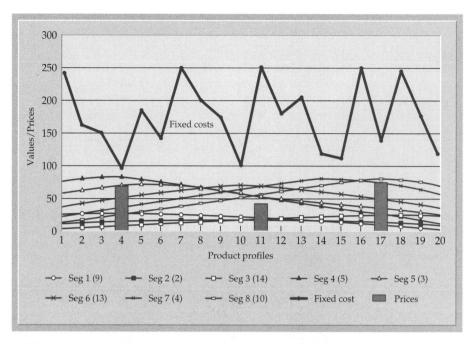

FIGURE 16-2   **Using Simulations to Optimize Product Mix and prices for Eight Market Segments (From Gregory Dobson and Shlomo Kalish, "Heuristics for Pricing and Positioning a Product Line Using Conjoint and Cost Data,"** *Management Science* **[February 1993], p. 170)**

ment 8 selected product 17. The beauty of this simulation approach is that it allows marketing managers to quickly evaluate a variety of price and product mix alternatives. Common applications of simulation in marketing have been to (1) help develop alternative marketing strategies, (2) provide inexpensive test markets to evaluate strategies, and (3) help control the implementation of marketing programs.

IMPLEMENTATION AND CONTROL

The success of marketing plans frequently depends on the level of execution that is achieved by the salespeople, dealers, and advertising agencies that implement programs in the real world. Even the most brilliant plan will fail if it is not implemented correctly. Effective implementation converts marketing plans into individual assignments and makes sure that they are executed on time. Business firms must have a system of control that quickly points out execution errors and helps managers take corrective action. An important first step is to decide what factors best explain the success or failure of an individual marketing plan. Depending on business conditions, a firm might emphasize market share, dollar volume, unit sales, dollar profit, or stockholder equity. Marketing control is basically a set of procedures that allows managers to compare the results of marketing plans with predetermined standards so that corrective action can be taken to ensure that objectives are met. Effective control requires a system that gathers data on market conditions and places them in the hands of executives who can make adjustments in plans and operating procedures.

A flow diagram that highlights the basic elements of the marketing control process is presented in Figure 16-3. The first few steps involve planning and are usually performed on an annual basis. Objectives are adopted; price, promotion, advertising, and distribution strategies are selected; and performance standards are set for sales quotas, selling expenses,

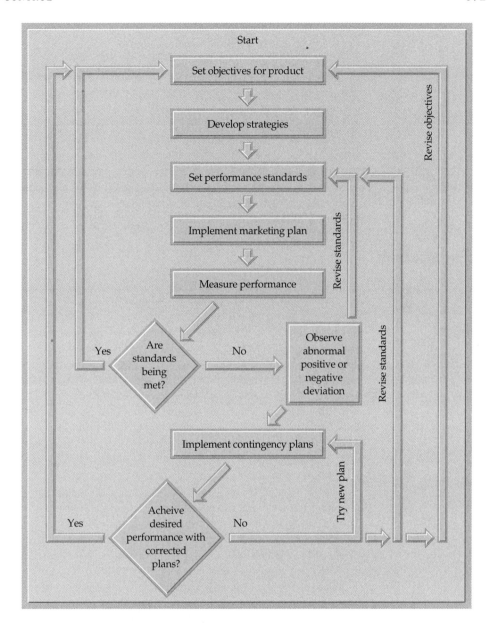

FIGURE 16-3 **Marketing Control Process**

and other control variables. Next, the marketing program is implemented over a span of time, and periodic measurements are taken to record the reactions of customers and competitors. The basic aim of the control process is to see whether the predetermined performance standards are being met. If they are, the successful results are fed back to the starting point and used to set the objectives for the next planning period (Figure 16-3).

When significant deviations from performance standards are observed, the manager has the choice of changing the standards or implementing contingency plans to attempt to correct the problem (Figure 16-3). For example, suppose that a new product, expected to attain a 3 percent market share after six months, actually captured 10 percent of the market. This suggests that the original estimate was low, and the manager should probably raise the annual forecast to 8 percent or more so that the production, advertising, and distribution efforts can be adjusted to reflect realized demand.

In the more typical situation in which sales fail to reach desired levels, managers can try a variety of short-run strategies to get the product back on target. These may take the form of cents-off coupons, new advertising themes or media, deals for retailers, changes in ad schedules, increased advertising, contests for salespeople, or simple changes in packaging or product specifications. If these tonics fail to do the job, the manager may have to revise the standards or objectives for the next planning period (Figure 16-3). In addition, managers can initiate special market research studies to determine why products do not reach long-run sales goals. These efforts may result in entirely new products, major changes in existing items, new channels, realignments in selling efforts, or a decision to drop the offending products entirely. An illustration showing how a new marketing plan helped save a company is described in Marketing in Action box 16-3.

Setting Standards

Performance standards are planned achievement levels for selected marketing variables that the firm expects to attain at stated intervals throughout the year. Managers do not have time to watch all dimensions of the marketing plan; they must select the most important performance factors to be monitored on a regular basis. In addition to traditional dollar sales, profit, and market share goals, most firms set standards for selling and advertising expenses. These are often expressed as a percentage of sales to simplify comparisons with past performance and the experience of other firms in the industry. For example, a company could measure the efficiency of its sales organization by setting a standard of 10 percent of revenue to cover branch office overhead, salaries of salespeople and sales managers, travel, commissions, bonuses, and customer entertainment. Other marketing factors that can be used for control purposes are shown in Table 16-3.

Measuring Performance

Marketing information systems provide the basic data used by control systems to compare planned performance with real-world results. A control system should permit assignment of responsibility for differences between planned and actual performance. Managers rely on a variety of special reports to point out deviations between standards and actual operations so that corrective action can be taken.

An example showing how a marketing control system operates is provided by the U.S. food company H.J. Heinz. The product was a frequently purchased item found in supermarkets. It was sold in several different sizes, and one size or another was promoted to the trade every four to six weeks. The impact of promotion on market share appeared to vary by container size and across sales districts. To study these effects, Heinz built some response functions for 27 market areas.

Newspaper features were the primary promotional tool used to draw customers' attention to the product. Heinz kept track of the number of features run, the share of the market of the retail chain, the size of the feature ad, and the percentage discount offered by the feature in relation to the average level of discounting to which the customers had become accustomed. These revealed that there was little evidence of any relationship among promotional spending and either the number of newspaper features or market share. The number of newspaper features for competitive products, as well as those for the product, did influence Heinz's market share.

Additional calculations suggested that most promotions were, on average, unprofitable. Accordingly, the number of promotions in most districts was decreased, and those promotions that were conducted were adjusted to include package sizes that seemed to be most

MARKETING IN ACTION *16-3*

Rescuing Quaker Oats

After Quaker Oats lost $1.4 billion on the sale of its Snapple beverage division, they hired a new CEO from Kraft Foods. Instead of selling off the company in pieces as Wall Street expected, the CEO instituted a new marketing plan. First he sold off two food-service divisions and combined Quaker's foods and beverage businesses into one organization, eliminating a layer of management. He also consolidated the sales forces and they now sell Gatorade and snack foods. To push its strongest brand, Gatorade, the company introduced new flavors such as Midnight Thunder, innovative packaging in the form of wide mouthed bottles, and a successful line of flavors under the Frost Label, a lighter-tasting drink. To sustain Gatorade growth, Quaker is focusing on getting the sports beverage into more places where people sweat. This involves expanding distribution for active thirst occasions with vending machines at golf courses, tennis centers, schools, and hospitals in warm weather states. The CEO is also shifting dollars from retail discounts to Gatorade advertising. Since the new CEO initiated his marketing plan, Quaker Oats' unit volume and profits have increased sharply. Also Quaker stock has jumped from $47 when the new manager arrived to $61. When the CEO took over, he was given options to buy 1.3 million shares at $47. The success of his marketing plan has provided him with a paper gain on his Quaker options of $1.8 million.

— *Good execution of a marketing plan can rescue a company in trouble.*

Source: Rekha Balu, "Like Oatmeal, Morrison Proves Good for Quaker," *The Wall Street Journal*, October 27, 1998, pp.B1, B6.

Courtesy Quaker Oats

TABLE 16-3   Performance Measures Used for Control Purposes

Customers	Awareness levels
	Inquiries
	Complaints
	Number of returns
	Warranty expense
Product	Rate of trial
	Repeat purchase rate
	Cannibalization rate
	Price relative to those of competitors
	Coupon redemption rate
Distribution	Average order and delivery time
	Percentage of stores carrying the product
	Months of inventory in dealers' hands
	Distribution costs per unit
Sales and advertising	Advertising cost per unit sold
	Turnover rate of sales force
	Sales calls per day
	Number of new accounts opened
	Sales per order
	Number of accounts lost

effectively promoted within a given district. During the first year in which these actions were taken, the total number of promotions was reduced by 40 percent, yet market share increased by more than three share points.

A marketing control system was designed to monitor Heinz's promotional activities. Each month the newly available data are entered into the system, and the current effectiveness of the promotions is evaluated. The purpose of the marketing control system is to detect changes in the effectiveness of any particular type of promotion. Heinz was concerned that rapidly rising prices in the general economy might make the consumer less loyal and more price conscious. As a result of the system, Heinz found that occasionally promotions for a particular size that had been successful in the past became ineffectual. Moreover, some promotions that had always been ineffective in a district became successful. The marketing control system thus accomplished its purpose in revealing changes in customers' habits.

SUMMARY

This chapter has shown why marketing plans are needed to help guide field marketing activities. In addition, we have explained who prepares marketing plans and how they are organized. The development of effective marketing programs depends on timely data.

The success of marketing planning in the real world frequently depends on how well the various elements of the marketing mix work together. Enlightened managers are now able to pretest the interactions of marketing variables by running examples through special business simulations. These simulations allow the manager to test combinations of marketing factors without spending the money or taking the risks associated with making changes in an actual competitive environment.

Computers can also be used to help monitor the implementation of marketing programs. The basic control process is a check for differences between desired performance standards and actual results. When negative deviations occur, simulation can be employed to determine what has gone wrong with the marketing plans and help develop new strategies.

In addition to monitoring current operations, you must prepare yourself for the future. This means that marketing programs should be audited periodically to make sure that the firm has the right products, personnel, and channels of distribution to fill customers' needs and meet the challenges offered by competitors.

NOTES

1. Nick Wingfield, "Free Search of Trademark Database Can Provide Clues to Companies' Plans," *The Wall Street Journal*, October 20, 1998, p. B8.
2. Thomas E. Weber, "Inside the Race to Grab High-Speed Connections: Cable Providers Could Become Rivals of AOL," *The Wall Street Journal*, October 22, 1998, pp. B1, B8.
3. Jonathan Friedland and Rekha Balu, "Head to Head: For Mighty Anheuser, No Rival Is Too Small—Even One It Owns," *The Wall Street Journal*, October 22, 1998, pp. A1, A10.

SUGGESTED READING

Albers, Sönke. "A Framework for Analysis of Sources of Profit Contribution Variance Between Actual and Plan," *International Journal of Research in Marketing*, Vol.15, No.2 (May 1998), pp. 109–122.

Cohen, William A. *The Marketing Plan* (New York: John Wiley, 1997).

REFERENCES

Gumpert, David E. *How to Really Create a Successful Marketing Plan* (Boston: Inc Publishing, 1996).

Hiebing, Roman G., and Scott W. Cooper. *The Successful Marketing Plan: A Disciplined and Comprehensive Approach* (Lincolnwood, IL: NTC Publishing 1997).

Larkin, Geraldine A. *12 Simple Steps to a Winning Marketing Plan* (Burr Ridge, IL: Probus Publishing Co., 1992).

QUESTIONS

1. In the third quarter of 1998, worldwide shipments of PCs increased 15 percent from the third quarter of the previous year. However, total worldwide revenue for PCs did not increase due to sinking prices. From 1996 to 1998 the average selling price for a PC dropped from $2,000 to $1,100. Meanwhile the five biggest PC marketers (Compaq, IBM, Dell, Hewlett-Packard, and Gateway) increased their share of the total world market from 37 percent to 40.6 percent. How should smaller PC producers adjust their marketing plans in response to these changes?

2. American power companies have been slow to buy new electrical generation equipment because of concerns about overcapacity and the uncertainties of deregulation. However, a shortage of power in the Midwest during a 1998 heat wave caused power companies to scramble to order new gas-powered turbines. Now the order books for turbine manufacturers are full and prices have increased. Should turbine builders, such as GE and ABB, adjust their marketing plans to reduce expenditures on marketing activities?

3. Ames Department Stores has purchased Hills Stores for $127 million to create a firm with sales over $4 billion a year from 456 stores. The combined firm will be the fourth largest U.S. discount store behind Wal-Mart, Kmart, and Target. By targeting lower-income and elderly customers, Ames has found a niche that sets it apart from Wal-Mart. The deal will also provide Ames with increased purchasing power and should mean lower prices for customers. Does Ames's plan to grow by merging two firms that have

recently filed for bankruptcy protection insure success in the future? What other adjustments to Ames's marketing plan do you recommend?

4. General Motors has signed a multibillion dollar 10-year deal to buy substantial amounts of aluminum from Alcan Aluminum Lt. The order suggests that GM plans to design much more aluminum into its vehicles, displacing steel. Why is GM substituting high-cost aluminum for steel and how will this change affect their plans to sell cars and trucks?

5. The nation's largest automobile insurance company has been granted a charter to operate a federal savings bank. State Farm plans to teach its 16,000 insurance agents to market products such as savings accounts, certificates of deposit, money market accounts, and mortgage and car loans to the company's insurance customers. They eventually plan to offer checking accounts. Why has State Farm taken this radical step to broaden their product offerings? What marketing synergies will occur as a result of this planned expansion?

6. Mercedes-Benz of Germany recently purchased America's third largest auto manufacturer, Chrysler. Why did Daimler, a producer of high-priced cares and trucks, want Chrysler that sells such low-priced cars as the Neon? How will the marketing plans of Chrysler be changed now that it is owned by Daimler?

7. Private labels now account for 21 percent of sales in the largest 15 U.S. grocery stores, up from 17 percent in 1992. During this period, a new private label company, American Italian Pasta Co., has grabbed 25 percent of the pasta market from national brands. What adjustments should the national brand firms make to their marketing plans to counter this growing threat to their food business?

8. Granola bars were introduced as a snack for health-conscious consumers. They were made from rolled oats, sugar, and dried fruit or nuts. Unfortunately, many consumers thought they tasted like cardboard, and sales were disappointing. Granola bar makers then added chocolate and peanut butter to their offerings and sales soared. The distinction between granola bars and candy bars has narrowed (Table 16-4). Consumers associate "granola" with "healthy." Granola bar makers reinforce this consumer perception by emphasizing "wholesome" and "goodness" in their advertising. Is the conduct of the granola makers ethical?

TABLE 16-4   Granola Bars Versus Candy Bars

		How Those Calories Break Down			
	Calories (per oz.)	Fat	Added Sugar	Complex Carbohydrates	Protein
Quaker Dips Granola Bars	158	40%	23%	29%	6%
Hershey's New Train Granola Bars	143	42	23	28	7
Nature Valley Chewy Granola Bars	138	38	21	35	7
Snickers	137	43	38	11	8
Milky Way	128	33	49	14	4

Source: Center for Science in the Public Interest.

APPENDIX SAMPLE MARKETING PLAN FOR COOK INC. ENDARTERECTOMY OSCILLATOR*

COMPANY SITUATION

Cook Inc. is a rapidly growing medical supply manufacturer. The company is currently profitable selling cardiovascular catheters, ureteral catheters, heart pacemakers, x-ray radiopaque dye, and stents. Cook sells its products throughout the world and markets catheters in the United States with a staff of 20 company salespeople. Their strongest market position is in their core cardiovascular catheter product lines. Cook's greatest strength is its highly trained staff of catheter designers and assembly workers. Recently the company has been given the opportunity to produce and market an endarterectomy oscillator developed by Dr. Everett Lerwick, a leading vascular surgeon. Endarterectomy oscillators move dissecting loops and debrading catheters back and forth inside arteries to help remove material that restricts the flow of blood. Oscillators are less invasive than other surgical procedures and can reduce the cost of treating partial arterial blockages.

ENVIRONMENT

Heart and vascular disease is a leading cause of death in America. New products that make it easier to treat these diseases and reduce death rates have been well received by physicians and governmental regulatory agencies. At the present time, there are no competing endarterectomy oscillators on the market. In addition, Dr. Lerwick's oscillator has a strong patent position that will prevent competitors from copying the present design. The Lerwick oscillator can be manufactured from standard components with the current staff and facilities of Cook Inc. We do not anticipate any threats from competitors, governmental regulators or existing laws that will prevent our product and sale of endarterectomy oscillators.

TARGET MARKETS

The current market potential for endarterectomy oscillators appears to be good. At the present time, artery blockages have to be treated with complex bypass surgery. The endarterectomy oscillator would replace the need for surgery and encourage collateral blood flow in surrounding tissue. If each hospital qualified to do this type of procedure bought only one oscillator and 20 percent of the cardiovascular surgeons purchased as well, total market potential would be 3500 units. This estimate is conservative because many of the hospitals have more than one operating room where cardiovascular surgery is performed. Thus, many hospitals would need more than one unit. If 30 percent of the hospitals bought two units, then total demand would be 4400 units.

A reasonable assumption in this case with respect to the expected life cycle of the oscillator would be about 10 years. This means that 10 percent penetration of the market each year would generate sales of 440 units and if each oscillator produced annual sales of $1,000 for dissecting loops and debriding catheters, sales revenue would be over $1 million per year. These are substantial revenues that could be added to Cook's sales receipts. Given the strong patent position on the oscillator, the target market potential is attractive.

OBJECTIVES

Cook has a reputation for selling high quality technologically advanced health care products. New items are expected to follow in this tradition to build sales and profits. The company favors product expansion that uses the existing manufacturing expertise, distribution channels and sales techniques. As a relatively small player in the medical equipment market, Cook does not require a number one or number two market share position to consider themselves successful.

STRATEGY

Each firm must have its own strategic vision. Cook looks to improve its market position through diversification and differentiation. Strategies for each element of the marketing mix for the endarterectomy oscillator are as follows.

---

* This marketing plan was prepared by Douglas J. Dalrymple from data supplied by Cook Inc. Some figures in the plan as well as some time sequences have been disguised. An executive summary has not been included to save space.

Product Design

The endarterectomy oscillator has been carefully developed and tested by Dr. Everett Lerwick, a leading vascular surgeon. The product was used in 90 successful operations over a period of five years. In addition, the long-run survival rate of patients has been encouraging. Lerwick's oscillator has proven to be durable, and Cook could expect continued sales of replacement loops and debriding catheters to go along with each machine.

In terms of design, the endarterectomy oscillator is fairly simple. The device has an electric motor whose circular motion is converted to oscillations in a 120° arc up to 8000 times per minute. The oscillations are transmitted through a handpiece with special loops that clear the material from the patient's arteries. Speed of oscillation is controlled by a foot pedal. This mechanical device has proven to be reliable, and there are few areas for product failure. All indications suggest that the endarterectomy oscillator is an excellent product that is ready to go to market.

Promotion

Extensive promotion will be needed to help acquaint surgeons with the new oscillator. Several rounds of direct mail are appropriate at a cost of $5000 each. In addition, six journal ads would help prepare the doctors for calls by the Cook sales force. Displays at four trade shows would seem to be a minimum to demonstrate to doctors how the new machine operates. These shows seem expensive ($2800), but they will require Cook to rent extra space and pay Dr. Lerwick's expenses. Trade shows are cost effective because large numbers of surgeons can be contacted in one location.

Distribution Channels

The use of the present distribution channels for the oscillator presents a number of problems for Cook. First, the product sells for a much higher price than the curent line of catheters that are purchased for $5 or $10 and then thrown away. The oscillator will require time-consuming personal sales calls to allow for demonstrations and closing. Moreover, the current salespeople are paid a salary and can sell large volumes of catheters much more easily than they can sell the new oscillator. In addition, the purchase of equipment is likely to be handled separately from supplies, and Cook will have to call on different people than those interested in catheters.

Sales force interest in the oscillator could be improved by offering a 10 percent sales commission, but this would reduce the profit potential. Another solution would be to assign one of the current salespeople or hire someone to be an oscillator specialist. This would raise fixed costs but probably could be justified by the strong market potential. Another possibility would be to manufacture the oscillator and then get an outside firm to sell it along with other products. If independent reps could be recruited to sell the oscillator for 10 to 15 percent of sales, then Cook would be advised to consider this channel of distribution. The problem for Cook is that independent reps are not interested in new products until it is clear that they have caught on in the marketplace. Reps do not want items that take a lot of time to build market acceptance. In addition, if development work has to be done, the reps will demand a margin of 30 to 40 percent of sales. If Cook has to pay 40 percent to the reps and 10 percent to Lerwick, then there will be very little profit unless a high price is charged.

Pricing

Pricing is a key decision because price will help determine the ultimate profitability of the product. Because the product is patented and hospitals are not expected to be sensitive to the price of this item, a skimming price is indicated. In this case, hospitals could easily charge off the cost of the oscillator to surgical patients over the course of a year. A skimming price of three to five times the cost would suggest selling prices between $1350 and $2250. Although these prices seem high, they are within the realm of possibility.

Because both fixed and variable cost elements are present, a multiple breakeven analysis is appropriate with selling prices of $1350, $1800, and $2250. Three different scenarios for sales force effort can also be considered. They are: (1) give salespeople no added incentive; (2) give salespeople an additional 10 percent commission; and (3) add an oscillator specialist. The resulting set of breakeven calculations is shown in the table in the Anticipated Results section.

With a selling price of $1350, the breakeven is less than one sales per week even when sales force effort is encouraged with a 10 percent commission. Adding a specialized salesperson increases the breakeven to about two sales per week at the same selling price. By increasing fixed costs, the addition of a salesperson increases the risk.

Strategic Choices

Introduction of the oscillator has a number of advantages for Cook. First, the market potential is strong, and the product is patented to keep competition at bay.

Second, the oscillator fits in well as a product line extension for the current line of catheters. Indeed, both the oscillator and Cook catheters can be used in the same surgical procedures. Furthermore, the product will be easy to manufacture with existing tools and labor. In addition, the oscillator can be sold with the same distribution channels used for the catheters. At prices over $1000, Cook makes good margins and the breakeven point is low. The key issue, however, is risk. Cook has spent nothing to develop the oscillator. In addition, production of the oscillators does not require new tooling, new equipment, new plant, or new technology, and promotional costs are modest. Thus, the risk to Cook if it takes on the product and it fails is very low. On the other hand, if the oscillator succeeds, profits will be good because Cook has so little money tied up in the project. The benefits of introducing the oscillator outweigh the risks: add the oscillator to the product line.

ACTION PROGRAM

Set an introductory price of $1350.
Sell extra dissecting loops at $65 each and charge $90 for the debriding catheter.
Sell the oscillator with the existing field sales force.
Promote the oscillator with direct mail and trade shows.
Avoid journal ads and special sales commissions.

ANTICIPATED RESULTS

A multiple breakeven analysis (Exhibit 1) shows that at a price of $1350, Cook only needs to sell 41 units to cover their costs.

Since this is only about one percent of the projected market of 3500 hospitals and cardiovascular surgeons, the oscillator should generate a handsome profit. Also shifting the $9600 ad money shown in the breakeven

EXHIBIT 1   Multiple Breakeven Analysis

Give Salespeople No Added Incentive			
Price	$ 1350	$ 1800	$ 2250
Royalty (10%)	135	180	225
Net revenue	1215	1620	2025
Variable production cost	450	450	450
Margin/unit	$ 765	$ 1170	$ 1575
Promotion	$ 30,800[a]	$ 30,800	$ 30,800
Breakeven volume	41	27	20
Sweeten with 10% Commission			
Price	$ 1350	$ 1800	$ 2250
Royalty (10%)	135	180	225
Net revenue	1215	1620	2025
Variable production cost	450	450	450
Commission (10%)	135	180	225
Total variable costs	585	630	675
Margin/unit	$ 630	$ 990	$ 1350
Promotion	$ 30,800	$ 30,800	$ 30,800
Breakeven volume	49	32	23
Add a Salesperson			
Price	$ 1350	$ 1800	$ 2250
Royalty (10%)	135	180	225
Net revenue	1215	1620	2025
Variable production cost	450	450	450
Margin/unit	$ 765	$ 1170	$ 1575
Promotion	30,800	30,800	30,800
Salesperson	50,000	50,000	50,000
Total fixed costs	$ 80,800	$ 80,800	$ 80,800
Breakeven volume	106	69	52

[a] 6 ads (@$1,600)	$ 9,600
4 conventions (@ $2,800)	11,200
5,000 direct mail brochures (@$2.00)	10,000
	$30,800

analysis to conventions and direct mail will make it easier to reach the breakeven volume of 41 units. Cook did not spend any money to design the oscillator, and it is anticipated that the breakeven volume will be reached during the first year of production.

CONTINGENCY PLAN

If the oscillator is selling at a rate of less than one per week at the end of the first year, discontinue selling it.

CASE 16-1 PROCTER & GAMBLE: FACELLE DIVISION FACIAL TISSUE*

Early in March 1992, Randall Beard was reviewing performance of the brands of facial tissue that Procter & Gamble had acquired in August 1991. "Now that we have had a few months to understand the tissue business in Canada," he thought, "it's time to build our plan for the future of the business. P&G hasn't spent $185 million in acquiring the Facelle division in order to stand still in the marketplace."

Although Procter & Gamble had global brands in some categories of paper products (e.g., Pampers, the leading disposable diaper), the Facelle acquisition was P&G's first step outside the U.S. in the tissue/towel business. For that reason, senior management would be closely watching the progress of the Facelle brands of facial tissue, paper towels, and bathroom tissue. In particular, the facial tissue market was especially challenging, as 1991 had seen more competitive product initiatives than the previous several years put together.

As associate advertising manager for Tissue, Towel and Facial Products, Randall Beard reported directly to Barbara Fraser, vice president and general manager of the Paper Products business in Canada. Together, the two would be responsible for several major decisions about the facial tissue brands, including positioning, product formulations, and promotion. For his forthcoming meeting with Fraser, Beard wanted to have a set of definite recommendations on the future of the brands.

THE PROCTER & GAMBLE COMPANY

Procter & Gamble originated in 1837, when William Procter and James Gamble, two immigrant soap and candle makers, formed a partnership in Cincinnati, Ohio. The partnership rapidly flourished, gaining a name as a principled manufacturer of high quality consumer goods sold at competitive prices. The Procter & Gamble Company was incorporated in 1890, and in every decade since incorporation, sales more than doubled. By 1992, P&G was a multinational company with annual sales of almost $30 billion (U.S.), profits exceeding $1.8 billion (U.S.), and a long-standing reputation for quality products, high integrity, strong marketing, and conservative management.

As Procter & Gamble grew, it increasingly focused on international markets. In 1992, P&G's brands were sold in more than 140 countries around the world. Major areas and representative brands included laundry and cleaning products (e.g., Tide, Cheer, Mr. Clean), paper products (Pampers, Luvs, Always, Bounty, Charmin), health care (Pepto-Bismol, Metamucil), oral care (Crest, Scope), food and beverage (Jif, Crisco), bar soaps (Ivory, Zest) and cosmetics (Oil of Olay, Max Factor, Cover Girl). Many of these brands were leaders in their categories.

In Canada, P&G operated as Procter & Gamble Inc., with 1992 sales expected to exceed $1.7 billion, and earnings before taxes of over $100 million. P&G Inc. operated as four divisions, of which Paper Products was one, organized on a category basis within

---

* This case was prepared by Professor Terry H. Deutscher solely to provide material for class discussion. The author does not intend to illustrate either effective or ineffective handling of a managerial situation. The author may have disguised certain names and other identifying information to protect confidentiality. One-time permission to reproduce granted by Ivey Management Services on February 1, 1999. Copyright © 1993, The University of Western Ontario. The University prohibits any form of reproduction, storage, or transmittal without written permission from the Richard Ivey School of Business. This material is not covered under authorization from CanCopy or any other reproduction rights organization.

each division (e.g., Tissue/Towel/Facial within Paper Products).

Procter & Gamble in Paper Products

Procter & Gamble first entered the consumer paper market in 1957 with its acquisition of Charmin Paper Company, a regional company with a strong presence in the north central U.S. In the early 1960s, P&G developed proprietary papermaking technologies which allowed it to deliver softness, strength and absorbency that were superior to conventionally manufactured products. This technology was used to strengthen the Charmin toilet tissue brand, leading to national expansion in the mid-sixties. Simultaneously, P&G launched Bounty towels, also employing the new technology, and subsequently expanded the brand to national distribution in 1972. Finally, P&G entered the facial tissue market in the early 1970s by launching the Puffs brand, which was initially sold as a regional brand, then expanded to the national market in 1990.

P&G built Charmin, Bounty and Puffs with similar strategies. First, proprietary technology was used to deliver products with superior performance at a competitive price. As well, consumers were offered "value-added" products which delivered additional benefits (e.g., Puffs Plus with lotion, Charmin Free with no inks, dyes or perfumes). Third, the brands were supported with successful advertising themes and consistently high media weights. Finally, P&G achieved competitive costs among premium brands by using Total Quality Methods to improve the papermaking process. Together, these strategies were extremely successful. Charmin and Bounty established clear market share leadership in their categories, with Puffs a close second (to Kimberly-Clark's Kleenex brand) in the facial tissue category.

The Facelle Acquisition

By 1991, P&G was sufficiently satisfied with its U.S. successes on Charmin, Bounty and Puffs that it was ready to take its first step in expanding the business. Canada was the logical first choice for that step, given its proximity to the U.S., the advent of free trade between Canada and the U.S., and the attendant opportunities for North American supply sourcing. At the time, P&G had only one paper plant in Canada, which manufactured diapers in Belleville, Ontario.

Early in 1991, an attractive acquisition opportunity developed for P&G. Canadian Pacific Forest Product Company, a large diversified paper company, was prepared to sell Facelle Paper Products, its tissue division. Facelle was a medium-sized manufacturer and mar-

keter of tissue, towel and sanitary products, headquartered in Toronto. In 1990, Facelle reported an operating profit of $13.4 million on sales of $170.5 million. The deal was concluded in August 1991; for $185 million, P&G bought the Facelle Co., its plant in Toronto, and its franchise for facial tissue, paper towels and bathroom tissue, including the Royale, Florelle, Pronto, Dove, Facettes, and Festival brands.

THE CONSUMER PAPER BUSINESS IN CANADA

The Canadian consumer paper market in 1992 was about 25 million cases, where a case represented a shipping unit of approximately equivalent size for the three principal types of tissue. In the facial tissue category, a case contained the equivalent of 48 boxes of 150 two-ply tissues. Of the 25 million cases, bathroom tissue accounted for 13 million, paper towels seven million, and facial tissue five million. Tissue products were inexpensive (usually less than $2.00 per package), they were widely used (in more than 95 percent of Canadian households), and they were frequently purchased (on average, once every two weeks). Brand switching was high, as there were many acceptable substitutes and the risk associated with product failure was low. The challenge for manufacturers was to differentiate their products enough on performance to build loyalty.

Retailing

Not surprisingly, retailers viewed paper as a low-profit, low-loyalty category, and they used it primarily to draw consumers into their stores. Traditional food stores typically carried a full line of paper products and featured them frequently. In recent years, however, mass merchandiser and drug chains had expanded their paper business substantially, focusing almost exclusively on price deals to attract customers to their stores. Recently, "club stores," with their emphasis on everyday low pricing, further squeezed retail and manufacturer margins. The vigorous retail competition had led to heavy featuring, where some brand was on sale virtually every week of the year, with resultant low profit margins. The challenge for manufacturers was to convince retailers to use their brands as the key feature items while trying to find ways to help retailers build profit.

Manufacturing

The paper business in Canada had a few very large national manufacturers and a few smaller regional players. This structure was driven, in part, by the sizable scale efficiencies that had been achieved in paper-making. Therefore, the industry was characterized by high capital and fixed costs. A single paper machine cost at least $100 million (U.S.), and at capacity it could satisfy about 10 percent of the Canadian market.

This cost structure, combined with the consumer and retail customer behaviors described above, strongly encouraged paper manufacturers to run their machines near capacity to maximize their contribution. Thus, most manufacturers marketed broad product lines in an attempt to compete in all segments of the market and utilize as much capacity as possible. Also, they competed intensely for the product features which drove volume at the retail level. It was common in the industry for one manufacturer to market both premium and price brands in all three of the Tissue, Towel and Facial categories, to supply retailers with private label products in the same categories, and to sell to the commercial and institutional markets as well. Furthermore, many retailers had moved to a "bidding" process that allocated featured promotions to the manufacturer with the most lucrative retail spending program.

The largest players in the Canadian consumer paper business were Scott Paper and Kimberly-Clark, both subsidiaries of successful large U.S. paper companies. In addition, there were several small regional players, of whom the largest was Irving Paper, operating in the Maritimes.

THE FACIAL TISSUE MARKET IN CANADA

A cost structure that Beard could envision for a national manufacturer competing aggressively in the facial tissue market is presented in Exhibit 1, based on the cost information presented above. Over half of the variable manufacturing cost of facial tissue was the cost of wood pulp.

The size of the facial tissue market in 1991 was 4,894,000 cases shipped, up 7 percent over 1990 sales. Market shares of the major producers, indexed to 1990 shares, are presented in Exhibit 2. They will be discussed in the following paragraphs.

Brand Developments in 1991

Facelle Brands   Shipments of the Facelle brands of facial tissue in 1991 were only 622,000 cases, or 84 percent of the 1990 results. Two brands, Royale and Florelle, accounted for most of Facelle's sales. Florelle and Royal were made from the same base tissue stock, with Royale having three layers or plys, while Florelle had only two. Until recently, the Royale brand had been the only 3-ply tissue on the market, and it enjoyed

EXHIBIT 1   Typical Cost Structure: Facial Tissue in Canada

	Cost per Case of 48 Units of 150-count two-ply tissue	
Net Revenue		$54
Off-invoice Allowance	$9[a]	
Co-op Allowance	10[b]	
Less: Total Discounts and Allowance		19
Net Sales		35
Less: Variable Manufacturing Cost (Including Delivery)		16[c]
Contribution		19
Manufacturing Fixed Cost	11	
Selling, Research, & Administration	3	
Marketing Support[d]	1	
Less: Total Fixed Costs		15
Profit		$ 4

[a] Average price reduction through the year, assuming feature price reductions of 25 percent were given on approximately 2/3 of the unit volume.
[b] Allowance for cooperative advertising and promotion. Some of these funds were actually used by retailers for this purpose, and the rest was retained by them.
[c] In March 1992, about 55 percent of the variable manufacturing cost of facial tissue was the cost of wood pulp. As a result, there was a substantial difference in profitability between the Florelle and Royale brands.
[d] Advertising, couponing, sampling. For many of the existing brands, less than $1 per case was spent on advertising support.

a brand image as the traditional, strong, premium quality facial tissue. Its market share increased very slightly during 1991. Florelle was a 2-ply tissue that had received little promotional attention. Not surprisingly, it had low awareness, trial and image. It had lost about one-third of its market share in 1991, down to 5.8 percent.

EXHIBIT 2   Facial Tissue Market Shares—1991

Company/Brand	Percentage Share of 1991 Shipments	Total P&G Index vs. 1990 Shares
Royale	6.9	101[a]
Florelle[b]	5.8	67
Total P&G	12.7	84
Kimberly-Clark	39.5	107
Scott	23.0	88
Irving	4.2	n.a.
All Others	20.6	98
	100.0	

[a] Index = (1991 share)/(1990 share) × 100. For example, the Royale index of 101 was calculated by dividing Royale's 1991 market share of 6.9 percent by their share of 6.8 per cent in 1990.
[b] In data throughout the case, Florelle numbers will include the Facettes brand. Facettes was a minor price brand.

Kimberly-Clark The Kleenex brand had enjoyed a very good year in 1991, gaining 2.5 share points to reach 39.5 percent of units shipped in the Canadian market. In fact, Kleenex's share reached 41.7 percent in the second half of the year. For several years in the late 1980s, Kimberly-Clark had made no significant changes in the Kleenex brand. However, there were several Kleenex product initiatives during 1991 which affected the brand's sales results. The new 300-tissue family size (2-ply) package, which had first been introduced in September 1989, had completed its national rollout in 1991; it achieved a share for the year of 8.2 percent, up from 3.1 percent in 1990. Also, the rollout of the 2-ply Kleenex 150, which replaced Kleenex 200s as the #1 stockkeeping unit (SKU) in the facial tissue category, was completed in 1991. Largely in support of this latter introduction, Kimberly-Clark increased merchandising support by 20 percent in food retailers and 13 percent in drug retailers. Finally, Kimberly-Clark introduced Kleenex Ultra, a 3-ply tissue which contained a silicone-based lotion, in the Ontario market in mid-1991.

Scott Scott's major brand, Scotties, fell from a share of 18.9 percent in 1990 to 15.9 percent in 1991. The main reason for the decline was the loss of trade support relative to Kleenex 150s. Scott relaunched the brand in September 1991, positioning it as a product with high content of recycled material, and supporting it with heavy advertising. As well, a 300-tissue family size of Scotties was launched in December 1991. Early indications were that the brand was recovering. Scott's secondary brand, White Swan (sold only in 150s), maintained a 7.1 percent share in 1991. Increased merchandising in drug channels led to a share gain there, which compensated for the share loss in food channels in the face of Kleenex 150s with its stronger brand image.

Irving Next to the aggressive developments in the Kleenex brand, the most significant competitive event in the facial tissue business in 1991 was the entry of Irving into the facial tissue market in the Maritime provinces and Quebec with its new Majesta brand. Majesta was packaged in an attractive format, and its feature pricing averaged 15 to 20 percent below Kleenex. It achieved a 4.2 percent national share in 1991.

All Others Overall, the other brands in the Canadian marketplace retained 98 percent of their cumulative market share in 1991. The group suffered some losses in the face of the merchandising support of Kleenex 150s, but these were balanced by gains in private label products in Western Canada.

Advertising

Advertising expenditures in the facial tissue category had historically been low, and quite inconsistent in "share of voice" and medium by manufacturer. Average industry annual expenditures were nearly $3.0 million over the last five years, with television accounting for 47 percent of spending, "out-of-home" (i.e., billboards, posters, and mass transit ads) 32 percent, consumer magazines 17 percent and daily newspapers four percent. Exhibit 3 summarizes copy and media strategy for the major brands in recent years, and share of advertising expenditures by brand.

Randall Beard believed that Kimberly-Clark had established a contemporary image for the Kleenex brand, but not a strong image for either softness or tissue strength. There had been no brand equity advertising[1] on the softness theme for the Kleenex brand since 1979, although there had been introductory campaigns for the softness upgrades to the basic product in 1989 and 1991, and the launch of the lotion line extension Kleenex Ultra in 1991.

Until the past year, when all Scotties' advertising was focused on the recycled paper relaunch behind an environmentally friendly position, Scotties had consistently advertised softness. This was somewhat ironic, because, according to P&G's tests of softness, the Scotties product was inferior on that dimension.

Royale had historically focused on the superior cold care afforded by the softness and strength of the 3-ply tissue. In 1991, ads for the product had emphasized softness, followed at year-end by the tactical cold season airing of an existing cold care execution.

By Procter & Gamble standards, advertising in the facial tissue category had not been strong. Not only were expenditures low, but only a small proportion of that spending was on brand equity. Furthermore, campaigns in the industry had tended to be of short duration, while P&G's extensive research on consumer advertising indicated that to be effective, advertising had to be sustained.

Consumer Promotion

Except for the Facelle brands, there was little consumer promotion activity in the category, relative to

---

[1] Brand equity advertising builds the franchise and image of a brand, rather than merely providing information about a feature or an upgrade.

EXHIBIT 3   Advertising Strategy of Facial Tissue Competitors

A. Copy Strategy

Brand	Years	Copy Strategy—Execution	Medium
Kleenex	1980–88	Heritage–family moments	TV, Print
		New packaging–pack shot	Print
	1989–91	Improved softness	TV
		Lotion–demonstration	TV, Print, OOH[a]
Scotties	1967–89	Softest cold care–"Scotties soften the blow"	TV
	1990	Caring softness–"Softer than a kiss"	TV
	1991	Environmentally friendly	Print, OOH
Royale	1973–86	Superior cold care–3-ply softness and strength	TV
	1988–90	New packaging	OOH
	1991	"Kitteny soft"	TV
	1992	Superior cold care–3-ply demonstration	TV

[a] OOH indicates advertising message delivered Outside Of Home (e.g. through billboards or mass transit advertising).

B. Share of Advertising Expenditure

Brand	Share of Advertising Spending			
	1988	1989	1990	1991
Royale	25%	52%	49%	16%
Kleenex	2%	35%	15%	18%
Kleenex Ultra	—	—	—	21%
Scotties	50%	13%	25%	33%
White Swan	3%	—	10%	6%
Majesta	—	—	1%	6%
Other	20%	—	—	—
TOTAL	100%	100%	100%	100%

the norms for other consumer packaged goods. In 1991, the three major facial tissue suppliers ran a total of 35 consumer promotions, with 21 of those for the Facelle brands (13 for Royale and eight for Florelle, respectively). Of the 35 promotions, 19 were coupons, and the other 16 a variety of sweepstakes, mail-in offers, samples, and cross-coupons. Altogether, P&G estimated, the 19 coupon promotions moved an incremental 42,000 cases of product for the three brands, or less than one percent of facial tissue shipments. In general, promotions did not pay for themselves because of the low absolute unit price of the product relative to the cost of the promotion. Therefore, promotions were likely to be used only as part of a more efficient group promotion, or as part of a strategy specifically directed at obtaining trial.

Pricing

While consumer promotions for facial tissues were relatively rare, price features were commonplace. There was always at least one brand on feature at any sizable food or drug retailer. In fact, the vast majority of facial tissues sold at retail during 1991 were feature-priced. Typical prices for the major brands during 1991 are shown in Exhibit 4.

ISSUES FOR THE FACELLE BRANDS

In planning the future of the Facelle brands, several problems had to be confronted. But first, Randall Beard reviewed a summary of the research which P&G had obtained in the seven months since acquiring the Facelle business.

The Royale Brand

Brand Image   Royale's long-term premium positioning, based upon its historically unique 3-ply product design and its softness claim, had built the leading brand image among its users in the product category. In judgments by a brand's users, Royale received an overall score of 85 on a scale of 100, marginally superior to Kleenex (at an average score of 82) and Scotties (81), and considerably ahead of the store brands (averaging 69).

EXHIBIT 4   Typical Prices—1991

Brand	Ply	Count	Typical Shelf Price	Typical Feature Price
P&G				
Royale	3	100	1.19	.89
Florelle	2	200	1.09	.79
Kimberley-Clark				
Kleenex	2	150	.99	.79
Kleenex	2	300	1.99	1.59
Kleenex-Ultra	3	100	.99	.79
Scott				
Scotties	2	150	.99	.69
Scotties	2	300	1.99	1.49
White Swan	2	150	.89	.59
Irving				
Majesta	2	150	.89	.63
Private Labels	2	150	.79	.49

Exhibit 5 compares four leading brands on a number of specific attributes of image. Royale enjoyed an image advantage for strength and thickness versus all other competition, but an image weakness for package design. Furthermore, it was seen as less fashionable than Kleenex and Scotties. The image data were particularly interesting to Beard and his product managers; despite low advertising spending in the category, historic campaigns appeared to have had a strong impact on brand image. For example, Scotties had a strong image for softness despite clearly inferior physical characteristics on that dimension relative to Royale and Kleenex. Almost ten years of advertising using the Little Softie character and the message "Scotties soft-ens the blow" had evidently produced a strong image for the brand as a soft, gentle tissue that was good for sore nose care.

Although Royale enjoyed a very favorable overall brand image, knowledge about the brand was not as high as Beard would have expected. For instance, among those who had used it in the past three months, 47 percent thought that Royale was a 2-ply tissue, and only 48 percent correctly assessed it as 3-ply.

Product Usage   Although Royale enjoyed a very favorable overall brand image, that image did not translate to market share, as Exhibit 6 demonstrates. Although half of households had used Royale some-

EXHIBIT 5   Brand Images by Attribute[a]

	Brand Rating			
Attribute	Royale	Kleenex	Scotties	Store Brands
• is soft	0	−	+	−
• good for sore nose care	0	0	+	−
• does not tear or fall apart when I blow my nose or sneeze	+	0	0	0
• is absorbent	+	−	0	0
• is thick	+	−	−	−
• contains lotion	0	+	0	0
• is 3-ply	+	−	−	0
• design/colors on box are attractive	−	+	+	−
• is caring	0	0	+	0
• is fashionable	−	+	0	−
• is contemporary	−	0	0	0
• is inexpensive	−	−	−	+

[a] In this chart, 0 represents a score that was not different from the average rating for all brands, − a score that was lower than the average rating, and + a score that was higher.

EXHIBIT 6   Trial and Usage by Brand

	Percent Usage by Brand			
	Royale	Kleenex	Scotties	Store Brands
1991 Market Share	6.9	39.5	15.9	20.6
Past 12 months used	51	91	52	29
Past 3 months used	34	79	33	22
Past 3 months usual brand	14	55	19	19
Loyalty: Used only this brand past 3 months	13	34	17	18
Share of total facial tissue usage past 12 months (among users of the brand)	14	45	36	80

time in the last year, only 14 percent claimed that it was their usual brand over the past three months. Qualitative research indicated that Royale was used as a part-time brand that was bought on feature or specifically for cold care, but seldom for regular usage around the household. This pattern was confirmed by the image data which showed significantly less agreement with the statement "is inexpensive" for Royale (32 percent) than Kleenex (52 percent), Scotties (42 percent), or store brands (83 percent).

Furthermore, as Exhibit 7 shows, Royale usage was heavily skewed to older consumers and smaller households.

Pricing vs. Kleenex   In the past, when the #1 SKU in the category was Kleenex 200s, feature price at retail on that product had been $0.99. Now, with the introduction of Kleenex 150s, feature price had dropped to $0.79, and sometimes lower in special promotions. In fact, in the past four months, average feature price for Kleenex had been $0.69, and for Royale $0.73. During this period, 80 percent of the Royale

sold at retail had been on feature. In the longer term, P&G estimated that the typical feature price for Kleenex 150s would be likely to increase modestly, but not dramatically. Furthermore, data from recent comparisons of Royale share at different levels of price disparity with Kleenex indicated higher price elasticity for Royale when its price exceeded Kleenex's by more than $.20.

Royale Price vs. Kleenex ($)	–.10	0.0	+.10	+.20	+.30	+.40
Royale Market Share (%)	7.2	7.0	6.8	6.2	5.2	4.1

The Florelle Brand

In 1991, 80 percent of facial tissue units sold were standard 2-ply tissue, the segment in which Facelle was represented by the Florelle brand. Specialty sizes (e.g., pocket packs, man-size, and cube format) represented 8 percent of units, and 3-ply tissue about 12 percent.

Exhibit 8 presents data from a November 1991 panel study of 2215 households on their attitudes towards brands of facial tissue. Only 3 percent of those surveyed claimed that Florelle was their usual brand. Not surprisingly for a brand which had received no advertising or consumer promotion, ratings of Florelle were not high. The obvious alternatives are to drop the Florelle brand, rejuvenate it with support, or continue it as an unsupported price brand.

The Softness Issue

A key success factor in the successful development of the Puffs brand in the United States was the effort that P&G invested in making the tissue softer. Softness is influenced by the process used in manufacturing the tissue, and the type of fiber employed. Longer fibers tend to make the resultant tissue stronger, but not as soft; shorter fibers, like eucalyptus, produce a softer tissue. A key issue in manufacturing facial tissue,

EXHIBIT 7   Demographic Characteristics by Brand

	Usual Brand		
	Royale	Kleenex	Scotties
Age Group	%	%	%
<24	3	5	2
25–50	48	68	63
>50	49	27	35
	100	100	100
Household Size			
1	16	10	8
2	42	32	35
>2	42	58	57
	100	100	100

EXHIBIT 8   Brand Attitudes

	All Users			Past 3 Months Brand Users
Brand	Average Value Rating	Average Overall Rating	% Who Purchased in Past 3 Months	Average Overall Rating
Florelle	53	58	10	73
Royale	71	78	30	85
Kleenex	73	80	75	82
Scotties	68	74	29	81
White Swan	61	66	14	77
Majesta	49	55	8	75
Store Brand	53	56	17	69

therefore, is how the softness/strength tradeoff is managed.

Data from P&G's experience in the U.S. market indicated that consumer preference as a function of strength followed an S-curve, where additional strength above the functional level did not provide any additional consumer benefit. On the other hand, softness did not level off in terms of diminishing returns on customer perceptions—at least at the levels of softness which could currently be obtained.

Relative tissue strength depended upon the conditions of the test, especially whether the tissue was wet or dry. A given brand of tissue, which had much higher dry strength than a second brand, would not necessarily have much higher wet strength. Procter & Gamble believed that dry strength (which affected ease of dispensing the tissue) was much less important than wet strength (which directly affected consumers' use of the product).

Exhibit 9 shows wet burst strength and softness for leading brands in the Canadian market. Softness was measured through tactile judgments of a panel of consumers, using Puffs as the standard zero-point on the scale.

EXHIBIT 9   Softness and Strength of Leading Brands of Facial Tissue

Brand	Softness[a]	Wet Burst Strength (g/sheet)
Royale	−2.5	69
Florelle	−2.1	32
Kleenex	−1.1	31
Kleenex Ultra	−0.5	76
Scotties	−2.0	57

[a] On this scale, Puffs tissues are rated at 0. Differences of 0.5 scale points or more are considered to be noticeable.

Commenting on this data, Randall Beard said, "This just reinforces what I have been told about Facelle's strategy prior to the acquisition. They chose to maximize strength—particularly dry strength—but that approach cost them severely on the softness dimension."

A study of customer dissatisfaction asked participants whether, in the past three months, they had experienced a problem with tissue breaking. Only one percent of Royale users had experienced a problem, vs. seven percent of Kleenex users.

In mid-1991, a blind paired comparison test was conducted with Royale and Kleenex Ultra. Attribute ratings on strength were the same for the two brands (8.5 on a 10-point scale), but Kleenex Ultra was rated significantly better on softness (9.1 vs. 7.4). When asked which brand they preferred overall, only 27 percent of participants chose Royale.

Beard was convinced that P&G needed to upgrade the softness of the Facelle products. By adding eucalyptus fiber and sacrificing some tissue strength, their softness could be significantly improved without the need for a major capital expenditure. In the long run, investments in process improvement could produce further softness enhancements, but the so-called "Eucalyptus Upgrade" could be done in a few months for a modest investment.

Accordingly, P&G carried out a pilot project to produce enough of the upgraded products for consumer acceptance testing. Early in 1992, "Single Product Blind Tests" (SPBT) were completed on the upgraded product, in both 2-ply and 3-ply form, as well as the current Royale, Florelle, Kleenex (Regular and Ultra), Scotties, and White Swan. In a SPBT, a sample of facial tissue with no identifying features is sent to a participant, who then uses the product for several weeks and answers a questionnaire about it. Participants in Facelle's SPBT were female heads of households whose first language was English. There were eight groups of participants, one for each brand. Group sizes ranged from 259 to 280 individuals. Results of this study are presented in Exhibit 10.

Overall ratings of the brands were found to be a function of consumer impressions of a tissue's softness and its thickness. A multiple regression with these two independent variables explained more than 95 percent of the variation in overall rating scores. The resultant equation is presented below:

$$\text{Overall rating} = 19.51 + (0.424 \times \text{Softness rating})$$
$$+ (0.359 \times \text{Thickness rating})$$

One issue in introducing an upgraded tissue was its perception by current Royale and Kleenex users. Would a new 2-ply product cannibalize sales of 3-ply Royale, or would it take share from Kleenex? Would a new 3-ply product be seen as an improvement by users of the current Royale tissue? Exhibit 11 compares ratings of the upgraded products by users of Royale and Kleenex, respectively, with similar users' ratings of the existing Royale and Florelle products. It is noteworthy that current Royale users who received the 2-ply upgrade in the SPBT were less favorably impressed with it than a group who actually received Royale in the blind test. In other words, the improved softness of the upgrade did not offset the reduction from three plies to two. The exhibit also enables a comparison of the group who received the 3-ply upgrade with the one

that received current Royale in the blind tests. In that situation, current Royale users rated the upgrade significantly higher on softness, slightly lower on strength and somewhat more favorably overall.

If the 2-ply upgrade were to be introduced, Randall Beard had to make a decision about what brand name would be used on it. Two apparent alternatives were Florelle (as an upgrade of the existing brand) and Royale (as a line extension). Furthermore, if the Royale name were chosen, a decision would have to be made about how to distinguish the 2-ply upgrade from the 3-ply upgrade of the traditional Royale brand. Another possibility would be to introduce the new product under the Puffs label that had been so successfully launched in the U.S. some twenty years earlier. Although Puffs had never been sold in Canada, there had been enough advertising spill-in from the U.S. that the brand was known to some Canadians. Exhibit 12 shows data on the image of Puffs among English and French Canadians.

CONCLUSION

Using the Puffs label in Canada would be a step toward making Puffs a North American brand, an alternative which would certainly have the blessing of the U.S. parent. However, the primary responsibility for the decision rested with Randall Beard and Barbara Fraser, and the choice had to be made soon if product, packaging and advertising and merchandising programs were to be ready for the fall cold season.

EXHIBIT 10   Consumer Evaluations of Facial Tissues in SPBT[a]

Brand	Overall[b]	Softness	Strength	Thickness	Absorbency
Facelle					
Royale:					
• current	82[c]	78	91	87	85
• 3-ply upgrade	88	93	90	87	85
Florelle:					
• current	73	70	74	68	70
• 2-ply upgrade	80	89	73	72	75
Kleenex					
Regular	75	82	68	65	71
Ultra	90	94	89	87	86
Scott					
Scotties	63	58	66	58	63
White Swan	62	50	74	63	65

[a] Ratings of English-speaking female heads of household, on a scale of 0–100 based on a single product blind test (SPBT) in home.

[b] Each respondent was asked: "Considering everything about the facial tissue sent to you, how would you rate it overall?"

[c] For this sample size, differences of more than 5 scale points across groups (i.e., within a column in the table) are significant at the .05 level.

EXHIBIT 11   SPBTª Ratings of Current Facelle Products and the Upgrades

	Users of Royale in Past 3 Months				Users of Kleenex in Past 3 Months			
Attribute Ratings	3-ply Upgrade	Current Royale	2-ply Upgrade	Current Florelle	3-ply Upgrade	Current Royale	2-ply Upgrade	Current Florelle
Overall	90	83	77	72	89	81	80	74
Softness	94	77	89	72	93	76	90	70
Strength	89	83	68	72	90	91	74	76
Thickness	90	88	68	63	88	86	72	69
Absorbency	87	85	74	69	86	84	75	71

ª Single Product Blind Test ratings. Each column in the table represents ratings by a group who received the indicated product in a blind test. Differences across columns of 6 scale points or more are statistically significant at the .05 level.

EXHIBIT 12   Canadian Consumer Evaluations of the Puffs Brand

	English HHs		French HHs	
	Royale %	Puffs %	Royale %	Puffs %
Awareness	97	40	97	11
TV Adv. Awareness	36	18	33	3
Trial (past 12 mos.)	51	9	57	3
Overall Rating	82	57	84	37
Judgment of Value	66	48	72	39
Of Those Aware				
% agreeing that the brand is good for nose care	42	77	30	33

"This is the year that we have to begin our move to make Facelle a major player in the market," said Randall Beard to himself, "and there are a number of issues we must face. Our long-term goal is a profitable leading share of the market, which is a long way from where we are now. To get there, it is essential that we establish a winning strategy for the Facelle Division brands." To do so, Beard felt, several inter-related questions had to be answered. What should be done about the Florelle brand? Should available technology from P&G be employed to increase the softness of Royale? What should be the position of the Facelle brand in the 2-ply segment? In fact, what brand should Facelle employ in that segment?

CASE 16-2   TIMOTEI (C)*

*I*n April 1988, Unilever established a new operating company, Elida Gibbs BV. Among the brands for which it was given responsibility was Timotei shampoo. As 1988 came to a close, the product manager for Timotei needed to prepare a strategic plan for 1989–1991 and a 1989 annual marketing plan for Timotei.

ELIDA GIBBS BV

In 1980 the personal products of Unilever were transferred to three operating companies: Lever-Sunlight BV, Unilever Export and Intertrade. Among these three companies Lever-Sunlight BV was by far the company which was most interested in the personal products, and it introduced two new products: Timotei shampoo in 1983 and the deodorant for men Axe in 1988. In 1986 Unilever, in light of the desired expansion in the direction of personal products, bought Cheseborough's Pond's division. Thus Unilever's range of personal products was extended by, among others, the brand Pond's "facial care" products and body lotion. Vaseline, a petroleum jelly product, was also added to the range of personal products of Unilever.

The responsibility for the sales of the personal products was divided among different agents, which caused too great a diffusion of interests. Consequently, advertising was limited. A study was conducted regarding this problem, and its conclusion was that it would be profitable to establish an independent operating company responsible for the marketing and sales of the personal products (Unilever has no personal-products factory in the Netherlands; production is elsewhere). At first, consideration was given to putting a division of Lever in charge of the personal products; however, the new concept did not correspond to the goals and culture of Lever.

One key aspect of the personal product concept is the fact that revenue or turnover (units × price) is more important than sales (units only). Historically, Lever has mainly concentrated on unit sales. Another aspect is the different method used to calculate the cost price.

The following price structure is typical of personal products:

Consumer price (CP)	180
Value Added Tax (VAT) + trade margin	80
Net proceeds of sales (NPS)	100
Cost of goods sold	40
Gross profit (GP)	60
Marketing appropriations (MA) (= advertising + promotion)	40
Profit before indirect cost (PBI)	20
Indirect costs	
Total profits	

In this cost price structure the objective is a GP of 60% of NPS, while this is 30% for the detergents of Lever. This shows that the difference between the new concept and Lever's traditional concept is rather large. Everything considered, adding the new concept to Lever would endanger the viability of the concept. Therefore, Elida Gibbs BV was founded in April 1988 and located in Schiedam. The characteristics of Elida Gibbs BV are 100% personal products; 30 million guilders of sales (out of factory), 1.2 million profit and 15 employees; simple organizational structure; and an average employee age of 29. Its organizational chart is shown in Exhibit 1.

The following Unilever brands were transferred to Elida Gibbs: Vinolia (toilet soap); Timotei (shampoo); Axe (among other things, men's deodorant); Signal (toothpaste). Cheseborough's Pond's, which was taken over by Unilever in 1986, was immediately transferred to Elida Gibbs and did not first go to Lever-Sunlight BV. In the meantime, its interests were looked after by an agent of Unilever. The brand portfolio of Elida Gibbs as of December 1988 is given in Exhibit 2.

THE MARKET 1987–1988

Throughout the years 1987 and 1988 the cosmetics market remained a growing market. Not only sales in units but sales in money continued to grow as well. Distribution levels remained more or less constant. This is evident from the figures in Exhibit 3. The sales

---

* This case was prepared by the Marketing and Marketing Research Team, Department of Economics, University of Groningen, the Netherlands. It has been edited by Leonard J. Parsons. Copyright © 1990 by the University of Groningen.

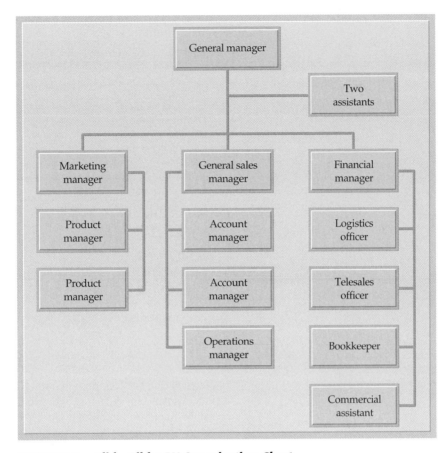

EXHIBIT 1   Elida Gibbs BV Organization Chart

of shampoo in guilders climbed from 128 million in 1986 to 134 million in 1987 and 141 million in 1988 (see Exhibit 4).

The market shares of Zwitsal, Head & Shoulders and, in particular, Schwarzkopf declined in this 2-year period (app. 2%). A possible explanation for the decline of Schwarzkopf could be the fact that Schauma has a different package, because of which the consumer no longer recognizes the familiar bottle. The market share of Timotei decreased a little, whereas the market share of the "other brands" grew strongly (see Exhibit 5). Competitive introductions and reintroductions during this period included:

EXHIBIT 2   Brand Portfolio Elida Gibbs, December 1988

Product	Market Share (volume)
Vinolia toilet soap	6
Vinolia bath foam	–
Timotei shampoo[a]	5.5
Timotei conditioner	4
Signal toothpaste	2
Axe aftershave, etc. (1988)	1
Axe deoderosol	6
Denim aftershave, etc.	15
Vaseline petroleum jelly	NA
Pond's facial care	7

[a] All sizes and variants.

1988 QT1	
Andrélon	Anti-dandruff shampoo
P&G	H&S every day shampoo
L'Oréal	Elsève with Jojoba
Schwarzkopf	Schauma, reintroduction

The average price of shampoos went up since 1986, from ƒ3.44 to ƒ3.55 (see Exhibit 6). There remains a price difference between the prices in the Food channel and the prices in the Drug-Perfumery channel (see Exhibit 7). For some brands this difference in price is minimal, such as, for instance, Timotei, Andrélon, Palmolive and Nivea. In Elsève's case the price in the Food channel is even higher than its price in the Drug-

EXHIBIT 3   Cosmetics Distribution Levels

A. Food

	1987	1988
By Volume		
Toilet soap	70%	70%
Shampoo	72	71
Toothpaste	75	75
Conditioner	61	NA
By Revenue		
Toilet soap	70	70
Shampoo	61	59
Toothpaste	65	65
Conditioner	51	NA

B. Drug

	1987	1988
By Volume		
Toilet soap	30%	30%
Shampoo	28	29
Toothpaste	24	25
Conditioner	39	NA
By Revenue		
Toilet soap	30%	30%
Shampoo	39	41
Toothpaste	35	35
Conditioner	49	NA

EXHIBIT 4   The Personal Products Market in the Netherlands

A. Food/Drug-Perfumery Unit Sales

In Millions of Units	1987	1988
Toilet soap (units)	74[a]	76
Shampoo (bottles)	38	39
Toothpaste (liters)	34	36
Bath foam (bottle)	20	22
Deodorant (bottle)	19	22

B. Food/Drug-Perfumery Revenue

In Millions of Guilders	1987	1988
Toilet soap	108	114
Shampoo	134	141
Toothpaste	98	107
Bath foam	94	109
Deodorant	85	95

[a] These figures can be compared to the 1986 numbers in Timotei (B) Exhibit 2.

Source: A. C. Nielsen.

Perfumery channel. Large differences in price can be seen in the cases of Head & Shoulders and Schwarzkopf.

The distribution figures for the years 1986–1988 remained practically constant (see Exhibit 8). As for sales, the relations between the Food Channel and the Drug-Perfumery channel are more or less as follows (Exhibit 9):

In volume: Food: Drug-Perfumery = 70:30.
In revenue: Food: Drug-Perfumery = 60:40.

These figures show that the Drug-Perfumery channel is gaining, both in terms of volume and money, at the expense of the Food channel.

The distribution figures are rather different for each brand in the various channels of distribution. For instance, Palmolive is underrepresented in the Drug-Perfumery channel, whereas Elsève is overrepresented in the Drug-Perfumery channel (see Exhibit 10). The distribution figures can be split up within the Food channel and the Drug-Perfumery channel. The Food channel can be divided into Chain Store I, Chain Store II and Food independent big. The Drug-Perfumery

channel can be decomposed into Drug-branch, Drug independent big and Drug independent small. Details can be found in Exhibits 11 and 12.

In Exhibit 13 the market shares of the various brands for the years 1987 and 1988 by channel of distribution can be found. These exhibits clearly show that some brands concentrate on one of the two channels. For instance, Elsève has a much larger market share in the Drug-Perfumery channel, whereas Palmolive has a much larger share in the Food channel. Most sales shares remain constant over the years. A striking exception is the market share of Schwarzkopf, which strongly decreased. It is also striking that the "other brands" have increased their market share in the Food channel as well as in the Drug-Perfumery channel.

TIMOTEI 1987–1988

In 1988 Elida Gibbs fixed the advisory price at ƒ3.25 and the trade margin amounted to approximately 30%. There has been a change as to the objective of the sales promotion:

1 promotion every 3 months
1 price-off a year (refund, 25% free, second bottle for half the price)
Other promotional activities are to support/improve the image of Timotei
Avoid a price-image

EXHIBIT 5 The Shampoo Market

A. 1987

Brand	Unit (ml)	Cons. Price	Market Share (%) Volume	Value
Zwitsal	200	4.15	9.7	11.5
Elsève	250	4.46	3.3	4.2
H & S	250	5.87	6.8	11.4
Nivea	250	3.22	3.7	3.4
Andrélon	250	3.95	13.3	15.0
Schwarzkopf	200	2.45	11.7	8.2
Palmolive	400	2.00	17.3	9.9
Timotei	200	3.15	4.9	4.4
Other brands			29.2	32.1

B. 1988

Brand	Unit (ml)	Cons. Price	Market Share (%) Volume	Value
Zwitsal	200	4.20	8.5	10.2
Elsève[a]	250	4.40	3.2	3.9
H & S	250	5.25	6.8	9.9
Nivea	250	3.60	3.3	3.4
Andrélon[a]	250	4.25	13.0	15.1
Schwarzkopf[a]	200	2.75	9.4	6.8
Palmolive[a]	400	1.99	17.6	9.9
Timotei[a]	200	2.99	4.8	4.2
On average in Food		2.95	71.0	59.0
On average in Drug	NA	4.98	29.0	41.0
Other brands (F + D)	200	3.95	33.3	36.8
Private labels (F + D)	NA	1.95	NA	NA

[a] More than one type/size.

Source: A. C. Nielsen.

EXHIBIT 6 Price of Shampoos (in guilders)

	F/D-Perfumery	Food	Drug-Perfumery
1986	3.44	2.89	4.85
1987	3.50	2.96	4.91
1988	3.55	2.95	4.98

Source: A.C. Nielsen.

EXHIBIT 7 Prices of Brands of Shampoo by Channel of Distribution in 1988 (in guilders)

	Food	Drug/Perfumery
Timotei	3.09	3.03
Andrélon	4.08	4.13
Elsève	4.36	4.31
Zwitsal	4.19	4.52
H & S	4.94	5.86
Schwarzkopf	2.39	3.04
Palmolive	1.99	1.99
Nivea	3.61	3.73
Timotei 200 ml	2.86	2.87
Timotei 400 ml	5.49	5.37

Source: A.C. Nielsen.

EXHIBIT 8   Shampoo Distribution

A. Numerical

Numerical	F/D-Perf.	Food	Drug-Perf.
1986	98.7	98.7	100
1987	99.2	99.0	100
1988	98.8	98.2	100

B. Weighted[a]

	F/D-Perf.	Food	Drug-Perf.
1986	100	100	100
1987	100	100	100
1988	100	100	100

[a] By store size in terms of sales.

Source: A. C. Nielsen.

EXHIBIT 9   Distribution by Channel

	Volume		Revenue	
	Food	Drug/Perf.	Food	Drug/Perf.
1987	72%	28%	61%	39%
1988	71	29	59	41

EXHIBIT 10   Distribution of Brands by Channel in 1988

A. Food

	Numerical	Weighted
Timotei	70%	92%
Andrélon	68	93
Elsève	20	46
Zwitsal	81	100
H & S	70	94
Schwarzkopf	68	89
Palmolive	89	94
Nivea	45	85
Timotei 200 ml	68	92
Timotei 400 ml	11	31

B. Drug/Perfumery

	Numerical	Weighted
Timotei	63%	84%
Andrélon	96	98
Elsève	88	88
Zwitsal	96	99
H & S	90	96
Schwarzkopf	78	90
Palmolive	33	66
Nivea	79	93
Timotei 200 ml	63	84
Timotei 400 ml	6	17

Source: A. C. Nielsen.

EXHIBIT 11   Distribution of Brands by Food Channel in 1988

A. Numerical

	CS I	CS II	Food Independent Large
Timotei	76.3%	90.0%	98.7%
Andrélon	77.7	88.2	98.7
Elsève	36.2	35.8	28.0
Zwitsal	100.0	99.0	100.0
H & S	78.7	90.8	99.8
Schwarzkopf	71.5	84.0	100.0
Palmolive	72.7	93.0	99.5
Nivea	59.2	81.3	89.2
Timotei 200 ml	76.0	89.8	99.0
Timotei 400 ml	30.7	8.6	26.2

B. Weighted

	CS I	CS II	Food Independent Large
Timotei	88.3%	94.7%	99.3%
Andrélon	88.2	95.7	100.0
Elsève	58.2	47.0	28.2
Zwitsal	100.0	100.0	100.0
H & S	88.3	99.2	100.0
Schwarzkopf	85.5	88.7	100.0
Palmolive	85.8	100.0	99.5
Nivea	75.7	81.3	94.5
Timotei 200 ml	88.2	94.7	99.2
Timotei 400 ml	52.8	6.6	33.2

Source: A. C. Nielsen.

EXHIBIT 12   Distribution of Brands by Drug/Perfumery Channel in 1988

A. Numerical

	Drug Branch	Drug Indep. Large	Drug Indep. Small
Timotei	97.2%	70.7%	50.8%
Andrélon	98.0	92.5	96.3
Elsève	99.0	93.3	81.8
Zwitsal	98.3	98.5	95.3
H & S	97.8	87.2	89.5
Schwarzkopf	97.2	74.7	74.2
Palmolive	97.2	15.0	20.7
Nivea	97.5	83.3	72.3
Timotei 200 ml	96.8	70.7	50.8

B. Weighted

	Drug Branch	Drug Indep. Large	Drug Indep. Small
Timotei	98.5%	73.8%	54.5%
Andrélon	99.0	96.5	97.7
Elsève	100.0	97.0	86.8
Zwitsal	99.3	98.3	97.5
H & S	99.0	92.5	90.7
Schwarzkopf	98.3	79.3	74.7
Palmolive	98.3	22.0	18.2
Nivea	99.0	89.0	79.5
Timotei 200 ml	98.3	73.8	54.5

Source: A. C. Nielsen.

EXHIBIT 13   Shampoo Market Shares by Channel

A. 1987

	Units		Guilders	
	Food	Drug/Perf.	Food	Drug/Perf.
Timotei	5.0%	4.6%	5.3%	2.9%
Andrélon	12.5	15.5	16.6	12.7
Elsève	1.9	7.0	2.9	6.2
Zwitsal	11.0	6.2	15.1	5.8
H & S	6.9	6.7	13.0	8.9
Schwarzkopf	12.5	9.6	10.0	5.3
Palmolive	22.2	4.8	15.0	1.9
Nivea	3.5	4.4	3.6	3.0
Others	24.6	41.1	18.6	53.1
Total (in 1000s)	27,680	10,717	ƒ81,898	ƒ52,596

B. 1988

	Units		Guilders	
	Food	Drug/Perf.	Food	Drug/Perf.
Timotei	5.0%	4.4%	5.2%	2.6%
Andrélon	12.5	14.3	17.3	11.8
Elsève	1.7	7.0	2.4	6.0
Zwitsal	9.5	5.9	13.5	5.4
H & S	6.9	6.5	11.6	7.5
Schwarzkopf	10.2	7.5	8.3	4.6
Palmolive	22.6	5.5	15.3	2.2
Nivea	3.3	3.1	4.1	2.3
Others	28.1	45.8	22.2	57.6
Total (in 1000s)	27,998	11,617	ƒ82,567	ƒ58,011

Source: A. C. Nielsen.

The 1987 and 1988 promotion schedules for regular Timotei shampoo (200 ml.) and conditioner are given in Exhibit 14. Promotional expenditures for 1987 amounted to 650 thousand guilders.

There were no Timotei commercials on TV in the years 1987 and 1988. Spending on print advertisements was 300 thousand guilders in 1987. See Exhibit 15 for an overview of the costs of the various media. The total recall of Timotei continued to increase in 1987, although the use of Timotei decreased (see Exhibit 16).

The results of Timotei were reasonably good until the end of 1987. Sales amounted to 534 thousand kilograms and market share 5.1 percent (volume) or 4.5 percent (revenue). In 1988 Timotei stabilized.

While waiting for the just released 1988 data to come on the computer screen, the manager reflected on Timotei's international situation. After the successful introduction of Timotei in Sweden, the product has gradually been introduced in more countries. Northern Europe took first place, with introductions in England, the Netherlands, Belgium, France and Germany. In Italy, for instance, Timotei was introduced in 1988. These introductions were all very successful, Timotei having average market shares of 7–8%. Subsequently, Timotei was also introduced in Asian countries.

Unfortunately, there has been a change in Timotei's success in various countries, among them Sweden and the Netherlands. This is partly caused by the fact that not all the countries are in the same stage of the product life cycle of the shampoo market. The Netherlands is in the maturity stage, whereas countries such as Japan—where Timotei is a big success—are still in the growth stage. This is a problem since, in principle, in all countries the same bottles, commercials and print advertising and the same advertising campaign are used. However, the various countries do have a certain amount of freedom. Proof of this is the fact that in

EXHIBIT 14   Promotion Schedule for Regular Timotei

A. 1987

Quarter	Weeks	Promotion	Shampoo[a]	Conditioner
1	5–8	On-pack barrette	X	
		On-pack comb		X
2	17–22	Umbrella (self-liquidating)	X	X
4	42–48	ƒ1. refund for 1 bottle	X	X
		ƒ2.50 refund for 2 bottles	X	X

B. 1988

Quarter	Weeks	Promotion	Shampoo[a]	Conditioner
1	2–5	Trio pack, 1 bottle free	X	
2	19–22	25% free	X	X
4	44–48	1 bottle conditioner free for two bottles	X	

[a] 200 ml size.

EXHIBIT 15   Media Costs 1988

Libelle	1/1 page full color	ƒ41,643
Margriet	1/1 page full color	ƒ33,965
Story	1/1 page full color	ƒ22,374
Telegraaf	2,000 mm	ƒ19,020
Alg. Dagblad	2,000 mm	ƒ11,640
NRC	2,000 mm	ƒ10,820
Volkskrant	2,000 mm	ƒ9,320
TV	Second	ƒ 500
Radio	Second	ƒ 80
Movie Theater	2 weeks national	ƒ60,000 (excl. VAT)
Bill Boards	Unit/month	ƒ 62 (250 units)
		ƒ 28 (5,000 units)

Source: Ad Media.

EXHIBIT 16   Recall of Timotei 1987

1987	Week			
	1	8	17	31
(% of total)				
Total recall	82.3	85.5	82.9	85.7
Unaided recall	18.4	19.9	17.2	16.8
Aided recall	63.9	65.6	65.8	68.9
Uses sometimes	8.8	6.7	6.8	5.9
Uses most of the time	6.6	6.7	5.8	5.3
Uses at the moment	5.9	6.2	6.3	4.6
Has already bought	40.0	41.3	37.4	38.4
Positive intention to buy	23.4	20.3	23.5	22.8
Received sample	—	—	—	—

Source: Burke-Inter/View.

some countries other Timotei products are put on the market in addition to the shampoos. In Sweden a complete range of Timotei products has been introduced. The idea was to improve Timotei's decreasing market share. This endeavor was not successful, however; Timotei's market share declined even further.

Other examples of new products in addition to the "normal" shampoos are the hair-care products in Japan and the complete range of hair products in England. In England there is also Timotei anti-dandruff available. This anti-dandruff shampoo is mild and natural, as opposed to most other anti-dandruff shampoos.

The task at hand is to prepare a strategic plan for 1989–1991 and an annual plan for 1989. The product manager wondered if there were changes in Dutch society that should be taken into account.

CASE INDEX

SUBJECT INDEX